Lecture Notes in Computer Science 7367

Commenced Publication in 1973
Founding and Former Series Editors:
Gerhard Goos, Juris Hartmanis, and Jan van Leeuwen

W0235151

Jun Wang   Gary G. Yen
Marios M. Polycarpou (Eds.)

Advances in Neural Networks – ISNN 2012

9th International Symposium on Neural Networks
Shenyang, China, July 11-14, 2012
Proceedings, Part I

 Springer

Volume Editors

Jun Wang
The Chinese University of Hong Kong
Department of Mechanical and Automation Engineering
Shatin, New Territories, Hong Kong
E-mail: jwang@mae.cuhk.edu.hk

Gary G. Yen
Oklahoma State University
School of Electrical and Computer Engineering
Stillwater, OK 74078, USA
E-mail: gyen@okstate.edu

Marios M. Polycarpou
University of Cyprus
Department of Electrical and Computer Engineering
75 Kallipoleos Avenue
1678 Nicosia, Cyprus
E-mail: mpolycar@ucy.ac.cy

ISSN 0302-9743   e-ISSN 1611-3349
ISBN 978-3-642-31345-5   e-ISBN 978-3-642-31346-2
DOI 10.1007/978-3-642-31346-2
Springer Heidelberg Dordrecht London New York

Library of Congress Control Number: 2012940272

CR Subject Classification (1998): F.1.1, I.5.1, I.2.6, I.2.8, I.2.10, I.2, I.4, I.5,
F.1, E.1, F.2

LNCS Sublibrary: SL 1 – Theoretical Computer Science and General Issues

Typesetting: Camera-ready by author, data conversion by Scientific Publishing Services, Chennai, India

Printed on acid-free paper

Springer is part of Springer Science+Business Media (www.springer.com)

Preface

This book and its sister volume constitute the proceedings of the 9th International Symposium on Neural Networks (ISNN 2012). ISNN 2012 was held in the beautiful city Shenyang in northeastern China during July 11–14, 2012, following other successful conferences in the ISNN series. ISNN has emerged as a leading conference on neural networks in the region with increasing global recognition and impact. ISNN 2012 received numerous submissions from authors in six continents (Asia, Europe, North America, South America, Africa, and Oceania), 24 countries and regions (Mainland China, Hong Kong, Macao, Taiwan, South Korea, Japan, Singapore, India, Iran, Poland, Germany, Finland, Italy, Spain, Norway, Spain, Russia, UK, USA, Canada, Brazil, Australia, and Tunisia). Based on rigorous reviews, 147 high-quality papers were selected by the Program Committee for presentation at ISNN 2012 and publication in the proceedings. In addition to the numerous contributed papers, three distinguished scholars (Kunihiko Fukishima, Erkki Oja, and Alessandro Sperduti) were invited to give plenary speeches at ISNN 2012. The papers are organized in many topical sections under coherent categories (mathematical modeling, neurodynamics, cognitive neuroscience, learning algorithms, optimization, pattern recognition, vision, image processing, information processing, neurocontrol and novel applications) spanning all major facets of neural network research and applications. ISNN 2012 provided an international forum for the participants to disseminate new research findings and discuss the state of the art of new developments. It also created a pleasant opportunity for the participants to interact and exchange information on emerging areas and future challenges of neural network research.

Many people made significant efforts to ensure the success of this event. The ISNN 2012 organizers are grateful to sponsors for their sponsorship; grateful to the National Natural Science Foundation of China for the financial support; and grateful to the Asian Pacific Neural Network Assembly, European Neural Network Society, IEEE Computational Intelligence Society, and IEEE Harbin Section for the technical co-sponsorship. The organizers would like to thank the members of the Program Committee for reviewing the papers. The organizers would particularly like to thank the publisher Springer for their agreement and cooperation in publishing the proceedings as two volumes of *Lecture Notes in Computer Science*. Last but not least, the organizers would like to thank all the authors for contributing their papers to ISNN 2012. Their enthusiastic contribution and participation are an essential part of the symposium, which made the event a success.

July 2012

Jun Wang
Gary G. Yen
Marios M. Polycarpou

ISNN 2012 Organization

ISNN 2012 was organized and sponsored by the Northeastern University and Institute of Automation of the Chinese Academy of Sciences. It was co-sponsored by the Chinese University of Hong Kong and University of Illinois at Chicago. It was technically cosponsored by the Asia Pacific Neural Network Assembly, and European Neural Network Society, IEEE Computational Intelligence Society, IEEE Harbin Section, and International Neural Network Society. It was financially supported by the National Natural Science Foundation of China.

General Chairs

Gary G. Yen   Stillwater, OK, USA
Huaguang Zhang   Shenyang, China

Advisory Committee Chairs

Tianyou Chai   Shenyang, China
Ruwei Dai   Beijing, China

Steering Committee Chairs

Marios Polycarpou   Nicosia, Cyprus
Paul Werbos   Wahshington, DC, USA

Organizing Committee Chair

Derong Liu   Beijing, China

Program Committee Chairs

Leszek Rutkowski   Czestochowa, Poland
Jun Wang   Hong Kong

Plenary Session Chairs

Cesare Alippi   Milan, Italy
Bhaskar DasGupta   Chicago, USA

Special Session Chairs

Haibo He   Rhode Island, USA
Zhigang Zeng   Wuhan, China

Finance Chair

Zeng-Guang Hou   Beijing, China

Publication Chairs

Amir Hussain   Stirling, UK
Zhanshan Wang   Shenyang, China
Qinglai Wei   Beijing, China

Publicity Chairs

Danchi Jiang   Hobart, Austria
Seiichi Ozawa   Kobe, Japan
Stefano Squartini   Ancona, Italy
Liang Zhao   Sao Paulo, Brazil

Registration Chairs

Jinhu Lu   Beijing, China
Dongbin Zhao   Beijing, China

Local Arrangements Chair

Zhiliang Wang   Shenyang, China

Electronic Review Chair

Tao Xiang   Chongqing, China

Secretary

Ding Wang   Beijing, China

Webmaster

Zheng Yan   Hong Kong

Program Committee

Jose Aguilar
Amir Atiya
Salim Bouzerdoum
Ivo Bukovsky
Xindi Cai
Jianting Cao
M. Emre Celebi
Jonathan Hoyin Chan
Rosa H.M. Chan
Songcan Chen
YangQuan Chen
Yen-Wei Chen
Li Cheng
Long Cheng
Xiaochun Cheng
Sung-Bae Cho
Sergio Cruces-Alvarez
Xuanju Dang
Mingcong Deng
Ming Dong
Wai-Keung Fung
Mauro Gaggero
Junbin Gao
Xiao-Zhi Gao
Chengan Guo
Ping Guo
Haibo He
Zhaoshui He
Zeng-Guang Hou
Chun-Fei Hsu
Huosheng Hu
Jinglu Hu
Xiaolin Hu
Guang-Bin Huang
Tingwen Huang
Danchi Jiang
Haijun Jiang
Yaochu Jin

Qi Kang
Rhee Man Kil
Sungshin Kim
Mario Koeppenm H.K.
  Kwan
James Kwok
Edmund M.K. Lai
Shutao Li
Tieshan Li
Yangmin Li
Hualou Liang
Yanchun Liang
Lizhi Liao
Aristidis Likas
Zhenwei Liu
Bao-Liang Lu
Jinhu Lu
Wenlian Lu
Jinwen Ma
Malik Magdon-Ismail
Danilo Mandic
Francesco Marcelloni
Francesco Masulli
Tiemin Mei
Dan Meng
Valeri Mladenov
Seiichi Ozawa
Jaakko Peltonen
Manuel Roveri
Tomasz Rutkowski
Sattar B. Sadkhan
Toshimichi Saito
Marcello Sanguineti
Gerald Schaefer
Furao Shen
Yi Shen
Daming Shi
Hideaki Shimazaki

Qiankun Song
Alessandro Sperduti
Stefano Squartini
John Sum
Johan Suykens
Roberto Tagliaferri
Norikazu Takahashi
Ying Tan
Toshihisa Tanaka
Ruck Thawonmas
Peter Tino
Christos Tjortjis
Ivor Tsang
Masao Utiyama
Bing Wang
Dan Wang
Dianhui Wang
Wenjia Wang
Wenwu Wang
Yiwen Wang
Zhanshan Wang
Zidong Wang
Qinglai Wei
Yimin Wen
Wei Wu
Cheng Xiang
Songyun Xie
Rui Xu
Jianqiang Yi
Xiao-Hua Yu
Jianghai Zhang
Jie Zhang
Kai Zhang
Yunong Zhang
Dongbin Zhao
Liang Zhao
Mingjun Zhong
Rodolfo Zunino

Reviewers

Esam Abdel-Raheem
Abdujelil
Angelo Alessandri
Raed Almomani
Jing An
Lucas Antiqueira
Young-Chul Bae
Ieroham S. Baruch
Abdelmoniem Bayoumy
Pablo Aguilera Bonet
Fabricio Aparecido Breve
Kecai Cao
Gary Chen
Haifeng Chen
Mou Chen
Yu Cheng
Yang Chenguang
Seong-Pyo Cheon
Chih-hui Chiu
Qun Dai
Ma Dazhong
Yongsheng Dong
Yang Dongsheng
Fanxiaoling
Paolo Gastaldo
Che Guan
Haixiang Guo
Xin Guo
Zhang Haihong
Xian-Hua Han
Huang He
Elsayed Hemayed
Kevin Ho
Jianwen Hu
Junhao Hu
Feng Jiang
Wei Jin
Snejana Jordanova

Yu Juan
Aman Kansal
Takuya Kitamura
Alessio Leoncini
Chi-Sing Leung
Bing Li
Fuhai Li
Wang Li
Yangmin Li
Yuanqing Li
Zhan Li
Zhuo Li
Cp Lim
Qiuhua Lin
Jinrong Liu
Xiaobing Liu
Yanjun Liu
Zhenwei Liu
Tao Long
Di Lu
Xiaoqing Lu
Qing Ma
Guyue Mi
Alex Moopenn
Wang Ning
Chakarida Nukoolkit
Shogo Okada
Woon Jeung Park
Rabie Ramadan
Thiago Christiano Silva
N. Sivakumaran
Angela Slavova
Qiankun Song
Jamie Steck
Wei Sun
Yonghui Sun
Ning Tan
Shaolin Tan

Liang Tang
Ban Tao
Tianming Hu
Ang Wee Tiong
Alejandro Toledo
Ding Wang
Guan Wang
Huiwei Wang
Jinliang Wang
Lijun Wang
Zhuang Wang
Kong Wanzeng
Jonathan Wu
Guangming Xie
Xinjiuju
Ye Xu
Dong Yang
Xubing Yang
Xianming Ye
Jiangqiang Yi
Jianchuan Yin
Yilong Yin
Juan Yu
Zhigang Zeng
Dapeng Zhang
Pengtao Zhang
Xianxia Zhang
Xin Zhang
Yu Zhang
Yunong Zhang
Qibin Zhao
Xudong Zhao
Yue Zhao
Zhenjiang Zhao
Ziyang Zhen
Yanqiao Zhu

Table of Contents – Part I

Mathematical Modeling

Neurodynamics

Cognitive Neuroscience

Learning Algorithms

Optimization

Erratum

Table of Contents – Part II

Pattern Recognition

Vision

Image Processing

Information Processing

Neurocontrol

Novel Applications

Attractor Neural Network Combined with Likelihood Maximization Algorithm for Boolean Factor Analysis*

Alexander A. Frolov[1], Dušan Húsek[2], and Pavel Yu. Polyakov[1,3]

[1] Institute of Higher Nervous Activity and Neurophysiology,
Russian Academy of Sciences, Butlerova 5a, 117 485 Moscow, Russia
aafrolov@mail.ru
[2] Institute of Computer Science, Academy of Sciences of the Czech Republic,
Pod Vodárenskou věží 2, 182 07 Prague 8, Czech Republic
dusan@cs.cas.cz
[3] VSB Technical University of Ostrava, Ostrava, Czech Republic

Abstract. When large data sets are analyzed, the pursuit of their appropriate representation in the space of lower dimension is a common practice. Boolean factor analysis can serve as a powerful tool to solve the task, when dealing with binary data. Here we provide a short insight into a new approach to Boolean factor analysis we have developed as an extension of our previously proposed method: Hopfield-like Attractor Neural Network with Increasing Activity. We have greatly enhanced its functionality, having complemented this method by maximizing the data set likelihood function. We have defined this Likelihood function on the basis of the data generative model proposed previously. As a result, in such a way we can obtain a full set of generative model parameters. We demonstrate the efficiency of the new method using the artificial signals, which are random mixtures of horizontal and vertical bars that are a benchmark for Boolean factor analysis. Then we show that the method can be used for real task solving when analyzing data from the Kyoto Encyclopedia of Genes and Genomes.

1 Introduction

Boolean Factor Analysis (BFA) implies that the components of the signals, factor loadings and factor scores are binary variables. In spite of the fact that binary data representations are typical in many fields, including social science, marketing, zoology, genetics, and medicine, BFA methods have only been rather moderately developed. We proposed earlier [1] a BFA method that is based on the Hopfield-like Attractor Neural Network with Increasing Activity (ANNIA). The method builds on the well known property of Hopfield network to create attractors of the network dynamics by assemblies of tightly connected neurons.

---

* This work was supported by the projects AV0Z10300504, GACR P202/10/0262, and IT4Innovations Centre of Excellence project, reg. no. CZ.1.05/1.1.00/02.0070.

J. Wang, G.G. Yen, and M.M. Polycarpou (Eds.): ISNN 2012, Part I, LNCS 7367, pp. 1–10, 2012.
© Springer-Verlag Berlin Heidelberg 2012

Since the neurons representing a factor are activated simultaneously each time when the factor appears in the patterns of the data set, and neurons representing different factors are rather seldom activated simultaneously, then - due to the Hebbian learning rule - the factor neurons become more tightly connected than the other neurons. So factors can be revealed as attractors of the network dynamics. In our previous paper [2], we demonstrated the method performance with artificial signals and with the sets of the real data. Recently we proposed a general blind information theoretic measure of BFA efficiency, which is the information gain provided by BFA [3]. Estimating the entropy of the data set when its hidden structure is revealed is based on the supposed generative model of signals, adequate for BFA. We have shown on artificial signals that the information gain is sensitive to both the noise in the signals and the errors in the BFA results. Thus, information gain seems to be a reliable basis for comparing different BFA methods and for detecting the presence of hidden factor structures in a given data set as well.

The offered BFA generative model provides also the possibility to improve ANNIA complementing it by the procedure of the likelihood maximization. We refer to the hybrid method as LANNIA. We estimate the efficiency of LAN-NIA using artificially generated signals and the Kyoto Encyclopedia of Genes and Genomes database (KEGG) containing full genome sequencing for 1368 organisms.

2   Generative Model of Signals Appropriate for BFA

Each pattern of a signal space is defined by a binary row vector $\mathbf{x} = [x_1, \ldots, x_N]$ where N is the dimensionality of the binary signal space. Every component of $\mathbf{x}$ takes value One or Zero. Each factor $\mathbf{f}_i = [f_{i1}, \ldots, f_{iN}]$ is a binary row vector of dimension N which components also take values One or Zero. Any vector $\mathbf{x}$ can be presented in the form

$$x_j = [\bigvee_{i=1}^{L} s_i \wedge f'_{ij}] \vee \eta_j, \tag{1}$$

where $\mathbf{s} = [s_1, \ldots, s_L]$ is a binary row vector of factor scores of dimension L, L being the total number of factors, $\mathbf{f}'_i = [f'_{i1}, \ldots, f'_{iN}]$ is a distorted version of factor $\mathbf{f}_i$ and $\boldsymbol{\eta}$ is a vector of specific factors. Each specific factor η_j is a random binary variable taking One with probability q_j. Factor distortion implies that One valued entries of $\mathbf{f}_i$ can transform to Zero with probability $1 - p_{ij}$ before mixing in the observed pattern. The probabilities of Zero valued entries of $\mathbf{f}_i$ to take One in the distorted version of the factor are assumed to be zero ($p_{ij} = 0$). We assume that factors appear in patterns (that is related scores s_i take Ones) independently with probabilities π_i ($i = 1, \ldots, L$).

The aim of Boolean factor analysis is to find the parameters of a generative model $p_{ij}, q_j, \pi_i, i = 1, \ldots, L, j = 1, \ldots, N$ and factor scores $\mathbf{s}_m$ ($m = 1, \ldots, M$) for all M patterns $\mathbf{x}_m$ of the observed data set.

The proposed generative model allows to define the BFA information gain. If factor structure of the signal space is unknown, then representing the jth component of vector $\mathbf{x}$ requires $h(p_j)$ bits of information, where $h(x) = -x \log_2 x - (1-x) \log_2(1-x)$ is Shannon function and p_j is the probability of the jth component's taking One. Representing the whole data set requires

$$H_0 = M \sum_{j=1}^{N} h(p_j) \tag{2}$$

bits of information. If the hidden factor structure of the signal space is detected that is all generative model parameters and all factor scores in the data set are found, then representing the whole data set requires

$$H = M \sum_{i=1}^{L} h(\pi_i) + \sum_{m=1}^{M} \sum_{j=1}^{N} h(P(x_{mj}|\mathbf{s}_m,)) \tag{3}$$

bits of information. The first term in (3) is the information required to represent the factor scores and the second term is the information required to represent all patterns of the data set when factor scores are given where

$$P(x_{mj}|\mathbf{s}_m) = x_{mj} - (2x_{mj} - 1)(1 - q_j) \prod_{i=1}^{L} (1 - p_{ij})^{s_{mi}} \tag{4}$$

is the probability of the jth component of mth signal $\mathbf{x}_m$ to take the value x_{mj}.

We define the relative information gain as

$$G = (H_0 - H)/H_0. \tag{5}$$

3 Likelihood Maximization (LM)

For the proposed generative model, the data set likelihood takes the form

$$\Lambda = \sum_{m=1}^{M} \Lambda_m, \tag{6}$$

where

$$\Lambda_m = \log[P(\mathbf{s}_m)P(\mathbf{x}_m|\mathbf{s}_m)], \tag{7}$$

$$P(\mathbf{x}_m|\mathbf{s}_m) = \prod_{j=1}^{N} P(x_{mj}|\mathbf{s}_m), \quad P(\mathbf{s}_m) = \prod_{i=1}^{L} \pi_i^{s_{mi}} (1 - \pi_i)^{1-s_{mi}},$$

and $P(x_{mj}|\mathbf{s}_m, \mathbf{\Theta})$ is given by (4).

To maximize Λ we suggest to use the iterative procedure which alternatively increase Λ with respect to a set of factor scores s_{mi} ($m = 1, \ldots, M, i = 1, \ldots, L$), while holding model parameters fixed (the E-step), and with respect to parameters, while holding s_{mi} fixed (the M-step).

At the M-step, when scores are fixed, p_{ij} and q_j can be found by maximization of Λ according to the following iterative procedure:

$$\Delta p_{ij} = \gamma_{ij}\frac{\partial\Lambda}{\partial p_{ij}}, \qquad \Delta q_j = \gamma_j\frac{\partial\Lambda}{\partial q_j}, \tag{8}$$

where γ_{ij} and γ_j are positive learning rates and $\partial\Lambda/\partial p_{ij}$ and $\partial\Lambda/\partial q_j$ can be easily found from (4), (6) and (7).

As we assume that the probabilities p_{ij} are sufficiently high for the components constituting the ith factor ($f_{ij} = 1$) and equal to zero for the other components ($f_{ij} = 0$), at each iteration cycle of step M we put $p_{ij} = 0$ if

$$p_{ij} < 1 - \prod_{l \neq i}(1 - \pi_l p_{lj}), \tag{9}$$

where the right side of the inequality is the probability that the jth attribute appears in the pattern due to other factors except $\mathbf{f}_i$.

The generative model parameters p_{ij} and q_j obtained at the M-step are used as the input for the next E-step to find factor scores. For each individual signal $\mathbf{x}_m$ of the data set, factor scores $\mathbf{s}_m$ can be found as those maximizing Λ_m. One of the possible procedures to maximize Λ is following. At each iterative step of this procedure the values $\Lambda_m|_{s_{mi}=1}$ and $\Lambda_m|_{s_{mi}=0}$ obtained by substituting $s_{mi} = 1$ and $s_{mi} = 0$ into (7) are compared. The value of s_{mi} that provides the greater $\Lambda_m|_{s_{mi}}$ is chosen and the procedure goes to another i until it converges. After computing $\mathbf{s}_m$ the procedure is applied to the next signal $\mathbf{x}_{m+1}$ until the data set is exhausted.

The scores found at the E-step are used as input to the next M-step. If, for some factors, all found loadings or scores are zeros, these factors are excluded from the list of found factors.

4   Hybrid LANNIA Method

As described in our previous papers [1,2], ANNIA itself performs BFA incompletely. It provides a precise solution for the factor loadings, an approximate solution for factor scores, and no results concerning the parameters of the generative model p_{ij} and q_j. In the combination ANNIA and LM the role of ANNIA is to provide LM the initial estimation of p_{ij}. Another aspect of the ANNIA and LM interaction is a suppression of the dominant attractors in ANNIA using the data provided by LM.

The LANNIA performance is illustrated below when solving the so called Bars Problem (BP) [4]. In this problem, each pattern of the data set is an $n \times n$ binary pixel image containing several of $L = 2n$ possible (one-pixel wide) horizontal and vertical bars (Fig. 1). Pixels constituting a bar take the values 1 and pixels not constituting it take the values 0. For each image, each bar could be chosen with the probability C/L, where C is the mean number of bars mixed in an image. At the point of intersection of a vertical and a horizontal bar, the pixel takes the value 1. The task is to recognize all bars as individual objects on the basis of a data set containing M images consisting of bar mixtures. As in the most papers where the BP was used as a benchmark, we set $C = 2$ and $n = 8$.

In terms of BFA, bars are factors. Factor loadings f_{ij} $(j = 1, \ldots, N)$ take value One for pixels constituting ith bar and value Zero for pixels not constituting it. Each image is a Boolean superposition of factors, and the factor score takes the value One or Zero depending on the presence or absence of a bar in the image. We consider the case of the homogeneously distributed noise in the images. Particularly, we put $p_{ij} = pf_{ij}$ and $q_j = q$. This means that pixels constituting a bar can take Zero with the equal probabilities $1 - p$ and any pixel can take One with the probability q due to the specific factor.

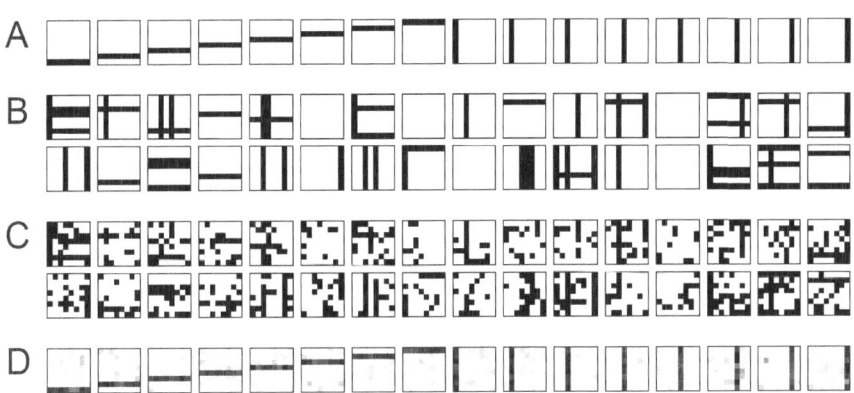

Fig. 1. A Sixteen vertical and horizontal bars in 8×8 pixel images. **B** Examples of images in the standard bars problem. Each image contains two bars on average. **C** Examples of noisy imaged ($p = 0.7$, $q = 0.2$). **D** Factors found by LANNIA when solving BP with the noisy images, the number of patterns in the data set is $M = 800$. In **D**, the black pixels correspond to $p_{ij} = 1$, the white pixels correspond to $p_{ij} = 0$, and the gray pixels corresponds to the intermediate values of p_{ij}.

The method ANNIA is based on the network of N neurons corresponding to N binary coordinates of a signal space. All patterns of the data set are stored in the network by the Hebbian learning rule. ANNIA reveals factors as attractors of the network dynamics in a two-run recall procedure. Its initialization starts by the presentation of a random initial pattern $\mathbf{x}^{in}$ with k_{in} active neurons. On the presentation of $\mathbf{x}^{in}$, the network activity $\mathbf{x}$ evolves to an attractor according to synchronous discrete time dynamics. At each time step, k_{in} winners with the highest synaptic excitations are activated. The excitations are calculated as $\mathbf{xJ}$, where $\mathbf{x}$ is the network state at the previous time step. When activity stabilizes at the initial level of activity k_{in}, then a neuron with the maximal excitation $T(k_{in})$ is selected over all not active neurons, and added to already active k_{in} neurons of the attractor. In fact, $T(k_{in})$ is a threshold of excitation for non-active neurons to activate only one of them. The obtained pattern with $k_{in} + 1$ active neurons is treated as the initial network state for the next iteration step, and the network activity evolves to an attractor at the new level of activity $k_{in} + 1$. The level of activity then increases to $k_{in} + 2$, and so on, until the number of active neurons reaches the final level k_{fin}.

At the end of each external step when the network activity stabilizes at the level of k active neurons, a Lyapunov function is calculated:

$$\lambda(k) = \mathbf{x}(t+1)\mathbf{J}\mathbf{x}^T(t)/k, \tag{10}$$

where $\mathbf{J}$ is the matrix of synaptic connections and $\mathbf{x}(t+1)$ and $\mathbf{x}(t)$ are the two network states in a possible cyclic attractor of length 2 (for a point attractor, $\mathbf{x}(t+1) = \mathbf{x}(t)$). In fact, $\lambda(k)$ is the mean synaptic excitation of k active neurons. The identification of factors is based on the analysis of the change of the Lyapunov function $\lambda(k)$ and the activation threshold $T(k)$ in the recall procedure [1].

The sizes of attraction basins around factors are distributed within a large range. When the initial network states are chosen randomly, as in the procedure described above, the network activity tends to converge to the factors with the largest attraction basins. To suppress the dominance of these factors we deleted them from the network memory by subtracting the matrix $\Delta\mathbf{J}^i$ from the matrix of synaptic connections $\mathbf{J}$ for each found factor where

$$\Delta J^i_{jk} = M\pi_i(1 - \pi_i)p_{ij}(1 - p^0_{ij})p_{ik}(1 - p^0_{ik}), \quad k \neq j, \qquad \Delta J^i_{jj} = 0, \tag{11}$$

p_{ij} is a probability that jth component takes One in ith found factor, p^0_{ij} is a probability that jth component takes One in signals not containing ith found factors. Probability p_{ij} is a parameter of the generative model, p^0_{ij} can be estimated as frequency of the jth attribute taking One in patterns of the data set not containing the ith factor. Since ANNIA does not provide direct estimates of generative model parameters required for the unlearning rule (11), they are obtained by using the LM procedure.

The LM procedure is initiated from E-step. To estimate the probabilities p_{ij} required to start LM procedure we use

$$p_{ij} = \begin{cases} h_{ij}/ \max_{k=1,\dots,N}\{h_{ik}\} & \text{if } h_{ij} > 0 \\ 0 & \text{if } h_{ij} \leq 0 \end{cases}, \tag{12}$$

where $\mathbf{h}_i = \mathbf{J}\mathbf{f}_i$ is a vector of synaptic excitations of neurons when ith found factor is activated in the network. This estimation seems to be reasonable because h_{ij} is proportional to p_{ij} [2]. After the LM convergence, the obtained probabilities p_{ij} and p^0_{ij} are used to suppress attractors for found factors. This allows to find by ANNIA the other factors with the lower Lyapunov function.

The parameters of the generative model and the factor scores obtained by LM are used to calculate the information gain provided by all found factors. The LANNIA continues until G stops to increase due to adding new found factors. This is the first criterion to terminate LANNIA.

The network dynamics can converge not only to the true attractors corresponding to the factors, but also to spurious attractors far from all factors. The

Lyapunov function for the spurious attractors is smaller than that for factors. To distinguish true and spurious attractors we used the procedure described in [1]. The appearance of only spurious attractors in the recall procedure indicates that all factors are found. This is the second criterion to terminate LANNIA.

The LANNIA performance is illustrated in Fig. 2 for the case of rather noisy images ($p = 0.7$ and $q = 0.2$). Twenty trajectories were run in ANNIA at the beginning of each LANNIA cycle. At the first cycle, 11 trajectories were identified as true (Fig. 2(a)). The increment of the information gain provided by LM at the first cycle amounted to 0.06. When the factors found were deleted from ANNIA at the end of the first LANNIA cycle, at the second cycle, ANNIA found three factors. The increment of the gain amounted to 0.015, that is proportional to the number of the found factors. At the third full LANNIA cycle, ANNIA found two factors and the gain increased for about 0.01. After deleting the factors found at the third cycle, all trajectories at ANNIA happened to be spurious and the procedure was terminated.

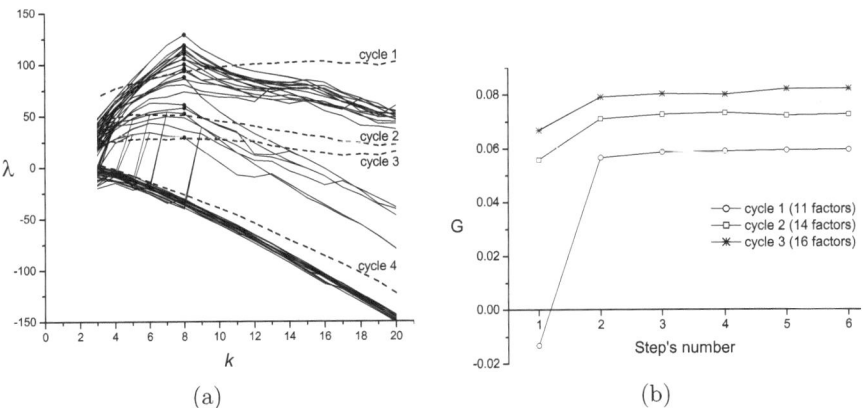

Fig. 2. Lyapunov function λ (a) and information gain G (b) for data set consisting of $M = 800$ noisy patterns ($p = 0.7$, $q = 0.2$). The dashed lines in (a) are the borders to distinguish true and spurious attractors.

The factors found by LANNIA are shown in Fig. 1(D). They almost coincide with bars shown in Fig. 1(A) but contain also pixels with small probabilities p_{ij}. Note that LANNIA revealed correctly the hidden factor structure of the data set even when the structure is practically invisible (see Fig. 1(C)). For this case the "theoretical" gain calculated for the precise generative model parameters amounts to 0.061. The gain obtained by LANNIA amounts to the same values, that is, it provides almost precise solution of BP.

5   LANNIA Application to the Genome Data Set Analysis

One of the important problems in a modern biology is to identify functions of proteins in the organisms. A fast growing of fully sequenced genomes makes it possible to reveal the protein function by comparing protein phylogenetic profiles of different organisms. The protein phylogenetic profile is defined as a binary pattern that encodes by Ones and Zeros the presence or, respectively, the absence of proteins in a given organism with the fully sequenced genome [5]. When two proteins show the correlated events of the presence or absence over the organisms, it is assumed that these proteins are also functionally correlated. This is based on the observation that a set of proteins is usually involved in each particular cellular process interacting in performing some function [6]. This leads to the concept of the modularity which assumes that the genome functionality can be partitioned into a collection of modules. Each module is a discrete entity of elementary components and performs an identifiable task, separable from the functions of the other modules [7]. Thus, revealing sets of proteins coherently appeared in different organisms may facilitate the search for functional modules in the genome structure. Since the concept of the genome functional modularity is completely compatible with the BFA generative model described here it was a challenge for us to apply LANNIA to reveal the hidden factor structure in some large genome data set.

For the BFA analysis we used the largest genome database KEGG [8], containing the fully sequenced genomes of $M = 1368$ organisms. LANNIA revealed 38 factors for four full cycles. Each cycle began by running twenty random trajectories in ANNIA. The Lyapunov functions along the eleven true trajectories at the first cycle of LANNIA are shown in Fig. 3(a). At the first cycle, the LM procedure converged for five steps and excluded two factors of eleven. The information gain provided by LM at each its step is shown in Fig. 3(b). At the fifth step, it amounts to $G = 0.27$. At the second full LANNIA cycle, ANNIA found fourteen factors. LM converged for four steps, excluded one factor and provided the gain increase up to $G = 0.31$. At the third and fourth full LANNIA cycles, ANNIA found thirteen and twelve factors, LM excluded six and three. At fifth cycle, the gain decreased and LANNIA was terminated. The maximal gain provided by LANNIA for the KEGG data set amounts to 0.32. The high gain obtained shows that, first, the genome data are actually adequate for BFA and, second, LANNIA provides the good BFA performance. The high information gain speeds in favor of the hypothesis of the modular genome structure [7].

Fig. 4 demonstrates the distribution of the factors over the organisms. All organisms are grouped in types according to the taxonomy of KEGG from animals to bacteria. Each type of the organisms is marked in Fig. 4 by the number. The factors are ranged according to the frequencies of their appearance in the data set. The factor number one appears in 22% of organisms and the factor number 38 appears in 5% of organisms. For the most factors, the frequencies of their appearance in the organisms are distributed around 0.1. In Fig. 4 the appearance of a given factor in a given organism is marked by the point. Thus, the frequency of appearance of each factor in the data set corresponds to the number of points in each horizontal line. Fig. 4 demonstrates that each type of the organisms is characterized by the specific set of factors. For example, animals are characterized by factors 20 and 37, fungi by factor 20, plants by factors

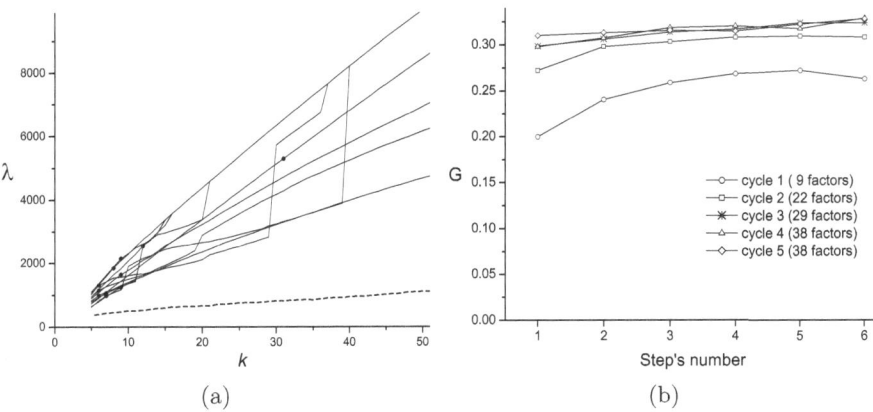

(a)   (b)

Fig. 3. Lyapunov function λ at the first cycle of LANNIA (a) and information gain (b) for the KEGG data set

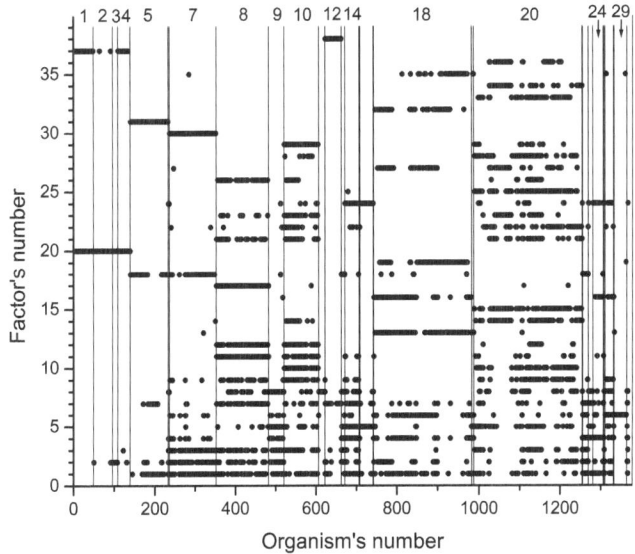

Fig. 4. Distribution of factors over types of organisms. Eukaryotes: 1 – Animals, 2 – Fungi, 3 – Plants, 4 – Protists; Prokaryotes: 5 – Archaea; 6-30 – Bacteria.

2, 20 and 37 and so on. Factor 20 was identified only in eukaria and never in prokaria. Oppositely factor 1 was identified in all types of prokaria but never in eukaria. Thus, the distribution of factors over the types of organisms seems to reflect some peculiarities of their functioning. It is interesting that LANNIA revealed only little effect of specific factors: only 472 proteins over 11451 taken into account have q_j exceeding 0.01. Thus, almost all organisms are completely described by common factors.

6   Discussion

Since LANNIA occurs to be perfect in BFA even with the very noisy artificial data, it was a challenge for us to apply the method to a large set of natural data. One of the important problems in modern biology is to identify functions of proteins in the organisms. When two proteins show correlated patterns of their presence or absence over the organisms, it is assumed that these proteins are also functionally correlated. Thus, revealing sets of the proteins coherently appeared in different organisms may facilitate the search for the functional modules in the genome structure. Since the concept of the genome functional modularity is completely compatible with the BFA generative model, we chose for LANNIA application the largest genome database KEGG [8], containing fully sequenced genomes of 1368 organisms. LANNIA revealed 38 factors which happened to be reasonably distributed over organisms so that each type of organisms contains the specific set of factors. The total information gain amounts to 0.32. The high information gain, first, confirms the hypothesis of the genome modular structure and, second, the high efficiency of LANNIA in processing natural data. The analysis of factor contents and their relation to known metabolic pathways is out of our competence and is not discussed here. However, we believe that the results obtained will attract the attention of genome researchers to BFA methods and, particularly, to LANNIA.

References

1. Frolov, A.A., Husek, D., Muraviev, I.P., Polyakov, P.Y.: Boolean factor analysis by attractor neural network. IEEE Transactions on Neural Networks 18(3), 698–707 (2007)
2. Frolov, A.A., Husek, D., Polyakov, P.Y.: Recurrent neural network based Boolean factor analysis and its application to automatic terms and documents categorization. IEEE Transactions on Neural Networks 20(7), 1073–1086 (2009)
3. Frolov, A., Husek, D., Polyakov, P.: Estimation of Boolean Factor Analysis Performance by Informational Gain. In: Snášel, V., Szczepaniak, P.S., Abraham, A., Kacprzyk, J. (eds.) Advances in Intelligent Web Mastering - 2. AISC, vol. 67, pp. 83–94. Springer, Heidelberg (2010)
4. Foldiak, P.: Forming sparse representations by local anti-hebbian learning. Biological Cybernetics 64, 165–170 (1990)
5. Pellegrini, M., Marcotte, E., Thompson, M., Eisenberg, D., Yeates, T.: Assigning protein functions by comparative genome analysis: protein phylogenetic profiles. Proceedings of the National Academy of Sciences of the United States of America 96(8), 4285 (1999)
6. Von Mering, C., Krause, R., Snel, B., Cornell, M., Oliver, S., Fields, S., Bork, P.: Comparative assessment of large-scale data sets of protein–protein interactions. Nature 417(6887), 399–403 (2002)
7. Ravasz, E., Somera, A., Mongru, D., Oltvai, Z., Barabási, A.: Hierarchical organization of modularity in metabolic networks. Science 297(5586), 1551 (2002)
8. Kanehisa, M., Goto, S., Kawashima, S., Nakaya, A.: The KEGG databases at GenomeNet. Nucleic Acids Research 30(1), 42 (2002)

Pruning Feedforward Neural Network Search Space Using Local Lipschitz Constants

Zaiyong Tang[1], Kallol Bagchi[2], Youqin Pan[1], and Gary J. Koehler[3]

[1] Dept. Marketing & Decision Sciences, Bertolon School of Business,
Salem State University, Salem, MA 01970, USA
[2] Dept. of Information & Decision Sciences, University of Texas at El Paso
El Paso, TX 79968, USA
[3] Dept. of Decision & Information Sciences, University of Florida
Gainesville, FL. 32611, USA

Abstract. Combination of backpropagation with global search algorithms such as genetic algorithm (GA) and particle swarm optimization (PSO) has been deployed to improve the efficacy of neural network training. However, those global algorithms suffer the curse of dimensionality. We propose a new approach that focuses on the topology of the solution space. Our method prunes the search space by using the Lipschitzian property of the criterion function. We have developed procedures that efficiently compute local Lipschitz constants over subsets of the weight space. Those Local Lipschitz constants can be used to compute lower bounds on the optimal solution.

Keywords: Feedforward neural networks, Lipschitz constant, search space.

1 Introduction

The backpropagation (BP) algorithm has been a widely used in training algorithm for feedforward neural networks (FNNs) [1]. However, the algorithm has some fundamental limitations. First of all, BP training may fail to converge. Secondly, many implementations of BP use gradient descent based search. In such cases BP may reach only a local minimum solution when it does converge. The local minimum may not represent an acceptable solution. Another often cited shortcoming of the BP algorithm is that it is generally slow and its performance may be inconsistent and unpredictable [2].

Evolutionary techniques have been developed to overcome the problem of solutions being trapped to local minima [3]. Genetic algorithm is a global optimization approach inspired by the process of natural evolution. Particle swarm optimization (PSO) [4] is another recently developed technique that searches global optimal solutions by evolving a swarm of particles. Each particle position represents a candidate solution, and the particles move in the solution space guided by their own best known positions and the best known position of the population. However, those evolutionary algorithms often suffer from the curse of dimensionality. That is, their performance

J. Wang, G.G. Yen, and M.M. Polycarpou (Eds.): ISNN 2012, Part I, LNCS 7367, pp. 11–20, 2012.

deteriorates quickly as the dimension of the search space increases. In order to improve the efficiency, many researchers have developed hybrid approaches that combine global and local search algorithms [5]. One of the advantages of the hybrid approaches is that evolutionary algorithms can be used to optimize the structure as well as the weights of the neural networks [6].

Another direction in searching for global optimal solution is to apply traditional global optimization methods to neural network training. Optimization of neural network weights is NP-complete [7]. Thus, obtaining global optimal solutions in practice is difficult. We need methods to explore the structure of the search space and guide the search process that converges effectively to the global optima. There has been scant research on exploring structure of the search space. Flores et al. notice that the search space grows quadratically with the number of variables in neural networks models [8]. They proposed to use statistical analysis to reduce the number of input variables, hence reducing the search space. Rempis and Pasemann suggested using constrained modularization to remove large parts of the search space. However, their focus is on the network topology rather than the weight space [9].

In this paper, we focus on the property of the search space. We show that an FNN is Lipschitzian. Thus various Lipschitz optimization methods (e.g., [10]) can be applied to neural network training. Lipschitz constants can be used in a branch-and-bound framework to compute lower bounds on the optimal solution within a current subset of weights [11]. We have developed procedures to compute Lipschitz constant over a given weight space. We show that by exploiting the structure of FNNs and the properties of the sigmoid activation function, computation of local Lipschitz constant can be carried out efficiently. Local Lipschitz constants can be used in a branch-and-bound framework to compute lower bounds to the optimal solution. They can also be used to identify subregions in the weight space that do not contain promising solutions.

2   An FNN Is Lipschitzian

Lipschitz optimization deals with the global optimization of a wide class of functions—the Lipschitz functions. In the following, we first give the definition of Lipschitz functions. Then we show that the standard sum-of-square error (SSE) criterion function of an FNN is Lipschitzian.

Definition 2.1. (Lipschitz function) A continuous function $F:M \rightarrow R$, $M \subseteq R^S$ is a Lipschitz function if there exists a constant $L = L(F,M) > 0$ such that

$$|F(x) - F(y)| \leq L \|x\text{-}y\|, \ \forall x, y \in M.$$

L is called a Lipschitz constant.

An FNN is trained using P known examples comprised of inputs x_p and targets t_p, both assumed to have all their components normalized over the interval [0,1].

Training attempts to minimize the sum of squared differences of the output computed by the FNN, o_p, with the target outputs, t_p:

$$F = \frac{1}{2} \sum_p \sum_k (t_{pk} - o_{pk})^2 .$$

Let $F(w, X)$ be the criterion function of an FNN, $w \in W$, where W is the weight set (We assume W is compact), and X is the training set. Since $F(w, X)$ is continuously differentiable, $F(w, X)$ is Lipschitzian if

$$L = \max \{ \| \nabla_w F(w, X) \| \mid w \in W \}$$

is finite.

Proposition 2.1. The standard sum of squared error (SSE) criterion function of a feedforward neural network with linear transfer function and sigmoid activation function is a Lipschitz function. (Proof can be requested from the authors).

3   Estimating the Lipschitz Constant of an FNN

Knowing the Lipschitz constant of a function F provides a way of computing lower bounds on the global minimum of F. Suppose we want to minimize F over M, let $\delta (M) \equiv \max \{ \| x - y \| \mid x, y \in M \}$ be the diameter of M. From the definition of Lipschitz function, we have

$$F(y) \geq F(x) - L \| x - y \| \geq F(x) - L\delta(M), \quad \forall x, y \in M .$$

If $F(x)$ is known for some $x \in M$, then $F(x) - L\delta(M)$ gives a lower bound to the global minimum of F over M.

Lemma 3.1. Let $x \in R^n$, and $F(x) = f(g(x))$, where $f:R^m \rightarrow R$, is Lipschitzian with Lipschitz constant L_f, and $g:R^n \rightarrow R^m$ with components g_i, $i=1,2,...,m$ being Lipschitzian with Lipschitz constants L_{g_i}. Then $F(x)$ has a Lipschitz constant L_F given by $L_F = L_f \sum_{i=1}^{m} L_{g_i}$.

3.1   One Hidden Layer with a Single Output

For a single-output FNN with one hidden layer, the output of the network is

$$o = f(w, x) = f\left(\sum_{j}^{h} w_j f_j \left(\sum_i w_{ij} x_{ij} + w_{0j} \right) + w_0 \right)$$

where h is the number of hidden units, and f_j's are activation functions in the hidden layer. Note that the output o can be written as a composite function $o = f(g(w, x))$, where

$$g = \sum_j^h w_j f_j \left(\sum_i w_{ij} x_{ij} + w_{0j} \right) + w_0.$$

Applying Lemma 3.1, we have

$$L_o = L_f L_g.$$

L_f is given by

$$L_f = \max \| \nabla_g f(w, x) \|$$
$$= \max \gamma f(1 - f), \ \forall w \in W$$

where γ is the learning rate. The function g can be rewritten as $g(f^H)$, where $g : R^h \to R$ transfers the hidden layer output to the output layer input. g can be written as

$$g = w_H f^H + w_o$$

where w_H is a vector of weights between the hidden layer and the output layer, and w_0 is the output unit bias. $f^H : R^n \to R^h$ maps the output from the input layer to the input of the hidden layer. The components of f^H are given by

$$f_j^H = f_j \left(\sum_i w_{ij} x_{ij} + w_{0j} \right), \quad j = 1, 2, ..., h.$$

Applying Lemma 3.1, we have

$$L_g = L_{g_o} \sum_j^h L_{f_j^H}$$

where L_{g_o} is given by

$$L_{g_o} = \max \| \nabla_f g \|$$
$$= \max \left(1 + \sum_j^h f_j^2 \right)^{\frac{1}{2}}.$$

Note that f_j^H in the hidden layer is equivalent to the output function of an FNN without a hidden layer. Hence, $L_{f_j^H}$ can be computed by

$$L_{f_j^H} = \max \gamma f_j (1 - f_j) \left(1 + \sum_i x_i^2 \right)^{\frac{1}{2}}.$$

Putting the above together, we have, for a single hidden layer FNN,

$$L_o = \max \gamma f (1-f) \max \left(1 + \sum_j^h f_j^2\right)^{\frac{1}{2}} \sum_j^h \max \gamma f_j (1 - f_j) \left(1 + \sum_i x_i^2\right)^{\frac{1}{2}} \tag{1}$$

and

$$L_{F_p} = \max |t_p - o_p| L_{o_p}, \quad \forall w \in W,$$

We observe that f and the f_j's are functions of the weights and maximizations are taken over the whole weight space, although, with the layered structure, the f_j's depend only on the hidden layer weights.

Recall that $L_F = \sum_p L_{F_p}$, thus

$$L_F = \sum_p \max |t_p - o_p| \max \gamma f (1-f) \max \left(1 + \sum_j^h f_j^2\right)^{\frac{1}{2}} \sum_j^h \max \gamma f_j (1 - f_j) \left(1 + \sum_i x_i^2\right)^{\frac{1}{2}} \tag{2}$$

3.2   Multiple Output Units and Hidden Layers

Let k be the index for the output neurons, then for each output neuron o_k, we have

$$L_{o_k} = \max \gamma f_k (1-f_k) \max \left(1 + \sum_j^h f_j^2\right)^{\frac{1}{2}} \sum_j^h \max \gamma f_j (1 - f_j) \left(1 + \sum_i x_i^2\right)^{\frac{1}{2}} \tag{3}$$

Consider the criterion function

$$F = \sum_p F_p = \frac{1}{2} \sum_p \sum_k (t_{pk} - o_{pk})^2$$

For each training pattern p, $F_p = f_s(f_o)$, where $f_s : R^K \rightarrow R$ maps the network output to a performance measure, and $f_o : R^h \rightarrow R^K$ maps the hidden layer output to the input to the output layer. Observe that each component of f_o is equivalent to the output function of a three layer FNN with a single output, the case discussed in the Section 3.1. Let o_k, $k = 1, 2, ..., K$ denote the component function of f_o, o_k is Lipschitzian with Lipschitz constant L_{o_k} given by Equation (3). By Lemma 3.1 the Lipschitz constant for F_p is

$$L_{F_p} = L_{f_s} \sum_k L_{o_k}$$

where L_{f_s} is given by

$$L_{f_s} = \max \| \nabla_o F_p \|$$

$$= \max \left(\sum_k (t_{pk} - o_{pk})^2 \right)^{\frac{1}{2}}$$

Thus for the criterion function F, we have a Lipschitz constant of

$$L_F = \sum_p \max\left(\sum_k (t_{pk} - o_{pk})^2\right)^{\frac{1}{2}} \sum_k L_{o_k} .$$ (4)

Extension of the procedure to estimating a Lipschitz constant for an FNN with more than one hidden layer can be carried out by applying the basic lemmas recursively, as illustrated above.

4   Computing Local Lipschitz Constant

The procedures outlined in Section 3 allow us to easily compute Lipschitz constant over subsets of the weight space. For clarity of exposition, we will consider computing the Lipschitz constant of a three layer FNN with a single output unit. The extension of this case to a general FNN is straight forward as discussed in the previous section. Using Equation (1), we can compute the Lipschitz constant of the criterion function with a given training pattern p by

$$L_o = \max \gamma f(1-f) \max\left(1 + \sum_j^h f_j^2\right)^{\frac{1}{2}} \sum_j^h \max \gamma f_j (1-f_j)\left(1 + \sum_i x_i^2\right)^{\frac{1}{2}}$$

$$L_{F_p} = \max |t_p - o_p| L_{o_p}, \ \forall w \in W$$

Hence four maximization problems need to be solved over a given weight subset. Solving those problems may seem to be difficult as the functions are nonlinear and nonconvex. However, by exploiting the properties of the sigmoid activation function and the special structure of the FNN, we can effectively solve those problems over a weight subset, when the weight subset is a hyper-rectangle in the weight space.

Let $W_{PE} \subseteq W \subset R^s$ (PE stands for partition element) be a hyper-rectangle over which L_{F_p} is to be computed. Also, let $\overline{w}$ and $\underline{w}$ be the upper vertex and the lower vertex of W_{PE}, respectively. $\overline{w}$ and $\underline{w}$ are defined as

$$\overline{w} \equiv \{\overline{w} \in W_{PE} \mid \overline{w}_i \geq w_i, i = 1,2,...,s, \forall w \in W_{PE}\}$$
$$\underline{w} \equiv \{\underline{w} \in W_{PE} \mid \underline{w}_i \leq w_i, i = 1,2,...,s, \forall w \in W_{PE}\}.$$ (5)

Lemma 4.1. For a standard sigmoid function $f(z) = 1/(1+e^{-z})$ over a finite interval $[a, b] \in R$, the maximum of its gradient (a Lipschitz constant) L_f is given by

$$L_f = f(1-f) = \begin{cases} f'(a) \ if \ a > 0 \\ f'(b) \ if \ b < 0 \\ 1/4 \ if \ a \leq 0 \leq b \end{cases}$$ (6)

Now let us consider the four maximization problems one at a time. First, consider the problem

$$P_1 = \max \gamma f_j (1 - f_j) \left(1 + \sum_i x_i^2 \right)^{\frac{1}{2}}.$$

For a given input pattern x_p, $\left(1 + \sum_i x_i^2 \right)^{\frac{1}{2}}$ is a constant. Since f_j, $j = 1, 2, ..., h$ are independent of each other, the maximization problem can be solved independently for each j. By Lemma 4.1, maximizing $f_j(1 - f_j)$ is determined by the interval $[a_j, b_j]$, where

$$a_j = \min \gamma \sum_i w_{ij} x_i + w_{0j}, \quad \forall w \in W_{PE},$$

and

$$b_j = \max \gamma \sum_i w_{ij} x_i + w_{0j}, \quad \forall w \in W_{PE}.$$

Since for each input we have $x \in [0,1]^n$, then

$$a_j = \gamma \sum_i \underline{w}_{ij} x_i + \underline{w}_{0j}$$

$$b_j = \gamma \sum_i \overline{w}_{ij} x_i + \overline{w}_{0j}$$

(7)

Using Lemma 4.1, P_1 is easily computed over W_{PE}.

$$P_1 = \sum_j \left(1 + \sum_i x_i^2 \right)^{\frac{1}{2}} P_{1_j}$$

Let

$$P_2 = \max \left(1 + \sum_j^h f_j^2 (w, x) \right)^{\frac{1}{2}}, \quad \forall w \in W_{PE}.$$

Since the sigmoid function is positive and monotonically increasing, we have

$$P_2 = \left(1 + \sum_j^h f_j^2 (b_j) \right)^{\frac{1}{2}}$$

The third maximization problem is

$$P_3 = \max f(w, x)(1 - f(w, x)), \quad \forall w \in W_{PE}.$$

We have

$$f(w, x) = f \left(\sum_j w_j f_j + w_0 \right),$$

To solve this, we need to partition the current hyper-rectangle into separate sets. Let J be the index set ($J = \{1,2,...,n\}$). We define

$$\overline{J} \equiv \{j \in J \mid \overline{w}_j > 0\}$$
$$\overline{J}' \equiv \{j \in J \mid \overline{w}_j \leq 0\}$$
$$\underline{J} \equiv \{j \in J \mid \underline{w}_j > 0\}$$
$$\underline{J}' \equiv \{j \in J \mid \underline{w}_j \leq 0\}$$

Then the input interval for f can be computed by

$$a = \gamma \sum_{j \in \underline{J}} \underline{w}_j f_j(a_j) + \sum_{j \in \underline{J}'} \underline{w}_j f_j(b_j) + \underline{w}_0$$
$$b = \gamma \sum_{j \in \overline{J}} \overline{w}_j f_j(b_j) + \sum_{j \in \overline{J}'} \overline{w}_j f_j(a_j) + \overline{w}_0$$

Note that the above equations are based on the facts that $f_j \in (0,1)$, and f_j is monotonically increasing. After the interval $[a, b]$ is computed, P_3 is determined by (6).

For the fourth maximization problem, we have

$$P_4 = \max |t_p - o_p(w,x)|, \ \forall w \in W_{PE}.$$

Notice that if the target values are binary, we will have

$$P_4 = \begin{cases} t_p - f(a) & \text{if } t_p = 1 \\ f(b) - t_p & \text{if } t_p = 0 \end{cases}$$

Even if the target value is not binary, computing P_4 would be easy since the interval $[a, b]$ used for P_3 could be used in a simple calculation, as only the end points of the interval need to be evaluated. Thus we have

$$L_o = P_1 P_2 P_3$$
$$L_{F_p} = P_4 L_o$$

5   Illustrative Example

Let us apply the above procedure to estimating the Lipschitz constant of the 2x2x1 XOR network. Table 1 shows Lipschitz constants computed for a number of subregions. Note that for the 2x2x1 XOR network, there are 9 adjustable weights (including both connection strength and bias).

Table 1. Lipschitz Constants over Weight Subsets

Weight Subset	Hyper-rectangle vertices	Lipschitz Constant
W_0	LV=(-10 -10 -10 -10 -10 -10 -10 -10 -10) UV=(10 10 10 10 10 10 10 10 10)	1.20388
W_1	LV=(0 0 0 0 0 0 -10 -10 -10) UV=(10 10 10 10 10 10 10 10 10)	0.89769
W_2	LV=(5 0 0 0 0 0 0 0 0) UV=(10 10 10 10 10 10 10 10 10)	0.01584
W_3	LV=(5 0 0 5 0 0 0 0 0) UV=(10 5 5 10 10 10 10 10 10)	0.00793
W_4	LV=(0 5 5 5 5 0 5 5 0) UV=(5 10 10 10 10 5 10 10 5)	0.00792
W_5	LV=(0 5 0 0 0 0 0 0 0) UV=(5 10 5 10 10 10 10 10 10)	0.17889
W_6	LV=(0 5 0 5 0 0 0 0 0) UV=(5 10 5 10 5 10 10 10 10)	0.01167
W_7	LV=(0 0 0 0 0 0 -5 -5 -5) UV=(5 5 5 5 5 5 5 5 5)	0.89769
W_8	LV=(2.5 2.5 0 0 0 0 0 0 0) UV=(5 5 5 5 5 5 5 5 5)	0.05438
W_9	LV=(2.5 2.5 2.5 2.5 0 0 0 0 0) UV=(5 5 5 5 5 5 5 5 5)	0.00880
W_10	LV=(-5 -5 -5 -5 -5 -5 -5 -5 -5) UV=(0 0 0 0 0 0 0 0 0)	0.74146

The results in Table 1 show that the local Lipschitz constants vary significantly over different weight subregions. These subregions are hyper-rectangles identified by the lower vertex (LV) and upper vertex (UV). With $W\_0 \equiv \{w \in R^9 \mid -10 \leq w_i \leq 10, i = 1, 2, ..., 9\}$, the local Lipschitz constant (1.20388) is equal (to five decimal places) to the loose Lipschitz constant computed by Equation 5. However, for some still relatively large weight subsets (e.g., W_3, W_4, W_9) the Lipschitz constants are quite small. Those local Lipschitz constants may be used to estimate lower bounds on the global criterion function. They may also be used in identifying subregions in the weight space that do not contain promising global optimal solutions, hence search space can be reduced

6   Conclusions

We have shown that the sum-of-squared error criterion function of a feedforward neural network is Lipschitzian. The special structure of feedforward neural networks makes it possible to estimate the Lipschitz constant in a recursive procedure. Furthermore, by exploiting the structure of the network and the properties of the sigmoid activation function, we have shown that the computation of local Lipschitz constant can be easily carried out.

Local Lipschitz constant can be used either to compute lower bounds on the optimal solution, or to describe approximately the topology of weight subsets. It is well known that the error surface of a feedforward neural network is composed mainly be flat plateaus and some deep valleys that contain local or global minimum solutions [12]. Our procedure provides a way to identify those flat areas and may be used to reduce the search space in neural network training. Implementation of the local Lipschitz constant procedure within a branch-and-bound framework can lead to a global convergent training algorithm for feedforward neural networks.

References

1. Rumelhart, D.E., Hinton, G.G., Williams, R.J.: Learning internal representations by error propagation. In: Parallel Distributed Processing: Exploration in the Microstructure of Cognition, pp. 318–362. MIT Press, Cambridge (1986)
2. Duch, W., Korczak, J.: Optimization and global minimization methods suitable for neural networks. Neural Computing Surveys 2, 163–212 (1999)
3. Yao, X.: Evolving artificial neural networks. Proceedings of the IEEE 89(9), 1423–1447 (1999)
4. Kennedy, J., Eberhart, R.: Particle swarm optimization. In: Proc. of IEEE Int. Conf. on Neural Networks, Perth, Australia, Piscataway, NJ, pp. 1942–1948 (1995)
5. Malviya, R., Pratihar, D.K.: Tuning of neural networks using particle swarm optimization to model MIG welding process. Swarm and Evolutionary Computation 1, 223–235 (2011)
6. Georgiopoulos, M., Li, C., Kocakb, T.: Learning in the feed-forward random neural network: A critical review. Performance Evaluation 68, 361–384 (2011)
7. Duch, W., Korczak, J.: Optimization and global minimization methods suitable for neural networks. In: Neural Computing Surveys, vol. 2, pp. 163–212. Lawrence Erlbaum Associates Inc., USA (1999)
8. Flores, J.J., Rodriguez, H., Graff, M.: Reducing the Search Space in Evolutive Design of ARIMA and ANN Models for Time Series Prediction. In: Sidorov, G., Hernández Aguirre, A., Reyes García, C.A. (eds.) MICAI 2010, Part II. LNCS (LNAI), vol. 6438, pp. 325–336. Springer, Heidelberg (2010)
9. Rempis, C.W., Pasemann, F.: Search Space Restriction of Neuro-Evolution Through Constrained Modularization of Neural Networks. In: Madani, K. (ed.) Artificial Neural Networks and Intelligent Information Processing, pp. 13–22 (2010)
10. Horst, R., Tuy, H.: Global Optimization: Deterministic Approaches. Springer, Berlin (1990)
11. Tang, Z., Koehler, G.J.: Deterministic global optimal FNN training algorithms. Neural Networks 7(2), 301–311 (1994)
12. Hush, D.R., Salas, J.M., Horne, B.: Error surfaces for Multi-layer perceptrons. In: International Joint Conference on Neural Networks, vol. 1, pp. 759–764. INNS/IEEE, Seattle (1991)

Context FCM-Based Radial Basis Function Neural Networks with the Aid of Fuzzy Clustering

Wook-Dong Kim, Sung-Kwun Oh, and Hyun-Ki Kim

Department of Electrical Engineering, The University of Suwon,
San 2-2 Wau-ri, Bongdam-eup, Hwaseong-si, Gyeonggi-do, 445-743, South Korea
ohsk@suwon.ac.kr

Abstract. In this paper, we introduce architecture of context FCM-based Radial Basis Function Neural Networks realized with the aid of information granulation using clustering algorithm based on FCM and context FCM. The output space is defined by FCM while the input space a clustered by means of context FCM. The connection weights of proposed model are represented as three types of polynomials. Weighted Least Square Estimation (WLSE) is used to estimate the coefficients of polynomial (connection weight). The performance of the proposed model are illustrated with by using two kinds of representative numerical dataset such as Automobile Miles per Gallon, (MPG dataset) and Boston Housing dataset and their results are compared with those reported in the previous studies.

Keywords: polynomial Radial Basis Function Neural Networks, K-means clustering, Particle Swarm Optimization, Differential Evolution algorithm.

1 Introduction

Dimensionality issues have emerged as an important topic in neuro-computing given our ultimate challenge to deal with real-world problems of high dimensionality [1]. In particular, nonlinear techniques using radial basis function neural networks received a great deal of attention. The radial basis function neural networks (RBF NNs) in neural network have been known to NNs is that form a unifying link among many different research area such as function approximation, regularization, noisy interpolation and pattern recognition. The major development direction and design strategies are introduced to make more efficient RBF NNs. An alternative dealing with the formation of the receptive fields on a basis of some experimental data comes through the use of various clustering techniques including its commonly encountered representatives such as K-Means and Fuzzy C-Means.

In our study, we introduce the architecture of context FCM-based RBF neural networks realized as the extended architecture of the conventional RBF NNs. The context values of context FCM are obtain through output space clustered by FCM.

J. Wang, G.G. Yen, and M.M. Polycarpou (Eds.): ISNN 2012, Part I, LNCS 7367, pp. 21–28, 2012.

The three types of polynomials are considered as connection weight such as linear, quadratic and modified quadratic. The coefficients of polynomial are obtained by Weighted Least Square Estimation.

Section 2 describes the architecture of the context FCM-based RBF NNs and section 3 presents a learning method applied to the construction of proposed model. Section 4 presents the experimental results. Finally, some conclusions are drawn in Section 5.

2   Context FCM-Based p-RBF Neural Networks

2.1   Architecture of Proposed Context FCM-Based p-RBF Neural Networks

The proposed context FCM-based p-RBF neural networks come as the combined structure of the conventional RBF NNs and clustering algorithm. As the context FCM algorithm take into the relationships between the regions of the input space and the output space, it helps the proposed model obtain the more stable and more precise output.

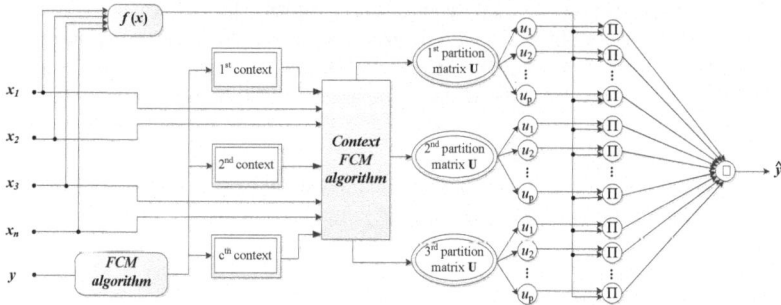

Fig. 1. Architecture of the context FCM-based RBF Neural Networks

The hidden layer of proposed model consists of context FCM algorithm. The partition matrix of context FCM becomes to be output of receptive fields of conventional RBF neural networks. Before using the context FCM directly, the outputs should be newly defined into context value to apply to context FCM algorithm. Although it exist a variety of methods to transform outputs into context values, the FCM algorithm is used in this studies.

The values of partition matrix $\mathbf{F}(\mathbf{y})$ of FCM are equals to context values of context FCM.

$$\mathbf{F}(\mathbf{y}) = \left\{ u_{ik} \in [0,1], \quad \sum_{i=1}^{c} u_{ik} = 1 \, \forall k, \quad 0 < \sum_{k=1}^{N} u_{ik} < N \, \forall i \right\} \qquad (1)$$

where, $i(i=1,\dots c)$ is the number of clusters; $k(k=1,\dots,N)$ denotes the number of data.

The detail procedure of context FCM algorithm is deal with the Section 2.1.

The connection weight of proposed model, three types of polynomials are considered. These are linear, quadratic and modified quadratic as follows.

Linear;
$$f_i(\mathbf{x}) = a_{i0} + \sum_{j=1}^{m} a_{ij} x_j \tag{2}$$

Quadratic;
$$f_i(\mathbf{x}) = a_{i0} + \sum_{j=1}^{m} a_{ij} x_j + \sum_{j=1}^{m} a_i(m+1) \cdot x_j^2 + a_{(2m+1)} x_1 x_2 + \cdots + a_{(m(m+3)/2)} x_{(m-1)} x_m \tag{3}$$

Modified Quadratic;
$$f_i(\mathbf{x}) = a_{i0} + \sum_{j=1}^{m} a_{ij} x_j + a_{(2m+1)} x_1 x_2 + \cdots + a_{(m(m+1)/2)} x_{(m-1)} x_m \tag{4}$$

The coefficients of the polynomials are evaluated by using WLSE. The output of each local model has the following form:

$$\hat{y}_i = \sum_{i=1}^{c} \hat{u}_i(\mathbf{x}) f_i(\mathbf{x}) \tag{5}$$

Where, $\hat{u}_i(\mathbf{x})$ is the ith value of partition matrix of context FCM, $f_i(\mathbf{x})$ is the ith polynomial function of connection weight.

2.2   Context Fuzzy C-Means Clustering Algorithm

The context-based clustering supporting the design of information granules is completed in the space of the input data while the build of the clusters is guided by a collection of some predefined fuzzy sets (so-called contexts) defined in the output space, cf. [3-4]. This helps reveal the relationships between the regions of the input space and the output space.

Let us introduce a family of the partition matrices induced by the j-th context and denote it by $\mathbf{U}(F_j)$,

$$\hat{\mathbf{U}}(F_j) = \left\{ \hat{u}_{ik} \in [0,1], \ \sum_{i=1}^{p} \hat{u}_{ik} = f_{jk} \ \forall k, \ 0 < \sum_{k=1}^{N} \hat{u}_{ik} < N \ \forall i \right\} \tag{6}$$

Recall that $p(2 \le p < N)$ is the number of clusters in input data and f_{jk} denotes a value of partition matrix of the j-th context obtained by FCM clustering.

The objective function of the context-based clustering is defined as follows:

$$V = \sum_{i=1}^{p} \sum_{k=1}^{N} \hat{u}_{ik}^{m} \| \mathbf{x}_k - \mathbf{z}_i \|^2 \tag{7}$$

where m>1 is a fuzzification coefficient (fuzzification factor).

The minimization of V is realized under the constraints expressed by (6) so in essence we end up with "C" separate clustering tasks implied by the respective contexts. Briefly speaking we have

$$Min\ V\ subject\ to\ \hat{\mathbf{U}}(F_j),\quad j = 1, 2, \cdots, C \tag{8}$$

The minimization of V as completed by the context-based FCM is realized by iteratively updating the values of the partition matrix and the prototypes.

The update of the partition matrix is completed as follows

$$\hat{u}_{ik} = \frac{f_{jk}}{\displaystyle\sum_{l=1}^{p}\left(\frac{\|\mathbf{x}_k - \mathbf{z}_i\|}{\|\mathbf{x}_k - \mathbf{z}_l\|}\right)^{2/(m-1)}}, i = 1, 2, \cdots, p,\quad k = 1, 2, \cdots, N \tag{9}$$

The prototypes ($\mathbf{z}_1$, $\mathbf{z}_2$, ..., $\mathbf{z}_c$) are calculated in the following form

$$\mathbf{z}_i = \frac{\displaystyle\sum_{k=1}^{N} \hat{u}_{ik}^m \mathbf{x}_k}{\displaystyle\sum_{k=1}^{N} \hat{u}_{ik}^m} \tag{10}$$

Completing the context-based clustering for all contexts, the partition matrix of context FCM is directly used as the output (fitness) of receptive fields of conventional RBF neural networks.

2.3   The Learning Method of WLSE

The weights between hidden layer and output layer are concerned with the estimation of the coefficients of the polynomial of the local model [2]. In the WLSE, we estimate the optimal coefficients of the model through the minimization of the objective function E.

$$Error(E) = \sum_{k=1}^{n}\sum_{i=1}^{c} \hat{\mathbf{U}}_i \cdot (y_k - f_i(\mathbf{x}))^2 \tag{11}$$

This matrix captures the activation levels with respect to the ith node. In this sense, we can consider the weighting factor matrix as activation levels of the corresponding local model. The optimal coefficients of the polynomial of ith local model are described as follows

$$\mathbf{a}_i = (\mathbf{X}^T \hat{\mathbf{U}}_i \mathbf{X})^{-1} \mathbf{X}^T \hat{\mathbf{U}}_i \mathbf{Y} \tag{12}$$

Notice that the coefficients of the polynomial of each local model have been computed independently using a subset of training data. Also, the computation can be implemented in parallel meaning that the computing overhead becomes independent from the number of cluster.

3   Experimental Results

In all experiments, we used re-sampling Cross-Validation that randomly divide data-set into the training (60%) and the testing (40%). To come up with a quantitative evaluation of the resulting neural network, we use the standard performance index of the Root Mean Square Error (RMSE) as follows (13).

$$RMSE = \sqrt{\frac{1}{n}\sum_{k=1}^{n}(y_k - \hat{y}_k)^2}$$ (13)

3.1   Automobile Miles Per Gallon Dataset (MPG)

We consider the well-known automobile MPG data (http://archive.ics.uci.edu/ml/datasets/auto+mpg) with the output being the automobile's fuel consumption expressed in miles per gallon. This dataset includes 392 input-output pairs (after removing incomplete data points). The number of input variables is 7 such as cylinder, displacement, horse power, weight, acceleration, model year, origin.

Table 1 shows the performance index of the proposed model. To assess an impact of the varying granularity of information, we carried out experiments by varying the number of contexts and clusters. For details, the clusters imply the number of clusters of FCM to transfer output space into partition matrix of FCM while the contexts describe the number of clusters of context FCM.

Table 1. Performance index of proposed models according to context and cluster

T	No. of contexts (p)	2		3		4	
	No. of clusters (c)	PI	EPI	PI	EPI	PI	EPI
L	2	2.35±0.07	2.87±0.13	**2.08±0.10**	**2.61±0.18**	**1.88±0.11**	**2.46±0.18**
	3	1.84±0.08	2.99±1.37	2.03±0.10	2.65±0.23	1.80±1.11	2.48±0.18
	4	2.25±0.06	2.85±0.20	1.95±0.12	2.69±0.28	1.72±0.13	2.62±0.28
M	2	1.95±0.07	2.89±0.16	1.71±0.08	2.77±0.16	1.47±0.10	2.58±0.10
	3	1.84±0.06	2.93±0.25	1.60±0.09	2.87±0.25	1.35±0.10	2.54±0.18
	4	1.76±0.06	2.95±0.19	1.51±0.08	3.07±0.28	1.25±0.08	2.73±0.24
Q	2	1.95±0.07	3.21±0.37	1.72±0.11	2.99±0.12	1.49±0.10	2.67±0.13
	3	**2.29±0.07**	**2.82±0.15**	1.61±0.12	3.01±0.19	1.38±0.10	2.65±0.22
	4	1.77±0.06	2.95±0.24	1.53±0.12	2.99±0.26	1.30±0.10	2.86±0.19

T : Polynomial type; **L** : Linear; **M** : Modified Quadratic; **Q** : Quadratic;

Fig.2 shows the output of local model expressed by linear combination of the partition matrix of context FCM and polynomial function, in which the coefficient of polynomial function is estimated through WLSE. The final output of model becomes the summation of local models. In particular, the major advantage of WLSE is that the performance of testing dataset is more stable than that of model based on the standard LSE. By considering local output, the WLSE improves the performance of testing dataset up to assigned numbers of clusters.

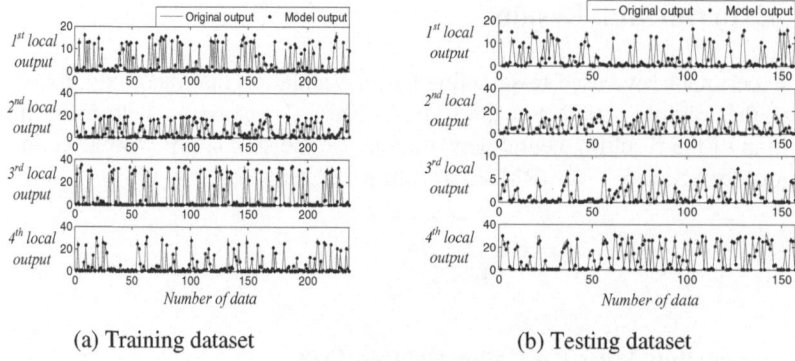

(a) Training dataset   (b) Testing dataset

Fig. 2.   Output of local model (c=2 , p=2, Linear)

Table 2 summarizes the performance of the proposed model when compared with other models. The performance of the best model is the values of PI and EPI are quantified to be 1.88(0.11) and 2.46(0.18), respectively and the optimized architecture of networks are produced by using p=4, c=2, and linear polynomial function.

Table 2. Comparative analysis of the performance of selected model

(AVG±STD)

Model		Number of nodes (rules)	Performance index	
			PI	EPI
RBFNN[5]		36	3.24±0.24	3.62±0.31
RBFNN with context-free clustering[5]		36	3.21±0.21	3.51±0.27
Linguistic modeling [5]	Without optimization	36	3.78±1.52	4.22±1.22
	One-loop optimization	36	2.90±0.52	3.17±1.01
	Multi-step optimization	36	2.86±0.83	3.14±1.01
Single PNN[6]		N/A	2.56±0.15	2.94±0.34
MARS[6]		N/A	2.72±0.10	3.05±0.21
TSK fuzzy model[6]		3	2.75±0.13	2.88±018
Fuzzy ensemble of parallel PNNs[6]		2	2.53±0.15	2.68±0.21
		8	2.51±0.09	2.65±0.13
K-Means based RBF NNs[7]	PSO	4	2.13±0.21	2.91±0.13
	DE	8	2.05±0.12	2.87±0.14
Proposed model	6 (p=3, c=2) Linear		**2.08±0.10**	**2.61±0.18**
	8 (p=4, c=2)		**1.88±0.11**	**2.46±0.18**
	6 (p=2, c=3) Quadratic		**2.29±0.07**	**2.82±0.15**

3.2   Boston Housing Dataset

This data set concerns about real estate in the Boston area .The median value of the house (MEDV) is considered as an output variable. The input variables consist of 13 variables.

Table 3 shows the values of the performance index according to the increase of number of clusters. The increase leads to the improvement of performance for training dataset, while, in case of the testing data set, the decreasing effect of performance takes place.

Table 3. Performance index of the proposed models according to the number of contexts and clusters

T	No. of Contexts / No. of Clusters	2		3		4	
		PI	EPI	PI	EPI	PI	EPI
L	2	2.78±0.19	3.71±0.44	**2.28±0.09**	**3.27±0.34**	**1.85±0.04**	**3.01±0.78**
	3	2.72±0.21	3.63±0.31	2.14±0.09	3.55±0.56	1.78±0.04	3.53±1.19
	4	**2.49±0.14**	**3.25±0.43**	2.10±0.08	3.66±0.75	0.83±0.02	4.23±0.81
M	2	1.49±0.06	4.51±0.85	1.26±0.05	4.57±0.66	1.02±0.03	4.16±0.32
	3	1.42±0.04	4.01±0.35	1.13±0.05	4.52±0.53	0.90±0.04	4.50±0.55
	4	1.32±0.05	4.35±0.51	1.08±0.07	4.56±0.71	0.86±0.04	4.31±0.51
Q	2	1.38±0.04	4.38±0.77	1.16±0.03	4.55±0.60	0.94±0.02	4.08±0.17
	3	1.30±0.03	4.18±0.50	1.03±0.03	4.66±0.58	0.83±0.02	4.23±0.81
	4	1.18±0.02	4.34±0.32	0.97±0.04	5.10±0.50	0.78±0.03	4.40±0.58

T : Polynomial type; **L** : Linear; **M** : Modified Quadratic; **Q** : Quadratic;

Table 4 summarizes the performance of the proposed model when compared with other models. The performance of the best model is the values of PI and EPI are quantified to be 1.85(0.04) and 3.01(0.78), respectively and the optimized architecture of networks are produced by using p=4, c=2, and linear polynomial function.

Table 4. Comparative analysis of the performance of selected model

(AVG±STD)

Model		Number of nodes (rules)	Performance index	
			PI	EPI
RBFNN[5]		25	6.36±0.24	6.94±0.31
RBFNN with context-free clustering[5]		25	5.52±0.25	6.91±0.45
Linguistic modeling [5]	Without optimization	25	5.21±0.12	6.14±0.28
	One-loop optimization	25	4.80±0.52	5.22±0.58
	Multi-step optimization	25	4.12±0.35	5.32±0.96
Single PNN[6]		N/A	3.72±0.35	5.54±3.46
MARS[6]		N/A	3.25±0.10	4.19±0.32
TSK fuzzy model[6]		3	3.67±0.26	4.27±0.46
Fuzzy ensemble of parallel PNNs[6]		11	2.60±0.13	3.36±0.41
		4	3.31±0.20	3.69±0.53
K-Means based RBF NNs[7]	PSO	6	1.99±0.04	3.97±0.75
	DE	8	2.02±0.09	3.83±0.79
Proposed model		6 (p=3, c=2)	**2.28±0.09**	**3.27±0.34**
		8 (p=4, c=2) Linear	**1.85±0.04**	**3.01±0.78**
		8 (p=2, c=4)	**2.49±0.14**	**3.25±0.43**

4   Concluding Remarks

In this paper, we have proposed context FCM-based Radial Basis Function neural networks. The proposed model is the extended architecture of conventional RBF NNs. The context values of context FCM are obtain through output space clustered by FCM. It helps reveal the relationships between the regions of the input space and the output space. The different number of the clusters for each context is useful in focusing attention on the specificity of models formed for particular regions of the input space. The connection weight of proposed model is represented as three types of polynomial, unlike in most conventional RBFNN constructed with constant as connection weight. Weighted Least Square Estimation (WLSE) is used to estimate the coefficients of polynomial. An effective mechanism of using variable number of clusters for each context deemed to be an effective design vehicle producing a meaningful distribution of information granules. .

Acknowledgements. This work(Grants No. 00047478) was supported by Business for Cooperative R&D between Industry, Academy, and Research Institute funded by Korea Small and Medium Business Administration in 2011 and also supported by the GRRC program of Gyeonggi province [GRRC SUWON2011-B2, Center for U-city Security & Surveillance Technology].

References

1. Frolov, A.A., Husek, D., Muraviev, I.P., Polyakov, P.Y.: A Boolean factor analysis by attractor neural network. IEEE Trans. Neural Network 3, 698–707 (2007)
2. Lloyd, S.P.: Least squares quantization in PCM. IEEE Trans. On Inf. Theory 28, 129–137 (1982)
3. Pedrycz, W.: Conditional fuzzy c-means. Pattern Recognition. Letters 17(6), 625–631 (1996)
4. Pedrycz, W., Kwak, K.C.: The development of incremental models. IEEE Trans. Fuzzy Systems 15(3), 507–518 (2007)
5. Pedrycz, W., Kwak, K.C.: Linguistic Models as a Framework of User-Centric System Modeling. IEEE Trans. 36, 727–745 (2006)
6. Roh, S.B., Oh, S.K., Pedrycz, W.: A fuzzy ensemble of parallel polynomial neural networks with information granules formed by fuzzy clustering. Knowledge-Based Systems 23, 202–219 (2010)
7. Oh, S.K., Kim, W.D., Pedrycz, W., Joo, S.J.: Design of K-means clustering-based polynomial radial basis function neural networks (pRBF NNs) realized with the aid of particle swarm optimization and differential evolution. Neurocomputing 78(1), 121–132 (2012)

Modeling Spectral Data Based on Mutual Information and Kernel Extreme Learning Machines

Li-Jie Zhao[1,3], Jian Tang[2,3], and Tian-you Chai[3]

[1] College of Information Engineering, Shenyang University of Chemical Technology,
Shenyang, China
zlj_lunlun@163.com
[2] Unit 92941, PLA, Huludao, China
tjian001@126.com
[3] Research Center of Automation, Northeastern University, Shenyang, China
tychai@mail.neu.edu.cn

Abstract. Effective modeling based on the high dimensional data needs feature selection and fast learning speed. Aim at this problem, a novel modeling approach based on mutual information and extreme learning machines is proposed in this paper. Simple mutual information based feature selection method is integrated with the fast learning kernel based extreme learning machines to obtain better modeling performance. In the method, optimal number of the features and learning parameters of models are selected simultaneously. The simulation results based on the near-infrared spectrum show that the proposed approach has better prediction performance and fast leaning speed.

Keywords: Feature reduction, Mutual information, Extreme learning machines, Spectral data.

1 Introduction

Feature selection has been addressed to solve the "curse of dimensionality" problems when modeling with high dimensional spectral data [1,2], which can avoid over-fitting, resist noise and strengthen prediction performance. Genetic algorithm-partial least square (GA-PLS) using for feature selection has been applied on many spectral data sets, which shows better result [3]. As the random initialization of the GA, the feature selection process has to be performed many times. Moreover, the PLS is inappropriate to capture the nonlinear characteristics. The mutual information (MI) is used to quantitative measure the mutual dependence of the two variables based on the probability theory and information theory. Thus, as one of the features selection method, the MI seems to be more comprehensively studied [4]. However, the popular used MI based method also needs lots of computational consume [5]. A simple MI based feature selection method is used in [6]. However, the MI threshold has to be selected based on the experience.

Many learning algorithm can be used to construct effective nonlinear model with the small number of samples and high dimension data, such as support vector

J. Wang, G.G. Yen, and M.M. Polycarpou (Eds.): ISNN 2012, Part I, LNCS 7367, pp. 29–36, 2012.

machines (SVM). However, the learning speed of SVM is slow and the model parameters are very sensitive to the prediction performance. The least square-support
vector machines (LS-SVM) can simplify the quadratic program (QP) problem of the
SVM to solve a set of linear equations in the sense of sub optimum. Although the
learning speed is improved, the sparse of the SVM is lost, and the sensitivity problem
of the models' learning parameters is not solved. The extreme leaning machines
(ELM)[7] obtained better learning speed than SVM by using the minimal norm least
square method instead of the standard optimization method. However, as the random-
ize initialization of the ELM algorithm, it is not suitable to construct the nonlinear
models with limited small samples. Kernel based ELM solves this problem successfully [8], which demonstrates better robustness with respect to model's parameters.

Therefore, this paper integrates the MI based feature selection and Kernel ELM
based learning algorithm together. The selection of the features and the model's parameter are looked as an optimize problem, whose objective to obtain the best prediction performance by select suitable MI threshold and ELM parameters. The proposed
approach is successfully used in estimating the level of saccharose of an orange juice
from its observed near-infrared spectrum.

2   MI and Kernel ELM Based Modeling Approach

2.1   Feature Selection Based on Mutual Information

In the information theory, entropy is a key measure of the information. As the information entropy can quantify the uncertainty of the random variables and scale the
amount of information shared by them effectively, it has been widely used in many
fields. The entropy in the information theory can be represented as:

$$H(X) = -\sum p(x) \log p(x) . \tag{1}$$

The mutual information (MI) is used to quantitatively measure the mutual dependence
of the two variables based on the probability theory and information theory, which is
defined as:

$$I(Y;X) = \sum\sum p(y,x) \log \frac{p(x,y)}{p(x)p(y)} = H(Y) - H(Y|X) . \tag{2}$$

where, $H(Y|X)$ is the conditional entropy at X is known. It can be calculated as:

$$H(Y|X) = -\sum\sum p(y|x) \log(p(y|x)) . \tag{3}$$

For the continuous random variables, the entropy and MI can be represented as:

$$H(Y|X) = -\sum\sum p(y|x) \log(p(y|x)) . \tag{4}$$

$$H(X) = -\int p(x) \log p(x) dx \tag{5}$$

$$H(\mathbf{Y} \mid \mathbf{X}) = -\iint_{x,y} p(y,x) \log(p(y \mid x)) dxdy \tag{6}$$

$$\mathbf{I}(\mathbf{Y};\mathbf{X}) = \iint_{x,y} p(y,x) \log \frac{p(x,y)}{p(x)p(y)} dxdy \tag{7}$$

Thus, as one of the features selection method, the MI seems to be more comprehensively studied [4]. Mutual information feature select (MIFS) algorithm was proposed in [9]. The MI between the each input feature and output variable are calculated. The input features with the bigger MI are selected, and as the same, the others features have the bigger MI with the selected feature are penalized. Using the greedy search method, the best input sub-set was obtained. Although this method can obtain best feature sub-set, it is time-consuming, especially for high dimensional spectral data. Therefore, a simple method based on MIFS was proposed in [6]. It is used in here: given a threshold value of the MI, if the MI values of the features are higher than threshold value, it is selected. However, how to select the optimal threshold value is a difficulty problem.

2.2   Nonlinear Modeling Based on Kernel ELM

ELM was originally proposed for the single-hidden layer feed forward networks (SLFNs) [7,10] and then extended to the generalized single-hidden layer feed forward network [11,12]. Recently, ELM has been extended to kernel cases and thus become a unifed learning model for feedforward neural networks and kernel learning including SVM [8]. The output of ELM is:

$$f(x) = \sum_{i=1}^{L} \beta_i G(\mathbf{a}_i, b_i, x) = \beta \cdot h(x). \tag{8}$$

where, $g_i = G(\mathbf{a}_i, b_i, x) = g(\mathbf{a}_i \cdot x + b_i)$ denotes the output function of the ith hidden node, $\mathbf{a}_i$ and b_i are the hidden layer parameters; β is the weight vector connecting the ith hidden node; $\mathbf{h}(x) = [G(\mathbf{a}_1, b_1, x), \cdots, G(\mathbf{a}_i, b_i, x)]$ is called the hidden layer feature mapping.

Different from traditional learning algorithms, ELM not only tends to reach the smallest training error but also the smallest norm of output weights. This can be represented as:

$$\begin{aligned} \text{minmize}: \quad & \sum \|\beta \cdot h(x_i) - y_i\|^2 \\ \text{and} \quad & \quad\quad\quad\quad\quad . \\ \text{minmize}: \quad & \|\beta\| \end{aligned} \tag{9}$$

Thus, from the standard optimization theory point of view, the above optimize problem can be solved using the simplified constrained-optimization problem. The objective can be written as [8]:

$$\text{minmize}: \quad L_p = \frac{1}{2}\|\beta\|^2 + C\frac{1}{2}\sum_{i=1}^{N}\xi_i^2 \qquad . \tag{10}$$

$$\text{Subject to}: \quad h(x_i)\beta = y_i - \xi_i \qquad i = 1,\cdots,N.$$

where, ξ_i is the training error; C is a user-specified parameter, which is called cost parameters in this paper.

Based on the KKT theorem, to train ELM is equivalent to solve the following dual optimization problem:

$$L_{P_{ELM}} = \frac{1}{2}\|\beta\|^2 + C\frac{1}{2}\sum_{i=1}^{N}\xi_i^2 - \sum_{i=1}^{N}\alpha_i(\mathbf{h}(x_i)\beta - y_i + \xi_i) \cdot \tag{11}$$

where each Lagrange multiplier α_i corresponds to the *ith* sample. We can have KKT optimal conditions as follows:

$$\frac{\partial(L_{P_{ELM}})}{\partial\beta} = 0 \rightarrow \beta = \sum_{i=1}^{N}\alpha_i(h(x_i)^{\mathrm{T}} = \mathbf{H}^{\mathrm{T}}\alpha \tag{12}$$

$$\frac{\partial(L_{P_{ELM}})}{\partial\xi_i} = 0 \rightarrow \alpha_i\xi_i \qquad i = 1,\cdots,N \tag{13}$$

$$\frac{\partial(L_{P_{ELM}})}{\partial\alpha_i} = 0 \rightarrow \mathbf{h}(x_i)\beta - y_i + \xi_i = 0 \qquad i = 1,\cdots,N \tag{14}$$

where $\alpha = [\alpha_i,\cdots,\alpha_N]^{\mathrm{T}}$.

For the case of little training samples, by substituting (10a) and (10b) to (10c), the aforementioned equations can be equivalently written as

$$\left(\frac{\mathbf{I}}{C} + \mathbf{H}\mathbf{H}^{\mathrm{T}}\right)\alpha = \mathbf{Y} \cdot \tag{15}$$

Then, the output function of ELM is

$$f(\mathbf{x}) = \mathbf{h}(\mathbf{x})\beta = \mathbf{h}(\mathbf{x})\mathbf{H}^{\mathrm{T}}\left(\frac{\mathbf{I}}{C} + \mathbf{H}\mathbf{H}^{\mathrm{T}}\right)^{-1}\mathbf{Y} \cdot \tag{16}$$

We apply Mercer's conditions on ELM, then kernel based ELM can be written as:

$$f(\mathbf{x}) = \begin{bmatrix} \mathbf{K}(\mathbf{x},\mathbf{x}_1) \\ \cdots \\ \mathbf{K}(\mathbf{x},\mathbf{x}_N) \end{bmatrix}\left(\frac{\mathbf{I}}{C} + K(\mathbf{x}_i,\mathbf{x}_j)\right)^{-1}\mathbf{Y} \cdot \tag{17}$$

Many kernel functions can be used, such as RBF kernel and poly kernel.

2.3   Nonlinear Modeling Based on MI and Kernel ELM

The modeling algorithm integrates the MI and Kernel ELM (MI-KELM), whose objective to obtain the best prediction performance by select suitable MI threshold and ELM parameters. Assume range of the MI values between the input features and output variable is θ_{min} to θ_{max}, and the selected MI threshold is denoted as θ_{sel}. Select the popular used RBF kernel

$$K(u,v) = \exp(-\frac{1}{2\gamma^2} \| u - v \|^2)$$ (18)

to construct the ELM kernel. Then, three parameters, namely, MI threshold θ_{sel}, cost parameters C and kernel radius γ need to be selected. The objective of the leaning algorithm in (10) can be rewritten as:

$$\text{minimize}: \quad L_p = \frac{1}{2} \| \beta \|^2 + C \frac{1}{2} \sum_{i=1}^{N} \xi_i^2$$

$$\text{Subject to}: \quad h(x_i)\beta = y_i - \xi_i \quad i = 1, \cdots, N. \cdot$$ (19)

$$\theta_{min} < \theta_{th} < \theta_{max}$$

In this paper, we do not discuss the solution of the above problem deeply. We just select the three parameters (θ_{sel}, C, γ) with the grid algorithm to minimize the root mean square error(RMSE). It is calculated as:

$$E_{rmse} = \sqrt{\frac{1}{N} \sum_{i=1}^{N} (y_i - \hat{y}_i)^2} = \sqrt{\frac{1}{N} \sum_{i=1}^{N} (y_i - f(x_i))^2} \,.$$ (20)

Given the search ranges of θ_{sel}, C and γ, then the best parameters can be obtained as long as (21) achieve minimum:

$$E_{rmse}(\theta_{sel}, C, \gamma) = \min(E_{rmse}).$$ (21)

Therefore, the MI-KLM based modeling algorithm can be described as follows:

Step1: Calculate the MI between the input features and out variable, obtain the ranges of the threshold θ_{sel};
Step2: Give the candidate parameters set θ_{sel}, C and γ;
Step3: Select parameters from the candidate parameters;
Step4: Use the selected parameters to construct kernel based ELM model, record the RMSE of the cross-validation model;
Step5: Repeat the step 3 and step4 with the grid search algorithm.
Step6: Select the final parameters with (18) and obtain the final model.

3   Application Study

In this section, the models based on MI-KLM for estimating the level of saccharose of an orange juice from its observed near-infrared spectrum are compared. The near-infrared spectral data come from http://www.ucl.ac.be, in which the data for learning and test are 150*700 and 68*700 respectively. The training data is shown in Fig. 1.

In this section, the performance of kernel based ELM using the full spectrum, and MI-KLM with different threshold values are carried out in MATLAB2009 environment running in a Pentium4, 2.66GHZ CPU with 768 RAM. Popular Gaussian kernel function are used to construct the final models based on ELM. The MI between each feature and the level of saccharose is calculated by the MutualInfo 0.9 package [5]. The results are shown in Fig. 2.

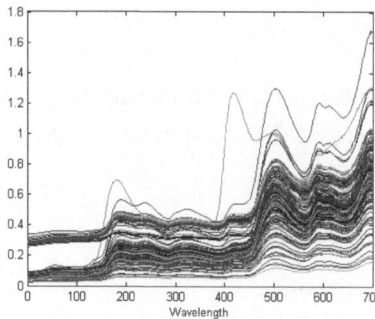

Fig. 1. Near-infrared spectrum

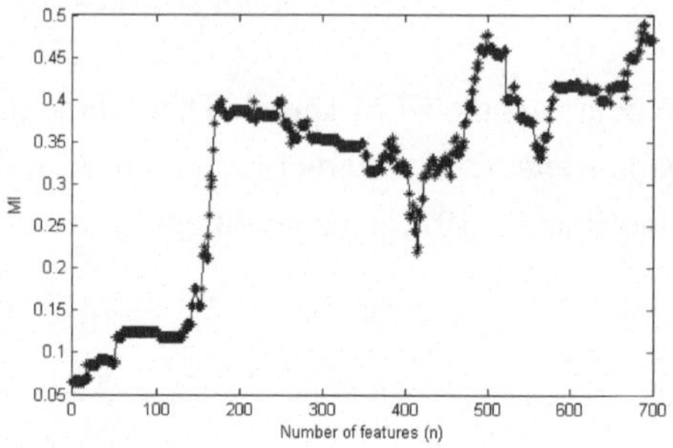

Fig. 2. MI values between NIR and level of saccharose

There are two parameters, namely, the cost parameters C and the kernel parameter r should be determined. In this paper, we have used 14 different values of C and 15 values of r resulting in a total of 210 pair of (C, r). The different values of C are $\{0.0001, 0.001, 0.01, 0.1, 1, 10, 100, 200, 400, 800, 1600, 3200, 6400, 10000\}$ and r are $\{0.0001, 0.001, 0.01, 0.1, 1, 10, 100, 200, 400, 800, 1600, 3200, 6400, 10000, 2000\}$. After extensive simulations, it is found that the performance of the KELM is actually not very sensitive to the cost parameters. The performance Performance of MI-KELM based the full spectrum and MI-KELM with threshold 0.3500 are shown in Fig. 3 and Fig. 4. It shows that the robustness of the cost parameters C in kernel based ELM model is better. The comparison among different threshold and method is shown Fig. 5, and the statistical results are shown in Table 1.

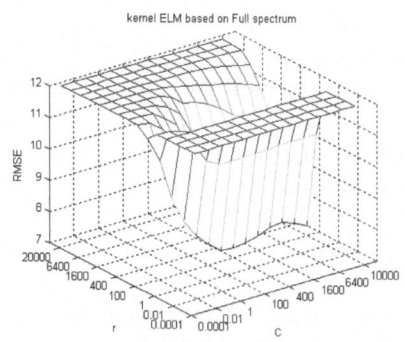

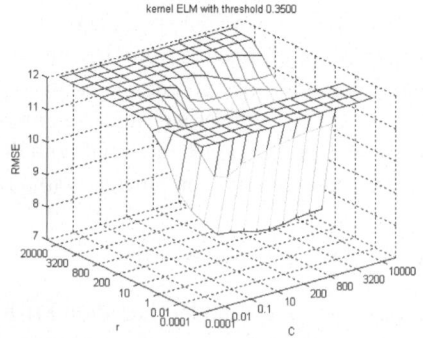

Fig. 3. Performance of kernel ELM based on full spectrum

Fig. 4. Performance of MI-KELM based on threshold 0.3500

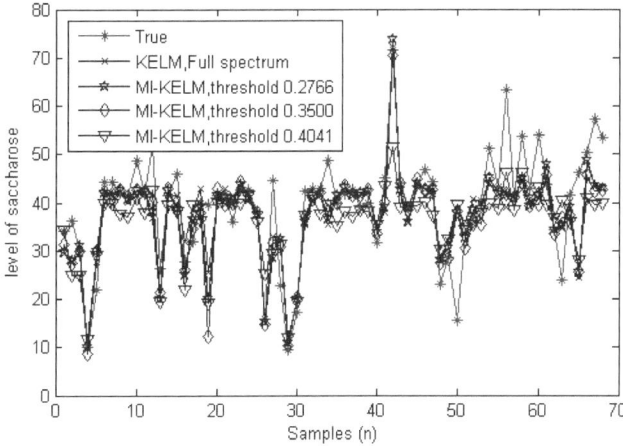

Fig. 5. Prediction results of the level of saccharose of an orange juice model

Table 1. Statistical Results of Different Approaches

Approach	MI threshold	Model Parameters (Nfea,C,r)	Training time	RMSE
ELM	Full spectrum	(700,9,7)	0.3304	7.5026
MI-KLM	0.2766	(522,200,10)	0.1702	7.3972
MI-KLM	0.3500	(370,1000,11)	0.1101	7.6340
MI-KLM	0.4041	(150,300,11)	0.06008	8.3775

The prediction results show that the MI-KELM algorithm has the fastest learning speed compare with the normal KELM approaches. With only half of the origin input features, the prediction accuracy is almost same with KELM model based on the full spectrum with lower complexity. The interpretation of the selected wavelength would be further addressed. With the extreme learning speed, this approach is useful in the online update the models. The trade-off between the learning speed and the predict accuracy also can be obtained by adjust the value of the threshold. More benchmark data should be used to test this approach further.

4   Conclusions

This paper presents a modeling approach for modeling the spectral data based on the mutual information and kernel extreme learning machines. The dimension of the spectrum is reduced based the information between the input features and the output variables. The kernel extreme learning machines are used to construct the final nonlinear model with the reduced features. The selection of the threshold value of the mutual information and the parameters of kernel extreme learning machines are integrated as one optimized problem. The proposed approach is validated by model the level of saccharose of an orange juice based on the near-infrared spectrum validates. Future research will address on how to select the parameters of the feature selection approach and the modeling algorithm more compactly and quickly. More simulations will be done to validate this approach further.

Acknowledgments. The work was supported by National Science Foundation for Post-doctoral Scientists of china (No.20100471464).

References

1. Jiménez-Rodríguez, L.O., Arzuaga-Cruz, E., Vélez-Reyes, M.: Unsupervised Linear Feature-Extraction Methods and Their Effects in the Classification of High-Dimensional Data. IEEE Transaction on Geoscience and Remote Sensing 45, 469–483 (2007)
2. Wang, L.: Feature Selection with Kernel Class Separability. IEEE Transactions on Pattern Analysis and Machine Intelligence 30, 1534–1546 (2008)
3. Leardi, R., Seasholtz, M.B., Pell, R.J.: Variable Selection for Multivariate Calibration Using a Genetic Algorithm: Prediction of Additive Concentrations in Polymer Films from Fourier Transform-infrared Spectral Data. Analytica Chimica Acta 461, 189–200 (2002)
4. Liu, H.W., Sun, J.G., Liu, L., Zhang, H.J.: Feature Selection with Dynamic Mutual Information. Pattern Recognition 42, 1330–1339 (2009)
5. Peng, H.C., Long, F.H., Ding, C.: Feature Selection Based on Mutual Information: Criteria of Max-dependency, Max-relevance, and Min-redundancy. IEEE Transactions on Pattern Analysis and Machine Intelligence 27, 1226–1238 (2005)
6. Tan, C., Li, M.L.: Mutual Information-induced Interval Selection Combined with Kernel Partial Least Squares for Near-infrared Spectral Calibration. Spectrochimica Acta Part A: Molecular and Biomolecular Spectroscopy 71, 1266–1273 (2008)
7. Huang, G.B., Zhu, Q.Y., Siew, C.K.: Extreme Learning Machine: Theory and Applications. Neurocomputing 70, 489–501 (2006)
8. Huang, G.B., Zhou, H.M., Ding, X.J., Zhang, R.: Extreme learning machines for regression and muticlass classification. IEEE Transaction on Systems Man and Cybernetics-part B: Cybernetics 42, 513–529 (2011)
9. Battiti, R.: Using mutual information for selecting features in supervised neural net learning. IEEE Transaction on Neural Network 5, 537–550 (1994)
10. Huang, G.B., Chen, L., Siew, C.K.: Universal Approximation Using Incremental Constructive Feedforward Networks with Random Hidden Nodes. IEEE Transactions on Neural Networks 17, 879–892 (2006)
11. Huang, G.B., Chen, L.: Convex Incremental Extreme Learning Machine. Neurocomputing 70, 3056–3062 (2007)
12. Huang, G.B., Chen, L.: Enhanced Random Search Based Incremental Extreme Learning Machine. Neurocomputing 71, 3460–3468 (2008)

A Hierarchical Neural Network Architecture for Classification

Jing Wang[1], Haibo He[1,*], Yuan Cao[2], Jin Xu[3], and Dongbin Zhao[4,*]

[1] Department of Electrical, Computer and Biomedical Engineering,
University of Rhode Island
Kingston, RI, 02881, USA
`{jwang,he}@ele.uri.edu`
[2] MathWorks, Inc.
Natick, MA, 01760, USA
`yuan.cao@mathworks.com`
[3] Department of Electrical and Computer Engineering
Stevens Institute of Technology
Hoboken, NJ, 07030, USA
`jxu4@stevens.edu`
[4] State Key Laboratory of Management and Control for Complex Systems
Institute of Automation, Chinese Academy of Sciences
Beijing, 100190, China
`dongbin.zhao@gmail.com`

Abstract. In this paper, a hierarchical neural network with cascading architecture is proposed and its application to classification is analyzed. This cascading architecture consists of multiple levels of neural network structure, in which the outputs of the hidden neurons in the higher hierarchical level are treated as an equivalent input data to the input neurons at the lower hierarchical level. The final predictive result is obtained through a modified weighted majority vote scheme. In this way, it is hoped that new patterns could be learned from hidden layers at each level and thus the combination result could significantly improve the learning performance of the whole system. In simulation, a comparison experiment is carried out among our approach and two popular ensemble learning approaches, bagging and AdaBoost. Various simulation results based on synthetic data and real data demonstrate this approach can improve the classification performance.

Keywords: hierarchical neural network, ensemble learning, classification, bagging, AdaBoost.

1 Introduction

Classification has been one of the key focuses of machine learning and data mining for several decades. Recent research suggested that ensemble learning could be an important technique to improve the classification performance of many base learning algorithms, such as neural network, decision tree, K-nearest neighbor, and others.

---

* This work was supported in part by the National Science Foundation under Grant ECCS 1053717 and the K. C. Wong Education Foundation, Hong Kong.

J. Wang, G.G. Yen, and M.M. Polycarpou (Eds.): ISNN 2012, Part I, LNCS 7367, pp. 37–46, 2012.

Ensemble learning has also been widely applied to different domains such as biomedical data mining [1][2], financial data prediction [3][4], power system data analysis [5][6], stream data learning[7][8], among others.

In general, as far as classification is concerned, ensemble learning aims to develop and combine multiple learning models/algorithms together for more accurate and robust classification performance in comparison to single model-based classification approaches [9][10]. Among various ensemble learning algorithms, bagging [11][12] and AdaBoost [13][14] are two popular approaches. In this work, we compare our approach to these two approaches to demonstrate the effectiveness of our method.

Briefly speaking, in bagging (abbreviation of bootstrap aggregating) algorithm, at each iteration a bootstrap sample $U_I^{(l)}$, $l = 1, 2, \ldots, L$ is randomly drawn, with replacement, from entire training set U_I according to a uniform distribution. $U_I^{(l)}$ is of the same size as U_I, therefore some instances may appear more than once while others will never appear in $U_I^{(l)}$ though the sampling frequency is a uniform distribution. A finite number of hypothesis $h^{(l)}, l = 1, 2, \ldots, L$ will be developed based on the bootstrap samples $U_I^{(l)}, l = 1, 2, \ldots, L$. The final hypothesis h^* is formed by combining L hypothesis through a combination scheme.

Freund and Schapire proposed two versions of AdaBoost algorithms, AdaBoost.M1 and AdaBoost.M2[13][14]. Similar to bagging, a boosting sample $U_I^{(l)}$, $l = 1, 2, \ldots, L$ is obtained through sampling the original training set U_I with replacement. However, in AdaBoost, the sampling frequency is no longer a uniform one. Instead, such sampling frequency (or weight distribution) will be adaptively changed according to the learnability of different data instance: data instances that are more difficult to learn (i.e., mis-classified) will carry higher weights compared to those instances that are easy to learn (i.e., correctly classified). Specifically, in AdaBoost.M1, the instances are drawn according to a distribution $\mathbf{D}^{(l)}$ that is related to the distribution $\mathbf{D}^{(l-1)}$ in previous iteration and predictive error in current iteration. In this way, the algorithm could adaptively adjust the weight of each instance and put more emphasis on instances that are hard to learn, while less emphasis on instances that are relatively easy to learn. In the case of multiple class classification problems, AdaBoost.M1 may stop early because of the strong constrain that $\varepsilon^{(l)}, l = 1, 2, \ldots, L$ must be smaller than $1/2$ in each iteration. To address this problem, AdaBoost.M2 was developed to learn from the pseudo-loss based on the mislabeled data set. Interested readers can refer to [11][13][14] for further details about bagging and AdaBoost.

2   Hierarchical Neural Network for Classification

In this work, motivated by the concept of ensemble learning, a hierarchical neural network with cascading architecture is proposed for pattern recognition. The system framework is illustrated in Fig.1, followed by a detailed description of the corresponding learning algorithm. The key idea of our approach is to develop a hierarchical neural network architecture by using the outputs of the hidden neurons at a higher level as the inputs to the neural network at a lower level. Because the outputs of hidden neurons could be considered as a kind of information coding of a specific input-output pair mapping, this architecture will hopefully improve the classification performance by providing each level with different feature representations. Backpropagation is the key to train and tune parameters in this approach. To further improve the accuracy and robustness of the system, a modified weighted majority vote scheme is developed to obtain the final predictive results.

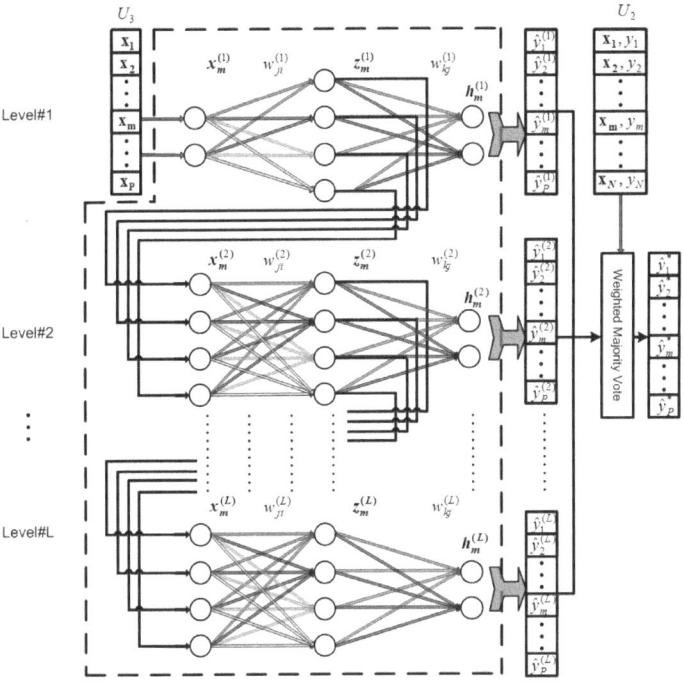

Fig. 1. Schematic of the hierarchical neural network

In Fig.1, the learning system contains L levels and one direction of data flow to accomplish the desired objective. The original data set is truncated into three subsets U_1, U_2, and U_3 for training, cross validation and testing. U_1, U_2, and U_3 contain M, N and P instances, respectively. An instance can be represented as $\{\mathbf{x_m}, y_m\}$, $(m = 1, 2, \ldots, M,\ N\ or\ P)$, where $\mathbf{x_m}$ is a vector in the n dimensional feature space $\mathbf{X}$, and $y_m \in \Omega = \{1, \ldots, C\}$ is the class identity label associated with $\mathbf{x_m}$.

In training stage, neural network at each level is trained sequentially and weights are tuned independently, without interfering with the weights tuning process in neighbor levels. It is recommended that weights should be initialized to certain random values with zero mean and variance σ_w^2 [15]. In our approach, all the input-hidden weights $w_{ji}^{(l)}$ and hidden-output weights $w_{kj}^{(l)}$ are randomly sampled from a Gaussian distribution with zero mean and variance $m^{1/2}$

$$w_{ji}^{(l)}, w_{kj}^{(l)} \sim N(0, m^{1/2}) \tag{1}$$

where m is the number of inputs to hidden neurons or the number of inputs to output neurons.

[Learning algorithm]: ***Hierarchical Neural Network***

(a) $\mathbf{x}_m^{(l)}$ refers to the m_{th} training data sample at the l_{th} level

(b) $\mathbf{z}_m^{(l)}$, $\mathbf{h}_m^{(l)}$, $\mathbf{t}_m$ refer to the hidden neuron output, real network output, and desired network output corresponding to $\mathbf{x}_m^{(l)}$

(c) $E_m^{(l)}$ is the squared error between real network output $\mathbf{h}_m^{(l)}$ and desired neural network output $\mathbf{t}_m$ at l_{th} level

(d) $w_{ji}^{(l)}$, $w_{kj}^{(l)}$ are the input-hidden weights and hidden-output weights

(e) nin, $nhidden$, $nout$ are the number of input, hidden and output neurons

Training

(1)   **for** $l = 1 : L$
(2)   **if** $l == 1$
(3)   Initialize weights for the neural network at the 1_{st} level
(4) $w_{ji}^{c(1)} \leftarrow randn(nin, nhidden)/sqrt(nin)$
(5) $w_{kj}^{(1)} \leftarrow randn(nhidden, nout)/sqrt(nhidden)$
(6) $x_m^{(1)} \leftarrow M$ instances in original training set $\boldsymbol{U_l}$
(7)   **else**
(8)   Initialize weights for the neural network at the l_{th} level
(9) $w_{ji}^{(l)} \leftarrow randn(nhidden, nhidden)/sqrt(nhidden)$
(10) $w_{kj}^{(l)} \leftarrow randn(nhidden, nout)/sqrt(nhidden)$
(11) $x_m^{(l)} = z_m^{(l-1)}$
(12)   **end**
(13)   Train neural network at the l_{th} level with $x_m^{(l)}$
(14)   **for** $m = 1 : M$
(15) $E_m^{(l)} = \frac{1}{2} \sum (\mathbf{t}_m - \mathbf{h}_m^{(l)})^2$
(16) $\Delta w_{ji}^{(l)} = -\eta \frac{\partial E_m^{(l)}}{\partial w_{ji}^{(l)}}, \Delta w_{kj}^{(l)} = -\eta \frac{\partial E_m^{(l)}}{\partial w_{kj}^{(l)}}$
(17) $w_{ji}^{(l)} \leftarrow w_{ji}^{(l)} + \Delta w_{ji}^{(l)}, w_{kj}^{(l)} \leftarrow w_{kj}^{(l)} + \Delta w_{kj}^{(l)}$
(18)   **end**
(19)   Calculate the hidden neuron outputs $z_m^{(l)}$ at the l_{th} level
(20) **end**

The main advantage of this procedure is to develop a neural network with cascading architecture by using the outputs at one level as the inputs at another level, which provides different levels/scales of feature representation for classification. Training set $\boldsymbol{U_l}$ is presented to the neural network at the highest (i.e., the first) level and then flows sequentially through all the other lower levels until it reaches the neural network at the lowest (i.e., the L_{th}) level in the architecture. More specifically, the hidden neuron output $z_m^{(l-1)}$ at the $(l-1)_{th}$ level is treated as an equivalent training set and connected to the input neurons at the l_{th} level, which is formulated as:

$$x_m^{(l)} = z_m^{(l-1)}, \ for \ l = 2, 3, \ldots, L \tag{2}$$

Therefore, the whole system is trained in such a sequential mode: training at l_{th} level starts after training at $(l-1)_{th}$ level is accomplished, and this process repeats until neural networks at L levels are well trained. The scaled conjugate gradient technique is also used in our work to accelerate the speed of computation.

Once all neural networks are trained, we use cross validation to evaluate the performance of networks and determine their voting weights for the final perdition result. In this stage, cross validation set U_2 propagates forward through each level cascadingly and develops L hypothesis $h_m^{(l)}(\mathbf{x_m}, y_m)$, $l = 1, 2, \ldots, L$. Corresponding error rate $\varepsilon^{(l)}$, $l = 1, 2, \ldots, L$ to each hypothesis are calculated and used to evaluate the performance of classifier at each level.

$$\varepsilon^{(l)} = \sum_{\hat{y}_m^{(l)} \neq y_m^{(l)}} D_m, l = 1, 2, \ldots, L, m = 1, 2, \ldots, N \tag{3}$$

where $\hat{y}_m^{(l)}$ is the predictive label sequence generalized from hypothesis $h_m^{(l)}(\mathbf{x_m}, y_m)$ and $y_m^{(l)}$ is the desired predictive label sequence. D_m is the distribution of cross validation set U_2, which is assumed as a uniform distribution and defined as $D_m = 1/N$ for all the instances in U_2. Intuitively, classifiers with lower error rate should be rewarded with higher voting weights than those with higher error rate. Therefore voting weight of the l_{th} classifier should be approximately proportional to $1/\varepsilon^{(l)}$. To achieve this, we first set $\beta^{(l)}$ as

$$\beta^{(l)} = \frac{\varepsilon^{(l)}}{1 - \varepsilon^{(l)}}, l = 1, 2, \ldots, L \tag{4}$$

During testing stage, the final predictive result for a given unlabeled instance $\mathbf{x_m}$ is obtained through a combination function to integrate L predictions $\hat{y}_m^{(l)}, l = 1, 2, \ldots, L$, generalized from each neural network. In our work, weighted majority vote is served as combination function

$$y_m^* = \arg\max_{k \in \Omega} \sum_{l : \hat{y}_m^{(l)} = k} \ln \frac{1}{\beta^{(l)}} \tag{5}$$

where $k \in \Omega, k = 1, 2, \ldots, C$ is the class label. The total vote that is received by each class is counted and then the class that receives the highest total vote is selected as the final predictive result.

3   Simulation Analysis

3.1   Data Set Description

In our study, comparison experiment is carried out on three ensemble learning algorithms: hierarchical neural network (hierarchical NN), bagging neural network(bagging

NN), and AdaBoost (we used AdaBoost.M2 in our current study) neural networks (AdaBoost NN). One synthetic data set and four real data sets from UCI repository are used to evaluate the performance of three different ensemble learning algorithms. The synthetic data set BiG1000 contains 2 classes of bivariate Gaussian random variables X_1 and X_2, with 500 instances in each class. BiG1000 is generated in Matlab according to the following distribution

$$X \sim N(\mu, \Sigma) \tag{6}$$

Different distributions can be obtained by changing the mean vector μ and covariance matrix Σ. In our simulation, $\mu_1 = [5.50 \; 4.50]^T$, $\mu_2 = [7.00 \; 7.00]^T$ and $\Sigma_1 = \begin{bmatrix} 2.50 & 1 \\ 1 & 2.50 \end{bmatrix}$, $\Sigma_2 = \begin{bmatrix} 1.50 & 1 \\ 1 & 2.50 \end{bmatrix}$. The distribution of the bivariate Gaussian variables used in this work is illustrated in Fig.2.

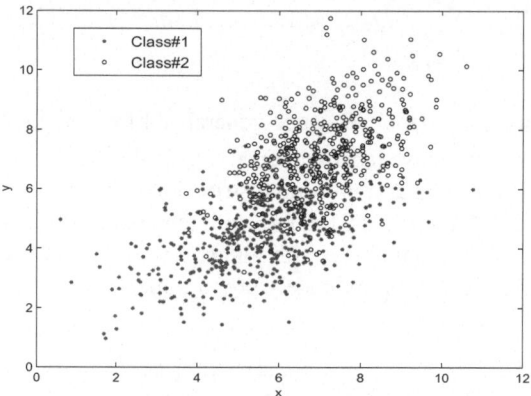

Fig. 2. Distribution of bivariate Gaussian variable

To examine the capability of our proposed hierarchical neural network in classification tasks over real-world data, four benchmarks from UCI repository [16] are selected to evaluate the three ensemble learning algorithms. Table 1 summarizes the major characteristics of the data sets used in our current simulation.

3.2   Simulation Procedure

In our simulation, training set U_1, cross validation set U_2 and testing set U_3 contain 50%, 25% and 25% instances of the original data set U, respectively. The number of total levels in hierarchical neural network is equivalent to the maximum number of iterations in bagging NN and AdaBoost NN, of which all are set to 25 in our current simulation.

In the hierarchical neural network, classifier at the l_{th} level is trained with the original training set U_1. In bagging neural network, the l_{th} classifier is trained with the l_{th}

Table 1. Summary of data set characteristics

#Data Set	Name	# Instances	# Features	# Classes
1	BiG1000	1000	2	2
3	Diabetes	768	8	2
5	Iris	150	4	3
4	Ecoli	336	7	8
3	Ionsphere	351	34	2

bootstrap sample $U_m^{(l)}$ obtained through sampling U_1 according to a uniform distribution. AdaBoost neural network accomplishes training in a similar way, each classifier is trained with a boosting sample U_1, but the sampling is based on a pseudo-loss of current hypothesis $h_m^{(l)}(\mathbf{x_m}, y_m)$.

During testing period, bagging neural network obtains the final result through majority vote by assigning each classifier an equal weight. Each classifier in AdaBoost neural network is assigned with a different weights according to pseudo-loss. In our scheme, a cross validation set U_2 is used to determine voting weight for each classifier and then weighted majority vote is applied on the individual results of l_{th} classifiers to obtain the final prediction result. The results presented following are all based on the average results of ten random experiments.

3.3 Simulation Results and Analysis

First, three ensemble learning algorithms are tested under the synthetic data set BiG1000. Training and testing error curves for the three approaches (i.e., bagging, AdaBoost, and hierarchical neural network) are illustrated in Fig. 3(a) and Fig. 3(b), respectively. As the number of neural networks increases, both training and testing error for our approach drop rapidly and the final testing error reaches 16.40% compared with 17.98%

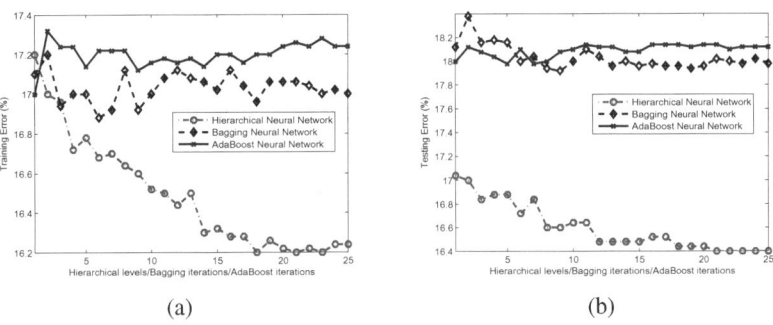

(a)   (b)

Fig. 3. Bivariate Gaussian variables: (a) Training error over 25 iterations/levels. (b) Testing error in 25 iterations/levels.

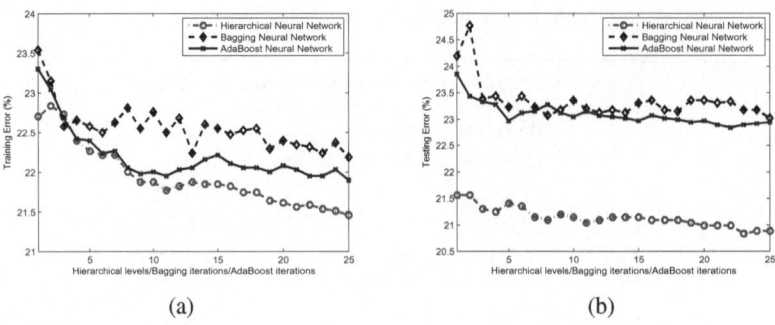

(a)   (b)

Fig. 4. UCI data set, Diabetes: (a) Training error over 25 iterations/levels. (b) Testing error in 25 iterations/levels.

Table 2. Testing Performance Comparison

Algorithm	BiG1000		Ionosphere		Diabetes		Ecoli		Iris	
	Mean	Std	Mean	Std	Mean	Std	Mean	Std	Mean	Std
Hierarchical NN	16.598	0.199	10.768	0.543	21.140	0.183	23.629	0.719	4.263	0.298
Bagging	18.030	0.101	14.127	1.080	23.356	0.361	24.607	1.690	4.869	0.285
AdaBoost	18.092	0.051	11.977	0.825	23.094	0.213	30.850	1.258	5.056	1.680

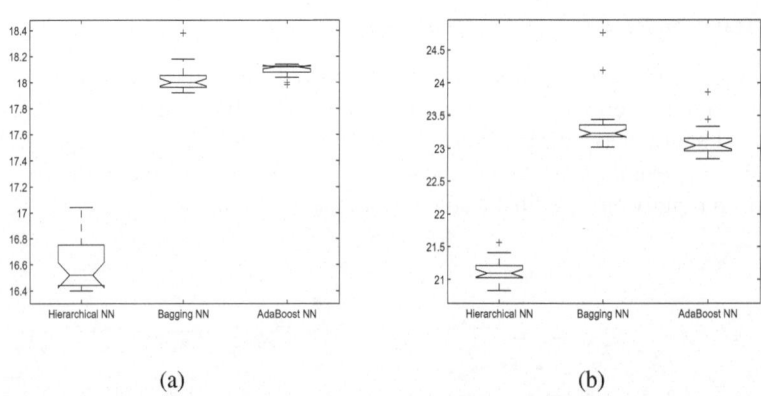

(a)   (b)

Fig. 5. Boxplot of the average testing error among Hierarchical NN, Bagging NN and AdaBoost NN (a) Data set #1 BIG1000 (b) Data set #2 Diabetes

and 18.12% that bagging and AdaBoost could reach. Next, the three approaches are evaluated on four real-world data sets. For space consideration, Fig. 4 demonstrates a snapshot of the classification performance of the Diabetes data set. The training and testing error curves in Fig. 4(a) and Fig. 4(b) show that our approach outperforms the other two approaches and reduces the testing error rate to 20.9% in this case. A numerical comparison of these three approaches over five data sets is listed in Table 2. For each column in

Table 2, the first and second number denotes the mean error and standard derivation of testing error over ten experiments. Furthermore, boxplot results of the three approaches on two data sets are illustrated in Fig. 5. We can see the boxplot results also prove that our approach performs much better than the other two approaches in the scenarios given above.

4   Conclusions

In this paper, we present a hierarchical neural network architecture to improve the predictive accuracy for classification problems. Detailed system level architecture with a specific learning algorithm is analyzed in detail. In order to demonstrate the effectiveness of our approach, simulation studies on both synthetic data and real-world data sets showed our approach can improve the classification performance in comparison with Bagging and AdaBoost method.

There are several interesting future research directions along this topic. First, our work in this paper mainly focuses on the architecture and algorithm development, as well as empirical studies. It would be interesting to investigate the theoretical aspect of such a hierarchical neural network structure in terms of it learning capability, efficiency, and robustness. Second, while simulations over a synthetic data and four UCI data sets showed promising results, large scale experiments and statistical tests are needed to fully justify the effectiveness of this approach. Also, how this architecture can handle the *imbalanced learning* problem (i.e., learning from imbalanced data, see survey paper [17]) will also be an interesting direction to study the classificaiton problem with complex data distributions. Third, in terms of specific learning strategies, in our current study, we adopted the scaled conjugate algorithm to tune weights at each level. It would also be interesting to observe how this architecture will perform when other learning techniques, such as classic backpropagation, quasi-Newton and Levenberg-Marquardt algorithms, among others, are adopted in this structure. Finally, as neural network architectures can be used in the design of autoencoder[18][19], it would also be interesting to see how this hierarchical architecture could be used to facilitate the autoencoder development.

References

1. Madabhushi, A., Feldman, M.D., Metaxas, D.N., Tomaszeweski, J., Chute, D.: Automated detection of prostatic adenocarcinoma from high-resolution ex vivo MRI. IEEE Transactions on Medical Imaging 24, 1611–1625 (2005)
2. Oh, S., Lee, M.S., Zhang, B.T.: Ensemble Learning with Active Example Selection for Imbalanced Biomedical Data Classification. IEEE/ACM Transactions on Computational Biology and Bioinformatics 8, 316–325 (2011)
3. Zhang, K.H., Li, A.G., Song, B.W.: Fraud Detection in Tax Declaration Using Ensemble ISGNN. In: WRI World Congress on Computer Science and Information Engineering, vol. 4, pp. 237–240 (2009)
4. Lin, W.Y., Hu, Y.H., Tsai, C.F.: Machine Learning in Financial Crisis Prediction: A Survey. IEEE Transactions on Systems, Man, and Cybernetics, Part C: Applications and Reviews (in press, 2012)

5. Chen, C.J., Chen, T.C., Ou, J.C.: Power System Stabilizer Using a New Recurrent Neural Network for Multi-Machine. In: Power and Energy Conference, pp. 68–72 (2006)
6. He, H., Cao, Y., Cao, Y., Wen, J.: Ensemble Learning for Wind Profile Prediction with Missing Values. Neural Computing & Applications 1–6 (2011)
7. He, H., Chen, S., Li, K., Xu, X.: Incremental Learning from Stream Data. IEEE Trans. Neural Networks 22(12), 1901–1914 (2011)
8. He, H., Chen, S.: IMORL: Incremental Multiple Objects Recognition and Localization. IEEE Trans. Neural Networks 19(10), 1727–1738 (2008)
9. Polikar, R.: Ensemble Based Systems in Decision Making. IEEE Circuits and Systems Magazine 6, 21–45 (2006)
10. Polikar, R.: Bootstrap Inspired Techniques in Computational Intelligence. IEEE Signal Processing Magazine 24, 56–72 (2007)
11. Breiman, L.: Bagging predictors. Machine Learning 24, 123–140 (1996)
12. Breiman, L.: Arching classifiers. Annals of Statistics 26, 801–849 (1998)
13. Freund, Y., Schapire, R.E.: Experiments with new boosting algorithm. In: Proceedings of the 13th the International Conference on Machine Learning, pp. 148–156 (1996)
14. Freund, Y., Schapire, R.E.: A decision-theoretic generalization of on-line learning and application to boosting. Journal of Computer and System Sciences 55, 119–139 (1996)
15. LeCun, Y.A., Bottou, L., Orr, G.B., Müller, K.-R.: Efficient BackProp. In: Orr, G.B., Müller, K.-R. (eds.) NIPS-WS 1996. LNCS, vol. 1524, pp. 9–50. Springer, Heidelberg (1998)
16. UCI Machine Learning Rerpository,
    http://archive.ics.uci.edu/ml/datasets.html
17. He, H., Garcia, E.A.: Learning from Imbalanced Data. IEEE Trans. Knowledge and Data Engineering 21(9), 1263–1284 (2009)
18. Hinton, G.E., Salakhutdinov, R.: Reducing the dimensionality of data with neural networks. Science 313, 504–507 (2006)
19. Lee, H., Grosse, R., Ranganath, R., Ng, A.Y.: Unsupervised Learning of Hierarchical Representations with Convolutional Deep Belief Networks. Communications of ACM 54, 95–103 (2009)

Discrete-Time ZNN Algorithms for Time-Varying Quadratic Programming Subject to Time-Varying Equality Constraint

Zhende Ke, Yiwen Yang, and Yunong Zhang[*]

School of Information Science and Technology
Sun Yat-sen University, Guangzhou 510006, China
zhynong@mail.sysu.edu.cn

Abstract. A special class of recurrent neural network (RNN), i.e., Zhang neural network (ZNN), has been proposed for a decade for solving online various time-varying problems. In this paper, we generalize and investigate a continuous-time ZNN model for online solution of the time-varying convex quadratic programming (QP) subject to a time-varying linear equality constraint. For the purpose of possible hardware (e.g., digital-circuit or digital-computer) realization, discrete-time ZNN models and numerical algorithms (i.e., discrete-time ZNN algorithms, in short) are proposed and developed by using Euler difference rules. Computer-simulation and numerical results demonstrate the efficacy and accuracy of the presented continuous-time ZNN model and the proposed discrete-time ZNN algorithms for solving online time-varying QP problems.

Keywords: Recurrent neural network (RNN), Quadratic programming (QP), Time-varying, Models, Discrete-time, Numerical algorithms.

1 Problem Formulation and Continuous-Time ZNN Model

Let us consider the following time-varying convex quadratic programming problem which is subject to a time-varying linear equality constraint:

$$\text{minimize} \quad x^T(t)P(t)x(t)/2 + q^T(t)x(t), \tag{1}$$

$$\text{subject to} \quad A(t)x(t) = b(t), \tag{2}$$

where Hessian matrix $P(t) \in R^{n \times n}$ is smoothly time-varying, positive-definite and symmetric for any time instant $t \in [0, +\infty) \subset R$. The coefficient vector $q(t) \in R^n$ is assumed smoothly time-varying as well. In (1) and (2), the time-varying decision vector $x(t) \in R^n$ is unknown and to be solved for at any time instant $t \in [0, +\infty)$. In equality constraint (2), the coefficient matrix $A(t) \in R^{m \times n}$ being of full row rank and vector $b(t) \in R^m$ are both assumed smoothly time-varying. According to the mathematical optimization method using Lagrange

---

[*] Corresponding author.

J. Wang, G.G. Yen, and M.M. Polycarpou (Eds.): ISNN 2012, Part I, LNCS 7367, pp. 47–54, 2012.

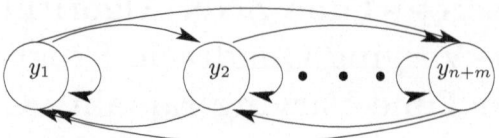

Fig. 1. Neurons' connection-architecture of CTZNN model (4)

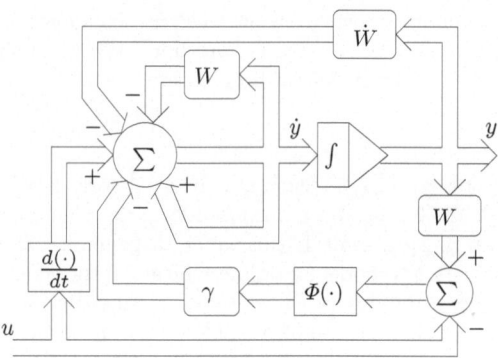

Fig. 2. Block diagram which realizes CTZNN model (4)

multipliers [1], time-varying QP problem (1)-(2) can be transformed into the following linear equation system:

$$W(t)y(t) = u(t), \tag{3}$$

where

$$W(t) := \begin{bmatrix} P(t) & A^T(t) \\ A(t) & \mathbf{0} \end{bmatrix} \in R^{(n+m)\times(n+m)},$$

$$y(t) := \begin{bmatrix} x(t) \\ \lambda(t) \end{bmatrix} \in R^{n+m}, \quad u(t) := \begin{bmatrix} -q(t) \\ b(t) \end{bmatrix} \in R^{n+m},$$

with $\lambda(t) \in R^m$ denoting the Lagrange-multiplier vector defined for (2).

Based on the authors' previous work [2], the implicit dynamic equation of a continuous-time ZNN (CTZNN) model for solving online the time-varying QP problem (1)-(2) is presented below:

$$W(t)\dot{y}(t) = -\dot{W}(t)y(t) - \gamma\Phi\big(W(t)y(t) - u(t)\big) + \dot{u}(t), \tag{4}$$

where, being the reciprocal of a capacitance parameter, the design parameter $\gamma > 0 \in R$ should be implemented as large as possible or selected appropriately for simulative purposes. In addition, $\Phi(\cdot) : R^{n+m} \rightarrow R^{n+m}$ denotes an activation-function (vector) array. More specifically, the array $\Phi(\cdot)$ is made of $(n + m)$ monotonically-increasing odd activation-functions $\phi(\cdot)$. Zhang *et al* have investigated and used six types of activation functions (i.e., linear activation functions, power activation functions, power-sum activation functions,

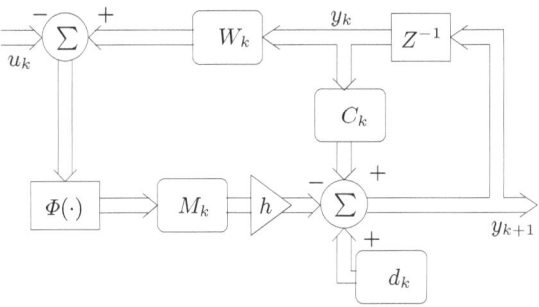

Fig. 3. Block diagram which realizes the K-DTZNN and U-DTZNN algorithms

sigmoid activation functions, power-sigmoid activation functions and hyperbolic sine activation functions) in the ZNN research [3]. Furthermore, the neurons' connection-architecture of CTZNN model (4) is depicted in Fig. 1, and Fig. 2 shows the corresponding block diagram of such a neural network model.

2 Discrete-Time ZNN Algorithms

For the purpose of possible hardware implementation via digital circuits or digital computers, it may be more preferable to discretize the CTZNN model (4) by using Euler difference rules. The discrete-time ZNN (DTZNN) models and numerical algorithms (i.e., discrete-time ZNN algorithms, in short) are thus generalized and developed for solving online time-varying QP problem (1)-(2) in this section. Note that almost no paper has been published on the time-varying QP problems solving via discrete-time algorithms in the literature at the present stage. This paper focuses on this time-varying optimization problem, and proposes three different discrete-time ZNN algorithms to solve it.

Situation 1. Assuming That $\dot{W}(t)$ and $\dot{u}(t)$ Are Known
With $\dot{W}(t)$ and $\dot{u}(t)$ known, we use W_k, $\dot{W}_k$, u_k, $\dot{u}_k$ standing for $W(t = k\tau)$, $\dot{W}(t = k\tau)$, $u(t = k\tau)$, $\dot{u}(t = k\tau)$, respectively, where $\tau > 0$ denotes the sampling gap, and $k = 0, 1, 2, \cdots$ denotes the iteration index. Using Euler forward-difference rule, we obtain the following discrete-time ZNN algorithm with $\dot{W}(t)$ and $\dot{u}(t)$ known (i.e., the K-DTZNN algorithm):

$$y_{k+1} = (I - \tau M_k \dot{W}_k)y_k - hM_k\Phi\big(W_k y_k - u_k\big) + \tau M_k \dot{u}_k, \qquad (5)$$

where y_k corresponds to the kth iteration/sampling of $y(t = k\tau)$, $M_k := W_k^{-1}$, $h := \tau\gamma > 0$ denotes the step-size (or termed, step-length), and $\Phi(\cdot)$ is defined as before. In addition, τ should be set appropriately small for better convergence and accuracy purposes. When linear activation functions are used, the aforementioned K-DTZNN algorithm (5) reduces to

$$y_{k+1} = \big((1 - h)I - \tau M_k \dot{W}_k\big)y_k + M_k(hu_k + \tau\dot{u}_k). \qquad (6)$$

Situation 2. Assuming That $\dot{W}(t)$ and $\dot{u}(t)$ Are Unknown
When the time-derivative information of time-varying coefficients [i.e., $\dot{W}(t)$ and $\dot{u}(t)$] is unknown in some real-world applications, we can use Euler backward-difference rule to approximate $\dot{W}_k$ and $\dot{u}_k$. Then, we have the following DTZNN algorithm with $\dot{W}(t)$ and $\dot{u}(t)$ unknown (i.e., the U-DTZNN algorithm):

$$y_{k+1} = M_k W_{k-1} y_k - h M_k \Phi (W_k y_k - u_k) + M_k (u_k - u_{k-1}), \qquad (7)$$

where h and $\Phi(\cdot)$ are defined as before. If we use the linear activation function array, the above U-DTZNN algorithm (7) reduces to

$$y_{k+1} = (M_k W_{k-1} - hI) y_k + (h+1) M_k u_k - M_k u_{k-1}. \qquad (8)$$

As a summary, we give Fig. 3 depicting the block diagram of K-DTZNN and U-DTZNN algorithms, where $C_k := I - \tau M_k \dot{W}_k$ and $d_k := \tau M_k \dot{u}_k$ for K-DTZNN algorithm (5); or $C_k := M_k W_{k-1}$ and $d_k := M_k (u_k - u_{k-1})$ for U-DTZNN algorithm (7).

Situation 3. Assuming That $\dot{W}(t)$ and $\dot{u}(t)$ Are Partially Known
Furthermore, there are another two situations, i.e., with $\dot{W}(t)$ unknown but $\dot{u}(t)$ known, and with $\dot{W}(t)$ known but $\dot{u}(t)$ unknown. In view of the similarity to aforementioned DTZNN algorithms, we just show the DTZNN algorithms with $\dot{W}(t)$ and $\dot{u}(t)$ partially known (i.e., the P-DTZNN algorithms) as below:

$$y_{k+1} = M_k W_{k-1} y_k - h M_k \Phi (W_k y_k - u_k) + \tau M_k \dot{u}_k, \qquad (9)$$

$$y_{k+1} = (I - \tau M_k \dot{W}_k) y_k - h M_k \Phi (W_k y_k - u_k) + M_k (u_k - u_{k-1}). \qquad (10)$$

3   Simulative and Numerical Verification

The previous sections presented the continuous-time ZNN model and discrete-time ZNN algorithms for online solution of time-varying convex QP problem subject to a time-varying linear-equality constraint. In this section, computer-simulation and numerical results are provided for substantiating the efficacy of the ZNN model and algorithms.

Example 1. Consider a time-varying convex QP problem subject to a time-varying linear-equality constraint, with the following coefficients:

$$P(t) = \begin{bmatrix} 4 + \cos(2t) & \sin(0.5t) & \sin(0.5t)/2 & \sin(0.5t)/3 \\ \sin(0.5t) & 6 + \sin(3t) & \sin(0.5t) & \sin(0.5t)/2 \\ \sin(0.5t)/2 & \sin(0.5t) & 8 & \sin(0.5t) \\ \sin(0.5t)/3 & \sin(0.5t)/2 & \sin(0.5t) & 10 + \cos(t) \end{bmatrix},$$

$$q(t) = - \begin{bmatrix} 1.5 \sin(2t) \\ 1.5 \sin(2t + 0.5\pi) \\ 1.5 \sin(2t + \pi) \\ 1.5 \sin(2t + 1.5\pi) \end{bmatrix}, \quad A(t) = \begin{bmatrix} \cos(t) \\ \cos(t - \pi/3) \\ \cos(t - 2\pi/3) \\ \cos(t - \pi) \end{bmatrix}^T, \quad b(t) = 1.5 \sin(2t).$$

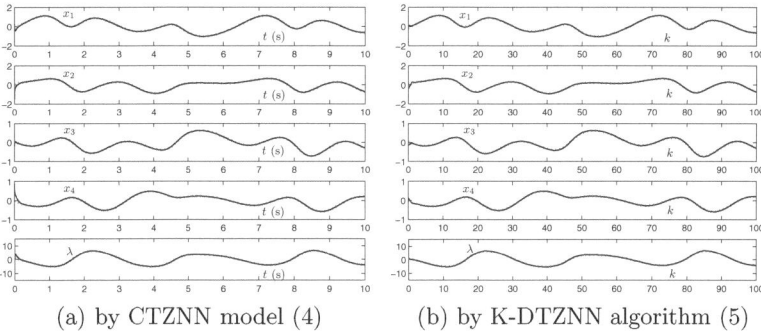

(a) by CTZNN model (4)   (b) by K-DTZNN algorithm (5)

Fig. 4. State trajectories of ZNN model and algorithm solving time-varying QP problem (1)-(2) in Example 1, where neural-network solution and theoretical solution are denoted respectively by solid curves and dotted curves

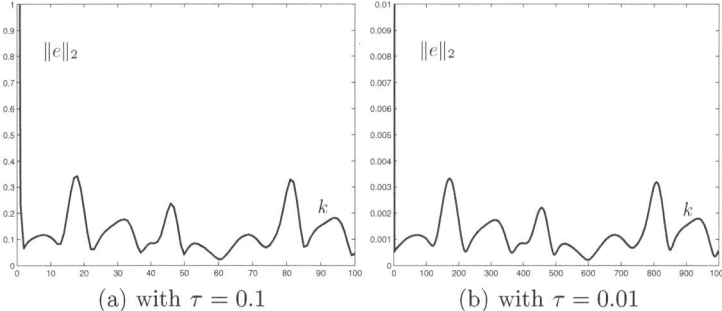

(a) with $\tau = 0.1$ (b) with $\tau = 0.01$

Fig. 5. Residual errors of K-DTZNN algorithm (5) solving the time-varying QP problem (1)-(2) with $h = 1$ in Example 1

The simulation results are presented in Figs. 4-6 and Table 1. Fig. 4(a) illustrates the simulation results of CTZNN model (4) using linear activation functions. As shown in Fig. 4(a), starting from an initial state randomly generated within $[-2, 2]^{4 \times 1}$, neural state $x(t)$ of CTZNN model (4) converges to the theoretical solution of the aforementioned time-varying QP problem. From this figure, we confirm the efficacy of the CTZNN model.

As presented previously, we discretized CTZNN model (4) for possible realization on digital circuits or computers, and three DTZNN algorithms [i.e., K-DTZNN algorithm (5), U-DTZNN algorithm (7) and P-DTZNN algorithm (9), for example] are generalized and developed for solving the time-varying QP problem (1)-(2). Figs. 4-6 and Table 1 illustrate the computer-testing results which are mainly of K-DTZNN algorithm (5) with different values of step-size h and sampling gap τ. As seen from Fig. 4(b), state x_k of the proposed K-DTZNN algorithm (5) converges to the theoretical solution. In addition, from Figs. 5 and 6, we see that good performance of K-DTZNN algorithm (5) can be achieved by using appropriate step-size h and sampling gap τ. Moreover, the

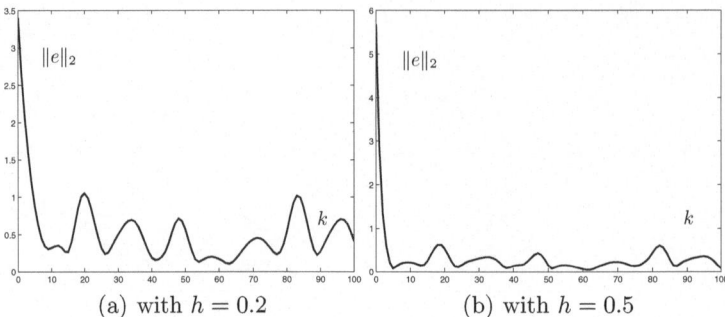

(a) with $h = 0.2$ (b) with $h = 0.5$

Fig. 6. Residual errors of K-DTZNN algorithm (5) solving the time-varying QP problem (1)-(2) with $\tau = 0.1$ in Example 1

Table 1. Errors of DTZNN solving the time-varying QP problem in Example 1

discrete-time ZNN algorithm	step-size h	maximal steady-state residual error			
		$\tau = 0.1000$	$\tau = 0.0100$	$\tau = 0.0010$	$\tau = 0.0001$
K-DTZNN algorithm (5)	$h = 0.2$	1.0539	1.6324×10^{-2}	1.6562×10^{-4}	1.6566×10^{-6}
	$h = 0.5$	0.6226	6.6159×10^{-3}	6.6259×10^{-5}	6.6264×10^{-7}
	$h = 0.8$	0.4263	4.1397×10^{-3}	4.1412×10^{-5}	4.1415×10^{-7}
	$h = 1.0$	0.3424	3.3119×10^{-3}	3.3130×10^{-5}	3.3132×10^{-7}
U-DTZNN algorithm (7)	$h = 0.2$	1.2149	1.8936×10^{-2}	1.9221×10^{-4}	1.9226×10^{-6}
	$h = 0.5$	0.7281	7.6761×10^{-3}	7.6895×10^{-5}	7.6904×10^{-7}
	$h = 0.8$	0.4914	4.8020×10^{-3}	4.8060×10^{-5}	4.8065×10^{-7}
	$h = 1.0$	0.3987	3.8425×10^{-3}	3.8448×10^{-5}	3.8452×10^{-7}
P-DTZNN algorithm (9)	$h = 0.2$	1.0788	1.6898×10^{-2}	1.7186×10^{-4}	1.7190×10^{-6}
	$h = 0.5$	0.6317	6.8618×10^{-3}	6.8755×10^{-5}	6.8761×10^{-7}
	$h = 0.8$	0.4350	4.2944×10^{-3}	4.2972×10^{-5}	4.2976×10^{-7}
	$h = 1.0$	0.3532	3.4358×10^{-3}	3.4378×10^{-5}	3.4381×10^{-7}

results illustrated in Table 1 show the relation between the maximal steady-state residual errors $\|e_k\|_2 := \|W_k y_k - u_k\|_2$ and the sampling-gap τ, which is in an $O(\tau^2)$ manner. That is to say, the steady-state residual error $\|e_k\|_2$ reduces by 100 times when the sampling-gap τ decreases by 10 times, which implies that τ can be selected appropriately small to satisfy effectively the usual precision we need in practice. Thus, we can have the important conclusion that the maximal steady-state residual errors of K-DTZNN algorithm (5) are of order $O(\tau^2)$. These demonstrate the efficacy of K-DTZNN algorithm (5) on time-varying QP problem (1)-(2) solving.

The numerical results of U-DTZNN algorithm (7) and P-DTZNN algorithm (9) are also depicted in Table 1. From this table, we can observe that the maximal steady-state residual errors of these two algorithms also show an $O(\tau^2)$ manner. Besides, U-DTZNN algorithm (7) performs slightly less better than K-DTZNN algorithm (5), in view of the former using the estimated time-derivative information of time-varying coefficients. In addition, by using

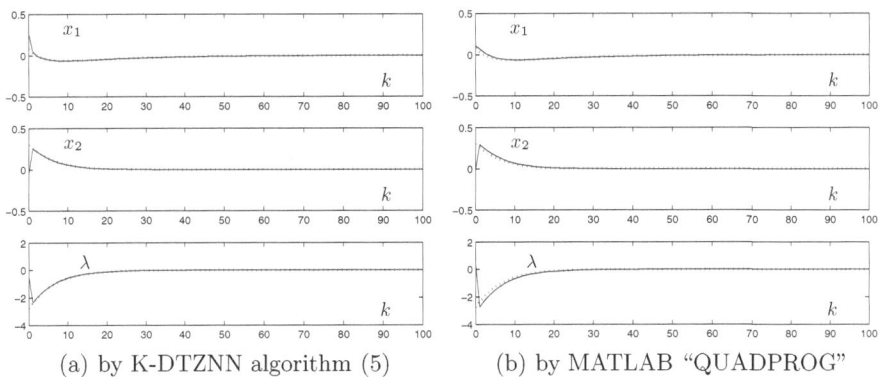

(a) by K-DTZNN algorithm (5)   (b) by MATLAB "QUADPROG"

Fig. 7. Trajectories of K-DTZNN algorithm (5) and MATLAB routine "QUADPROG" with $\tau = 0.1$ when solving the time-varying QP problem in Example 2

the accurate time-derivative information partially (e.g., with $\dot{u}_k$ known and $\dot{W}_k$ estimated), P-DTZNN algorithm (9) works better than U-DTZNN algorithm (7) but less better than K-DTZNN algorithm (5), as also seen from Table 1.

Example 2. In the above example, the time-varying coefficients are of the sinusoidal form. As another illustrative example, we consider the following time-varying coefficients in the exponential form:

$$P(t) = \begin{bmatrix} 8 & 2\exp(-0.5t) \\ 2\exp(-0.5t) & 10 \end{bmatrix}, \ q(t) = \begin{bmatrix} \exp(-0.5t) \\ \exp(-t) \end{bmatrix},$$

$$A(t) = \begin{bmatrix} 0.8\exp(-t) \ 1.5 \end{bmatrix}, \ b(t) = 0.5\exp(-2t).$$

It follows from equation (3) that we have

$$W(t) = \begin{bmatrix} 8 & 2\exp(-0.5t) & 0.8\exp(-t) \\ 2\exp(-0.5t) & 10 & 1.5 \\ 0.8\exp(-t) & 1.5 & 0 \end{bmatrix},$$

$$u(t) = \begin{bmatrix} -\exp(-0.5t), & -\exp(-t), & 0.5\exp(-2t) \end{bmatrix}^T.$$

Fig. 7(a) shows the state trajectories of K-DTZNN algorithm (5) with $\tau = 0.1$ for the time-varying QP problem solving. For comparative purposes, we also solve the above time-varying QP problem by using MATLAB optimization routine "QUADPROG" [4], of which the result is depicted in Fig. 7(b). From this figure, we see that state x_k of the proposed K-DTZNN algorithm (5) converges to the theoretical solution of the time-varying QP problem. Besides, the numerical results of these two methods with different sampling gap τ are presented in Table 2. As seen from this table and other simulation results, the maximal steady-state residual errors of MATLAB optimization method show an $O(\tau)$ manner (when applied to time-varying QP), while those of DTZNN algorithms (i.e., K-DTZNN,

Table 2. Errors of DTZNN algorithms (with $h = 1$) and MATLAB routine "QUAD-PROG" solving the time-varying QP problem in Example 2

discrete-time solver	maximal steady-state residual error			
	$\tau = 0.1000$	$\tau = 0.0100$	$\tau = 0.0010$	$\tau = 0.0001$
K-DTZNN (5)	4.5046×10^{-3}	3.1653×10^{-5}	3.0557×10^{-7}	3.0450×10^{-9}
U-DTZNN (7)	7.1685×10^{-3}	5.1472×10^{-5}	4.9815×10^{-7}	4.9653×10^{-9}
P-DTZNN (9)	5.5743×10^{-3}	3.7570×10^{-5}	3.6106×10^{-7}	3.5968×10^{-9}
"QUADPROG"	4.5118×10^{-2}	4.0497×10^{-3}	4.0111×10^{-4}	4.0073×10^{-5}

U-DTZNN and P-DTZNN algorithms) are all of order $O(\tau^2)$. In addition, better convergence and accuracy can be achieved by DTZNN algorithms for the same time-varying QP problem solving, as compared with the MATLAB optimization routine. This example also demonstrates the efficacy and advantages of the proposed DTZNN algorithms.

4   Conclusions

In this paper, we have generalized and investigated a special class of recurrent neural network (i.e., Zhang neural network) for online solution of time-varying convex QP problem subject to a time-varying linear equality. For the purposes of possible realization on digital circuits or computers, the discrete-time ZNN algorithms (i.e., K-DTZNN, U-DTZNN and P-DTZNN algorithms) have been proposed and investigated for such a time-varying quadratic-programming problem. Simulative and numerical results have demonstrated the efficacy and advantages of the proposed ZNN algorithms on time-varying QP problem solving.

Acknowledgements. This work is supported by the National Natural Science Foundation of China under Grants 61075121 and 60935001, and also by the Fundamental Research Funds for the Central Universities of China. Besides, please note that the authors of this paper are all jointly of the first authorship; and that the literal meanings of Chinese word "ZHANG" are 1) archer, 2) officer controlling bows and arrows, and 3) the act of sending arrows through a bow.

References

1. Zhang, Y., Li, Z.: Zhang neural network for online solution of time-varying convex quadratic program subject to time-varying linear-equality constraints. Physics Letters A 373(18-19), 1639–1643 (2009)
2. Zhang, Y., Ruan, G., Li, K., Yang, Y.: Robustness analysis of the Zhang neural network for online time-varying quadratic optimization. Journal of Physics A: Mathematical and Theoretical 43, 245202 (2010)
3. Zhang, Y., Yi, C.: Zhang Neural Networks and Neural-Dynamic Method. Nova Science Publishers, New York (2011)
4. The MathWorks, Inc.: MATLAB 7.0. Natick, MA (2004)

Patch Processing
for Relational Learning Vector Quantization

Xibin Zhu, Frank-Michael Schleif, and Barbara Hammer

CITEC centre of excellence, Bielefeld University, 33615 Bielefeld, Germany
xzhu@techfak.uni-bielefeld.de

Abstract. Recently, an extension of popular learning vector quantization (LVQ) to general dissimilarity data has been proposed, relational generalized LVQ (RGLVQ) [10,9]. An intuitive prototype based classification scheme results which can divide data characterized by pairwise dissimilarities into priorly given categories. However, the technique relies on the full dissimilarity matrix and, thus, has squared time complexity and linear space complexity. In this contribution, we propose an intuitive linear time and constant space approximation of RGLVQ by means of patch processing. An efficient heuristic which maintains the good classification accuracy and interpretability of RGLVQ results, as demonstrated in three examples from the biomdical domain.

1 Introduction

Learning vector quantization constitutes a popular supervised classification algorithm which represents classes in terms of prototypical vectors [11]. Since prototypes can directly be inspected in the same way as data points, it opens the way towards intuitive data analysis, unlike many black box alternatives such as feedforward networks or support vector machines. Prototype-based approaches are beneficial if human insight is crucial such as in the medical domain [16,2].

LVQ itself has been proposed on heuristic grounds and its mathematical investigation is difficult. Several alternatives have been developed which maintain the intuitive adaptation and classification scheme of LVQ but which can be derived from an objective function: important examples are generalized LVQ (GLVQ) which is based on the accumulated hypothesis margin of the classifier [17], or robust soft LVQ, which is based on probabilities in Gaussian mixture models [18]. While resulting in high-quality classification, basic LVQ and its extensions are restricted to Euclidean vector spaces.

In modern application scenarios, data are becoming more and more complex and dedicated dissimilarity measures are often used for their processing. Examples include dynamic time warping for time series, alignment for symbolic strings, graph or tree kernels for complex structures, the compression distance to compare sequences based on an information theoretic ground, and similar. These settings do not allow a vectorial representation of data at all, rather, data are given implicitly in terms of pairwise dissimilarities or relations; we refer to a 'relational data representation' in the following when addressing data sets which

J. Wang, G.G. Yen, and M.M. Polycarpou (Eds.): ISNN 2012, Part I, LNCS 7367, pp. 55–63, 2012.

are represented implicitly by means of pairwise dissimilarities d_{ij} of data; D denotes the corresponding matrix of dissimilarities.

Several popular unsupervised prototype-based clustering methods have been extended to relational data by means of an implicit embedding of data into pseudo-Euclidean space, see e.g. [8]. Recently, this technique has been transferred to supervised classification by means of GLVQ, resulting in relational GLVQ (RGLVQ) for general relational data matrices [10,9]. A very powerful technique results which determines prototypical representatives of given relational data such that priorly given categories are met by the cluster labels as much as possible. The scheme depends on the full dissimilarity matrix, thus it requires squared time and linear space complexity for training given n data samples. This makes the technique infeasible for large data sets.

In this contribution, we propose an approximation scheme which relies on a processing of the data in patches and a subsequent compression of the information by means of the learned prototypes. Assuming fixed patch sizes, a linear time and constant space learning technique results which allows us to deal with large dissimilarity data sets in reasonable time. We will demonstrate in three examples from the biomedical domain, that the resulting heuristic maintains the good classification accuracy of RGLVQ, while considerably speeding up the techniques. Now we first shortly review prototype based classification, generalized learning vector quantization and its relational counterpart. Then we explain the principle of patch processing and we demonstrate its performance.

2   Prototype Based Classification

Assume vectorial data $\boldsymbol{x}^i \in \mathbb{R}^n, i = 1, \ldots, m$ are given. Prototypes $\boldsymbol{w}^j \in \mathbb{R}^n, j = 1, \ldots, k$ decompose data into receptive fields $R(\boldsymbol{w}^j) = \{\boldsymbol{x}^i : \forall j'\ d(\boldsymbol{x}^i, \boldsymbol{w}^j) \leq d(\boldsymbol{x}^i, \boldsymbol{w}^{j'})\}$ based on the squared Euclidean distance $d(\boldsymbol{x}^i, \boldsymbol{w}^j) = \|\boldsymbol{x}^i - \boldsymbol{w}^j\|^2$. In a classification task, prototypes are equipped with class labels $c(\boldsymbol{w}^j) \in \{1, \ldots, L\}$. A given data point $\boldsymbol{x}^i$ is mapped to the class of its closest prototype. In a training scenario, training data $\boldsymbol{x}^i$ are labeled with priorly known classes $\boldsymbol{y}^i$ and the goal of a learning algorithm is to determine the prototype positions such that the classification error $E = \sum_{i,j:\boldsymbol{x}^i \in R(\boldsymbol{w}^j)} \delta(y^i, c(\boldsymbol{w}^j))$ is as small as possible where δ refers to the standard Kronecker-function.

Generalized Learning Vector Quantization. Since a direct optimization of these costs is hard, generalized learning vector quantization (GLVQ) [17] considers the related cost function

$$E_{GLVQ} = \sum_i \Phi\left(\frac{d(\boldsymbol{x}^i, \boldsymbol{w}^+(\boldsymbol{x}^i)) - d(\boldsymbol{x}^i, \boldsymbol{w}^-(\boldsymbol{x}^i))}{d(\boldsymbol{x}^i, \boldsymbol{w}^+(\boldsymbol{x}^i)) + d(\boldsymbol{x}^i, \boldsymbol{w}^-(\boldsymbol{x}^i))}\right)$$

where Φ is a differentiable monotonic function such as the hyperbolic tangent, and $\boldsymbol{w}^+(\boldsymbol{x}^i)$ refers to the prototype closest to $\boldsymbol{x}^i$ with the same label as $\boldsymbol{x}^i$, $\boldsymbol{w}^-(\boldsymbol{x}^i)$ refers to the closest prototype with a different label. This way, for every data point, its contribution to the cost function is small iff the distance to the closest prototype with a correct label is smaller than the distance to a wrongly labeled prototype, resulting in a correct classification of the point. It has been shown in [17] that these costs can be linked to the overall hypothesis margin of an LVQ classifier which directly influences its generalization ability.

A learning algorithm can be derived thereof by means of a stochastic gradient descent. After a random initialization of prototypes, data $\boldsymbol{x}^i$ are presented in random order and adaptation of the closest correct and wrong prototype takes place by means of the update rules

$$\Delta \boldsymbol{w}^+(\boldsymbol{x}^i) \sim -\,\Phi'(\mu(\boldsymbol{x}^i)) \cdot \mu^+(\boldsymbol{x}^i) \cdot \nabla_{\boldsymbol{w}^+(\boldsymbol{x}^i)} d(\boldsymbol{x}^i, \boldsymbol{w}^+(\boldsymbol{x}^i))$$
$$\Delta \boldsymbol{w}^-(\boldsymbol{x}^i) \sim \Phi'(\mu(\boldsymbol{x}^i)) \cdot \mu^-(\boldsymbol{x}^i) \cdot \nabla_{\boldsymbol{w}^-(\boldsymbol{x}^i)} d(\boldsymbol{x}^i, \boldsymbol{w}^-(\boldsymbol{x}^i))$$

where

$$\mu(\boldsymbol{x}^i) = \frac{d(\boldsymbol{x}^i, \boldsymbol{w}^+(\boldsymbol{x}^i)) - d(\boldsymbol{x}^i, \boldsymbol{w}^-(\boldsymbol{x}^i))}{d(\boldsymbol{x}^i, \boldsymbol{w}^+(\boldsymbol{x}^i)) + d(\boldsymbol{x}^i, \boldsymbol{w}^-(\boldsymbol{x}^i))},$$

$$\mu^+(\boldsymbol{x}^i) = \frac{2 \cdot d(\boldsymbol{x}^i, \boldsymbol{w}^-(\boldsymbol{x}^i))}{(d(\boldsymbol{x}^i, \boldsymbol{w}^+(\boldsymbol{x}^i)) + d(\boldsymbol{x}^i, \boldsymbol{w}^-(\boldsymbol{x}^i))^2},$$

$$\mu^-(\boldsymbol{x}^i) = \frac{2 \cdot d(\boldsymbol{x}^i, \boldsymbol{w}^+(\boldsymbol{x}^i)}{(d(\boldsymbol{x}^i, \boldsymbol{w}^+(\boldsymbol{x}^i)) + d(\boldsymbol{x}^i, \boldsymbol{w}^-(\boldsymbol{x}^i))^2}.$$

For the squared Euclidean norm, the derivative yields $\nabla_{\boldsymbol{w}^j} d(\boldsymbol{x}^i, \boldsymbol{w}^j) = -(\boldsymbol{x}^i - \boldsymbol{w}^j)$, leading to Hebbian update rules of the prototypes, i.e. they adapt the closest prototypes towards / away from a given data point depending on the correctness of the classification.

Relational Generalized Learning Vector Quantization. In the following, we assume that data $\boldsymbol{x}^i$ are not explicitly given as vectors, rather pairwise dissimilarities $d_{i,j} = d(\boldsymbol{x}^i, \boldsymbol{x}^j)$ are available. We assume symmetry $d_{ij} = d_{ji}$ and zero diagonal $d_{ii} = 0$. However, we do not require that d refers to a Euclidean data space, i.e. D does not need to be embeddable in Euclidean space, nor does it need to fulfill the conditions of a metric. The following observation constitutes the key to transfer GLVQ to this setting [7,8]: any such matrix D gives rise to a so-called pseudo-Euclidean embedding, i.e. a real-vector space equipped with a symmetric, but not necessarily positive semidefinite form where vectorial representations $\boldsymbol{x}^i$ give rise to the dissimilarity matrix D when computed based on the bilinear form. Further, assuming prototypes are represented as linear combinations of data points

$$\boldsymbol{w}^j = \sum_i \alpha_{ji} \boldsymbol{x}^i \text{ with } \sum_i \alpha_{ji} = 1,$$

dissimilarities can be computed by means of the formula

$$d(\boldsymbol{x}^i, \boldsymbol{w}^j) = \|\boldsymbol{x}^i - \boldsymbol{w}^j\|^2 = [D \cdot \alpha_j]_i - \frac{1}{2} \cdot \alpha_j^t D \alpha_j$$

where $\alpha_j = (\alpha_{j1}, \dots, \alpha_{jn})$ refers to the vector of coefficients describing $\boldsymbol{w}^j$.

This observation gives rise to an extension of GLVQ to relational data, relational GLVQ (RGLVQ), without actually computing the underlying pseudo-Euclidean embedding of data. We represent prototypes implicitly by means of coefficients α_j and adapt the cost function accordingly:

$$E_{\mathrm{RGLVQ}} = \sum_i \Phi \left(\frac{[D\alpha^+]_i - \frac{1}{2} \cdot (\alpha^+)^t D\alpha^+ - [D\alpha^-]_i + \frac{1}{2} \cdot (\alpha^-)^t D\alpha^-}{[D\alpha^+]_i - \frac{1}{2} \cdot (\alpha^+)^t D\alpha^+ + [D\alpha^-]_i - \frac{1}{2} \cdot (\alpha^-)^t D\alpha^-} \right),$$

where as before the closest correct and wrong prototype are referred to, indicated by the superscript $+$ and $-$, respectively. A stochastic gradient descent directly leads to adaptation rules for the coefficients α^+ and α^-: component l of these vectors is adapted by the rules

$$\Delta\alpha_l^+ \sim -\Phi'(\mu(\boldsymbol{x}^i)) \cdot \mu^+(\boldsymbol{x}^i) \cdot \frac{\partial \left([D\alpha^+]_i - \frac{1}{2} \cdot (\alpha^+)^t D\alpha^+\right)}{\partial \alpha_l^+}$$

$$\Delta\alpha_l^- \sim -\Phi'(\mu(\boldsymbol{x}^i)) \cdot \mu^-(\boldsymbol{x}^i) \cdot \frac{\partial \left([D\alpha^-]_i - \frac{1}{2} \cdot (\alpha^-)^t D\alpha^-\right)}{\partial \alpha_l^-}$$

where $\mu(\boldsymbol{x}^i)$, $\mu^+(\boldsymbol{x}^i)$, and $\mu^-(\boldsymbol{x}^i)$ are as above. The partial derivative yields

$$\frac{\partial [D\alpha_j]_i - \frac{1}{2} \cdot \alpha_j^t D\alpha_j}{\partial \alpha_{jl}} = d_{il} - \sum_{l'} d_{l'l}\alpha_{jl'}$$

After every adaptation step, normalization takes place to guarantee $\sum_i \alpha_{ji} = 1$. This way, a learning algorithm which adapts prototypes in a supervised manner similar to GLVQ is given for general dissimilarity data, whereby prototypes are implicitly embedded in pseudo-Euclidean space. We initialize α_{ij} with small random values such that the sum is one. It is possible to take class information into account by setting $\alpha_{ji} := 0$ if $c(\boldsymbol{w}^j) \neq \boldsymbol{y}^i$.

The resulting classifier represents clusters in terms of prototypes for general dissimilarity data. Although these prototypes correspond to vector positions in pseudo-Euclidean space, they can usually not be inspected directly because the pseudo-Euclidean embedding is not computed directly. For inspection, we use an approximation of the prototypes: we substitute a prototype by its K nearest exemplars as measured by the given dissimilarity.

Out-of-sample extension is as follows: given a novel data point $\boldsymbol{x}$ characterized by its pairwise dissimilarities $D(\boldsymbol{x})$ to the data used for training, the dissimilarity to the prototypes is given by $d(\boldsymbol{x}, \boldsymbol{w}^j) = D(\boldsymbol{x})^t \cdot \alpha_j - \frac{1}{2} \cdot \alpha_j^t D\alpha_j$. For an approximation of prototypes by exemplars, obviously, only the dissimilarities to these exemplars have to be computed, i.e. a very sparse classifier results.

3   Patch Relational Generalized Learning Vector Quantization

RGLVQ relies on the full dissimilarity matrix D and represents prototypes implicitly by means of coefficients α_{ji} referring of the contribution of data point $\boldsymbol{x}^i$

to prototype $\boldsymbol{w}^j$. Thus, the algorithm has squared time complexity and linear space complexity. Patch processing has been proposed as an alternative approximation scheme. It offers a powerful linear time and limited memory approximation for streaming data sets with a direct access to the dissimilarities, e.g. by means of a computation scheme for $d(\boldsymbol{x}^i, \boldsymbol{x}^j)$ [1]. In the article [8], it has been used to speed up relational prototype based clustering. The resulting technique is linear time and constant space. Here we extend it to RGLVQ.

The basic idea of patch processing is: A fixed size of the patches m is chosen, and data are separated into patches. Then the patches of data are processed consecutively using RGLVQ. Given a dissimilarity matrix, the patch p corresponds to the values of the matrix describing the pairwise dissimilarities along the diagonal: $d(\boldsymbol{x}^i, \boldsymbol{x}^j)$ where $i, j \in \{p \cdot m + 1, \ldots, (p+1) \cdot m\}$. In addition to this part, all previous patches are represented in compressed form by means of the prototypes found before. This way, the patch does not only represent data $\{\boldsymbol{x}^{pm+1} \ldots \boldsymbol{x}^{(p+1)m}\}$ but all data $\{\boldsymbol{x}^1 \ldots, \boldsymbol{x}^{(p+1)m}\}$ either explicitly or implicitly by taking into account the already extracted prototypes. To apply RGLVQ, the dissimilarities of data and these prototypes need to be available. In patch processing, these are retrieved on the fly.

Note that it is not clear how to compute these dissimilarities efficiently if prototypes are of the general form $\boldsymbol{w}^j = \sum_i \alpha_{ji} \boldsymbol{x}^i$: this representation would, eventually, refer to the full dissimilarity matrix. Therefore, after processing a patch, we approximate a prototype by its K-approximation for fixed K. The K-approximation $\boldsymbol{w}^j_K$ of a prototype $\boldsymbol{w}^j$ based on a given set of points E corresponds to the closest K data points in E: $\boldsymbol{w}^j_K := \{\boldsymbol{x}^i \in E \,|\, d(\boldsymbol{x}^i, \boldsymbol{w}^j) \leq d(\boldsymbol{x}^{i'}, \boldsymbol{w}^j)$ for all but K indices $i\}$. This way, the dissimilarity matrix considered in step p corresponds to a fixed size $m + kK$ matrix, k being the number of prototypes.

Algorithm 1. Principled algorithm for patch clustering

1: **init:** $E := \emptyset$;   ▷ exemplars/K-approximated prototypes
2:     $m_i := 1$ for $\boldsymbol{x}_i \in E$;   ▷ multiplicities
3:     $p := 1$;   ▷ patch number
4: **repeat**
5:     $P_{m,m} := \{d(\boldsymbol{x}_i, \boldsymbol{x}_j)\} \,|\, i, j \in \{p \cdot m + 1, \ldots, (p+1) \cdot m\}\}$;   ▷ patch size m
6:     $P_{m,|E|} := \{d(\boldsymbol{x}_i, \boldsymbol{x}_j) \,|\, p \cdot m < i \leq (p+1) \cdot m, \boldsymbol{x}_j \in E\}$;
7:   ▷ dissimilarities of patch and exemplars
8:     $P_{|E|,|E|} := \{d(\boldsymbol{x}_i, \boldsymbol{x}_j) \,|\, \boldsymbol{x}_i, \boldsymbol{x}_j \in E\}$;   ▷ dissimilarities of exemplars
9:     $P := \begin{pmatrix} P_{m,m} & P_{m,|E|} \\ P_{m,|E|}^t & P_{|E|,|E|} \end{pmatrix}$;   ▷ full matrix for loop
10:     $m_i :=$ multiplicities for $\boldsymbol{x}_i \in E$;   ▷ multiple points
11:     $m_i := 1$ for other x_i;   ▷ standard points
12:     perform Patch RGLVQ with multiplicities for P and m_i;
13:     approximate prototypes by K closest exemplars;
14:         $E :=$ set of exemplars obtained this way;   ▷ new exemplars
15:         $m_i :=$ size of receptive field/K counted with multiplicities for $\boldsymbol{x}_i \in E$;
16:     p:=p+1;   ▷ next patch
17: **until** all dissimilarities are considered

Exemplars/K-approximated prototypes representing the previous clustering results represent a large set of data. Thus, it is vital to weight their relevance correspondingly. In the patch algorithm, this problem is solved by assigning a multiplicity to these prototypes which corresponds to the size of its receptive field divided by K. This means, we assume that the corresponding prototypes are contained in the data set not only once but multiple times. Note that RGLVQ can easily be extended to deal with sets where data points are equipped with multiplicities. For a points x^i with multiplicity m_i its contribution to the costs is simply multiplied by m_i. Hence the corresponding step width of a gradient descent algorithm is simply multiplied with m_i. The resulting algorithm, Patch RGLVQ, is depicted in Algorithm 1.

4   Experiments

We evaluate the algorithm for three benchmark data sets where data are characterized by pairwise dissimilarities:

1. The Copenhagen chromosomes data set constitutes a benchmark from cytogenetics [13]. 4,200 human chromosomes from 22 classes (the autosomal chromosomes) are represented by grey-valued images. These are transferred to strings measuring the thickness of their silhouettes. These strings are compared using edit distance with insertion/deletion costs 4.5 [15].
2. The vibrio data set consists of 1,100 samples of vibrio bacteria populations characterized by mass spectra. The spectra contain approx. 42,000 mass positions. The full data set consists of 49 classes of vibrio-sub-species. The mass spectra are preprocessed with a standard workflow using the BioTyper software [14]. As usual, mass spectra display strong functional characteristics due to the dependency of subsequent masses, such that problem adapted similarities such as described in [3,14] are beneficial. In our case, similarities are calculated using a specific alignment measure as provided by the BioTyper software[14].
3. The *SwissProt* data set consists of 10,988 samples of protein sequences in 32 classes taken as a subset from the full database [4]. The considered subset of the SwissProt database refers to the release 37 mimicking the setting as proposed in [12]. The full database consists of 77,977 protein sequences varying between 30 to more than 1000 amino acids depending on the sequence. The 32 most common classes such as Globin, Cytochrome a, Cytochrome b, Tubulin, Protein kinase st, etc. provided by the Prosite labeling [5] where taken leading to 10,988 sequences. Due to this choice, an associated classification problem maps the sequences to their corresponding prosite labels. These sequences are compared using Smith-Waterman which computes a local alignment of sequences [6]. Popular alternatives could rely on global alignment as provided by Needleman-Wunsch, or linear time heuristics such as BLAST or FASTA [6]. This database is the standard source for identifying and analyzing protein sequences such that an automated classification and processing technique would be very desirable.

Table 1. Results on three data sets: RGLVQ, RGLVQ with Nyström, and Patch RGLVQ are evaluated in a repeated cross-validation. The classification accuracy, and the speedup factor according to the CPU time are reported.

	RGLVQ	Nyström-RGLVQ using 10%	Patch - RGLVQ $K = 1$	$K = 3$	$K = 5$
Vibrio	1.0	0.992	0.999	1	1
Chromosomes	0.927	0.782	0.867	0.840	0.828
SwissProt	0.823	0.834	0.833	0.824	0.822
speed-up factor	1	7.6	26.2	20	13.2

These three data sets constitute typical examples of non-Euclidean data which occur in biomedical domains. The dissimilarity measures are inherently non-Euclidean and cannot be embedded isometrically in a Euclidean vector space.

We compare the results of RLVQ for the full dissimilarity matrix and patch processing. For comparison, we report the result of a Nyström approximation of the full dissimilarity matrix. This approximation constitutes a standard low rank approximation of a similarity or dissimilarity matrix, which has been introduced in the context of kernel methods in [19]. For RGLVQ, it has been proposed in the contribution [10]. Like patch processing, it leads to a linear time approximation technique. The setting is as follows in the experiments:

- *Evaluation*: We evaluate the result by means of the classification accuracy obtained in a ten-fold cross-validation with 10 repeats (Chromosomes, Vibrio), or a 2-fold cross-validation with 10 repeats (SwissProt).
- *RGLVQ*: RGLVQ is initialized randomly, and training takes place for 5 epochs. We use 49 (Vibrio), 63 (Chromosomes), and 64 (SwissProt) prototypes evenly distributed among the classes.
- *Patch processing*: For patch processing, ten patches are chosen. The value K for the K-approximation for patch processing is taken in $\{1, 3, 5\}$.
- *Nyström approximation*: A fraction of 10% of the data is used.
- *Implementation:* For all data sets, we use a 12 Intel(R) Xeon X5690 machine with 3.47GHz processors and 48 GB DDR3 1333MHz memory. All experiments are implemented in Matlab.[1]

For Vibrio and SwissProt, the classification accuracy obtained with a linear time approximation is the same as for full RGLVQ. For Chromosomes, it decreases by 6% using patch approximation as compared to almost 25% for the Nyström approximation. Interestingly, all patch approximations already yield a high quality when approximating the prototypes by its closest exemplar ($K = 1$). This approximation has the side effect that classes can directly be inspected in terms of this representative exemplar, i.e. interpretable models result. We measure the speed-up of the technique for the SwissProt data set which deals with close to

---

[1] The Matlab code of the proposed algorithms can be obtained from Xibin Zhu (xzhu@techfak.uni-bielefeld.de) on request.

$11,000^2$ entries. Original RGLVQ takes 24481 seconds CPU time (i.e. almost seven hours), which can be accelerated by a factor 26 to 15 minutes using patch processing – the Nyström approximation requires considerably more time.

5 Conclusions

In this contribution, we proposed a linear time constant space approximation scheme for supervised prototype based classification by means of relational LVQ. Apart from a considerable speed-up, training does no longer rely on the full dissimilarity matrix; rather a linear subpart is required depending on the chosen patch scheme and the prototypes. Since the computation of the full matrix often constitutes a major bottleneck for complex dissimilarity measures such as alignment, this fact offers even greater application potential. The method has been demonstrated in three examples from the biomedical domain, among those a large portion of the polular SwissProt data set for proteins.

Acknowledgement. Financial support from the Cluster of Excellence 277 Cognitive Interaction Technology funded in the framework of the German Excellence Initiative is gratefully acknowledged.

References

1. Alex, N., Hasenfuss, A., Hammer, B.: Patch clustering for massive data sets. Neurocomputing 72(7-9), 1455–1469 (2009)
2. Arlt, W., et al.: Urine steroid metabolomics as a biomarker tool for detecting malignancy in adrenal tumors. Journal of Clinical Endocrinology and Metabolism 96(12), 3775–3784 (2011)
3. Barbuddhe, S.B., Maier, T., Schwarz, G., Kostrzewa, M., Hof, H., Domann, E., Chakraborty, T., Hain, T.: Rapid identification and typing of listeria species by matrix-assisted laser desorption ionization-time of flight mass spectrometry. Applied and Environmental Microbiology 74(17), 5402–5407 (2008)
4. Boeckmann, B., Bairoch, A., Apweiler, R., Blatter, M.-C., Estreicher, A., Gasteiger, E., Martin, M., Michoud, K., O'Donovan, C., Phan, I., Pilbout, S., Schneider, M.: The swiss-prot protein knowledge base and its supplement trembl in 2003. Nucleic Acids Research 31, 365–370 (2003)
5. Gasteiger, E., Gattiker, A., Hoogland, C., Ivanyi, I., Appel, R., Bairoch, A.: Expasy: the proteomics server for in-depth protein knowledge and analysis. Nucleic Acids Res. 31, 3784–3788 (2003)
6. Gusfield, D.: Algorithms on Strings, Trees, and Sequences: Computer Science and Computational Biology. Cambridge University Press (1997)
7. Hammer, B.: Learning with Recurrent Neural Networks. LNCIS, vol. 254. Springer (2000)
8. Hammer, B., Hasenfuss, A.: Topographic mapping of large dissimilarity datasets. Neural Computation 22(9), 2229–2284 (2010)
9. Hammer, B., Mokbel, B., Schleif, F.-M., Zhu, X.: Prototype-Based Classification of Dissimilarity Data. In: Gama, J., Bradley, E., Hollmén, J. (eds.) IDA 2011. LNCS, vol. 7014, pp. 185–197. Springer, Heidelberg (2011)

10. Hammer, B., Mokbel, B., Schleif, F.-M., Zhu, X.: White Box Classification of Dissimilarity Data. In: Corchado, E., Snášel, V., Abraham, A., Woźniak, M., Graña, M., Cho, S.-B. (eds.) HAIS 2012, Part III. LNCS, vol. 7208, pp. 309–321. Springer, Heidelberg (2012)

11. Kohonen, T. (ed.): Self-Organizing Maps, 3rd edn. Springer-Verlag New York, Inc. (2001)

12. Kohonen, T., Somervuo, P.: How to make large self-organizing maps for nonvectorial data. Neural Networks 15, 945–952 (2002)

13. Lundsteen, C., Phillip, J., Granum, E.: Quantitative analysis of 6985 digitized trypsin g-banded human metaphase chromosomes. Clinical Genetics 18, 355–370 (1980)

14. Maier, T., Klebel, S., Renner, U., Kostrzewa, M.: Fast and reliable maldi-tof ms–based microorganism identification. Nature Methods (3) (2006)

15. Neuhaus, M., Bunke, H.: Edit distance based kernel functions for structural pattern classification. Pattern Recognition 39(10), 1852–1863 (2006)

16. Schleif, F.-M., Hammer, B., Kostrzewa, M., Villmann, T.: Exploration of mass-spectrometric data in clinical proteomics using learning vector quantization methods. Briefings in Bioinformatics 9(2), 129–143 (2008)

17. Schneider, P., Biehl, M., Hammer, B.: Adaptive relevance matrices in learning vector quantization. Neural Computation 21(12), 3532–3561 (2009)

18. Seo, S., Obermayer, K.: Soft learning vector quantization. Neural Computation 15, 1589–1604 (2002)

19. Williams, C., Seeger, M.: Using the Nyström method to speed up kernel machines. In: Advances in Neural Information Processing Systems 13, pp. 682–688. MIT Press (2001)

A Neural Network Model
for Currency Arbitrage Detection

Zheng Zhang

College of Mathematics and Information,
China West Normal University, Nanchong 637002, China

Abstract. The currency arbitrage detection is to find a proper currency conversion sequence that can make the most currency arbitrage. In this paper, the currency arbitrage detection is described as a energy function. And then a Lotka-Volterra (LV) recurrent neural network (RNN) is proposed to obtain the minimum points of the energy function. Simulations demonstrate that the proposed LV RNN is a practical and effective model for the currency arbitrage detection.

Keywords: currency arbitrage detection, Energy Function, Minimum Points, Lotka-Volterra Recurrent Neural Networks, Stable Attractors.

1 Introduction

Converting one currency to or from any other one currency is based on the current day's exchange rates. The currency exchange rate includes the ask price and bid price. The ask price represents what has to be paid in the quote currency to obtain one unit of the base currency when buying a currency. However, the bid price represents what will be obtained in the quote currency when selling one unit of the base currency. In general, there always exist losses when converting money from a base currency to another and then back. However, if there is discrepancy in the exchange rates among different financial centers, a longer chain of currency conversions may result in a gain in the base currency. Such an opportunity is termed as a currency arbitrage [1].

Currency arbitrage detection means to obtain the most currency arbitrage through detecting a currency conversion sequence from given several currencies. So, the problem of the currency arbitrage detection can be described as a optimization problem. Neural network is a efficient method for solving optimization problems. In [2], Hopfield and Tank applied Hopfield network to solve traveling salesman problem. Since then, many other neural networks were proposed to solve the optimization problems, see, e.g., [3–6]. In [7], the competitive layer model (CLM) was implemented by a Lotka-Volterra (LV) recurrent neural network (RNN). The CLM of the LV RNN has the capability of feature binding which can be used to solve different optimization problems. In this paper, a LV RNN model modified from [7] is proposed to solve the problem of currency arbitrage.

J. Wang, G.G. Yen, and M.M. Polycarpou (Eds.): ISNN 2012, Part I, LNCS 7367, pp. 64–71, 2012.

The paper is organized as follows. Section 2 briefly introduces the LV RNN model in [7]. In Section 3, the LV RNN model for currency arbitrage detection is described in detail. Simulations are presented in Section 4 to demonstrate that the propose LV RNN model is efficient for detecting currency arbitrage. Finally, conclusions are given in Section 5.

2   The Lotka-Volterra Recurrent Neural Networks

The LV RNN model was firstly proposed in [8]. It was derived from the conventional membrane dynamics of neurons with a sigmoid response function. LV RNNs possess good dynamical properties and have many potential applications in WTA, winner-share-all (WSA) and k-winner-take-all (k-WTA) problems [9,10]. In [11], some properties of permitted and forbidden sets of LV RNNs are reported. More general dynamical properties can be found in [12,13]. Some hardware implementations of LV RNNs are now available [10]. In [7], a LV RNN was proposed to implement the CLM. The CLM contains L layers, and there are N neurons in each layer. The corresponding energy function of the CLM is described by

$$E(x) = \frac{C}{2} \sum_{i=1}^{N} \left(\sum_{\beta=1}^{L} x_{i\beta} - h_i \right)^2 - \frac{1}{2} \sum_{\alpha=1}^{L} \sum_{i,j=1}^{N} w_{ij} x_{i\alpha} x_{j\alpha} \tag{1}$$

for $x \in \mathbb{R}_+^{NL}$. Where, the symbols $\alpha, \beta (1 \leq \alpha, \beta \leq L)$ are layer indexes, and the symbols $i, j (1 \leq i, j \leq N)$ are row indexes. h_i is input for row i. Here, w_{ij} denotes the similar between the neuron $i\alpha$ and the neuron $j\alpha$. Those neurons that are more similar will have lager w_{ij}. The CLM has the capability of feature binding, which can bind similar features into same layers. The LV RNN that implements the CLM can be described as follows,

$$\dot{x}_{i\alpha}(t) = x_{i\alpha}(t) \left[C \left(h_i - \sum_{\beta=1}^{L} x_{i\beta}(t) \right) + \sum_{j=1}^{N} w_{ij} x_{j\alpha}(t) \right] \tag{2}$$

for $t \geq 0$ and $1 \leq i \leq N, 1 \leq \alpha \leq L$. In [7], the obtained theories shown that the LV RNN (2) is convergence in $x \in \mathbb{R}_+^{NL}$ space, and that the set of the minimum points of the energy function (1) is equal to the set of stable attractors of (2). In addition, for each stable attractor, in each row there is only one neuron whose value is greater than 0, the values of other neurons are equal to 0. Refer to [7] for details.

3   The LV RNN Model for Currency Arbitrage Detection

Inspired by the work of [7], in this paper, a new LV RNN model for currency arbitrage detection is proposed. It assumes that there are N currencies. Let

r_{ij} denote the currency exchange rate for converting currency i to currency j, where $i, j = 1, 2, \cdots, N$. Obviously, $r_{ij} \neq r_{ji}$ when $i \neq j$. R is called as currency exchange rate matrix. For example, Table 1 shows the exchange rates among 5 currencies on January 9, 2012. Therefore,

$$R = \begin{bmatrix} 1 & 0.783 & 0.645 & 1.022 & 77.19 \\ 1.278 & 1 & 0.824 & 1.305 & 98.62 \\ 1.55 & 1.213 & 1 & 1.583 & 119.638 \\ 0.979 & 0.766 & 0.632 & 1 & 75.566 \\ 0.013 & 0.01 & 0.008 & 0.013 & 1 \end{bmatrix}.$$

If the currency conversion sequence is $1 \rightarrow 3 \rightarrow 2 \rightarrow 5 \rightarrow 4 \rightarrow 1$, then the obtained currency arbitrage is $r_{13} \cdot r_{32} \cdot r_{25} \cdot r_{54} \cdot r_{41} = 0.982$. It means that there is 0.018 USA dollars losses if converting one USA dollar according to the currency conversion sequence.

The aim of currency arbitrage detection is to detect a currency conversion sequence $i \rightarrow j \rightarrow k \rightarrow l \rightarrow \cdots \rightarrow p \rightarrow q \rightarrow i$ such that $r_{ij} \cdot r_{jk} \cdot r_{kl} \cdots r_{pq} \cdot r_{qk} > 1$ and the currency arbitrage is to be the maximum. However, how to obtain a currency conversion sequence that results in a most currency arbitrage? For N currencies, the currency arbitrage problem can be mapped into a neural network consisting of $N \times N$ neurons. The current state of the neuron $i\alpha$ is denoted by $x_{i\alpha}$, where $i(1 \leq i \leq N)$ is the currency index and $\alpha(1 \leq \alpha \leq N)$ is the order in the conversion sequence. The neural network is shown in Fig. 1. The neuron i in each column connects with the neuron j in the next column through $log(r_{ij})$, $i, j = 1, 2, \cdots, N$. Denote $T = \{x | \forall \alpha, \exists i, x_{i\alpha} > 0, x_{j\alpha} = 0, (i \neq j)\}$. Then T is the set of currency conversion sequences, any one of T consists a currency conversion sequence. The Fig.2 shows one stable attractor x^* of neural network. The gray color for the neuron $i\alpha$ denotes $x_{i\alpha} > 0$, white means $x_{i\alpha} = 0$. Obviously, $x^* \in T$. Therefore, the obtained currency conversion sequence from x^* is: $2 \rightarrow 3 \rightarrow 1 \rightarrow i \rightarrow \ldots \rightarrow j \rightarrow N \rightarrow 2$.

From the view of mathematical programming, the currency arbitrage problem can be described as a quadratic programming problem with linear constraints

$$\begin{cases} \min -\sum_{\alpha=1}^{N} \sum_{i,j=1, i\neq j}^{N} log(r_{ij}) x_{i\alpha} x_{j(\alpha+1)}, \\ \text{s.t.} \sum_{\alpha=1}^{N} x_{i\alpha} = 1, \quad (1 \leq i \leq N) \\ \sum_{i=1}^{N} x_{i\alpha} = 1, \quad (1 \leq \alpha \leq N), \\ x \in T \end{cases} \quad (3)$$

(the $\alpha + 1$ subscript is given modulo N).

Detecting currency arbitrage means finding the optimum points in the non-negative orthant of $\mathbb{R}^{NN}$ space, denoted by $\mathbb{R}_+^{NN}$.

In order to guarantee obtaining a valid exchange sequence, we need to add more constraint terms. Then, equation (3) can be rewritten as another equivalent

Table 1. Exchange rates on January 9, 2012

	USD	EUR	GBP	CAD	JPY
USD	1	0.783	0.645	1.022	77.19
EUR	1.278	1	0.824	1.305	98.62
GBP	1.55	1.213	1	1.583	119.638
CAD	0.979	0.766	0.632	1	75.566
JPY	0.013	0.01	0.008	0.013	1

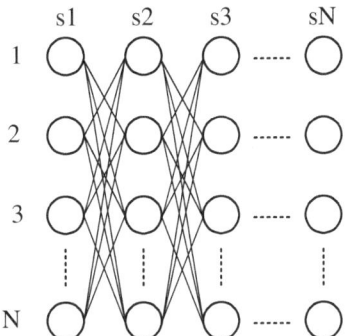

Fig. 1. Structure of neural network

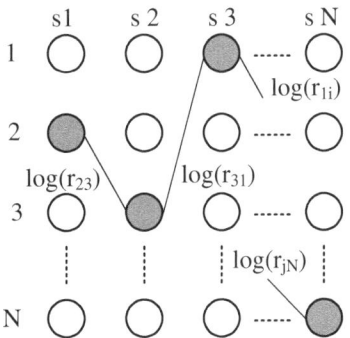

Fig. 2. A stable attractor of neural network

optimization problem

$$
\begin{cases}
\min \dfrac{a}{2} \sum_{\alpha=1}^{N} \left(\sum_{j=1}^{N} x_{j\alpha} - 1 \right)^{2} + \dfrac{b}{2} \sum_{\alpha=1}^{N} \sum_{i,j=1}^{N} w_{ij} x_{i\alpha} x_{j\alpha} \\
\quad -c \sum_{\alpha=1}^{N} \sum_{i,j=1}^{N} log(r_{ij}) x_{i\alpha} x_{j(\alpha+1)}, \\
\text{s.t. } x_{i\alpha} \geq 0, \quad (1 \leq i \leq N; 1 \leq \alpha \leq N)
\end{cases}
\tag{4}
$$

where $a > 0$, $b > 0$ and $c > 0$ are some sufficiently large constants. In equation (4), the first two items are constraints, which ensure that in each column there is only one active neuron. The third item is optimization objective. Let w_{ij} be

$$w_{ij} = \begin{cases} 0, \text{ if } i = j \\ 1, \text{ if } i \neq j \end{cases}$$

where $1 \leq i, j \leq N$. Thus, Detecting currency arbitrage is then equivalent to finding a optimum point of (4) in the $\mathbb{R}_+^{NN}$ space. Therefore, according to equation (4), the energy function of detecting currency arbitrage can be defined by

$$E(x) = \frac{a}{2} \sum_{\alpha=1}^{N} \left(\sum_{j=1}^{N} x_{j\alpha} - 1 \right)^2 + \frac{b}{2} \sum_{\alpha=1}^{N} \sum_{i,j=1}^{N} w_{ij} x_{i\alpha} x_{j\alpha} \qquad (5)$$

$$-c \sum_{\alpha=1}^{N} \sum_{i,j=1}^{N} log(r_{ij}) x_{i\alpha} x_{j(\alpha+1)}$$

for $x \in \mathbb{R}_+^{NN}$. Detecting currency arbitrage requires finding minimum points of the above energy function $E(x)$ in the $\mathbb{R}_+^{NN}$ space. Denote

$$E_{i\alpha}(x) = \frac{\partial E(x)}{\partial x_{i\alpha}} = a \left(\sum_{j=1}^{N} x_{j\alpha} - 1 \right) + b \sum_{j=1}^{N} w_{ij} x_{j\alpha}$$

$$-c \sum_{j=1}^{N} log(r_{ij}) x_{j(\alpha+1)} - c \sum_{j=1}^{N} log(r_{ji}) x_{j(\alpha-1)} \qquad (6)$$

(the $\alpha + 1$ and $(\alpha - 1)$ subscripts are given modulo N).

Therefore, based on equation (5) and (6), a LV RNN can be designed to find the minimum point of the energy function (5). The proposed LV RNN model can be described as follows.

$$\dot{x}_{i\alpha}(t) = x_{i\alpha}(t) \left[-a \left(\sum_{j=1}^{N} x_{j\alpha}(t) - 1 \right) - b \sum_{j=1}^{N} w_{ij} x_{j\alpha}(t) \right.$$

$$\left. +c \sum_{j=1}^{N} log(r_{ij}) x_{j(\alpha+1)}(t) + c \sum_{j=1}^{N} log(r_{ji}) x_{j(\alpha-1)}(t) \right], t \geq 0 \qquad (7)$$

for $t \geq 0$ and $1 \leq i \leq N, 1 \leq \alpha \leq N$. $x(t)$ denotes the state of the network at time t.

The LV RNN model can be used to obtain minimum points of the energy function $E(x)$ in $\mathbb{R}_+^{NN}$ space. Therefore, the LV RNN model can be used to detect currency arbitrage from the currency exchange matrix R.

4   Simulations

In this section, we will test the performance of the LV RNN for detecting currency arbitrage by simulations. Before running the LV RNN for detecting currency arbitrage from R, the initial state and the parameters a, b and c of the LV RNN model have to be set. It is considered that small disturbances are needed at the beginning to break the symmetry of the neural network. So, the initial state $x(0)$ is randomly generated by $x_{i\alpha} = 1 + \kappa \cdot u$. Where $i, \alpha = 1, 2, \cdots, N$, κ is a small value and u is a uniform random value in $[0, 1]$. In addition, for the above example shown in Table 1, in order to ensure that there only one active neuron in each column, set $a = 500$, $b = 500$ and $c = 5$. Under given initial state and parameters setting, the currency arbitrage detection can be completed by running the LV RNN (7) until it converges to a stable attractor. Fig. 3(a)-3(e) show the trajectories of neurons in the column from 1 to 5. The trajectory of each neuron is convergent. In each column, only one neuron has state value that is larger than 0, other state values are equal to 0. Fig. 3(f) shows the corresponding energy function of the LV RNN. The energy function reaches it's one minimum point along with the convergence of the LV RNN.

The obtained stable attractor of the LV RNN is shown bellow

$$
x^* = \begin{pmatrix}
0.0000 & 0.9827 & 0.0000 & 0.0000 & 1.0000 \\
0.0000 & 0.0000 & 0.0000 & 0.0000 & 0.0000 \\
0.0000 & 0.0000 & 0.0000 & 0.0000 & 0.0000 \\
0.0000 & 0.0000 & 1.0174 & 0.0000 & 0.0000 \\
1.0003 & 0.0000 & 0.0000 & 1.0002 & 0.0000
\end{pmatrix}.
$$

From the stable attractor x^*, The obtained currency conversion sequence from the exchange matrix R is $5 \to 1 \to 4 \to 5 \to 1 \to 5$. The conversion sequence can make 0.0075 on each initial JPY, USD or CAD.

5   Conclusions

This paper proposes a LV RNN model to detect currency arbitrage. Through running the LV RNN until it converges to it's one stable attractor, the energy function which describes the problem of currency arbitrage detection also reach it's one of minimum points. Therefore, from the stable attractor, we can obtain a currency conversion sequence which can make the most currency arbitrage. Simulations demonstrate that the proposed LV RNN can be used to detect currency arbitrage.

Acknowledgments. A Project Supported by Scientific Research Fund of SiChuan Provincial Education Department(12ZA172). This work was also partly supported by the Foundation of the China West Normal University under Grant 09A016 and 10A003.

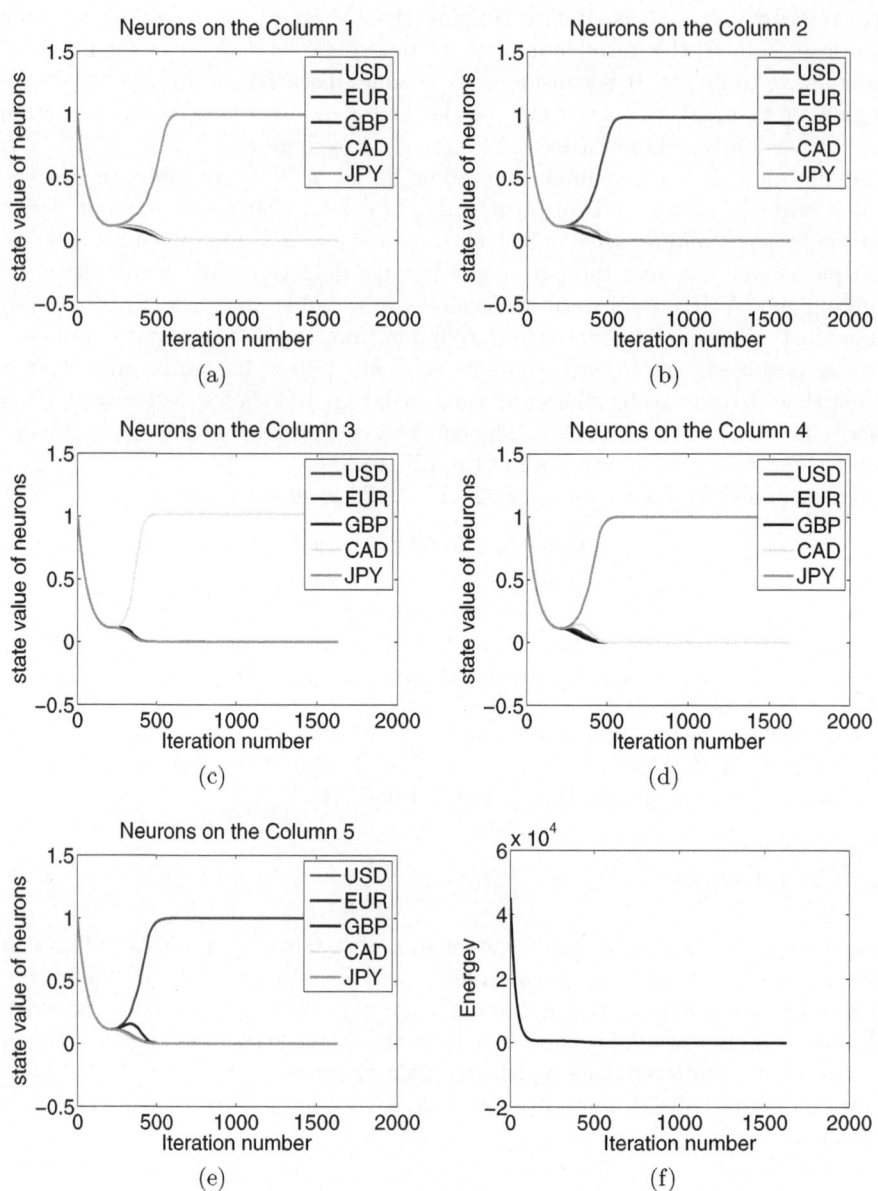

Fig. 3. The trajectories of the LV RNN

References

1. Soon, W.M., Ye, H.Q.: Currency arbitrage detection using a binary integer programming model. International Journal of Mathematical Education in Science and Technology 42(3), 369–376 (2011)
2. Hopfield, J.J., Tank, D.W.: "Neural" computation of decisions in optimization problem. Biol. Cybern. 52(3), 141–152 (1985)
3. Tang, H.J., Tan, K.C., Yi, Z.: A columnar competitive model for solving combinatorial optimization problems. IEEE Trancsaction on Neural Networks 15(6), 1568–1573 (2004)
4. Qu, H., Yi, Z., Tang, H.J.: Improving local minima of columnar competitive model for TSPs. IEEE Tansactions on Circuits and Systems-I: Regular Papers 53(6), 1353–1362 (2006)
5. Teoh, E.J., Tan, K.C., Tang, H.J., Xiang, C., Goh, C.K.: An asynchronous recurrent linear threshold network approach to solving the traveling salesman problem. Neurocomputing 71, 1359–1372 (2008)
6. Budinich, M.: A self-organising neural network for the travelling salesman problem that is competitive with simulated annealing. Neural Computation 8(2), 416–424 (1996)
7. Yi, Z.: Foundations of implementing the competitive layer model by Lotka-Volterra recurrent neural networks. IEEE Transactions on Neural Networks 21(3), 494–507 (2010)
8. Fukai, T., Tanaka, S.: A simple neural network exhibiting selective activation of neuronal ensembles: from winner-take-all to winner-share-all. Neural Computation 9(1), 77–97 (1997)
9. Asai, T., Fukai, T., Tanaka, S.: A subthreshold MOS circuit for the Lotka-Volterra neural network porducing the winner-take-all solutions. Neural Networks Letter 12, 211–216 (1999)
10. Asai, T., Ohtani, M., Yonezu, H.: Analog integrated circuits for the Lotka-Volterra competitive neural networks. IEEE Trans. Neural Networks 10(5), 1222–1231 (1999)
11. Hahnloser, R.H., Seung, H.S., Slotine, J.J.: Permitted and forbidden sets in symmetric threshold-linear networks. Neural Computation 15(3), 621–638 (2003)
12. Yi, Z., Tan, K.K.: Convergence analysis of recurrent neural networks. Kluwer Academic Publishers (2004)
13. Yi, Z., Tan, K.K.: Dynamical stability conditions for Lotka-Volterra recurrent neural networks with delays. Physical Review E 66, 011910 (2002)

A Rank Reduced Matrix Method
in Extreme Learning Machine

Shuxia Lu, Guiqiang Zhang, and Xizhao Wang

Key Lab. of Machine Learning and Computational Intelligence,
College of Mathematics and Computer Science, Hebei University, Baoding, Hebei, China
{cmclusx,zhangguiqiang81}@126.com, wangxz@hbu.cn

Abstract. Extreme learning machine (ELM) is a learning algorithm for single-hidden layer feedforward neural networks (SLFNs) which randomly chooses hidden nodes and analytically determines the output weights of SLFNs. but when dealing with large datasets, we need more hidden nodes to enhance training and testing accuracy, in this case, this algorithm can't achieve high speed any more, sometimes its training can't be executed because the bias matrix is out of memory. We focus on this issue and use the Rank Reduced Matrix (MMR) method to calculate the hidden layer output matrix, the result showed this method can not only reach much higher speed but also better improve the generalization performance whenever the number of hidden nodes is large or not.

Keywords: Extreme learning machine, Singular value decomposition, Rank reduced matrix.

1   Introduction

Extreme learning machine (ELM) [1] represents one of the recent successful approaches in machine learning. It not only has been successfully applied to many real world applications but also has been shown to generate good generalization performance at high learning speed. But unfortunately, when dealing with large datasets, certain problems arise, including the huge amount of memory required for storing the bias matrix, so a lot of varieties of ELM was proposed by researchers for solving both generalization performance and learning speed problems in the last few years. For instance, in [2] a sequential learning algorithm referred to as on line sequential extreme learning machine (OS-ELM) that can handle both additive and RBF nodes in a unified framework is introduced. Similar to [2], in [3] propose a simple and efficient approach named error minimized extreme learning machine (ELM) to automatically determine the number of hidden nodes in generalized single-hidden-layer feedforward networks (SLFNs) which need not be neural alike. In [4] a structure-adjustable online learning neural network (SAO-ELM) based on the extreme learning machine (ELM) with quicker learning speed and better generalization performance is proposed. And in [5] proposed pruned-ELM, this algorithm uses statistical methods to measure the relevance of hidden nodes, beginning from an

J. Wang, G.G. Yen, and M.M. Polycarpou (Eds.): ISNN 2012, Part I, LNCS 7367, pp. 72–79, 2012.
© Springer-Verlag Berlin Heidelberg 2012

initial large number of hidden nodes, irrelevant nodes are then pruned by considering their relevance to the class labels. This approach leads to compact network classifiers that generate fast response and robust prediction accuracy on unseen data.

Unlike the above varieties of ELM, since ELM can be referred to a linear system, we can improve the algorithm which used to compute the Moore-Penrose generalized inverse, there are several methods for computing the Moore-Penrose inverse matrix proposed by learners in the last few years, Toutounian and Ataei [6] presented the CGS-MPi algorithm based on the conjugate Gram-Schmidt process and the Moore-Penrose inverse of partitioned matrices, and they concluded that this algorithm is a robust and efficient tool for computing the Moore-Penrose inverse of large sparse and rank deficient matrices. Also, in the recent work [7] Petkovic and Stanimirovic proposed a new iterative method based on Penrose equations. In addition, Greville's method [8] is a classic method, and many varieties were proposed. But the most popular method is the Singular Value Decomposition (SVD) method, this method is very accurate but also time-consuming since it requires a large mount of computational resources, especially in the case of large matrices, in order to train ELM on large datasets we used a new algorithm Rank Reduced Matrix (RRM) based on [9] to precisely compute the Moore-Penrose generalized inverse of the hidden layer output matrix. Our algorithm based on an efficient reducing the ranks of a matrix, through calculating the lower rank matrix ensure the efficacy of our algorithm.

We begin this paper with a brief review of ELM. Then we introduce our method in section 3. Section 4 briefly presents our fast training algorithm that also allows us to process large datasets and compare the experimental results with the SVD algorithm. In section 5, we give our conclusions and show our future work.

2   Review of ELM

The extreme learning machine (ELM) [1] is a single hidden layer feed forward network where the input weights are chosen randomly and the output weights are calculated analytically. In general, a multi-category classification problem can be stated in the following manner. Suppose, we have N observation samples $\{x_i, y_i\}$, If the sample x_i is as signed to the class label C_k then the k th element of y_i is one ($y_{ik} = 1$) and other elements are -1. Here, we assume that the samples belong to C distinct classes. The function $Y = F(X)$ which predicting the class label with the desired accuracy is called a classifier function.

Standard SLFNs with $\tilde{N}$ hidden nodes and activation function $g(x)$ are mathematically modeled as

$$\sum_{i=1}^{\tilde{N}} \beta_i g(x_j) = \sum_{i=1}^{\tilde{N}} \beta_i g(w_i \cdot x_j + b_i) = o_j, \quad j = 1,...,N . \tag{1}$$

where w_i is the weight vector connecting the ith hidden node and the input nodes, β_i is the weight vector connecting the ith hidden node and the output nodes, and b_i

is the threshold of the ith hidden node, $w_i \cdot x_j$ denotes the inner product of w_i and x_j. The output nodes are chosen linear usually. That standard SLFN with $\tilde{N}$ hidden nodes with activation function $g(x)$ can approximate these N samples with zero error means that $\sum_{j=1}^{\tilde{N}} \| o_j - t_j \| = 0$, there exist b_i, w_j satisfies

$$\sum_{i=1}^{\tilde{N}} \beta_i g(w_i \cdot x_j + b_i) = t_j, \quad j = 1, ..., N. \tag{2}$$

this equation can be written compactly as

$$H\beta = T. \tag{3}$$

where

$$H(w_1, ..., w_{\tilde{N}}, b_1, ..., b_{\tilde{N}}, x_1, ..., x_{\tilde{N}}) = \begin{bmatrix} g(w_1 \cdot x_1 + b_1) & .... & g(w_{\tilde{N}} \cdot x_1 + b_{\tilde{N}}) \\ .... & .... & .... \\ g(w_1 \cdot x_N + b_1) & .... & g(w_{\tilde{N}} \cdot x_N + b_{\tilde{N}}) \end{bmatrix}_{N \times \tilde{N}}, \tag{4}$$

$$\beta = \begin{bmatrix} \beta_1^T \\ \vdots \\ \beta_{\tilde{N}}^T \end{bmatrix}_{\tilde{N} \times m}, \text{ and } T = \begin{bmatrix} t_1^T \\ \vdots \\ t_N^T \end{bmatrix}_{N \times m}. \tag{5}$$

Here, H is called the hidden layer output matrix of the neural network; the ith column of H is the ith hidden neuron output with respect to inputs X. For most practical problems, it is assumed that the numbers of hidden neurons are always less than the number of samples in the training set. In ELM algorithm, for a given number of hidden neurons, it is as summed that the input weights w and bias b of hidden neurons are selected randomly. H is a non square matrix and there may not exist w_i, b_i, β_i $(i = 1, ..., N)$ such that $H\beta = T$, the smallest norm least squares solution of the above linear system is $\hat{\beta} = H^\dagger T$, where $H^\dagger$ is the Moore-Penrose generalized inverse of matrix H.

From above theory, if we want to get good generalization performance, the most important step is to accurately calculate the Moore-Penrose generalized inverse $H^\dagger$.

3   The Rank Reduced Matrix (MMR) Method in ELM

Assume the symmetric positive $n \times n$ matrix $H^T H$, whose rank is $r \le n$, we know that there is a unique upper triangular matrix S with exactly $n - r$ zero rows, can satisfy the following form $S^T S = H^T H$. To compute S is a simple extension of the usual Cholesky factorization of non-singular matrices. Removing the zero rows from S, we obtain a simple $r \times n$ matrix, using R^T to denote, and we get the following equation

$$H^T H = S^T S = RR^T .$$ (6)

note that one can as well directly compute the matrix R, it is a very simpler method from which we can obtain H^+, finally, we have

$$(H^T H)^+ = (RR^T)^+ = R(R^T R)^{-1}(R^T R)^{-1} R^T .$$ (7)

Thus the main operations are the full rank Cholesky factorization of $H^T H$ and the inversion of $R^T R$. On a serial processor, these operations are of complexity order $o(n^3)$ and $o(r^3)$, respectively. However, in a parallel architecture, with as many processors as necessary, the time complexity for the Cholesky factorization of $H^T H$ could reduce to $o(n)$, while the time complexity for the inversion of the symmetric positive definite matrix $R^T R$ could reduce to $o(\log r)$.

A new ELM based on the RRM method can be summarized as follows.

Algorithm. ELM based on the RRM method
Given a training set $\mathbb{N} = \{(x_i, t_i) \mid x_i \in R^n, t_i \in R^m, i = 1, ..., N\}$, activation function $g(x)$, and hidden node number $\widetilde{N}$,

Step 1: Randomly assign input weight w_i and bias b_i $(i = 1, ..., \widetilde{N})$.
Step 2: Calculate the Moore-Penrose generalized inverse of matrix H
    (1) Formulate $H^T H$.
    (2) Utilize the Cholesky factorization of $H^T H$, obtain $S^T S$ which satisfies $S^T S = H^T H$.
    (3) Remove the zero rows from S, obtain a simple product matrix RR^T which satisfies $S^T S = RR^T$.
    (4) From above, we obtain $H^T H = S^T S = RR^T$, and then calculate

$$H^+ = R(R^T R)^{-1}(R^T R)^{-1} R^T H^T .$$ (8)

Step 3: Calculate the output weight β

$$\beta = H^+ T = R(R^T R)^{-1}(R^T R)^{-1} R^T H^T T .$$ (9)

where $T = [t_1, ..., t_N]^T$.

The Singular Value Decomposition (SVD) algorithm can transform the origin problem to eigenvalue problem, but it is a pity that the eigenvalue problem may have more sensitivity to disturbance, so it is not stable to solve the Moore-Penrose generalized inverse of matrix H.

4   Performance Evaluation

In this section, we compare the performance of two methods for the computation of Moore-Penrose inverse matrices which used in ELM on several data sets from the UCI machine learning repository [10] in classification areas. All the simulations are carried out in MATLAB7.1 environment running in a Intel(R) Pentium(R) Dual E2180@2.0GHZ, 2.0GHZCPU, with the memory of 0.99GB, and all the experiments we select *sine* function as activation function, the better result is in italic type.

Table 1. Description of data sets used in experiments

Date sets	Training samples	Testing samples	Attributes
Mushroom	2820	2821	22
Shuttle	29000	29000	9
Sat	3217	3218	32
Segment	1500	810	19
Digit	2810	2810	64
Letter	10000	10000	16

Table 2. Comparison between the two methods when the numbers of hidden nodes are small

Data sets	Methods		Nodes					
			20	60	100	140	180	200
Mushroom	RRM	Test	*0.9096*	0.9741	0.9890	0.9947	*0.9989*	*0.9989*
		Time	*0.0156*	*0.0625*	*0.1250*	*0.2031*	*0.3281*	*0.3906*
	SVD	Test	0.9061	*0.9780*	*0.9900*	*0.9961*	0.9968	0.9975
		Time	*0.0156*	0.1250	0.3281	0.5469	0.8281	0.9219
Shuttle	RRM	Test	*0.9509*	*0.9831*	0.9922	0.9932	0.9949	0.9957
		Time	*0.1875*	*0.7500*	*1.4688*	*2.4219*	*3.5313*	*4.1563*
	SVD	Test	0.9497	0.9818	*0.9927*	*0.9933*	*0.9952*	*0.9959*
		Time	0.3594	2.0625	5.0104	7.7188	10.9844	12.1406
Sat	RRM	Test	*0.8111*	0.8523	*0.8735*	0.8763	0.8773	0.8804
		Time	*0.0156*	*0.0781*	*0.1563*	*0.2430*	*0.3750*	*0.4219*
	SVD	Test	0.8109	*0.8549*	0.8705	*0.8766*	*0.8797*	*0.8810*
		Time	0.0313	0.1406	0.4063	0.6400	0.9375	1.0525
Segment	RRM	Test	0.8575	*0.9218*	0.9373	*0.9457*	0.9461	0.9489
		Time	*0.0125*	*0.0344*	*0.0781*	*0.1250*	*0.1875*	*0.2282*
	SVD	Test	*0.8585*	0.9153	*0.9378*	0.9464	*0.9486*	*0.9501*
		Time	0.0156	0.0469	0.1406	0.2562	0.4063	0.4844

Table 3. Comparison when the numbers of hidden nodes are much large

Data sets	Methods		Nodes					
			200	600	800	1000	1200	1400
Digit	RRM	Test	0.8164	0.9338	0.9445	0.9466	0.9552	0.9594
		Time	0.5313	4.5156	8.7656	15.0781	23.3594	34.5625
	SVD	Test	0.8148	0.9386	0.9429	0.9450	0.9514	0.9578
		Time	1.2969	12.9688	27.1094	44.4688	73.1875	107.0469
Letter	RRM	Test	0.8130	0.9072	0.9225	0.9352	0.9415	0.9478
		Time	1.5881	11.3906	20.5000	32.6631	48.3594	68.1094
	SVD	Test	0.8120	0.9061	0.9222	0.9349	0.9418	0.9466
		Time	4.2656	29.9531	54.5469	84.8125	128.6719	181.9688

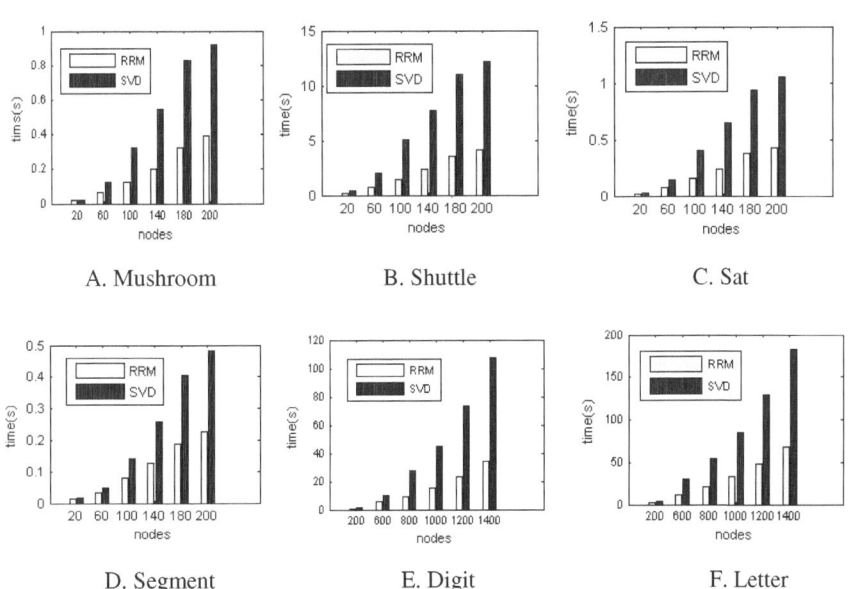

A. Mushroom   B. Shuttle   C. Sat

D. Segment   E. Digit   F. Letter

Fig. 1. Comparison of the time consuming between two methods used in ELM. Each graph shows the result on a unique data set in the tables, from graph A to F, represents Mushroom, Shuttle, Sat, Segment, Digit and Letter respectably.

For the experiment, each date set was tested for 10 times, the data showed are the average of the results which were summarized in Table 2 and Table 3. Table 2 shows performance on four large data sets when the number of hidden nodes is not very large, the speed of ELM based on the RRM method is surpasses twice than ELM based on the SVD method except Mushroom data set when the hidden nodes are too small (20 nodes), but the accuracy is very close, sometimes the RRM method get the better performance. Table 3 shows the performance of ELM based on the RRM method and the SVD method on two large data sets when the number of hidden nodes is very large, seen from the table, 200 nodes can not get better training and testing accuracy.

The result on time consuming between two methods used in ELM is showed by Figure 1, ELM based on the RRM method yields the same or better error rates on 6 data sets compared to ELM based on the SVD method. It is very clear that whenever the number of hidden nodes large or not, our method is at least two times faster than the SVD method, we had also tested increase the nodes to 1600 or even larger, the advantages of ELM based on the RRM method is much more apparent, this method remain reach the same or better result but much faster than ELM based on the SVD method.

5   Conclusions

This paper used a simple and efficient method (RRM) for computing the Moore-Penrose generalized inverse of the hidden layer output matrix used in ELM, the experiments showed, ELM based on our method is at least two times faster than the ELM based on SVD method in dealing with small datasets and our algorithm reach the same or better train accuracy and testing accuracy, but when we deal with large datasets and we need more hidden nodes to improve generalization performance of ELM, the result is very extinguishable, our method is still mush faster this could greatly speed up the application run time in many problem domains, so the new method will be extensively used for ELM training.

In the future, we plan to modify more efficient method to speed up the speed of ELM on the condition of reaching the same or better result compared to other methods.

Acknowledgments. This research is supported in part by the National Natural Science Foundation of China (No. 61170040), the Natural Science Foundation of Hebei Province (No. F2011201063, F2010000323), the Plan of the Natural Science Foundation of Hebei University (doctor project) (No.Y2008122).

References

1. Huang, G.B., Zhu, Q.Y., Siew, C.K.: Extreme Learning Machine Theory and Applications. Neurocomputing 70, 489–501 (2006)
2. Liang, N.Y., Huang, G.B., Saratchandran, P., Sundararajan, N.: A Fast and Accurate Online Sequential Learning Algorithm for Feedforward Networks. IEEE Trans. Neural Networks 17(6), 1411–1423 (2006)
3. Feng, G.R., Huang, G.B., Lin, Q.P., Gay, R.: Error Minimized Extreme Learning Machine with Growth of Hidden Nodes and Incremental Learning. IEEE Trans. Neural Networks 20(8), 1352–1357 (2009)
4. Li, G.H., Liu, M., Dong, M.Y.: A New Online Learning Algorithm for Structure-adjustable Extreme Learning Machine. Computers and Mathematics with Applications 60, 377–389 (2010)

5. Rong, H.J., Ong, Y.S., Tan, A.H., Zhu, Z.X.: A Fast Pruned-extreme Learning Machine for Classification Problem. Neurocomputing 72, 359–366 (2008)
6. Toutounian, F., Ataei, A.: A New Method for Computing Moore-Penrose Inverse Matrice. Journal of Computational and Applied Mathematics 228, 412–417 (2009)
7. Petkovic, M.D., Stanimirovic, P.S.: Iterative Method for Computing the Moore-Penrose Inverse Based on Penrose Equations. Journal of Computational and Applied Mathematics 235, 1604–1613 (2011)
8. Israel, A.B., Greville, T.N.E.: Generalized Inverses: Theory and Applications, 2nd edn. Springer, New York (2003)
9. Courrieu, P.: Fast Computation of Moore-Penrose Inverse Matrices. Neural Information Processing-Letters and Reviews 8(2), 25–29 (2005)
10. Murphy, P.M., Aha, D.W.: UCI repository of machine learning databases (1992)

Research of Dynamic Load Identification Based on Extreme Learning Machine

Wentao Mao[1,2,*], Mei Tian[3], Guirong Yan[2], and Xianfang Wang[1]

[1] College of Computer and Information Technology, Henan Normal University,
Xinxiang City, 453007, China
[2] State Key Laboratory for Strength and Vibration, Xi'an Jiaotong University, China
[3] Management Institute, Xinxiang Medical University, China
maowt.mail@gmail.com

Abstract. In this paper, the problem of multiple-input multiple-output dynamic load identification is addressed. First, from dynamic theory point of view, load identification is proved as a nonlinear multiple-input multiple-output regression problem which can be solved directly in black-box modeling manner from perspective of data analysis. Second, considering the good effect on multiple-input multiple-output problem, a recently proposed excellent machine learning algorithm, referred to as extreme learning machine, is introduced. Finally, a new identification method based on extreme learning machine is proposed to improve identification performance. Experiments on cylinder stochastic vibration system are conducted, demonstrating comparable results and encouraging performance of the proposed method compared with support vector machine based method in terms of identification accuracy, computational cost and numerical stability. A conclusion can also be drawn that extreme learning machine is better applicable to small-sample multiple-input multiple-output problem than support vector machine because of its ability to discover the dependencies among all outputs.

Keywords: Load identification, Extreme learning machine, Inverse problem, MIMO model.

1 Introduction

Dynamic load identification is an important branch of inverse problem, and always plays an important role in the fields of machinery fault diagnosis, machine design and structural vibration control[1,2], etc. Generally speaking, the actual loads acting on structure are usually difficult to be measured directly in practical applications. Modal transform method and direct inversion method are two representative and widely used identification methods. These two methods both require some key system features and dynamic responses of structure, e.g., displacement, speed, acceleration, strain, etc[3]. More specifically, the later method only requires priori information of Frequency Response Function(FRF) matrix and response spectrum at the cost of high computational cost and the existing of generalized inverse of FRF matrix. However, measurement errors tends to cause ill-posed FRF matrix existing in resonance region, and inversion

---

* Corresponding author.

J. Wang, G.G. Yen, and M.M. Polycarpou (Eds.): ISNN 2012, Part I, LNCS 7367, pp. 80–89, 2012.

error will be generally inevitable. Although some methods, such as regularization and vibration equation decoupling, are adopted to reduce inversion error, the numerical precision and stability are usually not as good as expected[4].

According to dynamic theory, the relatedness between load and response only depends on the structure itself, so the problem of load identification is suited to be viewed as nonlinear black-box modeling from perspective of data analysis. Therefore, a new idea was introduced: application of machine learning algorithms for dynamic load identification[5]. Cao et al.[6] utilized neural networks to identify the loads acting on aircraft wings. The key idea is to establish a regression model by means of the collected response and load signals. Similarly, Mao et al.[7] utilized support vector machine(SVM) regression to get high load identification accuracy. Hu et al.[8] proposed a new LS-SVM model selection method based on particle swarm optimization to improve identification performance.

However, there are some problems in the above researches. Traditional neural networks can hardly get satisfactory results with small-size training data because of overfitting. Despite the successful applications for small-sample problems, SVM still has two issues to be considered: many computational costs for solving quadratic programming and some hyper-parameters to be tuned. These issues will restrict the wider applications of SVM. Additionally, classical SVM runs in single-input single-output(SISO) or multiple-input single-output(MISO) structure. If multiple measuring points are considered simultaneously, load identification will be transformed into a multiple-input multiple-output(MIMO) system which needs to consider all measuring points at the same time instead of building a different regression model for each point, so it is more in accord with the nature of load identification. At the same time, classical SVM fails to model MIMO system.

Based on the above discussions, in order to improve the performance of load identification, it is necessary to choose an efficient modeling algorithm whose three features are required: fast learning speed, simple architecture of algorithm (fewer hyper-parameters) and MIMO structure. As a pioneer research, Huang[10] developed an efficient and simple MIMO learning algorithm, called Extreme Learning Machine(ELM), which has its roots in feedforward neural network. When facing the classification of mental tasks[11] and DNA gene[12], ELM ELM has shown its benefit in comparison with backpropagation neural networks(BPNNs) and SVM. As tested by many researches[13,12,11], ELM can meet three requirements mentioned above. However, to our best knowledge, there are few researches to evaluate ELM's performance for MIMO problem. Therefore, this paper chooses ELM as MIMO modeling algorithm and proposes a new identification method for dynamic load identification. As evaluated on cylinder stochastic vibration system, this method can improve identification accuracy with higher learning speed than the one using SVM with model selection.

The rest of this paper is organized as follows. In Section 2, we provide a theoretical analysis about MIMO load identification system from dynamic theory. In Section 3, we give a brief review to ELM. Section 4 is devoted to computer experiments on cylinder stochastic vibration system, followed by a conclusion of the paper in the last section.

2   Principle of Dynamic Load Identification

In our previous works[7,8], load identification has been theoretically proved as a black-box modeling process. And in our another work[9], the modeling process of load identification has been generalized in MIMO manner. For sake of paper's integrity, the theoretical analysis of MIMO modeling in frequency domain is also elaborated.

Let $\mathbf{F} = [F_1, \cdots , F_n]^T$ be a set of load signals acting on n driving points, and $\mathbf{X} = [x_1, \cdots , x_m]^T$ be a set of response signals collected from m measuring points. Accordingly, $\mathbf{S}_{FF}(\omega)$ and $\mathbf{S}_{xx}(\omega)$ are cross-power spectrum density matrices which are calculated from $\mathbf{F}$ and $\mathbf{X}$, respectively. For linear deterministic system, the relationship between $\mathbf{F}$ and response $\mathbf{X}$ can be described as:

$$\mathbf{F} = \mathbf{G}_{m \times n}^{-1} \mathbf{X} \tag{1}$$

where $\mathbf{G}_{m \times n}$ is composed of FRFs on m points. And for linear stochastic system, the relationship between $\mathbf{S}_{FF}(\omega)$ and $\mathbf{S}_{xx}(\omega)$ can be described as:

$$\mathbf{S}_{xx}(\omega) = \mathbf{H}(\omega)\mathbf{S}_{FF}(\omega)\mathbf{H}(\omega)^T \tag{2}$$

where $\mathbf{H}(\omega)$ is FRF matrix:

$$\mathbf{H}(\omega) = (\mathbf{K} - \omega^2 \mathbf{M} + i\omega \mathbf{C})^{-1} \tag{3}$$

where $\mathbf{M}$, $\mathbf{K}$, $\mathbf{C}$ are mass matrix, stiffness matrix and damping matrix, respectively. Therefore the following equation can be obtained:

$$\mathbf{S}_{FF}(\omega) = [\mathbf{H}(\omega)^T \mathbf{H}(\omega)]^{-1} \mathbf{H}(\omega)^T \mathbf{S}_{xx}(\omega)[\mathbf{H}(\omega)\mathbf{H}(\omega)^T]\mathbf{H}(\omega) \tag{4}$$

Suppose that $\mathbf{S}_{FF}(\omega) = \phi(\mathbf{F})$ and $\mathbf{S}_{xx}(\omega) = \varphi(\mathbf{X})$, where the forms of $\phi(\cdot)$ and $\varphi(\cdot)$ are not concerned here. Therefore, equation (4) can be converted to the following equation:

$$\mathbf{F} = \phi^{-1}\left([\mathbf{H}(\omega)^T \mathbf{H}(\omega)]^{-1} \mathbf{H}(\omega)^T \varphi(\mathbf{X})[\mathbf{H}(\omega)\mathbf{H}(\omega)^T]\mathbf{H}(\omega)\right) \tag{5}$$

According to equations (1) and (5), there is a determinate functional relationship between load $\mathbf{F}$ and response $\mathbf{X}$ in linear system, as follows:

$$\mathbf{F} = f(\omega, \mathbf{X}) \tag{6}$$

where $f(\cdot)$ is either linear or nonlinear function and only depends on system's characteristics. In $f(\cdot)$, input $\mathbf{X}$ and output $\mathbf{F}$ are of m and n dimension respectively. So it is a MIMO regression model. Figure 1 shows the framework of MIMO load identification.

3   Brief introduction of ELM

For MIMO system, a traditional modeling method is neural network. As stated in section 1, the performance of neural network generally depends on the initial value

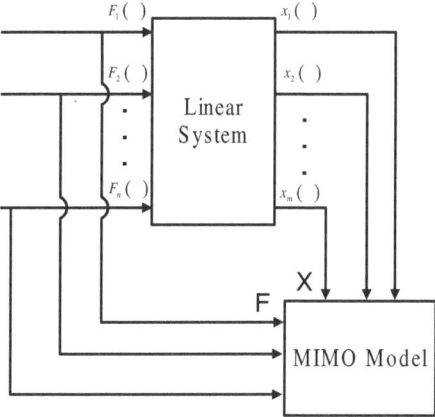

Fig. 1. Framework of MIMO load identification

of neurons and sample size. As an excellent MIMO regression tool, ELM extends single-hidden layer feedforward neural network(SLFN) to "generalized" hidden node case where its generalization performance and learning speed are both improved than traditional neural networks[13]. ELM can analytically determine the output weights by a simple matrix inversion procedure while the input weights and hidden layer biases are generated randomly[14]. Based on the above advantages, ELM is chosen as the basic MIMO regression algorithm in Figure 1. Here we briefly introduce ELM.

Given a set of $i.i.d$ training samples $\{(\mathbf{x}_1, \mathbf{t}_1), \cdots, (\mathbf{x}_N, \mathbf{t}_N)\} \subset \mathbb{R}^n \times \mathbb{R}^m$, standard SLFNs with $\tilde{N}$ hidden nodes can be mathematically formulated as[13]:

$$\sum_{i=1}^{\tilde{N}} \beta_i g_i(\mathbf{x}_j) = \sum_{i=1}^{\tilde{N}} \beta_i g_i(\mathbf{w}_i \cdot \mathbf{x}_j + b_i) = \mathbf{o}_j, \ j = 1, ..., N \tag{7}$$

where $g(x)$ is activation function, $\mathbf{w}_i = [w_{i1}, w_{i2}, ..., w_{in}]^T$ is input weight vector connecting the ith hidden node and input nodes, $\boldsymbol{\beta}_i = [\beta_{i1}, \beta_{i2}, ..., \beta_{im}]^T$ is the output weight vector connecting the ith hidden node and output nodes, b_i is bias of the ith hidden node. Huang[13] has rigorously proved that then for N arbitrary distinct samples and any $(\mathbf{w}_i, b_i)$ randomly chosen from $\mathbb{R}^n \times \mathbb{R}^m$ according to any continuous probability distribution, if the activation function $g : \mathbb{R} \mapsto \mathbb{R}$ is infinitely differentiable in any interval, the hidden layer output matrix $\mathbf{H}$ of a standard SLFN with N hidden nodes and is invertible and $\|\mathbf{H}\boldsymbol{\beta} - \mathbf{T}\| = 0$ with probability one . Then given $(\mathbf{w}_i, b_i)$, training a SLFN equals finding a least-squares solution of the following equation[13]:

$$\mathbf{H}\boldsymbol{\beta} = \mathbf{T} \tag{8}$$

where:

$$\mathbf{H}(\mathbf{w}_1, ..., \mathbf{w}_{\tilde{N}}, b_1, ..., b_{\tilde{N}}, \mathbf{x}_1, ..., \mathbf{x}_{\tilde{N}}) = \begin{bmatrix} g(\mathbf{w}_1 \cdot \mathbf{x}_1 + b_1) & \cdots & g(\mathbf{w}_{\tilde{N}} \cdot \mathbf{x}_1 + b_{\tilde{N}}) \\ \vdots & \cdots & \vdots \\ g(\mathbf{w}_1 \cdot \mathbf{x}_N + b_1) & \cdots & g(\mathbf{w}_{\tilde{N}} \cdot \mathbf{x}_N + b_{\tilde{N}}) \end{bmatrix}_{N \times \tilde{N}}$$

$$\boldsymbol{\beta} = [\beta_1, ..., \beta_{\tilde{N}}]^T$$

$$\mathbf{T} = [\mathbf{t}_1, ..., \mathbf{t}_N]^T$$

Considering most cases that $\tilde{N} \ll N$, $\boldsymbol{\beta}$ cannot be computed through the direct matrix inversion. Therefore, Huang[13] calculated the *smallestnorm* least-squares solution of equation (8):

$$\hat{\boldsymbol{\beta}} = \mathbf{H}^\dagger \mathbf{T} \qquad (9)$$

where $\mathbf{H}^\dagger$ is the Moore-Penrose generalized inverse of matrix $\mathbf{H}$[13]. The framework of ELM is stated as follows[13]:

- Step 1. Randomly generate input weight and bias $(\mathbf{w}_i, b_i)$, $i = 1, \cdots, \tilde{N}$.
- Step 2. Compute the hidden layer output matrix $\mathbf{H}$.
- Step 3. Compute the output weight $\hat{\boldsymbol{\beta}} = \mathbf{H}^\dagger \mathbf{T}$.

[13] provides a rigorously theoretical prove. The output of ELM can be computed by $(\mathbf{w}_i, b_i)$ and $\hat{\boldsymbol{\beta}}$:

$$f(\mathbf{x}_j) = \sum_{i=1}^{\tilde{N}} \hat{\beta}_i g_i(\mathbf{w}_i \cdot \mathbf{x}_j + b_i) = \hat{\boldsymbol{\beta}} \cdot h(\mathbf{x}_j)$$

4   Load Identification Based on ELM

Cylinder shell performs as a typical structure in the fields of aeronautics and mechanical manufacture. In this section, a number of experiments are conducted to show the benefits of ELM when used in load identification on a cylinder shell vibration system. Because SVM is a promising tool for small-sample problem and model selection can provide best learning performance, ELM is compared with the SVM based method with model selection which was proposed by Hu in [8]. This method, named as PSO-SVM in this paper, adopts leave-one-out error bound of LS-SVM and utilizes particle swarm optimization to choose the best hyper-parameters. Gaussian RBF kernel is thus used and defined as $K(x, x') = \exp(-\frac{\|x-x'\|^2}{2\sigma^2})$. In ELM, the activation function is sigmoidal function: $g(x) = \frac{1}{1+\exp(-x)}$. Note that the results of ELM shown in this paper are the mean values of 30trails. All the simulations for PSO-SVM and ELM are carried out in MATLAB7.04 environment running in a Core2, 2.66GHz CPU and 3.37GB RAM. Each of the input variables x and output y are rescaled linearly to the range $[-1, +1]$.

4.1   Data Source

The cylinder shell vibration system has been partly introduced in our previous work[7,8] For the sake of paper's integrity, we describe this system and data collection process briefly.

The cylinder shell vibration system is composed of a cylinder shell, a clamp and a shaker, as shown in Figure 2.

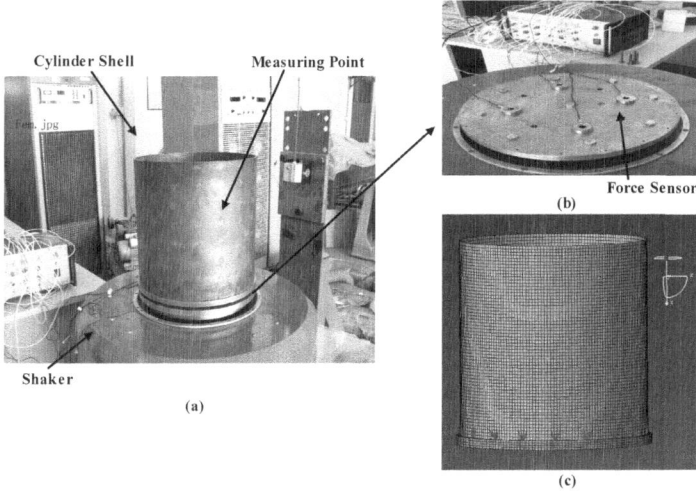

Fig. 2. Experimental setup of cylinder shell vibration system: (a) cylinder structure assembled on the shaker, (b) four force sensors and (c) finite element model.

The cylinder shell shown in Figure 2(a) is made of steel, with the outer diameter of 370mm, the inner diameter of 365mm, and the height of 370mm. The clamp is made of steel, with the height of 10mm, the diameter of 380mm, and connected with cylindrical shell by 18 bolts. The whole structure is fixed on the shaker through four force sensors. Four accelerometers are placed randomly on the cylinder shell to measure the vibration in axial directions in term of acceleration. Modal analysis is performed using both finite element simulation and impact test in advance. Accelerometers are placed on shell and the acceleration signals are recorded and preprocessed by LMS Test.Lab. 30 groups of drive currents with various spectrum patterns are added to drive the shaking table. Actual stochastic loads are recorded by the four force sensors, as shown in Figure 2(b). Correspondingly, 30 groups of accelerations are recorded as response and then transformed into the power spectral densities (PSD) with sampling frequency of 4096Hz and frequency interval of 1Hz.

4.2 Identification Framework

To establish the MIMO identification model with $n=4$ and $m=4$ in Figure 1, a group of observations are selected randomly for test, and other 29 groups are used for training. It is worth noting that equation (6) is based on the single frequency ω, so the target load should be identified frequency by frequency in the whole band. Denote by x_{ji}^{k} the response value of j node produced by ith training load on k Hz. The framework of load identification based on ELM model selection is illustrated in Figure 3.

4.3 Numerical Results

In this section, three evaluation indices, root mean square error(RMSE), average relative error(ARE) and maximum relative error(MRE), are adopted to test the proposed method, as listed in Table 1.

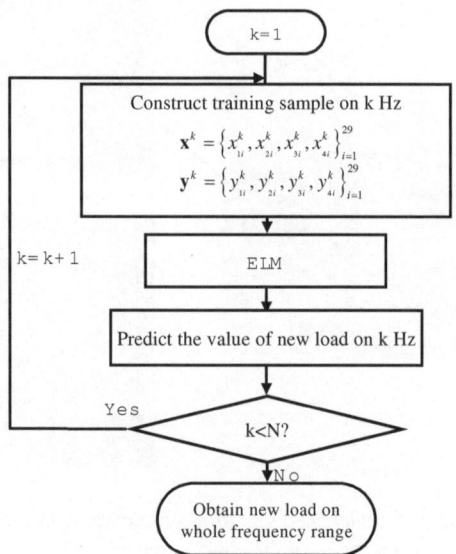

Fig. 3. Framework of load identification based on ELM

Table 1. Three error evaluation indices of load identification

Error	RMSE	APE	MPE
Expression	$\sqrt{\dfrac{\sum_{i=1}^{n}(y_i-\hat{y}_i)^2}{n}}$	$\dfrac{1}{n}\sum_{i=1}^{n}\dfrac{|y_i-\hat{y}_i|}{|y_i|}$	$\max\dfrac{|y_i-\hat{y}_i|}{|y_i|}, i=1,\ldots,n$

Denote by force 1 to 4 the actual loads measured by four force sensors. Select randomly the 29th load to identify, and the identification performances of PSO-SVM and ELM with five neurons for force 1 to 4 are illustrated in Figure 4 and Figure 5, respectively. The corresponding identification errors are listed in Table 2.

As shown in Table 2, ELM gets higher precision than the traditional method in terms of all three error indices. These results are fairly satisfying. Especially for RMSE and ARE which could better reflect identification performance, ELM can obtain errors far less than PSO-SVM. Furthermore, we compare the computational costs of ELM and PSO-SVM. It takes **0.0156**s CPU time for ELM and **0.4531**s for PSO-SVM at single frequency on average. With lower identification error, ELM shows more benefits.

Based on the above results, we find that ELM is more likely to get better generalization performance than SVM for small-sample MIMO system. The possible reason is that ELM tries to exploit the dependencies between all outputs and considers the generalization ability of every output model simultaneously. According to equation (9), contains all outputs' information and thus discovers the inner dependencies. Therefore, ELM tends to make each output less vulnerable to the interference such as noises than SVM which focuses on single output at one moment. As illustrated in Figure 4 and Figure 5, the load curve identified by ELM fits the true load curve closer than PSO-SVM, especially at main central peak and two side peaks. Although the prediction curve of

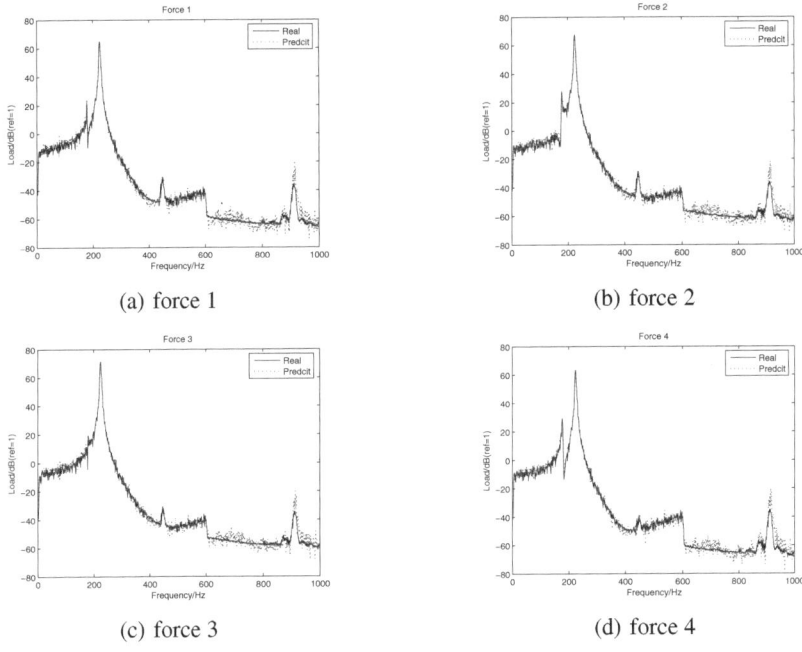

Fig. 4. Identification performance of PSO-SVM

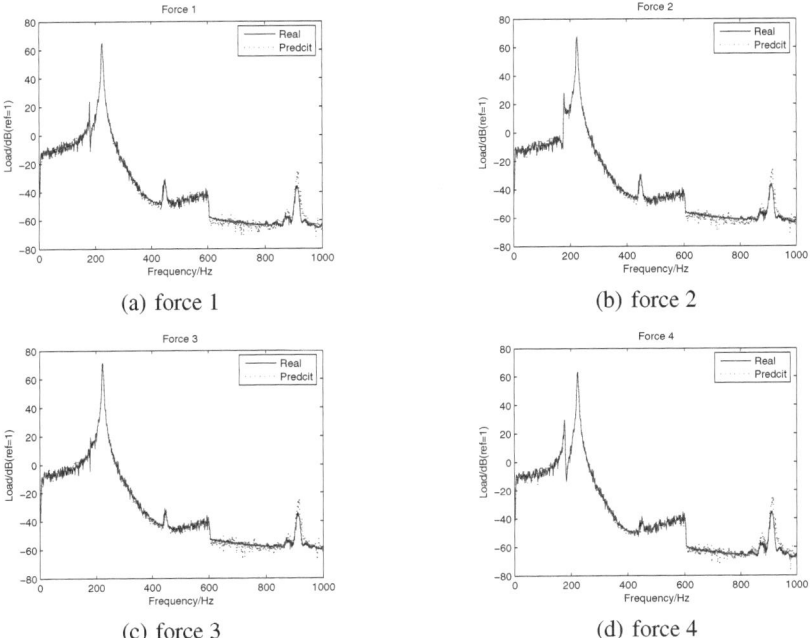

Fig. 5. Identification performance of ELM

Table 2. Comparative results of load identification

Datasets	PSO-SVM			ELM		
	RMSE	APE(%)	MPE(%)	RMSE	APE(%)	MPE(%)
Force 1	0.7146	28.89	447.33	0.3524	19.80	369.55
Force 2	0.8779	28.51	422.80	0.4947	18.78	381.31
Force 3	1.3501	27.45	427.16	0.6727	18.14	345.01
Force 4	0.6009	30.74	479.06	0.3216	20.66	428.37

PSO- SVM can approximate the true load to a certain extent, it fluctuates at side peaks and some frequencies, which demonstrates ELM performs more stable and accurate than the traditional method for small-sample MIMO problem.

We further study the effect of the number of neurons on generalization performance. We run a series of simulations, in which we gradually increase the number of neurons. After repeating 30 trials, Figure 6 shows the ARE errors on four outputs with different number of neurons.

As shown in Figure 6, the performance of ELM is not sensitive to the number of neurons in a relative large range(from 4 to 12). Hence it is easy for users to choose or adjust the network structure. On the contrary, in order to obtain good performance, SVMs need many computational costs to choose proper hyper-parameters and kernel functions, which are usually in empirical manner or depend on optimization method.

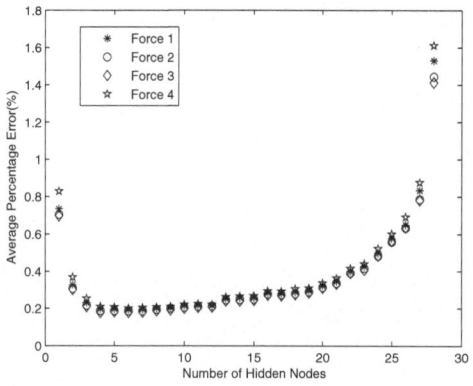

Fig. 6. APE error on four outputs with different number of neurons

5 Conclusions

Considering the superior performance of ELM, this paper introduces ELM and proposes a new MIMO identification framework. In numerical experiments we found ELM can apply especially to small-sample MIMO problem much better than SVM. The reason is ELM can well discover the dependencies among all outputs and can contain more useful information of the target. From a practical point of view, ELM better meets the needs of load identification and outperforms the present methods in terms of identification accuracy, computational cost and numerical stability.

Acknowledgement. This work was supported by Key Scientific and Technological Project of Henan Province, China(NO.112102210412) and Foundation and Advanced Technology Research Program of Henan Province, China(NO.112300410111).

References

1. Chan, T.H.T., Yu, L., Law, S.S.: Comparative studies on moving force identification from bridge strains in laboratory. J. Sound. Vib. 235, 87–104 (2000)
2. Möller, P.W.M.: Load identification through structural modification, J. Appl. Mech. 66, 236–241 (1999)
3. Stevens, K.K.: Force identification problems- an overview. In: Proceeding of SEM Spring Conference on Experimental Mechanics 1987, pp. 838–844. Society for Experimental Mechanics, Houston (1987)
4. Uhl, T.: The inverse identification problem and its technical application. Arch. Appl. Mech. 77, 325–337 (2007)
5. Sjoberg, J., Zhang, Q., Ljung, L.: Nonlinear black-box modeling in system identification: an unified overview. Automatica 31, 1691–1724 (1995)
6. Cao, X., Sugiyama, Y., Mitsui, Y.: Application of artificial neural networks to load identification. Comput. Struct. 69, 63–78 (1998)
7. Mao, W., Hu, D., Yan, G.: A new SVM regression approach for mechanical load identification. Int. J. Appl. Electrom. 33, 1001–1008 (2010)
8. Hu, D., Mao, W., Zhao, J., Yan, G.: Application of LSSVM-PSO to Load Identification in Frequency Domain. In: Deng, H., Wang, L., Wang, F.L., Lei, J. (eds.) AICI 2009. LNCS, vol. 5855, pp. 231–240. Springer, Heidelberg (2009)
9. Mao, W., Tian, T., Yan, G.: Research of load identification based on multiple-input multiple-output SVM model selection. Proceedings of the Institution of Mechanical Engineers, Part C: Journal of Mechanical Engineering Science (in press, 2012)
10. Huang, G.-B., Zhu, Q., Siew, C.K.: Extreme learning machine: a new learning scheme of feedforward neural networks. In: Proceedings of International Joint Conference on Neural Networks(IJCNN 2004), pp. 985–990. IEEE Press, Budapest (2004)
11. Liang, N., Saratchandran, P., Huang, G.-B.: Classification of mental tasks from EEG signals using extreme learning machine. Int. J. Neural. Syst. 16, 29–38 (2006)
12. Huang, G.-B., Ding, X., Zhou, H.: Optimization method based extreme learning machine for classification. Neurocomputing 74, 155–163 (2010)
13. Huang, G.-B., Zhou, H., Siew, C.K.: Extreme learning machine: theory and applications. Neurocomputing 70, 489–501 (2006)
14. Huang, G.-B., Wang, D., Lan, Y.: Extreme Learning Machines: A Survey. Int. J. Mach. Lean. Cyber. 2, 107–122 (2011)

Fuzzy Relation-Based Polynomial Neural Networks Based on Hybrid Optimization

Wei Huang[1] and Sung-Kwun Oh[2]

[1] School of Computer and Communication Engineering, Tianjin University of Technology,
Tianjin 300191, China
[2] Department of Electrical Engineering, The University of Suwon, San 2-2, Wau-ri,
Bongdam-eup, Hwaseong-si, Gyeonggi-do, 445-743, South Korea
ohsk@suwon.ac.kr

Abstract. This paper introduces hybrid optimized fuzzy relation-based polynomial neural network (HOFRPNN), a novel architecture that is constructed by using a combination of fuzzy rule-based models, polynomial neural networks (PNNs) and a hybrid optimization algorithm. The proposed hybrid optimization algorithm is developed by a combination of a space search algorithm and an improved complex method. The structure of HOFRPNN comprises of a synergistic usage of fuzzy-rule-based polynomial neuron that are essentially fuzzy rule-based models and polynomial neural networks that is an extended group method of data handling (GMDH). The architecture of HOFRPNN is an essentially modified PNN whose basic nodes are fuzzy-rule-based polynomial neurons rather than conventional polynomial neurons. Moreover, the hybrid optimization algorithm is utilized to optimize the structure topology of HOFRPNN. A comparative study demonstrates that the proposed model exhibits higher accuracy and superb predictive capability when compared with some previous models reported in the literature.

Keywords: Hybrid optimized fuzzy relation-based polynomial neural network (HOFRPNN), hybrid optimization, fuzzy rule-based models, polynomial neural networks (PNNs).

1   Introduction

Nowadays, computational intelligence technologies such as neural networks, fuzzy sets and evolutionary computing have given rise to a number of new methodologies that have been widely used when modeling complex systems [1-2]. Variety efficient modeling techniques that allow for a selection of pertinent variables and a formation of highly representative datasets have been presented. However, the problem of effectively modeling high dimensionality of the system such as a system with huge input variables is still a difficulty. To construct models with high approximation capabilities, the most promising and successful approaches are augmenting fuzzy systems with learning and adaptation mechanisms, especially neural fuzzy systems and genetic fuzzy models hybridize the approximate inference method of fuzzy models by augmenting them with the learning capabilities of neural networks and evolutionary algorithms [3]. Fuzzy sets highlight the role of any prior knowledge

J. Wang, G.G. Yen, and M.M. Polycarpou (Eds.): ISNN 2012, Part I, LNCS 7367, pp. 90–97, 2012.

about the model, yet it is also bring about some problems. For example, a vast amount of data for estimating all model's parameters are required when dealing with high-order nonlinear and multivariable equations of the model. To alleviate the problems, one of efficient approaches is group method of data handling (GMDH) initialized by Ivakhnenko [4] in 1960s. It is a vehicle for identifying nonlinear relations between input and output variables, which is essential to refer to some developments that have happened over time. Then Ichihashi [5] further proposed new GMDH models in 1994 and 1998, respectively. In these models, their partial descriptions are represented by the radial basis functions networks. In 2000s, Oh et al. [6] developed various structures of self-organizing polynomial neural networks. Some enhancements to these models have been also proposed [7], yet the problem of resulting in optimal networks architecture of fuzzy polynomial neural networks remains open.

This study is concerned with the design of neuro-fuzzy models. We proposed a hybrid optimized fuzzy relation-based polynomial neural network (HOFRPNN) based on fuzzy rule-based model, polynomial network and a hybrid optimization algorithm. The proposed hybrid algorithm combines a space search algorithm with an improved complex method. This combination addresses the needs of global optimization and supports local convergence of the algorithm. In the design of HOFRPNN, fuzzy rule-based models are formed as basic nodes of input layer in polynomial neural networks, while the hybrid algorithm is exploited to optimize the architecture of networks.

2   Hybrid Optimization Algorithm

In our previous study, we propose a space search algorithm (SSA) [8] that is a heuristic algorithm whose search method comes with the analysis of the solution space. It has been proven that is an efficient algorithm when dealing with the optimization of the fuzzy models. SSA search the new space by means of randomly generating a new solution (individual) located in this space, where the new space is generated from the selected solutions in the current solution set (population). This mechanism helps to form new solutions with higher fitness. However, SSA must maintain a balance between the exploration of a side area of the solution space so as to avoid premature convergence, and the exploitation of beneficial aspect of existing solutions in order to improve them. Based on this observation, we may induce that SSA may rapidly approach a near-optimal solutions without reaching it in a feasible length of time. It is evident that a strategy with strong local optimization is needed for alleviating the disadvantage of SSA.

The improved complex method (ICM) [9] is a powerful auto-tuning algorithm that may reach a local optimum according to the initial vales for exploration of the solution space. That is to say, obtaining the global solution depends on the configuration of initial values. If the initial value is near from the global optimum, this method may reach the desired low error state faster in comparison with SSA.

With this understanding, we propose a hybrid algorithm combines SSA and ICM for dealing with the optimization of fuzzy models. In this hybrid algorithm, SSA find the hills (near-optimal solutions), and then hill-climber (the improved complex method) climbs them. It is clear that the proposed hybrid algorithm overcomes limitations and shortcomings of each method used separately. The flowchart of hybrid algorithm outlining main development phases are shown in Figure 1.

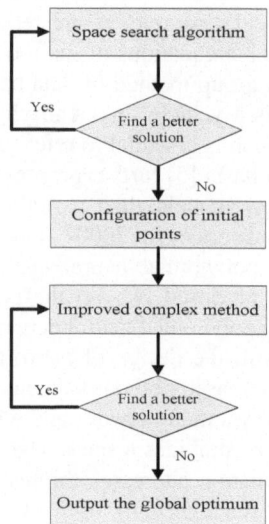

Fig. 1. A general flowchart of the hybrid optimization algorithm

3   A Design of the HOFRPNN

The HOFRPNN is a synergy between two other general constructs such as fuzzy rule-based model [10] and PNN [5], where their structures of networks are optimized by the hybrid algorithm.

3.1   Fuzzy Rule-Based Model

Fuzzy modeling has been utilized in many fields and the identification of fuzzy rules is one of most important parts in the development of rule-based fuzzy system. Generally, the identification procedure for fuzzy rule-based models (FRBM) is split into the identification activities dealing with two parts, namely premise part and consequence part of rules. Here the identification of premise part is the same as conventional models, while the consequence part of the rule that is extended form of a typical fuzzy rule in the TSK (Takagi-Sugeno-Kang) fuzzy model has the form.

$$R^j : If \ x_1 \ is \ A_{1c} \ and \ \cdots \ and \ x_k \ is \ A_{kc} \ then \ y_j = f_j(x_1,\cdots,x_k) \tag{1}$$

Type 1 (Simplified Inference): $f_j = a_{j0}$

Type 2 (Linear Inference): $f_j = a_{j0} + a_{j1}x_1 + \cdots + a_{jk}x_k$

Type 3 (Quadratic Inference):

$$f_j = a_{j0} + a_{j1}x_1 + \cdots + a_{jk}x_k + a_{j(k+1)}x_1^2 + \cdots + a_{j(2k)}x_k^2 + a_{j(2k+1)}x_1x_2 +$$
$$\cdots + a_{j((k+2)(k+1)/2)}x_{k-1}x_k$$

Type 4 (Modified Quadratic Inference):

$$f_j = a_{j0} + a_{j1}x_1 + \cdots + a_{jk}x_k + a_{j(k+1)}x_1 x_2 + \cdots + a_{j(k(k+1)/2)}x_{k-1}x_k$$

The calculations of the numeric output of the model, based on the activation (matching) levels of the rules there, rely on the following expression.

$$y^* = \frac{\sum_{j=1}^{n} w_{ji}y_i}{\sum_{j=1}^{n} w_{ji}} = \frac{\sum_{j=1}^{n} w_{ji}(f_j(x_1,\cdots,x_k))}{\sum_{j=1}^{n} w_{ji}} = \sum_{j=1}^{n} \hat{w}_{ji}(f_j(x_1,\cdots,x_k)) \tag{2}$$

Here, as the normalized value of w_{ji}, we use an abbreviated notation to describe an activation level of rule R^j to be in the form

$$\hat{w}_{ji} = \frac{w_{ji}}{\sum_{j=1}^{n} w_{ji}}, \quad \hat{w}_{ji} = \frac{A_{j1}(x_{1i}) \times \cdots \times A_{jk}(x_{ki})}{\sum_{j=1}^{n} A_{j1}(x_{1i}) \times \cdots \times A_{jk}(x_{ki})} \tag{3}$$

Where R^j is the j-th fuzzy rule, x_k represents the input variables, A_{kc} is a membership function of fuzzy sets, a_{jk} is a constant, n is the number of fuzzy rules, y^* is the inferred output value, w_{ji} is the premise fitness matching R^j (activation level).

The consequence parameters a_{jk} can be determined by the standard least-squares method that leads to the expression

$$\hat{\mathbf{a}} = (\mathbf{X}^T\mathbf{X})^{-1}\mathbf{X}^T\mathbf{Y} \tag{4}$$

In the case of Type 2 we have

$$\hat{\mathbf{a}} = [a_{10} \cdots a_{n0}\, a_{11} \cdots a_{n1} \cdots a_{1k} \cdots a_{nk}]^T, \quad \mathbf{X} = [\mathbf{x}_1 \quad \mathbf{x}_2 \quad \cdots \quad \mathbf{x}_i \quad \cdots \quad \mathbf{x}_m]^T,$$

$$\mathbf{x}_i^T = [\hat{w}_{1i} \cdots \hat{w}_{ni}\, x_{1i}\hat{w}_{1i} \cdots x_{1i}\hat{w}_{ni} \cdots x_{ki}\hat{w}_{1i} \cdots x_{ki}\hat{w}_{ni}] \quad \mathbf{Y} = [y_1 \quad y_2 \quad \cdots \quad y_m]^T$$

3.2   Hybrid Optimized Fuzzy Rule-Based Polynomial Neural Networks

The PNN algorithm is an augmenting of GMDH method and utilizes a class of polynomials such as linear, modified quadratic, cubic, etc. Here we combine the PNN and fuzzy rule-based models to construct fuzzy rule-based polynomial neural networks (FRBPNN). Unlike the conventional PNN, each node of FRBPNN is a FRBM. The architecture of FRBPNN is visualized in Figure 2.

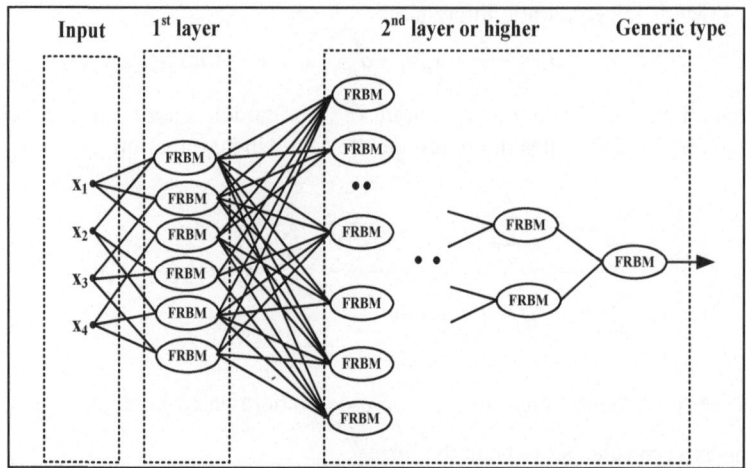

Fig. 2. A general topology of fuzzy rule-based polynomial neural network

As shown in Figure 2, each node of the FRBPNN is a fuzzy rule-based model and the output of node is regarded as input for the next layer. We use two performance indexes as the standard root mean squared error (RMSE) and mean squared error (MSE)

$$PI(or\ E\_PI) = \begin{cases} \sqrt{\dfrac{1}{m}\sum_{i=1}^{m}(y_i - y_i^*)^2}, & (RMSE) \\ \dfrac{1}{m}\sum_{i=1}^{m}(y_i - y_i^*)^2. & (MSE) \end{cases} \tag{5}$$

Where y^* is the output of the fuzzy model, m is the total number of data, and i is the data number.

The design framework of the HOFRPNN involves the following steps.

Step 1. Set the number of nodes for the next layer, where the number is denoted p. In particular, the input of the first layer equals to the number of input variables in the original dataset.

Step 2. Select p nodes with best fitness as the input for the next layer.

Step 3. Construct FRBM nodes.

 Step 3.1. Set values of four parameters (the number of input variables to be used, a specific subset of input variables, the number of membership functions, and polynomial type) for the structure identification of fuzzy rule-based model. The values of four parameters are selected by the hybrid optimization algorithm.

 Step 3.2. Estimate the apexes of membership function. The apexes are firstly obtained by using hard clustering method (HCM), and then are adjusted by the hybrid optimization algorithm.

Step 3.3. Output the FRBM.

Step 4. Repeat step 2 and step 3 until the termination condition is satisfied.
Step 5. Output the result of HOFRPNN.

4   Experimental Studies

This section includes comprehensive numeric studies illustrating the design of the HOFRPNN. We use two well-known data sets. PI denotes the performance index for training data, and E_PI for testing data. The numeric values of the parameters of SSA and improved complex method were either predetermined or selected experimentally. More specifically, we used the following values of the parameters: both maximum generations of SSA and ICM are 100; the number of solutions for generating new space of SSA is set as 8; the reflection, expansion, and contraction coefficients of ICM are set as 0.55, 0.5 and 2, respectively. In HOFRPNN, the number of input nodes (FRBM) for next layer (the second of higher layer) is fixed as 20.

4.1   Gas Furnace Process

The first well-known dataset is time series data of a gas furnace utilized by Box and Jenkins [8-14]. The time series data is comprised of 296 input-output pairs resulting from the gas furnace process has been intensively studied in the previous literature. The Gas dataset is split into two parts. The first 148 pairs are used as the training data, and the remaining 148 pairs are the testing data set for assessing the predictive performance. MSE is considered as a performance index. Table 1 illustrates the results of comparative analysis of the proposed model when being contrasted with other models. PI_t denotes the performance index for total process data. It indicates that the proposed model outperforms several previous fuzzy models known in the literature.

Table 1.   Comparative analysis of selected models (GAS)

Model	PI_t (MSE)	PI (MSE)	E_PI (MSE)
Pedrycz's model [9]	0.776		
Tong's model [10]	0.469		
Xu's model [11]	0.328		
Sugeno's model [12]	0.355		
Oh et al.'s Model [13](Simplified)		0.024	0.328
Oh et al.'s Model [13] (Linear)		0.021	0.364
HCM+GA[14] (Simplified)		0.022	0.333
HCM+GA[14] (Linear)		0.020	0.264
Huang et al.'s model [8]		0.015	0.258
Our model	0.071	0.019	0.123

4.2   Automobile Miles Per Gallon (MPG) Data

Next we consider automobile MPG data (ftp://ics.uci.edu/pub/machine-learning-databased/auto-mpg) with the output being the automobile's fuel consumption expressed in miles per gallon. The data set includes 392 input-output pairs (after removing incomplete instances) where the input space involves 8 input variables. The automobile MPG data is divided into two separate parts. The first one (consisting of 235 pairs) is used for training. The remaining part (consisting of 157 pairs) serves as a testing set. To come up with a quantitative evaluation of the fuzzy model, we use the standard RMSE performance index.

The detail results of HOFRPNN are illustrated in Figure 3. It shows that both the training error and the testing error gradually decrease after the second layer. The identification error of the proposed model is also compared with the performance of some other models; refer to Table 2. It is clear that the performance of the proposed model is better in the sense of its approximation and prediction abilities.

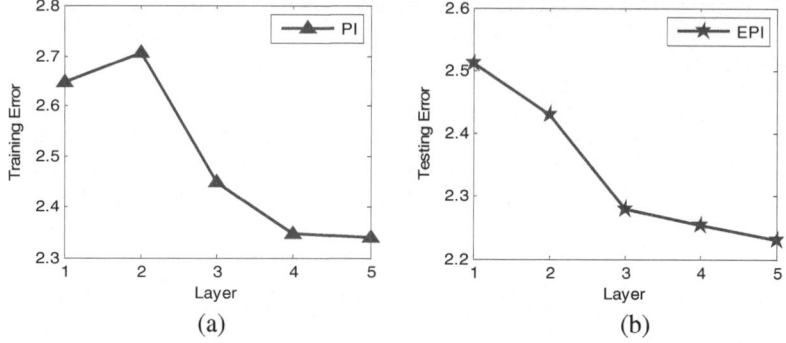

(a)   (b)

Fig. 3. Performance index of HOFRPNN (MPG): (a) Training error; and (b) Testing Error

Table 2. Comparative analysis of selected models (MPG)

Model	PI (RMSE)	E_PI (RMSE)
RBFNN [15]	3.24	3.62
Functional RBFNN[15]	2.41	2.82
Linguistic model [16]	2.86	3.24
Our model	2.34	2.23

5   Conclusions

This study introduces a new architecture HOFRPNN that is based on fuzzy rule-based models, polynomial neural networks and a hybrid optimization algorithm. In the proposed HOFRPNN, fuzzy rule-based models forming the nodes of the input layer of the polynomial neural network, while a hybrid algorithm combined SSA and ICM is presented to optimize the input nodes (FRBM) of each layer. Experimental studies involving two well-known datasets quantify a superb performance of the HORBMPNN in comparison with some existing fuzzy and neruo-fuzzy models.

Acknowledgments. This work was supported by the GRRC program of Gyeonggi province [GRRC SUWON2011-B2, Center for U-city Security & Surveillance Technology] and also National Research Foundation of Korea Grant funded by the Korean Government (NRF-2010-D00065).

References

1. Sommer, V., Tobias, P., Kohl, D., Sundgren, H., Lundstrom, L.: Neural Networks and Abductive Networks for Chemical Sensor Signals: A Case Comparison. Sens. Actuators B, Chem. 28, 217–222 (1995)
2. Cherkassky, V., Gehring, D., Mulier, F.: Comparison of Adaptive Methods for Function Estimation from Samples. IEEE Transactions on Neural Networks 7, 969–984 (1996)
3. Woei, W.T., Hong, H.: A Generic Neurofuzzy Model-Based Approach for Detecting Faults in Induction Motors. IEEE Trans. Ind. Electron. 52, 1478–1489 (2005)
4. Ivakhnenko, A.G.: Polynomial Theory of Complex Systems. IEEE Trans. Syst., Man, Cybern. B, Cybern. SMC 1, 364–378 (1971)
5. Ohtani, T., Ichihashi, H., Miyoshi, T., Nagasaka, K.: Orthogonal and Successive Projection Methods for the Learning of Neurofuzzy GMDH. Information Sciences 110, 5–24 (1998)
6. Oh, S.K., Pderycz, W.: The Design of Self-Organizing Polynomial Neural Networks. Information Sciences 141, 237–258 (2002)
7. Park, B.J., Pedrycz, W., Oh, S.K.: Fuzzy Polynomial Neural Networks: Hybrid Architectures of Fuzzy Modeling. IEEE Transactions on Fuzzy Systems 10, 607–621 (2002)
8. Huang, W., Ding, L., Oh, S.K., Jeong, C.W., Joo, S.C.: Identification of Fuzzy Inference System Based on Information Granulation. KSII Transactions on Internet and Information Systems 4, 575–593 (2010)
9. Pedrycz, W.: An Identification Algorithm in Fuzzy Relational System. Fuzzy Sets Syst. 13, 153–167 (1984)
10. Tong, R.M.: The Evaluation of Fuzzy Models Derived from Experimental Data. Fuzzy Sets Syst. 13, 1–12 (1980)
11. Xu, C.W., Zailu, Y.: Fuzzy Model Identification Self-learning for Dynamic System. IEEE Trans. Syst., Man, Cybern. B, Cybern. 17, 683–689 (1987)
12. Sugeno, M., Yasukawa, T.: Linguistic Modeling Based on Numerical Data. In: IFSA 1991 Brussels, Computer, Management & System Science, pp. 264–267. IEEE Press (1991)
13. Oh, S.K., Pedrycz, W.: Identification of Fuzzy Systems By means of An Auto-Tuning Algorithm and Its Application to Nonlinear Systems. Fuzzy Sets and Syst. 115, 205–230 (2000)
14. Park, B.J., Pedrycz, W., Oh, S.K.: Identification of Fuzzy Models with the Aid of Evolutionary Data Granulation. IEE Proc. Control Theory and Applications 148, 406–418 (2001)
15. Pedrycz, W., Park, H.S., Oh, S.K.: A Granular-Oriented Development of Functional Radial Basis Function Neural Networks. Neurocomputing 72, 420–435 (2008)
16. Pedrycz, W., Kwak, K.C.: Linguistic models as a framework of user-centric system modeling. IEEE Trans. Syst., Man Cybern. –PART A: Systems and Humans 36, 727–745 (2006)

Time-Varying Moore-Penrose Inverse Solving Shows Different Zhang Functions Leading to Different ZNN Models

Yunong Zhang*, Yunjia Xie, and Hongzhou Tan

School of Information Science and Technology
Sun Yat-sen University, Guangzhou 510006, China
zhynong@mail.sysu.edu.cn

Abstract. A novel class of recurrent neural network (RNN), termed Zhang neural network (ZNN), has been proposed for solving online time-varying problems by Zhang *et al* since 2001. In this paper, by defining different Zhang functions (ZFs), we construct different ZNN models correspondingly solving for time-varying Moore-Penrose inverse (MPI). As an error-monitoring function, ZF is the basis of the ZNN design method and can be positive, zero, negative, bounded or even unbounded (including lower-unbounded). Computer simulation results further illustrate the excellent convergence performance of the proposed ZNN models for online time-varying MPI solving.

Keywords: Moore-Penrose inverse (MPI), Zhang neural network (ZNN), time-varying (TV), Zhang function (ZF).

1 Introduction

The online solution of Moore-Penrose inverse (MPI) as a fundamental problem is usually encountered in scientific research and engineering fields; such as, ocean data assimilation [1], kinematic redundancy control [2], acoustic field control [3] and fault tolerant control [4]. In mathematics, we have the following.

- If matrix $A \in R^{m \times n}$ (with $m < n$) is full-rank, i.e. rank(A)=m, then matrix A has a unique Moore-Penrose right inverse (MPRI) A^+, which is given as

$$A^+ := A^{\mathrm{T}}(AA^{\mathrm{T}})^{-1} \in R^{n \times m}. \tag{1}$$

- Similarly, if matrix $A \in R^{m \times n}$ (with $m > n$) is full-rank, i.e. rank(A)=n, then matrix A has a unique Moore-Penrose left inverse (MPLI) A^+, i.e.,

$$A^+ := (A^{\mathrm{T}}A)^{-1}A^{\mathrm{T}} \in R^{n \times m}. \tag{2}$$

In equations (1) and (2), we use the superscript ^{T} to denote the transpose of a matrix or a vector, and use the superscript $^{-1}$ to denote the inverse of a

---

* Corresponding author.

J. Wang, G.G. Yen, and M.M. Polycarpou (Eds.): ISNN 2012, Part I, LNCS 7367, pp. 98–105, 2012.

matrix. In this paper, we take the time-varying MPRI problem as an example to investigate the efficacy of the ZNN method for solving the time-varying MPI problem. Matrix $A \in R^{m \times n}$ hereafter is defined as a full-rank matrix with $m < n$, of which the MPRI A^+ satisfies the following equations:

$$A^+ A A^{\mathrm{T}} = A^{\mathrm{T}} \in R^{n \times m} \text{ and } A A^+ = I \in R^{m \times m}.$$

Owing to the important role of MPI, many efforts have been contributed towards the fast solution of MPI and many related algorithms have been proposed [4,5,6]. However, these numerical or neural-dynamics methods are designed just to deal with the static MPI problem and may not be efficient enough for the time-varying MPI solving. When matrix A is time-varying, these methods may not work well (specifically speaking, they are less effective and less efficient).

In this paper, we develop and investigate a special class of recurrent neural network [termed Zhang neural network (ZNN)] solving for time-varying MPRI (being a sub-case of time-varying MPI). The ZNN design method is based on a matrix-valued error-monitoring function and guarantees that the resultant ZNN models can have the global/exponential convergence performance. After three years' thinking and preparing, we propose the newest result that different error-monitoring functions, i.e., Zhang functions (ZFs), lead to different ZNN models solving for the MPI. Through computer simulations, we substantiate the excellent convergence of the ZNN models solving online for time-varying MPI.

2   ZFs and ZNN Models

In this section, we introduce different ZNN models based on different ZFs for online solution of the time-varying MPRI.

Let us consider the problem of time-varying MPRI in the general form of

$$A(t)X(t) = I \in R^{m \times m}, \tag{3}$$

where $A(t) \in R^{m \times n}$ (with $m < n$) is defined as a smoothly time-varying coefficient matrix, $I \in R^{m \times m}$ is the identify matrix, and $X(t) \in R^{n \times m}$ is the unknown time-varying MPRI matrix which we want to obtain. Note that time instant $t \in [t_0, T] \subseteq [0, +\infty)$.

In order to solve for the time-varying MPRI of matrix $A(t)$, we construct the ZNN models by the following steps of the ZNN method.

Firstly, define an indefinite ZF as the error-monitoring function to control the computing process of time-varying MPRI. Here, the word "indefinite" means that such an error-monitoring function (i.e., ZF) can be positive, zero, negative, unbounded and even lower-unbounded. In addition, ZF is denoted by $E(X(t), t)$ with $\dot{E}(X(t), t)$ being the time-derivative of $E(X(t), t)$.

Secondly, in order to force $E(X(t), t)$ to converge to zero, we make $\dot{E}(X(t), t)$, i.e., the time-derivative of $E(X(t), t)$, as below:

$$\dot{E}(X(t), t) := \frac{\mathrm{d}E(X(t), t)}{\mathrm{d}t} = -\gamma E(X(t), t), \tag{4}$$

where the design parameter γ is designed to be positive and should be set as large as the hardware would permit. It is worth pointing out that γ is used to scale the convergence rate of the resultant ZNN models, which will be further discussed and shown in the simulations.

Thirdly, by substituting the ZF, i.e., the error-monitoring function, into ZNN design formula (4), a corresponding ZNN model is obtained.

Specifically, facing the time-varying MPRI problem (3), we define ZFs as

$$E(X(t), t) = A(t)X(t) - I, \tag{5}$$

$$E(X(t), t) = A(t) - X^+(t), \tag{6}$$

$$E(X(t), t) = X(t)A(t)A^{\mathrm{T}}(t) - A^{\mathrm{T}}(t), \tag{7}$$

$$E(X(t), t) = X(t)A(t) - I. \tag{8}$$

Via the ZNN design formula (4), different ZFs lead to different ZNN models.

A. Combining ZNN design formula (4) and ZF (5), we have

$$\dot{A}(t)X(t) + A(t)\dot{X}(t) = -\gamma(A(t)X(t) - I),$$

$$A(t)\dot{X}(t) = -\dot{A}(t)X(t) - \gamma(A(t)X(t) - I), \tag{9}$$

and then

$$A^{\mathrm{T}}(t)A(t)\dot{X}(t) = -A^{\mathrm{T}}(t)\dot{A}(t)X(t) - \gamma\left(A^{\mathrm{T}}(t)A(t)X(t) - A^{\mathrm{T}}(t)\right). \tag{10}$$

It is worth noting that $A^{\mathrm{T}}(t)A(t)$ is singular (in view of $m < n$). Hence, ZNN model (10) can not be used directly to obtain the time-varying MPRI $A^+(t)$. In order to make ZNN model (10) computable and make $X(t)$ converge to the unique solution, we can add a bias term $\lambda I \in R^{n \times n}$ with $\lambda > 0 \in R$ to $A^{\mathrm{T}}(t)A(t)$. Therefore, by defining $C(t) = A^{\mathrm{T}}(t)A(t) + \lambda I$, ZNN model (10) is modified as

$$C(t)\dot{X}(t) = -A^{\mathrm{T}}(t)\dot{A}(t)X(t) - \gamma\left(C(t)X(t) - A^{\mathrm{T}}(t)\right), \tag{11}$$

which is the final ZNN model (11) based on ZF (5) solving for time-varying MPRI. Additionally, design parameter λ should be set appropriately small for the convergence of ZNN model (11) to the solution.

B. By considering ZF (6) and following the ZNN design formula (4), the time-derivative of $E(X(t), t)$ is obtained with a minimum-norm derivation:

$$\dot{E}(X(t), t) = \dot{A}(t) + X^+(t)\dot{X}(t)X^+(t) = -\gamma\left(A(t) - X^+(t)\right).$$

Reformulating the above equation (with XX^+ replaced by I), we have the following new ZNN model aiming at solving for the time-varying MPRI:

$$\dot{X}(t) = -X(t)\dot{A}(t)X(t) - \gamma\left(X(t)A(t)X(t) - X(t)\right), \tag{12}$$

which is the ZNN model (12) based on ZF (6). Note that ZNN model (12) is also the Getz and Marsden (G-M) dynamic system [8] for time-varying MPRI

Table 1. Different ZFs leading to different ZNN models for time-varying MPRI solving

Zhang function	ZNN model
$E = AX - I$	$C\dot{X} = -A^{\mathrm{T}}\dot{A}X - \gamma\left(CX - A^{\mathrm{T}}\right)$
$E = A - X^{+}$	$\dot{X} = -X\dot{A}X - \gamma(XAX - X)$
$E = XAA^{\mathrm{T}} - A^{\mathrm{T}}$	$\dot{X}AA^{\mathrm{T}} = -X\left(\dot{A}A^{\mathrm{T}} + A\dot{A}^{\mathrm{T}}\right) + \dot{A}^{\mathrm{T}} - \gamma\left(XAA^{\mathrm{T}} - A^{\mathrm{T}}\right)$
$E = XA - I$	$\dot{X}AA^{\mathrm{T}} = -X\dot{A}A^{\mathrm{T}} - \gamma\left(XAA^{\mathrm{T}} - A^{\mathrm{T}}\right)$

solving. In other words, the G-M dynamic system is found to be a special case of the ZNN models. In addition, such a G-M dynamic system requires the initial state $X(0)$ to be close enough to the theoretical initial MPRI $A^{+}(0)$.

C. Combining the ZNN design formula (4) and ZF (7), we have

$$\dot{X}(t)A(t)A^{\mathrm{T}}(t) = -X(t)\left(\dot{A}(t)A^{\mathrm{T}}(t) + A(t)\dot{A}^{\mathrm{T}}(t)\right)$$
$$+\dot{A}^{\mathrm{T}}(t) - \gamma\left(X(t)A(t)A^{\mathrm{T}}(t) - A^{\mathrm{T}}(t)\right). \tag{13}$$

Hence, we have the ZNN model (13) for time-varying MPRI solving.

D. With the ZNN design formula (4) and ZF (8) combined, we have

$$\dot{X}(t)A(t)A^{\mathrm{T}}(t) = -X(t)\dot{A}(t)A^{\mathrm{T}}(t) - \gamma\left(X(t)A(t)A^{\mathrm{T}}(t) - A^{\mathrm{T}}(t)\right). \tag{14}$$

The ZNN model (14) based on ZF (8) is thus obtained.

As a result, we have obtained four different ZNN models, i.e., ZNN models (11)–(14), corresponding to four different ZFs, i.e., ZFs (5)–(8). For readers' convenience, we summarize these ZFs and ZNN models in Table 1.

3   Convergence Characteristics

In this section, we present and compare the following propositions on the convergence characteristics of the ZNN models.

Proposition 1. *Consider a smoothly time-varying full-rank matrix $A(t) \in R^{m \times n}$ with $m < n$. The matrix state $X(t)$ of the theoretical ZNN model (9) based on ZF (5) starting from any initial state $X(0) \in R^{n \times m}$ globally converges to the time-varying matrix $A^{+}(t)$ which is the MPRI of matrix $A(t)$.*

Proposition 2. *Consider a smoothly time-varying full-rank matrix $A(t) \in R^{m \times n}$ with $m < n$. The matrix state $X(t)$ of the practical ZNN model (11) based on ZF (5) starting from a randomly-generated initial state $X(0) \in R^{n \times m}$ converges to the time-varying matrix $A^{+}(t)$ which is the MPRI of matrix $A(t)$.*

Proposition 3. *Consider a smoothly time-varying full-rank matrix $A(t) \in R^{m \times n}$ with $m < n$. Starting from an initial state $X(0) \in R^{n \times m}$ which is close enough*

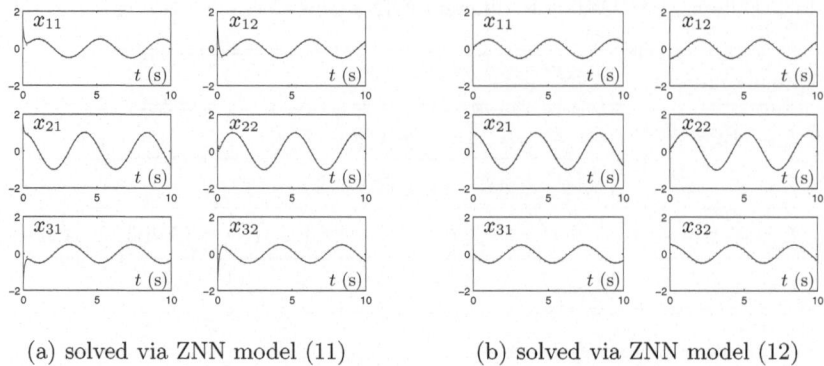

(a) solved via ZNN model (11)   (b) solved via ZNN model (12)

Fig. 1. State trajectories of ZNN models (11) and (12) with $\gamma = 10$ and $\lambda = 10^{-8}$

to the theoretical initial MPRI $A^+(0)$, the matrix state $X(t)$ of ZNN model (12) based on ZF (6) converges to the time-varying matrix $A^+(t)$ which is the MPRI of matrix $A(t)$.

Besides, the propositions on the convergence characteristics of ZNN models (13) and (14) have been given in the previous work [7]. Therefore, we do not detail these two ZNN models [i.e., ZNN models (13) and (14)] in this paper.

4   Computer Simulations

In this section, we have three examples to verify the efficacy and superiority of ZNN models (11) and (12) and discuss how the design parameter γ and λ effect the convergence performance of the above two ZNN models.

Example 1. Let us consider the following time-varying full-rank matrix

$$A(t) = \begin{bmatrix} \sin(1.5t)\cos(1.5t) & -\sin(1.5t) \\ -\cos(1.5t)\sin(1.5t) & \cos(1.5t) \end{bmatrix}, \tag{15}$$

with its time-varying theoretical MPRI given below for comparative purposes (i.e., to check the correctness of ZNN solutions):

$$A^+(t) = \begin{bmatrix} 0.5\sin(1.5t) & -0.5\cos(1.5t) \\ \cos(1.5t) & \sin(1.5t) \\ -0.5\sin(1.5t) & 0.5\cos(1.5t) \end{bmatrix}.$$

We exploit ZNN models (11) and (12) to solve for the MPRI of (15) with $\gamma = 10$ and $\lambda = 10^{-8}$. In Fig. 1, the neural states $X(t)$ of ZNN models (11) and (12) are respectively shown, with the theoretical solution denoted by the dash-dotted curves. From the simulation results, we see that the state trajectories of ZNN model (11) always converge to the trajectories of the time-varying theoretical MPRI; in contrast, there exists appreciable difference between the trajectories of the time-varying theoretical MPRI and the state trajectories of ZNN model

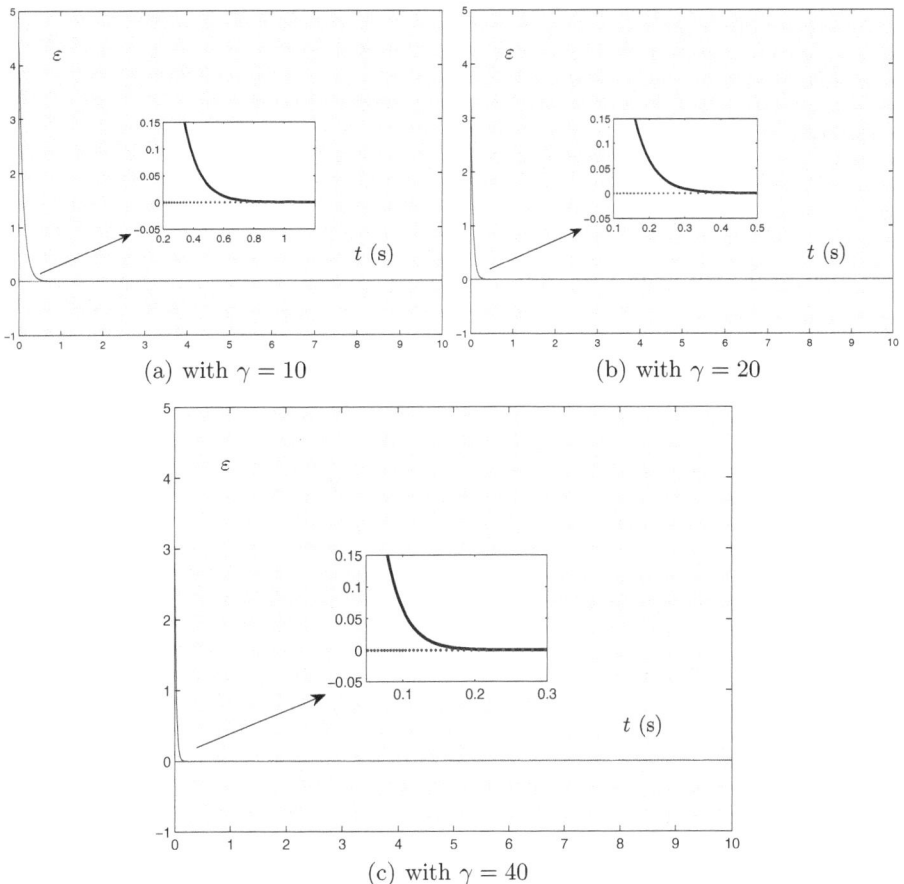

Fig. 2. Solution errors $\varepsilon = \|X(t) - A^+(t)\|_F$ of ZNN model (11) solving for the time-varying MPRI of (16) with $\lambda = 10^{-8}$ fixed and with different values of γ tested

(12) (which is also the G-M dynamic system). Thus, the difference and efficacy of the proposed ZNN models (resulting from different ZFs) are demonstrated.

Example 2. In this example, we consider a time-varying full-rank matrix

$$A(t) = \begin{bmatrix} 0.5\sin(t) & -\cos(t) & 0.5\sin(t) \\ 0.5\cos(t) & \sin(t) & 0.5\cos(t) \end{bmatrix}, \tag{16}$$

with its theoretical MPRI given below for comparison:

$$A^+(t) = \begin{bmatrix} \sin(t) & \cos(t) \\ -\cos(t) & \sin(t) \\ \sin(t) & \cos(t) \end{bmatrix}.$$

About ZNN model (11) solving for the time-varying MPRI of (16) with $\lambda = 10^{-8}$ and different values of γ, the solution errors $\varepsilon = \|X(t) - A^+(t)\|_F$ are displayed

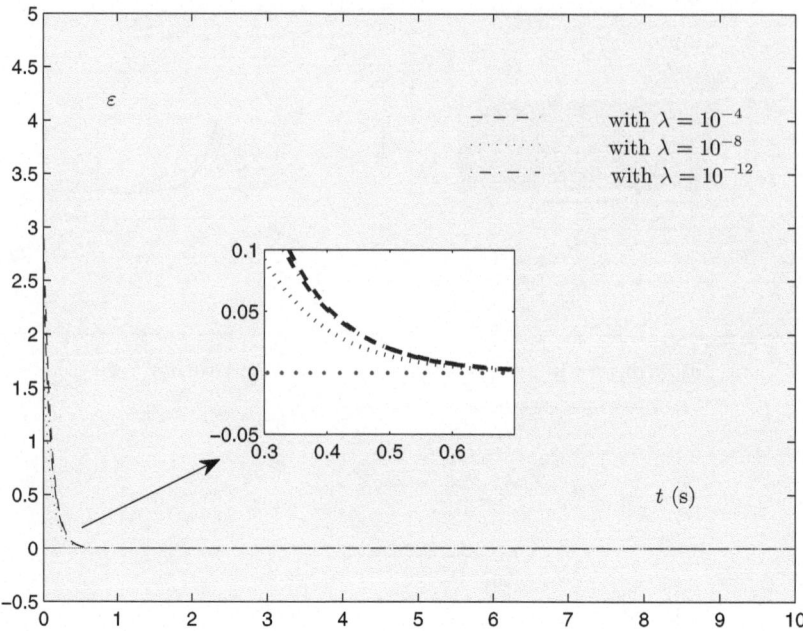

Fig. 3. Solution errors $\varepsilon = \|X(t) - A^+(t)\|_F$ of ZNN model (11) solving for the time-varying MPRI of (15) with $\gamma = 10$ fixed and with different values of λ tested

in Fig. 2, where symbol $\| \cdot \|_F$ denotes the Frobenius norm of a matrix. When $\gamma = 10$, the solution error ε converges to zero in about 0.7 second; and when $\gamma = 20$ and $\gamma = 40$, the convergence time of the solution error toward zero is shortened to about 0.35 second and 0.15 second, respectively. Therefore, we can set γ appropriately large to expedite the ZNN-solution process.

Example 3. For comparative purposes, we set the value of λ to be 10^{-4}, 10^{-8} and 10^{-12} in this example to solve the time-varying MPRI of (15). As shown in Fig. 3, the solution errors of ZNN model (11) (with $\gamma = 10$) all converge to zero rapidly. Though different values of λ are used, the convergence time is almost the same. Thus, we come to the conclusion that, when design-parameter λ is set appropriately small, ZNN model (11) can achieve the same excellent convergence performance, i.e., solving online for the time-varying MPRI accurately.

5   Conclusions

A new class of recurrent neural network, termed Zhang neural network (ZNN), has been generalized and developed in this paper to solve for the time-varying Moore-Penrose right inverse (MPRI). By defining different Zhang Functions (ZFs) as the error-monitoring functions, we have surprisingly discovered, proposed and developed different ZNN models solving online for the time-varying MPRI.

The propositions and computer-simulations have been given further, which have demonstrated well the difference and efficacy of the proposed ZNN models in terms of solving online for the time-varying MPRI.

Acknowledgments. This work is supported by the National Natural Science Foundation of China under Grants 61075121 and 60935001, and also by the Fundamental Research Funds for the Central Universities of China. Besides, the corresponding author, Yunong, would like to thank the coauthors of this paper by sharing the following thoughts: 1) "The obvious is that which is never seen until someone expresses it simply" (Gibran), 2) "It is difficult to establish elegantly a novel computational scheme or model, and it is also difficult to prove rigorously such a scheme or model. If we can complete both tasks, it is very good; but, it is also good if we just complete one", 3) "Especially, when we walk long and far, we need to think more about where and why we start and/or end the journey", 4) "The door or way to another world or space is thinking", and 5) "People with great wisdom and/or bravery shall return to their homeland".

References

1. Fieguth, P.W., Menemenlis, D., Fukumori, I.: Mapping and pseudoinverse algorithms for ocean data assimilation. IEEE Trans. Geosci. Remote Sensing 4, 43–51 (2003)
2. Park, J., Choi, Y., Chung, W.K., Youm, Y.: Multiple tasks kinematics using weighted pseudo-inverse for kinematically redundant manipulators. In: Proc. 2001 IEEE Conference on Robotics & Automation, Seoul, Korea, pp. 4041–4047 (2001)
3. Hu, J., Qian, S., Ding, Y.: Improved pseudoinverse algorithm and its application in controlling acoustic field generated by phased array. J. Syst. Simul. 22, 1111–1116 (2010)
4. Staroswiecki, M.: Fault tolerant control: the pseudo-inverse method revisited. In: Proc. 16th IFAC World Congress, Prague, Czech Republic (2005)
5. Guo, P., Lyu, M.R.: A pseudoinverse learning algorithm for feedforward neural networks with stacked generalization applications to software reliability growth data. Neurocomputing 56, 101–121 (2004)
6. Song, J., Yam, Y.: Complex recurrent neural network for computing the inverse and pseudo-inverse of the complex matrix. Appl. Math. Comput 93, 195–205 (1998)
7. Zhang, Y., Yang, Y., Tan, N., Cai, B.: Zhang neural network solving for time-varying full-rank matrix Moore-Penrose inverse. Computing 92, 97–121 (2011)
8. Getz, N.H., Marsden, J.E.: Dynamical methods for polar decomposition and inversion of matrices. Linear Alg. Appl. 258, 311–343 (1997)

A Multi-object Segmentation Algorithm
Based on Background Modeling and Region Growing

Kun Zhang, Cuirong Wang, and Baoyan Wang

Northeastern University at Qinhuangdao, 066004, Hebei, China
zkhbqhd@163.com

Abstract. A multi-object segmentation algorithm based on Background Modeling and Region Growing (named as BMRG) algorithm is proposed in this paper. For multi-object segmentation, the algorithm uses Chebyshev inequality and the kernel density estimation method to do background modeling firstly. Then in order to classify image pixels as background points, foreground points and suspicious points, an adaptive threshold algorithm is proposed accordingly. After using background subtraction to get the ideal foreground image, region growing method is used for multi-object segmentation. Here, we improved the region growing method by introducing the growth seed concept for multi-object segmentation, which is calculated from the sparse matrix of quad-tree decomposition. Experimental results show that Chebyshev inequalities can quickly distinguish the foreground and background points. Multi-object segmentation results are satisfactory through seed-based region growing method. Comparison and analysis the experimental results show that the proposed BMRG algorithm is feasible, rapid and effective.

Keywords: Chebyshev inequality, adaptive threshold, kernel density estimation, region growing, multi-object segmentation.

1   Introduction

With the computer hardware and software technology continues to mature, a variety of multimedia technology begins to flourish, so does the network video monitoring system. In order to deal with the massive recorded video content, it requires an intelligent video surveillance system to analyze the critical target automatically. The detection and segmentation of moving objects from a video stream is a basic and fundamental problem of tracking and traffic control etc..

Image segmentation is always a chief, classical and knotty problem in image analysis and pattern recognition field. It also plays an important role in object recognition system. Main segmentation methods include histogram threshold [1], features clustering [2] [3], area-based method [4], neural network [5] etc.. Recent image segmentation approaches have provided interactive methods that implicitly define the segmentation problem relative to a particular task of content localization. This approach to image segmentation requires users (or preprocessor) guidance of the working algorithm to define the desired object to be extracted. For example, frame difference method [6], background subtraction [7] and optical flow method [8]. Background models which can be applied to light illumination and background slow changes are Kalman filtering and Gaussian mixture model [9]. Elgammal [10]

J. Wang, G.G. Yen, and M.M. Polycarpou (Eds.): ISNN 2012, Part I, LNCS 7367, pp. 106–115, 2012.

proposed kernel density estimation method for each pixel location in the video sequence to establish non-parametric probability model, using a number of neighboring frames sample value constructed close to the actual probability distribution. Jiandong Gu [11] proposed the moving object segmentation with the combination of kernel density estimates and the edge information when foreground and background are similar in color aspect. Qin, A. K. [12] proposed a MRF-based multivariate segmentation algorithm named MIRGS, which uses RKM-based initialization and region growing method, consistently provides accurate initial conditions at low computational cost.

This paper is organized as follows. In Section 2, we explain the related work of our algorithm, including Chebyshev inequality, the kernel density estimation and region growing. Section 3 describes the proposed algorithm in detail. Section 4 provides the experimental results and the analysis. Finally, there are conclusion and references.

2   Related Work

In order to complete multi-object segmentation from the monitor image, the first job we have to do is foreground image extraction based on background modeling. In this paper we improve the moving object segmentation algorithm [13] for the multi-object segmentation algorithm, here an adaptive threshold background modeling algorithm is proposed, pixels are classified as background points, foreground points and suspicious points. After foreground image getting, we use seed-based region growing method to complete the multi-object segmentation. Introduce the quad-tree decomposition method to get some coefficient matrix, and the above region growing seed is the calculation result of such sparse matrix.

Chebyshev inequality can distinguish the background pixels and foreground pixels quickly. Pixels which features are not significant are defined as suspicious points and we use kernel density estimation method to complete further pixels judge.

Let random variable X with its expectation $E(x) = \mu$ and its variance $D(x) = \sigma^2$, for any positive number $\varepsilon > 0$, there is the Chebyshev inequality

$$P\{|X - \mu| \geq \varepsilon\} \leq \frac{\sigma^2}{\varepsilon^2} \quad (\text{or } P\{|X - \mu| < \varepsilon\} \geq 1 - \frac{\sigma^2}{\varepsilon^2}) \tag{1}$$

Chebyshev inequality gives a lower bound for the probability of $P\{|X - \mu| < \varepsilon\}$. If we define a random variable X to represent the value of each pixel for foreground segmentation, the probability of event $\{|X - \mu| < \varepsilon\}$ can be estimated by the Chebyshev inequality which reflects the changing circumstances about the corresponding value of video image pixels.

The kernel density estimation technique is a particular nonparametric technique that estimates the underlying density, avoids having to store the complete data, and it is quite general. In this technique, the underlying probability density function is estimated as

$$\hat{f}(x) = \sum_i \alpha_i K(x - x_i) \tag{2}$$

Let $x_1, x_2, \cdots, x_N$ be a sample of intensity values for a pixel. Given this sample, we can obtain an estimate of the pixel intensity probability density function at any intensity value using kernel density estimation. Given the observed intensity x_t at time t, we can estimate the probability of this observation as

$$P_r(x_t) = \frac{1}{N} \sum_{i=1}^{N} \frac{1}{\sqrt{2\pi\sigma^2}} e^{-\frac{1}{2} \frac{(x_t-x_i)^2}{\sigma^2}}$$ (3)

Here we choose the kernel function K to be Gaussian. If we assume that this local-in-time distribution would be Gaussian $N(\mu, \sigma^2)$, then the distribution for the deviation $(x_i - x_{i+1})$ would be Gaussian $N(0, 2\sigma^2)$. The kernel function bandwidth σ can be estimated as

$$\hat{\sigma} = \frac{m}{(0.68\sqrt{2})}, m = median(|x_i - x_{i+1}|), \sigma = \max(1, \hat{\sigma})$$ (4)

Segmentation of images with uneven regions has long been a hard nut in image processing. Not only the contrasts among regions are different, but also the gradual changing grey values are varied in the same region in a wide range. These problems present segmentation with difficulties. It is needed to perform detection respectively for these different target areas. To complete the multi-object segmentation pre-detection is especially important. If we can pre-select and determine a seed point for each target, then multi-object segmentation can be done by parallel region growing based on the seed. Because of quad-tree decomposition can get a representative image sparse matrix, so we can use such sparse matrix to find the seed points for region growing. In view of the above methods, in this paper we proposed a multi-object segmentation algorithm based on Background Modeling and Region Growing algorithm which is named as BMRG algorithm.

3   Multi-object Segmentation Algorithm

In this section, we describe the proposed BMRG algorithm in detail. The algorithm uses pixel intensity (greyscale or colour) as the basic feature for the background modelling and region growing. Let $X_1, X_2, \cdots, X_N$ be a sample of adjacent N-frame video images, the location of the pixel in the image is marked as (i, j), $X_1(i, j), X_2(i, j), \cdots, X_N(i, j)$ represent the pixel gray values in the given position (i, j) for these images. The BMRG algorithm is as follows:

(1) Calculate the sample mean $\bar{X}(i, j)$ and sample second-order centre distance $S(i, j)$ for each pixel.

$$\bar{X}(i, j) = \frac{1}{N} \sum_{k=1}^{N} X_k(i, j), \quad S(i, j) = \frac{1}{N} \sum_{k=1}^{N} (X_k(i, j) - \bar{X}(i, j))^2$$ (5)

Here, $\bar{X}(i, j)$ and $S(i, j)$ are the maximum likelihood estimators of the expectation $E(X(i, j)) = \mu(i, j)$ and variance $D(X(i, j)) = \sigma^2(i, j)$. That is

$$\hat{\mu}(i, j) = \bar{X}(i, j), \hat{\sigma}^2(i, j) = S(i, j)$$ (6)

(2) Calculate $\sigma_k^2(i,j) = (X_k(i,j) - \bar{X}(i,j))^2$ and $P\{|X_k(i,j) - \hat{\mu}(i,j)| < \varepsilon\} \geq 1 - \dfrac{\sigma_k^2(i,j)}{\varepsilon^2}$ for

the frame $X_k (k=1,2,\cdots,N)$. The calculation results of $1 - \hat{\sigma}^2(i,j)/\varepsilon^2$ for different ε values show in Table 1.

Table 1. Different calculation results according to different ε

ε	$\hat{\sigma}$	$1.225\,\hat{\sigma}$	$1.414\,\hat{\sigma}$	$1.581\,\hat{\sigma}$	$1.732\,\hat{\sigma}$	$1.871\,\hat{\sigma}$	$2\,\hat{\sigma}$
$\hat{\sigma}^2/\varepsilon^2$	1	0.667	0.5	0.4	0.333	0.286	0.25
$1 - \hat{\sigma}^2/\varepsilon^2$	0	0.333	0.5	0.6	0.667	0.714	0.75

If $\sigma_k^2(i,j) < \hat{\sigma}^2(i,j)$ or $1 - \sigma_k^2(i,j)/\varepsilon^2 > 1 - \hat{\sigma}^2(i,j)/\varepsilon^2$, the gray value change of pixel $X_k(i,j)$ is smaller than the variance , this pixel is more likely to be a background point. If $\sigma_k^2(i,j) > \hat{\sigma}^2(i,j)$ or $1 - \sigma_k^2(i,j)/\varepsilon^2 < 1 - \hat{\sigma}^2(i,j)/\varepsilon^2$,   this pixel is more likely to be a foreground point.

(3) For each $X_k(i,j)(k=1,2,\cdots,N)$ the adaptive classification threshold setting formula is as follows:

$$\begin{cases} T_1 = \dfrac{(1 - \hat{\sigma}^2(i,j)/\varepsilon_1^2) + 0.5}{2}, & \varepsilon_1 = 1.414\hat{\sigma}(i,j) + \theta_1\hat{\sigma}(i,j) \\ T_2 = \dfrac{(1 - \hat{\sigma}^2(i,j)/\varepsilon_2^2) + 0.5}{2} & \varepsilon_2 = 1.414\hat{\sigma}(i,j) - \theta_2\hat{\sigma}(i,j) \end{cases} \quad (0 < \theta_1, \theta_2 < 1) \quad (7)$$

Adaptive threshold T_1, T_2 can changed with the change of $\hat{\sigma}$ for a given θ_1, θ_2. Different video frames conditions, the above-mentioned formula can calculate the foreground and background distinguish threshold T_1, T_2 effectively. Adjust the coefficients θ_1 and θ_2 make $0 < |\varepsilon_1 - \varepsilon_2| < 2\hat{\sigma}$, the greater θ_1 the larger T_1, but the greater θ_2 the smaller T_2.

(4) Use the following formula for $X_k(i,j)(k=1,2,\cdots,N)$ to classify background points, foreground points and suspicious points.

$$C_k^1(i,j) = \begin{cases} 1 & (1 - \dfrac{\sigma_k^2(i,j)}{\varepsilon^2}) \geq T_1 \\ 0 & (1 - \dfrac{\sigma_k^2(i,j)}{\varepsilon^2}) \leq T_2 \end{cases} \quad \varepsilon = 1.414\hat{\sigma} \quad (8)$$

When $C_k^1(i,j)=1$, the pixel is classified as background point. When $C_k^1(i,j)=0$, the pixel is classified as foreground point. The pixel is classified as suspicious point When $T_2 < (1 - \dfrac{\sigma_k^2(i,j)}{\varepsilon^2}) < T_1$, for suspicious point we use density estimation method for further discrimination. If $T_1 = T_2 = 0.5$, the suspicious point set is empty, at this time the BMRG algorithm uses only Chebyshev inequality for background subtraction, and if $T_1 = 1$, $T_2 = 0$, all pixels are suspicious points, the BMRG algorithm uses only kernel density estimation for background subtraction.

(5) Calculate $P_r(X_k) = \dfrac{1}{N} \sum\limits_{i=1}^{N} \dfrac{1}{\sqrt{2\pi\hat{\sigma}^2}} e^{-\frac{1}{2}\frac{(X_k - X_i)^2}{\hat{\sigma}^2}}$ for suspicious point, set threshold T_3 and classification function:

$$C_k^2(i, j) = \begin{cases} 1 & P_r(x_k) \geq T_3 \\ 0 & P_r(x_k) < T_3 \end{cases} \tag{9}$$

When $C_k^2(i, j) = 1$, the suspicious point is further identified as a background point. When $C_k^2(i, j) = 0$, the suspicious point is further identified as foreground point.

(6) Update the background pixel value using the following formula:

$$\begin{cases} H_N^1(i, j) = \sum\limits_{k=1}^{N} X_k(i, j) \cdot C_k^1(i, j), \ Q_N^1 = \sum\limits_{k=1}^{N} C_k^1(i, j), & (i, j) \notin K \\ H_N^2(i, j) = \sum\limits_{k=1}^{N} X_k(i, j) \cdot C_k^2(i, j), \ Q_N^2 = \sum\limits_{k=1}^{N} C_k^2(i, j), & (i, j) \in K \\ B_N(i, j) = \dfrac{H_N^1(i, j) + H_N^2(i, j)}{Q_N^1(i, j) + Q_N^2(i, j)}, & (i, j) \in K \cup \bar{K} \end{cases} \tag{10}$$

Here, $B_N(i, j)$ means the pixel value in the position (i, j) of the background image (marked as B_N) for the sample $X_1, X_2, \cdots, X_N$, K is a collection of suspicious point location. It can be seen that the background image updating is based on the real-time sample $X_1, X_2, \cdots, X_N$. Therefore, real-time background modeling can be achieved simply by adding new real-time adjacent N-frame video images and ignoring previous samples.

(7) Complete the foreground image segmentation through background subtraction method. These foreground images are marked as $F_k (k = 1, 2, \cdots, N)$. T_3 and T_4 are empirical values, generally based on the specific test data to select.

$$F_k(i, j) = \begin{cases} X_k(i, j) & X_k(i, j) - B_N(i, j) \geq T_4 \\ 255 & X_k(i, j) - B_N(i, j) < T_4 \end{cases} \quad (k = 1, 2, \cdots, N) \tag{11}$$

(8) Obtain sparse matrix $D_k (k \in [1, N])$ of the foreground image $F_k (k \in [1, N])$ by quad-tree decomposition. The quad-tree decomposition density can be seen through the sparse matrix, so the center of high decomposition density region should be defined as multi-object region growing seed. If the number of those seeds is Ω_k, then mark these seeds as $Seed_k^{\omega} (\omega = 1, 2, \cdots, \Omega_k)$.

(9) Around $Seed_k^{\omega} (\omega = 1, 2, \cdots, \Omega_k)$, generate four suspicious seeds marked as $g_{Seed_k^{\omega}}^{r} (r = 1, 2, 3, 4)$. If the location of $Seed_k^{\omega}$ is (i, j) in the foreground image F_k, then set $g_{Seed_k^{\omega}}^{r}(i, j)$ to represent its pixel gray value. For each $g_{Seed_k^{\omega}}^{r} (r = 1, 2, 3, 4)$, generate a small 3×3 image area which contains nine pixels, the gray-scale value of these pixels are being marked as $g_{Seed_k^{\omega}}^{r}(u, v), \begin{cases} u = i - 1, i, i + 1 \\ v = j - 1, j, j + 1 \end{cases}$ (shown in Fig. 1).

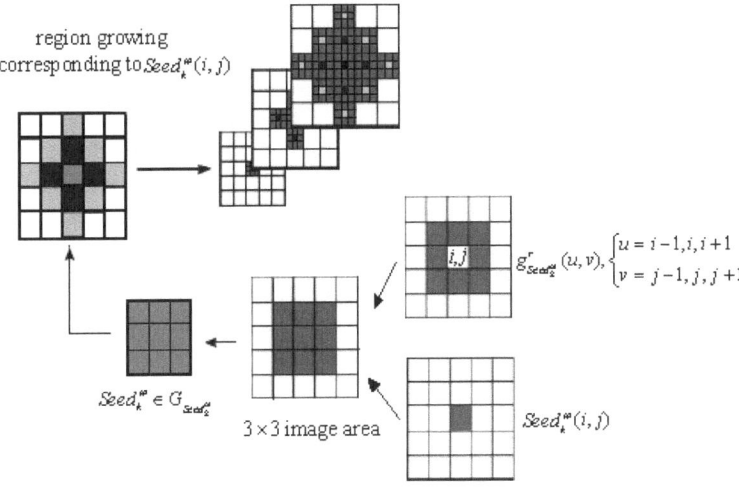

Fig. 1. Seed-based region growing chart

(10) Detect the gray value of each pixel in the small 3×3 area of $g^r_{Seed_k^\omega}\ (r = 1, 2, 3, 4)$.

$$\begin{cases} g^r_{Seed_k^\omega} \in G_{Seed_k^\omega} & \text{if not all } g^r_{Seed_k^\omega}(u, v) = 255, \\ g^r_{Seed_k^\omega} \notin G_{Seed_k^\omega} & \text{if all } g^r_{Seed_k^\omega}(u, v) = 255, \end{cases} \qquad (12)$$

Here $G_{Seed_k^\omega}$ means a collection which is generated by $Seed_k^\omega$, set $Seed_k^\omega \in G_{Seed_k^\omega}$ initially. If $g^r_{Seed_k^\omega} \in G_{Seed_k^\omega}$ and it is different from the original seed and other elements in the collection $G_{Seed_k^\omega}$, then such $g^r_{Seed_k^\omega}$ becomes a new growth seed (just like $Seed_k^\omega$), repeats the above seed growth algorithm (9) and (10). With the growth of these seeds, the region grows by these small 3×3 image areas accordingly.

(11) Iteration of seed collection is marked as $G^I_{Seed_k^\omega}\ (I = 1, 2, 3, \cdots)$, if $G^I_{Seed_k^\omega} = G^{I+1}_{Seed_k^\omega}$, it means that no new seeds are added to the collection $G_{Seed_k^\omega}$, at this time region growing end (corresponding to the $Seed_k^\omega$).

(12) Complete the multi-object segmentation by region growing corresponding to different seeds. Calculate the center coordinates of $G_{Seed_k^\omega}(\omega = 1, 2, \cdots, \Omega_k)$ to combined repeat segmentation.

The above description of the algorithm is based on pixel gray value, but it does not mean the proposed BMRG algorithm is only suitable for grayscale images. For color images, the calculation is similar to the grayscale in each different color channel, it only needs simple adjustments.

4   Experimental Results

To demonstrate the feasibility and effectiveness of the BMRG algorithm, in this paper, we use the Intel (R) Core (TM)2 6300 CPUs, 1.86GHz, 1GB memory PC, use the Java language programming in the Eclipse development platform. The video images are captured from 336×448 traffic surveillance video (shown in Fig. 2).

(1) 20th-frame image   (2) 30th-frame image   (3) 40th-frame image   (4) 50th-frame image

Fig. 2. Surveillance video images

Here we chose greyscale images for example to carry out the experiments. The background modeling experimental results of the BMRG algorithm about different threshold settings is shown in Fig. 3.

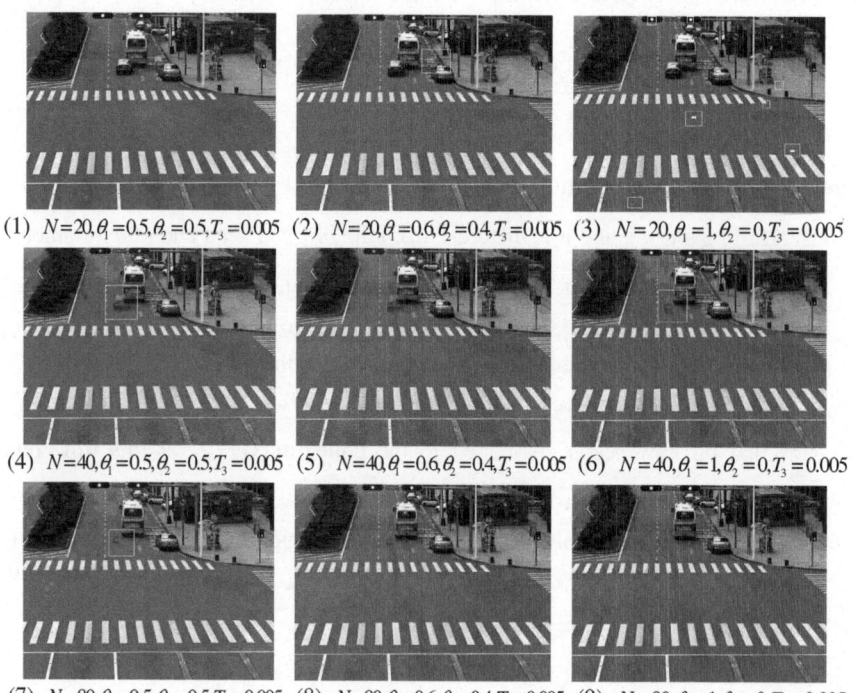

(1) $N=20, \theta_1=0.5, \theta_2=0.5, T_3=0.005$ (2) $N=20, \theta_1=0.6, \theta_2=0.4, T_3=0.005$ (3) $N=20, \theta_1=1, \theta_2=0, T_3=0.005$

(4) $N=40, \theta_1=0.5, \theta_2=0.5, T_3=0.005$ (5) $N=40, \theta_1=0.6, \theta_2=0.4, T_3=0.005$ (6) $N=40, \theta_1=1, \theta_2=0, T_3=0.005$

(7) $N=80, \theta_1=0.5, \theta_2=0.5, T_3=0.005$ (8) $N=80, \theta_1=0.6, \theta_2=0.4, T_3=0.005$ (9) $N=80, \theta_1=1, \theta_2=0, T_3=0.005$

Fig. 3. Background modeling experimental results

On the basis of a large number of experimental data, we compare and analysis the experimental results of different threshold settings. From the Fig.3 it can be seen that for the same parameter θ_1, θ_2, T_3 settings, the greater the number of samples N the experimental effect is more ideal (shown in Fig.3-(1),(4),(7)), for the same N, T_3 settings, the larger θ_1 and the smaller θ_2 the experimental effect is more ideal (shown in Fig.3-(4),(5),(6)). However, when N is small, there will be some empty area of the background image (shown in Fig.3-(3)). Therefore, according to different background modeling requirements, adjust the parameters properly, the BMRG algorithm can achieve an ideal background modeling results (shown in Fig.3-(8),(9)).

In order to test the experimental results of the BMRG algorithm, we chose the frame-difference algorithm [6] and the original kernel density estimation algorithm [10] for comparison. For the same video frame images, experimental results of background modeling for three different algorithms are shown in Fig. 4-(1),(2),(3).

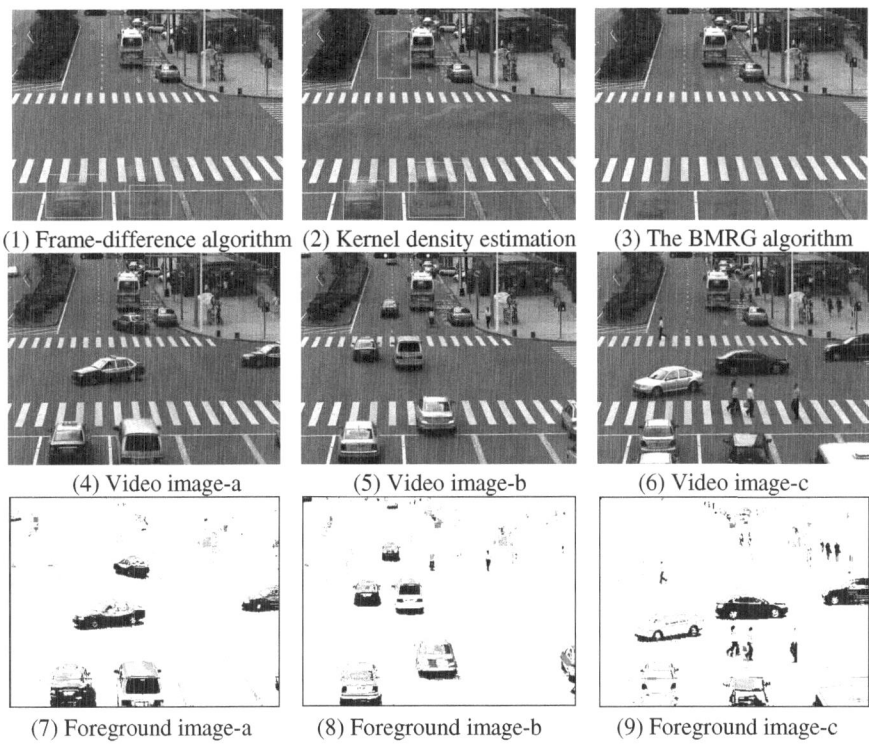

(1) Frame-difference algorithm	(2) Kernel density estimation	(3) The BMRG algorithm
(4) Video image-a	(5) Video image-b	(6) Video image-c
(7) Foreground image-a	(8) Foreground image-b	(9) Foreground image-c

Fig. 4. Background modeling and foreground image extraction experimental results

From Fig. 4, we can see that the BMRG algorithm has the best experimental result. It can get good foreground images (shown in Fig.4-(7),(8),(9)), but also can save computation cost, this is another superiority of our algorithm. The comparison chart of algorithm running time is shown in Fig. 5.

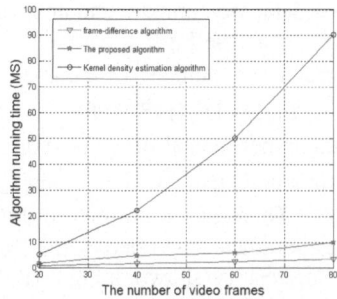 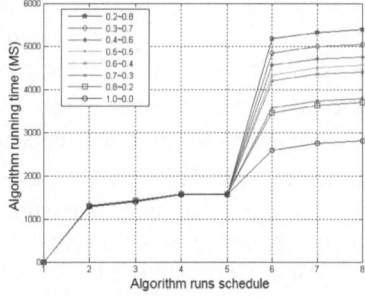

(1) Three algorithms run-time comparison chart   (2) Different θ_1, θ_2 algorithm run-time chart

Fig. 5. Algorithm running time comparison charts

In the same number of frame images, compared with frame difference method and kernel density estimation algorithm, the background modelling time of our algorithm is far less than the kernel density estimation method, only slightly higher than the frame-difference algorithm. Consider both real-time and effectiveness, the advantages of our algorithm is obviously.

Quad-tree decomposition to find seeds and regional growth for multi-object segmentation experimental results are shown in Fig.6.

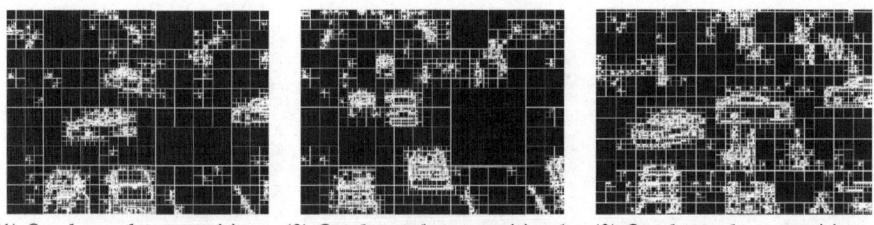

(1) Quad-tree decomposition-a (2) Quad-tree decomposition-b   (3) Quad-tree decomposition-c

(4) Multi-object segmentation result

Fig. 6. Region growing algorithm for multi-object segmentation

From Fig.6 we can seen that multi-object segmentation results are very satisfactory on the basis of the desired foreground image. The proposed BMRG algorithm can save computation time through parallel region growing of different seeds, and the redundancy of the seeds is good for our algorithm to avoid segmentation omission. In summary, the BMRG algorithm not only can extract the desired background image but also can get satisfactory multi-object segmentation image. Especially, this algorithm is time savings which makes it more suitable for a real-time monitoring system.

5   Conclusion

In this paper, relating to the moving object segmentation we proposed a combination of background modelling and region growing algorithm for multi-object segmentation. The application of Chebyshev inequality, setting of the adaptive threshold algorithm, the seed-based region growing method related with quad-tree decomposition are innovations of the proposed BMRG algorithm. The experimental results show that the background modelling results are significantly better than the frame difference algorithm, and it can save more running time than the kernel density estimation method. Multi-object segmentation results by region growing are very satisfactory. Therefore, the BMRG algorithm is feasible, rapid and effective and is suitable for a real-time monitoring system.

References

1. Kaiyan, L., Junhui, W., Lihong, X.: Discussion of color image segmentation. Journal of Image and Graphics 10 (2005)
2. Yin, G., Dayou, L., Hong, Q., He, L.: A cluster way of K mean. Journal of Software 19(11), 2814–2821 (2008)
3. Ubukata, T., Terabayashi, K., Moro, A., Umeda, K.: Multi-Object Segmentation in a Projection Plane Using Subtraction Stereo. In: 2010 International Conference on Pattern Recognition, pp. 3296–3299 (2010)
4. Verma1, O.P., Hanmandlu, M., Susan, S., et al.: A Simple Single Seeded Region Growing Algorithm for Color Image Segmentation using Adaptive Thresholding. In: 2011 International Conference on Communication Systems and Network Technologies, pp. 500–503 (2011)
5. Xiaofang, L., Dansong, C., Xianglong, T., Jiafeng, L.: Multi-object Segmentation Based on Pulse Coupled Neural Network. In: 2008 IEEE Conference on Cybernetics and Intelligent Systems, vol. 1, pp. 744–748 (2008)
6. Badenas, J., Bober, M., Pla, F.: Segmenting traffic scenes from grey level and motion information. Pattern Analysis and Applications 4, 28–38 (2001)
7. Csaba, B., David, S.: Multiple object tracking by hierarchical association of spatio—temporal data. In: 17th IEEE International Conference on Image Processing, pp. 41–44 (2010)
8. Shuifa, Z., Wensheng, Z., Huan, D., Liu, Y.: Background modeling and object detecting based on optical flow velocity field. Journal of Image and Graphics 16, 236–243 (2011)
9. Jean, G., Akio, K., Avinash, C.K.: A multi-Kalman filtering approach for video Tracking of human-delineated objects in cluttered environments. Computer Vision and Image Understanding 102, 260–316 (2006)
10. Elgammal, A., Duraiswami, R., Harwood, D., et al.: Back ground and foreground modeling using nonparametric kernel density estimation for visual surveillance. Proceedings of the IEEE 90, 1151–1163 (2002)
11. Jiandong, G., Zhi, L., Zhaoyang, Z.: A Novel Moving Object Segmentation Algorithm Using Kernel Density Estimation and Edge Information. Journal of Computer-aided Design & Computer Graphics 21, 223–228 (2009)
12. Qin, A.K., David, A.: Multivariate Image Segmentation Using Semantic Region Growing With Adaptive Edge Penalty. IEEE Transactions on Image Processing 19, 2157–2170 (2010)
13. Kun, Z., Cuirong, W.: A Novel Moving Object Segmentation Algorithm Based on Chebyshev Inequality. In: Proceedings of 2011 International Conference on Opto-Electronics Engineering and Information Science, pp. 1346–1350 (2011)

Reflectance Estimation Using Local Regression Methods

Wei-Feng Zhang[1], Peng Yang[2], Dao-Qing Dai[3], and Arye Nehorai[2]

[1] Department of Applied Mathematics, South China Agricultural University,
483 Wushan Road, Guangzhou 510642, China
zhangwf@scau.edu.cn
[2] Preston M. Green Department of Electrical and Systems Engineering,
Washington University in St. Louis, St. Louis, MO 63130, USA
[3] Center for Computer Vision and Department of Mathematics,
Sun Yat-Sen (Zhongshan) University, Guangzhou 510275, China

Abstract. Regression methods have been widely used in the problem of spectral reflectance estimation from camera responses, due to their simple application without needing prior knowledge of the imaging system. These methods can be called global regression methods since the regression functions are trained on all the training samples. Recently, local learning methods have received considerable attention due to their capability in exploiting the local manifold structure of data. In this paper, we propose a set of reflectance estimation methods based on local regression methods. These methods can be seen as the local versions of the traditional global regression methods. The training set is confined to the test point's k-nearest neighbors. Experimental results show that the local ridge regression has the best generalization performance in the compared methods.

Keywords: Ridge regression, Local learning, Reflectance estimation.

1 Introduction

The spectral reflectance of a natural object is the amount of incident light reflected for each wavelength in the visible spectrum. Commonly used color imaging systems, such as three-channel digital cameras, measure the integral responses of object reflectance, incident illuminant and imaging sensor sensitivities. The generated RGB responses are not reliable acquisition of colorimetric information, since they are device and illuminant dependent. Different digital cameras and illuminant conditions will produce different RGB responses for the same scene. The most accurate and informative way to describe a color is to use its spectral reflectance. Therefore in applications which require accurate color reproduction, such as digital archiving of art painting and remote sensing tasks, knowing the spectral reflectance is very important.

Reflectance can be measured directly by spectrophotometers. However, these sophisticated equipments are often very expensive and only equipped by specialized labs. Therefore developing accurate spectral reflectance estimation methods from camera responses has attracted increasing attention in recent years.

J. Wang, G.G. Yen, and M.M. Polycarpou (Eds.): ISNN 2012, Part I, LNCS 7367, pp. 116–122, 2012.

Spectral reflectances of natural objects are typically smooth continuous functions of wavelength. In practice, they are usually discretized by uniformly sampling in the visible wavelengths from 400-700 nm. If the sampling interval is 10nm, the reflectance can be seen as a 31-dimensional vector $\mathbf{r} \in \mathbb{R}^{31}$. The 3-dimensional RGB camera response $\mathbf{x} \in \mathbb{R}^3$ can then be seen as the result of mapping the high-dimensional reflectance space into a low-dimensional RGB space. The problem of reflectance estimation therefore attempts to build inverse models that can map $\mathbf{x}$ back into $\mathbf{r}$. If there is no constraint on the properties of spectral reflectance, it is impossible to build reasonable inverse models. Fortunately, smoothness of reflectance functions ensure that the high dimensional reflectance vectors are located in a relatively low-dimensional subspace. This enables a lot of reasonable reflectance estimation methods proposed [1–9].

Regression methods are widely used for reflectance estimation by building the functional relationship between the RGB responses and reflectance values. It is not necessary to know the spectral power distribution of the illumination or the spectral sensitivities of the sensors, which are difficult to obtain in practice. With only the spectral reflectance and camera responses of a set of training samples, the regression model can be built, which is more applicable than other methods. Hardeberg used linear regression for reflectance estimation [1]. Connah *et al.* extended the work using the nonlinear polynomial regression with regularization [2]. Heikkinen *et al.* showed that kernel ridge regression methods surpassed the performance of the former regression methods [5]. Zhang *et al.* proposed a reflectance estimation method using support vector regression and a composite model, which can improve the accuracy when the training set is small [6].

Recently, local learning methods have received increasing attention [8–13]. It has been shown that local learning models can exploit the local manifold structure of data and perform more efficiently than the global learning models. Here, we describe a set of local regression methods for reflectance estimation. The proposed methods can be seen as local versions of the traditional global regression methods, where the training set is confined to the testing point's k-nearest neighbors. We show that local ridge regression outperforms conventional global kernel regression for reflectance estimation.

2   Regression Methods to Estimate Spectral Reflectance

The relationship between the reflectance $\mathbf{r} \in \mathbb{R}^{31}$ and camera responses $\mathbf{x} \in \mathbb{R}^3$ can be modeled as

$$\mathbf{x} = \mathbf{SLr} + \mathbf{e}, \tag{1}$$

where $\mathbf{S}$ is a 3×31 matrix of spectral sensitivities of the camera sensors, $\mathbf{L}$ is a 31×31 diagonal matrix having the illuminant's spectral power distribution in the diagonal, and $\mathbf{e}$ is a 3×1 column vector of system noise. For abbreviation, Eq. (1) is usually expressed as

$$\mathbf{x} = \mathbf{Mr} + \mathbf{e}, \tag{2}$$

where $\mathbf{M} = \mathbf{SL}$ denotes the spectral responsivity matrix.

Assume we have a training set $S = \{(\mathbf{x}_i, \mathbf{r}_i), \mathbf{x}_i \in \mathbb{R}^3, \mathbf{r}_i \in \mathbb{R}^{31}, i = 1, \ldots, n\}$ of input-output pairs of camera responses $\mathbf{x}_i$ and reflectance vector $\mathbf{r}_i$. The problem setting of regression methods is to learn a set of functions

$$\hat{r}_j = f_j(\mathbf{x}), \qquad j = 1, \ldots, 31 \tag{3}$$

separately for each sampled wavelength. When new input $\mathbf{x}$ is presented, the target reflectance $\mathbf{r}$ can be estimated as $\hat{\mathbf{r}} = (\hat{r}_1, \ldots, \hat{r}_{31})^T$.

2.1   Global Regression Methods

The conventional regression based reflectance estimation methods use all the training samples to build the functions in Eq. (3), which means all the testing data will be predicted by the same model. Since the reflectance vectors are located in a higher dimensional space than the RGB response vectors, the functional relationship between $\mathbf{x}$ and r_j should be nonlinear. Therefore the regression functions in Eq. (3) should be chosen to flexible enough to represent the nonlinear relationship. The earliest and simplest regression model is the linear model

$$f(\mathbf{x}) = \mathbf{w}^T \mathbf{x}. \tag{4}$$

Hardeberg used this model for reflectance estimation [1]. The coefficient $\mathbf{w}$ can be searched by least squares approach which minimizes

$$\mathcal{L}(f, S) = \sum_{i=1}^{n} (r_{ij} - \mathbf{w}^T \mathbf{x}_i), \tag{5}$$

or by ridge regression method which minmizes

$$\mathcal{L}(f, S) = \sum_{i=1}^{n} (r_{ij} - \mathbf{w}^T \mathbf{x}_i) + \lambda \|\mathbf{w}\|_2^2. \tag{6}$$

Connah *et al.* extended the linear model to nonlinear using polynomial expansion of camera responses [2]. They proved that nonlinear estimation method provided better performance than linear model.

Heikkinen *et al.* proposed the nonlinear method of kernel ridge regression for reflectance estimation [5]

$$\min_{f \in \mathcal{H}_K} H[f] = \sum_{i=1}^{n} (r_{ij} - f(\mathbf{x}_i))^2 + \gamma \|f\|_K^2, \tag{7}$$

where $\|f\|_K^2$ is the norm in a reproducing kernel Hilbert space (RKHS) $\mathcal{H}_K$ defined by kernel function $K(\mathbf{x}, \mathbf{z})$. The solution has the form

$$f(\mathbf{x}) = \sum_{i=1}^{n} c_i K(\mathbf{x}_i, \mathbf{x}). \tag{8}$$

The results in [5] showed that the kernel model surpassed the performance of the polynomial model.

2.2   Local Regression Methods

Local learning methods, such as the well-known k-nearest neighbors method (KNN) and many new algorithms [8–13], have the same setting that only a small subset of the training samples is used to train the model for each testing pattern. Recent studies have shown that naturally occurring data usually locates on a lower dimensional manifold in the embedded high-dimensional space [10]. The given training data very rarely are evenly distributed in the input space. The global learning methods attempt to discover the global structure of the data space, which is unreasonable with the limited training data. The local learning methods can not only exploit the local manifold structure of data but also perform more efficiently than the global learning models.

Here we propose the local regression methods for reflectance estimation. For a given camera response $\mathbf{x}$, let $\{\mathbf{x}_1, \ldots, \mathbf{x}_k\}$ be its k nearest neighbors from the training set in the sense of Euclidean distance, and $\{\mathbf{r}_1, \ldots, \mathbf{r}_k\}$ be the corresponding reflectances of $\{\mathbf{x}_1, \ldots, \mathbf{x}_k\}$. We train the regression models in Eq. (5), (6) and (7) with only these few examples. Then apply the resulting regression models to the testing pattern $\mathbf{x}$. These reflectance estimation methods are named as local linear least squares regression (LLLSR), local ridge regression (LRR), and local kernel ridge regression (LKRR), respectively.

3   Experimental Results

We provide an experiment on the spectral reflectance data from [14], showing the results for reflectance estimation. Camera responses are simulated based on the Sony DXC-930 3CCD camera measured by Barnard *et al.* [15]. The spectral sensitivity curves of the three channels are shown in Fig. 1. The illumination light is assumed to be the CIE illuminant D65. To exemplify the practicability and the superiority of our methods, we compare the performance of our three local regression methods with the corresponding three global regression methods: linear least squares regression (LLSR); ridge regression (RR); kernel ridge regression (KRR). The classical Gaussian kernel

$$K(\mathbf{x}, \mathbf{z}) = \exp\left(-\frac{\|\mathbf{x} - \mathbf{z}\|^2}{2\sigma^2}\right) \tag{9}$$

is used for both the local and global kernel regression methods.

Three reflectance datasets are used as training set, validation set, and test set. The training set is used to build the regression functions with given parameters. The optimal parameters are chosen to minimize the root mean square error (RMSE) on the validation set. This can help to minimize over-fitting on the training set, making the method generalize well to novel data. Finally the generalization performance is evaluated using the test set, which consists of novel samples for which the model is not trained. The information of the experimental datasets is shown in Table 1.

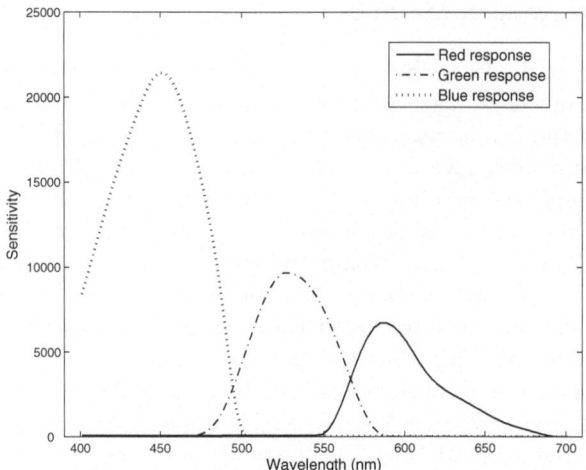

Fig. 1. Spectral sensitivity curves of Sony DXC-930 3CCD camera

Table 1. Summary of experimental datasets

Dataset	Name	Size
Training set	Munsell Matte	1269
Validation set	Agfa IT8.7/2	288
Test set	Paper	426

Table 2 shows the RMSE values and colorimetric errors (ΔE_{ab} color difference with CIE 1964 observer and CIE illuminant D65 and A [6]) between the measured and reconstructed reflectances on test set. In this case we add no noise to the simulated RGB responses. We also compare the situation with additive independent Gaussian noise of zero mean and variance 0.01. The results are shown in Table 3. The parameters in different methods are chosen from predefined sets. For the local regression methods, the number of nearest neighbors $k = 20$ always give satisfying results. For the regularization methods, we chose $\lambda = 0.0001$. For the Gaussian kernel, we chose kernel width $\sigma = 0.3$. The results in Table 2 and 3 are given by this parameter setting.

As can be seen, both the local linear least squares regression and local ridge regression perform better than the three global regression methods. They can provide lower mean reflectance errors and mean colorimetric errors. The performance of global linear least squares regression is close to that of the global ridge regression, while the local ridge regression is a little better than the local linear least squares regression. In the three global regression methods, kernel ridge regression performs better than the two linear regression methods, which exemplifies the results in [5]. This is due to the functional relationships in the global setting are essentially nonlinear, and the nonlinear approximation ability of kernel regression is more suitable here. However, in the local learning setting,

Table 2. Estimation errors on the test set without noise. In each row the best result is labeled in bold type.

Error term		LLSR	RR	KRR	LLLSR	LRR	LKRR
	Mean	0.0502	0.0502	0.0489	0.0448	**0.0447**	0.0492
RMSE	Max	0.2503	0.2503	**0.1440**	0.1893	0.1909	0.2171
	Min	**0.0034**	**0.0034**	0.0082	**0.0034**	**0.0034**	0.0071
	Mean	1.7991	1.7992	1.6563	1.5517	**1.5473**	1.8550
ΔE_{ab}(D65)	Max	15.743	15.744	**7.7811**	8.8800	9.4990	12.440
	Min	**0.0177**	**0.0177**	0.0511	0.0208	0.0930	0.0559
	Mean	3.2568	3.2568	2.4144	2.1665	**2.1604**	2.4858
ΔE_{ab}(A)	Max	23.1836	23.182	**8.6975**	12.0962	12.808	16.0874
	Min	0.0924	0.0925	0.0879	0.0810	0.0983	**0.0344**

Table 3. Estimation errors of on the test set with noise. In each row the best result is labeled in bold type.

Error term		LLSR	RR	KRR	LLLSR	LRR	LKRR
	Mean	0.0504	0.0504	0.0488	0.0446	**0.0445**	0.0506
RMSE	Max	0.2502	0.2502	**0.1470**	0.1897	0.1904	0.2618
	Min	0.0055	0.0055	0.0054	0.0041	**0.0038**	0.0090
	Mean	2.1710	2.1710	1.9488	1.8505	**1.8291**	2.6352
ΔE_{ab}(D65)	Max	16.293	16.294	12.144	**11.156**	11.801	22.025
	Min	0.1552	0.1551	**0.0963**	0.1143	0.1130	0.2060
	Mean	3.4372	3.4372	2.6901	2.3697	**2.3663**	3.1696
ΔE_{ab}(A)	Max	25.004	25.003	17.075	**14.1817**	14.9216	25.162
	Min	0.1415	0.1416	**0.0736**	0.1936	0.1850	0.1976

kernel regression performs worse than the two linear regression methods, and even worse than the global kernel regression. The reason may be that the training size is too small in the local setting, and thus the nonlinear kernel regression overfits easily.

4   Conclusions

In this paper, we propose a class of reflectance estimation methods from RGB camera responses using local regression methods. The local regression methods focus on the lcoal reflectance estimation performance rather than trying to build a global model that fits all the training samples. They can exploit the local manifold structure of data and perform more efficiently than the global regression models. Experimental results show that the local ridge regression method outperforms the other global and local regression methods compared in this paper.

Acknowledgments. This work was supported in part by the National Natural Science Foundation of China (NSFC, grants 60903094, 11171354 and 90092007).

Peng Yang and Arye Nehorai are supported by National Science Foundation, NSF Grants CCF-1014908 and CCF-0963742, and AFOSR Grant FA9550-11-1-0210.

References

1. Hardeberg, J.Y.: Filter Selection for Multispectral Color Image Acquistion. J. Imaging Sci. Technol. 48, 105–110 (2004)
2. Connah, D., Hardeberg, J.Y.: Spectral Recovery Using Polynomial Models. In: Proc. SPIE, vol. 5667, pp. 65–75 (2005)
3. Shimano, N., Terai, K., Hironaga, M.: Recovery of Spectral Reflectances of Objects being Imaged by Multispectral Cameras. J. Opt. Soc. Am. A 24, 3211–3219 (2007)
4. Shen, H.L., Xin, J.H.: Estimation of Spectral Reflectance of Object Surfaces with the Consideration of Perceptual Color Space. Opt. Lett. 32, 96–98 (2007)
5. Heikkinen, V., Jetsu, T., Parkkinen, J., Hauta-Kasari, M., Jaaskelainen, T., Lee, S.D.: Regularized Learning Framework in the Estimation of Reflectance Spectra from Camera Responses. J. Opt. Soc. Am. A 24, 2673–2683 (2007)
6. Zhang, W.F., Dai, D.Q.: Spectral Reflectance Estimation from Camera Responses by Support Vector Regression and a Composite Model. J. Opt. Soc. Am. A 25, 2286–2296 (2008)
7. Lansel, S., Parmar, M., Wandell, B.A.: Dictionaries for Sparse Representation and Recovery of Reflectances. In: Proc. SPIE, Comp. Imaging VII., vol. 7246, p. 72460D (2009)
8. Zhang, W.F., Tang, G., Dai, D.Q., Nehorai, A.: Estimation of Reflectance from Cameara Responses by the Regularized Local Linear Model. Opt. Lett. 36, 3933–3935 (2011)
9. Lansel, S.: Local Linear Learned Method for Image and Reflectance Estimation. Doctoral Dissertation, Standford University (2011)
10. Roweis, S.T., Saul, L.K.: Nonlinear Dimensionality Reduction by Locally Linear Embedding. Science 290, 2323–2326 (2000)
11. Wu, M., Schölkopf, B.: A Local Learning Approach for Clustering. In: Advances in Neural Information Processing Systems 19, pp. 1529–1536. MIT Press (2007)
12. Gupta, M.R., Garcia, E.K., Chin, E.: Adaptive Local Linear Regression with Application to Printer Color Mangement. IEEE T. Image. Process. 17, 936–945 (2008)
13. Ladický, L., Torr, P.H.S.: Locally Linear Support Vector Machines. In: Proceddings of the 28th International Conference on Machine Learning (2011)
14. Spectral Database. University of Joensuu Color Group, http://spectral.joensuu.fi/
15. Barnard, K., Martin, L., Funt, B., Coath, A.: A Data Set for Color Research. Color Res. Appl. 27, 147–151 (2002)

Applying a Novel Decision Rule to the Semi-supervised Clustering Method Based on One-Class SVM

Lei Gu[1,2]

[1] JiangSu Province Support Software Engineering R&D Center for Modern Information Technology Application in Enterprise, Suzhou, China, 215104
[2] School of Computer Science and Technology, Nanjing University of Posts and Telecomunications, Nanjing, China, 210046
gulei@njupt.edu.cn

Abstract. Semi-supervised clustering takes advantage of some labeled data called seeds to bring a great benefit to the clustering of unlabeled data. This paper presents a novel semi-supervised clustering method based on one-class support vector machine, which applies a novel decision rule to assigning the class label to one data point. To investigate the effectiveness of our approach, experiments are done on one artificial data set and two real datasets. Experimental results show that the proposed method can improve the clustering performance significantly compared to other semi-supervised clustering algorithms when using a very small amount of seeds.

Keywords: Semi-supervised clustering, One-class SVM, Decision rule.

1 Introduction

The aim of data clustering methods is to divide data into several homogeneous groups called clusters, within each of which the similarity or dissimilarity between data is larger or less than data belonging to different groups[1]. Unsupervised clustering partitions all unlabeled data into a certain number of groups on the basis of one chosen similarity or dissimilarity measure[2,3]. Different measure of the similarity or dissimilarity can lead to various clustering methods such as k-means[4], fuzzy c-means[5], mountain clustering, subtractive clustering[6] and neural gas[7]. In these traditional clustering algorithms, k-means, which can be easily implemented, is the best-known squared error- based clustering algorithm. Recently, a novel kernel method for clustering based on one-class Support Vector Machine(SVM) was presented in [8]. This kernel-based clustering method can be implemented in a similar way to the classical k-means and use a one-class support vector machine as the description of each cluster rather than the center of several data. Experiments on real datasets show that the clustering algorithm in [8] is valid and can have encouraging performance.

Semi-supervised clustering can also divide a collection of unlabeled data into several groups. However, a small amount of labeled data is allowed to be applied to aiding and biasing the clustering of unlabeled data in semi-supervised clustering unlike

J. Wang, G.G. Yen, and M.M. Polycarpou (Eds.): ISNN 2012, Part I, LNCS 7367, pp. 123–131, 2012.

the unsupervised clustering, and so a significant increase in clustering performance can be obtained by the semi-supervised clustering[9]. The popular semi-supervised clustering methods are composed of two categories called the similarity-based and search-based approaches respectively[10]. In similarity-based methods, an existing clustering algorithm employs a specific similarity measure trained by labeled data. In search-based methods, the clustering algorithms modify the objective function under the aid of labeled data such that better clusters are found[10]. A number of semi-supervised clustering approaches published until now belongs to the search-based methods. For example, [11] presented a semi-supervised clustering with pair-wise constraints and [10] gave an active semi-supervised fuzzy clustering.

It is noticeable that semi- supervised clustering by seeding was proposed in [9]. [9] introduced a clustering method viewed as the semi-supervised variants of k-means and also called Constrained K-Means(CKM). Furthermore, In [12], we also demonstrated a novel semi-supervised clustering method called CCOSVM, which introduced the semi-supervised clustering technique inspired by CKM into the presented clustering based on one-class support vector machine in [8]. In CKM and CCOSVM, labeled data is regarded as the seeds. Although the seeds can be used for the initializations of CKM and CCOSVM and have an important effect on constructing the centers and spheres in the clustering processes of CKM and CCOSVM, they can not affect the decision rule applied to assigning the class label to one data point. So this paper proposes a novel semi-supervised clustering method called CCOSVM_NDR, which applies a novel decision rule to CCOSVM according to the seeds. Experimental results show that our approach can obtain the better clustering performance when using a very small amount of seeds.

The remainder of this paper is organized as follows. Section 2 reports the CCOSVM clustering algorithm. In Section 3, the CCOSVM_NDR clustering method is formulated. Experimental results are shown in Section 4, and Section 5 gives our conclusions.

2   The CCOSVM Clustering Algorithm

CCOSVM is one of the semi-supervised clustering algorithms. In CCOSVM, each cluster is iteratively described by a one-class support vector machine. Therefore, we introduce one-class support vector machine related to CCOSVM here at first[12].

One-class support vector machine is a kernel-based data domain description method. It tries to find the smallest sphere containing all input data in the feature space. Let $X^m = \{x_1^m, x_2^m, \cdots, x_n^m\}$ be a nonempty set of cluster m in the d-dimensional space R^d. Now we construct a smallest sphere S_m for cluster m that can enclose all points x_i^m ($x_i^m \in X^m, i = 1, 2, \cdots, n$). This problem is considered as a quadratic optimization as follows:

$$\min_{a, R} R \ \ s.t. \ \left(x_i^m - a\right)^T \left(x_i^m - a\right) \leq R^2, i = 1, 2, \cdots, n \tag{1}$$

where a is the center of the sphere S_m and R is its radius. The constraints introduce slack variables ξ_i as follows:

$$\min_{a,R,\xi_i} R + C\sum_{i=1}^{n} \xi_i \ \ s.t. \ \left(x_i^m - a\right)^T \left(x_i^m - a\right) \le R^2 + \xi_i \tag{2}$$

where $\forall i, \xi_i \ge 0$ and the variable C gives the trade-off between the volume of the sphere and the number of target objects rejected. This is a convex optimization problem. Therefore, we can use Lagrange multipliers to guarantee it to converge to the global minimum:

$$L\left(R,a,\xi_i\right) = R^2 - \sum_{i=1}^{n} \beta_i \, \xi_i + C\sum_{i=1}^{n} \xi_i - \sum_{i=1}^{n} \alpha_i \left(R^2 + \xi_i - \left(x_i^m - a\right)^T \left(x_i^m - a\right)\right) \tag{3}$$

where $\forall_i, \alpha_i \ge 0, \beta_i \ge 0$. The minimization problem of Eq.(3) can be transformed into the maximization problem of the Wolfe dual form[13] as follows:

$$L = \sum_{i=1}^{n} \alpha_i \left(x_i^m \cdot x_i^m\right) - \sum_{i=1}^{n}\sum_{j=1}^{n} \alpha_i \alpha_j \left(x_i^m \cdot x_j^m\right) \tag{4}$$

with the constraints $\forall_i, 0 \le \alpha_i \le C$ and $\sum_{i=1}^{n} \alpha_i = 1$.

In real-world applications, data is not spherically distributed, even when the most outlying data points are excluded. To make more flexible descriptions of a class, the kernel functions can be applied to transforming the data examples into a high-dimensional feature space F by a nonlinear mapping $\Phi : R^d \to F$ instead of the Euclidean inner product often used as a similarity measure in a variety of fields, like pattern classification and data clustering. Let K be a positive kernel function. The inner product in F can be computed through the kernel function K in R^d:

$$K\left(x_i, x_j\right) = \Phi\left(x_x\right) \cdot \Phi\left(x_j\right) \tag{5}$$

After solving the problem of Eq.(4) by using the Karush-Kuhn-Tucker conditions[14], we can get the smallest sphere S_m of cluster m. When the smallest sphere of each cluster is attained, we finish the training process of one-class support vector machine in one iteration step of CCOSVM.

Although the centers of the smallest spheres can not be explicitly expressed, they are regarded as the clusters presented by the smallest spheres in CCOSVM. Let x be any point from X ($X = \left\{X^1, \cdots, X^m, \cdots, X^M\right\}$) and M be the number of clusters. The distance D between x and the center of the sphere S_m can be calculated as the following formula:

$$D(x,S_m) = K(x,x) - 2\sum_{i=1}^{n} \alpha_i K(x_i^m, x) + \sum_{i=1}^{n}\sum_{j=1}^{n} \alpha_i \alpha_j K(x_i^m, x_j^m) \qquad (6)$$

Consequently, CCOSVM assigns x to one cluster m by the following decision rule:

$$m = \arg \min_{h=1,2,\cdots,M} D(x,S_h) \qquad (7)$$

where M is the number of clusters, $D(x,S_h)$ can be computed by Eq.(6), $D(x,S_h) < \rho$ and ρ is a parameter explained in [8] and [15].

Next, Given the number of clusters M, the unlabeled data set X, the seed set W ($W \subseteq X$) that can be divided into M groups on the basis of data labels (each subgroup should contain at least two labeled data for the implementation of one-class support vector machine), we get a M partitioning $\{W_1, W_2, \cdots W_M\}$ of W.

Finally, the procedure for CCOSVM is presented as follows[12]:

Step1. Let $\{W_1, W_2, \cdots W_M\}$ be the initial data sets. For each W_m ($m = 1,2,\cdots,M$), Obtain a smallest sphere S_m encircling all elements in W_m by training the one-class support vector machine.

Step2. Firstly, assign each data x ($x \in X$ and $x \in W$) to one cluster m ($m = 1,2,\cdots,M$) on the basis of its label. Secondly, according to Eq.(7), assign each data x ($x \in X$ and $x \notin W$) to one cluster m viewed as the smallest sphere S_m in the feature space. Finally, gain a M partitioning $\{X^1, X^2, \cdots, X^m\}$ of the whole X.

Step3. If the division $\{X^1, X^2, \cdots, X^m\}$ is not changed, goto Step5.

Step4. After train a one-class support vector machine for each X^m to get the smallest sphere S_m enclosing all elements in X^m, goto Step2.

Step5. End CCOSVM.

3   The Proposed Method CCOSVM_NDR

The proposed method CCOSVM_NDR is outlined as follows:

Step1. Let $G = 1$ and MAX be the maximum iteration times of CCOSVM_NDR. In experiments of this paper, we set $MAX = 100$.

Step2. Let a M partitioning $\{W_1, W_2, \cdots W_M\}$ of the seed set W be the initial data sets. For each W_m ($m = 1,2,\cdots,M$), Obtain a smallest sphere S_m

encircling all elements in W_m by training the one-class support vector machine.

Step3. Firstly, assign each data x ($x \in X$ and $x \notin W$) to one cluster m according to the following Eq.(8) regarded as a novel decision rule:

$$m = \begin{cases} \arg \min_{h=1,2,\cdots,M} D(x, S_h) & \text{if } \min_{h=1,2,\cdots,M} D(x, S_h) \leq \min_{t=1,2,\cdots,M} d(x, W_t) \\ \arg \min_{t=1,2,\cdots,M} d(x, W_t) & \text{if } \min_{h=1,2,\cdots,M} D(x, S_h) > \min_{t=1,2,\cdots,M} d(x, W_t) \end{cases} \qquad (8)$$

$$d(x, W_t) = \min_{p=1}^{T} \left(K(x, x) - 2K(x, y_p) + K(y_p, y_p) \right), \forall y_p \in W_t \qquad (9)$$

where $d(x, W_t)$ and $D(x, S_h)$ can be computed by Eq.(9) and Eq.(6) respectively. Moreover, T is the size of W_t in Eq.(9) and K is the same kernel function with Eq.(6) . Secondly, assign each data x ($x \in X$ and $x \in W$) to one cluster m on the basis of its label. At last, gain a M partitioning $\{ X^1, X^2, \cdots, X^m \}$ of the whole X .

Step4. If the division $\{ X^1, X^2, \cdots, X^m \}$ is not changed, goto Step8.

Step5. If G is equal to MAX , goto Step8.

Step6. Let $G = G + 1$.

Step7. After train a one-class support vector machine for each X^m to get the smallest sphere S_m enclosing all elements in X^m , goto Step3.

Step8. End CCOSVM_NDR.

Although both CCOSVM and CCOSVM_NDR use a small amount of labeled data called the seeds for initializations, different decision rules are applied to labeling the data point. Because the distances between unlabeled data points and the labeled seeds are considered in decision rule Eq.(8) of CCOSVM_NDR, CCOSVM_NDR can gain a better decision boundaries than CCOSVM.

4   Experimental Results

To demonstrate the effectiveness of the above CCOSVM_NDR algorithm, we compared it with other semi-supervised clustering methods, such as COSVM and CKM, on one artificial data set shown in Fig.1 and two UCI real datasets[16] referred to as Iris and Sonar respectively. The artificial data set collects 150 2-dimensional cases belonging to three classes. Iris data set contains 150 cases with 4-dimensional feature from three classes. Sonar data set is a 60-dimensinal dataset with 208 instances of two classes. All experiments were done by Matlab on WindowsXP operating system.

The Gaussian kernel function Eq.(10) was applied to two kernel-based methods.

$$K\left(x_i, x_j\right) = \exp\left(-\left\|x_i - x_j\right\|^2 / 2\delta\right) \tag{10}$$

We used the better kernel parameter for each dataset in each clustering algorithm respectively, such as $\delta = 5$ on the artificial data set, $\delta = 10$ on Iris data set and $\delta = 2.2$ on Sonar data set. For CCOSVM and CCOSVM_NDR, we used the same kernel parameters, set the regularization parameter $C = 1$ according to [8] and employ the same modification with [15], in which the parameter ρ related to Eq.(7) was not used. A Matlab's function called quadprog was used to solve the quadratic optimization problems for CCOSVM and CCOSVM_NDR. On each dataset, the seeds with very small size are randomly extracted from the whole data to compare their contributions to the clustering performance of CKM, CCOSVM and CCOSVM_NDR and we randomly generated $P\%$ ($P = 4, 5, \cdots, 10$) of the whole data as seeds. Furthermore, Given the clustering accuracies $Q\%$ on unlabeled data, because the labels of seeds are known, the clustering accuracies of the whole dataset consisting of unlabeled data and labeled seeds could be calculated by $Q\% \cdot (100 - P)\% + P\%$. On each dataset CKM, CCOSVM and CCOSVM_NDR were run 20 times for different P ($P = 4, 5, \cdots, 10$).

We report in Fig.2, Fig.3 and Fig.4 the average accuracies of the whole dataset obtained over these 20 runs. Firstly, In Fig.2, although CCOSVM obtains the better performance than CKM, we can see that CCOSVM_NDR achieves the best clustering performance compared with them. Secondly, Fig.3 and Fig.4 show that there are not the drastic distinctions between CCOSVM and CKM, but CCOSVM_NDR can present good advantage over other two clustering algorithms. Finally, Fig.2, Fig.3 and Fig.4 demonstrate CCOSVM_NDR outperforms CKM and CCOSVM when a very small amount of seeds is used in the semi-supervised clustering processes.

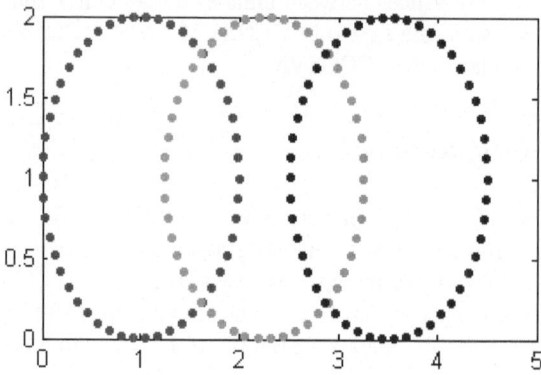

Fig. 1. The artificial data set

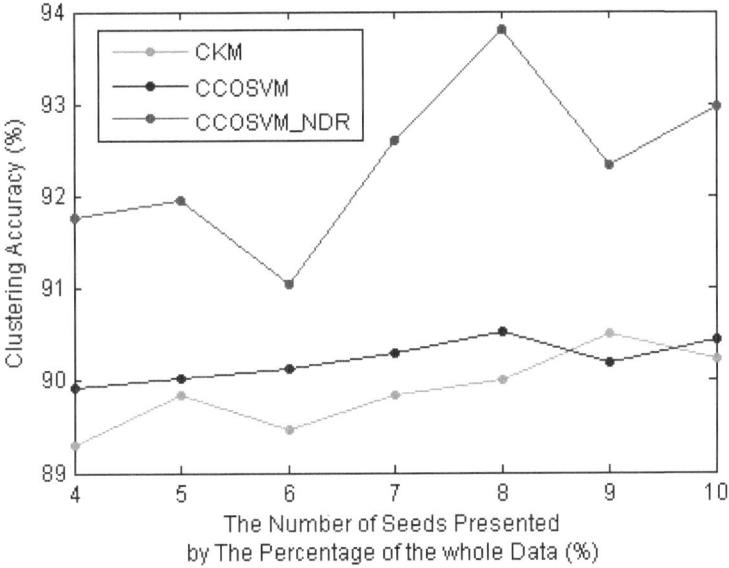

Fig. 2. Comparison of clustering accuracies on Iris data set

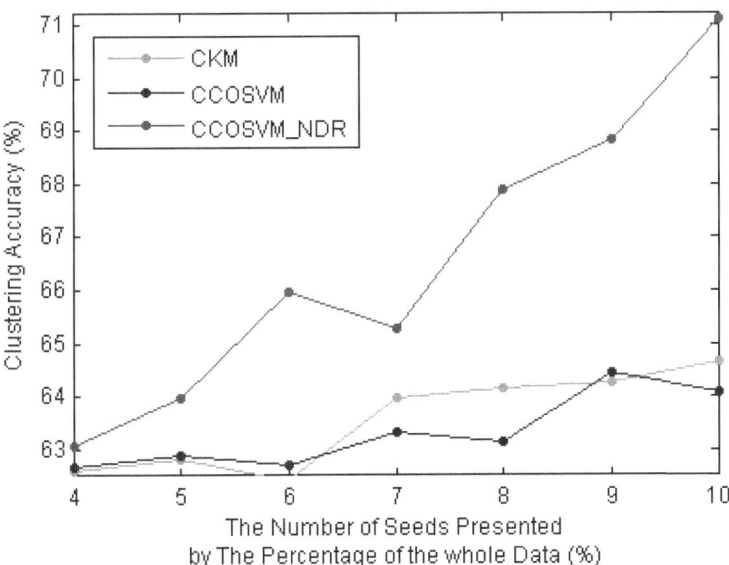

Fig. 3. Comparison of clustering accuracies on the artificial data set

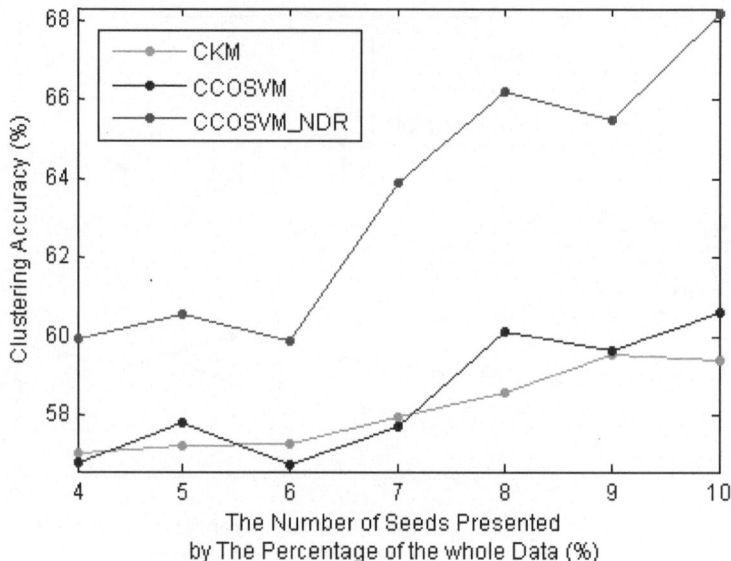

Fig. 4. Comparison of clustering accuracies on Sonar data set

5   Conclusions

In this paper, we propose the novel kernel-based semi-supervised clustering methods CCOSVM_NDR. Compared with CCOSVM, CCOSVM_NDR applies a novel decision rule to assigning one class label to a data point. Experiments are carried out on one artificial data set and two real data sets. In comparison to CKM and CCOSVM, our proposed method has been demonstrated their superiority when using a very small amount of seeds.

Acknowledgements. This research is supported by the Opening Project of Jiang-Su Province Support Software Engineering R&D Center for Modern Information Technology Application in Enterprise (No. SX201101). This research is also supported by the Scientific Research Foundation of Nanjing University of Posts and Telecommunications (No. NY210078), and the Foundation of Key Laboratory of Advanced Process Control for Light Industry(Jiangnan University), Ministry of Education, China (No. APCLI1003), and the Foundation of Key Laboratory of Embedded System and Service Computing(Tongji University), Ministry of Education, China (No.2011-01), and the Foundation of Guangxi Key Lab of Wireless Wideband Communication & Signal Processing (No.21107).

References

1. Fillippone, M., Camastra, F., Masulli, F., Rovetta, S.: A survey of kernel and spectral methods for clustering. Pattern Recognition 41(1), 176–190 (2008)
2. Jain, A.K., Murty, M.N., Flyn, P.J.: Data clustering: a review. ACM Computing Surveys 31(3), 256–323 (1999)

3. Xu, R., Wunsch, D.: Survey of clustering algorithms. IEEE Transactions on Neural Networks 16(3), 645–678 (2005)
4. Tou, J.T., Gonzalez, R.C.: Pattern recognition principles. Addison-Wesley, London (1974)
5. Bezdek, J.C.: Pattern recognition with fuzzy objective function algorithms. Plenum Press, New York (1981)
6. Kim, D.W., Lee, K.Y., Lee, D., Lee, K.H.: A kernel-based subtractive clustering method. Pattern Recognition Letters 26(7), 879–891 (2005)
7. Martinetz, T.M., Berkovich, S.G., Schulten, K.J.: Neural-gas network for vector quantization and its application to time-series prediction. IEEE Transactions on Neural Networks 4(4), 558–569 (1993)
8. Camastra, F., Verri, A.: A novel kernel method for clustering. IEEE Transaction on Pattern Analysis and Machine Intelligence 27(5), 801–805 (2005)
9. Basu, S., Banerjee, A., Mooney, R.J.: Semi-supervised clustering by seeding. In: Proceedings of the Nineteenth International Conference on Machine Learning, pp. 27–34 (2002)
10. Grira, N., Crucianu, M., Boujemaa, N.: Active semi-supervised fuzzy clustering. Pattern Recognition 41(5), 1834–1844 (2008)
11. Basu, S., Banjeree, A., Mooney, R.J.: Active semi-supervised for pairwise constrained clustering. In: Proceedings of the 2004 SIAM International Conference on Data Mining, pp. 333–344 (2004)
12. Gu, L., Sun, F.C.: Two novel kernel-based semi-supervised clustering methods by seeding. In: Proceedings of the 2009 Chinese Conference on Pattern Recognition (2009)
13. Wolfe, P.: A duality theorem for nonlinear programming. Q. Appl. Math. 19, 239–244 (1961)
14. Kukn, H.W., Tucker, A.W.: Nonlinear programming. In: Proceedings of Second Berkeley Symposium on Mathematical Statistics and Probability, pp. 481–492 (1951)
15. Bicego, M., Figueiredo, M.A.T.: Soft clustering using weighted one-class support vector machines. Pattern Recognition 42(1), 27–32 (2009)
16. UCI Machine Learning Repository,
    http://www.ics.uci.edu/~mlearn/MLSummary.html

State Estimation of Markovian Jump Neural Networks with Mixed Time Delays*

He Huang and Xiaoping Chen

School of Electronics and Information Engineering,
Soochow University, Suzhou 215006, P.R. China
cshhuang@gmail.com, xpchen@suda.edu.cn

Abstract. This paper is concerned with the state estimation problem of Markovian jump neural networks with discrete and distributed delays. A stochastic Lyapunov functional with a triple-integral term is constructed to handle it. A delay-dependent design criterion is derived such that the resulting error system is mean square exponentially stable with a prescribed decay rate. The gain matrices of the state estimator and the decay rate can be obtained by solving some coupled linear matrix inequalities.

Keywords: Markovian jump neural networks, state estimation, mixed delays, decay rate.

1 Introduction

The research of neural networks has gained rapid development during the past decades. Various kinds of neural networks have been proposed and successfully applied in many areas such as combinatorial optimization, image processing, adaptive control and pattern recognition, etc. Due to the finite switching speeds of the amplifiers, time delays are inevitable in the VLSI implementation of neural networks. It has been well-recognized that the existence of time delays may lead to instability and poor performance of the underlying neural networks. As a result, stability analysis of delayed neural networks has received considerable attention and a great number of interesting stability conditions have been available in the literature (see, e.g., [3, 17, 18]).

On the other hand, neural networks frequently display information latching [14]. Generally, the information latching problem can be efficiently resolved by extracting finite-state representations. That is, the neural networks with information latching may have finite modes which can switch from one to another governing by a Markov chain. Consequently, the Markovian jump neural networks were proposed [9] and the stability analysis was investigated in [19–21].

As suggested in [15], in a relatively large-scale neural network, it may be difficult (or even impossible) to acquire the complete information of the neuron states. Therefore, in some practical applications of neural networks, it is

---

* This work was jointly supported by the National Natural Science Foundation of China under Grant No. 61005047 and the Natural Science Foundation of Jiangsu Province of China under Grant No. BK2010214.

J. Wang, G.G. Yen, and M.M. Polycarpou (Eds.): ISNN 2012, Part I, LNCS 7367, pp. 132–139, 2012.

necessary to estimate the neuron states via available measurements. Recently, the state estimation problem was widely studied for delayed neural networks [6–8, 10–12]. It should be noted that most of the related works in the above literature were devoted to the neural networks without Markovian jump. Although some results on the state estimation of Markovian jump neural networks were reported in [4, 16], this issue has not yet been fully studied and remains to be challenging. This motivates the present study.

In this paper, our attention focuses on designing a state estimator to Markovian jump neural networks with discrete and distributed delays. The activation function and nonlinear disturbance are assumed to be sector-bounded, which are more general than those satisfying Lipschitz condition. By choosing a stochastic Lyapunov functional with a triple-integral term, a delay-dependent criterion is derived under which the resulting error system is mean square exponentially stable with a prescribed decay rate. It is shown that the gain matrices of the state estimator and the decay rate can be obtained by solving linear matrix inequalities (LMIs) [2]. Comparing with [4], there are two advantages in our developed approach: (i) since the decay rate is determined, the transient process of the resulting error system can be better characterized; (ii) as observed in [1, 13], the introduction of a triple-integral term can reduce the conservatism in the design criterion. It is expected that our result is less conservative than the one in [4].

2   Problem Formulation

The Markovian jump neural network with discrete and distributed delays is described by the following equations:

$$\dot{x}(t) = -A(r_t)x(t) + B(r_t)\sigma(x(t)) + B_1(r_t)\sigma(x(t-h))$$

$$+D(r_t)\int_{t-d}^{t}\sigma(x(s))ds + J(r_t), \tag{1}$$

$$x(s) = \varphi(s), \quad s \in [-\max\{h,d\}, 0], \quad r(0) = r_0, \tag{2}$$

where $x(t) = [x_1(t), x_2(t), \ldots, x_n(t)]^T \in \mathbb{R}^n$ is the state vector associated with n neurons; $\sigma(x(t)) = [\sigma_1(x_1(t)), \sigma_2(x_2(t)), \ldots, \sigma_n(x_n(t))]^T$ is the activation function. $\{r_t\}$ is a continuous-time Markovian process with right continuous trajectories and taking values in a finite set $S = \{1, 2, \ldots, N\}$. The transition probabilities are given by

$$\Pr\{r(t+\Delta) = j | r(t) = i\} = \begin{cases} \pi_{ij}\Delta + o(\Delta), & i \neq j \\ 1 + \pi_{ii}\Delta + o(\Delta), & i = j \end{cases}$$

where $\Delta > 0, \lim_{\Delta \to 0+} o(\Delta)/\Delta = 0, \pi_{ij} \geq 0$ for $j \neq i$ is the transition rate from mode i at time t to mode j at time $t + \Delta$, and for each $i \in S$,

$$\pi_{ii} = -\sum_{j=1, j\neq i}^{N} \pi_{ij}. \tag{3}$$

The scalars $h > 0$ and $d > 0$ are respectively the discrete and distributed delays. $\varphi(s) \in \mathcal{C}([-\max\{h, d\}, 0]; \mathbb{R}^n)$ is the initial function and $r_0 \in S$ is the initial mode. For a fixed system mode i, $A(r_t), B(r_t), B_1(r_t)$ and $D(r_t)$ are real known matrices where $A(r_t) = \mathrm{diag}(a_1(r_t), a_2(r_t), \ldots, a_n(r_t)) > 0$, $B(r_t), B_1(r_t), D(r_t)$ are connection weight matrices. $J(r_t)$ is a constant external input vector.

As discussed in [15], it is difficult to directly obtain the complete information of the neuron states. Consequently, to facilitate the practical applications of neural networks, one needs to propose an efficient algorithm to estimate them from the available network measurements. It is the objective of this study. Here, the measurement is assumed to be of the form:

$$y(t) = C(r_t)x(t) + \phi(t, x(t)) \tag{4}$$

with $C(r_t) \in \mathbb{R}^{m \times n}$ being a constant matrix and $\phi(t, x(t))$ being a nonlinear disturbance on the measurement. For convenience, for each $r_t = i$, we respectively denote $A(r_t), B(r_t), B_1(r_t), C(r_t), D(r_t)$ by $A_i, B_i, B_{1i}, C_i, D_i$.

For each $i \in S$, a causal full-order state estimator is constructed to the above delayed Markovian jump neural network:

$$\dot{\hat{x}}(t) = -A_i\hat{x}(t) + B_i\sigma(\hat{x}(t)) + B_{1i}\sigma(\hat{x}(t - h))$$

$$+D_i \int_{t-d}^{t} \sigma(\hat{x}(s))ds + J_i + K_i[y(t) - C_i\hat{x}(t) - \phi(t, \hat{x}(t))], \tag{5}$$

$$\hat{x}(s) = 0, \quad s \in [-\max\{h, d\}, 0], \quad r(0) = r_0, \tag{6}$$

where $\hat{x}(t) \in \mathbb{R}^n$ is the estimation of the neuron state $x(t)$, and $K_i(i = 1, 2, \ldots, N)$, to be determined, are the estimator gain matrices.

Let the error signal be $e(t) = x(t) - \hat{x}(t)$, then one can immediately obtain the error system from (1) and (5) as

$$\dot{e}(t) = -(A_i + K_iC_i)e(t) + B_if(t) + B_{1i}f(t - h) + D_i \int_{t-d}^{t} f(s)ds - K_ig(t) \tag{7}$$

with $f(t) = \sigma(x(t)) - \sigma(\hat{x}(t))$, $g(t) = \phi(t, x(t)) - \phi(t, \hat{x}(t))$.

Throughout this paper, the two assumptions are made:

Assumption 1. *The activation function $\sigma(\cdot)$ satisfies*

$$[\sigma(u) - \sigma(v) - \Sigma_1(u - v)]^T[\sigma(u) - \sigma(v) - \Sigma_2(u - v)] \leq 0 \tag{8}$$

for all $u, v \in \mathbb{R}^n$, where $\Sigma_1, \Sigma_2 \in \mathbb{R}^{n \times n}$ are known constant matrices.

Assumption 2. *The nonlinear disturbance $\phi(\cdot)$ satisfies*

$$[\phi(t, u) - \phi(t, v) - \Phi_1(u - v)]^T[\phi(t, u) - \phi(t, v) - \Phi_2(u - v)] \leq 0 \tag{9}$$

for all $u, v \in \mathbb{R}^n$ with $\Phi_1, \Phi_2 \in \mathbb{R}^{n \times n}$ being known constant matrices.

Before ending this section, the mean square exponential stability definition and a useful lemma are given.

Definition 1. *The error system* (7) *is said to be mean square exponentially stable if there exist scalars $\alpha > 0$ and $\lambda > 0$ such that*

$$\mathbb{E}|e(t)|^2 \leq \alpha e^{-\lambda t}\|\varphi\|^2 \tag{10}$$

holds for any initial conditions $\varphi \in \mathcal{C}(-[\max\{h,d\},0];\mathbb{R}^n)$ and $r_0 \in S$, where $\|\varphi\| = \sup_{-\max\{h,d\}\leq s\leq 0}|\varphi(s)|$ and $|\cdot|$ is the Euclidean norm. Then, the scalars α and λ are respectively called the decay coefficient and decay rate.

Lemma 1 ([13]). *For any constant matrix $W > 0$, scalars $\alpha_2 > \alpha_1 > 0$, and vector function $\omega(t)$ such that the following integrations are well defined, then*

$$-\frac{1}{2}(\alpha_2^2 - \alpha_1^2)\int_{-\alpha_2}^{-\alpha_1}\int_{t+\theta}^{t}\omega^T(s)W\omega(s)dsd\theta$$

$$\leq -\int_{-\alpha_2}^{-\alpha_1}\int_{t+\theta}^{t}\omega^T(s)dsd\theta W\int_{-\alpha_2}^{-\alpha_1}\int_{t+\theta}^{t}\omega(s)dsd\theta.$$

3   Main Result

This section is dedicated to designing a state estimator (5) for the delayed Markovian jump neural network (1). By constructing a stochastic Lyapunov functional with a tripe-integral term, a delay-dependent design criterion is derived under which the error system (7) is mean square exponentially stable with a prescribed decay rate. Let

$$F_1 = \frac{\Sigma_1^T\Sigma_2 + \Sigma_2^T\Sigma_1}{2}, \quad F_2 = -\frac{\Sigma_1^T + \Sigma_2^T}{2}, G_1 = \frac{\Phi_1^T\Phi_2 + \Phi_2^T\Phi_1}{2},$$

$$G_2 = -\frac{\Phi_1^T + \Phi_2^T}{2}, \quad \lambda_h = \frac{e^{\lambda h} - 1}{\lambda}, \quad \lambda_d = \frac{e^{\lambda d} - 1}{\lambda}, \quad \bar{\lambda} = \frac{e^{\lambda h} - \lambda h - 1}{\lambda^2},$$

then one has

Theorem 1. *For given scalars $h > 0, d > 0$ and $\lambda > 0$, the error system* (7) *is mean square exponentially stable with a prescribed decay rate λ if there exist real matrices $P_i > 0, Q_i = \begin{bmatrix} Q_{1i} & Q_{2i} \\ * & Q_{3i} \end{bmatrix} > 0, Q = \begin{bmatrix} Q_1 & Q_2 \\ * & Q_3 \end{bmatrix} > 0, R > 0, S > 0, X > 0, Y > 0, E_i$ and positive scalars $\epsilon_{1i} > 0, \epsilon_{2i} > 0, \epsilon_{3i} > 0$ such that the following LMIs are satisfied for $i = 1, 2, \ldots, N$:*

$$\begin{bmatrix} \Omega_{11}^i & \frac{1}{h}R & \Omega_{13}^i & P_iB_{1i} & P_iD_i & \Omega_{16}^i & \frac{2}{h}X & \Omega_{18}^i \\ * & \Omega_{22}^i & 0 & \Omega_{24}^i & 0 & 0 & 0 & 0 \\ * & * & \Omega_{33}^i & 0 & 0 & 0 & 0 & B_i^TP_i \\ * & * & * & \Omega_{44}^i & 0 & 0 & 0 & B_{1i}^TP_i \\ * & * & * & * & -\frac{1}{d}S & 0 & 0 & D_i^TP_i \\ * & * & * & * & * & -\epsilon_{3i}I & 0 & -E_i^T \\ * & * & * & * & * & * & -\frac{2}{h^2}X - \frac{1}{h}Y & 0 \\ * & * & * & * & * & * & * & \Omega_{88}^i \end{bmatrix} < 0, \tag{11}$$

$$e^{\lambda h}\sum_{j=1}^{N}\pi_{ij}Q_j \leq Q, \tag{12}$$

where $*$ represents the symmetric block in a symmetric matrix, and

$$\Omega_{11}^i = \lambda P_i - P_i A_i - A_i^T P_i - E_i C_i - C_i^T E_i^T + \sum_{j=1}^N \pi_{ij} P_j$$

$$+ e^{\lambda h} Q_{1i} + \lambda_h Q_1 - \frac{1}{h} R - 2X + \lambda_h Y - \epsilon_{1i} F_1 - \epsilon_{3i} G_1,$$

$$\Omega_{13}^i = P_i B_i + e^{\lambda h} Q_{2i} + \lambda_h Q_2 - \epsilon_{1i} F_2,$$

$$\Omega_{16}^i = -E_i - \epsilon_{3i} G_2, \quad \Omega_{18}^i = -A_i^T P_i - C_i^T E_i^T,$$

$$\Omega_{22}^i = -Q_{1i} - \frac{1}{h} R - \epsilon_{2i} F_1, \quad \Omega_{24}^i = -Q_{2i} - \epsilon_{2i} F_2,$$

$$\Omega_{33}^i = -\epsilon_{1i} I + e^{\lambda h} Q_{3i} + \lambda_h Q_3 + \lambda_d S,$$

$$\Omega_{44}^i = -Q_{3i} - \epsilon_{2i} I, \quad \Omega_{88}^i = -2P_i + \lambda_h R + \bar{\lambda} X.$$

Moreover, the gain matrices K_i can be designed as

$$K_i = P_i^{-1} E_i. \tag{13}$$

Proof. It follows from $[P_i - (\lambda_h R + \bar{\lambda} X)](\lambda_h R + \bar{\lambda} X)^{-1}[P_i - (\lambda_h R + \bar{\lambda} X)] \geq 0$ that $-P_i(\lambda_h R + \bar{\lambda} X)^{-1} P_i \leq -2P_i + \lambda_h R + \bar{\lambda} X$. Pre- and post-multiplying (11) by $\mathrm{diag}\{I, I, I, I, I, I, I, (\lambda_h R + \bar{\lambda} X) P_i^{-1}\}$ and its transpose, respectively, and noting (13) yield

$$\begin{bmatrix} \Xi_{11}^i & \frac{1}{h} R & \Omega_{13}^i & P_i B_{1i} & P_i D_i & \Xi_{16}^i & \frac{2}{h} X & \Xi_{18}^i \\ * & \Omega_{22}^i & 0 & \Omega_{24}^i & 0 & 0 & 0 & 0 \\ * & * & \Omega_{33}^i & 0 & 0 & 0 & 0 & B_i^T Z \\ * & * & * & \Omega_{44}^i & 0 & 0 & 0 & B_{1i}^T Z \\ * & * & * & * & -\frac{1}{d} S & 0 & 0 & D_i^T Z \\ * & * & * & * & * & -\epsilon_{3i} I & 0 & -K_i^T Z \\ * & * & * & * & * & * & -\frac{2}{h^2} X - \frac{1}{h} Y & 0 \\ * & * & * & * & * & * & * & -Z \end{bmatrix} < 0, \tag{14}$$

with

$$\Xi_{11}^i = \lambda P_i - P_i A_i - A_i^T P_i - P_i K_i C_i - C_i^T K_i^T P_i + \sum_{j=1}^N \pi_{ij} P_j$$

$$+ e^{\lambda h} Q_{1i} + \lambda_h Q_1 - \frac{1}{h} R - 2X + \lambda_h Y - \epsilon_{1i} F_1 - \epsilon_{3i} G_1,$$

$$\Xi_{16}^i = -P_i K_i - \epsilon_{3i} G_2, \quad \Xi_{18}^i = -(A_i + K_i C_i)^T Z, \quad Z = \lambda_h R + \bar{\lambda} X.$$

From (8) and (9), one can get that for any scalars $\epsilon_{1i} > 0, \epsilon_{2i} > 0$ and $\epsilon_{3i} > 0$,

$$\epsilon_{1i}[f(t) - \Sigma_1 e(t)]^T [f(t) - \Sigma_2 e(t)] \leq 0, \tag{15}$$

$$\epsilon_{2i}[f(t-h) - \Sigma_1 e(t-h)]^T [f(t-h) - \Sigma_2 e(t-h)] \leq 0, \tag{16}$$

$$\epsilon_{3i}[g(t) - \Phi_1 e(t)]^T [g(t) - \Phi_2 e(t)] \leq 0. \tag{17}$$

Furthermore, (12) guarantees

$$\int_{t-h}^{t} e^{\lambda(s+h)}\xi^T(s)\Big(\sum_{j=1}^{N}\pi_{ij}Q_j\Big)\xi(s)ds - e^{\lambda t}\int_{t-h}^{t}\xi^T(s)Q\xi(s)ds \leq 0. \quad (18)$$

Let $e_t = e(t+s)$, $-\max\{h,d\} \leq s \leq 0$ and $\xi(t) = [e^T(t), f^T(t)]^T$. Construct a stochastic Lyapunov functional candidate as

$$V(e_t, i, t) = e^{\lambda t}e^T(t)P_i e(t) + \int_{t-h}^{t} e^{\lambda(s+h)}\xi^T(s)Q_i\xi(s)ds$$

$$+ \int_{-h}^{0}\int_{t+\theta}^{t} e^{\lambda(s-\theta)}\xi^T(s)Q\xi(s)dsd\theta$$

$$+ \int_{-h}^{0}\int_{t+\theta}^{t} e^{\lambda(s-\theta)}\dot{e}^T(s)R\dot{e}(s)dsd\theta$$

$$+ \int_{-d}^{0}\int_{t+\theta}^{t} e^{\lambda(s-\theta)}f^T(s)Sf(s)dsd\theta$$

$$+ \int_{-h}^{0}\int_{\theta}^{0}\int_{t+\beta}^{t} e^{\lambda(s-\beta)}\dot{e}^T(s)Z\dot{e}(s)dsd\beta d\theta$$

$$+ \int_{-h}^{0}\int_{t+\theta}^{t} e^{\lambda(s-\theta)}e^T(s)Ye(s)dsd\theta. \quad (19)$$

By calculating the weak infinitesimal generator $\mathcal{L}V(e_t, i, t)$ of the random process $\{(e_t, r_t), t \geq 0\}$ acting on $V(e_t, i, t)$, one has

$$\mathcal{L}V(e_t, i, t) = e^{\lambda t}\Big\{ e^T(t)\Big[\lambda P_i - P_i(A_i + K_iC_i) - (A_i + K_iC_i)^T P_i + \sum_{j=1}^{N}\pi_{ij}P_j\Big]e(t)$$

$$+2e^T(t)P_iB_if(t) + 2e^T(t)P_iB_{1i}f(t-h) + 2e^T(t)P_iD_i\int_{t-d}^{t}f(s)ds$$

$$-2e^T(t)P_iK_ig(t) + \xi^T(t)\Big[e^{\lambda h}Q_i + \lambda_hQ\Big]\xi(t) - \xi^T(t-h)Q_i\xi(t-h)$$

$$+\dot{e}^T(t)\Big[\lambda_hR + \lambda_1X\Big]\dot{e}(t) - \int_{t-h}^{t}\dot{e}^T(s)R\dot{e}(s)ds + \lambda_d f^T(t)Sf(t)$$

$$- \int_{t-d}^{t}f^T(s)Sf(s)ds - \int_{-h}^{0}\int_{t+\theta}^{t}\dot{e}^T(s)X\dot{e}(s)dsd\theta + \lambda_h e^T(t)Ye(t)$$

$$- \int_{t-h}^{t}e^T(s)Ye(s)ds\Big\} + \int_{t-h}^{t} e^{\lambda(s+h)}\xi^T(s)\Big(\sum_{j=1}^{N}\pi_{ij}Q_j\Big)\xi(s)ds$$

$$-e^{\lambda t}\int_{t-h}^{t}\xi^T(s)Q\xi(s)ds. \quad (20)$$

Then, by applying Lemma 1 and Jensen's inequality [5] and combining (15)-(20) together, it is easy to derive that

$$\mathcal{L}V(e_t, i, t) \leq \zeta^T(t)[\Lambda_{1i} + \Lambda_{2i}^T Z \Lambda_{2i}]\zeta(t), \tag{21}$$

where

$$\Lambda_{1i} = \begin{bmatrix} \Xi_{11}^i & \frac{1}{h}R & \Omega_{13}^i & P_i B_{1i} & P_i D_i & \Xi_{16}^i & \frac{2}{h}X \\ * & \Omega_{22}^i & 0 & \Omega_{24}^i & 0 & 0 & 0 \\ * & * & \Omega_{33}^i & 0 & 0 & 0 & 0 \\ * & * & * & \Omega_{44}^i & 0 & 0 & 0 \\ * & * & * & * & -\frac{1}{d}S & 0 & 0 \\ * & * & * & * & * & -\epsilon_{3i}I & 0 \\ * & * & * & * & * & * & -\frac{2}{h^2}X - \frac{1}{h}Y \end{bmatrix},$$

$$\Lambda_{2i} = \begin{bmatrix} -(A_i + K_i C_i) & 0 & B_i & B_{1i} & D_i & -K_i & 0 \end{bmatrix},$$

$$\zeta(t) = \begin{bmatrix} e^T(t) & e^T(t-h) & f^T(t) & f^T(t-h) & \int_{t-d}^t f^T(s)ds & g^T(t) & \int_{t-h}^t e^T(s)ds \end{bmatrix}^T.$$

By Schur complement, it follows from (14) that $\mathcal{L}V(e_t, i, t) \leq 0$ for $t > 0$. Now, the mean square exponential stability of the resulting error system (7) can be proven by following the similar line in the proof of Theorem 1 in [21]. The procedure is omitted and the proof is completed.

Remark 1. Theorem 1 presents a design criterion to a state estimator for the delayed Markovian jump neural network (1). In [4], the state estimation problem was studied for Markovian jump neural networks with mixed delays, where a delay-dependent condition was established. However, the condition in Theorem 1 can guarantee the mean square exponential stability of the error system and the decay rate λ can be obtained by solving some couple LMIs. That is, by our developed approach, the transient process of the error system can be better described. On the other hand, comparing with [4], a triple-integral term is taken into account in the stochastic Lyapunov functional (19). As suggested in [1, 13], the introduction of a triple-integral term can well reduce the conservatism of the design criterion.

Remark 2. No free weighting matrix is involved in the LMIs (11) and (12). It implies that less computation demand is required in our design criterion.

4   Conclusion

In this paper, the state estimation problem has been studied for a class of Markovian jump neural networks with discrete and distributed delays. By introducing a triple-integral term in the stochastic Lyapunov functional, a delay-dependent condition has been developed under which the resulting error system is mean square exponentially stable with a prescribed decay rate. It has been shown that the gain matrices and the decay rate can be obtained by solving some LMIs.

References

1. Ariba, Y., Gouaisbaut, F.: Delay-dependent stability analysis of linear systems with time-varying delay. In: 46th IEEE Conf. on Decision and Control, New Orleans, LA, UAS, pp. 2053–2058 (2007)
2. Boyd, S., El Ghaoui, L., Feron, E., Balakrishnan, V.: Linear Matrix Inequalities in System and Control Theory. SIAM, Philadelphia (1994)
3. Chen, T., Rong, L.: Delay-independent stability analysis of Cohen-Grossberg neural networks. Phys. Lett. A 317, 436–449 (2003)
4. Chen, Y., Zheng, W.X.: Stochastic state estimation for neural networks with distributed delays and Markovian jump. Neural Netw. 25, 14–20 (2012)
5. Gu, K., Kharitonov, V.L., Chen, J.: Stability of Time-delay Systems. Birkhauser, Massachusetts (2003)
6. He, Y., Wang, Q.-G., Wu, M., Lin, C.: Delay-dependent state estimation for delayed neural networks. IEEE Trans. Neural Netw. 17, 1077–1081 (2006)
7. Huang, H., Feng, G.: State estimation of recurrent neural networks with time-varying delay: A novel delay partition approach. Neurocomputing 74, 792–796 (2011)
8. Huang, H., Feng, G., Cao, J.: State estimation for static neural networks with time-varying delay. Neural Networks 23, 1202–1207 (2010)
9. Kovacic, M.: Timetable construction with Markovian neural network. Eur. J. Oper. Res. 69, 92–96 (1993)
10. Liu, X., Cao, J.: Robust state estimation for neural networks with discontinuous activations. IEEE Trans. Syst. Man Cyber. B 40, 1425–1437 (2010)
11. Liu, Y., Wang, Z., Liu, X.: Design of exponential state estimators for neural networks with mixed time delays. Phys. Lett. A 364, 401–412 (2007)
12. Park, J.H., Kwon, O.M.: State estimation for neural networks of neutral-type with interval time-varying delays. Appl. Math. Comput. 203, 217–223 (2008)
13. Sun, J., Liu, G.P., Chen, J., Rees, D.: Improved delay-range-dependent stability criteria for linear sytems with time-varying delays. Automatica 46, 466–470 (2010)
14. Tino, P., Cernansky, M., Benuskova, L.: Markovian architectural bias of recurrent neural networks. IEEE Trans. Neural Netw. 15, 6–15 (2004)
15. Wang, Z., Ho, D.W.C., Liu, X.: State estimation for delayed neural networks. IEEE Trans. Neural Netw. 16, 279–284 (2005)
16. Wu, Z., Su, H., Chu, J.: State estimation for discrete Markovian jumping neural networks with time delay. Neurocomputing 73, 2247–2254 (2010)
17. Zeng, Z., Huang, D., Wang, Z.: Global stability of a general class of discrete-time recurrent neural networks. Neural Processing Lett. 22, 33–47 (2005)
18. Zeng, Z., Huang, T., Zheng, W.: Multistability of recurrent neural networks with time-varying delays and the piecewise linear activation function. IEEE Trans. Neural Netw. 21, 1371–1377 (2010)
19. Zhang, H., Wang, Y.: Stability analysis of Markovian jumping stochastic Cohen-Grossberg neural networks with mixed time delays. IEEE Trans. Neural Netw. 19, 366–370 (2008)
20. Zhao, Y., Zhang, L., Shen, S., Gao, H.: Robust stability criterion for discrete-time uncertain Markovian jumping neural networks with defective statistics of mode transitions. IEEE Trans. Neural Netw. 22, 164–170 (2011)
21. Zhu, Q., Cao, J.: Exponential stability of stochastic neural networks with both Markovian jump parameters and mixed time delays. IEEE Trans. Syst. Man Cybern. 41, 341–353 (2011)

Lattice Boltzmann Model for Nonlinear Heat Equations

Qiaojie Li, Zhoushun Zheng, Shuang Wang, and Jiankang Liu

School of Mathematics and Statistics, Central South University,
Changsha 410083, P.R. China
2009zhengzhoushun@163.com

Abstract. In this paper, a lattice Boltzmann scheme with an amending function for the nonlinear heat equations with the form $\partial_t \phi = \alpha \nabla^2 \phi + \psi(\phi)$ which directly to solve some important nonlinear equations, including Fisher equation, Newell-Whitehead equation and FitzHugh-Nagumo equation is proposed. Detailed simulations of these equations are performed, and it is found that the numerical results agree well with the analytical solutions or the numerical solutions reported in previous studies.

Keywords: Lattice Boltzmann method, Fisher equation, Newell-Whitehead equation, FitzHugh-Nagumo equation.

1 Introduction

The lattice Boltzmann method(LBM) was originally developed as a natural extension to the lattice gas automata for modeling fluid flow based on kinetic theory[1]. Compared with the conventional computational fluid dynamics approach, the LBM is easy for programming, intrinsically parallel, and it is also easy to incorporate complicated boundary condtions. As a new mesoscopic numerical approach, LBM has attracted more and more attentions for simulating complex fluid flows[2,3,4]. The lattice Boltzmann models can also be used as partial differential equation(PDE) solvers. By chosing appropriate collision operator or equilibrium distribution, the lattice Boltzmann model is able to recover the PDE of interest. Recently, it has been developed to simulate linear and nonlinear PDE such as Laplace equation[5], Poisson equation[6,7], the shallow equation [8], Burgers equation[9], Korteweg-de Vires equation[10], Wave equation[11,12], reaction-diffusion equation[13,14], convection-diffusion equation[15,16] and even some complex equations[17,18]. The LB models for advection and anisotropic dispersion equation have been proposed[19,20], among them the model by Ginzburg[21] is generic. Shi and Guo[22] studied the LBM for nonlinear convection-diffusion equation deeply, and applied it to the common real and complex-valued nonlinear evolutionary equations.

The nonlinear heat equations play fundamental role in a great number of various models of reaction-diffusion processes, mathematical biology, chemistry, genetics and many, many others. In this paper, we present a lattice Bhatnagar-Gross-Krook(LBGK) model for nonlinear heat equations with source term through selecting equilibrium distribution function and relaxation time properly. The LBM for nonlinear heat equations with source term is applied directly to solve some important nonlinear equations, including Fisher equation(FE), Newell-Whitehead equation(NWE) and FitzHugh-Nagumo

J. Wang, G.G. Yen, and M.M. Polycarpou (Eds.): ISNN 2012, Part I, LNCS 7367, pp. 140–148, 2012.
© Springer-Verlag Berlin Heidelberg 2012

equation(FHNE). Detailed simulations of these equations are carried out for accuracy test. Numerical reasults agree well with the analytical solutions, which show that the LBM is also an effective numerical solver for nonlinear systerms.

The rest of the paper is organized as follows. In Section 2, the lattice Boltzmann model is described. Numerical examples are simulated in section 3. Summary and conclusion are presented in section 4.

2 Lattice Boltzmann Model

The nonlinear heat equations with source term considered in this paper can be written as

$$\partial_t \phi = \alpha \nabla^2 \phi + \psi(\phi), \tag{1}$$

where ∇ is the gradient operator with respect to the spatial coordinate x; ϕ is a scalar function of time t and position x; $\psi(\phi)$ is the source term. When $\psi(\phi) = a\phi(1 - \phi)$ Eq.(1) is Fisher equation, $\psi(\phi) = a\phi - b\phi^3$ is Newell-Whitehead equation and $\psi(\phi) = \phi(1 - \phi)(a - \phi)$ is Newell-Whitehead equation.

2.1 Equilibrium Distribution Functions and Their Higher-Order Moments

The lattice Boltzmann model used on this study is the three-velocity LBGK model. The directions of the discrete velocity are defined as c_i which is $\{c_0, c_1, c_2\} = \{0, c, -c\}$ and c is a constant. The lattice Boltzmann equation with an amending function is given as follows

$$f_i(x + c_i\Delta t, t + \Delta t) - f_i(x, t) = \Omega_i + \Omega_i', \tag{2}$$

where $\Omega_i = -\frac{1}{\tau}(f_i(x, t) - f_i^{eq}(x, t))$ and $\Omega_i' = \Delta t\psi_i$ is an amending function which is to derive the source term. $f_i(x, t)$ and $f_i^{eq}(x, t)$ are defined as the distribution and equilibrium distribution function, respectively. τ is the dimensionless relaxation time; $\Delta x = c_i\Delta t$ and Δt are the lattice spacing and time step.

To solve Eq.(1) using the lattice Boltzmann Eq.(2) without additional assumptions, we must give appropriate $f_i^{eq}(x, t)$ and $\psi_i(x, t)$. As pointed in the general parallel analysis of LBM for convection diffusion and fluid flow in Ref.[24], reasonable constraints of moments of the equilibrium distribution $f_i^{eq}(x, t)$ must be satisfied. Keeping this in mind and following the common LBGK model, we take the equilibrium distribution function such that

$$\sum_i f_i = \sum_i f_i^{eq} = \phi, \quad \sum_i c_i f_i^{eq} = 0, \quad \sum_i c_i c_i f_i^{eq} = c_s^2 \phi, \tag{3}$$

where $c_s^2 = c^2/3$ is so called sound speed in the LBM for fluid which depend on the lattice model we used. Solving these Eqs.(3) determine the equilibrium distribution functions which read

$$f_i^{eq}(x, t) = \omega_i \phi, \tag{4}$$

where $\omega_0 = 2/3$, $\omega_1 = \omega_2 = 1/6$. Meanwhile, the corresponding source term ψ_i is taken as

$$\psi_i = \omega_i \psi, \tag{5}$$

such that

$$\sum_i \psi_i = \psi. \tag{6}$$

2.2 Recovery of the Macroscopic Equations

The macroscopic equation can be recovered in the multiscaling analysis using an small expansion parameter ϵ which is proportional to the ratio of the lattice spacing to the characteristic macroscopic length. To do this, the Chapman-Enskog expansion in time and space is applied:

$$f_i = f_i^{eq} + \epsilon f_i^{(1)} + \epsilon^2 f_i^{(2)}, \psi_i = \epsilon^2 \psi_i^{(2)}, \partial_t = \epsilon \partial_{t_1} + \epsilon^2 \partial_{t_2}, \nabla = \epsilon \nabla_1. \tag{7}$$

From Eq.(7), (3) and (5), it follows that

$$\sum_i f_i^{(k)} = 0 \, (k \geq 1), \sum_i \psi_i^{(2)} = \psi^{(2)}. \tag{8}$$

Applying the Taylor expansion to Eq.(2), we get

$$D_i f_i + \frac{\Delta t}{2} D_i^2 f_i + O(\Delta t^2) = -\frac{1}{\tau \Delta t}(f_i - f_i^{eq}) + \psi_i, \tag{9}$$

where $D_i = \partial_t + c_i \cdot \nabla$ and denote $D_{1i} = \partial_{t_1} + c_i \cdot \nabla_1$. Substituting Eq.(7) into Eq.(9) and treating the terms in order of ϵ and ϵ^2 separately gives

$$O(\epsilon): \; D_{1i} f_i^{eq} = -\frac{1}{\tau \Delta t} f_i^{(1)}, \tag{10}$$

$$O(\epsilon^2): \; \partial_{t_2} f_i^{eq} + D_{1i} f_i^{(1)} + \frac{\Delta t}{2} D_{1i}^2 f_i^{eq} = -\frac{1}{\tau \Delta t} f_i^{(2)} + \psi_i^{(2)}. \tag{11}$$

Applying Eq.(10) to the left side of Eq.(11), we can rewrite Eq.(11) as

$$\partial_{t_2} f_i^{eq} + (1 - \frac{1}{2\tau}) D_{1i} f_i^{(1)} = -\frac{1}{\tau \Delta t} f_i^{(2)} + \psi_i^{(2)}. \tag{12}$$

Summing Eq.(10) and (12) over i and using Eq.(3) and Eq.(8) we obtain

$$\partial_{t_1} \phi = 0, \tag{13}$$

$$\partial_{t_2} \phi + (1 - \frac{1}{2\tau}) \nabla_1 \cdot (\sum_i c_i f_i^{(1)}) = \psi^2. \tag{14}$$

Using Eq.(10) and (3), we get that

$$\sum_i c_i f_i^{(1)} = -\tau \Delta t \sum_i c_i D_{1i} f_i^{eq} = -\tau \Delta t c_s^2 \nabla_1 \phi. \tag{15}$$

Then substituting Eq.(15) into Eq.(14), we have

$$\partial_{t_2}\phi = c_s^2(\tau - \frac{1}{2})\Delta t \nabla_1^2 \phi + \psi^{(2)}. \tag{16}$$

Therefore, summing Eq.(13)$\times\epsilon$ and Eq.(16)$\times\epsilon^2$ and taking $\alpha = c_s^2(\tau - \frac{1}{2})\Delta t$, we get that

$$\partial_t\phi = \alpha\nabla^2\phi + \psi(\phi). \tag{17}$$

The nonlinear heat equation is exactly recovered.

3   Numberical Simulation Results

In this section, we present the results of our LBM numerical experiments for the relevant equations. In comparison with the analytical solutions and results derived by existing literature, the efficiency of proposed model is validated. In all simulations, the nonequilibrium extrapolation scheme proposed by Guo[25] for the boundary condtion was used. The following global relative error is used to measure the accuracy:

$$GRE = \frac{\sum_i |u(x_i, t) - u^\star(x_i, t)|}{\sum_i |u^\star(x_i, t)|},$$

where $u(x_i, t)$ and $u^\star(x_i, t)$ are the numerical solution and analytical one, respectively, and the summaton is taken over all grid point.

Example 1. Fisher equation with the form $u_t = u_{xx} + 6u(1 - u)$. The initial value is

$$u(x, 0) = \frac{1}{(1 + e^x)^2}.$$

The exact solution is given in Ref.[26]

$$u(x, t) = \frac{1}{(1 + e^{x-5t})^2}.$$

The simulation is conducted for x in $[0,20]$ with $\Delta x = 0.1$, $\Delta t = 0.001$, $c = 100$, $\tau = 0.8$. The results are shown in Fig.1 and Fig.2. It can be found that the LBGK results are in excellent agreement with the analytical solution. The global relative errors at different time are listed in Table 1.

Table 1. The GRE for solutions of Fisher equation at different times

t	t=0.5	t=1	t=1.5	t=2
GRE	9.8202E-03	2.2853E-03	1.9430E-03	1.7972E-03

Example 2. Newell-Whitehead equation with the form $u_t = u_{xx} + au - bu^3$. When a=-8, b=2, the equation have the following analytical solution[27]

$$u(x, t) = \frac{2\sin(2x + c_1)}{\cos(2x + c_1) + c_2 e^{12t}},$$

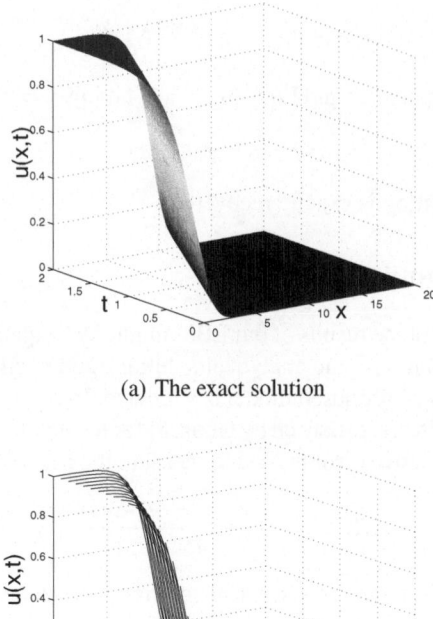

(a) The exact solution

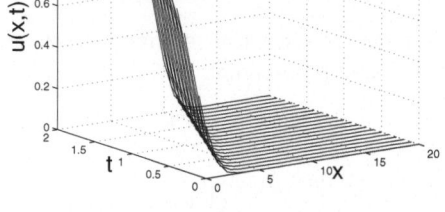

(b) The LBM result

Fig. 1. The surface figures of the Fisher equation. (a) The exact solution; (b) The LBM result at different time.

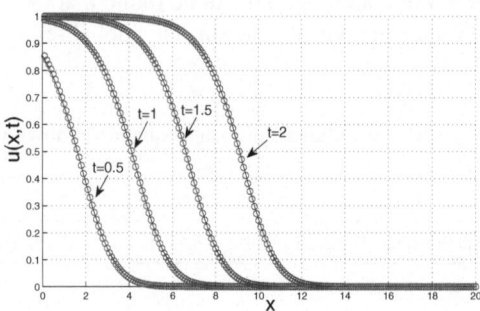

Fig. 2. Comparison of exact of solution and LBM results. Solid line show exact solutions; circles show LBM result. Parameters are $c = 100$, lattice size $M = 200$, and $\tau = 0.8$.

where c_1, c_2 are arbitrary constants. In the simulation, we set $c_1 = 0, c_2 = 2$ and the other parameters in present model are $\Delta x = 0.1$, $\Delta t = 0.0005, c = 200, \tau = 0.65$. The initial condition is determined by the analytical solution. The global relative error $GRE = 6.3633e - 03$. Detailed numerical results are present in Fig.3 and Table 2.

Example 3. FitzHugh-Nagumo equation[28] with the form $u_t = u_{xx} + u(1 - u)(4 - u)$. The exact solution is

$$u(x, t) = \frac{Ae^{z_1} + 4Be^{z_2}}{Ae^{z_1} + Be^{z_2} + C},$$

where $z_1 = \frac{\sqrt{2}}{2}x - \frac{7}{2}t, z_2 = 2\sqrt{2}x + 4t$, A, B, C are arbitrary constants. In the simulation, we set $A = B = C = 1$ and the other parameters in present model are $\Delta x = 0.05$, $\Delta t = 0.0005, c = 100, \tau = 1.1$. The initial condition is determined by the analytical

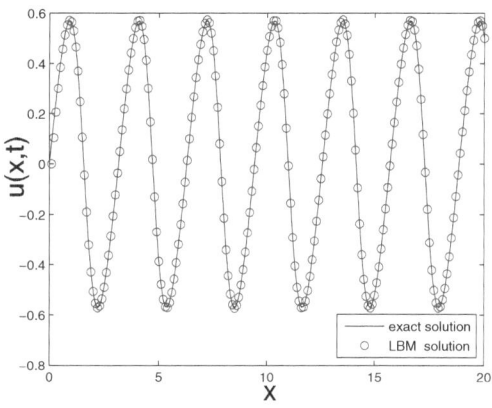

Fig. 3. Comparison of exact of solution and LBM results at $t = 0.05$. Solid line show exact solutions; circles show LBM result. Parameters are $c = 200$, lattice size $M = 200$, and $\tau = 0.65$.

Table 2. Comparisons between numerical solution and analytical solution at $t = 0.05$

x_i	LBM solution	Analytical solution	Absolute error:$\mid u(x_i) - u^\star(x_i) \mid$
0	0.000000	0.000000	0.000000
2	-0.506855	-0.506122	7.3348E-04
4	0.567531	0.565552	1.9796E-03
6	-0.239997	-0.239110	8.8708E-04
8	-0.214033	-0.214327	2.9382E-04
10	0.452341	0.450579	1.7618E-03
12	-0.446914	-0.445175	1.7396E-03
14	0.201756	0.202045	2.8926E-04
16	0.247172	0.246257	9.1521E-04
18	-0.566101	-0.564108	1.9935E-03
20	0.500529	0.500529	0.000000

solution. Detailed numerical results are present in Fig.4. The global relative error GRE = 8.6920e−04. On the other hand, as shown in Fig.5, the proposed model is nearly a second order scheme on precision(the slope of the line is about 1.95).

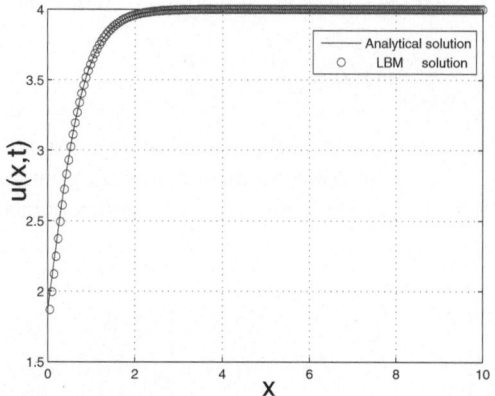

Fig. 4. Comparison of exact of solution and LBM results at t = 0.05. Solid line show exact solutions; circles show LBM result. Parameters are c = 100, lattice size M = 200, and τ = 1.1.

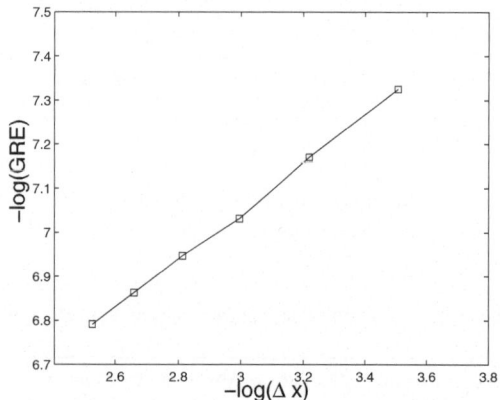

Fig. 5. The relation between GRE and lattice spacing

4   Conclusion

In the current study, a new lattice Boltzmann model is proposed to solve 1D nonlinear heat equation. The efficiency and accuracy of the proposed model are validated through detail numerical simulation with Fisher equation, Newell-Whitehead equation and FitzHugh-Nagumo equation. It can be found that the LBGK result are in excellent agreement with the analytical solution. It should be point out that in order to attain better accuracy the lattice Boltzmann model requires a relatively small time step Δt and the proper range is from 10^{-3} to 10^{-4}. The selection of τ should be carefully due to the stability. Detailed stability analysis of present model is needed in further study.

Acknowledgments. This study was financially support by the National Natural Science Foundation of China(Grant No. 50874123 and No. 51174236) and National Basic Research Program of China(Grant No. 2011CB606306).

References

1. Frisch, U., Hasslacher, B., Pomeau, Y.: Lattice gas automata for the Navier-Stokes equations. Phys. Rev. Lett. 56, 1505–1508 (1986)
2. Chen, S.Y., Doolen, G.D.: Lattice Boltzmann method for fluid flows. Annu. Fluid Mech. 3, 314–322 (1998)
3. Benzi, R., Succi, S., Vergassola, M.: The lattice Boltzmann equation: theory and applications. Phys.Rep. 222, 147–197 (1992)
4. Chen, H., Kandasamy, S., Orszag, S., Shock, R., Succi, S.: Extended Boltzmann kinetic equation for turbulent flow. Science 301, 633–636 (2003)
5. Zhang, J.Y., Yan, G.W., Dong, Y.F.: A new lattice Boltzmann model for the laplace equation. Appl. Math. Comput. 215, 539–547 (2009)
6. Cai, Z.H., Shi, B.C.: A novel lattice Boltzmann model for the poisson equation. Appl. Math. Model. 32, 2050–2058 (2008)
7. Hirabayashi, M., Chen, Y., Ohashi, H.: The lattice BGK model for the Poisson equation. JSME Int. J. Ser. B 44, 45–52 (2001)
8. Zhou, J.G.: Lattice Boltzmann Methods for Shallow Water Flows. Springer, Berlin (2000)
9. Shen, Z., Yuan, G., Shen, L.: Lattice Botlzmann method for Burgers equation. Chin. J. Comput. Phys. 17, 166–172 (2000)
10. Zhang, J.Y., Yan, G.W.: A lattice Boltzmann model for the KortewegCde Vries equation with two conservation laws. Comput. Phys. Commun. 180, 1054–1062 (2009)
11. Yan, G.W.: A lattice Boltzmann equation for waves. J. Comput. Phys. 161, 61–69 (2000)
12. Zhang, J.Y., Yan, G.W., Shi, X.B.: Lattice Boltzmann model for wave propagation. Phys. Rev. E 80, 026706 (2009)
13. Dawson, S.P., Chen, S.Y., Doolen, G.D.: Lattice Boltzmann computations for reaction-diffusion equations. J. Chem. Phys. 98, 1514–1523 (1993)
14. Yu, X.M., Shi, B.C.: A lattice Boltzmann model for reaction dynamical systems with time delay. Appl. Math. Comput. 181, 958–963 (2006)
15. van der Sman, R.G.M., Ernst, M.H.: ConvectionCdiffusion lattice Boltzmann scheme for irregular lattices. J. Comput. Phys. 160, 766–782 (2000)
16. Guo, Z.L., Shi, B.C., Wang, N.C.: Fully Lagrangian and Lattice Boltzmann methods for the advection-diffusion equation. J. Sci. Comput. 14, 291–300 (1999)
17. Shi, B.: Lattice Boltzmann Simulation of Some Nonlinear Complex Equations. In: Shi, Y., van Albada, G.D., Dongarra, J., Sloot, P.M.A. (eds.) ICCS 2007. LNCS, vol. 4487, pp. 818–825. Springer, Heidelberg (2007)
18. Zhang, J.Y., Yan, G.W.: Lattice Boltzmann model for the complex Ginzburg-Landau equation. Phys. Rev. E 81, 066705 (2010)
19. Zhang, X.X., Bengough, A.G., Crawford, J.W., Young, I.M.: A lattice BGK model for advection and anisotropic dispersion equation. Adv. Water Resour. 25, 1–8 (2002)

20. Rasin, I., Succi, S., Miller, W.: A multi-relaxation lattice kinetic method for passive scalar diffusion. J. Comput. Phys. 206, 453–462 (2005)
21. Ginzburg, I.: Equilibrium-type and link-type lattice Boltzmann models for generic advection and anisotropic-dispersion equation. Adv. Water Resour. 28, 1171–1195 (2005)
22. Shi, B.C., Guo, Z.L.: Lattice Botlzmann model for nonlinear convevtion-diffusion equations. Phys. Rev. E 79, 016701 (2009)
23. Qian, Y.H., Succi, S., Orszag, S.A.: Recent advances in lattice Boltzmann computing. Annu. Rev. Comput. Phys. 3, 195–242 (1995)
24. van der Sman, R.G.M.: Galilean invariant lattice Boltzmann scheme for natural convection on square and rectangular lattices. Phys. Rev. E 74, 026705 (2006)
25. Guo, Z.L., Zheng, C.G., Shi, B.C.: Non-equilibrium extraploation method for velocity and pressure boundary conditions in the lattice Boltzmann method. Chin. Phys. 11, 366–374 (2002)
26. Wazwaz, A.M., Gorguis, A.: An analytic study of Fisher's equation by using Adomian decomposition method. Appl. Math. Comput. 154, 609–620 (2004)
27. Clarkson, P.A., Mansfield, E.L.: Symmetry reductions and exact solutions of a class of nonlinear heat equations. Physica D 70, 250–288 (1994)
28. Nucci, M.C., Clarkson, P.A.: The nonclassical method is more general than the direct method for symmetry reductions. An example of the Fitzhugh-Nagumo equation. Phys. Lett. A 164, 49–56 (1992)

A Modified One-Layer Spiking Neural Network Involves Derivative of the State Function at Firing Time*

Wenyu Yang, Jie Yang, and Wei Wu**

School of Mathematical Sciences, Dalian University of Technology, Dalian, China
wuweiw@dlut.edu.cn

Abstract. Usual spiking neural network with a hidden layer whose input and output are all spike times is very powerful for performing classification on real-world data. In this paper, we investigate the performance of a modified one-layer spiking neural network that involves both the spike time and derivative of the state function at firing time. It is shown by numerical experiments that a modified one-layer spiking neural network using same or fewer encoding neurons is almost as good as a usual spiking neural network with a hidden layer for solving some benchmark problems.

Keywords: Spiking neuron, Firing time, Derivative of the state function.

1 Introduction

In recent years, spiking neural networks (SNNs) that are more biologically plausible and often referred to as the third generation of neural networks [1] have experienced an increasingly large amount of research attention. They model the precise time of spikes motivated by the discoveries of information processing mechanism inside brain. SNNs have been applied extensively and successfully for practical application [2]-[7] such as auto-associator, pattern recognition, classification and clustering.

In generally, a spiking neuron fires when the internal neuron state variable influenced by the spike times of its presynaptic neurons reaches a given threshold. The firing time is usually taken as the output of the spiking neuron. For a method of supervised learning in SNNs, the goal of learning is to learn a set of target firing times for a set of training samples. In the working process, a spiking neuron has to go through an iterative-like procedure before it gives a response to an input, while the classical feedforward neuron only needs a single operation to do the same. Hence, it seems reasonable that we expect to extract more information, for a given input, from one working process of the spiking neuron. If the firing time t^a,

---

* Research funded by National Natural Science Foundation of China (11171367) and the Fundamental Research Funds for the Central Universities of China.
** Corresponding author.

which indicates when the state function reaches the threshold value, is the most important information extracted from the input, then from a mathematical point of view, the second important information should be the derivative $x'(t^a)$, which indicates how fast the state function reaches the threshold value. Therefore, we proposed a modified spiking neuron in [8] (called a novel spiking perceptron there) such that the output is a linear combination of the firing time t^a and the derivative $x'(t^a)$. An advantage of the modified spiking neuron is shown by the fact that the XOR problem can be solved by a single modified spiking neuron in [8], but not by the classical spiking perceptron or the usual feedforward perceptron. The aim of this paper is to show a somehow surprising merit of the one-layer modified spiking neural network constructed by the modified spiking neurons that it is as powerful as a usual spiking neural network with a hidden layer for performing classification on real-world data.

This paper is divided into four sections. We introduce the structure of the modified one-layer spiking neural network in section 2. Section 3 describes the error-backpropagation algorithm. In section 4, we test the performance of the modified one-layer spiking neural network on some benchmark problems.

2   The Modified One-Layer Spiking Neural Network

In the classical spiking neuron model, the output of a neuron is described by the firing time of the spike it produced. The firing time t of the postsynaptic neuron is defined as the time when the internal neuron state variable $x(t)$ reaches a given threshold v:

$$t^a = \{t \mid x(t) = v \wedge x'(t) \geq 0\} \tag{1}$$

We assume that each spiking neuron fires at most once during a single simulation time window. The state variable $x_j(t)$ is influenced by the spike times t_i of its presynaptic neurons i as follows:

$$x_j(t) = \sum_{i=1}^{n} \sum_{k=1}^{K} w_{ij}^k \varepsilon(t - t_i - d_{ij}^k) \tag{2}$$

where w_{ij}^k is the kth synaptic weight between the presynaptic neuron i and the postsynaptic neuron j, d_{ij}^k is a given synaptic delay of the kth synaptic sub-connection between presynaptic neuron i and the postsynaptic neuron j, and $\varepsilon(t)$ is a spike-response function chosen as:

$$\varepsilon(t) = \begin{cases} \dfrac{t}{\tau} e^{1 - \frac{t}{\tau}} & \text{if} \quad t > 0 \\[2ex] 0 & \text{else} \end{cases} \tag{3}$$

where τ is the time decay constant that determine the rise and decay of the response function.

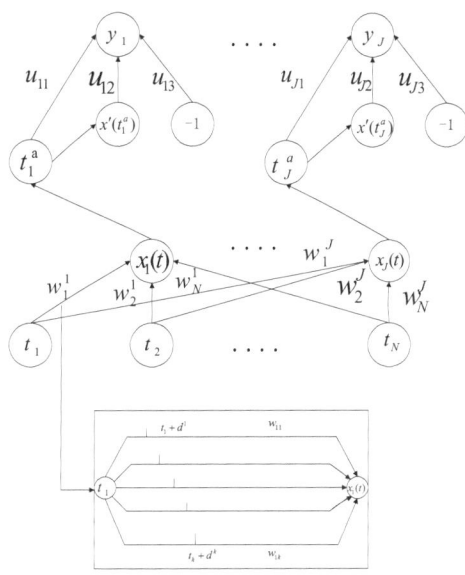

Fig. 1. Architecture of the modified one-layer spiking neural network

For a given input, the spiking neuron will check successively the values of the state function $x(t)$ at a time series $\{t^1, t^2, \cdots, \}$ until a threshold value is reached at a firing time t^a (cf. (1)). Compared with a usual feedforward neuron, the spiking neuron takes more workload to get a response for a given input. Hence, it seems reasonable that we expect to extract more information from one working process of the network. Therefore, the output y_j of our modified one-layer spiking neural network is defined as the value of a nonlinear function $f(\cdot)$ at a linear combination of the firing time t_j^a, which indicates when the state function reaches the threshold value, and the derivative $x'(t_j^a)$, which indicates how fast the state function reaches the threshold value:

$$y_j = f(u_{j1}t_j^a + u_{j2}x'(t_j^a) - u_{j3}), \quad j = 1, \cdots, J \tag{4}$$

where J is the number of the output nodes; t^a is the firing time computed by (1); and the weights u_{j1} and u_{j2}, the threshold u_{j3}, and the weights w_{ij}^k are determined through learning as described in the next section. In particular, the nonlinear function $f(\cdot)$ is selected as the sigmoid function

$$f(x) = \frac{1}{1 + e^{-x}} \tag{5}$$

The architecture of the one-layer modified neural network is shown in Fig.1.

3 Error-Backpropagation Training Algorithm

We derive a online gradient descent learning rule for the modified one-layer spiking neural network in a analogous way as SpikeProp. Given a training pattern set $\{\mathbf{t}^{(s)}, \mathbf{o}^{(s)}\}_{s=1}^{S} \in R^n \times R^J$, where $\mathbf{o}^{(s)}$ is the desired output for the input $\mathbf{t}^{(s)}$. A training sequence $\{\mathbf{t}^T, \mathbf{o}^T\}_{T=1}^{\infty}$ is generated by repeating the training set $\{\mathbf{t}^{(s)}, \mathbf{o}^{(s)}\}_{s=1}^{S} \in R^n \times R^J$ infinite times. At the T-th step of the training, we uses the gradient descent method to minimize the instantaneous error function

$$E = E(W^T, U^T) = \frac{1}{2J} \sum_{j=1}^{J} (y_j^T - O_j^T)^2 \tag{6}$$

where $\mathbf{y} = (y_1, \ldots, y_J)$ is the actual output of the neuron for the input $\mathbf{t}$ with

the weights $W = \begin{pmatrix} w_{11}^1 \cdots w_{11}^K \cdots w_{n1}^1 \cdots w_{n1}^K \\ w_{12}^1 \cdots w_{12}^K \cdots w_{n2}^1 \cdots w_{n2}^K \\ \cdots\cdots\cdots\cdots\cdots\cdots\cdots \\ w_{1J}^1 \cdots w_{1J}^K \cdots w_{nJ}^1 \cdots w_{nJ}^K \end{pmatrix}$

and $U = \begin{pmatrix} u_{11} \, u_{12} \, u_{13} \\ u_{21} \, u_{22} \, u_{23} \\ \cdots\cdots\cdots \\ u_{J1} \, u_{J2} \, u_{J3} \end{pmatrix}$. Then, the present weights are updated by

$$u_{jl}^{T+1} = u_{jl}^T + \triangle u_{jl}^T \tag{7}$$

and

$$(w_{ij}^k)^{T+1} = (w_{ij}^k)^T + (\triangle w_{ij}^k)^T \tag{8}$$

where

$$\triangle u_{jl}^T = -\eta_1 \frac{\partial E}{\partial u_{jl}^T} \tag{9}$$

$$(\triangle w_{ij}^k)^T = -\eta_2 \frac{\partial E}{\partial (w_{ij}^k)^T} \tag{10}$$

and η_1 and η_2 are the learning rates.

The computation of $\partial E/\partial u_{jl}^T$ in (9) is an easy job by using (4):

$$\frac{\partial E}{\partial u_{jl}^T} = \frac{\partial E}{\partial y_j^T} \frac{\partial y_j^T}{\partial u_{jl}^T} \tag{11}$$

Note that the derivative of the sigmoid function (5) is $f'(x) = (1 - f(x))f(x)$. We denote $(y_j^T - O_j^T)(1 - y_j^T)y_j^T$ as I_j. Hence

$$\frac{\partial E}{\partial u_{j1}^T} = \frac{1}{J} I_j t^a \tag{12}$$

$$\frac{\partial E}{\partial u_{j2}^T} = \frac{1}{J} I_j x'(t^a) \tag{13}$$

and

$$\frac{\partial E}{\partial u_{j3}^T} = -\frac{1}{J}I_j \tag{14}$$

Next, we compute $\partial E/\partial (w_{ij}^k)^T$. Using the chain rule, we have

$$\frac{\partial E}{\partial w_{ij}^k} = \frac{1}{J}\frac{\partial E}{\partial y_j}\left(\frac{\partial y_j}{\partial t^a}\frac{\partial t^a}{\partial w_{ij}^k} + \frac{\partial y_j}{\partial x'(t^a)}\frac{\partial x'(t^a)}{\partial w_{ij}^k}\right) \tag{15}$$

Here the superscript T have been removed for sake of clear representation. To compute the term $\partial t^a/\partial w_{ij}^k$, Bohte et al. [11] used chain ruler $\partial t^a/\partial w_{ij}^k = \partial t^a/\partial x(t) \cdot \partial x(t)/\partial w_{ij}^k$ and assumed that there was a linear relationship between the firing time t^a and the state $x(t)$ around $t = t^a$. In terms of this assumption, the Frechet derivative of the functional

$$\frac{\partial t^a}{\partial x(t)} = \frac{-1}{x'(t)}, \text{ at } t = t^a \tag{16}$$

Therefore

$$\frac{\partial t^a}{\partial w_{ij}^k} = \frac{-1}{x'(t)}\frac{\partial x(t)}{\partial w_{ij}^k}, \text{ at } t = t^a \tag{17}$$

However, we have proved that (17) is mathematically correct in [12], without the help of the linearity assumption. From (2) the derivative of the state variable is computed as

$$x'(t^a) = \sum_{i=1}^{n} w_{ij}^k \varepsilon'(t^a - t_i - d_i^k) \tag{18}$$

where

$$\varepsilon'(t^a - t_i - d_i^k)$$
$$= \begin{cases} \frac{1}{\tau}e^{1-\frac{t^a-t_i-d_i^k}{\tau}}(1 - \frac{t^a - t_i - d_i^k}{\tau}) & \text{if } t^a - t_i - d_i^k > 0 \\ 0 & \text{else} \end{cases} \tag{19}$$

Then (15) is rewritten as

$$\frac{\partial E}{\partial w_{ij}^k} = \frac{1}{J}I_j[-u_{j1}\frac{1}{x'(t^a)}\varepsilon(t^a - t_i - d_i^k) \\ + u_{j2}\varepsilon'(t^a - t_i - d_i^k)], \text{ at } t = t^a \tag{20}$$

4   Numerical Simulation

In this section, we perform experiments with the modified one-layer spiking neural network on three benchmark problems: the Wisconsin breast-cancer dataset, the Iris dataset and Landsat dataset. The inputs of the three benchmark problems are continuous and real value. Hence, encoding scheme (population coding) [11] is used here.

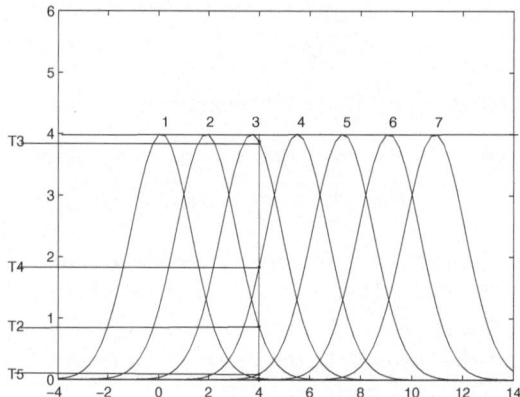

Fig. 2. Population encoding scheme to convert a component variable $\xi = 4$ to a vector $T(\xi) = (0, T_2, T_3, T_4, T_5, 0, 0)$

The method of population coding can increase the dimension of a input vector. Briefly, each vector component is encoded separately into a m-component vector by $m > 2$ Gaussian functions. For a component variable ξ of the input vector, we can compute the ith component of a new m-component vector according to the Gaussian function $g_i(\xi)$ in the following way:

$$\begin{aligned} T_i(\xi) &= g_i(\xi) \times C \\ &= e^{-\frac{(\xi - \mu_i)^2}{2\sigma^2}} \times C \end{aligned} \tag{21}$$

where the center μ_i of the Gaussian function is set to be $Min(\xi) + (2i - 3)/2 \cdot (Max(\xi) - Min(\xi))/(m - 2)$, the width $\sigma = 1/\beta(Max(\xi) - Min(\xi))/(m - 2)$, and C is the length of coding interval. Following Bohte et.al [11], we set the adjustment factor $\beta = 1.5$. The coding of a component variable ξ of the input vector by $m = 7$ Gaussian functions is depicted in Fig.2.

The Wisconsin breast cancer data consists of 699 instances in which 16 instances containing missing data. There are 2 classes: begin and malignant and 9 attributes which are in the same range $[1, 10]$. We encode each attribute with 7 Gaussian functions, following Bohte et al. [11], we encode the missing variable as not fire. In addition, we encode each attribute with 5 Gaussian functions. We choose the learning rates $\eta_1 = 0.1$ and $\eta_2 = 0.01$, and the up limit of the epoch to be 50. 3-fold cross-validation use here and 2-fold cross-validation used in [11].

The Iris data set contains 3 classes : Versicolor, Virginica, and Setosa. The first two classes are not linearly separable. The dataset consists of 150 instances with 4 attributes. We encode each attribute with 12 Gaussian functions as Bohte et al. did in [11]. In addition, we encode each attribute with 10 Gaussian functions. The learning rates η_1 and η_2 are set to be 0.1 and 0.01, respectively, and the up limit of the epoch is 200. We use 3-fold cross-validation and Bohte et al. used 2-fold cross-validation.

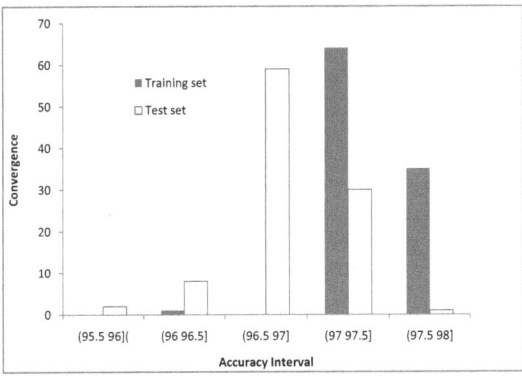

Fig. 3. Learning Wisconsin breast cancer dataset: number of runs out of 100 that converged in different accuracy intervals

To investigate the performance of the modified one-layer spiking neural network on a larger dataset, we use Landsat dataset consisting of 6435 instances which contain pixel values in 3×3 neighbourhoods described by 4 spectral bands in a satellite image. The dataset divided into 6 classes according to the central pixel in the 3×3 neighbourhoods. As Bohte et al. did in [11], We average the spectral bands in the 3×3 neighbourhoods and each band is encoded by 25 Gaussian functions. In addition, we encode each attribute with 20 Gaussian functions. We choose the learning rates $\eta_1 = 0.1$ and $\eta_2 = 0.01$, and the up limit of the epoch to be 150. The method of k-fold cross-validation is not used here, following Bohte et al. [11], for the dataset is large.

Table 1. The average results over 100 runs on each training set

Benchmark problem	Input	Hidden	Output	Epochs	Accuracy	
					Training set	Test set
Wisconsin breast cancer dataset	63	–	2	45	97.47%	96.89%
Iris dataset	48	–	3	188	97.30%	95.70%
Landsat dataset	100	–	6	88	85.48%	84.82%

In the three experiments, τ is set to be 7 and the length of coding interval to be 4. The output weights U are initialized as random numbers close to zero. While executing the experiments, we find that it is not necessary to use reference neurons. Hence the number of input neurons is less using the same encoding neurons in [11]. In this paper, when the value of instantaneous error function is less than a given small number E_0 or the pattern fails to make the neuron fire in the given simulation time window, we do not really update the weights. We set $E_0 = 0.003$ here. For the three benchmark problems, the number of the runs, out of the total 100 runs, that converged in different accuracy intervals

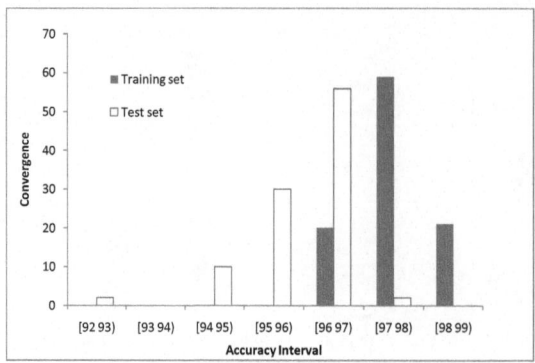

Fig. 4. Learning Iris dataset: number of runs out of 100 that converged in different accuracy intervals

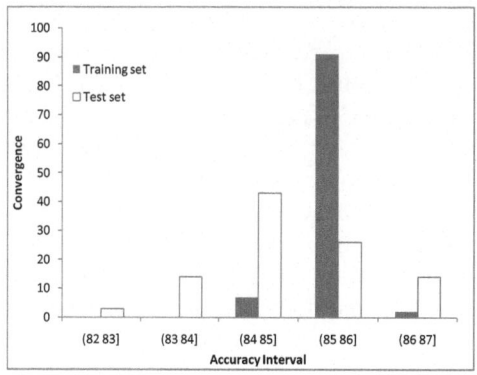

Fig. 5. Learning Landsat dataset: number of runs out of 100 that converged in different accuracy intervals

Table 2. The average results over 10 runs on each training set with fewer encoding neurons

Benchmark problem	Inputs	Hidden	Outputs	Epochs	Accuracy	
					Training set	Test set
Wisconsin breast cancer dataset	45	–	2	43	97.45%	96.97%
Iris dataset	40	–	3	164	96.93%	95.30%
Landsat dataset	80	–	6	69	85.12%	84.96%

Table 3. The average results over 10 runs in [11]

Benchmark problem	Inputs	Hidden	Outputs	Iterations	Accuracy	
					Training set	Test set
Wisconsin breast cancer dataset	64	15	2	1500	97.6% ± 0.2	97.0% ± 0.6
Iris dataset	50	10	3	1000	97.4% ± 0.1	96.1% ± 0.1
Landsat dataset	101	25	6	60000	87.0% ± 0.5	85.3% ± 0.3

are plotted in Figs. 3, 4 and 5, respectively, and the results averaged over 100 runs are summarized in Table 1. The results averaged over 10 runs with fewer encoding neurons are summarized in Table 2. We see that our average results with the modified one-layer neural network using same or fewer encoding neurons are almost as good as the corresponding results averaged over 10 runs in [11] shown in Table 3.

5   Conclusion

Proposed in this paper is a modified one-layer spiking neural network, of which the output is a linear combination of t^a, the firing time, and $x'(t^a)$, the derivative of the state function at the firing time. The modified one-layer spiking neural network can be viewed as a network constructed by classical spiking neurons connected with classical feedforward neurons. In the working process, a spiking neuron has to go through an iterative-like procedure before it gives a response to an input, while the classical feedforward neuron only needs a single operation to do the same. Hence, the modified one-layer spiking neural network does not increase very much the computational time than a usual one-layer spiking neural network in the working process. As indicated in our numerical experiments for the three benchmark problems, the accuracy of a modified one-layer spiking neural network using same or fewer encoding neurons is comparable to a spiking neural network with a hidden layer.

References

1. Maass, W.: Networks of spiking neurons: the thid generation of neural network. Neural Networks 10, 1659–1671 (1997)
2. Ghosh-Dastidar, S., Adeli, H.: A new supervised learning algorithm for multiple spiking neural networks with application in epilepsy and seizure detection. Neural Networks 22(10), 1419–1431 (2009)
3. Ghosh-Dastidar, S., Adeli, H.: Improved spiking neural networks for EEG classification and epilepsy and seizure detection. Integrated Computer-Aided Engineering 14(3), 187–212 (2007)
4. González-Nalda, P., Cases, B.: Topos: Spiking neural networks for temporal pattern recognition in complex real sounds. Neurocomputing 71(4-6), 721–732 (2008)
5. Wysoski, S.G., Benuscova, L., Kasabov, N.: Fast and adaptive network of spiking neurons for multi-view visual pattern recongnition. Neurocomputing 71(13-15), 2563–2575 (2008)
6. Natschlager, T., Berthold, R.: Pattern analysis with spiking neurons using delay coding. Neurocomputing 26-27, 463–469 (1999)
7. Wysoski, S.G., Benuskova, L., Kasabov, N.: Evolving spiking neural networks for audiovisual information processing. Neural Networks 23(7), 819–835 (2010)
8. Yang, J., Yang, W., Wu, W.: A novel spiking perceptron can solve XOR problem. Neural Network World 21, 45–50 (2011)
9. Wu, O.X., McGinnity, T.M., et al.: Learning under weight constraints in networks of temproral encoding spiking neurons. Neurocomputing 69, 1912–1922 (2006)

10. Booij, O., tat Nguyen, H.: A gradient descent rule for spiking neurons emitting multiple spikes. Information Processing Letters 95, 552–558 (2005)
11. Bohte, S.M., Kok, J.N., La Poutré, H.: Error-backpropagation in temporally encoded networks of spiking neurons. Neurocomputing 48(1-4), 17–37 (2002)
12. Yang, J., Yang, W., Wu, W.: A remark on the error-backpropagation learning algorithm for spiking neural networks. Appiled Mathematics Letters accepted (2012)

Modeling and Monitoring of Multimodes Process

Yingwei Zhang[*] and Chuang Wang

State Laboratory of Synthesis Automation of Process Industry,
Northeastern University, Shenyang, Liaoning 110004, P.R. China

Abstract. in the paper, a new monitoring approach is proposed for handling the dynamic problem in the industrial batch process. Compared to conventional method, the contributions are as follows:1) Multimodes are separated correctly since the cross-mode correlations are considered and the common information is extracted.2) a manifold learning approach(LLE) is implemented to extract the common information.3）after that two different subspaces are separated, the common and specific subspace models are built and analyzed respectively. The monitoring is carried out in subspace. The corresponding confidence regions are constructed according to their models respectively.

Keywords: multimodes process monitoring, subspace separation, manifold learning.

1 Introduction

In order to ensure the safety and quality of products, the monitoring of the process performance has become a key issue. Multivariate statistical process monitoring (MSPM) has been intensively researched in the last few decades, which have been applied widely in industrial processes. In particular, principal component analysis (PCA) and partial least squares (PLS) have achieved great success in process monitoring [1]-[7]. Kernel principal component analysis (KPCA) [8] and kernel partial least squares (KPLS) [9],[10] have been used to deal with nonlinear fault detection problem. Multi-way principal component analysis (MPCA) has been applied to batch processes [11]-[14]. However, in the industrial processes, the system has different operation conditions, control objectives or raw materials. Therefore, there are often different production modes, which make multimode batch processes more complicated [15]. Multi-scale principal component analysis (MSPCA) is used for fault detection and diagnosis in some multimode batch processes. Using wavelets, the data model is decomposed at different scales. Contributions from each scale are collected in separate matrices, and a new model is then constructed at each scale [16]. Under different assumptions, many researchers proposed a variety of methods to solve the dynamic problems[14]-[17]. Although these methods can be applied to adapt the online process changes, they still lack the ability of coping with processes with multiple operating modes. Recently, the novel models were built based on modified PCA methods [1],[4]. In [1], the fault probabilities can be determined. In [4], the

---

[*] Corresponding author.

J. Wang, G.G. Yen, and M.M. Polycarpou (Eds.): ISNN 2012, Part I, LNCS 7367, pp. 159–168, 2012.

unbalanced feature extraction cannot be avoided. Zhao et al. [18],[19] proposed a multiple principal component analysis model, which adopted principal angles to measure the similarities of any two models. Measuring the differences between normal and faulty states can identify the faulty variables since the faults are formed into a new operating region.

In the present work, new statistical analysis and online monitoring approaches are proposed for handling the problem of multimode in batch processes. The basic idea is that the similarity and dissimilarity of different modes are first analyzed. That is to analyze different types of correlations from the cross-mode viewpoint. The common part is the similar variable correlations over modes, and the specific part is the correlations which are not shared by all modes. By analyzing both common part and specific part, this method can identify the different operating modes and can effectively diagnose faults of multimode process. The contributions of the proposed method are as follows: 1) Multiple modeling may give each mode a higher resolution, but it neglects the cross-mode correlations and may result in some false alarms. In the proposed approach, the multimodes are separated correctly since the cross-mode correlations are considered. 2) When the multimodes are separated, the common information is extracted. 3) Compared to conventional method, the expensive computing load is avoided since only the specific information is calculated when a mode is monitored online.

The remainder of the paper is organized as follows. LLE algorithm is introduced and a corresponding modeling method of multimode processes is proposed in Section 2. A monitoring method of multimode processes is proposed in Section 3. The proposed monitoring approach is applied to a fused process in Section 4. Conclusions are summarized in Section 5.

2   Modeling of Multimode Processes

2.1   Introduction of LLE

Manifold learning is an important research topic in machine learning. To discover the underlying low-dimensional structure hidden in high-dimensional data is the goal of manifold learning. Many algorithms have been developed [20]-[22], including locally linear embedding (LLE)[20], Laplacian Eigenmap(LE)[23], local tangent alignment(LTSA)[24], semidefinite embedding[25], and other extensions. The LLE algorithm is based on simple geometric intuitions. Essentially, the algorithm attempts to compute a low dimensional embedding with the property that nearby points in the high dimensional space remain nearby and similarly co-located with respect to one another in the low dimensional space. Indeed, the LLE algorithm operates entirely without recourse to measures of distance or relation between faraway data points. It is theoretically elegant and easy in implementation. The utility of LLE has been witnessed in many applications, such as image super resolution, data visualization and soon. According to the LLE algorithm's goal, the underlying low-dimensional structure hidden in high-dimensional data can be found. Using the above thought, this paper applies the LLE algorithm to extract the common information that is the public properties between modes from the across-mode datasets. Through the extraction of common change information of the various models, each mode is divided into common information part and special information part and modeled respectively.

The main step of LLE algorithm [26]:

Suppose that $\Phi(\mathbf{X}) \in \mathbb{R}^{m \times n}$ is the data points. In order to facilitate with this paper, mapping the data from the original space to the feature space as $\mathbf{X} \rightarrow \Phi(\mathbf{X})$.

First, for $\Phi(x_i) \in \Phi(\mathbf{X})$, identify its nearest k neighbors in $\Phi(\mathbf{X})$ with Euclidean distance metric.

Second, linearly reconstruct $\Phi(x_i)$ with its $k-1$ neighbors:

$$\Phi(x_i) = \Phi(x_{i_1}) \approx \sum_{j=2}^{k} w_j^{(i)} \Phi(x_{i_j}) \tag{1}$$

Third, linearly reconstruct the low-dimensional coordinate of $\Phi(x_i)$ with the same weights

$$\Phi(y_i) = \Phi(y_{i_1}) \approx \sum_{j=2}^{k} w_j^{(i)} \Phi(y_{i_j}) \tag{2}$$

Finally, solve the following optimization problem:

$$\min_{\Phi(\mathbf{Y})\Phi(\mathbf{Y})^{\mathrm{T}}=\mathbf{I}_d} tr\left(\Phi(\mathbf{Y})\mathbf{A}\Phi(\mathbf{Y})^{\mathrm{T}}\right) \tag{3}$$

where $\mathbf{A} = (\mathbf{I}_n - \mathbf{W})^{\mathrm{T}}(\mathbf{I}_n - \mathbf{W})$, $\mathbf{W}$ collects the weight vectors $\{\mathbf{w}_i\}$ evaluated on the n neighborhoods. The optimum $\Phi(\mathbf{Y})$ for the d-dimensional global embedding can be obtained via the eigenvalue decomposition of $\mathbf{A}$.

2.2   Modeling of the Multimodes Process

In the measurement data, suppose that there are M industrial production patterns in the same production line. Therefore the multiple datasets of the same production line $\Phi(\mathbf{X}^m) = [\Phi(\mathbf{x}_1^m), \cdots, \Phi(\mathbf{x}_n^m)] \in (J \times n)$, where J denotes the number of variables, and $m = 1, 2, \cdots, M$ denote different modes.

Without loss of generality, the case of two modes which are called mode A and mode B is discussed here. What's more, supposing that there are the same numbers of variables between the two modes. Then, the two modes' measurement data are got:

$$\Phi(\mathbf{X}) = \begin{bmatrix} \Phi(x_{11}^A) & \Phi(x_{12}^A) & \cdots & \Phi(x_{1n}^A) \\ \Phi(x_{21}^A) & \Phi(x_{22}^A) & \cdots & \Phi(x_{2n}^A) \\ \vdots & \vdots & & \vdots \\ \Phi(x_{N1}^A) & \Phi(x_{N2}^A) & \cdots & \Phi(x_{Nn}^A) \\ \Phi(x_{11}^B) & \Phi(x_{12}^B) & \cdots & \Phi(x_{1n}^B) \\ \Phi(x_{21}^B) & \Phi(x_{22}^B) & \cdots & \Phi(x_{2n}^B) \\ \vdots & \vdots & & \vdots \\ \Phi(x_{N1}^B) & \Phi(x_{N2}^B) & \cdots & \Phi(x_{Nn}^B) \end{bmatrix} \in \mathbb{R}^{2N \times n}$$

in which, N is the number of variables, n is the number of samples.

According to the essence of the LLE algorithm, the low-dimensional structure: $\Phi(\mathbf{Y}) \in \mathbb{R}^{N \times n}$. It can be assumed that the low-dimensional characterization mentioned above is equal to the common information of the multimode. Here, the common information is noted for $\Phi(\mathbf{X}^c)$.

Applying KPCA to $\Phi(\mathbf{X}^c)$, the global and common matrix $\mathbf{P}_c$ and the common score matrix $\mathbf{T}^c$ can be obtained. Then, mode A and mode B can be separated into two different parts, one common subspace and the residual part called the specific subspace. They are described as fellow:

$$\begin{cases} \Phi(\mathbf{X}_A) = \Phi(\mathbf{X}^c) + \Phi(\mathbf{X}_A^s) \\ \Phi^T(\mathbf{X}_A^c) = (\mathbf{T}^c \mathbf{P}_c^T)^T = \mathbf{P}_c(\mathbf{T}^c)^T = \mathbf{P}_c \mathbf{P}_c^T \Phi^T(\mathbf{X}_A) \\ \Phi^T(\mathbf{X}_A^s) = \Phi^T(\mathbf{X}_A) - \Phi^T(\mathbf{X}^c) = (\mathbf{I} - \mathbf{P}_c \mathbf{P}_c^T)\Phi^T(\mathbf{X}_A) \end{cases} \quad (4)$$

$$\begin{cases} \Phi(\mathbf{X}_B) = \Phi(\mathbf{X}^c) + \Phi(\mathbf{X}_B^s) \\ \Phi^T(\mathbf{X}_B^c) = (\mathbf{T}^c \mathbf{P}_c^T)^T = \mathbf{P}_c(\mathbf{T}^c)^T = \mathbf{P}_c \mathbf{P}_c^T \Phi^T(\mathbf{X}_B) \\ \Phi^T(\mathbf{X}_B^s) = \Phi^T(\mathbf{X}_B) - \Phi^T(\mathbf{X}^c) = (\mathbf{I} - \mathbf{P}_c \mathbf{P}_c^T)\Phi^T(\mathbf{X}_B) \end{cases} \quad (5)$$

3   Monitoring of Multimode Processes

In the common subspace, the common basis vectors actually denote the initial and basic correlations underlying the subspace. While the residual subspace have no common information and are specific to each mode. Therefore it has revealing the dissimilarity with other modes. Therefore, different model structures should be designed in each specific subspace respectively. The KPCA is performed to separate the systematic and residual information:

$$
\begin{cases}
\mathbf{T}_1^s = \Phi\left(\mathbf{X}_A^s\right)\mathbf{P}_A^s = \Phi\left(\mathbf{X}_A\right)\left(\mathbf{I}-\mathbf{P}_A\mathbf{P}_A^{\mathrm{T}}\right)\mathbf{P}_A^s \\
\Phi\left(\hat{\mathbf{X}}_A^S\right) = \mathbf{T}_A^s\left(\mathbf{P}_A^s\right)^T \\
\mathbf{E}_1^S = \Phi\left(\mathbf{X}_A^s\right)-\Phi\left(\hat{\mathbf{X}}_A^s\right)
\end{cases}
\tag{6}
$$

$$
\begin{cases}
\mathbf{T}_B^s = \Phi\left(\mathbf{X}_B^s\right)\mathbf{P}_B^s = \Phi\left(\mathbf{X}_B\right)\left(\mathbf{I}-\mathbf{P}_B\mathbf{P}_B^{\mathrm{T}}\right)\mathbf{P}_B^s \\
\Phi\left(\hat{\mathbf{X}}_B^s\right) = \mathbf{T}_B^s\left(\mathbf{P}_B^s\right)^{\mathrm{T}} \\
\mathbf{E}_B^s = \Phi\left(\mathbf{X}_B^s\right)-\Phi\left(\hat{\mathbf{X}}_B^s\right)
\end{cases}
\tag{7}
$$

Where $\mathbf{P}_A^s(N\times R_A^s)$ and $\mathbf{P}_B^s(N\times R_B^s)$ are the specific PCA loadings, revealing the major specific variation directions and R_A^s is the retained PC number. $\mathbf{E}_A^s$ is the specific residuals, also the final modeling errors.

Generally, $\mathbf{P}_A^s(N\times R_A^s)$ and $\mathbf{P}_B^s(N\times R_B^s)$ should be more different over datasets. From another viewpoint, since $\mathbf{P}_A^s$ and $\mathbf{P}_B^s$ result from the basic PCA model, it means that those PCA loadings can also be expressed as one form of linear combination of the original measurement and thus can be regarded as one type of basis vectors.

By calculating the Hotelling-T^2 of the common features, the faults in common information can be detected. If there are no faults in the common features, the calculation of the specific Hotelling-T^2 can reveal the faults in the specific features. And the calculation of SPE can help to detect the process faults

4   Illustration Example

The electro-fused magnesia furnace (EFMF) is one of the main equipment used to produce electro-fused magnesia belongs to a kind of mine hot electric arc furnace. With the development of technology of melting, EFMF has already gotten extensive application in the industry. EFMF refining technology can enhance the quality and increase the production variety. The whole equipment of the EFMF has transformer, short net, electrode holder, electrode, furnace, etc. Operating board besides the furnace controls electrode up and down. The furnace shell is round, slightly tapered, facilitate melting in processing. There are rings on the furnace wall and trolley under the furnace. When melting process has completed, move the trolley to cool. The EFMF smelting process is shown in Fig.1.

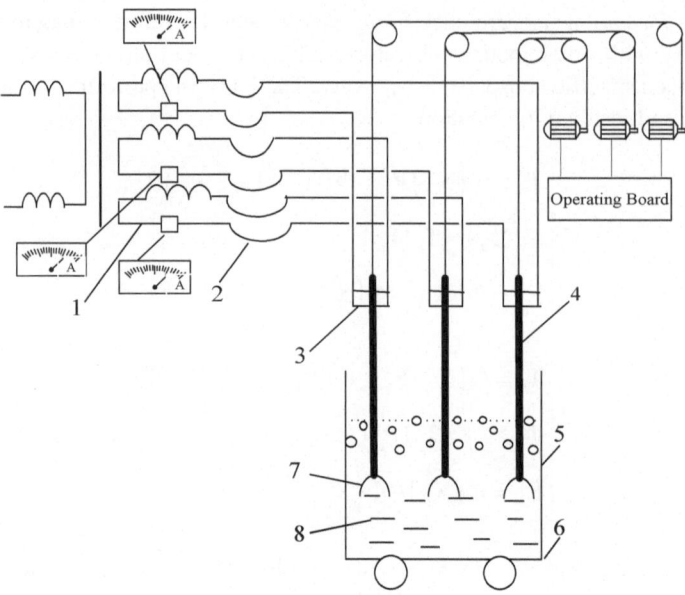

1-transformer, 2-short circuit network, 3-electrode holder, 4-electrode, 5-furnace shell, 6-trolley, 7-electric arc, 8-burden

Fig. 1. Diagram of electro-fused magnesium furnace

In the melting process, voltage flicker is a kind of power quality problems, which occurs in the power system when the gas aggregates quickly in the magnesia. The EFMF in this paper takes the light-burned magnesia as the raw material. It makes use of the heat generated both by the burden resistance when the current through the burden and the arc between the electrodes and the burden to melt the burden, and then obtain the fused magnesia crystals with higher purity. The materials are powdery magnesium in mode A. The materials are massive magnesium in mode B.

In total, 40 normal batch runs are generated in mode A and 40 normal batches runs in mode B, after the data processing in the above section, the data sets $\Phi(\mathbf{X}_A)$ and $\Phi(\mathbf{X}_B)$ are obtained. Here, a batch run is used to test the feasibility of the method. There are 3 variables in both modes. First of all, 200 normal samples are used to be tested in the proposed process monitoring method. As is shown in Fig.2 (a), the T^2 statistics of testing data in the common subspace is not beyond the control limit. From the Fig.2 (b), the T^2 statistics of the specific part of model A is not beyond the control limit, but the T^2 statistics of the specific part of model B is partly beyond the control limit. Correspondingly, from the Fig.2 (c), the SPE statistics of test data in the model A almost has no phenomenon of overrunning and the SPE statistics of test data in the model B is beyond the control limit. Therefore, the test data can be judged to belong to model A normal dataset, then the current work mode of the fused magnesia furnace is ascertained.

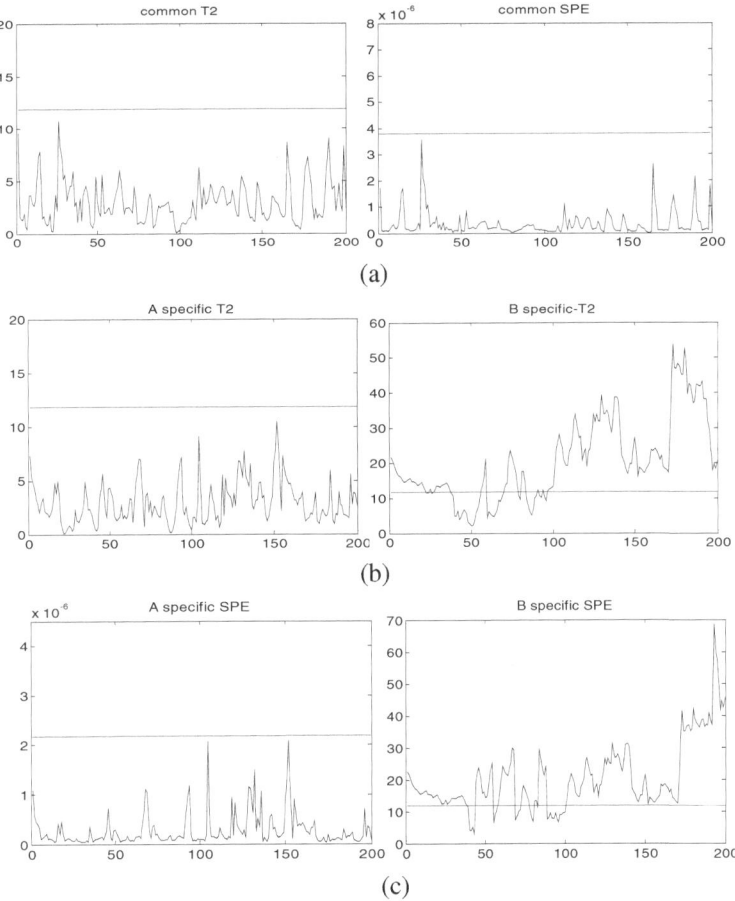

Fig. 2. The proposed method monitoring results of the two different modes for (a) common part T^2 statistic; (b) specific part T^2 statistic; (c) residual statistic

Next, an abnormal batch run, which belongs to mode A, is applied in proposed method. Process faults are introduced from the 145th sample. As is shown in Fig.3, the three detection figures all have overrun phenomenon, this is showed that the fault is detected. At the same time, it is stated the fault is not only occurred in the common part, but also occurred in the special part.

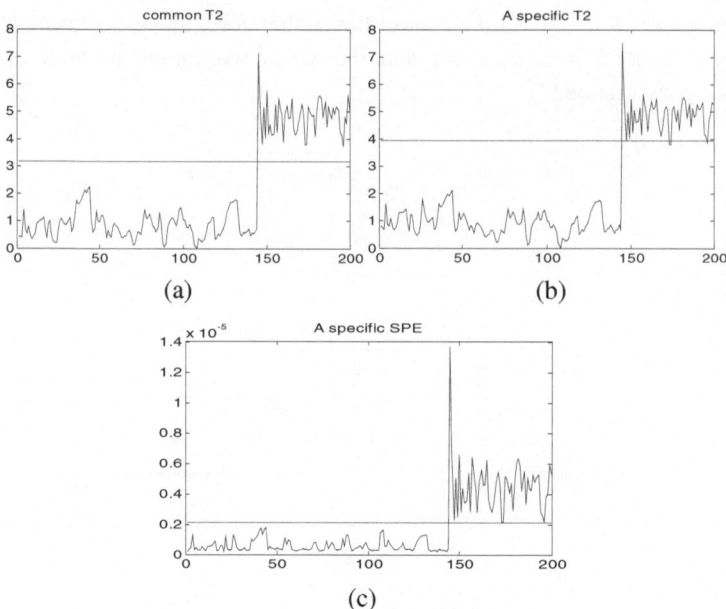

Fig. 3. Monitoring results by mode A for (a) Common part T^2 statistic; (b) Specific part T^2 statistic; (c) Residual statistic

5   Conclusion

In this work, a new method was proposed for detection of multi-mode batches. Since the cross-mode correlations were considered, the multimodes were separated more correctly in the proposed method. And the similarity and dissimilarity of different modes were first analyzed. By use of the LLE algorithm, the common information among modes is extracted easily. The common information was the similar variable correlations over modes, and the specific information was the difference in each mode. By dataset decomposition and subspace separation, the underlying variations of different modes can be analyzed more comprehensively. For the new dataset, through the proposed method, what mode it belongs to is ensured firstly. Then, making use of the process statistics, the fault detection can be accurate and obvious. What's more, all the data in this paper is nonlinear, the kernel trick is introduced and applied commendably into the proposed method.

References

1. Ge, Z., Gao, F.R., Song, Z.H.: Two-dimensional Bayesian monitoring method for nonlinear multimode processes. Chemical Engineering Science 66, 5173–5183 (2011)
2. Wang, X., Kruger, U., Lennox, B.: Recursive partial least squares algorithms for monitoring complex industrial processes. Control Engineering Practice 11, 613–632 (2003)

3. Kruger, U., Dimitriadis, G.: Diagnosis of process faults in chemical systems using a local partial least squares approach. AIChE J. 54, 2581–2596 (2008)

4. Zhao, C.H., Mo, S.Y., Gao, F.R.: Statistical analysis and online monitoring for handling multiphase batch processes with varying durations. Journal of Process Control 21, 817–829 (2011)

5. Zhang, Y.W., Qin, S.J.: Improved nonlinear fault detection technique and statistical analysis. AIChE J. 54, 3207–3220 (2008)

6. AlGhazzawi, A., Lennox, B.: Monitoring a complex refining process using multivariate statistics. Control Engineering Practice 16, 294–307 (2008)

7. Zhang, Y.W., Zhou, H., Qin, S.J., Chai, T.Y.: Decentralized fault diagnosis of large-scale processes using multiblock kernel partial least squares. IEEE Transactions on Industrial Informatics 6, 3–12 (2010)

8. Zhang, Y.W., Qin, S.J.: Nonlinear Fault Detection Technique and Statistical Analysis. AIChE J. 54, 3207–3220 (2008)

9. Zhang, Y.W., Zhang, Y.: Fault detection of non-Gaussian processes based on modified independent component analysis. Chemical Engineering Science 65, 4630–4639 (2010)

10. Zhang, Y.W., Teng, Y.D., Zhang, Y.: Complex process quality prediction using modified kernel partial least squares. Chemical Engineering Science 65, 2153–2158 (2010)

11. Nomikos, P.: Detection and diagnosis of abnormal batch operations based on multi-way principal component analysis. ISA Transaction 35, 259–266 (1996)

12. He, N., Wang, S., Xie, L.: An improved adaptive multi-way principal component analysis for monitoring streptomycin fermentation process. Chinese Journal of Chemical Engineering 12, 96–101 (2004)

13. Gallagher, N.B., Wise, B.M.: Application of multi-way principal components analysis to nuclear waste storage tank monitoring. Computers and Chemical Engineering 20, S739–S744 (1996)

14. Lee, J., Yoo, C., Lee, L.: Online batch process monitoring using a consecutively updated multiway principal analysis model. Journal of Biotechnology 108, 61–77 (2004)

15. Singhai, A., Seborg, D.E.: Evaluation of a pattern matching method for the Tennessee Eastman challenge process. J. Process Control 16, 601–613 (2007)

16. Bakshi, B.R.: Multiscale PCA with application to multivariate statistical process monitoring. AIChE J. 44, 1596–1610 (1998)

17. Fu, J., He, H.B., Zhou, X.M.: Adaptive learning and control for MIMO system based on adaptive dynamic programming. IEEE Transactions on Neural Networks 22, 1133–1148 (2011)

18. Wang, F.Y., Jin, N., Liu, D.R., Wei, Q.L.: Adaptive dynamic programming for finite-horizon optimal control of discrete-time nonlinear systems with λ_A -error bound. IEEE Transactions on Neural Networks 22, 24–36 (2011)

19. Han, M., Fan, J.C., Wang, J.: "A dynamic feedforward neural network based on Gaussian particle swarm optimization and its application for predictive control. IEEE Transactions on Neural Networks 22, 1457–1468 (2011)

20. Flury, B.K.: Two generalizations of the common principal component model. Biometrika 74(1), 59–69 (1987)

21. Roweis, S., Saul, L.: Nonlinear dimensionality reduction by locally linear embedding. Science 290, 2323–2326 (2000)

22. Ham, J., Lee, D.D., Mika, S., Schokopf, B.: A kernel view of the dimensionality reduction of manifolds. In: Proc. Int. Conf. Mach. Learn., Banff, AB, Canada, pp. 369–376 (2004)

23. de Silva, V., Tenenbaum, J.B.: Global versus local methods in nonlinear dimensionality reduction. In: Advances in Neural Information Processing Systems 15, pp. 721–728. MIT Press, Cambridge (2003)
24. Belkin, M., Niyogi, P.: Laplacian eigenmaps for dimensionality reduction and data representation. Neural Compute. 15, 1373–1396 (2003)
25. Zhang, Z., Zha, H.: Principal manifolds and nonlinear dimensionality reduction via tangent space alignment. SIAM J. Sci. Compute. 26, 313–338 (2004)
26. Weinberger, K.Q., Sha, F., Saul, L.K.: Learning a kernel matrix for nonlinear dimensionality reduction. In: Proc. Int. Conf. Mach. Learn., Banff, AB, Canada, pp. 888–905 (2004)

Data-Based Modeling and Monitoring for Multimode Processes Using Local Tangent Space Alignment

Yingwei Zhang[*] and Hailong Zhang

State Laboratory of Synthesis Automation of Process Industry, Northeastern University,
Shenyang, Liaoning 110004, P.R. China

Abstract. In the paper, a new online monitoring approach is proposed for handling the multimode monitoring problem in the industrial batch processes.
Compared to conventional method, the contributions are as follows: 1) The
LTSA algorithm is applied to the multi-mode batches process. And a common
subspace is extracted via the new method proposed instead of extracting the
common subspaces of each mode. 2) After those two different subspaces are
separated, the common and specific subspace models are built and analyzed respectively. The monitoring is carried out in subspace. The corresponding confidence regions are constructed according to their models respectively.

Keywords: LTSA, common and specific correlations, multimode process
monitoring.

1   Introduction

In order to ensure safety of the equipment and quality of product, the monitoring of the
process performance has become a key issue. Multivariate statistical process control
(MSPC) has been intensively researched in the last few decades. In particular, principal
component analysis (PCA), partial least squares (PLS) have been applied widely in
industrial processes[1]-[6], and some improved methods, such as kernel principal
component analysis (KPCA) [7]has achieved great success in process monitoring and
fault diagnosis. Recently, monitoring the batch processes is needed for various reasons
such as safety, waste-stream reduction, consistency and quality improvement. Multi-way principal component analysis (MPCA) has been developed to deal with such
batch processes.

However, in the industrial processes, the same production line is often used to
produce different products. Therefore, there are often different production modes in the
same production line, which makes dynamical multimode batch processes more complicated [8]. However, the MSPM methods are not available for the dynamical multimode processes. These methods may cause false alarms, even when the process is
operating under another nominal steady-state mode. Recently, recursive or adaptive
PCA and PLS methods have been proposed [9] [10]. Although these methods can be
applied to treat the online process changes, they still lack the ability of coping with

---

[*] Corresponding author.

J. Wang, G.G. Yen, and M.M. Polycarpou (Eds.): ISNN 2012, Part I, LNCS 7367, pp. 169–178, 2012.
© Springer-Verlag Berlin Heidelberg 2012

processes with multiple operating modes. Alternatively, model library based methods have been introduced. Predefined models match their corresponding operating modes, but the effect of this method is not satisfactory.

Manifold learning is an important research topic in machine learning. The goal of manifold learning is to discover the underlying low-dimensional structure hidden in high-dimensional data. Many algorithms have been developed[11][12][13][14], including Isomap [15], locally linear embedding (LLE)[16], manifold charting, Laplacian Eigenmap (LE)[17], Hessian LLE, local tangent space alignment (LTSA)[18], semi-definite embedding, conformal eigenmap, and other extensions. The usage of manifold learning has been demonstrated in many aspects, including image processing, computer vision, pattern recognition, visualization, and other applications.

LTSA [18] is another fundamental algorithm in manifold learning. LTSA employs locally linear transformations to map neighboring data points onto the low-dimensional manifold. In usage, locally linear transformation is proven to be an effective method to treat the neighboring data points for graph-based learning. In digital matting, locally linear transformations are applied to image windows, through which an effective matting for complex natural images is developed [19].

In this work, an online monitoring method is proposed for handling the problem of multimode in batch processes. The nonlinear similarity and dissimilarity of different modes are analyzed. And the method of LTSA is used to obtain the low-dimensional embedding of the data points. When the mode switches, the specific monitoring model is changed accordingly. By analyzing both common part and specific part, the different operating modes are identified and the faults of multimode process are diagnosed.

The rest of this paper is organized as follows. The LTSA algorithm is proposed in section 2. The Monitoring of multimode processes is proposed and analysed in section 3. The simulation results are given to show the effectiveness of the proposed method in section 4. Finally, conclusions are summarized in section 5.

2   The Main Steps of LTSA Algorithm

In the measurement data, suppose that there are M industrial production patterns in the same production line. Therefore the multiple datasets $\mathbf{X}^m = [\mathbf{x}_1^{\ m}, \cdots, \mathbf{x}_{N_m}^{\ m}]^T \in (N_m \times J)$, where J denotes the number of variables, and $m = 1, 2, \cdots, M$ denote different modes. The proposed algorithm maps the data from the original space to the feature space as $\mathbf{X}^m \to \Phi(\mathbf{X}^m)$. And $\mathrm{N}_i = \left\{ \Phi\left(\mathbf{x}_{i_j} \right) \right\}_{j=1}^{k}$ are centered nonlinear mapping of the input variables, and suppose that $\sum_{j=1}^{N_m} \Phi(\mathbf{x}_j^{\ m}) = 0$. The main steps of LTSA can be summarized as follows[20]:

First, for $\Phi(\mathbf{x}_i^{\ m}) \in \Phi(\mathbf{X}^m)$, identify its k nearest neighbors in $\Phi\left(\mathbf{X}^m \right)$ with Euclidean distance metric, and collect them in $\mathrm{N}_i = \left\{ \Phi\left(\mathbf{x}_{i_j} \right) \right\}_{j=1}^{k}$.

Second, project k data points in $\mathbf{N}_i$ into the tangent space of the manifold at $\Phi(\mathbf{x}_i)$.

$$\mathbf{t}_j^{(i)} = \mathbf{Q}_i^T \left(\Phi(\mathbf{x}_{i_j}) - \mathbf{C}_i \right), \qquad j = 1,2,3...,k \qquad (1)$$

where $\mathbf{t}_j^{(i)}$ is called a local coordinate of $\Phi(\mathbf{x}_{i_j})$, $\mathbf{C}_i = \dfrac{1}{k}\sum\limits_{j=1}^{k}\Phi(\mathbf{x}_{i_j})$ is the mean vec-

tor, and $\mathbf{Q}_i \in \mathbb{R}^{m \times d}$ is a tangent space projection matrix. $\mathbf{Q}_i$ can be estimated by performing the optimal rank-d approximation of the centered data matrix.

Third, linearly align the local coordinates into a single global coordinate system in $\mathbf{R}^d$

$$\Phi(\mathbf{y}_{i_j}) \approx \mathbf{L}_i \mathbf{t}_j^{(i)} + \mathbf{b}_i, \qquad j = 1, 2, ..., k \qquad (2)$$

where $\mathbf{L}_i \in \mathbf{R}^{d \times d}$ is an affine transformation matrix and $\mathbf{b}_i$ is a translation vector in $\mathbf{R}^d$.

Obviously, these two linear transformations above can be combined together into a single transformation. Based on (1) and (2), we have

$$\Phi(\mathbf{y}_{i_j}) = \mathbf{L}_i \mathbf{Q}_i^T \left(\Phi(\mathbf{x}_{i_j}) - \mathbf{C}_i \right) + \mathbf{b}_i, \qquad j = 1, 2, ..., k \qquad (3)$$

Formally taking $\mathbf{Q}_i \mathbf{L}_i^T$ in (3) as a transformation matrix, we can obtain a linear transformation as follows:

$$\mathbf{g}_i(\mathbf{x}) = \mathbf{W}_i^T(\mathbf{x} - \mathbf{C}_i) + \mathbf{b}_i \qquad (4)$$

where $\mathbf{W}_i \in \mathbb{R}^{m \times d}, \mathbf{b}_i \in \mathbb{R}^d$, and $\mathbf{C}_i$ is the mean vector of data points in $\mathbf{N}_i$, According to (3) and (4), we see that $\mathbf{W}_i$ will be estimated as $\mathbf{W}_i = \mathbf{Q}_i \mathbf{L}_i^T$.

Now, we consider to directly solve the $\mathbf{W}_i$ under the least squares regression framework. In this framework, it is unnecessary to perform the rand-d approximation. Straightforwardly, we hope that each $\Phi(\mathbf{x}_{i_j})$ can be directly mapped as $\Phi(\mathbf{y}_{i_j})$

$$\Phi(\mathbf{y}_{i_j}) \approx \mathbf{g}_i\left(\Phi(\mathbf{x}_{i_j}) \right) \qquad (5)$$

The least squares regression problem is given as follow:

$$\min \sum_{j=1}^{k} \left\| \Phi(\mathbf{y}_{i_j}) - \mathbf{g}\left(\Phi(\mathbf{x}_{i_j}) \right) \right\|_2^2 + \lambda \left\| \mathbf{W}_i \right\|_2^2 \qquad (6)$$

According to (6), we can obtain the object function $\mathbf{G}(\mathbf{W}_i, \mathbf{b}_i)$:

$$\min \sum_{j=1}^{k} \left\| \mathbf{W}_i^T \left(\Phi(\mathbf{x}_{i_j}) - \mathbf{C}_i \right) + \mathbf{b}_i - \mathbf{g}\left(\Phi(\mathbf{x}_{i_j}) \right) \right\|_2^2 + \lambda \left\| \mathbf{W}_i \right\|_2^2 \qquad (7)$$

Let $\mathbf{\Phi}\left(\mathbf{X}_i^{(c)}\right) = \left[\mathbf{g}\left(\mathbf{\Phi}\left(\mathbf{x}_{i_1}\right)\right) - \mathbf{C}_i, \mathbf{g}\left(\mathbf{\Phi}\left(\mathbf{x}_{i_2}\right)\right) - \mathbf{C}_i, \dots, \mathbf{g}\left(\mathbf{\Phi}\left(\mathbf{x}_{i_k}\right)\right) - \mathbf{C}_i\right] \in \mathbb{R}^{m \times k}$ be the

centralized data matrix and $\mathbf{\Phi}(\mathbf{Y}_i) = \left[\mathbf{\Phi}\left(\mathbf{y}_{i_1}\right), \mathbf{\Phi}\left(\mathbf{y}_{i_2}\right), \dots, \mathbf{\Phi}\left(\mathbf{y}_{i_k}\right)\right] \in \mathbb{R}^{d \times k}$ collect the k

low-dimensional data points.

The optimization $\mathbf{W}_i$ should meet the following conditions [20]:

$$
\begin{cases}
\dfrac{\partial G(\mathbf{W}_i, \mathbf{b}_i)}{\partial \mathbf{W}_i} = 0 \\[3mm]
\dfrac{\partial G(\mathbf{W}_i, \mathbf{b}_i)}{\partial \mathbf{b}_i} = 0
\end{cases} \tag{8}
$$

Solving the above optimization problem, we can get the optimal $\mathbf{W}_i$ and $\mathbf{b}_i$

$$
\mathbf{W}_i = \left(\mathbf{\Phi}\left(\mathbf{X}_i^{(c)}\right)\mathbf{\Phi}\left(\mathbf{X}_i^{(c)}\right)^T + \lambda\mathbf{I}_m\right)^{-1}\mathbf{\Phi}\left(\mathbf{X}_i^{(c)}\right)\mathbf{\Phi}(\mathbf{Y}_i)^T \tag{9}
$$

$$
\mathbf{b}_i = \frac{1}{k}\mathbf{\Phi}(\mathbf{Y}_i)\mathbf{e}_k \tag{10}
$$

After the optimal $\mathbf{W}_i$ and $\mathbf{b}_i$ are estimated, the sum of k squared errors can be
evaluated as

$$
\varepsilon_i = \sum_{j=1}^{k}\left\|\mathbf{\Phi}\left(\mathbf{y}_{i_j}\right) - \left(\mathbf{W}_i^T\left(\mathbf{\Phi}\left(\mathbf{x}_{i_j}\right) - \mathbf{C}_i\right) + \mathbf{b}_i\right)\right\|_2^2 \tag{11}
$$

Based on (9) and (10), then we can get ε_i

$$
\varepsilon_i = \mathrm{tr}\left(\mathbf{\Phi}(\mathbf{Y}_i)\mathbf{L}\mathbf{G}_i\mathbf{G}_i\mathbf{L}\mathbf{\Phi}(\mathbf{Y}_i)^T\right) \tag{12}
$$

Where $\mathbf{G}_i = \mathbf{I}_k - \mathbf{\Phi}\left(\mathbf{X}_i^{(c)}\right)^T\left(\mathbf{\Phi}\left(\mathbf{X}_i^{(c)}\right)\mathbf{\Phi}\left(\mathbf{X}_i^{(c)}\right)^T + \lambda\mathbf{I}_m\right)^{-1}\mathbf{\Phi}\left(\mathbf{X}_i^{(c)}\right)$. We can con-

struct an objective function to learn the global embedding, which has the form as

$$
\mathbf{E}_{ltsa}(\mathbf{Y}) = \sum_{i=1}^{n}\mathrm{tr}\left(\mathbf{\Phi}(\mathbf{Y}_i)\mathbf{L}\mathbf{G}_i\mathbf{G}_i\mathbf{L}\mathbf{\Phi}(\mathbf{Y}_i)^T\right) \tag{13}
$$

Finally, solve the following problem to obtain the low-dimensional embedding:

$$
\min_{\mathbf{Y}^T\mathbf{Y}=\mathbf{I}_d}\mathrm{tr}\left(\mathbf{\Phi}(\mathbf{Y}_i)\mathbf{L}\mathbf{G}_i\mathbf{G}_i\mathbf{L}\mathbf{\Phi}(\mathbf{Y}_i)^T\right) \tag{14}
$$

where $\mathbf{\Phi}(\mathbf{Y}_i)$ is matrix of the low-dimensional coordinates of the data points in

$\mathbf{N}_i = \left\{\mathbf{\Phi}\left(\mathbf{x}_{i_j}\right)\right\}_{j=1}^{k}$, and $\mathbf{\Phi}(\mathbf{Y}_i) = \left[\mathbf{\Phi}\left(\mathbf{y}_{i_1}\right), \mathbf{\Phi}\left(\mathbf{y}_{i_2}\right), \dots, \mathbf{\Phi}\left(\mathbf{y}_{i_k}\right)\right] \in \mathbb{R}^{d \times k}$.

Given a set of n data points $\Phi(\mathbf{X}) = \{\Phi(\mathbf{x}_1), \Phi(\mathbf{x}_2), ..., \Phi(\mathbf{x}_n)\} \subset \mathbb{R}^m$, the task of manifold learning is to find a low-dimensional embedding $\Phi(\mathbf{y}) = \{\Phi(\mathbf{y}_1), \Phi(\mathbf{y}_2), ..., \Phi(\mathbf{y}_n)\} \subset \mathbb{R}^d$, which can explore the intrinsic structure hidden in the high-dimensional data in $\Phi(\mathbf{X})$. Here, $\Phi(\mathbf{y}_i)$ is a low-dimensional coordinate of $\Phi(\mathbf{x}_i)$, and $d < m$ .we can deem that $\Phi(\mathbf{y}_i)$ can replace the common subspace $\Phi(\mathbf{X}^c)$ .To be convenient, we define $\Phi(\mathbf{Y}_i)$ as $\Phi(\mathbf{Y}_c)$.

3   Monitoring of Multimode Processes

And after the above calculation, each data set can be divided into two different types of correlations. And the similar variable correlations over datasets belong to the common operation part, and the specific part reflects the correlations which are not shared by the two datasets. As we know the common subspace $\Phi(\mathbf{Y}_c)$, we can calculate the basis matrix $\mathbf{P}$ of each mode. And the dataset $\Phi(\mathbf{X}_1)$ can be separated into two different parts, one common subspace $\Phi(\mathbf{Y}_c)$, and the residual part $\Phi(\mathbf{X}_1^S)$, called the specific subspace.

$$\begin{cases} \Phi(\mathbf{X}_1) = \Phi(\mathbf{Y}_c) + \Phi(\mathbf{X}_1^S) \\ \Phi(\mathbf{Y}_c) = \mathbf{T}_1^C \mathbf{P}_1^T \\ \Phi(\mathbf{X}_1^S) = \Phi(\mathbf{X}_1) - \Phi(\mathbf{Y}_c) \end{cases} \tag{15}$$

After the above subspace separation, the data set $\Phi(\mathbf{X}_1)$ is divided to two different types of correlations from the cross-mode viewpoint. The common dataset $\Phi(\mathbf{Y}_c)$ and the specific dataset $\Phi(\mathbf{X}_1^S)$ are separated. With the same method, $\Phi(\mathbf{X}_2)$ can be also separated into $\Phi(\mathbf{Y}_c)$ and $\Phi(\mathbf{X}_2^S)$ as follows :

$$\begin{cases} \Phi(\mathbf{X}_2) = \Phi(\mathbf{Y}_c) + \Phi(\mathbf{X}_2^S) \\ \Phi(\mathbf{Y}_c) = \mathbf{T}_2^C \mathbf{P}_2^T \\ \Phi(\mathbf{X}_2^S) = \Phi(\mathbf{X}_2) - \Phi(\mathbf{Y}_c) \end{cases} \tag{16}$$

where $\mathbf{T}_1^C$ and $\mathbf{T}_2^C$ are the linear combination coefficients corresponding to the common subspace. Which are actually calculated by direct projecting $\Phi(\mathbf{X}_1)$ and $\Phi(\mathbf{X}_2)$ onto the common dataset $\Phi(\mathbf{Y}_c)$.

In the common subspace, the common basis vectors actually denote the initial and basic correlations underlying the subspace. While the residual subspace have no common information and are specific to each mode. Therefore it has revealing the dissimilarity with other modes. Therefore, different model structures should be designed in each specific subspace respectively. The traditional PCA decomposition is performed to separate the systematic and residual information:

$$\begin{cases} \mathbf{T}_1^S = \mathbf{\Phi}\left(\mathbf{X}_1^S\right)\mathbf{P}_1^S = \mathbf{\Phi}\left(\mathbf{X}_1\right)\left(\mathbf{I} - \mathbf{P}_1\mathbf{P}_1^T\right)\mathbf{P}_1^S \\ \mathbf{\Phi}\left(\hat{\mathbf{X}}_1^S\right) = \mathbf{T}_1^S\left(\mathbf{P}_1^S\right)^T \\ \mathbf{E}_1^S = \mathbf{\Phi}\left(\mathbf{X}_1^S\right) - \mathbf{\Phi}\left(\hat{\mathbf{X}}_1^S\right) \end{cases} \tag{17}$$

$$\begin{cases} \mathbf{T}_2^S = \mathbf{\Phi}\left(\mathbf{X}_2^S\right)\mathbf{P}_2^S = \mathbf{\Phi}\left(\mathbf{X}_2\right)\left(\mathbf{I} - \mathbf{P}_2\mathbf{P}_2^T\right)\mathbf{P}_2^S \\ \mathbf{\Phi}\left(\hat{\mathbf{X}}_2^S\right) = \mathbf{T}_2^S\left(\mathbf{P}_2^S\right)^T \\ \mathbf{E}_2^S = \mathbf{\Phi}\left(\mathbf{X}_2^S\right) - \mathbf{\Phi}\left(\hat{\mathbf{X}}_2^S\right) \end{cases} \tag{18}$$

where $\mathbf{P}_1^S\left(J \times R_1^S\right)$ and $\mathbf{P}_2^S\left(J \times R_2^S\right)$ are the specific PCA loadings, reveal the major specific variation directions and R_1^S is the retained PC number. $\mathbf{E}_1^S$ and $\mathbf{E}_2^S$ are the specific residuals, also the final modeling errors.

4   Illustration Example

The electro-fused magnesia furnace (EFMF) is one of the main equipment used to produce electro-fused magnesia belongs to a kind of mine hot electric arc furnace. With the development of technology of melting, EFMF has already gotten extensive application in the industry. EFMF refining technology can enhance the quality and increase the production variety. The whole equipment of the EFMF has transformer, short net, electrode holder, electrode, furnace, etc. Operating board besides the furnace controls electrode up and down. The furnace shell is round, slightly tapered, facilitate melting in processing. There are rings on the furnace wall and trolley under the furnace. When melting process has completed, move the trolley to cool. The EFMF smelting process is shown in Figure 1.

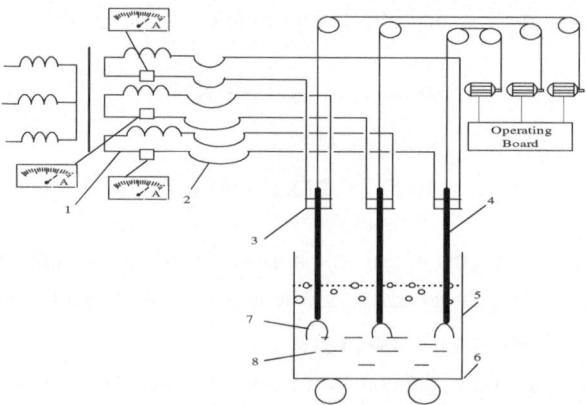

Fig. 1. Diagram of electro-fused magnesium furnace:1-transformer, 2-short circuit network, 3-electrode holder,4-electrode, 5-furnace shell, 6-trolley, 7-electric arc, 8-burden

In the melting process, voltage flicker is a kind of power quality problems, which occurs in the power system when the gas aggregates quickly in the magnesia. The EFMF in this paper takes the light-burned magnesia as the raw material. It makes use of the heat generated both by the burden resistance when the current through the burden

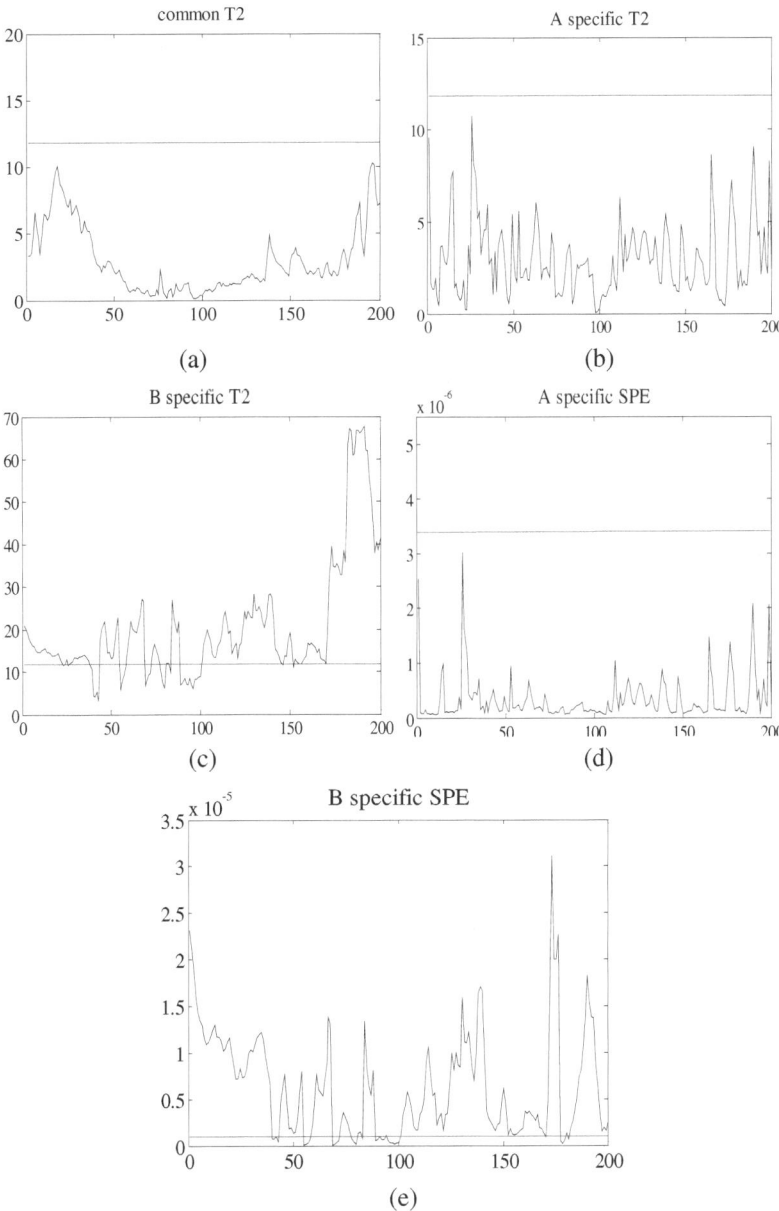

Fig. 2. Monitoring results by different modes for (a) common systematic information; (b) and (c) specific systematic information; (d) and (e) residual information

and the arc between the electrodes and the burden to melt the burden, and then obtain the fused magnesia crystals with higher purity. The materials are powdery magnesium in mode A. The materials are massive magnesium in mode B.

In total, 40 normal batch runs are generated in mode A and 40 normal batches runs in mode B, after the data processing in the above section, the data sets $\Phi(\mathbf{X}_A)$ and $\Phi(\mathbf{X}_B)$ are obtained. There are 3 variables in both dataset $\Phi(\mathbf{X}_A)$ and in dataset $\Phi(\mathbf{X}_B)$. First, a batch run is used to test the feasibility of the method. As is shown in Figures 2 (a), the consecutive T^2 statistics values can be enclosed by the confidence region. Then the group affiliation can be further checked by monitoring specific systematic information as shown in Figure 2 (b) and (c). Obviously, due to use of different specific parts, the out-of-control indications in mode B are more obvious compared with those shown in mode A. For example, the T^2 values occur in mode B. Combining their monitoring results in both subspaces, the affiliation of the two modes is definitely fixed and the operation status is also checked for systematic information in both subspaces. Finally, the residual information is supervised and shown in Figure 2 (d) and (e), which also indicates that the current batch is operating normally.

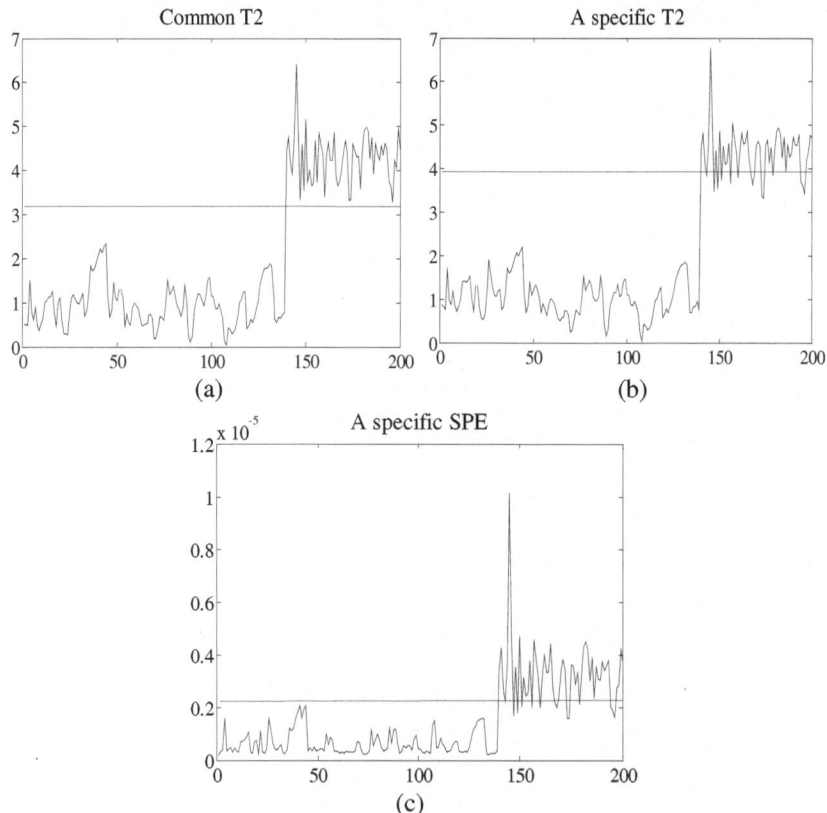

Fig. 3. Monitoring results by different modes for (a) common systematic information; (b) specific systematic information; (c) residual information

At the same time, from above analysis, the electro-fused magnesia furnace is working in which mode can be judged. From the Figure 2, T^2 of the common and the specific part are enclosed by the confidence region in mode A, and SPE of mode A also shows there are no faults. While T^2 of the specific go beyond the confidence region in mode B, SPE shows the test data is normal. From the test results of mode A, the test data is deemed to be a normal data. From the test results of mode B, the common part of mode B is under control, but the specific part of mode B is abnormal. That means the test data is normal data belongs to mode A.

Then an abnormal batch run, which belongs to mode A, is applied in proposed method. Process faults are introduced from the 140th sample. As is shown in Figure 3 (a), in the common part, there are some samples which are not enclosed by the confidence region, and some part of the faults is not very obvious. Further checked by monitoring specific systematic information is obvious that there are faults which start from 140 approximately in Figure 3 (b). And the residual information is supervised which reveals the faults in the batch in Figure 3 (c). Generally, clear and stable alarms are revealed especially by the T^2 monitoring system in specific systematic subspace, which means the abnormal behavior mainly disturbs the specific part of information.

In the proposed method, the common information is used for the overall analysis and the specific information is used for the local analysis.

5   Conclusion

In this work, a new method was proposed for analysis of multi-mode batches. Since the cross-mode correlations were considered, the multimode was separated more correctly in the proposed method. The LTSA algorithm is applied to the multi-mode batches process. And a common subspace is extracted via the new method proposed. However, in the conventional method, two different common subspace are extracted from mode A and mode B. The common information was the similar variable correlations over modes, and the specific information was the difference in each mode. And then he underlying variations of different modes can be analyzed more comprehensively by dataset decomposition and subspace separation. The strengths of the proposed strategy laid in not only the effective monitoring but also the appealing analysis results and comprehension for multi-mode problem. Fault detection can be accurate and obvious. The case of electro-fused magnesia furnace illustrated its effectiveness. What's more, considering the nonlinearity of data, the kernel trick may be introduced into the proposed method, which can deal with the nonlinear problem.

References

1. Ge, Z., Gao, F.R., Song, Z.H.: Two-dimensional Bayesian monitoring method for nonlinear multimode processes. Chemical Engineering Science 66, 5173–5183 (2011)
2. Wang, X., Kruger, U., Lennox, B.: Recursive partial least squares algorithms for monitoring complex industrial processes. Control Engineering Practice 11, 613–632 (2003)

3. Kruger, U., Dimitriadis, G.: Diagnosis of process faults in chemical systems using a local partial least squares approach. AIChE J. 54, 2581–2596 (2008)
4. Zhao, C.H., Mo, S.Y., Gao, F.R.: Statistical analysis and online monitoring for handling multiphase batch processes with varying durations. Journal of Process Control 21, 817–829 (2011)
5. Zhang, Y.W., Qin, S.J.: Improved nonlinear fault detection technique and statistical analysis. AIChE J. 54, 3207–3220 (2008)
6. Zhang, Y.W., Zhou, H., Qin, S.J., Chai, T.Y.: Decentralized fault diagnosis of large-scale processes using multiblock kernel partial least squares. IEEE Transactions on Industrial Informatics 6, 3–12 (2010)
7. Zhang, Y.W., Qin, S.J.: Nonlinear Fault Detection Technique and Statistical Analysis. AIChE J. 54(12), 3207–3220 (2008)
8. Singhai, A., Seborg, D.E.: Evaluation of a pattern matching method for the Tennessee Eastman challenge process. J. Process Control 16, 601–613 (2007)
9. Qin, S.J.: Recursive PLS algorithms for adaptive data monitoring. Comput. Chem. Eng. 22, 503–514 (1998)
10. Li, W., Yue, H.H., Valle-Cervantes, S., Qin, S.J.: Recursive PCA for adaptive process monitoring. J. Process Control 10, 471–486 (2000)
11. de Silva, V., Tenenbaum, J.B.: Global versus local methods in nonlinear di-mensionality reduction. In: Advances in Neural Information Processing Systems 15, pp. 721–728. MIT Press, Cambridge (2003)
12. Ham, J., Lee, D.D., Mika, S., Schokopf, B.: A kernel view of the dimensionality reduction of manifolds. In: Proc. Int. Conf. Mach. Learn., Banff, AB, Canada, pp. 369–376 (2004)
13. Lee, J.A., Verleysen, M.: Nonlinear Dimensionality Reduction. Springer, New York (2007)
14. Yan, S., Xu, D., Zhang, B., Zhang, H.: Graph embedding: A general framework for di-mensionality reduction. In: Proc. IEEE Comput. Soc. Conf. Comput. Vis. Pattern Recog., San Diego, CA, pp. 830–837 (2005)
15. Tenenbaum, J.B., de Silva, V., Langford, J.C.: A global geometric framework for nonlinear dimensionality reduction. Science 290(5500), 2319–2323 (2000)
16. Roweis, S., Saul, L.: Nonlinear dimensionality reduction by locally linear embedding. Science 290(5500), 2323–2326 (2000)
17. Belkin, M., Niyogi, P.: Laplacian eigenmaps for dimensionality reduction and data representation. Neural Comput. 15(6), 1373–1396 (2003)
18. Zhang, Z., Zha, H.: Principal manifolds and nonlinear dimensionality reduction via tangent space alignment. SIAM J. Sci. Comput. 26(1), 313–338 (2004)
19. Levin, A., Lischinski, D., Weiss, Y.: A closed form solution to natural image matting. In: Proc. Int. Conf. Comput. Vis. Pattern Recog., New York, pp. 61–68 (2006)
20. Xiang, S., Nie, F., Pan, C., Zhang, C.: Regression Reformulations of LLE and LTSA With Locally Linear Transformation. IEEE Transactions on Systems 41(5), 1250–1262 (2011)

Modeling Rate-Dependent and Thermal-Drift Hysteresis through Preisach Model and Neural Network Optimization Approach[*]

Shunli Xiao[1] and Yangmin Li[1,2,**]

[1] Department of Electromechanical Engineering, University of Macau, Macao, China
[2] School of Mechanical Engineering, Tianjin University of Technology, Tianjin, China
ymli@umac.mo

Abstract. Smart material actuators like Piezoelectric(PZT) are widely used in Micro/Nano manipulators, but their hysteresis behaviors are complex and difficult to model. Most hysteresis models are based on elementary quasistatic operators and are not suitable for modeling rate-dependent or thermal-drift behaviors of the actuators. This work proposes a Preisach model based neurodynamic optimization model to account for the complex hysteresis behaviors of the smart material actuator system. Through simulation study, the rate-dependent and the thermal-drift behaviors are simulated via Bouc-Wen model. The μ-density function of the Preisach model is identified on-line through neurodynamic optimization method to suit for the varied rate of the input signals. The output of the actuator system is predicated in realtime based on the on-line identified μ-density plane. It is shown experimentally that the predicated hysteresis loops match the simulated PZT loops very well.

Keywords: Hysteresis, Preisach Model, Bouc-Wen Model, Neurodynamic optimization.

1 Introduction

Smart material actuators like piezoceramic (PZT) with advantages of high output force, large bandwidth and fast response time have found increasing applications in micro/nono technology. Nevertheless, like many other intelligent materials, the PZT possesses a natural hysteresis characteristics which brings a severe positioning error to the system and affects the performance of the system especially for those cases requiring precise micromanipulation [1]. Even worse, the hysteresis is rate-dependent, that means, increasing with the rate of input driving signal of the PZT, the hysteretic loop is varied and becomes larger and rounder. This characteristics not only bring errors to the system, but also causes

---

[*] This work was supported in part by National Natural Science Foundation of China (Grant No. 61128008), Macao Science and Technology Development Fund (Grant No. 016/2008/A1), and Research Committee of University of Macau (Grant No. MYRG203(Y1-L4)-FST11-LYM).
[**] Corresponding author.

J. Wang, G.G. Yen, and M.M. Polycarpou (Eds.): ISNN 2012, Part I, LNCS 7367, pp. 179–187, 2012.

troubles to the compensator and controller, because it brings difficulty in modeling and even causes some close-loop controller instability.

Various methods were developed to model the hysteresis problems, such as the Preisach model [2], Maxwell model [3], Duhem model [4], Bouc-Wen model [5], Prandtl-Ishlinskii model [6][7], Ishlinskii hysteresis (IM) model [8][9], and ANN models [10], etc. But most of those works are focused on canceling stationary hysteresis problems, however, many applications of the PZT are in the situations of dynamic environment, and the hysteresis behavior are drifting caused by the thermal property of the PZT. Therefore, finding a model with characteristics of less time consuming, rate-dependent and high accuracy compensation for a real time control system is very necessary. In this research, the numerical expression of the classical Preisach model is introduced, the μ density function is identified on-line via neural network optimization method, and the performance of the μ density functions are verified by numerical simulation experiment. The good agreement between the measured and predicted curves shows that the classical Preisach model is an effective way for modeling the hysteresis of the piezoceramic actuator system. The proposed method can be extended to model electromagnetic actuators as well [11].

2   Experimental Setup and Simulation Model

The experimental setup is shown in Fig.1. The dSPACE is a realtime system running in Matlab simulink(real time instrument)RTI environment. The adopted dSPACE is with DS1005 DSP board and DS2001 and DS2002 in the chases, but only DS1005 board is used here to run the simulation models in current research. It is adopted to simulate the hysteresis as well as the realtime on-line predication ability of the proposed rate-dependent and thermal-drift hysteresis model in a real time environment.

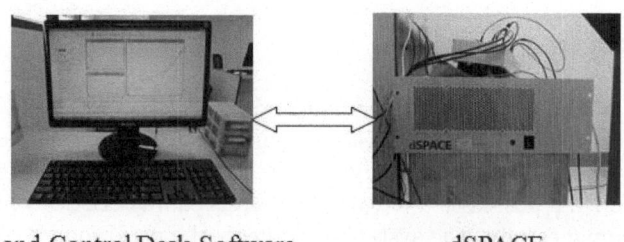

PC and Control Desk Software   dSPACE

Fig. 1. Realtime simulation hardware

Bouc-Wen model is adapted to simulate the piezoelectric actuators, which can be described as follows [5]:

$$y(t) = \dot{u} - h$$
$$\dot{h} = \alpha \dot{u} - \beta |\dot{u}|h - \gamma \dot{u}|h| \tag{1}$$

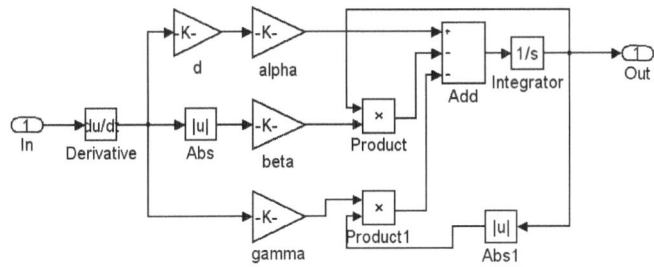

Fig. 2. Structure of the Bouc-Wen model

where y is the output displacement, h denotes the hysteresis loop in terms of displacement whose magnitude and shape are determined by parameters α, β and γ. A rate-dependent and thermal-drift hysteresis can be simulated by tuning the parameters as shown in Fig.2.

To study the rate-dependent property of the smart material actuators like PZT, the rate-dependent hysteresis behaviors are simulated via Bouc-Wen model through changing the parameters of α, β and γ for different input signals with different frequencies. The simulated relationship between response and the input signals can be observed in Fig.3(a). It shows that the higher frequency, the larger hysteresis loop, which means that the hysteresis problem of the PZT is rate-dependent. It is a typically rate-dependent hysteresis loop which can be found in literature or obtain through experiment easily. Furthermore, as we can always meet the phenomenon as shown in Fig.3(b) that the hysteresis loops drift after a long time running of the PZT or electromagnetic actuators. Since no exact reasons are found for that phenomenon, we just call it thermal-drifting.

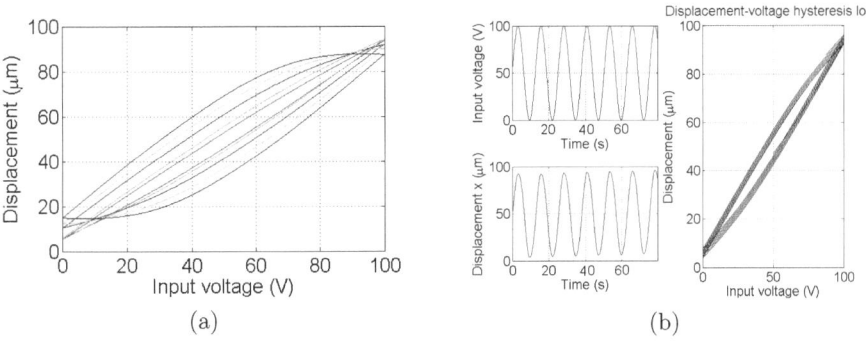

Fig. 3. Simulation of hysteresis loops via Bouc-Wen model, (a) Rate-dependent hysteresis loops, (b) Thermal-drift hysteresis loops

3   Introduction to Preisach Hysteresis Model

After the hysteresis behaviors of the PZT are simulated through Bouc-Wen model, Preisach model is used to model the complex hysteresis behaviors. Even though the Bouc-Wen model can be used to model the hysteresis problems, seldom hysteresis loops are symmetry and regular in the real situation. Aiming for suiting the most hysteresis behaviors of the smart materials like PZT, Preisach model is selected to model the complex hysteresis loops in terms of rate-dependent and thermal-drifting hysteresis characteristics.

The Preisach hysteresis model originates from the process of investigating the physical mechanisms of magnetization. At the beginning, the Preisach model is regarded as a physical model of hysteresis, which is in fact a general numerical method for Preisach problems in wide fields. As a mathematical principle, many rules and properties are investigated systemically. Mathematically, the classical Preisach model can be written as follows[12]:

$$y(t) = \int \int_{\alpha \geq \beta} \mu(\alpha, \beta) \gamma_{\alpha\beta}[u(t)] d\alpha d\beta \tag{2}$$

where $y(t)$ is the output of the system, $\mu(\alpha, \beta)$ is a density weighting function, $\hat{\gamma}_{\alpha\beta}[u(t)]$ is the hysteresis operator with output of +1 or -1, and α and β represent increase and decrease switching step of values of the input $u(t)$, respectively, as shown in Fig.4.

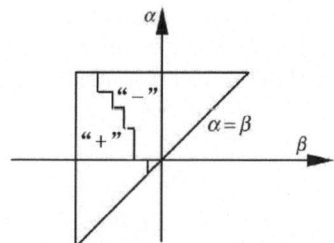

Fig. 4. μ weight density function plane and the memory curve

The result of $\gamma_{\alpha\beta}[u(t)]$ is set to +1 or -1 as the input value runs up over the switching value α or goes down below the switching value β. The product of the weighting function $\mu(\alpha, \beta)$ and the operator is integrated over the triangle T, which is the predication value of the corresponding hysteresis loop.

4   Off-Line Pre-identification of the Density Plane for Preisach Model

For some μ-density weight functions known hysteresis system, the predication of the output to construct the hysteresis loop is a easy work, but for some known hysteresis loops measured by experiment, the identification of the density weight function $\mu(\alpha, \beta)$ is always a hard work [13]. Many methods can be used to identify the density weight function, a numerical method is adopted in this paper. Both the input function $u(t)$ and the μ weight density function are expressed in a discrete way and arranged in a vector according to the rules how and when these μ weights are integrated. Let Y be the output vector $Y = [y_1, y_2, \cdots, y_n]$, A_i be the vector of Preisach operator at the time t_1, vector X is used to denote the values of each partition x_i in μ-density plane, then, the output at time t_1 can be $y(t_1) = A_1 X + c + \varepsilon$. Notice that $A = [A_1, A_2, \cdots, A_n, 1]$, $X = [x_1, x_2, \cdot, x_n, c]$, the identification problem of the Preisach model is to find the vector X using the input and output data measured from the experiment to fit the linear equation $Y = AX + \varepsilon$. Then, the most important thing is to find a way to solve for X that will best suit for the measurement data under the condition of $x_i \geq 0$. Although the Lagrange multiplier theorem can tackle this problem, we can adopt the least square optimization method to solve it also. According to the least square principle, we can minimize the function

$$f(X) = \frac{1}{2}||AX - Y||^2 \tag{3}$$

under the inequality constraint condition of $g(X) = X > 0$.

Although the adopted least square optimization method can identify the density weight function precisely and remove effectively the influences of the sensor noises, it is really time consuming. It can only be used as the pre-identified the density weight function off-line. Aiming for constructing an on-line and less time consuming model of the PZT, a neuro-dynamic realtime online optimization method will be developed.

5   On-Line Realtime Neurodynamic Optimization

Although many researches focused on the identification problems of the hysteresis, most of them are based on off-line stationary identified method. It is hard to be used into rate-independent and thermal-drift hysteresis behaviors. In this research, the identified method should be less time consuming in real time environment. In this research, a neural network dynamic optimization method is adopted. Just the same as the most studied traditional dynamic system approach, it typically consists of three steps: to establish a dynamic system first, then to study the convergence of ODE solution, at last to solve the dynamic system numerically. For example, this problem can be solved by MATLAB routing "quadprog" function or other linear optimization programs as the last section presented. In the current research, the realtime solutions of optimization problems are demanded. However, traditional algorithms for digital computers may not be able to provide the solutions on-line in realtime. Therefore, the search for realtime on-line solutions becomes not only important but also essential. In the neural network optimization approach, even the traditional neural networks optimization method such as Genetic Algorithm(ga) method is also time consuming, an attractive and very promising neural network optimization approach based on simplified dual networks was introduced in [14][15], which can provide realtime on-line solutions for optimization problems. As shown in Fig.5, a typical architecture of the simplified dual network associated with the recursive algorithm constructs a realtime neural dynamic optimization method. It is suitable for both typical Quadratic Programming(QP) and Linear Programming(LP) optimization problem to acquire realtime solutions. In this research, the optimization problems as described in Eq.3 can be solved by the developed method easily in realtime environment.

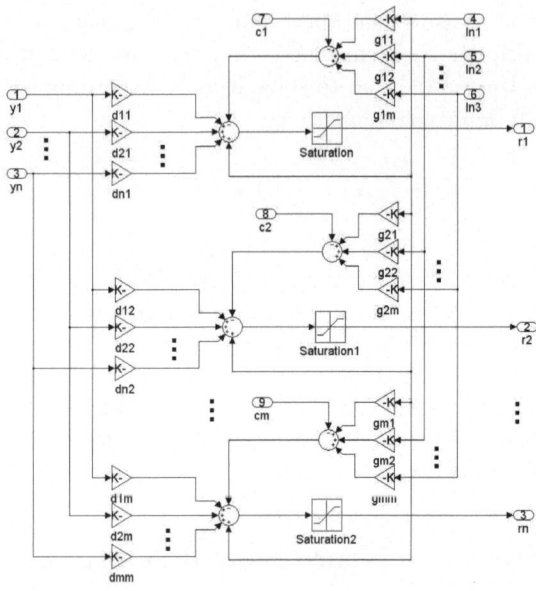

Fig. 5. Architecture of the simplified dual network

6   Numerical Simulation Tests and Discussions

After all the hysteresis simulator and the on-line realtime optimization algorithms for the μ-density function of the Preisach model are prepared well, the numerical tests can be made and run in dSPACE under MATLAB simulink environment. A typical identified μ-density plane can be shown in Fig.6, then the predicated hysteresis loop can be seen in Fig.7. It can be observed that the predicated loops matched the simulated hysteresis loops very well. As shown in Fig.8, the predicated output also matches the simulated output very well, except at the bottom and top end of the loops. The deviation at the bottom and top end of the loops may mainly comes from the numerical discrete process of the

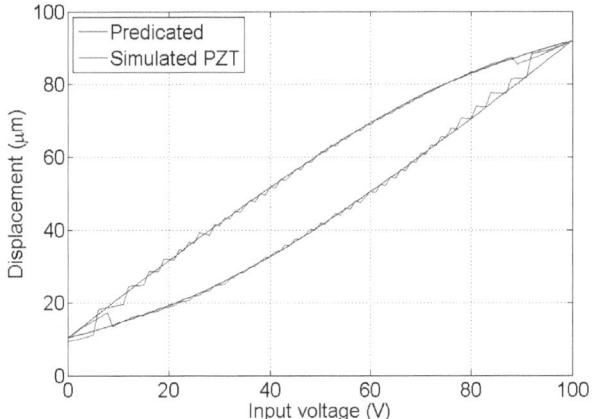

Fig. 6. Typical identified μ density function of Preisach model

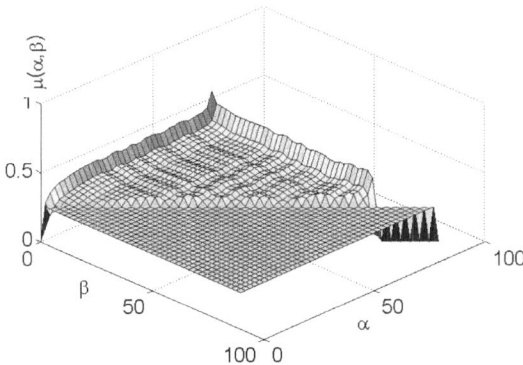

Fig. 7. Performance of the predicated loop through identified μ density function

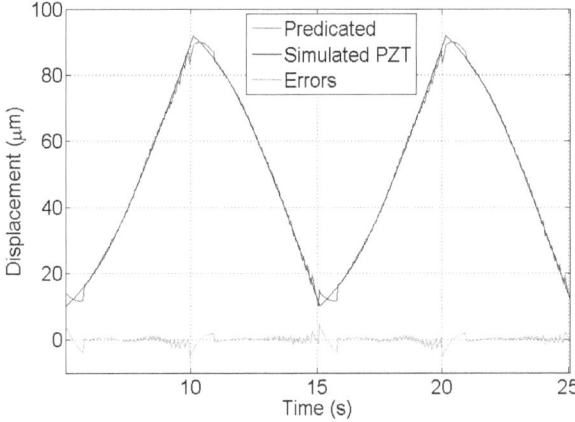

Fig. 8. Performance of the Predicated output through identified μ density function

hysteresis model. For thermal drifting problems, since the hysteresis loops can be predicated via the on-line identified Preisach model in realtime, the predicated the hysteresis problem about thermal drifting characters can be predicated in the long time running.

7   Conclusion

Errors caused by the hysteresis issue of a PZT bring much troubles to its applications in high precision field, especially the hysteresis problems are rate-dependent and thermal-drift which will further limit its performance in micro dynamic trajectory tracking. Based on neural network parameter identified optimization method, we present a rate-dependent Preisach model to predicate the output of the PZT under dynamic situation for compensation. A dual simplified neural network architecture is used to identify the μ-density function of the Preisach model on-line. The proposed method is tested through numerical simulation experiment in realtime system. The rate-dependent and thermal-drift hysteresis problems are simulated by Bouc-Wen model. The proposed predication model is constructed in MATLAB simulink realtime instrument(RTI) environment and running in dSPACE. The results show that it can predicate the hysteresis in realtime. In the experiment, two aspects of the influence to the hysteresis problems considered are the rate-dependent and thermal-drift, many other factors such as moisture and creep for any kinds of smart materials can be included into the model to further increase the accuracy. Furthermore, if the proposed method is used as feed-forward compensator and feedback close-loop controller is added on the whole cascade compensator and PZT system, the accuracy can be increased significantly. Then, the proposed compensator can be widely applied in all kinds of situations with hysteresis problems.

References

1. Xiao, S., Li, Y., Zhao, X.: Design And Analysis of a Novel Micro-Gripper With Completely Parallel Movement of Gripping Arms. In: IEEE Conference on Industrial Electronics and Applications, Beijing, China, pp. 2121–2126 (2011)
2. Weibel, F., Michellod, Y., Mullhaupt, P., Gillet, D.: Real-Time Compensation of Hysteresis in a Piezoelectric-Stack Actuator Tracking a Stochastic Reference. In: Proceedings of the American Control Conference, pp. 2939–2944 (2008)
3. Goldfarb, M., Celanovic, N.: Modeling Piezoelectric Stack Actuators for Control of Micromanipulation. IEEE Transactions on Control Systems Technology 17(3), 69–79 (1997)
4. Stepanenko, Y., Su, C.-Y.: Intelligent Control of Piezoelectric Actuators. In: Proc. IEEE Conf. Decision Control, Tampa, FL, pp. 4234–4239 (1998)
5. Lin, C.-J., Yang, S.R.: Precise Positioning of Piezo-Actuated Stages Using Hysteresis-Observer Based Control. Mechatronics 16(7), 417–426 (2006)
6. Kuhnen, K.: Modeling, Identification and Compensation of Complex Hysteretic Nonlinearities: A Modified Prandtl-Ishlinskii Approach. European Journal of Control 9(4), 407–418 (2003)

7. Bashash, S., Jalili, N.: Robust Multiple Frequency Trajectory Tracking Control of Piezoelectrically Driven Micro/Nanopositioning Systems. IEEE Transactions on Control Systems Technology 15(5), 867–878 (2007)
8. Ha, J.-L., Kung, Y.-S., Fung, R.-F., Hsien, S.-C.: A Comparison of Fitness Functions for The Identification of a Piezoelectric Hysteretic Actuator Based on the Real-Coded Genetic Algorithm. Sensors and Actuators A 132(2), 643–650 (2006)
9. Lee, S.-H., Ozer, M.B., Royston, T.J.: Piezoceramic Hysteresis in the Adaptive Structural Vibration Control Problem. Journal of Intelligent Material Systems and Structures 13(2-3), 117–124 (2002)
10. Lin, F.-J., Shieh, H.-J., Huang, P.-K., Teng, L.-T.: Adaptive Control with Hysteresis Estimation and Compensation Using RFNN for Piezo-Actuator. IEEE Transactions on Ultrasonics, Ferroelectrics, and Frequency Control 53(9), 1649–1661 (2006)
11. Xiao, S., Li, Y., Zhao, X.: Design and Analysis of a Novel Flexure-based XY Micropositioning Stage Driven by Electromagnetic Actuators. In: International Conference on Fluid Power and Mechatronics, Beijing, China, pp. 953–958 (2011)
12. Mayergoyz, I.: Mathematical Models of Hysteresis and Their Applications, 2nd edn. Academic Press (August 29, 2003)
13. Shirley, M.E., Venkataraman, R.: On the Identification of Preisach Measures. In: Proceedings of the SPIE, Smart Structures and Materials, Modeling, Signal Processing, and Control, vol. 5049, pp. 326–336 (2003)
14. Liu, S., Wang, J.: A Simplified Dual Neural Network for Quadratic Programming with Its KWTA Application. IEEE Transaction on Neurial Networks 17(6), 1500–1511 (2006)
15. Xia, Y.: A New Neural Network for Solving Linear and Quadratic Programming Problems. IEEE Transaction On Neurial Networks 1(6), 1544–1547 (1996)

The Neuron's Modeling Methods
Based on Neurodynamics

Xiaoying He[1], Yueping Peng[2], and Haiqing Gao[3]

[1] School of Management and Economics, Xi'an Technological University, 710032 Xi'an, China
He99@sohu.com
[2] Information Engineering Department, Engineering University of Chinese Armed Police Force,
710086 Xi'an, China
Percy001@163.com
[3] School of Management, Yulin University, 719000 Yulin, China
Liuzhuzhu@126.com

Abstract. In the paper, based on the neurodynamics theory, the neuron's dynamic description and how to build the neuron's dynamic model are analyzed and generalized from the dynamics angle. The building methods and the building procedures of the neuron model based on neurodynamics and electrophysiology are systematically put forward. The modeling methods and the modeling procedures are systematical summaries and sublimations of the neuron's modeling theories and achievements in recent years, and have the important guiding significance for the neuron's modeling based on the neurodynamics theory.

Keywords: Neurodynamics, Neuron, Model, Electrophysiology.

1 Introduction

In 1952, Hodgkin and Huxley recorded the squid gigantic axon's rest potential and active potential from the intracellular by the glasscapillary electrode for the first time, and based on these recorded data's processing quantitatively, they built the famous Hodgkin-Huxley(H-H) model which can describe precisely the discharge actions of the squid gigantic axon membrane[1-4]. The H-H neuron model describes quantitatively the action potential of the neuron membrane, and is the basic model of all excitable cells. The H-H neuron model also establishes the theoretical basis for the neuron dynamic model's building. Based on the H-H model, people have measured the related parameters of the neuron by the electrophysiological experiments. These parameters include dynamic parameters, discharge frequency, the maximum conductance of the neuron's currents, and so on. Based on the measured experiment data, people have built all kinds of neuron model resembling the H-H model and meeting the actual demands[5-19].

However, it is very difficult to build a perfect neuron model meeting the actual demands. The primal problem is how to get accurately the values of the parameters.

J. Wang, G.G. Yen, and M.M. Polycarpou (Eds.): ISNN 2012, Part I, LNCS 7367, pp. 188–195, 2012.

Because the individual neuron has the difference each other, even if the measured neurons are from the same neuron kind, the measured values of the same parameter may have the large difference, which consumedly affects valuing of the model's parameter. Moreover, the measured difference sometimes causes the error of the parameter's value. In addition, some parameters of the neuron can't be measured at all, so people often estimate these parameters' values by the fine-tuning process[20]. But the gotten values of the parameters in this way are accurate or not, which has been a dispute so far.

From the neurodynamics angle, a perfect neuron model can not only copy the electrophysiological characteristics of the neuron, but also meet the dynamic bifurcation characteristics of the neuron. So based on the neurodynamics theory, we can get the related parameters' values of the neuron by getting the neuron's dynamic bifurcation process about the given parameter such as the neurotransmitter, the drug blocker, and so on, instead of the complex process of the former getting the parameters' values of the neuron by the electrophysiological experiments. Moreover, if some currents of the neuron are omitted or some parameters of the neuron are wrongly estimated, the neuron's dynamic bifurcation process isn't affected. So the process of getting the related parameters' values of the neuron by getting the neuron's the dynamic bifurcation process is more accurate. In this sense, it is of more practical use to give priority to getting the neuron's the dynamic bifurcation process about the given parameter in the neuron's modeling process. However, it is very difficult to realize this priority method, and it may be a dream by far[20].

In the paper, based on the neurodynamics theory and the electrophysiological theory, the neuron's dynamic description is firstly analyzed from the dynamics angle; then the modeling methods and the modeling procedures of the neuron are systematically analyzed and generalized.

2   The Neuron's Dynamic Description

The neuron is the basic unit of structure and function in the nervous system. From the neurodynamics angle, the neuron is a dynamic system, which is made up of a set of variables which change with time and describe the state's changing rule of the neuron. For an example, H-H neuron model is a four-dimension dynamic system, whose state variables are composed of the membrane potential variable, the voltage-gating activation variable of the persist potassium current, the voltage-gating activation variable of the instantaneous sodium current, and the voltage-gating inactivation variable of the instantaneous sodium current. The state's changing rule of the H-H neuron model is described by the four-dimension constant coefficient differential equation set which are consisted of the four above variables.

According to the action function and the time scale of the dynamic state variables describing the neuron's dynamic characteristics, they can usually be divided into four kinds: the membrane potential variable, the excitable variable, the recovery variable, and the adaptable variable.

The membrane potential variable describes the membrane potential's changing rule of the neuron. All neuron dynamic models include the membrane potential variable. Because many ionic channels of the neuron have the voltage-gating characteristics, the description variables of many ion currents' dynamic characteristics also have the close relation to the membrane potential.

The excitable variable's function is to make the neuron's depolarization, and to complete the action potential's ascending phase process. The usual excitable variables include the sodium current's voltage-gating activation variable, the quick potassium current's voltage-gating inactivation variable, and so on.

The recovery variable's function is to make the neuron's repolarization, and to complete the action potential's descending phase process. The usual recovery variables include the sodium current's voltage-gating inactivation variable, the quick potassium current's voltage-gating activation variable, and so on.

The adaptable variable can buildup gradually during the neuron's discharge process, and affect the neuron's excitability. The usual adaptable variables include the voltage-gating slow current's activation variable, the calcium-activated slow current's activation variable, and so on.

The neuron model can produce the action potential, which should include the membrane potential variable, the excitable variable, and the recovery variable. The adaptable variable isn't the indispensable variable for all neuron models. But for these neuron models which can reveal the dynamic characteristics such as bursting, they should include the adaptable variable. For examples, the usual H-H neuron model hasn't the adaptable variable; But the Hindmarsh-Rose neuron model (HR neuron model)[19, 21] has the adaptable variable, and can produce the bursting discharge actions.

For the voltage-gating current such as persistent potassium current and instantaneous sodium current of the neuron model, they can often be described by formula (1):

$$I = g_{MAX} m^a h^b (V - E) \tag{1}$$

Where

I —— The voltage-gating current;

g_{MAX} —— The maximum conductance of the current's corresponding ion channel;

m —— The activation variable, whose value represents probability of activation gate to be open;

a —— The number of activation gates per channel;

h —— The inactivation variable, whose value represents probability of inactivation gate to be open;

b —— The number of inactivation gates per channel;

V —— The neuron's membrane potential;

E —— The Nernst potiential.

3   The Neuron's Modeling Methods and Procedures Based on Neurodynamics

The neuron model's building successfully is based on the neurodynamics theory and the electrophysiological experimental data of the neuron's related ion channels. Under the condition of the neuron's related electrophysiological experimental data's being given, the neuron's dynamic modeling procedures are as follows:

At First, the involved current kinds of the studied neuron and their corresponding dynamic general equations are decided.

Secondly, based on the electrophysiological experimental data, the parameters' values of the currents' dynamic general equations are solved by the mathematical methods.

Thirdly, the dynamic equation set of the neuron model are built by all currents' solved dynamic equations. Based on the electrophysiological experimental data, the neuron model dynamic equations have been tested and revised until the test results are agreed to the electrophysiological experimental data and the neuron's dynamic characteristics.

3.1   Decision of the Involved Current Kinds of the Studied Neuron and Their Corresponding Dynamic General Equations

The different neurons usually have different current kinds, so the involved current kinds of the studied neuron and their corresponding dynamic general equations should be firstly decided. If the studies neuron is very new, there may be not the research data and results to refer to. But the involved current kinds of the studied neuron can be decided by the electrophysiological experiments. Under the condition of the neuron's involved current kinds' being known, each current's dynamic general equation can be written down according to the dynamic characteristics of the current. For examples, the neuron's usual currents include the leakage current, the instantaneous sodium current, the persistent sodium current, the delayed rectifier potassium current, and so on. Their dynamic characteristics can all be described by the corresponding dynamic general equations. Taking example for the instantaneous sodium current (I_{Na}), the dynamic general equation is as follows:

$$I_{Na} = g_{Na} m^3 h(V - V_{Na}) \qquad (2)$$

Where

g_{Na} —— The maximum conductance of the instantaneous sodium channel;

m —— The activation variable of the instantaneous sodium channel, which decides the open state of the instantaneous sodium channel;

h —— The inactivation variable of the instantaneous sodium channel, which decides the close state of the instantaneous sodium channel;

V_{Na} —— The Nernst potiential of the instantaneous sodium channel;

V —— The neuron's membrane potential.

3.2   The Parameter Values' Decision of the Currents' Dynamic General Equations

After each current' dynamic general equation of the studied neuron is decided, the next work is to decide the typical value of each current general equation's parameters. Values of some parameters such as the Nernst potential of ion channels often are known, which don't need to be solve. However, for different kinds of neurons, Values of some parameters such as the activation/inactivation variables' half-maximal activation/inactivation voltages and their activation/inactivation time constants are usually different. They need to be solved by the electrophysiological experiment data. For the voltage-gating activation/inactivation variables of each current, their dynamic equation description forms are the same. The description general equation is as follows:

$$\frac{dx}{dt} = \frac{x_\infty(V) - x}{\tau_x(V)} \tag{3}$$

Where

 x —— The activation/inactivation variable;
 V —— The neuron's membrane potential;
 $x_\infty(V)$ —— The stead-state activation/inactivation function;
 $\tau_x(V)$ —— The activation/inactivation time constant function.

Based on formula (3), taking example for the instantaneous sodium current (I_{Na}) described by formula (2), the activation variable(m) and the activation variable(m) can respectively be described by formula (4) and formula (5).

$$\frac{dm}{dt} = \frac{m_\infty(V) - m}{\tau_m(V)} \tag{4}$$

$$\frac{dh}{dt} = \frac{h_\infty(V) - h}{\tau_h(V)} \tag{5}$$

Where

 $m_\infty(V)$ —— The stable state activation function;
 $\tau_m(V)$ —— The activation time constant function;
 $h_\infty(V)$ —— The stable state inactivation function;
 $\tau_h(V)$ —— The inactivation time constant function.

It must be noted that because ion channels have often voltage-gating characteristics, $m_\infty(V)$, $\tau_m(V)$, $h_\infty(V)$, and $\tau_h(V)$ are related to the neuron's membrane potential V, and are the functions of membrane potential V.

 In fact, to decide the parameters' values of each current's dynamic general equation is essentially to decide the expressions of $m_\infty(V)$, $\tau_m(V)$, $h_\infty(V)$, and $\tau_h(V)$. They can be solved from the electrophysiological experimental data by the fitting algorithms. For the activation variables and the inactivation variables, their parameters' solving process and solving methods are the same. In the following, Taking example for the activation variables, it is showed how to decide the stable state activation function $m_\infty(V)$ and the activation time constant function $\tau_m(V)$.

The stable state activation function $m_\infty(V)$ is often described by the Boltzmann function, and is as follows:

$$m_\infty(V) = \frac{1}{1 + \exp(\dfrac{V_{1/2} - V}{k})} \tag{6}$$

Where

$V_{1/2}$ —— Voltage at half-maximal activation. For the inactivation variables, it is called Voltage at half-maximal inactivation;

k —— The slope factor. For the activation variable, k is positive, and for the inactivation variable, k is negative.

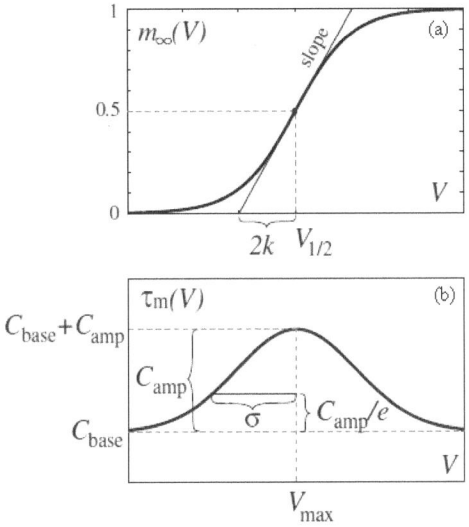

Fig. 1. The curve of the stable state activation function $m_\infty(V)$ and the curve of activation time constant function $\tau_m(V)$. (a) The curve of the stable state activation function $m_\infty(V)$. (b) The curve of the activation time constant function $\tau_m(V)$.

The parameter $V_{1/2}$ and k can be solved from the curve of the stable state activation function $m_\infty(V)$, which is gotten from the electrophysiological experimental data by the fitting of Boltzmann function. The curve of $m_\infty(V)$ is showed in Fig.1 (a)[20]. From Fig.1 (a), we can solve $V_{1/2}$ and k, and decide the stable state activation function $m_\infty(V)$. In addition, the smaller the absolute value of the slope factor k is, the steeper the activation/inactivation variable curve is.

The voltage-gating activation time constant $\tau_m(V)$ can often be estimated and described by the Gaussian function, and it is as follows:

$$\tau_m(V) = C_{base} + C_{amp} \exp[-(V_{max} - V)/\sigma^2] \qquad (7)$$

Where C_{base}, C_{amp}, V_{max}, and σ are showed in Fig.1 (b) [20].

The related parameters of formula (7) can be gotten from the curve of the activation time constant $\tau_m(V)$, which is gotten from the electrophysiological experimental data by the fitting of Gaussian function and is showed in Fig.1 (b). From Fig.1 (b), we can get the related parameters of formula (7), and decide the activation time constant $\tau_m(V)$.

After solving the stable state activation function $m_\infty(V)$ and the activation time constant function $\tau_m(V)$, we can decide the dynamic equation of activation variable m by formula (4).

The solving processes of the other variables such as the inactivation variable h are the same as or similar to the solving process of the activation variable m, and we don't introduce any longer. Therefore, to decide the parameters of the current equations is finally to solve the curve of the stable state activation/ inactivation function and the curve of the activation/inactivation time constant function from the electrophysiological experimental data by the data fitting algorithms.

3.3   The Neuron Model's Building, Testing and Revising

Under solving the related currents' dynamic equations of the neurons, we can build the neuron model's equation set by all currents' solved dynamic equations. In generally, the built neuron model need to be repeatedly tested and be revised to meet the modeling conditions and requirements. In the testing and revising process of the neuron model, not only it is based on the electrophysiological experimental data, but also it must meet the dynamic characteristics of the neuron.

It must be noted that above modeling procedures and methods are very complicated. In actual application, based on the existing neuron model, we can modify the neuron model equations' parameters by the actual electrophysiological experimental data, and get a revised new neuron model. Then, based on the revised neuron model, we can analyze and discuss its dynamic characteristics.

4   Conclusion

In the paper, based on the neurodynamics theory, the neuron's dynamic description and how to build the neuron's dynamic model are analyzed and generalized from the dynamics angle. The building methods and the building procedures of the neuron model based on neurodynamics and electrophysiology are systematically put forward. The modeling methods and the modeling procedures are systematical summaries and sublimations of the neuron's modeling theories and achievements in recent years, and have the important guiding significance for the neuron's modeling based on the neurodynamics theory.

References

1. Hodgkin, A.L., Huxley, A.F.: Currents carried by sodium and potassium ions through the membrane of the giant axon of Loligo. Journal of Physiology 116, 449–472 (1952)
2. Hodgkin, A.L., Huxley, A.F.: The components of membrane conductance in the giant axon of Loligo. Journal of Physiology 116, 473–496 (1952)
3. Hodgkin, A.L., Huxley, A.F.: The dual effect of membrane potential on sodium conductance in the giant axon of Loligo. Journal of Physiology 116, 497–506 (1952)
4. Hodgkin, A.L., Huxley, A.F.: A quantitative description of membrane and its application to conduction and excitation in nerve. Journal of Physiology 117, 500–544 (1952)
5. Frankenhaeuser, B., Huxley, A.F.: The action potential in the myelinated nerve fivre of Xenpous laevis as computed on the basis of voltage clamp data. Journal of Physiology 171(4), 302–315 (1964)
6. Adrian, R.H., Chandler, W.K., Hodgkin, A.L.: Voltage clamp experiments in striated muscle fibres. Journal of Physiology 208(5), 607–644 (1970)
7. Adrian, R.H., Peachey, L.D.: Reconstruction of the action potential of frog sartorius muscle. Journal of Physiology 235(1), 103–131 (1973)
8. Noble, D.: A modification of the Hodgkin-Huxley equation applicable to Purkinje fibre action and pacemaker potentials. Journal of Physiology 160(3), 317–352 (1962)
9. McAllister, R.E., Noble, D., Tsien, R.W.: Reconstruction of the electrical activity of cardiac Purkinje fibers. Journal of Physiology 251(1), 1–58 (1975)
10. Beeler, G.W., Reuter, H.: Reconstruction of the action potential of ventricular myocardial fibres. Journal of Physiology 235(1), 103–131 (1977)
11. Morris, C., Lecar, H.: Voltage oscillations in the barnacle giant muscle fiber. Biophysical Journal 35(2), 193–213 (1981)
12. Chay, T.R., Keizer, J.: Minimal model for membrane oscillations in the pancreatic beta-cell. Biophysical Journal 42(2), 181–190 (1983)
13. Rinzel, J., Lee, Y.S.: Dissection of a model for neuronal parabolic bursting. Journal of Mathematical Biology 25(7), 653–675 (1987)
14. Butera, R.J., Rinzel, J., Smith, J.C.: Models of respiratory rhythm generation in the pre-Botzinger complex. I. Bursting pacemaker neurons. Journal of Neurophysiology 81(4), 382–397 (1999)
15. Dayan, P., Abbott, L.F. (eds.): Theoretical Neuroscience: Computational and Mathematical Modeling of Neural Systems. MIT Press, Cambridge (2002)
16. Brunel, N., Meunier, C., Fregnac, Y.: Neuroscience and computation. Journal of Physiology-Paris 97(4), 387–390 (2003)
17. Ermentrout, G.: Type I membranes, phase resetting curves, and synchrony. Neural Computation 8(10), 979–1001 (1996)
18. Ermentrout, G., Kopell, N.: Parabolic bursting in an excitable system coupled with a slow oscillation. SIAM Journal on Applied Mathematics 46(3), 223–253 (1986)
19. Hindmarsh, J.L., Rose, R.M.: A mode of neuronal bursting using three coupled first order differential equations. Proceedings of the Royal Society of London, Series B, Biological Sciences 221(1222), 87–102 (1984)
20. Izhikevich, E.M.: Dynamical Systems in Neuroscience: The Geometry of Excitability and Bursting. The MIT Press (2005)
21. Hindmarsh, J.L., Rose, R.M.: A mode of the nerve impulse using two first-order differential equations. Nature 296, 162–164 (1982)

Stability Analysis of Multiple Equilibria for Recurrent Neural Networks

Yujiao Huang, Huaguang Zhang, Zhanshan Wang, and Mo Zhao

School of Information Science and Engineering, Northeastern University,
Shenyang, Liaoning 110819, China
hyj0507@126.com, {zhanghuaguang,wangzhanshan}@ise.neu.edu.cn,
zhaomo2008@163.com

Abstract. This paper is concerned with the dynamical stability analysis of multiple equilibrium points in recurrent neural networks with piecewise linear nondecreasing activation functions. By a geometrical observation, conditions are obtained to ensure that n-dimensional recurrent neural networks with r-stair piecewise linear nondecreasing activation functions can have $(2r + 1)^n$ equilibrium points. Positively invariant regions for the solution flows generated by the system are established. It is shown that this system can have $(r + 1)^n$ locally exponentially stable equilibrium points located in invariant regions. Moreover, the result is presented that there exist $(2r+1)^n - (r+1)^n$ unstable equilibrium points for the system. Finally, an example is given to illustrate the effectiveness of the results.

Keywords: recurrent neural network, stability, instability, activation function.

1 Introduction

In an associative memory neural network, the addressable memories or patterns are stored as stable equilibrium points or stable periodic orbits. Thus, it is required that neural networks exhibit more than one stable equilibrium point or more than one exponentially attractive periodic orbit instead of a single globally stable equilibrium point. In recent years, some sufficient conditions for multistability and multiperiodicity of recurrent neural networks have been studied in the literature, see [1]-[17] and references therein.

It is well known that the activation functions play an important role in the dynamical analysis of recurrent neural networks. The storage capacity of patterns and associative memories relies heavily on the structures of activation functions. It was shown that the n-neuron recurrent neural networks with one step piecewise linear activation functions could have 2^n locally exponentially stable equilibrium points located in saturation regions (see [7]-[9], [16]). In order to increase storage capacity, a stair-style activation function can be redefined with k steps. In [17], multistability for n-neuron neural networks with k-stair activation functions was discussed. It was shown that this system could have $(4k - 1)^n$ equilibrium

J. Wang, G.G. Yen, and M.M. Polycarpou (Eds.): ISNN 2012, Part I, LNCS 7367, pp. 196–205, 2012.
© Springer-Verlag Berlin Heidelberg 2012

points and $(2k)^n$ of them were locally exponentially stable. In [13], the authors investigated the neural networks with a class of nondecreasing piecewise linear activation functions with $2r$ corner points, and n-neuron dynamical system could have and only have $(2r+1)^n$ equilibrium points under some conditions, of which $(r+1)^n$ were locally exponentially stable and others were unstable.

There are two generally kinds of methods to study the multistability for neural networks. The one is based on decomposition of state space, and the other one is based on a geometrical observation. In [9], the authors studied multistability and multiperiodicity issues for Cohen-Grossberg neural networks by decomposition of state space. Similar approach was used in [10], [12]-[17]. Through decomposition of state space, the result in the literature relies strongly on the piecewise linearity and saturations of the standard activation function as well as subsequent partition of the phase space. In [6], by a geometrical observation, the multistability was discussed for the Hopfield neural networks with smooth sigmoidal activation functions. Similar approach was used in [7] [8]. The theory therein is primarily based upon an observation on the structures of the equations. It is thus rather general and can be applied to at least the Hopfield-type neural networks and the cellular neural networks. The analysis is valid for the networks with various activation functions, including the typical sigmoidal ones and the saturated linear ones, as well as some unbounded activation functions. In fact, a geometrical observation depends on the configuration of the activation functions instead of the precise form of the functions. Thus, the theorems are pertinent in neural networks as well.

Motivated by the above discussions, the purpose of this paper is to establish some sufficient conditions for multistability of the following recurrent neural networks with r-stair piecewise linear nondecreasing activation functions employing a geometrical observation: for $i = 1, 2, \cdots, n$.

$$\frac{dx_i(t)}{dt} = -x_i(t) + \sum_{j=1}^{n} a_{ij} f(x_j(t)) + u_i \tag{1}$$

where $\mathbf{x} = (x_1, x_2, \cdots, x_n)^T \in \mathbb{R}^n$ is the state vector; a_{ij} is the connection weight from neuron j to neuron i; $\mathbf{u} = (u_1, u_2, \cdots, u_n)^T \in \mathbb{R}^n$ is an input vector; $f(\cdot)$ is a activation function.

The main contributions of this technical note are as follows. 1) We use a geometrical observation to discuss multistability in recurrent neural networks with piecewise linear nondecreasing activation functions with $2r$ ($r \geq 1$) corner points. This system can store many more patterns or associative memories. It is meaningful in applications. 2) The existing conditions assuring existence of multiple equilibrium points of neural networks were obtained in the literature. Some of the equilibrium points were stable. However, few papers mentioned the dynamical behaviors of the remaining equilibrium points. In [13], authors indicated that the remaining equilibrium points were unstable. However, they didn't give detailed proof about the result for recurrent neural networks with activation function with $2r$ ($r \geq 1$) corner points. This paper provides detailed proof.

2   Paper Preparation

Existence and stability of stationary patterns for neural networks certainly depend on the characteristics of activation functions. To be more general, we consider a class of nondecreasing piecewise linear activation functions with $2r$ corner points, $r = 1, 2, \cdots$, which can be described by

$$
f(\xi) = \begin{cases}
m_1, & \xi \in (-\infty, p_1) \\
\frac{m_2 - m_1}{q_1 - p_1}(\xi - p_1) + m_1, & \xi \in [p_1, q_1] \\
m_2, & \xi \in (q_1, p_2) \\
\frac{m_3 - m_2}{q_2 - p_2}(\xi - p_2) + m_2, & \xi \in [p_2, q_2] \\
m_3, & \xi \in (q_2, p_3) \\
\cdots \\
\frac{m_{r+1} - m_r}{q_r - p_r}(\xi - p_r) + m_r, & \xi \in [p_r, q_r] \\
m_{r+1}, & \xi \in (q_r, +\infty)
\end{cases} \tag{2}
$$

where m_k, $k = 1, 2, \cdots, r+1$ are increasing constant series with $-\infty < m_1 < m_2 < \cdots < m_{r+1} < +\infty$; p_k, q_k, $k = 1, 2, \cdots, r$ are constants with $-\infty < p_1 < q_1 < p_2 < q_2 < \cdots < p_r < q_r < +\infty$.

Notably the stationary equation of system (1) is

$$
G_i(\mathbf{x}) := -x_i + \sum_{j=1}^{n} a_{ij} f(x_j) + u_i = 0, \ i = 1, 2, \cdots, n. \tag{3}
$$

Based on a geometrical observation, we shall consider the above activation functions and formulate sufficient conditions for the existence of multiple stationary solutions for system (1). We propose the first condition:

$$
(\mathbb{H}1): \ a_{ii} \max_{k \in 1, 2, \cdots, r} \{ \frac{m_{k+1} - m_k}{q_k - p_k} \} > 1
$$

We define, for $i = 1, 2, \cdots, n$

$$
\hat{g}_i(\zeta) = -\zeta + a_{ii} f(\zeta) + J_i^+ \tag{4}
$$

$$
\check{g}_i(\zeta) = -\zeta + a_{ii} f(\zeta) + J_i^- \tag{5}
$$

where $\zeta \in \mathbb{R}$, $J_i^+ = \sum_{j=1, j \neq i}^{n} m_{r+1} |a_{ij}| + u_i$, $J_i^- = \sum_{j=1, j \neq i}^{n} m_1 |a_{ij}| + u_i$, $r = 1, 2, \cdots$. It follows that $\check{g}_i(x_i) \leq G_i(\mathbf{x}) \leq \hat{g}_i(x_i)$ for all $\mathbf{x} = (x_1, x_2, \cdots, x_n)^T$, $i = 1, 2, \cdots, n$. We introduce a family of single neuron equations, for $i = 1, 2, \cdots, n$

$$
g_i(\zeta) := -\zeta + a_{ii} f(\zeta) + J_i
$$

where $\zeta \in \mathbb{R}$, $J_i^- \leq J_i \leq J_i^+$. Consider the second parameter condition which is used to establish existence of multiple equilibrium points for system (1):

$$
(\mathbb{H}2): \ \hat{g}_i(p_j) < 0, \ \check{g}_i(q_j) > 0, \ i = 1, 2, \cdots, n, \ j = 1, 2, \cdots, r.
$$

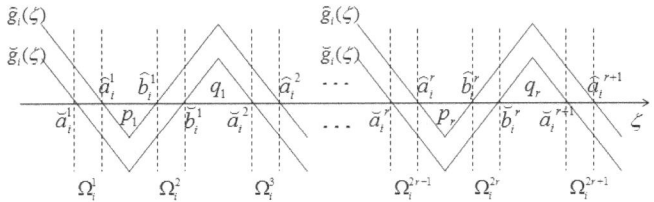

Fig. 1. The configuration of functions $\hat{g}_i(p_j)$ and $\check{g}_i(q_j)$

The configuration that motivates (ℍ2) is depicted in Fig.1.

Under assumptions (ℍ1) and (ℍ2), there exist points $\hat{a}_i^j, \hat{b}_i^j, \hat{a}_i^{r+1}, j = 1, 2, \cdots, r$ with $\hat{a}_i^1 < \hat{b}_i^1 < \hat{a}_i^2 < \hat{b}_i^2 < \cdots < \hat{a}_i^r < \hat{b}_i^r < \hat{a}_i^{r+1}$ such that $\hat{g}(\hat{a}_i^j) = \hat{g}(\hat{b}_i^j) = \hat{g}(\hat{a}_i^{r+1}) = 0, i = 1, 2, \cdots, n, j = 1, 2, \cdots, r, r = 1, 2, \cdots$ as well as $\check{a}_i^j, \check{b}_i^j, \check{a}_i^{r+1}, j = 1, 2, \cdots, r$ with $\check{a}_i^1 < \check{b}_i^1 < \check{a}_i^2 < \check{b}_i^2 < \cdots < \check{a}_i^r < \check{b}_i^r < \check{a}_i^{r+1}$ such that $\check{g}(\check{a}_i^j) = \check{g}(\check{b}_i^j) = \check{g}(\check{a}_i^{r+1}) = 0, i = 1, 2, \cdots, n, j = 1, 2, \cdots, r, r = 1, 2, \cdots$. Denote

$$[\check{a}_i^1, \hat{a}_i^1] = [\check{a}_i^1, \hat{a}_i^1]^1 \times [\hat{b}_i^1, \check{b}_i^1]^0 \times \cdots \times [\check{a}_i^{r+1}, \hat{a}_i^{r+1}]^0$$

$$[\hat{b}_i^1, \check{b}_i^1] = [\check{a}_i^1, \hat{a}_i^1]^0 \times [\hat{b}_i^1, \check{b}_i^1]^1 \times \cdots \times [\check{a}_i^{r+1}, \hat{a}_i^{r+1}]^0$$

$$\cdots$$

$$[\check{a}_i^{r+1}, \hat{a}_i^{r+1}] = [\check{a}_i^1, \hat{a}_i^1]^0 \times [\hat{b}_i^1, \check{b}_i^1]^0 \times \cdots \times [\check{a}_i^{r+1}, \hat{a}_i^{r+1}]^1$$

Denote

$$\Phi_1 = \{\prod_{i=1}^n [\check{a}_i^1, \hat{a}_i^1]^{\delta_i^{(1)}} \times [\hat{b}_i^1, \check{b}_i^1]^{\delta_i^{(2)}} \times \cdots \times [\check{a}_i^{r+1}, \hat{a}_i^{r+1}]^{\delta_i^{(2r+1)}} : (\delta_i^{(1)}, \delta_i^{(2)}, \cdots, \delta_i^{(2r+1)})$$

$$= (1, 0, \cdots, 0) \text{ or } (0, 1, \cdots, 0) \text{ or} \cdots \text{ or } (0, 0, \cdots, 1).$$

$$\Phi_2 = \{\prod_{i=1}^n [\check{a}_i^1, \hat{a}_i^1]^{\delta_i^{(1)}} \times [\hat{b}_i^1, \check{b}_i^1]^0 \times \cdots \times [\check{a}_i^{r+1}, \hat{a}_i^{r+1}]^{\delta_i^{(r+1)}} : (\delta_i^{(1)}, \delta_i^{(2)}, \cdots, \delta_i^{(r+1)})$$

$$= (1, 0, \cdots, 0) \text{ or } (0, 1, \cdots, 0) \text{ or} \cdots \text{ or } (0, 0, \cdots, 1).$$

$$\Phi_3 = \{\prod_{i=1}^n [\check{a}_i^1, \hat{a}_i^1]^0 \times [\hat{b}_i^1, \check{b}_i^1]^{\delta_i^{(1)}} \times \cdots \times [\check{a}_i^{r+1}, \hat{a}_i^{r+1}]^0 : (\delta_i^{(1)}, \delta_i^{(2)}, \cdots, \delta_i^{(r)})$$

$$= (1, 0, \cdots, 0) \text{ or } (0, 1, \cdots, 0) \text{ or} \cdots \text{ or } (0, 0, \cdots, 1).$$

$$\Phi_4 = \Phi_1 - \Phi_2 - \Phi_3.$$

where $r = 1, 2, \cdots, N_1 \cup N_2 = \{1, 2, \cdots, n\}, N_1 \cap N_2 = \emptyset$. It is easy to see that Φ_1 is composed of $(2r+1)^n$ regions, Φ_2 is composed of $(r+1)^n$ regions, Φ_3 is composed of r^n regions, and Φ_4 is composed of $(2r+1)^n - (r+1)^n - r^n$ regions.

Now, we will discuss the existence of multiple equilibrium points.

Proposition 1: There exist $(2r+1)^n$ equilibrium points for system (1) with activation function (2), under conditions (ℍ1) and (ℍ2).

Proof: The equilibrium points of system (1) are roots of stationary equation (3). For any given $\tilde{\mathbf{x}} = (\tilde{x}_1, \tilde{x}_2, \cdots, \tilde{x}_n)^T \in \Phi_1$, we solve

$$-x_i + a_{ii} f(x_i) + \sum_{j=1, j \neq i}^{n} a_{ij} f(\tilde{x}_j) + u_i = 0 \qquad (6)$$

for $i = 1, 2, \cdots, n$. Note that the graph of equation (6) is a vertical shift and lies between $\hat{g}_i$ and $\check{g}_i$ due to (4) and (5). Therefore, there exist $2r + 1$ solutions to equation (6), which lie in regions Ω_i^j, $j = 1, 2, \cdots, 2r + 1$ respectively for each i. We define a mapping $H: \Phi_1 \to \Phi_1$ by $H(\tilde{\mathbf{x}}) = \underline{\mathbf{x}} = (\underline{x}_1, \underline{x}_2, \cdots, \underline{x}_n)^T$, where $\underline{x}_i$ is the solution of (6) lying in Ω_i^j, $i = 1, 2, \cdots, n$, $j = 1, 2, \cdots, 2r + 1$. Since f is continuous, the map H is continuous. From Brouwer's fixed point theorem, there exists one fixed point $\bar{\mathbf{x}} = (\bar{x}_1, \bar{x}_2, \cdots, \bar{x}_n)^T$ of H, which is also a zero of (3). Hence, there exist $(2r + 1)^n$ equilibrium points for system (1), and each of them lies in one of the $(2r + 1)^n$ regions Φ_1. The proof is completed. $\qquad \square$

3   Main Result

In this section, we first establish some positively invariant sets for system (1) and discuss stability of the equilibrium points in each invariant set. Moreover, we also study stability of the equilibrium points which are not in positively invariant sets.

Theorem 1: Under conditions (ℍ1) and (ℍ2), each subset of Φ_2 is positively invariant with respect to the solution flow generated by system (1) with activation function (2).

Proof: Consider any initial condition $\phi = (\phi_1, \phi_2, \cdots, \phi_n)^T \in \Phi_2$. We claim that the solution $\mathbf{x}(t, \phi)$ remains in Φ_2 for all $t > 0$. If it is not true, then there exists a component $x_i(t)$ which is firstly (or one of the first ones) escaping from one subset of Φ_2. Without loss of generality, suppose $x_i(t)$ firstly escapes from $[\check{a}_i^{k_0}, \hat{a}_i^{k_0}]$ ($k_0 \in \{1, 2, \cdots, r + 1\}$). Then there exists a $t_1 > 0$ such that either $x_i(t_1) = \hat{a}_i^{k_0} + \varepsilon_0$, $(dx_i/dt)(t_1) > 0$ or $x_i(t_1) = \check{a}_i^{k_0} - \varepsilon_0$, $(dx_i/dt)(t_1) < 0$, where $\varepsilon_0 > 0$. For the first case, we derive from system (1) that

$$\frac{dx_i(t_1)}{dt} = -x_i(t_1) + a_{ii} f(x_i(t_1)) + \sum_{j=1, j \neq i}^{n} a_{ij} f(x_j(t_1)) + u_i$$

$$= -(\hat{a}_i^{k_0} + \varepsilon_0) + a_{ii} f(\hat{a}_i^{k_0} + \varepsilon_0) + \sum_{j=1, j \neq i}^{n} a_{ij} f(x_j(t_1)) + u_i$$

$$\leq -(\hat{a}_i^{k_0} + \varepsilon_0) + a_{ii} f(\hat{a}_i^{k_0} + \varepsilon_0) + \sum_{j=1, j \neq i}^{n} m_{r+1} |a_{ij}| + u_i$$

$$= \hat{g}_i(\hat{a}_i^{k_0} + \varepsilon_0)$$

$$< 0$$

This yields a contradiction to $(dx_i/dt)(t_1) > 0$. Hence, $x_i(t) \leq \hat{a}_i^{k_0}$ for all $t > 0$. With the similar proof, we can get that $x_i(t) \geq \check{a}_i^{k_0}$ for all $t > 0$. Therefore, each subset of Φ_2 is positively invariant with respect to the solution flow generated by system (1) with activation functions (2). The proof is completed.   □

In the following, we shall consider local exponential stability of system (1) with the activation function (2) in the invariant sets.

Theorem 2: If assumptions (ℍ1) and (ℍ2) hold, then there exist $(r+1)^n$ locally exponentially stable equilibrium points for system (1).

Proof: Assume $\bar{\mathbf{x}}$ is an equilibrium point lying in any subset Θ of Φ_2. Let $\mathbf{x}(t) = \mathbf{x}(t; \phi)$ be the solution to system (1) with initial condition $\phi \in \Theta$. Under the transformation $\mathbf{y}(t) = \mathbf{x}(t) - \bar{\mathbf{x}}$, system (1) becomes

$$\frac{dy_i(t)}{dt} = -y_i(t) + \sum_{j=1}^{n} a_{ij}[f(x_j(t)) - f(\bar{x}_j)] \tag{7}$$

where $\mathbf{y} = (y_1, y_2, \cdots, y_n)^T$. In Theorem 1, we have proven that each subset of Φ_2 is positively invariant with respect to the solution flow. Therefore, Θ is invariant and $\mathbf{x}(t, \phi) \in \Theta$. From $\bar{\mathbf{x}} \in \Theta$ and configuration of activation function, we can get that

$$f(x_j(t)) - f(\bar{x}_j) = 0 \tag{8}$$

where $i, j = 1, 2, \cdots, n$. It follows from (7) and (8) that

$$\frac{dy_i(t)}{dt} = -y_i(t), \quad i = 1, 2, \cdots, n$$

which implies $\bar{\mathbf{x}}$ in Θ is stable exponentially. Since Φ_2 has $(r + 1)^n$ elements, there are $(r + 1)^n$ locally exponentially stable equilibrium points for system (1). The proof is completed.   □

From Proposition 1 and Theorem 2, we have derived that there were $(2r + 1)^n$ equilibrium points for system (1), and $(r+1)^n$ of which were locally exponentially stable. Now, we will discuss what happens about the remaining $(2r+1)^n - (r+1)^n$ equilibrium points.

Theorem 3: If assumptions (ℍ1) and (ℍ2) hold, then there exist $(2r + 1)^n - (r + 1)^n$ unstable equilibrium points for system (1).

Proof: (i) Assume $\bar{\mathbf{x}}$ is an equilibrium point lying in any subset Θ of Φ_3. Let $\mathbf{x}(t) = \mathbf{x}(t; \phi)$ be the solution to system (1) with initial condition $\phi \in \Theta$. The linearized equation of system (1) at the equilibrium point $\bar{\mathbf{x}}$ is

$$\frac{dy_i(t)}{dt} = -y_i(t) + \sum_{j=1}^{n} a_{ij} \frac{m_{k_j+1} - m_{k_j}}{q_{k_j} - p_{k_j}} y_j(t) \tag{9}$$

where $i, j = 1, 2, \cdots, n$, $k_j \in \{1, 2, \cdots, r\}$, $r = 1, 2, \cdots$. System (9) can be rewritten as follows,

$$\frac{dy(t)}{dt} = Ay(t)$$

where

$$A = \begin{pmatrix} -1 + a_{11} \frac{m_{k_1+1} - m_{k_1}}{q_{k_1} - p_{k_1}} & a_{12} \frac{m_{k_2+1} - m_{k_2}}{q_{k_2} - p_{k_2}} & \cdots & a_{1n} \frac{m_{k_n+1} - m_{k_n}}{q_{k_n} - p_{k_n}} \\ a_{21} \frac{m_{k_1+1} - m_{k_1}}{q_{k_1} - p_{k_1}} & -1 + a_{22} \frac{m_{k_2+1} - m_{k_2}}{q_{k_2} - p_{k_2}} & \cdots & a_{2n} \frac{m_{k_n+1} - m_{k_n}}{q_{k_n} - p_{k_n}} \\ \cdots & \cdots & \cdots & \cdots \\ a_{n1} \frac{m_{k_1+1} - m_{k_1}}{q_{k_1} - p_{k_1}} & a_{n2} \frac{m_{k_2+1} - m_{k_2}}{q_{k_2} - p_{k_2}} & \cdots & -1 + a_{nn} \frac{m_{k_n+1} - m_{k_n}}{q_{k_n} - p_{k_n}} \end{pmatrix}$$

where $k_i \in \{1, 2, \cdots, r\}$, $i = 1, 2, \cdots, n$, $r = 1, 2, \cdots$. According to condition (H1), the trace

$$\text{trace}(A) = \sum_{i=1}^{n} [-1 + a_{ii} \frac{m_{k_i+1} - m_{k_i}}{q_{k_i} - p_{k_i}}] > 0$$

where $k_i \in \{1, 2, \cdots, r\}$, $i = 1, 2, \cdots, n$, $r = 1, 2, \cdots$, we conclude that there must be an eigenvalue λ_0 of A such that $Re(\lambda_0) > 0$. Thus, $\bar{x}$ is one unstable equilibrium point.

(ii) Assume $\bar{x}$ is an equilibrium point lying in any subset Θ of Φ_4. Denote $N_1 = \{i | \dot{f}(\bar{x}_i) = 0\}$, $N_2 = \{i | \dot{f}(\bar{x}_i) \neq 0\}$, then $N_1 \cup N_2 = \{1, 2, \cdots, n\}$, $N_1 \cap N_2 = \emptyset$. Let $\mathbf{x}(t) = \mathbf{x}(t; \phi)$ be the solution to system (1) with initial condition $\phi \in \Theta$. The linearized equation of system (1) at the equilibrium point $\bar{x}$ is

$$\frac{dy_i(t)}{dt} = -y_i(t) + \sum_{j \in N_2} a_{ij} \frac{m_{k_j+1} - m_{k_j}}{q_{k_j} - p_{k_j}} y_j(t) \tag{10}$$

where $i = 1, 2, \cdots, n$, $k_j \in \{1, 2, \cdots, r\}$, $j \in N_2$, $r = 1, 2, \cdots$. System (10) can be rewritten as follows,

$$\frac{dy(t)}{dt} = By(t) \tag{11}$$

The characteristic equation of coefficient matrix B of (11) can be written as

$$|\lambda I - B| = \prod_{i \in N_1} (\lambda + 1)|\lambda I - C| = 0$$

where matrix C is made up of the ith row and the ith column of matrix B for $i \in \{1, 2, \cdots, n\} \setminus N_1$. Because

$$\text{trace}(C) = \sum_{i \in N_2} [-1 + a_{ii} \frac{m_{k_i+1} - m_{k_i}}{q_{k_i} - p_{k_i}}] > 0$$

there must be an eigenvalue λ of C such that $Re(\lambda) > 0$. So, the matrix B has one eigenvalue with positive real-part at least. Thus, $\bar{x}$ is one unstable equilibrium point.

Since there exist $(2r + 1)^n - (r + 1)^n$ subsets in $\Phi_3 \cup \Phi_4$, system (1) has $(2r + 1)^n - (r + 1)^n$ unstable equilibrium points.   □

4   Illustrative Example

In this section, an example of system (1) is presented to illustrate our result.

Example 1: Consider the following recurrent neural networks with a piecewise linear activation function

$$\begin{cases} \dot{x}_1(t) = -x_1(t) + 2f(x_1(t)) + 0.04f(x_2(t)) + 0.1 \\ \dot{x}_2(t) = -x_2(t) + 0.07(x_1(t)) + 2f(x_2(t)) + 0.1 \end{cases} \tag{12}$$

where the activation function is described by

$$f(\xi) = \begin{cases} -5, & \xi \in (-\infty, -5) \\ 2\xi + 5, & \xi \in [-5, -3] \\ -1, & \xi \in (-3, -1) \\ \xi, & \xi \in [-1, 1] \\ 1, & \xi \in (1, 3) \\ 2\xi - 5, & \xi \in [3, 5] \\ 5, & \xi \in (5, +\infty) \end{cases} \tag{13}$$

Hence,

$$\hat{g}_1(\zeta) = -\zeta + 2f(\zeta) + 0.9$$
$$\check{g}_1(\zeta) = -\zeta + 2f(\zeta) - 0.7$$
$$\hat{g}_2(\zeta) = -\zeta + 2f(\zeta) + 0.95$$
$$\check{g}_2(\zeta) = -\zeta + 2f(\zeta) - 0.75$$

Herein, the parameters satisfy our conditions
   Condition ($\mathbb{H}1$):

$$a_{11} \max_{r=1,2,3} \{ \frac{m_{r+1} - m_r}{q_r - p_r} \} = 4 > 1$$

$$a_{22} \max_{r=1,2,3} \{ \frac{m_{r+1} - m_r}{q_r - p_r} \} = 4 > 1$$

   Condition ($\mathbb{H}2$):

$$\hat{g}_1(p_1) = -4.1 < 0, \quad \hat{g}_1(p_2) = -0.1 < 0$$
$$\hat{g}_1(p_3) = -0.1 < 0, \quad \hat{g}_2(p_1) = -4.05 < 0$$
$$\hat{g}_2(p_2) = -0.05 < 0, \quad \hat{g}_2(p_3) = -0.05 < 0$$
$$\check{g}_1(q_1) = 0.3 > 0, \quad \check{g}_1(q_2) = 0.3 > 0$$
$$\check{g}_1(q_3) = 4.3 > 0, \quad \check{g}_2(q_1) = 0.25 > 0$$
$$\check{g}_2(q_2) = 0.25 > 0, \quad \check{g}_2(q_3) = 4.25 > 0$$

The dynamics of this system are illustrated in Fig.2, where evolutions of 320 initial conditions have been tracked. There are 16 locally exponentially stable equilibrium points in the system, as confirmed by our results. The simulation demonstrates convergence to these 16 equilibrium points from initial states ϕ lying in the respective basin for the equilibrium.

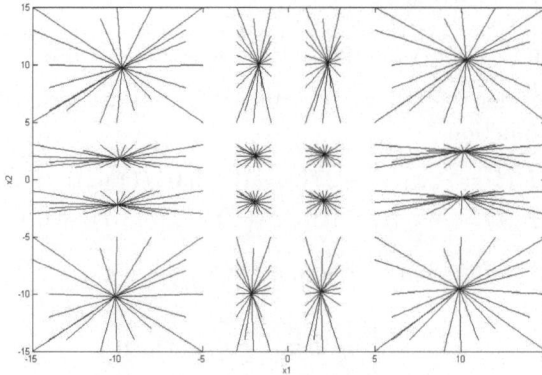

Fig. 2. Illustration for the dynamics of system (12)

5   Conclusion

In this paper, we have discussed the multistability problem for n-neuron recurrent neural networks with r-stair activation functions. With a geometrical observation, parameter conditions ($\mathbb{H}1$) and ($\mathbb{H}2$) assuring the existence of $(2r+1)^n$ equilibrium points for n-dimensional recurrent neural networks with r-stair activation functions have been derived. Under the same conditions, $(r+1)^n$ out of these $(2r+1)^n$ equilibrium points are locally exponentially stable, and others are unstable.

Acknowledgments. This work was supported by the National Natural Science Foundation of China (61034005, 61074073), the Program for New Century Excellent Talents in University of China (NCET-10-0306), the Fundamental Research Funds for the Central Universities (N110604005).

References

1. Morita, M.: Associative memory with non-monotone dynamics. Neural Networks 6(1), 115–126 (1993)
2. Yi, Z., Tan, K.: Multistability of Discrete-Time Recurrent Neural Networks With Unsaturating Piecewise Linear Activation Functions. IEEE Transactions on Neural Networks 15(2), 329–336 (2004)
3. Zhang, L., Yi, Z., Yu, J.: Multiperiodicity and Attractivity of Delayed Recurrent Neural Networks With Unsaturating Piecewise Linear Transfer Functions. IEEE Transactions on Neural Networks 19(1), 158–167 (2008)
4. Zhang, L., Yi, Z., Yu, J., Heng, P.A.: Some multistability properties of bidirectional associative memory recurrent neural networks with unsaturating piecewise linear transfer functions. Neurocomputing 72(13-15), 3809–3817 (2009)
5. Zhang, L., Yi, Z., Yu, J., Heng, P.A.: Activity Invariant Sets and Exponentially Stable Attractors of Linear Threshold Discrete-Time Recurrent Neural Networks. IEEE Transactions on Automatic Control 54(6), 1341–1347 (2009)

6. Cheng, C., Lin, K., Shih, C.: Multistability in recurrent neural networks. SIAM Journal on Applied Mathematics 66(4), 1301–1320 (2006)
7. Cheng, C., Lin, K., Shih, C.: Multistability and convergence in delayed neural networks. Physica D: Nonlinear Phenomena 225(1), 61–64 (2007)
8. Huang, G., Cao, J.: Multistability in bidirectional associative memory neural networks. Physics Letters A 372(16), 2842–2854 (2008)
9. Cao, J., Feng, G., Wang, Y.: Multistability and multiperiodicity of delayed Cohen-Grossberg neural networks with a general class of activation functions. Physica D: Nonlinear Phenomena 237(13), 1734–1749 (2008)
10. Huang, Y., Zhang, X.: Multistability properties of linear threshold discrete-time recurrent neural networks. International Journal of Information and Systems Sciences 7(1), 1–10 (2010)
11. Chen, T., Amari, S.: New theorems on global convergence of some dynamical systems. Neural Networks 14(4), 251–255 (2001)
12. Wang, L., Lu, W., Chen, T.: Multistability and new attraction basins of almost periodic solutions of delayed neural networks. IEEE Transactions on Neural Networks 20(3), 1581–1593 (2009)
13. Wang, L., Lu, W., Chen, T.: Coexistence and local stability of multiple equilibria in neural networks with piecewise linear nondecreasing activation functions. Neural Networks 23(2), 189–200 (2010)
14. Zeng, Z., Huang, D., Wang, Z.: Memory pattern analysis of cellular neural networks. Physics Letters A 342(1-2), 114–128 (2005)
15. Zeng, Z., Wang, J.: Multiperiodicity of discrete-time delayed neural networks evoked by periodic external inputs. IEEE Transactions on Neural Networks 17(5), 1141–1151 (2006)
16. Zeng, Z., Wang, J.: Multiperiodicity and exponential attractivity evoked by periodic external inputs in delayed cellular neural networks. Neural Computation 18(4), 848–870 (2006)
17. Zeng, Z., Huang, T., Zheng, W.: Multistability of Recurrent Neural Networks with Time-varying Delays and the Piecewise Linear Activation Function. IEEE Transactions on Neural Networks 21(8), 1371–1377 (2010)

Addressing the Local Minima Problem
by Output Monitoring and Modification Algorithms

Sin-Chun Ng[1], Chi-Chung Cheung[2], Andrew kwok-fai Lui[1], and Hau-Ting Tse[1]

[1] School of Science and Technology, The Open University of Hong Kong,
30 Good Shepherd Street, Homantin, Hong Kong
scng@ouhk.edu.hk
[2] Department of Electronic and Information Engineering,
The Hong Kong Polytechnic University, Hunghom, Hong Kong
encccl@polyu.edu.hk

Abstract. This paper proposes a new approach called output monitoring and modification (OMM) to address the local minimum problem for existing gradient-descent algorithms (like BP, Rprop and Quickprop) in training feed-forward neural networks. OMM monitors the learning process. When the learning process is trapped into a local minimum, OMM changes some incorrect output values to escape from such local minimum. This modification can be repeated with different parameter settings until the learning process converges to the global optimum. The simulation experiments show that a gradient-descent learning algorithm with OMM has a much better global convergence capability than those without OMM but their convergence rates are similar. In one benchmark problem (application), the global convergence capability was increased from 1% to 100%.

Keywords: local minimum problem, back-propagation, Rprop, Quickprop.

1 Introduction

Gradient descent algorithms are the most widely used class of algorithms for training multi-layer feed forward neural networks, and back-propagation algorithm (BP) [1] is the most popular gradient descent algorithm. BP is a first-order method that minimizes the error function using the steepest descent algorithm. BP is simple and has low computational complexity; however, it suffers from slow convergence rate due to the premature saturation, sometimes referred as the "flat spot" problem [2, 3]. If the learning process is get trapped in a flat spot, the weight adjustment of the algorithm will become very slow or even stopped. Furthermore, BP will easily get trapped in local minima and cannot converge to the global optimum, especially for non-linearly separable problems such as the exclusive-or (XOR) problem [4, 5]. To overcome these problems, different kinds of modified BP algorithms have been proposed to improve its performance. Quickprop [6] and Rprop [7] are the most popular fast learning methods because they are direct, computationally cheap, and easy to implement. Although Quickprop and Rprop can greatly improve the learning speed of BP, their performance is still limited by the local minimum problem.

J. Wang, G.G. Yen, and M.M. Polycarpou (Eds.): ISNN 2012, Part I, LNCS 7367, pp. 206–216, 2012.

The problem of local minima is caused by gradient descent algorithm which is used for searching the global optimal solution [5]. Training is believed to have reached the local minimum when the error function does not have an obviously change through a large number of epochs because the change of weight become negligible. The output of the neural network will remain unchanged due to the insignificant change of weight. Therefore the target value of error can never be reached and thus the training will be failed.

Some algorithms have recently been developed to solve the local minimum problem [8-10]. Mutation is a common operation used in genetic algorithms (GA), which is employed in BP to generate the mutant weights during the weight update rule to compare with the trained weights updated by the training [8]. If the mutant weights have a better performance than the actual weights, the trained weights will be replaced by the mutant weights. It is hoped that the training process can escape from local minima by using mutation. However, this approach can only be used with a small learning rate and the mutation effect is not effective in a learning process with a large learning rate. An algorithm has been used in adapting the activation function to avoid the hidden neurons reaching saturation [9]. However, the results for real-case problems were not given. DWM (Deterministic Weight Modification) is another algorithm used to solve the local minimum problem [10]. It produces a variation on the weights in a deterministic way to escape from a local minimum. When the weight update rule is applied, several sets of weights will be generated based on the estimation of the location of the global minimum. The best set of weights which has the best performance will replace the original weights. Therefore, the performance of the training process has not only improved the speed but also the global convergence capability. Note that these three algorithms cannot totally solve the local minimum problem.

This paper proposes a new method called Output Monitoring and Modification (OMM) which can be applied to gradient-descent learning algorithms to address the local minimum problem. It monitors the learning process and changes some incorrect output nodes in a systematic manner when it is trapped into a local minimum. This method can be repeated with different parameters until the global optimum is found. The paper is organized as follows. Section 2 describes some popular gradient descent algorithms. Section 3 introduces the OMM methodology and also its variation, OMM-R (OMM with Reiteration). Section 4 shows the simulation results of the proposed algorithms and compares them with other gradient descent algorithms. Conclusions are drawn in Section 5.

2 Gradient Descent Algorithms

Consider a network with three layers (including input, hidden and output layers) having N input neurons, K hidden neurons and M output neurons. Assume ω_{km} is the weight between the m-th output neurons and the k-th hidden neuron, and $\overline{\omega}_{nk}$ is the weight between the k-th hidden neurons and the n-th input neuron. The desired output for the m-th output neuron due to the p-th input pattern is given as t_{pm}. The input for the n-th input neuron due to the p-th input pattern is denoted as x_{pn}. Using the above definition, the output of the k-th node in the hidden layer is given by:

$$\bar{o}_{pk} = f(\textstyle\sum_{n=1}^{N} \bar{\omega}_{nk}\, x_{pn}) \tag{1}$$

where f is the activation (sigmoid) function defined as

$$f(x) = 1/(1+e^{-x}). \tag{2}$$

Similarly, the output of the m-th node in the output layer is:

$$o_{pm} = f(\textstyle\sum_{k=1}^{K} \omega_{km}\, \bar{o}_{pk}) \tag{3}$$

The first derivative of the sigmoid function is:

$$f'(x) = e^{-x}/(1+e^{-x})^2 = f(x)(1-f(x)). \tag{4}$$

The sum of the squared error of the system is given as:

$$E = \tfrac{1}{2}\textstyle\sum_{p=1}^{P}\sum_{m=1}^{M}(t_{pm} - o_{pm})^2 \tag{5}$$

The gradient descent method is designed to change the current weights ω_{km} and $\bar{\omega}_{nk}$ iteratively such that the system error function E is minimized. The weight updates are proportional to the partial derivative of E.

The partial derivative of E with respect to ω_{km} is:

$$\frac{\partial E}{\partial \omega_{km}} = \frac{\partial E}{\partial o_{pm}} \cdot \frac{\partial o_{pm}}{\partial \omega_{km}} \tag{6}$$

where
$$\frac{\partial E}{\partial o_{pm}} = o_{pm} - t_{pm} \quad \text{and} \quad \frac{\partial o_{pm}}{\partial \omega_{km}} = o_{pm}(1-o_{pm})\bar{o}_{pk} \tag{7}$$

And the partial derivative of E with respect to $\bar{\omega}_{nk}$ is:

$$\frac{\partial E}{\partial \bar{\omega}_{nk}} = \sum_{m=1}^{M} \frac{\partial E}{\partial o_{pm}} \cdot \frac{\partial o_{pm}}{\partial \bar{o}_{pk}} \cdot \frac{\partial \bar{o}_{pk}}{\partial \bar{\omega}_{nk}} \tag{8}$$

Where
$$\frac{\partial o_{pm}}{\partial \bar{o}_{pk}} = o_{pm}(1-o_{pm})\,\omega_{km} \quad \text{and} \quad \frac{\partial \bar{o}_{pk}}{\partial \bar{\omega}_{nk}} = \bar{o}_{pk}(1-\bar{o}_{pk})\,x_{pn} \tag{9}$$

The weight change for the t-th epoch can be expressed as follows, where μ is the learning rate of the gradient method.

$$\Delta\omega_{km}(t) = \mu\textstyle\sum_{p=1}^{P}\delta_{pm}\bar{o}_{pk} \quad \text{where} \quad \delta_{pm} = (t_{pm} - o_{pm})o_{pm}(1-o_{pm}) \tag{10}$$

$$\Delta\bar{\omega}_{nk}(t) = \mu\textstyle\sum_{p=1}^{P}\bar{\delta}_{pk}\, x_{pn} \quad \text{where} \quad \bar{\delta}_{pk} = \bar{o}_{pk}(1-\bar{o}_{pk})\textstyle\sum_{m=1}^{M}\delta_{pm}\,\omega_{km} \tag{11}$$

When the learning process is about to converge or is trapped by a local minimum, the change of the system error is very small. It implies that most of the actual outputs

o_{pm} or/and $\overline{o}_{pk}$ approach extreme values (i.e., 0 or 1) at that moment. Thus the back-propagated error signals δ_{pm} and $\overline{\delta}_{pk}$ including the factors $o_{pm}(1-o_{pm})$ and $\overline{o}_{pk}(1-\overline{o}_{pk})$ respectively turn out to be very small and hence the effect of the true error signal ($t_{pm}-o_{pm}$) become very weak. When any one of the outputs is extremely different from the target output, that is, the true error signal ($t_{pm}-o_{pm}$) is large, but the factor $o_{pm}(1-o_{pm})$ will produce a small and negligible value which in turn makes the error signals to be insignificant values and there is a small or even no change of weights. This is the case where a local minimum is formed.

Although BP can be used to find the global optimum, the time required to complete the training through BP is too long. Thus, many gradient descent algorithms (such as Quickprop [6] and Rprop [7]) have been developed based on BP and are aimed at enhancing the efficiency of training. These fast algorithms can successfully enhance the efficiency of the training process in terms of speed and accuracy, but the local minimum problem still exists. In order to address the problem, we first investigate the cause of local minima and then design a suitable solution to tackle the problem. The solution could be applied to those gradient descent algorithms such as BP, Quickprop, and Rprop to improve their global convergence capability.

3   Output Monitoring and Modification Methodology

3.1   An Extreme Error

Generally, since a sigmoid function is used as an activation function, the range of the output value in a neural network is between 0 and 1. An extreme error is defined as the difference between an output node and its target value where their values are in two opposite extremes, meaning the value of an output node is close to 0 while its target value is 1, or vice versa. Fig. 1 is an example to show there is an extreme error in the output nodes. This result in Fig. 1 was produced when Rprop was applied in the 5-bit counting problem [2]. In Fig. 1, the fifth output node produces an extreme value which is totally different from its target output. The rest of the output nodes have reached the target value. In other words, the extreme error has occurred at that output node when the learning process is trapped into a local minimum.

The reason causing an extreme error is the calculation of the weight update of gradient descent algorithms using the partial derivative of the error with respect to weights (i.e., $\partial E/\partial \omega_{km}$ and $\partial E/\partial \overline{\omega}_{nk}$ in Equations (10) and (11)). To obtain the partial derivative of error with respect to weights, the error signal of all output nodes in each pattern should be added together. When an output node has an extreme error, it will be wrongly considered as a correct value by the weight update rule because the overall value of the error signal produces a very small value which cannot be used to correctly identify the extreme error. Therefore, the change of weights will become negligible and this situation will remain unchanged after that, i.e., the learning process is trapped into a local minimum.

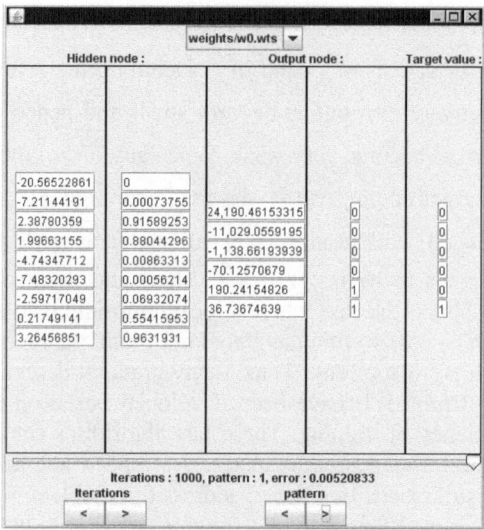

Fig. 1. Example of an extreme error

3.2   Output Monitoring and Modification (OMM)

The existence of an extreme error is a common source of the local minimum problem found in many datasets. Based on this observation, Output Monitoring and Modification (OMM) algorithm is proposed to address the local minimum problem by removing extreme errors in a systematic manner. When an extreme error exists, the change of weights becomes insignificant because the weight update equations simply neglect the extreme error. Thus, a possible way to solve this problem is to introduce a non-extreme value for the output node to be further exploited in the calculation. To do so, the algorithm is divided into two parts: output monitoring, and modification.

In the output monitoring algorithm, the existence of a local minimum is identified by monitoring the change of the system error. When the difference between the target output and the actual output is greater than a threshold (say *diff_threshold*), it is considered to be an extreme error. The corresponding output node and the pattern will be recorded, and then modified in the output modification algorithm. *diff_threshold* was set as 0.95 in this paper.

After the output node of extreme error has been recorded, the output value will be modified to a non-extreme value in the output modification phase. The modification will be handled at the calculation of error signal (before the weight update rule). The OMM algorithm is described as follows:

Fig. 3 shows an example of output modification. In Fig. 3, one of the output nodes has an extreme error and the original sum value (i.e., *Sum*) of this output node is 6. After applying the sigmoid function, an extreme output value of 0.9975 is produced but its target value is 0. By applying the output modification algorithm, *Sum* is divided by λ ($\lambda = 2$ in this case) to obtain the result of 3. The output value of 0.9526 is produced by the sigmoid function, which will be different from the original output value. The new output will be adapted through the original weight update rule so that the extreme error can be rectified.

FOR all patterns p

    FOR all output nodes m

        IF $(\left| t_{pm} - o_{pm} \right| > diff\_threshold)$

            $Sum \leftarrow -\ln\left(\dfrac{1 - o_{pm}}{o_{pm}} \right)$ where Sum is the reversed sigmoid function

            $Sum \leftarrow Sum / \lambda$ where λ = reducing factor

            $o_{pm} \leftarrow 1/(1 + e^{-Sum})$

        ENDIF

    ENDFOR

END FOR

Fig. 2. Output monitoring and modification

The division is applied to the sum value of the feed forward calculation but not the actual output because the division can yield a greater variation than assigning a desired value to the output. Moreover, according to the sigmoid function, the sign of the sum value determines whether the output value is greater than 0.5 or not, which means there must be a change of sign when the value of an output node attempts to reach the target value from the extreme error. Using division can ensure that the correction of the output node is done by the learning process instead of the modification phase, since the sign of the number remains unchanged when it is divided by a positive number.

In the above algorithm, the reducing factor λ can be set as a positive number greater than 1. A large number can have a better effect but it may introduce more interruption during the training. The default setting was 2, which is shown to be effective from simulation results.

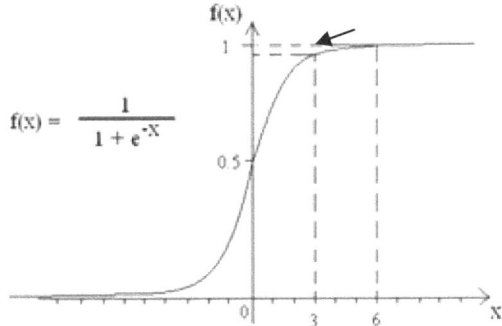

$$f(x) = \frac{1}{1 + e^{-x}}$$

Fig. 3. Example of output modification

3.3   OMM with Reiteration (OMM-R)

It can be seen in Section 4 that the global convergence capability of existing gradient descent algorithms with OMM is much better than those without OMM. However, the local minimum problem cannot be totally solved by using one single reducing factor. To overcome this problem, we can reiterate OMM systematically using different reducing factors. It resets the learning process to the initial stage and starts over again with another reducing factor. In some cases, an extreme error may not cause the local minimum problem, or it is necessary that such an extreme value occurs in a certain period of time during the whole learning process. Therefore, the reiteration phase provides an opportunity to clarify whether or not removing an extreme error can solve the local minimum problem.

In the reiteration phase, the original gradient descent algorithm will be used first, and the training process will be returned to the initial stage when the learning process is trapped into a local minimum. When the system error does not produce an observable change in a number of epochs, the training process will return to initial stage and apply the optimization algorithm with other reducing factors. Note that the factor λ is increased in the reiteration phase. The OMM with reiteration algorithm is shown in Fig. 4. In this algorithm, the local minimum criterion is met when the absolute difference between the current error and previous error is smaller than 10^{-5} in 1000 consecutive epochs (i.e. Count >= 1000). The criterion should be carefully set because if the difference is too large, it may affect the normal training process since the change of the system error will be reduced when the training is about to finish. Conversely, if a Count value is set too large, it may waste many epochs checking if the local minimum criterion is met.

IF ($|E(n) - E(n-1)| < 10^{-5}$)   //locate local minimum

    Count = Count + 1;

ELSE

    Count = 0

ENDIF

IF (Count >= 1000)   // a local minimum criterion is satisfied

    Load the initial set of weights

    $\lambda \leftarrow \lambda * 2$

    start OMM

    Count = 0

ENDIF

Fig. 4. The algorithm of OMM with reiteration

4   Numerical Results

This section shows experimental results of OMM applied in some gradient descent algorithms (BP, QuickProp and Rprop) for addressing the local minimum problem. The new algorithm will be used to train all problem sets and the results will be compared with other gradient descent algorithms. Their performance is compared in terms of the average convergence rate and the global convergence capability. The average convergence rate is the average number of epochs in completing the training to global minimum, while the convergence percentage (i.e., the global convergence capability) represents the percentage of successful training achieving the global minimum.

4.1   Application of OMM to Different Learning Algorithms

The OMM algorithm is embedded into various gradient descent algorithms to solve the 5-bit counting problem [2]. Assume (I, H, J) has a network configuration with I input nodes, H hidden nodes and J output nodes respectively. The network configuration for 5-bit counting is (5, 9, 6). The training is considered to be successful if the system error is smaller than 0.001 in 3000 epochs. Table 1 shows the values of the parameter setting in different gradient descent algorithms.

Table 2 shows the results of using OMM in various algorithms for solving the 5-bit counting problem based on 30 different sets of initial weights. The results show that the OMM approach is applicable to different gradient descent algorithms and can enhance the training performance of different gradient descent algorithms in terms of the convergence percentage. However it cannot remove all extreme errors that caused the local minima problem. For example, OMM applied in Quickprop cannot achieve 100% global convergence. It would be worthwhile to apply the reiteration phase in order to improve the performance further, which will be shown later in this section.

To summarize, OMM can overcome the extreme error problem in different gradient descent algorithms but it is better to have a systematic way to record the output for modification. Moreover, the results of Rprop illustrate that the most significant improvement is not only in the percentage of successful training but also in the average convergence rate. Thus, the OMM approach will be applied in Rprop in further experiments.

Table 1. Parameter setting of different gradient descent algorithms

Learning algorithm	Parameter
BackPropagation	Learning rate = 0.5 Momentum = 0.5
QuickProp	Maximum growth factor = 1.75 Mode switch threshold = 0.0
Rprop	Learning rate = 0.1 Increase of step size = 1.005 Decrease of step size = 0.5 Maximum of delta weight = 50 Minimum of delta weight = 0.000001

Table 2. Performance of OMM embedded in different gradient descent algorithms for the 5-bit counting problem in 3000 epochs

Learning algorithm	Average convergence rate	Convergence percentage
BackPropagation	>3000	0%
BackPropagation(OMM)	2706.24	96.67%
QuickProp	399	26.67%
QuickProp(OMM)	334.8	33.33%
Rprop	>3000	0%
Rprop(OMM)	215.53	100%

4.2   OMM with Reiteration (OMM-R)

In order to improve OMM performance further, the reiteration phase will be triggered when the training is trapped in a local minimum. The training will start with $\lambda = 1$ (i.e., the original Rprop) and then λ will be multiplied by 2 if the local minimum criterion is met. The training process will go to the initial stage and start over again with different values of λ. The algorithm is implemented based on Rprop with the default parameters. OMM is embedded into Rprop to solve real-case problems including Thyroid, Wine, Breast cancer and Iris, which can be found in UCI machine learning repository [11]. The results are compared with the original Rprop.

The network configurations of Thyroid, Wine, Breast cancer and Iris are (5, 15, 3), (13, 23, 3), (9, 20, 1) and (4, 15, 3) respectively. Training is considered to be successful if the system error is smaller than 0.001 in 30,000 iterations. The results based on 100 different sets of initial weights are shown in Table 3. The convergence percentage has increased greatly for difficult problems, especially Breast cancer and Iris. With the reiteration phase (OMM-R), the percentage of successful training has increased up to about 100% in most of the problem sets. That means OMM-R can effectively tackle the local minimum problem. However, the number of epochs to converge has also increased greatly, which is expected because the cases that usually cannot converge using the original Rprop should take more epochs to converge to the global optimum.

Table 4 shows the performance of OMM-R in terms of the global convergence capability. When the change time is 0, it is the original Rprop algorithm. When change time is 1, it means that the algorithm will return one time to the initial stage when the local minimum criteria are met and the value of λ will increase two times in OMM during the reiteration phase. It can be seen that the training can achieve up to 97% of global convergence in most cases within less than three returning processes. Since it is expected that some difficult extreme error problems will need more effort to solve, OMM with reiteration provides a more systematic and effective way to tackle the local minimum problem.

Table 3. Performance of OMM and OMM-R to solve real case problems

Problem set	Learning algorithm	Average convergence rate	Convergence percentage
Thyroid	Rprop	316.27	98%
	Rprop (OMM)	383.64	100%
	Rprop(OMM-R)	383.64	100%
Wine	Rprop	784.06	62%
	Rprop (OMM)	584.0	81%
	Rprop(OMM-R)	2965.5	98%
Breast Cancer	Rprop	1550.0	1%
	Rprop (OMM)	1374.47	87%
	Rprop(OMM-R)	2612.74	100%
Iris	Rprop	3906.0	19%
	Rprop (OMM)	10144.42	97%
	Rprop(OMM-R)	13510.44	100%

Table 4. Performance of OMM-R for different problems with different change time

Change time / λ	Percentage of global convergence			
	Thyroid	Wine	Breast cancer	Iris
0 / 1	98	62	1	19
1 / 2	100	86	93	92
2 / 4		96	100	96
3 / 8		97		98
4 / 16		97		99
5 / 32		97		100
9 / 512		98		

5   Conclusions

This paper proposed using output monitoring and modification (OMM) in gradient descent algorithms to address the local minimum problem. OMM records the output nodes having the extreme error and then modifies the value to a non-extreme value to tackle the local minimum problem. The reiteration phase provides another chance for the training process to increase the level of modification to tackle the local minimum problem. With this new approach, the time and cost to train a neural network can be greatly reduced with a high percentage of successful training. The simulation results verified that most of the local minimum problems have been solved by using the proposed approach.

References

[1] Rumelhart, D.E., Hinton, G.E., Williams, R.J.: Learning internal representations by error propagation. In: Parallel Distributed Processing: Exploration in the Microstructure of Cognition, vol. 1, MIT Press, Cambridge (1986)

[2] Van Ooyen, A., Nienhuis, B.: Improving the convergence of the back-propagation algorithm. Neural Networks 5, 465–471

[3] Vitela, J.E., Reifman, J.: Premature Saturation in Backpropagation Networks: Mechanism and Necessary Conditions. Neural Networks 10(4), 721–735 (1997)

[4] Blum, E.K., Li, L.K.: Approximation theory and feedforward networks. Neural Networks 4, 511–515 (1991)

[5] Gori, M., Tesi, A.: On the problem of local minima in back-propagation. IEEE Trans. On Pattern Analysis and Machine Intelligence 14(1), 76–86 (1992)

[6] Fahlman, S.E.: Fast learning variations on back-propagation: An empirical study. In: Touretzky, D., Hinton, G., Sejnowski, T. (eds.) Proc. the 1988 Connectionist Models Summer School, Pittsburgh, pp. 38–51 (1989)

[7] Riedmiller, M., Braun, H.: A direct adaptive method for faster back-propagation learning: The RPROP Algorithm. In: Proc. of Int. Conf. on Neural Networks, vol. 1, pp. 586–591 (1993)

[8] Yuceturk, A.C., Herdağdelen, A., Uyanik, K.: A solution to the problem of local minima in backpropagation algorithm. In: Proc. of the Fourteenth International Symposium on Computer and Information Sciences, Kusadasi, Turkey, pp. 1081–1083 (1999)

[9] Wang, X.G., Tang, Z., Tamura, H., Ishii, M., Sun, W.D.: An improved backpropagation algorithm to avoid the local minima problem. Neurocomputing 56, 455–460 (2004)

[10] Ng, S.C., Cheung, C.C., Leung, S.H.: Magnified Gradient Function with Deterministic Weight Evolution in Adaptive Learning. IEEE Trans. on Neural Networks 15(6), 1411–1423 (2004)

[11] Frank, A., Asuncion, A.: UCI Machine Learning Repository. University of California, School of Information and Computer Science, Irvine, CA (2012),
http://archive.ics.uci.edu/ml/

Stability Analysis and Hopf-Type Bifurcation of a Fractional Order Hindmarsh-Rose Neuronal Model

Min Xiao

School of Mathematics and Information Technology,
Nanjing Xiaozhuang University, Nanjing 210017, China
candymanxm2003@yahoo.com.cn

Abstract. In this paper, the dynamical behaviors of a fractional order Hindmarsh-Rose neuronal model are studied. First, based on the stability theory of fractional order systems, some sufficient conditions for the stability and Hpof-type bifurcation are given for such fractional order system. Then, the frequency and amplitude of periodic oscillations are determined by numerical simulations. It is shown that the frequency of oscillations incurs a small variation with respect to different values of the order, while the amplitude of oscillations gets larger as the order is increased. Numerical simulations are performed to verified the theoretical results.

Keywords: Fractional order Hindmarsh-Rose neuronal model, Stability, Hopf-type bifurcation.

1 Introduction

Fractional calculus as an extension of ordinary calculus is a mathematical topic with more than 300 years of history. Even though fractional calculus has a long history, its application to physics and engineering has attracted lots of attention only in the last few decades [1]. It has been found that many systems in interdisciplinary fields can be elegantly described with the help of fractional derivatives. Many systems are known to display fractional-order dynamics, such as viscoelastic systems [2], dielectric polarization [3], electrode-electrolyte polarization [4], electromagnetic waves [5], quantitative finance [6], and quantum evolution of complex systems [7].

There are many definitions of fractional derivatives. The widely accepted definition of a fractional derivative of the order $\alpha \in R^+$ is the Caputo definition

$$D_t^\alpha f(t) = \frac{1}{\Gamma(m - \alpha)} \int_0^t \frac{f^{(m)}(s)}{(t - s)^{\alpha - m + 1}} ds, \tag{1}$$

where m is the first integer larger than α, i.e., $m - 1 < \alpha \leq m$ and $\Gamma(\cdot)$ is the gamma function. For details of the basic definitions and properties of the fractional calculus theory, see for instance [1]. This paper is based on the Caputo definition.

J. Wang, G.G. Yen, and M.M. Polycarpou (Eds.): ISNN 2012, Part I, LNCS 7367, pp. 217–224, 2012.

Although the integer order models can be considered as a special form of the more general fractional order models, there are basic differences between fractional order and integer order models. The main difference between them arises from an inherent attribute of fractional derivatives. In fact, the fractional derivatives are not local operators in opposition with integer derivatives that are local operators [1]. In other words, the fractional derivative of a function depends on its whole past values. This property makes a fractional order model behave like a system with an infinite memory or long memory. Recently many mathematicians and applied researchers have tried to model real processes using the fractional order differential equations. In biology, it has been deduced that the membranes of cells of biological organisms have fractional order electrical conductance [8] and then are classified in a group of noninteger order systems. Also, it has been shown that modeling the behavior of brainstem vestibule-oculumotor neurons by fractional order models has more advantages than classical integer order modeling [9].

Dynamical characteristics for a variety of neural network models has become a subject of extensive research activity [10,11,12]. However, these neural network models do not take into account the fractional order derivatives. In this paper, we extend an integer order Hindmarsh-Rose neuronal model to a fractional order system. We explore the capabilities of a fractional order Hindmarsh-Rose model to exhibit different dynamical behaviors, including the stability, bifurcations and oscillations. We focus primarily on the effect of the fractional orders on the dynamics of the neural model. It has been shown that the dynamics of fractional order systems is not invariant in contrary to the integer order systems.

2   Preliminaries

This section presents the stability theorems in fractional order systems and the introduction to the model under study.

2.1   Stability Theorems

We state two stability theorems for fractional order systems with commensurate orders.

Lemma 1. *([13]) The following linear autonomous system:*

$$D_t^\alpha x = Ax, \quad x(0) = x_0, \tag{2}$$

where $0 < \alpha \leq 1$, $x \in R^n$ and A is an $n \times n$ matrix, is asymptotically stable if and only if $|\arg(\lambda)| > \alpha\pi/2$ is satisfied for all eigenvalues (λ) of matrix A. In this case, each component of the states decays towards 0 like $t^{-\alpha}$. Also, this system is stable if and only if $|\arg(\lambda)| \geq \alpha\pi/2$ is satisfied for all eigenvalues (λ) of matrix A with those critical eigenvalues satisfying $|\arg(\lambda)| = \alpha\pi/2$ having geometric multiplicity of one.

Lemma 2. *([14]) For the nonlinear fractional-order system:*

$$D_t^\alpha x = g(x), \qquad (3)$$

where $0 < \alpha \le 1$, $x \in R^n$ and g is a smooth nonlinear function, the equilibrium x_0 is locally asymptotically stable if $|\arg(\lambda)| > \alpha\pi/2$ is satisfied for all eigenvalues (λ) of the Jacobian matrix $J = \partial g/\partial x$ evaluated at the equilibrium x_0, where x_0 satisfies $g(x_0) = 0$.

2.2   Model Descriptions

Motivated by FitzHugh-Nagumo model [15,16], Tsuji et. al [17] proposed a two-dimensional Hindmarsh-Rose type neuronal model by introducing a generalized quadratic function into the FHN model. The equation is as follows:

$$\dot{x} = c(x - \frac{x^3}{3} - y + I),$$
$$\dot{y} = \frac{x^2 + dx - by + a}{c}, \qquad (4)$$

where x and y denote the cell membrane potential and a recovery variable, respectively. I represents the external stimulus. a, b, c and d are parameters. System (4) may exhibit typical nonlinear phenomena such as the Hopf and saddle-node bifurcations, separatrix loops, and oscillations [17]. We are concerned with the following fractional order system as the extended Hindmarsh-Rose neuronal model in the rest of the paper:

$$D_t^\alpha x = c(x - \frac{x^3}{3} - y + I),$$
$$D_t^\alpha y = \frac{x^2 + dx - by + a}{c}, \qquad (5)$$

where $\alpha \in (0, 1]$. The fractional order system (5) is reduced to the integer order system (4) when $\alpha = 1$.

3   Main Results

In this section, we investigate the stability, Hopf bifurcations and oscillations for the fractional order Hindmarsh-Rose model (5).

3.1   Local Stability

It is well known the the order cannot change the number and location of equilibria of (5). Let $E_0 = (x_0, y_0)$ be the equilibrium of (5), i.e., it is the solution of equation

$$x - \frac{x^3}{3} - y + I = 0,$$
$$x^2 + dx - by + a = 0. \qquad (6)$$

The Jacobian matrix of (5) at equilibrium E_0 is

$$J = \begin{bmatrix} c(1 - x_0^2) & -c \\ \dfrac{2x_0 + d}{c} & -\dfrac{b}{c} \end{bmatrix}, \tag{7}$$

with the characteristic equation

$$\lambda^2 + m\lambda + n = 0, \tag{8}$$

where

$$m = \frac{b}{c} - c(1 - x_0^2), \qquad n = 2x_0 + d - b(1 - x_0^2). \tag{9}$$

Theorem 1. *For (5), the following results hold.*

(*i*) *If $m > 0$ and $n > 0$, then the equilibrium E_0 of (5) is locally asymptotically stable for all $\alpha \in (0, 1]$.*

(*ii*) *If $n < 0$ or $0 < n < \frac{1}{4}m^2$ and $m < 0$, then the equilibrium E_0 of (5) is unstable for all $\alpha \in (0, 1]$.*

(*iii*) *If $n > \frac{1}{4}m^2$, $m < 0$ and*

$$\arctan \frac{-\sqrt{4n^2 - m^2}}{m} > \frac{\alpha\pi}{2}, \tag{10}$$

then the equilibrium E_0 of (5) is locally asymptotically stable.

(*iv*) *If $n > \frac{1}{4}m^2$, $m < 0$ and*

$$\arctan \frac{-\sqrt{4n^2 - m^2}}{m} < \frac{\alpha\pi}{2}, \tag{11}$$

then the equilibrium E_0 of (5) is unstable.

Proof. (i) If $m > 0$ and $n > 0$, (8) has two roots with negative real parts by the Routh-Hurwitz criterion [18]. Hence, the conclusion (i) holds.

(ii) If $n < 0$ or $0 < n < \frac{1}{4}m^2$ and $m < 0$, (8) has at least one positive real root. The conclusion (ii) holds.

(iii) If $n > \frac{1}{4}m^2$, $m < 0$, (8) has a pair of complex conjugate eigenvalues $\lambda_{1,2}$ with positive real parts:

$$\lambda_{1,2} = \frac{-m \pm i\sqrt{4n^2 - m^2}}{2}.$$

It is straightforward to obtain that

$$|\arg(\lambda_{1,2})| = \arctan \frac{-\sqrt{4n^2 - m^2}}{m}.$$

Hence, by Lemma 2, we have that the equilibrium E_0 of (5) is locally asymptotically stable if (10) is satisfied.

(iv) This conclusion follows directly from (11). This completes the proof.

According to the conclusion of Theorem 1, we can draw the bifurcation diagram in the parameter plane as in Figure 1.

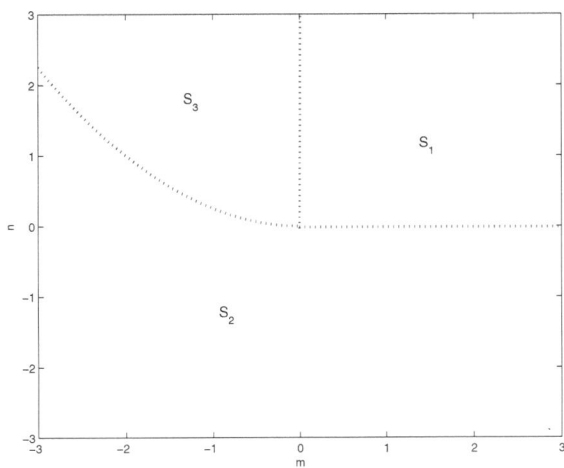

Fig. 1. The curves $n = \frac{1}{4}m^2$, $m = 0$ and $n = 0$ divide the (m, n)-plane into three regions, read S_1, S_2 and S_3. S_1 is an absolutely stable region; S_2 is an unstable region for all $\alpha \in (0, 1]$; S_3 is a conditionally stable region, and there is a stability switch for the fractional order α being located in the region S_3.

3.2 Hopf Bifurcation

From Theorem 1, we can easily derive the following theorem.

Theorem 2. *Suppose that $n > \frac{1}{4}m^2$ and $m < 0$. Then (5) undergoes a Hopf bifurcation at the equilibrium E_0 when the fractional order α passes through the critical value*

$$\alpha^* = \frac{2}{\pi} \arctan \frac{-\sqrt{4n^2 - m^2}}{m}. \tag{12}$$

Proof. For $n > \frac{1}{4}m^2$ and $m < 0$, when $\alpha = \alpha^*$, the characteristic equation (8) has a pair of conjugate complex roots $\lambda_{1,2}$ settled on the stability margin $|\arg(\lambda)| = \alpha^*\pi/2$. It can be seen that when α varies near α^*, $\lambda_{1,2}$ cross the stability boundary. Hence, a Hopf bifurcation occurs. This completes the proof.

Remark 1. Theorem 2 develops a method to construct fractional order neural oscillations by regulating the order α. In detail, system (5) converges to the equilibrium E_0 when α is smaller than α^*, namely, there is no occurrence of oscillations; while a Hopf bifurcation may occur as α passes through a critical point, α^*, where a family of oscillations bifurcate from the equilibrium E_0.

3.3 Oscillation Region

Theorem 3. *If the parameters $(a, b, c, d, I) \in \Omega$, where*

$$\Omega = \left\{ (a, b, c, d, I) \,\middle|\, n > \tfrac{1}{4}m^2, m < 0, \alpha^* < \alpha \leq 1 \right\}, \tag{13}$$

then system (5) has oscillations.

Remark 2. The freedom in choosing a, b, c, d, I and α in (5) allows us to determine the distribution of eigenvalues and fractional order, respectively, and so influences the amplitude and frequency of the corresponding oscillation.

4 Numerical Simulations

In this section, we will provide some simulation results to confirm our analysis about the fractional order Hindmarsh-Rose model (5). The numerical approach is based on the Adams-Bashforth-Moulton algorithm [19].

Let us fix as $a = -1, b = 1.4, c = 3, d = 1.8$ and $I = 0$, which are used for the integer order model (4) in [17]. We vary the order α to study the dynamical behavior of the fractional order system (5). It follows from (12) that

$$\alpha^* = 0.8104278382522. \tag{14}$$

From Theorems 1 and 2, it is known that when $\alpha < \alpha^*$, the trajectories converge to the equilibrium E_0 as shown in Figure 2(a), while with α being increased to pass α^*, the equilibrium E_0 loses its stability and a Hopf-type bifurcation

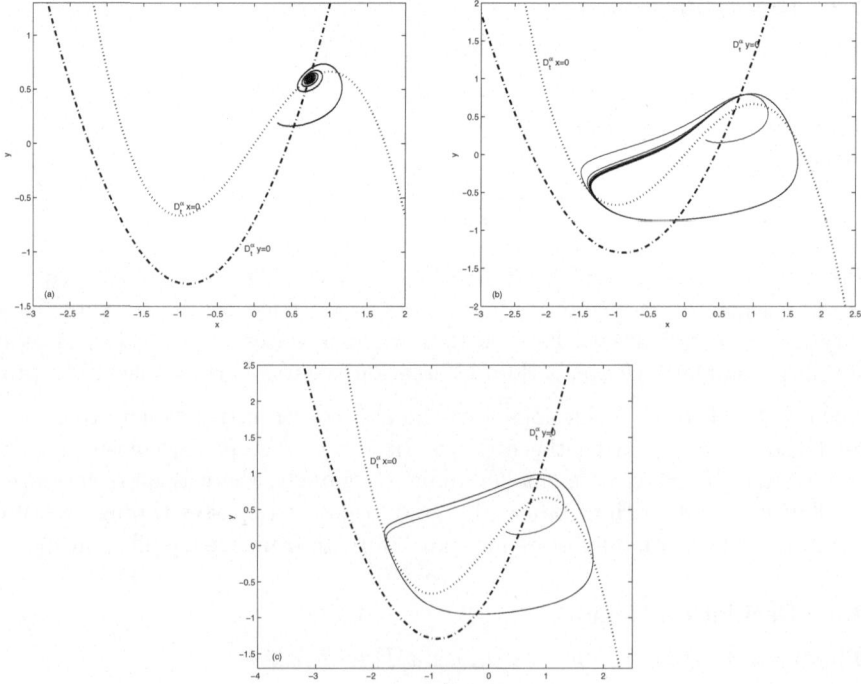

Fig. 2. Phase portraits of (5) with parameters $a = -1, b = 1.4, c = 3, d = 1.8$ and $I = 0$. (a): Stable equilibrium point, where $\alpha = 0.8 < \alpha^*$; (b): Periodic oscillation, where $\alpha = 0.87 > \alpha^*$; (c): Periodic oscillation, where $\alpha = 1 > \alpha^*$.

occurs as shown in Figure 2(b) and (c). It should be noted that the equilibrium E_0 which is unstable (see Figure 2(c)) in the integer order model (4) [17] can become asymptotically stable (see Figure 2(a)) in our fractional order model (5).

Figure 3(a) shows that the frequency of the oscillations incurs a small variation with respect to different values of α, and it decreases with the system parameter b. Figure 3(b) displays that the amplitude of the oscillations gets larger as the order α is increased, and it decreases with the system parameter b.

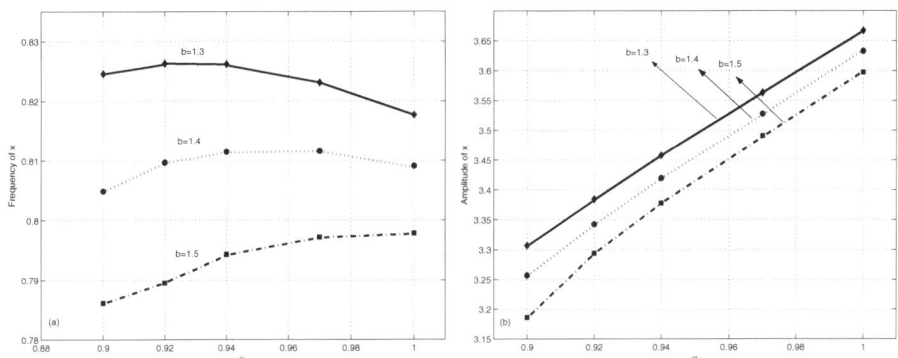

Fig. 3. The frequency and amplitude of x of the oscillations in system (5) with $0.9 \leq \alpha \leq 1$ and $b = 1.3, 1.4$ and 1.5.

5   Concluding Remarks

In this paper, the stability and Hopf bifurcation of a fractional order Hindmarsh-Rose model are studied. Based on the stability theory of fractional order systems, some sufficient criteria for the stability and Hpof bifurcation are obtained. We have demonstrated that under certain conditions, when the order α varies, the equilibrium point E_0 loses its stability and a Hopf bifurcation occurs, which is a family of periodic oscillations bifurcating from the equilibrium E_0 when α passes a critical value, say α^*. It is worth noting that fractional order α and system parameter b can effectively affect the frequency and amplitude of fractional order oscillations. The frequency of the oscillations incurs a small variation with respect to different values of α, and it decreases with the system parameter b. The amplitude of the oscillations gets larger as the order α is increased, and it decreases with the system parameter b. By choosing appropriate fractional order α and system parameter b, one can achieve the oscillation with the desired frequency and amplitude.

Acknowledgement. This work is supported by the China Postdoctoral Science Foundation funded project under Grant 20090461056, and the Jiangsu Ordinary University Natural Science Research Project under Grant 11KJD120002.

References

1. Podlubny, I.: Fractional Differential Equations. Academic Press, New York (1999)
2. Bagley, R.L., Calico, R.A.: Fractional Order State Equations for the Control of Viscoelastically Damped Structures. J. Guid. Control Dyn. 14, 304–311 (1991)
3. Sun, H.H., Abdelwahad, A.A., Onaral, B.: Linear Approximation of Transfer Function with a Pole of Fractional Order. IEEE Trans Autom. Control AC 29, 441–444 (1984)
4. Ichise, M., Nagayanagi, Y., Kojima, T.: An Analog Simulation of Noninteger Order Transfer Functions for Analysis of Electrode Process. J. Electroanal. Chem. 33, 253–265 (1971)
5. Heaviside, O.: Electromagnetic Theory. Chelsea, New York (1971)
6. Laskin, N.: Fractional Market Dynamics. Phys. A 287, 482–492 (2000)
7. Kusnezov, D., Bulgac, A., Dang, G.D.: Quantum Levy Processes and Fractional Kinetics. Phys. Rev. Lett. 82, 1136–1139 (1999)
8. Cole, K.S.: Electric Conductance of Biological Systems. In: Proc. Cold Spring Harbor Symp. Quant. Biol., New York, pp. 107–116 (1993)
9. Anastasio, T.J.: The Fractional Order Dynamics of Brainstem Vestibuleoculumotor Neurons. Biol. Cybern. 72, 69–79 (1994)
10. Gopalsamy, K., Leung, I.: Convergence under Dynamical Thresholds with Delays. IEEE Trans. Neural Netw. 8, 341–348 (1997)
11. Xu, X., Hua, H.Y., Wang, H.L.: Stability Switches, Hopf Bifurcation and Chaos of a Neuron Model with Delay-Dependent Parameters. Phys. Lett. A 354, 126–136 (2006)
12. Cao, J., Xiao, M.: Stability and Hopf bifurcation in a Simplified BAM Neural Network with Two Time Delays. IEEE Trans. Neural Netw. 18, 416–430 (2007)
13. Matignon, D.: Stability Results for Fractional Differential Equations with Applications to Control Processing. In: Proceedings IMACS-SMC 1996, Lille, France, pp. 963–968 (1996)
14. Ahmed, E., El-Sayed, A., El-Saka, H.: Equilibrium Points, Stability and Numerical Solutions of Fractional Order Predator-Prey and Rabies Models. J. Math. Anal. Appl. 325, 542–553 (2007)
15. FitzHugh, R.: Impulses and Physiological State in Theoretical Models of Nerve Membrane. Biophy. J. 1, 445–467 (1961)
16. Nagumo, J., Arimoto, S., Yoshizawa, S.: An Active Pulse Transmission Line Simulating Nerve Axon. In: Proc. IRE, vol. 50, pp. 2061–2070 (1962)
17. Tsuji, S., Ueta, T., Kamakami, H., Fujii, H., Aihara, K.: Bifurcations in Two-Dimensional Hindmarsh-Rose Type Model. Int. J. Bifurc. Chaos 17, 985–998 (2007)
18. Gantmacher, F.R.: The Theory of Matrices. Chelsea, New York (1959)
19. Diethelm, K., Ford, N.J., Freed, A.D.: A predictor-corrector approach for the numerical solution of fractional differential equations. Nonlin. Dynam. 29, 3–22 (2002)

Study on Decision Algorithm of Neurons' Synchronization Based on Neurodynamics

Xiaoying He[1] and Yueping Peng[2]

[1] School of Management and Economics,
Xi'an Technological University,710032 Xi'an, China
He99@sohu.com
[2] Information Engineering Department,
Engineering University of Chinese Armed Police Force, 710086 Xi'an, China
Percy001@163.com

Abstract. In the paper, based on the neurodynamics theory and the existing neuron synchronization's research findings, the dynamic phase function which can describe the neuron's discharge characteristics is defined and revised, and the neuron synchronization decision algorithm and procedure based on the dynamic phase function is put forward. The synchronization characteristics and rule of the two uncoupled HR neurons are discussed by the synchronization decision algorithm. Compared with other decision indexes and algorithms, the neuron synchronization decision algorithm based on the dynamic phase function can not only judge the three common synchronization types: asynchronization, the generalized synchronization, and the phase synchronization, but also quantitatively solve the critical value of the neurons' realizing synchronization such as the stimulation current amplitude.

Keywords: The phase function, Neuron, Synchronization, Neurodynamics.

1   Introduction

In recent years, with the development and the integrity of the neurodynamics theory[1], the neurons' synchronization research has been deepened, and lots of synchronization concepts, decision indexes, and decision methods have been put forward[2-11].

However, some synchronization decision indexes are only suitable for the given synchronization types, and some synchronization decision indexes have flaws, so they can't describe and judge all neuron synchronization phenomena. The synchronization error of the neurons' membrane potential is good for the complete synchronization, and isn't suitable for the phase synchronization and the generalized synchronization. Interspike intervals(ISIs) of the neurons' membrane potential are suitable for the phase synchronization, and can't sometimes distinguish between the complete synchronization and the phase synchronization. In lots of literatures, the maximal condition Lyapunov exponent has been used to judge the chaos systems' synchronization. When the maximal condition Lyapunov exponent is negative, the

J. Wang, G.G. Yen, and M.M. Polycarpou (Eds.): ISNN 2012, Part I, LNCS 7367, pp. 225–234, 2012.

chaos systems realize synchronization. But that the maximal condition Lyapunov exponent is negative is the essential condition that systems realize synchronization, and it isn't the sufficient condition[12,13]. The cross-correlation function can effectively judge the common nonlinear systems' synchronization. But for the many time scale neuron systems, the cross-correlation function only effectively judge the bursting synchronization, and can't judge other synchronizations[12]. In addition, the defined phase function of the common nonlinear system can't represent the neuron's typical discharge characteristics. So it has only the reference significance, and can't be put into practical application. By far, there are few literatures to present systematically the neurons' synchronization judging methods and procedures, especially for the uncoupled neurons.

In the paper, based on the neurodynamics theory and the existing neuron synchronization's research findings, the dynamic phase function which can describe the neuron's discharge characteristics is defined and revised, and the neuron synchronization decision algorithm and procedure based on the dynamic phase function is put forward. Then, we take the two uncoupled Hindmarsh-Rose neuron (HR neuron) system[14,15] as the object, and study the two uncoupled HR neurons' synchronization characteristics and rule by the algorithm.

2   The Neuron's Synchronization and Its Classfication

Based on the neurodynamics theory, the neurons' synchronization can be defined: Two (or more) different (the same) neurons' discharge behaviors approach to accord under their inside or outside condition's changing and affecting. In recent ten years, with the nonlinear science's development, people have known the chaos more deeply. The chaos's synchronization and controlling of the neurons and their network have been developed the hot research field. These following concepts about the neurons' synchronization are often referred: the complete synchronization, the phase synchronization, the generalized synchronization, the lag synchronization, and the imperfect phase synchronization. In the paper, the three following synchronization concepts are used: the complete synchronization, the phase synchronization, and the generalized synchronization.

Based on the neurodynamics theory, the complete synchronization can be defined: Two (or more) different (the same) neurons' membrane potentials become the same under their inside or outside condition's changing and affecting. So the complete synchronization is also named as the state synchronization. The membrane potential absolute synchronization error ($err = |x_1 - x_2|$, x_i is the neuron's membrane potential.) is often used to judge the neurons' complete synchronization. the phase synchronization can be defined: Two (or more) different (the same) neurons' membrane potential phases become the same under their inside or outside condition's changing and affecting; Namely, neurons' membrane potentials have the sure time delay difference, and the time delay difference isn't zero. The phase synchronization is also named as the spike synchronization. When the neurons realize the phase synchronization, they discharge at the same time, and their discharge frequency is the same. But their membrane potentials' change is different, and has the sure time delay difference, and their amplitudes may be also different. The phase difference and ISI are often used to judge the neurons' phase synchronization. The generalized synchronization is that Two (or more) different (the same) neurons' membrane potentials aren't completely the same, but meet a complex sure function relation. The generalized synchronization is named as the frequency synchronization, the intermittent the phase synchronization, the intermittent discharge synchronization, and the burst synchronization. The phase difference, ISI, and the cross-correlation function are used to judge neurons' generalized synchronization.

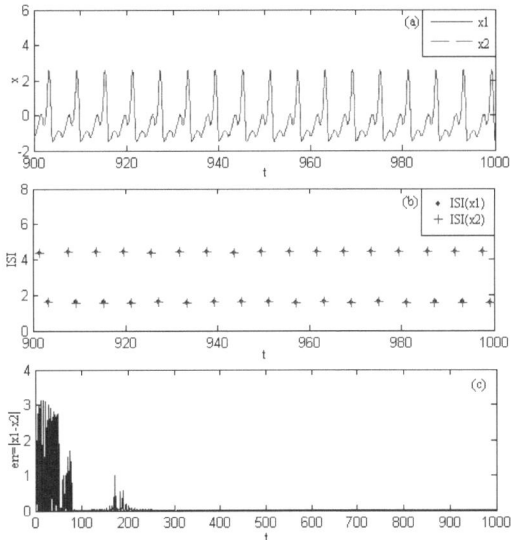

Fig. 1. The process of the two uncoupled HR neurons realizing complete synchronization. (a) The membrane potential changing chart of the two neurons with time. (b) The membrane potential's ISI changing chart of the two neurons with time. (c) The membrane potential absolute synchronization error changing chart of the two neurons with time.

Limited to the length, Fig.1 only shows the complete synchronization process of the two uncoupled HR neurons. In Fig.1, the two HR neurons' parameter r is respectively 0.0085 and 0.009. The stimulation current is the half wave sine current, whose amplitude and period is respectively 6 and 2. The values of these two neurons' parameters (except r) are showed in reference[21]. From Fig.1, the two neurons realize the complete synchronization at 250.

3   The Neuron's Dynamic Phase Function and Synchronization Decision Algorithm

The phase of the chaos system's orbit can not only be totally defined and described by the Hilbert transform[16], but also be locally defined and described in the orbit tangent space or the orbit projection space[17-20]. With the nonlinear science's development and application, based on the existing research findings, a more flexible phase definition is put forward[12]:

There is a chaos system: $\dot{x} = F(x)$, which has the two inside independent variables: $s_1(t)$ and $s_2(t)$. These two variables are defined as:

$$s_1(t) = s_1(x, \dot{x}, \ddot{x}, ...)$$ (1)

$$s_2(t) = s_2(x, \dot{x}, \ddot{x}, ...)$$ (2)

If the chaos system has only one center of rotation on the $s_1 - s_2$ projection space, the phase function can be defined as:

$$\phi(t) = \arctan \frac{s_1(t) - s_{1c}}{s_2(t) - s_{2c}}$$ (3)

Where

(s_{1c}, s_{2c}) —— The center of rotation of the system's orbit attractor. For example, if the chaos system' orbit rotates point of origin in the $s_1 - s_2$ projection space, the center of rotation (s_{1c}, s_{2c}) is (0, 0).

It is needed to emphasized that the phase function $\phi(t)$ is defined in the whole real axis, but isn't in one period($[\pi, \pi]$).

For the neuron, the orbit phase function can be defined by formula (3). But the observed data of the neuron are often the membrane potential, so the variables $s_1(t)$ and $s_2(t)$ need to be gotten from the membrane potential of the neuron. We can get $x(t - \tau)$ (τ is the time delay.) by the time delay method, so the variables $s_1(t)$ and $s_2(t)$ are made up of the membrane potential $x(t)$, the membrane potential delay $x(t - \tau)$, and their each order derivative functions. We can reconstruct the phase space by $x(t), x(t - \tau)$, and their each order derivative functions, and get the corresponding phase plane of the phase function $\phi(t)$. Because $x(t), x(t - \tau)$, and their each order derivative functions are infinite, we can theoretically get thousands of phase planes of the phase function. But the typical simple planes are $x(t) - x(t - \tau)$, $\dot{x}(t) - \dot{x}(t - \tau)$, $x(t) - \dot{x}(t)$, $\dot{x}(t) - \ddot{x}(t)$, and so on. At application, according to the neuron having only one center of rotation in these reconstructed phase planes and calculating simple, we can select one phase plane meeting conditions.

The neuron has the special characteristics which the common nonlinear system hasn't. For example, The HR neuron model has plenty of discharge patterns such as the period discharge, bursting discharge, and the chaos discharge[21-23]. Moreover, the HR neuron model has only one center of rotation[12]. Fig.2 shows the orbit attractor of the HR Neuron model on the phase plane of $x(t) - x(t - \tau)$, $\dot{x}(t) - \dot{x}(t - \tau)$, $x(t) - \dot{x}(t)$, and $\dot{x}(t) - \ddot{x}(t)$. In Fig.2, values of the HR model's parameters are as follows: r =0.013, I=3, $\tau = 0.5$, and other parameters are showed in reference[21]. From Fig.1 of reference[21], the HR neuron model is the chaos discharge pattern. From Fig.2, in these phase planes, the orbit attractor of the HR neuron model has only one center of rotation, so the orbit dynamic phase function of the HR neuron can be defined and described by the form of formula (3).

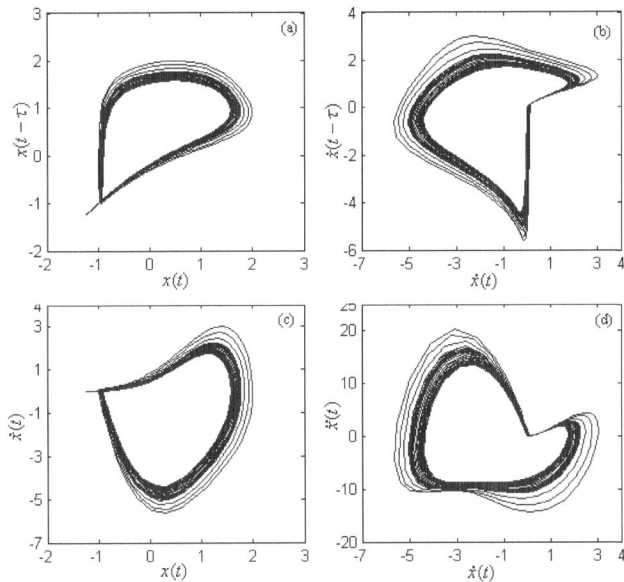

Fig. 2. The attractors of the HR neuron model in the different phase planes. (a) $x(t) - x(t - \tau)$. (b) $\dot{x}(t) - \dot{x}(t - \tau)$. (c) $x(t) - \dot{x}(t)$. (d) $\dot{x}(t) - \ddot{x}(t)$.

The neuron has plenty of discharge actions, and the definition of the neuron phase function $\phi(t)$ should represent the discharge characteristics of the neuron. So we define: As the neuron model does a spike, the neuron phase function $\phi(t)$ correspondingly adds 2π. Based on above definition, the dynamic phase function $\phi(t)$ of the neuron at t can be defined as:

Taking example for the $\dot{x}(t) - \dot{x}(t - \tau)$ phase plane, the neuron has only one center of rotation in this plane, and the initial observed time is t_0. The neuron has discharged n times from t_0 to t, and the dynamic phase function $\phi(t)$ of the neuron at t time is as follows:

$$\phi(t) = \arctan \frac{\dot{x}(t - \tau) - s_{1c}}{\dot{x}(t) - s_{2c}} + 2n\pi \tag{4}$$

Where

n——The neuron's discharge times from the initial observed time t_0 to t time;

$\dot{x}(t)$——The first derivative of the membrane potential $x(t)$;

τ —— Time delay ;

(s_{1c}, s_{2c}) —— The center of rotation of the neuron's orbit attractor.

Taking example for the HR neuron model, the phase function is based on the $\dot{x}(t) - \dot{x}(t - \tau)$ phase plane, and the center of rotation is (-0.1, 0). The delay time τ is 0.5. The HR neuron has discharged n times from t_0 to t, and the dynamic phase function $\phi(t)$ of the HR neuron at t time can be defined as:

$$\phi(t) = \arctan \frac{\dot{x}(t - 0.5)}{\dot{x}(t) + 0.1} + 2n\pi \tag{5}$$

Where

n —— The HR neuron's discharge times from the initial observed time t_0 to t time;

$\dot{x}(t)$ —— The first derivative of the membrane potential $x(t)$.

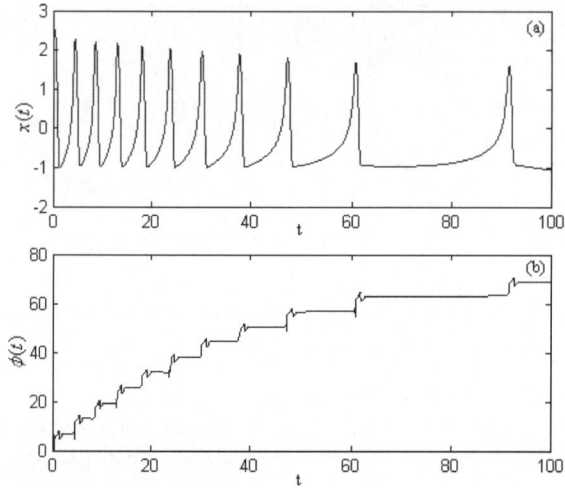

Fig. 3. the changing chart of the HR neuron's membrane potential and the corresponding dynamic phase function from 0 to 100. (a) The changing chart of the HR neuron's membrane potential from 0 to 100. (b) The changing chart of the HR neuron's dynamic phase function from 0 to 100.

Fig.3 shows the changing chart of the HR neuron's dynamic phase function described by formula (5) from 0 to 100. In Fig.3, Values of the neuron model's parameters are as follows: r =0.014, I=3, and other parameters are showed in reference[21]. From Fig.3, When the neuron discharges quickly, the phase function of the neuron also changes quickly; When the neuron doesn't discharge, the phase function of the neuron changes very slowly; The neuron discharges once, the phase function of the neuron increases 2π.

Based on formula (4), the absolute phase difference $|\Delta\phi(t)|$ is defined:

$$|\Delta\phi(t)| = |\phi_1(t) - \phi_2(t)| \tag{6}$$

Where

$\phi_i(t)$—— The dynamic phase function of neuron i; i=1, 2.

Based on the existing neuron synchronization's research findings and the above definition of the dynamic phase function, the neuron synchronization decision algorithm and procedure based on the dynamic phase function is put forward:

(1) When the maximum absolute phase difference of these two neurons ($|\Delta\phi(t)|_{max}$) is more than 4π, these two neurons don't realize synchronization.

(2) When the maximum absolute phase difference of these two neurons ($|\Delta\phi(t)|_{max}$) is no more than 4π for some small time intervals and is more than 2π, these two neurons can be viewed as the generalized synchronization.

(3) When the maximum absolute phase difference of these two neurons ($|\Delta\phi(t)|_{max}$) is no more than 2π, these two neurons realize the phase synchronization.

(4) When the maximum absolute phase difference of these two neurons ($|\Delta\phi(t)|_{max}$) approximates to zero, these two neurons maybe realize the complete synchronization; When the membrane potential absolute synchronization error ($err = |x_1 - x_2|$, x_i is the neuron's membrane potential.) approximates to zero, these two neurons realize the complete synchronization.

It must be noted that the maximum absolute phase difference of these two neurons ($|\Delta\phi(t)|_{max}$) must approximate to zero when they realize the complete synchronization. But these two neurons mustn't realize the complete synchronization when the maximum absolute phase difference of these two neurons ($|\Delta\phi(t)|_{max}$) approximates to zero. So that the maximum absolute phase difference ($|\Delta\phi(t)|_{max}$) is zero is the necessary condition that the two neurons realize the complete synchronization, and isn't the sufficient condition.

4   Synchronization of Two Uncoupled HR Neurons

The equation set of two uncoupled HR neurons' model is:

$$\dot{x}_i = y_i - a_i x^3_i + b_i x^2_i - z_i + (I_i + I_s(t))$$

$$\dot{y}_i = c_i - d_i x^2_i - y_i$$

$$\dot{z}_i = r_i[s_i(x_i - X_i) - z_i] \qquad \text{(i=1, 2)} \tag{7}$$

Where

$(x_1,\ y_1,\ z_1)$ —— Time variables of neuron 1;

$(x_2,\ y_2,\ z_2)$ —— Time variables of neuron 2;

$(a_1,\ b_1,\ c_1,\ d_1,\ r_1,\ s_1,\ I_1,\ X_1)$ —— Parameters of neuron 1;
$(a_2,\ b_2,\ c_2,\ d_2,\ r_2,\ s_2,\ I_2,\ X_2)$ ——Parameters of neuron 2.

Formula (7) is nondimensional. At numerical calculation, the values of these two neurons' parameters (except r) are as follows: $a_1=a_2=1.0$, $b_1=b_2=3.0$, $c_1=c_2=1.0$, $d_1=d_2=5.0$, $s_1=s_2=4.0$, $X_1=X_2=-1.56$, $I_1=I_2=3.0$; And the values of the initial states of these two neurons are respectively (1.0, 0.2, 0.2) and (-1.0, 0.8, 0.3); The discharge threshold value is -0.25, and if the membrane potential is more than -0.25, the neuron will produce one discharge process. Total stimulation current includes two parts: the bias current(I_1 and I_2) and the input stimulation current $I_S(t)$. The main function of the bias current(I_1 and I_2) is to make the neuron the discharge state. The input stimulation current begins to stimulate the synchronization system model after the bias current(I_1 and I_2) has been working for some time.

The difference between two uncoupled HR neurons is realized by the values of parameter r. The physical meaning of parameter r is presented in reference[21]. According to the difference of these two neurons' parameter r, there are three cases: the parameter r is the same, a little different($|r_1-r_2|\le 0.0005$), and much different($|r_1-r_2|\ge 0.003$). In Fig.1 of reference[21], you can set these two neurons at different discharge patterns by controlling values of the parameter r_i (i=1, 2). Values of two neurons' parameter r and their corresponding initial discharge patterns are showed in Table 1.

Table 1. The two neurons' parameter r and their initial discharge patterns

Case	Values of r_1 and r_2	The initial discharge pattern of neuron 1	The initial discharge pattern of neuron 2
The same	$r_1=r_2=0.013$	Chaos	Chaos
A little different	$r_1=0.017$, $r_2=0.0171$	Period 4	Period 4
Much different	$r_1=0.014$, $r_2=0.0085$	Chaos	Chaos

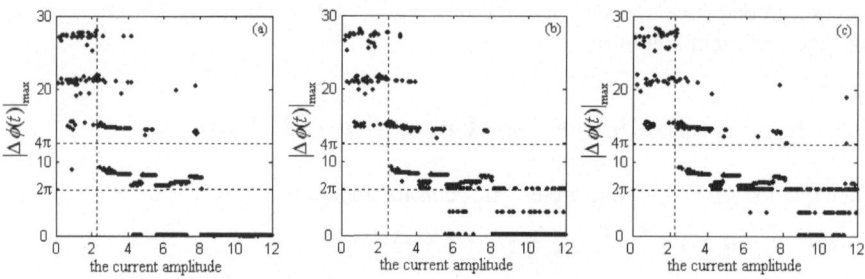

Fig. 4. The changing diagram of $|\Delta\phi(t)|_{max}$ with the stimulation current amplitude changing, where the period of the stimulation current is 2, and the changing step of the stimulation amplitude is 0.02. (a) The parameter r of these two neurons is the same: $r_1=r_2=0.013$. (b) The parameter r of these two neurons is a little different: $r_1=0.017$ and $r_2=0.0171$. (c) The parameter r of these two neurons is much different: $r_1=0.014$ and $r_2=0.0085$.

In the two uncoupled HR neuron model, the half wave sine current is taken as $I_S(t)$ and Its initial phase is zero. It stimulates the system model after the bias current has been working for 200. The simulation time of the system model is often 0~4000. In order to represent the neurons' synchronization process under the stimulation current amplitude's changing, the three group models are solved by above neuron synchronization decision algorithm, and the results are showed in Fig.4.

From Fig.4, when the period of the stimulation current is 2 and the stimulation amplitude changes from 0 to 12 according to the step 0.02, Whatever different or the same the parameter r is, these two neurons' discharge patterns begin with asynchronization($\left|\Delta\phi(t)\right|_{max} > 4\pi$), and gradually realize the phase synchronization ($\left|\Delta\phi(t)\right|_{max} \leq 2\pi$) state via the generalized synchronization($2\pi < \left|\Delta\phi(t)\right|_{max} \leq 4\pi$) process. When the current amplitude is near 2.2, and these two neurons go into the generalized synchronization(the intermittent discharge synchronization) state, so the current amplitude critical value of these two neurons realizing synchronization is about 2.2, which has nothing to do with the neurons' parameter and the initial state. In addition, the bigger the stimulation current amplitude is, the easier the neurons realize synchronization.

In this way, compared with other decision indexes and algorithms, the neuron synchronization decision algorithm based on the dynamic phase function can not only judge the three common synchronizations types: asynchronization, the generalized synchronization, and the phase synchronization, but also quantitatively solve the critical value of the neurons' realizing synchronization such as the stimulation current amplitude.

5   Conclusion

Based on the neurodynamics theory and the existing neuron synchronization's research findings, the dynamic phase function which can describe the neuron's discharge characteristics is defined and revised, and the neuron synchronization decision algorithm and procedure based on the dynamic phase function is put forward. The synchronization characteristics and the rule of the two uncoupled HR neurons are discussed by the synchronization decision algorithm. Compared with other decision indexes and algorithms, the neuron synchronization decision algorithm based on the dynamic phase function can not only judge the three common synchronizations types: asynchronization, the generalized synchronization, and the phase synchronization, but also quantitatively solve the critical value of the neurons' realizing synchronization such as the stimulation current amplitude.

References

1. Izhikevich, E.M.: Dynamical Systems in Neuroscience: The Geometry of Excitability and Bursting. The MIT Press (2005)
2. Neiman, A.B., Russell, D.F.: Synchronization of noise-induced bursts in noncoupled sensory neurons. Phys. Rev. Lett. 88(13), 138103-1–138103-4 (2002)

3. He, D., Shi, P., Stone, L.: Noise-induced synchronization in realistic models. Physical Review: E 67(2), 0272011–0272013 (2003)
4. Schafer, C., Rosenblum, M.G., Abel, H.H., et al.: Synchronization in the human cardiorespiratory system. Phys. Rev. E 60(1), 857–870 (1999)
5. Park, J.H.: Chaos synchronization between two different chaotic dynamical systems. Chaos, Solitons & Fractals 27(2), 549–554 (2006)
6. Rosemblum, M.G., Pikovsky, A.S., Kurths, J.: Phase Synchronization of Chaotic Oscillators. Chaos Phys. Rev. Lett. 76, 1804–1808 (1996)
7. Roscnblm, M.G., Pikovsky, A.S., Kurths, J.: From Phase to Lag Synchronization in Coupled Chaotic Oscillators. Phys. Rev. Lett. 78, 4193–4197 (1997)
8. Kocarev, L., Parlitz, U.: General Approach for Chaotic Synchronization with Applications to Communication. Phys. Rev. Lett. 74, 5028–5032 (1995)
9. Rulkov, N.F., Sushchik, M.M., Tsimring, L.S., et al.: Generalized synchronization of chaos in directionally coupled chaotic systems. Phys. Rev. E 51, 980–984 (1995)
10. Lee, D.-S., Kye, W.-H., Rim, S., Kwon, T.-Y., Kim, C.-M.: Generalized Phase Synchronization In Unidirectionally Coupled Chaotic Oscillators. Phys. Rev. E 67, 045201 (2003)
11. Zaks, M.A., Park, E.H., Rosenblum, M.G., et al.: Alternating Locking Ratios in Imperfect Phase Synchronization. Phys. Rev. Lett. 82, 4228–4232 (1999)
12. Shuai, J.-W., Durand, D.M.: Phase synchronization in two coupled chaotic neurons. Physics Letters: A 264(12), 289–296 (1999)
13. Wu, Y., Xu, J., He, D., Jin, W.: Study on nonlinear characteristic of two synchronizing uncoupled Hindmarsh-Rose neurons. Acta Physica Sinica 54(7), 3457–3464 (2005)
14. Hindmarsh, J.L., Rose, R.M.: A mode of the nerve impulse using two first-order differential equation. Nature 296, 162–164 (1982)
15. Hindmarsh, J.L., Rose, R.M.: A mode of neuronal bursting using three coupled first order differential equations. Proceedings of the Royal Society of London, Series B, Biological Sciences 221(1222), 87–102 (1984)
16. Rosenblum, M.G., Pikovsky, A.S., Kurths, J.: Phys. Rev. Lett. 76, 1804 (1996)
17. Osipov, G.V., Pikovsky, A.S., Rosenblum, M.G., Kurths, J.: Phys. Rev. E 55, 2353 (1997)
18. Rosenblum, M.G., Pikovsky, A.S., Kurths, J.: Phys. Rev. Lett. 78, 4193 (1997)
19. Pikovsky, A.S., Rosenblum, M.G., Osipov, G.V., Kurths, J.: Physica D 104, 219 (1997)
20. Lee, K.J., Kwak, Y., Lim, T.K.: Phys. Rev. Lett. 81, 321 (1998)
21. Peng, Y., Jian, Z., Wang, J.: Study on Discharge Patterns of Hindmarsh-Rose Neurons Under Slow Wave Current Stimulation. In: Jiao, L., Wang, L., Gao, X.-b., Liu, J., Wu, F. (eds.) ICNC 2006. LNCS, vol. 4221, pp. 127–134. Springer, Heidelberg (2006)
22. Peng, Y., et al.: Synchrony of two uncoupled neurons under half wave sine current stimulation. Communications in Nonlinear Science and Numerical Simulation 14(4), 1570–1575 (2009)
23. Peng, Y.: Study on the Synchrony Intensity Threshold of Two Uncoupled Neurons under Different Currents' Stimulation. In: Liu, D., Zhang, H., Polycarpou, M., Alippi, C., He, H. (eds.) ISNN 2011, Part I. LNCS, vol. 6675, pp. 42–51. Springer, Heidelberg (2011)

The SMC Approach to Global Synchronization of the Cellular Neural Networks with Multi-delays and Distributed Delays

Guoliang Cai[1,*], Qin Yao[1], and Xianbin Wu[2]

[1] Nonlinear Scientific Research Center, Jiangsu University, Zhenjiang, Jiangsu 212013, China
glcai@ujs.edu.cn, yaoqin11kuaile@163.com
[2] Junior College, Zhejiang Wanli University, Ningbo, Zhejiang, 315100, China
wxb3210@zwu.edu.cn

Abstract. This paper is further to investigate the global synchronization of the cellular neural networks with both multi-delays and distributed delays. Based on the Lyapunov stability theorem, by using the LMI technique and designing a sliding mode control (SMC) approach, a less conservative yet sufficient condition is derived to guarantee the global stability of the error system with both delay-independent and delay-dependent situations. The feasible SMC law is designed such that the trajectory of the error system is globally driven onto the specified sliding surface. The global synchronization is obtained at last.

Keywords: cellular neural networks, delays, global synchronization, global stability, sliding mode control.

1 Introduction

Cellular neural networks (CNNs) were introduced by Chua and Yang [1] in 1988, and have become a new subject of the natural and social sciences. Since Chua and Roska have presented the cellular neural networks with time delays (DCNNs) in 1992, the cellular neural networks have got their tremendous development and become an important branch of the neural networks. Recently, DCNNs have widely used in detection of the mobile objects, pattern classification and signal processing. Especially with the development of bioinformation, DCNNs has largely applied to the fields about image analysis, associative memories and cell simulations in nowadays. It is well known that time delays may cause instability, divergence or oscillation in many systems. Thus the stability analysis of DCNNs and neural networks has become an important topic of theoretical studies [2-8]. The global exponential stability of cellular neural networks with time-varying delays was studied in papers [9-12]. Many delay-independent and delay-dependent stability criteria for networks have been proposed over the past years, mainly based on Razumikhin techniques, the Lyapunov functional and linear matrix inequality (LMI) formulation [13-18].

---

[*] Corresponding author.

J. Wang, G.G. Yen, and M.M. Polycarpou (Eds.): ISNN 2012, Part I, LNCS 7367, pp. 235–245, 2012.
© Springer-Verlag Berlin Heidelberg 2012

The main advantages of the sliding mode control (SMC) theory are as follows: fast response, good transient performance and robustness to variations of system parameters. In paper [19], the authors studied the synchronization problem for non-identical chaotic neural networks with time delays, where the mismatched parameters were considered. An integral sliding mode control approach was proposed to address it. Then, by using the SMC method, paper [20] successfully considered the global synchronization of non-parameter perturbations of multi-delay Hopfield neural networks. Next, paper [21] investigated the synchronization problems of chaotic neural networks with mixed time delays also by SMC approach. In our paper, we will use the modified SMC approach to study the global synchronization of the cellular neural networks with multi-delays and distributed delays, where both delay-independent and delay-dependent are simultaneously taken into account. Based on the Lyapunov stability theory, some sufficient conditions for the global synchronization of the DCNNs is derived.

This paper is organized as follows: In section 2, system description and preliminaries are stated and a lemma and a corollary are listed. The SMC approach will be developed to address the synchronization problem of the DCNNs in section 3. We first properly construct an integral sliding surface. Then both delay-independent and delay-dependent conditions are derived, where an integral sliding mode controller is designed to guarantee the reachability of the specified sliding surface. We give the conclusions of this study in section 4.

2   Model Description and Preliminaries

In this paper, we first consider the following cellular neural networks with multi-delays and distributed delays:

$$\dot{x}_i(t) = -d_i x_i(t) + \sum_{j=1}^{n} a_{ij} f_j(x_j(t)) + \sum_{j=1}^{n} b_{ij} f_j(x_j(t - \tau_{ij}(t)))$$
$$+ \sum_{j=1}^{n} c_{ij} \int_{-\infty}^{t} K_{ij}(t-s) f_j(x_j(s)) ds + I_i. \qquad i = 1, 2, ..., n. \tag{1}$$

or in a compact form:

$$\dot{x}(t) = -Dx(t) + Ag(x(t)) + \sum_{j=1}^{n} B_j g(x(t - \tau_j))$$
$$+ \sum_{j=1}^{n} C_j \int_{-\infty}^{t} K_j(t-s) g(x(s)) ds + I. \qquad i = 1, 2, ..., n. \tag{2}$$

where $x_i(t) = (x_{i1}(t), x_{i2}(t), ..., x_{in}(t))^T \in R^n$ is the state vector of the ith neuron at time t. $D = (d_i)_{n \times n}$ indicates the feedback control of neurons; $A = (a_{ij})_{n \times n}$ and $B_j = (b_{ij})_{n \times 1}$ are connection weight and multi-delayed connection weight matrices, respectively; $f(x_i) = 0.5(|x_i + 1| + |x_i - 1|)$ is the activation and bounded function, $\tau_{ij}(t)$ is the multi-delay and satisfies $1 - \dot{\tau}_j \leq 1$, $C_j = (c_{ij})_{n \times 1}$ is the connection weight parameter of the distributed delay. $I=(I_1,I_2,...,I_n)^T$ is the external input vector. The nuclear coefficient $K_{ij} : [0, \infty) \to [0, \infty)$ is sectional continuous in $[0, \infty)$ and satisfies

$$\int_0^\infty K_{ij}(s)ds = 1, \qquad i, j = 1, 2, ..., n.$$

It is assumed that the measured output of system (1) is dependent on both the state and the multi-delay and distributed delay state with the following form:

$$z(t) = Ex(t) - \sum_{j=1}^n Mx(t-\tau_j) + \sum_{j=1}^n Q \int_{-\infty}^t K_j(t-s)g(x(s))ds \qquad j = 1, 2, ..., n. \quad (3)$$

where $z(t) \in R^m, E, M, Q \in R^{m \times n}$ are constant matrices.

Let (1) be the drive system. The response system is represented by

$$\dot{y}_i(t) = -\hat{d}_i y_i(t) + \sum_{j=1}^n \hat{a}_{ij} \hat{f}_j(y_j(t)) + \sum_{j=1}^n \hat{b}_{ij} \hat{f}_j(y_j(t-\tau_{ij}(t)))$$

$$+ \sum_{j=1}^n \hat{c}_{ij} \int_{-\infty}^t \hat{K}_{ij}(t-s) \hat{f}_j(y_j(s))ds + \hat{I}_i + u_i(t). \qquad i = 1, 2, ..., n. \quad (4)$$

or in a compact form:

$$\dot{y}(t) = -\hat{D}x(t) + \hat{A}\hat{g}(y(t)) + \sum_{j=1}^n \hat{B}_j \hat{g}(y(t-\tau_j))$$

$$+ \sum_{j=1}^n \hat{C}_j \int_{-\infty}^t \hat{K}_j(t-s) \hat{g}(x(s))ds + \hat{I} + u(t). \qquad i = 1, 2, ..., n. \quad (5)$$

where $y(t) \in R^n$ is the state vector of the response system, $u(t)$ is the sliding mode controller to be designed. The purpose of this study is to propose a method to designing a suitable controller such that: $\|x(t)-y(t)\| \to 0$ as $t \to \infty$. Define the error signal $e(t) = x(t)-y(t)$, then the error system of (2) and (5) can be obtained as follow:

$$\dot{e}(t) = -De(t) + A\varphi(e(t)) + \sum_{j=1}^n B_j \varphi(e(t-\tau_j)) + \sum_{j=1}^n C_j \int_{-\infty}^t K_j(t-s)\varphi(e(s))ds + I - \hat{I}$$

$$+ (\hat{D}-D)y(t) - \hat{A}\hat{g}(y(t)) - \sum_{j=1}^n \hat{B}_j \hat{g}y(t-\tau_j) - \sum_{j=1}^n \hat{c}_j \int_{-\infty}^t \hat{K}_j(t-s)\hat{g}(y(s))ds$$

$$+ Agy(t) + \sum_{j=1}^n B_j g(y(t-\tau_j)) + \sum_{j=1}^n c_j \int_{-\infty}^t K_j(t-s)g(y(s))ds. \qquad j = 1, 2, ..., n.$$

where $\varphi(e(t))=g(x(t))-g(y(t))$. Let

$$R(t) = I - \hat{I} + (\hat{D}-D)y(t) - \hat{A}\hat{g}(y(t)) - \sum_{j=1}^n \hat{B}_j \hat{g}y(t-\tau_j) - \sum_{j=1}^n \hat{c}_j \int_{-\infty}^t \hat{K}_j(t-s)\hat{g}(y(s))ds$$

$$+ Agy(t) + \sum_{j=1}^n B_j g(y(t-\tau_j)) + \sum_{j=1}^n c_j \int_{-\infty}^t K_j(t-s)g(y(s))ds.$$

Then we have

$$\dot{e}(t) = -De(t) + A\varphi(e(t)) + \sum_{j=1}^{n} B_j\varphi(e(t-\tau_j)) + \sum_{j=1}^{n} C_j \int_{-\infty}^{t} K_j(t-s)\varphi(e(s))ds + R(t). \quad (6)$$

In order to meet the proof of the theorem, different from the assumptions about the activation functions in papers [19], [20] and [21], we don't make assumptions. We use the following lemma.

Lemma 1. [22] $\forall$ $x(t)=(x_1(t), x_2(t),\ldots, x_n(t))^{\mathrm{T}}$, $y(t)=(y_1(t), y_2(t),\ldots, y_n(t))^{\mathrm{T}} \in R^n$, there exists a positive definite matrix $P \in R^{n \times n}$, the following matrix inequality holds

$$2x^{\mathrm{T}} y \leq x^{\mathrm{T}} Px + y^{\mathrm{T}} P^{-1}y.$$

Corolary 1. $\forall$ $x(t)=(x_1(t), x_2(t),\ldots, x_n(t))^{\mathrm{T}}$, $y(t)=(y_1(t), y_2(t),\ldots, y_n(t))^{\mathrm{T}} \in R^n$, $\forall$ Q is a constant matrix, we get the next matrix inequality

$$2x^{\mathrm{T}}Qy \leq x^{\mathrm{T}}QQ^{\mathrm{T}}x + y^{\mathrm{T}} y. \quad (7)$$

Proof. $\forall$ $x(t)=(x_1(t), x_2(t),\ldots, x_n(t))^{\mathrm{T}}$, $y(t)=(y_1(t), y_2(t),\ldots, y_n(t))^{\mathrm{T}} \in R^n$, from the Lemma 1, we have

$$2x^{\mathrm{T}}Qy = 2(Q^{\mathrm{T}}x)^{\mathrm{T}} y \leq (Q^{\mathrm{T}}x)^{\mathrm{T}} P(Q^{\mathrm{T}}x) + y^{\mathrm{T}}P^{-1}y = x^{\mathrm{T}}QPQ^{\mathrm{T}}x + y^{\mathrm{T}} P^{-1}y$$

then let $P=I$, we get

$$2x^{\mathrm{T}}Qy \leq x^{\mathrm{T}}QQ^{\mathrm{T}}x + y^{\mathrm{T}} y.$$

3   SMC Design

For the DCNNs in Eq. (2), a sliding mode controller is to be chosen so that: (i) the sliding motion is globally asymptotically stable; (ii) the state trajectory in Eq. (2) is globally driven onto the specified sliding surface and maintained there for all subsequent time.

To utilize the information of the measured output $z(t)$ sufficiently, a suitable sliding surface is constructed as

$$S(t) = e(t) - \int_0^t [-De(s) + A\varphi(e(s)) + \sum_{j=1}^{n} B_j\varphi(e(s-\tau_j)) + \sum_{j=1}^{n} C_j \int_{-\infty}^{t} K_j(s-\rho)\varphi(e(\rho))d\rho$$

$$- K(z(s) - Ey(s) + \sum_{j=1}^{n} My(s-\tau_j) - \sum_{j=1}^{n} Q\int_{-\infty}^{t} K_j(s-\rho)g(y(\rho))d\rho)]ds. \quad (8)$$

where the gain matrix $K \in R^{m \times n}$ is to be designed. From Eq. (6), one can obtain

$$e(t) = e(0) + \int_0^t [-De(s) + A\varphi(e(s)) + \sum_{j=1}^{n} B_j\varphi(e(s-\tau_j))$$

$$+ \sum_{j=1}^{n} C_j \int_{-\infty}^{t} K_j(s-\rho)\varphi(e(\rho))d\rho - u(s) + R(s)]ds. \quad (9)$$

Substitute (9) to (8), then one can get

$$S(t) = e(0) + \int_0^t [KEe(s) - \sum_{j=1}^n KMe(s - \tau_j)) + \sum_{j=1}^n KQ \int_{-\infty}^s K_j(s - \rho)\varphi(e(\rho))d\rho - u(s) + R(s)]ds.$$

where $e(0)$ is an initial condition of the error system (6).

According to the SMC theory, after the error system driving onto the specified sliding surface, the sliding mode controller is a strong nonlinear input, so it is difficult to analyze. But if we use a continuous equivalent input instead of the switching input, then the analysis can be simplified. When the state trajectories of the error system (6) enter into the sliding surface, we have: $S(t)=0$ and $\dot{S}(t)=0$. Then we get the following equivalent control law

$$u(t) = KEe(t) - \sum_{j=1}^n KMe(t - \tau_j)) + \sum_{j=1}^n KQ \int_{-\infty}^t K_j(t - s)\varphi(e(s))ds + R(t). \quad (10)$$

By substituting (10) into (6), the sliding mode dynamics can be obtained and represented by

$$\dot{e}(t) = -(D + KE)e(t) + A\varphi(e(t)) + \sum_{j=1}^n KMe(t - \tau_j) + \sum_{j=1}^n B_j\varphi(e(t - \tau_j))$$

$$+ \sum_{j=1}^n (C_j - KQ) \int_{-\infty}^t K_j(t - s)\varphi(e(s))ds. \quad (11)$$

The next work is to study the stability of the system (11). Both delay-independent and delay-dependent criteria are taken into account such that the system (11) is globally stable, then the DCCNs of (1) and (4) may achieve global synchronization. The next theorem is obtained.

Theorem 1. *For given scalars $\tau_j > 0$ ($j=1,2,\ldots,n$), the sliding mode dynamics (11) is globally asymptotically stable, if one of the following conditions is held:*

(i) *(Delay-independent condition) there exist real matrices $P=P^T > 0$, $H_{1j}= H_{1j}^T > 0$,*
    $H_{2j}= H_{2j}^T > 0$, $H_{3j}= H_{3j}^T > 0$, such that

$$N_j = \begin{pmatrix} \Phi_{11} + \Phi_{21} + \Phi_{31} + \Phi_{41} + \Phi_{51} & -\sum_{j=1}^n H_{1j} & \sum_{j=1}^n H_{2j} & -\sum_{j=1}^n H_{2j} & \sum_{j=1}^n H_{3j} & -\sum_{j=1}^n H_{3j} \\ * & I & 0 & 0 & 0 & 0 \\ * & * & I & 0 & 0 & 0 \\ * & * & * & I & 0 & 0 \\ * & * & * & * & I & 0 \\ * & * & * & * & * & 0 \end{pmatrix} < 0. \quad (12)$$

where $*$ always denotes the symmetric block in a symmetric matrix, and

$$\Phi_{11} = -P(D+KE) - (D+KE)^{\mathrm{T}} P + \sum_{j=1}^{n} H_{1j}, \quad \Phi_{21} = (PKM)(PKM)^{\mathrm{T}}, \quad \Phi_{31} = (PA)(PA)^{\mathrm{T}},$$

$$\Phi_{41} = (P\sum_{j=1}^{n} B_j)(P\sum_{j=1}^{n} B_j)^{\mathrm{T}}, \quad \Phi_{51} = (P\sum_{j=1}^{n}(C_j - KQ))(P\sum_{j=1}^{n}(C_j - KQ))^{\mathrm{T}}.$$

(ii) (Delay-dependent condition) there exist real matrices $P=P^{\mathrm{T}}>0$, $H_{1j}= H_{1j}^{\mathrm{T}}>0$, $H_{2j}= H_{2j}^{\mathrm{T}}>0$, $H_{3j}= H_{3j}^{\mathrm{T}}>0$, $R=R^{\mathrm{T}}$, and $r>0$ such that:

$$\Gamma_j = \begin{pmatrix} \Phi_{11}+\Phi_{21}+\Phi_{31}+\Phi_{41}+\Phi_{51}+\Xi_{11} & -\sum_{j=1}^{n}H_{1j} & \sum_{j=1}^{n}H_{2j} & -\sum_{j=1}^{n}H_{2j} & \sum_{j=1}^{n}H_{3j} & -\sum_{j=1}^{n}H_{3j} \\ * & \Xi_{22} & 0 & 0 & 0 & 0 \\ * & * & \Xi_{33} & 0 & 0 & 0 \\ * & * & * & \Xi_{44} & 0 & 0 \\ * & * & * & * & \Xi_{55} & 0 \\ * & * & * & * & * & 0 \end{pmatrix} < 0. \quad (13)$$

where τ_j is the delay, the matrix K can be designed by (12) and (13), respectively, and

$$\Xi_{11} = -r(D+KE)\sum_{j=1}^{n}\tau_j R, \quad \Xi_{22} = I + rKM\sum_{j=1}^{n}\tau_j R, \quad \Xi_{33} = I + rA\sum_{j=1}^{n}\tau_j R,$$

$$\Xi_{44} = I + r\sum_{j=1}^{n}\tau_j RB_j, \quad \Xi_{55} = I + r\sum_{j=1}^{n}\tau_j R(C_j - KQ).$$

Proof. We first prove that system (11) is globally asymptotically stable under condition (i). Design the Lyapunov function as: $V_1(t)= V_{11}(t)+ V_{12}(t)+ V_{13}(t)+ V_{14}(t)$, where

$$V_{11}(t) = e^{\mathrm{T}}(t)Pe(t), \qquad V_{12}(t) = \sum_{j=1}^{n}\int_{t-\tau_j}^{t} e^{\mathrm{T}}(s)H_{1j}e(s)\mathrm{d}s,$$

$$V_{13}(t) = \sum_{j=1}^{n}\int_{t-\tau_j}^{t} \varphi^{\mathrm{T}}(e(s))H_{2j}\varphi(e(s))\mathrm{d}s, \qquad (14)$$

$$V_{14}(t) = \sum_{j=1}^{n}\int_{t-\tau_j}^{t} (\int_{-\infty}^{t} K_j(s-\rho)\varphi(e(\rho))\mathrm{d}\rho)^{\mathrm{T}} H_{3j}(\int_{-\infty}^{t} K_j(s-\rho)\varphi(e(\rho))\mathrm{d}\rho)\mathrm{d}s.$$

Calculating the derivative of (14) along the trajectories of (11), we get

$$\dot{V}_{11}(t) = 2e^{\mathrm{T}}(t)P\dot{e}(t)$$

$$\leq e^{\mathrm{T}}(t)[-P(D+KE)-(D+KE)^{\mathrm{T}}P + \sum_{j=1}^{n} H_{1j}]e(t) + 2e^{\mathrm{T}}(t)P\sum_{j=1}^{n} KMe(t-\tau_j)$$

$$+ 2e^{\mathrm{T}}(t)PA\varphi(e(t)) + 2e^{\mathrm{T}}(t)P\sum_{j=1}^{n}(C_j - KQ)\int_{-\infty}^{t} K_j(t-s)\varphi(e(s))\mathrm{d}s \qquad (15)$$

$$+ 2e^{\mathrm{T}}(t)P\sum_{j=1}^{n} B_j\varphi(e(t-\tau_j)).$$

By the Corollary 1, we have

$$\dot{V}_{11}(t) \leq e^{\mathrm{T}}(t)[\Phi_{11} - \sum_{j=1}^{n} H_{1j} + \Phi_{21} + \Phi_{31} + \Phi_{41} + \Phi_{51}]e(t) + e(t-\tau_j)^{\mathrm{T}}e(t-\tau_j)$$

$$+ \varphi^{\mathrm{T}}(e(t))\varphi(e(t)) + \varphi^{\mathrm{T}}(e(t-\tau_j))\varphi(e(t-\tau_j)) \qquad (16)$$

$$+ (\int_{-\infty}^{t} K_j(t-s)\varphi(e(s))\mathrm{d}s)^{\mathrm{T}}(\int_{-\infty}^{t} K_j(t-s)\varphi(e(s))\mathrm{d}s).$$

$$\dot{V}_{12}(t) = \sum_{j=1}^{n}[e^{\mathrm{T}}(t)H_{1j}e(t) - (1-\dot{\tau}_j)e^{\mathrm{T}}(t-\tau_j)H_{1j}e(t-\tau_j)]$$

$$\leq \sum_{j=1}^{n}[e^{\mathrm{T}}(t)H_{1j}e(t) - e^{\mathrm{T}}(t-\tau_j)H_{1j}e(t-\tau_j)]. \qquad (17)$$

$$\dot{V}_{13}(t) = \sum_{j=1}^{n}[\varphi^{\mathrm{T}}(e(t))H_{2j}\varphi(e(t)) - (1-\dot{\tau}_j)\varphi^{\mathrm{T}}(e(t-\tau_j))H_{2j}\varphi(e(t-\tau_j))]$$

$$\leq \sum_{j=1}^{n}[\varphi^{\mathrm{T}}(e(t))H_{2j}\varphi(e(t)) - \varphi^{\mathrm{T}}(e(t-\tau_j))H_{2j}\varphi(e(t-\tau_j))]. \qquad (18)$$

$$\dot{V}_{14}(t) = \sum_{j=1}^{n}[(\int_{-\infty}^{t} K_j(t-s)\varphi(e(s))\mathrm{d}s)^{\mathrm{T}}H_{3j}(\int_{-\infty}^{t} K_j(t-s)\varphi(e(s))\mathrm{d}s)$$

$$-(1-\dot{\tau}_j)(\int_{-\infty}^{t} K_j(t-\tau_j-s)\varphi(e(s))\mathrm{d}s)^{\mathrm{T}}H_{3j}(\int_{-\infty}^{t} K_j(t-\tau_j-s)\varphi(e(s))\mathrm{d}s)] \qquad (19)$$

$$\leq \sum_{j=1}^{n}[(\int_{-\infty}^{t} K_j(t-s)\varphi(e(s))\mathrm{d}s)^{\mathrm{T}}H_{3j}(\int_{-\infty}^{t} K_j(t-s)\varphi(e(s))\mathrm{d}s)$$

$$-(\int_{-\infty}^{t} K_j(t-\tau_j-s)\varphi(e(s))\mathrm{d}s)^{\mathrm{T}}H_{3j}(\int_{-\infty}^{t} K_j(t-\tau_j-s)\varphi(e(s))\mathrm{d}s)].$$

Then we have

$$\dot{V}_1(t) \leq \sum_{j=1}^{n} \Sigma_j^{\mathrm{T}}(t)N_j\Sigma_j(t).$$

$$\Sigma_j(t) = [e^{\mathrm{T}}(t), e^{\mathrm{T}}(t-\tau_j), \varphi^{\mathrm{T}}(e(t)), \varphi^{\mathrm{T}}(e(t-\tau_j)), (\int_{-\infty}^{t} K_j(t-s)\varphi(e(s))\mathrm{d}s)^{\mathrm{T}}, (\int_{-\infty}^{t} K_j(t-\tau_j-s)\varphi(e(s))\mathrm{d}s)^{\mathrm{T}}]^{\mathrm{T}}.$$

Choose a suitable K, then follow from (12), we have

$$\dot{V}_1(t) \leq \sum_{j=1}^{n} \Sigma_j^T(t) N_j \Sigma_j(t) < 0.$$

Therefore, the sliding mode dynamics (11) is globally asymptotically stable.

For case (ii), we design the following Lyapunov function: $V_1(t) = V_{11}(t) + V_{12}(t) + V_{13}(t) + V_{14}(t) + V_{15}(t)$, where $V_{11}(t)$, $V_{12}(t)$, $V_{13}(t)$, $V_{14}(t)$ are the same with (14) and

$$V_{15}(t) = r \sum_{j=1}^{n} \int_{-\tau_j}^{0} \int_{t+\sigma}^{t} \dot{e}^T(s) R \dot{e}(s) \, ds \, d\sigma.$$

$$\dot{V}_{15}(t) = r \dot{\tau}_j \int_{t+\sigma}^{t} \dot{e}^T(s) R \dot{e}(s) \, ds + r \tau_j \dot{e}^T(t) R \dot{e}(t) - r \int_{t-\tau_j}^{t} \dot{e}^T(s) R \dot{e}(s) \, ds$$

$$\leq r \sum_{j=1}^{n} \tau_j \dot{e}^T(t) R \dot{e}(t).$$

(20)

Calculating (11) along with (20), then combine with (16), (17), (18) and (19), thus we have

$$\dot{V}_2(t) \leq \sum_{j=1}^{n} \Sigma_j^T(t) \Gamma_j \Sigma_j(t).$$

Choose a suitable K, then follow from (13), we get

$$\dot{V}_2(t) \leq \sum_{j=1}^{n} \Sigma_j^T(t) \Gamma_j \Sigma_j(t) < 0.$$

Therefore, the sliding mode dynamics (11) is globally asymptotically stable. Thus the proof is completed.

Theorem 1 presents the global stability of system (11), both delay-independent and delay-dependent criteria are investigated. The conservatism is reduced and the result guarantees the global synchronization of systems (1) and (4). Compare with the result of [20], our method not only solve the multi-delays condition but also finish off the distributed delays condition.

In order to guarantee the reachability of the specific switching surface, we choose a feasible SMC law as follows.

Theorem 2. *Consider the error system (6). Assume that the sliding function is given by (8) with P, K and r, where P, K and r are the suitable solution to (12) and (13). Let $\theta > 0$ be a constant scalar, if the SMC law is designed as follows:*

$$u(t) = KEe(t) - \sum_{j=1}^{n} KMe(t-\tau_j)) + \sum_{j=1}^{n} KQ \int_{-\infty}^{t} K_j(t-s) \varphi(e(s)) \, ds - \omega(t) \text{sgn}(S(t)). \quad (21)$$

with the switching gain $\omega(t)$ being taken as

$$\omega(t) = -\theta - [\|\hat{D} - D\| + \|\hat{A}\|\|\hat{g}\| + \sum_{j=1}^{n}\|\hat{c}_j\|\|\hat{K}_j\|\|\hat{g}\| + \|A\|\|g\| + \sum_{j=1}^{n}\|c_j\|\|K_j\|\|g\|]\|y(t)\|$$

(22)

$$- \sum_{j=1}^{n}\|B_j\|[\|\hat{g}\| + \|g\|]\|y(t - \tau_j)\| - \|I - \hat{I}\|.$$

The trajectories of the error system can be globally driven onto the sliding surface S(t)=0.

Proof. We are in a position to design a feasible SMC law to guarantee the reachability of the sliding surface. It is follows from (8) and (21) that

$$\dot{S}(t) = R(t) + \omega(t)\,\mathrm{sgn}\,(S(t)).$$

(23)

By designing the following Lyapunov function:

$$V_3(t) = \frac{1}{2}S^{\mathrm{T}}(t)S(t),$$

by (22), one can obtain that

$$\dot{V}_3(t) = S^{\mathrm{T}}(t)[R(t) + \omega(t)\mathrm{sgn}(S(t))]$$

$$\leq \|S(t)\|\left([\|\hat{D} - D\| + \|\hat{A}\|\|\hat{g}\| + \sum_{j=1}^{n}\|\hat{c}_j\|\|\hat{K}_j\|\|\hat{g}\| + \|A\|\|g\| + \sum_{j=1}^{n}\|c_j\|\|K_j\|\|g\|]\|y(t)\| \right.$$

$$\left. + \sum_{j=1}^{n}\|B_j\|[\|\hat{g}\| + \|g\|]\|y(t - \tau_j)\| + \|I - \hat{I}\| + \omega(t)\|S(t)\|_1 \right)$$

$$= -\theta\|S(t)\|.$$

It means that $\dot{V}_3(t) < 0,$ for any $S(t) \neq 0$. So the trajectory of the error system (6) is globally driven onto the specified sliding surface and maintained there for all subsequent time. Therefore, the DCNNs (1) can achieve global synchronization with (4). This completes the proof.

The designed SMC law can be regarded as an output error feedback control plus a high-gain compensation law which is used to cope with the global synchronization of the neural networks, and this approach can also use for other complex networks.

4   Conclusions

In this paper, the global synchronization of the cellular neural networks with both multi-delays and distributed delays has been investigated effectively. Based on the Lyapunov stability theorem, by using the LMI technique, the SMC approach is successfully used to guarantee the global stability of the error system, which includes both delay-independent and delay-dependent conditions. The SMC law has been derived such that the trajectory of the error system is globally driven onto the specified sliding surface. There are rich consequences of the synchronization of

DCNNs in literature, but one may find that the method presented in this paper is much general and effectiveness compared with someone [13-18]. Consequently, it is a more comprehensive way to apply to the practice.

Acknowledgments. This work was supported by the National Nature Science foundation of China (Nos. 70571030, 11102180), the Society Science Foundation from Ministry of Education of China (Nos. 12YJAZH002, 08JA790057), the Priority Academic Program Development of Jiangsu Higher Education Institutions, the Advanced Talents' Foundation of Jiangsu University (Nos. 07JDG054, 10JDG140), and the Students' Research Foundation of Jiangsu University (No. 10A147). Especially, thanks for the support of Jiangsu University.

References

1. Chua, L.O., Yang, L.: Cellular Neural Networks: Theory. IEEE Trans. Circuits Syst. I. 35, 1257–1272 (1998)
2. Singh, V.: A Generalized LMI-based Approach to the Global Asymptotic Stability of Delayed Cellular Neural Networks. IEEE Trans. Neural Netw. 15, 223–225 (2004)
3. Chen, A.P., Cao, J.D., Huang, L.H.: Global Robust Stability of Interval Cellular Neural Networks With Time-varying Delays. Chaos Solitons Fractals 23, 787–799 (2005)
4. Huang, L.H., Huang, C.X., Liu, B.W.: Dynamics of a Class of Cellular Neural Networks With Time-varying Delays. Phys. Lett. A. 345, 330–344 (2005)
5. Hu, S.Q., Liu, D.R.: On the global output convergence of a class of recurrent neural networks with time-varying inputs. Neural Netw. 18, 171–178 (2005)
6. Wang, Z., Liu, Y., Liu, X.: Stability Analysis for Stochastic Cohen-Grossberg Neural Networks with Mixed Time Delays. IEEE Trans. Neural Netw. 17, 814–820 (2006)
7. Dai, L.M., Wang, G.Q.: Implementation of Periodicity Ratio in Analyzing Nonlinear Dynamic Systems: A Comparison With Lyapunov Exponent. J. Compu. Nonli. Dyn. 3(1), 011006 (2008)
8. Cai, G.L., Yao, Q., Shao, H.J.: Global synchronization of weighted cellular neural networks with time-varying coupling delays. Commun. Nonlinear Sci. Numer. Simul. (2012), doi:10.1016/j.cnsns.2012.02.010
9. Liu, D.R., Xiong, X.X.: Identification of motifs with insertions and deletions in protein sequences using self-organizing neural networks. Neural Netw. 18, 8355–8842 (2005)
10. Jiang, H.J., Teng, Z.D.: A New Criterion on the Global Exponential Stability for Cellular Neural Networks With Multiple Time-varying Delays. Phys. Lett. A. 338, 461–471 (2005)
11. Gau, R.S., Lien, C.H., Hsieh, J.G.: Global Exponential Stability for Uncertain Cellular Neural Networks With Multiple Time-varying Delays via LMI Approach. Chaos Solitons Fractals 32, 1258–1267 (2007)
12. Ma, K.Y., Yu, L., Zhang, W.A.: Global Exponential Stability of Cellular Neural Networks With Time-varying Discrete and Distributed Delays. Neurocomputing 72, 2705–2709 (2009)
13. Zhang, Q., Wei, X.P., Xu, J.: Delay-dependent Exponential Stability of Cellular Neural Networks With Time-varying Delays. Chaos Solitons Fractals 23, 1363–1369 (2005)
14. He, Y., Liu, G.P., Rees, D.: New Delay-dependent Stability Criteria for Neural Networks With Time-varying Delay. IEEE Trans. Neural Netw. 18, 310–314 (2007)

15. Cai, G.L., Shao, H.J., Yao, Q.: A Linear Matrix Inequality Approach to Global Synchronization of Multi-Delay Hopeld Neural Networks with Parameter Perturbations. Chin. J. Phys. 50, 86–99 (2012)
16. Mou, S., Gao, H., Lam, J., Qiang, W.: A New Criterion of Delaydependent Asymptotic Stability for Hopfield Neural Networks With Time Delay. IEEE Trans. Neural. Netw. 19, 532–535 (2008)
17. Wang, D., Liu, D.R., Wei, Q.L.: Finite-horizon neuro-optimal tracking control for a class of discrete-time nonlinear systems using adaptive dynamic programming approach. Neurocomputing 78, 14–22 (2012)
18. Zhang, Q., Wei, X.P., Xu, J.: Delay-dependent Exponential Stability Criteria for Non-autonomous Cellular Neural Networks With Time-varying Delays. Chaos Solitons Fractals 36, 985–990 (2008)
19. Huang, H., Feng, G.: Synchronization of Nonidentical Chaotic Neural Networks with Time Delays. Neural Netw. 22, 869–874 (2009)
20. Shao, H.J., Cai, G.L., Wang, H.X.: A Linear Matrix Inequality Approach to Global Synchronisation of Non-parameters Perturbations of Multi-delay Hopfield Neural Network. Chin. Phys. B. 19, 110509.1–110509.6 (2010)
21. Gan, Q.T., Xu, R., Kang, X.B.: Synchronization of Chaotic Neural Networks with Mixed Time Delays. Commun. Nonlinear Sci. Numer. Simul. 16, 966–974 (2011)
22. Cao, J.D., Lu, J.Q.: Adaptive Synchronization of Neural Networks With or Without Time-varying Delays. Chaos 16, 013133 (2006)

A Novel Feature Sparsification Method
for Kernel-Based Approximate Policy Iteration

Zhenhua Huang, Chunming Liu, Xin Xu, Chuanqiang Lian, and Jun Wu

Institute of Automation, National University of Defense Technology,
Changsha, 410073, P.R. China
zhenhuahuang10@gmail.com

Abstract. In this paper, we present a novel feature sparsification approach for a class of kernel-based approximate policy iteration algorithms called KLSPI. We firstly introduce the relative approximation error in the sparsification process based on the approximate linear dependence (ALD) analysis. The relative approximation error is used as the criterion for selecting the kernel-based features. An improved KLSPI algorithm is also proposed by integrating the new sparsification method with KLSPI. Experimental results on the Inverted Pendulum problem demonstrate that the proposed sparsification method can obtain a smaller size of kernel dictionary than the previous ALD method. Furthermore, by using the more representative samples as the kernel dictionary, the precision of value function approximation has been increased. The improved KLSPI algorithm can also achieve better learning efficiency and policy quality than the original one. The feasibility and validity of the new method are proven.

Keywords: reinforcement learning, sparsification, kernel methods, approximate linear dependence, kernel-based least-squares policy iteration.

1 Introduction

Reinforcement learning (RL) is a machine learning framework for sequential decision making under uncertainties [1]. The environment of RL is typically modeled as a Markov decision process (MDP). While solving an MDP problem, most RL algorithms approximate the value functions by observing data generated from the states transitions and the rewords [2]. So RL provides a model-free methodology, which is very promising to solve the optimization in complex sequential decision-making problems. Although the research field becomes more mature, the approximation and generalization ability are still open issues in RL [6].

In 1988 Richard S. Sutton proposed a widely used RL method called temporal-difference (TD) learning [1]. By combining the theory of linear least-squares function approximation with the TD learning method, Bradtke and Andrew G. Barto in 1996 introduced two new algorithms called Least-Squares TD (LSTD) and Recursive Least-Squares TD (RLSTD) [4]. Later in 2003 Michail G. Lagoudakis and Ronald Parr proposed an approach called least-squares policy iteration (LSPI) which combines value function approximation with linear architectures and approximate policy

J. Wang, G.G. Yen, and M.M. Polycarpou (Eds.): ISNN 2012, Part I, LNCS 7367, pp. 246–255, 2012.

iteration [2]. Moreover, based on LSPI algorithm a new method called Kernel-based Least-Squares policy iteration (KLSPI) [3] was proposed by Xu, which adopts the kernel-function as the approximator to solve value function approximation problems in MDP. The computational cost of the kernel methods is one of the most concerned problems. Xu presented a spasification procedure [3] by approximating linear dependence analysis on the whole samples to obtain a kernel dictionary, the size of which is smaller than the samples' number. However, how to select a proper and representative kernel dictionary from the original samples is a difficult issue since that few knowledge about the sparsity level σ will be presented, which plays an important role in the spasification procedure.

To overcome such difficulty, an approximate linear dependence (ALD) method based on the relative approximation error is presented in this paper. Besides, an improved Kernel-based Least-squares Policy Iteration (KLSPI) algorithm comes into being by integrating the proposed novel ALD method. Finally, an experiment on the Inverted Pendulum is performed to evaluate the new method.

The rest of the paper is organized as follows. Section 2 introduces the framework of the approximate linear dependence (ALD) analysis in KLSPI and gives an overview about the main steps of the spasification procedure. Section 3 describes the the ALD approach based on the relative approximation error and the corresponding improved KLSPI algorithm. Section 4 describes some experimental results and the evaluations. Finally, some conclusions are drawn in Section 5.

2   Approximate Linear Dependence (ALD) Analysis in KLSPI

In Least-square policy iteration algorithm (LSPI) [7], the approximation state-action value function is represented by

$$\tilde{Q}(x,a) = \sum_{i=1}^{k} \alpha_i \varphi_i(x,a) \tag{1}$$

where $\varphi_i(x,a)$ ($i=1,2,\ldots,k$) are basis functions and α_i are the coefficients.

Let S denote the original state space. A kernel function is a mapping from $S \times S$ to R. A Mercer kernel is a definite kernel function. According to the Mercer theorem [5], there exists a Hilbert space H and a mapping φ from S to H such that

$$k(s_i,s_j) = <\varphi(s_i),\varphi(s_j)> \tag{2}$$

where $<\bullet,\bullet>$ is the inner product in H.

By introducing the kernel function $k(s,s_i)$ as the basis functions, the state-action value of KLSPI can be expressed as follows [3]:

$$\tilde{Q}(s) = \sum_{i=1}^{m} \alpha_i k(s,s_i) \tag{3}$$

where s and s_i are the combined features of state-action pairs (x, a) and (x_i, a_i), respectively, α_i ($i=1, 2, \ldots, m$) are the corresponding coefficients.

An important problem in KLSPI is how to obtain the proper dictionary and decrease the computation complexity as well as the memory cost of the kernel methods [8]. When using kernel methods the number of adjustable parameters for the solutions is equal to the number of sample data points. It's awful to apply kernel methods on the whole samples. An essential step for KLSPI is the sparsification to obtain a proper and smaller kernel dictionary. A sparsification approach called approximate linear dependence (ALD) analysis was introduced by Xu in [3]. After the ALD analysis, all the feature vectors of the data samples can be approximately represented by the linear combinations of the feature vectors in the dictionary within a given precision [9].

The optimal value of δ_m can be computed by

$$\delta_m = \mathbf{k}_{mm} - \mathbf{k}_{m-1}^{\mathrm{T}}(s_m)\mathbf{K}_{m-1}^{-1}\mathbf{k}_{m-1}(s_m). \tag{4}$$

The second step is to update the dictionary by comparing the value of δ_m corresponding to s_m with a predefined threshold σ. If $\delta_m > \sigma$, s_m will be added into the dictionary, i.e., $D_m = D_{m-1} \cup s_m$; otherwise the current dictionary will be not changed.

After the sparsification, the feature vectors produced by the elements in kernel dictionary are employed to replace these of the whole data set and the following vectors with reduced dimensions can be obtained [10]:

$$\Phi^{d_m} = (\phi^T(s_1), \phi^T(s_2), ..., \phi^T(s_{d_m}))^T \tag{5}$$

$$k^{d_m}(s_i) = (k(s_1, s_i), k(s_2, s_i), ..., k(s_{d_m}, s_i))^T \tag{6}$$

where d_m is the size of the kernel dictionary after the ALD approach. Then the equation (3) can be transformed to

$$\tilde{Q}(s) = \sum_{i=1}^{d_m} \alpha_i k(s, s_i). \tag{7}$$

Using the kernel machine, the least-squares solution to the TD learning problem can be represented as [4]:

$$\alpha = (A_t^d)^{-1} b_t^d \tag{8}$$

where

$$A_t^d = A_{t-1}^d + k^d(s_t)[k^d(s_t) - \gamma k^d(s_{t+1})]^T$$
$$b_t^d = b_{t-1}^d + k^d(s_t)r_t. \tag{9}$$

After knowing the coefficient α in (7) the optimal state-action value can be obtained using

$$Q^*(s, a) = \max_\pi Q^\pi(s, a) = \max_a \sum_{i=1}^{d_m} \alpha_i k(s(x, a), s(x_i, a)). \tag{10}$$

Besides, the corresponding optimal policy is represented as

$$\pi^*(x) = \arg\max Q^*(x, a). \tag{11}$$

3   ALD Based on Relative Approximation Error for KLSPI

In this section we will firstly introduce the origin of the basic ideas, then a novel sparsification approach of ALD based on relative approximation error instead of the absolute one will be presented. Besides, an improved KLSPI algorithm using the new ALD approach in the sparsification procedure will be proposed.

3.1   The Origin of the Basic Ideas

Assume the projection of $\varphi(x)$ on plane II can be represented as $\sum \alpha_i \varphi_i(x)$, where $\varphi_i(x)$ could be seen as the basis functions of the plane II. Two lemmas can be concluded.

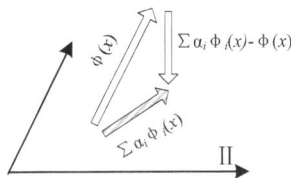

Fig. 1. The projection of vector $\varphi(x)$ on plane II

Lemma 1: $\|\varphi(x) - \sum \alpha_i \varphi_i(x)\|^2 + \|\sum \alpha_i \varphi_i(x)\|^2 = \|\varphi(x)\|^2$.

Lemma 2: $0 \le \dfrac{\|\varphi(x) - \sum \alpha_i \varphi_i(x)\|^2}{\|\varphi(x)\|^2} \le 1$.

3.2   ALD Based on Relative Approximation Error in KLSPI

ALD analysis is performed as follows: given an obtained dictionary set $D_{m-1} = \{s_j\}$ ($j=1, 2, \ldots, d_{m-1}$), for a new sample s_m, the ALD method introduces an approximately linearly dependent condition [3] for the new feature vector $\varphi(s_m)$,

$$\delta_m = \min_c \left\| \sum_j c_j \varphi(s_j) - \varphi(s_m) \right\|^2 \le \sigma, \ 0 < \delta_m < \infty \tag{12}$$

where $c = [c_j]$ and σ is a threshold parameter determining the sparsity level.

The parameter σ can be referred to the sparsity level, which should be adjusted properly to determine the size of the kernel dictionary and the approximation ability of the basis functions. δ_m is regarded as the absolute approximation error of the $\varphi(s_m)$ approximated using the basis functions $\varphi(s_j)$. The purpose is to compute the c_j by minimizing the absolute approximation error. Obviously we have few knowledge of δ_m, including its bound. In this paper, the method is termed as the ALD approach based on absolute approximation error.

In the paper a novel ALD method based on relative approximation error instead of the absolute one is presented. By introducing the new method the value of the sparsity level can be bounded in [0, 1], which eases the difficulty on the value selection of σ.

Combining Lemma 1 and 2, a novel bounded sparsity level ρ_m is introduced by replacing absolute error with the relative one. The corresponding approximately linearly dependent condition can be represented as follows:

$$\rho_m = \min_c \frac{\left\| \sum_j c_j \varphi(s_j) - \varphi(s_m) \right\|^2}{\| \varphi(s_m) \|^2} \leq \sigma, \ 0 \leq \rho_m \leq 1. \tag{13}$$

The previous ALD method adopts the absolute approximation error of a new state s_m using the kernel dictionary $D_{m-1} = \{s_j\}$ ($j=1,2,\ldots,d_{m-1}$). However, what the new criterion in (13) we introduce emphasizes is the relative approximation error.

By replacing the absolute error with the relative one, the improved ALD approach need smaller size of the kernel dictionary under the same sparsity level than the previous one. What's more, using the same size kernel dictionary the former method has greater nonlinear approximation ability at some extent than the latter one.

Algorithm 1: ALD approach based on relative approximation error
1. Given:
   - Samples D={ $(s_i, a_i, s_{i'}, r_i) \mid i = 1,2,\ldots,n$};
   - A heat kernel function $k(\cdot,\cdot)$, including its parameters;
   - Parameter σ as the sparsity level.
2. Sparsification:
   - Initialization: $i=1$, the dictionary $Dic = \{s_1\}$;
   - Loop for the entire data samples:
     - $i=i+1$;
     - For a new state s_i, calculate ρ_i using (15);
     - If $\rho_i < \sigma$, s_i will not be added into Dic, otherwise $Dic = \{s_1, s_i\}$;
3. Output Dic;

Fig. 2. The main steps of the ALD approach based on relative approximation error

The sparsification procedure of the proposed ALD approach consists of two main steps. Above all, the following optimization solutions should be calculated:

$$\begin{aligned} \rho_m &= \min_c \frac{\left\| \sum_j c_j \varphi(s_j) - \varphi(s_m) \right\|^2}{\| \varphi(s_m) \|^2} \\ &= \min_c \left\{ \frac{\sum_{i,j} c_i c_j \langle \varphi(s_i), \varphi(s_j) \rangle - 2\sum_i c_i \langle \varphi(s_i), \varphi(s_m) \rangle + \langle \varphi(s_m), \varphi(s_m) \rangle}{\langle \varphi(s_m), \varphi(s_m) \rangle} \right\} \\ &= \min_c \left\{ \frac{\sum_{i,j} c_i c_j k(s_i, s_j) - 2\sum_i c_i k(s_i, s_m) + k(s_m, s_m)}{k(s_m, s_m)} \right\} \\ &= \min_c \left\{ \mathbf{c}^T \frac{\mathbf{K}_{m-1}}{\mathbf{k}_{mm}} \mathbf{c} - 2\mathbf{c}^T \frac{\mathbf{k}_{m-1}(s_m)}{\mathbf{k}_{mm}} + 1 \right\}. \end{aligned} \tag{14}$$

where $[K_{m-1}]_{i \cdot j} = k(s_i, s_j)$, s_i ($i = 1, 2, \ldots, d(m-1)$) are the elements in the current dictionary, $d(m-1)$ is the length of the data dictionary, $k_{m-1}(s_m) = [k(s_1, s_m), k(s_2, s_m), \ldots, k(s_{d(m-1)}, s_m)]^T$, $c = [c_1, c_2, \ldots, c_d]^T$ and $k_{mm} = k(s_m, s_m)$.

Then the optimal value of ρ_m can be computed by

$$\rho_m = 1 - \mathbf{k}_{m-1}^T(s_m) \mathbf{k}_{mm}^{-1} \mathbf{K}_{m-1}^{-1} \mathbf{k}_{m-1}(s_m). \tag{15}$$

The second step is to update the dictionary by comparing the value of ρ_m corresponding to the new sample s_m with σ. If $\rho_m > \sigma$, s_m will be added into the dictionary; otherwise the current dictionary will be not changed. Algorithm 1 in Fig.2 shows the main framework of the ALD based on the relative approximation error. The introduced ALD method can be realized on condition that $k_{mm} \neq 0$. Therefore, the kernel function we select is a heat kernel function which can be represented as

$$k(s_i, s_j) = \alpha(s_i, s_j) exp(-\|s_i - s_j\|^2 / T) \tag{16}$$

where $\alpha(s_i, s_j) = \varepsilon + \|s_i\|_2 * \|s_j\|_2$ is predefined, and ε is a constant parameter.

Fig.3 shows the framework of the improved KLSPI algorithm.

Algorithm 2: the improved KLSPI algorithm
1. Given:
   - Samples D={ $(s_i, a_i, s_{i'}, r_i)$ | $i = 1, 2, \ldots, n$} collected by a random policy;
   - Heat kernel function as (16), ε and T of the heat kernel;
   - the terminate criterion and other parameters used for policy iteration.
2. Policy iteration:
   Let iteration number $j = 0$;
   2.1. Sparsification starts:
   - Initialization: $i=1$, the dictionary $Dic = \{s_1\}$;
   - Loop for the entire data samples:
     ➢ $i=i+1$;
     ➢ For a new state s_i, compute ρ_i in (15).
     ➢ If $\rho_i < \sigma$, s_i will not be added into Dic, otherwise $Dic = \{s_1, s_i\}$.
   - Output Dic; Sparsification ends.
   2.2. Compute A_t^d and b_t^d simultaneously.
   - Initialization: $t = 0$, $A_t^d = 0$, and $b_t^d = 0$;
   - Loop for the entire data samples:
     ➢ $t=t+1$;
     ➢ For the current sample (s_t, a_t, r_t, x_{t+1}) , using (6) to compute the kernel-based feature vectors of state-action pairs.
     ➢ Use (9) to calculate A_t^d and b_t^d.
   2.3. Obtain the solution of the KLSTD-Q using $\alpha = (A_t^d)^{-1} b_t^d$.
   2.4. Update the policy by

   $$\pi[j+1] = \arg \max_a Q^{\pi[j]}(s, a).$$

   2.5. $j = j+1$, return to 2.1 until the termination condition is satisfied.

Fig. 3. The procedure of the improved Kernel-based Least-Squares Policy Iteration

4   Experiments and Evaluations

In this paper, a traditional problem of Inverted Pendulum is used to evaluate the proposed method, which requires balancing an inverted pendulum of unknown length and mass at the upright position by applying forces F to the cart which is attached to. This problem is shown in Fig.4.

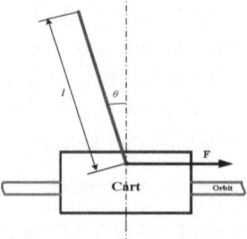

Fig. 4. The inverted pendulum

There are two variables in the state space: θ, the vertical angle of the pendulum, and $\dot{\theta}$, the angle velocity of the pendulum. Three actions are assumed as -10, 0, or 10 Newtons, and an uniform noise which obeys standard normal distribution is added to the chosen action. The transitions are governed by the nonlinear dynamics of the system and depend on the current state and the current noisy control u [2].

$$\ddot{\theta} = \frac{g\sin(\theta) - \alpha ml\dot{\theta}^2 \sin(2\theta)/2 - \alpha\cos(\theta)u}{4l/3 - \alpha ml\cos^2(\theta)} \qquad (17)$$

where g is the gravity constant ($g = 9.8m/s^2$), m is the mass of the pendulum ($m = 2.0kg$), l is the length of the pendulum ($l = 0.5m$), and $\alpha = 1.0/(m + M_{cart})$, M_{cart} is the mass of the cart ($M_{cart} = 8.0kg$). The simulation step was set to 0.1 seconds. The episodes ends and a penalty reward of -1 is given when $|\theta| \geq \pi/2$. All other actions result in a reward of 0. In the experiment, a heat kernel function as (16) was selected as the kernel function, where points s_i and s_j in S are $(\theta_i, \dot{\theta}_i)$ and $(\theta_j, \dot{\theta}_j)$ respectively.

In the improved KLSPI algorithm, the main parameters were listed in Table 1:

Train samples were collected by a random policy, in which three actions was chosen uniformly at random. 10732 samples were gathered in 1200 episodes with the started state (0, 0). Each episode ends once the $|\theta| > 90°$. Besides, two different values of the parameter ε were set as 1.5 and 5.0 in order to validate the generalization of the proposed improved ALD method. The experimental results are shown as below.

Table 1. Parameters setting in the improved KLSPI

Parameters of improved KLSPI	Value
discount factor	0.90
max iteration number	10
epsilon	10^{-8}
T in heat kernel	0.8^2
max steps	50

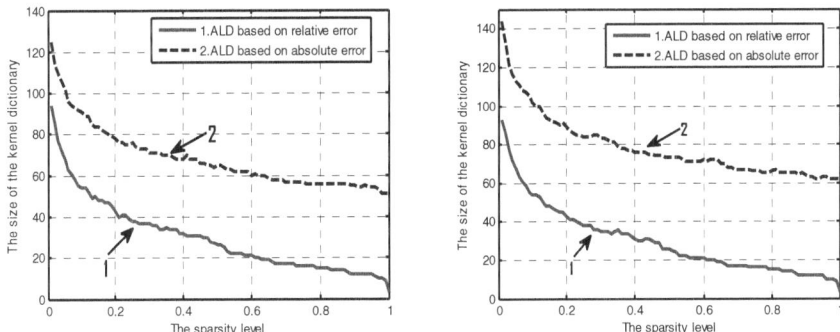

Fig. 5. The size of the kernel dictionary using two ALD methods varies with the sparsity level. In the left plot ε was 1.5 and 5.0 in the right one

We tested the sparsity level from 0.01 to 1, which increases 0.01 per time. The size of the dictionary was recorded with each sparsity level. Results in Fig.5 show the size of the kernel dictionary obtained by the proposed improved ALD method is much smaller than that using the original one under the same sparsity level. The sparsity level in the former method can be bounded to [0, 1] by replacing the absolute approximation error with the relative one. Different values of σ to perform the sparsification procedure can be selected from [0, 1]. Besides, the dictionary size of the solid red lines changes faster with the sparsity level than that of the blue dot ones.

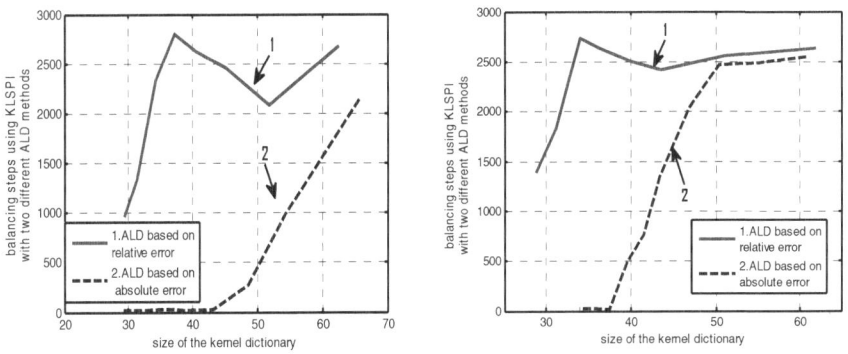

Fig. 6. The balancing steps of the pendulum using the improved and unimproved KLSPI algorithm varies with the size of the dictionary obtained by the two different sparsification methods. Parameter ε in the left plot was set to 1.5 and 5.0 in the right one

We recorded the average balancing steps of the pendulum under the interval about [30, 65] of the dictionary size. To remove randomness in the simulation results, we got the results by median average over 30 learning runs. It is illustrated in the Fig.6 the inverted pendulum controlled by integrating the improved ALD sparsification procedure into KLSPI algorithm could balance much more steps than that by the previous algorithm under the same size of the dictionary. In other words, the dictionary obtained by ALD approach based on relative approximation error performs better on the value function approximation than that gained by the original ALD method. When the size of the dictionary is small the unimproved ALD works poor. It only works better when increasing the dictionary size at the cost of the computation complexity and memory. However, the improved ALD can perform better using the dictionary of the both small and big size.

In order to evaluate the proposed method comprehensively, another experiment was done as follows: different numbers of sampling episodes were chosen as 50, 100, 150, … , 600. Samples were collected randomly. Each episode starts from the state (0, 0) and ends once the $|\theta|>\pi/2$ or the simulation steps reach to 3000. Furthermore, we got the results by median average over 30 learning runs to remove randomness. In the experiment through adjusting the parameter σ the size of the dictionary can be kept the same almost. The setting of each parameter can be seen from Table 2.

Table 2. Two sets of parameters setting in ALD based on relative/absolute error

(a)		(b)	
ALD based on relative error	**ALD based on absolute error**	**ALD based on relative error**	**ALD based on absolute error**
$\varepsilon=1.1$	$\varepsilon=1.1$	$\varepsilon=5.0$	$\varepsilon=5.0$
$\sigma=0.1$	$\sigma=0.26$	$\sigma=0.25$	$\sigma=1.8$
size of Dic=30	size of Dic=30	size of Dic=37	size of Dic=37

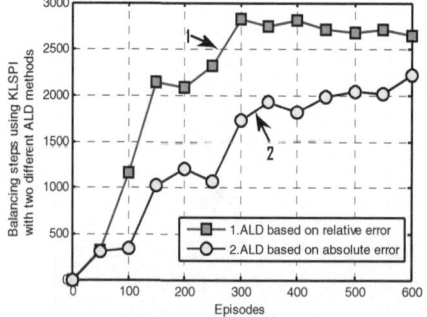 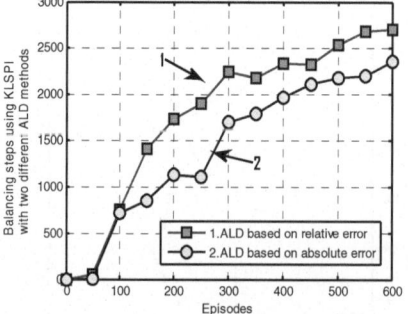

Fig. 7. Performance of the improved and original KLSPI algorithm using two sparsification methods. The above two figures depict the average steps with the increasing episodes, where parameters in Table 2.(a)/(b) corresponds to the left/right plot, respectively.

Fig.7 shows how the number of the episodes and the new method impact the results of balancing steps. After about 100 episodes the improved ALD approach converges much faster than the original one does. Besides, the converging steps of the former (corresponding to the red curve 1) are about 2600 steps, about 400 more than the blue curve's.

Therefore, it is evident that the relative error instead of the absolute one in ALD analysis makes the kernel-based approximate policy iteration algorithm not only use less size of the dictionary which saves certain computation complexity and memory cost but also approximate the optimal value-function more precisely.

5   Conclusion

In this paper, a novel ALD based on the relative approximation error instead of the absolute error is proposed to ease the difficulty of the sparsity level selection in KLSPI algorithm. By integrating the new sparsification operation an improved KLSPI algorithm is introduced as well. The experiments on the Inverted Pendulum problem illustrate the new ALD method can obtain much smaller size of the dictionary than the previous approach under the same level of sparsification. To some content the cost of the computation complexity and memory cost has been decreased. Besides, both the precision of the value function approximation in KLSPI and the quality of the learned control policy have also been improved. Although the results in this paper are encouraging, more experiments need to be carried out extensively to validate the new approach. Moreover, some more theories about the kernel function and its ability in value function approximation need to be discussed more thoroughly in the future.

Acknowledgments. This work is supported in part by the National Natural Science Foundation of China under Grant 61075072 and 90820302, the Fork Ying Tung Education Foundation under Grant 114005, and the Program for New Century Excellent Talent under Grant NCET-10-0901.

References

[1] Sutton, R., Barto, A.: Reinforcement learning:an introduction. MIT Press, Cambridge (1998)

[2] Boyan, J.: Technical update: Least-squares temporal difference learning. Mach. Learn. 49(2-3), 233–246 (2002)

[3] Xu, X., et al.: Kernel-based Least-Squares Policy Iteration for Reinforcement Learning. IEEE Trans. on Neural Networks 18, 973–992 (2007)

[4] Xu, X., et al.: Efficient Reinforcement Learning Using Recursive Least-Squares Methods. Journal of Artificial Intelligence Research 16, 259–292 (2002)

[5] Cristianini, N., Shawe-Taylor, J.: An Introduction to Support Vector Machines. Cambridge Univ. Press, Cambridge (2000)

[6] Kaelbling, L.P., et al.: Reinforcement learning: A survey. J. Artif. Intell. Res. 4, 237–285 (1996)

[7] Lagoudakis, M.G., Parr, R.: Least-squares policy iteration. J.Mach. Learn. Res. 4, 1107–1149 (2003)

[8] Ormoneit, S.: Kernel-based reinforcement learning. Machine Learning 49(2), 161–178 (2002)

[9] Schölkopf, B., Smola, A.: Learning With Kernels. MIT Press, Cambridge (2002)

[10] Tsitsiklis, J.N., Roy, B.V.: An analysis of temporal difference learning with function approximation. IEEE Trans. Autom. Control. 42(5), 674–690 (1997)

Quasi-synchronization of Different Fractional-Order Chaotic Systems with External Perturbations and Its Application

Zhen Zhang and Haijun Jiang

College of Mathematics and System Sciences, Xinjiang University,
Urumqi 830046, Xinjiang, P.R. China
jianghai@xju.edu.cn,zs0866@163.com

Abstract. In this paper, based on the fractional comparison principle, a scheme for quasi-synchronization of different fractional-order chaotic systems with external perturbations is constructed. Subsequently, the scheme is applied to achieve quasi-synchronization between fractional-order Lorenz and Chen systems with external perturbations. The proposed method in this paper can be easily extended to achieve quasi-synchronization for other different fractional-order chaotic systems. Meanwhile numerical simulation results show the effectiveness of the derived results.

Keywords: Quasi-synchronization, External perturbation, Fractional-order system.

1 Introduction

Since Pecora and Carroll [1] proposed the concept of chaotic synchronization, chaos synchronization has been widely explored and investigated in various fields such as physical science, biological science, chemical science, medical science, and secure communications [2-5]. A variety of approaches have been investigated to synchronize chaotic systems, such as Lyapunov method, linear and nonlinear feedback control, adaptive control, impulsive control, and so on [6-11].

Recently, study on the dynamics of fractional-order differential systems has greatly attracted interest of many researchers. It is demonstrated that some fractional-order differential systems behave chaotically, such as fractional-order Chen system [12], fractional-order Lü system [14], fractional-order Chua's system [13], fractional-order Rössler system [15], and fractional-order Lorenz system [16]. All systems mentioned above are expound with proper parameters that make the fractional-order system exhibits chaos by numerical simulation.

Moreover, synchronization of chaotic fractional-order differential systems starts to attract increasing attention due to its potential applications in secure communication and control processing. There are many methods of chaos synchronization, such as the PC method, the APD technique, the one-way method and the bidirectional coupled means [17-20]. Most of these methods for achieving synchronization are derived via the Laplace transformation theory.

J. Wang, G.G. Yen, and M.M. Polycarpou (Eds.): ISNN 2012, Part I, LNCS 7367, pp. 256–265, 2012.

However, many existing synchronization methods have ignored the uncertainties. In real applications, system dynamics are always exposed to external noises, which may cause failure in using of those means. Therefore, it is necessary to investigate quasi-synchronization of fractional-order chaotic systems by using some different methods. Moreover, to the best of our knowledge, no results have been reported for quasi synchronization between two different fractional-order chaotic systems. Motivated by the above discussion, in this paper, the quasi-synchronization for different fractional-order chaotic systems with external perturbations are investigated based on the fractional comparison principle.

This paper is organized as follows. In Section 2, preliminaries about fractional-order systems are given. In Section 3, a quasi-synchronization criterion for different fractional-order chaotic systems with external perturbations is presented. In Section 4, the proposed scheme is applied to achieve the quasi-synchronization between fractional-order Lorenz and Chen systems with external perturbations and numerical simulation results are presented to show the effectiveness of the obtained results. Finally, the paper is concluded in section 5.

2   Preliminaries

To discuss fractional-order chaotic systems, we usually need to solve fractional-order differential equation. For the fractional differential operator, there are three common definitions [21-23]: Grünwald-Letnikov (GL) definition, Riemann-Liouville (RL) definition and Caputo definition.

The best-known RL definition of fractional-order, which is described by

$$_aD_t^q f(t) = \frac{1}{\Gamma(n-q)} \frac{d^n}{dt^n} \int_a^t \frac{f(\tau)}{(t-\tau)^{q-n+1}} d\tau, \tag{1}$$

where n is an integer such that $n - 1 < q < n$, $\Gamma(.)$ is the Γ-function.

The Caputo definition can be written as

$$_aD_t^q f(t) = \frac{1}{\Gamma(n-q)} \int_a^t \frac{f^{(n)}(\tau)}{(t-\tau)^{q-n+1}} d\tau, \tag{2}$$

where n is an integer such that $n - 1 < q < n$, $\Gamma(.)$ is the Γ-function.

Lemma 1. (Fractional comparison principle [24]).   Let $_0^C D_t^q x(t) \geq_0^C D_t^q y(t)$ and $x(0) = y(0)$, where $q \in (0, 1)$. Then $x(t) \geq y(t)$.

3   Main Results

Consider two nonlinear fractional-order chaotic systems, i.e., drive system and response system. The drive system is given by

$$\frac{d^q x}{dt^q} = Ax + f(x) + d_1(t), \tag{3}$$

where $0 < q < 1$, $x = (x_1, x_2, \cdots, x_n)^T \in R^n$ denotes the state vector of drive system, $A \in R^{n \times n}$ is a constant coefficient matrix, $f : R^n \longrightarrow R^n$ is a continuous nonlinear vector function, and $d_1(t) = (d_{11}, d_{12}, \cdots, d_{1n})^T$ is an external perturbation vector.

The response system is described by

$$\frac{d^q y}{dt^q} = By + g(y) + d_2(t) + u, \tag{4}$$

where $0 < q < 1$, $y = (y_1, y_2, \cdots, y_n)^T \in R^n$ denotes the state vector of response system, $B \in R^{n \times n}$ is a constant coefficient matrix, $g : R^n \longrightarrow R^n$ is a continuous nonlinear vector function, $d_2(t) = (d_{21}(t), d_{22}(t), \cdots, d_{2n}(t))^T$ is an external perturbation vector, and $u = (u_1, u_2, \cdots, u_n)^T \in R^n$ is a controller which will be designed later.

Now, we give the definition of quasi-synchronization between systems (3) and (4).

Definition 1. Let Ω denotes a region in the phase space that contains the chaotic attractor of drive system (3) and response system (4). The drive and response systems (3) and (4) are said to be quasi-synchronized with error bound $\varepsilon > 0$ if there exists a $T \geq t_0$ such that for all $t \geq T$, $x_0, y_0 \in \Omega$,

$$\|e(t)\| \leq \varepsilon,$$

where $\|.\|$ is ∞-norm, $e = y - x$ is the synchronization error vector between systems (3) and (4) and x_0, y_0 are initial values of the drive systems (3) and response system (4), respectively.

Subtracting (3) from (4), the error system can be got

$$\frac{d^q e}{dt^q} = Be + (B - A)x + g(y) - f(x) + \bar{d}(t) + u, \tag{5}$$

where $\bar{d}(t) = d_2(t) - d_1(t) = (\bar{d}_1(t), \bar{d}_2(t), \cdots, \bar{d}_n(t))^T$.

Define the controller u as

$$u = f(x) - g(y) + (A - B)x + v, \tag{6}$$

where $v = (v_1, v_2, \cdots, v_n)^T \in R^n$ is an input vector function. With the choice of u, the error system (5) becomes

$$\frac{d^q e}{dt^q} = Be + \bar{d}(t) + v. \tag{7}$$

In fact, there are numerous choices for the control input vector v. Here, we choose

$$v = Ce, \tag{8}$$

where $C = -B + diag(-k_1, -k_2, \cdots, -k_n)$ and $k_i > 0$ $(i = 1, 2, \cdots, n)$ are free parameters. Hence, the error system can be written as

$$\frac{d^q e}{dt^q} = De + \bar{d}(t), \tag{9}$$

where $D = diag(-k_1, -k_2, \cdots, -k_n)$.

Theorem 1. systems (3) and (4) are quasi-synchronized with error bound ε under the controller (6) if the following conditions are satisfied:

(H_1) $\bar{d}_i(t)$ are bounded, i.e.,

$$|\bar{d}_i(t)| \leq \tilde{d}_i, \quad i = 1, 2, \cdots, n, \tag{10}$$

(H_2)

$$k_i > \frac{\hat{d}}{\varepsilon}, \quad i = 1, 2, \cdots, n, \tag{11}$$

where $\hat{d} = max\{\tilde{d}_1, \tilde{d}_2, \cdots, \tilde{d}_n\}$ and ε is a quasi-synchronized bound which is determined according to the practical requirement.

Proof. Define $p_i(t)$ as the ratio between $\bar{d}_i(t)$ and $e_i(t)$, i.e.,

$$p_i(t) = \frac{\bar{d}_i(t)}{e_i(t)}, \tag{12}$$

then, the perturbation vector can be rewritten as

$$\bar{d}(t) = p(t)e, \tag{13}$$

where $p(t) = diag(p_1(t), p_2(t), \cdots, p_n(t))$, then the error system becomes

$$\frac{d^q e}{dt^q} = \bar{D}e, \tag{14}$$

where $\bar{D} = diag(-k_1 + p_1(t), -k_2 + p_2(t), \cdots, -k_n + p_n(t))$.

For a specified index i, consider the following two cases.

(1) $e_i(t_0) < \varepsilon$.

If $\forall \ t \geq t_0$, $e_i(t) < \varepsilon$, the quasi-synchronization is realized. Otherwise there has a constant $T_1 > t_0$ such that

$$e_i(T_1) = \varepsilon,$$

which together with (H_1), we have

$$p_i(T_1) \leq \frac{\tilde{d}_i}{\varepsilon}. \tag{15}$$

From (H_2) and (14), we have

$$\left.\frac{d^q e_i(t)}{dt^q}\right|_{t=T_1} < 0. \tag{16}$$

Then in view of lemma 1, there exists a $T_2 > T_1$ such that

$$e_i(t) < e_i(T_1) = \varepsilon, \quad t \in (T_1, T_2). \tag{17}$$

If $T_2 = \infty$, the quasi-synchronization is realized. Otherwise, there has a $T_3 > T_2$ such that

$$e_i(T_3) = \varepsilon, \tag{18}$$

similar to the discussion of T_1, we have

$$\left.\frac{d^q e_i(t)}{dt^q}\right|_{t=T_3} < 0. \tag{19}$$

Hence, repeated such a way, for all $t \geq T_1$,

$$e_i(t) \leq \varepsilon.$$

(2) $e_i(t_0) > \varepsilon$.
Evidently,

$$\left. \frac{d^q e_i(t)}{dt^q} \right|_{t=t_0} < 0. \tag{20}$$

In fact, the above inequality is true for all t satisfying $e_i(t) \geq \varepsilon$. Then there has a $T_4 > t_0$ such that $e_i(T_4) = \varepsilon$ and $e_i(t) > \varepsilon$ for $t_0 \leq t < T_4$. Similar to the discussion of case (1), we have

$$e_i(t) \leq \varepsilon, \quad t \geq T_4. \tag{21}$$

In conclude, there exists a $T \geq t_0$ such that for all $t \geq T$, $\|e(t)\| \leq \varepsilon$ which implies that systems (3) and (4) are quasi-synchronized with error bound ε. The proof is completed.

Remark 1. It is noted that the result obtained on quasi-synchronization here for fractional-order chaotic systems with external perturbations is more useful, because it is obvious that the system dynamics are always exposed to external noises.

Remark 2. According to our assumption, ε is arbitrary value which is selected by the designer. It is clear that the smaller ε is, the better quasi-synchronization can be derived, but the higher control energy is needed.

4   Numerical Simulations

In this section, the above-mentioned scheme is applied to derive the quasi-synchronization between fractional-order Lorenz and Chen systems with external perturbations.

The fractional-order Lorenz system [16,25] is described by

$$\begin{cases} \dfrac{d^q x}{dt^q} = \sigma(y - x), \\ \dfrac{d^q y}{dt^q} = \gamma x - xz - y, \\ \dfrac{d^q z}{dt^q} = xy - \mu z, \end{cases} \tag{22}$$

where $(\sigma, \gamma, \mu) = (10, 28, 8/3)$, $q \geq 0.993$, system (22) exhibits chaotic behavior. When $q = 0.995$, the chaotic attractor is shown in Fig. 1.

The fractional-order Chen system [26] is given by

$$\begin{cases} \dfrac{d^q x}{dt^q} = a(y - x), \\ \dfrac{d^q y}{dt^q} = (c - a)x - xz + cy, \\ \dfrac{d^q z}{dt^q} = xy - bz, \end{cases} \tag{23}$$

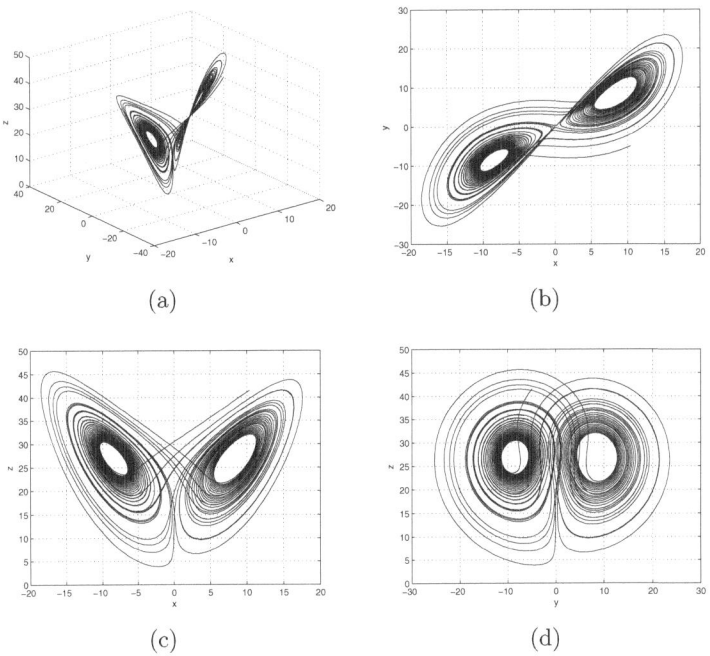

(a)   (b)

(c)   (d)

Fig. 1. Phase portraits of novel family of chaotic system (22) in (a) the $x - y - z$ space; and projected on (b) the $x - y$ plane, (c) the $x - z$ plane, and (d) $y - z$ plane

where $(a, b, c) = (35, 3, 28)$, $q \geq 0.83$, system (23) exhibits chaotic behavior. When $q = 0.995$, the chaotic attractor is shown in Fig. 2.

In the following, we consider the external perturbations in (22), the modified model is viewed as the drive system, which is descried by

$$\frac{d^q x}{dt^q} = Ax + f(x) + d_1(t),\tag{24}$$

where $x = (x_1, y_1, z_1)^T$, $d_1(t) = (0.3sin(t) + 3, 0.5sin(t) + 5, 0.4sin(t) + 4)^T$,

$$A = \begin{pmatrix} -a & a & 0 \\ c - a & c & 0 \\ 0 & 0 & -b \end{pmatrix}.$$

When $q = 0.995$, the phase portrait of system (24) is presented in Fig. 3 with $x_0 = (2, 1, 3)^T$, which shows that system(26) has a chaotic attractor.

The response system is given as

$$\frac{d^q y}{dt^q} = By + g(y) + d_2(t) + u,\tag{25}$$

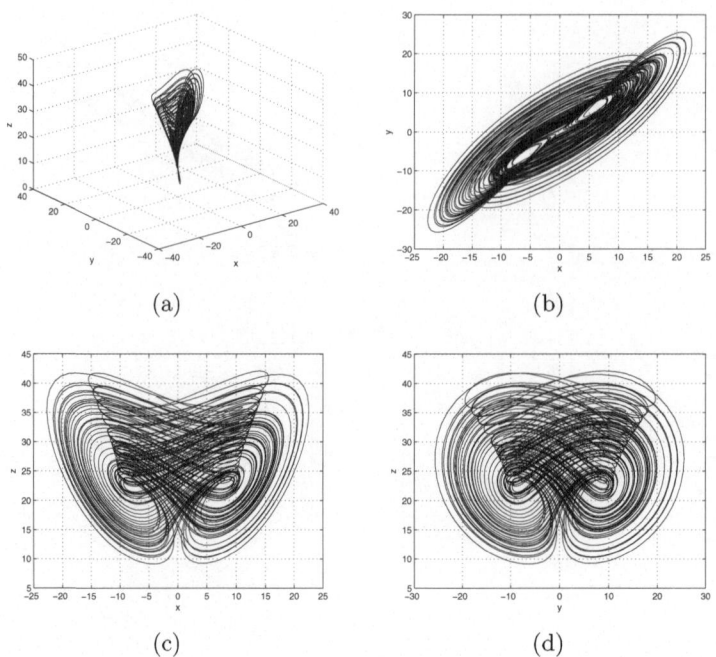

Fig. 2. Phase portraits of novel family of chaotic system (23) in (a) the $x-y-z$ space; and projected on (b) the $x-y$ plane, (c) the $x-z$ plane, and (d) $y-z$ plane

where $y = (x_2, y_2, z_2)^T$, $d_2(t) = (0.3cos(t) + 3, 0.5cos(t) + 5, 0.4cos(t) + 4)^T$,

$$B = \begin{pmatrix} -a & a & 0 \\ c-a & c & 0 \\ 0 & 0 & -b \end{pmatrix}.$$

According to the scheme given in section 3, one can obtain

$$\frac{d^q e}{dt^q} = \bar{D}e,$$

where $e = y - x$, $\bar{D} = diag(-k_1 + p_1(t), -k_2 + p_2(t), -k_3 + p_3(t))$.

For example, the fractional order q is taken to be 0.995 for which the drive system (24) is chaotic. According to Theorem 1, $\hat{d} = max\{\tilde{d}_1, \tilde{d}_2, \tilde{d}_3\} = max\{0.6, 1, 0.8\} = 1$. Choose $\varepsilon = 0.1$ and then control parameters k_1, k_2, k_3 should be selected such that $k_i > \frac{\hat{d}}{\varepsilon} = \frac{1}{0.1} = 10$ for i=1,2,3. Here, we choose $k_1 = k_2 = k_3 = 11$. Similarly, choose $\varepsilon = 0.2$ and then control parameters k_1, k_2, k_3 should be selected such that $k_i > \frac{\hat{d}}{\varepsilon} = \frac{1}{0.2} = 5$ for i=1,2,3. Here, we choose $k_1 = k_2 = k_3 = 6$. Numerical simulation results in Figs. 4,5 illustrate that the quasi-synchronization between drive system (24) and response system (25) has occurred with given different initial values when $\varepsilon = 0.1$ and $\varepsilon = 0.2$, respectively.

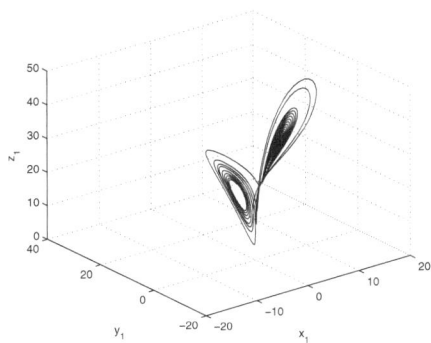

Fig. 3. Chaotic attractors of the drive system (24) with the order $q = 0.995$

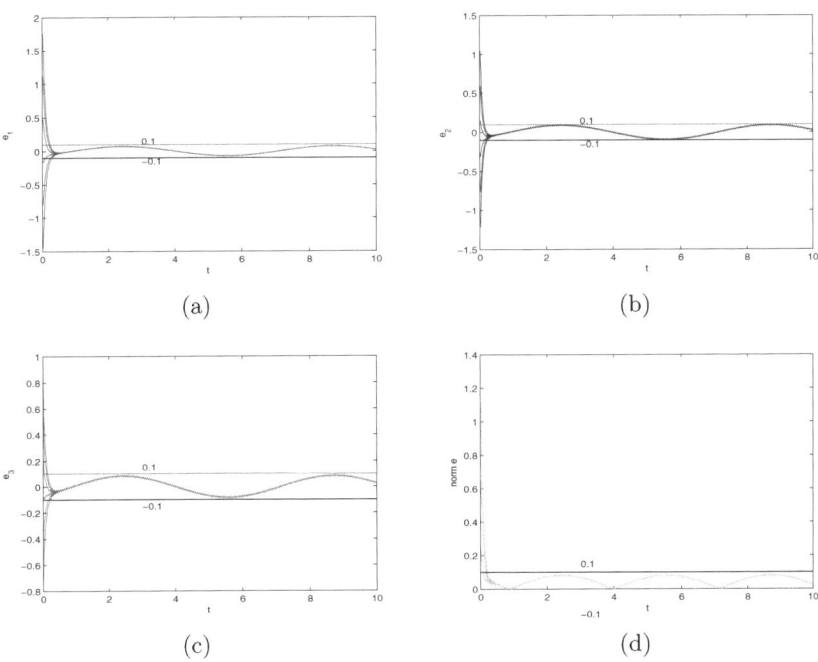

Fig. 4. Quasi-synchronization results between drive system (23) and response system (24) with different initial values when $\varepsilon = 0.1$

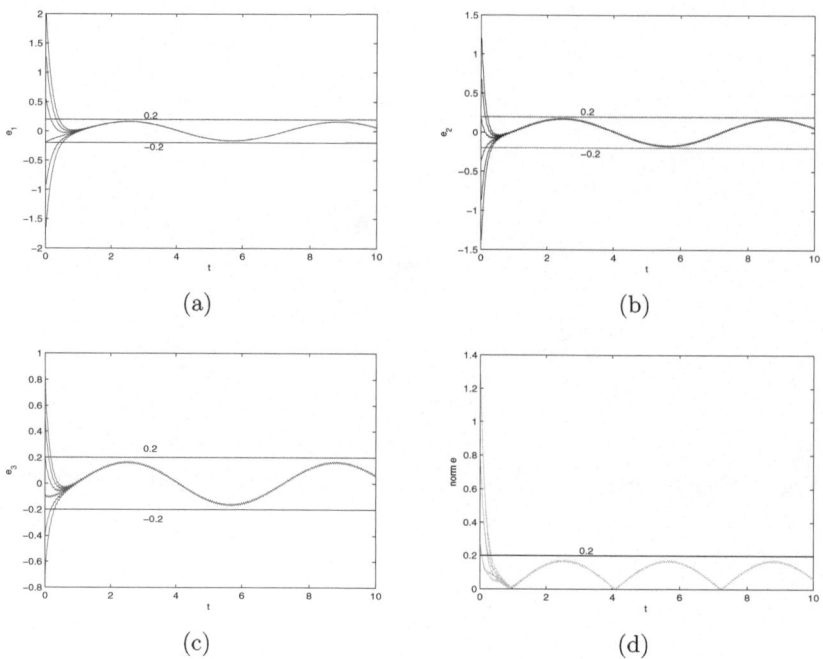

Fig. 5. Quasi-synchronization results between drive system (23) and response system (24) with different initial values when $\varepsilon = 0.2$

Acknowledgments. This work was supported by the National Natural Science Foundation of People's Republic of China (Grant Nos.10961022, 10901130 and 61164004), the Natural Science Foundation of Xinjiang (Grant No. 2010211A07).

References

1. Carroll, T.L., Pecora, L.M.: Synchronizing chaotic system. IEEE Trans. Circuits Syst. I 38, 453–456 (1991)
2. Lakshmanan, K., Murali, M.: Chaos in nonlinear oscillators: controlling and synchronization. World Scientific, Singapore (2004)
3. Han, S.K., Kerrer, C.: Dephasing and bursting in coupled neural oscillators. Phys. Rev. Lett 75, 3190–3193 (1995)
4. Blasius, B., Huppert, A., Stone, L.: Complex dynamics and phase synchronization in spatially extended ecological systems. Nature 339, 354–359 (1999)
5. Moez, F.: An adaptive chaos synchronization scheme applied to secure communication. Chaos Solitons Fract. 18, 141–148 (2003)
6. Momani, S., Odibat, Z.: Numerical comparison of methods for solvig linear differential equations of fractional order. Chaos Solitons Fract. 31, 1248–1255 (2007)
7. Ahmad, W., Sprott, C.: Chaos in fractional-order autonomous nonlinear systems. Chaos Solitons Fract. 16, 339–351 (2003)
8. Chen, C., Yau, H., Peng, C.: Design of extended backstepping sliding mode controller for uncertain chaotic systems. Int. J. Nonlinear Sci. Numer. Simul. 8, 137–145 (2007)

9. Yau, H., Kuo, C., Yan, J.: Fuzzy sliding mode control for a class of chaos synchronization with uncertainties. Int. J. Nonlinear Sci. Numer. Simul. 7, 333–338 (2006)

10. Deng, W., Li, C.: Chaos synchronization of the fractional Lü system. Physica A 353, 61–72 (2005)

11. Wang, J., Zhang, Y.: Designing synchronization schemes for chaotic fractional-order unified systems. Chaos Solitons Fract. 30, 1265–1272 (2006)

12. Li, C., Chen, G.: Chaos in the fractional-order Chen system and its control. Chaos Solitons Fract. 22, 549–554 (2004)

13. Hartley, T.T., Lorenzo, C.F., Qammar, H.K.: Chaos in a fractional-order Chua system. IEEE Trans. 42, 485–490 (1995)

14. Lu, J.G.: Chaotic dynamics of the fractional-order Lu system and its synchronization. Phys. Lett. A 354, 305–311 (2006)

15. Li, C., Chen, G.: Chaos hyperchaos in the fractional-order Rössler equations. Phys. A 341, 55–61 (2004)

16. Grigorenko, I., Grigorenko, E.: Chaotic dynamics of the fractional Lorenz system. Phys. Rev. Lett. 91 (2003)

17. Sira-Ramirez, H., Cruz-Hernandez, C.: Synchronization of chaotic systems: a generalized Hamiltonian systems approach. Int. J. Bifurcation Chaos 11, 1381–1395 (2001)

18. Petráš, I.: Control of fractional-order Chua's system. J. Electron. Eng. 53, 219–222 (2002)

19. Wang, J.W., Xiong, X.H., Zhang, Y.B.: Extending synchronization scheme to chaotic fractional-order Chen systems. Physica A 370, 279–285 (2006)

20. Li, C.P., Yan, J.P.: The synchronization of three fractional differential equations. Chaos Solitons Fract. 32, 751–757 (2007)

21. Butzer, P.L., Westphal, U.: An introduction to fractional calculus. World Scientific, Singapore (2000)

22. Kenneth, S.M., Bertram, R.: An introduction to the fractional calculus and fractional differential equations. Wiley-Intescience, New York (1993)

23. Podlubny, I.: Fractional differential equations. Academic press, San Diego (1999)

24. Li, Y., Chen, Y.Q.: Stability of fractional-order nonlinear dynamic systems: Lyapunov direct method and generalized Mittag-Leffler stability. Int. J. Computers and Mathematics with Applications 59, 1810–1821 (2010)

25. Wu, X., Shen, S.: Chaos in the fractional-order Lorenz system. Int. J. Comput Math. 86, 1274–1282 (2009)

26. Li, C., Peng, G.: Chaos in Chen's system with a fractional order. Chaos Solitons Fractals 22, 443–450 (2004)

Synchronization of Complex Interconnected Neural Networks with Adaptive Coupling

Zhanshan Wang[1], Yongbin Zhao[1], and Shuxian Lun[2]

[1] School of Information Science and Engineering, Northeastern University
Shenyang, Liaoning, 110004, People's Republic of China
wangzhanshan@ise.neu.edu.cn
[2] College of Engineering, Bohai University, Jinzhou 121000,
People's Republic of China

Abstract. An decentralized adaptive coupling adjusting law is proposed to synchronize a class of complex interconnected neural networks with delayed coupling. The proposed method can sufficient use the neighbor information of the nodes to adjust the connection strengths of the coupled matrix adaptively, which will lead to the self-synchronization of the complex networks without the external control influence on the networks. Some remarks are used to show the effectiveness of the proposed method.

Keywords: complex interconnected neural networks, synchronization, adaptive coupling, decentralized control, delayed coupling.

1 Introduction

Synchronization is an important property of complex dynamical systems, such as food-webs, ecosystems, metabolic pathways, the Internet, the World Wide Web, social networks, and global economic markets. In general, a complex network is a large set of interconnected nodes by edges, in which each node is a fundamental unit with detailed contents. Over the past few decades, synchronization of complex networks consisting of coupled nodes with identical topological structures has been extensively investigated in various fields of science and engineering due to the fact that it not only can well explain many natural phenomena observed, but also has many promising potential applications in image processing, secure communication, etc [1]–[12]. The earlier studies of synchronization in networks concentrated on regular networks such as lattices with nearest neighbor or short range couplings or globally coupled networks, recently it has been recognized that some complex systems have underlying structures that are described by networks which are not regular but have some random element. This has led to the study of synchronization properties of different not regular networks. In spite of several studies of synchronization on networks, most of the studies have concentrated on static networks where the nodes and edges (couplings) are constant in time.

However, in several naturally occurring networks the topology of the networks changes with time, especially for the purpose of synchronization. Generally, there are mainly two kinds of synchronization methods. One is the self-synchronization, the other is the controlled synchronization. For the external

J. Wang, G.G. Yen, and M.M. Polycarpou (Eds.): ISNN 2012, Part I, LNCS 7367, pp. 266–273, 2012.

control case, it can change the dynamics of the coupled system to implement the synchronization. This is the mostly concerned methods in the synchronization problems. For the control gain, it can also be designed adaptively to meet the synchronization requirement. Reference [1] gave a controller gain adjusting law under the assumption of 1-order leading asymptotically stable condition. In practice, the assumption is too strong to be applied. References [8,7,2,10] aimed to design an adaptive controller to realize the synchronization, in which the controller gain was adjusted adaptively by design a adaptive law. Reference [2] studied the adaptive law of the coupled interconnected matrix, in which the state feedback controller was designed and only the self-node information was used. If there is no any external stimuli on the systems and the synchronization is achieved, it is called the self-synchronization. Self-synchronization can also be cast into several case, for example, the fixed connection and the variable connection, in which the latter mainly refers to adaptive synchronization of the connection strength or matrix. Reference [3,4,9] studied the adaptive law of the coupling strength. Reference [12] proposed a decentralized control method to adjust the connected matrix. It is the advantage of the adaptive coupling method to save the energy and improve the efficiency compared with the controlled synchronization method. It is the self-organization, self-regulation and self-learning of the adaptive coupling to realize the desired collective dynamics of the complex. The application of adaptive coupling method has been applied in position synchronization of multiple motion axes and posteriori error estimates for the symmetric finite element and boundary element coupling for a nonlinear interface problem [5,6], which showed the effectiveness of the adaptive coupling method.

It should be noted that as pointed out in [12], decentralized control method has many features in the complex network systems, in which the classical centralized control method will lose its dominant role. However, the decentralized adaptive method was only first applied to the complex networks without delayed coupling. For the practical consideration, the delayed coupling exists and may effect the dynamics of the whole system. Therefore, inspired by the work in [12], this paper will study a synchronization problem of complex interconnected neural networks with adaptive delayed coupling.

2 Problem Description and Preliminaries

In this paper we will discuss the following complex networks with N identical nodess,

$$\dot{x}_i(t) = -Cx_i(t) + Af(x_i(t)) + Bf(x_i(t-\tau)) + J(t)$$
$$+ c_1 \sum_{j=1}^{N} G_{ij}^1(t)\Gamma_1 x_j(t) + c_2 \sum_{j=1}^{N} G_{ij}^2(t)\Gamma_1 x_j(t-\tau), \quad (1)$$

where $x_i(t) = (x_{i1}(t), \cdots, x_{in}(t))^T$, $C > 0$, A and B are interconnection matrices, $f(x_i(t)) = (f_1(x_{i1}(t)), \cdots, f_n(x_{in}(t)))^T$ is the activation function, $\tau > 0$ is the time delay, $i = 1, \cdots, N$.

Assumption 21. The activation function $f_i(x_i(t))$ is bounded and continuous, which satisfies $|f_i(x_i(t))| \leq G_i^b$, $G_i^b > 0$ is a positive constant,

$$0 \leq \frac{f_i(\eta) - f_i(v)}{\eta - v} \leq \delta_i, \tag{2}$$

for any $\eta \neq v, \eta, v \in \Re$, and $\delta_i > 0$, $i = 1, \cdots, n$. Let $\Delta = \mathrm{diag}(\delta_1, \cdots, \delta_n)$.

Let the synchronization state $\bar{x} = \frac{1}{N} \sum_{j=1}^{N} x_j$, then one has

$$\dot{\bar{x}}(t) = \frac{1}{N} \sum_{j=1}^{N} \Big[- Cx_i(t) + Af(x_i(t)) + Bf(x_i(t - \tau)) + J(t) \Big]. \tag{3}$$

Define the synchronization error $e_i(t) = x_i(t) - \bar{x}$, then we have the following error dynamical system, $i = 1, \cdots, N$,

$$\dot{e}_i(t) = - Cx_i(t) + Af(x_i(t)) + Bf(x_i(t - \tau)) + J(t)$$

$$- \frac{1}{N} \sum_{j=1}^{N} \Big[- Cx_i(t) + Af(x_i(t)) + Bf(x_i(t - \tau)) + J(t) \Big]$$

$$+ c_1 \sum_{j=1}^{N} G_{ij}^1(t)\Gamma_1 e_j(t) + c_2 \sum_{j=1}^{N} G_{ij}^2(t)\Gamma_2 e_j(t - \tau) \tag{4}$$

In the sequel, we will design the adaptive coupling adjusting law $\dot{G}_{ij}^1(t)$ and $\dot{G}_{ij}^2(t)$ to guarantee the synchronization of the network nodes.

Note that the purpose of designing the adaptive coupling adjusting law $\dot{G}_{ij}^1(t)$ and $\dot{G}_{ij}^2(t)$ is to estimate the coupling strength among the different nodes. That is, we only estimate the magnitudes of $G_{ij}^1(t)$ and $G_{ij}^2(t)$ for $i \neq j$. For the case of $i = j$, we use the results of $G_{ij}^1(t)$ and $G_{ij}^2(t)$ with $i \neq j$ to compute $G_{ii}^1(t)$ and $G_{ii}^2(t)$, which is used to guarantee the diffusive condition of the coupling matrices, i.e., $G_{ii}^1(t) = - \sum_{j=1, j \neq i}^{N} G_{ij}^1(t)$ and $G_{ii}^2(t) = - \sum_{j=1, j \neq i}^{N} G_{ij}^2(t)$.

Lemma 1. (see [13]) Let X, Y and P be real matrices with appropriate dimensions, P is a positive definite symmetric matrix. Then for any positive scalar $\epsilon > 0$, the following inequality holds,

$$X^T Y + Y^T X \leq \epsilon^{-1} X^T P^{-1} X + \epsilon Y^T P Y. \tag{5}$$

3   Main Results

Now we state our main results in this section.

Theorem 1. Suppose that Assumption 21 holds. The complex networks (1) is synchronized under the following coupling adjusting laws,

$$\dot{G}_{ij}^1 = -\alpha_{ij}(x_i - x_j)^T \Gamma_1 (x_i - x_j), \tag{6}$$

$$\dot{G}_{ij}^2 = -\beta_{ij}(x_i(t) - \bar{x})^T \Gamma_2 (x_j(t - \tau) - \bar{x}), \tag{7}$$

if there exist sufficiently large positive constants $\bar{\alpha}_{ij}, \bar{\beta}_{ij}$ such that the following condition holds,

$$
\begin{bmatrix} I_N \otimes H - \alpha \otimes \Gamma_1 & 0 \\ 0 & -\beta \otimes \Gamma_2 \end{bmatrix} < 0, \tag{8}
$$

where $\bar{\alpha}_{ij} = \bar{\alpha}_{ji}$ and $\bar{\beta}_{ij} = \bar{\beta}_{ji}$ are positive constants, $\alpha = (\bar{\alpha}_{ij}), \beta = (\bar{\beta}_{ij})$.

Proof. Let us consider the Lyapunov functional $V(t) = V_1(t) + V_2(t)$, where

$$
\begin{aligned}
V_1(t) = & \sum_{i=1}^{N} e_i^T(t)e_i(t) + \sum_{i=1}^{N} \sum_{j=1, j\neq i}^{N} \frac{c_1}{2\alpha_{ij}}(G_{ij}^1(t) + \bar{\alpha}_{ij})^2 \\
& + \sum_{i=1}^{N} \sum_{j=1, j\neq i}^{N} \frac{c_2}{2\beta_{ij}}(G_{ij}^2(t) + \bar{\beta}_{ij})^2
\end{aligned} \tag{9}
$$

$$
V_2(t) = \sum_{i=1}^{N} \int_{t-\tau}^{t} e_i^T(s)Me_i(s)ds, \tag{10}
$$

where $\bar{\alpha}_{ij} = \bar{\alpha}_{ji}$ and $\bar{\beta}_{ij} = \bar{\beta}_{ji}$ are nonnegative constants, $\bar{\alpha}_{ij} = 0$ if and only if $G_{ij}^1(t) = 0$, $\bar{\beta}_{ij} = 0$ if and only if $G_{ij}^2(t) = 0$, positive semi-definite matrix M will be defined later.

The derivative of $V_1(t)$ is as follows

$$
\begin{aligned}
\dot{V}_1(t) = & 2\sum_{i=1}^{N} e_i^T(t)\dot{e}_i(t) + \sum_{i=1}^{N} \sum_{j=1, j\neq i}^{N} \frac{c_1}{\alpha_{ij}}(G_{ij}^1(t) + \bar{\alpha}_{ij})\dot{G}_{ij}^1(t) \\
& + \sum_{i=1}^{N} \sum_{j=1, j\neq i}^{N} \frac{c_2}{\beta_{ij}}(G_{ij}^2(t) + \bar{\beta}_{ij})\dot{G}_{ij}^2(t) \\
= & 2\sum_{i=1}^{N} e_i^T(t)\Big\{ -Cx_i(t) + Af(x_i(t)) + Bf(x_i(t-\tau)) + J(t) \\
& - \frac{1}{N}\sum_{j=1}^{N}\Big[-Cx_i(t) + Af(x_i(t)) + Bf(x_i(t-\tau)) + J(t)\Big] \\
& + c_1\sum_{j=1}^{N} G_{ij}^1(t)\Gamma_1 e_j(t) + c_2\sum_{j=1}^{N} G_{ij}^2(t)\Gamma_2 e_j(t-\tau)\Big\} \\
& + c_1\sum_{i=1}^{N} \sum_{j=1, j\neq i}^{N} (G_{ij}^1(t) + \bar{\alpha}_{ij})(x_i - x_j)^T\Gamma_1(x_i - x_j) \\
& + c_2\sum_{i=1}^{N} \sum_{j=1, j\neq i}^{N} (G_{ij}^2(t) \\
& + \bar{\beta}_{ij})(x_i(t-\tau) - x_j(t-\tau))^T\Gamma_2(x_i(t-\tau) - x_j(t-\tau))
\end{aligned} \tag{11}
$$

Adding and subtracting $-C\bar{x}(t) + Af(\bar{x}(t)) + Bf(\bar{x}(t-\tau)) + J(t)$ in (11), we have

$$
\begin{aligned}
2\sum_{i=1}^{N} e_i^T &\Big\{ -Cx_i(t) + Af(x_i(t)) + Bf(x_i(t-\tau)) + J(t) \\
&- \Big[-C\bar{x}(t) + Af(\bar{x}(t)) + Bf(\bar{x}(t-\tau)) + J(t) \Big] \Big\} \\
&= \sum_{i=1}^{N} e_i^T \Big[-2Ce_i + A(f(x_i(t)) - f(\bar{x})) + Bf(x_i(t-\tau) - f(\bar{x})) \Big] \\
&\leq \sum_{i=1}^{N} \Big[-2e_i^T Ce_i + e_i^T A(f(x_i(t)) - f(\bar{x})) + e_i^T Bf(x_i(t-\tau) - f(\bar{x})) \Big] \\
&\leq \sum_{i=1}^{N} \Big[-2e_i^T Ce_i + \epsilon_1 e_i^T AA^T e_i + \epsilon_1^{-1} e_i^T \Delta\Delta e_i \\
&\qquad\quad + \epsilon_2 e_i^T BB^T e_i + \epsilon_2^{-1} e_i(t-\tau)^T \Delta\Delta e_i(t-\tau) \Big],
\end{aligned}
\tag{12}
$$

where we have applied Lemma 1 and Assumption 21.

Since

$$
\sum_{i=1}^{N} e_i = \sum_{i=1}^{N}(x_i - \bar{x}) = \sum_{i=1}^{N} x_i - \sum_{i=1}^{N} \bar{x} = \sum_{i=1}^{N} x_i - N\bar{x} = 0,
\tag{13}
$$

then

$$
\begin{aligned}
\sum_{i=1}^{N} e_i^T &\Big\{ -C\bar{x}(t) + Af(\bar{x}(t)) + Bf(\bar{x}(t-\tau)) + J(t) \\
&- \frac{1}{N}\sum_{j=1}^{N}\Big[-Cx_j(t) + Af(x_j(t)) + Bf(x_j(t-\tau)) + J(t) \Big] \Big\} = 0,
\end{aligned}
\tag{14}
$$

Note that the following equalities hold,

$$
\begin{aligned}
\sum_{i=1}^{N}\sum_{j=1,j\neq i}^{N} & c_1(G_{ij}^1(t) + \bar{\alpha}_{ij})(x_i - x_j)^T \Gamma_1(x_i - x_j) \\
&= \sum_{i=1}^{N}\sum_{j=1,j\neq i}^{N} c_1(G_{ij}^1(t) + \bar{\alpha}_{ij})(e_i - e_j)^T \Gamma_1(e_i - e_j) \\
&= -2\sum_{i=1}^{N}\sum_{j=1}^{N} c_1 G_{ij}^1(t) e_i^T \Gamma_1 e_j - 2\sum_{i=1}^{N}\sum_{j=1}^{N} c_1 \bar{\alpha}_{ij} e_i^T \Gamma_1 e_j,
\end{aligned}
\tag{15}
$$

$$\sum_{i=1}^{N}\sum_{j=1,j\neq i}^{N} c_2(G_{ij}^2(t) + \bar{B}_{ij})(x_i(t) - \bar{x})^T \Gamma_2(x_j(t-\tau) - \bar{x})$$

$$= \sum_{i=1}^{N}\sum_{j=1,j\neq i}^{N} c_2(G_{ij}^2(t) + \bar{B}_{ij})e_i^T(t)\Gamma_2 e_j(t-\tau)$$

$$= -2\sum_{i=1}^{N}\sum_{j=1}^{N} c_2 G_{ij}^2(t)e_i^T(t)\Gamma_2 e_j(t-\tau) - 2\sum_{i=1}^{N}\sum_{j=1}^{N} c_2 \bar{B}_{ij} e_i^T(t)\Gamma_2 e_j(t-\tau). \quad (16)$$

The derivative of $V_2(t)$ is as follows,

$$\dot{V}_2(t) = \sum_{i=1}^{N} e_i^T(t)M e_i(t) - \sum_{i=1}^{N} e_i^T(t-\tau)M e_i(t-\tau). \quad (17)$$

Combining (12)-(17) into (11), one has

$$\dot{V}_1(t) \leq \sum_{i=1}^{N} \Big[-e_i^T C e_i + \epsilon_1 e_i^T AA^T e_i + \epsilon_1^{-1} e_i^T \Delta\Delta e_i$$

$$+ \epsilon_2 e_i^T BB^T e_i + \epsilon_2^{-1} e_i(t-\tau)^T \Delta\Delta e_i(t-\tau) \Big]$$

$$+ 2\sum_{i=1}^{N} e_i^T(t)\Big[c_1 \sum_{j=1}^{N} G_{ij}^1(t)\Gamma_1 e_j(t) + c_2 \sum_{j=1}^{N} G_{ij}^2(t)\Gamma_2 e_j(t-\tau) \Big]$$

$$- 2\sum_{i=1}^{N}\sum_{j=1}^{N} c_1 G_{ij}^1(t)e_i^T \Gamma_1 e_j - 2\sum_{i=1}^{N}\sum_{j=1}^{N} c_1 \bar{\alpha}_{ij} e_i^T \Gamma_1 e_j$$

$$- 2\sum_{i=1}^{N}\sum_{j=1}^{N} c_2 G_{ij}^2(t)e_i^T(t)\Gamma_2 e_j(t-\tau) - 2\sum_{i=1}^{N}\sum_{j=1}^{N} c_2 \bar{B}_{ij} e_i^T(t)\Gamma_2 e_j(t-\tau)$$

$$+ \sum_{i=1}^{N} e_i^T(t)M e_i(t) - \sum_{i=1}^{N} e_i^T(t-\tau)M e_i(t-\tau). \quad (18)$$

If we take $M = \epsilon_2^{-1}\Delta\Delta$, then we have

$$\dot{V}_1(t) \leq \sum_{i=1}^{N} e_i^T \Big[-2C + \epsilon_1 AA^T + \epsilon_1^{-1}\Delta\Delta + \epsilon_2 BB^T + \epsilon_2^{-1}\Delta\Delta \Big] e_i$$

$$- 2\sum_{i=1}^{N}\sum_{j=1}^{N} c_1 \bar{\alpha}_{ij} e_i^T \Gamma_1 e_j - 2\sum_{i=1}^{N}\sum_{j=1}^{N} c_2 \bar{B}_{ij} e_i(t-\tau)^T \Gamma_2 e_j(t-\tau)$$

$$\leq e^T(I_N \otimes H - \alpha \otimes \Gamma_1)e - e^T(t-\tau)\beta \otimes \Gamma_2 e(t-\tau), \quad (19)$$

where $\alpha = (\bar{\alpha}_{ij})$, $\beta = (\bar{B}_{ij})$, $H = -2C + \epsilon_1 AA^T + \epsilon_1^{-1}\Delta\Delta + \epsilon_2 BB^T + \epsilon_2^{-1}\Delta\Delta$.

Remark 1. From the proof procedure, it is obvious that the parameters $\bar{\alpha}_{ij}$ and $\bar{\beta}_{ij}$ always exist if their magnitudes are large enough. Therefore, the adopted adaptive laws can guarantee the synchronization of the whole nodes.

For the case of no delayed coupling, we can have the following corollary.

Corollary 1. Suppose that Assumption 21 holds. The complex networks (1) without delayed coupling is synchronized under the following coupling adjusting law,

$$\dot{G}_{ij}^1(t) = -\alpha_{ij}(x_i - x_j)^T \Gamma_1(x_i - x_j). \tag{20}$$

Remark 2. For the Corollary 1, the result is just the main result in [12]. However, in the proof procedure of the main result, some transformations on the interconnected matrix are used to re-formulate the synchronization. In contrast, the transformation of the interconnected matrix can be canceled and some matrix inequality can be directly applied.

Remark 3. In this paper, the synchronization state of the whole nodes are assumed to be $\bar{x} = \frac{1}{N} \sum_{j=1}^N x_j$. Based on this premise, the decentralized adaptive adjusting law is designed. For the synchronization case of $x_1 = x_2 = \cdots, = x_N$, how to design the decentralized adaptive coupling law is not an easy work because the information on the relations among the node states is little and can not be utilized correspondingly.

4   Conclusions

For a class of interconnected delayed neural networks with delayed coupling, a decentralized adaptive coupling law is designed to synchronize the whole states. The outstanding feature of the proposed method is that it can sufficiently use the neighbor information of the nodes to adjust the whole states of the complex networks. Some challenging problems are still not solved in this direction. For example, how to guarantee the persistent excitation of adaptive mechanism, how to measure the delayed state information as the feedback action, etc.

Acknowledgements. This work was supported by National Natural Science Foundation under Grants 61074073, 61034005 and 60974071, Program for New Century Excellent Talents in University of China under Grant NCET-10-0306, and the Fundamental Research Funds for the Central Universities under Grants N110504001 and N100104102.

References

1. Zhang, R., Hu, M., Xu, Z.: Synchronization in complex networks with adaptive coupling. Physics Letters A 368, 276–280 (2007)
2. Wu, X., Lu, H.: Outer synchronization of uncertain general complex delayed networks with adaptive coupling. Neurocomputing 82, 57–166 (2012)

3. Hu, C., Yu, J., Jiang, H., Teng, Z.: Synchronization of complex community networks with nonidentical nodes and adaptive coupling strength. Physics Letters A 375, 873–879 (2011)
4. Liu, H., Chen, J., Lu, J., Cao, M.: Generalized synchronization in complex dynamical networks via adaptive couplings. Physica A: Statistical Mechanics and its Applications 389, 1759–1770 (2010)
5. Sun, D.: Position synchronization of multiple motion axes with adaptive coupling control. Automatica 39, 997–1005 (2003)
6. Carstensen, C., Zarrabi, D., Stephan, E.: On the h-adaptive coupling of fe and be for viscoplastic and elasto-plastic interface problems. Journal of Computational and Applied Mathematics 75, 345–363 (1996)
7. Xu, Y., Zhou, W., Fang, J., Sun, W.: Adaptive synchronization of the complex dynamical network with non-derivative and derivative coupling. Physics Letters A 374, 1673–1677 (2010)
8. Sun, W., Chen, S., Guo, W.: Adaptive global synchronization of a general complex dynamical network with non-delayed and delayed coupling. Physics Letters A 372, 6340–6346 (2008)
9. Huang, L., Wang, Z., Wang, Y., Zuo, Y.: Synchronization analysis of delayed complex networks via adaptive time-varying coupling strengths. Physics Letters A 373, 3952–3958 (2009)
10. Bian, Q., Yao, H.: Adaptive synchronization of bipartite dynamical networks with distributed delays and nonlinear derivative coupling. Communications in Nonlinear Science and Numerical Simulation 16, 4089–4098 (2011)
11. Li, Z., Jiao, L., Lee, J.: Robust adaptive global synchronization of complex dynamical networks by adjusting time-varying coupling strength. Physica A: Statistical Mechanics and its Applications 387, 1369–1380 (2008)
12. Yu, W., De Lellis, P., Chen, G., di Bernardo, M., Kurths, J.: Distributed adaptive control of synchronization in complex networks. IEEE Transactions on Automatic Control (to appear)
13. Wang, Z., Zhang, H., Liu, D., Feng, J.: LMI Based Global Asymptotic Stability Criterion for Recurrent Neural Networks with Infinite Distributed Delays. In: Yu, W., He, H., Zhang, N. (eds.) ISNN 2009. LNCS, vol. 5551, pp. 463–471. Springer, Heidelberg (2009)

Quasi-synchronization of Delayed Coupled Networks with Non-identical Discontinuous Nodes*

Xiaoyang Liu[1] and Wenwu Yu[2,3,**]

[1] School of Computer Science & Technology,
Jiangsu Normal University, Xuzhou 221116, China
liuxiaoyang1979@gmail.com
[2] Department of Mathematics, Southeast University, Nanjing 210096, China[***]
wenwuyu@gmail.com
[3] School of Electrical and Computer Engineering,
RMIT University, Melbourne VIC 3001, Australia

Abstract. This paper is concerned with the quasi-synchronization issue of linearly coupled networks with discontinuous nonlinear functions in each isolated node. Under the framework of Filippov systems, the existence and boundedness of solutions for such complex networks can be guaranteed by the matrix measure approach. A design method is presented for the synchronization controllers of coupled networks with non-identical discontinuous systems. Numerical simulations on the coupled chaotic systems are given to demonstrate the effectiveness of the theoretical results.

Keywords: Quasi-synchronization, Filippov systems, Discontinuous functions, Non-identical nodes.

1 Introduction

Over the past decades, complex networks have been studied intensively in various fields, such as physics, mathematics, engineering, biology, and sociology [1,2]. A complex network is a large set of interconnected nodes, which represent individuals in the system and among them, the edges, represent the connections. Each node is a fundamental unit having specific contents and exhibiting dynamical behavior. A complex network can exhibit complicated dynamics which may be

---

* This work was supported by the National Natural Science Foundation of China under Grant No. 61104145, the Natural Science Foundation of Jiangsu Province of China under Grant No. BK2011581, the Research Fund for the Doctoral Program of Higher Education of China under Grant No. 20110092120024, the Fundamental Research Funds for the Central Universities of China, and the scientific research support project for teachers with doctor's degree, Jiangsu Normal University under Grant No. 11XLR19.
** Corresponding author.
*** Corresponding address.

J. Wang, G.G. Yen, and M.M. Polycarpou (Eds.): ISNN 2012, Part I, LNCS 7367, pp. 274–284, 2012.

absolutely different from those of a single node. Hence, the investigation of complex dynamical networks is of great importance, and many large-scale systems in nature and human societies, such as biological neural networks, the Internet, the WWW, electrical power grids, etc., can be described by complex networks.

On the other hand, synchronization, a typical collective behavior in nature, means two or more systems share a common dynamical behavior, which can be induced by coupling or by external forces. Synchronization certainly is a basis to understand an unknown dynamical system from one or more well-known dynamical systems [3–7]. However, it is known that dynamical systems with discontinuous and/or unbounded nonlinear functions do frequently arise in the real applications. For the well known neural networks, there have been extensive results on the global stability of neural networks with discontinuous activations in the existing literature [8–14]. In these references, the first problem to be resolved is giving the definition of solution for the discontinuous systems under the framework of Filippov solution. By constructing the Filippov set-valued map, the differential equation could be transformed into a differential inclusion, which is also called as the Filippov regularization (the details can be founded in Definition 2). Such a notion has been utilized as a feasible approach in the field of mathematics and control for discontinuous dynamical systems.

The behavior of a network is determined by two main features: the dynamics of the isolated nodes, and the connections between the nodes. In order to analyze the network synchronization, most works in the literature assume that all the node dynamics are identical which mainly origins from physical connections in biology, physics and social science [15, 16]. Nowadays, the interest of synchronization issue is shifting to networks of coupled non-identical dynamical systems mainly due to the above assumption that the identical nodes is a highly unlikely circumstance for technological networks in the real world. Indeed, almost all complex dynamical networks in engineering have different nodes [17]. In addition, the behavior of networks with non-identical nodes is much more complicated than the identical-node case. For instance, there does not exist a common equilibrium for all nodes even if each isolated node has an equilibrium. Therefore, a network with non-identical nodes still show some kind of synchronization behaviors which are far from being fully understood. Certain reasonable and satisfactory boundedness [15, 18] of state motion errors between different nodes can be taken as useful synchronization properties, which is usually called as quasi-synchronization [19].

Motivated by the above discussions, we aim (i) to formulate a mathematical model considering discontinuous dynamics of each isolated node for the coupled complex networks; (ii) to use the concept of Filippov solution to describe the solutions' existence and boundedness of coupled networks; (iii) to utilize matrix measure method to cope with the quasi-synchronization issue of network with non-identical nodes.

2 Model Formulation and Preliminaries

In this paper, we consider a complex dynamical network consisting of N linearly coupled identical nodes. Each node is an n-dimensional system composed of linear and nonlinear terms. The i-th node can be described by following differential equation:

$$\dot{x}_i(t) = Dx_i(t) + Bf(x_i(t)), \ i = 1, 2, \cdots, N, \tag{1}$$

where $x_i(t) = (x_{i1}(t), x_{i2}(t), \cdots, x_{in}(t))^T \in \mathbb{R}^n (i = 1, 2, \cdots, N)$ is the state vector representing the state variables of node i at time t; $D \in \mathbb{R}^{n \times n}$, $B \in \mathbb{R}^{n \times n}$; and $f(x_i(t)) = [f_1(x_i), f_2(x_i), \cdots, f_n(x_i)]^T : \mathbb{R}^n \to \mathbb{R}^n$.

Consider the dynamical behavior of the complex dynamical network described by the following linearly coupled differential equations:

$$\dot{x}_i(t) = Dx_i(t) + Bf(x_i(t)) + c \sum_{j=1}^{N} a_{ij} \Gamma x_j(t), \ i = 1, 2, \cdots, N, \tag{2}$$

where Γ is the inner coupling positive definite matrix between two connected nodes i and j; c is the coupling strength; a_{ij} is defined as follows: if there is a connection from node j to node i $(j \to i)$, then $a_{ij} = a_{ji} > 0$; otherwise, $a_{ij} = a_{ji} = 0 (j \neq i)$; and the diagonal elements of matrix A are defined by

$$a_{ii} = - \sum_{j=1, j \neq i}^{N} a_{ij}. \tag{3}$$

Unlike the previous studies on synchronization of complex networks, the nonlinear function f of each isolated node in this paper does not hold the Lipschitz condition [4, 19, 20] or QUAD condition [7] any more. Moreover, the basic continuous conditions are also removed. The marked difference between this paper and the existing work is that the node dynamics in our model are admitted to be discontinuous.

From the theoretical point of view, the basic and natural question is about the solution of the discontinuous dynamical systems. The existence of solutions for discontinuous dynamical systems is a delicate problem, as can be seen from our previous work [11, 12]. Firstly, we need some preliminaries to introduce the new definition for the solutions.

Definition 1. Class $\mathcal{F}$ of functions: we call $f \in \mathcal{F}$, if for all $i = 1, 2, \cdots, n$, $f_i(\cdot)$ satisfies: $f_i(\cdot)$ is continuously differentiable, except on a countable set of isolated points $\{\rho_k^i\}$, where the right and left limits $f_i^+(\rho_k^i)$ and $f_i^-(\rho_k^i)$ exist, $k = 1, 2, \cdots$.

In the following, we apply the framework of Filippov [21] in discussing the solution of each node (1) with the discontinuous function f.

Definition 2. A set-valued map is defined as

$$F(x_i) = \bigcap_{\delta > 0} \bigcap_{\mu(N)=0} K[f(B(x_i, \delta) \setminus N)], \tag{4}$$

where $K(E)$ is the closure of the convex hull of set E, $B(x_i, \delta) = \{y : \|y - x_i\| \leq \delta\}$, and $\mu(N)$ is Lebesgue measure of set N. A solution in the sense of Filippov of equation (1) with initial condition $x_i(s) = \theta_s$, $\forall s \in [-\tau, 0]$, is an absolutely continuous function $x_i(t), t \in [0, T]$, which satisfies differential inclusion:

$$\frac{dx_i}{dt} \in Dx_i(t) + B\mathbb{F}(x_i), \quad a.e. \ t \in [0, T], i = 1, \cdots, N. \tag{5}$$

where $\mathbb{F}(x_i) \overset{\triangle}{=} K[f(x_i)] = (K[f_1(x_i)], \cdots, K[f_n(x_i)])$, and $K[f_j(x_i)] = [\min \{f_j(x_i^-), f_j(x_i^+)\}, \max\{f_j(x_i^-), f_j(x_i^+)\}]$, $i = 1, \cdots, N, j = 1, \cdots, n$.
It is obvious that, for all $f \in \mathcal{F}$, the set-valued map $x_i(t) \hookrightarrow Dx_i(t) + B\mathbb{F}(x_i(t))$ has nonempty compact convex values. Furthermore, it is upper-semi-continuous [22] and hence it is measurable. By the measurable selection theorem [23], if $x_i(t)$ is a solution of (1), then there exists a measurable function $\alpha_i(t) \in K[f(x_i(t))]$ such that for $a.e. \ t \in [0, +\infty)$, the following equations hold:

$$\dot{x}_i(t) = Dx_i(t) + B\alpha_i(t), \quad for \ a.e. \ t \in [0, T), i = 1, \cdots, N. \tag{6}$$

In [11, 12], we have considered the existence and stability (and then the uniqueness) of such solutions for each node. In this paper, we will not repeat the existence results, which can also be found in [9, 10, 13, 14]. We will discuss the uniform boundedness of the complex dynamical networks (2) in the next section.

Next, we introduce the concept of matrix measure which is the main tool in the deduction of this paper.

Definition 3. The matrix measure of a real square matrix $A = (a_{ij})_{n \times n}$ is as follows:

$$\mu_p(A) = \lim_{\varepsilon \to 0^+} \frac{\|\mathbf{I} + \varepsilon A\|_p - 1}{\varepsilon},$$

where $\| \cdot \|_p$ is an induced matrix norm on $\mathbb{R}^{n \times n}$, $\mathbf{I}$ is the identity matrix, and $p = 1, 2, \infty$.

3   Uniform Boundedness of Complex Networks

In this section, we establish some basic results on uniform boundedness of solutions in the sense of Filippov for the complex networks (2) under the next hypothesis called as the growth condition [23].

The growth condition (**g.c.**): for $f \in \mathcal{F}$, there exist constants M_1 and M_2, with $M_1 \geq 0$ such that

$$\|\mathbb{F}(x_i)\|_p = \sup_{\xi \in \mathbb{F}(x_i)} \|\xi\|_p \leq M_1 \|x_i\|_p + M_2, \ p = 1, 2, \infty, \ i = 1, 2, \cdots, N. \tag{7}$$

Let $A \otimes B$ denote the Kronecker product of matrices A and B, $\mathbf{D} = I_N \otimes D$, $\mathbf{B} = I_N \otimes B$, $\mathbf{\Gamma}_1 = A \otimes \Gamma_1$, $x(t) = (x_1^T(t), x_2^T(t), \cdots, x_N^T(t))^T$ and $\mathbf{f}(x(t)) = (f^T(x_1(t)), f^T(x_2(t)), \cdots, f^T(x_N(t)))^T$. The linearly coupled dynamical system (2) can be rewritten as

$$\dot{x}(t) = \mathbf{D}x(t) + \mathbf{B}\mathbf{f}(x(t)) + c_1\mathbf{\Gamma}_1 x(t). \tag{8}$$

Definition 4. The complex system (8) is uniformly bounded with a bound $\omega > 0$ if there exist $\delta_0 > 0$ and $T \geq 0$ such that if $\|x(0)\|_p^\tau \leq \delta_0$ then $\|x(t)\|_p \leq \omega$ for all $t \geq T$, where $\|x(0)\|_p^\tau = \max\limits_{-\tau \leq z \leq 0} \|x(z)\|_p$.

Theorem 1. Under the growth condition (**g.c.**), the complex network (8) will be uniformly bounded, if there exist $\sigma > 0$ and one matrix measure $\mu_p(\cdot)$, $p = 1, 2, \infty$ such that

$$\mu_p(\mathbf{D} + c_1 \mathbf{\Gamma}_1) + M_1 \|\mathbf{B}\|_p \leq -\sigma < 0. \tag{9}$$

Proof. The proof is omitted for simplicity due to page limit.

4   Quasi-synchronization of Coupled Networks

In the above section, model (2) is a complex dynamical network without delayed coupling. In this section, we consider the synchronization issue of linearly delayed coupled networks with non-identical nodes:

$$\dot{x}_i(t) = D_i x_i(t) + B_i f(x_i(t)) + c_1 \sum_{j=1}^N a_{ij} \Gamma_1 x_j(t) + c_2 \sum_{j=1}^N a_{ij} \Gamma_2 x_j(t - \tau),$$

$$i = 1, 2, \cdots, N, \tag{10}$$

which is a general complex network model. It means that each node communicates with other non-identical nodes at time t as well as at time $t - \tau$.

Our goal is to synchronize the states of networks (10) on the manifold

$$\dot{s}(t) = Ds(t) + Bf(s(t)), \tag{11}$$

by introducing a controller $u_i(t) \in \mathbb{R}^n$, $i = 1, 2, \cdots, N$, into each individual node, where $s(t)$ can be any desired state, for example, an equilibrium point, a nontrivial periodic orbit, or even a chaotic orbit. That is, by adding a suitable designed feedback controller to complex networks (10), there exists a constant $t_1 > 0$ such that $x_1(t) = x_2(t) = \cdots = x_N(t) = s(t)$, for any $t \geq t_1$. The controlled complex networks (10) can be written as :

$$\dot{x}_i(t) = D_i x_i(t) + B_i f(x_i(t)) + c_1 \sum_{j=1}^N a_{ij} \Gamma_1 x_j(t) + c_2 \sum_{j=1}^N a_{ij} \Gamma_2 x_j(t - \tau)$$

$$+ u_i(t). \tag{12}$$

Subtracting (11) from (12), we obtain the following error dynamical systems:

$$\dot{e}_i(t) = \dot{x}_i(t) - \dot{s}(t)$$

$$= D_i e_i(t) + B_i g_i(t) + c_1 \sum_{j=1}^N a_{ij} \Gamma_1 x_j(t) + c_2 \sum_{j=1}^N a_{ij} \Gamma_2 x_j(t - \tau) + u_i(t)$$

$$+ \Delta D_i s(t) + \Delta B_i f(s(t)), \tag{13}$$

where $\Delta D_i = D_i - D$, $\Delta B_i = B_i - B$, $g_i(t) = f(x_i(t)) - f(s(t))$.

Based on (3), we have

$$\sum_{j=1}^{N} a_{ij} \Gamma_1 s(t) = \sum_{j=1}^{N} a_{ij} \Gamma_2 s(t - \tau) = 0. \tag{14}$$

Consider the state-feedback control law

$$u_i(t) = k_i e_i(t). \tag{15}$$

By Kronecker product, (14) and (15), the error system (13) can be rewritten as

$$\dot{e}(t) = \mathbb{D}e(t) + \mathbb{B}\mathbf{g}(t) + c_1 \mathbf{\Gamma}_1 e(t) + c_2 \mathbf{\Gamma}_2 e(t - \tau) + \mathbf{K}e(t) + \Delta \mathbb{D}\mathbf{S}(t)$$
$$+ \Delta \mathbb{B}\mathbf{f}(\mathbf{S}(t)), \tag{16}$$

where $\mathbb{D} = \mathrm{diag}(D_1, D_2, \cdots, D_N)$, $\mathbb{B} = \mathrm{diag}(B_1, B_2, \cdots, B_N)$, $\mathbf{K} = \mathrm{diag}(k_1, k_2, \cdots, k_N)$, $\Delta \mathbb{D} = \mathrm{diag}(\Delta D_1, \Delta D_2, \cdots, \Delta D_N)$, $\Delta \mathbb{B} = \mathrm{diag}(\Delta B_1, \Delta B_2, \cdots, \Delta B_N)$, $\mathbf{\Gamma}_2 = A \otimes \Gamma_2$, $\mathbf{S}(t) = (s^T(t), s^T(t), \cdots, s^T(t))^T$, and $\mathbf{g}(t) = (g_1^T(t), g_2^T(t), \cdots, g_N^T(t))^T$.

Definition 5. [15, 18]. Complex networks (10) and (11) is quasi-synchronized, if there exists a compact set $\Omega \subset \mathbb{R}^{Nn}$ so that $e(t_0) \in \Omega$ and there exists a bound B and a time $T(B, e(t_0))$, which are both independent of $t_0 > 0$, such that $\|e(t)\|_p \leq B$, $p = 1, 2, +\infty$, $\forall t \geq t_0 + T$.

Before proceeding to the main results, we further assume that the set-valued map $\mathbb{F}$ satisfies:

(**L.**) Suppose $0 \in K[f(0)]$ and there exist constants $\bar{M}_1$ and $\bar{M}_2 \geq 0$ such that for all $\iota(t) \in K[f(x(t))]$, $\kappa(t) \in K[f(y(t))]$, the following holds:

$$\|\iota(t) - \kappa(t)\|_p \leq \bar{M}_1 \|x(t) - y(t)\|_p + \bar{M}_2, \quad p \in \{1, 2, \infty\}.$$

Remark 1. Under the assumption (**L.**), the growth condition (**g.c.**) holds. Hence, based on the Theorem 1, the synchronization manifold (11) will be uniformly bounded. In other words, for each orbit in system (11), $\forall \mathbf{S}_0 \in \mathbb{R}^{Nn}$, there exist a time T and a constant $\omega > 0$ such that $\|\mathbf{S}(t)\|_p \leq \omega$, $\forall t \geq T$.

Theorem 2. Under the condition (**L.**), if there exists one matrix measure $\mu_p(\cdot)$, $p = 1, 2, \infty$ such that (9) and (17) hold

$$\mu_p(\mathbb{D} + c_1 \mathbf{\Gamma}_1 + \mathbf{K}) + M_1 \|\mathbb{B}\|_p + c_2 \|\mathbf{\Gamma}_2\|_p \leq -\bar{\sigma} < 0, \quad \forall t \geq T. \tag{17}$$

Then, complex network (10) quasi-synchronizes (11). Moreover, the bounds on synchronization error can be smaller by increasing the control gain $\mathbf{K}$.

Proof. Consider another positive radially unbounded auxiliary functional for the error system (16) as

$$V_2(t) = \|e(t)\|_p. \tag{18}$$

By the Chain Rule in [26], calculating the upper right-hand derivative of $V_2(t)$ along the positive half trajectory of Eq. (16), we have

$$
\begin{aligned}
D^+V_2(t) &= \overline{\lim}_{h\to0^+} \frac{\|e(t+h)\|_p - \|e(t)\|_p}{h} \\
&\leq \overline{\lim}_{h\to0^+} \frac{\|\mathbf{I} + h(\mathbb{D} + c_1\mathbf{\Gamma}_1 + \mathbf{K})\|_p - 1}{h} \|e(t)\|_p + \|\mathbb{B}\beta(t)\|_p \\
&\quad + c_2\|\mathbf{\Gamma}_2 e(t-\tau)\|_p + \|\Delta\mathbb{D}S(t)\|_p + \|\Delta\mathbb{B}F(\mathbf{S}(t))\|_p.
\end{aligned} \tag{19}
$$

where $\beta(t) = (\beta_1^T(t), \beta_2^T(t), \cdots, \beta_N^T(t))^T$, and $\beta_i(t) \in K[g_i(t)]$, $i = 1, 2, \cdots, N$. Based on the condition (**L.**) and Theorem 1, when $t \geq T$, we have

$$
\begin{aligned}
D^+V_2&(x(t)) \\
&\leq (\mu_p(\mathbb{D} + c_1\mathbf{\Gamma}_1 + \mathbf{K}) + \bar{M}_1\|\mathbb{B}\|_p)\|e(t)\|_p + c_2\|\mathbf{\Gamma}_2\|_p \cdot \max_{t-\tau\leq z\leq t} \|e(z)\|_p \\
&\quad + \bar{M}_2\|\mathbb{B}\|_p + \omega\|\Delta\mathbb{D}\|_p + \omega\bar{M}_1\|\Delta\mathbb{B}\|_p + \bar{M}_2\|\Delta\mathbb{B}\|_p.
\end{aligned} \tag{20}
$$

Then, by (17) and the generalized Halanay inequalities, one obtains

$$
\|e(t)\|_p \leq \frac{\bar{\gamma}}{\bar{\sigma}} + (\sup_{-\infty\leq z\leq 0} \|e(z)\|_p - \frac{\bar{\gamma}}{\bar{\sigma}}) \cdot e^{-\bar{\mu}^*(t-t_0)}, \tag{21}
$$

where $\bar{\gamma} = \bar{M}_2(\|\mathbb{B}\|_p + \|\Delta\mathbb{B}\|_p) + \omega(\|\Delta\mathbb{D}\|_p + \|\Delta\mathbb{B}\|_p)$ and $\bar{\mu}^* > 0$.

Therefore, for the given sufficient small $\varepsilon > 0$, there exists $\bar{T} \geq 0$ such that

$$
\|e(t)\|_p \leq \frac{\bar{\gamma}}{\bar{\sigma}} + \varepsilon, \ \forall\, t \geq \bar{T}. \tag{22}
$$

This completes the proof of Theorem 2.

Remark 2. From the matrix measure and Definition 5, we can see that it can have positive as well as negative values, whereas a norm can assume only non-negative ones. Due to these special properties, the results obtained via matrix measure usually are less restrictive than the one using the norm. Furthermore, the matrix measure approach appears simple and clear, which can be verified and applied easily.

5 Numerical Examples

Example 1. Consider the following linearly coupled network model:

$$
\dot{x}_i(t) = Dx_i(t) + Bf(x_i(t)) + c_1 \sum_{j=1}^{N} a_{ij}\Gamma_1 x_j(t) + c_2 \sum_{j=1}^{N} a_{ij}\Gamma_2 x_j(t-\tau),
$$

$$
i = 1, 2, 3, \ (23)
$$

where $x_i(t) = (x_{i1}(t), x_{i2}(t), x_{i3}(t))^T$, $c_1 = c_2 = 1$, $D = \text{diag}(-1, -1, -1)$, $\tau = 1$, the discontinuous function

$$f(x_{i1}(t), x_{i2}(t), x_{i3}(t)) = \begin{cases} -\frac{11}{21}x_{i1}(t) + 3x_{i2}(t) + \frac{9}{7}\text{sign}(x_{i1}(t)), \\ \frac{2}{3}x_{i1}(t) + 5x_{i2}(t) + \frac{1}{3}x_{3i}(t), \\ -\frac{1}{3}x_{i1}(t) - 10x_{i2}(t) + \frac{1}{3}x_{i3}(t), \end{cases}$$

$$B = \begin{bmatrix} 3 & 0 & 0 \\ 0 & 2 & 1 \\ 0 & 1 & 2 \end{bmatrix}, A = \begin{bmatrix} -0.2 & 0.1 & 0.1 \\ 0.1 & -0.1 & 0 \\ 0.1 & 0 & -0.1 \end{bmatrix}, \Gamma_1 = \begin{bmatrix} 1 & 0.5 & 0.4 \\ 0.8 & 1 & 0.3 \\ 0.2 & 0.7 & 0.9 \end{bmatrix}, \Gamma_2 = \begin{bmatrix} 0.6 & 0.3 & 0.4 \\ 0.5 & 1 & 0.3 \\ 0.2 & 0.5 & 0.9 \end{bmatrix}.$$

Based on the detailed discussion in [24], the isolated node dynamics behavior is chaotic (the generalized Chua circuit). From Theorem 1, the linearly coupled network (23) is uniformly bounded, as shown by Fig. 1.

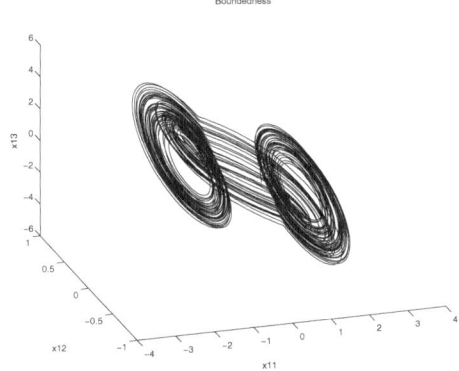

Fig. 1. Trajectories of one node in the coupled networks

Example 2. Consider the following linearly coupled network model with non-identical nodes:

$$\dot{x}_i(t) = D_i x_i(t) + B_i f(x_i(t)) + c_1 \sum_{j=1}^{N} a_{ij} \Gamma_1 x_j(t) + c_2 \sum_{j=1}^{N} a_{ij} \Gamma_2 x_j(t - \tau),$$

$$i = 1, 2, 3, (24)$$

where the values of c_1, c_2, A, Γ_1, Γ_2, τ and f are same as those in Example 1,

$$B_1 = \begin{bmatrix} 3.01 & 0 & 0 \\ 0 & 2 & 1.02 \\ 0 & 1 & 1.99 \end{bmatrix}, B_2 = \begin{bmatrix} 2.99 & 0 & 0 \\ 0 & 1.99 & 1.01 \\ 0 & 1 & 2 \end{bmatrix}, B_3 = \begin{bmatrix} 3 & 0 & 0 \\ 0 & 2 & 0.99 \\ 0 & 1.01 & 2.01 \end{bmatrix},$$

$D_1 = diag(-0.99, -0.97, -0.99)$, $D_2 = diag(-1.01, -1, -0.99)$, and $D_3 = diag(-1, -0.99, -1.01)$. The manifold that we want to synchronize to is:

$$\dot{s}(t) = Ds(t) + Bf(s(t)), \tag{25}$$

where the parameters D and B are the same as those in Example 1. Designing the feedback controller $u(t) = \mathbf{K}e(t) = k * \mathbf{I}e(t)$, where $\mathbf{I}$ is the identity matrix with proper dimensions. Based on Theorem 2, the coupled network (24) quasi-synchronizes (25), just as shown as Figs. 2-3.

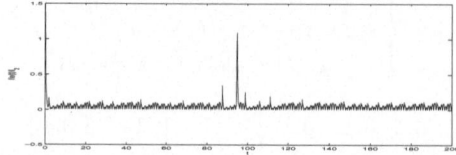

Fig. 2. The quasi-synchronization error $\|e(t)\|_2$ with $k = -5$ in Example 2

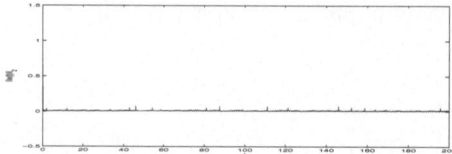

Fig. 3. The quasi-synchronization error $\|e(t)\|_2$ with $k = -20$ in Example 2

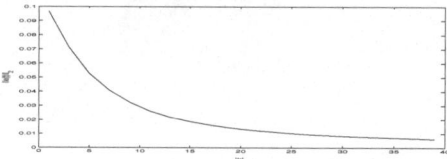

Fig. 4. The trend of quasi-synchronization error $\|e(t)\|_2$ with the increasing $|k|$

Fig. 4 shows the trend of $\|e(t)\|_2$ with the decreasing gain k. However, for the coupled complex networks with non-identical discontinuous node dynamics, the complete synchronization ($\|e(t)\|_2 \to 0$) can't be realized even for a given sufficiently large $|k|$, unless $|k| \to \infty$.

6   Conclusions

This paper has introduced a general delayed coupled complex networks model with nonlinear functions of possessing jumping discontinuities. Based on the concept of Filippov solution, boundedness and quasi-synchronization problems of such networks have been studied by the matrix measure approach and the generalized Halanay inequalities. Easily testable conditions have been established to ensure synchronization for linearly coupled networks with non-identical nodes. These results are novel since there are few works on the synchronization control of complex networks with discontinuous non-identical systems.

References

1. Strogatz, S.H.: Exploring Complex Networks. Nature 410, 268–276 (2001)
2. Watts, D.J., Strogatz, S.H.: Collective Dynamics of "Small-World" Networks. Nature 393, 440–442 (1998)
3. Pecora, L.M., Carroll, T.L.: Synchronization in Chaotic Systems. Phys. Rev. Lett. 64, 821 (1990)
4. Liang, J., Wang, Z., Liu, Y., Liu, X.: Robust Synchronization of an Array of Coupled Stochastic Discrete-Time Delayed Neural Networks. IEEE Trans. Neural Networks. 19, 1910–1921 (2008)
5. Luo, A.C.J.: A Theory for Synchronization of Dynamical Systems. Communications in Nonlinear Science and Numerical Simulation 14, 1901–1951 (2009)
6. Jost, J., Joy, M.P.: Spectral Properties and Synchronization in Coupled Map Lattices. Phys. Rev. E. 65, 016201 (2001)
7. Lu, W., Chen, T.: New Approach to Synchronization Analysis of Linearly Coupled Ordinary Differential Systems. Physica D 213, 214–230 (2006)
8. Cortés, J.: Discontinuous Dynamical Systems. IEEE Control Systems Magazine 28, 36–73 (2008)
9. Forti, M., Nistri, P.: Global Convergence of Neural Networks with Discontinuous Neuron Activations. IEEE Trans. Circ. Syst. I. 50(11), 1421–1435 (2003)
10. Forti, M., Nistri, P., Papini, D.: Global Exponential Stability and Global Convergence in Finite Time of Delayed Neural Networks with Infinite Gain. IEEE Trans. Neural Networks 16(6), 1449–1463 (2005)
11. Liu, X.Y., Cao, J.D.: Robust State Estimation for Neural Networks with Discontinuous Activations. IEEE Transactions on Systems, Man, and Cybernetics: Part B 40(6), 1425–1437 (2010)
12. Liu, X.Y., Cao, J.D.: Complete Periodic Synchronization of Delayed Neural Networks with Discontinuous Activations. International Journal of Bifurcation and Chaos 20(7), 2151–2164 (2010)
13. Lu, W., Chen, T.: Dynamical Behaviors of Cohen-Grossberg Neural Networks with Discontinuous Activation Functions. Neural Networks 18(3), 231–242 (2005)
14. Lu, W., Chen, T.: Almost Periodic Dynamics of a Class of Delayed Neural Networks with Discontinuous Activations. Neural Computation 20, 1065–1090 (2008)
15. Hill, D.J., Zhao, J.: Global Synchronization of Complex Dynamical Networks with Non-Identical Nodes. In: Proc. IEEE Conference on Decision and Control, pp. 817–822 (2008)
16. Newman, M., Barabasi, A.L., Watts, D.J.: The Structure and Dynamics of Networks. Princeton University Press, Princeton (2006)
17. Hill, D.J., Chen, G.R.: Power Systems as Dynamic Networks. In: Proc. IEEE International Symposium on Circuits and Systems, pp. 722–725 (2006)
18. Das, A., Lewis, F.L.: Distributed Adaptive Control for Synchronization of Unknown Nonlinear Networked Systems. Automatica 46, 2014–2021 (2010)
19. Huang, T.W., Li, C.D., Yu, W.W., Chen, G.R.: Synchronization of Delayed Chaotic Systems with Parameter Mismatches by Using Intermittent Linear State Feedback. Nonlinearity 22, 569–584 (2009)
20. Lu, J., Ho, D.W.C., Wu, L.: Exponential Stabilization of Switched Stochastic Dynamical Networks. Nonlinearity 22, 889–911 (2009)
21. Filippov, A.F.: Differential Equations with Discontinuous Right-Hand Side. Kluwer Academic Publishers, Boston (1988)

22. Aubin, J.P., Cellina, A.: Differential Inclusions, Set-Valued Functions and Viability Theory. Springer, Berlin (1984)
23. Aubin, J.P., Frankowska, H.: Set-Valued Analysis. Birkhäuser, Boston (1990)
24. Danca, M.: Chaotifying Discontinuous Dynamical Systems via Time-Delay Feedback Algorithm. International Journal of Bifurcation and Chaos 14(7), 2321–2339 (2004)
25. Song, Q.K., Cao, J.D.: Global Dissipativity Analysis on Uncertain Neural Networks with Mixed Time-Varying Delays. Chaos. 18, 043126 (2008)
26. Clarke, F.: Optimization and Nonsmooth Analysis. Wiley, New York (1983)

Hybrid Synchronization of Two Delayed Systems with Uncertain Parameters

Zhen Zheng, Manchun Tan*, and Qunfang Wang

Department of Mathematics, Jinan University, Guangzhou 510632, China
tanmc@jnu.edu.cn

Abstract. This paper is concerned with the hybrid synchronization of two different delayed chaotic systems with uncertain parameters. A synchronization and anti-synchronization integrated processing method is employed. Suitable nonlinear controller and adaptive law of parameters are designed to realize the hybrid anti-synchronization and identify the uncertain parameters by the adaptive controlling method. Numerical simulations show the effectiveness of the developed approach.

Keywords: delayed chaotic system, hybrid synchronization, adaptive control method, uncertain parameters.

1 Introduction

Synchronization of chaotic systems was proposed by Pecora and Carroll, which depended on the conception of drive-response in 1990. About two decades later, the control and synchronization of chaotic system had caused wide public concern, as the result of the huge potential application in information processing, secure communications, chemical reactions, laser physics, etc [1-3]. Another interesting phenomenon discovered is anti-phase synchronization, which is noticeable in periodic oscillators. The anti-synchronization is the synchronization of anti-phase, but the hybrid synchronization of two systems is that the different state variables of the two systems can reach either synchronization or anti-synchronization [4-6]. In the past few decades, a series of effective approaches have been proposed for the synchronization of chaotic systems, such as drive-response control [7], pulse control [8], linear and nonlinear feedback control [9-10], adaptive control [11-12] and so on. Although there are approaches to the synchronization and anti-synchronization problem of the hyperchaotic system with uncertain parameters at present, there are few studies on hybrid synchronization of the different delayed systems with uncertain parameters. Recently, the conception of two dynamic full state hybrid projective synchronization was proposed. Since the time delay phenomenon always exist and affect the dynamical behavior of the chaotic system in practical application, achieving the hybrid delay synchronization of different hyperchaotic systems will expand the communication range and make a more broad application prospect accordingly.

---

* Correspondding author.

J. Wang, G.G. Yen, and M.M. Polycarpou (Eds.): ISNN 2012, Part I, LNCS 7367, pp. 285–292, 2012.
© Springer-Verlag Berlin Heidelberg 2012

Motivated by the above discussion, the aim of this paper is to investigate the different systems with time delays based on the model of [13], and the hybrid synchronization problem of the two different chaotic systems with uncertain parameters and time delays is solved by adaptive control. The controller of adaptive hybrid synchronization is designed, which depend on Lyapunov stability theory and the analysis and proof to the adaptive law of parameters for the controller. At last, the hybrid synchronizaticl problems of Chen and Lü hyperchaotic systems with time delays show the effectiveness of the method.

2   Problem Description

Consider the drive chaotic system in the form of

$$\dot{x}(t) = f(x(t)) + F(x(t - \tau))\alpha, \tag{1}$$

where $x \in \Omega_1 \subset R^n$ is the state vector, $\alpha \in R^m$ is the unknown constant parameter vector of the system, $x(t - \tau) = (x_1(t - \tau_1), x_2(t - \tau_2), \cdots, x_n(t - \tau_n))^T, \tau_i > 0 (i = 1, 2, \cdots, n)$ are lag time, $f(.) : R^n \to R^n$, $F(.) : R^n \to R^{n \times m}$. The response system is assumed by

$$\dot{y}(t) = g(y(t)) + G(y(t - \tau))\beta + u(t), \tag{2}$$

where $y \in \Omega_2 \subset R^n$ is the state vector, $\beta \in R^q$ is the unknown constant parameter vector of the system, $y(t - \tau) = (y_1(t - \tau_1), y_2(t - \tau_2), \cdots, y_n(t - \tau_n))^T, \tau_i > 0 (i = 1, 2, \cdots, n)$ is lag time, $g(.) : R^n \to R^n$, $G(.) : R^n \to R^{n \times q}$, $u(t)$ is control input vector.

Definition 1. [14] For drive system (1) and response system (2), the two dynamical systems are said to be hybrid synchronization if there exist two new vectors composed of partial system variables x

$$x_r = (x_{n1}, x_{n2}, \cdots, x_{nr}), x_s = (x_{m1}, x_{m2}, \cdots, x_{ms}),$$

where $ni(i = 1, \cdots, r), mj(j = 1, \cdots, s) \in \{1, 2, \cdots, n\}, ni \neq mj$, and $r + s = n$, such that the following equations hold:

$$\lim_{t \to \infty} ||y_i + x_i|| = 0, i \in n_i, \lim_{t \to \infty} ||y_j - x_j|| = 0, j \in m_j.$$

Let $e(t) = x(t) + My(t)$ be the anti-synchronization error vector, where M is a n diagonal matrix, and the diagonal elements are 1 or -1. From Eqs.(1) and (2), we get the error dynamical system as follows

$$\dot{e}(t) = f(x(t)) + F(x(t - \tau))\alpha + M[g(y(t)) + G(y(t - \tau))\beta + u(t)]. \tag{3}$$

Our goal is to design a controller $u(t)$ such that the error system (3) with initial conditions can achieve asymptoticl stability, i.e.,

$$\lim_{t \to \infty} ||e(t)|| = \lim_{t \to \infty} ||My(t, y_0) + x(t, x_0)|| = 0,$$

where $||.||$ is the Euclidean norm.

3   Control Law Design

Lemma 1. [15] Let $V(x) : R^n \rightarrow R$ be such that on $\Omega = \{x \in R^n : 0 < V(x) \le L\}$, we have $\dot{V}(x) \le 0$. Define $\Upsilon = \{x \in R^n : \dot{V}(x) = 0\}$. Then, if Υ contains no other trajectories other than $x = 0$, then the origin 0 is asymptotically stable.

Theorem 1. If the nonlinear control is selected as

$$u(t) = M^{-1}[-f(x(t)) - F(x(t-\tau))\tilde{\alpha}(t) - ke(t)] - g(y(t)) - G(y(t-\tau))\tilde{\beta}(t) \quad (4)$$

and the adaptive laws of parameters are taken as

$$\frac{d\tilde{\alpha}(t)}{dt} = Q^{-1}[F(x(t-\tau))]^T Pe(t) + Q^{-1}(\alpha - \tilde{\alpha}(t)), \quad (5)$$

$$\frac{d\tilde{\beta}(t)}{dt} = R^{-1}[MG(y(t-\tau))]^T Pe(t) + R^{-1}(\beta - \tilde{\beta}(t)), \quad (6)$$

then the drive-response systems (1) and (2) are hybrid synchronization, where $\tilde{\alpha}(t)$ and $\tilde{\beta}(t)$ are, respectively, estimations of the unknown parameters α and β, $k > 0$ is a constant, and P, Q, R are positive definite constant matrixes.

Proof. Consider the Lyapunov function

$$V(e, \tilde{\alpha}, \tilde{\beta}) = \frac{1}{2}\{e(t)^T Pe(t) + (\alpha - \tilde{\alpha}(t))^T Q(\alpha - \tilde{\alpha}(t)) + (\beta - \tilde{\beta}(t))^T R(\beta - \tilde{\beta}(t))\}. \quad (7)$$

From Eqs.(3)-(6) we can get the equation of the time derivative of V along the trajectory of the error dynamical systems as follows

$$\dot{V}(t) = \dot{e}(t)^T Pe(t) + (\alpha - \tilde{\alpha}(t))^T Q(-\dot{\tilde{\alpha}}(t)) + (\beta - \tilde{\beta}(t))^T R(-\dot{\tilde{\beta}}(t))$$
$$= -ke(t)^T Pe(t) + \{(\alpha - \tilde{\alpha}(t))^T [F(x(t-\tau))]^T + (\beta - \tilde{\beta}(t))^T [MG(y(t-\tau))]^T\}Pe(t) - (\alpha - \tilde{\alpha}(t))^T QQ^{-1}[F(x(t-\tau))]^T Pe(t) - (\beta - \tilde{\beta}(t))^T RR^{-1}[MG(y(t-\tau))]^T Pe(t) - (\alpha - \tilde{\alpha}(t))^T (\alpha - \tilde{\alpha}(t)) - (\beta - \tilde{\beta}(t))^T (\beta - \tilde{\beta}(t))$$
$$= -ke(t)^T Pe(t) - (\alpha - \tilde{\alpha}(t))^T (\alpha - \tilde{\alpha}(t)) - (\beta - \tilde{\beta}(t))^T (\beta - \tilde{\beta}(t)) \le 0.$$

Since $V(t)$ is positive definite, and $\dot{V}(t)$ is negative semi-definite, $V(0)$ is constant, so there exist L so that $V(x) \le L$, It's easy to see that $\dot{V}(t) = 0$ holds if only if $(\alpha - \tilde{\alpha}(t)) = 0, (\beta - \tilde{\beta}(t)) = 0$, and $e(t) = 0$.

From **Lemma 1** we get : $\lim_{t \to \infty} ||e(t)|| = \lim_{t \to \infty} ||(\alpha - \tilde{\alpha}(t))|| = \lim_{t \to \infty} ||(\beta - \tilde{\beta}(t))|| = 0$, in the sense that

$$\lim_{t \to \infty} ||e(t)|| = \lim_{t \to \infty} ||My(t, y_0) + x(t, x_0)|| = 0.$$

So the error system (3) is globally asymptotically stable. This completes the proof.

4   The Hybrid Synchronization of Chen and Lü Systems

The hyperchaotic Lü system is given by:

$$
\begin{cases}
\dot{x}_1(t) = a_1(y_1(t - \tau_1) - x_1(t - \tau_1)) + w_1(t) \\
\dot{y}_1(t) = -x_1(t)z_1(t) + c_1y_1(t - \tau_2) \\
\dot{z}_1(t) = x_1(t)y_1(t) - b_1z_1(t - \tau_3) \\
\dot{w}_1(t) = x_1(t)z_1(t) + r_1w_1(t - \tau_4)
\end{cases}
\tag{8}
$$

where $x_1(t), y_1(t), z_1(t)$ and $w_1(t)$ are state variables, $\tau_i > 0 (i = 1, 2, \cdots, n)$ are lag time, $a_1, b_1, c_1,$ and r_1 are constants. The system (8) exhibits hyperchaotic behavior, when $a_1 = 36, b_1 = 3, c_1 = 20, -0.35 \le r_2 \le 1.3$ [15-16].

Consider the response Chen system as follows

$$
\begin{cases}
\dot{x}_2(t) = a_2(y_2(t - \tau_1) - x_2(t - \tau_1)) + w_2(t) \\
\dot{y}_2(t) = d_2x_2(t - \tau_2) - x_2(t)z_2(t) + c_2y_2(t - \tau_2) \\
\dot{z}_2(t) = x_2(t)y_2(t) - b_2z_2(t - \tau_3) \\
\dot{w}_2(t) = y_2(t)z_2(t) + r_2w_2(t - \tau_4)
\end{cases}
\tag{9}
$$

where $x_2(t), y_2(t), z_2(t)$ and $w_2(t)$ are state variables, $\tau_i > 0 (i = 1, 2, \cdots, n)$ are lag time, $a_2, b_2, c_2, d_2,$ and r_2 are constants. The system (9) have hyperchaotic behavior, when $a_2 = 35, b_2 = 3, c_2 = 12, d_2 = 7, 0.085 \le r_2 \le 0.798$ [17].

In order to observe the hybrid anti-synchronous phenomenon of the system (8) and (9) , take $M = diag(-1, 1, -1, 1)$. Applying the controller to system (9), we have

$$
\begin{cases}
-\dot{x}_2(t) = -a_2(y_2(t - \tau_1) - x_2(t - \tau_1)) - w_2(t) - u_1 \\
\dot{y}_2(t) = d_2x_2(t - \tau_2) - x_2(t)z_2(t) + c_2y_2(t - \tau_2) + u_2 \\
-\dot{z}_2(t) = -x_2(t)y_2(t) + b_2z_2(t - \tau_3) - u_3 \\
\dot{w}_2(t) = y_2(t)z_2(t) + r_2w_2(t - \tau_4) + u_4
\end{cases}
\tag{10}
$$

where $u_i(i = 1, 2, 3, 4)$ are four control functions.

By adding Eq.(8) to Eq.(10), we get

$$
\begin{cases}
\dot{e}_1(t) = a_1(y_1(t - \tau_1) - x_1(t - \tau_1)) + w_1(t) - a_2(y_2(t - \tau_1) - x_2(t - \tau_1)) - w_2(t) - u_1 \\
\dot{e}_2(t) = -x_1(t)z_1(t) + c_1y_1(t - \tau_2) + d_2x_2(t - \tau_2) - x_2(t)z_2(t) + c_2y_2(t - \tau_2) + u_2 \\
\dot{e}_3(t) = x_1(t)y_1(t) - b_1z_1(t - \tau_3) - x_2(t)y_2(t) + b_2z_2(t - \tau_3) - u_3 \\
\dot{e}_4(t) = x_1(t)z_1(t) + r_1w_1(t - \tau_4) + y_2(t)z_2(t) + r_2w_2(t - \tau_4) + u_4
\end{cases}
\tag{11}
$$

where $e_1(t) = x_1(t) - x_2(t), e_2(t) = y_2(t) + y_1(t), e_3(t) = z_1(t) - z_2(t), e_4(t) = w_2(t) + w_1(t)$. Our goal is to find proper control functions $u_i(i = 1, 2, 3, 4)$ and parameter update rule, such that the error system (11) can achieve global asymptotic stability, in the sense that,

$$
\lim_{t \to \infty} ||e(t)|| = 0, e = [e_1, e_2, e_3, e_4]^T.
$$

From **Theorem 1** we can choice the nonlinear controller for (3), adaptive laws of parameters for (4) and (5). where

$$F(x(t-\tau)) = diag(y_1(t-\tau_1) - x_1(t-\tau_1), y_1(t-\tau_2), -z_1(t-\tau_3), w_1(t-\tau_4)),$$

$$f(x(t)) = (w_1(t), -x_1(t)z_1(t), x_1(t)y_1(t), x_1(t)z_1(t))^T,$$

$$g(y(t)) = (w_2(t), -x_2(t)z_2(t), x_2(t)y_2(t), y_2(t)z_2(t))^T,$$

$$G(y(t-\tau)) = \begin{pmatrix} y_2(t-\tau_1) - x_2(t-\tau_1) & 0 & 0 & 0 & 0 \\ 0 & y_2(t-\tau_2) & x_2(t-\tau_2) & 0 & 0 \\ 0 & 0 & 0 & -z_2(t-\tau_3) & 0 \\ 0 & 0 & 0 & 0 & w_2(t-\tau_4) \end{pmatrix}.$$

For $t \leq 0$, let $(x_1(t)), y_1(t), z_1(t), w_1(t))) = (5, 8, -1, -3), ((x_2(t)), y_2(t)), z_2(t)$, $w_2(t))) = (-2, -3, 8, 10)$. $\tau_1 = \tau_2 = 1, \tau_3 = \tau_4 = 0.5$, $k_1 = k_2 = k_3 = k_4 = 9$. $Q = E_{(4\times 4)}$, $R = E_{(5\times 5)}$, $E_{(i\times i)}$ is unit matrix, $P = diag(2, 2, 2, 2)$, $\alpha = (a_1, c_1, b_1, r_1)^T = (36, 20, 3, 1.3)^T$, $\beta = (a_2, c_2, d_2, b_2, r_2)^T = (35, 12, 7, 3, 0.5)^T$. $\tilde{\alpha}(t) = (\tilde{\alpha}_1(t), \tilde{\alpha}_2(t), \tilde{\alpha}_3(t), \tilde{\alpha}_4(t))^T = (5, 7, 11, 9)^T$, $\tilde{\beta}(t) = (\tilde{\beta}_1(t), \tilde{\beta}_2(t), \tilde{\beta}_3(t), \tilde{\beta}_4(t), \tilde{\beta}_5(t))^T = (2, 6, 10, 4, 8)^T$.
The results of simulation of two systems are shown in Fig.1-3.

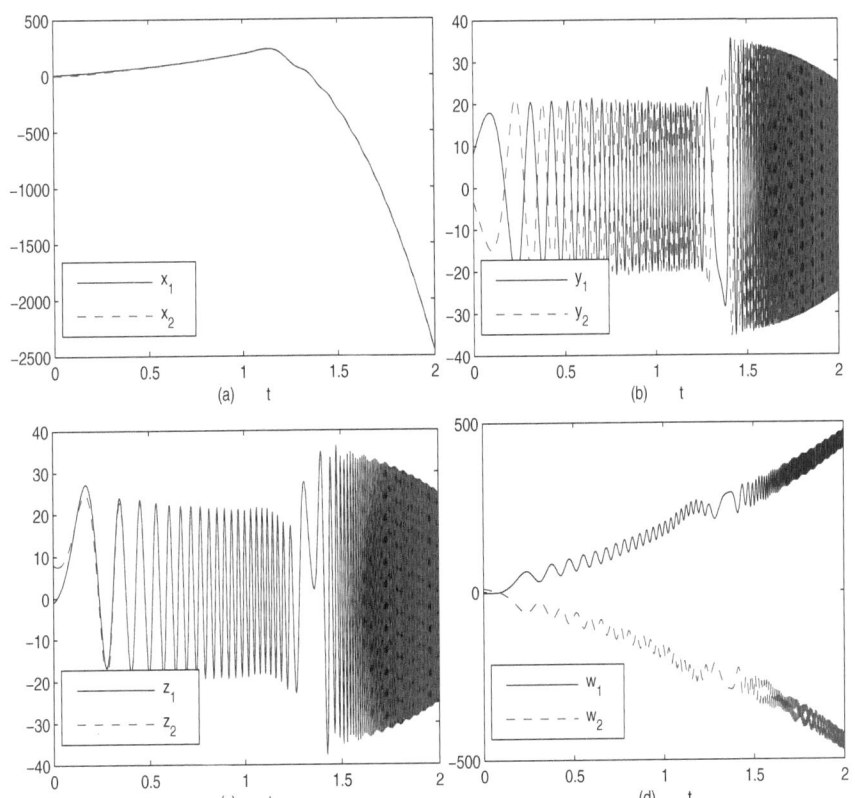

Fig. 1. State trajectories of Lü system(8) and Chen system(10)

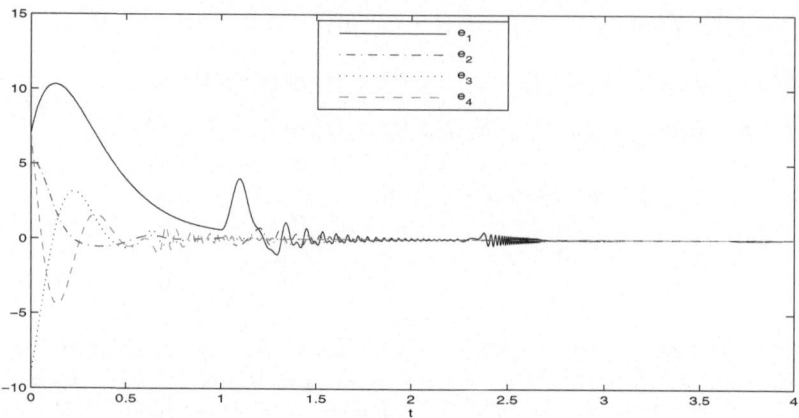

Fig. 2. State trajectories of the error system(11)

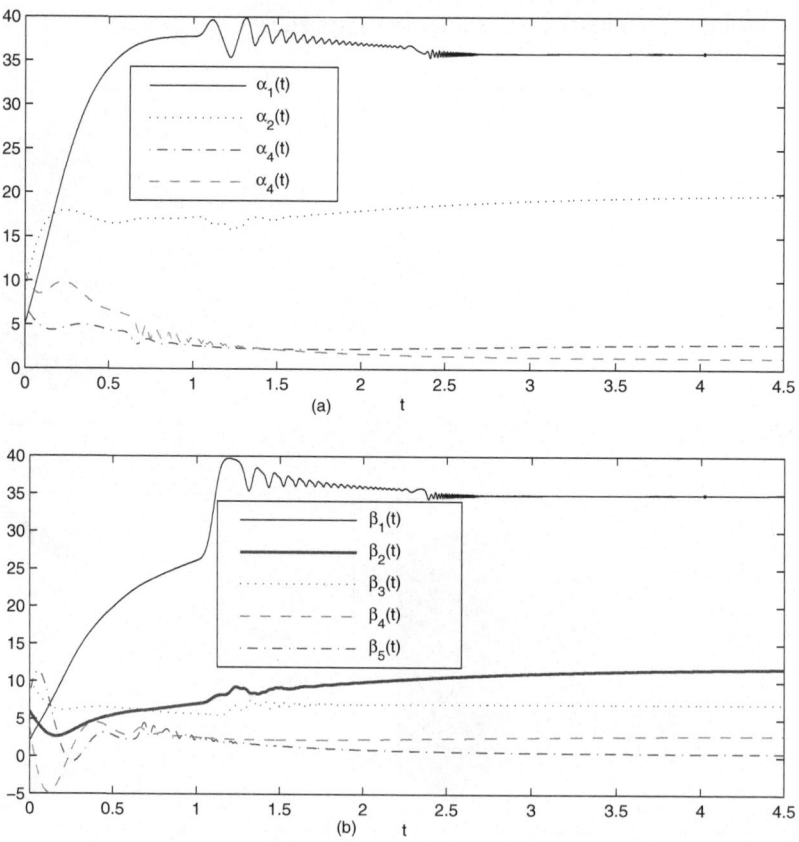

Fig. 3. Estimations trajectories of the parameters of the two systems

Fig.1(a) and (c) show that the state trajectories of the two systems tend to synchronization as the time is increasing. Meanwhile, Fig.1(b) and (d) show that the state trajectories of the two systems achieve anti-synchronization as the time is increasing. The state trajectories of the error system converge to zero quickly as the time is increasing in Fig.2. The estimations value of parameters tend to the true value gradually as the time is increasing in Fig.3.

5   Conclusion

In this paper, by structuring Lyapunov function and the adaptive control method, a new sufficient condition of hybrid synchronization of two different delayed hyperchaotic systems with uncertain parameters is derived. The results of the numerical simulation also prove the validity and feasibility of this method.

Acknowledgments. The research is supported by grants from the Natural Science Foundation of Guangdong Province in China (No. 9151001003000005), and the Foundation of Science and Technology of Guangdong Province in China (No. 2009B011400046).

References

1. Ott, E., Grebogi, C., Yorke, A.J.: Controlling chaos. Physical Review Letters 64, 1190–1196 (1990)
2. Boccaletti, S., Grebogi, C., Lai, Y.C., et al.: The control of chaos theory and applications. Physics Reports 329, 103–197 (2000)
3. Yan, X.M., Liu, D.: Based on the observer not sure the hyperchaotic Ln the active control system. Xian University of Science and Technology Journal 26(1), 1–6 (2010)
4. Hu, G., Zhang, Y., Cerdeira, H.A., Chen, S.: From low-dimensional synchronous chaos to high-dimensional desynchronous spatiotemporal chaos in coupled systems. Phys. Rev. Lett. 85, 3377–3380 (2000)
5. Ho, M.C., Hung, Y.C., Chou, C.H.: Phase and anti-phase synchronization of two chaotic systems by using active control. Phys. Lett. A. 296, 43–48 (2002)
6. Uchida, A., Liu, Y., Fischer, I., Davis, P.: Chaotic antiphase dynamics and synchronization in multimode semiconductor lasers. Phys. Rev. A. 64, 023801–023807 (2001)
7. Yang, X.S., Duan, C.K., Liao, X.X.: A note on mathematica aspects of drive-response type synchronization. Chaos, Solitons and Fraetals 10(9), 1457–1462 (1999)
8. Li, C.D., Liao, X.F., Zhang, R.: Impulsive synchronization of nonlinear coupled chaotic systems. Physics Letters A 328(1), 47–50 (2004)
9. Zeng, X.P., Ruan, J., Li, L.J.: Synchronization of chaotic systems by feedback. Communications in Nonlinear Science and Numerical Simulation 4(2), 162–166 (1999)
10. Park, J.H.: Chaos synchronization of a chaotic system via nonlinear control. Chaos Solitons and Fractals 25, 579–584 (2005)

11. Chen, S., Hu, J., Wang, C., et al.: Adaptive synchronization of uncertain Rossler hyperchaotic system based on parameter identification. Physics Letters A 321, 50–55 (2004)
12. Gao, T., Chen, Z., Yuan, Z., et al.: Adaptive synchronization of a new hyperchaotic system with uncertain parameters. Chaos, Solitons and Fractals 33, 922–928 (2007)
13. AL-Sawalha, M.M., Noorani, M.S.N.: Adaptive anti-synchroization of two identical and different hyperchaotic system with uncertain parameters. Communications in Nonlinear Science and Numerical Simulation 15, 1036–1047 (2010)
14. Li, R.: A special full-state hybrid projective synchronization in symmetrical chaotic systems. Applied Mathematics and Computation 200, 321–329 (2008)
15. Mei, S.W., Shen, T.L., Liu, K.Z.: Modern robust control theory and application. Tsinghua University, Beijing (2008)
16. Yuxia, L., Waace, K., Chen, G.: Generating hyperchaos via state feedback control. Int. J. Bifurcat Chaos 15, 3367–3375 (2005)
17. Park, J.: Adaptive synchronization of hyperchaotic Chen system with uncertain parameters. Chaos, Solitons and Fractal 26, 959–964 (2005)
18. Chen, A., Lu, J., Yu, S.: Generating hyperchaotic Lü attractor via state feedback control. Physical A 364, 103–110 (2006)

Adaptive Projective Synchronization and Function Projective Synchronization of Chaotic Neural Networks with Delayed and Non-delayed Coupling

Guoliang Cai[1,*], Hao Ma[1], and Yuxiu Li[2]

[1] Nonlinear Scientific Research center, Jiangsu University, Zhenjiang, Jiangsu 212013, China
glcai@ujs.edu.cn, 597795513@qq.com
[2] School of Mechanical Engineering, Jiangsu University, Zhenjiang, Jiangsu 212013, China
jxdw@ujs.edu.cn

Abstract. This paper is involved with adaptive projective synchronization and function projective synchronization of nonlinearly coupled chaotic neural networks with time-varying delayed and non-delayed. Based on the Lyapunov stability theorem and adaptive control method, adaptive control law is presented. Especially, the parameters of this paper are very few, which is different from other papers and easily applied to practice.

Keywords: chaotic neural networks, Lyapunov stability theorem, projective synchronization, function projective synchronization, time-varying delayed.

1   Introduction

In recent years, neural networks have been investigated widely [1-3] because of their extensive applications in pattern identify, auto control, image processing, military application, decision support system, and many other fields. Peculiarly, time delays often exist in practice, such as confidential communication. So the neural networks with time delays have attracted more and more attention. Synchronization is a ubiquitous phenomenon in nature, roughly speaking, if two networks have something in common, a synchronization phenomenon will occur between them when they interact. It is an important part of the research of neural networks. In the past two decades, some new types of synchronization have appeared in the literatures, such as projective synchronization [4-5], stochastic synchronization [6-7], function projective synchronization [8], impulsive synchronization [9-10], and so on.

Projective synchronization, which was first proposed by Mainieri and Rehacek [11] in partially linear systems and improved by many researchers [12-15], is the most noticeable one, where neural networks will be synchronized up to a scaling factor. Recently, function projective synchronization was introduced [16], where the drive and response neural networks can be synchronized up to a scaling function matrix. What we have done is that design an adaptive controller such that the projective

---

* Corresponding author.

J. Wang, G.G. Yen, and M.M. Polycarpou (Eds.): ISNN 2012, Part I, LNCS 7367, pp. 293–301, 2012.
© Springer-Verlag Berlin Heidelberg 2012

synchronization and function projective synchronization of a chaotic neural networks with delayed and non-delayed coupling are achieved.

The rest of this paper is organized as follows: Section 2 gives neural networks model and preliminaries. In Section 3, adaptive projective synchronization and function projective synchronization are presented for chaotic neural networks with delayed and non-delayed coupling, respectively. The conclusion is finally drawn in section 4.

2   Neural Networks Model and Preliminaries

In this paper, we consider the following neural networks with delayed and non-delayed coupling as drive neural networks:

$$\dot{x}_i(t) = -c_i x_i(t) + \sum_{j=1}^{N} a_{ij} f_j(x_j(t)) + \sum_{j=1}^{N} b_{ij} g_j(x_j(t-\tau)) + I_i \quad i = 1, 2, ..., N \quad (1)$$

where $x(t) = (x_1(t), x_2(t), ..., x_N(t))^T \in R^N$ is the state vector of the ith neuron at time t, N corresponds to the number of neurons, $\tau > 0$ is the coupling delay, $C = \text{diag}(c_1, c_2, ..., c_N) > 0$ is a positive diagonal matrix, obviously, we can know that $c_i > 0, i = 1, 2, ..., N$. $A = (a_{ij})_{N \times N}$ and $B = (b_{ij})_{N \times N}$ are the connection weight matrix and the delayed connection weight matrix, respectively, which satisfy $a_{ij} = a_{ji} \geq 0$, for $i \neq j$, $a_{ii} = -\sum_{j=1, j\neq i}^{N} a_{ij}$, and $b_{ij} = b_{ji}$, for $i \neq j$, $b_{ii} = -\sum_{j=1, j\neq i}^{N} b_{ij}, i, j = 1, 2, ..., N$. The external input $I = (I_1, I_2, ..., I_N) \in R^N$ is a constant external input vector. The two functions of the equation (1) $f(x(t)) = (f_1(x(t)), f_2(x(t)), ..., f_N(x(t)))^T \in R^N$, and $g(x(t)) = (g_1(x(t)), g_2(x(t)), ..., g_N(x(t)))^T \in R^N$, denote the activation functions of the neurons. Let $C([-\pi, 0], R^N)$ be the Banach space of continuous functions that map the interval $[-\tau, 0]$ into R^N with norm $\|\phi\| = \sup_{-\tau \leq \theta \leq 0} \|\phi(\theta)\|$. The initial conditions of the functional differential equation (1) are given by $x_i(t) = \phi_i(t) \in C([-\tau, 0], R^N)$. It is assumed that equation (1) has a unique solution for these initial conditions.

Now we introduce some useful lemmas and assumptions that will be required throughout this paper as follows:

Lemma 1. (i) *The real parts of the eigenvalues of A and B in this paper are all negative except for the eigenvalue* 0 *with multiplicity* 1.

(ii) *A has a right eigenvector* $(1, 1, ..., 1)^T$ *corresponding to the eigenvalue* 0.

Lemma 2 [17]. *Let Q and R be two symmetric matrices, and matrix S has suitable dimension. Then*

$$\begin{pmatrix} Q & S \\ S^T & R \end{pmatrix} < 0, \text{ if and only if both } R < 0 \text{ and } Q - SR^{-1}S^T < 0.$$

Lemma 3 [18]. *If $G = (g_{ij})_{N \times N}$ is an irreducible matrix that satisfies $g_{ij} = g_{ji} > 0$ for $i \neq j$ and $g_{ii} = -\sum\limits_{j=1, j \neq i} g_{ij}$ for $i = 1, 2, ..., N$, then all the eigenvalues of the matrix*

$$\tilde{G} = \begin{pmatrix} g_{11} - \varepsilon_1 & \cdots & g_{1N} \\ \vdots & \ddots & \vdots \\ g_{N1} & \cdots & g_{NN} - \varepsilon_N \end{pmatrix}$$

are negative, where $\varepsilon_1, \varepsilon_2, ..., \varepsilon_N$ are nonnegative constants and $\sum\limits_{i=1}^{N} \varepsilon_i > 0$.

Lemma 4 [19]. *Suppose that the matrix $A = (a_{ij})_{N \times N}$ satisfies $a_{ij} = a_{ji} \geq 0$, for $i \neq j$, $a_{ii} = -\sum\limits_{j=1, j \neq i}^{N} a_{ij}$ $i, j = 1, 2, ..., N$. Then for two arbitrary vectors $x = (x_1, x_2, ..., x_N)^T$ and $y = (y_1, y_2, ..., y_N)^T$, we have*

$$x^T A y = -\sum\limits_{j>i} a_{ij}(x_j - x_i)(y_j - y_i).$$

For convenience in later proof, we make the following assumptions:

Assumption 1. *For $j = 1, 2, ..., N$, the neuron activation functions satisfy*

$$\alpha \leq \frac{f_j(x_j(t)) - \lambda f_j(y_j(t))}{x_j(t) - \lambda y_j(t)} \leq \beta, \quad \forall x_j(t) \neq y_j(t),$$

for all $x_j(t), y_j(t) \in R$, where α, β are appropriate positive constants.

Assumption 2. *For $j = 1, 2, ..., N$, the neuron activation functions satisfy*

$$\xi \leq \frac{f_j(y_j(t)) - \varphi(t) f_j(x_j(t))}{y_j(t) - \varphi(t) x_j(t)} \leq \eta, \quad \forall x_j(t) \neq y_j(t),$$

for all $x_j(t), y_j(t) \in R$, where ξ, η are appropriate positive constants.

Assumption 3. *Both A and B of system (1) are irreducible.*

3   Adaptive Projective Synchronization and Function Projective Synchronization Analysis

In this section, we will describe the method for adaptive projective synchronization between chaotic neural networks (1) and (2), then we describe the method for function projective synchronization between chaotic neural networks (1) and (7).

3.1   Adaptive Projective Synchronization Analysis

For simplicity, we refer to model (1) as the drive chaotic neural networks, and make the following equations as response chaotic neural networks:

$$
\begin{cases}
\dot{y}_i(t) = -c_i y_i(t) + \sum_{j=1}^{N} a_{ij} f_j(y_j(t)) + \sum_{j=1}^{N} b_{ij} g_j(y_j(t-\tau)) + I_i + u_i, & i = 1, 2, \ldots, r \\
\dot{y}_i(t) = -c_i y_i(t) + \sum_{j=1}^{N} a_{ij} f_j(y_j(t)) + \sum_{j=1}^{N} b_{ij} g_j(y_j(t-\tau)) + I_i, & i = r+1, r+2, \ldots, N
\end{cases}
\tag{2}
$$

where $y_i(t) = (y_{i1}(t), y_{i2}(t), \ldots, y_{in}(t))^{\mathrm{T}} \in R^n$ is the response state vector of the ith neuron at time t, $u_i (i = 1, 2, \ldots, r)$ are nonlinear controllers to be designed, the notations c_i, I_i, a_{ij}, b_{ij}, f_j and g_j are same as the neural networks (1).

Let the vector error state be $e_i(t) = x_i(t) - \lambda y_i(t)$, where λ is a scaling factor, it is said that neural networks (1) and (2) are projective synchronization, if there exists a scaling factor λ, such that $\lim_{t \to \infty} \|e_i(t)\| = \lim_{t \to \infty} \|x_i(t) - \lambda y_i(t)\| = 0$.

Then the error cellular neural networks of (1) and (2) can be obtained:

$$
\begin{cases}
\dot{e}_i(t) = -c_i e_i(t) + \sum_{j=1}^{N} a_{ij} \left(f_j(x_j(t)) - f_j(y_j(t)) \right) + \sum_{j=1}^{N} b_{ij} \left(g_j(x_j(t-\tau)) - g_j(y_j(t-\tau)) \right) - u_i, & i = 1, 2 \ldots, r \\
\dot{e}_i(t) = -c_i e_i(t) + \sum_{j=1}^{N} a_{ij} \left(f_j(x_j(t)) - f_j(y_j(t)) \right) + \sum_{j=1}^{N} b_{ij} \left(g_j(x_j(t-\tau)) - g_j(y_j(t-\tau)) \right), & i = r+1, \ldots, N
\end{cases}
\tag{3}
$$

By using adaptive controlling method, we get the following theorem:

Theorem 1. *Consider neural networks (2) and (1). The neural networks (2) and (1) can realize projective synchronization, if we choose the adaptive controller and update law such that:*

$$
u_i(t) = -l_i \left(f_i(x_i(t)) - \lambda f_i(y_i(t)) \right) \qquad i = 1, 2, \ldots, r
\tag{4}
$$

where $\dot{l}_i = \varepsilon_i e_i^{\mathrm{T}}(t) P e_i(t)$ $i = 1, 2, \ldots, r$, ε_i *are positive constants and* $l_i(0) > 0$.

Proof. Choose the following Lyapunov function:

$$V(t) = \frac{1}{2}\sum_{i=1}^{N} e_i^{\mathrm{T}}(t) P e_i(t) + \sum_{j=1}^{N} p_j \int_{t-\tau}^{t} \tilde{e}_j^{\mathrm{T}}(s) Q_j \tilde{e}_j(s) ds + (\lambda-1)\frac{\alpha}{2}\sum_{i=1}^{r}\frac{(l_i-l_i^*)^2}{\varepsilon_i} \tag{5}$$

$P = \mathrm{diag}(p_1, p_2, ..., p_N)$, $(p_i > 0, i = 1, 2, ..., N)$ is a positive definite diagonal matrix, $Q \in R^{N \times N}$ is also a positive definite diagonal matrix, where $l_1^*, l_2^*, ..., l_r^*$ are positive constants that will be defined below. Then we get:

$$\dot{V}(t) = \sum_{i=1}^{N} e_i^{\mathrm{T}}(t) P \dot{e}_i(t) + \sum_{j=1}^{N} p_j\left(\tilde{e}_j^{\mathrm{T}}(t) Q_j \tilde{e}_j(t) - \tilde{e}_j^{\mathrm{T}}(t-\tau) Q_j \tilde{e}_j(t-\tau)\right)$$

$$+ (\lambda-1)\alpha \sum_{i=1}^{r} l_i e_i^{\mathrm{T}}(t) P e_i(t)$$

$$= \sum_{i=1}^{N} e_i^{\mathrm{T}}(t) P\left(-c_i e_i(t) + \sum_{j=1}^{N} a_{ij}\left(f_j x_j(t)\right) - \lambda f_j\left(y_j(t)\right)\right)$$

$$+ \sum_{i=1}^{N} e_i^{\mathrm{T}}(t) P \sum_{j=1}^{N} b_{ij}\left(g_j\left(x_j(t-\tau)\right) - \lambda g_j\left(y_j(t-\tau)\right)\right)$$

$$- \sum_{i=1}^{r} e_i^{\mathrm{T}}(t) P \lambda u_i + \sum_{j=1}^{N} p_j\left(\tilde{e}_j^{\mathrm{T}}(t) Q_j \tilde{e}_j(t) - \tilde{e}_j^{\mathrm{T}}(t-\tau) Q_j \tilde{e}_j(t-\tau)\right)$$

$$+ (\lambda-1)\alpha \sum_{i=1}^{r}(l_i - l_i^*) e_i^{\mathrm{T}}(t) P e_i(t)$$

$$< - \sum_{i=1}^{N} e_i^{\mathrm{T}}(t) c_i P e_i(t) - \alpha \sum_{j=1}^{N} p_j \sum_{k>m} \tilde{a}_{mk}\left(e_{mj}(t) - e_{kj}(t)\right)\left(e_{mj}(t) - e_{kj}(t)\right)$$

$$+ \sum_{j=1}^{N} p_j \tilde{e}_j^{\mathrm{T}}(t) B\left(g_j\left(x_j(t-\tau)\right) - \lambda g_j\left(y_j(t-\tau)\right)\right) - \alpha \sum_{i=1}^{r} l_i e_i^{\mathrm{T}} p e_i(t)$$

$$+ \sum_{j=1}^{N} p_j\left(\tilde{e}_j^{\mathrm{T}}(t) Q_j \tilde{e}_j(t) - \tilde{e}_j^{\mathrm{T}}(t-\tau) Q_j \tilde{e}_j(t-\tau)\right)$$

$$< - \sum_{i=1}^{N} c_i e_i^{\mathrm{T}}(t) P e_i(t) + \sum_{j=1}^{N} p_j \tilde{e}_j^{\mathrm{T}}(t)\left(\alpha\overline{A}+Q_j\right)\tilde{e}_j(t) + \sum_{j=1}^{N} p_j \tilde{e}_j^{\mathrm{T}}(t) B\left(g_j\left(\tilde{x}_j(t-\tau)\right) - \lambda g_j\left(\tilde{y}_j(t-\tau)\right)\right)$$

$$- \frac{1}{\beta}\sum_{j=1}^{N} p_j\left(g_j\left(\tilde{x}_j(t-\tau)\right) - \lambda g_j\left(\tilde{y}_j(t-\tau)\right)\right)^{\mathrm{T}} Q\left(g_j\left(\tilde{x}_j(t-\tau)\right) - \lambda g_j\left(\tilde{y}_j(t-\tau)\right)\right)$$

$$= - \sum_{i=1}^{N} c_i e_i^{\mathrm{T}}(t) P e_i(t) + \sum_{j=1}^{N} p_j\left(\tilde{e}_j^{\mathrm{T}}(t); g_j\left(\tilde{x}_j(t-\tau)\right) - \lambda g_j\left(\tilde{y}_j(t-\tau)\right)\right)^{\mathrm{T}} H_j$$

$$\left(\tilde{e}_j^{\mathrm{T}}(t); g_j\left(\tilde{x}_j(t-\tau)\right) - \lambda g_j\left(\tilde{y}_j(t-\tau)\right)\right)$$

where $\Lambda = \mathrm{diag}(l_1, ..., l_r, 0, ..., 0)$, and $H_j = \begin{pmatrix} \alpha\overline{A}+Q_j & \frac{1}{2}B \\ \frac{1}{2}B & -\frac{1}{\beta^2}Q_j \end{pmatrix}$, we denote

$$\bar{A} = \begin{pmatrix} a_{11} - l_1^*/c & \cdots & a_{1r} & a_{1,r+1} & \cdots & a_{1N} \\ \vdots & \ddots & \vdots & \vdots & \cdots & \vdots \\ a_{r1} & \cdots & a_{rr} - l_r^*/c & a_{r,r+1} & \cdots & a_{rN} \\ a_{r+1,1} & \cdots & a_{r+1,r} & a_{r+1,r+1} & \cdots & a_{r+1,N} \\ \vdots & \ddots & \vdots & \vdots & \ddots & \vdots \\ a_{N1} & \cdots & a_{Nr} & a_{N,r+1} & \cdots & a_{NN} \end{pmatrix}$$

By choosing the suitable values of $l_1^*, l_2^*, ..., l_r^*$ and following from lemma 2 that if $\alpha \bar{A} + Q_j + \frac{1}{4}\beta^2 BQ_J^{-1}BI_N < 0$, then $H_j < 0$.

Therefore if $Q_j = \frac{1}{2}\beta\left(-\lambda_{\min}(B)\right)^{\frac{1}{2}} I_N$, then we get:

$$\alpha \bar{A} + Q_j + \frac{1}{4}\beta^2 BQ_J^{-1}BI_N = \alpha \bar{A} + \beta\left(-\lambda_{\min}(B)\right)^{\frac{1}{2}} I_N < 0 \tag{6}$$

So H_j is negative definite, we have $\dot{V}(t) < -\sum_{i=1}^{N} c_i e_i^{\mathrm{T}}(t) Pe_i(t)$,

where $c_i > 0, i = 1, 2, ..., N$.

Therefore, these neural networks which we have discussed are projective synchronization. So, theorem 1 is proved.

3.2   Function Projective Synchronization Analysis

In this section, we consider model (1) as the drive chaotic neural networks, and make the following equations as response chaotic neural networks:

$$\dot{y}_i(t) = -c_i y_i(t) + \sum_{j=1}^{N} a_{ij} f_j\left(y_j(t)\right) + \sum_{j=1}^{N} b_{ij} g_j\left(y_j(t-\tau)\right) + I_i + u_i, \quad i = 1, 2, ..., N \tag{7}$$

where $y_i(t) = \left(y_{i1}(t), y_{i2}(t), ..., y_{in}(t)\right)^{\mathrm{T}} \in R^n$ is the response state vector of the ith neuron at time t, $u_i (i = 1, 2, ..., r)$ are controllers to be designed, the notations c_i, I_i, a_{ij}, b_{ij}, f_j and g_j are same as the neural networks (1).

Let the vector error state be $e_i(t) = y_i(t) - \varphi(t) x_i(t)$, where $\varphi(t)$ is an n-order diagonal matrix, $\varphi(t) = \mathrm{diag}\left(\varphi_1(t), \varphi_2(t), ..., \varphi_N(t)\right)$ and $\varphi_i(t)$ is a continuously differentiable function, $\varphi_i(t) \neq 0$ for all t. It is said that neural networks (1) and (7) are function projective synchronization, if there exists a scaling function matrix $\varphi(t)$, such that $\lim_{t \to \infty} \|e_i(t)\| = \lim_{t \to \infty} \|y_i(t) - \varphi(t) x_i(t)\| = 0$.

Then the error cellular neural networks of (1) and (7) can be obtained:

$$\dot{e}_i(t) = -c_i e_i(t) + \sum_{j=1}^{N} a_{ij}\left(f_j\left(y_j(t)\right) - \varphi(t)f_j\left(x_j(t)\right)\right)$$

$$+ \sum_{j=1}^{N} b_{ij}\left(g_j\left(y_j(t-\tau)\right) - \varphi(t)g_j\left(x_j(t-\tau)\right)\right) - \dot{\varphi}(t)x + u_i \tag{8}$$

Theorem 2. *For a given scaling function matrix $\varphi(t)$, the neural networks (7) and (1) can realize function projective synchronization by the control law as shown below:*

$$u_i(t) = -l_i\left(f_i\left(y_i(t)\right) - \varphi(t)f_i\left(x_i(t)\right)\right) + \dot{\varphi}(t)x \qquad i = 1,2,...,N \tag{9}$$

where $l_i = \varepsilon_i e_i^{\mathrm{T}}(t)Pe_i(t)$ $i = 1,2,...,r$, ε_i are positive constants and $l_i(0) > 0$.

Proof. Choose the following Lyapunov function:

$$V(t) = \frac{1}{2}\sum_{i=1}^{N} e_i^{\mathrm{T}}(t)Pe_i(t) + \sum_{j=1}^{N} p_j \int_{t-\tau}^{t} \tilde{e}_j^{\mathrm{T}}(s)Q_j\tilde{e}_j(s)ds \tag{10}$$

$P = \mathrm{diag}(p_1, p_2,..., p_N)$, $(p_i > 0, i = 1,2,...,N)$ is a positive definite diagonal matrix, $Q \in R^{N\times N}$ is a positive definite diagonal matrix. Then we get:

$$\dot{V}(t) = \sum_{i=1}^{N} e_i^{\mathrm{T}}(t)P\dot{e}_i(t) + \sum_{j=1}^{N} p_j\left(\tilde{e}_j^{\mathrm{T}}(t)Q_j\tilde{e}_j(t) - \tilde{e}_j^{\mathrm{T}}(t-\tau)Q_j\tilde{e}_j(t-\tau)\right)$$

$$= \sum_{i=1}^{N} e_i^{\mathrm{T}}(t)P\left[-c_i e_i(t) + \sum_{j=1}^{N} a_{ij}\left(f_j\left(y_j(t)\right) - \varphi(t)f_j\left(x_j(t)\right)\right)\right]$$

$$+ \sum_{i=1}^{N} e_i^{\mathrm{T}}(t)P\sum_{j=1}^{N} b_{ij}\left(g_j\left(y_j(t-\tau)\right) - \varphi(t)g_j\left(x_j(t-\tau)\right)\right)$$

$$+ \sum_{i=1}^{N} e_i^{\mathrm{T}}(t)Pu_i - \sum_{i=1}^{N} e_i^{\mathrm{T}}(t)P\dot{\varphi}(t) + \sum_{j=1}^{N} p_j\left(\tilde{e}_j^{\mathrm{T}}(t)Q_j\tilde{e}_j(t) - \tilde{e}_j^{\mathrm{T}}(t-\tau)Q_j\tilde{e}_j(t-\tau)\right)$$

$$< -c_i\sum_{i=1}^{N} e_i^{\mathrm{T}}(t)Pe_i(t) - \xi\sum_{j=1}^{N} p_j\sum_{k>m}\tilde{a}_{mk}\left(e_{mj}(t) - e_{kj}(t)\right)\left(e_{mj}(t) - e_{kj}(t)\right)$$

$$+ \sum_{j=1}^{N} p_j\tilde{e}_j^{\mathrm{T}}(t)B\left(g_j\left(y_j(t-\tau)\right) - \varphi(t)g_j\left(x_j(t-\tau)\right)\right) - \alpha\sum_{i=1}^{r} l_i e_i^{\mathrm{T}}pe_i(t)$$

$$+ \sum_{j=1}^{N} p_j\left(\tilde{e}_j^{\mathrm{T}}(t)Q_j\tilde{e}_j(t) - \tilde{e}_j^{\mathrm{T}}(t-\tau)Q_j\tilde{e}_j(t-\tau)\right)$$

$$< -\sum_{i=1}^{N} c_i e_i^{\mathrm{T}}(t)Pe_i(t) + \sum_{j=1}^{N} p_j\tilde{e}_j^{\mathrm{T}}(t)\left(\xi\tilde{A} + Q_j\right)\tilde{e}_j(t)$$

$$+ \sum_{j=1}^{N} p_j\tilde{e}_j^{\mathrm{T}}(t)B\left(g_j\left(\tilde{y}_j(t-\tau)\right) - \varphi(t)g_j\left(\tilde{x}_j(t-\tau)\right)\right)$$

$$- \frac{1}{\eta^2}\sum_{j=1}^{N} p_j\left(g_j\left(\tilde{y}_j(t-\tau)\right) - \varphi(t)g_j\left(\tilde{x}_j(t-\tau)\right)\right)^{\mathrm{T}} Q_j\left(g_j\left(\tilde{y}_j(t-\tau)\right) - \varphi(t)g_j\left(\tilde{x}_j(t-\tau)\right)\right)$$

$$= -\sum_{i=1}^{N} c_i e_i^{\mathrm{T}}(t) Pe_i(t) + \sum_{j=1}^{N} p_j \left(\tilde{e}_j^{\mathrm{T}}(t); g_j \left(\tilde{y}_j (t-\tau) \right) - \varphi(t) g_j \left(\tilde{x}_j (t-\tau) \right) \right)^{\mathrm{T}} H_j$$

$$\left(\tilde{e}_j^{\mathrm{T}}(t); g_j \left(\tilde{y}_j (t-\tau) \right) - \varphi(t) g_j \left(\tilde{x}_j (t-\tau) \right) \right)$$

where we denote $\tilde{A} = \begin{pmatrix} a_{11} - l_1/c & \cdots & a_{1N} \\ \vdots & \ddots & \vdots \\ a_{N1} & \cdots & a_{NN} - l_N/c \end{pmatrix}$, and

$$H_j = \begin{pmatrix} \alpha \tilde{A} + Q_j & \dfrac{1}{2} B \\ \dfrac{1}{2} B & -\dfrac{1}{\beta^2} Q_j \end{pmatrix}.$$

Same as Theorem 1, let $Q_j = \dfrac{1}{2} \beta \left(-\lambda_{\min}(B) \right)^{\frac{1}{2}} I_N$, we can get $H_j < 0$.

Therefore we have $\dot{V}(t) < -\sum_{i=1}^{N} c_i e_i^{\mathrm{T}}(t) Pe_i(t)$, where $c_i > 0$, $i = 1, 2, ..., N$.

So we have $\lim_{t \to \infty} \left\| e_i(t) \right\| = \lim_{t \to \infty} \left\| y_i(t) - \varphi(t) x_i(t) \right\| = 0$, therefore, the theorem 2 is proved. We can obtain that neural networks (7) is function projective synchronization with (1).

4   Conclusions

This paper investigated adaptive projective synchronization and function projective synchronization of delayed chaotic neural networks. On the basis of Lyapunov stability theory, we designed some simple controllers and update laws, which are different from that in other literatures. This method can be easily generalized to other neural networks and applied to practice.

Acknowledgments. This work was supported by the National Nature Science foundation of China (Nos. 70571030, 11102180), the Society Science Foundation from Ministry of Education of China (Nos. 12YJAZH002, 08JA790057), the Priority Academic Program Development of Jiangsu Higher Education Institutions, the Advanced Talents' Foundation of Jiangsu University (Nos. 07JDG054, 10JDG140), and the Students' Research Foundation of Jiangsu University (No. 10A147). Especially, thanks for the support of Jiangsu University.

References

1. Liu, D.R., Xiong, X.X.: Identification of Motifs with Insertions and Deletions in Protein Sequences Using Self-organizing Neural Networks. Neural. Netw. 18, 835–842 (2005)
2. Shao, H.J., Cai, G.L., Wang, H.X.: An Linear Matrix Inequality Approach to Global Synchronization of Non-parameters Perturbations of Multi-delay Hopfield Neural Network. Chin. Phys. B. 19, 1–6 (2010)

3. Zhou, J., Xiang, L., Liu, Z.R.: Global Synchronization in General Complex Delayed Dynamical Networks and Its Applications. Phys. A. 385, 729–742 (2007)
4. Zheng, S., Bi, Q.S., Cai, G.L.: Adaptive Projective Synchronization in Complex Networks with time-varying coupling delay. Phys. Lett. A. 373, 1553–1559 (2009)
5. Zhang, D., Xu, J.A.: Projective Synchronization of Different Chaotic Time-delayed Neural Networks Based on Integral Sliding Mode Controller. Appl. Math. Comput. 217, 164–174 (2010)
6. Yang, X.S., Zhu, Q.X., Huang, C.X.: Lag Stochastic Synchronization of Chaotic Mixed Time-delayed Neural Networks with Uncertain Parameters or Perturbations. Neurocomputing 74, 1617–1625 (2011)
7. Feng, J., Wang, S.Q., Wang, Z.S.: Stochastic Synchronization in An array of Neural Networks with Hybrid Nonlinear Coupling. Neurocomputing 74, 3808–3815 (2011)
8. Cai, G.L., Wang, H.X., Zheng, S.: Adaptive Function Projective Synchronization of Two Different Hyperchaotic Systems with Unknown Parameters. Chin J. Phys. 47, 662–669 (2009)
9. Tang, Y., Wong, W.K., Fang, J.A., Miao, Q.Y.: Pinning Impulsive Synchronization of Stochastic Delayed Coupled Networks. Chin. Phys. B. 20, 1056–1088 (2011)
10. Zheng, S., Dong, G.G., Bi, Q.S.: Impulsive Synchronization of Complex Networks with Non-delayed Coupling. Phys. Lett. A. 373, 4255–4259 (2009)
11. Mainieri, R., Rehacek, J.: Projective Synchronization in Three-dimensioned Chaotic Systems. Phys. Rev. Lett. 82, 3042–3045 (1999)
12. Wang, X.Y., Men, J.A.: Generalized Projective Synchronization of Chaotic Networks Observer-based Approach. Int. J. Mod. Phys. B. 24, 3351–3363 (2010)
13. Cai, G.L., Yao, Q., Shao, H.J.: Global synchronization of weighted cellular neural networks with time-varying coupling delays. Commun. Nonlinear Sci. Numer. Simul. 17, 3843–3847 (2012)
14. Xu, X.J., Lu, H.T.: Generalized Projective Synchronization Between Two Different General Complex Dynamical Networks with Delayed Coupling. Phys. Lett. A. 374, 3932–3941 (2010)
15. Cai, G.L., Shao, H.J., Yao, Q.: A Linear Matrix Inequality Approach to Global Synchronization of Multi-Delay Hopeld Neural Networks with Parameter Perturbations. Chin. J. Phys. 50, 86–99 (2012)
16. Chen, L.P., Chai, Y., Wu, R.C.: Modified Function Projective Synchronization of Chaotic Neural Networks with Delays Based on Observer. Int. J. Mod. Phys C. 22, 169–180 (2011)
17. Zhou, J., Chen, T.P.: Synchronization in General Complex Delayed Dynamical Networks. IEEE Trans. Circuits Syst. I. 53, 733–744 (2006)
18. Guo, W.L., Austin, F., Chen, S.H.: Global Synchronization of Nonlinearly Coupled Complex Networks with Non-delayed and Delayed Coupling. Commun. Nonlinear Sci. Numer. Simul. 15, 1631–1639 (2010)
19. Chai, W.W., Chua, L.O.: Synchronization in an Array of Linearly Coupled Dynamical Systems. IEEE Trans. Circuits Syst. I. 42, 430–447 (1995)

Global Asymptotic Synchronization of Coupled Interconnected Recurrent Neural Networks via Pinning Control

Zhanshan Wang[1], Dakai Zhou[1], Dongsheng Ma[1], and Shuxian Lun[2]

[1] School of Information Science and Engineering, Northeastern University,
Shenyang, Liaoning, 110004, People's Republic of China
wangzhanshan@ise.neu.edu.cn
[2] College of Engineering, Bohai University, Jinzhou 121000,
People's Republic of China

Abstract. Global asymptotic synchronization problem of a coupled interconnected recurrent neural networks with linearly delayed coupled has been investigated. By using the state feedback and delayed state feedback pinning control method, two different pinning synchronization criteria have been established. One is based on the matrix eigenvalue of the coupled matrix, the other is based on the matrix inequality of the known networks information. Some remarks on the synchronization criteria are used to show the characteristics of the proposed results.

Keywords: Interconnected recurrent neural networks, delayed couple, global asymptotic synchronization, pinning control.

1 Introduction

Many large-scale systems in nature and human societies, such as biological neural networks, ecosystems, metabolic pathways, electrical power grids, etc., can be described by networks with the nodes representing individuals in the system and the edges representing the connections among them. Recently, the study of various complex networks has attracted increasing attention from researchers in various fields of physics, mathematics, engineering, biology, and sociology.

Synchronization is a kind of typical collective behavior exhibited in many natural systems [1–4]. Recently, synchronization of all dynamical nodes in a complex network has aroused wide attention. In the case where the whole network cannot synchronize by itself, some controllers may be designed and applied to force the network to synchronize [5–12, 14–16]. Because a large numbers of nodes exist in real world complex networks, there are two kind of synchronization control schemes in the literature. One is the all nodes control, i.e., control action is added to every node, the other is the pinning control, i.e., control action is pinned on a small fraction of the network nodes. As is known, a complex network normally has a large number of nodes. It would take great cost to control a complex network by applying the controllers to all nodes. However, the all nodes control

J. Wang, G.G. Yen, and M.M. Polycarpou (Eds.): ISNN 2012, Part I, LNCS 7367, pp. 302–311, 2012.

scheme may have the advantages such as easy to design the synchronization controller and require a small control gain. In contrast, it is impractical to control a complex network by applying the controllers to all nodes due to a large number of nodes. To reduce the number of controllers, a natural approach is to control a network by pinning part of nodes. However, because the part state variables of the nodes are utilized in the pinning controller, it is not easy to directly design the controller due to the singularity of the feedback gain matrix. Scientific and Technical innovation is just rooted from these practical fundamental challenges. Therefore, both all nodes control and pinning control have their own advantages and disadvantages. How to choose these two synchronization control schemes depends on the scale of the controlled complex networks. In general, if the number of the nodes is large enough, it is better to use pinning control to realize the synchronization. The more nodes are pinned, the smaller the feedback strength is needed.

Pinning control of complex networks has received increasing interests in recent years [9–12, 14–16]. Reference [10] first proposed an test method to pin a complex linearly coupled dynamical network to its equilibrium, in which the feedback gain was implicitly required to satisfy a eigenvalue condition. Reference [11] proposed an effective method for the same complex networks model in [10] to realize the pinning synchronization, in which a positive semi-definite matrix is used to judge the synchronization by choosing the feedback gain matrix. The methods in [10, 11] provide two different kind of pinning control design methods. However, the number of pinning nodes in [10, 11] are required to be δN, which may be greater than 1. Then it is natural to raise the problem whether one can pin the coupled network by introducing a single negative feedback controller (the simplest control)? The answer can not be found in [10, 11], while in [12] Chen et al. studied pinning complex networks using a single controller and established some single pinning control schemes for different cases of complex networks. The main contribution of [12] is that a rigorous proof is presented to pin a complex network by adding a single linear controller to one node with symmetric or asymmetric coupling matrix. An extended pinning result has been presented in [13], in which a single impulse pinning control scheme is used to realize the pinning synchronization. Moreover, in the method of [10], either the feedback control gain or the coupling strength has to be large enough, both of which are difficult to put into practice [19]. In [19], the feedback control gain can not be infinite or large enough by adding a relaxation factor in the method proposed in [10], which improve the implementation effect in practice.

However, above researches are only for the complex networks without delayed term and delayed coupled. As an extension and improvement of the result in [10], we will consider the global asymptotic synchronization problem of coupled interconnected recurrent neural networks with delayed coupling via pinning control method. Some remarks are used to show the effectiveness of the proposed results.

The rest of the paper is organized as follows. In Section 2, the problem formulation is stated. In Section 3, we present the main result for global asymptotic synchronization of coupled interconnected recurrent neural networks via pinning control. Some remarks are used to compare our results with the previous ones. Finally, conclusions are made in Section 4.

2 Problem Formulation

Consider the following coupled interconnected recurrent neural networks with delays,

$$\dot{x}_i(t) = - Cx_i(t) + Ag(x_i(t)) + Bg(x_j(t - \tau(t))) + J(t)$$

$$+ \sum_{j=1}^{n} G_{ij}^0 \Gamma_0 x_j(t) + \sum_{j=1}^{n} G_{ij}^1 \Gamma_1 x_j(t - \tau(t)), \qquad (1)$$

where $u_i(t)$ is the neural state, $a_i > 0$, w_{ij} and w_{ij}^1 are connection weight coefficients and delayed connection weight coefficients, respectively, U_i is the constant external input, time-varying delay satisfies $0 \leq \tau(t) \leq \tau_M$, $\dot{\tau}(t) \leq \mu < 1$, $g_j(u_j(t)))$ is the activation function, $\sum_{j=1}^{N} G_{ij}^0 = \sum_{j=1}^{N} G_{ij}^1 = 0$, $G_{ij}^k \geq 0$ if $i \neq j$, $G_{ij}^k < 0$ if $i = j$, $i,j = 1, \ldots, N$.

The isolated node networks are as follows,

$$\dot{x}_i(t) = - Cx_i(t) + Ag(x_i(t)) + Bg(x_j(t - \tau(t))) + J(t). \qquad (2)$$

If all the states of coupled system (1) can approach the same trajectories when the internal interconnection matrices satisfy some constrained condition, we call this phenomena as self-synchronization. The distinctive feature of self-synchronization is that no external control input is required. In general, self-synchronization can only reach the instrinc dynamics of the coupled systems. In contract, if one wants all the states of the coupled system to synchronize a specified dynamics by a designer, external control input is necessary to fulfill this task. This kind of synchronization can be called as controlled synchronization. Controlled synchronization have more powerful capability to master the dynamics of the coupled system than the self-synchronization. One of the promising controlled synchronization methods is pinning control. In this case, the coupled system (1) with external controller $u_i(t)$ can be described as follows,

$$\dot{x}_i(t) = - Cx_i(t) + Ag(x_i(t)) + Bg(x_j(t - \tau(t))) + J(t)$$

$$+ \sum_{j=1}^{n} G_{ij}^0 \Gamma_0 x_j(t) + \sum_{j=1}^{n} G_{ij}^1 \Gamma_1 x_j(t - \tau(t)) + u_i(t). \qquad (3)$$

Suppose that $s(t)$ is a unique solution of the homogenous system with the initial condition $\in C$ if it satisfies the isolated node equation (2), where $s(t)$ may be an equilibrium point, a periodic orbit, an aperiodic orbit, or a chaotic orbit in the phase space.

Definition 1. [17, 18]: The controlled delayed dynamical network (1) is said to achieve asymptotical synchronization, for any ϕ, if the solution $x_i(t)(i = 1, 2, \ldots N)$ through ϕ satisfies

$$\text{limit}_{t \to \infty} \|x_i(t) - s(t)\| = 0. \qquad (4)$$

Assumption 21. The activation function $g_j(u_j(t))$ satisfies

$$0 \leq (g_j(\zeta) - g_j(\xi))/(\zeta - \xi) \leq \delta_j$$

for $\forall \zeta \neq \xi,\ \zeta, \xi \in \Re,\ \delta_j > 0,\ j = 1, \ldots, n$

3   Main Results

In order to study the controlled synchronization of the coupled system (3), we define the synchronization error vectors as $e_i(t) = x_i(t) - s(t), i = 1, \cdots, N$, then we have the following synchronization error system,

$$\dot{e}_i(t) = - Ce_i(t) + Af(e_i(t)) + Bf(e_j(t - \tau(t)))$$
$$+ \sum_{j=1}^{n} G_{ij}^0 \Gamma_0 e_j(t) + \sum_{j=1}^{n} G_{ij}^1 \Gamma_1 e_j(t - \tau(t)) + u_i(t), \tag{5}$$

where $f(e_i(t)) = g(e_i(t) + s(t)) - g(s(t))$.

In order to realize the synchronization, we take the following pinning control action,

$$u_i(t) = -d_i^0(x_i(t) - s(t)) - d_i^1(x_i(t - \tau(t)) - s(t)), i = 1, \cdots, l, \tag{6}$$

where $d_i^k > 0, d_i^k \neq 0$ for $i = 1, \cdots, l, d_i^k = 0$ for $i = l+1, \cdots, N, k = 0, 1$.

Substituting (6) into (5), we have

$$\dot{e}_i(t) = - Ce_i(t) + Af(e_i(t)) + Bf(e_j(t - \tau(t)))$$
$$+ \sum_{j=1}^{N} G_{ij}^0 \Gamma_1 e_j(t) + \sum_{j=1}^{N} G_{ij}^1 \Gamma_2 e_j(t - \tau(t)) - d_i^0 e_i(t) - d_i^1 e_i(t - \tau(t)). \tag{7}$$

Theorem 1. Suppose that Assumption 21 holds. For some $\epsilon_0 > 0$, if there exists a natural number $1 \leq l \leq N - 1$ such that $L + \|\Gamma_0\|(\lambda_{l+1} + \epsilon_0) < 0$, then the coupled complex networks (3) is synchronized under the pinning control (6), or the synchronization system (7) is globally asymptotically stable under the pinning control (6), where λ_i is the maximal eigenvalue of the i-th minor matrix M_i of matrix $\frac{\tilde{G}^0 + (\tilde{G}^0)^T}{2} + \frac{\tilde{G}^1 + (\tilde{G}^1)^T}{2\|\Gamma_0\|}$, which is obtained by removing the 1st, $\cdots$, $i - 1$th row-column pairs of $\frac{\tilde{G}^0 + (\tilde{G}^0)^T}{2} + \frac{\tilde{G}^1 + (\tilde{G}^1)^T}{2\|\Gamma_0\|}$, and $\tilde{G}^0$ is a modified matrix of G^0 by replacing the diagonal elements G_{ii}^0 by $\tilde{G}_{ii}^0 = \frac{\rho_m}{\|\Gamma_0\|} G_{ii}^0$, $\tilde{G}^1$ is a modified matrix of G^1 by replacing the diagonal elements G_{ii}^1 by $\tilde{G}_{ii}^1 = |G_{ii}^1|$, $L = \|A\|\|\Delta\| + 0.5\|BB^T\| + \|\Gamma_1^T \Gamma_1\|\|\tilde{G}^1\| + 0.5\|\Delta^2\| - \lambda_{\min}(C)$.

Proof. Consider the following Lyapunov functional

$$V = \frac{1}{2} \sum_{i=1}^{N} e_i^T(t)e_i(t) + h \sum_{i=1}^{N} \int_{t-\tau(t)}^{t} e_i^T(s)e_i(s)ds, \tag{8}$$

where $h > 0$ is a constant to be determined later.

The derivative of $V(t)$ along the trajectories of system (7) is as follows,

$$
\begin{aligned}
\dot{V}(t) &= \sum_{i=1}^{N} e_i^T(t)\dot{e}_i(t) + h\sum_{i=1}^{N}\left[e_i^T(t)e_i(t) - e_i^T(t-\tau(t))e_i(t-\tau(t))\right] \\
&= \sum_{i=1}^{N} e_i^T(t)\Big[-Ce_i(t) + Af(e_i(t)) + Bf(e_j(t-\tau(t))) \\
&\quad + \sum_{j=1}^{N} G_{ij}^0 \Gamma_0 e_j(t) + \sum_{j=1}^{N} G_{ij}^1 \Gamma_1 e_j(t-\tau(t)) - d_i^0 e_i(t) - d_i^1 e_i(t-\tau(t))\Big] \\
&\quad + h\sum_{i=1}^{N}\left[e_i^T(t)e_i(t) - e_i^T(t-\tau(t))e_i(t-\tau(t))\right].
\end{aligned}
\tag{9}
$$

Note that the following inequalities hold,

$$
-e_i^T(t)Ce_i(t) + e_i^T Af(e_i(t)) \leq -\lambda_{min}(C)e_i^T(t)e_i(t) + \|A\|\|\Delta\|e_i^T(t)e_i(t), \tag{10}
$$

$$
e_i^T(t)Bf(e_i(t-\tau(t))) \leq 0.5\|BB^T\|e_i^T(t)e_i(t) + 0.5\|\Delta^2\|e_i^T(t-\tau(t))e_i(t-\tau(t)), \tag{11}
$$

$$
\begin{aligned}
&\sum_{i=1}^{N}\sum_{j=1}^{N} e_i^T(t)G_{ij}^0 \Gamma_0 e_j(t) \\
&= \sum_{i=1}^{N}\sum_{j=1,j\neq i}^{N} e_i^T(t)G_{ij}^0 \Gamma_0 e_j(t) + \sum_{i=1}^{N} e_i^T(t)G_{ii}^0 \frac{\Gamma_0 + \Gamma_0^T}{2}e_i(t) \\
&\leq \sum_{i=1}^{N}\sum_{j=1,j\neq i}^{N} G_{ij}^0\|\Gamma_0\|\|e_i^T(t)\|\|e_j(t)\| + \sum_{i=1}^{N} e_i^T(t)G_{ii}^0 \frac{\Gamma_0 + \Gamma_0^T}{2}e_i(t) \tag{12}
\end{aligned}
$$

$$
\begin{aligned}
&\sum_{i=1}^{N}\sum_{j=1}^{N} e_i^T(t)G_{ij}^1 \Gamma_1 e_j(t-\tau(t)) \\
&= \sum_{i=1}^{N}\sum_{j=1,j\neq i}^{N} e_i^T(t)G_{ij}^1 \Gamma_1 e_j(t-\tau(t)) + \sum_{i=1}^{N} e_i^T(t)G_{ii}^1 \Gamma_1 e_i(t-\tau(t)) \\
&\leq \sum_{i=1}^{N}\sum_{j=1,j\neq i}^{N} G_{ij}^1\left[e_i^T(t)e_i(t) + e_j^T(t-\tau(t))\Gamma_1^T \Gamma_1 e_j(t-\tau(t))\right]
\end{aligned}
$$

$$\leq + \sum_{i=1}^{N} e_i^T(t) G_{ii}^1 \Gamma_1 e_i(t - \tau(t))$$

$$+ \sum_{i=1}^{N} \sum_{j=1, j \neq i}^{N} G_{ij}^1 \left[e_i^T(t) e_i(t) + e_j^T(t - \tau(t)) \Gamma_1^T \Gamma_1 e_j(t - \tau(t)) \right]$$

$$+ \sum_{i=1}^{N} |G_{ii}^1| \left[e_i^T(t) e_i(t) + e_i^T(t - \tau(t)) \Gamma_1^T \Gamma_1 e_i(t - \tau(t)) \right]. \tag{13}$$

Substituting (10)-(13) into (9), one has

$$\dot{V}(t) = \sum_{i=1}^{N} \Big[-\lambda_{min}(C) e_i^T(t) e_i(t) + \|A\| \|\Delta\| e_i^T(t) e_i(t)$$

$$+ 0.5 \|BB^T\| e_i^T(t) e_i(t) + 0.5 \|\Delta^2\| e_i^T(t - \tau(t)) e_i(t - \tau(t)) \Big]$$

$$+ \sum_{i=1}^{N} \sum_{j=1, j \neq i}^{N} G_{ij}^0 \|\Gamma_0\| e_i^T(t) e_j(t) + \sum_{i=1}^{N} e_i^T(t) G_{ii}^0 \frac{\Gamma_0 + \Gamma_0^T}{2} e_i(t)$$

$$+ \sum_{i=1}^{N} \sum_{j=1, j \neq i}^{N} G_{ij}^1 \left[e_i^T(t) e_i(t) + e_i^T(t - \tau(t)) \Gamma_1^T \Gamma_1 e_i(t - \tau(t)) \right]$$

$$+ \sum_{i=1}^{N} |G_{ii}^1| \left[e_i^T(t) e_i(t) + e_i^T(t - \tau(t)) \Gamma_1^T \Gamma_1 e_i(t - \tau(t)) \right]$$

$$- \sum_{i=1}^{N} e_i^T(t) d_i^0 e_i(t) - \sum_{i=1}^{N} e_i^T(t) d_i^1 e_i(t - \tau(t))$$

$$+ h \sum_{i=1}^{N} \left[e_i^T(t) e_i(t) - e_i^T(t - \tau(t)) e_i(t - \tau(t)) \right]$$

$$= \sum_{i=1}^{N} e_i^T(t) \Big[(\|A\| \|\Delta\| + 0.5 \|BB^T\| + h - \lambda_{min}(C)) I_N + \|\Gamma_0\| \sum_{j=1}^{N} \tilde{G}_{ij}^0$$

$$+ \sum_{j=1}^{N} \tilde{G}_{ij}^1 \Big] e_i(t) - h \sum_{i=1}^{N} e_i^T(t - \tau(t)) e_i(t - \tau(t))$$

$$+ \sum_{i=1}^{N} 0.5 \|\Delta^2\| e_i^T(t - \tau(t)) e_i(t - \tau(t)) - \sum_{i=1}^{l} e_i^T(t) d_i^0 e_i(t)$$

$$+ \|\Gamma_1^T \Gamma_1\| \sum_{i=1}^{N} \sum_{j=1}^{N} e_i^T(t - \tau(t)) \tilde{G}_{ij}^1 e_i(t - \tau(t)) - \sum_{i=1}^{l} e_i^T(t) d_i^1 e_i(t - \tau(t))$$

$$= e^T(t) (L I_N + \|\Gamma_0\| \tilde{G}^0 + \tilde{G}^1 - D_0) e(t)$$

$$+ e^T(t - \tau(t)) (0.5 \|\Delta^2\| I_N + \|\Gamma_1^T \Gamma_1\| \tilde{G}^1 - h I_N - D_1) e(t - \tau(t)), \tag{14}$$

where $\tilde{G}_{ii}^0 = \frac{\rho_m}{\|\Gamma_0\|}G_{ii}^0, \tilde{G}_{ij}^0 = G_{ij}^0, \tilde{G}_{ii}^1 = |G_{ii}^1|, \tilde{G}_{ij}^1 = G_{ij}^1, \rho_m = \lambda_{min}(\frac{\Gamma_0+\Gamma_0^T}{2})$,
$L = \|A\|\|\Delta\| + 0.5\|BB^T\| + h - \lambda_{min}(C), D_0 = \text{diag}(d_1^0, d_2^0, \cdots, d_l^0, 0, \cdots, 0)$,
$D_1 = \text{diag}(d_1^1, d_2^1, \cdots, d_l^1, 0, \cdots, 0), e(t) = (\|e_1(t)\|, \cdots, \|e_N(t)\|)^T, e(t - \tau(t)) = (\|e_1(t - \tau(t))\|, \cdots, \|e_N(t - \tau(t))\|)^T$.

If we take $h = \|\Gamma_1^T\Gamma_1\|\|\tilde{G}^1\| + 0.5\|\Delta^2\| > 0$, from (14) we can have

$$\dot{V}(t) = e^T(t)\left(LI_N + \|\Gamma_0\|\frac{\tilde{G}^0 + (\tilde{G}^0)^T}{2} + \frac{\tilde{G}^1 + (\tilde{G}^1)^T}{2} - D_0\right)e(t). \qquad (15)$$

Assume that $\tilde{\lambda}_1$ is the maximal eigenvalue of the matrix $\frac{\tilde{G}^0 + (\tilde{G}^0)^T}{2} + \frac{\tilde{G}^1 + (\tilde{G}^1)^T}{2\|\Gamma_0\|} - \frac{D_0}{\|\Gamma_0\|}$, then we can choose the proper d_i^0 such that $\tilde{\lambda}_1 \leq \lambda_{l+1} + \epsilon_0$ from Lemma 1 in [19]. Therefore,

$$\dot{V}(t) = e^T(t)\left(LI_N + \|\Gamma_0\|\frac{\tilde{G}^0 + (\tilde{G}^0)^T}{2} + \frac{\tilde{G}^1 + (\tilde{G}^1)^T}{2} - D_0\right)e(t)$$
$$\leq (L + \|\Gamma_0\|(\lambda_{l+1} + \epsilon_0))e^T e. \qquad (16)$$

According to the condition in Theorem 1, we can obtain $\dot{V}(t) < 0$ for any $e \neq 0$. Thus, the synchronization error vectors approach to zero as the time approaches to the infinity. It indicates that the coupled complex networks achieves the global asymptotic synchronization under the pinning control law (6).

Remark 1. If we take the pinning control (6) as

$$u_i(t) = -d_i^0(x_i(t) - s(t)), i = 1, \cdots, l, \qquad (17)$$

where $d_i^0 > 0$, $d_i^0 \neq 0$ for $i = 1, \cdots, l$, $d_i^0 = 0$ for $i = l + 1, \cdots, N$, $k = 0, 1$, we can have the same result as that in Theorem 1. The details are omitted.

Remark 2. The same synchronization results between different pinning controls (6) and (17) can be stated as follows. Due to the singularity of diagonal matrices D_0 and D_1, the inequality reduction of $e^T(t - \tau(t))(0.5\|\Delta^2\|I_N + \|\Gamma_1^T\Gamma_1\|\tilde{G}^1 - hI_N - D_1)e(t - \tau(t))$ in (14) will ignore the effects of $-e^T(t - \tau(t))D_1e(t - \tau(t)) \leq \lambda_{min}(D_1)e^T(t - \tau(t))e(t - \tau(t)) = 0$. This is the fundamental reason why both pinning control (6) and (17) can lead to the same synchronization criteria in scalar form.

In order to show the different effects of different pinning controls (6) and (17), we have the following synchronization result in the matrix form.

Theorem 2. Suppose that Assumption 21 holds. The coupled complex networks (3) is synchronized under the pinning control (6), or the synchronization system (7) is globally asymptotically stable under the pinning control (6), if the following condition is satisfied,

$$I_N \otimes L_1 + (\|\Gamma_0\|\tilde{G}^0 + \tilde{G}^1) \otimes I_n < 0, \qquad (18)$$
$$0.5I_N \otimes \Delta^2 + (\|\Gamma_1^T\Gamma_1\|\tilde{G}^1 - D_1) \otimes I_n - I_N \otimes H < 0, \qquad (19)$$

where

$$\tilde{G}^0 = (G_{ij}^0)_{n \times N}, \tilde{G}^1 = (G_{ij}^1)_{n \times N},$$

$$L_1 = 0.5BB^T + H + 0.5A^T A + 0.5\Delta^T \Delta - C - D_0,$$

$$D_0 = \mathrm{diag}(d_1^0, d_2^0, \cdots, d_l^0, 0, \cdots, 0), D_1 = \mathrm{diag}(d_1^1, d_2^1, \cdots, d_l^1, 0, \cdots, 0),$$

$$e(t) = (e_1^T(t), e_2^T(t), \cdots, e_N^T(t))^T,$$

$$e(t - \tau(t)) = (e_1^T(t - \tau(t)), e_2^T(t - \tau(t)), \cdots, e_N^T(t - \tau(t)))^T.$$

Proof. Consider the following Lyapunov functional

$$V_2 = \frac{1}{2}\sum_{i=1}^{N} e_i^T(t)e_i(t) + \sum_{i=1}^{N}\int_{t-\tau(t)}^{t} e_i^T(s)He_i(s)ds, \tag{20}$$

where $H > 0$ is a positive definite symmetric matrix to be determined later.
The derivative of $V_2(t)$ along the trajectories of system (7) is as follows,

$$\dot{V}_2(t) = \sum_{i=1}^{N} e_i^T(t)\dot{e}_i(t) + \sum_{i=1}^{N}\left[e_i^T(t)He_i(t) - e_i^T(t - \tau(t))He_i(t - \tau(t))\right]$$

$$= \sum_{i=1}^{N} e_i^T(t)\left[-Ce_i(t) + Af(e_i(t)) + Bf(e_j(t - \tau(t)))\right.$$

$$+ \sum_{j=1}^{N} G_{ij}^0 \Gamma_0 e_j(t) + \sum_{j=1}^{N} G_{ij}^1 \Gamma_1 e_j(t - \tau(t)) - d_i^0 e_i(t) - d_i^1 e_i(t - \tau(t))\Big]$$

$$+ \sum_{i=1}^{N}\left[e_i^T(t)He_i(t) - e_i^T(t - \tau(t))He_i(t - \tau(t))\right]. \tag{21}$$

Note that the following inequalities hold,

$$- e_i^T(t)Ce_i(t) + e_i^T Af(e_i(t)) \le e_i^T(t)(0.5A^T A + 0.5\Delta^T \Delta - C)e_i(t), \tag{22}$$

$$e_i^T(t)Bf(e_i(t - \tau(t))) \le 0.5e_i^T(t)BB^T e_i(t) + 0.5e_i^T(t - \tau(t))\Delta^2 e_i(t - \tau(t)). \tag{23}$$

Substituting (22), (23), (12)-(13) into (21), one has

$$\dot{V}_2(t) = \sum_{i=1}^{N} e_i^T(t)\Big[0.5BB^T + H + 0.5A^T A + 0.5\Delta^T \Delta - C + \|\Gamma_0\|\sum_{j=1}^{N}\tilde{G}_{ij}^0$$

$$+ \sum_{j=1}^{N}\tilde{G}_{ij}^1\Big]e_i(t) - \sum_{i=1}^{N} e_i^T(t - \tau(t))He_i(t - \tau(t))$$

$$+ \sum_{i=1}^{N} 0.5e_i^T(t - \tau(t))\Delta^2 e_i(t - \tau(t))$$

$$+ \|\Gamma_1^T \Gamma_1\|\sum_{i=1}^{N}\sum_{j=1}^{N} e_i^T(t - \tau(t))\tilde{G}_{ij}^1 e_i(t - \tau(t))$$

$$-\sum_{i=1}^{l} e_i^T(t)d_i^0 e_i(t) - \sum_{i=1}^{l} e_i^T(t)d_i^1 e_i(t - \tau(t))$$
$$=e^T(t)(I_N \otimes L_1 + (\|\Gamma_0\|\tilde{G}^0 + \tilde{G}^1) \otimes I_n)e(t)$$
$$+ e^T(t - \tau(t))(0.5I_N \otimes \Delta^2 + (\|\Gamma_1^T \Gamma_1\|\tilde{G}^1 - D_1) \otimes I_n - I_N \otimes H)e(t - \tau(t)),$$
$$\tag{24}$$

where $\tilde{G}^0 = (\tilde{G}_{ij}^0)_{n \times N}$, $\tilde{G}^1 = (\tilde{G}_{ij}^1)_{n \times N}$.

Note the conditions (18) and (19) in Theorem 2, we can obtain $\dot{V}_2(t) < 0$ for any $e \neq 0$. Thus, the synchronization error vectors approach to zero as the time approaches to the infinity. It indicates that the coupled complex networks achieves the global asymptotic synchronization under the pinning control law (6).

Remark 3. Under the pinning control (6), synchronization criterion in Theorem 2 sufficiently utilizes the delayed feedback information to realize the pinning synchronization. The main difference between Theorem 1 and Theorem 2 is the expression form of synchronization criterion, the former is in the scalar form while the latter is in the matrix form. It is the matrix inequality form that makes the corresponding synchronization criterion be able to use more known information to realize the pinning control.

Remark 4. For the positive definite matrix H, one can use the matrix inequalities (18) and (19) to solve it. In this case, the feasibility space will be expanded. One can also fix the H in advance. For example, according to inequality (24), one can choose $H = N\Delta$. Different choice of H, one can have different pinning synchronization criterion with different level of conservativeness.

4   Conclusions

Pinning control method and all node control method have their own features in the practical design. In general, the pinning control is most suitable for the large scale complex networks with more nodes. Therefore, the pinning control synchronization has gained much attention in recent years. In this paper, by using the state feedback and delayed state feedback, two different pinning synchronization criteria have been established. One is based on the matrix eigenvalue of the coupled matrix, the other is based on the matrix inequality of the known networks information. comparisons among the pinning control methods are made to show the the characteristics of the proposed results.

Acknowledgements. This work was supported by National Nature Science Foundation under Grants 60974071, 61074073 and 61034005, Program for New Century Excellent Talents in University of China under Grant NCET-10-0306, and the Fundamental Research Funds for the Central Universities under Grants N110504001 and N100104102.

References

1. Watts, D., Strogatz, S.: Collective dynamics of small-world networks. Nature 393, 440–442 (1998)
2. Pecora, L., Carroll, T.: Master stability function for synchronized coupled systems. Phys. Rev. Lett. 80, 2109–2112 (1998)
3. Wu, C., Chua, L.: Synchronization in an array of linearly coupled dynamical systems. IEEE Trans. Circ. Syst-I 42, 430–447 (1995)
4. Pastor-Satorras, R., Vespignani, A.: Epidemic spread in scale-free networks. Phys. Rev. Lett. 86, 3200–3203 (2001)
5. Wang, X., Chen, G.: Synchronization in scale-free dynamical networks: robustness and fragility. IEEE Trans. Circ. Syst-I 49, 54–62 (2002)
6. Zhou, J., Chen, T.: Synchronization in general complex delayed dynamical networks. IEEE Trans. Circ. Syst-I 53, 733–744 (2006)
7. Lu, J., Yu, X., Chen, G.: Chaos synchronization of general complex dynamical networks. Physica A 33, 281–302 (2004)
8. Wu, J., Jiao, L.: Synchronization in complex dynamical networks with nonsymmetric coupling. Physica D 237, 2487–2498 (2008)
9. Zhan, M., Gao, J., Wu, Y.: Chaos synchronization in coupled systems by applying pinning control. Phys. Rev. E 76, 036203 (2007)
10. Wang, X., Chen, G.: Pinning control of scale-free dynamical networks. Physica A 310, 521–531 (2002)
11. Li, X., Wang, X., Chen, G.: Pinning a complex dynamical network to its equilibrium. IEEE Trans. Circ. Syst-I 51, 2074–2087 (2004)
12. Chen, T., Liu, X., Lu, W.: Pinning complex networks by a single controller. IEEE Trans. Circ. Syst-I 54, 1317–1326 (2007)
13. Zhou, J., Wu, Q., Xiang, L.: Pinning complex delayed dynamical networks by a single impulse controller. IEEE Trans. Circ. Syst-I 58, 1–12 (2011)
14. Zhou, J., Wu, X., Yu, W.: Pinning synchronization of delayed neural networks. Chaos 18, 043111 (2008)
15. Zhao, J., Lu, J., Zhang, Q.: Pinning a complex delayed dynamical network to a homogenous trajectory. IEEE Trans. Circ. Syst-II 56, 514–517 (2009)
16. Guo, W., Austin, F., Chen, S.: Pinning synchronization of the complex networks with non-delayed and delayed coupling. Phys. Lett. A 373, 1565–1572 (2009)
17. Lu, J., Yu, X., Chen, G.: Chaos synchronization of general complex dynamical networks. Phys. A 334, 281–302 (2004)
18. Lu, J., Chen, G.: A time-varying complex dynamical network models and its controlled synchronization criteria. IEEE Trans. Autom. Control 50, 841–846 (2005)
19. Zhao, J., Lu, J., Wu, X.: Pinning control of general complex dynamical networks with optimization. Science China - Information Sciences 53, 813–822 (2010)

Mean Square Stability of Stochastic Impulsive Genetic Regulatory Networks with Mixed Time-Delays

Zhanheng Chen[1] and Haijun Jiang[2]

[1] Department of Mathematics and statistics, YiLi Normal University,
YiNing, 835000, China
Czh918czh@163.com
[2] College of Mathematics and System Sciences, Xinjiang University,
Urumqi, 830046, China
jianghai@xju.edu.cn

Abstract. In this paper, we investigate a class of stochastic impulsive genetic regulatory networks with mixed time-delays. By using Lyapunov-Krasovskii functional method, LMI method and mathematical induction, some sufficient conditions are derived ensuring the globally exponential stability of the equilibrium point of the genetic regulatory networks in mean square. It is believed that these results are significant and useful for the design and applications of stochastic impulsive genetic regulatory networks. Finally, an example is given to illustrate the results obtained in this paper.

Keywords: Genetic regulatory networks, Stochastic, Impulsive, Mean square stability.

1 Introduction

Nowadays, genetic regulatory network has became an important new area of research in the biological and biomedical sciences [1-3]. The construction of a gene regulatory networks with a basic biological function is a focus of synthetic biology and genetic engineering [4, 5]. Thus, understanding the architectures and the design principles of gene networks will fundamentally advance the study of core problems of synthetic biology.

Recently, several computational models have been applied to investigate the behaviours of genetic regulatory networks (GRNs): Bayesian network models [6, 7], Petri net models [8, 9], the Boolean models [10, 11] and the differential equation models [12-15], etc. The differential equation model describes the rates of change in the concentrations of gene products, such as mRNAs and proteins, as continuous values. Several typical GRNs have been studied experimentally and theoretically [16-21].

Due to small numbers of transcriptional factors and other key signaling proteins, there is considerable experimental evidence that stochastic noise plays a

J. Wang, G.G. Yen, and M.M. Polycarpou (Eds.): ISNN 2012, Part I, LNCS 7367, pp. 312–321, 2012.
© Springer-Verlag Berlin Heidelberg 2012

very important role in gene regulation [21]. Additionally, Time delays usually exist in transcription, translation processes especially in a eukaryotic cell and one can see some experimental results [22, 23]. Moreover, impulsive effects are also likely to exist in the networks system. So, in the applications and designs of networks, these unavoidable uncertainties must be integrated into the system model.

Analyzing stability behaviors is an important task in both theoretical studies and bioengineering applications on GRNs. Therefore, it is of great significance to consider the stability of GRNs and sufficient stability conditions have been proposed in [17, 24-28] and references therein. Motivated by the above discussions, in this paper, we investigate a class of stochastic impulsive genetic regulatory networks with mixed time-delays. By using Lyapunov-Krasovskii functional method, LMI method and mathematics induction, some sufficient conditions are derived for the globally exponential stability of the equilibrium point of the genetic regulatory networks in mean square. It is believed that these results are significant and useful for the design and applications of stochastic impulsive genetic regulatory networks.

2   Model Description and Preliminaries

Throughout this paper, R_+ denotes the set of nonnegative real numbers, Z denotes the set of positive integers. Let $(\Omega, \mathscr{F}, \{\mathscr{F}_t\}_{t\geq 0}, P)$ be a complete probability space with a filtration $\{\mathscr{F}_t\}_{t\geq 0}$ satisfying the usual conditions (i.e., the filtration contains all P-null sets and is right continuous) and $\mathbb{E}(\cdot)$ be the mathematical expectation.

Consider the following stochastic impulsive genetic regulatory networks:

$$
\begin{cases}
dM_i(t) = \Big(- a_i M_i(t) + \sum_{j=1}^{n} \omega_{ij} \widetilde{g}_j(P_j(t - \tau_j(t))) \\
\qquad + \sum_{j=1}^{n} b_{ij} \int_{-\infty}^{t} k_j(t - s)\widetilde{g}_j(P_j(s))ds + I_i \Big)dt \\
\qquad + \sum_{j=1}^{n} \widetilde{\delta}_{ij}(M_i(t), P_i(t))d\omega_j(t), & t \neq t_k, \\
M_i(t) = \widetilde{H}_{ik}(M_i(t^-)), & t = t_k, \\
dP_i(t) = [-c_i P_i(t) + d_i M_i(t - \sigma_i(t)) \\
\qquad + e_i \int_{-\infty}^{t} k_i(t - s)M_i(s)ds]dt, & t \neq t_k, \\
P_i(t) = \widetilde{I}_{ik}(P_i(t^-)), & t = t_k,
\end{cases}
\tag{1}
$$

where $i = 1, 2, \cdots, n$, $M_i(t), P_i(t)$ are the concentrations of mRNA and protein of the ith node; a_i, c_i are the degradation rates of the mRNA and protein; d_i, e_i are constant matrices; $\widetilde{g}_j(P_j(t)) = \widetilde{f}_j(P_j(t)) = (P_j(t/\beta_j)^{H_j}/[1+(P_j(t)/\beta_j)^{H_j}]$ are the Hill form regulatory functions; $W = (\omega_{ij}) \in R^{n\times n}$ and $B = (b_{ij}) \in R^{n\times n}$ are the coupling matrixs of the genetic network, I_i is the basal transcriptional rate of the repressor of gene i; $k \in Z, t \in R_+$, time sequence $\{t_k\}$ satisfies $0 < t_1 < t_2 < \cdots < t_k < t_{k+1} < \cdots$ and $\lim_{k \to \infty} t_k = \infty$; $\delta(m(t), p(t)) = (\delta_{ij}(m(t), p(t)))_{n \times n}$ is the diffusion coefficient matrix; $\omega(t) = (\omega_1(t), \omega_2(t), \cdots, \omega_n(t))^T$ is zero-mean Brown motion defined on a complete probability space $(\Omega, \mathscr{F}, \{\mathscr{F}_t\}_{t \geq 0}, P)$ with a filtration $\{\mathscr{F}_t\}_{t \geq 0}$ satisfying $\mathbb{E}d(\omega(t)) = 0$ and $\mathbb{E}d(\omega^2(t)) = dt$; $H_{ik}(M_i(t_k^-))$ and $\tilde{I}_{ik}(P_i(t_k^-))$ represent impulsive perturbations of mRNA and protein of the ith node at time t_k, where $M_i(t_k^-)$ and $P_i(t_k^-)$ denote the left limit of $M_i(t_k)$ and $P_i(t_k)$, respectively.

In this paper, for system (1) we introduce the following assumptions.

(H_1) Each function $g_j(u)(j = 1, 2, \cdots, n)$ is monotonically increasing and there exists constant $l_j > 0$ for $a, b \in R$ and $a \neq b$ such that $0 \leq \frac{g_j(a) - g_j(b)}{a - b} \leq l_j$.

(H_2) The kernels $K_{ij}(i, j = 1, 2, \cdots, n)$ are real-valued non-negative continuous integrable defined on $[0, \infty)$ and satisfy $\int_0^\infty K_{ij}(s)ds = 1$ and $\int_0^\infty sK_{ij}(s)ds < \infty$.

(H_3) $H_{ik}(m)$ and $I_{ik}(p)(i = 1, 2, \cdots, n, \ k \in Z)$ are Lipschitz continuous functions with Lipschitz constants S_{ik} and R_{ik}, respectively.

(H_4) For the noise intensity matrix $\delta(m, p) = (\delta_{ij}(m_i, p_i))_{n \times n}$, there exist matrices $H_1 > 0, H_2 > 0$ such that $trace[\delta(m, p)\delta^T(m, p)] \leq m^T H_1 m + p^T H_2 p$ and $\delta(0, 0) \equiv 0$.

(H_5) $0 < \tau(t) < \tau, 0 < \sigma(t) < \sigma, \dot{\tau}(t) \leq \varrho < 1, \dot{\sigma}(t) \leq \zeta < 1$.

Consider the following deterministic system

$$\begin{cases} dM_i(t) = [-a_i M_i(t) + \sum_{j=1}^n \omega_{ij} \tilde{g}_j(P_j(t - \tau_i(t))) \\ \qquad + \sum_{j=1}^n b_{ij} \int_{-\infty}^t k_j(t - s)\tilde{g}_j(P_j(s))ds + I_i]dt, \\ dP_i(t) = [-c_i P_i(t) + d_i M_i(t - \sigma_i(t)) + e_i \int_{-\infty}^t k_i(t - s)M_i(s)ds]dt, \end{cases} \quad (2)$$

It is obvious that, from the well-known Brouwer's fixed point theorem and assumption (H_1), system (2) has at least one equilibrium point which is denoted by $(m^{*T}, p^{*T})^T = (m_1^*, m_2^*, \cdots, m_n^*, p_1^*, p_2^*, \cdots, p_n^*)^T$.

We further introduce the following assumption.

(H_6) $\delta(m^*, p^*) = 0, H_{ik}(M_i^*) = M_i^*, I_{ik}(P_i^*) = P_i^*$ for all $i = 1, 2, \cdots, n$ and $k \in Z$.

Therefore, $(m^{*T}, p^{*T})^T$ also is the equilibrium point of system (1). Let $m_i(t) = M_i(t) - m_i^*, p_i(t) = P_i(t) - p^*, g_j(p_j(t)) = \tilde{g}_j(P_j(t)) - g_j(p^*), f_j(p_j(t)) = \tilde{f}_j(P_j(t)) - f_j(p^*), \delta_{ij}(m_i(t), p_i(t)) = \tilde{\delta}_{ij}(M_i(t), P_i(t)) - \delta_{ij}(m^*, p^*), H_{ik}(m_i(t^-)) = \tilde{H}_{ik}(M_i(t^-)) - H_{ik}(m^*), I_{ik}(p_i(t^-)) = \tilde{I}_{ik}(P_i(t^-)) - I_{ik}(p^*)$. Denote $m(t) = (m_1(t), \cdots, m_n(t))^T, p(t) = (p_1(t), p_2(t), \cdots, p_n(t))^T, g(p(t - \tau(t)) = (g_1(p_1(t - \tau_1(t))), \cdots, g_n(p_n(t - \tau_n(t))))^T, f(p(t)) = (f_1(p_1(t)), \cdots, f_n(p_n(t)))^T, H_k(m(t_k)) = (H_{1k}(m_1(t_k)), \cdots, H_{nk}(m_n(t_k)))^T, I_k(p(t_k)) = (I_{1k}(p_1(t_k)), \cdots, I_{nk}(p_n(t_k)))^T, A = diag(a_1, \cdots, a_n), W = (\omega_{ij})_{n \times n}, B = (b_{ij})_{n \times n}, K(t - s) = diag\Big(k_1(t - s), \cdots, k_n(t - s)\Big), C = diag(c_1, c_2, \cdots, c_n),$

$D = diag(d_1, d_2, \cdots, d_n)$, time delays $\tau(t) = (\tau_1(t), \tau_2(t), \cdots, \tau_n(t))^T$ and $\sigma(t) = (\sigma_1(t), \sigma_2(t), \cdots, \sigma_n(t))^T$, $E = diag(e_1, e_2, \cdots, e_n)$. System (1) can be rewritten in the following vector-matrix form

$$
\begin{cases}
dm(t) = [-Am(t) + Wg(p(t - \tau(t))) \\
\qquad + B \displaystyle\int_{-\infty}^{t} K(t-s)f(p(s))ds]dt \\
\qquad + \delta(m(t), p(t))d\omega(t), & t \neq t_k, \\
m(t) = H_k(m(t^-)), & t = t_k, \\
dp(t) = [-Cp(t) + Dm(t - \sigma(t)) \\
\qquad + E \displaystyle\int_{-\infty}^{t} K(t-s)m(s)ds]dt, & t \neq t_k, \\
p(t) = I_k(p(t^-)), & t = t_k.
\end{cases}
\tag{3}
$$

Evidently, the globally exponential stability of the origin of system (3) is equivalent to the globally exponential stability of the equilibrium point $(m^{*T}, p^{*T})^T$ of system (1).

3 Main Results

In this section, based on LMI and Lyapunov functional methods, we study the globally exponential stability of the origin of system (3) in mean square.

Theorem 1. *Under* $(H_1) - (H_6)$, *equilibrium* $(m^{*T}, p^{*T})^T$ *of system (1) is unique and globally exponentially stable in mean square, if the following conditions hold:*

(i) There exist positive definite matrices N_1, N_2, Q_1, Q_2, Q_3, *positive diagonal matrices* Π, $L = diag(L_1, \cdots, L_n)$, $R = diag(r_1, \cdots, r_n)$ *and constants* $\rho > 0, \alpha > 0$ *such that*

$$N_1 \leq \rho I, \tag{4}$$

$$
\Omega = \begin{bmatrix}
\Delta_{11} & 0 & 0 & 0 & 0 & 0 & 0 & 0 & 0 \\
0 & \Delta_{22} & 0 & \Pi & 0 & 0 & \Pi & 0 & 0 \\
0 & 0 & \Delta_{33} & 0 & 0 & 0 & 0 & 0 & 0 \\
0 & \Pi & 0 & -2\Pi L^{-1} + Q_2 & 0 & 0 & 0 & 0 & 0 \\
0 & 0 & 0 & 0 & \Delta_{55} & 0 & 0 & 0 & 0 \\
0 & 0 & 0 & 0 & 0 & \Delta_{66} & 0 & 0 & 0 \\
0 & \Pi & 0 & 0 & 0 & 0 & -2\Pi L^{-1} + L & 0 & 0 \\
0 & 0 & 0 & 0 & 0 & 0 & 0 & -L & 0 \\
0 & 0 & 0 & 0 & 0 & 0 & 0 & 0 & -R
\end{bmatrix} < 0 \tag{5}
$$

and

$$N_1 B + B^T N_1 < 0, \quad N_2 E + E^T N_2 < 0, \tag{6}$$

where $\Delta_{11} = \alpha N_1 - N_1 A - A^T N_1 + \rho H_1 + Q_1 + R + N_1$, $\Delta_{22} = \alpha N_2 - N_2 C - C^T N_2 + \rho H_2 + Q_3 + N_2$, $\Delta_{33} = D^T N_2 D - e^{-\alpha\sigma}(1-\zeta)Q_1$, $\Delta_{55} = W^T N_1 W - e^{-\alpha\tau}(1-\varrho)Q_2$, $\Delta_{66} = -e^{-\alpha\tau}(1-\varrho)Q_3$, $L^{-1} = diag\{L_1^{-1}, L_2^{-1}, \cdots, L_n^{-1}\}$.

(ii) There exists a constant $\theta \in (0, 2\alpha)$ such that$\ln \tilde{\rho}_k \leq \theta(t_k - t_{k-1})$ for $k = 1, 2, \cdots$, where $\tilde{\rho}_k = \max\{\max_{1 \leq i \leq n} S_{ik}^2, \max_{1 \leq i \leq n} R_{ik}^2, 1\}$.

Proof. Based on system (3), we construct the following Lyapunov-Krasovskii functional:

$$V(t) = V_1(t) + V_2(t) + V_3(t) + V_4(t) + V_5(t) + V_6(t), \tag{7}$$

where

$$V_1(t) = e^{\alpha t} m^T(t) N_1 m(t) + e^{\alpha t} p^T(t) N_2 p(t), \quad V_2(t) = \int_{t-\sigma(t)}^t e^{\alpha s} m^T(s) Q_1 m(s) ds,$$

$$V_3(t) = \int_{t-\tau(t)}^t e^{\alpha s} g^T(p(s)) Q_2 g(p(s)) ds, \quad V_4(t) = \int_{t-\tau(t)}^t e^{\alpha s} p^T(s) Q_3 p(s) ds,$$

$$V_5(t) = \sum_{i=1}^n l_i \int_0^\infty k_i(\eta) \int_{t-\eta}^t e^{\alpha r} f_i^2(p_i(r)) dr d\eta,$$

$$V_6(t) = \sum_{i=1}^n r_i \int_0^\infty k_i(\eta) \int_{t-\eta}^t e^{\alpha s} m_i^2(s) ds d\eta.$$

For $t \neq t_k$, by Itô's formula, we have

$$dV(t) = [\mathscr{L}V_1 + \mathscr{L}V_2 + \mathscr{L}V_3 + \mathscr{L}V_4 + \mathscr{L}V_5 + \mathscr{L}V_6]dt$$
$$+ 2e^{\alpha t} m^T(t) N_1 \delta(m(t), p(t)) d\omega, \tag{8}$$

where $\mathscr{L}V_i (i = 1, 2, 3, 4, 5, 6)$ are the infinitesimal operators, and

$$\mathscr{L}V_1 = \alpha e^{\alpha t} m^T(t) N_1 m(t) + 2e^{\alpha t} m^T(t) N_1 [-Am(t) + Wg(p(t-\tau(t)))$$

$$+ B \int_{-\infty}^t K(t-s) f(p(s)) ds] + \alpha e^{\alpha t} p^T(t) N_2 p(t)$$

$$+ 2e^{\alpha t} p^T(t) N_2 [-Cp(t) + Dm(t-\sigma(t)) + E \int_{-\infty}^t K(t-s) m(s) ds]$$

$$+ e^{\alpha t} trace[\delta^T(m(t), p(t)) N_1 \delta(m(t), p(t))],$$

$$\mathscr{L}V_2 = e^{\alpha t} m^T(t) Q_1 m(t) - e^{\alpha(t-\sigma(t))} (1 - \dot{\sigma}(t)) m^T(t-\sigma(t)) Q_1 m(t-\sigma(t)),$$

$$\mathscr{L}V_3 = e^{\alpha t} g^T(p(t)) Q_2 g(p(t))$$

$$- e^{\alpha(t-\tau(t))} (1 - \dot{\tau}(t)) g^T(p(t-\tau(t))) Q_2 g(p(t-\tau(t))),$$

$$\mathscr{L}V_4 = e^{\alpha t} p^T(t) Q_3 p(t) - e^{\alpha(t-\tau(t))} (1 - \dot{\tau}(t)) p^T(t-\tau(t)) Q_3 p(t-\tau(t)),$$

$$\mathscr{L}V_5 = \sum_{i=1}^n l_i \int_0^\infty k_i(\eta) e^{\alpha t} f_i^2(p_i(t)) d\eta - \sum_{i=1}^n l_i \int_0^\infty k_i(\eta) e^{\alpha(t-\eta)} f_i^2(p_i(t-\eta)) d\eta,$$

$$\mathscr{L}V_6 = \sum_{i=1}^n r_i \int_0^\infty k_i(\eta) e^{\alpha t} m_i^2(t) d\eta - \sum_{i=1}^n r_i \int_0^\infty k_i(\eta) e^{\alpha(t-\eta)} m_i^2(t-\eta) d\eta.$$

Using assumption (H_4), (H_5), Hölder inequality, we have

$$2m^T(t)N_1Wg(p(t-\tau(t)))$$
$$\leq m^T(t)N_1m(t) + g^T(p(t-\tau(t)))W^TN_1Wg(p(t-\tau(t))),$$
$$2p^T(t)N_2Dm(t-\sigma(t)) \leq p^T(t)N_2p(t) + m^T(t-\sigma(t))D^TN_2Dm(t-\sigma(t)),$$
$$trace[\delta^T(m(t),p(t))N_1\delta(m(t),p(t))] \leq \rho m^T(t)H_1m(t) + \rho p^T(t)H_2p(t),$$
$$-\sum_{i=1}^{n} l_i \int_0^\infty k_i(\eta)e^{\alpha(t-\eta)}f_i^2(p_i(t-\eta))d\eta$$
$$\leq -\left(\int_{-\infty}^t K(t-s)e^{-\alpha(t-s)}f(p(s))ds\right)^T Le^{\alpha t}\left(\int_{-\infty}^t K(t-s)e^{-\alpha(t-s)}f(p(s))ds\right),$$
$$-\sum_{i=1}^{n} r_i \int_0^\infty k_i(\eta)e^{\alpha(t-\eta)}m_i^2(t-\eta)d\eta$$
$$\leq -\left(\int_{-\infty}^t K(t-s)e^{-\alpha(t-s)}m(s)ds\right)^T Re^{\alpha t}\left(\int_{-\infty}^t K(t-s)e^{-\alpha(t-s)}m(s)ds\right).$$

By (H_1), for any diagonal positive matrix Π, we can get

$$2p^T(t)\Pi f(p(t)) - 2f^T(p(t))\Pi L^{-1}f(p(t)) \geq 0,$$
$$2p^T(t)\Pi g(p(t)) - 2g^T(p(t))\Pi L^{-1}g(p(t)) \geq 0.$$

Combining the above inequalities, we have

$$
\begin{aligned}
dV(t) \leq e^{\alpha t}\Big\{ &m^T(t)[\alpha N_1 - N_1A - A^TN_1 + \rho H_1 + Q_1 + R + N_1]m(t) \\
&+p^T(t)[\alpha N_2 - N_2C - C^TN_2 + \rho H_2 + Q_3 + N_2]p(t) \\
&+m^T(t-\sigma(t))[D^TN_2D - e^{-\alpha\sigma}(1-\zeta)Q_1]m(t-\sigma(t)) \\
&+g^T(p(t))[-2\Pi L^{-1} + Q_2]g(p(t)) + 2p^T(t)\Pi g(p(t)) \\
&+g^T(p(t-\tau(t)))[W^TN_1W - e^{-\alpha\tau}(1-\varrho)Q_2]g(p(t-\tau(t))) \\
&+p^T(t-\tau(t)))[-e^{-\alpha\tau}(1-\varrho)Q_3]p(t-\tau(t))) \\
&+f^T(p(t))[-2\Pi L^{-1} + L]f(p(t)) + 2p^T(t)\Pi f(p(t)) \\
&+\left(\int_{-\infty}^t K(t-s)e^{-\alpha(t-s)}f(p(s))ds\right)^T(-L)\left(\int_{-\infty}^t K(t-s)e^{-\alpha(t-s)}f(p(s))ds\right) \\
&+\left(\int_{-\infty}^t K(t-s)e^{-\alpha(t-s)}m(s)ds\right)^T(-R)\left(\int_{-\infty}^t K(t-s)e^{-\alpha(t-s)}m(s)ds\right) \\
&+m^T(t)[N_1B + B^TN_1]\int_{-\infty}^t K(t-s)f(p(s))ds \\
&+p^T(t)[N_2E + E^TN_2]\int_{-\infty}^t K(t-s)m(s)ds\Big\}dt \\
&+2e^{\alpha t}m^T(t)N_1\delta(m(t),p(t))d\omega.
\end{aligned}
$$

$$(9)$$

Taking the mathematical expectation of both sides of (9), by (5) and (6) we have

$$\frac{d\mathbb{E}V(t)}{dt} \leq 0. \tag{10}$$

For any $t \in [0, t_1)$, by (10) and noting $\tilde{\rho}_k \geq 1 (k = 1, 2, \cdots)$, we have

$$\mathbb{E}V(t) \leq \mathbb{E}V(0), \tag{11}$$

$$\begin{aligned}
\mathbb{E}V(t_1) \leq {} & \mathbb{E}\Big(e^{\alpha t_1} m^T(t_1) S_1^T N_1 S_1 m(t_1) + e^{\alpha t_1} p^T(t_1) R_1^T N_2 R_1 p(t_1) \\
& + \int_{t_1 - \sigma(t_1)}^{t_1} e^{\alpha s} m^T(s) Q_1 m(s) ds + \int_{t_1 - \tau(t_1)}^{t_1} e^{\alpha s} g^T(p(s)) Q_2 g(p(s)) ds \\
& + \int_{t_1 - \tau(t_1)}^{t_1} e^{\alpha s} p^T(s) Q_3 p(s) ds + \int_0^\infty K(\eta) \int_{t_1 - \eta}^{t_1} e^{\alpha r} f^T(p(r)) L f(p(r)) dr d\eta \\
& + \int_0^\infty K(\eta) \int_{t_1 - \eta}^{t_1} e^{\alpha s} m^T(s) R m(s) ds d\eta \Big) \\
\leq {} & \tilde{\rho}_1 \mathbb{E}V(t_1^-)
\end{aligned} \tag{12}$$

For $t \in [t_1, t_2)$, by (10)-(12) and noting $\tilde{\rho}_k \geq 1 (k = 1, 2, \cdots)$, we have

$$\mathbb{E}V(t) \leq \mathbb{E}V(t_1) \leq \tilde{\rho}_1 \mathbb{E}V(t_1^-) \leq \mathbb{E}V(0) \tag{13}$$

and

$$\mathbb{E}V(t_2) \leq \tilde{\rho}_2 \mathbb{E}V(t_2^-). \tag{14}$$

For $t \in [t_2, t_3)$, by (11), (13) and (14), we have

$$\mathbb{E}V(t) \leq \mathbb{E}V(t_2) \leq \tilde{\rho}_2 \mathbb{E}V(t_2^-) \leq \tilde{\rho}_2 \tilde{\rho}_1 \mathbb{E}V(0) \tag{15}$$

Therefore, by mathematical induction, for all $t \in [t_k, t_{k+1})$, we have

$$\mathbb{E}V(t) \leq \tilde{\rho}_k \tilde{\rho}_{k-1} \cdots \tilde{\rho}_2 \tilde{\rho}_1 \mathbb{E}V(0). \tag{16}$$

Using assumption (H_1), we have

$$\mathbb{E}V(0) \leq U \sup_{s \in (-\tau, 0]} \mathbb{E}\|p(s)\|^2, \tag{17}$$

where

$$\begin{aligned}
U = \max \Big\{ & \lambda \max(N_1) + \sigma \lambda \max(Q_1) + \frac{\lambda \max(R)\|\lambda\|^2}{\alpha}, \\
& \lambda \max(N_2) + \tau \|Q_2\| \|\mu\|^2 + \tau \max \lambda(Q_3) + \frac{\|L\| \|\lambda\|^2}{\alpha} \Big\}
\end{aligned}$$

By (16), (17) and condition (ii), for any $t \in [t_k, t_{k+1})$, we have

$$\mathbb{E}\|m(t)\|^2 + \mathbb{E}\|p(t)\|^2 \leq \frac{U}{\lambda} e^{-(\alpha - \theta)t} \Big(\sup_{s \in (-\sigma, 0]} \mathbb{E}\|m(s)\|^2 + \sup_{s \in (-\tau, 0]} \mathbb{E}\|p(s)\|^2 \Big), \tag{18}$$

where $\tilde{\lambda} = \min\{\lambda_{\min}(N_1), \lambda_{\min}(N_2)\}$, which implies the equilibrium $(m^{*T}, p^{*T})^T$ of system (1) is globally exponentially stable in mean square. This completes the proof. $\square$

Remark 1. Note that condition (i) of Theorem 1 is a linear matrix inequality, its solvability can be readily checked by using the LMI toolbox. Different from the conventional stability criteria that depend on the matrix norm computation, no tuning of parameters will be needed when employing our LMI-based stability criteria.

4 An Example

In model (1), choose $f_{ij}(p_j) = g_{ij}(p_j) = \frac{p_j^2}{1+p_j^2}$ for $i = 1, 2$, the Hill coefficient is 2, $k_{ij}(s) = e^{-s}$, $|\Phi_{ik}| \leq 1, |\Psi_{ik}| \leq 1$, $\tau(t) = \sigma(t) = \frac{e^t}{2(1+e^t)}$. Obviously, $\tau = \sigma = \frac{1}{2}, \zeta = \varrho = \frac{1}{8}$.

Choose $A = diag(15, 10)$, $C = diag(10, 12)$, $\Pi = I, H_1 = 0.2I, H_2 = 0.1I$, and $W = \begin{bmatrix} 0.2 & 0.3 \\ 0.1 & 0.2 \end{bmatrix}, B = \begin{bmatrix} -0.3 & 0 \\ 0 & -0.4 \end{bmatrix}, D = \begin{bmatrix} -0.2 & -0.4 \\ 0.3 & 0.2 \end{bmatrix}, E = \begin{bmatrix} -0.1 & 0 \\ 0 & -0.5 \end{bmatrix}$.

By using the Matlab LMI Toolbox, it is found that there exist $\alpha = 0.9783, \rho = 43.0535$,

$L = \begin{bmatrix} 0.1759 & 0 \\ 0 & 0.1815 \end{bmatrix}, R = \begin{bmatrix} 34.2181 & 0 \\ 0 & 36.0695 \end{bmatrix}, N_1 = \begin{bmatrix} 6.3478 & -0.3386 \\ -0.3386 & 11.7601 \end{bmatrix},$

$N_2 = \begin{bmatrix} 5.2091 & 2.2104 \\ 2.2104 & 5.5370 \end{bmatrix}, Q_1 = \begin{bmatrix} 105.3993 & 6.2685 \\ 6.2685 & 139.0873 \end{bmatrix}, Q_2 = \begin{bmatrix} 108.2729 & 38.0222 \\ 38.0222 & 148.8690 \end{bmatrix},$

$Q_3 = \begin{bmatrix} 58.1637 & 32.0613 \\ 32.0613 & 78.6495 \end{bmatrix}$ such that the conditions in Theorem 1 hold. Therefore, the equilibrium of system (1) is unique and globally exponentially stable in mean square.

Acknowledgments. This work was supported by The National Natural Science Foundation of P.R. China (61164004), The Natural Science Foundation of Xinjiang (2010211A07), The Major Scientific Research Programmes of Yili Normal University (2012ZD005).

References

1. Bower, J., Bolouri, H.: Computational Modelling of Genetic and Biochemical Networks. MIT Press, Cambridge (2001)
2. Davidson, E.: Genomic Regulatory Systems. Academic Press, San Diego (2001)
3. Kitano, H.: Foundations of Systems Biology. MIT Press, Cambridge (2001)
4. Hood, L., Galas, D.: The digital code of DNA. Nature 421, 444–448 (2003)
5. Wang, Y., Shen, J., Niu, B., Liu, Z., Chen, L.: Robustness of interval gene networks with multiple time-varying delays and noise. Neurocomputing 72, 3303–3310 (2009)
6. Friedman, N., Linial, M., Nachman, I., Pe'er, D.: Using Bayesian networks to analyze expression data. J. Comput. Biol. 7, 601–620 (2000)

7. Hartemink, A.J., Gifford, D.K., Jaakkola, T.S., Young, R.A.: Bayesian Methods for Elucidating Genetic Regulatory Networks. IEEE Intel. Syst. Biol. 17, 37–43 (2002)
8. Chaouiya, C., Remy, E., Ruet, P., Thieffry, D.: Petri net modelling of biological regulatory networks. J. Disc. 6, 165–177 (2008)
9. Hardy, S., Robillard, P.N.: Modelling and simulation of molecular biology systems using Petri nets: modelling goals of various approaches. J. Bioinform. Comput Biol. 2, 595–613 (2004)
10. Somogyi, R., Sniegoski, C.: Modeling the complexity of genetic networks: Understanding multigenic and pleiotropic regulation. Complexity 1, 45–63 (1996)
11. Weaver, D.C., Workman, C.T., Storm, G.D.: Modeling regulatory networks with weight matrices. In: Proc. Pacific Symposium on Biocomputing, vol. 4, pp. 113–123 (1999)
12. Bolouri, H., Davidson, E.H.: Modelling transcriptional regulatory networks. BioEssay 24, 1118–1129 (2002)
13. Jong, H.D.: Modelling and simulation of genetic regulatory systems: A literature review. J. Comput. Biol. 9, 67–103 (2002)
14. Chen, L., Aihara, K.: Stability of genetic regulatory networks with time delay. IEEE Trans. Circuits Syst. I 49, 602–608 (2002)
15. Smolen, P., Baxter, D.A., Byrne, J.H.: Mathematical modeling of gene networks review. Neuron 26, 567–580 (2000)
16. Becskei, A., Serrano, L.: Engineering stability in gene networks by autoregulation. Nature 405, 590–593 (2000)
17. Li, C., Chen, L., Aihara, K.: Stochastic Stability of Genetic Networks With Disturbance Attenuation. IEEE Trans. Circuits Syst. II, Exp. Briefs 54, 892–896 (2007)
18. Chen, L., Aihara, K.: Stability of genetic regulatory networks with time delay. IEEE Trans. Circuits Syst. I 49, 602–608 (2002)
19. Gardner, T., Cantor, C.R., Collins, J.J.: Construction of a genetic toggle switch in Escherichia Coli. Nature 403, 339–342 (2000)
20. Isaacs, F.J., Hasty, J., Cantor, C.R., Collins, J.J.: Prediction and measurement of an autoregulatory genetic module. Proc of Natl. Acad. Sci 100, 7714–7719 (2003)
21. Tian, T., Burragea, K., Burragea, P.M., Carlettib, M.: Stochastic delay differential equations for genetic regulatory networks. J. Comput. Appl. Math. 205, 696–707 (2007)
22. Lewis, J.: Autoinhibition with transcriptional delay: a simple mechanism for the zebra fish somitogenesis oscillator. Curr. Biol. 13, 1398–1408 (2003)
23. Hirata, H., Yoshiura, S., Ohtsuka, T., Bessho, Y., Harada, T., Yoshikawa, K., Kageyama, R.: Oscillatory expression of the bHLH factor Hes1 regulated by a negative feedback loop. Science 298, 840–843 (2002)
24. Li, C., Chen, L., Aihara, K.: Stability of genetic networks with SUM regulatory logic: Lur'e system and LMI approach. IEEE Trans. Circuits Syst. I 53, 2451–2458 (2006)
25. He, W., Cao, J.: Robust stability of genetic regulatory networks with distributed delay. Cognitive Neurodynamics 2, 355–361 (2008)
26. Cao, J., Ren, F.: Exponential Stability of Discrete-Time Genetic Regulatory Networks With Delays. IEEE Trans. Neural Networks 19, 520–523 (2008)
27. Liu, Y., Wang, Z., Liu, X.: On global exponential stability of generalized stochastic neural networks with mixed time-delays. Neurocomputing 70, 314–326 (2006)
28. Mao, X.: Attraction, stability and boundedness for stochastic differential delay equations. Nonlinear Analysis 47, 4795–4806 (2001)

29. Mao, X.: Stochastic Differential Equations and Their Applications. Horwood, Chichester (1997)
30. Boyd, S., Ghaoui, L.E., Feron, E., BalaKrishnan, V.: Linear matrix inequalities in systems and control theory. SIAM Studies in Applied Mathematics, Philadelphia (1994)

Mesh Exponential Stability of Look-Ahead Vehicle Following System with Time Delays

Qiankun Song[1] and Jiye Zhang[2]

[1] Department of Mathematics, Chongqing Jiaotong University,
Chongqing 400074, China
qiankunsong@163.com
[2] Traction Power State Key Laboratory, Southwest Jiaotong University,
Chengdu 610031, China

Abstract. In this paper, the problem on the mesh stability for a class of look-ahead vehicle following system with time delays is investigated under the assumption that all isolated subsystems are exponentially stable. Based on the vector Lyapunov function method and inequality technique, several criteria for checking the global exponential stability and global exponential mesh stability are obtained.

Keywords: Mesh stability, Look-ahead system, Infinite dimension, Time delay.

1 Introduction

The stability and control of interconnected system are considered in many high technological fields such as automated highway systems, unmanned aerial vehicles and autonomous underwater vehicles [1]-[3]. Swaroop and Hedrick investigated the string stability for a class of infinite interconnected systems and obtained a sufficient condition by using Lyapunov method [4]. A significant amount of researches have been done on the concept of string stability [4]-[10]. It is concerned in interconnected systems that how to damp or eliminate the disturbances when they travel in the system. Intuitively, mesh stability is the property of damping disturbances as they travel away from the source in an interconnected system. Seiler, Pant and Hedrick proposed the concept of mesh stability on the base of string stability, and obtained a sufficient condition for checking the mesh stability of linear systems [11]. In [12], the mesh stability of nonlinear interconnected system was defined, and obtained a set of sufficient conditions to mesh stability of look-ahead interconnected system. Mesh stability was shown to be robust with respect to structural and singular perturbation. Recently, the authors studied the global exponential mesh stability of a class of look-ahead vehicle following system [13]. However, the effect of delay on the mesh stability is not considered. It is well known that the existence of delay can causes oscillation or instability in vehicle control systems, Therefore, the study of mesh stability for look-ahead vehicle following system with time delays is of both theoretical and practical importance.

J. Wang, G.G. Yen, and M.M. Polycarpou (Eds.): ISNN 2012, Part I, LNCS 7367, pp. 322–327, 2012.
© Springer-Verlag Berlin Heidelberg 2012

Motivated by the above discussions, the objective of this paper is to investigate the mesh stability for look-ahead vehicle following system with time delays. Based on the vector Lyapunov function method and inequality technique, a criterion for checking the global mesh exponential stability is obtained. The presented condition is in terms of system parameters and have important leading significance in the design and applications of mesh stability for look-ahead vehicle following system with time delays.

2   Preliminaries

Definition 1. *An interconnected system is called look-ahead, if the (i,j)th subsystem is connected only to the subsystems (k,l) such that $k \leq i$ and $l \leq j$.*

From [9], we know that the look-ahead vehicle following system with time delays can be described by a system of ordinary differential equations

$$\begin{cases} \dot{x}_1(t) = f_1(x_1(t),0,0), \\ \dot{x}_i(t) = f_i(x_i(t), x_{i-1}(t-\tau), \dot{x}_{i-1}(t-\tau)), \quad i = 2,3,\cdots,N. \end{cases} \tag{1}$$

where $x_i(t) \in \mathbb{R}^n$, $f_i : \mathbb{R}^n \times \mathbb{R}^n \times \mathbb{R}^n \to \mathbb{R}^n$ and $f_i(0,0,0) = 0$, τ is a positive constant.

For presentation convenience, in the following, we denote

$$x = (x_1^T, x_2^T, \cdots, x_N^T)^T, \quad \|x(0)\|_\infty = \max_{1 \leq i \leq N} \|x_i(0)\|,$$

$$\|x(t)\|_\infty = \max_{1 \leq i \leq N} \|x_i(t)\|_\infty, \quad \|x(t)\|_\infty^k = \max_{i \leq k} \|x_i(t)\|_\infty.$$

Definition 2. *The origin $x = 0$ of the dynamical system (1) is globally exponentially mesh stable if*
(a). all isolated subsystems are exponentially stable;
(b). $\forall \varepsilon > 0$, $\exists \delta > 0$, such that $\|x(0)\|_\infty < \delta$ implies $\|x(t)\|_\infty < \varepsilon$;
(c). $\forall i \in \{2,3,\cdots,N\}$, $\exists \delta > 0$, $\|x_i(t)\|_\infty \leq \|x(t)\|_\infty^{i-1}$.

Remark 1. The mesh stability is different from ordinary defined stabilities, which is harder in conditions. It is mainly used in error control, such as the car following systems. If the biggest error occures in the frist car, then the mesh stability will guarantee the disturbances is damped as they travel in the system, and the string will travel as expected formation.

Throughout this paper, we make the following assumptions:

(H1). For any isolated subsystem $\dot{x}_i(t) = f_i(x_i(t),0,0)$ of system (1), there are a C^1 function $V_i(x_i)$ and positive constants $\alpha_{1i}, \alpha_{2i}, \beta_{1i}$ and β_{2i}, such that

$$\alpha_{1i}\|x_i(t)\|^2 \leq V_i(x_i) \leq \alpha_{2i}\|x_i(t)\|^2, \tag{2}$$

$$\frac{\partial V_i}{\partial x_i} f_i(x_i,0,0) \leq -\beta_{1i}\|x_i(t)\|^2, \tag{3}$$

$$\|\frac{\partial V_i}{\partial x_i}\| \leq \beta_{2i}\|x_i(t)\| \tag{4}$$

for $\forall x_i(t) \in \mathbb{R}^n$, $i \in \{1,2,\cdots,N\}$.

(H2). There exist three positive constants L_1, L_2 and L_3 such that

$$\|f_i(y_1, y_2, y_3) - f_i(z_1, z_2, z_3)\| \leq \sum_{i=1}^{3} L_i \|y_i - z_i\|. \tag{5}$$

3   Main Results

Theorem 1. *Assume that the conditions* **(H1)** *and* **(H2)** *hold, then the interconnected system* (1) *is globally exponentially stable if*

$$\frac{(L_2 + L_1 L_3)}{2} \sum_{j=1}^{i-1} \frac{\alpha_{1,i-j} + \alpha_{2i}}{\alpha_{1,i-j}} L_3^{j-1} < \frac{\beta_{1i}}{\beta_{2i}}, \quad i = 2, 3, \cdots, N. \tag{6}$$

Proof. From assumption **(H1)**, we know that there is a C^1 function $V_i(x_i)$ and

$$
\begin{aligned}
\frac{dV_i(x_i(t))}{dt} &= \frac{\partial V_i}{\partial x_i} f_i(x_i(t), x_{i-1}(t-\tau), \dot{x}_{i-1}(t-\tau)) \\
&= \frac{\partial V_i}{\partial x_i} f_i(x_i(t), 0, 0) \\
&\quad + \frac{\partial V_i}{\partial x_i} \Big[f_i(x_i(t), x_{i-1}(t-\tau), \dot{x}_{i-1}(t-\tau)) - f_i(x_i(t), 0, 0) \Big] \\
&\leq -\beta_{1i} \|x_i(t)\|^2 + \beta_{2i} \|x_i(t)\| \\
&\quad \times \|f_i(x_i(t), x_{i-1}(t-\tau), \dot{x}_{i-1}(t-\tau)) - f_i(x_i(t), 0, 0)\|. \tag{7}
\end{aligned}
$$

From assumption **(H2)** and (7), we have that

$$
\begin{aligned}
\frac{dV_i(x_i(t))}{dt} &\leq -\beta_{1i} \|x_i(t)\|^2 \\
&\quad + \beta_{2i} \|x_i(t)\| \Big[L_2 \|x_{i-1}(t-\tau)\| + L_3 \|\dot{x}_{i-1}(t-\tau)\| \Big]. \tag{8}
\end{aligned}
$$

From assumption **(H2)** and (1), we can get that

$$
\begin{aligned}
\|\dot{x}_{i-1}(t-\tau)\| &= \|f_{i-1}(x_{i-1}(t-\tau), x_{i-2}(t-2\tau), \dot{x}_{i-2}(t-2\tau)) - f_{i-1}(0, 0, 0)\| \\
&\leq L_1 \|x_{i-1}(t-\tau)\| + L_2 \|x_{i-2}(t-2\tau)\| + L_3 \|\dot{x}_{i-2}(t-2\tau)\| \\
&\leq L_1 \|x_{i-1}(t-\tau)\| + (L_2 + L_1 L_3) \sum_{j=2}^{i-1} L_3^{j-2} \|x_{i-j}(t-j\tau)\|. \tag{9}
\end{aligned}
$$

It follows from (8) and (9) that

$$
\begin{aligned}
\frac{dV_i(x_i(t))}{dt} &\leq -\beta_{1i} \|x_i(t)\|^2 \\
&\quad + (L_2 + L_1 L_3)\beta_{2i} \|x_i(t)\| \sum_{j=1}^{i-1} L_3^{j-1} \|x_{i-j}(t-j\tau)\|. \tag{10}
\end{aligned}
$$

Using the inequalities $2ab \leq \frac{1}{2}(a^2 + b^2)$, we have

$$\frac{dV_i(x_i(t))}{dt} \leq -\left[\beta_{1i} - \frac{(L_2 + L_1 L_3)\beta_{2i}}{2} \sum_{j=1}^{i-1} L_3^{j-1}\right]\|x_i(t)\|^2$$

$$+ \frac{(L_2 + L_1 L_3)\beta_{2i}}{2} \sum_{j=1}^{i-1} L_3^{j-1}\|x_{i-j}(t - j\tau)\|^2. \qquad (11)$$

By (2) and (11), we get

$$\frac{dV_i(t)}{dt} \leq -\frac{1}{\alpha_{2i}}\left[\beta_{1i} - \frac{(L_2 + L_1 L_3)\beta_{2i}}{2} \sum_{j=1}^{i-1} L_3^{j-1}\right] V_i(t)$$

$$+ \frac{(L_2 + L_1 L_3)\beta_{2i}}{2} \sum_{j=1}^{i-1} \frac{L_3^{j-1}}{\alpha_{1,i-j}} V_{i-j}(t - j\tau). \qquad (12)$$

From Halanay differential inequality and (6), we know that the interconnected system (1) is globally exponentially stable. The proof is completed.

Theorem 2. *Assume that the conditions* **(H1)** *and* **(H2)** *hold, then the interconnected system (1) is globally exponentially mesh stable if*

$$(L_2 + L_1 L_3)\frac{\beta_{2i}}{\beta_{1i}} \sum_{j=1}^{i-1} \frac{\alpha_{1,i-j} + \alpha_{2i}}{\alpha_{1,i-j}} L_3^{j-1} \leq \left(\frac{\alpha_{1i}}{\alpha_{2i}}\right)^{\frac{1}{2}}, \quad i = 2, 3, \cdots, N. \qquad (13)$$

$$\|x_i(0)\|_\infty \leq \|x(0)\|_\infty^{i-1}, \quad i = 1, 2, \cdots, N. \qquad (14)$$

Proof. Since $\alpha_{1i} \leq \alpha_{2i}$, from condition (13), we know that inequality (6) holds. Thus the interconnected system (1) is globally exponentially stable.

From (10), we have that

$$\frac{dV_i(x_i(t))}{dt} \leq -\|x_i(t)\|\left[\beta_{1i}\|x_i(t)\|\right.$$

$$\left. -(L_2 + L_1 L_3)\beta_{2i} \sum_{j=1}^{i-1} L_3^{j-1}\|x_{i-j}(t - j\tau)\|\right]$$

$$\leq -\|x_i(t)\|\left[\beta_{1i}\|x_i(t)\| - \left((L_2 + L_1 L_3)\beta_{2i} \sum_{j=1}^{i-1} L_3^{j-1}\right)\|x\|_\infty^{i-1}\right]. (15)$$

Let

$$g_i = (L_2 + L_1 L_3)\frac{\beta_{2i}}{\beta_{1i}} \sum_{j=1}^{i-1} \frac{\alpha_{1,i-j} + \alpha_{2i}}{\alpha_{1,i-j}} L_3^{j-1}\|x\|_\infty^{i-1}, \quad c_i = \left(\frac{\alpha_{2i}}{\alpha_{1i}}\right)^{\frac{1}{2}}. \qquad (16)$$

Then $c_i \geq 1$. Define the following sets in state space:

$$B_{i1} = \{x_i : \|x_i\| \leq g_i\}, \quad B_{i2} = \{x_i : \|x_i\| \leq c_i g_i\}.$$

If $x_i \in \mathbb{R}^n \backslash B_{i1}$, then $\frac{dV_i(x_i(t))}{dt} < 0$. Thus, for any $y \in \mathbb{R}^n \backslash B_{i2}$ and $z \in B_{i1}$, we have $\|y\| > c_i g_i$ and $\|z\| \leq g_i$. Therefor, we get

$$V_i(z) \leq \alpha_{2i} \|z\|^2 \leq \alpha_{2i} g_i^2 < \frac{\alpha_{2i}}{c_i^2} \|y\|^2 = \alpha_{1i} \|y\|^2 \leq V_i(y). \tag{17}$$

In the following, we will prove that if $x_i(0) \in B_{i1}$, then for any $t \geq 0$, $x_i(t) \in B_{i2}$.

When $c_i = 1$, then $B_{i1} = B_{i2}$. Suppose that there exists t_2 such that $x_i(t_2) \in \mathbb{R}^n \backslash B_{i2}$, then there also exists t_1 $(t_1 < t_2)$ satisfying $x_i(t_1) \in \partial(B_{i2})$. For any $t \in [t_1, t_2]$, we know that $\frac{dV_i(x_i(t))}{dt} \leq 0$, thus $V_i(x_i(t_1)) \geq V_i(x_i(t_2))$, which is in contradiction with (17). So, for any $t \geq 0$, $x_i(t) \in B_{i2}$.

When $c_i > 1$, then $B_{i1} \subset B_{i2}$. Suppose that there exists t_2 such that $x_i(t_2) \in \mathbb{R}^n \backslash B_{i2}$, then there also exists t_1 $(t_1 < t_2)$ satisfying $x_i(t_1) \in B_{i1}$. For any $t \in [t_1, t_2]$, we know that $\frac{dV_i(x_i(t))}{dt} \leq 0$, thus $V_i(x_i(t_1)) \geq V_i(x_i(t_2))$, which is in contradiction with (17). So, for any $t \geq 0$, $x_i(t) \in B_{i2}$.

Therefore, if $x_i(0) \in B_{i1}$, then for any $t \geq 0$, $x_i(t) \in B_{i2}$. This implies that

$$\|x_i(t)\| \leq c_i g_i = \left(\frac{\alpha_{2i}}{\alpha_{1i}}\right)^{\frac{1}{2}} (L_2 + L_1 L_3) \frac{\beta_{2i}}{\beta_{1i}} \sum_{j=1}^{i-1} \frac{\alpha_{1,i-j} + \alpha_{2i}}{\alpha_{1,i-j}} L_3^{j-1} \|x\|_\infty^{i-1} \tag{18}$$

for any $t \geq 0$. By condition (13) and inequality (18), we get that

$$\|x_i(t)\| \leq \|x\|_\infty^{i-1}$$

for any $t \geq 0$. It can be seen that the interconnected system (1) is globally exponentially mesh stable. The proof is completed.

4   Conclusions

In this paper, the global exponential stability and global exponential mesh stability for a class of look-ahead vehicle following system with time delays have been investigated. Based on the vector Lyapunov function method and inequality technique, several criteria for checking the global exponential stability and global exponential mesh stability have been obtained.

Acknowledgments. This work was supported by the National Natural Science Foundation of China under Grants 60974132 and 11172247, and in part by the Natural Science Foundation Project of CQ CSTC2011BA6026, the Scientific & Technological Research Projects of CQ KJ110424.

References

1. Chu, K.C.: Decentralized Control of High-Speed Vehicular String. Transportation Science 8, 361–384 (1974)
2. Fenton, B.J.: An Overview of Systems Studies of Automated Highway Systems. IEEE Transactions on Vehicular Technology 40, 82–99 (1991)
3. Barbieri, E.: Stability Analysis of A Class of Interconnected Systems. Journal of Dynamic System Measurements Control 115, 546–551 (1993)
4. Swaroop, D., Hedrick, J.K.: String Stability for A Class of Nonlinear Systems. IEEE Transactions on Automatic Control 41, 349–357 (1996)
5. Eyre, J.: A Simplified Framework for String Stability Analysis of Automated Vehicle. Vehicle System Dynamics 30, 375–405 (1998)
6. Zhang, J.Y., Yang, Y.R., Zeng, J.: String Stability of Infinite Interconnected System. Applied Mathematics and Mechanics 21, 715–719 (2000)
7. Socha, L.: Stochastic Stability of Interconnected String Systems. Chaos, Solitons and Fractals 19, 949–955 (2004)
8. Zhang, J.Y., Suda, Y., Iwasa, T., Komine, H.: Vector Liapunov Function Approach to Longitudinal Control of Vehicles in A Platoon. JSME International Journal(Series C) 47, 653–658 (2004)
9. Ren, D.B., Zhang, J.Y., Sun, L.F.: Stability Analysis of Vehicle Following System with Delays Based on Vector Liapunov Function. Journal of Traffic and Transportation Engineering 7, 89–92 (2007)
10. Shi, J.Z., Zhang, J.Y., Xu, X.H.: String Stability of Stochastic Interconnected Systems with Time Delays. Acta Automatica Sinica 36, 1744–1751 (2010)
11. Seiler, P., Pant, A., Hedrick, J.K.: Preliminary Investigation of Mesh Stability for Linear Systems. IMECE99/DSC-7B-1 (1999)
12. Pant, A., Seiler, P., Hedrick, K.: Mesh Stability of Look-Ahead Interconnected Systems. IEEE Transactions on Automatic Control 47, 403–407 (2002)
13. Cao, Z.L., Li, T., Zhang, J.Y.: Mesh Exponential Stability of Look-Ahead Interconnected System. Applied Mechanics and Materials 29-32, 847–850 (2010)

Global Dissipativity of Neural Networks with Time-Varying Delay and Leakage Delay

Zhenjiang Zhao[1] and Qiankun Song[2]

[1] Department of Mathematics, Huzhou Teachers College, Huzhou 313000, China
[2] Department of Mathematics, Chongqing Jiaotong University,
Chongqing 400074, China
qiankunsong@163.com

Abstract. In this paper, the problem on global dissipativity is investigated for neural networks with time-varying delays and leakage delay as well as generalized activation functions. By constructing appropriate Lyapunov-Krasovskii functionals and using linear matrix inequality (LMI) technique, a new delay-dependent criterion for checking the global dissipativity of the addressed neural networks is established in terms of LMIs, which can be checked numerically using the effective LMI toolbox in MATLAB. The proposed dissipativity criterion does not require the monotonicity of the activation functions and the differentiability of the time-varying delays, which means that our result generalizes and further improves those in the earlier publications.

Keywords: Neural networks, Global dissipativity, Time-varying delays, Leakage delay.

1 Introduction

The dissipativity in dynamical systems is a more general concept and it has found applications in the areas such as stability theory, chaos and synchronization theory, system norm estimation, and robust control [1]. Recently, the dissipativity of neural networks was considered [2], some sufficient conditions on the dissipativity of delayed neural networks were derived, for example, see [2]-[11] and references therein. In [2]-[4], authors analyzed the dissipativity of neural network with constant delays, and derived several sufficient conditions for the global dissipativity of neural network with constant delays. In [5], authors considered the global dissipativity and global robust dissipativity for neural network with both time-varying delays and unbounded distributed delays, several sufficient conditions for checking the global dissipativity and global robust dissipativity were obtained. In [6]-[7], by using linear matrix inequality technique, authors investigated the global dissipativity of neural network with both discrete time-varying delays and distributed time-varying delays. In [8], authors proposed the concept on global dissipativity of stochastic neural networks with constant delay, and gave several criteria for checking the global dissipativity of stochastic neural networks with constant delay. In [9], the global dissipativity of discrete-time neural networks with time-varying delay was investigated.

J. Wang, G.G. Yen, and M.M. Polycarpou (Eds.): ISNN 2012, Part I, LNCS 7367, pp. 328–335, 2012.

However, to the best of the authors' knowledge, there are no results on the problem of dissipativity for neural networks with leakage delay. As pointed out in [10], neural networks with leakage delay is a class of important neural networks, time delay in the leakage term also has great impact on the dynamics of neural networks because time delay in the stabilizing negative feedback term has a tendency to destabilize a system [10]-[12]. Therefore, it is necessary to further investigate the dissipativity problem for neural networks with leakage delay.

Motivated by the above discussions, the objective of this paper is to study the problem on global dissipativity for neural networks with time-varying delays and leakage delay as well as generalized activation functions. By employing appropriate Lyapunov-Krasovskii functionals and using LMI technique, we obtain a new sufficient condition for checking the global dissipativity of the addressed neural networks.

2   Problem Formulation and Preliminaries

In this paper, we consider the following neural network:

$$\dot{x}(t) = -Cx(t - \delta) + Af(x(t)) + Bf(x(t - \tau(t))) + u \tag{1}$$

for $t \geq 0$, where $x(t) = (x_1(t), x_2(t), \cdots, x_n(t))^T \in R^n$ is state vector of the network at time t, n corresponds to the number of neurons; $C = \mathrm{diag}(c_1, c_2, \cdots, c_n)$ is a positive diagonal matrix, $A = (a_{ij})_{n \times n}$ and $B = (b_{ij})_{n \times n}$ are interconnection weight matrices; $f(x(t)) = (f_1(x_1(t)), f_2(x_2(t)), \cdots, f_n(x_n(t)))^T$ denotes neuron activation at time t; $u = (u_1, u_2, \cdots, u_n)^T$ is a external input vector; δ and $\tau(t)$ denote the leakage delay and time-varying delay, respectively.

Throughout this paper, we make the following assumptions:

(H1).([13]) For any $j \in \{1, 2, \cdots, n\}$, $f_j(0) = 0$ and there exist constants F_j^- and F_j^+ such that

$$F_j^- \leq \frac{f_j(\alpha_1) - f_j(\alpha_2)}{\alpha_1 - \alpha_2} \leq F_j^+$$

for all $\alpha_1 \neq \alpha_2$.

(H2).([12]) The leakage delay δ and time-varying delays $\tau(t)$ satisfy the following conditions

$$0 \leq \delta, \quad 0 \leq \tau(t) \leq \tau,$$

where δ and τ are constants.

The initial condition associated with model (1) is given by

$$x(s) = \phi(s), \qquad s \in [-\rho, 0],$$

where $\phi(s)$ is bounded and continuously differential on $[-\rho, 0]$, $\rho = max\{\delta, \tau\}$.

Definition 1. ([2]) Neural network (1) is said to be a globally dissipative, if there exists a compact set $S \subseteq R^n$, such that $\forall x_0 \in R^n$, $\exists T(x_0) > 0$, when

$t \geq t_0 + T(x_0)$, $x(t, t_0, x_0) \subseteq S$, where $x(t, t_0, x_0)$ denotes the solution of (1) from initial state x_0 and initial time t_0. In this case, S is called a globally attractive set. A set S is called a positive invariant, if $\forall x_0 \in S$ implies $x(t, t_0, x_0) \subseteq S$ for $t \geq t_0$.

To prove our result, the following lemmas that can be found in [7] are necessary.

Lemma 1. *([7]) For any constant matrix $W \in R^{m \times m}$, $W > 0$, scalar $0 < h(t) < h$, vector function $\omega : [0, h] \to R^m$ such that the integrations concerned are well defined, then*

$$\left(\int_0^{h(t)} \omega(s)ds \right)^T W \left(\int_0^{h(t)} \omega(s)ds \right) \leq h(t) \int_0^{h(t)} \omega^T(s)W\omega(s)ds.$$

Lemma 2. *([7]) Given constant matrices P, Q and R, where $P^T = P$, $Q^T = Q$, then*

$$\begin{bmatrix} P & R \\ R^T & -Q \end{bmatrix} < 0$$

is equivalent to the following conditions

$$Q > 0 \quad \text{and} \quad P + RQ^{-1}R^T < 0.$$

3   Main Result

For presentation convenience, in the following, we denote

$$F_1 = \mathrm{diag}(F_1^-, F_2^-, \cdots, F_n^-), \quad F_2 = \mathrm{diag}(F_1^+, F_2^+, \cdots, F_n^+),$$

$$F_3 = \mathrm{diag}(F_1^- F_1^+, \cdots, F_n^- F_n^+), \quad F_4 = \mathrm{diag}(\frac{F_1^- + F_1^+}{2}, \cdots, \frac{F_n^- + F_n^+}{2}).$$

Theorem 1. *Suppose that (H1) and (H2) hold. If there exist eight symmetric positive definite matrices P_i ($i = 1, 2, \cdots, 8$), four positive diagonal matrices D, H, R and S, and four matrices Q_i ($i = 1, 2, 3, 4$) such that the following LMI holds:*

$$\Omega = \begin{bmatrix}
\Omega_{11} & \Omega_{12} & Q_4 & 0 & P_1C & \Omega_{16} & \Omega_{17} & Q_2B & Q_2 & Q_4 & 0 & 0 \\
* & \Omega_{22} & 0 & 0 & 0 & P_1C & \Omega_{27} & Q_1B & 0 & 0 & Q_1 & 0 \\
* & * & \Omega_{33} & Q_3 & 0 & 0 & 0 & F_4S & 0 & 0 & 0 & Q_3 \\
* & * & * & -P_4 & 0 & 0 & 0 & 0 & 0 & 0 & 0 & 0 \\
* & * & * & * & -P_2 & \Omega_{56} & 0 & 0 & 0 & 0 & 0 & 0 \\
* & * & * & * & * & -P_3 & 0 & 0 & 0 & 0 & 0 & 0 \\
* & * & * & * & * & * & -R & 0 & 0 & 0 & 0 & 0 \\
* & * & * & * & * & * & * & -S & 0 & 0 & 0 & 0 \\
* & * & * & * & * & * & * & * & -P_7 & 0 & 0 & 0 \\
* & * & * & * & * & * & * & * & * & -\frac{1}{\tau}P_5 & 0 & 0 \\
* & * & * & * & * & * & * & * & * & * & -P_6 & 0 \\
* & * & * & * & * & * & * & * & * & * & * & -\frac{1}{\tau}P_5
\end{bmatrix} < 0, \quad (2)$$

where $\Omega_{11} = -P_1C - CP_1 + P_2 + \delta^2 P_3 + P_4 - Q_2C - CQ_2 - Q_4 - Q_4^T - F_3R + P_8$,
$\Omega_{12} = P_1 - F_1D + F_2H - CQ_1^T - Q_2$, $\Omega_{16} = CP_1C$, $\Omega_{17} = Q_2A + F_4R$, $\Omega_{22} = \tau P_5 - Q_1 - Q_1^T$, $\Omega_{27} = D - H + Q_1A$, $\Omega_{33} = -Q_3 - Q_3^T - F_3S$, $\Omega_{56} = -CP_1C$,
then model (1) is globally dissipative, and

$$S = \left\{ z: \quad \|z\| \leq \sqrt{\frac{u^T(P_6 + P_7)u}{\lambda_{min}(P_8)}}, \quad z \in \mathbb{R}^n \right\} \tag{3}$$

is a positive invariant and globally attractive set.

Proof. From assumption (H1), we know that

$$\int_0^{x_i(t)} (f_i(s) - F_i^- s)ds \geq 0, \quad \int_0^{x_i(t)} (F_i^+ s - f_i(s))ds \geq 0, \quad i = 1, 2, \cdots, n.$$

Let $D = \text{diag}(d_1, d_2, \cdots, d_n)$, $H = \text{diag}(h_1, h_2, \cdots, h_n)$, and consider the following Lyapunov-Krasovskii functional as

$$V(t) = V_1(t) + V_2(t) + V_3(t) + V_4(t), \tag{4}$$

where

$$V_1(t) = \left(x(t) - C \int_{t-\delta}^t x(s)ds \right)^T P_1 \left(x(t) - C \int_{t-\delta}^t x(s)ds \right), \tag{5}$$

$$V_2(t) = 2 \sum_{i=1}^n d_i \int_0^{x_i(t)} (f_i(s) - F_i^- s)ds + 2 \sum_{i=1}^n h_i \int_0^{x_i(t)} (F_i^+ s - f_i(s))ds, \tag{6}$$

$$V_3(t) = \int_{t-\delta}^t x^T(s)P_2x(s)ds + \delta \int_{-\delta}^0 \int_{t+\xi}^t x^T(s)P_3x(s)ds d\xi, \tag{7}$$

$$V_4(t) = \int_{t-\tau}^t x^T(s)P_4x(s)ds + \int_{-\tau}^0 \int_{t+\xi}^t \dot{x}^T(s)P_5\dot{x}(s)ds d\xi. \tag{8}$$

Calculating the time derivative of $V_i(t)$ $(i = 1, 2, 3, 4)$, we obtain

$$\dot{V}_1(t) = 2 \left(x(t) - C \int_{t-\delta}^t x(s)ds \right)^T P_1 \left(\dot{x}(t) - Cx(t) + Cx(t - \delta) \right), \tag{9}$$

$$\dot{V}_2(t) = 2\dot{x}^T(t)D(f(x(t)) - F_1x(t)) + 2\dot{x}^T(t)H(F_2x(t) - f(x(t)))$$
$$= 2x^T(t)(-F_1D + F_2H)\dot{x}(t) + 2\dot{x}^T(t)(D - H)f(x(t)), \tag{10}$$

$$\dot{V}_3(t) = x^T(t)(P_2 + \delta^2 P_3)x(t) - x^T(t - \delta)P_2x(t - \delta) - \delta \int_{t-\delta}^t x^T(s)P_3x(s)ds$$
$$\leq x^T(t)(P_2 + \delta^2 P_3)x(t) - x^T(t - \delta)P_2x(t - \delta)$$
$$- \left(\int_{t-\delta}^t x(s)ds \right)^T P_3 \left(\int_{t-\delta}^t x(s)ds \right), \tag{11}$$

$$\dot{V}_4(t) = x^T(t)P_4x(t) - x^T(t - \tau)P_4x(t - \tau) + \tau \dot{x}^T(t)P_5\dot{x}(t)$$
$$- \int_{t-\tau}^t \dot{x}^T(s)P_5\dot{x}(s)ds, \tag{12}$$

in deriving inequalities (11), we have made use of Lemma 1. It follows from inequalities (9)-(12) that

$$\dot{V}(t) \leq x^T(t)(-2P_1C + P_2 + \delta^2 P_3 + P_4)x(t) + 2x^T(t)(P_1 - F_1D + F_2H)\dot{x}(t)$$

$$+2x^T(t)P_1Cx(t-\delta) + 2x^T(t)CP_1C\int_{t-\delta}^{t} x(s)ds + \tau\dot{x}^T(t)P_5\dot{x}(t)$$

$$-2\dot{x}^T(t)P_1C\int_{t-\delta}^{t} x(s)ds + 2\dot{x}^T(t)(D-H)f(x(t)) - x^T(t-\delta)P_2x(t-\delta)$$

$$-2x^T(t-\delta)CP_1C\int_{t-\delta}^{t} x(s)ds - x^T(t-\tau)P_4x(t-\tau)$$

$$-\left(\int_{t-\delta}^{t} x(s)ds\right)^T P_3\left(\int_{t-\delta}^{t} x(s)ds\right) - \int_{t-\tau}^{t} \dot{x}^T(s)P_5\dot{x}(s)ds. \tag{13}$$

From model (1), we have

$$0 = 2\left(\dot{x}^T(t)Q_1 + x^T(t)Q_2\right)\left[-\dot{x}(t) - Cx(t)\right.$$

$$\left.+Af(x(t)) + Bf(x(t-\tau(t))) + u\right]$$

$$\leq x^T(t)(Q_2P_7^{-1}Q_2^T - 2Q_2C)x(t) - 2x^T(t)(CQ_1^T + Q_2)\dot{x} + 2x^T(t)Af(x(t))$$

$$+2x^T(t)Bf(x(t-\tau(t))) + \dot{x}^T(t)(Q_1P_6^{-1}Q_1^T - 2Q_1)\dot{x}$$

$$+2\dot{x}^T(t)Af(x(t)) + 2\dot{x}^T(t)Bf(x(t-\tau(t))) + u^T(P_6 + P_7)u. \tag{14}$$

By Newton-Leibniz formulation and assumption (**H2**), we have

$$0 - -2x^T(t - \tau(t))Q_3\left(x(t-\tau(t)) - x(t-\tau) - \int_{t-\tau}^{t-\tau(t)} \dot{x}(s)ds\right)$$

$$\leq -2x^T(t-\tau(t))Q_3x(t-\tau(t)) + 2x^T(t-\tau(t))Q_3x(t-\tau)$$

$$+\tau x^T(t-\tau(t))Q_3P_5^{-1}Q_3^Tx(t-\tau(t)) + \int_{t-\tau}^{t-\tau(t)} \dot{x}^T(s)P_5\dot{x}(s)ds. \tag{15}$$

and

$$0 = -2x^T(t)Q_4\left(x(t) - x(t-\tau(t)) - \int_{t-\tau(t)}^{t} \dot{x}(s)ds\right)$$

$$\leq -2x^T(t)Q_4x(t) + 2x^T(t)Q_4x(t-\tau(t))$$

$$+\tau x^T(t)Q_4P_5^{-1}Q_4^Tx(t) + \int_{t-\tau(t)}^{t} \dot{x}^T(s)P_5\dot{x}(s)ds. \tag{16}$$

In addition, for positive diagonal matrices $R > 0$ and $S > 0$, we can get from assumption (**H1**) that [13]

$$\begin{bmatrix} x(t) \\ f(x(t)) \end{bmatrix}^T \begin{bmatrix} F_3R & -F_4R \\ -F_4R & R \end{bmatrix} \begin{bmatrix} x(t) \\ f(x(t)) \end{bmatrix} \leq 0 \tag{17}$$

and

$$\begin{bmatrix} x(t-\tau(t)) \\ f(x(t-\tau(t))) \end{bmatrix}^T \begin{bmatrix} F_3 S & -F_4 S \\ -F_4 S & S \end{bmatrix} \begin{bmatrix} x(t-\tau(t)) \\ f(x(t-\tau(t))) \end{bmatrix} \leq 0. \qquad (18)$$

It follows from (13) to (18) that

$$\begin{aligned}
\dot{V}(t) \leq{}& x^T(t)\Big[-2P_1 C + P_2 + \delta^2 P_3 + P_4 + Q_2 P_7^{-1} Q_2^T - 2Q_2 C - 2Q_4 \\
&+\tau Q_4 P_5^{-1} Q_4^T - F_3 R\Big] x(t) \\
&+2x^T(t)\Big[P_1 - F_1 D + F_2 H - C Q_1^T - Q_2\Big]\dot{x}(t) + 2x^T(t)Q_4 x(t-\tau(t)) \\
&+2x^T(t)P_1 C x(t-\delta) + 2x^T(t)C P_1 C \int_{t-\delta}^{t} x(s)ds \\
&+2x^T(t)\Big[Q_2 A + F_4 R\Big]f(x(t)) + 2x^T(t)Q_2 B f(x(t-\tau(t))) \\
&+\dot{x}^T(t)\Big[\tau P_5 + Q_1 P_6^{-1} Q_1^T - 2Q_1\Big]\dot{x}(t) - 2\dot{x}^T(t)P_1 C \int_{t-\delta}^{t} x(s)ds \\
&+2\dot{x}^T(t)\Big[D - H + Q_1 A\Big]f(x(t)) + 2\dot{x}^T(t)Q_1 B f(x(t-\tau(t))) \\
&+x^T(t-\tau(t))\Big[-2Q_3 + \tau Q_3 P_5^{-1} Q_3^T - F_3 S\Big]x(t-\tau(t)) \\
&+2x^T(t-\tau(t))Q_3 x(t-\tau) + 2x^T(t-\tau(t))F_4 S f(x(t-\tau(t))) \\
&-x^T(t-\tau)P_4 x(t-\tau) - x^T(t-\delta)P_2 x(t-\delta) \\
&-2x^T(t-\delta)C P_1 C \int_{t-\delta}^{t} x(s)ds - \left(\int_{t-\delta}^{t} x(s)ds\right)^T P_3 \left(\int_{t-\delta}^{t} x(s)ds\right) \\
&-f^T(x(t))R f(x(t)) - f^T(x(t-\tau(t)))S f(x(t-\tau(t))) + u^T(P_6 + P_7)u \\
={}& -x^T(t)P_8 x(t) + u^T(P_6 + P_7)u + \xi^T(t)\Pi\xi(t), \qquad (19)
\end{aligned}$$

where

$$\xi(t) = \Big(\ x^T(t), \dot{x}^T(t), x^T(t-\tau(t)), x^T(t-\tau), x^T(t-\delta), \int_{t-\delta}^{t} x^T(s)ds, f^T(x(t)),$$

$$f^T(x(t-\tau(t)))\Big)^T,$$

$$\Pi = \begin{bmatrix}
\Pi_{11} & \Pi_{12} & Q_4 & 0 & P_1 C & C P_1 C & Q_2 A + F_4 R & Q_2 B \\
* & \Pi_{22} & 0 & 0 & 0 & P_1 C & D - H + Q_1 A & Q_1 B \\
* & * & \Pi_{33} & Q_3 & 0 & 0 & 0 & F_4 S \\
* & * & * & -P_4 & 0 & 0 & 0 & 0 \\
* & * & * & * & -P_2 & -C P_1 C & 0 & 0 \\
* & * & * & * & * & -P_3 & 0 & 0 \\
* & * & * & * & * & * & -R & 0 \\
* & * & * & * & * & * & * & -S
\end{bmatrix}$$

with $\Pi_{11} = -P_1C - CP_1 + P_2 + \delta^2 P_3 + P_4 + Q_2 P_7^{-1} Q_2^T - Q_2C - CQ_2 - Q_4 - Q_4^T + \tau Q_4 P_5^{-1} Q_4^T - F_3R + P_8$, $\Pi_{12} = P_1 - F_1D + F_2H - CQ_1^T - Q_2$, $\Pi_{22} = \tau P_5 + Q_1 P_6^{-1} Q_1^T - Q_1 - Q_1^T$, $\Pi_{33} = -Q_3 - Q_3^T + \tau Q_3 P_5^{-1} Q_3^T - F_3S$.

It is easy to verify the equivalence of $\Pi < 0$ and $\Omega < 0$ by using Lemma 2. Thus, one can derive from condition (2) and inequality (19) that

$$\dot{V}(t) \leq -x^T(t) P_8 x(t) + u^T(P_6 + P_7)u$$
$$\leq -\lambda_{min}(P_8)\|x(t)\|^2 + u^T(P_6 + P_7)u < 0, \tag{20}$$

when $x(t) \in \mathbb{R}^n \backslash S$. Therefore, neural network (1) is globally dissipative and S is an attractive set. The proof is completed.

4   Conclusions

In this paper, the global dissipativity has been investigated for neural networks with time-varying delays and leakage delay as well as generalized activation functions. By constructing appropriate Lyapunov-Krasovskii functionals and employing linear matrix inequality technique, a new delay-dependent criterion for checking the global dissipativity of the addressed neural networks has been established in terms of LMI, which can be checked numerically using the effective LMI toolbox in MATLAB.

Acknowledgments. This work was supported by the National Natural Science Foundation of China under Grants 60974132 and 11172247, and in part by the Natural Science Foundation Project of CQ CSTC2011BA6026, the Scientific & Technological Research Projects of CQ KJ110424.

References

1. Hale, J.: Asymptotic Behavior of Dissipative Systems. American Mathematical Society, New York (1989)
2. Liao, X.X., Wang, J.: Global Dissipativity of Continuous-time Recurrent Neural Networks with Time Delay. Physics Review E 68, 1–7 (2003)
3. Arik, S.: On The Global Dissipativity of Dynamical Neural Networks with Time Delays. Physics Letters A 326, 126–132 (2004)
4. Song, Q.K., Zhao, Z.J.: Global Dissipativity of Neural Networks with Both Variable and Unbounded Delays. Chaos, Solitons and Fractals 25, 393–401 (2005)
5. Lou, X.Y., Cui, B.T.: Global Robust Dissipativity for Integro-differential Systems Modeling Neural Networks with Delays. Chaos, Solitons and Fractals 36, 469–478 (2008)
6. Cao, J.D., Yuan, K., Ho, D.W.C., Lam, J.: Global Point Dissipativity of Neural Networks with Mixed Time-varying Delay. Chaos 16, 013105 (2006)
7. Song, Q.K., Cao, J.D.: Global Dissipativity Analysis on Uncertain Neural Networks with Mixed Time-varying Delays. Chaos 18, 043126 (2008)
8. Wang, G.J., Cao, J.D., Wang, L.: Global Dissipativity of Stochastic Neural Networks with Time Delay. Journal of the Franklin Institute 346, 794–807 (2009)

9. Song, Q.K.: Stochastic Dissipativity Analysis on Discrete-time Neural Networks with Time-varying Delays. Neurocomputing 74, 838–845 (2011)
10. Gopalsamy, K.: Leakage Delays in BAM. Journal of Mathematical Analysis and Applications 325, 1117–1132 (2007)
11. Li, C.D., Huang, T.W.: On The Stability of Nonlinear Systems with Leakage Delay. Journal of the Franklin Institute 346, 366–377 (2009)
12. Li, X.D., Cao, J.D.: Delay-dependent Stability of Neural Networks of Neutral Type with Time Delay in The Leakage Term. Nonlinearity 23, 1709–1726 (2010)
13. Liu, Y.R., Wang, Z.D., Liu, X.H.: Global Exponential Stability of Generalized Recurrent Neural Networks with Discrete and Distributed Delays. Neural Networks 19, 667–675 (2006)

Novel Results on Mesh Stability for a Class of Vehicle Following System with Time Delays

Qiankun Song[1] and Jiye Zhang[2]

[1] Department of Mathematics, Chongqing Jiaotong University,
Chongqing 400074, China
qiankunsong@163.com
[2] Traction Power State Key Laboratory, Southwest Jiaotong University,
Chengdu 610031, China

Abstract. In this paper, the problem on the mesh stability for a class of vehicle following system with time delays is investigated. Based on the vector Lyapunov function method and inequality technique, several criteria for checking the global exponential stability and global exponential mesh stability are obtained. An example is provided to illustrate the effectiveness of the developed theoretical results.

Keywords: Mesh stability, Vehicle following system, Infinite dimension, Time delay.

1 Introduction

In automatic vehicle following systems, vehicles are dynamically coupled by feedback control laws [1]-[5]. An important aspect of an automated highway system design is the synthesis of an automated vehicle following system. Associated with automated vehicle following system is the problem of the stability of a string of vehicle [6]. Loosely speaking, the string stability of an interconnected system implies uniform boundedness of the state of all the systems [6]-[7]. Recent years, some researches have been done on string stability for vehicle following systems [6]-[12]. It is concerned in interconnected systems that how to damp or eliminate the disturbances when they travel in the system. Intuitively, mesh stability is the property of damping disturbances as they travel away from the source in an interconnected system. In [13], authors proposed the concept of mesh stability on the base of string stability, and obtained a sufficient condition for checking the mesh stability of linear systems. In [14], the mesh stability of nonlinear interconnected system was defined, and obtained a set of sufficient conditions to mesh stability of look-ahead interconnected system. Mesh stability was shown to be robust with respect to structural and singular perturbation. Very Recently, the authors studied the global exponential mesh stability of a class of look-ahead vehicle following system [15]. However, the effect of delay on the mesh stability is not considered in [14]-[15]. It is well known that the existence of delay can causes oscillation or instability in vehicle control systems, Therefore, the study of mesh

J. Wang, G.G. Yen, and M.M. Polycarpou (Eds.): ISNN 2012, Part I, LNCS 7367, pp. 336–342, 2012.

stability for vehicle following system with time delays is of both theoretical and practical importance.

Motivated by the above discussions, the objective of this paper is to investigate the mesh stability for vehicle following system with time delays. Based on the vector Lyapunov function method and inequality technique, a criterion for checking the global mesh exponential stability is obtained. The presented condition is in terms of system parameters and have important leading significance in the design and applications of mesh stability for vehicle following system with time delays.

2   Preliminaries

In this paper, we consider the following vehicle following system with time delays

$$\begin{cases} \dot{x}_1(t) = f_1(x_1(t)), \\ \dot{x}_i(t) = f_i(x_i(t), x_{i-1}(t-\tau), \cdots, x_2(t-\tau), x_1(t-\tau)), \quad i = 2, 3, \cdots, N. \end{cases} \tag{1}$$

where $x_i(t) \in \mathbb{R}^n$, $f_i : \mathbb{R}^n \times \mathbb{R}^n \times \cdots \times \mathbb{R}^n \to \mathbb{R}^n$ and $f_i(0, 0, \cdots, 0, 0) = 0$, τ is a positive constant.

For presentation convenience, in the following, we denote

$$x = (x_1^T, x_2^T, \cdots, x_N^T)^T, \quad \|x(0)\|_\infty = \max_{1 \le i \le N} \|x_i(0)\|,$$

$$\|x(t)\|_\infty = \max_{1 \le i \le N} \|x_i(t)\|_\infty, \quad \|x(t)\|_\infty^k = \max_{i \le k} \|x_i(t)\|_\infty.$$

Definition 1. *The origin $x = 0$ of the dynamical system (1) is globally exponentially mesh stable if*
(a). all isolated subsystems are exponentially stable;
(b). $\forall \varepsilon > 0$, $\exists \delta > 0$, such that $\|x(0)\|_\infty < \delta$ implies $\|x(t)\|_\infty < \varepsilon$;
(c). $\forall i \in \{2, 3, \cdots, N\}$, $\exists \delta > 0$, $\|x_i(t)\|_\infty \le \|x(t)\|_\infty^{i-1}$.

Remark 1. The mesh stability is different from ordinary defined stabilities, which is harder in conditions. It is mainly used in error control, such as the car following systems. If the biggest error occures in the frist car, then the mesh stability will guarantee the disturbances is damped as they travel in the system, and the string will travel as expected formation.

Throughout this paper, we make the following assumptions:

(H1). For any isolated subsystem $\dot{x}_i(t) = f_i(x_i(t), 0, \cdots, 0, 0)$ of system (1), there are a C^1 function $V_i(x_i)$ and positive constants α_{1i}, α_{2i}, β_{1i} and β_{2i}, such that

$$\alpha_{1i}\|x_i(t)\|^2 \le V_i(x_i) \le \alpha_{2i}\|x_i(t)\|^2, \tag{2}$$

$$\frac{\partial V_i}{\partial x_i} f_i(x_i, 0, \cdots, 0, 0) \le -\beta_{1i}\|x_i(t)\|^2, \tag{3}$$

$$\|\frac{\partial V_i}{\partial x_i}\| \le \beta_{2i}\|x_i(t)\| \tag{4}$$

for $\forall x_i(t) \in \mathbb{R}^n$, $i \in \{1, 2, \cdots, N\}$.

(H2). For any $i \in \{1, 2, \cdots, N\}$, there exist positive constants $L_{ij}(j = 1, 2, \cdots, i)$ such that

$$\|f_i(y_i, y_{i-1}, \cdots, y_1) - f_i(z_i, z_{i-1}, \cdots, z_1)\| \leq \sum_{j=1}^{i} L_{ij} \|y_j - z_j\|. \qquad (5)$$

3   Main Results

Theorem 1. *Assume that the conditions* **(H1)** *and* **(H2)** *hold, then the interconnected system (1) is globally exponentially stable if*

$$\sum_{j=1}^{i-1} (1 + \frac{\alpha_{2i}}{\alpha_{1j}}) L_{ij} < \frac{2\beta_{1i}}{\beta_{2i}}, \quad i = 2, 3, \cdots, N. \qquad (6)$$

Proof. From assumption **(H1)**, we know that there is a C^1 function $V_i(x_i)$ and

$$\begin{aligned}
\frac{dV_i(x_i(t))}{dt} &= \frac{\partial V_i}{\partial x_i} f_i(x_i(t), x_{i-1}(t - \tau), \cdots, x_2(t - \tau), x_1(t - \tau)) \\
&= \frac{\partial V_i}{\partial x_i} f_i(x_i(t), 0, \cdots, 0) \\
&\quad + \frac{\partial V_i}{\partial x_i} \Big[f_i(x_i(t), x_{i-1}(t - \tau), \cdots, x_1(t - \tau)) - f_i(x_i(t), 0, \cdots, 0) \Big] \\
&\leq -\beta_{1i} \|x_i(t)\|^2 + \beta_{2i} \|x_i(t)\| \\
&\quad \times \|f_i(x_i(t), x_{i-1}(t - \tau), \cdots, x_1(t - \tau)) - f_i(x_i(t), 0, \cdots, 0)\|. \quad (7)
\end{aligned}$$

From assumption **(H2)** and (7), we have that

$$\frac{dV_i(x_i(t))}{dt} \leq -\beta_{1i} \|x_i(t)\|^2 + \beta_{2i} \|x_i(t)\| \sum_{j=1}^{i-1} L_{ij} \|x_j(t - \tau)\|. \qquad (8)$$

Using the inequalities $2ab \leq \frac{1}{2}(a^2 + b^2)$, we have

$$\frac{dV_i(x_i(t))}{dt} \leq -\Big[\beta_{1i} - \frac{\beta_{2i}}{2} \sum_{j=1}^{i-1} L_{ij} \Big] \|x_i(t)\|^2 + \frac{\beta_{2i}}{2} \sum_{j=1}^{i-1} L_{ij} \|x_j(t - \tau)\|^2. \qquad (9)$$

By (2) and (9), we get

$$\frac{dV_i(t)}{dt} \leq -\frac{1}{\alpha_{2i}} \Big[\beta_{1i} - \frac{\beta_{2i}}{2} \sum_{j=1}^{i-1} L_{ij} \Big] V_i(t) + \frac{\beta_{2i}}{2} \sum_{j=1}^{i-1} \frac{L_{ij}}{\alpha_{1j}} V_j(t - \tau). \qquad (10)$$

From Halanay differential inequality and (6), we know that the interconnected system (1) is globally exponentially stable. The proof is completed.

Theorem 2. *Assume that the conditions* (**H1**) *and* (**H2**) *hold, then the inter-connected system* (1) *is globally exponentially mesh stable if*

$$\sum_{j=1}^{i-1}(1+\frac{\alpha_{2j}}{\alpha_{1j}})L_{ij} \leq \frac{\beta_{1i}}{\beta_{2i}}\left(\frac{\alpha_{1i}}{\alpha_{2i}}\right)^{\frac{1}{2}}, \quad i=2,3,\cdots,N. \tag{11}$$

$$\|x_i(0)\|_\infty \leq \|x(0)\|_\infty^{i-1}, \quad i=1,2,\cdots,N. \tag{12}$$

Proof. Since $\alpha_{1i} \leq \alpha_{2i}$, from condition (11), we know that inequality (6) holds. Thus the interconnected system (1) is globally exponentially stable.

From (8), we have that

$$\frac{dV_i(x_i(t))}{dt} \leq -\|x_i(t)\|\left[\beta_{1i}\|x_i(t)\| - \beta_{2i}\sum_{j=1}^{i-1}L_{ij}\|x_j(t-\tau)\|\right]$$

$$\leq -\|x_i(t)\|\left[\beta_{1i}\|x_i(t)\| - \left(\beta_{2i}\sum_{j=1}^{i-1}L_{ij}\right)\|x\|_\infty^{i-1}\right]. \tag{13}$$

Let

$$g_i = \frac{\beta_{2i}}{\beta_{1i}}\sum_{j=1}^{i-1}(1+\frac{\alpha_{2j}}{\alpha_{1j}})L_{ij}\|x\|_\infty^{i-1}, \quad c_i = \left(\frac{\alpha_{2i}}{\alpha_{1i}}\right)^{\frac{1}{2}}. \tag{14}$$

Then $c_i \geq 1$. Define the following sets in state space:

$$B_{i1} = \{x_i : \|x_i\| \leq g_i\}, \quad B_{i2} = \{x_i : \|x_i\| \leq c_i g_i\}.$$

If $x_i \in \mathbb{R}^n \backslash B_{i1}$, then $\frac{dV_i(x_i(t))}{dt} < 0$. Thus, for any $y \in \mathbb{R}^n \backslash B_{i2}$ and $z \in B_{i1}$, we have $\|y\| > c_i g_i$ and $\|z\| \leq g_i$. Therefor, we get

$$V_i(z) \leq \alpha_{2i}\|z\|^2 \leq \alpha_{2i}g_i^2 < \frac{\alpha_{2i}}{c_i^2}\|y\|^2 = \alpha_{1i}\|y\|^2 \leq V_i(y). \tag{15}$$

In the following, we will prove that if $x_i(0) \in B_{i1}$, then for any $t \geq 0$, $x_i(t) \in B_{i2}$.

When $c_i = 1$, then $B_{i1} = B_{i2}$. Suppose that there exists t_2 such that $x_i(t_2) \in \mathbb{R}^n \backslash B_{i2}$, then there also exists t_1 $(t_1 < t_2)$ satisfying $x_i(t_1) \in \partial(B_{i2})$. For any $t \in [t_1, t_2]$, we know that $\frac{dV_i(x_i(t))}{dt} \leq 0$, thus $V_i(x_i(t_1)) \geq V_i(x_i(t_2))$, which is in contradiction with (15). So, for any $t \geq 0$, $x_i(t) \in B_{i2}$.

When $c_i > 1$, then $B_{i1} \subset B_{i2}$. Suppose that there exists t_2 such that $x_i(t_2) \in \mathbb{R}^n \backslash B_{i2}$, then there also exists t_1 $(t_1 < t_2)$ satisfying $x_i(t_1) \in B_{i1}$. For any $t \in [t_1, t_2]$, we know that $\frac{dV_i(x_i(t))}{dt} \leq 0$, thus $V_i(x_i(t_1)) \geq V_i(x_i(t_2))$, which is in contradiction with (15). So, for any $t \geq 0$, $x_i(t) \in B_{i2}$.

Therefore, if $x_i(0) \in B_{i1}$, then for any $t \geq 0$, $x_i(t) \in B_{i2}$. This implies that

$$\|x_i(t)\| \leq c_i g_i = \left(\frac{\alpha_{2i}}{\alpha_{1i}}\right)^{\frac{1}{2}}\frac{\beta_{2i}}{\beta_{1i}}\sum_{j=1}^{i-1}(1+\frac{\alpha_{2j}}{\alpha_{1j}})L_{ij}\|x\|_\infty^{i-1} \tag{16}$$

for any $t \geq 0$. By condition (11) and inequality (16), we get that

$$\|x_i(t)\| \leq \|x\|_\infty^{i-1}$$

for any $t \geq 0$. It can be seen that the interconnected system (1) is globally exponentially mesh stable. The proof is completed.

4   Example

Consider the following system:

$$\begin{cases} \ddot{x}_1(t) + 0.4\dot{x}_1(t) + 0.03x_1 = 0 \\ \ddot{x}_2(t) + 0.4\dot{x}_2(t) + 0.03x_2 - 0.2\dot{x}_1(t-1) - 0.02x_1(t-1) = 0 \\ \ddot{x}_3(t) + 0.4\dot{x}_3(t) + 0.03x_3 - 0.2\dot{x}_2(t-1) - 0.02x_2(t-1) = 0 \end{cases} \quad (17)$$

with initial conditions

$$x_1(0) = 0.6, \quad x_2(0) = 0.5, \quad x_3(0) = 0.4,$$

$$\dot{x}_1(0) = 0.1, \quad \dot{x}_2(0) = -0.2, \quad \dot{x}_3(0) = -0.3.$$

Let $y_i(t) = \dot{x}_i(t) + 0.1x_i(t)$ $(i = 1, 2, 3)$, then model (17) is rewritten as

$$\begin{cases} \dot{y}_1(t) = -0.3y_1 \\ \dot{y}_2(t) = -0.3y_2 + 0.2y_1(t-1) \\ \dot{y}_3(t) = -0.3y_3 + 0.2y_2(t-1) \end{cases} \quad (18)$$

with initial conditions

$$y_1(0) = 0.7, \quad y_2(0) = 0.3, \quad y_3(0) = 0.1,$$

then $f_1(z_1) = -0.3z_1$, $f_2(z_2, z_1) = -0.3z_2 + 0.2z_1$, $f_3(z_3, z_2, z_1) = -0.3z_3 + 0.2z_2$. It is easy to see that assumption **(H2)** is satisfied with $L_{11} = 0.3$, $L_{21} = 0.2$, $L_{22} = 0.3$, $L_{31} = 0$, $L_{32} = 0.2$, $L_{33} = 0.3$.

Taking Lyapunov functions $V_i(y_i) = y_i^2$, we can check that assumption **(H1)** holds, and $\alpha_{1i} = \alpha_{2i} = 1$, $\beta_{1i} = 6$, $\beta_{2i} = 2$.

And we can check that the conditions in Theorem 1 and Theorem 2 are also satisfied. So system (18) are globally exponentially stable and globally exponentially mesh stable. Therefore, there are positive constants $M > 0$ and $\varepsilon > 0$ such that

$$|y_i(t)| \leq Me^{-\varepsilon t}, \quad i = 1, 2, 3. \quad (19)$$

From the definitions of $y_i(t)$, we can get that

$$x_i(t) = x_i(0)e^{-0.1t} + \int_0^t y_i(s)e^{-0.1(t-s)}ds, \quad i = 1, 2, 3. \quad (20)$$

Thus,

$$|x_i(t)| - |x_{i-1}(t)| = (|x_i(0)| - |x_{i-1}(0)|)e^{-0.1t}$$
$$+ \int_0^t (|y_i(s)| - |y_{i-1}(s)|)e^{-0.1(t-s)}ds, \quad i = 1, 2, 3. \quad (21)$$

By using initial conditions of system (17) and the mesh stability of system (18), we get that

$$|x_i(t)| \le |x_{i-1}(t)|, \quad i = 2, 3. \tag{22}$$

From (19) and (20), we have that

$$|x_i(t)| = |x_i(0)|e^{-0.1t} + \int_0^t |y_i(s)|e^{-0.1(t-s)} ds$$

$$\le |x_i(0)|e^{-0.1t} + M \int_0^t e^{-\varepsilon s - 0.1(t-s)} ds, \quad i = 1, 2, 3. \tag{23}$$

If $\varepsilon \ne 0.1$, then

$$|x_i(t)| \le |x_i(0)|e^{-0.1t} + \frac{M}{|0.1 - \varepsilon|}|e^{-\varepsilon t} - e^{-0.1t}|, \quad i = 1, 2, 3, \tag{24}$$

hence, $|x_i(t)| \longrightarrow 0$ as $t \longrightarrow +\infty$.
If $\varepsilon = 0.1$, then

$$|x_i(t)| \le |x_i(0)|e^{-0.1t} + Mte^{-0.1t}, \quad i = 1, 2, 3, \tag{25}$$

hence, $|x_i(t)| \longrightarrow 0$ as $t \longrightarrow +\infty$. So system (17) is globally exponentially mesh stable.

5   Conclusions

In this paper, the global exponential stability and global exponential mesh stability for a class of vehicle following system with time delays have been investigated. Based on the vector Lyapunov function method and inequality technique, several criteria for checking the global exponential stability and global exponential mesh stability have been obtained. An example has been given to verify the theoretical results.

Acknowledgments. This work was supported by the National Natural Science Foundation of China under Grants 60974132 and 11172247, and in part by the Natural Science Foundation Project of CQ CSTC2011BA6026, the Scientific & Technological Research Projects of CQ KJ110424.

References

1. Caudill, R.E., Garrard, W.L.: Vehicle Follower Longitudinal Control for Automated Transit Vehicles. Journal of Dynamic System, Measurements and Control 99, 241–248 (1977)
2. Fenton, B.J.: An Overview of Systems Studies of Automated Highway Systems. IEEE Transactions on Vehicular Technology 40, 82–99 (1991)
3. Hedrick, J.K., Swaroop, D.: Dynamic Coupling in Vehicles under Automatic Control. Vehicle System Dynamics 23, 209–217 (1994)

4. Barbieri, E.: Stability Analysis of A Class of Interconnected Systems. Journal of Dynamic System Measurements Control 115, 546–551 (1993)
5. Shladover, S.E.: Review of the State of Development of Advanced Vehicle Control Systems(AVCS). Vehicle System Dynamics 24, 551–595 (1995)
6. Swaroop, D., Hedrick, J.K.: String Stability for A Class of Nonlinear Systems. IEEE Transactions on Automatic Control 41, 349–357 (1996)
7. Eyre, J.: A Simplified Framework for String Stability Analysis of Automated Vehicle. Vehicle System Dynamics 30, 375–405 (1998)
8. Zhang, J.Y., Yang, Y.R., Zeng, J.: String Stability of Infinite Interconnected System. Applied Mathematics and Mechanics 21, 715–719 (2000)
9. Socha, L.: Stochastic Stability of Interconnected String Systems. Chaos, Solitons and Fractals 19, 949–955 (2004)
10. Zhang, J.Y., Suda, Y., Iwasa, T., Komine, H.: Vector Liapunov Function Approach to Longitudinal Control of Vehicles in A Platoon. JSME International Journal(Series C) 47, 653–658 (2004)
11. Ren, D.B., Zhang, J.Y., Sun, L.F.: Stability Analysis of Vehicle Following System with Delays Based on Vector Liapunov Function. Journal of Traffic and Transportation Engineering 7, 89–92 (2007)
12. Shi, J.Z., Zhang, J.Y., Xu, X.H.: String Stability of Stochastic Interconnected Systems with Time Delays. Acta Automatica Sinica 36, 1744–1751 (2010)
13. Seiler, P., Pant, A., Hedrick, J.K.: Preliminary Investigation of Mesh Stability for Linear Systems. IMECE99/DSC-7B-1 (1999)
14. Pant, A., Seiler, P., Hedrick, K.: Mesh Stability of Look-Ahead Interconnected Systems. IEEE Transactions on Automatic Control 47, 403–407 (2002)
15. Cao, Z.L., Li, T., Zhang, J.Y.: Mesh Exponential Stability of Look-Ahead Interconnected System. Applied Mechanics and Materials 29-32, 847–850 (2010)

Robust Stability Analysis of Fuzzy Cohen-Grossberg Neural Networks with Mixed Time-Varying Delay[*]

Yougang Wang and Deyou Liu

College of Science, Yanshan University, Qinhuangdao, 066004, China
wangyougang1234@126.com

Abstract. In this paper, based on the ideas of T-S fuzzy, the T-S fuzzy Cohen-Grossberg neural network model with mixed time-varying is presented. By using Lyapunov functional approach, some sufficient conditions are obtained to guarantee the T-S fuzzy Cohen-Grossberg neural networks to be globally asymptotically stable for all admissible parametric uncertainties. A numerical example is provided to illustrate the usefulness of the theoretical result.

Keywords: Cohen-Grossberg neural networks, Mixed time-varying delays, Global robust asymptotic stability, T-S fuzzy model, Lyapunov functional, Linear matrix inequality.

1   Introduction

In recent years, neural networks have received increasing interest due to their wide range of applications in many scientific fields, for example, information processing, pattern recognition, associative memory and optimization calculation. In applications of neural networks, network stability is a prerequisite for the application of them. Therefore, the stability system has received great attention of researchers in and abroad, sees, e.g. [1-12]. The Cohen-Grossberg neural network is a very important class neural network, which has attracted increasing interest ever since it was proposed and studied in 1983 by Cohen and Grossberg in [1].The stability problems have been studied in these recent publications see, e.g. [2-7] [8-10]. In [8], by using Lyapunov functional and LMI approach, the stability for Cohen-Grossberg neural network with discrete and distributed time delays was analyzed.

In hardware implementation of the neural networks, due to unavoidable factors, such as modeling error, external perturbation and parameter fluctuation, the neural networks model certainly involve uncertainties such as perturbations and component variations, which will change the stability of neural networks. These parameter uncertainties of neural networks require analyzing the robust stability of neural

---

[*] This work was supported by the Natural Science Foundation of Hebei Province of China (A2011203103) and the Hebei Province Education Foundation of China (2009157).

J. Wang, G.G. Yen, and M.M. Polycarpou (Eds.): ISNN 2012, Part I, LNCS 7367, pp. 343–351, 2012.

networks. Under parameter uncertainties, stability criteria obtained is expressed by using strict LMIs, which can be easily checked.

Motivated by the above discussion, combing the theories of T-S systems and Cohen-Grossberg neural network with time delays, the fuzzy Cohen-Grossberg neural networks with mixed time-varying delays is proposed. To the best of our knowledge, up to now, there are a few researchers to deal with the stability of the fuzzy Cohen-Grossberg neural networks. The purpose of this paper is to prove the global asymptotic stability for the fuzzy Cohen-Grossberg neural networks with mixed time-varying delays by constructing a suitable Lyapunov functional and LMI approach. The provided results are new and extend the existing results.

The rest of this paper is organized as follows. In Section 2, the model description and some preliminaries are introduced. Some sufficient conditions will be derived by combining the Lyapunov-Krasovskii approach with the LIMs technique in Section 3. A numerical example will be presented to demonstrate our proposed in Section 4.Fina -lly in Section 5, we will give some conclusions of the results.

Notation: Throughout this paper, we denote A^T and A^{-1} the transpose and the inverse of any square matrix A. We use $A > 0 (A < 0)$ to denote a positive (negative) definite matrix A ; and I (respectively, 0) denote the identity matrix (respectively, zero matrix) of appropriate dimension. R denotes the set of real numbers; R^n denotes the n – dimensional Euclidean space; $R^{m \times n}$ denotes the set of all $m \times n$ real matrices; and $diag(\cdot)$ denotes a block diagonal matrix. The symbol $*$ within the matrix represents the symmetric term of the matrix.

2   Model Description and Preliminaries

The Cohen-Grossberg neural networks with mixed time-varying delays can be described by the following delay differential equations:

$$\frac{dx}{dt} = -a(x(t))[b(x(t)) - A\overline{g}(x(t)) - B\overline{g}(x(t - \tau(t))) - C\int_{t-d(t)}^{t} \overline{f}(x(s))ds + I] \qquad (1)$$

Where $x(t)$ corresponds to the state of the ith unit at time t . $A \in R^{n \times n}, B \in R^{n \times n}$ and $C \in R^{n \times n}$ denote the connection weight matrix, the discrete and distributively delayed connection weight matrix. $\tau(t)$ and $d(t)$ are the time varying delays, $\tau(t)$ and $d(t)$ are nonnegative, bounded and differentiable functions and satisfied ($0 \le \tau(t) \le \tau_m$, $\dot{\tau}(t) \le \tau < 1$, $0 \le d(t) \le d_m$, $\dot{d}(t) \le d < 1$)(a), $I = [I_1, I_2, ..., I_n]$ is a constant vector and denotes the external input.

It is well known that bounded activation functions always guarantee the existence of an equilibrium point for neural networks (1). For notational convenience, we shift the equilibrium $x^* = [x_1^*, x_2^*, \cdots, x_n^*]^T$ to the origin by transformation $u(t) = x(t) - x^*$, which yields the following system:

$$\frac{du}{dt} = -\alpha(u(t))[\beta(u(t)) - Af(u(t)) - Bf(u(t - \tau(t))) - C\int_{t-d(t)}^{t} g(u(s))ds] \tag{2}$$

Where $f(u(t)) = (f_1(u_1(t)), \cdots, f_n(u_n(t)))^T$, $g(u(t)) = (g_1(u_1(t)), \cdots, g_n(u_n(t)))^T$

$f_i(u_i(t)) = \overline{g}(u_i(t) + x_i^*) - \overline{g}(x_i^*), g_i(u_i(t)) = \overline{f}(u_i(t) + x_i^*) - \overline{f}(x_i^*).$

Plant Rule k

IF { $u_1(t)$ and $v_1(t)$ are η_1^k } and $\cdots$ and { $u_p(t)$ and $v_p(t)$ are η_p^k }

THEN

$$\frac{du}{dt} = -\alpha(u(t))[\beta(u(t)) - (A_k + \Delta A_k)f(u(t)) - (B_k + \Delta B_k)f(u(t - \tau(t)))$$
$$- (C_k + \Delta C_k)\int_{t-d(t)}^{t} g(u(s))ds] \tag{3}$$

Where η_i^k $(i = 1, 2, \ldots, p, k = 1, 2, \cdots, r)$ are fuzzy sets $(u_1(t), u_2(t)), \ldots, u_p(t), v_1(t),$

$v_2(t), \ldots, v_p(t)$) is the premise vector, r is the number of IF-THEN rules.

Let $\mu_k(t)$ be the normalized membership function of the inferred fuzzy set $M_k(t)$,

i.e.

$$\mu_k(t) = \frac{M_k(t)}{\sum_{k=1}^{r} M_k(t)}, M_k(t) = \prod_{l=1}^{p} \eta_l^k(z_l(t)) \tag{4}$$

Where $\eta_i^k(z_i(t))$ is the grade membership of $z_i(t)$ in η_i^k. It is assumed that

$$M_k(t) \geq 0, k = 1, 2, \ldots, r, \sum_{k=1}^{r} M_k(t) > 0, \mu_k(t) \geq 0, k = 1, 2, \ldots, r, \sum_{k=1}^{r} \mu_k(t) = 1 \tag{5}$$

for all t. Therefore, it implies

$$\frac{du}{dt} = \sum_{k=1}^{r} \mu_k(t)\{-\alpha(u(t))[\beta(u(t)) - \overline{A}_k f(u(t)) - \overline{B}_k f(u(t - \tau(t))) - \overline{C}_k \int_{t-d(t)}^{t} g(u(s))ds]\} \tag{6}$$

Where $\overline{A}_k = A_k + \Delta A_k, \overline{B}_k = B_k + \Delta B_k$, and $\overline{C}_k = C_k + \Delta C_k$, ΔA_k, ΔB_k, ΔC_k denote the time-varying parameter uncertainties.

Throughout this paper, we have the following assumptions.

(H1). There exists positive diagonal matrix $L = diag(l_1, l_2, \cdots, l_n) > 0$ and, $K = diag(k_1,$ $k_2, \cdots, k_n)$, such that the activation $f_i(\cdot)$ and $g_i(\cdot)$ satisfy:

$$|f_i(x) - f_i(y)| \leq l_i|x - y|, |g_i(x) - g_i(y)| \leq k_i|x - y| \tag{7}$$

for all $x, y \in R, i = 1, 2, \cdots, n$.

(H2). The parametric uncertainties $\Delta A_k, \Delta B_k$, and ΔC_k are unknown, but norm bounded. The uncertainties are of the following form:

$$\begin{bmatrix} \Delta A_k & \Delta B_k & \Delta C_k \end{bmatrix} = M_k F(t) \begin{bmatrix} E_k^A & E_k^B & E_k^C \end{bmatrix} \tag{8}$$

in which E_k^A, E_k^B, E_k^C and M_k are known real constant matrices with appropriate dimensions. The uncertain matrix $F(t)$ satisfies $F^T(t)F(t) \leq I$ for $\forall t \in R$, where I is the identity matrix of appropriate dimension.

To give our main results in the next section, we need the following lemmas.

Lemma 1 (Schur Complement [12]): For a given matrix

$$S = \begin{bmatrix} s_{11} & s_{12} \\ s_{12}^T & s_{22} \end{bmatrix} < 0 \tag{9}$$

Where $s_{11} = s_{11}^T, s_{22} = s_{22}^T$ is equivalent to any one of the following conditions•

(1) $s_{22} < 0, s_{11} - s_{12} s_{22}^{-1} s_{12}^T < 0$,   (2) $s_{11} < 0, s_{22} - s_{12}^T s_{11}^{-1} s_{12} < 0$ $\tag{10}$

Lemma 2 (Jensen's Inequality [13]): For any constant matrix $V \in R^{m \times m}, V > 0$, scalar $0 < r(t) < r$, vector function v $[0, r] \to R^m$ such that the integrations concerned are well defined, then

$$r(t) \int_0^{r(t)} v^T(s) V v(s) ds \geq \left(\int_0^{r(t)} v(s) ds \right)^T V \left(\int_0^{r(t)} v(s) ds \right) \tag{11}$$

Lemma 3 ([14]): If U, V , and W are real matrices of appropriate dimension with M satisfying $M = M^T$, then

$$M + UVW + W^T V^T U^T < 0 \tag{12}$$

for all $V^T V \leq I$, if and only if there exists a positive constant ε such that

$$M + \varepsilon^{-1} U U^T + \varepsilon W^T W < 0 \tag{13}$$

3   Main Result

In this section, we will discuss the global robust asymptotic stability for fuzzy Cohen-Grossberg neural networks (6) under T-S fuzzy rule. Sufficient conditions are derived by means of an appropriate Lyapunov-Krasovskii function. Stability criteria obtained here are expressed by using strict LMIs, which can be easily checked in practice.

Theorem 1. Under the assumptions (H1) and (H2), the origin of the T-S fuzzy neural networks system (6) is globally asymptotically stable if there exist appropriately dimension matrices, $P = diag(p_1, \cdots, p_n) > 0$, $Q_i = Q_i^T > 0, i = 1, 2, 3$, $\Gamma = diag(\gamma_1, \cdots \gamma_n) > 0$, $H = diag(h_1, h_2, \cdots, h_n) > 0$, $\varepsilon_i > 0, (i = 1, \cdots, 6)$ such that the following conditions hold for $k = 1, 2, \cdots, r$ .Let $\pi = P - \Gamma H$

$$\Sigma_k = \begin{bmatrix} \Phi_{11} & \Phi_{12} & \Phi_{13} & 0 & PC_k - \Gamma H & \pi M_k \\ * & \Phi_{22} & HB_k & 0 & HC_k & 0 \\ * & * & \Phi_{33} & 0 & 0 & 0 \\ * & * & * & \Phi_{44} & 0 & 0 \\ * & * & * & * & \Phi_{55} & 0 \\ * & * & * & * & * & \Phi_{66} \end{bmatrix} < 0 \qquad (14)$$

$\Phi_{11} = -2P - 2\Gamma HA_k L + 2PA_k L + L^T (\tau_m Q_1 + Q_2)L + d_m K^T Q_2 K, +\varepsilon_1 (E_k^A L)^T E_k^A L$

$\Phi_{12} = L^T A_k^T H^T + \Gamma H$, $\Phi_{13} = \phi_{13}$, $\Phi_{22} = \phi_{22} + \varepsilon_2 (E_k^A)^T E_k^A + (\varepsilon_5^{-1} + \varepsilon_6^{-1}) M_k^T M_k$,

$\Phi_{33} = PB_k - \Gamma HB_k + (\varepsilon_3 + \varepsilon_5)(E_k^B)^T E_k^B$, $\Phi_{44} = \phi_{44}$, $\Phi_{55} = \phi_{55} + (\varepsilon_4 + \varepsilon_6)(E_k^C)^T E_k^C$,

$\Phi_{66} = -(\varepsilon_1^{-1} + \varepsilon_3^{-1} + \varepsilon_4^{-1})I$.

Proof: We use the following Lyapunov functional to derive the stability result:

$$V(t) = V_1(t) + V_2(t) + V_3(t)$$

$$V_1 = \sum_{i=1}^{n} 2 p_i \int_0^{u_i(t)} \frac{s}{\alpha_i(s)} ds + \sum_{j=1}^{n} 2 h \int_0^{u_j(t)} \frac{\beta_j(s) - \gamma_j s}{\alpha_i(s)} ds \qquad (15)$$

$$V_2 = \int_{-\tau(t)}^0 \int_{t+\theta}^t f^T(u(s))Q_1 f(u(s)) ds d\theta + \int_{-d(t)}^0 \int_{t+\theta}^t g^T(u(s))Q_2 g(u(s)) ds d\theta$$

$$V_3 = \int_{t-\tau(t)}^t f^T(u(s))Q_3 f(u(s)) ds$$

Using Jensen's Inequality and (7), we have:

$$|f(u(t))| \le L|u(t)|, |g(u(t))| \le K|u(t)| \qquad (16)$$

$$-\int_{t-\tau(t)}^t f^T(u(s))Q_1 f(u(s)) \le -\tau_m^{-1} \left(\int_{t-\tau(t)}^t f(u(s))ds \right)^T Q_1 \left(\int_{t-\tau(t)}^t f(u(s))ds \right) \qquad (17)$$

$$-\int_{t-d(t)}^t g^T(u(s))Q_2 g(u(s)) \le -d_m^{-1} \left(\int_{t-d(t)}^t g(u(s))ds \right)^T Q_2 \left(\int_{t-d(t)}^t g(u(s))ds \right)$$

Calculating the derivative of $V(t)$ along the trajectories of the system (6) and applying (a), (15), (16) and (17). Finally, we have

$$\dot{V}(t) \le \sum_{k=1}^{r} \mu_k(t)\{u^T(t)[-2P-2\Gamma H\bar{A}_k L+2P\bar{A}_k L+L^T(\tau_m Q_1+Q_3)L+d_m K^T Q_2 K]u(t)$$

$$-\beta^T(u(t))2H\beta(u(t))-f^T(u(t-\tau(t)))(1-\tau)\,Q_3 f(u(t-\tau(t)))$$

$$-\left(\int_{t-\tau(t)}^t f(u(s))ds\right)^T (1-\tau)\tau_m^{-1}Q_1\left(\int_{t-\tau(t)}^t f(u(s))ds\right)$$

$$-\left(\int_{t-d(t)}^t g(u(s))ds\right)^T (1-d)d_m^{-1}Q_2\left(\int_{t-d(t)}^t g(u(s))ds\right)$$

$$+2u^T(t)(L^T\bar{A}_k^T H^T+\Gamma H)\beta(u(t))+2u^T(P\bar{B}_k-\Gamma H\bar{B}_k)f(u(t-\tau(t)))$$

$$+2u^T(t)(P\bar{C}_k-\Gamma H\bar{C}_k)\int_{t-d(t)}^t g(u(s))ds+2\beta^T(u(t))H\bar{B}_k f(u(t-\tau(t)))$$

$$+2\beta^T(u(t))H\bar{C}_k\int_{t-d(t)}^t g(u(s))ds\}=\sum_{k=1}^{r}\mu_k(t)(\varsigma(t)\Omega\varsigma^T(t)\le 0$$

Where

$$\varsigma(t)=\left[u^T(t) \quad \beta^T(u(t)) \quad f^T(u(t-\tau(t))) \quad \left(\int_{t-\tau(t)}^t f(u(s))ds\right)^T \quad \left(\int_{t-d(t)}^t g(u(s))ds\right)^T\right]^T \tag{18}$$

And

$$\bar{\Sigma}_k = \begin{bmatrix} \phi_{11} & \phi_{12} & \phi_{13} & 0 & P\bar{C}_k-\Gamma H \\ * & \phi_{22} & H\bar{B}_k & 0 & H\bar{C}_k \\ * & * & \phi_{33} & 0 & 0 \\ * & * & * & \phi_{44} & 0 \\ * & * & * & * & \phi_{55} \end{bmatrix} < 0 \tag{19}$$

$\phi_{11}=-2P-2\Gamma H\bar{A}_k L+2P\bar{A}_k L+L^T(\tau_m Q_1+Q_2)L+d_m K^T Q_2 K$, $\phi_{12}=L^T\bar{A}_k^T H^T+\Gamma H$, $\phi_{13}=P\bar{B}_k-\Gamma H\bar{B}_k$, $\phi_{22}=-2H$, $\phi_{44}=-(1-\tau)\tau_m^{-1}Q_1$, $\phi_{33}=-(1-\tau)Q_3$, $\phi_{55}=-(1-d)d_m^{-1}Q_2$

From the negative definiteness of $\bar{\Sigma}_k$, we known the trivial solution of (6) is globally asymptotically stable.

Next we prove the equivalence of conditions (19) and (14).From conditions in (H2) and (12), (13), $\bar{\Sigma}_k$ can be rewritten as

$$\overline{\Sigma}_k \leq \begin{bmatrix} \varphi_{11} & \varphi_{12} & \varphi_{13} & 0 & PC_k - \Gamma H \\ * & \varphi_{22} & HB_k & 0 & HC_k \\ * & * & \varphi_{33} & 0 & 0 \\ * & * & * & \varphi_{44} & 0 \\ * & * & * & * & \varphi_{55} \end{bmatrix} \tag{20}$$

$$+\varepsilon_1^{-1}\Omega_0\Omega_0^T + \varepsilon_1\Omega_1\Omega_1^T + \varepsilon_2^{-1}\Omega_5\Omega_5^T + \varepsilon_2\Omega_2\Omega_2^T + \varepsilon_3^{-1}\Omega_0\Omega_0^T + \varepsilon_3\Omega_3\Omega_3^T$$
$$+\varepsilon_4^{-1}\Omega_0\Omega_0^T + \varepsilon_4\Omega_4\Omega_4^T + \varepsilon_5^{-1}\Omega_6\Omega_6^T + \varepsilon_5\Omega_3\Omega_3^T + \varepsilon_6^{-1}\Omega_6\Omega_6^T + \varepsilon_6\Omega_4\Omega_4^T$$

Where $\Omega_0 = \begin{bmatrix} M_k^T\pi & 0 & 0 & 0 & 0 \end{bmatrix}^T$, $\Omega_1 = \begin{bmatrix} E_k^A L & 0 & 0 & 0 & 0 \end{bmatrix}^T$,

$\Omega_2 = \begin{bmatrix} 0 & E_k^A & 0 & 0 & 0 \end{bmatrix}^T$, $\Omega_3 = \begin{bmatrix} 0 & 0 & E_k^B & 0 & 0 \end{bmatrix}^T$, $\Omega_4 = \begin{bmatrix} 0 & 0 & 0 & 0 & E_k^C \end{bmatrix}^T$,

$\Omega_5 = \begin{bmatrix} M_k^T L & 0 & 0 & 0 & 0 \end{bmatrix}^T$, $\Omega_6 = \begin{bmatrix} 0 & HM_k^T & 0 & 0 & 0 \end{bmatrix}^T$. $\phi_{13} = PB_k - \Gamma HB_k$

$\phi_{11} = -2P - 2\Gamma HA_k L + 2PA_k L + L^T(\tau_m Q_1 + Q_2)L + d_m K^T Q_2 K$, $\phi_{12} = L^T A_k^T H^T + \Gamma H$

Rearranging (20), we have:

$$\Theta = \begin{bmatrix} \Psi_{11} & \Phi_{12} & \Phi_{13} & 0 & PC_k - \Gamma H \\ * & \Phi_{22} & HB_k & 0 & HC_k \\ * & * & \Phi_{33} & 0 & 0 \\ * & * & * & \Phi_{44} & 0 \\ * & * & * & * & \Phi_{55} \end{bmatrix} < 0 \tag{21}$$

Where $\Psi_{11} = \varphi_{11} + \varepsilon_1(E_k^A L)^T E_k^A L + \varepsilon_2^{-1} L M_k M_k^T L + (\varepsilon_1^{-1} + \varepsilon_3^{-1} + \varepsilon_4^{-1})\pi M_k M_k^T \pi$.

By Lemma 1, (21) is equivalent to (14). Thus we conclude that the equilibrium point of system (6) is globally asymptotically stable. This completes the proof of Theorem 1.

Remark. When $r = 1$, system (6) is simplified to the general Cohen-Grossberg neural networks with mixed time delays and uncertainties. Recently, the authors of [2], [3], [5], [7] have been studied the Cohen-Grossberg neural networks with mixed time delays. Thus our results make more general case of those results in the literature.

4   An Illustrative Example

In this section, we give an example to illustrate the proposed stability criterion. Consider the plant rule for $r = 2$. The T-S fuzzy Cohen-Grossberg neural networks with mixed time-varying delays is of the following form:

Plant Rules:
Rule1: IF { $u_1(t)$ and $v_1(t)$ are η^1 }, **THEN**

$$\frac{du}{dt} = -\alpha(u(t))[\beta(u(t))-(A_1+\Delta A_1)f(u(t))-(B_1+\Delta B_1)f(u(t-\tau(t)))$$

$$-(C_1+\Delta C_1)\int_{t-d(t)}^{t}g(u(s))ds] \tag{22}$$

Rule2: IF { $u_2(t)$ and $v_2(t)$ are η^2 }, **THEN**

$$\frac{du}{dt} = -\alpha(u(t))[\beta(u(t))-(A_2+\Delta A_2)f(u(t))-(B_2+\Delta B_2)f(u(t-\tau(t)))$$

$$-(C_2+\Delta C_2)\int_{t-d(t)}^{t}g(u(s))ds] \tag{23}$$

With $f(x)=\tanh(x), g(x)=\tanh(x), b(x)=x$, $\tau=0.5, d=0.5, \tau_m=1, d_m=1$ .The
memberships functions for Rule 1 and Rule 2 are $\eta^1=1/e^{-2u_1(t)}$, $\eta^2=1-\eta^1$.

$$A_1=\begin{bmatrix}0.2 & 0 \\ 0 & 0.1\end{bmatrix} B_1=\begin{bmatrix}0.1 & 0.1 \\ 0.3 & 0.2\end{bmatrix} C_1=\begin{bmatrix}0.1 & 0.4 \\ 0.5 & 0.2\end{bmatrix} A_2=\begin{bmatrix}0.4 & 0 \\ 0 & 0.3\end{bmatrix} B_2=\begin{bmatrix}0.3 & 0.1 \\ 0.4 & 0.2\end{bmatrix}$$

$$C_2=\begin{bmatrix}0.3 & 0.1 \\ 0.6 & 0.2\end{bmatrix} L=\begin{bmatrix}0.5 & 0 \\ 0 & 0.5\end{bmatrix} K=\begin{bmatrix}0.6 & 0 \\ 0 & 0.6\end{bmatrix} M_k=\begin{bmatrix}0.2 & 0 \\ 0 & 0.2\end{bmatrix} I=\begin{bmatrix}1 & 0 \\ 0 & 1\end{bmatrix}$$

$$E_k^A=\begin{bmatrix}0.5 & 0.5\end{bmatrix} E_k^B=\begin{bmatrix}0.2 & 0.2\end{bmatrix} E_k^C=\begin{bmatrix}0.3 & 0.3\end{bmatrix}.$$

By using the Matlab LMI toolbox, we solve the LMI (14), a feasible solution is

$$P=\begin{bmatrix}305.2278 & 0 \\ 0 & 297.6336\end{bmatrix}, Q_1=\begin{bmatrix}303.0784 & 5.1611 \\ -501611 & 302.4519\end{bmatrix}, Q_2=\begin{bmatrix}336.1400 & 3.5941 \\ 3.5941 & 336.4772\end{bmatrix}$$

$$Q_3=\begin{bmatrix}416.4329 & 24.7841 \\ 24.7841 & 419.1993\end{bmatrix}, \Gamma=\begin{bmatrix}302.7188 & 0 \\ 0 & 302.7188\end{bmatrix}, H=\begin{bmatrix}30.9333 & 0 \\ 0 & 31.1908\end{bmatrix}$$

$\varepsilon_1=297.6046, \varepsilon_2=268.3142, \varepsilon_3=287.1995, \varepsilon_4=298.1409, \varepsilon_5=287.1955,$

$\varepsilon_6=298.1409$.

This implies that the conditions of Theorem 1 are satisfied. Therefore the T-S fuzzy
neural networks system (6) is globally asymptotically stable for all admissible
uncertainties.

5   Conclusion

In this paper, fuzzy Cohen-Grossberg neural networks with mixed time-varying delays has been proposed by combining the theory of T-S fuzzy model and Cohen-Grossberg neural networks, several conditions expressed in the form of LMI for the robust stability of the fuzzy Cohen-Grossberg neural networks with mixed time-varying delays have been obtained. An illustrative example has been also given to demonstrate the effectiveness of the results.

References

1. Cohen, M.A., Grossberg, S.: Absolute stability and global pattern formation and parallel memory storage by competitive neural networks. IEEE Trans. Syst., Man, Cybern. 13, 815–826 (1983)
2. Lu, K., Xu, D., Yang, Z.: Global attraction and stability for Cohen-Grossberg neural networks with time delays. Neural Netw. 19, 1538–1549 (2006)
3. Yuan, K., Cao, J.: An analysis of global asymptotic stability of delayed Cohen–Grossberg neural networks via nonsmooth analysis. IEEE Trans. Circuits Syst. I, Reg. Papers 52, 1854–1861 (2005)
4. Huang, H., Qu, Y., Li, H.: Robust stability analysis of switched Hopfield neural networks with time-varying delay under uncertainty. Phys. Lett. A 345, 345–354 (2005)
5. Lu, W., Chen, T.: New conditions on global stability of Cohen–Grossberg neural networks. Neural Comput. 15, 1173–1189 (2003)
6. Cao, J., Song, Q.: Stability in Cohen-Grossberg type BAM neural networks with time-varying delays. Nonlinearity 19, 1601–1617 (2006)
7. Cao, J., Li, X.: Stability in delayed Cohen–Grossberg neural networks. LMI Optimization Approach Physica D 54–65 (2005)
8. Li, T., Fei, S., Guo, Y., Zhu, Q.: Stability analysis on Cohen-Grossberg neural networks with both time-varying and continuously distributed delays. Nonlinear Anal., Real Word Appl. 10, 2600–2612 (2009)
9. Huang, T.W.: Exponential stability of fuzzy cellular neural networks with distributed delay. Phys. Lett. A 351, 48–52 (2006)
10. Zhang, Y., Heng, P.A.: Stability of fuzzy control systems with bounded uncertain delays. IEEE Trans. Fuzzy Systems 10, 92–97 (2002)
11. Lou, X., Cui, B.: Robust asymptotic stability of uncertain fuzzy BAM neural networks with time-varying delays. Fuzzy Sets and Systems 158, 2746–2756 (2007)
12. Boyd, S., El Ghaoui, L., Feron, E., Balakrishnan, V.: Linear Matrix Inequalities in System and Control Theory. SIAM, Philadephia (1994)
13. Gu, K., Kharitonov, V., Chen, J.: Stability of Time-Delay Systems. Birkhäuser, Boston (2003)
14. Xie, L.: Output feedback H∞ control of systems with parameter uncertainty. Int. J. Control 63, 741–750 (1996)

Adaptive Stochastic Robust Convergence of Neutral-Type Neural Networks with Markovian Jump Parameters

Cheng-De Zheng[1], Chao-Ke Gong[1], and Zhanshan Wang[2]

[1] School of Science, Dalian Jiaotong University, Dalian, 116028, P.R. China
{chd4211853,chaoke886}@163.com
[2] School of Information Science and Engineering, Northeastern University,
Shenyang, 110004, P.R. China
zhanshan_wang@163.com

Abstract. The adaptive stochastic robust convergence and stability in mean square are investigated for a class of uncertain neutral-type neural networks with both Markovian jump parameters and mixed delays. The mixed delays consists of discrete and distributed time-varying delays. First, by employing the Lyapunov method and a generalized Halanay-type inequality, a delay-independent condition is derived to guarantee the state variables of the discussed neural networks to be globally uniformly exponentially stochastic convergent to a ball in the state space with a pre-specified convergence rate. Next, by applying the Jensen integral inequality and a novel Lemma, a delay-dependent criterion is developed to achieve the globally stochastic robust stability in mean square. The proposed conditions are all in terms of linear matrix inequalities, which can be solved numerically by employing the LMI toolbox in Matlab.

Keywords: Lyapunov method, adaptive robust convergence, robust stability in mean square, Markovian jump.

1 Problem Description and Preliminaries

Consider the following uncertain neutral-type neural networks with both Markovian jump parameters and mixed delays:

$$\dot{u}(t) = - D(t, \eta(t))u(t) + A(t, \eta(t))f(u(t)) + B(t, \eta(t))f(u(t - \tau(t, \eta(t))))$$

$$+ C(t, \eta(t)) \int_{t-\sigma(t,\eta(t))}^{t} f(u(s))\mathrm{d}s + L(t, \eta(t))\dot{u}(t - \omega(t, \eta(t))) + \phi(t, \eta(t)),$$

$$u(t) = \varphi(t), \qquad t \in [-\check{\tau}, 0], \qquad (1)$$

where $u(t) = [u_1(t), u_2(t), ..., u_n(t)]^T \in \mathbb{R}^n$ is the state vector associated with the neurons, the positive diagonal matrix $D(t, \eta(t)) = D(\eta(t)) + \Delta D(t, \eta(t))$ is the self-feedback term, $A(t, \eta(t)) = A(\eta(t)) + \Delta A(t, \eta(t)), B(t, \eta(t)) = B(\eta(t)) + \Delta B(t, \eta(t)), C(t, \eta(t)) = C(\eta(t)) + \Delta C(t, \eta(t)), L(t, \eta(t)) = L(\eta(t)) + \Delta L(t, \eta(t))$

J. Wang, G.G. Yen, and M.M. Polycarpou (Eds.): ISNN 2012, Part I, LNCS 7367, pp. 352–360, 2012.

are the interconnection matrices representing the weight coefficients of the neurons. $D(\eta(t))$ is a known positive diagonal matrix, $A(\eta(t)), B(\eta(t)), C(\eta(t)),$ $L(\eta(t))$ are known real constant matrices. $\Delta D(t, \eta(t)), \Delta A(t, \eta(t)),$ $\Delta B(t, \eta(t)), \Delta C(t, \eta(t)), \Delta L(t, \eta(t))$ are the time-varying structured uncertainties. $f(u(t)) = [f_1(u_1(t)), \ f_2(u_2(t)), ..., f_n(u_n(t))]^T \in \mathbb{R}^n$ denotes the neural activation function. The bounded function $\tau(t, \eta(t)), \sigma(t, \eta(t)), \omega(t, \eta(t))$ represents unknown time-varying delays with $0 \leq \tau(t, \eta(t)) \leq \bar{\tau}(\eta(t)) \leq \bar{\tau}, \dot{\tau}(t, \eta(t)) \leq$ $\tau_d(\eta(t)) \leq \tau_d, 0 \leq \sigma(t, \eta(t)) \leq \bar{\sigma}(\eta(t)) \leq \bar{\sigma}, 0 \leq \omega(t, \eta(t)) \leq$ $\bar{\omega}(\eta(t)) \leq \bar{\omega}, \dot{\omega}(t, \eta(t)) \leq \omega_d(\eta(t)) \leq \omega_d$ where $\bar{\tau}(\eta(t)), \bar{\tau}, \bar{\sigma}(\eta(t)), \bar{\sigma}, \bar{\omega}(\eta(t)), \bar{\omega}$ are positive scalars. $\tilde{\tau} = \max\{\bar{\tau}, \bar{\sigma}, \bar{\omega}\}$. $\varphi(t)$ is a real-valued initial vector function that is continuous on the interval $[-\tilde{\tau}, 0]$. $\phi(t, \eta(t)) = X(\eta(t))u(t) + Y(\eta(t))u(t - \tau(t, \eta(t))) \in \mathbb{R}^n$ is the control vector. $\{\eta(t), t \geq 0\}$ is a homogeneous, finite-state Markovian process with right continuous trajectories and taking values in finite set $\mathcal{N} = \{1, 2, ..., N\}$ with given probability space $(\Omega, \mathbb{F}, \mathbb{P})$ and the initial model η_0. Let $\Pi = [\pi_{ij}]_{N \times N}$ denote the transition rate matrix with transition probability:

$$\mathbb{P}(\eta(t + \delta) = j | \eta(t) = i) = \begin{cases} \pi_{ij}\delta + o(\delta), & i \neq j, \\ 1 + \pi_{ii}\delta + o(\delta), & i = j, \end{cases}$$

where $\delta > 0, \lim_{\delta \to 0^+} \frac{o(\delta)}{\delta} = 0$ and π_{ij} is the transition rate from mode i to mode j satisfying $\pi_{ij} \geq 0$ for $i \neq j$ with

$$\pi_{ii} = - \sum_{j=1, j \neq i}^{N} \pi_{ij}, \quad i, j \in \mathcal{N}.$$

For convenience, each possible value of $\eta(t)$ is denoted by $i(i \in \mathcal{N})$ in the sequel. Then we have

$$D_i = D(\eta(t)), \quad A_i = A(\eta(t)), \quad B_i = B(\eta(t)), \quad C_i = C(\eta(t)), \quad L_i = L(\eta(t)),$$
$$\Delta D_i(t) = \Delta D(t, \eta(t)), \quad \Delta A_i(t) = \Delta A(t, \eta(t)),$$
$$\Delta B_i(t) = \Delta B(t, \eta(t)), \quad \Delta C_i(t) = \Delta C(t, \eta(t)), \quad \Delta L_i(t) = \Delta L(t, \eta(t)).$$

Throughout this paper, we make the following assumptions:

Assumption 1: The time-varying structured uncertainties are assumed to be of the form:

$$[\ \Delta D_i(t) \ \ \Delta A_i(t) \ \ \Delta B_i(t) \ \ \Delta C_i(t) \ \ \Delta L_i(t) \ ]$$
$$= E[\ F_{1i}(t)G_{1i} \ \ F_{2i}(t)G_{2i} \ \ F_{3i}(t)G_{3i} \ \ F_{4i}(t)G_{4i} \ \ F_{5i}(t)G_{5i} \ ].$$

where $E, G_{ji}(j = 1, ..., 5)$ are known real constant matrices, $F_{ji}(t)(j = 1, ..., 5)$ are unknown time-varying matrix functions satisfying $F_{ji}(t)^T F_{ji}(t) \leq I$ for any $t > 0$.

Assumption 2: Each neural activation function $f_j(\cdot)(j = 1, 2, ..., n)$ is bounded and satisfies the following condition

$$f_j(0) = 0, \quad \gamma_j \leq \frac{f_j(\xi) - f_j(\zeta)}{\xi - \zeta} \leq \lambda_j, \quad \forall \ \xi, \zeta \in \mathbb{R}, \ \xi \neq \zeta,$$

where γ_j, λ_j are known real constants.

For notational simplicity, we denote $\Gamma = \text{diag}\{\gamma_1, \gamma_2, ..., \gamma_n\}$, $\Lambda = \text{diag}\{\lambda_1, \lambda_2, ..., \lambda_n\}$, $\Theta = \text{diag}\{\theta_1, \theta_2, ..., \theta_n\}$, where $\theta_j = \max\{|\gamma_j|, |\lambda_j|\}$.

Now, we give the following definitions.

Definition 1.[24] Define a ball $\mathbb{B}(r) = \{x \in \mathbb{R}^n : ||x|| \leq r\}$. The uncertain system (1) is said to be globally uniformly exponentially convergent to the ball $\mathcal{B}(r)$ at a rate $\beta > 0$, if for any solution $u(t)$ of system (1), any given positive number ζ, there exists a positive number $\nu = \nu(\zeta)$ such that

$$\| u(t) \| \leq r + \nu e^{-\beta(t-t_0)},$$

for any $t \geq t_0$, $\varphi(t) \in C([-\check{\tau}, 0], \mathbb{R}^n)$, and $\| \varphi \| \leq \zeta$.

If $r = 0$, then the system is globally exponentially stable with a convergence rate β.

Definition 2.[30] Markovian system (1) is said to be stochastically stable if the following condition is satisfied for any $\varphi(t) \in \mathcal{C}^p_{\mathbb{F}_0}\left([-\check{\tau}, 0]; \mathbb{R}^n\right)$ and $\eta_0 \in \mathcal{N}$

$$\lim_{t \to +\infty} \mathbb{E}|u(t, \varphi(t), \eta_0)|^2 = 0,$$

where $u(t, \varphi(t), \eta_0)$ is the solution of system (1) at time t under the initial state $\varphi(t)$ and initial mode η_0.

The development of the work in this paper requires the following lemmas.

Lemma 1. *Let $g(t, \eta(t))$ be a continuous function with $g(t, \eta(t)) \geq 0$ for all $t \geq t_0 - \vartheta$, and suppose that*

$$\sup_{t_0 - \vartheta \leq s \leq t_0} g(s, \eta(s)) \leq \delta,$$

where δ is a positive constant. Assume that $g(t, \eta(t))$ satisfies the following inequality

$$\mathbb{E}\pounds g(t, \eta(t)) \leq -\kappa_1 \mathbb{E}g(t, \eta(t)) + \kappa_2 \sup_{t-\vartheta \leq s \leq t} \mathbb{E}g(s, \eta(s)) + \kappa_3, \qquad \forall t \geq t_0,$$

where $\pounds$ is the weak infinitesimal generator [30,34], κ_1, κ_2, and κ_3 are positive constants. If $0 < \kappa_2 < \kappa_1$, then

$$\mathbb{E}g(t, \eta(t)) \leq \chi + \delta e^{-\varrho(t-t_0)}, \qquad \forall t \geq t_0,$$

where $\chi = \kappa_3/(\kappa_1 - \kappa_2)$ and ϱ is the unique solution to $\varrho = \kappa_1 - \kappa_2 e^{\varrho\vartheta}$.

Lemma 1 is a modified version of those in references [16,24,33], which can be easily proved by the same method as in [16].

Lemma 2 (see[6], Jensen integral inequality). *For any positive symmetric constant matrix $M \in \mathbb{R}^{n\times n}$, scalars $r_1 < r_2$ and vector function $\varpi : [r_1, r_2] \to \mathbb{R}^n$ such that the integrations concerned are well defined, the following matrix inequality holds:*

$$\left(\int_{r_1}^{r_2} \varpi(s)\mathrm{d}s\right)^T M \left(\int_{r_1}^{r_2} \varpi(s)\mathrm{d}s\right) \leq (r_2 - r_1)\int_{r_1}^{r_2} \varpi^T(s)M\varpi(s)\mathrm{d}s.$$

Motivated by [23], we established the following Lemma 3, which plays an important role in obtaining our delay-dependent stability result.

Lemma 3. If $\lambda_j \leq 1$, $\lambda_j + \mu_j \leq 4(j = 1, 2)$, $\underline{\theta} \leq \theta(t) \leq \bar{\theta}$, $\underline{\tau} \leq \nu(t) \leq \bar{\nu}$, $\alpha, \beta, \gamma, \delta \geq 0$, then we have

$$- \frac{\alpha}{\theta(t) - \underline{\theta}} - \frac{\beta}{\bar{\theta} - \theta(t)} - \frac{\gamma}{\nu(t) - \underline{\nu}} - \frac{\delta}{\bar{\nu} - \nu(t)}$$

$$\leq \max \left\{ -\frac{\lambda_1 \alpha + \mu_1 \beta}{\bar{\theta} - \underline{\theta}} - \frac{\lambda_2 \gamma + \mu_2 \delta}{\bar{\nu} - \underline{\nu}}, -\frac{\lambda_1 \alpha + \mu_1 \beta}{\bar{\theta} - \underline{\theta}} - \frac{\mu_2 \gamma + \lambda_2 \delta}{\bar{\nu} - \underline{\nu}} \right.$$

$$\left. -\frac{\mu_1 \alpha + \lambda_1 \beta}{\bar{\theta} - \underline{\theta}} - \frac{\lambda_2 \gamma + \mu_2 \delta}{\bar{\nu} - \underline{\nu}}, -\frac{\mu_1 \alpha + \lambda_1 \beta}{\bar{\theta} - \underline{\theta}} - \frac{\mu_2 \gamma + \lambda_2 \delta}{\bar{\nu} - \underline{\nu}} \right\}. \quad (2)$$

Remark 1. If we set $\lambda_j = \mu_j = 1(j = 1, 2)$, then Lemma 3 degenerates into the one which are used in [17,28]. Through the following numerical example, we will obtain less conservative result from Lemma 3.

Notations: Throughout this paper, let W^T, W^{-1} denote the transpose and the inverse of a square matrix W, respectively. Let $W > 0(< 0)$ denote a positive (negative) definite symmetric matrix, I stand for the identity matrix, the symbol "*" denote a block that is readily inferred by symmetry. The shorthand $\mathrm{col}\{M_1, M_2, ..., M_k\}$ denotes a column matrix with the matrices $M_1, M_2, ..., M_k$. $\mathrm{diag}\{\cdot\}$ stands for a diagonal or block-diagonal matrix. For $\chi > 0, \mathcal{C}([-\chi, 0]; \mathbb{R}^n)$ denotes the family of continuous functions ϕ from $[-\chi, 0]$ to $\mathbb{R}^n$ with the norm $||\phi|| = \sup_{-\chi \leq s \leq 0} |\phi(s)|$. Moreover, let $(\Omega, \mathbb{F}, \mathbb{P})$ be a complete probability space with a filtration $\{\mathbb{F}_t\}_{t \geq 0}$ satisfying the usual conditions and $\mathbb{E}\{\cdot\}$ representing the mathematical expectation. Denote by $\mathcal{C}^p_{\mathbb{F}_0}([-\chi, 0]; \mathbb{R}^n)$ the family of all bounded, $\mathbb{F}_0$-measurable, $\mathcal{C}([-\chi, 0]; \mathbb{R}^n)$-valued random variables $\xi = \{\xi(s) : -\chi \leq s \leq 0\}$ such that $\sup_{-\chi \leq s \leq 0} \mathbb{E}|\xi(s)|^p < \infty$. For any $x = [x_1, x_2, ..., x_n]^T \in \mathbb{R}^n$, the notation $\| x \|$ denotes the Euclidean norm with $\| x \| = \sqrt{\sum_{j=1}^n x_j^2}$. Matrices, if not explicitly stated, are assumed to have compatible dimensions.

2 Main Result

As well known, for stochastic systems, Itô's formula plays an important role in the stability analysis of stochastic systems and we cite some related results here [1]. Consider a general system with Markovian jump

$$\dot{x}(t) = \varsigma(t, x(t), \eta(t)), \quad (3)$$

on $t \geq t_0$ with initial value $x(t_0) = x_0 \in \mathbb{R}^n$, where $\varsigma : \mathbb{R}^+ \times \mathbb{R}^n \times \mathcal{N} \to \mathbb{R}^n$. Nonnegative function $V(t, x(t), \eta(t))$ are defined on $\mathbb{R}^+ \times \mathbb{R}^n \times \mathcal{N}$, which are continuously differentiable once in t and twice in x. Let $\mathcal{L}$ be the weak infinitesimal generator of the random process $\{x(t), \eta(t)\}_{t \geq t_0}$ along the system (3) (see [14,22,27]), i.e.

$$\pounds V(t, x_t, i) := \lim_{\delta \to 0+} \left[\mathbb{E} \left\{ V(t + \delta, x_{t+\delta}, \eta(t + \delta)) | x(t), \eta(t) = i \right\} - V(t, x_t, \eta(t) = i) \right], \tag{4}$$

then, by the generalized Itô's formula, one can get

$$\mathbb{E}V(t, x(t), i) = \mathbb{E}V(t_0, x(t_0), i) + \mathbb{E}\int_{t_0}^{t} \pounds V(s, x(s), i) \mathrm{d}s.$$

In order to get our main results, we propose the following Lemma:

Lemma 4. For each $i \in \mathcal{N}$, we have

$$\pounds \left\{ \sum_{j=1}^{n} q_{ji} \int_{0}^{u_j(t)} [f_j(s) - \gamma_j s] \, \mathrm{d}s \right\}$$

$$= [f(u(t)) - \Gamma u(t)]^T Q_i \dot{u}(t) + \sum_{k=1}^{N} \pi_{ik} \sum_{j=1}^{n} \left\{ q_{jk} \int_{0}^{u_j(t)} [f_i(s) - \gamma_j s] \mathrm{d}s \right\}, \tag{5}$$

$$\pounds \left\{ \sum_{j=1}^{n} z_{ji} \int_{0}^{u_j(t)} [\lambda_j s - f_j(s)] \, \mathrm{d}s \right\}$$

$$= [\Lambda u(t) - f(u(t))]^T Z_i \dot{u}(t) + \sum_{k=1}^{N} \pi_{ik} \sum_{j=1}^{n} \left\{ z_{jk} \int_{0}^{u_j(t)} [\lambda_j s - f_j(s)] \mathrm{d}s \right\}, \tag{6}$$

where $Q_i = \mathrm{diag}\{q_{1i}, q_{2i}, ..., q_{ni}\}$, $Z_i = \mathrm{diag}\{z_{1i}, z_{2i}, ..., z_{ni}\}$ are positive diagonal matrices.

First, we consider model (1) with $C(t, \eta(t)) = L(t, \eta(t)) = 0$, that is,

$$\dot{u}(t) = -D_i(t)u(t) + A_i(t)f(u(t)) + B_i(t)f(u(t - \tau_i(t)) + \phi_i(t),$$
$$u(t) = \varphi(t), \qquad t \in [-\bar{\tau}, 0]. \tag{7}$$

Now, we begin to state our delay-independent exponential convergence result.

Theorem 1. *Under the Assumptions 1, 2, the uncertain neural network (7) is globally uniformly exponentially convergent to the ball $\mathbb{B}(r)$ at a rate $\iota/2$ for any $0 \le \tau_i(t) \le \bar{\tau}_i \le \bar{\tau}$, $\dot{\tau}_i(t) \le \tau_{di}$, where*

$$r = \sqrt{\frac{\varepsilon_0 \epsilon \rho \bar{\tau}}{(\alpha - 1)\beta \varrho_0}},$$

with $\varepsilon_0 = \max_{i \in \mathcal{N}}\{\varepsilon_{0i}\}$, $\varrho_0 = \min_{i \in \mathcal{N}}\{\lambda_m(P_i)\}$, and $\iota > 0$ is the unique solution of the following equation:

$$\iota = \alpha\beta + \rho - (\beta + \rho)e^{2\iota\bar{\tau}},$$

if there exist symmetric definite positive matrices P_i, M, K_i, diagonal positive matrices $W, H_i, J_i, R_i, S_i, Q_i, Z_i$, positive scalars $\beta, \rho, \varepsilon_{ji}$ $(j = 0, 1, 2, 3)$ such that the following inequalities hold

$$\beta\left[P_i + (Q_i + Z_i)(\Lambda - \Gamma)\right] \le S_i, \tag{8}$$

$$\beta\Theta W\Theta - \rho S_i + \beta M \le 0, \tag{9}$$

$$(1 + \rho\bar{\tau}_i)(K_i + \Theta W\Theta) - \beta P_i \le 0, \tag{10}$$

$$\begin{bmatrix} S_i + \psi_{1i} & 0 & \psi_{2i} & \bar{P}_i B_i & \bar{P}_i E_i & \bar{P}_i E_i & \bar{P}_i E_i & \bar{P}_i \\ * & \psi_{3i} - K_i & 0 & \frac{1}{2}J_i(\Lambda + \Gamma) & 0 & 0 & 0 & 0 \\ * & * & \psi_{4i} & \bar{Q}_i B_i & \bar{Q}_i E_i & \bar{Q}_i E_i & \bar{Q}_i E_i & \bar{Q}_i \\ * & * & * & \psi_{5i} - H_i & 0 & 0 & 0 & 0 \\ * & * & * & * & -\varepsilon_{1i}I & 0 & 0 & 0 \\ * & * & * & * & * & -\varepsilon_{2i}I & 0 & 0 \\ * & * & * & * & * & * & -\varepsilon_{3i}I & 0 \\ * & * & * & * & * & * & * & -\varepsilon_{0i}I \end{bmatrix} < 0, \tag{11}$$

where

$$\bar{P}_i = P_i - \Gamma Q_i + \Lambda Z_i, \quad \bar{Q}_i = Q_i - Z_i,$$

$$\psi_{1i} = -\bar{P}_i(D_i - X_i) - (D_i - X_i^T)\bar{P}_i + M - \Lambda R_i \Gamma$$
$$+ \varepsilon_{1i}G_{1i}^T G_{1i} + \sum_{j=1}^{N}\left[\pi_{ij}P_j + \pi'_{ij}(Q_j + Z_j)(\Lambda - \Gamma)\right],$$

$$\psi_{2i} = \bar{P}_i A_i - (D_i - X_i^T)\bar{Q}_i + \frac{1}{2}(\Lambda + \Gamma)R_i,$$

$$\psi_{3i} = -(1 - \tau_{di})M - \Lambda J_i \Gamma + \sum_{j=1}^{N}\pi'_{ij}\bar{\tau}_j M,$$

$$\psi_{4i} = W + \bar{Q}_i A_i + A_i^T \bar{Q}_i - R_i + \varepsilon_{2i}G_{2i}^T G_{2i},$$

$$\psi_{5i} = -(1 - \tau_{di})W - J_i + \varepsilon_{3i}G_{3i}^T G_{3i} + \sum_{j=1}^{N}\pi'_{ij}\bar{\tau}_j W, \quad \pi'_{ij} = \max\{\pi_{ij}, 0\},$$

and the adaptive controller is designed as $\phi(t) = X_i u(t) + v(t)$, *where* $v(t)$ *is a vector function of* t *such that* $v(t)^T v(t) \le \epsilon I$, *and* ϵ *is a positive scalar which can be freely chosen.*

Next, we propose the following delay-dependent stability criterion.

Theorem 2. *Under the Assumptions* 1, 2, *the uncertain neural network* (1) *is globally robustly asymptotically stable in the mean square for any* $0 \le \tau_i(t) \le \bar{\tau}_i$, $\dot{\tau}_i(t) \le \tau_{di} < 1$, $0 \le \sigma_i(t) \le \bar{\sigma}_i$, $0 \le \omega_i(t) \le \bar{\omega}_i$, $\dot{\omega}_i(t) \le \omega_{di} < 1$, *if there exist symmetric definite positive matrices* $P_i, M, U_l(l = 1, 2, 3)$, *diagonal positive matrices* $W, J_i, R_i, S_i, Q_i, Z_i$, *positive scalars* $\beta, \rho, \varepsilon_{ji}$ $(j = 1, ..., 5)$ *such that the following inequalities hold*

$$\hat{\Phi}_i - 2\mathcal{I}_1^T \bar{U}_1 \mathcal{I}_1 - 2\mathcal{I}_3^T \bar{U}_2 \mathcal{I}_3 < 0, \tag{12}$$

$$\hat{\Phi}_i - 2\mathcal{I}_1^T \bar{U}_1 \mathcal{I}_1 - 2\mathcal{I}_4^T \bar{U}_2 \mathcal{I}_4 < 0, \tag{13}$$

$$\hat{\Phi}_i - 2\mathcal{I}_2^T \bar{U}_1 \mathcal{I}_2 - 2\mathcal{I}_3^T \bar{U}_2 \mathcal{I}_3 < 0, \tag{14}$$

$$\hat{\Phi}_i - 2\mathcal{I}_2^T \bar{U}_1 \mathcal{I}_2 - 2\mathcal{I}_4^T \bar{U}_2 \mathcal{I}_4 < 0, \tag{15}$$

where

$$\hat{\Phi}_i = \begin{bmatrix} \Phi_i + \mathcal{A}_i(\bar{\tau}_i^2 U_1 + U_3)\mathcal{A}^T & \mathfrak{B}_i \\ * & -\Upsilon_i \end{bmatrix},$$

$$\mathcal{I}_1 = \operatorname{col}\{I_n, -I_n, 0_{11n \times n}\}, \quad \mathcal{I}_2 = \operatorname{col}\{0_n, I_n, 0_{4n \times n}, -I_n, 0_{6n \times n}\},$$

$$\mathcal{I}_3 = \operatorname{col}\{0_{4n \times n}, I_n, 0_{8n \times n}\}, \quad \mathcal{I}_4 = \operatorname{col}\{0_{7n \times n}, I_n, 0_{5n \times n}\},$$

$$\bar{U}_1 = \Big(1 - \sum_{j=1}^{N} \pi_{ij}\bar{\tau}_j\Big)U_1, \qquad \bar{U}_2 = \Big(1 - \sum_{j=1}^{N} \pi_{ij}\bar{\sigma}_j\Big)U_2.$$

with

$$\Phi_i = (\Phi_{lji})_{8n \times 8n},$$

$$\Phi_{11i} = \psi_{1i} - \bar{U}_1, \ \Phi_{12i} = \bar{P}Y_i + \bar{U}_1, \ \Phi_{13i} = \psi_{2i}, \ \Phi_{14i} = \bar{P}B_i, \ \Phi_{15i} = \bar{P}C_i,$$

$$\Phi_{16i} = \bar{P}L_i, \ \Phi_{22i} = \psi_{3i} - 2\bar{U}_1, \ \Phi_{23i} = Y_i\bar{Q}_i, \ \Phi_{24i} = \frac{1}{2}J_i(\Lambda + \Gamma),$$

$$\Phi_{27i} = \bar{U}_1, \ \Phi_{33i} = \psi_{4i} + \bar{\sigma}_i^2 U_2, \ \Phi_{34i} = \bar{Q}_i B_i, \ \Phi_{35i} = \bar{Q}_i C_i,$$

$$\Phi_{36i} = \bar{Q}_i L_i, \quad \Phi_{44i} = \psi_{5i}, \quad \Phi_{55i} = \varepsilon_{4i} G_{4i}^T G_{4i} - \bar{U}_2,$$

$$\Phi_{66i} = \varepsilon_{5i} G_{5i}^T G_{5i} - (1 - \omega_{di})U_3 + \sum_{j=1}^{N} \pi'_{ij}\bar{\omega}_j, \ \Phi_{77i} = -\bar{U}_1, \ \Phi_{88i} = -\bar{U}_2,$$

$$\mathcal{A}_i = \operatorname{col}\{X_i - D_i, Y_i, A_i, B_i, C_i, L_i, 0_{n \times n}, C_i\}, \ \mathfrak{B}_i = [\mathcal{B}_i \ \mathcal{B}_i \ \mathcal{B}_i \ \mathcal{B}_i \ \mathcal{B}_i],$$

$$\mathcal{B}_i = \operatorname{col}\{P_i, 0_n, \bar{Q}_i, 0_{5n \times n}\}E_i, \quad \Upsilon_i = \operatorname{diag}\{\varepsilon_{1i}I, \varepsilon_{2i}I, \varepsilon_{3i}I, \varepsilon_{4i}I, \varepsilon_{5i}I\},$$

and the adaptive controller is designed as $\phi_i(t) = X_i u(t) + Y_i u(t - \tau_i(t))$.

3   Conclusion

This paper deals with the adaptive stochastic robust convergence and stability in mean square for a class of uncertain neutral-type neural networks with both Markovian jump parameters and mixed delays. The mixed delays consists of discrete and distributed time-varying delays. First, by employing the Lyapunov method and a generalized Halanay-type inequality, a delay-independent condition is derived to guarantee the state variables of the discussed neural networks to be globally uniformly exponentially stochastic convergent to a ball in the state space with a pre-specified convergence rate. Next, by applying the Jensen integral inequality and a novel Lemma, a delay-dependent criterion is developed to achieve the globally stochastic robust stability in mean square. The proposed conditions are all in terms of linear matrix inequalities, which can be solved numerically by employing the LMI toolbox in Matlab. Finally, two illustrated examples are given to show the effectiveness and usefulness of the obtained results.

References

1. Arnold, L.: Stochastic Differential Equations: Theory and Applications. Wiley, New York (1972)
2. Balasubramaniam, P., Rakkiyappan, R.: Delay-dependent robust stability analysis for Markovian jumping stochastic Cohen-Grossberg neural networks with discrete interval and distributed time-varying delays. Nonlinear Anal. Hybrid Systems 3, 207–214 (2009)
3. Chen, H., Zhang, Y., Hu, P.: Novel delay-dependent robust stability criteria for neutral stochastic delayed neural networks. Neurocomputing 73, 2554–2561 (2009)
4. Chen, W., Lu, X.: Mean square exponential stability of uncertain stochastic delayed neural networks. Phys. Lett. A 372, 1061–1069 (2008)
5. Fu, J., Zhang, H., Ma, T.: Delay-probability-distribution-dependent robust stability analysis for stochastic neural networks with time-varying delay. Progress in Natural Science 19, 1333–1340 (2009)
6. Gu, K.: An integral inequality in the stability problem of time-delay systems. In: Proc. 39th IEEE Conf. Decision and Control, pp. 2805–2810 (2000)
7. Han, W., Liu, Y., Wang, L.: Robust exponential stability of Markovian jumping neural networks with mode-dependent delay. Commun. Nonlinear Sci. Numer. Simulat. 15, 2529–2535 (2010)
8. Li, T., Song, A., Fei, S.: Robust stability of stochastic Cohen-Grossberg neural networks with mixed time-varying delays. Neurocomputing 73, 542–551 (2009)
9. Liu, H., Ou, Y., Hua, J., Liu, T.: Delay-dependent stability analysis for continuous-time BAM neural networks with Markovian jumping parameters. Neural Netw. 23, 315–321 (2010)
10. Liu, H., Zhao, L., Zhang, Z., Ou, Y.: Stochastic stability of Markovian jumping Hopfield neural networks with constant and distributed delays. Neurocomputing 72, 3669–3674 (2009)
11. Liu, K., Zhang, H.: An improved global exponential stability criterion for delayed neural networks. Nonlinear Anal. Real World Appl. 10, 2613–2619 (2009)
12. Liu, Y., Wang, Z., Liang, J., Liu, X.: Stability and synchronization of discrete-time Markovian jumping neural networks with mixed mode-dependent time delays. IEEE Trans. Neural Netw. 20, 1102–1116 (2009)
13. Ma, Q., Xu, S., Zou, Y.: Stability and synchronization for Markovian jump neural networks with partly unknown transition probabilities. Neurocomputing 74, 3404–3411 (2011)
14. Mao, X.: Exponential stability of stochastic delay interval systems with Markovian switching. IEEE Trans. Autom. Contr. 47(10), 1604–1612 (2002)
15. Mariton, M.: Jump Linear Control Systems. Marcel-Dekker, New York (1990)
16. Oucgeriah, S.: Adaptive robust control of a class of dynamic delay systems with unknown uncertainty bounds. Int. J. Adapt. Control Signal Process. 15, 53–63 (2001)
17. Qian, W., Li, T., Cong, S., Fei, S.: Improved stability analysis on delayed neural networks with linear fractional uncertainties. Appl. Math. Comput. 217, 3596–3606 (2010)
18. Salamon, D.: Control and Observation of Neutral Systems. Pitman Advanced Publication, Boston (1984)
19. Sanchez, E.N., Perez, J.P.: Input-to-state stability (ISS) analysis for dynamic NN. IEEE Trans. Circuits Syst. I 46, 1395–1398 (1999)

20. Shen, H., Xu, S., Zhou, J., Lu, J.: Fuzzy H_∞ filtering for nonlinear Markovian jump neutral systems. Int. J. Systems Sci. 42, 767–780 (2011)
21. Tino, P., Cernansky, M., Beunskova, L.: Markovian architectural bias of recurrent neural networks. IEEE Trans. Neural Netw. 15(1), 6–15 (2004)
22. Wang, Z., Liu, Y., Liu, X.: Exponential stabilization of a class of stochastic system with Markovian jump parameters and mode-dependent mixed time-delays. IEEE Trans. Autom. Contr. 55(7), 1656–1662 (2010)
23. Wu, Y., Wu, Y., Chen, Y.: Mean square exponential stability of uncertain stochastic neural networks with time-varying delay. Neurocomputing 72, 2379–2384 (2009)
24. Xiong, W., Song, L., Cao, J.: Adaptive robust convergence of neural networks with time-varying delays. Nonlinear Anal. Real World Appl. 9, 1283–1291 (2008)
25. Xu, S., Lam, J., Mao, X.: Delay-dependent H_∞ control and filtering for uncertain Markovian jump systems with time-varying delays. IEEE Trans. Circuits Syst. I 54, 2070–2078 (2009)
26. Xu, S., Chen, T., Lam, J.: Robust H_∞ filtering for uncertain Markovian jump systems with mode-dependent time delays. IEEE Trans. Autom. Control 48, 900–908 (2003)
27. Yuan, C., Lygeros, J.: Stabilization of a class of stochastic differential equations with Markovian switching. Syst. Control Lett. 54, 819–833 (2005)
28. Yue, D., Tian, E., Zhang, Y., Peng, C.: Delay-distribution-dependent stability and stabilization of T-S fuzzy systems with probabilistic interval delay. IEEE Trans. Syst. Man Cybern. Part B 39, 503–516 (2009)
29. Zhang, B., Xu, S., Zong, G., Zou, Y.: Delay-dependent exponential stability for uncertain stochastic Hopfield neural networks with time-varying delays. IEEE Trans. Circuits Syst. I. 56(6), 1241–1247 (2009)
30. Zhang, H., Wang, Y.: Stability analysis of Markovian jumping stochastic Cohen-Grossberg neural networks with mixed time delays. IEEE Trans. Neural Netw. 19(2), 366–370 (2008)
31. Zhang, H., Wang, Z., Liu, D.: Robust stability analysis for interval Cohen-Grossberg neural networks with unknown time-varying delays. IEEE Trans. Neural Netw. 19(11), 1942–1955 (2008)
32. Zhang, L., Boukas, E.: Stability and stabilization of Markovian jump linear systems with partly unknown transition probabilities. Automatica 45, 463–468 (2009)
33. Zheng, F., Wang, Q., Lee, T.H.: Adaptive robust control of uncertain time delay systems. Automatica 41, 1375–1383 (2005)
34. Zhu, Q., Cao, J.: Robust exponential stability of markovian jump impulsive stochastic Cohen-Grossberg neural networks with mixed time delays. IEEE Trans. Neural Netw. 21(8), 1314–1325 (2010)

A New Global Asymptotic Stability of Cellular Neural Network with Time-Varying Discrete and Distributed Delays

Lin Zhu

Nanchang Institute Of Technology, NanChang,
330099, P.R. China
rigss84@yahoo.com.cn
http://www.springer.com/lncs

Abstract. This paper is concerned with the global asymptotic stability of cellular neural network with time-varying discrete and distributed delays. A novel criterion for the stability using the Lyapunov stability theory and linear matrix inequality(LMI) framework is presented. The result is less conservative than those established in the earlier references.

Keywords: Global asymptotic stability, Lyapunov method, Linear matrix inequality, Cellular neural network.

1 Introduction

In recent years, artificial neural networks have been widely studied due to their extensive applications in pattern recognition, image processing, association memories, optimal computation and other areas. Time delays are unavoidably encountered in implementation of artificial networks. As is well known, time delays may degrade system performance and induce oscillation in a network, causing instability. So, it is very important to study time delays effects on stability and convergent dynamics of neural networks.So far numerous works on global asymptotic stability of equilibrium of the networks have been investigated, see for example [1-3], and references cited therein. On the other hand, in order to deal with moving images, one must introduce the time delays in the signal transmission among the cells. This leads to the model of delayed cellular neural networks(DCNNs). Thus the stability analysis of DCNNs has become an important topic of theoretical studies in neural networks[4-7].

In this paper, we deal with the problem of global asymptotic stability of cellular neural network with time-varying discrete and distributed delays. By constructing a suitable Lyapunov-Krasovskii function, a new condition for global asymptotic stability is given in terms of LMIs. The resulting criteria are applicable to both fast and slow time-varying delay.

J. Wang, G.G. Yen, and M.M. Polycarpou (Eds.): ISNN 2012, Part I, LNCS 7367, pp. 361–368, 2012.
© Springer-Verlag Berlin Heidelberg 2012

2   Problem Statement

Consider the following delayed neural networks with n neurons:

$$\begin{cases} \dot{y}(t) = -Ay(t) + +W_0 f(y(t)) + W_1 f(y(t-h(t))) + W_2 \int_{t-\tau(t)}^{t} f(y(s))ds + J \\ y(t) = \varphi(t), t \in [-\bar{d}, 0] \end{cases}$$

(1)

where $y(t) = [y_1(t), y_2(t), \ldots, y_n(t)]^T \in R^n$ is the neuron state vector, $f(y(t)) = [f_1(y(t)), f_2(y(t)), \ldots, f_n(y(t))]^T$ is the activation functions with $f_i(0) = 0 J \in R^n$ is a constant input vector, $A = diag(a_1, a_2, \ldots, a_n) a_i > 0$, W_0, W_1, W_2 are the interconnection matrices representation the weight coefficients of the neurons. $\varphi(t)$ is the initial value. The time delay $h(t)$ is a time-varying continuous function and $\tau(t)$ is the distributed time delay, that satisfies

$$h_1 \le h(t) \le h_2, \dot{h}(t) \le \mu, 0 \le \tau(t) \le \bar{\tau}$$

(2)

where $0 \le h_1 < h_2$ The activation function $y(t)$ is nondecreasing, bounded and globally Lipschitz; that is

$$0 \le \frac{f_i(\xi_1) - f_i(\xi_2)}{\xi_1 - \xi_2} \le k_i, i = 1, 2, \ldots, n$$

(3)

One can easily prove that there exists at least one equilibrium point y^* to the origin. Assume that $y^* = (y_1^*, y_2^*, \ldots, y_n^*)^T$ is an equilibrium point of the system (1), the transformation

$$x(.) = y(.) - y^*$$

The transformation puts system (1) into the following form

$$\begin{cases} \dot{x}(t) = -Ax(t) + +W_0 g(x(t)) + W_1 g(x(t-h(t))) + W_2 \int_{t-\tau(t)}^{t} g(x(s))ds \\ x(t) = \phi(t), t \in [-\bar{d}, 0] \end{cases}$$

(4)

where $x(t) = [x_1(t), x_2(t), \ldots, x_n(t)]^T \in R^n$ is the state vector of the transformed system and $g(x(t)) = [g_1(x(t)), g_2(x(t)), \ldots, g_n(x(t))]^T$, $g_j(x_j(t)) = f_j(x_j(t) + y_j^*) - f_j(y^*)$, $g_i(0) = 0$. From (3) one can see that the activation function satisfies

$$0 \le \frac{g_i(\xi_1) - g_i(\xi_2)}{\xi_1 - \xi_2} \le k_i, i = 1, 2, \ldots, n$$

(5)

The following lemmas will be used for deriving main result.

Lemma1. (Schur complement) For a symmetric matrix

$$S = \begin{pmatrix} S_{11} & S_{12} \\ S_{21} & S_{22} \end{pmatrix}$$

the following conditions are equivalent: $(i) S < 0$; $(ii) S_{11} < 0$ and $S_{22} - S_{12}^T S_{11}^{-1} S_{12} < 0$; $(iii) S_{22} < 0$ and $S_{11} - S_{12} S_{22}^{-1} S_{12}^T < 0$.

Lemma2. For any vectors $a, b \in R^n$ and any positive definite matrix $Y \in R^{n \times n}$, the following inequality holds:

$$2a^T b \leq a^T Y a + b^T Y^{-1} b$$

Lemma3. Assume that $a \in R^{n_a}, b \in R^{n_b}, N \in R^{n_a \times n_b}$, for any constant matrix $X \in R^{n_a \times n_a}, Y \in R^{n_b \times n_b}, Z \in R^{n_b \times n_b}$, the following inequality holds:

$$-2a^T N b \leq \begin{bmatrix} a \\ b \end{bmatrix}^T \begin{bmatrix} X & Y - N \\ * & Z \end{bmatrix} \begin{bmatrix} a \\ b \end{bmatrix}, \begin{bmatrix} X & Y \\ * & Z \end{bmatrix} \geq 0$$

Lemma4. For any constant matrix $\Sigma \in R^{n \times n} \Sigma = \Sigma^T > 0$, scalar $\gamma > 0$, vector function $\omega : [0, \gamma] \to R^n$ such that the integrations concerned are well defined, then

$$\left(\int_0^\gamma \omega(s) ds \right)^T \Sigma \left(\int_0^\gamma \omega(s) ds \right) \leq \gamma \int_0^\gamma \omega^T(s) \Sigma \omega(s) ds$$

3   Main Result

Theorem1. For given $h_1 \leq h(t) \leq h_2, \dot{h}(t) \leq \mu, 0 \leq \tau(t) \leq \bar{\tau}, \alpha > 0$, $K = diag(k_1, k_2, \ldots, k_n)$, system (4) is globally asymptotically stable if there exist positive matrices $P, Q_i, (i = 1, 2, 3, 4), X, Y, S, Z_j(j = 1, 2), D = diag(d_1, d_2, \ldots, d_n)$, and any matrices $M_j, N_j (j = 1, 2)$, satisfying the following LMIs:

$$\begin{bmatrix} (1,1) & PW_0 & PW_1 + Y^T & PW_2 & M_1 & -N_1 & N_1 - M_1 & h_{12}N_1 & h_{12}M_1 & -A^T V \\ * & (2,2) & DW_1 & DW_2 & 0 & 0 & 0 & 0 & 0 & W_0^T V \\ * & * & (3,3) & 0 & 0 & 0 & 0 & 0 & 0 & W_1^T V \\ * & * & * & -S & 0 & 0 & 0 & 0 & 0 & W_2^T V \\ * & * & * & * & -Q_1 & 0 & M_2^T & 0 & 0 & 0 \\ * & * & * & * & * & -Q_2 & -N_2^T & 0 & 0 & 0 \\ * & * & * & * & * & * & (7,7) & h_{12}N_2 & h_{12}M_2 & 0 \\ * & * & * & * & * & * & * & -Z_2 & 0 & 0 \\ * & * & * & * & * & * & * & * & -Z_2 & 0 \\ * & * & * & * & * & * & * & * & * & -V \end{bmatrix} < 0 \tag{6}$$

$$\begin{bmatrix} X & Y \\ * & Z_1 \end{bmatrix} \geq 0 \tag{7}$$

where

$(1,1) = -PA - A^T P + \sum_{i=1}^{3} Q_i$

$(2,2) = DW_0 + W_0^T D - 2DAK^{-1} + Q_4 + \bar{\tau}^2 S$

$(3,3) = -(1 - \mu)Q_4 + h_2 X - Y K^{-1} - K^{-1} Y^T$

$(7,7) = -(1 - \mu)Q_3 + N_2 + N_2^T - M_2 - M_2^T$

$h_{12} = h_2 - h_1$

Proof: Consider the following Lyapunov-Krasovskii

$V(x(t)) = V_1(x(t)) + V_2(x(t)) + V_3(x(t)),$ *where*

$V_1(x(t)) = x^T(t)Px(t) + 2\sum_{i=1}^n d_i \int_0^{x_i(t)} g_i(s)ds$

$V_2(x(t)) = \int_{t-h_1}^t x^T(s)Q_1x(s)ds + \int_{t-h_2}^t x^T(s)Q_2x(s)ds + \int_{t-h(t)}^t x^T(s)Q_3x(s)ds$
$\qquad + \int_{t-h(t)}^t g^T(x(s))Q_4g(x(s))ds$

$V_3(x(t)) = \bar{\tau}\int_{-\bar{\tau}}^0 \int_{t+\theta}^t g^T(x(s))Sg(x(s))dsd\theta + \int_{-h_2}^0 \int_{t+\theta}^t \dot{x}^T(s)Z_1\dot{x}(s)dsd\theta$
$\qquad + \int_{-h_2}^{-h_1} \int_{t+\theta}^t \dot{x}^T(s)Z_2\dot{x}(s)dsd\theta$

we have

$$
\begin{aligned}
\dot{V}_1 =\ & 2x^T(t)P[-Ax(t) + W_0g(x(t)) + W_1g(x(t-h(t))) + W_2\int_{t-\tau(t)}^t g(x(s))ds] \\
& +2g^T(x(t))D[-A \times x(t) + W_0g(x(t)) + W_1g(x(t-h(t))) \\
& +W_2\int_{t-\tau(t)}^t g(x(s))ds] \\
\le\ & 2x^T(t)P[-Ax(t) + W_0g(x(t)) + W_1g(x(t-h(t))) \\
& +W_2\int_{t-\tau(t)}^t g(x(s))ds] + 2g^T(x(t))D[W_0 \times g(x(t)) + W_1g(x(t-h(t))) \\
& +W_2\int_{t-\tau(t)}^t g(x(s))ds] - 2g^T(x(t))DAK^{-1}g(x(t))
\end{aligned}
$$
$$\text{(8)}$$

$$
\begin{aligned}
\dot{V}_2 =\ & x^T(t)Q_1x(t) - x^T(t-h_1)Q_1x(t-h_1) + x^T(t)Q_2x(t) \\
& -x^T(t-h_2)Q_2x(t-h_2) + x^T(t)Q_3x(t) \\
& -(1-\dot{h}(t))x^T(t-h(t))Q_3x(t-h(t)) + g^T(x(t))Q_4g(x(t)) \\
& -(1-\dot{h}(t))g^T(x(t-h(t)))Q_4g(x(t-h(t))) \\
\le\ & x^T(t)\sum_{i=1}^3 Q_ix(t) - \sum_{i=1}^2 x^T(t-h_i)Q_ix(t-h_i) \\
& -(1-\mu)x^T(t-h(t))Q_3x(t-h(t)) + g^T(x(t))Q_4 \times g(x(t)) \\
& -(1-\mu)g^T(x(t-h(t)))Q_4g(x(t-h(t)))
\end{aligned}
$$
$$\text{(9)}$$

$$
\begin{aligned}
\dot{V}_3 =\ & \bar{\tau}^2 g^T(x(t))Sg(x(t)) - \bar{\tau}\int_{t-\bar{\tau}}^t g^T(x(s))Sg(x(s))ds + h_2\dot{x}^T(s)Z_1\dot{x}(s) \\
& -\int_{t-h_2}^t \dot{x}^T(s)Z_1\dot{x}(s)ds \\
& +(h_2-h_1)\dot{x}^T(s)Z_2\dot{x}(s) - \int_{t-h_2}^{t-h_1} \dot{x}^T(s)Z_2\dot{x}(s)ds
\end{aligned}
$$
$$\text{(10)}$$

By applying lemma 4 and $0 \le \tau(t) \le \bar{\tau}$, we have

$$
\begin{aligned}
-\bar{\tau}\int_{t-\bar{\tau}}^t g^T(x(s))Sg(x(s))ds &\le -\tau(t)\int_{t-\tau(t)}^t g^T(x(s))Sg(x(s))ds \\
&\le -(\int_{t-\tau(t)}^t g^T(x(s))ds)^T S(\int_{t-\tau(t)}^t g^T(x(s))ds)
\end{aligned}
$$
$$\text{(11)}$$

Note that $h_1 \le h(t) \le h_2$, we have

$$
-\int_{t-h_2}^t \dot{x}^T(s)Z_1\dot{x}(s)ds \le -\int_{t-h(t)}^t \dot{x}^T(s)Z_1\dot{x}(s)ds \tag{12}
$$

By well-known Leibniz-Newton formula, we obtain that

$$2g^T(x(t-h(t)))[x(t)-x(t-h(t)) - \int_{t-h(t)}^t \dot{x}(s)ds] = 0 \qquad (13)$$

$$2[x^T(t)N_1 + x^T(t-h(t))N_2] \times [x(t-h(t))-x(t-h_2) - \int_{t-h_2}^{t-h(t)} \dot{x}(s)ds] = 0 \quad (14)$$

$$2[x^T(t)M_1 + x^T(t-h(t))M_2] \times [x(t-h_1)-x(t-h(t)) - \int_{t-h(t)}^{t-h_1} \dot{x}(s)ds] = 0 \quad (15)$$

By applying lemma 3 to (15), we have

$$-2\int_{t-h(t)}^t g^T(x(t-h(t)))\dot{x}^T(s)ds \le h_2 g^T(x(t-h(t)))Xg(x(t-h(t))) + 2g^T(x(t-h(t)))(Y -I)(x(t)-x(t-h(t))) + \int_{t-h(t)}^t \dot{x}^T(s)Z_1\dot{x}(s)ds$$
$$(16)$$

where

$$\begin{bmatrix} X & Y \\ * & Z_1 \end{bmatrix} \ge 0 \qquad (17)$$

Note that the following inequality holds

$$-2g^T(x(t-h(t)))Yx(t-h(t)) \le -2g^T(x(t-h(t)))YK^{-1}g(x(t-h(t))) \quad (18)$$

We have the following inequality

$$-\int_{t-h(t)}^t \dot{x}^T(s)Z_1\dot{x}(s)ds + 2g^T(x(t-h(t)))[x(t)-x(t-h(t)) - \int_{t-h(t)}^t \dot{x}(s)ds]$$
$$\le h_2 g^T(x(t-h(t)))Xg(x(t-h(t))) + 2g^T(x(t-h(t)))Yx(t)$$
$$-2g^T(x(t-h(t)))YK^{-1}g(x(t-h(t)))$$
$$(19)$$

Also, the following inequality holds

$$-\int_{t-h_2}^{t-h_1} \dot{x}^T(s)Z_2\dot{x}(s)ds = -\int_{t-h_2}^{t-h(t)} \dot{x}^T(s)Z_2\dot{x}(s)ds - \int_{t-h(t)}^{t-h_1} \dot{x}^T(s)Z_2\dot{x}(s)ds$$
$$(20)$$

Here

$$-\int_{t-h_2}^{t-h(t)} \dot{x}^T(s)Z_2\dot{x}(s)ds + 2[x^T(t)N_1 + x^T(t-h(t))N_2][x(t-h(t))$$
$$-x(t-h_2) - \int_{t-h_2}^{t-h(t)} \dot{x}(s)ds]$$
$$= 2[x^T(t)N_1 + x^T(t-h(t))N_2][x(t-h(t))-x(t-h_2)] + \xi^T(t)[h_{12}NZ_2^{-1}N^T]\xi(t)$$
$$-\int_{t-h_2}^{t-h(t)} [\xi^T(t)N + \dot{x}^T(s)Z_2]Z_2^{-1}[N^T\xi(t) + Z_2\dot{x}(s)]ds$$
$$\le 2[x^T(t)N_1 + x^T(t-h(t))N_2][x(t-h(t))-x(t-h_2)] + \xi^T(t)[h_{12}NZ_2^{-1}N^T]\xi(t)$$
$$(21)$$

Using the same way, we have

$$
\begin{aligned}
&- \int_{t-h(t)}^{t-h_1} \dot{x}^T(s) Z_2 \dot{x}(s) ds + 2[x^T(t) M_1 + x^T(t-h(t)) M_2][x(t-h_1) \\
&-x(t-h(t)) - \int_{t-h(t)}^{t-h_1} \dot{x}(s) ds] \\
&= 2[x^T(t) M_1 + x^T(t-h(t)) M_2][x(t-h_1) - x(t-h(t))] + \xi^T(t)[h_{12} M Z_2^{-1} M^T] \xi(t) \\
&\quad - \int_{t-h(t)}^{t-h_1} [\xi^T(t) M + \dot{x}^T(s) Z_2] Z_2^{-1} [M^T \xi(t) + Z_2 \dot{x}(s)] ds \\
&\leq 2[x^T(t) M_1 + x^T(t-h(t)) M_2][x(t-h_1) - x(t-h(t))] + \xi^T(t)[h_{12} M Z_2^{-1} M^T] \xi(t)
\end{aligned} \tag{22}
$$

where

$$
\xi(t) = \left[x^T(t)\, g^T(x(t))\, g^T(x(t-h(t))) (\textstyle\int_{t-\tau(t)}^t g(x(s)) ds)^T\, x^T(t-h_1)\, x^T(t-h_2)\, x^T(t-h(t)) \right]^T
$$

$$
N = \left[N_1^T\, 0\, 0\, 0\, 0\, 0\, N_2^T \right]^T, \quad M = \left[M_1^T\, 0\, 0\, 0\, 0\, 0\, M_2^T \right]^T
$$

Note that

$$
\dot{x}^T(s)[h_2 Z_1 + (h_2 - h_1) Z_2] \dot{x}(s) = \dot{x}^T(s) V \dot{x}(s) = \xi^T(t)[\Gamma^T V^{-1} \Gamma] \xi(t) \tag{23}
$$

where $V = h_2 Z_1 + (h_2 - h_1) Z_2$

$$
\Gamma = \left[-A^T V\, W_0^T V\, W_1^T V\, W_2^T V\, 0\, 0\, 0 \right]
$$

By putting (13),(14),(18),(20)-(25) into (12),we have

$$
\begin{aligned}
\dot{V}_3 \leq\ & \bar{\tau}^2 g^T(x(t)) S g(x(t)) - (\textstyle\int_{t-\tau(t)}^t g^T(x(s)) ds)^T S (\textstyle\int_{t-\tau(t)}^t g^T(x(s)) ds) \\
&+ h_2 g^T(x(t-h(t))) X g(x(t-h(t))) + 2 g^T(x(t-h(t))) Y x(t) \\
&- 2 g^T(x(t-h(t))) Y K^{-1} g(x(t-h(t))) + \xi^T(t)[\Gamma^T V^{-1} \Gamma] \xi(t) \\
&+ 2[x^T(t) N_1 + x^T(t-h(t)) N_2][x(t-h(t)) - x(t-h_2)] \\
&+ \xi^T(t)[h_{12} N Z_2^{-1} N^T] \xi(t) + 2[x^T(t) M_1 + x^T(t-h(t)) M_2][x(t-h_1) \\
&- x(t-h(t))] + \xi^T(t)[h_{12} M Z_2^{-1} M^T] \xi(t)
\end{aligned} \tag{24}
$$

Using (10),(11),(26),it can be shown that

$$
\dot{V} \leq \xi^T(t)
\begin{bmatrix}
(11)+\alpha P & PW_0 & PW_1+Y^T & PW_2 & M_1 & -N_1 & N_1 - M_1 \\
* & (22) & DW_1 & DW_2 & 0 & 0 & 0 \\
* & * & (33) & 0 & 0 & 0 & 0 \\
* & * & * & -S & 0 & 0 & 0 \\
* & * & * & * & -Q_1 & 0 & M_2^T \\
* & * & * & * & * & -Q_2 & -N_2^T \\
* & * & * & * & * & * & (77)
\end{bmatrix}
\xi(t)
$$
$$
+ \xi^T(t)[h_{12} N Z_2^{-1} N^T + h_{12} M Z_2^{-1} M^T + \Gamma^T V^{-1} \Gamma] \xi(t) \tag{25}
$$

By applying lemma 1,(25)is equivalent to

$$\dot{V} \le \xi^T(t) \begin{bmatrix} (11) & PW_0 & PW_1+Y^T & PW_2 & M_1 & -N_1 & N_1-M_1 & h_{12}N_1 & h_{12}M_1 & -A^TV \\ * & (22) & DW_1 & DW_2 & 0 & 0 & 0 & 0 & 0 & W_0^TV \\ * & * & (33) & 0 & 0 & 0 & 0 & 0 & 0 & W_1^TV \\ * & * & * & -S & 0 & 0 & 0 & 0 & 0 & W_2^TV \\ * & * & * & * & -Q_1 & 0 & M_2^T & 0 & 0 & 0 \\ * & * & * & * & * & -Q_2 & -N_2^T & 0 & 0 & 0 \\ * & * & * & * & * & * & (77) & h_{12}N_2 & h_{12}M_2 & 0 \\ * & * & * & * & * & * & * & -Z_2 & 0 & 0 \\ * & * & * & * & * & * & * & * & -Z_2 & 0 \\ * & * & * & * & * & * & * & * & * & -V \end{bmatrix} \xi(t) \tag{26}$$

According to the theorem, we get $\dot{V} < 0$. This completes our proof.

Remark 1. In Theorem 1,h_1 can not equal to 0,and from $(3,3),(7,7)$, we can have that μ can be any value. Therefore, Theorem 1 is applicable to both cases of fast and slow time-varying delay. In fact ,many results request that $h_1 = 0$ and $\mu < 1$,if $h_1 = 0$ and $\mu < 1$, we can have the following corollaries:

Corollary1. For given $0 \le h(t) \le h_2$, $\dot{h}(t) \le \mu < 1$, $0 \le \tau(t) \le \bar{\tau}$, $\alpha > 0$, $K = diag(k_1, k_2, \ldots, k_n)$,system (4)is globally asymptotically stable if there exist positive matrices $P,Q_i,(i = 2,3,4)$, and any matrices $X,Y,S,Z_1,D = diag(d_1, d_2, \ldots, d_n)$,satisfying the following LMIs:

$$\begin{bmatrix} (1,1) & PW_0 & PW_1+Y^T & PW_2 & 0 & 0 & -h_2A^TZ_1 \\ * & (2,2) & DW_1 & DW_2 & 0 & 0 & h_2W_0^TZ_1 \\ * & * & (3,3) & 0 & 0 & 0 & h_2W_1^TZ_1 \\ * & * & * & -S & 0 & 0 & h_2W_2^TZ_1 \\ * & * & * & * & -Q_2 & 0 & 0 \\ * & * & * & * & * & (6,6) & 0 \\ * & * & * & * & * & * & -h_2Z_1 \end{bmatrix} < 0 \tag{27}$$

$$\begin{bmatrix} X & Y \\ * & Z_1 \end{bmatrix} \ge 0 \tag{28}$$

where

$(1,1) = -PA - A^TP + Q_2 + Q_3$
$(2,2) = DW_0 + W_0^TD - 2DAK^{-1} + Q_4 + \bar{\tau}^2S$
$(3,3) = -(1-\mu)Q_4 + h_2X - YK^{-1} - K^{-1}Y^T$
$(6,6) = -(1-\mu)Q_3$

If $\mu = 0$ and $0 \le h(t) \le h_2$,according to Corollary 1, we can have the following corollary:

Corollary2. For given $0 \le h(t) \le h_2$, $0 \le \tau(t) \le \bar{\tau}$,$\alpha > 0$, $K = diag(k_1, k_2, \ldots, k_n)$,system (4)is globally asymptotically stable if there exist positive matrices $P,Q_i,(i = 2,3,4)$, and any matrices X,Y,S,Z_1, $D = diag(d_1, d_2, \ldots, d_n)$, satisfying the following LMIs:

$$\begin{bmatrix} (1,1) & PW_0 & PW_1 + Y^T & PW_2 & 0 & 0 & -h_2 A^T Z_1 \\ * & (2,2) & DW_1 & DW_2 & 0 & 0 & h_2 W_0^T Z_1 \\ * & * & (3,3) & 0 & 0 & 0 & h_2 W_1^T Z_1 \\ * & * & * & -S & 0 & 0 & h_2 W_2^T Z_1 \\ * & * & * & * & -Q_2 & 0 & 0 \\ * & * & * & * & * & -Q_3 & 0 \\ * & * & * & * & * & * & -h_2 Z_1 \end{bmatrix} < 0 \qquad (29)$$

$$\begin{bmatrix} X & Y \\ * & Z_1 \end{bmatrix} \geq 0 \qquad (30)$$

where

$$(1,1) = -PA - A^T P + Q_2 + Q_3 - \alpha P$$
$$(2,2) = DW_0 + W_0^T D - 2DAK^{-1} + Q_4 + \bar{\tau}^2 S$$
$$(3,3) = -Q_4 + h_2 X - YK^{-1} - K^{-1} Y^T$$

4   Conclusion

In this paper, a novel criterion for the global asymptotic stability of cellular neural network with time-varying discrete and distributed delays. The resulting criteria are applicable to both fast and slow time-varying delay.

References

1. Cao, J.: On stability of delayed cellular neural networks. Physics Letters A 261, 303–308 (1999)
2. Park, J.H.: A new stability analysis of delayed cellular neural networks. Applied Mathematics and Computation 181, 200–205 (2006)
3. Chen, C.J., Liao, T.L., Hwang, C.C.: Exponential synchronization of a class of chaotic neural networks. Chaos, Soliton, Fractals 24, 197–206 (2005)
4. Cao, J.: Global asymptotic stability of neural networks with transmission delays. International Journal of Systems Science 31, 1313–1316 (2000)
5. Liao, T.L., Wang, F.C.: Global stability for cellular neural networks with time delays. In: 11th IEEE Transaction on Neural Network, pp. 1481–1484. IEEE Press, New York (2000)
6. Arik, S.: An analysis of global asymptotic stability of delayed cellular neural networks. In: 13th IEEE Transaction on Neural Network, pp. 1239–1242. IEEE Press, New York (2002)
7. Park, J.H.: Robust stability of bidirectional associative memory neural networks with time delays. Physics Letters A 349, 494–499 (2006)

Localizing Sources of Brain Activity Relevant to Motor Imagery Brain-Computer Interface Performance, Using Individual Head Geometry

Alexander A. Frolov[1,*], Dušan Húsek[2], Pavel D. Bobrov[1,3], Alexey Korshakov[4], Lyudmila Chernikova[5], Rodion Konovalov[5], and Olesya Mokienko[1,5]

[1] Institute of Higher Nervous Activity and Neurophysiology, RAS,
Butlerova 5a, Moscow, Russia
aafrolov@mail.ru
[2] Institute of Computer Science, Academy of Sciences of the Czech Republic,
Pod Vodárenskou věží 2, Prague 8, Czech Republic
dusan@cs.cas.cz
[3] Faculty of Electronics and Informatics, VŠB-Technical University of Ostrava,
17. listopadu 15, Ostrava – Poruba, Czech Republic
[4] Russian Research Center Kurchatov Institute,
Kurchatov Square 46, Moscow, Russia
[5] Research Center of Neurology, RAMS,
Volokolamskoye highway, 80, Moscow, Russia

Abstract. It is shown that despite the fact that the motor imagery based brain computer interface does not rely on any particular feature of EEG signal defined a priori, system designed on the basis of EEG signal classifier is indeed controlled by the signals originating in the motor cortex. To prove this the most distinguishable EEG patterns were extracted by means of Independent Component Analysis with consequent cross-validation procedure used to select the independent components significant to the brain computer interface performance. Sources of the brain activity represented by the chosen independent components were located using single dipole approximation with individual head geometry model. These sources were found in the bottom of the central sulcus, area 3a, for each subject. These results are in good agreement with the outcome of fMRI study conducted under the same conditions.

Keywords: BCI, ICA, Bayesian classification, EEG inverse problem, motor imagery, mu rhythm, fMRI.

1 Introduction

Brain-computer interfacing has become an established technology during last years [15]. The most widespread BCI systems are those based on classification

* This work was supported by RFBR grants 10-04-00191 and 11-04-12025; by the project AV0Z10300504 and by IT4Innovations Centre of Excellence project, reg. No.CZ.1.05/1.1.00/02.0070.

J. Wang, G.G. Yen, and M.M. Polycarpou (Eds.): ISNN 2012, Part I, LNCS 7367, pp. 369–378, 2012.

of EEG patterns corresponding to performing some mental tasks chosen before-hand. In the following we consider a BCI based on performing Motor Imagery (MI) tasks, i.e. tasks involving human's kinesthetic imagining of moving his ex-tremities. Our interest in the BCI technology is motivated by its possible use as a tool for rehabilitation of people with post-stroke motor impairments [14]. Earlier we have designed such a system based on the basic Bayesian Classifier (BC) applied to the multi-channel EEG data directly. We have shown that this classifier provides an accuracy comparable with those that are based on more sophisticated techniques [9], while having much lower computational cost. The disadvantage of the classifier is that it does not provide a way to find physiolog-ically valid interpretation of classification in terms of the brain activity relevant to MI task.

That is why there are two questions addressed in the study. First, which are the patterns of EEG activity the most relevant to the BCI performance? Second, does the activity, the most relevant to the BCI control, originate from the sensorimotor cortex areas? A negative answer to the previous question could disprove the possibility to use BCI in rehabilitation.

In order to answer the previous questions we trained five subjects to control the BCI. Then we conducted an fMRI study for the subjects who had shown relatively high performance. In order to locate the sources of EEG activity un-derlying the BCI control we used the approach similar to the proposed in [2], involving the Independent Component Analysis (ICA) processing of the EEG signals before solving the inverse EEG problem. But we have incorporated the individual geometry model into the analysis of the sources and used only those independent components which are relevant to classification.

ICA provides representation of a multidimensional EEG signal $\mathbf{X}(t)$ (where components of $\mathbf{X}(t)$ represent electric potentials on N individual electrodes on the head surface) as a superposition of activities of independent components $\mathbf{X}(t) = \mathbf{W}\xi(t) = \mathbf{W}_1\xi_1 + \mathbf{W}_1\xi_2 + \cdots + \mathbf{W}_1\xi_N$. Columns $\mathbf{W}_i$ of matrix $\mathbf{W}$ specify the contribution of the corresponding independent component (or source) into each electrode potential, and the components ξ_i of the vector $\xi(t)$ specify source intensities at each time moment. The combination of active sources is supposed to be specific and individual for each mental task. Thus their activities during performing different task may be treated as independent.

2   Methods

Four male subjects aged 50 to 70 participated in the study. They formed the con-trol group in our current study of BCI efficiency as a procedure for rehabilitation of paralyzed patients. All subjects were right-handed and had no neurological diseases reported. The subjects have provided written participation consent. The experimental procedure was approved by the Board of Ethics at the Institute for Higher Nervous Activity and Neurophysiology, RAS. Also, one subject with the best BCI control abilities from the group of younger persons, previously investigated for BCI performance [9], was invited to take part in fMRI study.

2.1   Experimental Protocol

The subjects were trained to control the BCI for five consecutive days. Each day there were three experimental sessions: one session with no feedback, designed for classifier learning, and two sessions with feedback presented. The tasks were to relax and to perform a kinesthetic left or right hand grip imagining. The tasks to be performed were clued by changing the color of one of three markers placed around the center of monitor screen. The color was changed from gray into green to indicate an active task. Each command to imagine a movement was displayed for 15 seconds and was preceded by a relaxation period of 7 seconds. Each clue was preceded by a 3-second warning when the corresponding marker became blue. Four "relaxation - motor imagination" pairs presented in random order constituted a block, with two blocks constituting the first session and four blocks constituting the second and the third sessions.

EEG was recorded using 27 ActiCap (Munich, Germany) electrodes (Fz, F3, F4, Fcz, Fc3, Fc4, Cz, C1, C2, C3, C4, Cpz, Cp1, Cp2, Cp3, Cp4, Pz, P1, P2, P3, P4, Po3, Po4, Po8, Oz, O1, O2), Afz was used as reference. The data were digitized by 16 bit ADC NBL640 (NeuroBioLab, Russia) with sampling frequency 200 Hz and filtered within 6-28 Hz passband.

Two of the older subjects with the best BCI control and the younger subject were chosen for additional fMRI experiments to locate the areas of their brain activity during the motor imagery. fMRI recordings were made with 1.5 T MR scanner (Siemens, Erlangen, Germany). fMRI data were acquired using a T2*weighted EPI sequence (36 slices, TR=3800 ms, TE=50 ms, flip angle=90 degrees, 64×64 matrix, slice thickness 3 mm, voxel size= $3 \times 3 \times 3.7$ mm). A T1-weighted anatomical scan (176 slices, TR=1940 ms, TE=3 ms, scanning matrix 256×256, slice thickness 1 mm) was also acquired for each selected subject.

To compare the location of the brain areas active during motor imagery, revealed by EEG and fMRI studies, an additional (sixth) BCI session comprised of 10 blocks with no feedback was carried out for each subject just after fMRI. Positions of electrodes were identified with the aid of the Nexstim System (Finland). Precise localization of electrodes is one of the prerequisites for solving the inverse EEG problem using individual subject geometry.

2.2   Relevant Source Localization

To find EEG patterns, the most significant to the BCI performance, the data of the three sessions of each day were combined and decomposed into independent components using EEGLAB RunICA [7]. Then, combination of three independent components maximizing Cohen's κ by brute-force search was found. The κ index was estimated using the following cross-validation procedure. Ten blocks of the three sessions were randomly split into sets of seven and three blocks. The first set was used for classifier training and the second set was used for classifier testing. The κ index was computed as a result of 50 such splits. The cross-validation procedure was also applied to the records with no independent components excluded to estimate the subjects' performance.

The optimal components obtained for the EEG data recorded after the fMRI session were used for solving the EEG inverse problem. The problem was solved by fitting a single dipole to the independent component weights. This approach required solving the forward EEG problem. We used the Finite Element Method (FEM) which allows to take into account individual geometry of the brain and its covers. To apply FEM a 3d element mesh was generated from each subject's segmented anatomical MRI data. The data were segmented into regions containing White Matter (WM), Gray Matter (GM), Cerebrospinal Fluid (CSF), skull, and scalp by means of New Segmentation Tool of SPM8 toolbox for MAT-LAB. To obtain FEM mesh the segmented images were processed using our own tool, based on Computational Geometry Algorithms Library (CGAL) 3d mesh generation algorithms [1]. Upper bound size of the elements was 3 mm. Output mesh was imported into ANSYS software (ANSYS, Inc., PA, USA) which we used to solve the forward EEG problem. Electrical conductivities were assigned as follows: 0.14 S/m to WM, 0.33 S/m to GM, 1.79 S/m to CSF, 0.0132 S/m to the skull, and 0.35 S/m to the scalp [11].

3   Results

3.1   Independent Components the Most Relevant for BCI Control

For all subjects κ index, computed with all independent components taken into account, significantly exceeds zero (t-test, $P < 0.0001$). On average, over all subjects and all experimental days $\kappa = 0.37 \pm 0.06$, with maximum value equal to 0.60. Remarkably, average $\kappa = 0.43 \pm 0.05$, with maximum value equal to 0.64 when only the optimal component triples were considered. This observation suggests that the optimal triples contain independent components the most relevant to BCI performance.

Fig. 1 demonstrates spatial distributions of the component contribution into signal on EEG electrodes along with their spectrograms for the mental tasks performed during the experiment: relaxation and imagination of right or left hand movement. The data are shown for Subject 1 who demonstrated the best BCI control, day 5. These are typical components which were very stable and appeared in the triple of the most relevant components every day. Their intensities demonstrate event-related desynchronization and event-related synchronization, the well documented changes of the brain activity during MI [19]. As shown in Fig. 1, the intensity of the source located in the right hemisphere (marked $\mu1$ in Fig. 1) decreased drastically at the frequency of about 11 Hz during imagination of the left hand movement, while, on the contrary, the intensity of the source located in the left hemisphere (marked $\mu2$ in Fig. 1) increased. During imagining the right hand movement the changes of the intensities were opposite for each of the sources. It should be noted that ERD and ERS are much better exposed by these independent components than by EEG records.

As for the third component in the optimal triples, its spectrograms and contribution into EEG electrodes were different every day. Thus, only two components $\mu1$ and $\mu2$ can be considered to be the most relevant to BCI control.

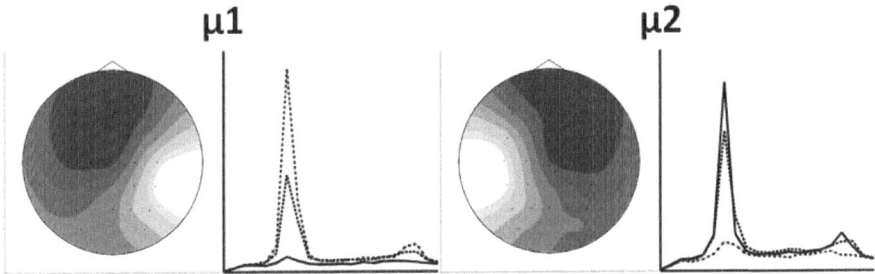

Fig. 1. Example of the optimal components obtained for Subject 1. Spatial distribution of the component contribution into EEG is given by columns of the ICA weighting matrix, **W**. The component spectrograms are shown in 5-25 Hz band. The dashed lines indicate relaxation, the solid lines indicate left hand MI, the dash-dotted lines indicate right hand MI.

3.2 Source Localization

Although it happened that the independent components identical to $\mu1$ and $\mu2$ depicted in Fig. 1 were identified at all subjects in all experimental days, still one could expect that they just originate from the results of formal mathematical transformations of the actual experimental data and consequently they have no physiological interpretation.

To clarify their nature we will show, first, that their contribution to EEG recordings can be explained by the current dipole source of brain activity located in the sensorimotor cortical areas, and, second, that locations of these dipolar sources are in agreement with clusters of task-relevant brain activity, identified in fMRI study.

We used contributions of the $\mu1$ and $\mu2$ components into signals on EEG channels for the dipole fitting. On average over all subjects and both hands the residual variance amounted only 8%. In Figs. 2, 3, 4 the obtained dipole locations are shown along with the fMRI topographic maps obtained by comparing local Blood-oxygen-level dependence (BOLD) responses during imagination of the left hand movement and the resting state. BOLD responses in these states were compared on a pixel-to-pixel basis with Student's test and thresholds at $P <$ 0.0001 by performing standard SPM8 fMRI processing steps. Only the sections through the found dipole positions are shown. Dipole positions and marked areas of fMRI activity are located very close to each other and to the "hand area", which is a segment of the central sulcus with a characteristic knob shape seen on axial slices [5]. However, the positions of dipoles happened to be a little deeper than areas of activity yielded by analysis of fMRI. Small discrepancy (up to 25 mm) between current dipole positions and centers of nearest clusters of BOLD response was also observed in the most studies of somatosensory response to hand electrical stimulation (see, for example, [6,4,25]. This may be explained by the fact that different processes are responsible for EEG and fMRI outcomes. EEG

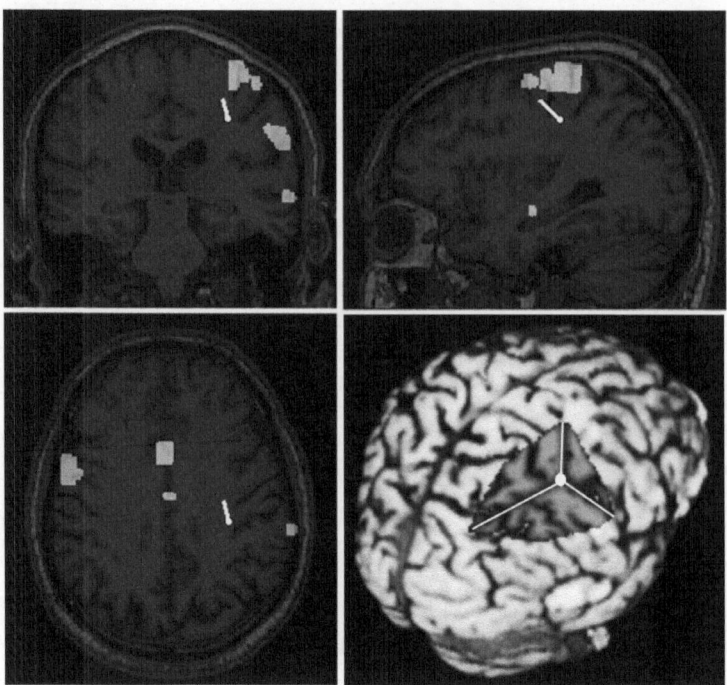

Fig. 2. Location and orientation of the dipole resulting as a solution of the inverse EEG problem for $\mu1$ component of Subject 1, along with the results of fMRI analysis. The component was estimated using the data of the additional BCI training session. Dipole location is marked by the white point. Its orientation is represented by projections onto each section. The cutoff shown in the right-bottom sub-figure has its origin at the dipole location and axes orthogonal to the sections. Voxels for which BOLD level was significantly higher during left hand MI compared to relaxation period are shown in white.

is the result of neuronal electric activity while fMRI relates to blood flow and oxygenation changes associated with the energetically dominant processes. If, for example, neuronal electric activity in the depth of central sulcus is less energy intensive than activity in the crown of pre- and postcentral gyrus than fMRI activity could be observed above the focus of neural electric activity. Moreover in our experiments performing the MI tasks results in an increase of BOLD signal, which is in accordance with the assumption, but at the same time to a decrease of magnitude of EEG signal, which is contrary to the assumption. Since relation between fMRI and neuronal electric activity is rather complex [16], then the brain areas where these two kinds of brain activity are maximally exposed could be slightly different. Hence, the small discrepancy of their positions does not provide evidence against the precision of dipole location. In our experiments the distance between dipole location and the COM of fMRI activity near central sulcus averaged over subjects and hands amounted to 15 ± 1.5 mm. For all

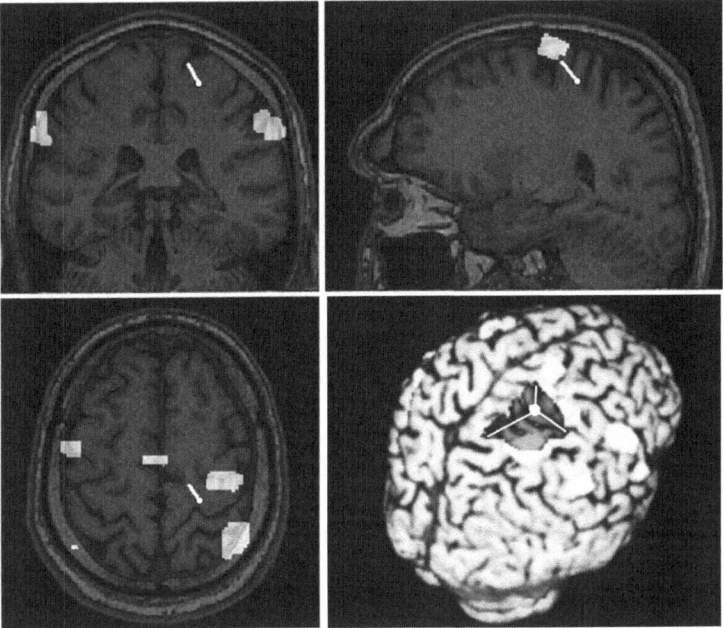

Fig. 3. Location and orientation of the dipole approximating $\mu 1$ for Subject 2

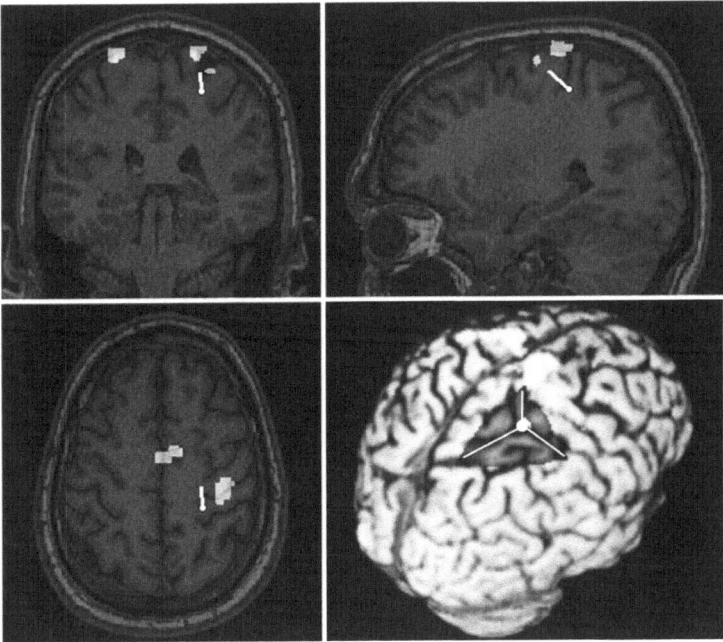

Fig. 4. Location and orientation of the dipole approximating $\mu 1$ for Subject 5

subjects and both hands the dipole was located near the bottom of the central sulcus (3 ± 2 mm at the sagittal sections), i.e. at the area 3a responsible for proprioceptive sensation [10].

4   Discussion

In the present work we have shown that despite the fact that the BC classifier does not rely on any particular feature of EEG signal, defined *a priori*, the MI BCI system designed on the basis of this classifier is indeed controlled by the signals originating in the sensorimotor cortex. The ICA plays an important role in the relevant source extraction, as shown in [2]. It allows for eliminating noise components and for estimating each source contribution into the registered signal, making possible to use a single dipole fitting procedure. Locating of the control signal sources is made possible by accounting for individual head geometry. The only thing we ignored was the WM anisotropy. Althoght it was shown in [12] that head model incorporating realistic anisotropic WM conductivity does not substantially improve the accuracy of EEG dipole localization, our next step is to take the anisotropy into account.

There is a long story of the debates concerning the brain areas involved into the motor imagination, especially the involvement of the primary sensorimotor cortex. Primary sensorimotor cortex fMRI activation during motor imagination was denied in [20,23], but was claimed in [22,8]. There were also many efforts to reveal whether SM1 activates during motor imagery, using EEG data [3,18,17]. Particularly in [18,17], conclusions on SM1 activation were drawn from the observation that ERD is maximally exposed at the electrodes related to SM1 activity. However, it is difficult to prescribe electrical activity to some particular brain area on the base of original EEG data. We believe that the approach we used allows to do this more accurately. The sources of the brain activity which are the most relevant for motor imagination happened to be located at the bottom of central sulcus, close to the Brodman area 3a which is responsible for proprioceptive sensation. This location corresponds to the internal feeling of the imagined hand movement according to reports of the subjects. However, our results do not provide an evidence against the presence of neural electric activity, specific to MI, in the primary motor cortex. We found the source of activity which demonstrates the most exposed ERD and ERS. As shown in [21], μ-rhythm is much more exposed in the primary somatosensory but not in primary motor cortex in immobile cat. Thus, one can expect that ERD and ERS in human could be also more exposed in the primary somatosensory cortex.

In addition to the foci of activity revealed by fMRI analysis, which are located near the primary sensorimotor cortex, we observed many other foci described by other researchers (see, for example, [8]). Also we obtained many independent components which were relevant to motor imagination other than two main components $\mu 1$ and $\mu 2$. Hence, the natural goal of our future research is to reveal the relations between other fMRI foci and other independent components.

References

1. Alliez, P., Rineau, L., Tayeb, S., Tournois, J., Yvinec, M.: 3D Mesh Generation. In: CGAL User and Reference Manual. CGAL Editorial Board, 3.9 edn. (2011), http://www.cgal.orgManuallatestdoc_htmlcgal_manualpackages.html#Pkg:Mesh_3
2. Baharan, K., Zhongming, L., Bin, H.: An EEG Inverse Solution based Brain-Computer Interface. International Journal of Bioelectromagnetism 7(2), 1–3 (2005)
3. Beisteiner, R., Hollinger, P., Lindinger, G., Lang, W., Berthoz, A.: Mental representations of movements. Brain potentials associated with imagination of hand movements. Electroecephalogr. Clin. Neurophysiol. 96, 183–193 (1995)
4. Christmann, C., Ruf, M., Braus, D.F., Flor, H.: Simultaneous electroencephalography and functional magnetic resonance imaging of primary and secondary somatosensory cortex in humans after electric stimulation. Neuroscience Letters 333, 69–73 (2002)
5. De Graaf, G., Frolov, A., Fiocchi, M., Nazarian, B., Anton, J.-L., Pailhous, J., Bonnard, M.: Preparing for a Motor Perturbation: Early Implication of Primary-Motor and Somatosensory Cortices. Human Brain Mapping 30, 575–587 (2009)
6. Del Grattaf, C., Della Penna, S., Ferretti, A., Franciotti, R., Pizzella, V., Tartaro, A., Torquati, K., Bonomo, L., Romani, G.L., Rossini, P.M.: Topographic organization of the human primary and secondary somatosensory cortices: comparison of fMRI and MEG findings. Neuroimage 17(3), 1373–1383 (2002)
7. Delorme, A., Makeig, S.: EEGLAB: an open source toolbox for analysis of single-trial EEG dynamics. Journal of Neuroscience Methods 134, 9–21 (2004)
8. Formaggio, E., Storti, S.F., Cerini, R., Fiaschi, A., Manganotti, P.: Brain oscillatory activity during motor imagery in EEG-fMRI coregistration. Magnetic Resonance Imaging 28(10), 1403–1412 (2010)
9. Frolov, A., Husek, D., Bobrov, P.: Comparison of four classification methods for brain computer interface. Neural Network World 21(2), 101–115 (2011)
10. Kaukoranta, E., Hamalainen, M., Sarvas, J., Hari, R.: Mixed and sensory nerve stimulations activate different cytoarchitectonic areas in the human primary somatosensory cortex SI. Exp. Brain Res. 63, 60–66 (1986)
11. Kim, T.S., Zhou, Y., Kim, S., Singh, M.: EEG distributed source imaging with a realistic finite-element head model. IEEE Trans. Nucl. Sci. 49, 745–752 (2002)
12. Lee, W.H., Liu, Z., Mueller, B.A., Limb, K., He, B.: Influence of white matter anisotropic conductivity on EEG source localization: Comparison to fMRI in human primary visual cortex. Clin. Neurophysiol. 120(12), 2071–2081 (2009)
13. Leuthardt, E., Schalk, G., Roland, J., Rouse, A., Moran, D.: Evolution of brain-computer interfaces: going beyond classic motor physiology. Neurosurgical Focus 27, E4 (2009)
14. del R. Millan, J., Mourino, J., Marciani, M.G., Babiloni, F., Topani, F., Canale, I., Heikkonen, J., Kaski, K.: Adaptive Brain Interfaces for Physically-Disabled People. In: 2nd Annual Int.Conf. of the IEEE Engineering in Medicine and Biology Science, Hong Kong, pp. 2008–2011 (1998)
15. del R. Millan, J., Rupp, R., Müller-Putz, G.R., Murray-Smith, R., Giugliemma, C., Tangermann, C., Vidaurre, M., Cincotti, F., Kbler, A., Leeb, R., Neuper, C., Müller, K.-R., Mattia, D.: Combining brain computer interfaces and assistive technologies: state-of-the-art and challenges. Frontiers in Neuroscience 4, Article 161 (2010)

16. Mulert, C., Lemieux, L. (eds.): EEG-fMRI. Physiological basis, techniques and application, 539 p. Springer (2010)
17. Neuper, C., Scherer, R., Reiner, M., Pfurtscheller, G.: Imagery of motor actions: Differential effects of kinesthetic and visual-motor mode of imagery in single-trial EEG. Cognitive Brain Reserch 25, 668–677 (2005)
18. Pfurtscheller, G., Neuper, C., Flotzinger, D., Pregenzer, M.: EEG-based discrimination between imagination of right and left hand movement. Electroencephalography and Clinical Neurophysiology 103, 642–651 (1997)
19. Pfurtscheller, G., Brunner, C., Schlogl, A., Lopes da Silva, F.: Mu rhythm (de) synchronization and EEG single-trial classification of different motor imagery tasks. NeuroImage 31, 153–159 (2006)
20. Rao, S.M., Binder, J.R., Bandettini, P.A., Hammeke, T.A., Yetkin, F.Z., Jesmanowicz, A., Lisk, L.M., Morris, G.L., Mueller, W.M., Estkowski, L.D., Wong, E.C., Haughton, V.M., Hyde, J.S.: Functional magnetic resonance imaging of complex human movements. Neurology 43, 2311–2318 (1993)
21. Rougeul-Buser, A., Buser, P.: Rhythms in the alpha band in cats and their behavioural correlates. International Journal of Psychophysiology 26, 191–203 (1997)
22. Sabbah, P., Simond, G., Levrier, O., Habib, M., Trabaud, V., Murayama, N., Mazoyer, B.M., Briant, J.F., Raybaud, C., Salamon, G.: Functional magnetic resonance imaging at 1.5 T during sensory motor and cognitive tasks. Eur. Neurol. 35, 131–136 (1995)
23. Sanes, J.N., Stern, C.E., Baker, J.R., Kwong, K.K., Donoghue, J.P., Rosen, B.R.: Human frontal motor cortical areas related to motor performance and mental imagery. Soc. Neurosci. Abstr. 18, 1208 (1993)
24. Stephan, K.M., Fink, G.R., Passingham, R.E., Silbersweig, D., Ceballos-Baumann, A.O., Frith, C.D., Frackowiak, R.S.J.: Functional anatomy of the mental representation of upper extremity movements in healthy subjects. Journal of Neurophysiology 73(1), 373–386 (1995)
25. Thees, S., Blabkenburg, F., Taskin, B., Curio, G., Villringer, A.: Dipole source localization and fMRI of simultaneously recorded data applied to somatosensory categorization. NeuroImage 18, 707–719 (2003)

Clustering Social Networks
Using Interaction Semantics and Sentics

Praphul Chandra[1], Erik Cambria[2], and Amir Hussain[3]

[1] Hewlett Packard Labs India, 560030, India
[2] National University of Singapore, 117411, Singapore
[3] University of Stirling, FK9 4LA, United Kingdom
praphul.chandra@hp.com, cambria@nus.edu.sg, ahu@cs.stir.ac.uk
http://sentic.net

Abstract. The passage from a static read-only Web to a dynamic read-write Web gave birth to a huge amount of online social networks with the ultimate goal of making communication easier between people with common interests. Unlike real world social networks, however, online social groups tend to form for extremely varied and multi-faceted reasons. This makes very difficult to group members of the same social network in subsets in a way that certain types of contents are shared with just certain types of friends. Moreover, such a task is usually too tedious to be performed manually and too complex to be performed automatically. In this work, we propose a new approach for automatically clustering social networks, which exploits interaction semantics and sentics, that is, the conceptual and affective information associated with the interactive behavior of online social network members.

Keywords: Social Network Analysis, Sentic Computing, NLP.

1   Introduction

Online social network representations often aggregate a user's social network into a common cluster of 'friends'. This approach is acceptable when the context of interaction is specific (e.g., LinkedIn [1]), but can lead to problems when the interaction context is broad and generic (e.g., Facebook [2]). The problem is further complicated by the fact that it is not always easy to demarcate the interaction context into 'specific' or 'generic'. Often, the interaction context is an emergent property of how users come to use the medium and different users choose to use it in different ways, e.g., some users may find it acceptable to add a family member as a LinkedIn contact whereas others may not.

Even when tools are available for users to be able to classify their friends into different clusters, they are rarely used [3]. Previous user studies have attributed this to (a) this process being time consuming and tedious; (b) the dynamic nature of the groups where individuals need to be added or removed from the group on a case-by-case basis [4]. This motivates the automatic clustering of a user's social network, which is updated dynamically based on user's social interactions.

J. Wang, G.G. Yen, and M.M. Polycarpou (Eds.): ISNN 2012, Part I, LNCS 7367, pp. 379–385, 2012.

For clustering social networks, we must differentiate between a user's ego-centric networks and a global socio-centric networks. Whereas, a user's ego-centric network only contains 'friends' of a particular user, the global socio-centric network is formed by combining the ego-centric networks of all users in the system. In this work, we focus initially on a user's ego-centric network. Later we show, how our approach may be extended to socio-centric networks. An automatic dynamic clustering of users' personal social network is useful to enable users to segregate their online social networks and reflect more accurately social networks in the real world. This is crucial, e.g., for meeting the privacy expectations of users (preventing unintended sharing). Clustering a user's social network is also useful for recommending potential group members during group communication and sharing – this is especially useful on mobile devices where interaction space is limited [3].

2   Related Work

In [3], Reto et al., use graph-clustering algorithms to cluster social networks based on edge density. They use a structural definition of cluster: "the density of edges within a cluster is larger than the density of edges connecting vertices from inside the cluster to vertices outside the cluster". Using this definition of cluster, they use an existing network clustering algorithm [5] to cluster a user's social network. Thus, their approach relies on analyzing the topology of the social graph that exists between a user's 'friends'.

An alternate approach for clustering social networks is used by Pal and McCallum [6]. Rather than using the topology of the social graph, the authors exploit the content of communication messages between users to cluster email recipients into groups. For each user, they build a model that maps keywords and phrases extracted from email messages to the recipients who are likely to receive an email containing those terms. Other approaches, which use neither the topology of the social graph nor the content of the communication messages, have also been used.

Bar-Yossef et al. [7] and Roth et al. [4] observe how users group their 'friends' when sending email messages. Based on past behavior of user's group communication messages, they develop ranking algorithms that can predict other similar users who can belong to a particular group specified as a seed-set of users. De Choudhury et al. [8] propose an approach to 'label' nodes in a social network as per their roles, e.g., "student", "faculty", or "director". They apply their approach on an email communication graph, filtering out infrequent email communications below a certain threshold.

Finally, there is significant literature on tie-strength, a notion first proposed by Granovetter [9]. However, the notion of tie strength is complementary to the problem we address. By assigning a weight to each link in the social graph, tie-strength in an ego-centric network determines the distance of a particular 'friend' from the given user – it can be seen as a distance metric in an ego-centric social network. On the other hand, the problem of clustering an ego-centric social network is concerned by grouping 'similar friends' together.

Fig. 1. The user is placed in the center of the map. People are placed closer to the user the more important they are, and are grouped depending on their tendency to be emailed together.

Our approach is most similar to [6] in that we exploit the contents of social interactions to cluster a user's social network. But rather than working on syntactics, we exploit interaction semantics and sentics [10], that is the conceptual and affective information associated with the interactive behavior of online social network members.

3   Our Approach

In our approach, the basic unit of analysis is the socio-interaction matrix, A. The elements of the socio-interaction matrix are the occurrences of each 'concept' in a particular social link:

$$A = [a_{ij}]$$

where a_{ij} denotes the frequency of concept, i in a social link, j. We assume that we have access to the content of interaction between users. This interaction may be in the form of email messages, chat messages, metadata of shared content (e.g., photos, videos, etc.). This content can then be mapped to a set of concepts from a concept space (see section 3.1).   The social links refer to the edges of a social network.

We then apply truncated singular value decomposition (TSVD) on this socio-interaction matrix to obtain a low-rank (k-dimension) approximation of A, i.e., $A_k = U_k \Sigma_k V_k^T$ and, hence, reduce the dimensionality of the socio-interaction space. The result of this process is a vector space, built by selecting the first k eigenvalues of Σ, which self-organizes social links as k-dimensional vectors, in a way that they can then be clustered in order to find semantic similarity between them. A similar approach is also used to find sentic similarity [11] between social links, i.e., to express how different users affectively interact with each other.

In one application of our approach, the social network we consider will be an un-weighted ego-centric social network, which will simply be a star graph from the user to each of his/her friends. Thus, in this application, we do not require knowledge about the network structure that exists between a user's friends or the interactions therein. This information may be hard to get since it is subject to privacy settings and expectations of users.

In an alternate application of our approach, the social network we consider will be an un-weighted socio-centric network containing social links between multiple users. This approach is more applicable when we do have access to the global information (as maybe the case for online social web services like Facebook). Our approach consists of three stages and we describe them in sections 3.1 – 3.3. We initially describe the application of our approach to an ego-centric network without assuming the availability of any information on the link structure between a user's social network and the semantics therein.

3.1   Adding Semantics to Social Interaction

We use the term 'social interaction' to include various types of interactions, e.g., text based communication (email, IM, wall-posts, etc.), sharing social media (photos, videos, etc.), exchange of goods (digital goods, e.g., e-cards, or physical goods, e.g., via eBay [5]). Social interaction semantics and sentics, then, refer to the conceptual and affective information contained in these social interactions. In particular, we currently focus on the text contained in these social interactions. This text may be unstructured (as in the case of emails, wall-posts, comments, etc.) or structured (as in the case of EXIF metadata for a photo).

In either case, the aim is to be able to map the text content of social interaction to a concept space. In the future, non-text content of social interaction can also form as a basis for determining the semantics of interaction but we do not focus on that in this work. The choice of the concept space is dependent on the application scenario. If the data set contains friends and family sharing personal emails and photos, a common sense knowledge base like ConceptNet [12] may be suitable.

On the other hand, if the social network represents a co-authorship network, a domain-ontology may be more applicable. In generic scenarios, Wikipedia may serve as the concept space as has been done in previous work. If the text content is structured, it may be mapped to the concept space using a rule-engine or simply treated as 'tags' in unstructured text.

Starting with unstructured text, a NLP module performs a first skim of the text and passes it to a semantic parser, whose aim is to deconstruct the lemmatized text into concepts. The retrieved concepts are then inserted into the socio-interaction matrix according to the protagonists of the interaction and, eventually, TSVD is applied to these data in order to find out how the different social links are related to each other.

3.2   Creating the Socio-interaction Matrix

Section 3.1 describes how a given social interaction can be mapped to a set of concepts from a concept space [13]. Given a particular user's interactions with his/her social network, the application of section 3.1 can lead to the formation of a labeled graph where each link between the user and a friend is labeled with a set of concepts from a concept space. This forms a raw M*N socio-interaction matrix, A', of the form:

	Friend-1	Friend-2	...	...	Friend-N
Concept-1	4	1	...	...	0
Concept-2	1	0	...	...	0
Concept-3	27	1	...	...	0
Concept-4	0	12	...	...	...
...	...	...	...	...	...
...	...	...	...	...	...
...	0	...	...	...	...
Concept-M	0	...	...	...	65

In this raw socio-interaction matrix, each element, a'_{ij} denotes the number of times a concept, i occurs in the interaction with a social link, j. This raw matrix may be used as is. However, in many cases, it is beneficial to apply some local weighting function. In our implementation, we use the notion of Concept Frequency-Inverse Social Frequency (CF-ISF) influenced by the common use of tf-idf in information retrieval. Using, CF-ISF, this raw socio-interaction matrix is converted to the socio-interaction matrix, A that we use in the rest of the work.

Concept frequency : $cf_{ij} = \dfrac{c_{ij}}{\sum\limits_{k} c_{kj}}$

Inverse Social frequency: $isf_i = \log \dfrac{|S|}{|s : c_i \in d|}$

where,

c_{ij} : the number of times concept i occurs in interaction with friend j

$\sum\limits_{k} c_{kj}$: sum of the number of occurrences of all concepts with friend j.

$|S|$: total number of friends the user has

$|s:c_i \in d|$: number of friends with which social interaction involved this concept

Thus, (Concept frequency – Inverse Social Frequency)$_{ij}$ is defined as:

$$cf_{ij} *isf_i = \frac{c_{ij}}{\sum_k c_{kj}} \log \frac{|S|}{|s:c_i \in d|}.$$

These (cf-isf)$_{ij}$ form the elements of the socio-interaction matrix, A, i.e., a_{ij} = (cf-isf)$_{ij}$

3.3   Reducing the Dimensionality of the Socio-interaction Matrix

The socio-interaction matrix is large even for a single user since the number of concepts in the concept space (M) is expectedly large. In ConceptNet, for example, the number of concepts exceeds 200,000 and in Wikipedia (which has been used as a concept space in earlier works), the number of entries is over 3 million.

To reduce the dimensionality of the socio-interaction matrix A, created in section 3.2, we use TSVD. Using SVD, any matrix, A can be factored into an orthonormal matrix U, a diagonal matrix Σ (consisting of s_{ii}) and an orthonormal matrix VT, so that:

$$A = U\Sigma V^T$$

Even though multiple such factorizations of the above form may exists, it can be shown that there exist non-unique matrices U and V such that $s_1 \geq s_2 \geq s_3... \geq s_N \geq 0$[6]. We refer to this as the singular value decomposition of A. In the SVD representation, the largest singular (s_1, s_2 etc.) values represent capture the principal components of the data.

The SVD representation allows a given matrix, A, to be represented by a matrix of lower rank, B, which best approximates A. The 'best approximation' is defined by minimizing the L2 norm of the error matrix between the original and the approximation. If we want to reduce the dimension of our socio-interaction matrix to k-dimensions, we can use the first k-principal components of Σ in the SVD to obtain:

$$A_k = U_k \Sigma_k V_k^T$$

Plotting social links in this (reduced) k-dimensional space leads to clustering of social links. This is one of the key results of our approach. Also, interestingly, concepts too can be plotted in this k-dimensional space thus giving a semantic context to a social cluster. As it has been done in related work, clustering social networks can be used for a variety of purposes, e.g., privacy, social query routing, automatic suggestion of list completion, etc. Our approach combines the use of a user's past communication pattern and the semantics and sentics of the communication therein.

4   Conclusions and Future Work

In this work, we proposed a new approach for automatically clustering social networks. In particular, we exploit the contents of social interactions to cluster a user's social network. But rather than working on syntactics, we exploit interaction semantics and sentics, that is the conceptual and affective information associated with the interactive behavior of online social network members. Preliminary tests on a toy social network (16 users) prove the in-principle effectiveness of the approach. In the future, we plan to perform a thorough evaluation of the system by using a real-world dataset (a real social network database), and further explore how the different user-interaction metadata can aid the clustering process.

References

1. LinkedIn (2011), `http://linkedIn.com`
2. Facebook (2011), `http://facebook.com`
3. Kuhn, M., Wirz, M.: Mobile social networking for enhanced group communication. In: International Conference on Supporting Group Work, Sanibel Island (2009)
4. Roth, M., Ben-David, A., Deutscher, D., Flysher, G., Horn, I., Leichtberg, A., Leiser, N., Matias, Y., Merom, R.: Suggesting friends using the implicit social graph. In: KDD, Washington (2010)
5. Gregory, S.: An Algorithm to Find Overlapping Community Structure in Networks. In: Kok, J.N., Koronacki, J., Lopez de Mantaras, R., Matwin, S., Mladenič, D., Skowron, A. (eds.) PKDD 2007. LNCS (LNAI), vol. 4702, pp. 91–102. Springer, Heidelberg (2007)
6. Golub, G., Van-Loan, C.: Matrix Computations, pp. 16–21. Johns Hopkins University Press (1983)
7. Bar-Yossef, O., Guy, I., Lempel, R., Maarek, Y., Soroka, V.: Cluster ranking with an application to mining mailbox networks. Knowledge and Information Systems 14(1), 101–139 (2008)
8. De Choudhury, M., Mason, W., Hofman, J., Watts, D.: Inferring relevant social networks from interpersonal communication. In: WWW, Raleigh (2010)
9. Granovetter, M.: The strength of weak ties: A network theory revisited. Sociological Theory 1, 201–233 (1983)
10. Cambria, E., Benson, T., Eckl, C., Hussain, A.: Sentic PROMs: Application of Sentic Computing to the Development of a Novel Unified Framework for Measuring Health-Care Quality. Expert Systems with Applications 39(12), 10533–10543 (2012)
11. Cambria, E., Hussain, A.: Sentic Computing: Techniques, Tools, and Applications. Springer, Heidelberg (2012)
12. Havasi, C., Speer, R., Alonso, J.: ConceptNet 3: a Flexible, Multilingual Semantic Network for Common Sense Knowledge. In: RANLP, Borovets (2007)
13. Cambria, E., Olsher, D., Kwok, K.: Sentic Activation: A Two-Level Affective Common Sense Reasoning Framework. In: AAAI, Toronto (2012)

Ontology-Based Semantic Affective Tagging

Marco Grassi and Francesco Piazza

Department of Information Engineering
Universitá Politecnica delle Marche - Ancona, 60131, Italy
{m.grassi,f.piazza}@univpm.it
http://www.semedia.dibet.univpm.it

Abstract. With the advent of Web 2.0, tagging has become a common practice over the Web and a valuable source of metadata that has been increasingly exploited for resource classification and retrieval. Several research efforts have been conducted in the recent years to improve the productivity of user created tags by providing them with a proper structure and semantics. Also several approaches have been proposed to add implicit tags to resources both by analyzing the media and measuring the physiological and physical signals produced by the humans interacting with the media. This paper discusses the application of Semantic Web technologies to foster Affective Tagging. In particular, a human emotion ontology is proposed to standardize the main emotion models and map together different representations. In addition, public knowledge bases exposed as Linked Data can be exploited not only to disambiguate words and concepts, overcoming some of the main issues related to the use of natural language, but also to reveal the affective valence of such tags.

Keywords: Semantic Tagging, Human Emotion Ontology, Semantic Web, Sentiment Analysis.

1 Introduction

Since the advent of Web 2.0, tagging has become a consolidated practice over the Web and is nowadays one of the most employed approaches on the Web for resource classification and retrieval [1].Several research efforts have been conducted in the recent years to improve the productivity of user created tags by providing a proper structure and semantic to tags, in order to overcome some of the limitations due to the ambiguity of natural language. Moreover, several approaches have been proposed to add implicit tags from resources both by analyzing the media and by measuring the physiological and physical signals produced by the humans interacting with the media. [2]. In addition, if till few years ago, resource classification was mostly oriented to topic categorization, recently the capability to classify resourcesaccording to their affective content is dragging a growing interest. Several application scenarios exist as: the studies of emotions that requires the fine-grain annotation of media according to the contained emotion; social marketing that aims to capture user opinion about products and brands

J. Wang, G.G. Yen, and M.M. Polycarpou (Eds.): ISNN 2012, Part I, LNCS 7367, pp. 386–393, 2012.

analyzing blog post; recommender systems to suggest music or videos according to user mood.

Tags have been extensively used for topic classification but their application for affective resource classification is currently still limited. Few systems allow to explicitly use emotion categories taken from controlled vocabularies as tags. Also, when they allow this they dont rely on standardized vocabularies with a well defined semantics, which makes difficult to reuse such tags in wider scenarios and by third party applications. In addition, often it's common practice to use, as tags, words that identify entities as actors, places, movies or events rather than concepts. Strings as "September 11" or "Monty Pythons" represent instances that belong to the common knowledge of users and have for them a clear connotation and underlying affective valence. By the way, this valence remains in most of the cases unrevealed to machines that rely for affect extraction on thesauri that dont contain the required background knowledge.

In recent years, the Linked Data Initiative has made available on the Web several knowledge bases, as Wikipedia and Wordnet, in a semantic aware format. Such knowledge bases have already been used in several applications to lookup for unambiguous named entities to be used as tags. This paper discusses the application of SW technologies to enhance both explicit and implicit "Affective Tagging" by revealing the affective valence of tags and making it available and easily processable by other applications. In particular, a human emotion ontology is proposed as source for explicit affective tags and background knowledge of emotions. Some approaches, based on Semantic Web and Sentiment Analysis, are then discussed that can allow to exploit public knowledge bases exposing Linked Data for Semantic Affective Tagging, allowing not only to disambiguate words and concepts in order to overcome some of the main issues related to the use of natural language but also to reveal the affective valence of the used tags.

2 The Semantic Web and the Linked Data Initiative

The Semantic Web (SW)[1] is an initiative by W3C that aims to improve the current Web in which the information can be expressed in a machine-understandable format and can be processed automatically by software agents. The SW enables data interoperability, allowing data to be shared and reused across heterogeneous device and applications. The SW bases on the Resource Description Framework (RDF) to define relations among different data, creating semantic networks. In SW ontologies are used to organize information and formally describe concepts and their relations in a domain of interest. Ontologies can be developed using specific ontology languages such as: the RDF Schema Language (RDFS) or the Web Ontology Language (OWL) Ontology for inference and knowledge base modeling.

Linked Data defines a set of good practices to publish structured data on the Web in a uniformly accessible way, in such a way that it is machine-readable, its

---

[1] See http://www.w3.org/2001/sw/ for Semantic Web initiative, related technologies and standards.

meaning is explicitly defined, it is linked to other external data sets, and can in turn be linked to/from external data sets. The Linked Data principles have been adopted by an increasing number of providers, especially from the Linking Open Data community project, which makes free and public data available as linked data. In October 2007, the Linked Data cloud consisted of 25 billion items, linked by around 400 million links. Data comes both from private and public providers and it embraces sectors and fields of knowledge including but not limited to: governmental and statistical data, encyclopedias, news and media, healthcare, life sciences, human sciences, geographic content.

3   Semantic Tagging

In most of the cases, tagging is based on natural language tags and without using restricted vocabularies. This approach is very intuitive and familiar for the user, giving them full freedom in adding tags, but it suffers from several issues related with the ambiguity of natural language [1]:

- *Base form variation*: different forms of the same word (e.g., plurals vs. singular forms, conjugations, misspellings) could be used as tags.
- *Polysemy*: tags could have ambiguous interpretation, e.g. the tag orange may be used to describe a fruit as well as a color.
- *Synonymy*: syntactically different tags may have the same meaning, e.g picture and image.
- *Specificity gap*: a tag could be a subclass of another tag, e.g. dog and animal, but considered as a completely different concept if analyzed only at syntactic level.

To overcome such issues, semantic tagging paradigm uses tags that have a clear meaning and are themselves a web resource, which have a description on the web which can be accessed by dereferencing its url. Several system have been developed that uses named entities coming from Linked Data knowledge bases as Dbpedia and Freebase as tags, as Faviki[2] a social bookmarking tool that allows using Wikipedia concepts as tags for Web pages. Also web services as Dbpedia Spotlight[3] and Zemanta[4] have been developed that allow to automatically extract named entities from text. Since this process is error prone, users is required to confirm the associations the system found between user-typed words and vocabulary terms. Such terms can then be added as tags.

4   Semlib Project

The SemLib project [5], see [3] for more details, aims to improve the current state of the art in DLs through the application of SW technologies for data representation and management. One of the main expected outputs of the SemLib

---

[2] Faviki: http://www.faviki.com/

[3] Dbpedia Spotlight: http://dbpedia.org/spotlight

[4] Zemanta: http://www.zemanta.com/

[5] Semlib Project http://www.semlibproject.eu/

project is the design and implementation of an annotation system able to enrich DLs content by means of semantically structured annotation. Resource annotation is supported at different granularity levels, allowing to annotate not only entire resources but also fragment of these, leveraging on Web standards such as XPointer[6] and Media Fragment URI[7] to unambiguously identify text excerpts in Web pages and subparts of images and audio-video resources. In order to provide support for different kind of users, different types of annotation are allowed, which can be structured according to different levels of complexity and provided with diverse expressive flavor and semantics, from natural language comments to semantic tags, coming from restricted vocabularies, to full subject-object-value statements based on domain ontologies. Some early experiments are currently conducted inside the Semlib project, to augment semantic tags with affective information as discussed in the following.

5   Human Emotion Ontology

Human Emotion Ontology (HEO) [4] standardizes the main emotion description models into a computational ontology. HEO is conceived as an high level ontology for human emotions, which supplies the most significant concepts and properties that are necessary to provide accurate human emotion descriptions, whose semantic is univocally defined and machine-interpretable. In HEO an emotion can be described both in a discrete way, by using the heo:hasEmotionCategory property, and in a dimensional way, by using the heo:hasDimension property. HEO has been developed in OWL-DL to take advantage of its expressiveness and its inference power in order to map the different models used in the emotion description. OWL-DL, in fact, allows a taxonomical organization of emotion categories and properties restriction to link emotion description made by category and dimension, providing inference capabilities without losing computational completeness and decidability.

HEO provides a wide set of discrete categories. In particular, all the vocabularies defined by EmotionML 1.0 [5] are included, ranging from Ekman's 6 archetypal emotions to the 24 FSRE categories by Fontaine, Scherer, Roesch and Ellsworth. Several additional emotion categories are also available between which also the categories defined by Wordnet Affect, which allows to connect it with Wordnet, as described in the next section.

HEO introduces the heo:hasIntensity property that can be used to define the intensity of the emotion defined through a discrete category, setting a value between 0 and 1. Several others dimensions can also be used to describe emotions belonging for example to the Activation-Evaluation or the Arousal-Valence-Dominance model. Several others emotion related features can also be described as action tendencies and appraisal.

Such wide collection of affective words that defines emotions and affective state and its taxonomic organization has been already used in Sentiment Analysis

---

[6] XML Pointer Language (XPointer): http://www.w3.org/TR/xptr/
[7] Media Fragments URI 1.0: http://www.w3.org/TR/media-frags/

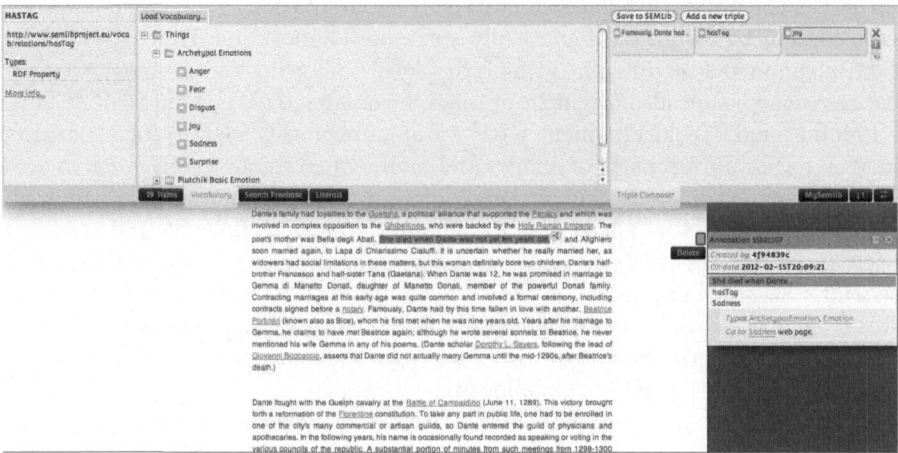

Fig. 1. Annotating page fragment using Semlib annotation system and HEO ontology

application [6]. It is also used in Semlib system to annotate affective information of web resources. HEO ontology can in fact be loaded in the annotation system and used to compose RDF statement, as shown in Fig. 1.

6   Enriching Wordnet Tags with Affective Information

Princeton University's WordNet [8] is one of the most widely used natural language processing resource today. Wordnet is a large lexical database of English, in which nouns, verbs, adjectives and adverbs are grouped into sets of cognitive synonyms (synsets), each expressing a distinct concept. Synsets are interlinked by means of conceptual-semantic and lexical relations.

In a 2006 W3C document, Mark van Assem et al. [9] proposed a standard conversion of Princeton Wordnet to RDF/OWL. Following this metodology, WordNet 3.0s knowledge base has been published as Linked data and an open SPARQL endpoint has been provided to allow semantic aware application to consume such information.

Using this accessible SPARQL endpoint, Wordnet can be used in Semlib for semantic tagging, allowing to disambiguate words according their sense. Listing 1.1 shows some of the information that is stored in the system when an annotation is created using a Wordnet tag.

Listing 1.1. Information encoded for a web page tagged using a disambiguated Wordnet's word sense

```
<http://www.example.com>   semlib:hasTag wordnet:wordsense-wrath-noun-1
wordnet:wordsense-wrath-noun-1 rdfs:label "wrath"
wordnet:synset-wrath-noun-1 wordnet:containsWordSense wordnet:wordsense-
    wrath-noun-1
wordnet:synset-wrath-noun-1 wordnet:gloss   "intense anger (usually on an
    epic scale)"
```

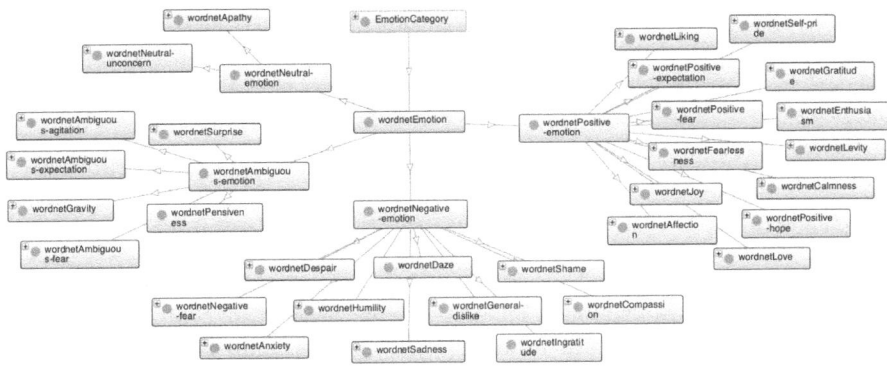

Fig. 2. Wordnet affective categories in HEO ontology

Strapparava and Valituti [10] developed WordNet-Affect, an extension of WordNet Domains, including a subset of synsets suitable to represent affective concepts correlated with affective words. Wordnet-Affect assigns to a number of WordNet synsets one or more affective labels (a-labels). In particular, the affective concepts representing emotional state are individuated by synsets marked with the a-label emotion. There are also other a-labels for those concepts representing moods, situations eliciting emotions, or emotional responses.

Wordnet-Affect introduces a wide number of emotion words organized in a taxonomical fashion, which have been linked to HEO ontology. For each of these words, in fact, HEO ontology defines a `heo:EmotionCategory`'s subclass. Such classes are organized in subclasses and superclasses following the Wornet-Affect synset taxonomy, as shown in Fig. 2.

Wordnet-Affect affective synsets are also additionally expanded with their hyponomies and similar synsets using `wordnet:hyponymOf` and `wordnet:similarTo`. Affective information for the resulting synsets are then encoded using HEO ontology as shown in Listing 1.2:

Listing 1.2. Affective information encoded for a web page tagged using a disambiguated Wordnet's word sense

```
wordnet:word-sense-wrath heo:isAssociatedToEmotion heo:wrath-emotion
heo:wrath-emotion heo:hasEmotionCategory heo:wnaWrath.
```

Once, information is encoded in this way, it becomes easy to search for resources according to the affective valence of their tags using SPARQL queries, as in Listing 1.3.

Listing 1.3. A SPARQL query example to retrieve resources according to their affective category

```
SELECT ?resource
WHERE {
    ?resource semlib:hasTag ?tag.
    ?tag heo:isAssociatedToEmotionCategory ?emotion
    ?emotion heo:hasEmotionCategory heo:Anger
}
```

In addition, the use HEO ontology makes possible to map emotions categories coming from different models and provides support for inference in search queries. In the example query, it's in fact worth to notice that, since in HEO ontology `heo:wnaWrath` has been defined as subclass of `heo:Anger`, also the page www.example.com will be retrieved as result.

7   Extracting Affect from Other Knowledge Bases

Wordnet is a powerful tool, which provides well-defined relationship between concepts, but lacks in instances. For example, it contains concepts as city, singer and movie, but no entities as Rome, Kurt Cobain or Pulp Fiction. Knowledge base as Dbpedia and Freebase are on the contrary very rich in instances but such instances lacks of the clean and carefully assembled hierarchy of thousands of Wordnet concepts. Its not surprising therefore that a great effort is currently undergoing to merge these knowledge base by mapping entities and categories belonging to different knowledge base.

Dbpedia is currently connected to Wordnet by the `dbpprop:wordnet_type`, which allows, at the time of writing, to link Dbpedia instances to 124 Wordnet concepts. Affective valence of such concept can be revealed using the same approach described in the previous section. This allows to extend the proposed affective tagging approach also to Dbpedia. At the current state of development, just a limited number of generic categories have been mapped to Wordnet, few of which have affective valence. Therefore, the proposed approach allows to extract affective information only from of a limited number of Dbpedia instances. By the way, as more categories will be introduced in Dbpedia and Wordnet mapping, more affective valence will be discoverable using the proposed approach, without requiring addition efforts. A similar activity is currently in progress in Freebase[8] to reconcile Freebase topics to Wordnet synsets.

Another approach, that will be investigated in the future is to extract affective valence of resources from Dbpedia and Freebase knowledge bases by applying Sentiment Analysis techniques over the textual descriptions that areprovided in the knowledge base for each resource. In particular, using Sentic Computing [11] which as already been used in combination with HEO ontology in sentiment analysis applications. Due to the considerable computational weight of processing this operation cannot be performed in real time when adding a tag. To overcome this limitation, knowledge bases entities should be processed offline and their affective valence stored in repositories to be accessed using simple SPARQL queries.

8   Conclusions

In this paper, the application of Semantic Web technologies to affective tagging has been discussed, in particular relying on a human emotion ontology and exploiting the formalized knowledge contained in Web available Linked Data knowledge bases.

---

[8] http://wiki.freebase.com/wiki/WordNet

Acknowledgements. The research leading to these results has received funding from the European Union's Seventh Framework Programme managed by REA-Research Executive Agency[9] ([FP7/2007-2013][FP7/2007-2011]) under grant agreement n. 262301. This work is also supported by COST 2102, EUCogII and SSPNET.

References

1. Andrews, P., Zaihrayeu, I., Pane, J.: A Classification of Semantic Annotation Systems. Semantic Web Journal (December 2011)
2. Kierkels, J.J.M., Pun, T.: Simultaneous exploitation of explicit and implicit tags in affect-based multimedia retrieval. In: 3rd International Conference on ACII 2009, pp. 1–6 (September 2009)
3. Morbidoni, C., Grassi, M., Nucci, M.: Introducing SemLib Project: Semantic Web Tools for Digital Libraries. In: International Workshop on Semantic Digital Archives - Sustainable Long-term Curation Perspectives of Cultural Heritage Held as Part of the 15th International Conference on Theory and Practice of Digital Libraries (TPDL), Berlin, September 29 (2011)
4. Grassi, M.: Developing HEO Human Emotions Ontology. In: Fierrez, J., Ortega-Garcia, J., Esposito, A., Drygajlo, A., Faundez-Zanuy, M. (eds.) BioID MultiComm 2009. LNCS, vol. 5707, pp. 244–251. Springer, Heidelberg (2009), doi:10.1007/978-3-642-04391-8_32
5. Baggia, P., Burkhardt, F., Pelachaud, C., Peter, C., Zovato, E.: Emotion Markup Language (EmotionML) 1.0. W3C Working Draft, April 7 (2011)
6. Grassi, M., Cambria, E., Hussain, A., Piazza, F.: Sentic Web: a New Paradigm for Managing Social Media Affective Information. To appear in: Cognitive Computation. Springer, Heidelberg (2011)
7. Grassi, M., Piazza, F.: Towards an RDF Encoding of ConceptNet. In: Liu, D. (ed.) ISNN 2011, Part III. LNCS, vol. 6677, pp. 558–565. Springer, Heidelberg (2011), doi:10.1007/978-3-642-21111-9_63
8. Miller, G., Beckwith, R., Fellbaum, C., Gross, D., Miller, K.: Introduction to Wordnet: An On-Line Lexical Database. J. Lexicography 3, 235–244 (1990)
9. van Assem, M., Gangemi, A., Schreiber, G.: RDF/OWL Representation of WordNet. Editor's Draft, April 23 (2006)
10. Strapparava, C., Valitutti, A.: WordNet-Affect: An Affective Extension of WordNet. In: Int. Conf. Language Resources and Evaluation, vol. 4, pp. 1083–1086 (2004)
11. Cambria, E., Erik: Sentic Computing: Techniques, Tools and Applications. In: Roelandse, M. (ed.). Springer, Berlin (in press)

---

[9] http://ec.europa.eu/research/rea

Dominance Detection in a Reverberated Acoustic Scenario

Emanuele Principi[1], Rudy Rotili[1], Martin Wöllmer[2], Stefano Squartini[1], and Björn Schuller[2]

[1] Dipartimento di Ingegneria dell'Informazione,
Università Politecnica delle Marche, Ancona, Italy
{e.principi,r.rotili,s.squartini}@univpm.it
[2] Institute for Human-Machine Communication,
Technische Universität München, Germany
{woellmer,schuller}@tum.de

Abstract. This work proposes a dominance detection framework operating in reverberated environments. The framework is composed of a speech enhancement front-end, which automatically reduces the distortions introduced by room reverberation in the speech signals, and a dominance detector, which processes the enhanced signals and estimates the most and least dominant person in a segment. The front-end is composed by three cooperating blocks: speaker diarization, room impulse responses identification and speech dereverberation. The dominance estimation algorithm is based on bidirectional Long Short-Term Memory networks which allow for context-sensitive activity classification from audio feature functionals extracted via the real-time speech feature extraction toolkit openSMILE. Experiments have been performed suitably reverberating the DOME dataset: the absolute accuracy improvement averaged over the addressed reverberated conditions is 32.68% in the most dominant person estimation task and 36.56% in the least dominant person estimation one, both with full agreement among annotators.

Keywords: Dominance Detection, Speech Dereverberation, Blind Channel Identification, Speaker Diarization.

1 Introduction

Recently, a certain attention has been paid by the scientific community to the development of automatic systems for dominance detection in small-groups [1]. Information coming from speech, but also from gesture, posture and face movements, can be extracted from the meeting activity and then be processed by expert algorithms in order to automatically detect the participants' level of dominance.

Dominance can be defined in multiple ways: it is often related to the notion of power, i.e. "the capacity to produce intended effects, and in particular, the ability to influence the behaviour of another person" [1]. This leads to defining dominance as a set of "expressive, relationally based communicative acts by

J. Wang, G.G. Yen, and M.M. Polycarpou (Eds.): ISNN 2012, Part I, LNCS 7367, pp. 394–402, 2012.

which power is exerted and influence achieved", "on behavioural manifestation of the relational construct of power", and "necessarily manifest" [1]. Dominance is directly related to the participant activity level [1]: persons with higher vocal and visual activity (e.g. body movement and gestures correlated with speaking activity) are often perceived as more dominant [2].

Several approaches have been proposed in the literature to address the dominance detection task. In [3], dominance is estimated calculating the speaking length of each speaker in a segment by means of the ICSI speaker diarization system. The system is able to work in real-time, but not online since the speaker diarization stage operates on the entire signals. The authors performed experiments on a subset of the AMI corpus using single distant microphone and headset signals. Reverberation and additive noise have not been taken into account. The methods proposed in [2,4] combine high level audio and visual features. They detect dominance levels either with a rule-based estimator, or with a Support Vector Machine classifier. Experiments are performed on the DOME dataset as considered herein [5] using individual headset microphones. In [6], two solutions for audio-visual activity and dominance detection are proposed: in the first, detection is performed using low level features and classification through Hidden Markov Models (HMM). In the second, a higher level feature containing the information about the current status of the group is added, and a two layer HMM system is employed for classification. Similarly to [3], experiments are conducted on a subset of the AMI corpus, this time employing individual headset microphones only, and annotated with participants' activity levels.

This paper addresses dominance detection in reverberated environments. Multiple distant microphones are used to acquire voices of meeting participants and the presence of the reverberation effect is dealt with by means of a recently proposed speech enhancement front-end [7]. Here, other sources of degradation, such as additive noise, are not considered. The enhanced signals are processed by the dominance detector stage which estimates the most and least dominant person in a segment using nonverbal vocalic cues. The full system block-scheme is shown in Fig. 1. The performance of the proposed framework are evaluated suitably reverberating the DOME dataset [5] with three different reverberation times: the obtained results show that both in estimating the most and least dominant person, the proposed framework achieves accuracies close to the non-reverberated condition ones.

The paper outline is the following. Sec. 2 briefly describes the speech enhancement front-end. Sec. 3 details the algorithm developed for dominance estimation. Sec. 4 discusses the experimental setup and the performed experiments. Finally, in Sec. 5 conclusions are drawn and future developments are proposed.

2   Speech Enhancement Front-End

The objective of the speech enhancement front-end is recovering the original clean speech sources. This is performed by means of a "context-aware" speech dereverberation approach, which includes the automatic identification of who

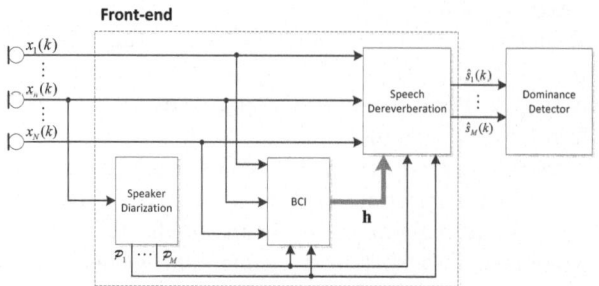

Fig. 1. Block diagram of the dominance detection framework

is speaking, the estimation of the unknown room IRs and the application of a knowledgeable dereverberation process to restore the original speech quality. To achieve such a goal, the framework proposed in [7] by some of the authors has been used. The framework consists of three stages: speaker diarization, blind channel identification and speech dereverberation.

Assuming M independent speech sources and N microphones, the relationship between them is described by an $M \times N$ MIMO FIR (Finite Impulse Response) system. According to such a model and denoting with $(\cdot)^T$ the transpose operator, the following equations (in the time and z domain) for the n-th microphone signal hold:

$$x_n(k) = \sum_{m=1}^{M} \mathbf{h}_{nm}^T \mathbf{s}_m(k, L_h), \qquad X_n(z) = \sum_{m=1}^{M} H_{nm}(z) S_m(z), \qquad (1)$$

where $\mathbf{h}_{nm} = [h_{nm,0}\ h_{nm,1}\ \dots\ h_{nm,L_h-1}]^T$ is the L_h-taps IR between the n-th microphone and m-th source $\mathbf{s}_m(k, L_h) = [s_m(k)\ s_m(k-1)\ \dots\ s_m(k-L_h+1)]^T$, with $(m = 1, 2, ..., M,\ n = 1, 2, ..., N)$.

The speaker diarization stage drives the BCI and dereverberation blocks so that they can operate into speaker-homogeneous regions. The algorithm consists of two phases, training and recognition. In the first, 19 Mel-Frequency Cepstral Coefficients (MFCC) plus their first and second derivatives are obtained from the input signals. Cepstral mean normalization is applied to deal with stationary channel effects. Speaker models are represented by mixture of Gaussians trained by means of the expectation maximization algorithm. The end accuracy at convergence and the number of Gaussians have been empirically determined on meetings IS1004a-d of the AMI corpus and set respectively to 10^{-4} and 100. In the recognition phase, the input signal is divided into non overlapping chunks, and feature vectors are extracted as in the training phase. Participants' identities are then determined using majority vote on the likelihoods.

The blind channel identification stage is based on the so-called Unconstrained Normalized Multi-Channel Frequency domain Least Mean Square algorithm (UNMCFLMS) [8], a technique that represents an appropriate choice in terms of estimation quality and computational cost. Though UNMCFLMS allows the estimation of long IRs, it requires a high input signal-to-noise ratio. Here, the noise free case has been assumed and future developments will consider improvements to make the algorithm more robust to the presence of noise.

The dereverberation stage is based on the Multi-channel Inverse Theorem (MINT) method. Given the SIMO system corresponding to source s_m, let us consider the polynomials $G_{s_m,n}(z), n = 1, 2, \ldots, N$ as the dereverberation filters to be applied to the SIMO outputs to provide the final estimation of the clean speech source s_m, according to the following:

$$\hat{S}_m(z) = \sum_{n=1}^{N} G_{s_m,n}(z)X_n(z). \tag{2}$$

The dereverberation filters can be obtained using the well known Bezout's Theorem. However, such a technique requires a matrix inversion that requires a high computational cost, especially in the case of long IRs. Therefore, in [7] the efficiency of the algorithm has been improved employing an adaptive approach.

3 Dominance Detector

Dominance detection is performed in three steps: in the first, feature vectors are extracted from the input signals every ten seconds. In the second, meeting participants' activity level is estimated by means of a Long Short-Term Memory network. In the third, the most and least dominant persons are estimated through a majority vote on the activities.

3.1 Speech Feature Extraction

For speech feature extraction, the online audio analysis toolkit openSMILE [9] is employed. We use the same set of 1 941 audio features as applied in [10]. It is composed of 25 energy and spectral related low-level descriptors (LLD) x 42 functionals, 6 voicing related LLD x 32 functionals, 25 delta coefficients of the energy/spectral LLD x 23 functionals, 6 delta coefficients of the voicing related LLD x 19 functionals, and 10 voiced/unvoiced durational features. The set of LLD covers a standard range of commonly used features in audio signal analysis and emotion recognition. The functional set has been based on similar sets, such as the one used for the Interspeech 2011 Speaker State Challenge, but has been carefully reduced to avoid LLD/functional combinations that produce values which are constant, contain very little information and/or a high amount of noise.

3.2 Most and Least Dominant Person Estimation Based on LSTM

Building on recent studies in the field of context-sensitive affective computing and human behaviour analysis [11], an activity classification framework that is based on bidirectional Long Short-Term Memory has been designed. The basic concept of Long Short-Term Memory (LSTM) networks was introduced in [12]

Table 1. Agreement statistics. "Full" indicates that three annotators agree, "Majority" indicates that two annotators agree, "None" indicates no agreement.

	Full	Majority	None
Most Dominant Person	58.62%	37.93%	3.45%
Least Dominant Person	53.45%	39.66%	6.89%

and can be seen as an extension of conventional recurrent neural networks that enables the modeling of long-range temporal context for improved sequence labeling. LSTM networks are able to store information in linear memory cells over a longer period of time and can learn the optimal amount of contextual information relevant for the classification task. An LSTM hidden layer is composed of multiple recurrently connected subnets (so-called *memory blocks*). Every memory block consists of self-connected *memory cells* and three multiplicative *gate* units (input, output, and forget gates). Since these gates allow for write, read, and reset operations within a memory block, an LSTM block can be interpreted as (differentiable) memory chip in a digital computer. Further details on the LSTM principle can be found in [13]. The most and least dominant persons in a meeting are estimated through a majority vote approach: the most (respectively, least) dominant person is the one that is classified as the most (respectively, least) active for the majority of segments.

4   Experiments

4.1   Corpus Description

Experiments have been conducted on the DOminance in MEetings dataset (DOME) [5], a subset of the AMI corpus [14] annotated with dominance levels. "Meeting Set 1" has been chosen in order to compare the obtained results with previous works on dominance estimation [2,3]. This set consists of 58 five minutes long segments extracted from 11 AMI scenario meetings. The total number of speakers is 20 and the female/male ratio is 42.86%. For each segment, dominance annotations have been performed by three annotators according to their level of perceived dominance. The distribution of agreement types is shown in Table 1.

Two main dominance tasks are defined in DOME: estimating the most dominant person and estimating the least dominant person. Based on the annotators' level of agreement, DOME defines four tasks:

- **FMD:** **F**ull agreement set, **M**ost **D**ominant person estimation task (34 segments).
- **FLD:** **F**ull agreement set, **L**east **D**ominant person estimation task (31 segments).
- **MMD:** **M**ajority agreement set, **M**ost **D**ominant person estimation task (56 segments).
- **MLD:** **M**ajority agreement set, **L**east **D**ominant person estimation task (54 segments).

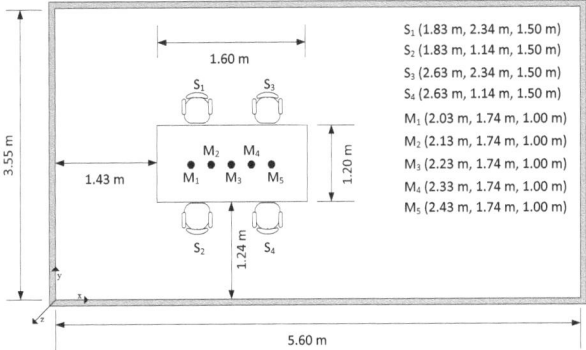

Fig. 2. Room setup: x, y and z coordinates are shown in brackets

4.2 Acoustic Scenario

The scenario under study is shown in Fig. 2: an array of five microphones is placed at the centre of the meeting table and four speakers are sitting around it. The number of microphones has been chosen taking into account that it must be greater than the number of speakers [8]. The inter-microphone distance is 10 cm and represents a good comprise between impulse response diversification, which increases with the inter-microphone distance, and the need for a reasonably sized array. It is worth highlighting that the UNMCFLMS and MINT algorithms do not suffer from the spatial aliasing problem as delay and sum beamformer [15]. Microphone signals have been created by manually removing cross-talk from the headset sources and convolving them with impulse responses 1024 taps long. RIRs have been generated using Habets' RIR Generator tool[1], and represent three different reverberation times (T_{60}): 120 ms, 240 ms and 360 ms. Cross-talk free individual headset sources will be denoted as "Clean" in the following sections.

4.3 Dominance Detector Training and Evaluation Procedure

The networks used for the experiments consist of 1 941 input nodes (one for each speech feature extracted from 10 s of speech), 128 memory blocks containing one memory cell each, and four output nodes that represent the likelihoods of the four activity classes.

We trained a BLSTM network on the transcribed meeting segments used in [6], excluding segments that also occur in the DOME corpus. This results in a training database consisting of 26 meeting segments of five minutes each. As test set, we used the whole DOME corpus. All features were mean and variance normalized prior to processing via BLSTM networks. Means and variances were calculated from the training set only. During training a learning rate of 10^{-5}

---

[1] http://home.tiscali.nl/ehabets/rirgenerator.html

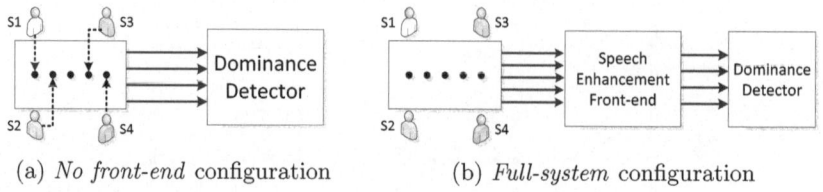

(a) *No front-end* configuration   (b) *Full-system* configuration

Fig. 3. System configurations. In (a), the central microphone is not used and the dashed arrows denote a logical link between speakers and microphones.

and a momentum of 0.9 are used. Zero mean Gaussian noise with standard deviation 0.6 was added to the inputs in the training phase in order to improve generalization. Prior to training, all weights were randomly initialised in the range from -0.1 to 0.1. Input and output gates used tanh activation functions, while the forget gates had logistic activation functions. Due to the observed fast convergence, training was aborted after 10 epochs.

4.4   Results

The system evaluation has been conducted considering two configurations, "No front-end" and "Full-system". In the first, the speech enhancement front-end is not present and the dominance detector operates on four microphone signals (Fig. 3a). Each microphone is logically associated to a single speaker, meaning that the dominance detector expects each signal to contain only one voice. The purpose of this experiment is to highlight the need for a front-end able to divide and dereverberate the inputs. The "Full-system" configuration represents the proposed framework as shown in Fig. 3b and described in Sec. 2.

The dominance detection accuracies obtained on "Clean" signals are 85.29% (FMD), 80.65% (FLD), 76.79% (MMD) and 62.96% (MLD). Similar results have been obtained in [3], where the DOME dataset has been used as well. In the most dominant person estimation tasks accuracies are very similar: 85% in FMD and 77% in MMD. In the least dominant person estimation tasks, they report a higher value in FLD (84%) and a lower value in MLD (59%). It is worth pointing out that differently from [3], the system described here operates entirely online.

Table 2 shows the dominance detection results on the three reverberated conditions. The "no front-end" configuration accuracies are very similar across the three T_{60}s, and significantly lower than the "Clean" condition ones. In the FMD task, the accuracy decreases by 31.37% on average while in the FLD task by 34.41%. A similar performance drop can be observed in the majority agreement tasks. This behaviour is due to both the reverberation effect, and to the presence of all the participants' voices in each input signal, which makes it impossible for the dominance detector to discriminates the four voices. The introduction of the speech enhancement front-end significantly improves the detection results, giving an accuracy improvement of 32.68% in the FMD task and of 36.56% in

Table 2. Dominance detection results. See Sec. 4.1 for the task labels description.

Accuracy (%)	Task	120 ms	240 ms	360 ms	Average
No front-end	FMD	50.00	55.88	55.88	53.92
	FLD	48.39	45.16	45.16	46.24
	MMD	53.57	55.36	51.79	53.57
	MLD	42.59	37.04	35.19	38.27
Full-system	FMD	82.35	85.29	91.18	86.61
	FLD	83.87	80.65	83.87	82.80
	MMD	76.79	76.79	82.14	78.57
	MLD	64.81	62.96	66.67	64.81

the FLD one. In the majority agreement results, the behaviour is similar: in the MMD task the improvement is 25.00%, while in the MLD task is 26.54%.

Note, finally, that both in the "Clean" and reverberated conditions, the majority agreement results are lower on average than the full agreement ones. This is due to the higher variability in the annotations and is consistent with [3].

5 Conclusion

This work presented a dominance detection framework able to operate in multi-talker reverberated acoustic scenarios. The overall framework is composed of two main blocks, a speech enhancement front-end and a dominance detector. The task of the first is to reduce the reverberation effect induced by the convolution between the meeting participant voice signals and the room impulse responses. This is performed using a recently proposed solution [7] composed of three stages: speaker diarization, room impulse response identification and speech dereverberation. The dominance detection algorithm is based on the speech feature extraction toolkit openSMILE. To exploit contextual information, a bidirectional Long Short-Term Memory network which produces the final estimate of the activity level for each speaker is employed. Experiments have been performed on the DOME dataset: results obtained on reverberated versions of the corpus have shown the effectiveness of the developed system, making it appealing for applications in real-life human-computer interaction scenarios.

Future developments will involve both the dominance estimator and the speech enhancement front-end. The first will be augmented with video features, which have been already successfully exploited in the literature [2,4]. The feature set could be also augmented with the speaking lengths of each participant coming from the speaker diarizer. In addition, the evaluation of the so-called bottleneck network architectures for enhanced BLSTM modelling of a participant's activity in meetings is planned. With regard to the front-end, the presence of additive noise will be considered and suitable procedures will be taken into account to reduce its impact. Moreover, the speaker diarization stage will be featured with an overlap-detector, which also allows to include a source separation stage within the front-end and exploit also the overlapped speech segments.

References

1. Gatica-Perez, D.: Automatic nonverbal analysis of social interaction in small groups: A review. Image and Vision Computing 27(12), 1775–1787 (2009)
2. Jayagopi, D., Hung, H., Yeo, C., Gatica-Perez, D.: Modeling dominance in group conversations using nonverbal activity cues. IEEE Trans. on Audio, Speech, and Language Processing 17(3), 501–513 (2009)
3. Hung, H., Huang, Y., Friedland, G., Gatica-Perez, D.: Estimating dominance in multi-party meetings using speaker diarization. IEEE Trans. on Audio, Speech, and Language Processing 19(4), 847–860 (2011)
4. Aran, O., Gatica-Perez, D.: Fusing audio-visual nonverbal cues to detect dominant people in group conversations. In: Proc. of Int. Conf. on Pattern Recognition, pp. 3687–3690 (August 2010)
5. Aran, O., Hung, H., Gatica-Perez, D.: A multimodal corpus for studying dominance in small group conversations. In: LREC Workshop on Multimodal Corpora: Advances in Capturing, Coding and Analyzing Multimodality, Malta (May 2010)
6. Hörnler, B., Rigoll, G.: Multi-modal activity and dominance detection in smart meeting rooms. In: Proc. of ICASSP, pp. 1777–1780 (2009)
7. Rotili, R., Principi, E., Squartini, S., Schuller, B.: A Real-Time Speech Enhancement Framework for Multi-party Meetings. In: Travieso-González, C.M., Alonso-Hernández, J.B. (eds.) NOLISP 2011. LNCS, vol. 7015, pp. 80–87. Springer, Heidelberg (2011)
8. Huang, Y., Benesty, J.: A class of frequency-domain adaptive approaches to blind multichannel identification. IEEE Trans. Speech Audio Process. 51(1), 11–24 (2003)
9. Eyben, F., Wöllmer, M., Schuller, B.: openSMILE - the Munich versatile and fast open-source audio feature extractor. In: Proc. of ACM Multimedia, Firenze, Italy, pp. 1459–1462 (2010)
10. Schuller, B., Valstar, M., Eyben, F., McKeown, G., Cowie, R., Pantic, M.: AVEC 2011–The First International Audio/Visual Emotion Challenge. In: D'Mello, S., Graesser, A., Schuller, B., Martin, J.-C. (eds.) ACII 2011, Part II. LNCS, vol. 6975, pp. 415–424. Springer, Heidelberg (2011)
11. Wöllmer, M., Schuller, B., Eyben, F., Rigoll, G.: Combining long short-term memory and dynamic bayesian networks for incremental emotion-sensitive artificial listening. IEEE Journal of Selected Topics in Signal Processing 4(5), 867–881 (2010)
12. Hochreiter, S., Schmidhuber, J.: Long short-term memory. Neural Computation 9(8), 1735–1780 (1997)
13. Graves, A., Schmidhuber, J.: Framewise phoneme classification with bidirectional LSTM and other neural network architectures. Neural Networks 18(5-6), 602–610 (2005)
14. Carletta, J., Ashby, S., Bourban, S., Flynn, M., Guillemot, M., Hain, T., Kadlec, J., Karaiskos, V., Kraaij, W., Kronenthal, M., Lathoud, G., Lincoln, M., Lisowska, A., McCowan, I., Post, W., Reidsma, D., Wellner, P.: The AMI Meeting Corpus: A Pre-announcement. In: Renals, S., Bengio, S. (eds.) MLMI 2005. LNCS, vol. 3869, pp. 28–39. Springer, Heidelberg (2006)
15. Johnson, D.H., Dudgeon, D.E.: Array Signal Processing. Prentice-Hall, Englewood Cliffs (1993)

Analysis of Attention Deficit Hyperactivity Disorder and Control Participants in EEG Using ICA and PCA

Ling Zou[1,3,*], Hui Pu[1], Qi Sun[2], and Wenjin Su[4]

[1] Faculty of Information Science & Engineering, Changzhou University,
Changzhou, Jiangsu, 213164, China
[2] School of Electronics & Information Engineering, Shenyang Aerospace University, Shenyang
110034, China
[3] State Key Laboratory of Robotics and System (HIT), Harbin Institute of Technology,
Harbin, Heilongjiang, 150001, China
[4] School of Information and Electronics, Beijing Institute of Technology,
Beijing, 100081, China
zouling@cczu.edu.cn

Abstract. This paper presents our preliminary EEG brain signals of children with attention deficit hyperactivity disorder (ADHD) in order to support a computer assisted diagnostic system. The EEG signals were recorded from 4 children including normal and children diagnosed with ADHD while performing Continuous Performance Test (CPT). Independent component analysis (ICA) was used as the preprocessing steps to remove artifacts associated with eye blinks, eye-movements and muscle noise. Then the Principal Component Analysis (PCA) was employed to select a subset of channels for EEG signals which are to preserve as much information present as compared to the full set of 128 channels as possible. The results would be used to classify ADHD study and lay the foundation of ADHD clinical diagnoses study.

Keywords: EEG, Attention Deficit Hyperactivity Disorder (ADHD), Continuous Performance Test (CPT), Principal Component Analysis (PCA), Independent Component Analysis (ICA).

1 Introduction

Attention deficit hyperactivity disorder (ADHD) is a childhood-onset, neuro developmental disorder [1]. ADHD is not a psychological problem but a kind of encephalopathy which occurs imbalance of brain development. Nowadays, a great number of countries have studied the electroencephalogram (EEG) activity of children with and without ADHD [2]. A task that used to estimate different executive processes impaired in ADHD is called cued-Go/Nogo task or Continuous Performance Test (CPT) task [3], in which subjects are requested to respond to a Go stimulus appeared immediately after cue stimulus, and inhibit responses on Nogo trials.

---

[*] Corresponding author.

J. Wang, G.G. Yen, and M.M. Polycarpou (Eds.): ISNN 2012, Part I, LNCS 7367, pp. 403–410, 2012.

The recorded EEG signals represent a mixture of overlapping brain and non-brain activities, such as cortical brain sources, physiological artifacts including eye movements, eye blinks and muscle activity, external artifacts and spatially irregular components of unknown origin. Up to now, contamination of EEG activity by the above artifacts remains a serious problem for EEG interpretation and analysis, especially for some patient groups since rejecting contaminated EEG segments may result in an unacceptable data loss. A critical point in EEG signal processing is the need for careful treatment and reduction of these artifacts which contaminate the EEG signals and can lead to wrong results and conclusions.

The most common reduction method is based on linear regression in the time or frequency domain. This method estimates and removes the influence of eye links or eye movements on the signals recorded by scalp electrodes from the EEG recordings. However, this technique has an inherent drawback that is the aforementioned bidirectional contamination. Independent component analysis (ICA) applied to concatenated collections of single-trial EEG data has proven to be an efficient method for separating distinct artifactual processes including eye blink, muscle and electrical artifacts [4]. Typical artifacts arising from eye movements, eye blinks and muscle tension have stereotyped scalp projections. Other artifacts like cortical brain sources or external artifacts, however, are difficult for ICA. We should carefully deal with the data of non-stereotyped artifacts. In the future, quicker and cleaner ICA method should be developed to remove EEG artifacts.

In most of the study, full scalp EEG recording is required, and signal averaging is required for latency estimation. However, this will require more huge set of measurement data in obtaining the results. Full channels data will lead into redundant data. Consequently, it is more difficult to reveal patterns in the data. Some optimization algorithms have been used to select the optimal channels [5] [6]. Principal component analysis (PCA) method has been widely used in feature extraction to reduce the dimensionality of original data by a linear transformation. PCA extracts dominant features, i.e. principal components (PCs), from a set of multivariate data; these dominant features contain most of the information of the original data. Therefore, the data size can be reduced significantly by using PCA while the dominant features of the original data will be maintained [7].

In this paper, ICA was used as the preprocessing steps to remove artifacts associated with eye blinks, eye-movements and muscle noise. Then PCA was employed to select a subset of channels for EEG signals which are to preserve as much information present as compared to the full set of 128 channels as possible. The results layed the foundation for the classification between ADHD and controls.

2   Methods

2.1   Independent Component Analysis

ICA is a statistical method that aims to find a linear transformation of the data that will make the outputs as independent as possible. In most practical situations, we have to process multidimensional observations of the form

$$x = As + n. \tag{1}$$

Where $x = (x_1, x_2, \cdots, x_L)^T$ is the observed m-dimensional random vector; $s = (s_1, s_2, \cdots, s_L)^T$ is an unknown is an unknown random vector with independent components representing the source; A is an unknown LxL constant mixing matrix and n is the additive noise.

The solution to the basic ICA problem can be expressed as the form:

$$u = Wx. \tag{2}$$

Where, W is the LxL demixing matrix, u are the independent components (ICs).

After carefully judgments, the artifact ICs were set as zero and we got the new ICs $\hat{u}$, The cleaned EEG data X were reconstructed by the projection of the new ICs onto the original data channels, which is given by

$$X = W^{-1}\hat{u}. \tag{3}$$

2.2   Principal Component Analysis

The PCA method was employed in the present study by using the following procedure.

Step 1: the cleaned EEG data X is arranged into an LxN matrix, where L is the number of the channels and N is the number of data samples (500 in this case).

$$X = [x_1 \quad x_2 \quad \cdots \quad x_L]^T. \tag{4}$$

Step 2: the covariance of matrix R is computed using

$$R = E[XX^T]. \tag{5}$$

Step 3: construct V and D, where V is the orthogonal matrix of eigenvectors of R and D is the diagonal matrix of its eigenvalues,

$$D = dig(d_1, \cdots, d_L). \tag{6}$$

Step 4: PCs are calculated using

$$Y = V^T X. \tag{7}$$

Step 5: the nth diagonal value of D is the variance of X along the nth PC. The PCs with most dominate variance values (99% of the total variance in this case) are selected to be part of the signal subspace, while the rest are considered to be part of the noise. In this study, the selected channels contribute 99% of the total variance, depicted in table 1.

3   Results

3.1   Experimental Setup and CPT Task

Continuous EEG data were recorded with a 128-channel Electrical Geodesics Inc. Net Station amplifier, via a dense array 128 electrode Geodesics Sensor Net (see Fig.1). The Vertex (Cz) was chosen as the reference, and impedances were kept below 70 kW as recommended for the EGI high input impedance amplifier. Sampling rate was 500 Hz with an on-line band pass filter of 0.3 to 30Hz. Children with ADHD (N=2) and normal control (N=2) had participated in this study. The children with ADHD were diagnosed at hospital.

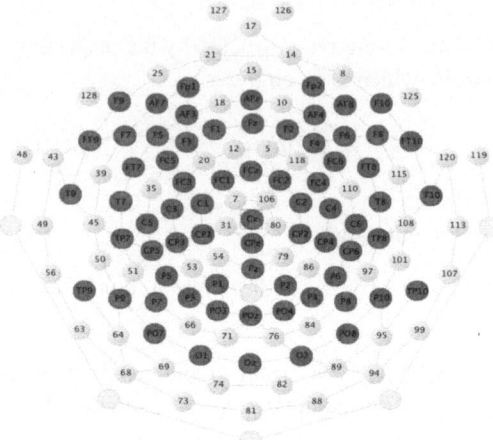

Fig. 1. Layout illustrating the approximate 10 – 10 equivalent on the 128-channel HydroCel GSN

The CPT task consisted of a sequence of 9 different digits. Subjects were asked to press the button when '9' appeared immediately after '1'.The experiment has 400 stimulations. Figure 2 shows the experiment paradigm. In the experiment, a number random display in the screen and each number represent one stimulation, which number range between 0 and 9. 1 represents the prompt cue. If 1 followed by 9 behind operators said GO, else said NOGO. And other case called background, BG.

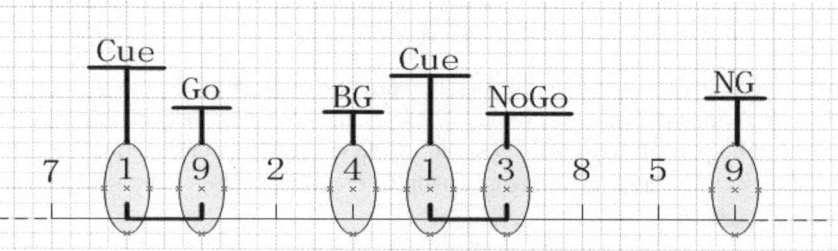

Fig. 2. Schematic representation of CPT task

3.2   Artifacts Removal by ICA Method

Due to limited space, we only showed the EEG raw data from 1 to 48 channels, displayed in Fig.3.Some obvious EOG artifacts could be found in frontal area (such as FP1, FP2 and AFZ, etc.).

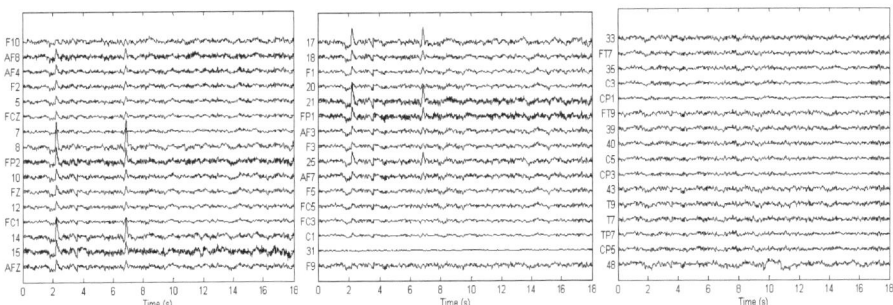

Fig. 3. An 18-sec portion of an EEG Raw Data containing prominent eye movements under the Nogo condition for an ADHD subject. Left: raw data from 1 to 16 electrodes; Middle: raw data from 17 to 32 electrodes; Right: raw data from 33 to 48 electrodes.

We used the extended Infomax-ICA method to deal with the 128 channels. Fig.4, Fig.5 and Fig.6 showed the corresponding independent components (ICs), topographies and the power spectra plot of single-trial for ICs. As we known, eye movements should project mainly to frontal sites with a low pass time course, eye blinks should project to frontal sites and have large punctuate activations, temporal muscle activity should project to temporal sites with a spectral peak above 20Hz.

We could judge that the ICs 1,2,3,4,5,6,7,8,12,13,14,15,20,21,23,24,25,26,27,28, 30,33,34,36,37,40,41,45,48,49,50,51,53,54,55,58,60,68,72,74,75,76,78,82,84,87,88,9 3,98,99,106,107,113,118 and 119 are the eye artifacts. The ICs 29, 38, 52, 56, 59, 61, 63,67,69,77, 89, 90, 96, 97, 101, 102, 103, 104, 105,108,111,115, 116, 120,126,127 and 128 are the muscle artifacts. The ICs 35, 39 and 43are the occipital artifacts. Then the above ICs are set as zero. After that, we could get the reconstructed EEG signals by ICA method, showed in Fig.7.

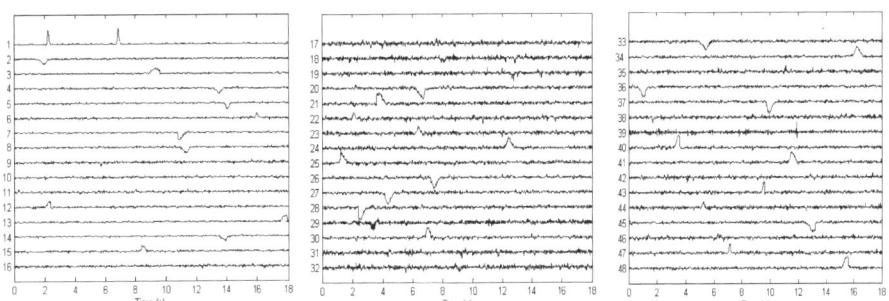

Fig. 4. Corresponding ICA component activations of the above 48 channel data

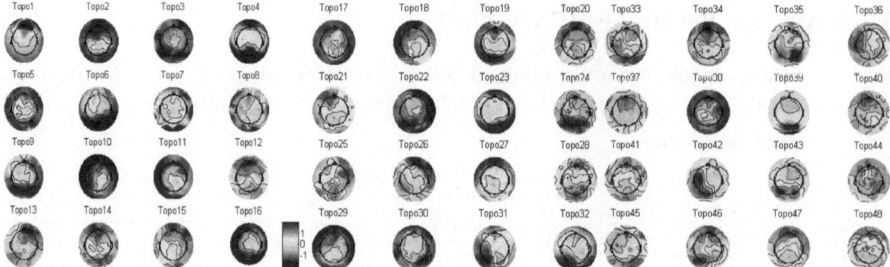

Fig. 5. Corresponding scalp maps of the above 48 ICs

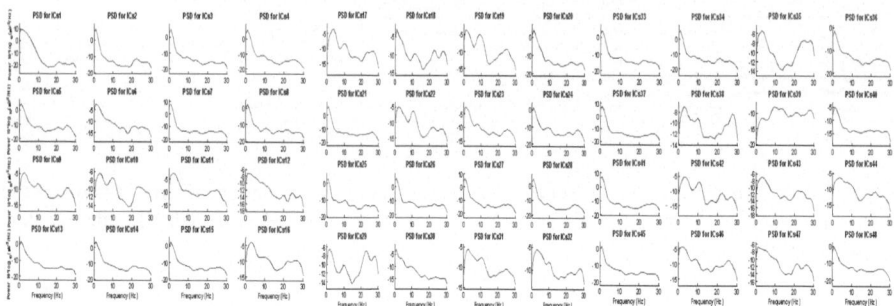

Fig. 6. The Power spectra plot of single-trial for ICs

3.3   EEG Channel Selection

Four subjects S_1-S_4 (2 ADHD children and 2 normal children) executed CPT task. Here, we focused on Go task and Nogo task. The PCA method was applied to the reconstructed EEG signals by ICA method and the PCs with 99% of the total variance were considered to be part of the EEG subspace. The results for the channel selection are shown in Table 1.Note that the individual best channels vary for each subject and task combination as expected. Bold channels were selected in Table 1 are related to the left/right postero-superior arrears [8].This result would lay the foundation for study of the neuropsychological and neuroanatomical differences between normal and ADHD participants.

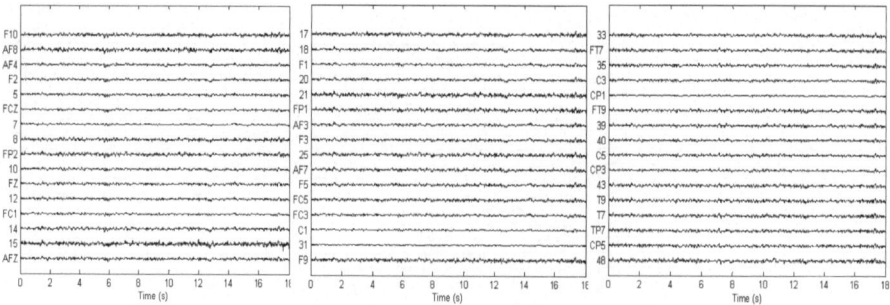

Fig. 7. The reconstructed EEG signals by ICA method

Table 1. Optimal EEG channels illustration

Subjects	tasks	Optimal EEG channels by selected PCs									
S_1	Go	84	59	22	15	58	90	21	83	76	65
		9	18	66	128	77	51	25	73	16	10
		89									
	Nogo	44	59	56	84	21	83	76	58	90	65
		14	60	66	51	77	64	69	52	22	49
		82	72	91							
S_2	Go	65	95	64	58	69	89	126	94	90	100
		127	70	66	99	96	48				
	Nogo	65	89	90	69	58	70	64	95	66	83
		96	88	82							
S_3	Go	58	65	59	90	83	84	66	50	96	76
		64									
	Nogo	89	82	42	69	65	74	36	61	83	70
		47	53	75	41	64	67	46			
S_4	Go	58	65	59	90	83	50	84	66	64	96
		76	68	51							
	Nogo	65	58	59	90	57	83	95	96	66	89
		64	70	50	63	56					

4 Discussion

This paper presents our preliminary EEG brain signals of children including normal and children diagnosed with ADHD while performing CPT tests in order to support a computer assisted diagnostic system. Firstly, The ICA method was proposed for removing artifacts from multi-channel EEG data, which appeared to be a promising tool for the analysis of highly correlated multi-channel EEG signals. Using ICA to remove artifacts from EEG recordings relies on expert knowledge and careful selection. Here, the features in the time-frequency-space domain were combined to judge the artifacts to ensure the results correct. Secondly, we proposed the PCA method to select optimal channels for further classification study of ADHD and normal subjects. In addition to reducing computational time, optimal channels selections results demonstrated that the important EEG sites centered in left/right postero-superior arrears when the subjects performed CPT tests. This study was a first attempt to select EEG channels of ADHD children by means of ICA and PCA methods.

Acknowledgments. This work was supported by the open project of the State Key Laboratory of Robotics and System (HIT), the Natural science fund for colleges and universities in Jiangsu Province (10KJB510003) and the Natural science fund in Changzhou City (CJ20110023). Thanks for the discussion of Prof. Xuan Dong and Doctor Suhong Wang from the first hospital of Changzhou City.

References

1. Faraone, S.V., Biederman, J., Mick, E.: The age-dependent decline of attention deficit hyperactivity disorder: A meta-analysis of follow-up studies. Psychol. Med. 36, 159–165 (2006)
2. Wiersema, R., van der Meere, J., Roeyers, H., Van Coster, R., Baeyens, D.: Event rate and event-related potentials in ADHD. J. Child. Psychol. Psyc. 47, 560–567 (2006)
3. Sikstrom, S., Soderlund, G.: Stimulus-dependent dopamine release in attention-deficit/hyperactivity disorder. Psychol. Rev. 114(4), 1047–1075 (2007)
4. Ling, Z., Suolin, D., Zhenghua, M., Changchun, Y.: Single-Trial Event Related Potentials Extraction by Using Independent Component Analysis. In: The 2nd International Conference on Biomedical Engineering and Informatics, vol. 2, pp. 1–5. IEEE, New York (2009)
5. Yu, S., Jianhua, D., Xiaochun, L., Qing, X.: EEG channel evaluation and selection by Rough Set in P300 BCI. J. Com. Infor. 6, 1727–1735 (2010)
6. Sabeti, M., Katebi, S.D., Boostani, R., Price, W.G.: A new approach for EEG signal classification of schizophrenic and control participants. Expert. Syst. Appl. 38, 2063–2071 (2011)
7. Ling, Z., Yingchun, Z., Laurence, T.Y., Renlai, Z.: Single Trial Evoked Potentials Study by Combining Wavelet Denoising and Principal Component Analysis Method. Journal of Clinical Neurophysiology 27(1), 17–24 (2010)
8. Zou, L., Zhou, R., Hu, S., Zhang, J., Li, Y.: Single Trial Evoked Potentials Study during an Emotional Processing Based on Wavelet Transform. In: Sun, F., Zhang, J., Tan, Y., Cao, J., Yu, W. (eds.) ISNN 2008, Part I. LNCS, vol. 5263, pp. 1–10. Springer, Heidelberg (2008)

A Systematic Independent Component Analysis Approach to Extract Mismatch Negativity

Fengyu Cong[1], Aleksandr Aleksandrov[2], Veronika Knyazeva[2],
Tatyana Deinekina[2], and Tapani Ristaniemi[1]

[1] Department of Mathematical Information Technology, University of Jyväskylä,
PL35(Agora), Jyväskylä, 40014, Finland
[2] Department of Higher Neural Activity and Psychophysiology, Saint Petersburg State
University, Saint Petersburg, Russia Federation
{Fengyu.Cong,Tapani.Ristaniemi}@jyu.fi, alexandrov@bio.pu.ru,
{werwulf.90,serpentera}@mail.ru

Abstract. This study systematically addressed how independent component analysis (ICA) can extract mismatch negativity (MMN) from EEG data elicited by a conventional oddball paradigm. MMN is usually observed from difference wave (DW) which is produced by subtracting the responses of the repeated standard stimuli from those of the deviant stimuli. This study performed ICA on the DW and the responses of standard and deviant stimuli individually. Results showed that ERPs with the latency around 120 ms in the estimated responses of the standard and the deviant stimuli were different, and the MMN extracted by ICA from the DW and that observed from the new DW between the estimated responses of the deviant and standard stimuli by ICA were not significantly different particularly at the frontal electrodes. We draw the conclusion that when ICA is used to extract the MMN of adults, there might be no difference to perform DW before or after ICA.

Keywords: Deviant, difference wave, event-related potential, independent component analysis, mismatch negativity, oddball, standard.

1   Introduction

Mismatch negativity (MMN) with a latency of 100-250 ms after the onset of the deviant stimulus is a brain event-related potential (ERP) elicited by an oddball paradigm and it is usually observed from difference wave (DW) which is produced by subtracting the brain responses of the repeated standard stimuli from those of the deviant stimuli which appear with relatively low probability [16], [19], [20]. Since MMN was found in 1978, it has been extensively used in cognitive studies, clinical neuroscience, and neuropharmacology [9], [10]. MMN is a small ERP and its peak amplitude is usually up to several microvolts [9], [19], hence, the signal to noise ratio (SNR) of EEG data may be very low in MMN experiments [14]. As a result, hundreds of single trials are usually collected for averaging to produce significant MMN in the experiment [9]. However, despite of such effort MMN may be not evident, especially in children's data. Thus, in the research of MMN, the group level analysis is mostly used, but the individual subject level analysis is desired [21]. Consequently, in order

J. Wang, G.G. Yen, and M.M. Polycarpou (Eds.): ISNN 2012, Part I, LNCS 7367, pp. 411–421, 2012.

to extract mismatch negativity from EEG data, researchers have been using different signal processing methods including digital filter [14], wavelet filter [3], independent component analysis (ICA) to extract MMN [4], [7], [13], [15], [18].

In [4], [7], [13], [15], the MMN was elicited by an uninterrupted sound and the responses of the standard stimuli and the deviant stimuli were uninterrupted either, hence, ICA was performed on the continuous responses elicited by the continuous stimuli. In these studies, the experiment stimuli were not of the conventional paradigm to elicit MMN. In [18], single-trial responses of deviant stimuli subtracted the grand averaged responses of the standard stimuli, and then, ICA was performed. So, what was decomposed was a special DW which was not conventionally defined.

Thus, it will be interesting to investigate what kind of components ICA can extract from the responses of the standard stimuli and from the responses of the deviant stimuli, and from the conventionally defined DW. After the desired components are extracted out from the responses of standard and deviant stimuli, they will be projected to the electrode field, and then a new DW between the projections will be calculated to observe MMN. Finally, we will examine whether the MMN extracted by the procedure of DW after ICA and the one by ICA after DW are identical or not.

2   Method

2.1   Data Description

EEG data were collected in the Saint Petersburg State University. Nine participants (about 22 years old) joined the experiment. The experimental task consisted of two tones with duration of 50 ms presented in the oddball paradigm including a standard tone with a frequency of 1000 Hz (85%) and a deviant tone with a frequency of 1200 Hz (15%). The participant had to respond on each deviant stimulus. The total number of stimuli was 1500. The inter-tone interval was 950 ms. EEG data were recorded by 11 electrodes (F3, Fz, F4, C3, Cz, C4, P3, Pz, P4, M1 and M2) following the extended international 10–20 System. The reference electrode was placed on the tip of the nose, and the ground electrode on the forehead. EOG was recorded from one electrode placed on the infraorbital ridges of the left eye. The signal was amplified (bandpass: 0.05-70 Hz) and digitized (sampling frequency: 250 Hz) and stored for off-line analysis. Responses to standard and deviant tones were analyzed in sweeps of 500 ms, including 50 ms before the stimulus onset. Epochs with the signal amplitude exceeding 100 μV were removed by WinEEG (v. 2.4, V. Ponomarev, Brain Institute, St. Petersburg, Russia). Then, the data of kept epochs were averaged for analysis.

2.2   General ICA Approach to Extract Brain Signals

ICA has been extensively used to study brain signals [22], and it is based on the linear transformation model associating EEG recordings ($\mathbf{x}$) along the scalp and electrical sources ($\mathbf{s}$) in the brain. The model without sensor noise can be expressed as

$$\mathbf{x} = \mathbf{As}, \tag{1}$$

where $\mathbf{x} = [x_1, x_2, \cdots, x_M]^T$, $\mathbf{s} = [s_1, s_2, \cdots, s_N]^T$, and $\mathbf{A}$ with the full column rank is usually called as the mixing matrix regarding ICA, and in this study we name it as the mapping matrix containing coefficients to map sources in the brain to points along the scalp. For any source, its mapping can be illustrated as

$$\mathbf{x}_r = \mathbf{a}_r \cdot s_r, \tag{2}$$

where, $\mathbf{x}_r = \left[x_{1,r}, x_{2,r}, \cdots, x_{M,r}\right]^T$, $\mathbf{a}_r$ is one column of $\mathbf{A}$, and $r \in [1, N]$. In this case, $\mathbf{x}_r$ is not the mixture like $\mathbf{x}$ in (1) any more, but is the sole information of one brain source. Hence, one goal to apply ICA is to achieve the mapping of one source in (2) from the mixture in (1) [5], [6]. For simplicity without losing generality, we assume $M = N$ here. In order to obtain (2), an unmixing matrix is first learned by ICA [12], and then it transforms the mixture in (1) into independent components as

$$\mathbf{y} = \mathbf{W}\mathbf{x}. \tag{3}$$

Subsequently, one component is selected according to the prior knowledge of the desired brain activity and is then projected back to the electrode field to correct the inherent variance indeterminacy of the extracted component by ICA [5], [6], [17] through

$$\mathbf{e}_k = \mathbf{b}_k \cdot y_k, \tag{4}$$

$$\mathbf{B} = \mathbf{W}^{-1}, \tag{5}$$

where $\mathbf{e}_k = \left[e_{1,k}, e_{2,k}, \cdots, e_{N,k}\right]^T$, $\mathbf{b}_k$ is one column of $\mathbf{B}$, y_k is one element of $\mathbf{y}$ and $k \in [1, N]$. By this way, we obtain the desired electrical brain activity's determined magnitude with the unit of the microvolt in the context of EEG recordings [5], [6], [17]. Furthermore, with the global matrix of ICA [1], [5], [6], a component can be interpreted as

$$y_k = \sum_{n=1}^{N} c_{kn} s_n, \tag{6}$$

$$\mathbf{C} = \mathbf{W}\mathbf{A}, \tag{7}$$

where c_{kn} is the (k, n) element of the global matrix $\mathbf{C}$. Then, (4) turns to

$$\mathbf{e}_k = \mathbf{b}_k \cdot \left(\sum_{n=1}^{N} c_{kn} s_n\right). \tag{8}$$

Under the global optimization of ICA, there is only one nonzero element in each row and each column matrix $\mathbf{C}$ [1], [5], [6], and then, (6) and (8) become

$$y_k = c_{kj} s_j, \tag{9}$$

$$\mathbf{e}_k = \mathbf{b}_k \cdot \left(c_{kj} s_j\right) \overset{\mathbf{BC}=\mathbf{A}}{=} \mathbf{a}_j \cdot s_j = \mathbf{x}_j, \tag{10}$$

Where $\mathbf{x}_j = \left[x_{1,j}, x_{2,j}, \cdots, x_{N,j}\right]^T$, and $j \in [1, N]$, $\mathbf{a}_j$ is one column of $\mathbf{A}$, and c_{kj} is the nonzero element of matrix $\mathbf{C}$.

In summary, when ICA is globally optimized to separate EEG recordings, we may theoretically gain the individual sources of brain activities with unknown scales and the determined mapping of individual sources along the scalp. However, what we may obtain in practice just approximate the counterparts in theory since ICA is often locally optimized practically [11], i.e., in any column or row of global matrix $\mathbf{C}$ of ICA there are probably more than one nonzero elements. Moreover, we cannot know the error between what we practically obtain and what we theoretically gain. Two lessons are necessary to follow: 1) if multi runs of ICA decomposition on EEG recordings are not stable, results are not acceptable; 2) although we cannot know the true source of brain activity, we may know the function of the brain activity, hence, the extracted source by ICA from EEG recordings should be evaluated by the function of the corresponding brain activity to validate whether what has been extracted are reliable or not [22].

2.3   Systematic ICA Approach to Extract MMN

Regarding the EEG data of MMN, responses of standard stimuli, and responses of deviant stimuli, and difference waveform of the two kinds of responses are available and are denoted by x_{st}, x_{dev}, and $x_{dw}(= x_{dev}-x_{st})$, respectively. Hence, in this study, ICA was individually performed on x_{st}, x_{dev}, and x_{dw}; and then, the independent components represented by y_{st}, y_{dev}, and y_{dw} were extracted by ICA from the corresponding data according to Eq. (3); next, desired components y_{st}, y_{dev}, and y_{dw} were selected and projected to the electrode field in terms of Eq. (4); finally, we obtained e_{st}, e_{dev}, and e_{dw} for each subject. Then, we define the estimated new DW by ICA is

$$d = e_{dev}-e_{st}. \tag{11}$$

The method using ICA after DW estimated e_{dw} and the method using DW after ICA estimated d. MMN peak amplitude and latency can be measured from them.

2.4   Data Processing and Analysis

Data processing was implemented for each subject individually in this study. In order to improve SNR and reduce the number of sources in the ordinary averaged EEG data [8], a Fast Fourier Transform (FFT) based digital filer [14] was used for removing interference to MMN. For the filter, the pass band was from 1 to 15 Hz and the number of points for FFT was 2500. Such a frequency band was referred to the previous publication about the frequency range of MMN [3]. Due to the low sampling frequency in data recording, there were only 125 samples in each epoch. Since 11 electrodes were used in the MMN experiment, we wanted to extract 11 components. Then, the number of samples was not enough to achieve this goal because the number of samples should be at least several times of the square of the number of extracted sources by ICA [17]. To facility ICA, we upsampled the data to 1500 Hz, and in each epoch, there were 750 samples which were much larger than the square of 11.

Subsequently, the filtered and resampled data were decomposed into 11 components by ICASSO which can estimate the stability of ICA decomposition [11]. After that, the components were downsampled into 250 Hz. ICASSO runs one ICA algorithm many times with individually and randomly initialized unmixing matrices; then, all the extracted components are clustered into the predefined number of clusters; finally, the component at the centroid of each cluster represents one component extracted by ICASSO and the stability index denoted by IQ is calculated for such a component [11]. The IQ ranges from '0' to '1'. When approaching to '1', it means that the corresponding component is extracted out in almost every run of ICA decomposition, indicating the stability of the ICA decomposition. Otherwise, it means the ICA decomposition is not stable. In this study, the IQs of 11 components were averaged to produce an averaged IQ as the criterion to evaluate the ICA decomposition because the projection of one component is really associated with all components [5], [6]. Regarding ICASSO, InfomaxICA [11] was run 100 times and 11 components were extracted at each run, and the default set of ICASSO for other parameters and algorithms was used. After the component with the latency the most nearest to 120 ms was selected and projected back to the electrode field, we finally obtained e_{st}, e_{dev}, e_{dw} and d as mentioned in the above section.

At last, the peak amplitudes and latencies of the component with the latency around 120 ms were measured from e_{st}, e_{dev}, e_{dw} and d. Regarding the peak amplitude, we gained two three-way matrices with the dimensions of 11 channels by 9 subjects by 2 methods or 2 stimuli types (DW after ICA Vs. ICA after DW or ST Vs. DEV). For the peak latency, we obtained two two-way matrices with the dimensions of 9 subjects and 2 methods or 2 stimuli types because the latency measured from e_{st}, e_{dev}, e_{dw} or d was invariable at different electrodes for one subject. For the analysis of the peak amplitude, a general linear model (GLM) repeated measures procedure for an 11×2 design was applied using the two factors including channels by the stimuli types or the methods. The latency was analyzed via one-way ANOVA.

3   Results

In order to show the components extracted from x_{st}, x_{dev}, and x_{dw}, we took the data of a typical subject for demonstration. Fig.1-a describes the ordinary averaged responses of standard stimuli and deviant stimuli and the corresponding filtered responses, and Fig.1-b, c & d display components extracted by ICA from the filtered responses of standard stimuli, the filtered responses of deviant stimuli, and from the

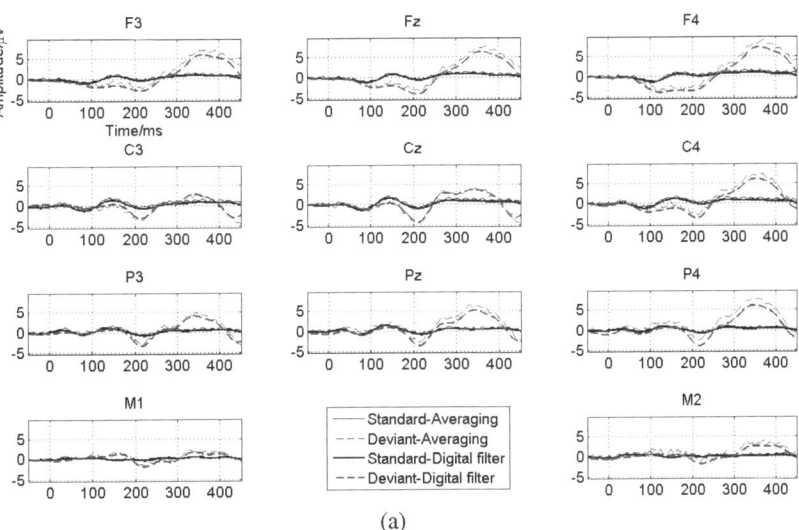

(a)

Fig. 1. Data of a typical subject for demonstration: a) ordinary averaged responses of standard stimuli and deviant stimuli and corresponding filtered responses, b) components extracted by ICA from filtered responses of standard stimuli, c) components from filtered responses of deviant stimuli, d) components from difference wave of filtered responses. The polarities and variances of components extracted by ICA are inherently indeterminate [12].

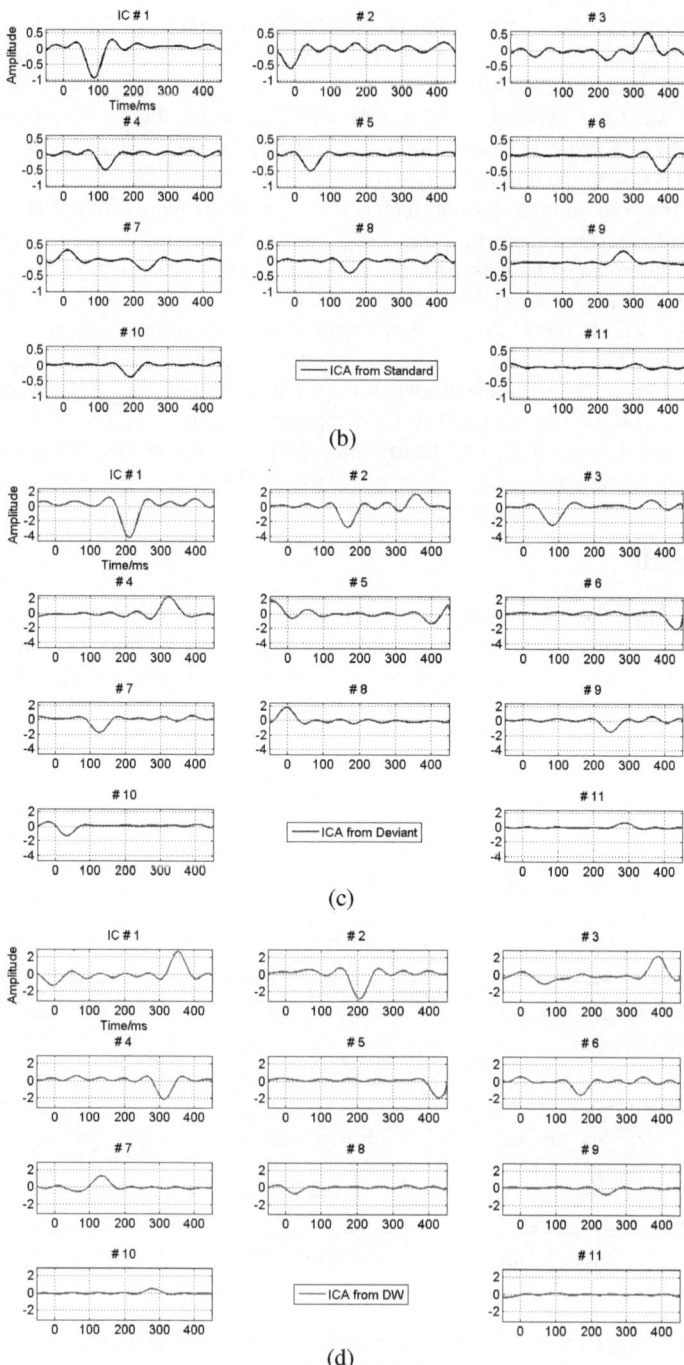

Fig. 1. (*continued*)

DW of the filtered deviant responses and the standard. Regarding the experiment design and MMN activity as mentioned earlier, the component # 4 in Fig.1-b, the component # 7 in Fig.1-c and the component # 7 in Fig.1-d were selected and projected back to the electrode field, and other components were discarded and were not analyzed since they were not the interest of this study. However, we still observe that, given certain latency, components with the similar temporal courses were extracted from different types of data, and without projecting them back to the electrode field we would not know whether their topographies could be similar or not.

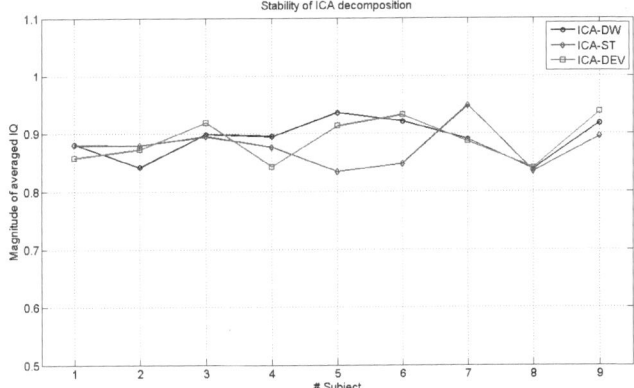

Fig. 2. Stability of ICA decomposition

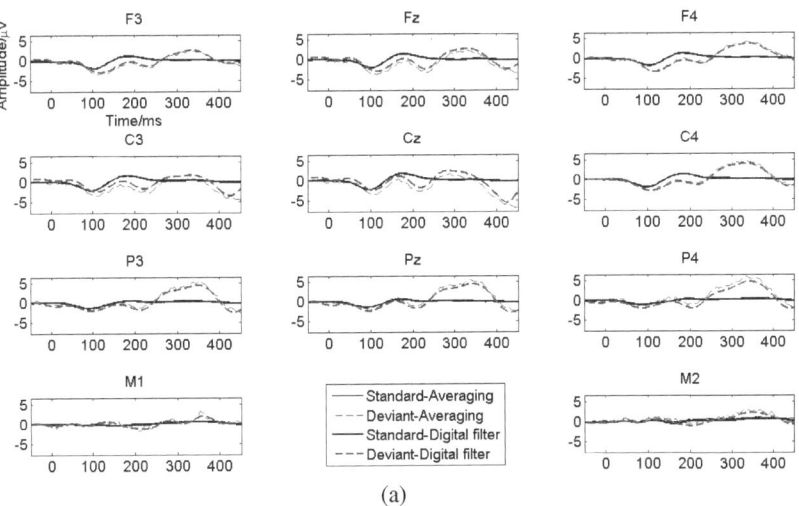

(a)

Fig. 3. Grand averaged waveforms: a) ordinary averaged responses and filtered responses, b) responses of standard and deviant stimuli estimated by ICA, c) new DW after ICA and estimation of ICA from DW of filtered responses

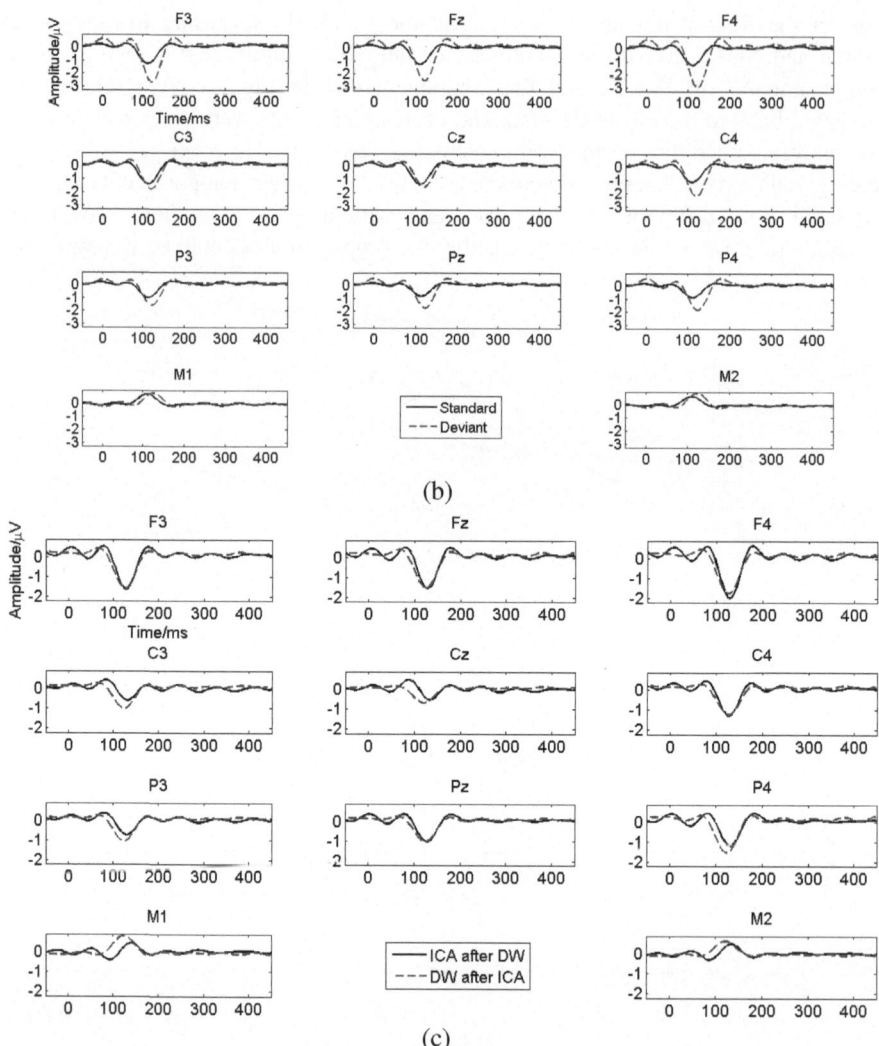

Fig. 3. (*continued*)

When ICA is used to decompose EEG, it is necessary to examine the stability of the ICA decomposition [22]. If the decomposition was not stable, the results would not be acceptable [4], [22]. Fig.2 shows the averaged IQ as defined in the last section for each subject. In terms of this figure, we can tell that the decomposition of the filtered EEG data under the model of 11-sensor-11-source in our study was stable and satisfactory and the results should be acceptable.

Fig.3 depicts the grand averaged waveforms under different conditions over nine subjects. Fig.3-a is for the ordinary averaged responses and filtered responses and Fig.3-b shows the estimated responses of standard and deviant stimuli by ICA, i.e., e_{st} and e_{dev} in Eq. (11), and Fig.3-c describes the new DW after ICA and the estimation of ICA from DW of the filtered responses, i.e., d and e_{dw} in section 2.3.

Regarding the ERPs with the latency around 120 ms measured from the estimated responses of standard and deviant stimuli by ICA, their peak latencies were significantly different (114.9 ms vs. 125.1 ms, and $F(1,8) = 7.8081$, $p = 0.0234$), and for their peak amplitudes, the significant interaction between stimulus types and channels ($F(10, 80) = 2.4684$ $p = 0.0125$) and the significant main effects of channels ($F(10,80) = 4.3194$, $p < 0.000$) and stimulus types ($F(1,8) = 5.1009$, $p = 0.0538$) were observed. As for the MMNs measured from the estimation of ICA from the DW of filtered responses and the new DW after ICA, their peak latencies were not significantly different (128.9 ms vs. 124.7 ms, $F(1,8) = 0.5886$, $p = 0.4650$), and for their peak amplitudes, the interaction between the estimation methods and channels ($F(10, 80) = 1.2312$ $p = 0.2844$) or the main effect of estimation methods ($F(1,8) = 3.7564$, $p = 0.0886$) was not significant, and the main effect of channels was significant ($F(10,80) = 2.5061$, $p = 0.0113$).

All of these effects can be observed from Fig.3 (b) and (c).

4   Conclusion

When ICA is applied to extract MMN elicited by an oddball paradigm, it can be performed on the responses of deviant and standard stimuli and the DW of the responses. Related to the MMN experimental design, the corresponding ERPs extracted by ICA from the responses of deviant and standard stimuli can be different in peak amplitudes and latencies; the MMN extracted by ICA from the DW of the raw responses and that observed from the new DW of the estimated responses of deviant and standard stimuli by ICA can be not significantly different particularly at the frontal electrodes. This indicates that the mixing matrix of Eq. (1) in the responses of the standard stimuli and the matrix in the responses of the deviant stimuli should be not significantly different, which may result from that the standard and the deviant stimuli in the experiment were adjacent in the experiment. However, regarding the MMN experimental design, the corresponding source in the responses of the standard stimuli and the one in the responses of the deviant stimuli may be different.

It should be noted that we assumed there were 11 sources in the filtered EEG data due to 11 electrodes used in EEG data collection. Although we could not examine whether there were 11 sources in the filtered EEG data directly through the model order selection [2], we still extracted 11 components through ICA and the decomposition was stable and satisfactory, indicating the assumption of 11 sources was reasonable. In the future, we will perform the similar data processing procedure on the EEG data elicited by an oddball paradigm and collected with a high-density array for further validating the idea proposed in this study.

Acknowledgments. CF. thanks the grant of FIRST (2011) from the international office of the University of Jyväskylä for supporting this study. AA., KV. and DF. are with the financial support of the Federal Target Program "Scientific and educational personnel of innovative Russia" GC 14.740.11.0232.

References

1. Cichocki, A., Amari, S.: Adaptive blind signal and image processing: Learning algorithms and applications. Revised edn. John Wile. & Sons Inc., Chichester (2003)
2. Cong, F., He, Z., Hämäläinen, J., et al.: Determining the Number of Sources in High-Density EEG Recordings of Event-Related Potentials by Model Order Selection. In: Proc. IEEE Workshop on Machine Learning for Signal Processing (MLSP) 2011, Beijing, China, September 18-21 (2011)
3. Cong, F., Huang, Y., Kalyakin, I., et al.: Frequency Response Based Wavelet Decomposition to Extract Children's Mismatch Negativity Elicited by Uninterrupted Sound. J. Med. Biol. Eng. (2011), doi:10.5405/jmbe.908
4. Cong, F., Kalyakin, I., Li, H., et al.: Answering Six Questions in Extracting Children's Mismatch Negativity through Combining Wavelet Decomposition and Independent Component Analysis. Cogn. Neurodynamics 5, 343–359 (2011)
5. Cong, F., Kalyakin, I., Ristaniemi, T.: Can Back-Projection Fully Resolve Polarity Indeterminacy of ICA in Study of ERP? Biomed. Signal Process. Control 6, 422–426 (2011)
6. Cong, F., Kalyakin, I., Zheng, C., et al.: Analysis on Subtracting Projection of Extracted Independent Components from EEG Recordings. Biomed. Tech. 56, 223–234 (2011)
7. Cong, F., Kalyakin, I., Huttunen-Scott, T., et al.: Single-Trial Based Independent Component Analysis on Mismatch Negativity in Children. Int. J. Neural Syst. 20, 279–292 (2010)
8. Cong, F., Leppanen, P.H., Astikainen, P., et al.: Dimension Reduction: Additional Benefit of an Optimal Filter for Independent Component Analysis to Extract Event-Related Potentials. J. Neurosci. Methods 201, 269–280 (2011)
9. Duncan, C.C., Barry, R.J., Connolly, J.F., et al.: Event-Related Potentials in Clinical Research: Guidelines for Eliciting, Recording, and Quantifying Mismatch Negativity, P300, and N400. Clin. Neurophysiol. 120, 1883–1908 (2009)
10. Garrido, M.I., Kilner, J.M., Stephan, K.E., et al.: The Mismatch Negativity: A Review of Underlying Mechanisms. Clin. Neurophysiol. 120, 453–463 (2009)
11. Himberg, J., Hyvarinen, A., Esposito, F.: Validating the Independent Components of Neuroimaging Time Series Via Clustering and Visualization. Neuroimage 22, 1214–1222 (2004)
12. Hyvarinen, A., Karhunen, J., Oja, E.: Independent component analysis. John Wile & Sons Inc., New York (2001)
13. Kalyakin, I., Gonzalez, M., Ivannikov, I., et al.: Extraction of the Mismatch Negativity Elicited by Sound Duration Decrements: A Comparison of Three Procedures. Data Knowl. Eng. 68, 1411–1426 (2009)
14. Kalyakin, I., Gonzalez, N., Joutsensalo, J., et al.: Optimal Digital Filtering Versus Difference Waves on the Mismatch Negativity in an Uninterrupted Sound Paradigm. Dev. Neuropsychol. 31, 429–452 (2007)
15. Kalyakin, I., Gonzalez, N., Karkkainen, T., et al.: Independent Component Analysis on the Mismatch Negativity in an Uninterrupted Sound Paradigm. J. Neurosci. Methods 174, 301–312 (2008)
16. Luck, S.J.: An introduction to the event-related potential technique. The MIT Press (2005)
17. Makeig, S., Jung, T.P., Bell, A.J., et al.: Blind Separation of Auditory Event-Related Brain Responses into Independent Components. Proc. Natl. Acad. Sci. U. S. A. 94, 10979–10984 (1997)

18. Marco-Pallares, J., Grau, C., Ruffini, G.: Combined ICA-LORETA Analysis of Mismatch Negativity. Neuroimage 25, 471–477 (2005)
19. Näätänen, R.: Attention and brain functions. Lawrence Erlbaum Associates, Hillsdale (1992)
20. Näätänen, R., Gaillard, A.W., Mantysalo, S.: Early Selective-Attention Effect on Evoked Potential Reinterpreted. Acta Psychol. (Amst) 42, 313–329 (1978)
21. Näätänen, R., Kujala, T., Kreegipuu, K., et al.: The Mismatch Negativity: An Index of Cognitive Decline in Neuropsychiatric and Neurological Diseases and in Ageing. Brain 134, 3432–3450 (2011)
22. Vigario, R., Oja, E.: BSS and ICA in Neuroinformatics: From Current Practices to Open Challenges. IEEE Reviews in Biomedical Engineering 1, 50–61 (2008)

A Study of Sickness Induced by Perceptual Conflict in the Elderly within a 3D Virtual Store and Avoidance

Cheng-Li Liu

Department of Management and Information Technology
Vanung University, Taoyuan, Taiwan
johnny@vnu.edu.tw

Abstract. Most virtual environments (VEs) lack information such as peripheral vision, responsiveness to limb-movement and, more often than not, subdued response to pleasantness. However, only a few studies in the literature have focused on the effects of age on VE sickness susceptibility and even less research was carried out focusing on the elderly. This study investigated the factors that contribute to sickness among the elderly when immersed into a 3D virtual store. The results of the first experiment showed that the rate of simulator sickness questionnaire (SSQ) scores increases significantly with navigational rotating speed and duration of exposure. In applying these findings, the fuzzy technology was used to develop a fuzzy sickness warning system with contributing factors. The results of the second experiment showed that the proposed system can efficiently combat sickness due to improper operating (i.e. faster rotation of the visual scene) or long exposure to a VE.

Keywords: Human-computer interaction, Sickness, Elderly, Virtual Store, Fuzzy sets.

1 Introduction

1.1 General Introduction

Increasingly, we are communicating electronically via the internet, and in particular through interaction with web based applications. Taking something for example, web stores are becoming popular and widespread. Its most killing applications for customers are that they can buy virtually anything from a web store. Just at this moment elderly society is coming, many older adults (i.e., the "silver tsunami" generation) have problems performing daily tasks because of restricted mobility, lack of transportation, inconvenience, and fear of crime [1]. Computers with an internet connection used at home can provide this population a new channel to access to information and services [2]. However, the traditional web stores introduce commodities only by 2D pictures and descriptive catalogue, which fall short in terms of reality and the interaction with commodities [3]. Nowadays, such problems can be solved utilizing the technology of virtual environments (VEs).

J. Wang, G.G. Yen, and M.M. Polycarpou (Eds.): ISNN 2012, Part I, LNCS 7367, pp. 422–430, 2012.
© Springer-Verlag Berlin Heidelberg 2012

1.2   Sickness in VEs

When people experience a VE which don't exactly match the real world, some users will exhibit symptoms that parallel those of classical motion sickness, both during and after the VE experience [4, 5]. This type of sickness is distinct from motion sickness in that the user is stationary, but has a compelling sense of motion induced through exposure to changing visual imagery [6, 7]. So et al. (2001) found that vection and sickness can be generated by watching moving scenes in a VE [8]. Vection sensation and sickness symptoms will increase in subjects exposed to a drum rotating at 60°/s around its vertical axis [9]. Additionally, rotating speeds from 10°/s to 200°/s around the lateral axis of an optokinetic projection of random-dots resulted in sickness symptoms after 3-8 sec. of exposure [10]. In a 3D web virtual store, the fore-and-aft, lateral and vertical directions represent the front-and-back, left-and- right and up-and-down directions relative to the user. Therefore, the effects of virtual scene rotation and speed on sickness should be discussed when the elderly immerse in a 3D web virtual store. In addition it is well known that exposure duration can influence sickness rates. Regan (1995) found that subjects experienced progressively more sickness symptoms as exposure duration in a VE continued over a 20 min [11]. Kennedy et al. (2000) reported that exposure duration and repeated exposures are significantly linearly related to sickness outcomes [12]. Taken together, these results confirm the logical and expected correspondence between sickness and exposure duration.

1.3   Objectives

When the reality and presence of VEs is improved with good 3D image quality and stereoscopic displays, however, the sickness for the elderly during exposure a 3D VEs with stereoscopic displays will be easily caused. The purpose of this study was to investigate the effects of virtual scene rotation and exposure duration on in the elderly during exposure a 3D virtual store. If we can determine the relative contributing effects, it will be a step forward towards designing a warning system with fuzzy sets for combating sickness.

2   Experiment I: Effects of Exposure Situations on Sickness

2.1   Participants, Apparatus and the Virtual Store

Thirty-two paid older people (F 13 and M 19 between 66 and 71 years of age and with an average age of 66.5 years) participated in the experiment. They were fully informed and had signed a consent form. All participants had normal vision or corrected-to-normal (i.e. acuity score between 0.83 and 1.11 in visual acuity test and normal color vision).The experimental environment was constructed by virtual developing software and presented on 15.6" 3D ready monitor with circular polarized glasses. The scene was designed as a store of automobile peripheral fitting for portable device, which contained as shown in Figure 1. All participants were exposed to the same VE. During the exposure period, participants were asked to search for and confirm some objects listed on a check sheet. In order to maintain participants' attention on this task, some of the objects listed on the check sheet would not appear in the VE, but participants didn't know. Therefore, participants might sustain attention on the screen to look for the assigned objects until simulation was terminated.

 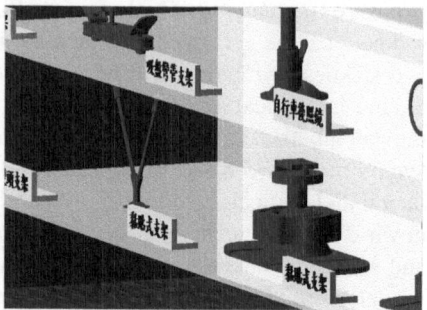

Fig. 1. The 3D simulated store (left) and products showed on the shelf (right)

2.2   Hypotheses

Based on the statements of introduction, therefore, it is reasonable to infer that exposure a VE with non-immersive stereoscopic display within different exposure situations would positively influence induction of sickness for the elderly. This study thus proposes the following hypotheses: (1) if elder users viewed a virtual store with moving scenes by means of a non-immersive stereoscopic display, they would experience symptoms of sickness; (2) the faster rotation of the visual scene and the longer exposure within a virtual store, the higher the levels of sickness would be. The first hypothesis is based on the assumption that sickness is a type of vection-induced motion sickness [13]. If sickness is a type of vection-induced motion sickness, then it is logical to expect that vection and its associated sickness will occur when users view a virtual store with moving scenes on a non-immersive stereoscopic display. The second hypothesis is based on the assumption that there will be more of a mismatch between the vection sensation and the vestibular cues under quick rotation for a prolonged period of exposure. Dichgans and Brandt (1972) reported a convergence of visual and vestibular information, which suggests that watching moving scenes will directly stimulate the vestibular neurons and cause conflicts when the sensory information is not the stimulus that the subject expected based on his/her experience [14]. Lo and So (2001) found that scene oscillations produce vection and induce sickness significantly [15]. Additionally, Kennedy et al. (2000) reported that duration is positively related to simulator sickness. Based on these results, vection in quick rotation for prolonged exposure duration are herein assumed to be associated with more sensory mismatch [16]. In order to verify these two hypotheses, an experiment with passive tasks was proceeded.

2.3   Questionnaires

The Simulator Sickness Questionnaire (SSQ), originally devised to evaluate computer based simulator systems, consists of a checklist of 16 sickness symptoms on three subscales representing separable but somewhat correlated dimensions of simulator sickness (i.e. nausea, oculomotor disturbances and disorientation) [16]. SSQ has been found to be valid, reliable measure and be the most popular subjective measure for both simulator sickness and side effects experienced in VEs [17, 18]. Therefore, SSQ was used to measure subjective symptoms of sickness in this study.

2.4   Experimental Design and Procedures

The experiment used a 4 (scene rotation speed) × 4 (scene inclination angle) × 4 (duration of exposure) within subject repeated measure design. In general, users in VEs would rotate scene around the vertical axis, but less around the lateral and the fore-and-aft axis. Reid et al. (1994) reported that vection generated during an exposure to a scene rotating around the vertical axis caused symptoms of nausea in over half of the participants. The elderly might be sensitive on scene rotating speed [19]. Therefore, it was designed with four levels of scene rotating speed around the vertical axis: 15°/s, 30°/s, 45°/s and 60°/s and four levels of inclination of scene in the lateral axis (clockwise): 0, 15, 30 and 45. Additionally, Liu (2009) found that 5 to 10 minutes after the start of exposure VEs with TFT-LCD, the rate of subjective symptoms of sickness accelerated significantly under scene rotation, then slightly increased for 15 to 20 minutes [20]. So the levels of exposure duration including 5 min., 10 min., 15 min. and 20 min were designed. In this experiment, a randomized block design with 4 × 4 Latin squares was used; four levels of the scene rotating speed block as the rows, four levels of the inclination angle of scene block as the columns and four levels of exposure duration are defined as treatments.

During the exposure, the VE was controlled by the program. First, the scene was rotated one circle at the door gate along vertical axis with the set rotating speed and angle. Second, the scene was moved forward along the fore-and-aft axis 5 seconds at 0.2 units of translate vector per second, then, rotated one circle. Third, the scene was turned right, then, moved forward to the end of the showroom. Fourth, the scene was moved back to the door gate, then, rotated one circle. Fifth, the scene was turned left, then, moved forwarded to the end of the showroom. Finally, the scene was returned to the door gate. The scene was halted for 5 seconds among each step. The circulation repeated until meeting experiment time. After the exposure, participants were asked to complete a post-exposure SSQ.

2.5   Experimental Design and Procedures

Measures of sickness (SSQ) were obtained from participants before and after VE exposure (see Table 1). For data analysis the difference between post-exposure and pre-exposure total sickness severity scores are used. There was significant difference found between before and after VE exposure (t(31) = 12.705, p = 0.000), showing participants' symptoms of sickness of post-exposure were significant than that of pre-exposure. The result supports the first hypothesis: a virtual store with scene moving through the use of non-immersive stereoscopic display would produce symptoms of sickness in the elderly. According to SSQ scores of post-exposure, we found that among the list of 16 symptoms of SSQ, over 50 percent of the subjects exposed virtual store reported an increase in fatigue, eyestrain, difficulty focusing and difficulty concentrating.

In addition Table 2 shows ANOVA for the effects of viewing a virtual store with moving scenes by means of non-immersive stereoscopic display on SSQ scores of post-exposure. The results indicates that the F of 7.278 for the SSQ scores for the effect of scene rotating speed was statistically significantly at p = 0.003, the F of 96.929 for SSQ scores for the effect of exposure duration was significant at p < 0.000, but the effect of scene inclination was not significant. Then the Scheffe's post hoc test, a multiple comparison statistical procedure, was used to determine where differences between groups exist after a significant F ratio has been obtained in ANOVA. The findings also indicated that the incidence and severity of sickness of the participants was low within 5 minutes of exposure, but increased significantly after 10 minutes and continued to increase until experiment finished. In addition, the results showed that the SSQ scores increased smaller at 30°/s and 45°/s than 15°/s, but larger at 60°/s.

Table 1. SSQ scores before and after VE Exposure

		SSQ ts*
Before VE Exposure	Mean	1.99
	SD	2.68
After VE Exposure	Mean	27.23
	SD	11.33

* indicates total scores in SSQ

Table 2. ANOVA for the effects of viewing a virtual store with moving scenes by means of non-immersive stereoscopic display on SSQ scores of post-exposure

Source	SS	DF	MS	F-value	P^a-value
Scene rotating speed	252.752	3	84.251	7.278	0.003*
Scene inclination	57.168	3	19.056	1.646	0.218
Exposure duration	3366.171	3	1122.057	96.929	0.000*
Rotation speed×Inclination angle×Exposure duration	113.177	6	18.863	1.629	0.203
Error	185.218	16	11.576		
Total	3974.485	31			

*Indicates significant difference at p <0.05

3   A Fuzzy Warning System for Combating Sickness

3.1   System Development

In this study, fuzzy sets were used to develop the fuzzy logic reasoning and warning system. There are two input variables (i.e. speed of navigation rotation and exposure duration) and one output variable (i.e. ratings of sickness) constructed in the module. There were two variables considered as input fuzzy sets: one is the fuzzy set $\tilde{S}$ which represents the linguistic notion "*Speed of navigation rotation*," around the vertical axis. The fuzzy set is described by three attributes: "Slow speed" (SS) (i.e. $\tilde{S}_{SS}(x)$), "Medium speed" (MS) (i.e. $\tilde{S}_{MS}(x)$) and "Quick speed" (QS) (i.e. $\tilde{S}_{QS}(x)$). Another is the fuzzy set $\tilde{D}$ which is defined as the linguistic notion "*Exposure duration.*" The fuzzy set is described by three attributes: "Short exposure duration" (SD) (i.e. $\tilde{D}_{SD}(y)$), "Medium exposure duration" (MD) (i.e. $\tilde{D}_{MD}(y)$) and "Long exposure duration" (LD) (i.e. $\tilde{D}_{LD}(y)$). $\tilde{S}_{SS}(x)$ and $\tilde{D}_{SD}(y)$ are L-shaped membership function; $\tilde{S}_{MS}(x)$ and $\tilde{D}_{MD}(y)$ are triangle-shaped membership function; $\tilde{S}_{QS}(x)$ and $\tilde{D}_{LD}(y)$ are Γ-shaped membership function. According to the study by Kennedy and Lane (1993), when the SSQ score is smaller than 7.5, the symptom of nausea occurs seldom. When the score is between 7.5 and 22.5, at least one symptom of nausea will occur. When the score is above 22.5, the symptoms of nausea increase quickly. Therefore, the SSQ score of 15 (i.e. middle value between 7.5 and 22.5) will be used to define the initial value of the parameter a_1 of $\tilde{S}$, the score of 22.5 will be used to define the initial value of parameter a_2 and the score 30 (i.e. 22.5 plus 7.5) will be used to define the initial value of parameter a_3. So how do we define these parameter values? The results of the previous experiment indicate that the mean SSQ score of the navigation rotating speed at level 15°/s was 20.27, at 30°/s was 23.28, at 45°/s was 27.19 and 60°/s was 31.62. Using the method of linear interpolation, corresponding SSQ score of 15, the crisp value of parameter a_1 could be estimated to be about 0.0 °/s. Similarly, corresponding SSQ score of 22.5, the crisp value of parameter a_2 was 27.0°/s; and corresponding SSQ score of 30, the crisp value of parameter a_3 was 54.51°/s. Additionally, the results of the experiment also shows that the mean SSQ score of exposure duration at the 5 min. level was 10.53, at the 10 min. level it was 23.67, at the 15 min. level it was 29.36 and at the 20 min. level it was 32.14. Similarly, the crisp value of parameter b_1 was estimated to be about 6.70 min., the crisp value of parameter b_2 was 9.55 min. and the crisp value of parameter b_3 was about 16.15 min. The output variable for sickness prediction, fuzzy set $\tilde{R}$, was defined as the linguistic notion "*Ratings of sickness*" included five attributes: "No symptoms" (NO), "Slight" (ST), "Mild" (MD), "Moderate" (MO) and "Serious" (SE). Therefore, we can define the five membership functions, $\mu_{R_{NO}}, \mu_{R_{ST}}, \mu_{R_{MD}}, \mu_{R_{MO}}, \mu_{R_{SE}}$ as membership functions in the continuous domain [0,100]. Finally, the IF-THEN rules are defined to process fuzzy reasoning. The processing stage was shown in Figure 2.

When the fuzzy warning system was completed, it will be linked to a voice device. As described in the previous section, the values 15, 22.5 and 30 are used to design the alarm for combating sickness. In other words, when the value of sickness rating (variable r) is higher than 15, the system will continuously sound a 5 second "BEEP" and the scene of virtual store will be locked for about 1 minute. When the value r is larger than 22.5, the system will continuously sound a 5 second "BEEP" and the scene will be locked for about 3 minutes. When the value r is higher than 30, the system will continuously make a 5 second "BEEP" and the operation will be stopped.

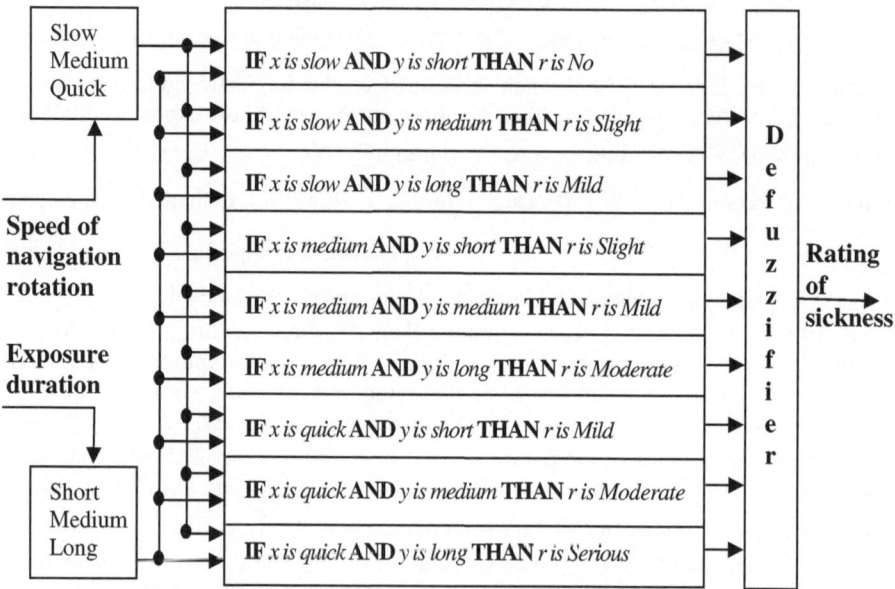

Fig. 2. The block diagram of fuzzy reasoning with IF-THEN rules

3.2   Second Experiment and Result

The second experiment used the same set of participants as those of the first experiment (i.e. thirty two participants). There were two experimental sets: one is with fuzzy warning system, another is none. Each participant was randomly assigned one of the two sets. During the exposure period, there were six target objects for which participants were required to search (see Table 3). However, only four of these objects were exhibited in the showroom. When the target object was found, participants could move the cursor over the object and push the left button on the control device to identify the object. If the object was the target, the system would beep once to notify the participant. At the same time, the participant was to write down the correct position on the check sheet (i.e., each showcase was numbered). If the participant determined that a particular target object was not exhibited in the showroom, the participant need to mark "X" in the corresponding column. In addition, participants were asked to complete the SSQ at ten minutes after beginning experiment and experiment finished. A test of differences between means showed that the post-exposure SSQ scores with the warning system were significantly smaller than those with 'no system' ($t(62) = -6.2870$, $p = 1.81E-8$). Additionally, we found that the SSQ scores with the fuzzy warning system were significantly smaller than those with 'no system' at experiment finished, ($t(15) = -3.8580$, $p = 0.0008$), but not significantly at ten minutes. The result confirmed our expectation that the fuzzy warning system for sickness reduction in the elderly exposed to a virtual store will produce better results for longer exposure durations.

Table 3. Sheet of target objects

No.	1	2	3	4	5	6
Objects						
Showing in the showroom or not?						

4   Conclusion

Sickness in VEs can present a significant problem for a number of individuals, especially for the elderly both during and after the VE exposure. The findings indicated that the sickness symptoms increased significantly with the increase in navigation rotating speed and exposure duration. Utilizing the contributing factors, a fuzzy sickness-warning system was developed. The experiment revealed that the proposed system can efficiently combat sickness due to improper operating (i.e. faster rotation of the visual scene) or long exposure to a VE. This finding will be also useful for research in estimating the severity levels of sickness in a particular VE.

Acknowledgement. The authors would like to thank the National Science Council of the Republic of China for financially supporting this work under Contract No. 100-2221-E-238-012.

References

1. Czaja, S., Lee, C.: Designing Computer Systems for Older Adults. In: The Human Computer Interaction Handbook 21, pp. 413–427 (2003)
2. Jones, S.: Generations Online in 2009, Pew Internet & American Life Project Report (2009)
3. Ding, J., Yu, L., Wang, Y., Pan, Z.: EasyHouse-I: A Virtual House Presentation System Based on Internet. In: Proceedings of the 11th International Conference on Human-Computer Interaction, Las Vegas (2005)

4. Bowman, D., Kruijff, E., LaViola, J.J., Poupyrev, I.: An Introduction to 3-D User Interface Design. Teleoperators and Virtual Environments 10, 96–108 (2001)
5. Rich, C.J., Braun, C.C.: Assessing the Impact of Control and Sensory Compatibility on Sickness in Virtual Environments. In: Proceedings of Human Factors and Ergonomics Society 40th Annual Meeting, Philadelphia (1996)
6. Stanney, K.M.: Handbook of Virtual Environments. Earlbaum, New York (2002)
7. Lathan, R.: Tutorial: A Brief Introduction to Simulation Sickness and Motion Programming. Real Time Graphics 9, 3–5 (2001)
8. So, H.Y., Lo, W.T., Ho, T.K.: Effects of Navigation Speed on Motion Sickness Caused by an Immersive Virtual Environment. Human Factors 43, 452–461 (2001)
9. Hu, S., Davis, M.S., Klose, A.H., Zabinsky, E.M., Meux, S.P., Jacobsen, H.A., Westfall, J.M., Gruber, M.B.: Effects of Spatial Frequency of a Vertically Striped Rotating Drum on Vection-Induced Motion Sickness. Aviation, Space, and Environmental Medicine 68, 306–311 (1997)
10. Muller, C.H., Wiest, G., Deecke, L.: Vertically Moving Visual Stimuli and Vertical Vection –A Tool Against Space Motion Sickness? In: Proceedings of the 4th European Symposium on Life Sciences Research in Space, Trieste (1990)
11. Regan, C.: An Investigation into Nausea and Other Side-Effects of Head-Coupled Immersive Virtual Reality. Virtual Reality 1, 17–32 (1995)
12. Kennedy, R.S., Stanney, K.M., Dunlap, W.: Duration and Exposure to Virtual Environments: Sickness Curves During and across Sessions. Presence: Teleoperators and Virtual Environments 9, 463–472 (2000)
13. McCauley, M.E., Sharkey, T.J.: Cybersickness: Perception of Self-Motion in Virtual Environments. Presence: Teleoperators and Virtual Environments 1, 311–318 (1992)
14. Dichgans, J., Brandt, T.: Visual-Vestibular Interaction: Effects on Self-Motion Perception and Postural Control. In: Held, R., Leibowitz, H.W., Teuber, H.-L. (eds.) Handbook of Sensory Physiology 8, pp. 755–804. Springer, Berlin (1972)
15. Lo, W.T., So, R.-H.Y.: Cybersickness in the Presence of Scene Rotational Movements along Different Axes. Applied Ergonomics 32, 1–14 (2001)
16. Kennedy, R.S., Lane, N.E.: Simulator Sickness Questionnaire: An Enhanced Method for Quantifying Simulator Sickness. The International Journal of Avivation Psychology 3, 203–220 (1993)
17. Kiryu, T., So, R.H.Y.: Sensation of Presence and Cybersickness in Applications of Virtual Reality for Advanced Rehabilitation. Journal of NeuroEngineering and Rehabilitation 4, 34 (2007)
18. Hale, K.S., Stanney, K.M.: Effects of Low Stereo Acuity on Performance, Presence and Sickness Within a Virtual Environment. Applied Ergonomics 37, 329–339 (2006)
19. Reid, K., Grundy, D., Khan, M.I., Read, N.W.: Gastric Emptying and The Symptoms of Vection-Induced Nausea. Eur. J. Gastroenterol. Hepatol. 7, 103–108 (1994)
20. Liu, C.L.: A Neuro-Fuzzy Warning System for Combating Cybersickness in The Elderly Caused by The Virtual Environment on a TFT-LCD. Applied Ergonomics 40, 316–327 (2009)

A Co-adaptive Training Paradigm for Motor Imagery Based Brain-Computer Interface

Bin Xia[1,*], Qingmei Zhang[1], Hong Xie[1], Shihua Li[1], Jie Li[2], and Lianghua He[2]

[1] Information Engineering College
Shanghai Maritime University, Shanghai, China
[2] College of Electronics and Information Engineering
Tongji University
Shanghai, China
binxia@shmtu.edu.cn

Abstract. In motor imagery based Brain-Computer Interface (MI-BCI), subjects should be trained to learn how to modulate the rhythm of EEG for a long time. In previous works, more researchers focused on adaptive BCI system and a few works studied neurofeedback-based subjects training. To achieve high training performance, system self-adaption and subjects training were considered simultaneously in recent works. In this work, we present a co-adaptive training paradigm which includes subjects training and BCI system training. For subjects training, we present a neurofeedback-based training paradigm applying the strength information of motor imagery. In system training, the classifier model is run-by-run updated by selecting good features from EEG data of several previous runs. The online and offline analysis demonstrate that the proposed training paradigm can achieve a better training performance than normal training paradigm.

Keywords: Brain-computer interface, co-adaptive training, support vector machine.

1 Introduction

Recently, motor imagery-based Brain-Computer Interface (MI-BCI) system has received more and more attention [1,2]. When subject imagines moving left or right hand, event related desynchronization (ERD) will be detected in contralateral sensorimotor cortex. The basic principle of motor imagery based BCI is to translate ERD phenomenon into commands[3]. To build a high performance

---

* The work was Supported by Innovation Program of Shang hai Municipal Education Commission (Grant No.12ZZ150) and the National Natural Science Foundation of China (Grant No. 60905065, 61105122), Shanghai Maritime University Foundation, the Ministry of Transport of the Peoples Republic of China (Grant No. 2010318810019),the Shanghai Phosphor Science Foundation, china (Grand No.10QA1407100,11QA1402900).

J. Wang, G.G. Yen, and M.M. Polycarpou (Eds.): ISNN 2012, Part I, LNCS 7367, pp. 431–439, 2012.
© Springer-Verlag Berlin Heidelberg 2012

in BCI system, there are two important factors: the ability to modulate Electroencephalogram(EEG) signals and signal processing algorithm. An outstanding signal processing algorithm may facilitate system to capture task related features in EEG signals and convert them into control commands effectively. No matter how outstanding the algorithms are, BCI cannot achieve good performance when subjects fail in self-modulating brain activity. Especially for the naive subjects of BCI, it is a tough task to control their own EEG patterns. Therefore, a suitable training program is necessary for naive subjects to help them to control their EEG pattern. Though subjects training is as important as system training, more works have focused on developing new algorithm to improve the performance of BCI in past decade[4,5]. On the other hand, a few works have studied the neurofeedback training of subjects [6,7]. In recent years, researchers began to pay more attention to co-adaptive training which considers subject's training and system adaptation simultaneously. Vidaurre et al investigated co-adaptive machine learning methods with a schema of supervised and unsupervised adaptation for three levels [8,9]. DiGiovanna et al introduced a co-adaptive Brain-Machine Interface (BMI) which enables continuous, synergistic adaptation between the BMI control algorithm and BMI user working in changing environments by reinforcement learning [10]. In [11], Li et al presented a bilateral training framework. The subjects and BCI system were trained alternately to achieve a dynamic equilibrium. At initial period of training, subjects obtain visual feedback by non-feedback training data model. However, they have no idea that which type of motor imagery is appropriate. As the experiment going on, subject is getting feeling of task-related motor imagery. Therefore, EEG feature is time-varying over time. In order to trace this variation, the classification model has to update timely so as to change again the feedback. Only in this way will the train performance be able to improve. The goal of this paper is to develop a co-adaptive training strategy based on system self-adaptation. In feedback training, feedback signals are refreshed by subjects' strength information of motor imagery (more details see 2.3 neurofeedback training paradigm). Meanwhile, system training is fulfilled via updating classification model which is trained by EEG feature from the previous runs according to a certain proportion.

2 Experimental Setup

2.1 Subjects

Ten healthy subjects (aged=22.4 ± 1.35; 8 males, 2 females), participated in this study. All were right-handed and had no BCI experience. They gave informed consent before the experiment started. After completion of the whole experiments, they received a fee for their participation. All participants were divided into experiment group and control group randomly.

2.2 The EEG Signal Recording and Preprocessing

The EEG signals are recorded using a 16-channel g.USBamp system, with electrodes placed according to the international $10 - 20$ system.13 channels are chosen(FC3 FCZ FC4 C5 C3 C1 CZ C2 C4 C6 CP3 CPZ CP4), the referenced and ground electrodes are respectively fixed on Fz and the left earlobe. All channel signals are acquired at a sampling frequency of 256Hz by passing a bandpass filter within $5 - 30$Hz.

2.3   Neurofeedback Training Paradigm

In this work, all subjects attended two-class motor imagery tasks (left hand vs right hand). During the whole experiment, each subject attended experiment every other day and training experiment lasted for fortnight. Each subject must complete 2 sessions every day, and in which one session consisted of 10 runs. Each run consisted of 20 trials, 10 trials for each class presented in randomized order. There was $5 - 10$ minutes rest time between two sessions. An experiment lasted about 1.5h including preparing time. The subjects were seated comfortably in an armchair, with their hands resting on the chair's arms or on the table in front of them during the whole trial.In the beginning of the experiment, the cue "ready"displayed at the center of screen and two sinks showed in left and right side of screen. When clicking "ok"on the interface, an arrow would turn up randomly pointing either to the left or to the right, meanwhile, a ball appeared in arrow pointed sink. The subject was instructed to imagine using the corresponding side hand to push up the ball. At this time, each subject had to continuously perform the motor imagery until the arrow was erased. This task time would last 3s, which was divided into 10 step time equably. The ball would move up H every step. H's value could be calculated as follow:

$$H = P \times L \times \frac{steptime}{tasktime} \tag{1}$$

Where P is the output probability of SVM per step time, L is the height of the sink. The ball would go up or down whether the outcome of classifier was in accord with task-related imagery or not. In addition, in this paradigm, we set rich visual feedback to encourage subjects. We marked the sink's half height, three-quarter height and total height h1, h2, h3, respectively. During a trial, if the ball arrived at certain height (h1, h2 or h3) at any time, simultaneously, the water-color would be changed from blue to red (h1) or green (h2), or yellow (h3), as shown in Fig.1. At the end of a trial, the performance of each trial would be measured by classifier again, and different score ("60","80","100") was also recorded according to the above different height. After a short pause (2s), the next trial started. In neurofeedback training experiment, we applied the same screen setting as descripting above for two groups. In system training, two different model training strategy are instructed for experiment and control group. The details of model training strategy will be described in following section.

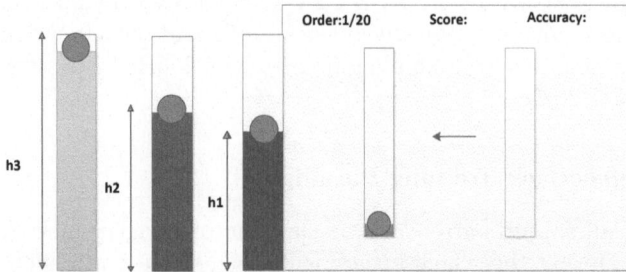

Fig. 1. Paradigm for feedback training, displaying a trial based on imagining left hand movement. Order means which trial is being conducted. Score and accuracy represent training performance in completed trials. The left three sinks only stands for the change of water color when the ball arrives at special position.

3   Classification Model Trained Framework

3.1   Feature Selection Based Model Training Strategy

In BCI system, Common Spatial Pattern (CSP) [12] was applied to extract the feature and a linear Support Vector Machine (SVM) [13] classifier was used to discriminate the EEG patterns between left hand and right hand motor imagery. During training period, task-related EEG features will vary over time. Therefore, the classification model should be self-adapted with EEG variation[11]. We apply a feature selection based adaption strategy for classifier model in this work. In the course of training model, the training data combined with chosen trials from the previous runs($i \leqslant 5$).When the number of runs is less than five, the proportion of training trials from previous runs is described as:

$$P(n) = \frac{X(n)}{5} \qquad (n = 1, 2, 3, 4, 5) \qquad (2)$$

$X(n)$'s value is 5 when n is the lastest run. $X(n)$'s value is orderly dropped by one from the lastest run to the previous runs. When the number of runs is more than five, the proportion of training trials from the lastest run to the previous fifth run is 1, $4/5$, $3/5$, $2/5$, $1/5$, respectively. The explanation of chosen trials in a run is as follows. If the trials are classified correctly, the higher the output probability of SVM is, the more possibility the trial is chosen. What's more, if the number of two-class candidate trials keeps balance, all of these trials will be ready to be chosen. In this study, the ratio of two-class trials is marked as r. If $3/5 \leqslant r \leqslant 1$ or $1 \leqslant r \leqslant 5/3$, we tentatively regard the candidate two-class trials as an balance level. Otherwise, the trials with the less number and the lower output probability of SVM will be in succession added. Like this, an update run comes into being. And then, the specific proportion of the chosen run is considered. The other chosen run will be formed a new run in a similar way. All update runs($\leqslant 5$) consist of a training set.

3.2   Non-feature Selection Based Model Training Strategy

For control group, we also applied an adaptive model training strategy without feature selection. To train a new model, the training data is consisted of the previous runs($i \leqslant 5$).These chosen runs data are all used to trained a new model rather than select according to P among them. Each model is updated after each run.

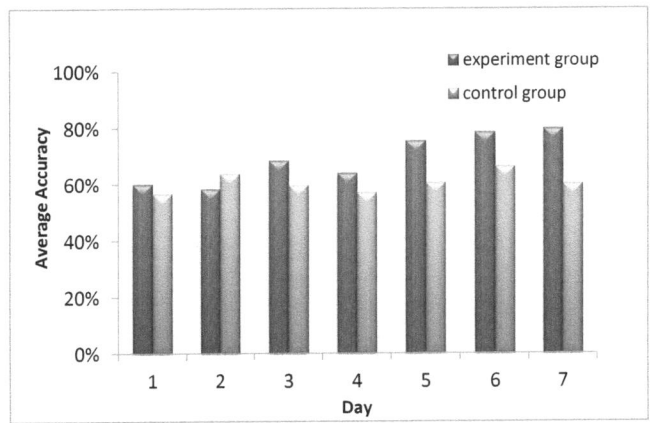

Fig. 2. The online training performance comparison between experiment group and control group

4   Results

4.1   Comparison of Training Performance

To compare the training performance between experiment group and control, the average classification accuracy (ACA) of whole group is calculated for each day. Fig. 2 shows the seven day's ACA of two groups. For experiment group, there exist an obviously ascending trend. At the end of experiment, the ACA achieved around 80% level, which is better than criterion training level 70%. On the contrary, the performance of control group always fluctuated under the criterion level. Fig.3 shows the detail of average accuracy for each subject. In Fig.3(a), most subjects' performance curves have a good ascending trend except for subject 5 in experiment group. For control group, the performances are different among subjects. But only subject 9 improved performance over time.

4.2   Off-Line Analysis for Model Training

In proposed paradigm, a feature selection based model training strategy was introduced. To further study the efficiency of model training, we have analyzed training strategy in offline state. To compare proposed model training with

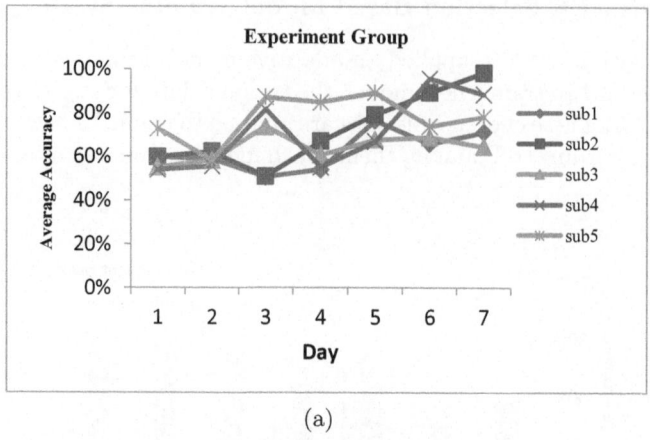

(a)

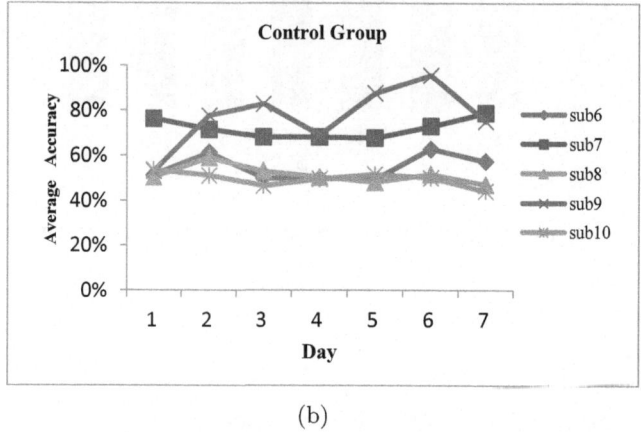

(b)

Fig. 3. Illustration of average accuracy of each subject

normal training method, we applied normal training method to experiment group and vice versa. As shown in Fig.4, average train accuracies are obviously improved using feature selection method for both groups.

5   Discussion and Conclusion

In motor imagery based BCI system, co-adaptive training is very of importance for the sake of improving BCI system performance in a short time. During the whole training period, two types of training are interactive. The core problem of bilateral training is how to provide right feedback for subjects. At the beginning of training, subjects try to do right motor imagery in different way. As a result, there exists good mode or bad mode in EEG data. If the BCI system can choose

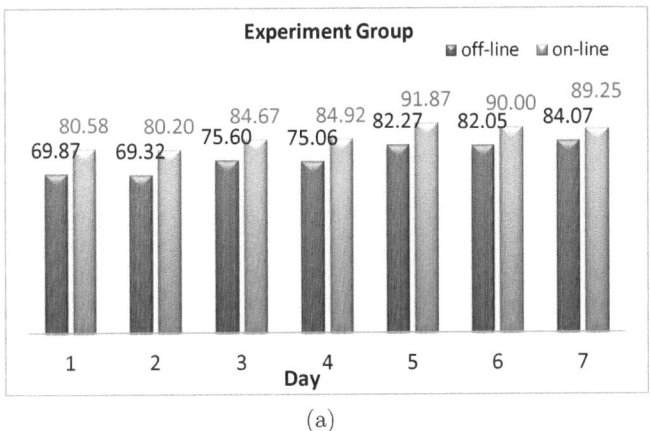

(a)

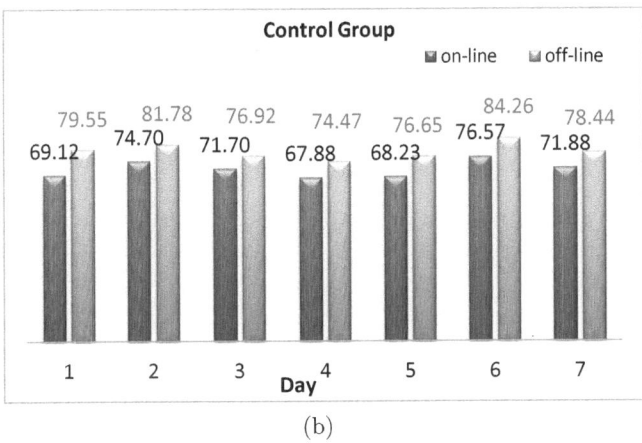

(b)

Fig. 4. Illustration of average train accuracies (%)using two different model training methods for both groups

the good mode and feedback to subject, it will instruct subject doing motor imagery in right way. In this paper, we proposed a feature selection based model training method, which generates feature in selection data. Feature distribution before and after data selecting is shown in Fig. 5. In the Fig.5 (a), the data is separable. By rejecting some intermediate data, the separability is improved (Fig.5 (c)). The separability is not good in Fig.5 (b). After data selecting, the data show good separability (Fig.5 (d)). In this study, we proposed a co-adaptive training strategy for MI BCI. Neurofeedback training of subjects and adaptive system training are combined in this training paradigm. Especially, to instruct subject training effectively, a feature selection method is introduced in system training. The experimental results demonstrate that this co-adaptive training based on feature screen training model is feasible.

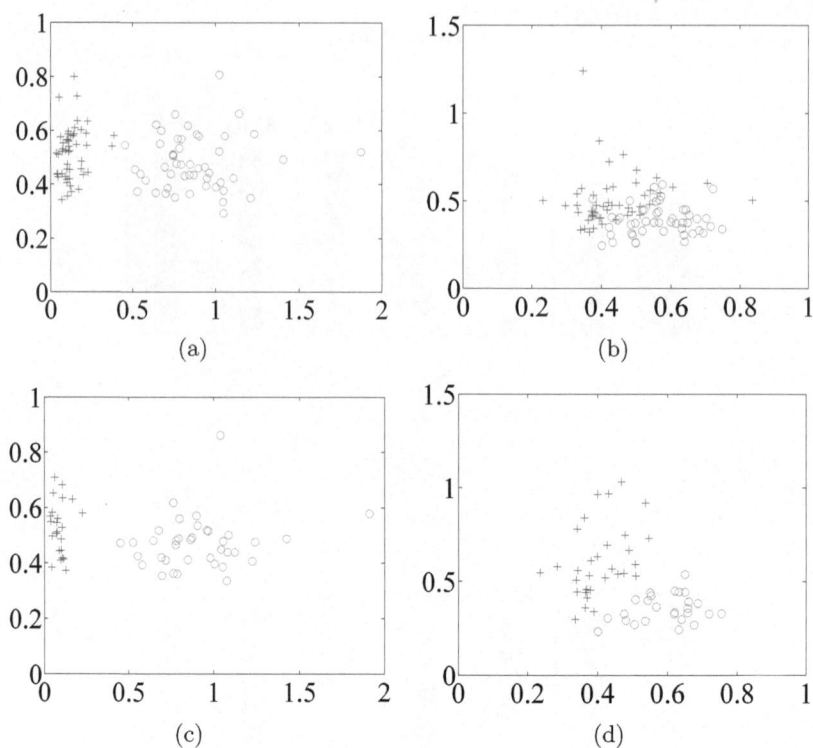

Fig. 5. Feature distribution. The first column displays the feature distribution of subject 3, and the second column shows subject 5's feature distribution. Figure (a) and (b) stands for feature distribution based non-feature selection training model strategy. Figure (c) and (d) shows selective feature distribution based feature selection training model strategy.

References

1. Neuper, C., Müller, G.R., Kübler, A., Birbaumer, N., Pfurtscheller, G.: Clinical application of an eeg-based brain–computer interface: a case study in a patient with severe motor impairment. Clinical Neurophysiology 114(3), 399–409 (2003)
2. Pfurtscheller, G., Neuper, C., Muller, G.R., Obermaier, B., Krausz, G., Schlogl, A., Scherer, R., Graimann, B., Keinrath, C., Skliris, D., et al.: Graz-bci: state of the art and clinical applications. IEEE Transactions on Neural Systems and Rehabilitation Engineering 11(2), 1–4 (2003)
3. Pfurtscheller, G., Neuper, C.: Motor imagery and direct brain-computer communication. Proceedings of the IEEE 89(7), 1123–1134 (2001)
4. Müller, K.-R., Krauledat, M., Dornhege, G., Curio, G., Blankertz, B.: Machine Learning and Applications for Brain-Computer Interfacing. In: Smith, M.J., Salvendy, G. (eds.) HCII 2007, Part I. LNCS, vol. 4557, pp. 705–714. Springer, Heidelberg (2007)

5. Müller, K.R., Tangermann, M., Dornhege, G., Krauledat, M., Curio, G., Blankertz, B.: Machine learning for real-time single-trial eeg-analysis: From brain-computer interfacing to mental state monitoring. Journal of Neuroscience Methods 167(1), 82–90 (2008)
6. Gruzelier, J., Egner, T.: Critical validation studies of neurofeedback. Child and Adolescent Psychiatric Clinics of North America 14(1), 83–104 (2005)
7. John Gruzelier, Ã., Egner, T., Vernon, D.: Validating the efficacy of neurofeedback for optimising performance. Event-related Dynamics of Brain Oscillations 159, 421 (2006)
8. Vidaurre, C., Sannelli, C., Müller, K.R., Blankertz, B.: Machine-learning-based coadaptive calibration for brain-computer interfaces. Neural Computation 23(3), 791–816 (2011)
9. Vidaurre, C., Blankertz, B.: Towards a cure for bci illiteracy. Brain Topography 23(2), 194–198 (2010)
10. DiGiovanna, J., Mahmoudi, B., Fortes, J., Principe, J.C., Sanchez, J.C.: Coadaptive brain–machine interface via reinforcement learning. IEEE Transactions on Biomedical Engineering 56(1), 54–64 (2009)
11. Li, J., Zhang, L.: Bilateral adaptation and neurofeedback for brain computer interface system. Journal of Neuroscience Methods 193(2), 373–379 (2010)
12. Muller-Gerking, J., Ramoser, H., Pfurtscheller, G.: Optimal spatial ltering of single trial eeg during imagined hand movement. Rehabilitation Engineering 8(4), 441–446 (2002)
13. Vapnik, V.N.: The nature of statistical learning theory. Springer (2000)

Overcoming the Local-Minimum Problem in Training Multilayer Perceptrons with the NRAE Training Method[*]

James Ting-Ho Lo[1], Yichuan Gui[2], and Yun Peng[2]

[1] Department of Mathematics and Statistics
jameslo@umbc.edu
[2] Department of Computer Science and Electrical Engineering
University of Maryland, Baltimore County
Baltimore, Maryland 21250, USA
{yichgui1,ypeng}@umbc.edu

Abstract. A method of training multilayer perceptrons (MLPs) to reach a global or nearly global minimum of the standard mean squared error (MSE) criterion is proposed. It has been found that the region in the weight space that does not have a local minimum of the normalized risk-averting error (NRAE) criterion expands strictly to the entire weight space as the risk-sensitivity index increases to infinity. If the MLP under training has enough hidden neurons, the MSE and NRAE criteria are both equal to nearly zero at a global or nearly global minimum. Training the MLP with the NRAE at a sufficiently large risk-sensitivity index can therefore effectively avoid non-global local minima. Numerical experiments show consistently successful convergence from different initial guesses of the weights of the MLP at a risk-sensitivity index over 10^6. The experiments are conducted on examples with non-global local minima of the MSE criterion that are difficult to escape from by training directly with the MSE criterion.

Keywords: Neural network, Training, Normalized risk-averting error, Global optimization, Local-minimum, Mean squared error, Hessian matrix.

1 Introduction

The local-minimum problem has plagued the development and application of the neural network approach based on the multilayer perceptron (MLP) and has attracted much attention since its inception [1,2,3,4,5,6,7,8,9]. A promising method to alleviate the problem was proposed in [10,11]. The method employs a new type of risk-averting error (RAE) criterion, which is a transformation of the standard mean squared error (MSE) criterion for training the MLP. By gradually

[*] This material is based upon work supported in part by the National Science Foundation under Grant ECCS1028048, but does not necessarily reflect the position or policy of the Government.

J. Wang, G.G. Yen, and M.M. Polycarpou (Eds.): ISNN 2012, Part I, LNCS 7367, pp. 440–447, 2012.

increasing the risk-sensitivity index, the convexity region of the RAE criterion expands strictly, thereby creating tunnels or wormholes for a local search method such as the conjugate gradient and quasi-Newton algorithm to escape non-global minima. However, the method has two shortcomings. First, the RAE is a sum of exponential functions of the risk sensitivity index. Computer overflow occurs in evaluating the RAE at a large risk sensitivity index. Second, it is not always easy to select an appropriate value of the risk-sensitivity index to start the gradual convexification. In the following, a remedy is discussed.

A standard formulation of training a multilayer perceptron (MLP) under supervision follows: A set of pairs, (x_k, y_k), $k = 1, ..., K$, of which the vectors x_k and the vectors y_k are related by an unknown function f

$$y_k = f(x_k) + \xi_k$$

where ξ_k are random noises. Find the weight vector w of a MLP $\hat{f}(x, w)$ such that the mean squared error (MSE) criterion,

$$Q(w) = \frac{1}{K} \sum_{k=1}^{K} \left\| y_k - \hat{f}(x_k, w) \right\|^2 \tag{1}$$

is minimized. If the MLP $\hat{f}(x_k, w)$ is nonlinear in w, the MSE criterion $Q(w)$ is usually nonconvex and has non-global local minima.

It is proven in [11] that the convexity region of $J_\lambda(w)/\lambda$, where $J_\lambda(w)$ is a new type of risk-averting error criterion,

$$J_\lambda(w) := \sum_{k=1}^{K} \exp\left(\lambda \left\| y_k - \hat{f}(x_k, w) \right\|^2 \right) \tag{2}$$

expands strictly as λ increases, and that $\lim_{\lambda \to 0} \frac{1}{\lambda} \ln\left[\frac{1}{K} J_\lambda(w) \right] = Q(w)$. Here := means "denote" or "be defined to be". These properties confirmed the effectiveness of the adaptive training method reported in [10] for avoiding poor local minima. However, note that the RAE is a sum of exponential functions of the risk sensitivity index λ.

The normalized RAE (NRAE)

$$C_\lambda(w) := \frac{1}{\lambda} \ln\left[\frac{1}{K} J_\lambda(w) \right]$$

is a strictly increasing function of $J_\lambda(w)/\lambda^2$, whose Hessian matrix is $H_\lambda(w)/\lambda^2$. A formula (i.e., equation (8) in [11]) for the Hessian matrix $H_\lambda(w)$ shows that $\lim_{\lambda \to \infty} H_\lambda(w)/\lambda^2$ is a positive semi-definite matrix. It follows that the convexity region of $J_\lambda(w)/\lambda^2$ expands to nearly the entire weight space as λ increases to nearly infinity. Moreover, $J_\lambda(w)/\lambda^2$ does not have a non-global local minimum in the convexity region for λ sufficiently large, although $\lim_{\lambda \to \infty} J_\lambda(w)/\lambda^2$ does not exist.

Since $C_\lambda(w)$ is a strictly increasing function of $J_\lambda(w)/\lambda^2$, it does not have a non-global local minimum in the convexity region of $J_\lambda(w)/\lambda^2$ for λ sufficiently large. As the convexity region of $J_\lambda(w)/\lambda^2$ expands to nearly the entire weight space as λ increases to nearly infinity, $C_\lambda(w)$ does not have a non-global minimum in nearly the entire weight space for λ sufficiently large. This is the first and primary reason for using $C_\lambda(w)$ as the training criterion.

As will be seen later in this paper, for $\lambda \gg 1$, $C_\lambda(w)$ and its gradient vector $g_\lambda(w) := \partial C_\lambda(w)/\partial w_j$ and Hessian matrix $H_\lambda(w) := [\partial^2 C_\lambda(w)/\partial w_i \partial w_j]$ can be computed without evaluating the exponential function $\exp\left(\lambda \left\| y_k - \hat{f}(x_k, w) \right\|^2\right)$, for $\lambda \gg 1$, $k = 1, \ldots, K$. This is the second reason for using $C_\lambda(w)$ as the training criterion.

If the MLP has enough hidden neurons to approximate the target function nearly perfectly, global minima of $C_\lambda(w)$ and the MSE criterion $Q(w)$ are both nearly 0. This is the third reason for using $C_\lambda(w)$ as the training criterion.

The method of training the MLP with $C_\lambda(w)$ is called the NRAE training method. The method is numerically tested for a number of large values of λ. Both $C_\lambda(w)$ and $Q(w)$ for the resultant MLP consistently converge to 0 for λ in the range 10^6 and 10^{11}. When λ exceeds 10^{11}, round-off errors occur and the NRAE training method could not be carried out. We expect to fix this numerical problem in the near future.

2   Evaluating NRAE and Its Derivatives

For notational simplicity, let

$$\hat{y}_k(w) := f(x_k, w)$$
$$\varepsilon_k(w) := y_k - \hat{y}_k(w) .$$

For a vector w, let $S(w) = \arg\max_{k \in \{1,\ldots,K\}} \left\| \varepsilon_k(w) \right\|^2$, which set may contain more than one elements if a tie exists, and $M(w) = \min_k \{k | k \in S(w)\}$. It follows that

$$\left\| \varepsilon_k(w) \right\|^2 \leq \left\| \varepsilon_{M(w)}(w) \right\|^2 .$$

Let

$$\eta_k(w) := e^{\lambda\left(\left\| \varepsilon_k(w) \right\|^2 - \left\| \varepsilon_{M(w)}(w) \right\|^2\right)}$$

then

$$\eta_k(w) \leq 1$$

$$\ln\left[\sum_{k=1}^{K} \eta_k(w)\right] \leq \ln K .$$

Hence

$$
C_\lambda(w) = \frac{1}{\lambda} \ln \left[\frac{1}{K} e^{\lambda \left\| \varepsilon_{M(w)}(w) \right\|^2} \sum_{k=1}^{K} \eta_k(w) \right]
$$

$$
= \frac{1}{\lambda} \ln \frac{1}{K} + \left\| \varepsilon_{M(w)}(w) \right\|^2 + \frac{1}{\lambda} \ln \left[\sum_{k=1}^{K} \eta_k(w) \right] \tag{3}
$$

$$
\leq \left\| \varepsilon_{M(w)}(w) \right\|^2
$$

and the terms in (3) are bounded by functions independent of λ and no register overflow occurs for $\lambda \gg 1$.

Consider the first-order derivative,

$$
\frac{\partial C_\lambda(w)}{\partial w_j} = \frac{1}{\lambda J_\lambda(w)} \frac{\partial J_\lambda(w)}{\partial w_j}
$$

$$
= \frac{1}{\lambda J_\lambda(w)} \left[-2\lambda \sum_{k=1}^{K} e^{\lambda \| \varepsilon_k(w) \|^2} \varepsilon_k^T(w) \frac{\partial \hat{y}_k(w)}{\partial w_j} \right] \tag{4}
$$

$$
= \frac{-2 \sum_{k=1}^{K} \eta_k(w) \varepsilon_k^T(w) \frac{\partial \hat{y}_k(w)}{\partial w_j}}{\sum_{k=1}^{K} \eta_k(w)}
$$

where

$$
\sum_{k=1}^{K} \eta_k(w) \leq K
$$

$$
\sum_{k=1}^{K} \eta_k(w) \varepsilon_k^T(w) \frac{\partial \hat{y}_k(w)}{\partial w_j} \leq \sum_{k=1}^{K} \varepsilon_k^T(w) \frac{\partial \hat{y}_k(w)}{\partial w_j}
$$

which is independent of λ. Hence, both the numerator and denominator of (4) can be handled without register overflow for $\lambda \gg 1$.

The Hessian matrix can be evaluated in a similar way.

3   Numerical Experiments

In this section, a function approximation task is implemented to demonstrate the effectiveness of the proposed NRAE training method. Before each training session starts, some parameters for MLPs are selected as follows. First, each synaptic weight in a weight vector is randomly selected from a uniform distribution between $-2.4/F_i$ and $2.4/F_i$, where F_i is the number of input neurons of the connected unit. Second, all input and output values defined in the training data are normalized into $[-1, 1]$. Third, the activation function in each training neuron is chosen as the hyperbolic tangent function $\varphi(v) = a \tanh(bv)$, where $a = 1.7159$ and $b = 2/3$.

3.1   Function Approximation

A function with three notches is defined by

$$y = f(x) = \begin{cases} 0 & \text{if } x \in [0, 1.0] \cup [2.2, 2.3] \cup [3.5, 4.5] \\ 0.25 & \text{if } x \in [2.8, 3.0] \\ 0.5 & \text{if } x \in [1.5, 1.7] \\ 1 & \text{otherwise} \end{cases} \tag{5}$$

where $x \in X = [0, 4.5]$. The input values x_k are obtained by random sampling 2000 non-repeatable numbers from X with a uniform distribution, and the corresponding output values y_k are computed by (5). The training data with 2000 (x_k, y_k) pairs is chosen to perform the three-notch function approximation. In our experiment, we randomly select five different initial weight vectors to start

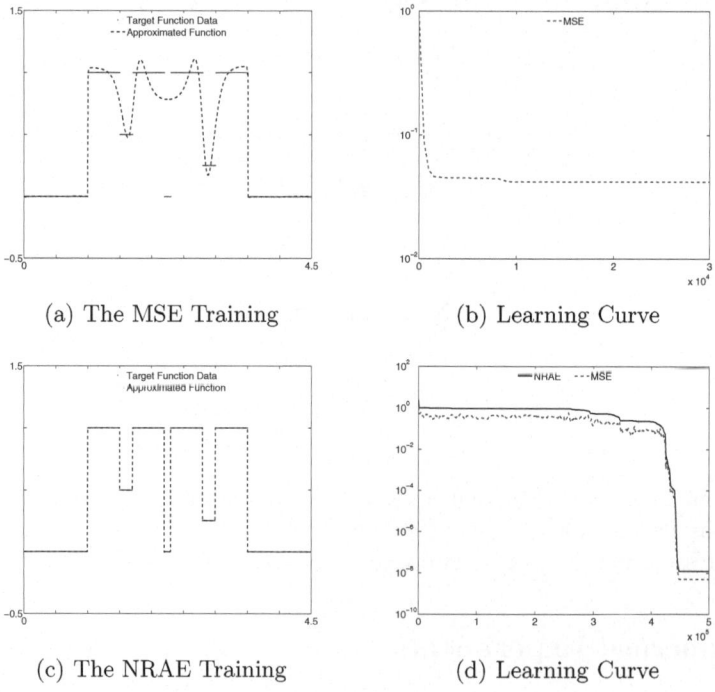

(a) The MSE Training   (b) Learning Curve

(c) The NRAE Training   (d) Learning Curve

Fig. 1. Results of the three-notch function approximation with the MSE and NRAE training. Figures on the left side column are function plots, and numbers on the horizontal and vertical axes in each subfigure denote the input and output of the function, respectively. Figures on the right side column are learning curves for the corresponding training criteria, and numbers on the horizontal and vertical axes in each subfigure denote the values of training epochs and errors, respectively. Here, the actual values of training errors are converted to the logarithmic numbers with respect to base 10. The represented NRAE training result and learning curves concerning the NRAE and MSE criteria are obtained when $\lambda = 10^6$.

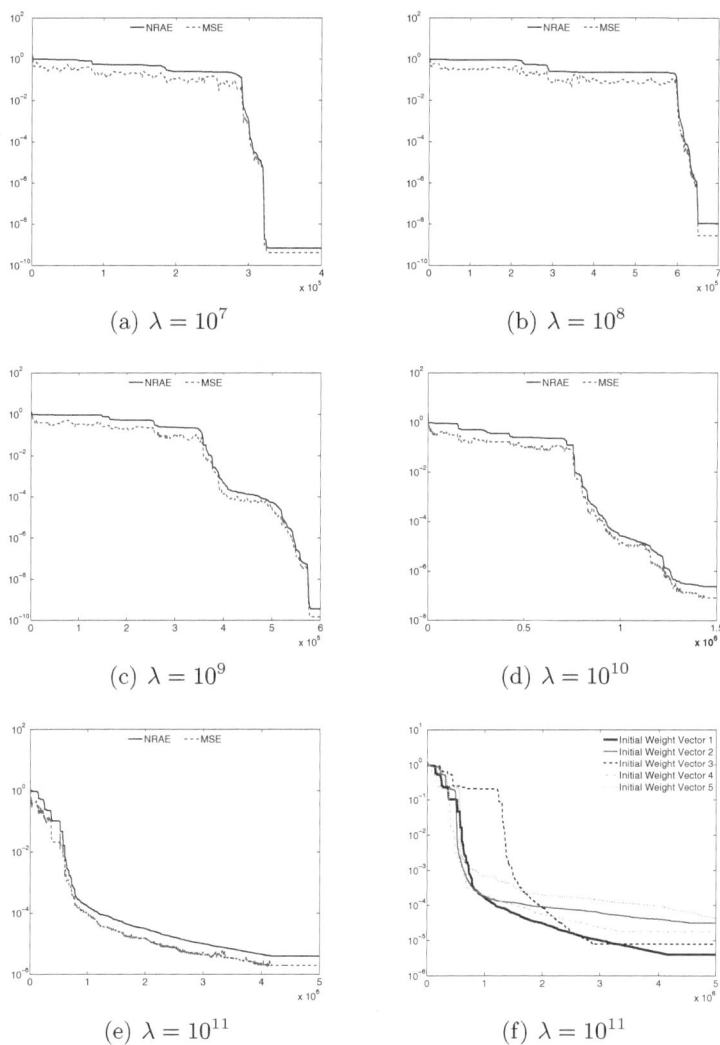

Fig. 2. Learning Curves for the three-notch function approximation with the NRAE training. Figures from Fig. 2(a) to Fig. 2(e) illustrate different trends of the NRAE training with respect to both the NRAE and MSE criteria as increasing of λ. Fig. 2(f) shows only the learning curves concerning the NRAE criterion for five different initial weight vectors when $\lambda = 10^{11}$. Numbers on the horizontal axis are the values of training epochs. Numbers on the vertical axis are the values of training errors which are converted to the logarithmic numbers with respect to base 10.

five training groups. In each training group, one standard MSE training session and six NRAE training sessions with the BP and BFGS algorithm are performed with the same initial weight vector. The values of λ are set respectively as $10^6, 10^7, 10^8, 10^9, 10^{10}$ and 10^{11} in all NRAE training sessions. MLPs with 1:16:1 architecture are initiated to both the MSE and NRAE training sessions. All training results are obtained when the deviation of objective function values between two consequent training epochs is less or equal to 10^{-15}.

3.2   Discussion

In this section, experimental results are demonstrated and discussed. First, as an example to visually show the training results, two approximated functions and learning curves separately obtained by the MSE and NRAE training method in one training group are selected and plotted in Fig. 1. Although six different values of λ are chosen to perform the NRAE training sessions in this selected training group, only one plot of the approximated function with $\lambda = 10^6$ is shown. Those approximated function plots achieved by other five NRAE training sessions with $\lambda = 10^7, 10^8, 10^9, 10^{10}$ and 10^{11} are exactly the same as Fig. 1(c), and learning curves for them are shown in Fig. 2. At last, a comparison of training errors achieved by different guesses of five initial weight vectors between the MSE and NRAE training sessions is illustrated in Fig. 3.

Since the three-notch function is intended to have typical non-global minima, the observations in our experimental results demonstrate that the NRAE training with a sufficiently large λ has the capability to avoid non-global local minima comparing with the MSE training. First, approximated function plots

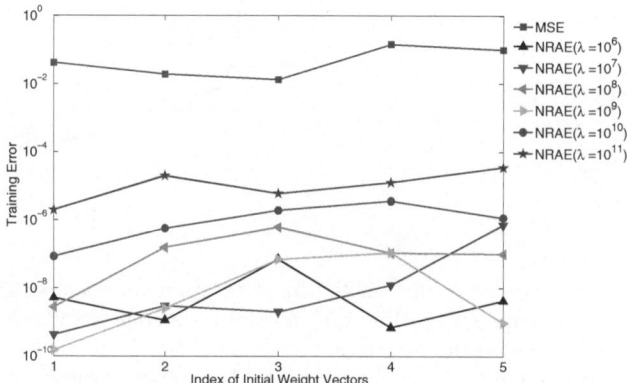

Fig. 3. Training errors of five different initial weight vectors for the three-notch function approximation with the MSE and NRAE training. Colors and symbols in the showed lines are used to distinguish the MSE and NRAE training methods, or describe independent NRAE training sessions with different values of λ. Here, all actual values on the vertical axis are converted to the logarithmic numbers with respect to base 10.

in Fig. 1(a) and Fig. 1(c) show that the NRAE training with a sufficiently large λ captures all significant features located in the target three-notch function, but the MSE training only finds few parts of those features. Second, learning curves in Fig. 1 and Fig. 2 present similar patterns for the NRAE training with sufficiently large values of λ to reach the global or nearly global minimum. Third, results in Fig. 3 indicate that the NRAE training sessions with sufficiently large values of λ consistently lead all trained MLPs to achieve satisfactory training errors, which are lower than the MSE training.

4   Conclusion

The NRAE training criterion does not have a non-global local minimum in nearly the entire weight space, provided that the risk sensitivity index λ of the NRAE is sufficiently large. We propose to use the NRAE criterion to train an MLPs that has enough hidden neurons to approximate the target function nearly perfectly. To select a sufficiently large λ, we start with a large number, say 10^6, as long as the computer can handle the NRAE with this λ and the local search optimization method (e.g., the BFGS and conjugate gradient method) applied to minimize this NRAE. If the NRAE criterion does not converge to zero, we increase the risk sensitivity index by multiplying it by 10. We continue increasing λ in this manner, if necessary, until the NRAE and MSE are nearly zero.

References

1. Aarts, E., Korst, J.: The Neuron. Oxford University Press (1989)
2. Zurada, J.M.: Introduction to Artificial Neural Networks. West Publishing Company, St. Paul (1992)
3. Hassoun, M.H.: Fundamentals of Artificial Neural Networks. MIT Press, Cambridge (1995)
4. Michalewicz, Z.: Genetic Algorithms + Data Structures = Evolution Programs, 3rd edn. Springer, New York (1999)
5. Principe, J.C., Euliano, N.R., Lefebvre, W.C.: Neural and Adaptive Systems: Fundamentals through Simulations. John Wiley and Sons, Inc., New York (2000)
6. Bishop, C.M.: Pattern Recognition and Machine Learning. Springer, New York (2006)
7. Du, K.L., Swamy, M.: Neural Networks in a Softcomputing Framework. Springer, New York (2006)
8. Press, W.H., Teukolsky, S.A., Vetterling, W.T., Flannery, B.P.: Numerical Recipes in C: The Art of Scientific Computing, 3rd edn. Cambridge University Press, New York (2007)
9. Haykin, S.: Neural Networks and Learning Machines, 3rd edn. Prentice Hall, Upper Saddle River (2008)
10. Lo, J.T.H., Bassu, D.: An adaptive method of training multilayer perceptrons. In: Proc. International Joint Conference on Neural Networks (IJCNN 2001), vol. 3, pp. 2013–2018 (July 2001)
11. Lo, J.T.H.: Convexification for data fitting. Journal of Global Optimization 46(2), 307–315 (2010)

Magnified Gradient Function to Improve First-Order Gradient-Based Learning Algorithms

Sin-Chun Ng[1], Chi-Chung Cheung[2], Andrew kwok-fai Lui[1], and Shensheng Xu[1]

[1] School of Science and Technology, The Open University of Hong Kong,
30 Good Shepherd Street, Homantin, Hong Kong
scng@ouhk.edu.hk
[2] Department of Electronic and Information Engineering,
The Hong Kong Polytechnic University, Hunghom, Hong Kong

Abstract. In this paper, we propose a new approach to improve the performance of existing first-order gradient-based fast learning algorithms in terms of speed and global convergence capability. The idea is to magnify the gradient terms of the activation function so that fast learning speed and global convergence can be achieved. The approach can be applied to existing gradient-based algorithms. Simulation results show that this approach can significantly speed up the convergence rate and increase the global convergence capability of existing popular first-order gradient-based fast learning algorithms for multi-layer feed-forward neural networks.

Keywords: magnified gradient function, gradient-based algorithms, back-propagation, Rprop, Quickprop.

1 Introduction

Nowadays, there are many different methods such as conjugate gradients [1], the Levenberg-Marquardt [2] algorithm and the Broyden-Fletcher-Goldfarb-Shanno (BFGS) [3] algorithms for training feedforward neural networks. These algorithms use the second-order derivatives to accelerate the learning process. They are efficient for small networks, however, for large networks, the memory requirements of these second-order methods are very huge, which make it impractical to compute the weight updates. In addition, these methods use approximations of the Hessian matrix which may become close to singular, and may produce inaccurate result during the training process.

Consequently, gradient descent methods are still the most widely used class of algorithms for training multi-layer feed forward neural networks. Back-propagation algorithm (BP) [4] is the most commonly used learning algorithm in the category of gradient descent methods. It is considered as a first-order method by minimizing the error function using the steepest descent algorithm. BP is simple and low computational; however, it suffers from very slow convergence rate owing to the premature saturation problem or referred as the "flat spot" problem [5]-[6]. If the algorithm is trapped in a flat spot, the learning process and weight adjustment of the

J. Wang, G.G. Yen, and M.M. Polycarpou (Eds.): ISNN 2012, Part I, LNCS 7367, pp. 448–457, 2012.

algorithm will become very slow or even suppressed because BP usually requires lots of iterations to leave the flat spot. Moreover, BP is easily trapped in local minima, especially for non-linearly separable problems such as the exclusive-or (XOR) problem [7]-[8]. BP may fail to find the global optimal solution in case of the entrapment of local minima. To overcome these problems, there are different kinds of modified BP have been proposed to improve its performance. Quickprop [9] and Rprop [10] are the most popular fast learning methods because they are direct, computationally cheap and easy to implement.

Quickprop uses successive values of the gradient of the error surface in weight space to estimate the location of a minimum and then changes the weights to move directly to this minimum. The gradient information of error function in weight space is used to predict the location of a minimum and change the weights to move directly to the global optimal solution, but directly move to the location of a minimum which implies that minimum could be a local minimum instead of the global optimal solution.

Rprop is a variable step size algorithm. The step size is the update value for a particular weight and each weight has its individual variable update value. The update values are calculated by the changes of the error gradient sign instead of the slope of the error function. If there is no change of error gradient sign, the update value is increased in order to have a larger step size; otherwise, the update value is decreased in order to step closer to the minimum which can prevent the error overshooting problem. Unfortunately, it is still easily trapped into local minima as it is a first-order gradient-based algorithm. The improved Rprop – iRprop [11] is one of popular variants of Rprop which applies a backtracking strategy and it improves the convergence speed of Rprop. However, iRprop will still get trapped in local minima where the system error will stay unchanged for a long time.

Although Quickprop, Rprop and iRprop can greatly improve the learning speed of BP, their performance is still hindered by the inherent problem of gradient descent methods – the convergence to a local minimum. The local minimum problem is the obstacle of the performance of first-order gradient-based algorithms, and it leads to poor global convergence capability. In this paper, we propose to magnify the derivative of gradient functions in existing first-order gradient-based fast learning algorithms to speed up their convergence rates and to increase their global convergence capabilities. Note that this approach can generally be applied to various first-order gradient-based fast learning algorithms such as BP, Quickprop, Rprop and iRprop.

This paper is organized as follows. Section 2 describes the basic operations of Magnified Gradient Function (MGF). Section 3 introduces the implementation of MGF into different first-order gradient-based fast learning algorithms. Section 4 shows the simulation results of the proposed method as compared with other fast learning algorithms. The conclusion is drawn in Section 5.

2   Magnified Gradient Function (MGF)

First-order gradient-based fast learning algorithms make use of the first order derivatives of the system error with respect to weights in their calculations. However, due to this unique characteristic, their performance is limited by the weak effect of the true error signal when the change of the system error is very small. Consider a network with three layers (input, hidden and output layers) having N input neurons, K

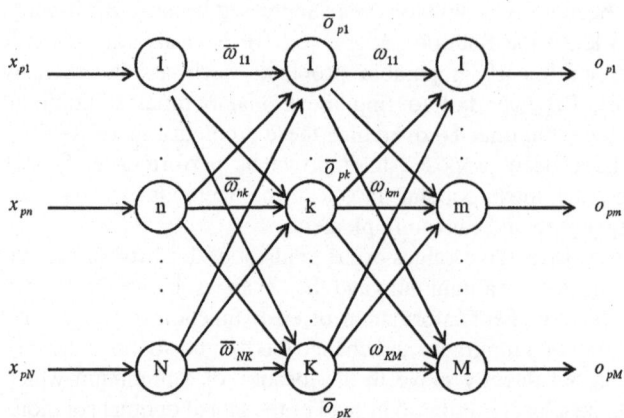

Fig. 1. The basic structure of a feed-forward network with a hidden layer

hidden neurons and *M* output neurons as shown in Fig. 1. Assume ω_{km} is the weight connecting the *m*-th output neurons and the *k*-th hidden neuron, and $\overline{\omega}_{nk}$ is the weight connecting the *k*-th hidden neurons and the *n*-th input neuron.

The desired output for the m-th output neuron due to the p-th input pattern is given by t_{pm}. The input for the n-th input neuron due to the p-th input pattern is denoted by x_{pn}. Using this definition, the output of the k-th node in the hidden layer is given by:

$$\overline{o}_{pk} = f(\sum_{n=1}^{N} \overline{\omega}_{nk} x_{pn}) \tag{1}$$

where *f* is the activation (sigmoidal) function defined as

$$f(x) = 1/(1 + e^{-x}). \tag{2}$$

Similarly, the output of the *m*-th node in the output layer is given by:

$$o_{pm} = f(\sum_{k=1}^{K} \omega_{km} \overline{o}_{pk}) \tag{3}$$

The derivative of the sigmoidal function is

$$f'(x) = e^{-x}/(1 + e^{-x})^2 = f(x)(1 - f(x)). \tag{4}$$

We define the sum of squared error of the system to be:

$$E = \tfrac{1}{2} \sum_{p=1}^{P} \sum_{m=1}^{M} (t_{pm} - o_{pm})^2 \tag{5}$$

The first order gradient descent method is designed to change the current weights ω_{km} and $\overline{\omega}_{nk}$ iteratively such that the system error function *E* is minimized. The weight updates are proportional to the partial derivative of *E*.

The partial derivative of *E* with respect to ω_{km} is:

$$\frac{\partial E}{\partial \omega_{km}} = \frac{\partial E}{\partial o_{pm}} \cdot \frac{\partial o_{pm}}{\partial \omega_{km}} \tag{6}$$

where

$$\frac{\partial E}{\partial o_{pm}} = o_{pm} - t_{pm} \tag{7}$$

and $\dfrac{\partial o_{pm}}{\partial \omega_{km}} = o_{pm}(1-o_{pm})\overline{o}_{pk} ;$ $\tag{8}$

And the partial derivative of E with respect to $\overline{\omega}_{nk}$ is:

$$\frac{\partial E}{\partial \overline{\omega}_{nk}} = \sum_{m=1}^{M} \frac{\partial E}{\partial o_{pm}} \cdot \frac{\partial o_{pm}}{\partial \overline{o}_{pk}} \cdot \frac{\partial \overline{o}_{pk}}{\partial \overline{\omega}_{nk}} \tag{9}$$

where $\dfrac{\partial o_{pm}}{\partial \overline{o}_{pk}} = o_{pm}(1-o_{pm})\omega_{km} ;$ $\tag{10}$

$$\frac{\partial \overline{o}_{pk}}{\partial \overline{\omega}_{nk}} = \overline{o}_{pk}(1-\overline{o}_{pk})x_{pn} \tag{11}$$

The weight change for the t-th epoch can be expressed as follows, where μ is the learning rate of the gradient method.

$$\begin{cases} \Delta\omega_{km}(t) = \mu\sum_{p=1}^{P}\delta_{pm}\overline{o}_{pk} \\ \text{where } \delta_{pm} = (t_{pm}-o_{pm})o_{pm}(1-o_{pm}) \end{cases} \tag{12}$$

$$\begin{cases} \Delta\overline{\omega}_{nk}(t) = \mu\sum_{p=1}^{P}\overline{\delta}_{pk}x_{pn} \\ \text{where } \overline{\delta}_{pk} = \overline{o}_{pk}(1-\overline{o}_{pk})\sum_{m=1}^{M}\delta_{pm}\omega_{km} \end{cases} \tag{13}$$

When the learning process is about to converge or is trapped by a local minimum, the change of the system error is very small. It implies that most of the actual outputs o_{pm} or/and $\overline{o}_{pk}$ approach extreme values (i.e., 0 or 1) at that moment. Thus the back-propagated error signals δ_{pm} and $\overline{\delta}_{pk}$ including the factors $o_{pm}(1-o_{pm})$ and $\overline{o}_{pk}(1-\overline{o}_{pk})$ respectively become very small and hence the effect of the true error signal $t_{pm}-o_{pm}$ is very weak.

This phenomenon causes two problems: (1) When the learning is going to be converged, the magnitude of $o_{pm}(1-o_{pm})$ or/and $\overline{o}_{pk}(1-\overline{o}_{pk})$ will become too small so that the output cannot be effectively adjusted by the true error signal and the learning becomes very slow moving towards the global optimal solution; (2) When the learning is trapped by a local minimum, the output also cannot be effectively adjusted by the true error signal and the learning becomes very slow such that it cannot escape from the local minimum or get stuck at the local minimum for prolonged time. It is noteworthy that the poor convergence was actually originated from the derivative of the activation function, i.e. eqns. (12) and (13), producing the term $o_{pm}(1-o_{pm})$ or $\overline{o}_{pk}(1-\overline{o}_{pk})$. Thus, some modifications to the derivative of $f(x)$ are necessary to improve the performance of first-order gradient based algorithms. We propose to magnify the gradient functions of first-order gradient-based fast learning algorithms so that the effect of the true error signal becomes strong when the actual output is approaching to 0 or 1. To magnify the gradient functions, we introduce a power factor, $1/S$ ($S \geq 1$), to the derivative of the sigmoidal function. The original derivative of the sigmoidal function is $f'(x) = f(x)(1 - f(x))$. By magnifying the derivative with the power factor, the modified derivative of the sigmoidal function is

$$f'(x, S) = [f(x)(1 - f(x))]^{1/S} \tag{14}$$

and the new error signals in eqns. (12) and (13) become:

$$\delta_{pm}^{(MGF)} = (t_{pm} - o_{pm})[o_{pm}(1 - o_{pm})]^{1/S} \tag{15}$$

and $$\overline{\delta}_{pk}^{(MGF)} = [\overline{o}_{pk}(i)(1 - \overline{o}_{pk})]^{1/S} \sum_{m=1}^{M} \delta_{pm} \omega_{km} . \tag{16}$$

Fig. 2 shows the effect of S on the magnified gradient function $f'(x, S)$. When $f(x)$ is close to 0 or 1, the value of $f'(x)$ (i.e., $f'(x, 1)$) is very small so that the effect of the true error signal is very weak. When the power factor is introduced, the value of the magnified derivative is much larger than the original one and the difference is larger when S increases.

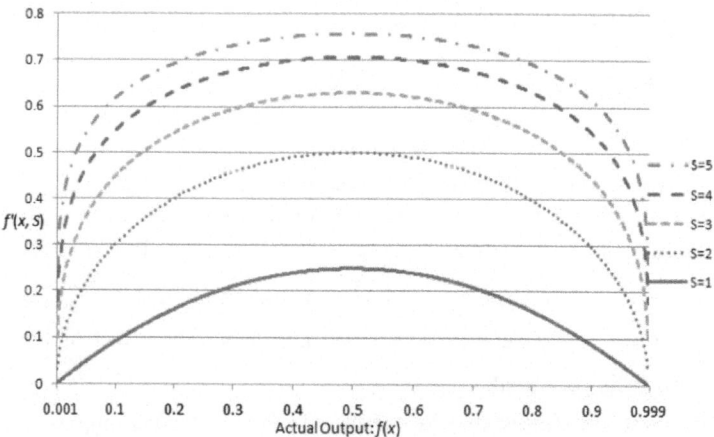

Fig. 2. The effect of S on the magnified gradient function $f'(x, S)$

Consider the following numerical example: when $f(x) = 0.5$, $f'(x, 2)$ is two times larger than $f'(x, 1)$; but when $f(x) = 0.001$, $f'(x, 2)$ is 30 times larger than $f'(x, 1)$. It shows that adding the power factor $1/S$ can successfully magnify $f'(x)$ and hence increase the effect of the local gradients. The magnification is very significant when the derivative is small. This characteristic is very important to solve the previous two problems: (1) When the learning is going to be converged, the effect of the true error signal will become stronger due to the magnified gradient function and thus the learning can still be fast with a further reduction of the system error. Hence the convergence rate is increased; (2) When the learning is trapped by a local minimum, the effect of the true error signal is still strong so that the output can be effectively adjusted by the true error signal and the learning can escape from the local minimum more easily. Thus the convergence rate and the global convergence capability can both be improved. Note that the use of the magnified gradient functions do not affect the gradient descent property of existing gradient-based fast learning algorithms since the sign of the partial derivatives $\partial E / \partial \omega_{km}$ or $\partial E / \partial \overline{\omega}_{nk}$ would be retained. In this paper, we propose the use of magnified gradient function can be employed generally to first-order gradient-based fast learning algorithms including BP and its variants such as Quickprop, Rprop and iRprop.

3   Application of MGF in Fast Learning Algorithms

3.1   MGF Applied in Quickprop

The Quickprop algorithm [9] was developed by S. E. Fahlman to improve the convergence of back-propagation (BP). Instead of simply using the gradient information or the first order derivative of the overall error to update the current weights, Quickprop uses successive values of the gradient of the error surface in weight space to estimate the location of a minimum. It then changes the weights to move directly towards this minimum. The main assumptions of the algorithm are that the error surface is concave, and the surface is locally quadratic.

Based on these assumptions, the weight update rule of the algorithm is:

$$\Delta \omega_{km}(t) = \frac{\partial E(t)/\partial \omega_{km}}{\partial E(t-1)/\partial \omega_{km} - \partial E(t)/\partial \omega_{km}} \Delta \omega_{km}(t-1) \tag{17}$$

From eqn. (17), the algorithm will take an infinite step and the network will behave chaotically when the difference of current and previous values of $\partial E / \partial \omega_{km}$ is near to zero. To avoid this problem, a new parameter is introduced − the "maximum growth factor", ϕ. No weight step is allowed to be greater than ϕ times the previous step for that weight. In that case, if the step calculated by the algorithm using eqn. (17) is too large, the step is set to the bound limited by $\phi \cdot \Delta \omega(t-1)$. The optimal value of ϕ suggested by Fahlman is 1.75, it works well for different sets of problems.

The original weight update rule of the back-propagation will still be followed and added to the value computed by the above quadratic formula (17).

$$\Delta \omega_{km}(t) = \mu \frac{\partial E(t)}{\partial \omega_{km}} + \alpha \Delta \omega_{km}(t-1) \tag{18}$$

where μ is the learning rate and α is the momentum.

Although the Quickprop algorithm can provide fast convergence rate as compared with standard back-propagation, it often gets trapped into local minima and then fails to converge to the global minimum. Here, the use of magnified gradient function in Quickprop is to change of the partial derivative terms $\partial E / \partial \omega_{km}$ and $\partial E / \partial \overline{\omega}_{nk}$ to include the power of $1/S$ as follows.

$$\frac{\partial E(t)}{\partial \omega_{km}}^{(MGF)} = \sum_{p=1}^{P} \delta_{pm}^{(MGF)} \overline{o}_{pk} \qquad (19)$$

$$\frac{\partial E(t)}{\partial \overline{\omega}_{nk}}^{(MGF)} = \sum_{p=1}^{P} \overline{\delta}_{pk}^{(MGF)} x_{pn} \qquad (20)$$

where the error signals $\delta_{pm}^{(MGF)}$ and $\overline{\delta}_{pk}^{(MGF)}$ are given in eqns. (15) and (16), respectively.

The use of MGF can greatly improve the performance of Quickprop especially when Quickprop is being stuck at local minimum and the error cannot be decreased any more. The simulation results of the new approach can be found in the next section.

3.2   MGF Applied in Rprop and iRprop

Rprop [10] proposed by Riedmiller and Braun is in effect a variable step size algorithm. Each weight has its own variable update step being adapted throughout the algorithm. In Rprop, the learning-rule is depended on the sign change of the partial derivative between the pervious ($\partial E(t-1)/\partial \omega_{km}$ and $\partial E(t-1)/\partial \overline{\omega}_{nk}$) and the current ($\partial E(t)/\partial \omega_{km}$ and $\partial E(t)/\partial \overline{\omega}_{nk}$) error descends gradient respectively and the weight updated rule is depended on the sign of current partial derivative ($\partial E(t)/\partial \omega_{km}$ and $\partial E(t)/\partial \overline{\omega}_{nk}$). In another word, the size of the partial derivative is not considered in Rprop but the sign. It is because the aim of Rprop is to avoid the problem of 'blurred adaptivity', which means the carefully adapted learning-rate is disturbed by the size of derivative.

When MGF is applied in Rprop, the partial derivatives $\partial E(t)/\partial \omega_{km}$ and $\partial E(t)/\partial \overline{\omega}_{nk}$ will be modified to $\frac{\partial E(t)}{\partial \omega_{km}}^{(MGF)}$ and $\frac{\partial E(t)}{\partial \overline{\omega}_{nk}}^{(MGF)}$ as shown in eqns. (19) and (20). The further steps like the learning-rule and the weight updated rule will remain unchanged. When the actual outputs o_{pm} or/and $\overline{o}_{pk}$ approach to extreme values (i.e. 0 or 1), the power factor $1/S$ will scale up the derivatives greatly. On a contrary, the derivative will be scaled up slightly when the actual output o_{pm} or $\overline{o}_{pk}$ has a medium value (i.e. 0.5).

iRprop [11] is one of the popular variants of Rprop which applies a backtracking strategy. The algorithm can improve the convergence speed of Rprop but will still get trapped in local minima as well. MGF can also be applied in iRprop using the same concept as that of Rprop.

4   Simulation Results

A number of experiments have been conducted on three benchmarking data sets, Iris, Wine, and Breast Cancer Wisconsin [13], to illustrate the performance of the magnified gradient functions (MGF) on different first-order gradient-based fast learning algorithms. Let (P-N-K-M) be a network configuration with P input patterns (instances), N input nodes, K hidden nodes and M output nodes respectively. The network configuration of the above three problems are (150-4-30-3), (178-13-23-3) and (699-9-

20-1) respectively. Table 1 summarizes the problem description and the network configuration used for the three data sets. These three data sets are real case problems and BP has difficulty in solving these problems in 5000 epochs. For these problems, all fast learning algorithms terminate when the system errors reach 10^{-3} within 10000 iterations. Simulation results are based on 100 independent runs for different sets of initial weights on three various first-order gradient-based fast learning algorithms: Quickprop [9], Rprop [10], and iRprop [11]. To apply MGF into these three algorithms, we set S to 5 and we call them MGF-QP, MGF-Rprop, and MGF-iRprop respectively. The performance comparison is shown in Tables 2-3. In the tables, 'Rate' means the average number of epochs to converge (i.e., $E = 0.001$), '%' means the percentage of the global convergence capability, 'Avg. Time' means the average time taken in seconds for successful runs. It was found that the MGF algorithms always outperform the original first-order fast algorithms in terms of both the convergence rate and the global convergence significantly. In Iris data set, the global convergence can improve greatly from 16% to 83% for the case of iRprop. In Wine data set, the convergence rate of the MGF is almost three times faster than the original ones; while in Breast Cancer Wisconsin data set, the global convergence capability of the modified ones has significantly improved from 5% to 95%. Moreover, the average times taken of the MGF algorithms for most of the cases are less than that of the original ones. It means our approach spends shorter time to converge in general. Figs. 3 and 4 show the performance comparison of Rprop and MGF-Rprop for typical runs in the Iris and breast cancer problem. It can be seen that the use of MGF in Rprop can quickly converge to global solution with a very fast convergence rate.

Table 1. Problem Description

Problem	Description	Network Architecture P-N-K-M
Iris	Classify the type of iris plant [13].	150-4-30-3
Wine	Classify the type of wines in the same region in Italy by the quantities of constituents [13].	178-13-23-3
Breast Cancer Wisconsin	Recognize the patients of breast cancer by the characteristics of the cell nuclei [13].	699-9-20-1

Table 2. Performance comparison of using MGF in various algorithms for Iris and Wine

	Iris			Wine		
	Rate	%	Avg. Time	Rate	%	Avg. Time
Quickprop (QP)	3897.26	27%	4.3587	1226.34	44%	1.6502
MGF-QP	2675.44	81%	4.1501	453.45	96%	0.7727
Rprop	3754.37	19%	4.2918	833.41	58%	1.1187
MGF-Rprop	2565.49	81%	4.0747	350.13	92%	0.5785
iRprop	2930.38	16%	3.3341	707.09	57%	0.9462
MGF-iRprop	1829.49	83%	2.9484	268.87	89%	0.4416

Table 3. Performance comparison of using MGF in various algorithms for Breast Cancer

	Breast Cancer		
	Rate	**%**	**Avg. Time**
Quickprop (QP)	1158.0	5%	4.0722
MGF-QP	983.04	95%	4.6331
Rprop	2151.0	2%	7.8900
MGF-Rprop	897.33	95%	4.2304
iRprop	806.0	6%	2.8385
MGF-iRprop	567.13	96%	2.6950

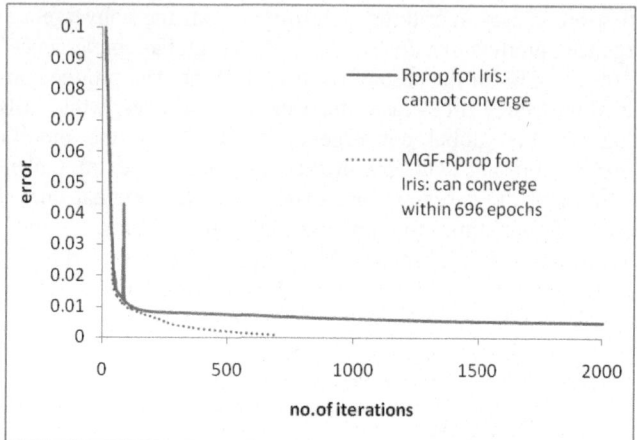

Fig. 3. The performance comparison of Rprop and MGF-Rprop for Iris

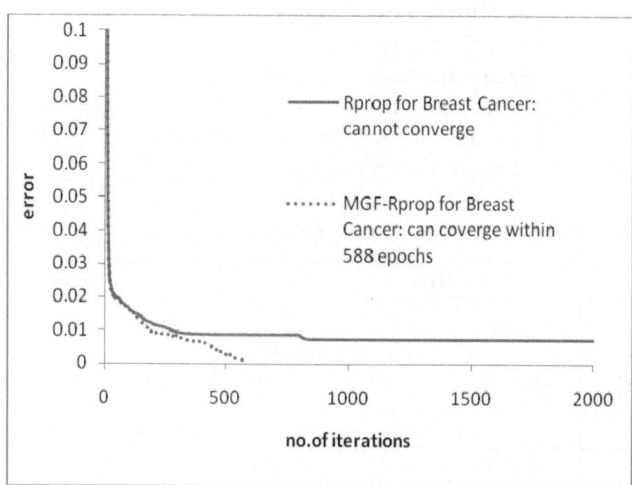

Fig. 4. The performance comparison of Rprop and MGF-Rprop for Breast cancer

5 Conclusions

This paper describes the limitations of existing first-order gradient-based fast learning algorithms and proposes an approach to solve the problems by magnifying their gradient functions. This approach can increase the effect of the true error signal so that a faster learning rate and a better global convergence capability can be achieved. Our simulation results show that our new approach of using magnified gradient function (MGF) can significantly improve the performance of existing algorithms in terms of the convergence rate and the global convergence capability.

Acknowledgment. This project is funded by The Open University of Hong Kong Research Grant (Project No. 09/1.3).

References

1. Moller, M.F.: A scaled conjugated gradient algorithm for fast supervised learning. Neural Networks 6, 525–533 (1993)
2. Hagan, M.T., Menhaj, M.B.: Training feedforward networks with the Marquardt algorithm. IEEE Trans. Neural Networks 5, 989–993 (1994)
3. Gill, P.E., Murray, W., Wright, M.H.: Practical Optimization. Academic Press, New York (1981)
4. Rumelhart, D.E., Hinton, G.E., Williams, R.J.: Learning internal representations by error propagation. In: Parallel Distributed Processing: Exploration in the Microstructure of Cognition, vol. 1, MIT Press, Cambridge (1986)
5. Van Ooyen, A., Nienhuis, B.: Improving the convergence of the back-propagation algorithm. Neural Networks 5, 465–471
6. Vitela, J.E., Reifman, J.: Premature Saturation in Backpropagation Networks: Mechanism and Necessary Conditions. Neural Networks 10(4), 721–735 (1997)
7. Blum, E.K., Li, L.K.: Approximation theory and feedforward networks. Neural Networks 4, 511–515 (1991)
8. Gori, M., Tesi, A.: On the problem of local minima in back-propagation. IEEE Trans. on Pattern Analysis and Machine Intelligence 14(1), 76–86 (1992)
9. Fahlman, S.E.: Fast learning variations on back-propagation: An empirical study. In: Touretzky, D., Hinton, G., Sejnowski, T. (eds.) Proc. the 1988 Connectionist Models Summer School, Pittsburgh, pp. 38–51 (1989)
10. Riedmiller, M., Braun, H.: A direct adaptive method for faster back-propagation learning: The RPROP Algorithm. In: Proc. of Int. Conf. on Neural Networks, vol. 1, pp. 586–591 (1993)
11. Igel, C., Husken, M.: Empirical evaluation of the improved Rprop learning algorithms. Neurocomputing 50, 105–123 (2003)
12. Ng, S.C., Cheung, C.C., Leung, S.H.: Magnified Gradient Function with Deterministic Weight Evolution in Adaptive Learning. IEEE Trans. on Neural Networks 15(6), 1411–1423 (2004)
13. Frank, A., Asuncion, A.: UCI Machine Learning Repository. University of California, School of Information and Computer Science, Irvine (2011)

Sensitivity Analysis with Cross-Validation for Feature Selection and Manifold Learning

Cuixian Chen, Yishi Wang, Yaw Chang, and Karl Ricanek

University of North Carolina Wilmington, USA
{chenc,wangy,changy,ricanekk}@uncw.edu

Abstract. The performance of a learning algorithm is usually measured in terms of prediction error. It is important to choose an appropriate estimator of the prediction error. This paper analyzes the statistical properties of the K-fold cross-validation prediction error estimator. It investigates how to compare two algorithms statistically. It also analyzes the sensitivity to the changes in the training/test set. Our main contribution is to experimentally study the statistical property of repeated cross-validation to stabilize the prediction error estimation, and thus to reduce the variance of the prediction error estimator. Our simulation results provide an empirical evidence to this conclusion. The experimental study has been performed on PAL dataset for age estimation task.

1 Introduction

The performance of a learning algorithm is generally measured in terms of prediction error, which provides the prediction capability over an independent test set. It is extremely important to have an accurate assessment to this test error, since it provides guidance on a reliable model selection and model assessment of learning methods or models. However, in most real-world practice, the expected prediction error can't be calculated exactly and hence it must be estimated. Extensive studies have been devoted to develop appropriate estimators of the prediction error, including hold-out validation, K-fold cross-validation, leave-one-out cross-validation, and repeated K-fold cross-validation. [12].

1.1 Cross-Validation

The ideal case is to have sufficient data so that we can divide the whole dataset into the training set, validation set and test set. After using the training set to build a model, we can use the validation set to estimate the prediction error for model selection. Finally, the test set is used for model assessment of the final chosen model. But it is generally not true in practice. With a small to moderate sample size, we can make use of resample techniques at the expense of higher computational cost: K-fold cross-validation (K-CV), Leave-one-out cross-validation (LOO-CV) and Bootstrap methods. Cross-validation has became the standard procedure for estimating the prediction error.

With K-fold cross-validation, the whole dataset is divided randomly into K non-overlapped subsets of roughly equal size, say $\mathcal{B}_1, \mathcal{B}_2, \cdots, \mathcal{B}_K$. Then for $k = 1, \cdots, K$,

J. Wang, G.G. Yen, and M.M. Polycarpou (Eds.): ISNN 2012, Part I, LNCS 7367, pp. 458–467, 2012.

a union of subsets, $\bigcup_{i=1:i\neq k}^{K} \mathcal{B}_i$ is used for learning a prediction rule and the remaining subset $\mathcal{B}_k$ for validation. The final prediction error is given by the average of the K estimates of the prediction errors from each loop. When K equals to the number of observations, it is called leave-one-out cross-validation (LOO-CV).

1.2 Comparison of Multiple Algorithms

It is desired to select a model/algorithm which provides the best performance for a specific dataset. In order to select the best method or model, it is often required to compare performance evaluation of a new proposed algorithm or model with existing state-of-art ones on some benchmark dataset. It is widely used in practice to compare the average accuracies of two algorithms. However, we will show in the paper that *when comparing a pair of algorithms using cross-validation, direct comparison of the average of estimated prediction error/accuracies can lead to misleading conclusions.* However, this strategy has been applied in computer vision extensively. Instead, it is suggested to employ appropriate statistical hypothesis tests for model selection.

Dietterich [5] applied four commonly used statistical tests to determine whether one learning algorithm outperforms another on a particular learning task, including 10-fold cross-validation and the paired t-test. They found out that such a test suffers from higher than expected type I error, which will attribute to high variance. Thus a new test 5×2-fold cross-validation is proposed to to overcome this difficulty. In this test 2-fold cross-validation is repeated five times resulting in 10 accuracy values. However, 5×2-fold cross-validation is shown to have less prediction power than the standard 10-fold cross validation.

Refaeilzadeh et al. [10] considered the problem of comparing two learning algorithms with feature selection under two cases: performing FS insider the CV or FS outside the CV. They compared bias analysis in details for both cases. Refaeilzadeh et al. [12] presented a survey on cross-validation with useful discussion on key application of cross-validation, including performance evaluation, model selection and parameter tuning.

1.3 Contribution of Work

In this paper we investigate the statistical properties of the K-fold crossvalidation prediction error estimator, and how to perform comparison of different learning algorithms with feature selection and manifold learning, using K-fold cross-validation. We investigate the comparison of multiple feature selection or manifold learning algorithms systematically in this paper.

The organization of this paper is laid out as follows: Section 2 reviews the techniques of model selection and manifold methods briefly. Section 3 provides the Data construction for simulation of this paper, including the measurement protocols, and the right way to use Cross-validation on feature selection and manifold learning. The experiment result and discussion on comparison of multiple feature selection or manifold learning algorithms using Cross-validation are presented in Section 4, and conclusions are drawn in final section of this paper.

2   Dimension Reduction and Variable Selection Analysis

Features from images consist of locations and gray levels. By using the AAM model, the original features are normalized. However, the normalized features are still highly multicollinear, and thus it is difficult to build an efficient model based on these features. Dimension reduction method is necessary since it can greatly reduce the dependency among the covariates, while still containing important normalized features.

The general setting for linear dimension reduction is: given a set of vectors $\{x_1, x_2, \ldots, x_m\} \subset \mathbb{R}^n$, we want to find a linear transformation matrix $A \in \mathbb{R}^{n \times l}$ that maps x_i to $z_i = A^T x_i \in \mathbb{R}^l$ ($l \ll n$) such that z_i "represents" x_i for all $1 \leq i \leq m$.

With the sample covariate matrix, PCA generates linear combinations of the vectors. The axes of the new coordinate system represent directions with maximum variabilities. However, PCA is focusing on the global structure among the features, without specific attention to the response. Also, the sole dependence of PCA on the covariance matrix makes it very sensitive to outliers. Hence, many authors consider dimension reduction approaches that could utilize local information of responses, and LPP as an example follows.

2.1   Locality Preserving Projections Implementation

The original Locality Preserving Projections (LPP) proposed by He and Niyogi [8]. Chen et al [3] developed a novel operator named "graph age preserving" (GAP) to build a neighborhood graph for LPP for age estimation, which is called **LPPG**. The basic idea is given as following: The age estimation problem comes with actual age associated with each x_i, and thus it is natural to use reported ages to create the graph G. We assume that two vectors x_i and x_j are related if their age difference is less than or equal to h for some $h \in \mathbb{N}$. Therefore, the edge set E is defined as:

$$(i, j) \in E, \text{ if and only if } |\text{age}(i) - \text{age}(j)| \leq h. \tag{1}$$

In this study, we use the simple-minded approach for the weighted adjacency matrix, that is, $W_{ij} = 1$ if $(i, j) \in E$ and zero otherwise. In order to compare the performances of various choices of features with Support Vector Regression (SVR) [17], we let $l = n$.

2.2   Least Angle Regression

Least Angle Regression (LAR) was proposed by Efron et al. [6] to select the best subset of variables for regression, and it is a computationally efficient algorithm. LAR is closely connected with Forward Stagewise Selection [7] and LASSO [16] and they all identify the best variable to be added in the model at each step. LAR employs a more democratic version of forward stepwise regression strategy.

3   Data Construction and Measurement Protocols

In this section we shall introduce the dataset used for empirical study of performance evaluation and measurement protocols for age estimate task.

3.1 Face Aging Databases

The Productivity Aging Laboratory (PAL) face database [9] is selected for this experiment due to its quality of images and diversity of ancestry. Only the frontal images with neutral facial expression are selected for our age estimation algorithm. It contains 540 images with ages ranging from 18 to 93 years old. It is worth mentioning that PAL contains adult face images of African-American, Asian, Caucasian, Hispanic and Indian.

3.2 Data Constructions and Experiment Setups

In PAL database, each image is annotated with 161 landmarks as shown in [11]. The annotated faces with shape and texture information are presented to the AAM system to obtain the encoded appearance features, a set of transformed features with dimension size 230. Here the AAM-Library tool [1] is utilized to implement the AAM system.

In this paper, we make use of manifold learning technique of LPPG and feature selection technique LAR in the following experiments. LPPG is used as a second fold of dimension reduction after obtaining features from AAM (PCA), and then selects features in sequential order. We call this approach "LPPG" (PCA+LPPG+sequential selection), where h ranges from 1 to 5, for the purpose of comparing various ways of defining the association matrix W as in equation (1). For simplicity, we only consider $h = 5$ in this paper. LAR is selected as one of two model selection techniques in this work due to the following reasons: (1) Empirical studies have shown that LAR is an effective model selection techniques for age estimation tasks in [3,4,13]. (2) [7] pointed out that LAR algorithm identifies the variable (predictor) which is most correlated to the evolving residuals at each step of selection. For example, LAR selects the predictor which is the most correlated to response (true age) in the first step. The direction chosen in this fashion keeps the correlations between residuals and selected features tied and monotonically decreasing. It may partially solve the correlation problem for the feature fusion.

For all approaches, we use SVR as the age estimation regressor. We use the contributed package "lars" in Matlab from Karl Sjstrand for the computation of LAR, which provides an ordered sequence of covariates entering SVR. We use the contributed package "Libsvm" [2] in Matlab for the computation of SVR. We use default parameters from Libsvm unless otherwise mentioned.

3.3 Performance Measure

The performance of age estimation is measured by the mean absolute error (MAE) and the cumulative score (CS). The MAE is defined as the average of the absolute errors between the estimated ages and the observed ages, i.e., $MAE = \sum_{i=1}^{N} |\hat{y}_i - y_i|/N$,

where $\hat{y}_i$ and y_i are the estimated age and observed age for the i-th test image respectively, and N is the total number of test images. The cumulative score is defined as the proportion of test images such that the absolute error is not higher than an integer j, $CS(j) = \sum_{i=1}^{N} I(|\hat{y}_i - y_i| \leq j)/N$ where $I(A) = 1$ when an event A is true; and 0 otherwise.

For 100 repeated 10-fold CV, we simply call it as 100 simulations. We further define the following notations. Let $\overline{MAE}$ be the mean of 100 MAEs. That is,

$$\overline{MAE} = \sum_{m=1}^{M} MAE_m/M, \tag{2}$$

where $MAE_m = \sum_{i=1}^{N} |\hat{y}_{mi} - y_{mi}|/N$.

Similarly, take $\overline{CS(j)}$ be the mean of 100 CSs at error level of j. That is,

$$\overline{CS(j)} = \sum_{m=1}^{M} CS_m(j)/M, \tag{3}$$

where $CS_m(j) = \sum_{i=1}^{N} I(|\hat{y}_{mi} - y_{mi}| \leq j)/N$.

3.4   How to Use Cross Validation on Subspace Learning or Feature Selection

When incorporating manifold learning or feature selection in regression/classifier construction, we should perform subspace learning or feature selection inside each cross-validation loop. For each iteration of cross-validation, subspace learning or feature selection are applied to the training set before regression/classifier construction. The procedure is outlines in the following algorithm:

Algorithm 1.. A Correct Way To Carry Out Cross-validation

Initialization:
Divide the sample into K cross-validation folds at random.

for $k = 1, 2, \cdots, K$ **do**
    (1) Learn a subspace, or find a subset of "good" predictors, using all of the samples except those in fold k.
    (2) Using just the subset of predictors, estimate the unknown tuning parameters and build a prediction rule, using all samples except those in fold k.
    (3) Use the prediction rule to estimate the prediction error for the sample in fold k.
end for

Output:
Take an average of the prediction errors over all K folds to produce the the cross-validation estimate of prediction error.

---

4   How to Compare Two Learning Algorithms Statistically?

It is a commonly asked question why we get different values for the cross validation accuracy even if we run the same script multiple times without any changes. The problem comes along the internal random factor of K-fold CV, that is, the data sampling must be made out of randomness that affects its outcome. It only ensures the sample proportion in each CV, not the sample consistency. Therefore, each time when we repeat the cross-validation process, we obtain different partitions of the training set. Consequently, we may end up with distinct prediction errors with large variation, unless we set the random seed to be a fixed number.

4.1   A Toy Simulation Example with 10-Fold Cross-Validation

For age estimation task, the evaluation protocols generally includes MAE and CS using 10-fold CV, or using Leave-one-person-out (LOPO) CV with multiple images for the same person in the dataset. However, is it enough to compare the MAE and CS from different learning algorithms to make a reliable decision on whether one technique is superior than another one? In order to explore this algorithm-comparison problem, we first consider the following toy simulation example. For simplicity and to avoid any selection bias, we will investigate the PAL dataset without involving any manifold learning or feature selection techniques. That is, we shall study the "AAM+SVR" approach with 10-fold CV on the PAL dataset with full dimensionality of $p = 230$. Rather than running the 10-fold CV only one time, we repeat the 10-fold CV for 100 times with different random seeds. Consequently, we shall have 100 different partitions in each simulation experiment.

The boxplot of the MAEs over 100 simulations is shown in Figure 1. The MAE ranges from 6.12 to 6.60, while the mean of 100 MAEs, $\overline{MAE} = 6.40$. The corresponding Cumulative Score curves are shown in Figure 2. The CS curves have certain variation at each error level. For instance, at error level of 10 years, $CS(10)$ ranges from 76.48% to 80%, while the mean of 100 CSs, $\overline{CS(10)} = 78.53\%$.

Therefore, even for the same learning method on a particular dataset, with different random partition, there are considerable variability in the measure protocols of MAE

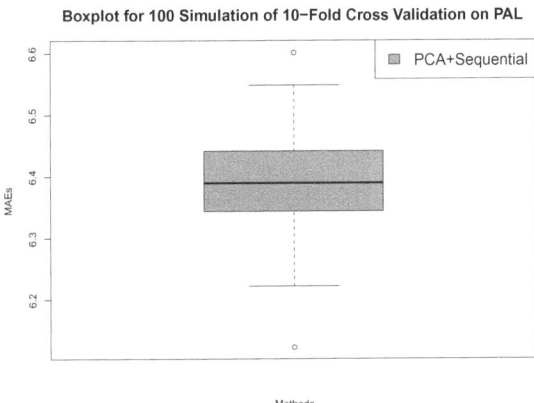

Fig. 1. Box plot of MAEs from 100-repeated 10-fold cross-validation with full feature on PAL dataset

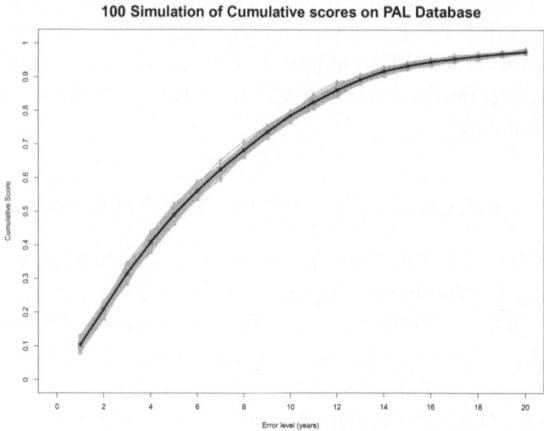

Fig. 2. Cumulative curves from 100-repeated 10-fold cross-validation with full feature on PAL dataset

and CS using 10-fold CV at the ranges of 0.48 years and 3.52%, respectively. In another word, if we select a lucky random seed, it produces $MAE = 6.123$ or $CS(10) = 76.48\%$. On contrast, we may be unlucky to have another random partition that produces $MAE = 6.601$ or $CS(10) = 80\%$ as our final outputs. It underscores the importance of MAE and CS when selecting the best model for age estimation task. Therefore, to compare two learning algorithms, the measuring protocols with MAE and CS are not enough to make a reliable conclusion. The next question is: *How to draw a reliable conclusion when comparing two learning algorithms?*

4.2   Repeated Cross-Validation

Single K-fold cross-validation might not be enough to obtain a reliable estimate on prediction error. To reduce variability and to mitigate any bias caused by a particular partition of training and test sets, it's better to repeat the cross-validation process multiple times with different partitions. Such a scheme is also useful when the amount of data is limited. Other methods include Leave-one-out (LOO)-CV and bootstrap to eliminate this bias. The LOO-CV is an unbiased estimation with larger variation, with an expensive computation cost. Bootstrap Sampling with replacement is another choice. Given a dataset with sample size N, randomly select a sample of size N with replacement as the training set. Then use the rest for testing, and repeat this process for certain times.

To investigate the statistical property of repeated cross-validation, we repeat 10-fold cross-validation 100 times with different partitioning, and then report the average of these 100 prediction error estimates on PAL dataset with feature selection method LAR and manifold learning method LPPG. The experimental results are shown in Figure 3 and Figure 4. The light blue curves are MAE curves for 100 simulations as model complexity is increased. The red curve is the estimate of expected mean absolute error

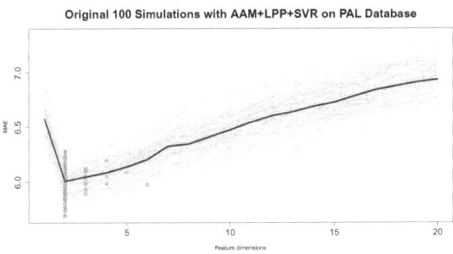

Fig. 3. 100-repeated 10-fold cross-validation with LPPG on PAL dataset

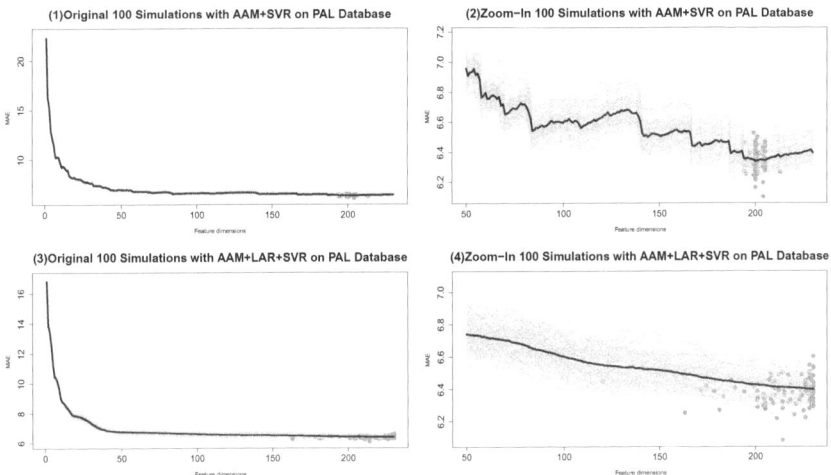

Fig. 4. 100-repeated 10-fold cross-validation with AAM and LAR on PAL dataset

of age estimators, that is, the average of 100 MAE curves at each model complexity. The orange dots are the *best* MAE for each MAE curve. Figure 3 gives the simulation results based on AAM+"LPPG"+SVR approach. Figure 4 (1)-(2) present the 100-simulation results based on AAM+SVR approach on PAL dataset, while (3)-(4) present simulation results based on AAM+"LAR"+SVR approach on PAL dataset. Due to the large range in MAEs, (1) and (3) can't reveal the pattern of feature selection clearly. Therefore we zoom in (1) and (3) as (2) and (4) respectively to reveal the variation in more details.

One can find that Figure 3 and Figure 4 (2), (4) show a large variation among 100 MAE curves. However, the locations (orange dots) of best MAE among each MAE curve clusters closer for sequential selection AAM+SVR approach and manifold learning AAM+"LPPG"+SVR approach than the feature selection AAM+"LAR"+SVR approach.

Table 1 gives the best $\overline{MAE}$ (year) with AAM, LAR and $LPPG$ using Method on PAL database. Here are some notations used in the table: $\overline{MAE}$ means the mean (average) of 100 MAEs; "std. of MAE" means the standard deviation of 100 MAEs;

Table 1. Best Mean MAEs (year) with LAR and $LPPG$ using Method on PAL database

Best $\overline{MAE}$ (year) with LAR and $LPPG$ on PAL database			
	AAM	LAR	$LPPG$
$\overline{MAE}$	6.34	6.39	6.01
std. of MAE	0.08	0.08	0.12
mean of SE.	0.68	0.68	0.71
std. of SE.	0.15	0.15	0.17
#-Var	200	230	2
Total-Var	230	230	20

"SE" means the stand error of MAEs among 10-fold CV; "mean of SE" means the mean of 100 SEs; "std. of SE" means the stand deviation of 100 SEs. One can find out that "LPPG" approach gives the best $\overline{MAE}$ among all three approaches. The other two approaches give similar results. However, for the standard deviation estimation of prediction errors (MAEs), "mean of SE" is much larger than "std. of MAE" and "std. of SE", while the latter two have similar scale ranges.

In cross-validation, the model must be completely retained for each fold of process. It is a wide accepted fact that there is considerable variability in the error, underscoring the importance of reporting the standard error of the CV estimate. It is supposed that the repeated cross-validation stabilizes the prediction error estimation, and therefore, it reduces the variance of the K-fold CV estimator, especially for small samples [14]. Our simulation results provides exactly an empirical evidence to this conjecture. Therefore, in order to estimate the prediction error, we will recommend to use repeated cross-validation to reduce variability.

5   Conclusion

In this paper, first, we experimentally study the selection bias caused by wrong cross-validation process with feature selection or manifold learning strategies, and recommend a correct way to carry out cross-validation. Next, we study the sensitivity to changes in the training/ test set using cross-validation. One of our findings is that different random partition of training/test sets may end up with significant different experimental results, which can easily lead to misleading conclusions if one merely compare two learning algorithms based on K-fold CV results. Finally we investigate the repeated CV to reduce the variability of prediction error. All experimental studies are performed on PAL dataset for age estimation task.

As suggested in [15], when comparing two or more learning algorithms, appropriate hypothesis testing should be performed instead of comparing only average accuracy of K-fold CV. Paired t-test is one such test taking into account the variance in accuracy estimates [5]. Based on our experimental study, due to variability, we *cannot* merely compare two numbers, merely based on MAE and CS. Further research of this work should be focused on finding appropriate parametric or non-parametric hypothesis testings. Even though the paired t-test is a simple and standard statistical hypothesis testing procedure, it is still challenging to find a appropriate estimator of standard deviation of prediction error when using cross-validation [15].

The future studies include investigating more experiments to understand the prediction errors based on cross-validation, repeated cross-validation; and also other resampling methods such as bootstrap and LOO-CV. It is also desired to run more experiments to investigate the predictive power based on various parametric and non-parametric hypothesis tests, such as paired student-t test, and rank test.

References

1. Aam-library, http://groups.google.com/group/asmlibrary?pli=1
2. Chang, C.-C., Lin, C.-J.: LIBSVM: a library for support vector machines (2001), http://www.csie.ntu.edu.tw/~cjlin/libsvm
3. Chen, C., Chang, Y., Ricanek, K., Wang, Y.: Face age estimation using model selection. In: CVPRW, pp. 93–99 (2010)
4. Chen, C., Yang, W., Wang, Y., Ricanek, K., Luu, K.: Facial feature fusion and model selection for age estimation. In: 9th International Conference on Automatic Face and Gesture Recognition (2011)
5. Dietterich, T.G.: Approximate statistical tests for comparing supervised classification learning algorithms. Neural Computation 10, 1895–1923 (1998)
6. Efron, B., Hastie, T., Johnstone, I., Tibshirani, R.: Least angle regression. Annal of Statistics 32, 407–499 (2004)
7. Hastie, T., Tibshirani, R., Friedman, J.: The Elements of Statistical Learning: Data Mining, Inference, and Prediction, 2nd edn. Springer, New York (2009)
8. He, X., Niyogi, P.: Locality preserving projections. In: Proceedings of Advances in Neural Information Processing Systems 16 (2003)
9. Minear, M., Park, D.C.: A lifespan database of adult facial stimuli. Behavior Research Methods, Instruments, & Computers 36, 630–633 (2004)
10. Refaeilzadeh, L.T.P., Liu, H.: On comaprison of feature selection algorithms. In: Proceedings of AAAI Workshop on Evaluation Methods for Machine Learning II, pp. 34–39 (2007)
11. Patterson, E., Sethuram, A., Albert, M., Ricanek, K.: Comparison of synthetic face aging to age progression by forensic sketch artist. In: IASTED International Conference on Visualization, Imaging, and Image Processing, Palma de Mallorca, Spain (2007)
12. Refaeilzadeh, P., Tang, L., Liu, H.: Cross-validation. In: Encyclopedia of Database Systems, pp. 532–538 (2009)
13. Ricanek, K., Wang, Y., Chen, C., Simmons, S.J.: Generalized multi-ethnic face age-estimation. In: BTAS (2009)
14. Rodriguez, J., Perez, A., Lozano, J.: Sensitivity analysis of k-fold cross validation in prediction error estimation. IEEE Transactions on Pattern Analysis and Machine Intelligence 32(3), 569–575 (2010)
15. Salzberg, S.: On comparing classifiers: Pitfalls to avoid and a recommended approach. Data Mining and Knowledge Discovery 1, 317–327 (1997)
16. Tibshirani, R.: Regression shrinkage and selection via the lasso. Journal of the Royal Statistical Society, Series B 58(1), 267–288 (1996)
17. Vapnik, V.: Statistical learning theory. Wiley Interscience, New York (1998)

Selective Ensemble of Support Vector Data Descriptions for Novelty Detection

Hong-Jie Xing and Xue-Fang Chen

Key Laboratory of Machine Learning and Computational Intelligence
College of Mathematics and Computer Science, Hebei University
Baoding 071002, Hebei Province, China
hjxing@hbu.edu.cn, chenxuefang0924@126.com

Abstract. Since support vector data description (SVDD) is regarded as a strong classifier, the traditional ensemble methods are not fit for directly combining the results of several SVDDs. Moreover, as is well-known, when many trained classifiers are available, it is better to ensemble some of them rather than all. In this paper, a selective ensemble method based on correntropy is proposed to deal with the foresaid problems. The base classifier used in the proposed ensemble is SVDD. Experimental results on two synthetic data sets and five benchmark data sets demonstrate that the proposed method is superior to its related approaches.

Keywords: SVDD, selective ensemble, novelty detection.

1 Introduction

An ensemble is generated by training multiple base classifiers for the same task and combining the results of them by certain methods [1]. Although an ensemble of classifiers often achieves better performance than one single classifier, the computational cost for obtaining the ensemble of these classifiers will become expensive when the number of base classifiers is large. Zhou et al. proved in [2] that it is better to ensemble part of the base classifiers rather than all of them. Till now, there emerge many selective ensemble methods [3,4,5]. They have been successfully used to tackle many real-world problems, such as face recognition, emotion recognition, news audio classification, among others. Nevertheless, to the best of our knowledge, the aforementioned selective ensemble approaches have not been applied to novelty detection.

Novelty detection is considered as one-class classification trained only with the normal data but used for classifying both the normal and novel data [6]. Support vector data description (SVDD) [7] is a generally used method as a one-class classifier in the novelty detection approaches. It establishes a hypersphere in the form of a kernel expansion to distinguish the normal data from the novel data. The kernel function in the decision function maps the data from the original space into a high-dimensional feature space while the explicit form of

J. Wang, G.G. Yen, and M.M. Polycarpou (Eds.): ISNN 2012, Part I, LNCS 7367, pp. 468–477, 2012.

the mapping is not needed according to the 'kernel trick' [8]. When the Gaussian kernel function is utilized, Tax and Duin proved that SVDD is equivalent to one-class support vector machine (OCSVM) [7].

To further improve the prediction accuracy rate of single one-class classifier, several one-class classifier ensemble methods have been proposed. Seguï et al. [9] proposed a weighted bagging based one-class classifier ensemble method. They utilized minimum spanning tree class descriptor as base classifiers. Zhang et al. [10] used locality preserving projection to reduce the dimensionality of the original data, trained several SVDDs upon the reduced data, and combined the outputs of the trained SVDDs. Hamdi and Bennani [11] proposed an ensemble of one-class classifiers by utilizing the orthogonal projection operator and the bootstrap strategy. Wilk and Wozniak [12] constructed the ensemble of one-class classifiers by fuzzy combiner. They utilized fuzzy rule based classifier as the base classifier, while used fuzzy error correcting output codes and fuzzy decision templates as the ensemble strategies.

Inspired by negative correlation learning (NCL) [13], we propose a novel selective ensemble method for SVDD to get the weights of base classifiers. The proposed ensemble strategy is based on the correntropy in information theoretic learning [14]. To the best of our knowledge, the selective ensemble approach for SVDD has not been reported. Moreover, we observe that our proposed selective ensemble can improve the results of the single SVDD.

The remainder of the paper is organized as follows. Section 2 reviews the traditional SVDD. Section 3 describes the selective ensemble of SVDDs in detail. Section 4 shows the experimental results of the proposed method and its related approaches on the two synthetic and five benchmark data sets. Finally, Section 5 concludes the paper.

2   SVDD

SVDD was proposed by Tax and Duin [7]. It finds the smallest sphere enclosing all the normal data. Given N normal data $\{\mathbf{x}_i\}_{i=1}^N$ with $\mathbf{x}_i \in \mathcal{R}^d$, the original optimization problem of SVDD is given by

$$\min_{R,a,\boldsymbol{\xi}} \ R^2 + C \sum_{i=1}^N \xi_i$$
$$s.t. \ \|\mathbf{x}_i - \mathbf{a}\|^2 \leq R^2 + \xi_i, \ i = 1, 2, \ldots, N$$
$$\xi_i \geq 0, \ i = 1, 2, \ldots, N, \tag{1}$$

where R is the radius of the enclosing sphere, C is the trade-off parameter, ξ_i is the slack variable, and $\mathbf{a}$ is the center of the enclosing sphere. The above optimization problem can be solved by the Lagrange multiplier method. Moreover, substituting the inner products in the dual optimization problem of (1) by kernel functions, we can get the following dual optimization problem with nonlinear kernels

$$\min_{\alpha} \sum_{i=1}^{N} \sum_{j=1}^{N} \alpha_i \alpha_j K(\mathbf{x}_i, \mathbf{x}_j) - \sum_{i=1}^{N} \alpha_i K(\mathbf{x}_i, \mathbf{x}_i)$$

$$s.t. \sum_{i=1}^{N} \alpha_i = 1$$

$$0 \le \alpha_i \le C, \quad i = 1, 2, \ldots, N. \tag{2}$$

For the choice of kernel functions $K(\cdot, \cdot)$, one can refer to literature [15].

Given a test sample $\mathbf{x}$, it can be classified as the normal data if the following condition holds

$$\|\mathbf{x} - \mathbf{a}\|^2 = K(\mathbf{x}, \mathbf{x}) - 2 \sum_{i=1}^{N} \alpha_i K(\mathbf{x}, \mathbf{x}_i) + \sum_{i=1}^{N} \sum_{j=1}^{N} \alpha_i \alpha_j K(\mathbf{x}_i, \mathbf{x}_j) \le R^2. \tag{3}$$

Otherwise, $\mathbf{x}$ is classified as the novel data.

3   Selective Ensemble of SVDDs

In this section, a new selective ensemble strategy based on correntropy is proposed for combining SVDDs. The half-quadratic optimization technique is utilized to solve the corresponding optimization problem.

3.1   Negative Correlation Learning

Negative correlation learning (NCL) is a neural network ensemble method [13]. Its error function consists of two parts. The first part is used for measuring individual training error of each network, while the second part is utilized to evaluate the the negative correlation of each network's error with errors for the rest of the ensemble. Given the training set $\{\mathbf{x}_i, y_i\}_{i=1}^{N}$, the ensemble error function of NCL is given by

$$\begin{aligned} E_{ens} &= \frac{1}{M} \sum_{i=1}^{N} \sum_{k=1}^{M} [f_k(\mathbf{x}_i) - y_i]^2 - \frac{1}{M} \sum_{i=1}^{N} \sum_{k=1}^{M} [f_k(\mathbf{x}_i) - f_{ens}(\mathbf{x}_i)]^2 \\ &= \frac{1}{M} \sum_{i=1}^{N} \sum_{k=1}^{M} [f_k(\mathbf{x}_i) - y_i]^2 - \sum_{i=1}^{N} \left\{ \frac{1}{M} \sum_{k=1}^{M} [f_k(\mathbf{x}_i) - f_{ens}(\mathbf{x}_i)]^2 \right\} \\ &= \frac{1}{M} \sum_{i=1}^{N} \sum_{k=1}^{M} [f_k(\mathbf{x}_i) - y_i]^2 - \sum_{i=1}^{N} Var(F_i), \end{aligned} \tag{4}$$

where $f_k(\mathbf{x}_i)$ denotes the output of the kth network upon the ith sample $\mathbf{x}_i$, $f_{ens}(\mathbf{x}_i)$ is the output of the network ensemble on $\mathbf{x}_i$, and $Var(F_i)$ is the variance of all the outputs of the networks in the ensemble on $\mathbf{x}_i$.

Moreover, the output of the ensemble upon $\mathbf{x}_i$ is given by

$$f_{ens}(\mathbf{x}_i) = \frac{1}{M}\sum_{k=1}^{M} f_k(\mathbf{x}_i), \tag{5}$$

which indicates that all the base classifiers (or regressors) have the same contribution to construct the ensemble.

3.2   NCL Based on Correntropy

For M SVDDs, the radius of their ensemble is defined as

$$\bar{r} = \sum_{k=1}^{M} w_k r_k = (\mathbf{w}, \mathbf{r}), \tag{6}$$

where r_i denotes the radius of the ith SVDD, $\mathbf{w} = (w_1, w_2, \ldots, w_M)^T$ is the weight vector for the M radii, $\mathbf{r} = (r_1, r_2, \ldots, r_M)^T$ is a vector consisting of the M radii, and $(\cdot, \cdot)$ denotes the inner product operator.

As declared in [14], correntropy is regarded as a new similarity measure. It is more robust against noises compared to the mean square error (MSE). Therefore, we utilize cross correntropy to replace the MSE in the first part of (4), while use auto-correntropy to substitute the variance in the second part. Therefore, the ensemble error function (4) can be rewritten as

$$\widetilde{E}_{ens} = V(R, \bar{r}) - V_W(k, l)$$
$$= \frac{1}{M}\sum_{k=1}^{M} \kappa_{\sigma_1}(r_k - \bar{r}) - \frac{1}{M^2}\sum_{k=1}^{M}\sum_{l=1}^{M} \kappa_{\sigma_2}(w_k - w_l), \tag{7}$$

where $\kappa_{\sigma_1}(\cdot)$ and $\kappa_{\sigma_2}(\cdot)$ are both kernel function. When they are taken as the Gaussian kernel function, (7) can be expressed as

$$\widetilde{E}_{ens} = \frac{1}{M}\sum_{k=1}^{M} \exp\left(-\frac{(r_k - \bar{r})^2}{2\sigma_1^2}\right) - \frac{1}{M^2}\sum_{k=1}^{M}\sum_{l=1}^{M} \exp\left(-\frac{(w_k - w_l)^2}{2\sigma_2^2}\right). \tag{8}$$

Considering the constraint $\sum_{k=1}^{M} w_k = 1$, we can get the following optimization problem:

$$\min \ \frac{1}{M}\sum_{k=1}^{M} \exp\left(-\frac{(r_k - \bar{r})^2}{2\sigma_1^2}\right) - \frac{1}{M^2}\sum_{k=1}^{M}\sum_{l=1}^{M} \exp\left(-\frac{(w_k - w_l)^2}{2\sigma_2^2}\right)$$
$$s.t. \ \sum_{k=1}^{M} w_k = 1. \tag{9}$$

To solve (9), the half-quadratic (HQ) optimization technique can be utilized. According to the theory of the convex conjugated function [16], we have

Proposition 1. *For* $G(z) = \exp\left(-\frac{z^2}{2\sigma^2}\right)$, *there exists a convex conjugated function* φ, *such that*

$$G(z) = \sup_{\alpha \in \mathcal{R}^-} \left(\alpha\frac{z^2}{2\sigma^2} - \varphi(\alpha)\right). \tag{10}$$

Moreover, for a fixed z, the supremum is reached at $\alpha = -G(z)$ [17].

Hence, according to Proposition 1 and the Lagrange multiplier method, the objective function of (9) can be augmented as

$$F(\mathbf{w}, \mathbf{P}, \mathbf{Q}) = \frac{1}{M}\sum_{k=1}^{M}\left[p_k\frac{(r_k - \bar{r})^2}{2\sigma_1^2} - \varphi(p_k)\right] -$$

$$\frac{1}{M^2}\sum_{k=1}^{M}\sum_{l=1}^{M}q_{kl}\left[\frac{(w_k - w_l)^2}{2\sigma_2^2} - \varphi(q_{kl})\right] - \lambda\left(\sum_{k=1}^{M}w_k - 1\right), \tag{11}$$

where $\mathbf{P}$ is a diagonal matrix with $\mathbf{P}_{kk} = p_k$ and $\mathbf{Q}$ is an $M \times M$ matrix with $\mathbf{Q}_{kl} = q_{kl}$. The local optimal solution of (11) can be calculated iteratively by

$$p_k^{\tau+1} = -\exp\left(-\frac{(r_k - \bar{r}^\tau)^2}{2\sigma_1^2}\right), \tag{12}$$

$$q_{kl}^{\tau+1} = -\exp\left(-\frac{(w_k^\tau - w_l^\tau)^2}{2\sigma_2^2}\right), \tag{13}$$

and

$$\mathbf{w}^{\tau+1} = \arg\min_{\mathbf{w}}\frac{1}{2}\mathbf{w}^T\left(\frac{1}{\sigma_1^2 M}\sum_{k=1}^{M}p_k^\tau\mathbf{R} - \frac{1}{\sigma_2^2 M^2}\mathbf{L}^\tau\right)\mathbf{w} - \left(\frac{1}{2\sigma_1^2 M}\sum_{k=1}^{M}p_k^\tau\mathbf{r} + \lambda\mathbf{1}\right)^T\mathbf{w}, \tag{14}$$

where τ denotes the τth iteration, the superscript T is the transposed operator, $\mathbf{R} = \mathbf{r}\mathbf{r}^T$ with $\mathbf{r} = (r_1, r_2, \ldots, r_M)^T$, $\mathbf{L} = \mathbf{D} - \mathbf{Q}$ is the Laplacian matrix with $\mathbf{D}_{kk} = \sum_{l=1}^{M}\mathbf{D}_{kl}$, and $\mathbf{1}$ is a column vector whose elements are all one.

4   Experimental Results

In the following experiments, the geometric mean (g-means) is utilized to measure the performance of the different methods. The expression of g-means is given by [18]

$$g = \sqrt{a^+ \times a^-}, \tag{15}$$

where a^+ and a^- denote the classification accuracy rates of a certain classifier upon the normal and novel data, respectively. Furthermore, let SESVDDs be the simplified notation of our proposed method in the following comparisons. For SVDD and SESVDDs, the Gaussian kernel function $K(\mathbf{x}, \mathbf{y}) = \exp\left(-\gamma\|\mathbf{x} - \mathbf{y}\|^2\right)$ are selected. For SESVDDs, its base classifiers are all constructed on the 80% samples randomly selected from each training set. During the course of training SESVDDs, the base classifiers with their weights less than $\frac{1}{M}$ are discarded. In addition, all the codes are implemented in Matlab.

4.1   Synthetic Data Sets

To test the effectiveness of the proposed ensemble method, two synthetic data sets are generated. The number of base classifiers in SESVDDs and the maximum number of iterations for the HQ optimization are both taken as 20. The description of the two data sets is as follows.

Sine-noise: 200 noise-free samples are randomly chosen from the sine curve along $y = \sin(\frac{3}{2}\pi x)$ with $x \in [0,3]$, while 50 noises are generated by $y = \sin(\frac{3}{2}\pi x) \pm \epsilon$ with $\epsilon \sim N(0,1)$. The parameter of the Gaussian kernel function and the trade-off parameter for SVDD are taken as $\gamma = 0.3$ and $C = 10$, respectively. The parameters of SESSVDs, i.e. the parameter of Gaussian kernel function γ, the trade-off parameter C, together with the width parameters σ_1 and σ_2 are taken as 0.3, 10, 0.9, and 20. The results of the two methods are shown in Fig. 1. The number of base classifiers in the trained SESVDDs is 2.

Square-noise: 200 noise-free samples are randomly selected in the square $\{(x,y)|x \in [0.3,2.7], y \in [0.3,0.6] \cup [2.4,2.7]\} \cup \{(x,y)|x \in [0.3,0.6] \cup [2.4,2.7], y \in [0.3,2.7]\}$, while 50 noises are randomly distributed in the area $\{(x,y)|x,y \in [0,3]\}$. The parameters of SVDD and SESVDDs are taken as $C = 0.3$, $\gamma = 40$, $\sigma_1 = 0.1$, and $\sigma_2 = 0.5$. The results of the two approaches are demonstrated in Fig. 2. The number of base classifiers in the obtained SESVDDs is 10.

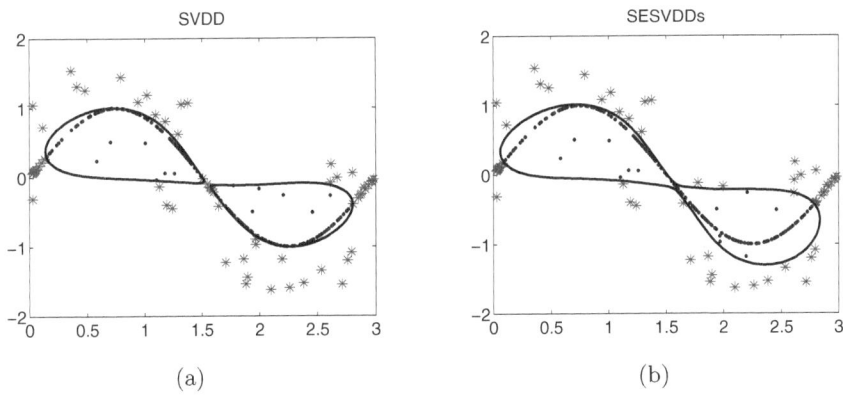

Fig. 1. The classification results of the two methods upon *Sine-noise*. (a) SVDD with g-means 0.8001. (b) SESVDDs with g-means 0.8138.

According to the results demonstrated in Figs. 1 and 2 together with the g-means of the two methods, one can easily find that the proposed SESVDDs is more robust against noises than SVDD upon the two synthetic data sets.

4.2   Benchmark Data Sets

In the following, the two methods, i.e. SVDD and SESVDDs are further compared on the five benchmark data sets chosen from the UCI machine learning

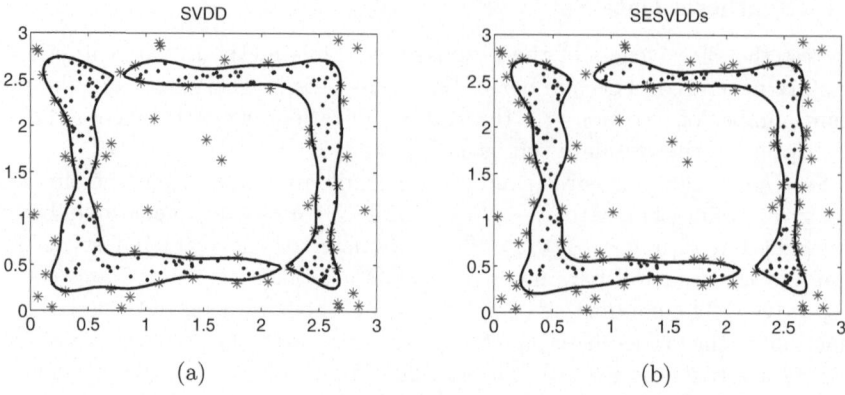

Fig. 2. The classification results of the two methods upon *Square-noise*. (a) SVDD with g-means 0.7869. (b) SESVDDs with g-means 0.8068.

repository [19]. The description of these data sets is included in Table 1. For SVDD, its parameters are carefully chosen to make it obtain the optimal performance. Then, these selected parameters are directly assigned to their counterparts of SESVDDs. Moreover, the values of the width parameters σ_1 and σ_2 are both adjusted to make SESVDDs obtain better performance. The original number of base classifiers in SESVDDs is set to be 50 for tackling all the data sets. It should be mentioned here that there may be several classes in the selected data sets. To make them fit for novelty detection, the samples in a certain class are chosen as the normal data, while the samples in the rest classes are utilized as the novel data. Thereafter, the normal data are used for training and all the data including the normal and novel data are utilized for testing.

Table 1. Details of the benchmark data sets used for comparing the different methods

Datasets	# features	# normal	# novel
Biomed	5	127	67
Survival	3	225	81
Balance scale	4	288	337
Breast cancer	9	458	241
Thyriod	21	3488	234

The selected parameters for SVDDs and SESVDDs are summarized in Table 2. To eliminate the randomness of selecting part of normal data for the base classifiers in SESVDDs, 20 repetitions are performed over SESVDDs on each data set. The average testing results of SVDDs and SESVDDs are included in Table 3. The standard variations of SVDDs upon the test sets of the five data sets are not demonstrated in Table 3 only because they are all zero, which means that SVDD is really a strong classifier.

Table 2. The settings of parameters for the different methods and the final number of base classifiers in the trained SESVDDs

Datasets	C	γ	σ_1	σ_2	# selected
Biomed	1	10	0.1	4.6	4
Survival	0.08	9	0.1	4	3
Balance scale	0.06	0.2	2.4	0.5	24
Breast cancer	0.07	0.1	0.4	1.3	11
Thyriod	0.01	2.6	2.2	2.2	24

Note: # selected–Number of selected base classifiers in the trained SESVDDs.

Table 3. Average g-means (percent) and the standard deviations (percent) of the four methods on the five data sets

Datasets	SVDD	Bagging[20]	AdaBoost[21]	SESVDDs
Biomed	64.32	39.80±5.09	45.09±4.24	65.60±6.91
Survival	62.15	58.86±1.38	58.92±0.49	63.61±3.74
Balance scale	71.67	70.97±0.53	70.37±1.03	73.99±0.53
Breast cancer	94.15	94.39±0.37	94.28±0.23	94.80±0.31
Thyriod	71.13	68.32±0.54	68.27±0.50	71.82 ±0.45

It can be observed from Table 3 that SESVDDs outperforms SVDD on all the five data sets. Moreover, SESVDDs achieves better classification performance compared to the traditional ensemble strategies, i.e. bagging and AdaBoost.

5   Conclusions

To improve the classification ability of SVDD, a selective ensemble of SVDDs based on correntropy is proposed. In the proposed ensemble strategy, the weights of base classifiers can be iteratively optimized. Once the ensemble completes, most elements in the weight vector will be zero or extremely small. Through discarding the base classifiers with zero or small weights, the selective ensemble of SVDDs can be implemented. Compared to the single SVDD, the ensemble of SVDDs by bagging, and the ensemble of SVDDs by AdaBoost, the proposed ensemble approach achieves better performance.

To make our proposed method more promising, there are two tasks for future investigation. First, the width parameters σ_1 and σ_2 in (7), the trade-off parameter C, and the parameter γ of the Gaussian kernel function are important parameters for the proposed ensemble. In the experiments, they are chosen by the 'trial and error' method, which is time-consuming. For selecting σ_1 and σ_2, the heuristic approaches, e.g. simultaneous regression-scale estimation [22], Silverman's rule [23], and Huber's rule [24] will be considered. Moreover, for choosing C and γ, the cross-validation method together with the grid search strategy can be adopted. Second, the correntropy based criteria are proved

476 H.-J. Xing and X.-F. Chen

to be more robust against noises in comparison with their corresponding MSE based criterions [14,25]. In future work, we will check the anti-noise ability of the proposed ensemble method.

Acknowledgments. This work is partly supported by the National Natural Science Foundation of China (Nos. 60903089; 61073121; 61170040) and the Foundation of Hebei University (Nos. 2008123; 3504020).

References

1. Huang, F., Xie, G., Xiao, R.: Research on Ensemble Learning. In: 2009 International Conference on Artificial Intelligence and Computational Intelligence, pp. 249–252. IEEE Press (2009)
2. Zhou, Z.-H., Wu, J., Tang, W.: Ensembling Neural Networks: Many Could Be Better Than All. Artificial Intelligence 137(1-2), 239–263 (2002)
3. Martínez-Muñoz, G., Suárez, A.: Pruning in Ordered Bagging Ensembles. In: The 23rd International Conference on Machine Learning, pp. 609–616 (2006)
4. Li, N., Zhou, Z.-H.: Selective Ensemble under Regularization Framework. In: Benediktsson, J.A., Kittler, J., Roli, F. (eds.) MCS 2009. LNCS, vol. 5519, pp. 293–303. Springer, Heidelberg (2009)
5. Zhang, L., Zhou, W.-D.: Sparse Ensembles Using Weighted Combination Methods Based on Linear Programming. Pattern Recognition 44(1), 97–106 (2011)
6. Tax, D.M.J., Duin, R.P.W.: Support Vector Domain Description. Pattern Recognition Letters 12(11-13), 1191–1199 (1999)
7. Tax, D.M.J., Duin, R.P.W.: Support Vector Data Description. Machine Learning 54(1), 45–66 (2004)
8. Schölkopf, B.: The Kernel Trick for Distances. In: Advances in Neural Information Processing Systems, vol. 13, pp. 301–307. MIT Press (2001)
9. Seguí, S., Igual, L., Vitrià, J.: Weighted Bagging for Graph Based One-Class Classifiers. In: El Gayar, N., Kittler, J., Roli, F. (eds.) MCS 2010. LNCS, vol. 5997, pp. 1–10. Springer, Heidelberg (2010)
10. Zhang, J., Lu, J., Zhang, G.Q.: Combining One Class Classification Models For Avian Influenza Outbreaks. In: The 2011 IEEE Symposium on Computational Intelligence in Multicriteria Decision-Making, pp. 190–196 (2011)
11. Hamdi, F., Bennani, Y.: Learning Random Subspace Novelty Detection Filters. In: The 2011 International Joint Conference on Neural Networks, pp. 2273–2280 (2011)
12. Wilk, T., Wozniak, M.: Soft Computing Methods Applied to Combination of One-Class Classifiers. Neurocomputing 75, 185–193 (2012)
13. Liu, Y., Yao, X.: Ensemble Learning via Negative Correlation. Neural Networks 12(10), 1399–1404 (1999)
14. Liu, W., Pokharel, P.P., Principe, J.C.: Correntropy:Properties and Applications in Nongaussian Signal Processing. IEEE Transactions on Signal Processing 55(11), 5286–5298 (2007)
15. Vapnik, V.N.: Statistical Learning Theory. Wiley, New York (1998)
16. Rockfellar, R.: Convex Analysis. Princeton University, Princeton (1970)
17. Yuan, X.-T., Hu, B.-G.: Robust Feature Extraction via Information Theoretic Learning. In: The 26th International Conference on Machine Learning, pp. 1–8 (2009)

18. Wu, M.R., Ye, J.P.: A Small Sphere and Large Margin Approach for Novelty Detection Using Training Data with Outliers. IEEE Transactions on Pattern Analysis and Machine Intelligence 31(11), 2088–2092 (2009)
19. Frank, A., Asuncion, A.: UCI Machine Learning Repository. University of California, Irvine, School of Information and Computer Sciences, Irvine, CA (2010), http://archive.ics.uci.edu/ml
20. Breiman, L.: Bagging Predictors. Machine Learing 24(2), 123–140 (1996)
21. Freund, Y., Schapire, R.E.: A Short Introduction to Boosting. Journal of Japanese Society for Artificial Intelligence 14(5), 771–780 (1999)
22. Mizera, I., Müller, C.H.: Breakdown Points of Cauchy Regression-Scale Estimators. Statistics & Probability Letters 57(1), 79–89 (2002)
23. Silverman, B.W.: Density Estimation for Statistics and Data Analysis. In: Monographs on Statistics and Applied Probability. Chapman and Hall, London (1986)
24. Rousseeuw, P.J.: Robust Regression and Outlier Detection. Wiley, New York (1987)
25. He, R., Zheng, W.-S., Hu, B.-G., Kong, X.-W.: A Regularized Correntropy Framework for Robust Pattern Recognition. Neural Computation 23, 2074–2100 (2011)

Tutorial and Selected Approaches on Parameter Learning in Bayesian Network with Incomplete Data

Mohamed Ali Mahjoub[1,2], Abdessalem Bouzaiene[2], and Nabil Ghanmy[2]

[1] Preparatory Institute of Engineer of Monastir,
Street Ibn Eljazzar 5019 Monastir, Tunisia
medali.mahjoub@ipeim.rnu.tn
[2] Sage (Advanced Systems in Electrical Engineering)
National School of Engineering of Sousse, Tunisia
bouzaieni@yahoo.fr, nabil.ghanmy@gmail.com

Abstract. Bayesian networks (BN) are used in a big range of applications but they have one issue concerning parameter learning. In real application, training data are always incomplete or some nodes are hidden. To deal with this problem many learning parameter algorithms are suggested foreground EM, Gibbs sampling and RBE algorithms. This paper presents a tutorial of basic concepts and in particular techniques and algorithms associated with learning in Bayesian network with incomplete data. We present also selected applications in the fields.

Keywords: Bayesian network, parameter learning, incomplete data.

1 Introduction

In recent years, Bayesian networks have become important tools for modeling uncertain knowledge. They are used in various applications such as information retrieval, data fusion, bioinformatics, and medical diagnostics [30]. Bayesian networks are graphical models that can apply these concepts in daily life by modeling a given problem as a causal structure as a graph indicating the independence between the different actors of the problem and using qualitative state which is in the form of conditional probability tables. The clarity of the semantics and comprehensibility by humans are the major advantages of using Bayesian networks for modeling applications. They offer the possibility of causal interpretation of models of learning. The concepts of learning in Bayesian network are devised into two types; the first one is to learn the parameters when the structure is known. The second one is to learn the structure and the parameters at the same moment. In this paper, we assume that the structure is known.

The parameter learning in this case is divided into two categories. If the training data are complete this problem is resolved by statistic approach or a Bayesian approach. In real application, to find complete training data is difficult for various reasons. When data are incomplete two classical approaches are usually used to

J. Wang, G.G. Yen, and M.M. Polycarpou (Eds.): ISNN 2012, Part I, LNCS 7367, pp. 478–488, 2012.

determine the parameters of a Bayesian network that include EM algorithm [1] and Gibbs Sampling.

In order to fully specify the Bayesian network and thus fully represent the joint probability distribution, it is necessary to specify for each node X the probability distribution for X conditional upon X's parents. The distribution of X conditional upon its parents may have any form. It is common to work with discrete or Gaussian distributions since that simplifies calculations. Sometimes only constraints on a distribution are known; we can then use the principle of maximum entropy to determine a single distribution, the one with the greatest entropy given the constraints.

Often these conditional distributions include parameters which are unknown and must be estimated from data; sometimes we use the maximum likelihood approach. Direct maximization of the likelihood (or of the posterior probability) is often complex when there are unobserved variables. A classical approach to this problem is the expectation-maximization algorithm which alternates computing expected values of the unobserved variables conditional on observed data, with maximizing the complete likelihood (or posterior) assuming that previously computed expected values are correct. Under mild regularity conditions this process converges on maximum likelihood values for parameters. A more fully Bayesian approach to learn parameters is to treat parameters as additional unobserved variables and to compute a full posterior distribution over all nodes conditional upon observed data, then to integrate out the parameters. This approach can be expensive and lead to large dimension models, so in practice classical parameter-setting approaches are more common.

The rest of this paper is organized as follows: in sections 2, we will present the fundamentals of Bayesian network. Section 3 deals with parameter learning with complete data. Approaches of parameter learning with incomplete data are discussed in section 4. Selected approaches are presented in section 5. Section 6 is conclusion.

2   Bayesian Network

A bayesian network is defined by a set of variables $\chi = \{X_1, X_2, ..., X_n\}$ that represent the actors of the problem and a set of edge that represent the conditional independence between these variables. If there is an arc from X_i to X_j then X_i is called parent of X_j and is noted by $pa(X_j)$. Each node is conditionally independent from all the other nodes given its parents. The conditional distribution of all nodes is described as:

$$P(\chi) = \prod_{i=1}^{n} P(X_i | pa(X_i))$$ (1)

Each node is described by a conditional probability table which we denote by the vector θ. The entire vector is composed by a set of parameters value $\theta_{i,j,k}$ and it's defined by:

$$\theta_{i,j,k} = P(X_i = x_k | pa(X_i) = x_j)$$ (2)

Where $i=1...n$ represents the range of all variables, $k=1...r_i$ describes all possible states taken by X_i and $j=1...q_i$ ranges all possible parent configurations of node X_i.

2.1   Inferring Unobserved Variables

Because a Bayesian network is a complete model for the variables and their relationships, it can be used to answer probabilistic queries about them. For example, the network can be used to find out updated knowledge of the state of a subset of variables when other variables (the *evidence* variables) are observed. This process of computing the *posterior* distribution of variables given evidence is called probabilistic inference. The posterior gives a universal sufficient statistic for detection applications, when one wants to choose values for the variable subset which minimize some expected loss function, for instance the probability of decision error. A Bayesian network can thus be considered a mechanism for automatically applying Bayes theorem to complex problems. The most common exact inference methods are: variable elimination, which eliminates the non-observed non-query variables one by one by distributing the sum over the product; clique tree propagation, which caches the computation so that many variables can be queried at one time and new evidence can be propagated quickly; and recursive conditioning and AND/OR search. All of these methods have complexity that is exponential in the network's tree width. The most common approximate inference algorithms are importance sampling, stochastic MCMC simulation, mini-bucket elimination, loopy belief propagation, generalized belief propagation, and variational methods.

2.2   Parameters Learning

The process of learning parameters in bayesian network is discussed in many papers. The goal of parameter learning is to find the most probable θ that explain the data. Let $D = \{D_1, D_2, ..., D_N\}$ be a training data where $D_l = \{x_1[l], x_2[l], ..., x_n[l]\}$ consists of instances of the bayesian network nodes. Parameter learning is quantified by the log-likelihood function denoted as $L_D(\theta)$. When the data are complete, we get the following equations:

$$L_D(\theta) = \log\{\prod_{i=1}^{N} P(x_1[l], x_2[l], ..., x_n[l]: \theta)\} \tag{3}$$

$$L_D(\theta) = \log\{\prod_{i=1}^{n} \prod_{l=1}^{N} P(x_i[l]|pa(x_i[l]): \theta)\} \tag{4}$$

The equation (3) and (4) are not applied where the training data is incomplete.

The task of learning parameters in the Bayesian network is of great importance today for their interest in decision-making. Approaches and applications that use Bayesian networks to attack more and more different areas in particular those based on the notion of uncertainty. This uncertainty is expressed by the conditional probability tables. The following paragraph gives a detailed definition of this table.

2.3   Conditional Probability Tables

A conditional probability table is a multidimensional vector denoted θ_i. This table contains the set of probabilities of the variable X_i for each of its possible values knowing each of the values taken by all of its parents $pa(X_i)$. Each component of the vector θ_i is expressed by the following equation.

$$\theta_{i,j,k} = P(X_i = x_k | pa(X_i = x_j))$$ (5)

The calculation of each θ_i in the Bayesian network was determined by the domain expert for the first applications of artificial intelligence tool. Nowadays, this mechanism is automatic and depends on the training set used. In this context, there are learning settings where data are complete or incomplete.

3   Learning Parameter with Complete Data

The learning base D is called complete if all variables in Bayesian networks are instantiated with their values. In this case, the calculation of conditional probability tables becomes easy. There are basically two categories in this case: the statistical approach and the Bayesian approach.

3.1   Statistical Approach

The statistical estimation is to determine the probability of an event by the frequency of occurrence of this event in the observation base D. The most common method in this context is the maximum likelihood is usually denoted by $L(\theta | D)$.

Consider the following data:

D learning data base, n nodes number, r_i the possible states of node,
q_i parent possible configurations of node,
X_i node, $pa(X_i)$ X_i node parent
$N_{i,j,k}$ evenment number in data base where X_i is in state x_k and its parents are in x_j configuration
$\Theta_{i,j,k}$ parameters where a variable X_i is in state x_k and its parents are in x_j configuration

The associated algorithm of maximum likelihood is based on the computing of the following probability :

$$P\left(X_i = x_k | pa(X_i = x_j)\right) = \theta_{i,j,k} = \frac{N_{i,j,k}}{\sum_k N_{i,j,k}}$$ (6)

3.2   Bayesian Approach

The Bayesian estimation is a straightforward application of Bayes rule. It consists in determining the posterior probability based on the a priori probability maintaining plausibility. This estimate is given by:

$$P(\theta | D) \propto P(D | \theta) * P(\theta)$$ (7)

There is also, in the Bayesian estimation, the frequency of occurrence of an event knowing his parents in the Bayesian network may be zero. But in reality this event may be encountered in real applications. The a priori probability in this case is multinomial. The combined distribution which keeps the same kind of prior distribution and the posterior distribution is the Dirichlet distribution which is given mathematically by:

$$p(\theta) = \prod_{i=1}^{n} \prod_{j=1}^{q_i} \prod_{k=1}^{r_i} \theta_{i,j,k}^{\alpha_{i,j,k}-1} \tag{8}$$

Where: $\alpha_{i,j,k}$ are the coefficients of the Dirichlet distribution associated with the prior rule : $P(X_i = x_k \mid pa(X_i) = x_j)$ where n is a random variable number, r_i is the possible states of node and q_i is the possible configurations of node parents.

One advantage of exponential distributions as the Dirichlet distribution is that it is possible to easily express the posterior distribution of parameters $P(\theta \mid D)$:

$$p(\theta|D) = \prod_{i=1}^{n} \prod_{j=1}^{q_i} \prod_{k=1}^{r_i} \theta_{i,j,k}^{N_{i,j,k}+\alpha_{i,j,k}-1} \tag{9}$$

The Bayesian approach called maximum a posteriori can deal with zero frequency using the Dirichlet coefficients. The operating principle of this approach is given by the following computing probability :

$$P\left(X_i = x_k \middle| pa\left(X_i = x_j\right)\right) = \theta_{i,j,k} = \frac{N_{i,j,k}+\alpha_{i,j,k}-1}{\sum_k N_{i,j,k}+\alpha_{i,j,k}-1}$$

These results are still possible if the data base of cases D has no element missing. In practice, having all variables instantiated is almost difficult to achieve. Hence the emergence of new algorithms for calculating conditional probabilities in the case of incomplete data. In the case where all variables are observed, the simplest method and most used is the statistical estimate. It estimats the probability of an event by the frequency of occurrence of the event in the database. This approach is called maximum likelihood (ML). The principle, somewhat different, of the Bayesian estimation is to find parameters most likely knowing that the data were observed. Using a Dirichlet distribution as a priori parameters which are written as:

$$p(\theta) \propto \prod_{i=1}^{n} \prod_{j=1}^{q_i} \prod_{k=1}^{r_i} \theta_{i,j,k}^{(\alpha_{i,j,k}-1)} \tag{10}$$

Where $\alpha_{i,j,k}$ are the parameters of the Dirichlet distribution associated with the prior distribution.

4   Learning Parameter with Incomplete Data

In the previous section, we presented approaches for estimating the conditional probability from complete data. In practice, this condition is not always assured. Indeed the absence of values is a rather frequent. This absence may be accidental or due to intensive removal. In a Bayesian network, the missing values can be divided by type into three categories:

- MCAR data: (Missing Completely At Random) The probability that data is missing does not depend on D. The lack of data is due entirely to chance.

- MAR data: (Missing At Random) The probability that data is missing depends on observed data. The lack of data is due to the presence of other values in some nodes.
- MNAR data: (Missing Not At Random) The probability that data is missing depends on both observed and missing data.

The resolution of data MCAR and MAR is easy to handle for the opportunity to correct the absence of such data in the training set, by cons MNAR data are sensitive to treatment because it is necessary to use external information for their manipulation. Several approaches to learning of parameters in Bayesian networks treat the case of missing data. We give in what follows an overview of some of these approaches.

4.1   EM Algorithm

Consideration of incomplete data is based on an iterative algorithm based on two steps: the expectation and maximization. The EM algorithm by Dempster wrote in 1977 estimated the parameters of a Bayesian network where the data base D is incomplete. A detailed description of this algorithm is given in [1] [13] [16] [7]. EM proceeds as follows: repeat the steps and hope to maximize the convergence. Each iteration guarantees the increase of a likelihood function that finally converges to a local maximum. The rapid convergence of this algorithm increases if the number of nodes with missing values decreases. This algorithm gives a better performance in four situations:

- Increasing the size of training data.
- Declining share of missing data.
- Increase the number of iterations.
- Using a priori information.

To tackle the complex problems, the EM algorithm has some extensions that improve one or two steps expectancy is maximization. Among these extensions, we quote:

- The GEM algorithm [1] was proposed by Dempster in 1977 which is a generalization of the EM algorithm to converge to a local maximum likelihood, it is not necessary to maximize each step but only simple improvement is sufficient.
- The EMC algorithm [9] The EM algorithm seeks to maximize the likelihood of the parameter θ, regardless of the classification made a posteriori using Bayes rule.
- The classification approach proposed by Govaert Celeux and in 1992 is to maximize, not the likelihood of the parameter, but directly completed likelihood.
- The SEM algorithm [8] To reduce the risk of falling into a local maximum likelihood Celeux Diebolt and in 1985 proposed to insert a step stochastic classification between stages E and M.

4.2   Robust Bayesian Estimator (RBE) Algorithm

The third algorithm is Robust Bayesian Estimator RBE [11]. It's composed of two steps Bound and Collapse. The first step consists of calculating a lower bound and an upper bound for each parameter in the bayesian network. The second step uses a convex combination to determine the value of $\theta_{i,j,k}$. RBE is considered a procedure that runs through all the data D recorded observations about the variables and then it allows to bound the conditional probability of a variable X_i. This procedure begins by identifying a virtual frequencies which help us to calculate the minimum and maximum number of observations that may have characteristics $X_i = x_k$ and pa $(X_i) = x_j$ in the database D. Virtual frequencies can be set to zero, which is called the Dirichlet distribution with parameters $\alpha_{i,j,k}$. A detailed example mentioned in [8] shows the use of these equations in calculating conditional probabilities by determining the minimum and maximum bounds of the interval. This phase of determining $min_{i,j,k}$ and $max_{i,j,k}$ depends only on the frequency of observed data in the database and virtual frequencies calculated by completing the records. The major advantage of this method is the independence of the distribution of missing data without trying to infer. To find the best parameters for this method, a second phase is necessary. It estimates the parameters using a convex combination from each distribution calculated for each given node. This convex combination can be determined either by external knowledge about the missing data, or by a dynamic estimate based on valid information in the database [6,7].

4.3   Gibbs Algorithm

The algorithm of Gibbs sampling (Geman, 1984) [15] is introduced by Heckerman. Gibbs sampling is described as a general method for probabilistic inference. It can be applied in all type of graphical models. Gibbs sampling generates a string of samples with accepting or rejecting some interesting points. In other words, Gibbs sampling consists in completing the sample by inferring the missing data from the available information. It's a method that converges slowly or has no solution if the number of hidden variables is very large. It's considered as a general method for probabilistic inference [15, 5]. This method is implemented for copying incomplete information and it is suggested for a large number of applications. Mr. In [11] authors have shown from their experimental results when missing data are MCAR or MAR type, the two EM algorithms and Gibbs sampling can use knowledge about the data to estimate tables of conditional probabilities, while the RBE algorithm can't in most cases give the same accuracy in the predictions correct. However, when missing data are MNAR, the three algorithms give false predictions for the learning mechanism of missing data. To reduce the disadvantages of EM algorithms and Gibbs sampling in learning settings, the incorporation of knowledge about the domain in the learning process is used. Its purpose, reducing the search space and escape local maxima. There are two basic approaches for incorporating knowledge. The first is to put constraints on the parameters and the second is to introduce qualitative influence between random variables

5   Some Approaches Dealing with Data Missing in Parameter Learning

In this section we present some examples of works dealing with parameter learning in Bayesian netwok in the case of missing data.

In [20] a method for estimating probabilities is presented which uses an entropy maximisation procedure to incorporate information regarding the nature of the missing data mechanism. If such information can be expressed by linear equalities of a nature elaborated below then explicit point estimates can usually be found. When data are missing at random the method is equivalent to a localised EM algorithm. The method appears to perform well for data missing at random but with considerable savings in computation time_ when compared to Gibbs sampling. In [21] the authors proposed a novel online learning method of Bayesian network parameters. It provides high flexibility through learning from incomplete data and provides high adaptability on environments through online learning. They have confirmed the performance of the proposed method through the comparison with Voting EM algorithm, which is an online parameter learning method proposed by Cohen, *et al*.

In [22] the authors consider the domain knowledge that constrains the values or relationships among subsets of parameters in a Bayesian network with known structure. They incorporate a wide variety of parameter constraints into learning procedures for Bayesian networks, by formulating this task as a constrained optimization problem. They present closed form solutions or fast iterative algorithms for estimating parameters subject to several specific classes of parameter constraints, including equalities and inequalities among parameters, constraints on individual parameters, and constraints on sums and ratios of parameters, for discrete and continuous variables. They're methods cover learning from both frequents and Bayesian points of view, from both complete and incomplete data. To validate the approach, they apply it to the domain of MRI brain image analysis.

In [23] the author presents a learning algorithm to incorporate domain knowledge into the learning to regularize the otherwise ill-posed problem, to limit the search space, and to avoid local optima. Specifically, the problem is formulated as a constrained optimization problem, where an objective function is defined as a combination of the likelihood function and penalty functions constructed from the qualitative domain knowledge. Then, a gradient-descent procedure is systematically integrated with the E-step and M-step of the EM algorithm, to estimate the parameters iteratively until it converges. The experiments show that algorithm improves the accuracy of the learned BN parameters significantly over the conventional EM algorithm.

In [24] the authors describe a new approach to unify constraints on parameters with training data to perform parameter estimation in Bayesian networks of known structure. The main contribution of this work is to allow an expert to specify her knowledge using *hard* constraints on estimations and *soft* constraints on priors, with no restrictions on the format of constraints besides convexity. As far as we know, no previous methods were able to handle such general situation. The idea can also be embedded into an iterative procedure to treat incomplete data, similar to the EM method. In [25] the authors present an iterative method to integrate qualitative constraints into two learning algorithms, APN and EM, by adding violation functions as a penalty term to the log likelihood function. They show that domain knowledge in the form of constraints can improve learning accuracy. In their experiments with synthetic data, this method yielded networks that satisfied the constraints almost perfectly. The accuracy of the learned networks was consistently superior to that of corresponding networks learned without constraints. However, this penalty-based method cannot guarantee to find the global maximum. In [26] the authors solve the learning problem by optimization techniques. They derive the closed form solutions with ML estimation for two kinds of constraints: inequalities between sums of parameters and upper bounds on sum of parameters within a CPT. They formalize the learning as a constraint optimization problem and derive closed form maximum likelihood parameter estimators There are two main limitations of their method: First, they assume one parameter can and only can have one constraint, and there is no overlap between parameters of different constraints. Second, their method cannot handle constraints from different CPTs. In [27] the authors have introduced the AI&M procedure for optimizing the likelihood, which provides an approach to learning from incomplete data under no assumptions on the coarsening mechanism. In the method AI&M (adjusting imputation and maximization) procedure the optimization is performed by operations in the space of data completions, rather than directly in the parameter space of the profile likelihood. Like EM, AI&M is a general algorithmic paradigm that can be instantiated over different types of probabilistic models. They have further proposed a particular instantiation of the AI&M procedure for learning parameters in Bayesian networks. Their results indicate that with AI&M one can obtain more accurate results than with EM when learning from non-mar data, especially in cases where our approximate implementation of the AI step does not introduce too large an error. That said, it must be born in mind that AI&M cannot overcome the fundamental problem that may have many global maxima, and the true parameter may not be identifiable. In [28] the authors propose an information-bottleneck EM (IB-EM) algorithm to learn the parameters of BNs with hidden nodes. They treat the learning problem as a tradeoff between two information-theoretic objectives, where the first one is to make the hidden nodes uninformative about the identity of specific instances, and the second one is to make the hidden variables informative about the observed attributes. However, although IB-EM has a better performance than the standard EM for some simple BNs, it is actually worse than EM for the complex hierarchical models. In order to limit the search space and escape from local maxima produced by executing EM algorithm, the authors present in [29] a learning parameter algorithm that is a fusion of EM and RBE algorithms. This algorithm incorporates the range of a parameter into the EM algorithm. The threshold EM algorithm is applied in brain tumor diagnosis and show some advantages and disadvantages over the EM algorithm

6   Conclusion

In recent years the use of probabilistic graphical models has been increasingly growing. The interest of these models lies in their understanding by laymen. In particular Bayesian networks are the most used models in this area. In addition, the problem of learning parameters and structure still retains an interest given its importance. This paper was interested in learning settings, especially in the case of missing data. Indeed, the lack of data is a very common phenomenon in practical problems. In addition to the algorithms EM, RBE and Gibbs sampling algorithms are still the most prevalent today. But hybridization of these presents in the future other learning techniques. For example, novel procedures can integrate with the E-step and M-step of the EM algorithm, to estimate the parameters iteratively until it converges.

References

1. Dempster, A.P., Laird, N.M., Rubin, D.B.: Maximum likelihood from incomplete data via the EM algorithm. Journal of the Royal Statistical Society, Series B 39, 1–38 (1977)
2. Feelders, A.D.: A new parameter learning method for bayesian network with qualitative influences. In: UAI, pp. 117–124 (2007)
3. Feelders, A.D., Van der Gaag, L.: Learning bayesian network parameters with prior knowledge about context-specific qualitative influences. In: Proceedings of the Twenty-First Conference Annual Conference on Uncertainty in Artificial Intelligence (UAI), pp. 193–200. AUAI Press, Arlington (2005)
4. Feelders, A.D.: Learning bayesian network under order constraints. In: Proceedings of the Twenty-First Conference Annual Conference on Uncertainty in Artificial Intelligence (UAI), pp. 37–53 (2006)
5. Yonghui, C.: Study of the case of learning bayesian network from incomplete data. In: International Conference on Information Management, Innovation Management and Industrial Engineering, ICIII, vol. 4, pp. 66–69 (December 2009)
6. de Campos, C.P.: Improving bayesian network parameter learning using constraints. In: International Conference on Pattern Recognition (ICPR), pp. 1–4 (2008)
7. Jensen, F.V., Lauritzen, S.L., Olesen, K.G.: Bayesian updating in recursive graphical models by local computations. Computational Statistical Quaterly 4, 269–282 (1990)
8. Celeux, G., Diebolt, J.: The SEM algorithm: a probabilistic teacher algorithm derived from the EM algorithm for the mixture problem. Comp. Statis. Quaterly 2, 73–82 (1985)
9. Celeux, G., Govaert, G.: A classification EM algorithm for clustering and two stochastic versions. Computational Statistics and Data Analysis 14(3), 315–332 (1992)
10. Ramoni, M., Sebastiani, P.: Robust Learning with Missing Data. Machine Learning 45, 147–170 (2001)
11. Ramoni, M., Sebastiani, P.: Robust Learning with Missing Data. Machine Learning 45, 147–170 (2001)
12. Friedman, N.: The Bayesian structural EM algorithm. In: Proceedings of the 14th Conference on Uncertainty in Artificial Intelligence (UAI), pp. 129–138. Morgan Kaufmann, San Francisco (1998)
13. Neal, R.M., Hinton, G.E.: A new view of the EM algorithm that justifies incremental, sparse and other variants. In: Learning in Graphical Models, pp. 355–368. Kluwer Academic Publishers (1998)

14. Niculescu, R.S., Mitchell, T.M.: Bayesian network learning with parameter constraints. Journal of Machine Learning Research 7, 1357–1383 (2006)
15. Geman, S., Geman, D.: Stochastic relaxation, Gibbs distributions, and the Bayesian restoration of images. IEEE Transactions on Pattern Analysis and Machine Intelligence (6), 721–741 (1984)
16. Lauritzen, S.L.: The EM algorithm for graphical association models with missing data. Computational Statistics and Data Analysis 19, 191–201 (1991)
17. Liao, W., Ji, Q.: Exploiting qualitative domain knowledge for learning bayesian network parameters with incomplete data. U.S. Army Research Office under grant number W911NF-06-1-0331 (2009)
18. Liao, W., Ji, Q.: Learning bayesian network parameters under incomplete data with domain knowledge. Pattern Recognition 42, 3046–3056 (2009)
19. Xiang, Y., Pant, B., Eisen, A., Beddoes, M.P., Poole, D.: Multiply sectioned Bayesian networks for neuromuscular diagnosis. In: PubMed., pp. 293–314 (1993)
20. Cowell, R.G., Dawid, A.P., Lauritzen, S.L., Spiegelhalter, D.J.: Bayesian Analysis in Probabilistic Networks. Springer (1999)
21. Lim, S., Cho, S.-B.: Online Learning of Bayesian Network Parameters with Incomplete Data (2004)
22. Niculescu, R.S., Mitchell, T.M.: Bayesian Network Learning with Parameter Constraints. Journal of Machine Learning Research 7, 1357–1383 (2006)
23. Liao, W.: Learning Bayesian Network Parameters Under Incomplete Data with Domain Knowledge (2007)
24. de Campos, C.P., Ji, Q.: Improving Bayesian Network Parameter Learning using Constraints. IEEE (2008)
25. Wittig, F., Jameson, A.: Exploiting qualitative knowledge in the learning of conditional probabilities of Bayesian networks. In: UAI, pp. 644–652 (2000)
26. Niculescu, R.S., Mitchell, T.M., Rao, R.B.: A theoretical framework for learning Bayesian networks with parameter inequality constraints. In: IJCAI (2007)
27. Jaeger, M.: The AI&M procedure for learning from incomplete data. In: Proceedings of the 22nd Conference on Uncertainty in Artificial Intelligence, pp. 225–232 (2006)
28. Elidan, G., Friedman, N.: The information bottleneck EM algorithm. In: Proceedings of the 19th Conference on Uncertainty in Artificial Intelligence, pp. 200–209 (2003)
29. Lamine, F.B., Kalti, K., Mahjoub, M.A.: The threshold EM algorithm for parameter learning in bayesian network with incomplete data. (IJACSA) International Journal of Advanced Computer Science and Applications 2(7), 86–90 (2011)
30. Mahjoub, M.A., Kalti, K.: Software Comparison Dealing with Bayesian Networks. In: Liu, D. (ed.) ISNN 2011, Part III. LNCS, vol. 6677, pp. 168–177. Springer, Heidelberg (2011)

Selective Ensemble Modeling Parameters of Mill Load Based on Shell Vibration Signal

Jian Tang[1,4], Li-Jie Zhao[2,4], Jia Long[3], Tian-you Chai[4], and Wen Yu[5]

[1] Unit 92941, PLA, Huludao, China
[2] College of Information Engineering,
Shenyang Institute of Chemical Technology, Shenyang, China
[3] Control Engineering of China, Northeastern University, Shenyang, China
[4] Research Center of Automation, Northeastern University, Shenyang, China
[5] Departamento de Control Automatico, CINVESTAV-IPN, Av.IPN 2508, México
{tjian001,jiajia0806-love}@126.com, zlj_lunlun@163.com,
tychai@mail.neu.edu.cn, yuw@ctrl.cinvestav.mx

Abstract. Load parameters inside the ball mill have direct relationships with the optimal operation of grinding process. This paper aims to develop a selective ensemble modeling approach to estimate these parameters. At first, the original vibration signal is decomposed into a number of intrinsic mode functions (IMFs) using empirical mode decomposition (EMD) adaptively. Then, frequency spectra of these IMFs are obtained via fast Fourier transform (FFT), and a serial of kernel partial least squares (KPLS) sub-models are constructed based on these frequency spectra. At last, the ensemble models are obtained by integrating the branch and band (BB) algorithm and the information entropy-based weighting algorithm. Experimental results based on a laboratory scale ball mill indicate that the propose approach not only has better prediction accuracy, but also can interpret the vibration signal more deeply.

Keywords: soft sensor, vibration frequency spectrum, empirical mode decomposition, selective ensemble modeling.

1   Introduction

The parameters of mill load (ML) inside the wet ball mill, such as mineral to ball volume ratio(MBVR), pulp density(PD), and charge volume ratio(CVR) have directly relationships with the grinding production rate (GPR) and the product quality of the grinding process [1]. Zeng et al constructed partial least square (PLS) and principle component regression (PCR) models between PD and characteristic frequency sub-bands based on the spectrum of the axis vibration and mill shell acoustical signals [2]. Shell vibration signal is more sensitive and less interference than the axis vibration and acoustic signals [3], which has been used to monitor the SAG mill [4]. Recently, a detailed experimental research was done on a laboratory scale ball mill, which shows that ML parameters have stronger relationships with the shell vibration frequency spectrum [5]. Based on the fact that shell vibration frequency spectrum can

J. Wang, G.G. Yen, and M.M. Polycarpou (Eds.): ISNN 2012, Part I, LNCS 7367, pp. 489–497, 2012.

be divided into low, medium, and high frequency bands evidently, a principal component analysis-support vector machines (PCA-SVM) approach was proposed [6]. However, principal components (PCs) don't take into account the correlations between the inputs and outputs [7].

Therefore, the vibration acceleration signal still cannot be decomposed and interpreted clearly. Empirical mode decomposition (EMD) was proposed by Huang [8], which has been widely used in the fault diagnosis [9]. Recently, bearing fault diagnosis method based on the EMD and the power spectral density (PSD) was proposed in [10]. More recently, an EMD, PSD, and PLS based approach was proposed to analyze the shell vibration signal [11]. However, the prediction performance is not satisfied. How to realize the nonlinear mapping and how to improve the modeling accuracy is still an open issue.

Zhou proposed a GASEN (Genetic Algorithm based Selective Ensemble) approach, which validated that ensembling many of the available neural networks can obtain better performance than ensembling all networks [12]. The problem of the selective ensemble can be considered as an optimal problem, and the objective is to maximize the prediction performance of the final ensemble model. Branch and bound (BB) algorithm is a powerful combinatorial optimization tool, and it and its variants have been successfully used to select the optimal features [13]. Based on the concept of information entropy, a weighting method was proposed [14].

Therefore, a novel selective modeling approach for modeling ML parameters based on EMD, FFT, kernel PLS (KPLS), BB, and weighting algorithm is proposed in this paper. At first, the original shell vibration signal is decomposed into a number of IMFs. Then, PSD of each IMF is obtained based on FFT technology, and KPLS based sub-models of different IMFs are constructed. At last, with the combination of BB and weighting algorithm, the optimal sub-models are selected to ensemble as the final soft sensor model.

2   Selective Ensemble Modeling Parameters of Mill Load

2.1   Strategy of Soft Sensor

The proposed soft sensor approach for ML parameters consists of data preprocessing module, sub-model module, and selective ensemble module, as shown in Fig. 1. The function of each module is shown as follows:

(1) Data preprocessing module: Decompose the original vibration signal and calculate the frequency spectrum of each IMF using EMD and FFT technology;
(2) Sub-model module: Construct ML parameters sub-models via KPLS algorithm;
(3) Selective ensemble module: Obtain the final soft sensor models by integrating combinational optimization algorithm and weighting algorithm.

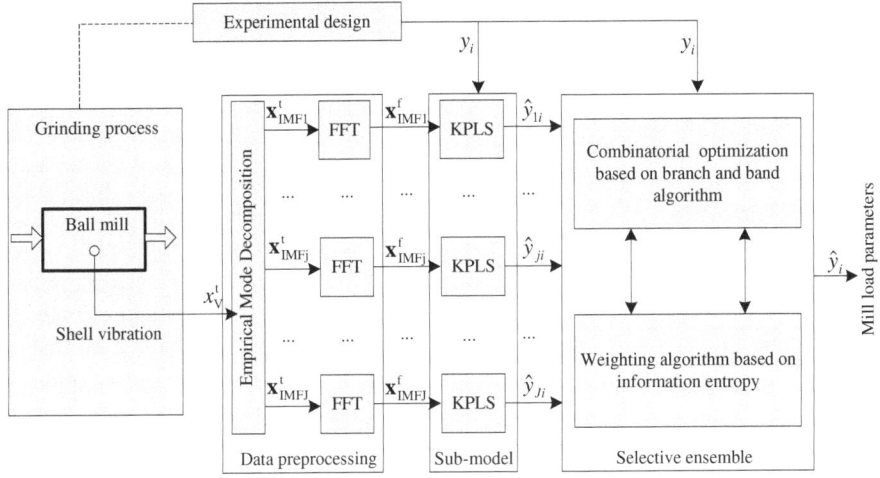

Fig. 1. Architecture of the selective ensemble modeling parameters of mill load

In Fig. 1, the superscirpt t and f represent the time and frequency domain signals respectively; the subscript V represents the shell vibration signal; $\mathbf{x}_V^t$ is the original time domain signal; $\mathbf{x}_{IMFj}^t$ and $\mathbf{x}_{IMFj}^f$ are the time and frequency domain signals of the jth IMF respectively; $j = 1, \cdots, J$, J is the number of the IMFs used to construct sub-models of ML parameters; $\hat{y}_{ji}$ is the output of ML parameters' sub-model; y_i and $\hat{y}_i$ are the real and estimate values of the final selective ensemble model; $i = 1, 2, 3$ represents MBVR, PD, and CVR respectively.

2.2   Data Preprocessing Module

The vibration signals of many rotational machinery devices satisfy the condition of EMD decomposition. The shell vibration signal of the ball mill are stable and periodic over a given time interval. Therefore, the shell vibration signal $\mathbf{x}_V^t$ can be decomposed into J_{all} IMFs plus a residue $r_{J_{all}}$ in this paper. These IMFs include different frequency bands from high to low. The residue can be either the mean trend or a constant. The following equation is gained:

$$\mathbf{x}_V^t = \sum_{j=1}^{J_{all}} \mathbf{x}_{IMFj}^t + r_{J_{all}} . \tag{1}$$

Although the IMFs of the shell vibration are different, the interested information for ML parameters still cannot be extracted effectively. However, evident features can be found in the frequency spectrum of each IMF. Therefore, the classic Welch's method is used to obtain the PSD of the first several IMFs respectively. Here, the frequency spectrum of the jth -IMF is denoted as $\mathbf{x}_{IMFj}^{f}$.

2.3   Sub-model Module

Modeling with the high dimensional frequency spectrum directly maybe lead to the "hushes phenomenon" and the "curse of dimensionality" problems. Using the latent variables of the input and output data to construct models, PLS algorithm realizes the dimension reduction and collinearity elimination simultaneously. However, it is a linear regression algorithm. Kernel PLS (KPLS) can solve this problem effectively [15]. Assume the number of the sample is k , frequency spectrum of the jth IMF is nonlinear mapped to a high dimension feature space, namely, the mapping is $\Phi : (\mathbf{x}_{IMFj}^{f})_{l} \rightarrow \Phi((\mathbf{x}_{IMFj}^{f})_{l})$; then, linear PLS algorithm is performed in this feature space; at last, the nonlinear model of the original input space is obtained.

To avoid the explicit nonlinear mapping, kernel trick $\mathbf{K}_{j} = ((\mathbf{x}_{IMFj}^{f})_{l})^{\mathrm{T}} \Phi((\mathbf{x}_{IMFj}^{f})_{m})$, $l, m = 1, 2, \cdots k$ is used. The kernel matrix of the jth IMF spectrum is centralized as the following equation:

$$\tilde{\mathbf{K}}_{j} = (\mathbf{I} - \frac{1}{k} 1_{k} 1_{k}^{\mathrm{T}}) \mathbf{K}_{j} (\mathbf{I} - \frac{1}{k} 1_{k} 1_{k}^{\mathrm{T}}) , \tag{2}$$

where, $\mathbf{I}$ is the unite matrix of k dimension; 1_{k} is a vector with value 1 and length k .

Based the nonlinear iterative partial least squares algorithm (NIPALS) and reproducing kernel Hilbert space (RKHS), the KPLS prediction output based on the training samples $\{(\mathbf{x}_{IMFj}^{f})_{l}\}_{l=1}^{k}$ can be represented as:

$$\hat{y}_{ij} = \Phi_{j} \mathbf{B}_{ij} = \tilde{\mathbf{K}}_{j} \mathbf{U}_{ij} (\mathbf{T}_{ij}^{\mathrm{T}} \tilde{\mathbf{K}}_{j} \mathbf{U}_{ij})^{-1} \mathbf{T}_{ij}^{\mathrm{T}} y_{i} . \tag{3}$$

The kernel matrix of the testing sample $\mathbf{K}_{\mathrm{test}, j}$ is scaled with:

$$\tilde{\mathbf{K}}_{\mathrm{test}, j} = (\mathbf{K}_{\mathrm{test}, j} \mathbf{I} - \frac{1}{k} 1_{kt} 1_{k}^{\mathrm{T}}) \mathbf{K}_{j} (\mathbf{I} - \frac{1}{k} 1_{k} 1_{k}^{\mathrm{T}}) , \tag{4}$$

where, $\mathbf{K}_{\mathrm{test}, j}$ is the kernel matrix of the testing samples; k_{t} is the number of the testing sample; 1_{kt} is a vector with value 1 and length k_{t} . The KPLS prediction output based on the testing samples can be represented as:

$$\hat{y}_{\mathrm{test}, ij} = \Phi_{\mathrm{test}, j} \mathbf{B}_{ij} = \tilde{\mathbf{K}}_{\mathrm{test}, j} \mathbf{U}_{ij} (\mathbf{T}_{ij}^{\mathrm{T}} \tilde{\mathbf{K}}_{ij} \mathbf{U}_{ij})^{-1} \mathbf{T}_{ij}^{\mathrm{T}} y_{i} , \tag{5}$$

2.4   Selective Ensemble Module

When the sub-models' weighting algorithm is determined, the selective ensemble modeling process is to select appreciate sub-models under the criterion of minimum prediction error of cross validation model. This can be considered as an optimal problem, denoted by the following equation: .

$$
\text{max} \quad J_{\text{obj(max)}} = \theta_{\text{th}} - \sqrt{\frac{1}{k}\sum_{l=1}^{k}(y_i^l - \sum_{j_{\text{sel}}=1}^{J_{\text{sel}}} w_{j_{\text{sel}}i}\,\hat{y}_{j_{\text{sel}}i}^l)^2} \quad , \tag{6}
$$

$$
s.t. \quad \sum_{j_{\text{sel}}=1}^{J_{\text{sel}}} w_{ij_{\text{sel}}} = 1, \quad 1 \le J_{\text{sel}} \le J
$$

where, θ_{th} is the thresh value, J_{sel} is the number of the selected sub-models and $\hat{y}_i^l$ is the estimate value of the final model , which is calculated with:

$$
\hat{y}_i^l = \sum_{j_{\text{sel}}=1}^{J_{\text{sel}}} w_{ij_{\text{sel}}}\,\hat{y}_{ij_{\text{sel}}}^l \quad , \tag{7}
$$

where $\sum_{j_{\text{sel}}=1}^{J_{\text{sel}}} w_{j_{\text{sel}}} = 1$, $w_{j_{\text{sel}}}$ is the weighting coefficients of the j_{sel}th sub-model. It is calculated based on the information entropy of the prediction error of cross validation model [14].

To select the optimal ensemble sub-models under the above criterion, only the enumeration algorithm and branch and bound (BB) algorithm can be used. Aiming to the low computing efficient of the enumeration algorithm, BB algorithm improves the searching efficiency by the branch and bound process. It and its variants have been used to select the optimal features successfully. Before using BB algorithm, the number of the selected sub-models needs to be known at first. Therefore, the optimal selective ensemble models are obtained by running the BB and weighting algorithm $(J-1)$ times. This process can be described as:

(1) Obtain the selective ensemble models with the number of the ensemble sub-models 1, 2, ... , $(J-1)$ respectively;
(2) Sort these ensemble models according to the prediction performance;
(3) Select the ensemble model with the best prediction performance as the final selective ensemble model.

3   Application Study

The experiments were performed on a laboratory scale ball mill, and the experimental details are described in [5]. After the original vibration signals are decomposed with EMD, the following parameters were used to calculate the PSD of each IMF: data length 32768, section number 32, and overlap fraction length 512. The time/frequency domain curves of these IMFs are shown in Figure.2~3.

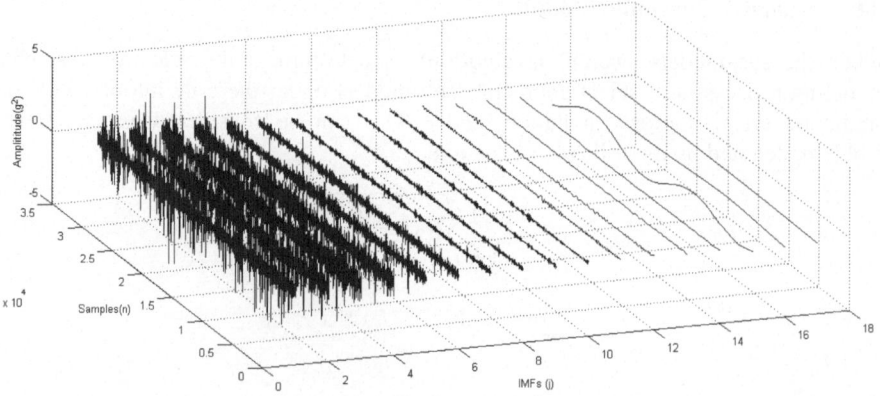

Fig. 2. Curves of IMFs for shell vibration signal

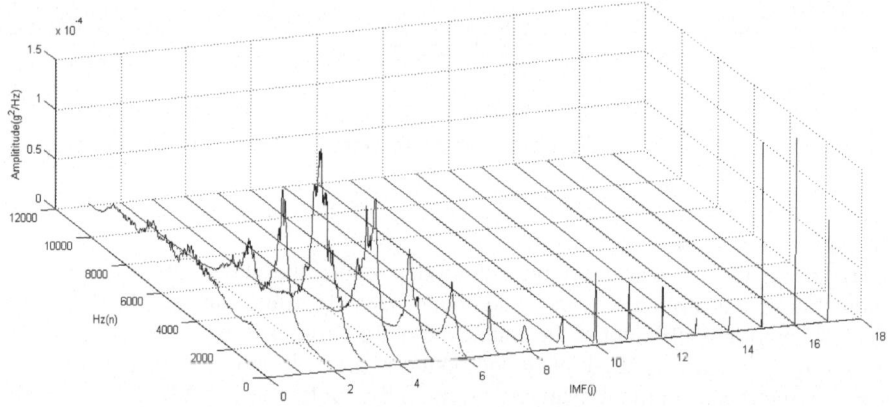

Fig. 3. Frequency spectrum curves of IMFs for shell vibration signal

The first IMF of the shell vibration signal has the minimum time scale, whose bandwidth is 2,000~12,000Hz. Its amplitude is the minimum one. Comparing with the PSD with only ball load in [5], it shows that the first IMF maybe is caused by the impaction among balls. The 16th IMF is a periodic signal with the largest amplitude, which is the low frequency disturbance produced by ball mill system itself. The bandwidth of the 2th IMF is mainly between 2000~6000Hz, whose amplitudes are ten times of the 1th IMF one, which is caused by the impaction of the balls.

Sub-models of ML parameters are carried out using 13 samples based the frequency spectrum of IMFs. The number of the latent variables of these sub-models is determined by the leave-one-out cross validation approach. Only the former 10 IMFs are used to construct the sub-models. The popular Gaussian kernel function is used. The prediction curves of the proposed approach (Weight sel ensemble), the best sub-model (Sub model best), and the fused all sub-models (Weight all ensemble) are shown in Fig.4~6. The statistical testing errors of the former 2 sub-models, the former 2 selective ensemble models, and the ensemble models are shown in Table 1.

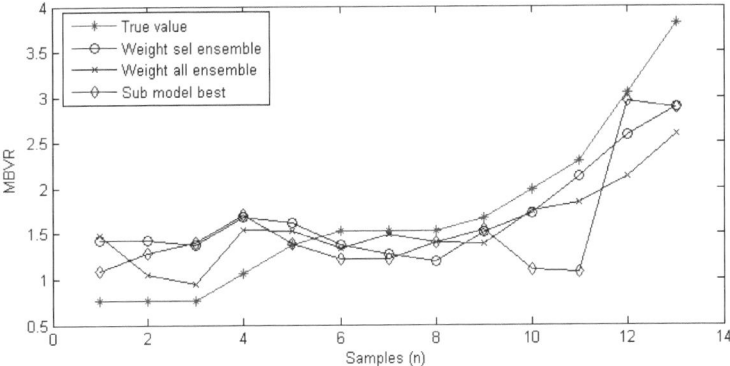

Fig. 4. Prediction results of the MBVR

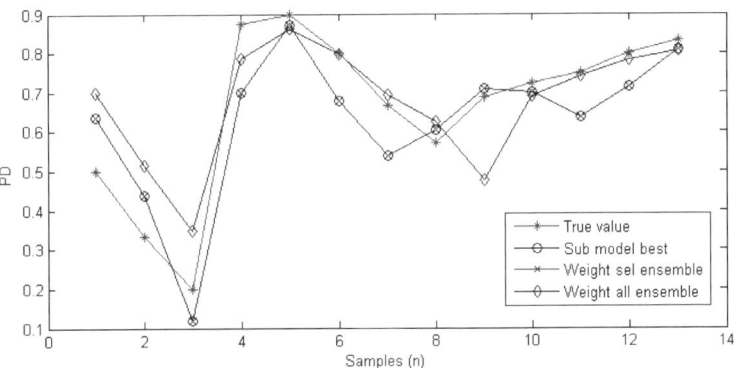

Fig. 5. Prediction results of the PD

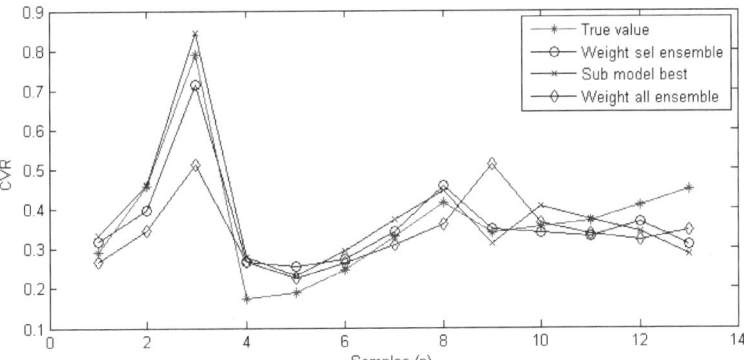

Fig. 6. Prediction results of the CVR

Table 1. Comparison of different soft sensor approaches

Approach	ML parameters		Sub models		Weight sel ensemble		Weight all ensemble
			1th	2th	1th	2th	ensemble
PLS-Based models	MBVR	RMSE	0.7376	0.7436	0.5601	0.7234	0.5601
		Sub_models	IMF9	IMF4	{all}	{9,4,1}	{all}
	PD	RMSE	0.1188	0.1361	0.1116	0.1156	0.1280
		Sub_models	IMF2	IMF6	{2,6}	{2,6,1}	{all}
	CVR	RMSE	0.07694	0.0830	0.07317	0.07694	0.1253
		Sub_models	IMF2	IMF1	{2,1}	{2}	{all}
KPLS-Based models	MBVR	RMSE	0.5905	0.5994	0.4864	0.4908	0.5287
		Sub_models	IMF2	IMF8	{2,8,1}	{2,8}	{all}
	PD	RMSE	0.09654	0.1215	0.09654	0.09884	0.1086
		Sub_models	IMF4	IMF2	{4}	{4,2}	{all}
	CVR	RMSE	0.06659	0.08041	0.06148	0.07383	0.1097
		Sub_models	IMF3	IMF2	{3,2}	{3,2,6}	{all}

Fig. 4~ Fig. 6 and Table 1 show that with KPLS algorithm, we obtain the best prediction performance for MBVR, PD, and CVR with sub-models {2,8,1}, {4} and {3,2} respectively. Table 2 shows that the frequency range of IMF4 is 100~4000Hz. With the analysis in [5], this range contains the nature vibration mode of the mill shell and the material, ball and water load, and the impact mode of the ball to mill shell. However, with PLS algorithm, the best prediction performance is obtained via ensemble the 2th and 6th IMF. The selective ensemble models based on KPLS also have better accuracy than PLS based models. It is shown that the KPLS can construct effective nonlinear model between the frequency spectrum and ML parameters. However, with the limited modeling samples and anomalous condition of the experiments, more experiment should be done to validate this approach.

4   Conclusions

A selective ensemble modeling approach for modeling the load parameters inside the ball mill based on EMD, FFT, KPLS, BB, and weighting algorithm is proposed in this paper. This approach solves the problems such as how to adaptively decompose the original vibration signal, how to extract the features of different IMFs, how to construct the nonlinear sub-models with frequency spectrum, and how to selective ensemble the sub-models effectively. A case study shows that the proposed approach is effective to analyze the shell vibration and model the ML parameters. However, more experiments should be done on the laboratory and industry ball mill to validate this approach further.

Acknowledgments. The work was supported by the Natural Science Foundation of China (No. 61020106003) and the National Science Foundation for Post-doctoral Scientists of china (No.20100471464).

References

1. Zhou, P., Chai, T.Y., Wang, H.: Intelligent Optimal-Setting Control for Grinding Circuits of Mineral Processing. IEEE Transactions on Automation Science and Engineering 6, 730–743 (2009)
2. Zeng, Y., Forssberg, E.: Monitoring Grinding Parameters by Vibration Signal Measurement-a Primary Application. Minerals Engineering 7, 495–501 (1994)
3. Gugel, K., Palcios, G., Ramirez, J., Parra, M.: Improving Ball Mill Control with Modern Tools Based on Digital Signal Processing (DSP) Technology. In: IEEE Cement Industry Technical Conference, pp. 311–318. IEEE Press, Dallas (2003)
4. Spencer, S.J., Campbell, J.J., Weller, K.R., Liu, Y.: Acoustic Emissions Monitoring of SAG Mill Performance. Intelligent Processing and Manufacturing of Materials 2, 936–946 (1999)
5. Tang, J., Zhao, L.J., Zhou, J.W., Yue, H., Chai, T.Y.: Experimental Analysis of Wet Mill Load Based on Vibration Signals of Laboratory-Scale Ball Mill Shell. Minerals Engineering 23, 720–730 (2010)
6. Tang, J., Zhao, L., Yu, W., Yue, H., Chai, T.: Soft Sensor Modeling of Ball Mill Load via Principal Component Analysis and Support Vector Machines. In: Zeng, Z., Wang, J. (eds.) Advances in Neural Network Research and Applications. Lecture Notes in Electrical Engineering, vol. 67, pp. 803–810. Springer, Heidelberg (2010)
7. Liu, J.L.: On-line Soft Sensor for Polyethylene Process with Multiple Production Grades. Control Engineering Practice 15, 769–778 (2007)
8. Huang, N.E., Shen, Z., Long, S.R.: The Empirical Mode Decomposition and the Hilbert Spectrum for Non-linear and Non Stationary Time Series Analysis. Proc. R. Soc. Lond. A. 454, 903–995 (1998)
9. McInerny, S.A., Dai, Y.: Basic Vibration Signal Processing for Bearing Fault Detection. IEEE Transactions on Education 46, 149–156 (2003)
10. Huang, P., Pan, Z.W., Qi, X.L., Lei, J.P.: Bearing Fault Diagnosis Based on EMD and PSD. In: Proceedings of the 8th World Congress on Intelligent Control and Automation, pp. 1300–1304. IEEE Press, Ji Nan (2010)
11. Tang, J., Zhao, L.J., Yue, H., Yu, W., Chai, T.Y.: Vibration Analysis Based on Empirical Mode Decomposition and Partial Least Square. Procedia Engineering 16, 646–652 (2011)
12. Zhou, Z.H., Wu, J., Tang, W.: Ensembling Neural Networks: Many Could be Better Than All. Artificial Intelligence 137, 239–263 (2002)
13. Narendra, P.M., Fukunaga, K.: A Branch and Bound Algorithm for Feature Subset Selection. IEEE Transactions on Computers C-26, 917–922 (1977)
14. Wang, C.S., Wu, M., Cao, W.H., He, Y.: Intelligent Integrated Modeling and Synthetic Optimization for Blending Process in Lead-Zinc Sintering. Acta Automatica Sinica 35, 605–612 (2009)
15. Rosipal, R., Trejo, L.J.: Kernel Partial Least Squares Regression in Reproducing Kernel Hilbert Space. Journal of Machine Learning Research 2, 97–123 (2002)

Selective Weight Update Rule for Hybrid Neural Network

Yoshitsugu Kakemoto[1] and Shinichi Nakasuka[2]

[1] JSOL Corp., 2-5-24, Harumi, Chuo-ku, Tokyo, Japan
[2] The University of Tokyo,7-3-1 Hongo, Bunkyo-ku, Tokyo, Japan

Abstract. VSF-Network,Vibration Synchronizing Function Network, is a hybrid neural network combining a chaos neural network with a hierarchical network. It is a neural network model which learns symbols. In this paper, the two theoretical backgrounds of VSF–Network are described. The first one is the incremental learning by CNN and the second background is ensemble learning. VSF-Network finds unknown parts of input data by comparing to learned pattern and it learns the unknown parts using unused part of the network. By the ensemble learning, the capability of VSF-network for recognizing combined patterns that are learned by every sub-network of VSF-network can be explained. Through the experiments, we show that VSF-network can recognize combined patterns only if it has learned parts of the patterns and show factors for affecting performance of the learning.

Index Terms: Ensemble Learning, Incremental learning, Chaos Neural network, Nonlinear Dynamics, Complex System.

1 Introduction

The purpose of our research is developing a model of symbol-generation with neural networks. We have reported our model and its performance in recent years[1,2]. In this paper, we show its backgrounds and the results of the experiments related to the backgrounds.

We human being perform cognitive operations for patterns abstracting data from our external environment and use them as symbol. Higher inference functions are the useful function for robots to work autonomously in external environment. Symbol is one of dominant background of the higher inference functions. We define the symbol-generation process as the process that a system abstracts input data and learns patterns considered as symbol.

Model of symbol-generation have been proposed in the past years. Inamura[3] has proposed a model of stochastic behavior recognition and symbol-generation. On the model, symbol is acquired through the following steps.

- Patterns are proto-symbols and they are acquired by abstracting input data.
- The relations among acquired proto-symbol are abstracted and maintained.

Not only the patterns abstracted from input data, relations among learned patterns also are key component of the process. In the field of semantics, many theories about symbol

J. Wang, G.G. Yen, and M.M. Polycarpou (Eds.): ISNN 2012, Part I, LNCS 7367, pp. 498–508, 2012.

have been also proposed. Chandler has proposed the model of the double articulation[4]. Semiotic codes have either single articulation, double articulation or non articulation. The double articulation enables a semiotic code to form an infinite number of meaningful combinations using a small number of low-level units.

The symbol generation has the following three steps.

1. At the first stage, patterns are learned by abstracting input data. The pattern is a prototype of a symbol or low-level units of symbol.
2. A combination of patterns is learned by refining learned low-level units or patterns.
3. The refined symbols and the combinations of them are maintained.

The key component of the process is incremental learning of patterns and the representation of pattern combination.

We have proposed VSF–Network for these process to learn symbols[5]. The network learns incrementally symbols by dividing itself into sub-networks. The sub-networks corresponds to a primary symbol, that is a proto-symbol. The ensemble of sub-networks represents relations among symbols.

In this paper, we describe basic framework of incremental learning of VSF–Network at the first. Followed by the section, we show our model of incremental learning using Chaos Neural Networks (CNN). Next, we show our consideration about the relation between function approximation by combining functions and ensemble learning Finally, we show the result and our consideration of experiments about basic performance of VSF–Network.

2 Incremental Learning and Pattern Recognition by CNN

2.1 Incremental Learning

For the neural network, the learning of symbol is an instance of incremental learning[6]. The reason for this that the neural network has to learn incrementally new patterns keeping learned patterns.

In the incremental learning by neural network, correlations among learned patterns take an important role for the learning. Lin[7] has proposed Negative Correlation Leaning model as a model of the incremental learning. If new patterns have no correlation with kept patterns, forgetting of kept patterns occurs. If a new pattern have some correlation with learned patterns, the forgetting of patterns dose not occurred but over learning occurs.

With VSF–Network, new patterns that have law correlation to learned patterns are learned by reusing a part of neurons in the neural network. VSF–Network learns patterns incrementally by dividing the network into sub-networks, if it has redundant neurons at the first step of incremental learning. Advantages of the learning comparing to the incremental learning by increasing neuron depending on are listed as follows.

- A learned neural network has redundant neurons. By these redundant neurons, an over-fitting for specific patterns is caused. With an increase in neurons, this problem is worsened.
- It is difficult to determine an appropriate number of neurons before learning.

2.2   Pattern Recognition by CNN

A candidate of reused neurons is the neurons that do not concern recognizing patterns. We apply CNN[8] for the identification of reused neurons. The i-th output x_i of CNN that has M-input neurons and N-chaotic neurons is determined by,

$$x_i(t+1) = f\left[\eta_i(t+1) + \zeta_i(t+1)\right] \tag{1}$$

In (1), diffusion term η_i and inhibitory term ζ_i are

$$\eta_i(t+1) = \sum_{j=1}^{N} w_{ij} \sum_{d=0}^{t} k_f^d x_j(t-d) \tag{2}$$

$$= k_n \eta_i(t) + \sum_{j=1}^{N} w_{ij} x_j(t) \tag{3}$$

$$\zeta_i(t+1) = -\alpha \sum_{d=0}^{t} k_r^d x_i(t-d) - \theta_i$$

$$= k_r \zeta_i(t+1) - \alpha x_i(t) - \theta(1-k_r)$$

In (2), w_{ij} is the connection weight between CN i and CN j. k_s, k_n and k_r is a parameter for the each term. α is the parameter and θ is the threshold for the inhibitory term. x_i is an output from an element i and the diffusion term η of CNN works as interactions on the CNN. This system is an instance of GCM[9], Globally Coupled Map. GCM is defined by (4) and it is a mapping on R^N ($N \geq 1$) that has two parameters a, ε[10].

$$F_{a,\varepsilon} : R^N \rightarrow R^N, x = (x_1, \cdots, x_N)^T \mapsto y = (y_1, \cdots, y_N)^T \tag{4}$$

$$y_i = (1-\varepsilon) g_a(x_i) + \frac{\varepsilon}{N} \sum_{j=1}^{N} g_a(x_j) \quad (1 \leq i \leq N) \tag{5}$$

For statuses of each element on a GCM, correlations among each element are defined by (6).

$$\lambda_{ij}(t) = \frac{1}{T} \sum_{n=t}^{t+T} C_n\left(\varepsilon^{spl}, g_i, g_j\right), \tag{6}$$

$$C_n\left(\varepsilon^{spl}, x_i, x_j\right) = H\left(\varepsilon^{spl} - |x_i - x_j|\right). \tag{7}$$

In (6), T is the time frame of retrieval by CNN, ε_{spl} is separation factor, g_i, g_j is status of each neuron i, j and H is Heaviside function.

Depending on the properties of CNN, we determine whether input data has unknown parts for memorized patterns. In the associative memory by CNN, we can find chaotic retrieval dynamics in addition to normal dynamics by associative memory[11]. The chaotic retrieval dynamics can be find when input pattern is a patchy pattern to stored patterns. This fact suggests that CNN can identify whether a pattern abstracted from input data matches a part of stored patter or not.

2.3   Capability of Function Approximation by Sub-Networks

Function approximation capability by neural networks has been researched from early of 90'. In these studies, The quantitative relation between number of units and the accuracy of approximation is discussed. The upper bound of the approximation error by layered neural network dose not depend on the dimension of inputs and it decreases according to the inverse number of hidden units [12,13,14] In these studies, unit is considered as basis function and target function is approximated by a combination of basis functions. Murata[15] proposed that the function approximation by multi-layered neural network is a combination of over-complete basis and discussed its approximation accuracy. We assume that inputs $x \in R^m$ are generated subject to probability density $\mu(x)$, and we can evaluate quantitatively the approximation accuracy of the with n hidden units in terms of the L^2-norm with repect to the probability density $\mu(x)$:

$$\|f_n(x) - f(x)\|^2_{L^2(R^m),\mu} = \int_{R^m} (f_n(x) - f(x))^2 \mu(x)\, dx.$$

For any arbitrary input distribution $\mu(x)$, the approximation error of bell-shaped three layered networks $f_n(x)$ can be bounded by:

$$\|f_n(x) - f(x)\|^2_{L^2(R^m),\mu} \leq C_T^2. \tag{8}$$

$$C_T = \int_{R^m} |\mathrm{Re}\, T(a,b)|\, dadb$$

Here, $T(a,b)$ is the transform of function f and it is

$$T(a,b) = \frac{1}{(2\pi)^m C_{\phi_d,\phi_c}} \int_{R^m} \overline{\phi_d(a \cdot x - b)} f(x)\, dx.$$

C_{ϕ_d,ϕ_c} is

$$C_{\phi_d,\phi_c} = \int_{R^m} \frac{\overline{\widehat{\phi_d}(w)}\, \widehat{\phi_c}(w)}{|w|^m}\, dw.$$

where $\overline{}$ denotes complex conjunction and $\widehat{}$ denotes the Fourier transform. The indexes d, c represent the decomposing and composing kernels of a bell-sharped function ϕ.

   A neural network is divided into the sub-networks with the selective weight update. The sub-network corresponds to proto-symbol. On our model, the combination of the symbols is represented by the ensemble of the sub-networks. The ensemble learning use multiple models to obtain better predictive performance than can be obtained from any of the constituent models[16]. If the sub-networks works as a weak learner, we can calculate an approximation of combination of proto-symbol by combining the sub-networks. From Eq.(8), we can conclude that a combination sub-networks $f_n, (i = 1, \cdots, n)$ approximates a function f less than certain errors C_T^2.

3   VSF-NETWORK

We have proposed VSF–Network[5,1]. VSF–Network is composed of BP–module that is a hierarchical network and CNN–module that is Chaos Neural Network. BP–module

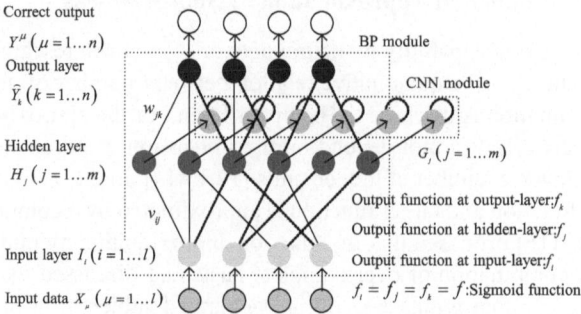

Fig. 1. An Overview of VSF-Network

is trained with the selective weight update rule. CNN–module finds known or unknown parts of an input data and an used part of hidden layer neurons of BP–module. In Fig.1, an overview of VSF–Network is shown.

3.1 Learning Procedure

VSF–Network works for the incremental learning only, so the learning of VSF–Network is assumed that the initial connection weights among layers have been learned before the its incremental learning. The learning of VSF–Network is performed as follows.

1. Data are provide to the input layer of BP–module.
2. The outputs of the hidden layer in BP–module are applied to CNN–module and they are used for the initial state of each neuron of CNN-module.
3. From the initial state, CNN–module performs the retrieval process based on the dynamics of (1) for times $t = 1, \cdots, T$. The consistent rates defined by (6) are calculated.
4. The rest process of the forward path on BP–Module is performed. The error $E_{k,\mu}$ between the output $\hat{Y}_k$ of BP-module and the target output Y^μ for the input data is calculated.
5. The connection weights among layers are updated based on the weight update rule defined by (9) and (10).

Because of variety of combination among symbol, the suitable weight set for the combination can not be settled before learning. In this case, the suitable weight is weights corresponding to the probability of patterns, hence we do not consider these factors.

3.2 Selecting Weights for Update

Based on the status on CNN, we can update weight in HNN selectively. Our policy for the weight updating is summarized as follows.

- For the neurons in the hidden layer, we keep the weights of neurons that show the synchronized behavior to other neurons.

– For the neurons in the hidden layer, we update the weights of neurons that show the unsynchronized behavior.

The delta rule for the HNN can be changed based on this selective weights update rule as follows. To emphasize the effects of CNN, we apply the correlations among weights by the term $cor_{ki,kj}$.

The weight update rule for the neuron j in hidden layer and the neuron i in input layer is defined as,

$$
\Delta W_{ij} = \begin{cases} \eta \frac{\partial E_{ij}}{\partial W_{ij}} & (\lambda_i \le P) \\ 0 & (\lambda_i > P) \end{cases},
$$
$$
\frac{\partial E_{ij}}{\partial W_{ij}} = \left(1.0 - |cor_{ki,kj}|\right)^{-1} \sum_{j=1}^{n} \frac{\partial E_{jk}}{\partial W_{jk}} f'\left(H_i^{\mu}\right).
$$
(9)

The update rule between neuron k in output layer and neuron j in hidden layer is also modified as,

$$
\Delta W_{jk} = \begin{cases} \eta \frac{\partial E_{jk}}{\partial W_{jk}} & (\lambda_i \le P) \\ 0 & (\lambda_i > P) \end{cases},
$$
$$
\frac{\partial E_{jk}}{\partial W_{jk}} = \left(\prod_{i=1}^{m}\left(1.0 - |cor_{ij}|\right)\right)^{-1} \sum_{j=1}^{n} E^{\mu} f'\left(O_k^{\mu}\right)
$$
(10)

In equations (9) and (10), the ΔW_{ij} is the delta value for the weight between the i-th input layer neuron and the j-th hidden layer neuron. ΔW_{jk} is the delta value for the weight between the j-th hidden layer neuron and the k-th output layer neuron. η is coefficient for update, E_{jk} is learning error, λ_i is degree of coincidence and P is the threshold for λ_i. $cor_{ki,kj}$ is Correlation between neuron ki and kj in hidden layer and H_i is Output from neuron i in the hidden layer.

4   Experiments and Discussion

Through two experiments, we examine capabilities of VSF–Network for the incremental learning. In this paper, we focus on two points of learning of VSF–Network. The first point is the basic capability of VSF-Network. The second point is correlations among input data. The correlation among input data concerns with the performances of the incremental learning as shown in the previous studies. A part of the incremental learning is finished before the incremental learning, if the learned data at the incremental learning phase have a correlation with the learned data at the preceding learning. We evaluate the effect of correlation among learning task for the incremental learning by VSF-Network.

4.1   Task for Experiment

The task for our experiments is learning of avoiding obstacles by a rover. It has the following three conditions of obstacle setting. We shows an overview of these conditions in Fig 2.

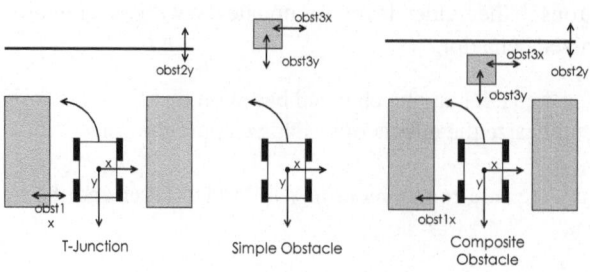

Fig. 2. Conditions of Task

- Condition 1: T-Junction obstacle
- Condition 2 : Combined obstacle
- Condition 3 : Simple obstacle

4.2   Experiment 1

The procedure and setting of the experiment are described as fellows.

- The initial step
    - The initial weight for BP–Module is learned by HNN using m records of from condition 1 of each task.
- The incremental learning step
    - We provide the patterns differ from the patterns that are assigned at the previous step. The input data is n records from the condition 2.
- The step for conforming learning performances.
    - We compare Mean Squired Error (MSE) of each trial of the incremental learning to show the effect of the learnings.
    - To confirm the combination form, the data combined the condition1 and condition 2 are used in this step.
- Number of learning
    - $m = 6000, n = 4000$

In the figure Fig.3, we show the changes of MSE with progress of of incremental learning for the task. For incremental learning of task1 and task2, the effect of VSF–network is observed in both tasks. VSF-Network learns new patterns incrementally and its weights are not destroyed. The combined patterns are learned without learning with the progress of incremental learning. After a certain number of incremental learning, MSE for every incremental learning reaches a equilibrium status. VSF–Network incrementally learns by reusing neurons which are considered as inconsequential neurons for identification of learned patterns. The incremental learning stops when redundant neuron is lost.

For the results of the task 1, we can find that MSE dose not show a major change comparing with the result of the task 2.

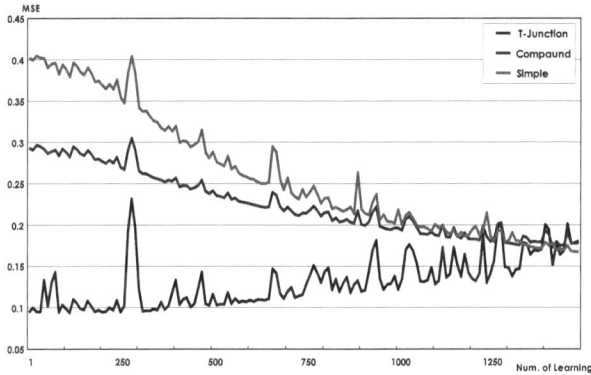

Fig. 3. Result of the Experiment 1

4.3 Experiment 2

By this experiment, we confirm the effects of the correlation between learned task and the task learned at the incremental learning phase. Using T-Junction obstacle, simple obstacle and combined obstacle data, we verify performances of VSF–Network.

To examine the correlations among data, we set up two kinds of incremental learning.

- Type 1: After the learning of T-Junction obstacle and simple obstacle, the network recognize combined obstacle.
- Type 2: After the learning of T-Junction obstacle and combined obstacle, the network recognize simple obstacle.

A correlation between T-Junction obstacle and simple obstacle is 0.34 and a correlation between T-Junction obstacle and combined obstacle is 0.68.

With the type 1 incremental learning and the type 2 incremental learning, we consider the effect of the correlation by applying following procedures.

- Setting initial weights
    - The initial weight between the input-hidden layer and the hidden-out layer for BP–Module is learned by HNN using 6000 records of the T-Junction.
- Incremental learning
    - At this step, we assign the patterns differ from the patterns that are assigned at the previous step. For the type 1 incremental learning, we apply the data of simple obstacle and apply the data of combined obstacle for the task 2. The number of records is 2000 for every incremental learning.

In the figure Fig.4, we show the progress of the type 2 incremental learning. The progress of the type 1 incremental learning is shown in the figure Fig.3.

The difference of these two results is the speed of the learning. For the task type 1, we can obtain the best result at $1,500$ trials, we can obtain the best result at $3,000$ trials for the task type 2. For the task type 1, we can obtain the best result at $1,500$ trials, we can obtain the best result at $3,000$ trials for the task type 2. The difference of the

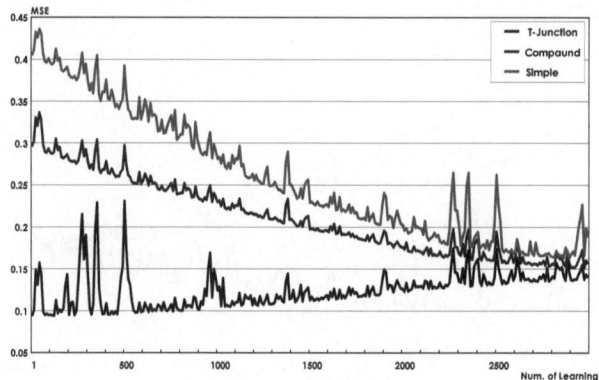

Fig. 4. Result of Experiment 2

learning speed is caused by the correlation between learning data in the initial learning phase and the incremental learning phase.

We also consider the relation between correlation among data and the learning speed based on the theory about information geometry[17]. VSF–Networks recognize the combination of proto-symbol by the combination of a number of sub-networks. On this experiment, an output from the network is

$$y = \sum_{i=1}^{n} \alpha^i h_i(x) \qquad (11)$$

With the combination of sub-networks $h_1(x), \ldots, h_n(x)$ weighted by α_i, the network identifies whether the output for an input is 1 or -1. Under the data set $\left\{(x_j, y_j)\right\}_{j=1}^{N}$ provided at the incremental learning phase, the propose of the learning by VSF-Network is the calculation of α_i that performs better.

Information geometrical interpretation of ensemble learning is described as follows[18] The ensemble learning is assumed to be a projection from a point in a space $\tilde{S}$ consisting of parameters of distribution functions of data sets to a point in the space of model m. We assume that model $M \subset \tilde{S}$ is a function of the exponential family. m-projection is specified because M is a e-flat sub-space in $\tilde{S}$. Because it is difficult to solve the projection, we replace it to the equivalent problem. The m–projection from the point for the data to M corresponds to a e–projection from a function $q_0(y|x) \in M$ to a model Q. The ensemble learning can be interpreted that it finally obtains the projection by calculating each points sequentially from the initial solution $q_0(y|x)$.

Let distributions $Q_1, Q_2 and Q_3$ are a subspace on space $\tilde{S}$ respectively. Under the condition, the correlations $R_{i,j}$ among data set i and j have a relation such that,

$$R_{13}(Q_1, Q_3) < R_{12}(Q_1, Q_2).$$

Let p_1, p_2, p_3 are e–projections on model $Q \subset S$ corresponding to each distribution and KL–divergence among each projection is $D^Q\left(p_i, p_j\right), (i, j = 1, \ldots, 3 \wedge i \neq j)$. Here,

$$D^Q(p_1, p_2) \leq D^Q(p_1, p_3)$$

We suppose a circle C_{13} on Q whose end points are p_1, p_3 and a circle C_{12} on Q whose end points are p_1, p_2 and $R_{12} \in R_{13}$. That is, Q_3 is not covered by the model form distribution Q_1, Q_2 and Q_2 is covered by the model form distribution Q_1, Q_3. This fact means that we have a relation,

$$E(Err(Q_1, Q_3)) \le E(Err(Q_1, Q_2))$$

between an expected error $E(Err(Q_1, Q_2))$ and an expected error $E(Err(Q_1, Q_3))$. The expected error $E(Err(Q_1, Q_2))$ is a mean error of recognition of Q_3 after the learning distributions Q_1, Q_2 and the expected error $E(Err(Q_1, Q_3))$ is a mean error of recognition of Q_2 after the learning distributions Q_1, Q_3. Hence, we can expect that a learning combination with low correlation data sets can reach the target model in fewer number of the learning if there is an expected model in the circle C_{13}.

5   Conclusion

In this paper, we show the theoretical backgrounds of VSF–Network. The background consists of two parts. The first background is incremental learning and CNN. VSF–Network can identify unknown parts of input data and a part of neurons for reusing based on a dynamics of CNN. It learns only unknown parts of input data.

Another background is ensemble learning. The ability of VSF–Network for recognizing combined patterns that are learned by every sub-network can be explained by the ensemble learning. Through the experiments, we show that VSF–Network can recognize the combined patterns only if it have learned parts of the patterns We show factors for affecting the incremental learning by VSF-Network.

The next step of our research concerns a detail consideration of the its dynamics. This points is related to the first background of VSF–Network and its capability for incremental learning.

References

1. Kakemoto, Y., Nakasuka, S.: Dynamics of Incremental Learning by VSF-Network. In: Alippi, C., Polycarpou, M., Panayiotou, C., Ellinas, G. (eds.) ICANN 2009. LNCS, vol. 5768, pp. 688–697. Springer, Heidelberg (2009)
2. Kakemoto, Y., Nakasuka, S.: Neural assembly generation by selective connection weight updating. In: Proc. IJCNN 2010 (2010)
3. Inamura, T., Tanie, H., Nakamura, Y.: Proto-symbol development and manipulation in the geometry of stochastic model for motion generation and recognition. Technical Report NC2003-65. IEICE (2003)
4. Chandler, D.: Semiotics for Beginners. Routledge (1995)
5. Kakemoto, Y., Nakasuka, S.: The learning and dynamics of vsf-network. In: Proc. of ISIC 2006 (2006)
6. Giraud-Carrier, C.: A note on the utility of incremental learning. AI Communications 13, 215–223 (2000)
7. Lin, M., Tang, K., Yao, X.: Incremental learning by negative correlation leaning. In: Proc. of IJCNN 2008 (2008)

8. Aihara, T., Tanabe, T., Toyoda, M.: Chaotic neural networks. Phys. Lett. 144A, 333–340 (1990)
9. Kaneko, K.: Chaotic but regular posi-nega switch among coded attractors by cluster size variation. Phys. Rev. Lett. 63, 219 (1989)
10. Komuro, M.: A mechanism of chaotic itinerancy in globally coupled maps. In: Dynamical Systems, NDDS 2002 (2002)
11. Uchiyama, S., Fujisaki, H.: Chaotic itinerancy in the oscillator neural network without lyapunov functions. Chaos 14, 699–706 (2004)
12. Jones, L.K.: A simple lemma on greedy approximation in hilbert space and convergence rates for projection pursuit regression and neural networktraining. Annals of Statistics 20(1), 608–613 (1992)
13. Barron, A.R.: Universal approximation bounds for superpositions of a sigmoidal function. IEEE Trans. Information Theory 39(3), 930–945 (1993)
14. Girosi, F., Anzellotti, G.: Convergence rates of approximation by translates. artificial intelligence laboratory technical report. Technical report, Massachusetts Institute of Technology (1992)
15. Murata, N.: Approximation bounds of three-layered neural networks – a theorem on an integral transform with ridge functions. Electronics and Communications in Japan 79(3), 23–33 (1996)
16. Opitz, D., Maclin, R.: Popular ensemble methods: An empirical study. Journal of Artificial Intelligence Research 11, 169–198 (1999)
17. Amari, S., Nagaoka, H.: Methods of Information Geometry. Oxford University Press (2007)
18. Akaho, S.: Information geometry in machine learning. Journal of the Society of Instrument and Control Engineers 44(5), 299–306 (2005)

Applying Ensemble Learning Techniques to ANFIS for Air Pollution Index Prediction in Macau

Kin Seng Lei and Feng Wan

Department of Electrical and Computer Engineering,
Faculty of Science and Technology, University of Macau,
Macau SAR, China
{ma76560,fwan}@umac.mo

Abstract. Nowadays, the conception on environmental protection is increasingly rising up and one of the critical environmental issues is the air pollution due to the rapidly growth of economy and population. Hence, a significant forecasting for the air pollution index (API) becomes important as it can act as the alarm for alerting our awareness in the air pollution issue. In this research, an architecture for ensembles of ANFIS (Adaptive Neuro-Fuzzy Inference System) is proposed for forecasting the Macau API and the performance of the proposed method is compared with the conventional ANFIS and the results is verified by the performance indexes, Root Mean Square Error (RMSE) and Average Percentage Error (APE), showing that a promising result can be achieved.

Keywords: API, ANFIS, Ensemble Learning, RMSE.

1   Introduction

The Macau Region, including the Macau Peninsula, Taipa Island and Coloane Island, is located south of Guangdong Province at the western bank of the Pearl River Estuary. It is neighboring to Gongpei of Zhuhai City, lying close to the South China Sea in the south. It is separated by a river from Wanchai of Zhuhai City in the west and faces Hong Kong in the east by the sea, with a distance of 42 nautical miles. Its total area covers 23.5 square kilometers. The population of Macau was rising up from 431,867 to 543,656 during the last decade while the Gross Domestic Product (GDP) was increasing from 6.1 billion MOP to 21.7 billion MOP. On the other words, the percentage growth of population and the GDP should be 20% and 350% respectively.

As a result of the dramatic growth of economy in Macau, air quality becomes a critical concern for us since the poor air quality has both chronic and serious effects on human health. The Macau Meteorological and Geophysical Bureau (SMG) was established at 1953 and started to monitor and report the last 24-hour air quality situation to the public in March of 1999 till now. In order to provide an easy understanding of air quality to the general public, the SMG used an Air Quality Index (AQI) system which classifies the air quality into six levels. The definition of the AQI

J. Wang, G.G. Yen, and M.M. Polycarpou (Eds.): ISNN 2012, Part I, LNCS 7367, pp. 509–516, 2012.

system presented in Macau is generally equivalent to the concept of the international API system.

The diffusion mechanism of air pollutants is very complicated and depends on several parameters, such as hydrocarbon (O_3), nitrogen dioxide (NO_2), suspended particulates (PM_{10}) and sulfur dioxides (SO_2), and so on. It is also strongly affected by both weather conditions (e.g. temperature, humidity, wind speed and direction.) and the presence of primary pollutants that react with each other. Therefore, it is hard to make a prediction for the API based on the traditional mathematical skills since its ill-defended and complicated structure. Thus many researchers have introduced lots of approaches to forecasting the API, and the most commonly used is Artificial Neural Network (ANN), which is a computational model based on biological neural network. ANN is generally trained by means of training data, and due to its generalization properties, hence it has been widely used for modeling and forecasting. Especially, it has been successfully applied in the field of air quality prediction in the past decade [1] [2]. From a different viewpoint, Takagi and Sugeno explored a systematical method to Fuzzy Inference [3]. It can apply the human knowledge and reasoning processes without employing precise quantitative analyses; however, there are still no standard methods existing for transforming the human knowledge or experience into the rule base of a fuzzy inference system. In addition, an effective method should be defined for fine tuning the membership functions so that the output error measure is minimized or a performance index is maximized.

In order to incorporate the concept of fuzzy logic into the neural network, Jang proposed another approach, that is, Adaptive Neuro-Fuzzy Inference System (ANFIS) [4], [5]. Generally speaking, ANFIS can be regarded as a basis for constructing a set of fuzzy if-then rules with appropriate membership functions which is based on the knowledge learning from the input/output data sets. Therefore, ANFIS combines the advantages of neural network and fuzzy logic: the neural networks have the better learning ability, parallel processing, adaptation, fault-tolerance and distributed knowledge representation, and the fuzzy logic techniques can deal with reasoning on a higher-level.

However, sample selection is a key concern as varies training data selection sometimes may not reflect the real distribution of the prediction model and the effectiveness of the prediction algorithm can not be assured. Therefore, how to choose a proper training data set is very important for time series prediction. In this paper, an ensemble structure is proposed as it comprises several Sub-ANFIS with different input selection so that the conclusion can be drawn by integrating the results of each ANFIS and the final result can be considered in a global view points. The proposed model is adopted for forecasting the Macau API and the simulating results compares with the signal ANFIS model via evaluating the performance index root mean square error (RMSE) against nine years measured data in the Macau city.

1.1   Paper Organization

In the next section, the basics theory of ANFIS and ensemble learning are addressed. Section 3 introduces the performance index for verifying the results obtained in this work. Section 4 performs the input selection for API issue. Section 5 discusses the results and the performance of the proposed model and finally, Section 6 draws out the conclusions of this paper.

2   Methodology Review

Previous researches revealed that it is inflexible to predict the air pollution index using traditional mathematical meteorological and dispersion models since it could only describe the relationship between pollutant emission, transmission and ambient air concentration of the air pollutant as a function of space and time, while the air quality could also be influenced by the condition of its neighboring region and numerous weather factors. Roughly speaking, all the related factors should be considered and addressed in the prediction model, which will be unfortunately a complicated non-linear function. As a result, many researchers suggested that the forecasting can be made by adopting the artificial intelligent techniques such as Artificial Neural Network (ANN), Fuzzy Inference System (FIS), and Adaptive Neuro-Fuzzy Inference System (ANFIS) because these methods have been verified that they are universal approximators. Among them, the ANFIS combines the advantages of ANN and FIS and therefore, this research focuses on the ANFIS model and the concept is discussed next.

2.1   Adaptive Neuro-fuzzy Inference System (ANFIS)

ANFIS can regard as a division of adaptive neural networks that are essentially equal to fuzzy inference systems. The basic structure of ANFIS can be expressed as a feedforward neural network with 5 layers:

Layer 1:   Every node i in this layer is an adaptive node with an appropriated membership function corresponds to the input to node i.

$$O_{1,i} = \mu_{A_i}(x) \tag{1}$$

Where x is the input to node i and A_i is a linguistic label associated with this node. $O_{1,i}$ is the membership grade which specifies the degree to which the given input satisfies the quantifier A_i. All the parameters in this layer are referred to as antecedent parameters.

Layer 2: Every node i in this layer is a fixed node whose output is the fire strengths of the rules. For instance:

$$O_{2,i} = w_i = \mu_{A_i}(x) \times \mu_B(y) \tag{2}$$

Layer 3: Every node i in this layer is a fixed node whose output is called normalized firing strength which represents the ratio of the ith rule's firing strength to the sum of all rules' firing strengths.

$$O_{3,i} = \overline{w}_i = \frac{w_i}{w_1 + w_2} \qquad (3)$$

Layer 4: Every node i in this layer is an adaptive node with node

$$O_{4,i} = \overline{w}_i f_i = \overline{w}_i (p_i x + q_i y + r_i) \qquad (4)$$

Where $\overline{w}_i$ is the output of the 3rd layer and (p_i, q_i, r_i) is the parameter set of this node. All the parameters in this layer are referred to as consequent parameters.

Layer 5: The singe node in this layer is a fixed node which computes the overall output as the summation of all incoming signals.

$$O_{5,i} = \sum_i \overline{w}_i f_i = \frac{\sum_i w_i f_i}{\sum_i w_i} \qquad (5)$$

Figure 1 illustrates a typical structure of the adaptive neuro-fuzzy inference system.

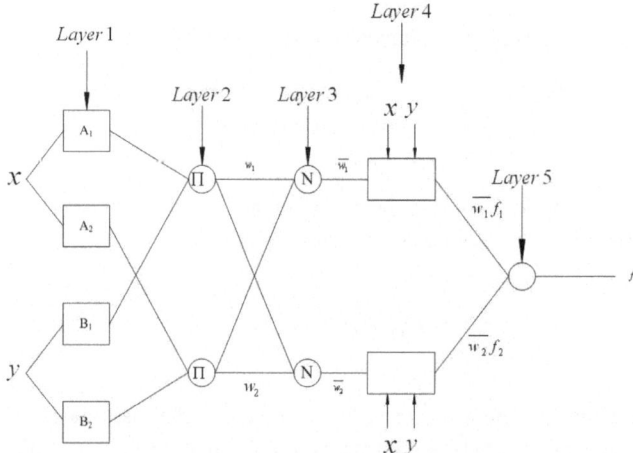

Fig. 1. General Structure for ANFIS

From the above ANFIS structure, it can be observed that the consequent parameters can be expressed as linear combinations if the values of the premise parameters were fixed. Such as

$$f = \overline{w}_i (p_i x + q_i y + r_i) = (\overline{w}_i x) p_i + (\overline{w}_i y) q_i + (\overline{w}_i) r_i \qquad (6)$$

In [4], Jang proposed a hybrid learning method which combines the gradient descent and least squares estimation. More specifically, these undefined linear parameters (p_i, q_i, r_i) can be identified by Least Squares Method where in the backward step the premise parameters are updated by gradient descent.

2.2   Ensemble learning

The general concept of ensemble learning is first proposed by Zhou where multiple component learners are trained for doing a same task. It has been widely used and successfully applied in different fields, including decision making, classification, medical diagnosis owing to its "global" characteristics. There are many methods to realize ensemble learning. In this paper, we use bootstrap sampling with replacement and random sample without replacement to construct the subsystems in the proposed ensemble system. [6]

   In Fig. 2, EN-ANFIS is constructed by five layers: input layers, sample layer, training layer, testing layer and output layer. In sample layer, each ANFIS (i) is trained by using random selected training data. Output (i) is the trained ANFIS (i). The testing data input to each Output (i) at the same time and the final out of EN-ANFIS is obtained by uniform weighting each outputs of all Sub-ANFIS units.

$$ENANFIS = \sum_{i=1}^{n} ANFIS_{i} / n \tag{7}$$

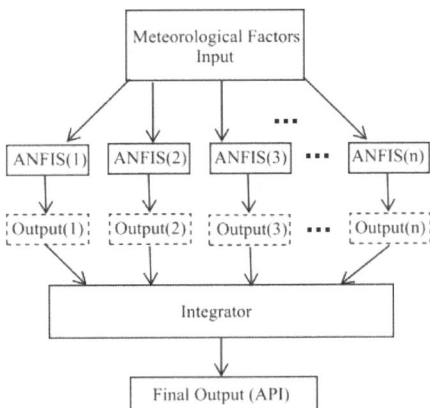

Fig. 2. The ensemble ANFIS structure

3   Performance Index

The root mean square error (RMSE) is employed as the performance index to check the predictive results of the proposed model.

$$RMSE = \sqrt{\frac{1}{N} \sum_{i=1}^{N} (a_i - p_i)^2}$$

(8)

Where a_i and p_i are the actual and predicted value of API on day i, N is the number of testing days.

4   Input Selection

The design inputs include the previous days' concentrations of particular matters (PM_{10}), sulphur dioxide (SO_2), nitrogen dioxide (NO_2), carbon monoxide (CO), and ozone (O_3), and for those are affecting to the API, also with some meteorological factors they are temperature, relative humidity, wind speed, solar radiation and pressure. Those daily record are provided by the Macau Meteorological and Geophysical Bureau (SMG) as 8-h average values and for the periods from 1994.4 to 2003.9.

5   Results and Discussion

From 1994.4 to 2003.9, we collected around 3400 data pairs. For conventional ANFIS, the first 3170 data sets are used for training while the others are used for testing. For EN-ANFIS, we only apply 30% of the training data that is 951 sets of data to each ANFIS unit. The training data using random sample are different but that of bootstrap have some repetitious data.

To ensure the same criteria for comparison, EN-ANFIS consists 8 ANFIS sub-units, all were trained by the hybrid-learning technique with the desired error 0.001 and employed the gaussmf as the membership function from considering the statistical aspect of prediction model.

Table 1. shows the mapping between the data accumulated over the past years for training and testing the API of the following year against the performances of EN-ANFIS, allANFIS and ANFIS units.

Table 1. Use of yearly progressively training sets and related performances

		RMSE	Training Time (s)	Number of Training data sets
Bootstrap sampling	ANFISmin	12.5271	11.54	951
	ANFISmax	13.7214	13.02	951
	ANFISmean	12.8312	12.21	951
Random sampling	ANFISmin	12.3897	12.08	951
	ANFISmax	14.2168	12.97	951
	ANFISmean	13.2011	12.55	951
EN-ANFIS (Bootstrap)		12.2351	12.78	951
EN-ANFIS (Random)		12.2072	12.79	951
allANFIS		12.0315	38.91	3400

Referring to Table.1., we can easily note that the prediction results of EN-ANFIS is always better than any ANFIS units whatever using different sampling technologies. On the other hand, the prediction accuracy of EN-ANFIS is almost similar to allANFIS. However, we can see that a significant improvement in the training time and number of training data adopting where EN-ANFIS consumes much less time and uses less training data pairs.

From the above discussion and analysis, we find that the EN-ANFIS shows an outstanding performance than any ANFIS units and the ensemble of each ANFIS units can achieve a similar performance with allANFIS. To reinforce this conclusion, the predicted API values and the actual API values is given in Fig. 3.

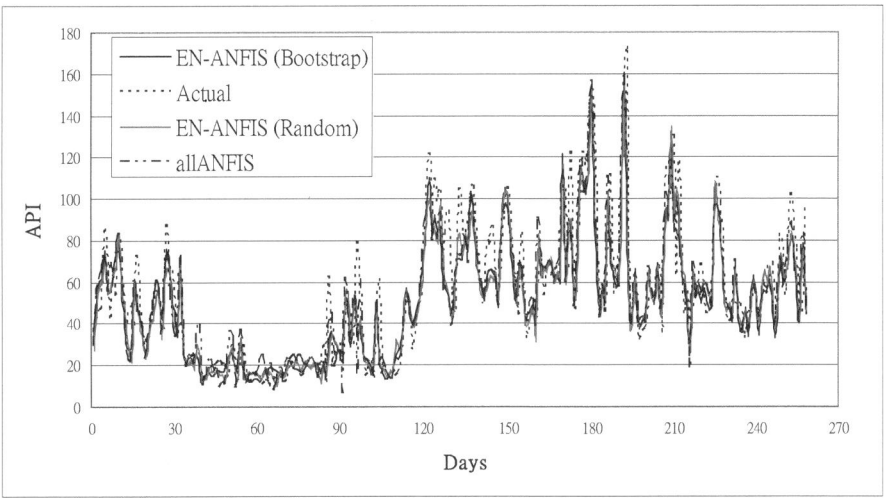

Fig. 3. The predicted and actual values of API during the testing stage

6   Conclusion

Ensemble learning incorporating with ANFIS is introduced in this paper for forecasting the API in Macau by adopting the daily metrological data sets measured from 1994.4 to 2002.12. The experimental results show that the proposed EN-ANFIS structure can not only perform much better than any ANFIS units but also can obtain an equivalent performance while comparing with the conventional ANFIS. However, EN-ANFIS is possible to use less training data sets and consumes less training time. It is proved that the proposed hybrid approach has great ability in handling the nonlinear problem and complex phenomena.

References

1. Boznar, M., Lesjack, M., Mlakar, P.: A neural network based method for short-term predictions of ambient SO2 concentrations in highly polluted industrial areas of complex Terrain. Atmospheric Environment 270B (2), 221–230 (1993)
2. Mok, K.M., Tam, S.C., Yan, P., Lam, L.H.: A neural network forecasting system for daily air quality index in Macau. In: Air Pollution VII, C.A (2000)
3. Takagi, T., Sugeno, M.: Fuzzy identification of systems and its applications to modeling and control. IEEE Trans. Syst., Man, Cybern. 15, 116–132 (1985)
4. Jang, J.S.: ANFIS: Adaptive-Network-Based Fuzzy Inference System. IEEE Trans. Syst., Man, Cybern. 23, 665–683 (1993)
5. Jang, J.–S.R.: Neuro-fuzzy and soft computing a computational approach to learning and machine intelligence, pp. 335–422. Prentice Hall, Upper Saddle River (1997)
6. Zhou, Z.H., Wu, J., Tang, W.: Ensembling neural networks: Many could be better than all. Artificial Intelligence 137(1-2), 239–263 (2002)
7. Wang, C., Zhang, J.P.: Time series prediction based on ensemble ANFIS. In: Proceedings of the Fourth International Conference on Machine Learning and Cybernetics, Guangzhou, August 18-21 (2005)
8. Talebizadeh, M., Moridnejad, A.: Uncertainty analysis for the forecast of lake level fluctuations using ensembles of ANN and ANFIS models. Expert Systems with Applications 38 (2011)

A PSO-SVM Based Model for Alpha Particle Activity Prediction Inside Decommissioned Channels

Mingzhe Liu[1,2,*], Xianguo Tuo[1,2], Jun Ren[2], Zhe Li[2], Lei Wang[2], and Jianbo Yang[2]

[1] State Key Laboratory of Geohazard Prevention and Geoenvironment Protection,
Chengdu University of Technology, Chengdu 610059, China
[2] College of Nuclear Technology and Automation Engineering,
Chengdu University of Technology, Chengdu 610059, China
`liumz@cdut.edu.cn`

Abstract. This paper presents a hybrid Support Vector Machine (SVM) and Particle Swarm Optimization (PSO) model for predicting alpha particles emitting contamination on the internal surfaces of decommissioned channels. Six measuring parameters (channel diameter, channel length, distance to radioactive source, radioactive strength, wind speed and flux) and one ionizing value have been obtained via experiments. These parameters show complex linear and nonlinear relationships to measuring results. The model used PSO to optimize SVM parameters. The comparison of computational results of the hybrid approach with normal BP networks confirms its clear advantage for dealing with this complex nonlinear prediction.

Keywords: Particle swarm optimization, support vector machine, alpha particles, radioactivity prediction.

1 Introduction

With the rapid development of nuclear industry over the last 50 years, nuclear decommissioning has become the hot topic within the industry worldwide. Most nuclear facility dismantling is involved in contaminated channel disassembling. Recently, a Long Range Alpha Detector (LRAD) technique has been used to measure alpha particles emitting contamination inside channels [1]-[7]. Normally, a LRAD measurement depends on six parameters, i.e., channel diameter, channel length, distance to radioactive source, radioactive source strength, wind speed and flux, except for the accuracy of the instrument itself. Our statistical analysis to LRAD experimental results has shown that distance to radioactive source and radioactive source strength have linear relationships to alpha activity while the rest parameters nonlinearly correspond to alpha activity. That is, there is a complex relationship between the parameter space and measuring results. Therefore, a nonlinear method should be used to deal

---

[*] Corresponding author.

J. Wang, G.G. Yen, and M.M. Polycarpou (Eds.): ISNN 2012, Part I, LNCS 7367, pp. 517–523, 2012.

with the uncertainty correction. To our best knowledge, this issue has been little studied using a hybrid method considering both linear and nonlinear characteristics so far. This paper presented a hybrid optimization algorithm to predict alpha particle activity by integrating support vector machines (SVM) with Particle Swarm Optimization (PSO).

SVM is a new machine learning tool and powerful to approximate any training data and generalizes better on given datasets [8]. Applying the SVM approach to a particular practical problem needs considering a number of questions based on the problem definition and the design involved in it. One of the major challenges is how to choose an appropriate kernel for the given application. Once the choice of kernel and optimization criterion has been made the key components of the system are in place [8]. There are many standard choices such as a Gaussian or polynomial kernel proposed in the literature, however if these prove ineffective for the special problem, other approaches seeking for good kernel functions will be taken into account.

In the usage of SVM, it is found that how to set the adjustment parameters c and kernel parameter g of SVM is a key issue since both two parameters play an important role to the algorithm performance [9]. Currently it still lacks a paradigmatic approach to guide how to choose two parameters. Some researchers proposed to use the gradient descent method to choose the SVM parameters [10]. However, this is restricted by the feature of core function being guided, and the search process is easily to fall into local minimum [11]. Some scholars also experimented with immune algorithm to optimize the parameters of SVM in order to reduce the blindness of parameter selection and to improve the prediction accuracy of SVM [12], but this method is more complex if realized. It is also suggested to use genetic algorithms to determine the SVM parameters [13], but it needs the manipulation of selection, crossover and mutation.

Particle Swarm Optimization (PSO) is a stochastic optimization algorithm on the basis of swarm intelligence [14]. Similarly with genetic algorithm, PSO is also a population-based random search optimization tools, differently, it is a process of the particles in the solution space following the optimal one to search. Therefore, the remarkable merits of PSO consist of parallel processing features, robust, simple and easy implementation, high computational efficiency, and a larger probability to find the best answer of overall situation of the optimizing problem. In this paper, we use PSO to optimize the SVM selection of parameters, and apply it to quantitative prediction of the alpha particle activity.

2   The Hybrid PSO-SVM Model

2.1   Particle Swarm Optimization Algorithm

As mentioned above, PSO is another optimum algorithm in the field of compute intelligent, which is also based on swarm intelligence. The algorithm was first proposed by Kennedy and Eberhart in 1995, and is a global optimization evolutionary algorithm [14-16]. Its basic concepts derived from the study of birds' predatory behavior. When birds are praying, the simplest and most effective way is to search the nearest distance between them and the food. PSO algorithm firstly initializes a group of particles in resoluble space, and each particle represents a potential optimum relation of set-valued optimization problem. By the three indexes: position, speed and fitness value, the particle characteristics are indicated. The fitness value comes from the calculation of fitness function whose value represents the quality of particles. Particles moves in the resoluble space and by tracking personal best and group best, they update individual positions to constantly correct the direction and governing speed so as to form positive feedback mechanism of group optimization. Personal best is optimal position of fitness value calculated by individual in experienced position. Group best is optimal position of fitness value searched by group.

For the Updated position of each particle every time, we calculate a fitness value to update the position of Pbest for personal best and Gbest for group best by comparing the fitness value of new particles; the fitness values of the individual extremum and groups extremum. And based on the different fitness of each particle to the environment, the individual will be gradually moved to the best range. Eventually, the optimal solution can be found [10].

Suppose there are n particles to form a community in a D-dimensional target search space, the position of the ith particle at time "t" is expressed as a D-dimensional vector

$$x_i = (x_{i1}(t), x_{i2}(t), \cdots, x_{iD}(t)), i = 1, 2, \cdots, n \qquad (1)$$

Meanwhile, the position of the ith particle in the D-dimensional search space also represents a potential solution to the problem. According to the objective function, the corresponding fitness value of position xi for each particle can be calculated and according to the size of the fitness value, the pros and cons of xi are measured. The "flying" velocity of the ith particle is also a D-dimensional vector, denoted by

$$v_i(t) = (v_{i1}(t), v_{i2}(t), \cdots, v_{iD}(t)), i = 1, 2, \cdots, n \qquad (2)$$

When the PSO algorithm is started, the first step is a random initialization of n particles' position and velocity; then, the second one is to find the optimal solution by iteration. In each iteration, by tracking two extremums (Pbest and Gbest), the particles update their speed and position. The optimal location of the ith particle has been searched and denoted as follows

$$p_i(t) = (p_{i1}(t), p_{i2}(t), \cdots, p_{iD}(t)) \qquad (3)$$

The whole particle swarm's best position has been found as follows

$$p_g(t) = (p_{g1}(t), p_{g2}(t), \cdots, p_{gD}(t)) \qquad (4)$$

In the (t+1)th iteration calculation, the particles update their velocity and position based on the Pbest and Gbest by the following update formula

$$v_{id}(t+1) = wv_{id}(t) + c_1 r_1(p_{id}(t) - x_{id}(t)) + c_2 r_2(p_{gd}(t) - x_{id}(t)) \qquad (5)$$

$$x_{id}(t+1) = x_{id}(t) + v_{id}(t+1) \qquad (6)$$

In the formula, w is inertia weight; v_{id} is the velocity of a particle; c_1 and c_2 are non-negative constants and called acceleration factors; r_1 and r_2 are random numbers distributed in the range of [0, 1]. To prevent particles from the blind search, it is generally recommended to confine their position and speed in ranges of $[-x_{max}, x_{max}]$ and $[-v_{max}, v_{max}]$. Let $f(x)$ the minimal target function (i.e., CV-MSE function), and then the current best position of the ith particle is determined by the formula below

$$p_{id}(t+1) = \begin{cases} p_{id}(t) & \text{if } f(x_{id}(t+1)) \geq f(p_{id}(t)) \\ x_{id}(t+1) & \text{if } f(x_{id}(t+1)) < f(p_{id}(t)) \end{cases} \tag{7}$$

The best position $p_g(t)$ experienced by all particles in the groups is called the global best position.   It can be written as follows

$$\begin{aligned} p_g(t) &\in \{p_1(t), p_2(t), \cdots p_m(t) \mid f(p_g(t))\} \\ &= \min\{f(p_1(t)), f(p_2(t)), \cdots, f(p_m(t))\} \end{aligned} \tag{8}$$

2.2   The SVM Parameter Optimization Process on PSO

SVM algorithm has two key parameters c and g, which have a great impact on the performance of prediction models; however, it is normally difficult to determine the appropriate values of c and g in advance. Since PSO has a strong global search capability, this paper explored the best one for SVM algorithm parameters c and g based on PSO algorithm. This hybrid algorithm can be written as follows:

1) Generate the particles and initialize the particle velocity by SVM;
2) Calculate particle fitness and search for Pbest and Gbest;

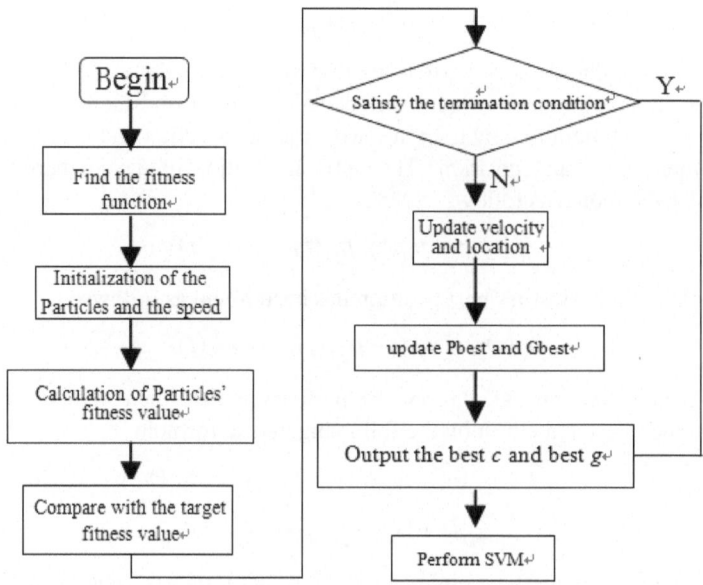

Fig. 1. A flow chart of the proposed hybrid model

3) Update particles' velocity and position, and calculate the particle fitness;

4) Update Pbest and Gbest;

5) According to 2), 3), 4), if the maximum number of iterations is reached or the mean square error gets to the initial set value, then we may end the particle search and output the particle positions. Otherwise go to 3) and repeat the iterative optimization. From the above mentioned steps, the best c and g can be obtained, and then SVM is performed for prediction. A flow chart of the proposed hybrid model is shown in Figure 1.

3   Computational Results and Analysis

According to literature investigation and actual situations, we determined six measuring factors, that is, channel diameter, channel length, distance to radioactive source, radioactivity strength, wind speed and flux, and the corresponding measuring result was alpha particle ionizing value which can directly reflect the degree of alpha particle contamination. Thus, the system includes 6 inputs and 1 output. 600 sampling data are collected, which 500 samples are used for model training, 50 samples for model testing and 50 samples for prediction.

Figure 2 shows the training and prediction results of 600 samples. The training results of the first 100 samples are illustrated; see the left picture of Figure 2. It can be seen that the model has a good fitness and prediction ability with some deviations from the measuring values. We checked the results carefully and found that most of those deviations occur at data change points, which indicates that the proposed model is not good at dealing with sharp data change. A future work will focus on improving prediction at extreme values. Figure 3 shows the relative errors between measuring and computational values. One can see that most of relative errors fall in [-0.03, 0.03] which is satisfied for prediction requirements. The right picture of Figure 3 also shows the fine selection of parameters and MSE values. Using the proposed model, we can roughly depict the picture of total alpha particle activity inside a contaminated channel.

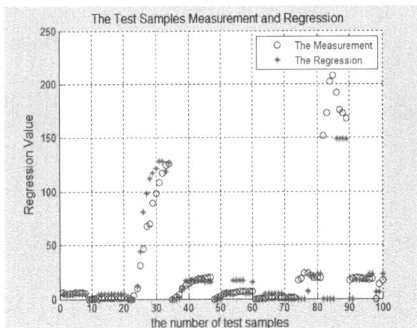 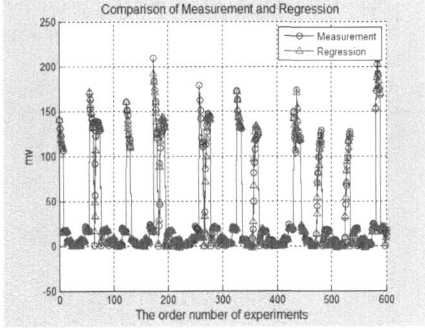

Fig. 1. Comparison between measurement and prediction results of 100 (left) and 600 (right) samples, respectively

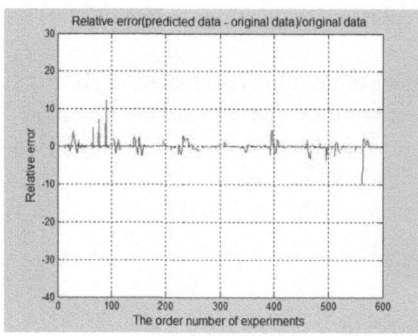 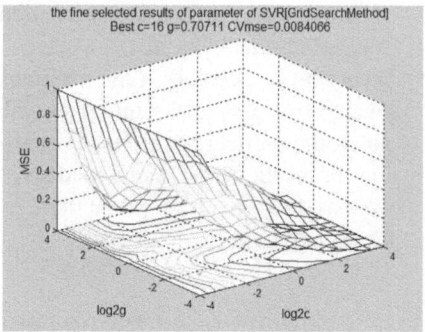

Fig. 2. (left) Relative prediction errors of 600 samples, and (right) MSE and parameter selection results

4   Conclusion

This paper introduced a hybrid PSO and SVM model to predict alpha particles activity inside decommissioned channels for nuclear waste disposal. The proposed model integrates linear and nonlinear regression models. The computational results indicate that the ensemble model can be used as an alternative solution for alpha particle activity correction. Once the six parameters are determined, the proposed model may give an approximate output, thus, an integrated picture of alpha particle activity inside contaminated channels can be obtained. However, the model cannot exactly predict extreme values in a certain degree which would be improved in the future work.

Acknowledgments. This work was supported by NSFC (Grant No. 41025015), SKLGP (Grant No. SKLGP2011Z006) and CDUT (Grant Nos. HY0084, HG0092).

References

1. MacArthur, D.W., Allander, K.S., Bounds, J.A., Butterfield, K.B.: Small Long-Range Alpha Detector(LRAD) with Computer Readout. Los Alamos National Laboratory publication LA- 12199-MS (1991)
2. MacArthur, D.W., Allander, K.S.: Long-Range Alpha Detectors. Los Alamos National Laboratory publication LA-12073-MS (1991)
3. MacArthur, D.W.: Long-range alpha detector (LRAD), LA-UR-91-3398 (1991)
4. MacArthur, D.W.: Long-range alpha detector for contamination monitoring, LA-UR-91-3396 (1991)
5. Bolton, R.D.: Radon Monitoring Using Long-Range Alpha Detector-Based Technology, LA-UR-94-3637 (1994)
6. Cheng, Y., Tuo, X.G., Huang, L.M., Li, Z., Yang, J.B., Zhou, C.W., Song, Q.Q.: Measuring energy loss of alpha particles in different vacuum conditions. Nuclear and Techniques 22 (2011)

7. Rawool-Sullivan, M.W., Allander, K.S., Bounds, J.A., Koster, J.E., MacArthur, D.W., Sprouse, L.L., Stout, D., Vaccarella, J.A., Vu, T.Q.: Field study of alpha characterization of a D&D site using long-range alpha detector. LA-UR-94-3632 (1994)
8. Cristianini, N., Shawe-Taylor, J.: An Introduction to Support Vector Machines and Other Kernel-based Learning Methods. Cambridge University Press (2000)
9. Guo, X.C., Yang, J.H., Wu, C.G., Wang, C.Y., Liang, Y.C.: A novel LS-SVMs hyper-parameter selection based on particle swarm optimization. Neurocomputing 71, 3211–3215 (2008)
10. Chapelle, O., Vapnik, V., Bousquet, O., Mukherjee, S.: Choosing multiple parameters for support vector machines. Machine Learning 46(209), 131–159
11. Youn, E., Koenig, L., Jeong, M.K., Baek, S.H.: Support vector-based feature selection using Fisher's linear discriminant and Support Vector Machine. Expert Systems with Applications 37, 6148–6156 (2010)
12. Wang, H., He, Z.: A Short-term load forecasting immune support vector machines. Power System Technology 23, 12–15 (2004)
13. Pourbasheer, E., Riahi, S., Ganjali, M.R., Norouzi, P.: Application of genetic algorithm-support vector machine (GA-SVM) for prediction of BK-channels activity. European Journal of Medicinal Chemistry 44, 5023–5028 (2009)
14. Clerc, M., Kennedy, J.: The particle swarm-explosion, stability, and convergence in a multidimensional complex space. IEEE Transactions on Evolutionary Computation 6, 58–73 (2002)
15. Rousseau, R.M.: Corrections for matrix effects in X-ray fluorescence analysis—A tutorial. Spectrochimica Acta Part B: Atomic Spectroscopy 61, 759–777 (2006)
16. Wu, J.S., Liu, M.Z., Jin, L.: A Hybrid Support Vector Regression Approach for Rainfall Forecasting Using Particle Swarm Optimization and Projection Pursuit Technology. International Journal of Computational Intelligence and Applications 9(2), 87–104 (2010)

Training Pool Selection for Semi-supervised Learning

Jian Ge[1,2], Tinghuai Ma[1,2,*], Qiaoqiao Yan[1,2], Yonggang Yan[1,2], and Wei Tian[1,2]

[1] Jiangsu Engineering Center of Network Monitoring,
[2] College of Computer & Software,
Nanjing University of Information Science & Technology, 210044, Nanjing, China
gejian0@163.com, {thma,tw}@nuist.edu.cn,
{xinfeiyanrjgc,wllyyg1}@126.com

Abstract. Semi-supervised leaning deals with methods for automatically exploiting unlabeled samples in addition to labeled set. The data selection is an important topic in active learning. It addresses the selection the valuable unlabeled data to label, considering that labeling data is a costly job. In this paper, we want to discuss in detail three aspects of technology in data selection, which includes how to select the unlabeled sample, how many unlabeled samples should be selected and how to define the capacity of the training pool. Experiments which use self-training based on *C4.5* show that while the *L* labeled ratio lager continuous, the initial error value becomes smaller. Also when *L* labeled ratio is less than 10%, the selection ratio value should be set in less than 0.8. The error value has no significant change while selection ratio value larger than 1.0.

Keywords: training pool, semi-supervised learning, data selection strategy, active learning.

1 Introduction

The explosion of available information during the last years has increased the interest of the Machine Learning community for different learning problems that have been raised in most of the information access applications [1]. Roughly speaking, there are three major techniques for this purpose [2], i.e., semi-supervised learning, transductive learning and active learning.

The data selection is an important topic in active learning [3]. It addresses the selecting the valuable unlabeled data to label, considering that labeling data is a costly job. The learning process iteratively queries unlabeled samples to select the most informative samples to annotate and update its learned models. Therefore, the unnecessary and redundant annotation is avoided. There are main three questions should be answered in this case. One is how to select the unlabeled samples, if there is a big size of unlabeled sample set. Another is how many unlabeled samples should be selected for augmenting the training samples. And the last is how to define the capacity of training pool.

---

* Corresponding author.

J. Wang, G.G. Yen, and M.M. Polycarpou (Eds.): ISNN 2012, Part I, LNCS 7367, pp. 524–532, 2012.

In this paper, we mainly answer above three questions. We summarize the literatures involved in semi-supervised learning and discuss the augmentation of training pool selection. The rest of paper is organized as follows: Semi-supervised learning is given in Section 2. In Section 3, we formalize the problem, and the training data selection is emphasized in Section 4. The results of our experiments are reported in Section 5. Finally, the related work and conclusions are given in Section 6.

2   Semi-supervised Learning

Semi-supervised learning [4] is a machine learning style between supervised learning and unsupervised learning. It deals with methods for automatically exploiting unlabeled data in addition to labeled data to improve learning performance, where no human intervention is assumed.

There are two basic assumptions in semi-supervised learning, that is, the cluster assumption and the manifold assumption. The former assumes that data with similar inputs should have similar class labels; the latter assumes that data with similar inputs should have similar outputs. These assumptions are closely related to the idea of low density separation, which has been taken by many semi-supervised learning algorithms.

Many semi-supervised learning algorithms have been developed. In general, they can be categorized into four categories, i.e., generative methods [5, 6], S3VMs (Semi-Supervised Support Vector Machines) [7, 8], graph-based methods [9, 10], and disagreement-based methods [11, 12].

In generative approaches, both labeled and unlabeled examples are assumed to be generated by the same parametric model. Thus, the model parameters directly link unlabeled examples and the learning objective. Methods in this category usually treat the labels of the unlabeled data as missing values of model parameters, and employ the EM (expectation–maximization) algorithm [23] to conduct maximum likelihood estimation of the model parameters.

S3VMs try to use unlabeled data to adjust the decision boundary learned from the small number of labeled examples, such that it goes through the less dense region while keeping the labeled data being correctly classified. Joachims proposed TSVM [24] (Transductive Support Vector Machine).

The first graph-based semi-supervised learning method is proposed by Blum and Chawla [25], which constructed a graph whose nodes are the training examples (both labeled and unlabeled) and the edges between nodes reflect certain relation, such as similarity, between the corresponding examples.

The disagreement-based semi-supervised learning was coined recently by Z-H Zhou [11] [12], in which multiple learners are trained for the same task and the disagreements among the learners are exploited during the learning process.

3   Problem Statement

Our work is especially motivated in training data selection, where we adopt the structure-activity high-throughput approaches. Hence, the pool-based active learning [13] setting is most appropriate. In this setting, the learner incurs a cost only when asking for the measurement of the target value of a particular instance, which must be selected from a known and finite pool. In principle, the learner may be able to exploit the distribution of the examples in the pool without cost. To some extent, this setting is therefore also a semi-supervised learning setting.

The problem sketched in section 2 can be more formally specified as follows:

```
Given:
- T, training data set
- U, unlabeled set
- U', a pool including u instances
1. Choosing u examples from U
   Loop for k iterations
2. Use T to train a classifier H //H may be a
classifier or classifiers combination
3. Pick the n unlabeled data which classifier H
agree with and add it to the collection of labeled
examples
4. Randomly choose n examples from U to replenish U'
End
```

From the above general semi-supervised learning style, training data selection is located in step1, 4 and 3. Step 1 and 4 is mainly responsible for choose the unlabeled data for classifying from huge observed data. Step 3 is mainly responsible for deciding whether the unlabeled data is suitable for being added into training data set *T*. In next section, it mainly discusses three key issues about the data selection strategies.

4   Selection Strategies

4.1   Training Data Selection

Different data selection strategies exist in active learning. Generally speaking, it mainly focuses on two aspects: (1) choosing classification boundary samples [14], (2) choosing the representative samples [15, 16].

Choosing the most reprehensive sample is the intuitive idea which is also called as entropy based method in [17]. As Guan Donghai [18] etc. mentioned, the candidate data first is clustered and the most closet data near center is chosen to represent its cluster.

Choosing classification boundary samples is from another viewpoint where is also named as margin based method in [19]. This selection strategy assumes that the samples located at the borders between clusters are more representative. If the boundary samples are classified exactly, other samples can be classified well.

Further more, Hybrid selection is adopt in selection strategy [16]. This strategy is a hybrid selection method combining the Center-based selection (CS) and Border-based selection (BS). It assumes that both the samples from CS and BS are representative. Combining them might provide better result than either alone.

In this paper, we mainly use the first selection strategy that is choose the representative sample, where it mainly assumes that unlabeled data set has the distribution with the labeled data set.

4.2   Number of Unlabeled Set

From the training set, the total unlabeled samples added into training set is $N_k = \sum_k u_i$, in which, u_i is the number of added unlabeled samples in i^{th} iteration.

Referring to the self-training algorithm, let n represents the total number of training data set D, r_l and r_u represent the samples ratio of labeled and unlabeled data set in D respectively. And also we define $r = \dfrac{|U'|}{|L|}$ as randomly selecting ratio in each iteration. Then we can get the number of training data in each iteration which is following as:

$$nr_l, nr_l(1+r), nr_l(1+r)^2, \cdots, nr_l(1+r)^{k-1}$$

So, the total training data number:

$$N_k = nr_l \sum_{i=0}^{k-1}(1+r)^i = nr_l \frac{(1+r)^k - 1}{r} \tag{1}$$

From the last iteration, we can get the constraint condition is as followed.

$$n - nr_l(1+r)^{k-1} \leq nr_l(1+r)^k \tag{2}$$

That is to say:

$$nr_l(1+r)^k \approx nr_u \tag{3}$$

Combining (1) (2) and (3), the formula about N_k is deduced as follows.

$$N_k = nr_l \frac{\dfrac{r_u}{r_l} - 1}{r} = nr_l \frac{1}{r}(\frac{1}{r_l} - 2) \tag{4}$$

In general, the number of labeled data set is far less than the number unlabeled data set, that is to say $r_l \leq r_u$, and then $r_l \leq 0.5$. At last, we can get expression about N_k is as follows.

$$N_k = \frac{n}{r} \tag{5}$$

Above all, one obvious conclusion is that the total training number N_k has a positive correlation with the number of training data set n, while it has an inverse relationship with selection ratio.

4.3   Capacity of Training Pool

At the step 1 in table 1, the capacity of U' is a key factor to affect the algorithm's efficiency. In one iteration, the training classification will be $2*|u|$ times. So, the number of $|u|$ decides the computational requirements.

Mohamed Farouk Abdel Hady etc. mentioned [20], in experimental evaluation the pool size u is set to 100, meanwhile the sample n to one and the number of nearest neighbors used to estimate local competence k is 10. Also in [21], Donghai Guan set the parameters used in the experiments as follows: iteration number k is 20 and the pool size u is 270. For the unlimited space U, there is not a clear idea about how to decide the capacity of U'. Obviously, it is not better classification performance while $|u|$ is increase. So in next section, we will do some experimental to test the capacity of U'.

5   Experimental Analysis

5.1   UCI Dataset

The experiments are based on the benchmark data sets form the Machine Learning Repository [22]. Information of these 9 datasets is tabulated in Table 1. These data sets are collected from different real-world applications in various domains.

Each data set is divided into labeled and unlabeled set. Self-training algorithm works on the unlabeled set and outputs the self-labeled training set, which then combines with the original labeled set to become an augmented training set. Afterwards the test set is classified by the supervised learning algorithm and the self-training algorithm respectively. Classification accuracy is the measure to evaluate the performance of data labeling function and self-training algorithm.

5.2   Configurations

The detailed process for each data set is as follows:

(1) Data set D is randomly partitioned into two parts: labeled set L and unlabeled set U.
(2) Ten trials derived from ten-fold cross-validation on L are used to evaluate the performance of every iterative classifier. At each trial, 90% of L is firstly selected and it is debited by T, used as training set. The remaining 10% of L is used as test to be classified by C4.5 based self-training algorithm. At each trial, we also calculate the predictive accuracy of ensemble-based data labeling function on U.

Table 1. UCI data sets in the experiments

Dataset	Attribute	Size	Class distribution
chess	6	28056	2796/27/78/246/81/198/471/592/683/1433/ 1712/1985/2854/3597/4194/2166/390
letter	16	20000	789/766/736/805/768/775/773/734/755/747/ 739/761/792/783/753/803/783/753/803/783/ 758/748/796/813/764/752/787/786/734
magic	11	19020	12332/6688
Nursery	8	12960	4320/2/328/4266/4044/
pendigits	16	10992	1143/1143/1144/1055/1144/ 1055/1056/1142/1055/1055
splice	61	3190	767/768/1655
segment	19	2310	330/330/330/330/330/330/330
car	6	1728	432/432/432/432
credit	2	1000	700/300

(3) The average classification accuracies of data labeling function and self-training algorithm are obtained by averaging all iterations classification accuracies.

(4) Considering that the partition of data set could influence this average classification accuracy, we execute the partition five times and get five classification values.

(5) Finally the report classification result is the further averaged value of these five values.

Two major parameters are able to influence this experiment. The first parameter determines data partitioning and it is the ratio between labeled data to whole data, referred to labeled ratio. It is set to 0.01, 0.05 and 0.1 in the experiment. The second parameter is selection ratio r, which is closely related to the size of U' and the size of labeled set L. Considering that the data sets obtained from the real applications might have different labeled ratios and selection ratios, we have performed several experiments varying two values to make the experiments comprehensively.

5.3   Result

The objectives of experiments in this part are two-fold: (1) whether there is any relationship between the labeled ratio and the performance of semi-supervised learning, and (2) whether there is any relationship between the selection ratio and the performance of semi-supervised learning.

The training set from UCI datasets unavoidable includes some noises. In this part, noises which may tend to degrade the quality of generalization model in training data are not considered in self-training algorithm. The labeled ratios are varied including 1%, 5%, 10%. The selection ratios are varied including 0.1 to 2.0, where the step size is 0.1.

We list the changing error value under different r value about nine datasets in which L labeled varied including 1%, 5% and 10% respectively in Fig. 1.

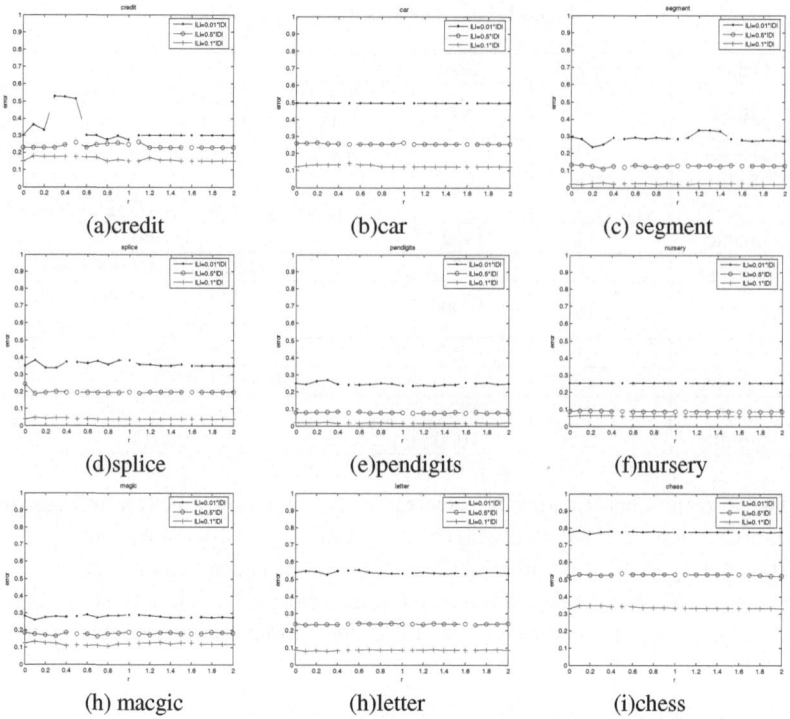

Fig. 1. classification performance on nine datasets vary in L labeled ratio

From figure 1, it can be seen that different ratio of L labeled has a great impact on the initial error value in each single data set. In other words, while the L labeled ratio lager continuous, the initial error value becomes smaller. Also from above figures, we can find when L labeled ratio is 1%, the learning performance may show better where r sets in 0.1-0.2; when L labeled ratio is 5%, the learning performance may show better where r sets in 0.1-0.7; when L labeled ratio is 10%, the learning performance may show better where r sets in 0.1-0.8. Meanwhile The error value has no significant change while r value larger than 1.0.

6   Conclusions and Future Work

To achieve the best possible classifier with a small number of labeled data, in this paper, three questions should be considered in semi-supervised learning. One is how to select the unlabeled samples, if there is a big size of unlabeled sample set. Another is how many unlabeled samples should be selected for augmenting the training samples. And the last is how to define the capacity of training pool. In this experiment, we can find that (1) when classification error has a small initial value in different L labeled ratio, in which it is not necessary to expand labeled samples to improve learning performance; (2) when L labeled ratio is less than 10%, the r value should be set in less than 0.8. The error value has no significant change while r value larger than 1.0.

In this paper, we only employ the single classifier based on C4.5 for experiment. In future, we will use more classifiers model and other algorithms to reduce the classification error.

Acknowledgments. This work was supported in part by the National Science Foundation (61173143) and the Special Fund for Meteorological Research in the Public Interest (GYHY201206030), and was also supported by A Project Funded by the Priority Academic Program Development of Jiangsu Higher Education Institutions (PAPD).

References

1. Krithara, A., Amini, M.-R., Goutte, C., Renders, J.-M.: An Extension of the Aspect PLSA Model to Active and Semi-Supervised Learning for Text Classification. In: Konstantopoulos, S., Perantonis, S., Karkaletsis, V., Spyropoulos, C.D., Vouros, G. (eds.) SETN 2010. LNCS, vol. 6040, pp. 183–192. Springer, Heidelberg (2010)
2. Zhou, Z.-H.: Learning with Unlabeled Data and Its Application to Image Retrieval. In: Yang, Q., Webb, G. (eds.) PRICAI 2006. LNCS (LNAI), vol. 4099, pp. 5–10. Springer, Heidelberg (2006)
3. Mackay, D.: Information-based objective functions for active data selection. Neural Computation 4(4), 305–318 (1992)
4. Blum, A., Mitchell, T.: Combining labeled and unlabeled data with co-training. In: 11th Annual Conference on Computational Learning Theory, pp. 92–100. ACM Press, New York (1998)
5. Miller, D.J., Uyar, H.S.: A mixture of experts classifier with learning based on both labeled and unlabelled data. In: Advances in Neural Information Processing Systems, pp. 571–577. MIT Press, Cambridge (1997)
6. Nigam, K., McCallum, A.K., Thrun, S., Mitchell, T.: Text classification from labeled and unlabeled documents using EM. Machine Learning 39, 103–134 (2000)
7. Chapelle, O., Zien, A.: Semi-supervised learning by low density separation. In: 10th International Workshop on Artificial Intelligence and Statistics, pp. 57–64. PASCAL EPrints, UK (2005)
8. Grandvalet, Y., Bengio, Y.: Semi-supervised learning by entropy minimization. In: Advances in Neural Information Processing Systems, pp. 529–536. MIT Press, Cambridge (2005)
9. Belkin, M., Niyogi, P.: Semi-supervised learning on Riemannian manifolds. Machine Learning 56(1-3), 209–239 (2004)
10. Belkin, M., Niyogi, P., Sindhwani, V.: On manifold regularization. In: 10th International Workshop on Artificial Intelligence and Statistics, pp. 17–24. PASCAL EPrints, UK (2005)
11. Blum, A., Mitchell, T.: Combining labeled and unlabeled data with co-training. In: 11th Annual Conference on Computational Learning Theory, pp. 92–100. ACM Press, New York (1998)
12. Zhou, Z.H., Li, M.: Semi-supervised learning by disagreement. Knowledge and Information Systems 24(3), 415–439 (2010)

13. De Grave, K., Ramon, J., De Raedt, L.: Active Learning for High Throughput Screening. In: Boulicaut, J.-F., Berthold, M.R., Horváth, T. (eds.) DS 2008. LNCS (LNAI), vol. 5255, pp. 185–196. Springer, Heidelberg (2008)

14. Schohn, G., Cohn, D.: Less is more: active learning with support vector machines. In: 17th International Conference on Machine Learning, pp. 839–846. Morgan Kaufmann, San Francisco (2000)

15. Xu, Z., Yu, G., Tresp, V., Xu, X., Wang, J.: Representative Sampling for Text Classification Using Support Vector Machines. In: Sebastiani, F. (ed.) ECIR 2003. LNCS, vol. 2633, pp. 393–407. Springer, Heidelberg (2003)

16. Lewis, D.D., Gale, W.A.: A sequential algorithm for training text classifiers. In: 17th ACM International Conference on Research and Development in Information Retrieval, pp. 3–12. Springer, New York (1994)

17. Dagan, I., Engelson, S.P.: Committee-based sampling for training probabilistic classifiers. In: The International Conference on Machine Learning, pp. 150–157. Morgan Kaufmann, San Francisco (1995)

18. Guan, D.H., Yuan, W.W., Lee, Y.-K., Gavrilov, A., Lee, S.: Improving Supervised Learning Performance by Using Fuzzy Clustering Method to Select Training Data. Journal of Intelligent & Fuzzy Systems 19, 321–334 (2008)

19. Krithara, A., Goutte, C., Amini, M.-R., Renders, J.-M.: Reducing the annotation burden in text classification. In: 1st International Conference on Multidisciplinary Information Sciences and Technologies, pp. 25–28. PASCAL EPrints, UK (2006)

20. Abdel Hady, M.F., Schwenker, F.: Combining Committee-Based Semi-supervised and Active Learning and Its Application to Handwritten Digits Recognition. In: El Gayar, N., Kittler, J., Roli, F. (eds.) MCS 2010. LNCS, vol. 5997, pp. 225–234. Springer, Heidelberg (2010)

21. Guan, D.H., Yuan, W.W., Lee, Y.-K.: Activity Recognition Based on Semi-supervised Learning. In: 13th IEEE International Conference on Embedded and Real-Time Computing Systems and Applications, pp. 465–475. IEEE Press, New York (2007)

22. UCI repository of machine learning databases, http://www.ics.uci.edu/learn/Repository.html

23. Dong, A., Bhanu, B.: A new semi-supervised EM algorithm for image retrieval. In: The IEEE International Conference on Computer Vision and Pattern Recognition, pp. 662–667. IEEE Press, New York (2003)

24. Joachims, T.: Transductive inference for text classification using support vector machines. In: The 16th International Conference on Machine Learning, pp. 200–209. Morgan Kaufmann, San Francisco (1999)

25. Blum, A., Chawla, S.: Learning from labeled and unlabeled data using graph mincuts. In: The 18th International Conference on Machine Learning, Williamston, pp. 19–26. Morgan Kaufmann, San Francisco (2001)

A Rapid Sparsification Method for Kernel Machines in Approximate Policy Iteration[*]

Chunming Liu, Zhenhua Huang, Xin Xu, Lei Zuo, and Jun Wu

Institute of Automation, National University of Defense Technology,
Changsha, 410073, P.R. China
lccmmm@126.com

Abstract. Recently approximate policy iteration (API) has received increasing attention due to its good convergence and generalization abilities in solving difficult reinforcement learning (RL) problems, e.g. least-squares policy iteration (LSPI) and its kernelized version (KLSPI). However, the sparsification of feature vectors, especially the kernel-based features, costs much computation and greatly influences the performance of API methods. In this paper, a novel rapid sparsification method is proposed for sparsifying kernel machines in API. In this method, the approximation error of a new feature vector is computed prior in the original space to decide if it is added to the current kernel dictionary, so the computational cost becomes a little higher when the collected samples are sparse, but remarkably lower when the collected samples are dense. Experimental results on the swing-up control of an double-link pendulum verify that the computational cost of the proposed algorithm is lower than that of the previous kernel-based API algorithm, and this performance becomes more and more obvious when the number of the collected samples increases and when the level of sparsification increases.

Keywords: reinforcement learning (RL), approximate policy iteration (API), Least Squares Policy Iteration (LSPI), kernel sparsification.

1   Introduction

Recently reinforcement learning (RL) has been widely studied not only in the neural network community but also in operations research. In RL, the learning agent interacts with an initially unknown environment and modifies its action policies to maximize its cumulative payoffs [1-2]. Thus, RL provides a general methodology to solve complex uncertain sequential decision problems, which are very challenging in many real-world applications. The environment in RL is typically modeled as a Markov decision process (MDP), which has been popularly studied in operations research [3]. A fundamental problem is to study theories and algorithms based on approximate value functions or policies since many real-world applications have large

---

[*] Supported by National Natural Science Foundation of China under Grant 61075072, & 90820302, the Program for New Century Excellent Talents in University under Grant NCET-10-0901.

J. Wang, G.G. Yen, and M.M. Polycarpou (Eds.): ISNN 2012, Part I, LNCS 7367, pp. 533–544, 2012.

or continuous state spaces. Until now, there are three main categories of research works on approximate RL, including value function approximation (VFA) [4], policy search [5-6], and actor-critic methods [7-8]. The value function approximation category has been studied the most popularly among these three classes of approximate RL methods. According to the basic properties of function approximators, there are two different kinds of value function approximation methods, i.e., linear [9-10] and nonlinear [11-13] VFA. Although RL with nonlinear VFA may have better approximation ability than linear VFA, the empirical results of RL applications using nonlinear VFA commonly lack a rigorous theoretical analysis and the nonlinear features are usually determined by manual selection.

As a popular method studied in operations research, policy iteration can be viewed as an actor-critic method since the value functions and the policies in it are approximated separately. To solve MDPs with large or continuous state spaces, API methods have been studied in some recent works. In [14], Michail G. Lagoudakis and Ronald Parr presented a model-free API algorithm called LSPI. As demonstrated in [14], the LSPI algorithm offers a RL method with better properties in convergence, stability, and sample complexity than previous RL algorithms. Nevertheless, its experiments also illustrated that, the approximation structure in value function and policy representation may have degenerated performance when the features are improperly selected. In [3], a kernel-based least squares policy iteration (KLSPI) algorithm was presented for MDPs with large or continuous state space, which can be used to realize adaptive feedback control of uncertain dynamic systems.

Although KLSPI is a very successful improvement of LSPI algorithm, it is analyzed in this paper that the sparsification process in KLSPI suffers much computational cost since a lot of kernel functions must be computed for every new input sample. If the approximation error of a new feature vector is computed prior in the original space to decide whether it is added to the kernel dictionary, then the computational cost may become a little higher when the collected samples are sparse, but remarkably lower when the collected samples are dense. Generally, in order to obtain a precisely approximated policy, the samples collected are dense. So in this paper, a novel rapid sparsification method is proposed for sparsifying kernel machines, and experimental results on a feedback control problem of uncertain nonlinear systems verify that the computational cost of the proposed algorithm becomes lower, and this performance becomes more and more obvious when the number of the collected samples increases and when the level of sparsification increases. Eventually by using the proposed algorithm, the efficiency of KLSPI is improved.

This paper is organized as follows. In Section 2, an introduction on MDPs as well as the previous LSPI learning algorithms is given. The novel rapid sparsification method for sparsifying kernel machines in KLSPI is presented in Section 3. In Section 4, experimental results on the swing-up control of an double-link pendulum system are provided to illustrate the effectiveness of the proposed algorithm. And Section 5 draws conclusions and suggests future work.

2   Markov Decision Processes and LSPI

According to the underlying formalism of RL problems is an MDP, the formalized MDP is depicted first, and then the famous LSPI algorithm is introduced.

2.1   Markov Decision Processes

An MDP is defined as a 4-tuple $\{ S, A, R, P \}$, where S is the state space of a finite set of states, A is the action space of a finite set of actions, R is the reward function and P is the state transition probability. $p(s,a,s')$ and $r(s,a,s')$ respectively represents the probability and reward of transferring from state s to state s' when taking action a. The policy of the MDP is defined as a function $\pi : S \rightarrow Pr(A)$, where $Pr(A)$ is a probability distribution in the action space. we assume that the underlying control problem is an MDP, and its rewards are discounted exponentially with a discount factor $\gamma \in [0,1)$. The MDP's objective is to estimate the optimal policy π^* satisfying the following equation:

$$J_{\pi^*} = \max_{\pi} J_{\pi} = \max_{\pi} E_{\pi}\left[\sum_{t=0}^{\infty} \gamma^t r(s_t, a_t, s_{t+1}) \right] \tag{1}$$

where $E_{\pi}[\cdot]$ stands for the expectation with respect to the policy π and the state transition probabilities, and J_{π} is the expected discounted total reward.

The state value function and the state-action value function for a stationary policy π are defined as:

$$V^{\pi}(s) = E_{\pi}\left[\sum_{t=0}^{\infty} \gamma^t r(s_t, a_t, s_{t+1}) \bigg| s_0 = s \right] \tag{2}$$

$$Q^{\pi}(s,a) = E_{\pi}\left[\sum_{t=0}^{\infty} \gamma^t r(s_t, a_t, s_{t+1}) \bigg| s_0 = s, a_0 = a \right] \tag{3}$$

The exact function $Q^{\pi}(s, a)$ must satisfy the Bellman equations [15]:

$$Q^{\pi}(s,a) = \sum_{s'} p(s,a,s') r(s,a,s') + \gamma \sum_{s',a'} p(s,a,s') \pi(a';s') Q^{\pi}(s',a') \tag{4}$$

where $\pi(a';s')$ represents the probability of action a' is taken by policy π in state s'.

The optimal state-action value function is defined as:

$$Q^*(s,a) = \max_{\pi} Q^{\pi}(s,a) \tag{5}$$

when $Q^*(s,a)$ is computed, the optimal policy π^* can be obtained easily by:

$$\pi^*(s) = \arg \max_{a} Q^*(s,a) \tag{6}$$

where the optimal policy π^* is a determined policy, which is defined as a projection from S to A.

2.2   The LSPI Algorithm

Policy iteration is a method of finding the optimal policy by iterating through a sequence of monotonically improving policies. Each iteration consists of two steps. The first step is to compute the state-action value function $Q^{\pi[m]}(s, a)$, and the other step is to improve policy $\pi[m]$ by a greedy method:

$$\pi[m+1](s) = \arg\max_a Q^{\pi[m]}(s,a) \tag{7}$$

These two steps are repeated until there is no change between the policies $\pi[m]$ and $\pi[m+1]$. After the convergence of policy iteration, the optimal policy may be obtained.

For large or continuous state space, to find the state-action value function $Q^{\pi}(s, a)$ for the current policy π is impractical. In order to solve such cases, a common class of approximators called linear architectures is introduced. The state-action value function $Q^{\pi}(s, a)$ is approximated as a linear weighted combination of M basis functions:

$$\phi(s,a) = \left(\underbrace{0,\cdots,0}_{M \cdot (l-1) \ zeros} , \phi_1(s), \phi_2(s), \cdots, \phi_M(s), \underbrace{0,\cdots,0}_{M \cdot (N_a-l) \ zeros} \right)^{\mathrm{T}} \tag{8}$$

$$\hat{Q}^{\pi}(s,a,w) = \phi(s,a)^{\mathrm{T}} \omega \tag{9}$$

where N_a is the size of the action space (actions are labeled from 1 to N_a), here action a is labeled as l, $\{\phi_i(s)\}$ are basis functions, and $\omega = (\omega_1, \omega_2, \cdots, \omega_{M \times Na})^{\mathrm{T}}$ is the weight vector.

Given a set of samples $D = \{(s_t, a_t, s_t', r_t) \mid t = 1, 2, \cdots, L\}$, let

$$\Phi = \begin{pmatrix} \phi(s_1, a_1)^{\mathrm{T}} \\ \cdots \\ \phi(s_t, a_t)^{\mathrm{T}} \\ \cdots \\ \phi(s_L, a_L)^{\mathrm{T}} \end{pmatrix} \quad \Phi' = \begin{pmatrix} \phi(s_1', \pi[t](s_1'))^{\mathrm{T}} \\ \cdots \\ \phi(s_t', \pi[t](s_t'))^{\mathrm{T}} \\ \cdots \\ \phi(s_L', \pi[t](s_L'))^{\mathrm{T}} \end{pmatrix} \quad R_e = \begin{pmatrix} r_1 \\ \cdots \\ r_t \\ \cdots \\ r_L \end{pmatrix}$$

Thus, the solution of this system is as follows [14]:

$$\begin{cases} \omega^{\pi[m]} = \left(\Phi^{\mathrm{T}} (\Phi - \gamma\Phi') \right)^{-1} \Phi^{\mathrm{T}} R_e \\ \pi[m+1](s) = \arg\max_a \phi(s,a)^{\mathrm{T}} \omega^{\pi[m]} \end{cases} \tag{10}$$

3   Sparsification of Kernel Machines for API Algorithms

In this section, the previous sequential sparsification process of kernel machines for LSPI is discussed, and then the rapid sparsification is proposed.

3.1   Sequential Sparsification of Kernel Machines for LSPI

In KLSPI, by introducing kernel machines in LSPI, the nonlinear approximation ability of API can be realized in an efficient way. In the KLSPI algorithm presented in [3], basis functions are described with kernel functions: $\{\phi_i(s) = k(s, s_j)\}$ $(0 \leq j \leq L, i = 1,2,\cdots,M)$, where $k(s, s_j)$ is a Mercer kernel function that is positive definite. For any finite set of features $\{s_1, s_2, \cdots, s_n\}$, the kernel matrix $K = [k(s_i, s_j)]_{n \times n}$ is positive definite. According to the Mercer Theorem [16], there exists a Hilbert space H and a mapping φ from S to H such that:

$$k\left(s_i, s_j\right) = < \varphi\left(s_i\right), \varphi\left(s_j\right) > \tag{11}$$

where $<\cdot,\cdot>$ is the inner product in H.

In the previous KLSPI algorithm, the following sequential sparsification procedure is used, which consists of the following steps:

Algorithm 1: Sequential sparsification of kernel functions

1: Given:
- A set of samples $D = \{(s_t, a_t, s_t', r_t) \mid t = 1,2,\cdots,L\}$.
- A kernel function $k(\cdot,\cdot)$ and its parameters.
- ε, which is an accuracy parameter determining the level of sparsity.

2: Initialize:
- Iteration number $t = 1$.
- Kernel dictionary $Dic_t = \{s_1\}$.

3: Loop for the whole set of states of samples:
- For the new feature s_t, compute the squared approximation error:

$$\delta_t = \min_c \left\| \sum_j c_j \varphi\left(s_j\right) - \varphi\left(s_t\right) \right\|_2^2 \left(s_j \in Dic_t\right) \tag{12}$$

- If $\delta_t < \varepsilon$
  $Dic_{t+1} = Dic_t$
  Else
  $Dic_{t+1} = Dic_t \cup s_t$
- Iteration number $t = t + 1$.

The sequential sparsification process was original proposed in [17] and it includes three main steps. In step 1, a set of samples are given at first, then a kernel function is chosen and the accuracy parameter determining the level of sparsity is set. The iteration number and kernel dictionary are initialized in step 2. At last, a loop is executed. In this loop, the squared approximation errors of every given sample are calculated with the current kernel dictionary, and in this procedure, the kernel dictionary is updated after the squared approximation error of any given sample is calculated. If the accuracy parameter is less than the squared approximation error, the corresponding feature is added to the kernel dictionary. Otherwise, the kernel dictionary will not be changed. During this process, the samples are tested according to their time ordering so it is called the sequential sparsification. In the following, we will develop a rapid sparsification process in order to reduce the computational cost.

3.2   Rapid Sparsification of Kernel Machines for LSPI

In the sequential sparsification process, if the squared approximation error δ_t is less than ε, the kernel dictionary is unchanged, else the new feature vector is added to the kernel dictionary. Let

$$\alpha = \max_{i,j,k} \left| \frac{\partial k(s_i, s_j)}{\partial s_{j,k}} \right| \qquad (13)$$

be the maximum of the kernel function's derivatives refers to all elements of all features, where s_i and s_j are arbitrary features in the state space S, and $s_{j,k}$ is the k'th element of s_j.

(*Lemma* 1) In Algorithm 1, if the new feature s_t satisfies:

$$2\alpha\rho_t < \varepsilon \qquad (14)$$

where

$$\rho_t = \min_j \left\| s_t - s_j \right\|_2 \left(s_j \in Dic_t \right) \qquad (15)$$

then the new feature s_t will not be added to the current kernel dictionary Dic_t.

Proof: For the current kernel dictionary Dic_t, the squared approximation error of the new feature s_t satisfies that:

$$\delta_t = \min_c \left\| \sum_j c_j \varphi(s_j) - \varphi(s_t) \right\|_2^2$$

$$\leq \min_j \left\| \varphi(s_j) - \varphi(s_t) \right\|_2^2$$

$$= \min_j \left(<\varphi(s_j), \varphi(s_j)> -2 <\varphi(s_t), \varphi(s_j)> + <\varphi(s_t), \varphi(s_t)> \right)$$

$$= \min_j \left(k(s_j, s_j) - 2k(s_t, s_j) + k(s_t, s_t) \right)$$

$$\leq 2\alpha \min_j \left\| s_t - s_j \right\|_2$$

$$= 2\alpha \rho_t$$

so the squared approximation error $\delta_t \leq 2\alpha\rho_t < \varepsilon$, and $Dic_{t+1} = Dic_t$, that is, the new feature s_t will not be added to the kernel dictionary Dic_t.

According to *Lemma* 1, for the new feature s_t and current kernel dictionary Dic_t, the value of ρ_t can be computed in original space first. If formula (14) is satisfied, there is no need to calculate the accurate value of the squared approximation error δ_t, so the computational cost can be decreased.

In order to decrease the computational cost of the sparsification process for kernel machines in API algorithms, we present a rapid sparsification process as follows:

Algorithm 2: Rapid sparsification of kernel functions

1: Given:
- A set of samples $D = \{(s_t, a_t, s_t', r_t) \mid t = 1, 2, \cdots, L\}$.
- A kernel function $k(\cdot, \cdot)$ and its maximal derivative refers to all elements of all features α.
- ε, which is an accuracy parameter determining the level of sparsity.

2: Initialize:
- Iteration number $t = 1$.
- Kernel dictionary $Dic_t = \{s_1\}$.

3: Loop for the whole set of states of samples:
- For the new feature s_t, compute its minimal distance ρ_t with Dic_t:
- If $2\alpha\rho_t < \varepsilon$
    $Dic_{t+1} = Dic_t$
  Else
    the squared approximation error is computed using formula (12).
    If $\delta_t < \varepsilon$
       $Dic_{t+1} = Dic_t$
    Else
       $Dic_{t+1} = Dic_t \cup s_t$
- Iteration number $t = t + 1$.

Different from the sequential sparsification algorithm, the maximal derivative of the given kernel function is given in step 1. In step 3, the distance of the new feature s_t and the current kernel Dic_t is computed to decide whether it is necessary to calculate the accurate value of the squared approximation error δ_t.

(*Lemma* 2) The kernel dictionary obtained by Algorithm 1 is the same as that obtained by Algorithm 2.

Proof: For the current kernel dictionary Dic_t, if the new feature s_t is added to Dic_t in Algorithm 1, then $\delta_t \geq \varepsilon$. In the same case in Algorithm 2, according to *Lemma* 1, $2\alpha\rho_t \geq \varepsilon$ (because $\delta_t \leq 2\alpha\rho_t$), so the squared approximation error is computed and $\delta_t \geq \varepsilon$, $Dic_{t+1} = Dic_t \cup s_t$. If the new feature s_t is not added to Dic_t in Algorithm 1, then $\delta_t < \varepsilon$. In the same case in Algorithm 2, if $2\alpha\rho_t < \varepsilon$, $Dic_{t+1} = Dic_t$, else the squared approximation error is computed and $\delta_t < \varepsilon$, $Dic_{t+1} = Dic_t$. Therefore, if the new feature s_t is added to Dic_t in Algorithm 1, it will be added to Dic_t in Algorithm 2, and if the new feature s_t is not added to Dic_t in Algorithm 1, it will not be added to Dic_t in Algorithm 2. Because the initialized dictionaries are the same in both algorithms, the kernel dictionary obtained by Algorithm 1 is the same as that obtained by Algorithm 2.

4　Experimental Results

In this subsection, a swing-up control problem of an double-link pendulum is studied to evaluate the effectiveness of the proposed algorithm. The double-link pendulum is also called an acrobot, which has been widely studied in control engineering [18-20]. As shown in Fig.1, the acrobot is a double-link pendulum (Link OA and AB) moving on a vertical plane, roughly analogous to a gymnast swinging on a high bar. The first joint (corresponding to the gymnast's hands on the bar) cannot exert torque, but the second joint (corresponding to the gymnast bending at the waist) can. It has two equilibrium points, which are the stable straight-down equilibrium point and the unstable straight-up equilibrium point. The control objective is to swing up the acrobot from the stable equilibrium point to the neighborhood of the unstable equilibrium and balance it there. Because of the complexity of the problem, the control of the acrobot is usually divided into two phases which are the swing-up control phase and the balancing control phase. In this paper, we will only consider the time-optimal swing-up control of the acrobot.

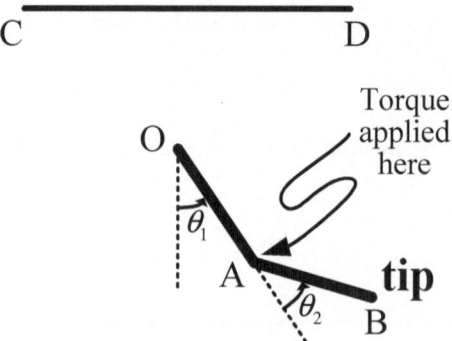

Fig. 1. The acrobot task

The system has four continuous state variables: two joint positions and two joint velocities. The dynamics model of the acrobot system is described by the following equations, which are only used for simulation.

$$\ddot{\theta}_1 = -\left(d_2\ddot{\theta}_2 + \phi_1\right)\big/d_1 \tag{16}$$

$$\ddot{\theta}_2 = \left(\tau + d_2\phi_1/d_1 - \phi_2\right) \tag{17}$$

where

$$d_1 = m_1 l_{c1}^2 + m_2\left(l_1^2 + l_{c2}^2 + 2l_1 l_{c2}\cos\theta_2\right) + I_1 + I_2 \tag{18}$$

$$d_2 = m_2\left(l_{c2}^2 + l_1 l_{c2}\cos\theta_2\right) + I_2 \tag{19}$$

$$\phi_1 = -m_2 l_1 l_{c2}\dot{\theta}_2^2\sin\theta_2 - 2m_2 l_1 l_{c2}\dot{\theta}_1\dot{\theta}_2\sin\theta_2 + \left(m_1 l_{c1} + m_2 l_1\right)g\cos\left(\theta_1 - \pi/2\right) + \phi_2 \tag{20}$$

$$\phi_2 = m_2 l_{c2}g\cos\left(\theta_1 + \theta_2 - \pi/2\right) \tag{21}$$

In the above equations, the parameters θ_i, $\dot{\theta}_i$, m_i, l_i, I_i, l_{ci} are the angle, the angle velocity, the mass, the length, the moment of inertia and the length of the center of mass for link i ($i = 1, 2$), respectively.

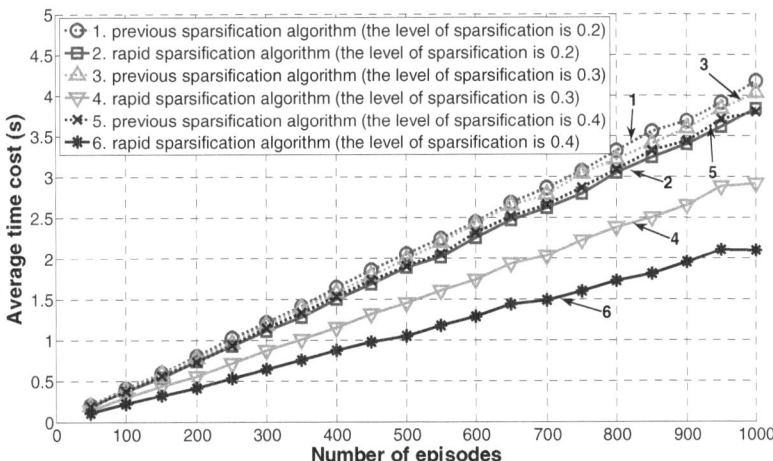

Fig. 2. The average time cost varies with the number of episodes for sample collection. This shows the computational cost of the proposed algorithm becomes lower, and this performance becomes more and more obvious when the number of the collected samples increases with the same level of sparsity (*the maximal squared approximation error of the whole samples*).

In the simulation, the parameters for the acrobot are chosen as $m_1 = m_2 = 1$kg, $I_1 = I_2 = 1$kgm^2, $l_{c1} = l_{c2} = 0.5$m, $l_1 = l_2 = 1$m and $g = 9.8$m/s^2. The control torque has two discrete values: [-1N, 1N]. The time step for simulation is 0.05s and the time interval for learning control is 0.2s. A learning episode is defined as the period that starts from the stable equilibrium, i.e., $_1 = _2 = 0$, and ends when the goal state is reached or a maximum time step of 1000 is accumulated. The reward of each step is -1, except that 100 when reaching the goal state.

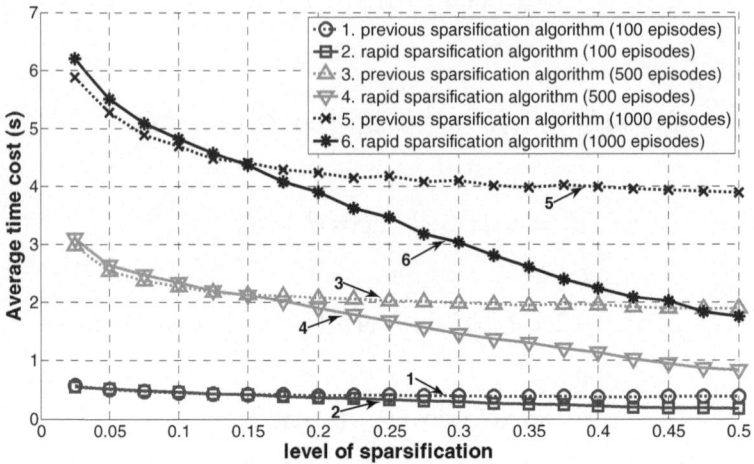

Fig. 3. The average time cost varies with the level of sparsification. This shows the computational cost of the proposed algorithm becomes lower, and this performance becomes more and more obvious when the level of sparsification increases with the same number of the collected samples.

As discussed in previous works [21-22], the swing-up control problem of the acrobot can be modeled as an MDP with four state variables: θ_1, θ_2, $\dot{\theta}_1$, $\dot{\theta}_2$. The initial training samples were generated by a random policy, where actions are selected with the same probability. The kernel function is selected as:

$$k\left(s_i, s_j\right) = e^{-\left[\left(\frac{\theta_{1i}-\theta_{1j}}{10.0}\right)^2 + \left(\frac{\theta_{2i}-\theta_{2j}}{10.0}\right)^2 + \left(\frac{\dot{\theta}_{1i}-\dot{\theta}_{1j}}{10.0}\right)^2 + \left(\frac{\dot{\theta}_{2i}-\dot{\theta}_{2j}}{10.0}\right)^2\right]} \tag{22}$$

where points s_i and s_j respectively are $(\theta_{1i}, \theta_{2i}, \dot{\theta}_{1i}, \dot{\theta}_{2i})$ and $(\theta_{1j}, \theta_{2j}, \dot{\theta}_{1j}, \dot{\theta}_{2j})$. and the maximal derivative of this kernel function is $\sqrt{2}e^{-0.5}/10$.

For each number of episodes of training samples from 50 to 1000 (the interval number is 50), 100 trials were executed to evaluate our proposed method and the previous sequential method. The average consumed times of the sparsification process in both algorithms are shown in Fig.2. For each level of sparsification from 0.025 to 0.5 (the interval level is 0.025), 100 trials were executed to evaluate our proposed method and the previous sequential method too. The average consumed times of the sparsification process in both algorithms are shown in Fig.3.

5   Conclusions and Future Work

In this paper, the rapid sparsification algorithm is proposed for kernel based API algorithms. In the proposed algorithm, the approximation error of a new feature vector is computed prior in the original space to decide whether it is added to the current kernel dictionary, so the computational cost becomes a little higher when the collected samples are sparse, but remarkably lower when the collected samples are dense. Experimental results on the swing-up control of an double-link pendulum verify that the computational cost of the proposed algorithm is lower than that of the previous kernel-based API algorithm, and this performance becomes more and more obvious when the number of the collected samples increases and when the level of sparsification increases. Although the results in this paper are very encouraging, how to construct suitable kernel functions, how to add more effective samples to the kernel dictionary and how to verify their optimality are to be studied in the future.

References

1. Sutton, R., Barto, A.: Reinforcement Learning. Introduction. MIT Press, Cambridge (1998)
2. Kaelbling, L.P., Littman, M.L., Moore, A.W.: Reinforcement learning: a survey. Journal of Artificial Intelligence Research 4, 237–285 (1996)
3. Xu, X., Hu, D.W., Lu, X.C.: Kernel based least-squares policy iteration. IEEE Transactions on Neural Networks 18(4), 973–992 (2007)
4. Bertsekas, D.P., Tsitsiklis, J.N.: Neurodynamic Programming. Athena Scientific, Belmont (1996)
5. Moody, J., Saffell, M.: Learning to trade via direct reinforcement. IEEE Transactions on Neural Networks 12(4), 875–889 (2001)
6. Baxter, J., Bartlett, P.L.: Infinite-horizon policy-gradient estimation. Journal of Artificial Intelligence Research 15, 319–350 (2001)
7. Barto, A.G., Sutton, R.S., Anderson, C.W.: Neuronlike adaptive elements that can solve difficult learning control problems. IEEE Transactions on System, Man, and Cybernetics 13, 835–846 (1983)
8. Konda, V.R., Tsitsiklis, J.N.: Actor-Critic Algorithm. In: Advances in Neural Information Processing Systems. MIT Press (2000)
9. Xu, X., He, H.G., Hu, D.W.: Efficient reinforcement learning using recursive least-squares methods. Journal of Artificial Intelligence Research 16, 259–292 (2002)
10. Boyan, J.: Technical update: least-squares temporal difference learning. Machine Learning 49(2-3), 233–246 (2002)
11. Crites, R.H., Barto, A.G.: Elevator group control using multiple reinforcement learning agents. Machine Learning 33(2-3), 235–262 (1998)
12. Tesauro, G.: TD-Gammon, a self-teaching backgammon program, achieves master-level play. Neural Computation 6, 215–219 (1994)

13. Zhang, W., Dietterich, T.: A reinforcement learning approach to job-shop scheduling. In: Proceedings of the Fourteenth International Joint Conference on Artificial Intelligence, pp. 1114–1120. Morgan Kaufmann (1995)
14. Lagoudakis, M.G., Parr, P.: Least-squares policy iteration. Journal of Machine Learning Research 4, 1107–1149 (2003)
15. Puterman, M.L.: Markov Decision Processes: discrete stochastic dynamic programming. John Wiley &. Sons, Inc., New York (1994)
16. Vapnik, V.: Statistical Learning Theory. Wiley Interscience, NewYork (1998)
17. Engel, Y., Mannor, S., Meir, R.: The kernel recursive least-squares algorithm. IEEE Transactions on Signal Processing 52(8), 2275–2285 (2004)
18. Hauser, J., Murray, R.M.: Nonlinear controllers for non-integratable systems: the acrobot example. In: Proceedings of American Control Conference, San Diego, USA, pp. 669–671 (1990)
19. Bortoff, S., Spong, M.W.: Psedolinearization of the acrobot using spline functions. In: Proceedings of the IEEE Conference on Decision and Control, Teuson, Arizona, pp. 593–598 (1992)
20. Spong, M.W.: The swing up control problem for the acrobot. IEEE Control System Magazine 15(1), 49–55 (1995)
21. Xu, X., He, H.G.: Residual-gradient-based neural reinforcement learning for the optimal control of an acrobot. In: Proceedings of the IEEE International Symposium on Intelligent Control, Vancouver, Canada, pp. 758–763 (October 2002)
22. Sutton, R.: Generalization in reinforcement learning: successful examples using sparse coarse coding. In: Advances in Neural Information Processing Systems 8, pp. 1038–1044. MIT Press (1996)

Computational Properties of Cyclic and Almost-Cyclic Learning with Momentum for Feedforward Neural Networks

Jian Wang[1,2], Wei Wu[1,*], and Jacek M. Zurada[2]

[1] Dalian University of Technology, Dalian, 116024, Liaoning, China
[2] University of Louisville, Louisville, 40292, Kentucky, U.S.
wangjiannl@mail.dlut.edu.cn,
wuweiw@dlut.edu.cn,
jacek.zurada@louisville.edu

Abstract. Two backpropagation algorithms with momentum for feedforward neural networks with a single hidden layer are considered. It is assumed that the training samples are supplied to the network in a cyclic or an almost-cyclic fashion in the learning procedure. A re-start strategy for the momentum is adopted such that the momentum coefficient is set to zero at the beginning of each training cycle. Corresponding weak and strong convergence results are presented, respectively. The convergence conditions on the learning rate, the momentum coefficient and the activation functions are much relaxed compared with those of the existing results. Numerical examples are implemented to support our theoretical results and demonstrate that ACMFNN does much better than CMFNN on both convergence speed and generalization ability.

Keywords: Backpropagation, momentum, cyclic, almost-cyclic, convergence.

1 Introduction

Backpropagation (BP) method is widely used for training feedforward neural networks (FNN) [1–3]. There are two popular ways of learning with training samples to implement the backpropagation algorithm: batch mode and incremental mode[4]. There are three incremental learning strategies according to the order that the samples are applied: online learning (completely stochastic order), almost-cyclic learning (special stochastic order) and cyclic learning (fixed order) [4–7].

It is well known that a general drawback of gradient-based BP methods is their slow convergence. Many modifications of this learning scheme have been proposed to overcome the difficulty [8, 9]. The backpropagation method with momentum is one of the popular variations [10]. This paper considers two backpropagation algorithms with momentum for feedforward neural networks with a

---

* This work was supported by the National Natural Science Foundation of China (11171367) and China Scholarship Council (CSC), China.

J. Wang, G.G. Yen, and M.M. Polycarpou (Eds.): ISNN 2012, Part I, LNCS 7367, pp. 545–554, 2012.
© Springer-Verlag Berlin Heidelberg 2012

single hidden layer, that is, cyclic learning with momentum for FNN (CMFNN) and almost-cyclic learning with momentum for FNN (ACMFNN).

We note that the convergence property for feedforward neural network learning is an interesting research topic which offers an effective guarantee in real application. For the gradient-based BP methods without momentum, the existing convergence results focus on online, almost-cyclic and cyclic learning algorithms. Deterministic convergence lies in almost-cyclic and cyclic learning mainly because every sample of the training set is fed exactly once in each training cycle [16, 17].

The convergence property of the BP methods with momentum has also been considered by researchers [18, 19]. For the batch learning backpropagation algorithm with momentum, a particular criterion to choose the momentum coefficients term is proposed in [20, 21] for BP neural networks with or without hidden layer, respectively, and the corresponding weak convergence (the gradient of the error function goes to zero) and strong convergence (the weight sequence goes to a fixed point) are proved. The cyclic learning with momentum is considered for feedforward neural networks without hidden layer in [22, 23], where some tight conditions are required to guarantee the convergence.

Unlike the corresponding restrictive conditions in [18–23], quite simple and general conditions are required in this paper on the learning rates and the momentum coefficients to guarantee the convergence. And these conditions are satisfied by all typical activation functions.

1. *The condition on the learning rate for cyclic and almost-cyclic learning with momentum is extended to a more general case:* $\sum_{m=0}^{\infty} \eta_m = \infty$, $\sum_{m=0}^{\infty} \eta_m^2 < \infty$ $(\eta_m > 0)$, *which is identical to those in [6, 7, 11–15] for online learning without momentum.*
2. *Our condition for the momentum coefficients μ_m to satisfy $\sum_{m=0}^{\infty} \mu_m^2 < \infty$ is more relaxed than those in [22, 23].*
3. *Our convergence results are valid for both cyclic learning and almost-cyclic learning with momentum.*
4. *We assume that the derivatives g' and f' of the activation functions are locally Lipschitz continuous.*
5. *The restrictive assumption on the stationary point set of the error function for the strong convergence in [16, 23] is relaxed, in that our only requirement on this set is that it does not contain any interior point.*

The detailed rigorous proofs of the weak and strong convergence results in this paper have been implemented in [24], however, the numerical performances of CMFNN and ACMFNN are absent. The main purpose of this paper is to illustrate the theoretical results of these two algorithms and then demonstrate the advantages of ACMFNN and CMFNN by performing classification and regression problems.

The remainder of this paper is organized as follows: In the next section, we formulate mathematically the cyclic and almost-cyclic learning with momentum for feedforward neural networks. The main convergence results are presented in

Section III, the performance of the presented two algorithms are reported and discussed in Section IV. In Section V, we conclude this paper with some remarks.

2   Cyclic and Almost-Cyclic Learning with Momentum

We consider a feedforward neural network with three layers. The numbers of neurons for the input, hidden and output layers are p, n and 1, respectively. Suppose that the training sample set is $\left\{ \mathbf{x}^j, O^j \right\}_{j=0}^{J-1} \subset \mathbb{R}^p \times \mathbb{R}$, where $\mathbf{x}^j$ and O^j are the input and the corresponding ideal output of the j-th sample, respectively. Let $\mathbf{V} = (v_{i,j})_{n \times p}$ be the weight matrix connecting the input and hidden layers, and write $\mathbf{v}_i = (v_{i1}, v_{i2}, \cdots, v_{ip})^T$ for $i = 1, 2, \cdots, n$. The weight vector connecting the hidden and output layers is denoted by $\mathbf{u} = (u_1, u_2, \cdots, u_n)^T \in \mathbb{R}^n$. To simplify the presentation, we combine the weight matrix $\mathbf{V}$ with the weight vector $\mathbf{u}$, and write $\mathbf{w} = \left(\mathbf{u}^T, \mathbf{v}_1^T, \cdots, \mathbf{v}_n^T \right)^T \in \mathbb{R}^{n(p+1)}$. Let g, $f : \mathbb{R} \to \mathbb{R}$ be given activation functions for the hidden and output layers, respectively. For convenience, we introduce the following vector valued function

$$G(\mathbf{z}) = (g(z_1), g(z_2), \cdots, g(z_n))^T, \quad \forall \, \mathbf{z} \in \mathbb{R}^n. \tag{1}$$

For any given input $\mathbf{x} \in \mathbb{R}^p$, the output of the hidden neurons is $G(\mathbf{Vx})$, and the final actual output is

$$y = f(\mathbf{u} \cdot G(\mathbf{Vx})). \tag{2}$$

For any fixed weight $\mathbf{w}$, the error of the neural networks is defined as

$$E(\mathbf{w}) = \frac{1}{2} \sum_{j=0}^{J-1} (O^j - f(\mathbf{u} \cdot G(\mathbf{Vx}^j)))^2 = \sum_{j=0}^{J-1} f_j(\mathbf{u} \cdot G(\mathbf{Vx}^j)), \tag{3}$$

where $f_j(t) = \frac{1}{2}(O^j - f(t))^2$, $j = 0, 1, \cdots, J-1$, $t \in \mathbb{R}$. The gradients of the error function with respect to $\mathbf{u}$ and $\mathbf{v}_i$ are, respectively, given by

$$E_{\mathbf{u}}(\mathbf{w}) = \sum_{j=0}^{J-1} f_j'(\mathbf{u} \cdot G(\mathbf{Vx}^j)) G(\mathbf{Vx}^j), \tag{4}$$

$$E_{\mathbf{v}_i}(\mathbf{w}) = \sum_{j=0}^{J-1} f_j'(\mathbf{u} \cdot G(\mathbf{Vx}^j)) u_i g'(\mathbf{v}_i \cdot \mathbf{x}^j) \mathbf{x}^j. \tag{5}$$

Write $E_{\mathbf{V}}(\mathbf{w}) = \left(E_{\mathbf{v}_1}(\mathbf{w})^T, \cdots, E_{\mathbf{v}_n}(\mathbf{w})^T \right)^T$, $E_{\mathbf{w}}(\mathbf{w}) = \left(E_{\mathbf{u}}(\mathbf{w})^T, E_{\mathbf{V}}(\mathbf{w})^T \right)^T$.

2.1   Cyclic Learning with Momentum of FNN (CMFNN)

With cyclic learning with momentum, a particular cycle is drawn at random from the set of all the possible cycles and then kept fixed at all times [4]. The detailed cyclic learning algorithm with momentum is presented as follows: Starting from an arbitrary initial weight $\mathbf{w}^0 = (\mathbf{u}^0, \mathbf{V}^0)$, the network weights are updated iteratively by

$$\begin{cases} \mathbf{u}^{mJ+1} = \mathbf{u}^{mJ} + \eta_m \nabla_0 \mathbf{u}^{mJ}, & j = 0, \\ \mathbf{u}^{mJ+j+1} = \mathbf{u}^{mJ+j} + \eta_m \nabla_j \mathbf{u}^{mJ+j} + \mu_m \left(\mathbf{u}^{mJ+j} - \mathbf{u}^{mJ+j-1} \right), j \neq 0. \end{cases} \tag{6}$$

$$\begin{cases} \mathbf{v}_i^{mJ+1} = \mathbf{v}_i^{mJ} + \eta_m \nabla_0 \mathbf{v}_i^{mJ}, & j = 0 \\ \mathbf{v}_i^{mJ+j+1} = \mathbf{v}_i^{mJ+j} + \eta_m \nabla_j \mathbf{v}_i^{mJ+j} + \mu_m \left(\mathbf{v}_i^{mJ+j} - \mathbf{v}_i^{mJ+j-1} \right), & j \neq 0. \end{cases} \quad (7)$$

where

$$\nabla_k \mathbf{u}^{mJ+j} = -f_k' \left(\mathbf{u}^{mJ+j} \cdot G^{mJ+j,\,k} \right) G^{mJ+j,k}, \quad (8)$$

$$\nabla_k \mathbf{v}_i^{mJ+j} = -f_k' \left(\mathbf{u}^{mJ+j} \cdot G^{mJ+j,k} \right) u_i^{mJ+j} g' \left(\mathbf{v}_i^{mJ+j} \cdot \mathbf{x}^k \right) \mathbf{x}^k, \quad (9)$$

$$G^{mJ+j,k} = G(\mathbf{V}^{mJ+j} \mathbf{x}^k), \quad (10)$$

$$y^{mJ+j,k} = f(\mathbf{u}^{mJ+j} \cdot G^{mJ+j,k}), \quad (11)$$

$$m \in \mathbb{N}; \ i = 1, 2, \cdots, n; \ j, \ k = 0, 1, \cdots, J - 1.$$

Here the parameters η_m and μ_m are the learning rate and the momentum coefficient, respectively.

2.2 Almost-Cyclic Learning with Momentum of FNN (ACMFNN)

With almost-cyclic learning with momentum, subsequent training cycles are drawn at random; almost-cyclic learning is online learning with training cycles instead of training patterns, i.e., the training samples are supplied in a stochastic order in each cycle. For the m-th training cycle, let $\{\mathbf{x}^{m,1}, \mathbf{x}^{m,2}, \cdots, \mathbf{x}^{m,J}\}$ be a stochastic order of the input vectors $\{\mathbf{x}^1, \mathbf{x}^2, \cdots, \mathbf{x}^J\}$. Similar to the above cyclic learning algorithm, starting from an arbitrary initial weight $\mathbf{w}^0 = (\mathbf{u}^0, \mathbf{V}^0)$, the network weights are updated iteratively by

$$\begin{cases} \mathbf{u}^{mJ+1} = \mathbf{u}^{mJ} + \eta_m \nabla_0^m \mathbf{u}^{mJ}, & j = 0, \\ \mathbf{u}^{mJ+j+1} = \mathbf{u}^{mJ+j} + \eta_m \nabla_j^m \mathbf{u}^{mJ+j} + \mu_m \left(\mathbf{u}^{mJ+j} - \mathbf{u}^{mJ+j-1} \right), & j \neq 0. \end{cases} \quad (12)$$

$$\begin{cases} \mathbf{v}_i^{mJ+1} = \mathbf{v}_i^{mJ} + \eta_m \nabla_0^m \mathbf{v}_i^{mJ}, & j = 0 \\ \mathbf{v}_i^{mJ+j+1} = \mathbf{v}_i^{mJ+j} + \eta_m \nabla_j^m \mathbf{v}_i^{mJ+j} + \mu_m \left(\mathbf{v}_i^{mJ+j} - \mathbf{v}_i^{mJ+j-1} \right), & j \neq 0. \end{cases} \quad (13)$$

where

$$\nabla_k^m \mathbf{u}^{mJ+j} = -f_k' \left(\mathbf{u}^{mJ+j} \cdot G^{mJ+j,m,k} \right) G^{mJ+j,m,k}, \quad (14)$$

$$\nabla_k^m \mathbf{v}_i^{mJ+j} = -f_k' \left(\mathbf{u}^{mJ+j} \cdot G^{mJ+j,m,k} \right) u_i^{mJ+j} g' \left(\mathbf{v}_i^{mJ+j} \cdot \mathbf{x}^{m,k} \right) \mathbf{x}^{m,k}, \quad (15)$$

$$G^{mJ+j,m,k} = G(\mathbf{V}^{mJ+j} \mathbf{x}^{m,k}), \quad (16)$$

$$y^{mJ+j,m,k} = f(\mathbf{u}^{mJ+j} \cdot G^{mJ+j,m,k}), \quad (17)$$

$$m \in \mathbb{N}; \ i = 1, 2, \cdots, n; \ j, \ k = 0, 1, \cdots, J - 1.$$

Remark: A re-start strategy for the momentum is adopted here: the momentum coefficient is set to zero at the beginning of each training cycle. Similar re-start strategy has been used in [25] for a conjugate gradient method.

3   Main Results

For any vector $\mathbf{x} = (x_1, x_2, \cdots, x_n)^T \in \mathbb{R}^n$, we write its Euclidean norm as $\|\mathbf{x}\| = \sqrt{\sum_{i=1}^{n} x_i^2}$. Let $\Omega_0 = \{\mathbf{w} \in \Omega : E_{\mathbf{w}}(\mathbf{w}) = 0\}$ be the stationary point set of the error function $E(\mathbf{w})$, where $\Omega \subset \mathbb{R}^{n(p+1)}$ is a bounded region satisfying (A4) below. Let $\Omega_{0,s} \subset \mathbb{R}$ be the projection of Ω_0 onto the s-th coordinate axis, that is,

$$\Omega_{0,s} = \left\{ w_s \in \mathbb{R} : \mathbf{w} = (w_1, \cdots, w_s, \cdots, w_{n(p+1)})^T \in \Omega_0 \right\} \tag{18}$$

for $s = 1, 2, \cdots, n(p+1)$. To analyze the convergence of the algorithm, we need the following assumptions.

(A1) $g'(t)$ and $f'(t)$ are continuous in any bounded closed interval;
(A2) $\eta_m > 0$, $\sum_{m=0}^{\infty} \eta_m = \infty$, $\sum_{m=0}^{\infty} \eta_m^2 < \infty$;
(A3) $\mu_m \geq 0$, $\sum_{m=0}^{\infty} \mu_m^2 < \infty$;
(A4) There exists a bounded region $\Omega \subset \mathbb{R}^n$ such that $\{\mathbf{w}^m\}_{m=0}^{\infty} \subset \Omega$;
(A5) $\Omega_{0,s}$ does not contain any interior point for every $s = 1, 2, \cdots, n(p+1)$.

Theorem 1. Assume that Conditions (A1-A4) are valid. Then, starting from an arbitrary initial value $\mathbf{w}^0$, the weight sequence $\{\mathbf{w}^m\}$ defined by (6) and (7) or by (12) and (13) satisfies the following weak convergence

$$\lim_{m \to \infty} \|E_{\mathbf{w}}(\mathbf{w}^m)\| = 0. \tag{19}$$

Moreover, if Assumption (A5) is also valid, there holds the strong convergence: There exists $\mathbf{w}^* \in \Omega_0$ such that

$$\lim_{m \to \infty} \mathbf{w}^m = \mathbf{w}^*. \tag{20}$$

4   Simulations

In this section, two different simulations are presented to verify the convergence property and compare the performance of CMFNN and ACMFNN on benchmark classifications and regression problem. The network architectures for each of the above problems are demonstrated below, respectively. In all cases, the logistic activation function $g(t) = 1/(1 + \exp(-2t))$, $(t \in \mathbb{R})$ is employed as the activation function of hidden layer for all of the preceding networks, while the output activation function is different and depends on the network output in terms of the following different applications. In the first example, we compare the performance between CMFNN and ACMFNN based on nine UCI benchmark problems. Four performance metrics which are often used for the performance analysis have been compared to demonstrate the advantages of ACMFNN. Besides the comparison between CMFNN and ACMFNN, the regression capability between BPFNN without momentum and CMFNN has also been compared on a nonlinear function. This regression simulation shows the good approximation ability of CMFNN which illustrate the theoretical results in this paper very well.

4.1   Example 1: Benchmark Classification Problems

The CMFNN and ACMFNN algorithms have been compared by using 9 bench-mark classification datasets from the UCI Machine Learning Repository [27] as shown in Fig. 1. In this example, 5-fold cross-validation has been performed.

Data Set	Data Size	Input Features	Classes
5 fold Cross Validation			
1. Monk's Problems	432	6	2
2. Liver Disorders	345	6	2
3. Breast Caner	286	9	2
4. Iris	150	4	3
5. Ionosphere	351	34	2
6. German Credit Data	1,000	20	2
7. Pima Indians	768	8	2
8. Sonar	208	60	2
9. Ecoli	336	7	8

Fig. 1. Benchmark classification datasets for Example 2

To compare the computational performance between CMFNN and ACMFNN, all of the learning parameters are identically chosen except for the order of the training. In this example, the initial learning rate and momentum factor are set to be 0.1 and 0.001, respectively. The stop criteria are set to be: $90,000$ training cycles or maximum error of $1e - 4$.

Data Sets	Algorithm	CPU time(s)	Iterations	Training Accuracy	Testing Accuracy
1. Monk's Problems	CMFNN	0.0632	103.5	0.7125	0.6570
	ACMFNN	0.0513	91.7	0.7280	0.6692
2. Liver Disorders	CMFNN	12.2148	1.8124e+004	0.7013	0.6723
	ACMFNN	11.9019	1.8015e+004	0.7251	0.6805
3. Breast Caner	CMFNN	4.8336	7.3468e+003	**0.9102**	**0.8503**
	ACMFNN	4.1854	6.9098e+003	**0.9093**	**0.8492**
4. Iris	CMFNN	8.7412	1.3861e+004	0.9830	0.9687
	ACMFNN	8.2246	1.2922e+004	0.9900	0.9809
5. Ionosphere	CMFNN	20.0930	2.9921e+004	0.7554	0.7291
	ACMFNN	17.3578	2.5917e+004	0.7639	0.7328
6. German Credit	CMFNN	34.8794	3.7665e+004	0.8134	0.7739
Data	ACMFNN	33.0461	3.3852e+004	0.8412	0.7958
7. Pima Indians	CMFNN	16.8625	2.3541e+004	0.7869	0.7429
	ACMFNN	15.9980	2.2997e+004	0.7980	0.7551
8. Sonar	CMFNN	18.7932	2.7512e+004	0.9638	0.9423
	ACMFNN	15.2910	2.2385e+004	0.9892	0.9650
9. Ecoli	CMFNN	0.0646	114.2	0.7309	0.6786
	ACMFNN	0.0597	98.5	0.7510	0.7012

Fig. 2. Comparison between CMFNN and ACMFNN for Example 1

Four performance metrics have been listed in Fig. 2, such as CPU time, Iterations, Training Accuracy and Testing Accuracy. It can be seen that the training times for ACMFNN are less than CMFNN on all of the datasets. This demonstrates that ACMFNN training runs much faster than CMFNN for the stochastic property. Training and testing accuracies are another two important factors to measure the performance of feedforward neural networks (FNN). Training accuracy represents the classification capability of FNN in training stage, while testing accuracy describes the generalization of FNN. From Fig. 2, we can see that ACMFNN shows better performance than CMFNN on most of the benchmark classification problems except for the "German Credit Data" set on training accuracy and "Pima Indians" set on testing accuracy. In brief, this example concludes that ACMFNN does better than CMFNN in terms of the stochastic property.

4.2   Example 2: Regression Problems

To show the performance significance of CMFNN and ACMFNN, the following regression simulation has been implemented. For simplicity, we only compare the BPFNN without momentum and CMFNN, thus omit the performance simulation of ACMFNN. In this simulation, a more complex nonlinear function (cf. [26]) has been employed to demonstrate the difference between BPFNN without momentum and CMFNN.

$$F(x) = 2x\sin(x) - 3, \qquad x \in [-7, 7]. \tag{21}$$

The training samples are generated as follows: 175 inputs are stochastically selected from the interval $[-7, 7]$ with the identical noise which belongs to $N(0, 0.1)$. The training samples are generated as following ways: 175 inputs $(x_i, i = 1, 2, \cdots, 100)$ are randomly chosen from the interval $[-7, 7]$ with the outputs: $F(x_i) + e_i$, where $e_i \in N(0, 0.1)$ is noise and $N(0, 0.1)$ stands for the normal distribution with expectation and variance being 0 and 0.1. Fig. 3 a) shows the training samples (" $*$ ") and the desired output function (" $-$ "). The same network architectures of BPFNN without momentum and CMFNN have been constructed with 2 inputs, 9 hidden neurons and 1 output neuron. Linear output function is used for the output layer. The initial weights have been randomly chosen in $[-1, 1]$. And the initial training parameters, learning rates, are set to be: $\eta = 0.03$, while momentum coefficients correspond with $\mu = 0.001$ for CMFNN and $\mu = 0$ for BPFNN without momentum, respectively.

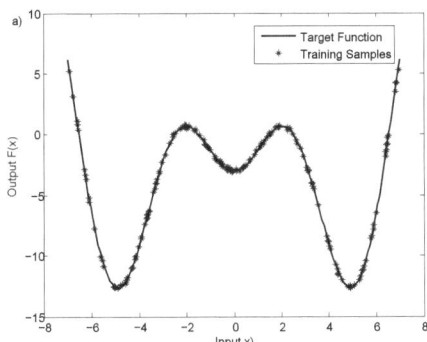

Fig. 3. Example 2, a) Target function and training samples

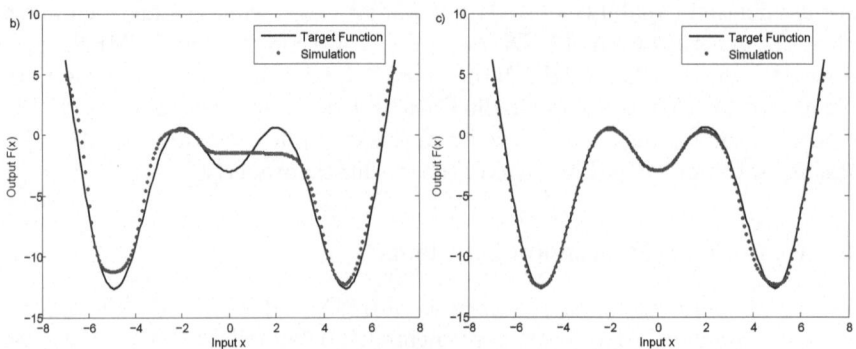

Fig. 4. Regression comparison between BPFNN without momentum and CMFNN for Example 2, b) BPFNN without momentum, c) CMFNN.

The stop conditions are set to be: $40,000$ cycles or error below $1e-3$. Comparing the informative figures Fig. 4 b) and c), we can see that CMFNN approximates the function (21) much better than BPFNN without momentum. It shows that the momentum term plays an important role in speeding up the training procedure and then improving the generalization capability for CMFNN. It is easy to predict that ACMFNN should be performed as well for the surviving stochastic property in the training procedure.

5   Conclusion

In this paper, the cyclic and almost-cyclic learning algorithms with momentum for three-layer BP neural networks are considered, and the weak and strong convergence results are presented. Compared with the existing convergence results, the assumptions to guarantee the convergence are much relaxed, and are valid for more extensive classes of feedforward neural networks. Two illustrative examples are performed to verify the theoretical results in this paper. The first example shows that ACMFNN does much better than CMFNN for most of the benchmark classification problems based on the four performance metrics, such as CPU time, iterations, training accuracy and testing accuracy. It is clear that stochastic property plays an important role in the training procedure of ACMFNN. The second example demonstrates that CMFNN can be a good regression solver, and performs much better than BPFNN without momentum.

References

1. Haykin, S.: Neural Networks: A Comprehensive Foundation, 2nd edn. Tsinghua University Press and Prentice Hall (2001)
2. Rumelhart, D.E., McClelland, J.L.: Parall Distributed Processing-Explorations in the Microstructure of Cognition. MIT Press, Cambridge (1986)
3. de Oliveira, E.A., Alamino, R.C.: Performance of the Bayesian Online Algorithm for the Perceptron. IEEE Trans. Neural Networ. 18, 902–905 (2007)

4. Heskes, T., Wiegerinck, W.: A Theoretical Comparison of Batch-Mode, On-Line, Cyclic, and Almost-Cyclic Learning. IEEE T Neural Networ. 7, 919–925 (1996)
5. Wilson, D.R., Martinez, T.R.: The general inefficiency of batch training for gradient descent learning. Neural Networks 16, 1429–1451 (2003)
6. Terence, D.S.: Optimal unsupervised learning in a single-layer linear feedforward neural network. Neural Networks 2, 459–473 (1989)
7. Finnoff, W.: Diffusion approximations for the constant learning rate backpropagation algorithm and resistance to local minima. Neural Computation 6, 242–254 (1994)
8. Hertz, J., Krogh, A., Palmer, R.G.: Introduction to the Theory of Neural Computation. Addison Wesley, Redwood City (1991)
9. Becker, S., Le Cun, Y.: Improving the convergence of back-propagation learning with second-order methods. In: Proc. of the 1988 Conneciiontst Models Summer School, San Mateo, pp. 29–37 (1989)
10. Hagan, M.T., Demuth, H.B., Beale, M.H.: Neural Network Design. PWS, Boston (1996)
11. Liang, Y.C., Feng, D.P., Lee, H.P.: Successive Approximation Training Algorithm for Feedforward Neural Networks. Neurocomputing 42, 11–322 (2002)
12. Chakraborty, D., Pal, N.R.: A novel training scheme for multilayered perceptrons to realize proper generalization and incremental learning. IEEE Trans. Neural Networ. 14, 1–14 (2003)
13. Fine, T.L., Mukherjee, S.: Parameter Convergence and Learning Curves for Neural Networks. Neural Computation 11, 747–769 (1999)
14. Bertsekas, D.P., Tsitsiklis, J.N.: Neuro-Dynamic Programming. Athena Scientific (1996)
15. Tadic, V., Stankovic, S.: Learning in neural networks by normalized stochastic gradient algorithm: Local convergence. In: Proceedings of the 5th Seminar Neural Networks Application Electronic Engineering, Yugoslavia (2000)
16. Wu, W., Shao, H.M., Qu, D.: Strong Convergence of Gradient Methods for BP Networks Training. In: Proc. Int. Conf. Neural Networks & Brains, pp. 332–334 (2005)
17. Wu, W., Feng, G.R., Li, X.: Training multilayer perceptrons via minimization of sum of ridge functions. Advances in Computational Mathematics 17, 331–347 (2002)
18. Bhaya, A., Kaszkurewicz, E.: Steepest descent with momentum for quadratic functions is a version of the conjugate gradient method. Neural Networks 17, 65–71 (2004)
19. Torii, M., Hagan, M.T.: Stability of steepest descent with momentum for quadratic functions. IEEE Trans. Neural Networks 13, 752–756 (2002)
20. Wu, W., Zhang, N.M., Li, Z.X.: Convergence of gradient method with momentum for back-propagation neural networks. Journal of Computational Mathematics 26, 613–623 (2008)
21. Zhang, N.M., Wu, W., Zheng, G.F.: Gonvergence of gradient method with momentum for two-layer feedforward neural networks. IEEE Trans. Neural Networks 17, 522–525 (2006)
22. Zhang, N.M.: Deterministic Convergence of an Online Gradient Method with Momentum. In: Huang, D.-S., Li, K., Irwin, G.W. (eds.) ICIC 2006. LNCS, vol. 4113, pp. 94–105. Springer, Heidelberg (2006)
23. Zhang, N.M.: An online gradient method with momentum for two-layer feedforward neural networks. Applied Mathematics and Computation 212, 488–498 (2009)

24. Wang, J., Yang, J., Wu, W.: Convergence of Cyclic and Almost-Cyclic Learning with Momentum for Feedforward Neural Networks. IEEE Trans. Neural Networks 22, 1297–1306 (2011)
25. Powell, M.J.D.: Restart procedure for the conjugate gradient method. Mathematical Programming 12, 241–254 (1977)
26. Ren, Y.J.: Numerical analysis and the implementations based on Matlab. Higer Education Press, Beijing (2007)
27. http://archive.ics.uci.edu/ml

A Hybrid Evolving and Gradient Strategy for Approximating Policy Evaluation on Online Critic-Actor Learning

Jian Fu[1], Haibo He[2], Huiying Li[1], and Qing Liu[1]

[1] School of Automation,Wuhan University of Technology,
Wuhan, Hubei 430070, China
pigeon1387@gmail.com, {cocoli_93,qliu2000}@163.com
[2] Department of Electrical, Computer and Biomedical Engineering,
University of Rhode Island, Kingston, RI 02881,USA
he@ele.uri.edu

Abstract. In this paper, we propose a novel strategy for approximating policy evaluation during online critic-actor learning procedure. We adopt the adaptive differential evolution with elites (ADEE) to optimize moving least square temporal difference with one step (MLSTD(0)) at the early stage which is good at global searching. Next we apply gradient method to perform local search efficiently and effectively. That solves the dilemma between explore and exploit in weight seeking for critic neural network. Simulation results on the online learning control of a cart pole benchmark demonstrate the efficiency of the presented method.

Keywords: adaptive dynamic programming, critic-actor learning, differential evolution, temporal difference.

1 Introduction

Adaptive dynamic programming(ADP)is a promising and effective approach to solving the complex sequential decision problem due to its ability of untangling the "the curse of dimensionality"effectively and efficiently.

Briefly speaking, the foundation for optimization over time in stochastic processes is the Bellman equation. Specifically, given a Markov Decision Process (MDPs) $M = (X, A, P, Q)$ with deterministic policy $\pi \in \Pi_{state}$.Where X is the set of states, A is the set of actions, P is the transition probability kernel, Q is the reward kernel, and $0 \leq \alpha < 1$ is the discount factor.

The objective of dynamic decision is to choose control sequence $u(t)$(generated by the policy π), so the cost function

$$V^*(x) = \min E\left[\sum_{t=0}^{\infty} \alpha^t R_{t+1} \,|X_0 = x\right], x \in X \tag{1}$$

is minimized. The process $(R_t; t \geq 1)$ is the reward part of the process $((X_t, A_t, R_{t+1}); t \geq 0)$ with the policy π .According to theorem of Bellman, it can be obtained by the fixed-point equation

J. Wang, G.G. Yen, and M.M. Polycarpou (Eds.): ISNN 2012, Part I, LNCS 7367, pp. 555–564, 2012.

$$V^{*}\left(x\right)=\min_{\beta\in A}\left\{r\left(x,\beta\right)+\alpha\sum_{y\in X}P\left(x,\beta,y\right)V^{*}\left(y\right)\right\} \tag{2}$$

In this way, the typical dynamic programming(DP) and tabular reinforcement learning (TDP)algorithms can obtain the Bellman optimality operator $T^{*}V^{*}=V^{*}$. However, DP needs the exact object model and TDP cannot handle MDPs with large and continuous state/action space.

ADP can successfully overcome the "the curse of dimensionality"to a great extent by using a function approaching structure such as neural network to approximate the cost function in order to get alike resolution of the Bellman equation.

However, explore and exploit of weight seeking is always a dilemma when we apply neural network to approximate the value function or action function. Especially, the issue becomes more prominent when ADP online learning in continuous MDPs space. Over the past decades, extensive efforts have been made to develop weight training method other than BP. There are genetic algorithms(GA) [1], evolutionary programming (EP)[2], particle swarm Optimization[3],and differential evolution[4,5]. Specifically, in the domain of reinforcement learning, GENITOR [6] and SANE[7]are two successful cases with GA, respectively. However, the search is employed only in policy function space. Xu[8]applied GA and residual gradient method alternatively to implement a policy evaluation in an Adaptive Heuristic Critic (AHC) structure.

In the paper, we present a novel approach, hybrid evolving and gradient strategy, to solve the dilemma ingeniously in the domain of actor-critic. Actor-critic is a class of ADP methods for MDPs with continuous space. The main motive of the approach in the paper is to provide a suitable initial weight for critic neural network (CNN). At the early stage, we search the weights in parallel. Specifically, we use differential evolution with elite to perform moving least square temporal difference with one step(MLSTD(0)) algorithms in the early stage of online learning. Afterwards, we switch the weight seeking method from differential evolution to classical back propagation. Thus it obtain a balance which are optimizing the weight in the large scope domain by differential evolution (DE) to increase the probability of "good" initial weight and refining the weight in the local area by BP to increase the probability of "fast" with lower computation consuming. To our best knowledge, this is the first study of investigating hybrid DE and gradient strategyfor CNN's approximate policy evaluation based on online critic-actor learning.

The rest of this paper is organized as follows. In Section2, a classical revised version of the actor-critic design and its implementation details is given. In Section3, we present DE (evolutionary computation) -BP (back propagation) algorithm and its integration into the online weight updating approach for CNN with MLSTD(0). Section4, we analyze experimental settings and results in detail based on a cart pole, a popular benchmark in the community. Finally, a conclusion is provided in Section5.

2   An Online Actor-Critic Design

Our proposed approach is based on the actor-critic architecture as presented in [9](see Fig. 1). In this structure,one can obtain the temporal difference by calculating the current cost-to-go approximation $J(k)$ and the previous value approximation $J(k-1)$. The binary reinforcement signal r ,"0" and "-1" representing "success"and "failure", is provided from the external environment which we mark as the reinforcement signal explicitly. Such a reinforcement signal indicates what is good and what is bad in an immediate sense, whereas a value function specifies what is good in the long term, which can be approximated by a critic network. Once a system state is determined, an action will be subsequently produced by the action network.All discussions in this article assume neural network with multi-layerperceptron (MLP) architecture is used in both the critic network and the action network design.

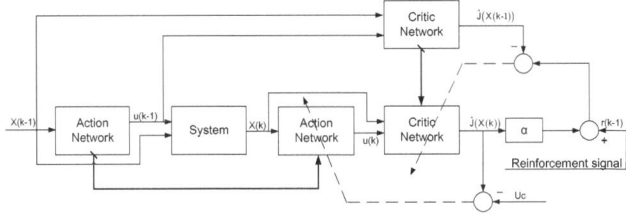

Fig. 1. Schematic diagram for implementation of online learning based on ADP

In the critic network, the output J can be defined as follows.

$$q_i(k) = \sum_{j=1}^{N_{cin}} w_{c_{ij}}^{(1)}(k) \cdot x_j(k), i = 1, \cdots, N_{ch} \tag{3}$$

$$p_i(k) = \frac{1 - \exp^{-q_i(k)}}{1 + \exp^{-q_i(k)}}, i = 1, \cdots, N_{ch} \tag{4}$$

$$J(k) = \sum_{i=1}^{N_{ch}} w_{c_i}^{(2)}(k) \cdot p_i(k) \tag{5}$$

Where q_i is the ith hidden node input of the critic network, p_i is the corresponding output of the hidden node q_i, $N_{cin}$is the total number of the input nodes in the critic network including the multiple action value u_k from the action network, and N_{ch} is the total number of the hidden nodes in the critic network.

The object function to be minimized in the critic network is

$$E_c(k) = \frac{1}{2}e_c^2(k) = \frac{1}{2}\{\alpha J(k) - [J(k-1) - r(k-1)]\}^2 \tag{6}$$

Next, we can investigate the action network. The associated equations for the action network are

$$h_i(k) = \sum_{j=1}^{N_{ain}} e_{a_{ij}}^{(1)}(k) \cdot x_j(k), i = 1, \cdots, N_{ah} \tag{7}$$

$$g_i(k) = \frac{1 - \exp^{-h_i(k)}}{1 + \exp^{-h_i(k)}}, i = 1, \cdots, N_{ah} \tag{8}$$

$$v_m(k) = \sum_{m=1}^{N_{ah}} w_{a_{mi}}^{(2)}(k) \cdot g_i(k), m = 1, \cdots, N_{aout} \tag{9}$$

$$u_m(k) = \frac{1 - \exp^{-v_m(k)}}{1 + \exp^{-v_m(k)}}, m = 1, \cdots, N_{aout} \tag{10}$$

Where h_i is the ith hidden node input of the action network, g_i is the ith hidden node output of the action network, v_m is the mth output node input of the action network, u_m is the mth output node output of the action network, N_{ain} is the total number of the input nodes in the action network, N_{ah} is the total number of the hidden nodes in the action network, and N_{aout} is the total number of the output nodes in the action network.

The purpose of adapting the action network is implicitly back propagating the error between the desired ultimate object U_c and approximate J function from the critic network.

The error of the action network is defined as

$$E_a(k) = \frac{1}{2}e_a^2(k) = \frac{1}{2}(J(k) - U_c)^2 = \frac{1}{2}(J(k))^2 \tag{11}$$

3   Integration of DE-BP Algorithm into ADP Design

Actor-critic architecture in the fig. 1 can be regarded as approximate policy iteration. The CNN and ANN conduct the procedures of policy evaluation and policy improvement, respectively. The former performances the TD learning to estimate the action value function under the policy given by ANN. And the latter produces a greedy policy under the value function presented by CNN. The iteration process is repeated until there is no change taken place any more. In other words, it is analogous to seeking the fixed point of operator T with newton iteration method in vector space[10].

Ideally, with the neural network as general approximator, we ordinarily randomly initialize the weights of the critic neural network (CNN) and the action neural network (ANN) at the beginning. Usually, a "good" estimation and an "appropriate" control value under the specific states make the principle of optimality equation balanced approximately. Furthermore, these "appropriate" operations will be reinforced through memory and association. Otherwise, they will be adjusted through tuning the weights in the neural network to balance the equation of the principle of optimality as much as possible.

However, the value function and the action function are unknown at priori, usually they are multimodal functions. It is well known that the popular gradient methods are prone to be stuck in local minimum. That results in the failure of online learning in the specific trail. And it is one of the reasons why the classical ADP approach takes relative more tries to attain the expected performance. Inappropriate initial weight pays for it, since it unavoidably leads the search into local minimum. Awkwardly, we need random the weight to expand the probability of searching the right approximation. At the same time it increases the probability of leading to local minimum as well.

Here, we present a novel strategy DE-BP to solve the dilemma ingeniously. The main idea is to provide a suitable initial weight for neural network to accomplish good approximation by iterative learning. At the early stage, we search the weights in parallel. Specifically, we use differential evolution with elite to performance LSTD(0) algorithms in the early stage of online learning. Afterward, with relative lower least square summation, we switch the weight seeking method from differential evolution to classical back propagation. Since the convergence of approximate policy iteration depends greatly on the approximation precision of the real value function. We just integrate this algorithm with CNN in the paper.

DE, introduced by Prince and Storn more than a decade ago, is a powerful population based stochastic search algorithm for global optimization.It perturbs the current generation population members with the scaled differences of randomly selected and distinct population members[11]. It makes few or no assumptions about the problem being optimized (gradient information is not needed) and can search very large spaces of candidate solutions.

We outline the algorithm of ADP with DE-BP weight seeking as follows:

[Algorithm]: *Outline of integrated DE-BP algorithm for ADP*

/* $u = ANN(w_a, x)$ is a neural network for control output calculation;
x: state vector;
w_a: weight of ANN;
u: control output of ANN;

$J = CNN(w_c, x, u)$ is a neural network for cost-to-go approximation;
w_c: weight of CNN;
J : total cost-to-go;

1) **While** TerminalContion **Do**
2) Initialize x, w_c, w_a;
3) **Repeat**
4) Employ the action u by ANN;
5) Obtain new x and immediate reward r via external environment;
6) Calculate the cost-to-go error E_c based on temporal difference;
7) **If** current counter< GivenThreshold, apply ADEE to minimize MLSTD(0) **Else** Employ backpropagation to train CNN to minimize error E_c;

8) Employ backpropagation method to train ANN to minimize the norm of $J - U_c$
9) **Until** CurrentState $\notin$ threshold
10) **End while**

Next we will describe two important parts inside: calculating MLSTD (0), optimizing MLSTD(0)with ADEE.

(1)definition and calculation of MLSTD(0)

In the paper, we present a moving least square algorithm to utilize regression via DE to seek proper initial weight of CNN, which conducts policy evaluation together with ANN alternately to search the fixed point of map.As for the learning procedure of CNN, the data set is generated online as a time series. We define a moving window with L data sampling. The data set produced with this window will perform a regression to minimize $\sum\limits_{t=1}^{L} \left[r_{t-1} - \left(\hat{J}(x_{t-1}) - \alpha \hat{J}(x_t) \right) \right]$. In our algorithm, there are five moving window matrixes: $\mathbf{inp} \in R^{(N_{cin}+N_{aout}) \times L}$, $\mathbf{inp}_{prev} \in R^{(N_{cin}+N_{aout}) \times L}$, $\gamma \in N_{[-1,0]}^{1 \times L}$, $\mathbf{J}_{prev} \in R^{1 \times L}$, $\mathbf{J} \in R^{1 \times L}$. They will be described in detail later. In order to avoid overfitting, only the data with prespective $TD(0)$ bigger than given threshold could be appended to the window. And there is a sampling counter to fulfill the counting.

Usually, the current sampling counter is lower than L. The new data set during this stage is just appended into the respective moving window matrixes.

As for the $\mathbf{inp}$, every column vector represents the mixture of state $\mathbf{x}$ and control $\mathbf{u}$ in the given time index. Fig. 2 depicts the vivid process of filling stage for it. We would like to point out that the superscript is sampling counter instead of time index.

Next we take the weight of the CNN as decision vector. Specifically, We reshape its weight matrixes $\mathbf{w}_c^{(1)}$, $\mathbf{w}_c^{(2)}$ into a weight vector like this form

$$\mathbf{x} = \left[w_{c11}^{(1)} \cdots w_{cN_{cin}1}^{(1)} \; w_{c21}^{(1)} \cdots w_{cN_{cin}N_{ch}}^{(1)} \; w_{c1}^{(2)} \; w_{c2}^{(2)} \cdots w_{cN_{ch}}^{(2)} \right] \tag{12}$$

Since DE is the population based stochastic search algorithm, we define the candidates set

$$\mathbf{X} = \begin{bmatrix} \mathbf{x}_1 \\ \mathbf{x}_2 \\ \vdots \\ \mathbf{x}_{NP} \end{bmatrix} \tag{13}$$

with the population NP.

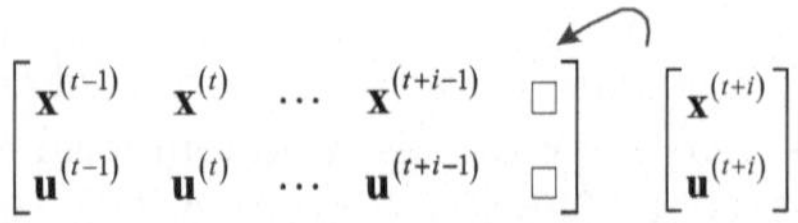

$$\begin{bmatrix} \mathbf{x}^{(t-1)} & \mathbf{x}^{(t)} & \cdots & \mathbf{x}^{(t+i-1)} & \square \\ \mathbf{u}^{(t-1)} & \mathbf{u}^{(t)} & \cdots & \mathbf{u}^{(t+i-1)} & \square \end{bmatrix} \quad \begin{bmatrix} \mathbf{x}^{(t+i)} \\ \mathbf{u}^{(t+i)} \end{bmatrix}$$

Fig. 2. Demonstration of filling of moving window

So we can calculate moving least square LSTD(0)in this way. As first, a candidate member $\mathbf{x}_i$ is sequentially chosen from $\mathbf{X}$. With this decision parameter and the moving window matrix $\mathbf{inp}$, we can obtain

$$\mathbf{J} = \left[\hat{J}_i \begin{pmatrix} x^{(t-1)} \\ u^{(t-1)} \end{pmatrix} \hat{J}_i \begin{pmatrix} x^{(t)} \\ u^{(t)} \end{pmatrix} \cdots \hat{J}_i \begin{pmatrix} x^{(t+L-2)} \\ u^{(t+L-2)} \end{pmatrix} \right] \tag{14}$$

Also, we have similar definition for $\mathbf{J}_{prev}$. According to the formula of one time backward TD(0), we have

$$\left[TD_i^{(t)} \ TD_i^{(t+1)} \cdots TD_i^{(t+L-1)} \right] \tag{15}$$

$$\left[\alpha \hat{J}_i \begin{pmatrix} x^{(t-1)} \\ u^{(t-1)} \end{pmatrix} - \hat{J}_i \begin{pmatrix} x^{(t)} \\ u^{(t)} \end{pmatrix} + \gamma^{(t-1)} \cdots \alpha \hat{J}_i \begin{pmatrix} x^{(t+L-2)} \\ u^{(t+L-2)} \end{pmatrix} - \hat{J}_i \begin{pmatrix} x^{(t+L-1)} \\ u^{(t+L-1)} \end{pmatrix} + \gamma^{(t+L-2)} \right] \tag{16}$$

$$= \alpha \mathbf{J}_{pre} - \mathbf{J} + \gamma \tag{17}$$

Finally, moving least square LSTD(0) is attained as follows,

$$MLSTD\,(0) = \begin{cases} \frac{1}{2} \sum\limits_{j=t}^{t+L-1} \left(TD_i^{(j)} \right) t_{current} \geq t + L - 1 \\ \frac{1}{2} \sum\limits_{j=t}^{t_{current}} \left(TD_i^{(j)} \right) t_{current} < t + L - 1 \end{cases} \tag{18}$$

with widow length as L.

(2) minimize of MLSTD(0)with ADEE

In order to perform the searching progress efficiently and seamlessly with critic -actor structure, we put forward ADEE (adaptive differential evolution with elites) algorithm. We depict in detail how to minimize the MLSTD(0) by employing JADEE . Similar to the approach presented by Zhang [12], ADEE comprises current -to-pbest mutation, binomial crossover method,standard selection and parameter adaption. Besides we introduce strategy of elite inheritance which is good at exploring with the benefit of fast convergence. Also, ADEE can be regarded as an implicitly parallel process of online policy evaluation with given policy sequence output.

The pseudo codefor optimizing MLSTD(0)by ADEE during the policy evaluation period is listed as following:

Begin
Set μ_{CR}, μ_F initial value
For g=1 to G
Set $Set_F = \emptyset, Set_{CR} = \emptyset$
If firstSampling within condition
$\mathbf{x}_1 \leftarrow$ Current weight of CNN;

Randomly initialize $\mathbf{x}_2, \cdots \mathbf{x}_{NP}$
Else
$\mathbf{x}_1, \cdots \mathbf{x}_q \leftarrow$ Elites generated in the previous sampling within condition
Randomly initialize $\mathbf{x}_{q+1}, \cdots \mathbf{x}_{NP}$
For i=1 to NP
Generate $CR_i = rand_{Gausian} \left(\mu_{CR}, 0.1 \right), F_i = rand_{Caucy} \left(\mu_F, 0.1 \right)$
Randomly choose $x_{best,g}^p$ as one of 100p% best vector
$v_{i,g} = x_{i.g} + F_i \left(x_{best,g}^p - x_{i,g} \right) + F_i \left(x_{r1,g} - x_{r2,g} \right)$ where $x_{i.g} \neq x_{r1,g} \neq x_{r2,g}$
Generate $j_{rand} = rand_{int} \left(1, D \right)$
$$u_{j,i,g} = \begin{cases} v_{j,i,g} & rand\left(0,1\right) \leq CR_i \text{ or } j = j_{rand}, \\ x_{j,i,g} & otherwise, \end{cases}$$
If $MLSTD \left(0 \right) : \mathbf{x}_{i,g} \leq MLSTD \left(0 \right) : \mathbf{u}_{i,g}$
$\mathbf{x}_{i,g+1} = \mathbf{x}_{i,g+1}$
Else $\mathbf{x}_{i,g+1} = \mathbf{u}_{i,g}$
End
Sort $\mathbf{X}$ in ascending order with respect to itsMLSTD(0)
Elites $\leftarrow \mathbf{x}_1, \cdots \mathbf{x}_q$
End
New weight of CNN $\leftarrow \mathbf{x}_1$
End

4   Case Study with Cart Polebenchmark

The proposed approach mentioned above is now tested on a single cart-pole problem, which is unstable with multivariable and exhibits non-negligible non-linearities. The objective is to balance a single pole mounted on a cart, which can move either to the right or to the left on abounded, horizontal track. The goal for the controller is to provide a force (applied to the cart) of a fixed magnitudein either the right or the left direction so that the pole stands balanced and avoids hitting the track boundaries. This kind of pendulum is generally used to evaluate the performance of newcontrol strategies. Here we consider the same system model as [13].

The cart-pole system used in the current study is descried as

$$\frac{d^2\theta}{dt^2} = \frac{g\sin\theta + \cos\theta \left[\frac{-F - ml\dot{\theta}^2 \sin\theta + \mu_c \text{sgn}(\dot{x})}{m_c + m} \right] - \frac{\mu_p \dot{\theta}}{ml}}{l \left(\frac{4}{3} - \frac{m\cos^2\theta}{m_c + m} \right)} \tag{19}$$

$$\frac{d^2x}{dt^2} = \frac{F + ml \left[\dot{\theta}^2 \sin\theta - \ddot{\theta} \cos\theta \right] - \mu_c \text{sgn} \left(\dot{x} \right)}{m_c + m} \tag{20}$$

g $9.8m/s^2$, acceleration due to gravity;
m_c $1.0kg$, mass of cart;
m $0.1kg$, mass of pole;

Table 1. performance evaluation of BP vs DE-BP method

Noise type	BP method		DE-BP method	
	Success rate	♯ of trial	Success rate	♯ of trial
Noise free	100%	7.1	100%	5.7
U.*5% a.*	96.7%	30.9	100%	25.2
U. 10% a.	100%	50.8	100%	44.3
U. 5% s.†	100%	12.5	100%	8.1
U. 10% s.	100%	17.3	100%	9.9
G.‡σ^2 (0.1) s.	100%	33.8	100%	21.5
G. σ^2 (0.2) s.	100%	50.3	100%	24.4

* a. : actuators are subject to the noise
† s. : sensors are subject to the noise
* U. : Uniform noise
‡ G. : Gaussian noise

l 0.5m, half-pole length;
μ_c 0.0005m, coefficient of friction of cart on track;
μ_p 0.000002m, coefficient of friction of pole on cart;
F ±10 $Newtons$, force applied to cart's center of mass;

This model provides four state variables:1)position of the cart on the track; 2)angle of the pole with respect to the vertical position;3)cart velocity;4)angular velocity.In our current study, a run consists of a maximum of 1000 consecutive trials. It is considered successful if the last trial(trial number less than 1000) of the run has lasted 6000 timesteps. Otherwise, if the controller is unable to learn to balance the cart-pole within 1000 trials (i.e., none of the 1000 trials has lasted over 600 000 time steps), then the run is considered unsuccessful. In our simulations, we have used 0.02 s for eachtime step, and a trial is a complete process from start to fall.A pole is considered fallen when the pole is outside the range of [12 12]and/or the cart is beyond the range of [2.4 2.4]m in reference to the central position on the track.

In our DE-BP method, we choose window length as 5, population as 5 times dimension of CNN's weight vector,and elites as 10% of population.

5   Conclusions

In this paper, we propose a hybrid evolving and gradient strategy for approximate policy evaluation on online critic-actor learning. Detailed actor-critic architecture with DE-BP algorithm is presented, followed by a case study based on the cart pole which is a popular benchmark in the community for adaptive learning and control. Various simulation results subjected to different types of noise conditions demonstrate the effectiveness of this approach.

References

1. Xin, Y.: Evolving artificial neural networks. Proceedings of the IEEE 87(9), 1423–1447 (1999)
2. Yao, X., Liu, Y.: A new evolutionary system for evolving artificial neural networks. IEEE Transactions on Neural Networks / A Publication of the IEEE Neural Networks Council 8(3), 694–713 (1997)
3. Garro, B.A., Sossa, H., Vázquez, R.A.: Evolving Neural Networks: A Comparison between Differential Evolution and Particle Swarm Optimization. In: Tan, Y., Shi, Y., Chai, Y., Wang, G. (eds.) ICSI 2011, Part I. LNCS, vol. 6728, pp. 447–454. Springer, Heidelberg (2011)
4. Ilonen, J., Kamarainen, J.K., Lampinen, J.: Differential evolution training algorithm for feed-forward neural networks. Neural Processing Letters 17(1), 93–105 (2003)
5. Slowik, A., Bialko, M.: Training of artificial neural networks using differential evolution algorithm. In: Conference on Human System Interactions, vol. 1 and 22008, pp. 60–65 (2008)
6. Whitley, D., et al.: Genetic reinforcement learning for neurocontrol problems. Machine Learning 13(2), 259–284 (1993)
7. Moriarty, D.E., Mikkulainen, R.: Efficient reinforcement learning through symbiotic evolution. Machine Learning 22(1), 11–32 (1996)
8. Xu, X., et al.: Evolutionary adaptive-critic methods for reinforcement learning. In: Cec 2002: Proceedings of the 2002 Congress on Evolutionary Computation, vol. 1 and 2, pp. 1320–1325 (2002)
9. Fu, J., He, H., Zhou, X.: Adaptive learning and control for MIMO system based on adaptive dynamic programming. IEEE Transactions on Neural Networks 22(7), 1133–1148 (2011)
10. Liu, K.: Applied markov decision process. Tinghua University Press, Beijing (2004)
11. Das, S., Suganthan, P.: Differential evolution: a Survey of the state-of-the-art. IEEE Transactions on Evolutionary Computation 15(1), 27–54 (2011)
12. Zhang, J., Sanderson, A.: JADE: Adaptive Differential Evolution With Optional External Archive. IEEE Transactions on Evolutionary Computation 13(5), 945–958 (2009)
13. Barto, A.G., Sutton, R., Anderson, C.: Neuronlike adaptive elements that can solve difficult learning control problems. IEEE Transactions on Systems, Man, & Cybernetics (1983)

Preventing Error Propagation in Semi-supervised Learning

Thiago C. Silva and Liang Zhao

Department of Computer Science, Institute of Mathematics and Computer Science,
University of São Paulo, São Carlos, SP, Brazil, 13560-970
{thiagoch,zhao}@icmc.usp.br

Abstract. Semi-supervised learning is a machine learning approach that is able to employ both labeled and unlabeled samples in the training process. In these cases, the reliability of the labels is a crucial factor, because mislabeled samples may propagate wrong labels to a portion of or even the entire data set. This paper has the objective of addressing the error propagation problem originated by these mislabeled samples by presenting a mechanism embedded in a network-based (graph-based) semi-supervised learning method. Such a technique is based on a combined random-preferential walk of particles in a network constructed from the input data set. The particles of the same class cooperate among them, while the particles of different classes compete with each other to propagate class labels to the whole network. Computer simulations conducted on real-world data sets reveal the effectiveness of the model.

Keywords: Stochastic competitive learning, semi-supervised learning, error propagation, random walk, preferential walk, complex networks.

1 Introduction

In many real situations, only a small subset of data items can be effectively labeled. This is because the labeling process is often expensive, time consuming, and requires intensive human involvement. In order to treat such partially labeled data sets, semi-supervised learning methods are designed to characterize the input data by using both labeled and unlabeled data [1]. Many semi-supervised learning methods, such as Transductive Support Vector Machines [2], can identify data classes of well-defined forms, but usually fail to identify classes of irregular forms. Thus, assumptions on the class distributions have to be made. Unfortunately, such information is usually unknown a priori. In order to overcome this problem, graph-based methods have been developed in the last years [3,1,4]. The main advantage of graph-based methods is the ability of identifying classes of arbitrary distributions.

Recently, Silva and Zhao proposed a network-based semi-supervised learning model using particle competition and cooperation mechanisms [5]. The model considers a large-scale network, in which each labeled data item corresponds to a particle. The particles walk in the network to dominate as many nodes as possible.

J. Wang, G.G. Yen, and M.M. Polycarpou (Eds.): ISNN 2012, Part I, LNCS 7367, pp. 565–572, 2012.
© Springer-Verlag Berlin Heidelberg 2012

Particles with different labels compete with each other and particles with the same label cooperate each other. Each particle can perform a random walk by choosing any neighbor to visit, a preferential walk by choosing the node with the highest domination to visit, or a combination of them. Finally, each particle team propagates its label to all the vertices of a community (a community is defined as a subgraph whose nodes are densely connected within itself, but sparsely connected with the remainder of the network). The system is represented by a non-linear stochastic dynamical system. It shows high precision in data label propagation and, at the same time, presents low computational complexity.

The quality of the training data is a fundamental issue in semi-supervised learning because, in this case, less labeled data is available and errors (wrong labels) may easily be propagated to a portion of or the entire data set. Most algorithms just assume that the input label information is completely reliable, but in practice mislabeled samples are commonly found in the data sets due to instrumental errors, corruption from noise, or even human mistakes in the labeling process. Though this is an important topic, it has not received much attention from researchers and there are still few works devoted to the study of semi-supervised learning from imperfect data [6,7].

In this paper, we introduce a mechanism for preventing error propagation via the particle competition and cooperation model proposed in [5]. The study of this topic is important due to the following factors: (i) In many real situations, we have difficulty to get the labels of the whole data set; however, it is easy to have the labels of some of the data items. This means that semi-supervised learning is quite a common mechanism in learning systems. (ii) We believe that machine learning techniques consisting only of deterministic rules are insufficient. This is because the number of rules required to completely describe even a very specific environment can be prohibitively high. Thus, our conjecture is that a certain level of randomness or chaos is essential for the learning process of autonomous systems. Such a randomness represents the "I don't know" state and serves as a novelty finder. (iii) In real situations, wrong or conflicting information appears frequently. Thus, a learner cannot be blind-confident on all the information or knowledge that it has at its disposal. Humans and other animals can easily compensate for imperfect data in their learning process. Behavioral experiments show that animals can successfully learn from conditioning even when they are inconsistently rewarded. The ability of treating wrong or conflicting information is essential for autonomous learning systems. One of the ways to treat wrongly labeled data, and consequently preventing their propagation, is presented in this paper.

2   Background: Particle Competition Technique (PCM)

In this section, we review the particle-based competitive learning technique [5]. Consider a graph $\mathcal{G} = \langle \mathcal{V}, \mathcal{E} \rangle$, where $\mathcal{V} = \{v_1, \ldots, v_V\}$ is the set of vertices (or nodes) and $\mathcal{E} = \{e_1, \ldots, e_L\} \subset \mathcal{V} \times \mathcal{V}$ is the set of links (or edges). In the proposed competitive learning model, a set of particles $\mathcal{K} = \{1, \ldots, K\}$ is inserted into the vertices of the network in a random manner. Each particle can be conceptualized as a flag carrier with its main objective being to conquer new vertices, while defending its current dominated vertices. In this case, a competition process will naturally take place amongst the particles. When a particle visits an arbitrary vertex, it strengthens its own domination level on that vertex and, simultaneously, weakens the domination levels of all other rival particles on the same vertex. At the end, each particle dominates a community.

In this model, each particle $k \in \mathcal{K}$ can perform two distinct types of movements: (i) a random movement term, modeled by the matrix $\mathbb{P}_{\text{rand}}^{(k)}$, which permits the particle to venture throughout the network, without accounting for the defense of the previously dominated vertices; and (ii) a preferential movement term, modeled by the matrix $\mathbb{P}_{\text{pref}}^{(k)}$, which is responsible for inducing the particle to reinforce the vertices that are owned by itself, i.e., the particle prefers visiting its dominated vertices, instead of a randomly selected one. With the intent of keeping track of the current states of all particles, the following stochastic vector: $S(t) = [S^{(1)}(t), \ldots, S^{(K)}(t)]$ is introduced, where the kth-entry, $S^{(k)}(t) \in \{0, 1\}$, indicates whether the particle k is active ($S^{(k)}(t) = 0$) or exhausted ($S^{(k)}(t) = 1$) at time t. When it is active, the movement policy consists of a combined behavior of randomness and preferential movements. When it is exhausted, the particle switches its movement policy to a new transition matrix, here referred to as $\mathbb{P}_{\text{rean}}^{(k)}(t)$. This matrix is responsible for taking the particle back to its dominated territory, in order to reanimate the corresponding particle by recharging its energy. This is called the *reanimation procedure*. After the energy has been properly recharged, the particle can again perform the combined random-preferential movement in the network. The transition matrix of particle k is given by:

$$\mathbb{P}_{\text{transition}}^{(k)}(t) \triangleq (1 - S^{(k)}(t)) \left[\lambda \mathbb{P}_{\text{pref}}^{(k)}(t) + (1 - \lambda) \mathbb{P}_{\text{rand}}^{(k)} \right] + S^{(k)}(t) \mathbb{P}_{\text{rean}}^{(k)}(t), \quad (1)$$

where $\lambda \in [0, 1]$ indicates the desired fraction of preferential movement that all particles in the network will perform. Specifically, $\mathbb{P}_{\text{transition}}^{(k)}(i, j, t)$ indicates the probability that particle k performs a transition from vertex i to j at time t. For a detailed derivation of the matrices shown in (1), refer to [5].

3   Detection and Prevention of Error Propagation via Competitive Learning

In this section, the main contributions of this paper are discussed. Specifically, we show how to adapt the previous competitive model so as to detect and also prevent error propagation.

3.1   Detecting Incorrectly Labeled Vertices

In order to detect possible mislabeled vertices, consider the stochastic vector $D(t) = [D^{(1)}(t), \ldots, D^{(K)}(t)]$, where the kth-entry, $D^{(k)}(t)$, stores the number of times that particle k has become exhausted until time t. The main idea of introducing this variable is described in the following. Consider the networked data in Fig. 1, in which there are two perceivable classes, namely red and blue. The white vertices denote unlabeled vertices, whereas the colored vertices, labeled vertices. Observe that, within the region of the red class, there is a mislabeled blue vertex. In the competitive model, for each labeled vertex, a representative particle is formed. In this way, the vertices in the vicinity of the mislabeled vertices are expected to be in constant competition among the two red particles and the single mislabeled blue particle. Therefore, it is expected that the blue particle will be stranded in the small region centered at the mislabeled vertex. By virtue of the combination of random and preferential walking of the particle, it will eventually try to venture far away from its represented vertex. Since the surrounding region is expected to be heavily dominated by the red team, this "false" representative particle will get exhausted very often. Hence, the number of times that a particle becomes exhausted is a good indicator whether the vertex that it is representing is a mislabeled one or not. If the particle is constantly getting exhausted, it is possibly representing a mislabeled vertex. Otherwise, it is probably representing a correctly labeled vertex.

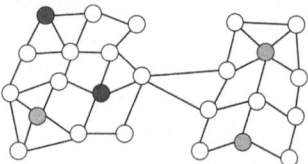

Fig. 1. A networked data example. Observe that there is a mislabeled blue vertex within the region that is probably from the red class.

In view of this, the update rule of of each entry of $D(t)$ is expressed by:

$$D^{(k)}(t) = D^{(k)}(t-1) + S^{(k)}(t), \tag{2}$$

where $S^{(k)}(t+1)$ is the internal system variable already presented in Sect. 2. A natural question that arises from this scenario is: how can we quantify when a particle is getting exhausted more times than the others? In order to solve this problem, first we quantify the average number of times that the particles have become exausted at time t as follows:

$$\langle D(t) \rangle = \frac{1}{K} \sum_{u=1}^{K} D^{(u)}(t). \tag{3}$$

In view of the statistical stochastic variable introduced in (3), any particle k such that:

$$(1 - e^{-\frac{t}{\tau}})D^{(k)}(t) \geq (1 + \alpha)\langle D(t)\rangle \tag{4}$$

holds is considered to be getting exhausted more than the other particles. τ is the time constant of the exponencial decaying function.

3.2 Preventing the Label Propagation from Incorrectly Labeled Vertices

Consider that vertex i has been pinpointed as a mislabeled vertex. In order to prevent its fake label propagation, it is going to have its stochastic vector $N_i(t)$ altered ($N_i(t)$ denotes the number of visits that vertex i received from all particles until time t), in such a way to reflect how the neighborhood is being dominated at time t. Motivated by the fact that if vertex i is considered as a wrongly labeled vertex, then its neighborhood is probably being dominated by rival particles, we simply restart $N_i(t)$ as the average number of visits received by its neighbors. Mathematically, for all $k \in \mathcal{K}$, we have:

$$N_i^{(k)}(t) = \frac{1}{V_i} \sum_{j=1}^{V} a_{i,j} N_j^{(k)}(t), \tag{5}$$

where V_i denotes the number of neighbors of vertex i. An important difference from the modified model and the original model is that the former is capable of re-labeling labeled vertices, while the latter is not. This new feature is processed when (5) is applied.

3.3 The New Competitive Learning System

The new internal state of the proposed stochastic dynamical system is given by: $X(t) = [p(t)\ N(t)\ E(t)\ S(t)\ D(t)]^T$. Denote wrong$(k_i, t) = (1 - e^{-\frac{t}{\tau}})D^{(k_i)}(t) \geq (1 + \alpha)\langle D(t)\rangle$, then the proposed dynamical system is given by:

$$\phi: \begin{cases} p^{(k)}(t+1) = j, \quad j \sim \mathbb{P}_{\text{transition}}^{(k)}(t) \\ N_i^{(k)}(t+1) = \mathbb{1}_{[\text{wrong}(k_i,t)]}\left[\frac{1}{V_i}\sum_{j=1}^{V} a_{i,j} N_j^{(k)}(t)\right] \\ \qquad\qquad + \mathbb{1}_{[\neg\text{wrong}(k_i,t)]}\left[N_i^{(k)}(t) + \mathbb{1}_{[p^{(k)}(t+1)=i]}\right] \\ E^{(k)}(t+1) = \begin{cases} \min(\omega_{\max}, E^{(k)}(t) + \Delta), \text{if owner}(k,t) \\ \max(\omega_{\min}, E^{(k)}(t) - \Delta), \text{if } \neg\text{owner}(k,t) \end{cases} \\ S^{(k)}(t+1) = \mathbb{1}_{[E^{(k)}(t+1)=\omega_{\min}]} \\ D^{(k)}(t+1) = D^{(k)}(t) + S^{(k)}(t+1) \end{cases} \tag{6}$$

where k_i denotes the representative particle of vertex i. In the following, we present the meaning of the first four expressions shown in the competitive dynamical system ϕ (the fifth expression has already been introduced):

- *Particle's Transition Rule (1st Expression)*: Provides the update rule for the localizations of the particles ($p^{(k)}(t)$ denotes the localization of particle k). This is performed using the transition matrix shown in (1).
- *Update Rule of the Number of Visits (2nd Expression)*: Supplies the update rule of the number of visits received by all vertices in the model. The two indicators are exclusive: either one or another is active in a given time. The first indicator accounts for adding 1 on those vertices that are being visited by particles, while the second is responsible for resetting the counting of this vector.
- *Update Rule of the Particle's Energy (3rd Expression)*: Here, we introduce the vector: $E(t) = [E^{(1)}(t), \ldots, E^{(K)}(t)]$, where the kth-entry, $E^{(k)}(t) \in [\omega_{\min}, \omega_{\max}]$, denotes the energy level of particle k at time t. In the second expression of system ϕ, owner(k, t) $= \left(\arg \max_{m \in \mathcal{K}} \left(\bar{N}^{(m)}_{p^{(k)}(t)}(t) \right) = k \right)$. $\Delta > 0$ symbolizes the increment or decrement of energy that each particle receives at time t.
- *Update Rule of the Particle's State (4th Expression)*: Here, the update rule that governs $S(t)$ is given. As we have stated, an arbitrary particle k will be transported back to its domain only if its energy drops to a threshold $\omega_{\min}$. With that in mind, it is natural that each entry of $S^{(k)}(t)$ must monitor the current energy value of its corresponding particle k. If this energy ever drops to the given threshold, the switch must be enabled. Analogously, if the particle still has an energy value greater than this threshold, then the switch should be disabled. This behavior is exactly expressed in the third expression of the competitive system ϕ.

4   Computer Simulations

In this section, computer simulations are conducted in order to assess the effectiveness of the proposed model on error-prone environments.

4.1   Setting Up the Proposed Algorithm and Environment

Following the line and analysis realized in [5], the PCM is able to supply decent accuracy rates when $\Delta \in [0.05, 0.4]$ and $\lambda \in [0.2, 0.8]$ both on artificial and real-world data sets. Based on that, in the next computer simulations, the PCM's parameters are fixed to $\Delta = 0.1$, $\lambda = 0.6$, and $\tau = 10$, unless we provide a note orienting otherwise.

In the semi-supervised scheme, a set of pre-labeled examples $\mathcal{L} = \{l_1, \ldots, l_{|\mathcal{L}|}\} \subset \mathcal{V}$ is provided. Each labeled instance $l_i, i \in \{1, \ldots, |\mathcal{L}|\}$ holds a label that is contained in the set $\mathcal{C}$. The remaining non-labeled set is denoted as $\mathcal{U} = \mathcal{V} \backslash \mathcal{L}$. In order to introduce labeled instances with wrong labels (error-prone environment), we deliberately exchange the labels of some instances in the labeled set $\mathcal{L}$. The proportion of instances changed is denoted as q and the set of mislabeled samples is given by $\mathcal{Q} \in \mathcal{L}$. For example, if $q = 0.1$, then 10% of the labeled instances are incorrectly labeled.

4.2   Simulations on Real-World Data Sets

We conduct computer simulations using the proposed technique and 3 state-of-art competing techniques: LP, LNP, and the original particle competition model (PCM) with no error detection [8,9,10]. We apply these algorithm on two data sets from the UCI Machine Learning Repository [11]: Iris and Letter Recognition. The former is composed of three equal-sized classes, each of which comprising 50 samples, totalizing 150 samples. The latter is composed of 20000 samples divided into 26 unbalanced classes, each representing a different letter of the English alphabet. Thus, the Letter Recognition data set can be considered as a large-scale data set.

Figures 2a and 2b show the behavior of the accuracy rate vs. the proportion of mislabeled samples q. One can verify that, as q grows, all algorithms start to produce smaller accuracy rates. However, the proposed technique (proposed PCM) is able to outperform all the compared algorithms, by virtue of the detection and prevention mechanisms embedded into the competitive model. One point that is worth mentioning is, when the environment is error-free ($q = 0$), then the proposed and original PCMs supply very similar results. This is expected, since the labeled samples are hoped to lie within densely connected groups; therefore, the owner switching mechanism introduced in (4) will rarely be satisfied. The proposed PCM is able to maintain decent accuracy rate because of the competition mechanism realized by the particles. In an error-prone environment, we can conceive the algorithm as having two types of competition taking place simultaneously: competition of particles spreading correctly and incorrectly labeled samples. Since the competition is always taking place indirectly (through the accumulated domination levels of each vertex and particles' movement policy), then these two types of label spreading are always in confront. As it is expected to one have more correctly labeled samples than incorrectly labeled ones, then the competition will naturally extinct the propagation of the mislabeled samples as the system progresses in time.

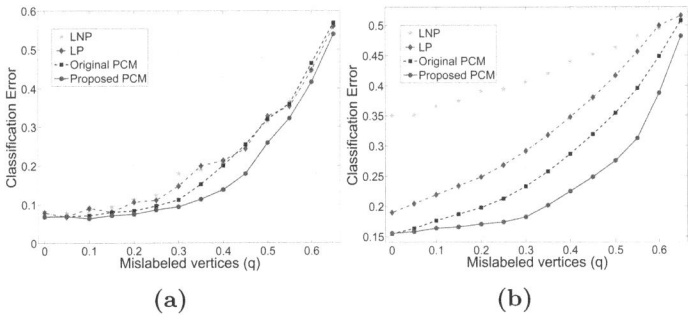

(a)   (b)

Fig. 2. Behavior of the classification error as the proportion of wrongly labeled vertices increases on two real-world data sets. (a) Iris data set and (b) Letter Recognition Data Set.

5   Final Remarks

This paper proposes a new method for detecting and preventing error propagation through particle competition. In this model, several particles, each of which representing a class, navigate in the network to explore their territory and, at the same time, attempt to defend their territory against rival particles. If several particles propagate the same class label, then a team is formed, and a cooperation process amongst these particles occurs. The error detection mechanism is realized by weighting the domination levels of the vertices in relation to the current iteration. When the dynamical competitive system begins, there is a penalizing factor which prevents the detection of false positives. This has been introduced in order to diminish the dependency of the proposed error propagation model on the initial location of the labeled samples. As the system evolves, this penalization ceases to exist and the plain domination level that each vertex has is used in the error propagation inference. Once a vertex is declared as mislabeled, the proposed technique resets its domination levels as the average value of its neighborhood, so as to conform to the cluster assumption that the proposed algorithm holds on to. Computer simulations conducted on real-world data sets confirm that the model is effective in noisy environments.

Acknowledgments. This work is supported by the State of São Paulo Research Foundation (FAPESP) and the Brazilian National Council of Technological and Scientific Development (CNPq).

References

1. Chapelle, O., Schölkopf, B., Zien, A. (eds.): Semi-supervised Learning. Adaptive computation and machine learning. MIT Press, Cambridge (2006)
2. Vapnik, V.N.: Statistical Learning Theory. Wiley Interscience, New York (2008)
3. Zhu, X.: Semi-supervised learning literature survey. Technical Report 1530, Computer Sciences, University of Wisconsin-Madison (2005)
4. Silva, T.C., Zhao, L.: Semi-supervised learning guided by the modularity measure in complex networks. Neurocomputing 78(1), 30–37 (2012)
5. Silva, T.C., Zhao, L.: Network-based stochastic semisupervised learning. IEEE Transactions on Neural Networks and Learning Systems 23(3), 451–466 (2012)
6. Hartono, P., Hashimoto, S.: Learning from imperfect data. Appl. Soft Comput. 7(1), 353–363 (2007)
7. Amini, M.R., Gallinari, P.: Semi-supervised learning with an imperfect supervisor. Knowl. Inf. Syst. 8(4), 385–413 (2005)
8. Zhou, D., Bousquet, O., Lal, T.N., Weston, J., Schölkopf, B.: Learning with local and global consistency. In: Advances in Neural Information Processing Systems, vol. 16, pp. 321–328. MIT Press (2004)
9. Wang, F., Zhang, C.: Label propagation through linear neighborhoods. IEEE Transactions on Knowledge and Data Engineering 20(1), 55–67 (2008)
10. Quiles, M.G., Zhao, L., Alonso, R.L., Romero, R.A.F.: Particle competition for complex network community detection. Chaos 18(3), 033107 (2008)
11. Frank, A., Asuncion, A.: UCI machine learning repository (2010)

An Incremental Approach to Support Vector Machine Learning

Jing Jin

Department of Computer Science and Engineering,
Nanjing University of Aeronautics and Astronautics,
davidxh2012@126.com

Abstract. In this paper we proposed a novel approach for incremental support vector machine training. The original problem of SVM is a quadratic programming(QP) problem, the result of which reduces to a linear combination of training examples. This result inspires us that SVM can be viewed as a two layer neural network, the structure of the first layer of which is determined by the kernel function chosen and the training examples, and what remains mutable is coefficients and bias of the second. In our method we train the weights of support vectors and bias using the same stochastic gradient descent algorithm as perceptron training. In contrast with perceptron training, we picked the hinge loss function rather than the square of errors as the target function, since in hinge loss function correctly classified training examples has no effect on the decision surface.

Keywords: incremental SVM, neural network, online training.

1   Introduction

Classification problem involves constructing a rule for classifying vector into two categories based on the training set whose categories are known prior. Support vector machines(SVM)[4] first maps input vector to a feature space, the dimension of which is as high as the size of training set. Then it constructs a hyperplane in feature space and maximizes the margin between itself and points in the training set. The hyperplane is then used to bisects vectors of unknown category. The following are several advantages of SVM:

1. It implemented a form of structural risk minimization[4].In this way it tries to find a comprise between the minimization of empirical risk and the prevention of overfitting.
2. This is a convex quadratic programming problem, in which case any minimum solution is global minimum.

Usually SVM is trained under batch mode, in which case training set must be known a prior. When new training data comes, SVM must be trained from scratch. In real world applications, training data often comes sequentially and the size of training data set will grow huge soon, in this case the batch mode

J. Wang, G.G. Yen, and M.M. Polycarpou (Eds.): ISNN 2012, Part I, LNCS 7367, pp. 573–579, 2012.

will cause considerable computational cost and requires much more resources to store matrix, which often makes the batch mode infeasible. Training SVM incrementally is a scenario in which examples come one by one, in contrast with batch mode in which all examples are available at one time. It is advantageous in situations when resource is limited and data are not available at once. Early work on this subject[1,2,3,5,8] gives approximate solution. An exact solution was found by Cauwenberghs and Poggio[6], this method updates the optimal solution and keeps it under K-T conditions when an example is added or removed. However, as far as we know, there is not any successful applications that adopted this algorithm. Shilton[7] proposed an approach using the active set method to solve the quadratic programming problem and as a result of the incremental nature of the active set method, their approach turned into an incremental one successfully. In our method we view the SVM solution as a two layer RBF neural network, the first layer of which is determined by the training set and kernel chosen, since the remainder is a one layer perceptron and can be trained incrementally, we proposed our approach of incremental SVM training. The rest of this paper is organized as follows: In section 2 we reviewed the basic ideas of SVM. In section 3 we described and explained the outline of our algorithm. In section 4 we conducted several experiments and compared the result with SVM training using batch mode implemented using libsvm. Section 5 includes some conclusion and discussions.

2   SVM Basics

The original problem of SVM is

$$\min_{\beta,\beta_0} \frac{1}{2}\|\beta\|^2 + C\sum_{i=1}^{n}\xi_i$$

$$s.t. \quad \forall i \quad y_i(x_i^T\beta + \beta_0) \geq 1 - \xi_i \tag{1}$$

$$\xi_i \geq 0$$

$$where \quad C > 0$$

Under the Kuhn-Tucker condition we can conclude that the optimal separating function reduces to a linear combination of dot product on the training examples,namely

$$\beta = \sum_{i=1}^{n}\alpha_i y_i x_i^T, \forall i \quad 0 \leq \alpha_i \leq C \tag{2}$$

Replacing the dot product with a kernel function we get the discriminant function as follows:

$$f(x) = \sum_{i=1}^{n}\alpha_i y_i K(x, x_i) + b, \forall i \quad 0 \leq \alpha_i \leq C \tag{3}$$

Thus by substituting $(1 - y_i f(x_i))_+$ for the loss function the original problem can be written as

$$\min_{0 \leq \alpha \leq C1, b} \frac{1}{2} \alpha^T Y^T K Y \alpha + C \sum_{i=1}^{n} (1 - y_i f(x_i))_+$$

$$where \quad Y_{ij} = \begin{cases} y_i & \text{if } i = j \\ 0 & \text{otherwise} \end{cases} \tag{4}$$

$$K_{ij} = K(x_i, x_j)$$

$$\alpha = \begin{bmatrix} \alpha_1 & \alpha_2 & \cdots & \alpha_n \end{bmatrix}^T$$

which is a much simpler optimization problem on α. This formulation 4 inspires us that we can solve this problem by searching the feasible region using conventional approach like gradient descent.

3   Method

From the perspective of RBF neural network, one aporia is to find out an effective way to determine the hidden layer, including the number of nodes and the structure. SVM can be viewed as a solution to this. The formulation 3 first maps the input vector into a n dimensional feature space through kernel function, where n is the size of the training set, then it sums them up by giving each item of the feature vector a weight with a bias. Since the structure and the number of nodes in the hidden layer is determined, which is the kernel function chosen and the number of training examples correspondingly, what remains is to work out the weights of the items of the feature vector and the bias. Standard SVM solves this using numerical ways, which is infeasible for large data sets in practical because of the limitation of resources like physical memory. In fact, after mapping the input vector into feature space, what remains is just a linear constrained perceptron, so we can adopt the learning methods we used in perceptron training, usually the stochastic gradient descent algorithm.

Explanation of the Algorithm. Algorithm 1 describes the outline of the algorithm. Since there exists abudant proof of the great performance of hinge loss function, so we use it as loss function here, namely

$$\mathbf{W_i} = (1 - y_i f(x_i))_+$$
$$where \quad (\alpha)_+ = \max[0, \alpha] \tag{5}$$

When using kernel function, the following equations are clear:

$$\frac{\nabla f(x_i)}{\nabla \alpha_j} = y_j K(x_i, x_j) \tag{6}$$

$$g_{\alpha_i} = \frac{\nabla \mathbf{W}}{\nabla \alpha_j} = -y_i y_j K(x_i, x_j) \tag{7}$$

$$g_b = \frac{\nabla \mathbf{W}}{\nabla \mathbf{b}} = -y_i \tag{8}$$

$$when \quad y_i f(x_i) < 1$$

Algorithm 1. Incremental SVM algorithm

Initialize α with random values less than C
  $b \leftarrow 0$
  $k \leftarrow 0$
  while $k < M$ **do**
    for $i = 1$ *to* N **do**
      if $(y_i * (kernel_i * \alpha) + b) > margin$ **then**
        $\alpha_i = 0$
      else
        $b \leftarrow b + p * y_i$
        $\alpha \leftarrow \alpha + p * y_i * kernel_i$
        for $j = 1$ *to* N **do**
          if $\alpha_j > C$ **then**
            $\alpha_j = C$
          else if $\alpha_j < C$ **then**
            $\alpha_j = 0$
          end if
        end for
      end if
    end for
    if $\triangle acc < threshold$ **then**
      break;
    end if
  end while

When $y_i f(x_i) < 1$, it means that this training example is either in the margin or misclassified by the current discriminant function in both cases this example is a support vector and the coefficients should be adapted, otherwise the training example is correctly classified and not a support vector, the weight on it should be set to 0. In the algorithm, p denotes the learning rate. Since this is a linear constrained problem, we need to pull the weights back into the feasible region when it exceeds the limitation, e.t. it turns negative or grows larger than c. The convergence of our algorithm is determined by two conditions: whether the accuracy still improves and the iterative steps exceeds the maximum number. In Algorithm 1, M is the number of maximum iterative steps and can be predefined, $\triangle acc$ is the absolution difference of accuracy between two adjacent steps, if the difference is too small, it means that the accuracy has turned stable and the algorithm converged.

Incremental Learning. The application of our method to incremental learning problem is straightforward. Suppose we have obtained the optimal solution for an existing training set and we wish to add additional training points. First we need to update the kernel matrix, this will not cause much computation since we just need to calculate the kernel function between new training points and existing points. Then we set the initial weights of new examples to 0, and iterate several until the algorithm converges.

4   Experiments

4.1   Data Set

We conducted ten experiments on different data sets ,including eight from our lab and two(adult and mushroom) from the UCI repository[9], and compared its accuracy with standard svm using libsvm. Tabel 4 lists the data set used for training and testing. For the data sets excluding adult, we achieved a very high accuracy without much effort. However, for the adult data set, which is unbalanced,it was difficult to achieve an error rate less than 20% using both our incremental svm and libsvm. To show that our algorithm requires much less memory than the standard svm method, we introduced another data set,i.e. patents, which contains more than 3,000,000 training examples.

4.2   Implementation

In the implementation of our algorithm we first calculated the kernel matrix and save it on hard disk. For both the sake of efficiency and convenience, we used to the memory map file mechanism to manipulate the matrix in local file as a matrix in memory.For the implementation of standard svm, we picked libsvm. For both methods, we picked linear kernel and set margin and C to 1. For the incremental svm, the learning rate p and maximum step number differs slightly on different data sets. Table 4 shows the result accuracy on different data sets.It can be seen from the table that our method can achieve a high accuracy in most cases(the adult data set excluded). For the adult data set, however, it is difficult to achieve a error rate less than 20%.

We showed the memory usage of two methods on the large data sets with more 3,000,000 training examples in figure 4.2. In this figure the horizontal axis is the number of training examples used while the vertical axis is the 10-based logarithm of the number of bytes used by each method, and it's obvious our method requires less than 1% memory space than the standard svm. When the

Table 1. Data Sets

Data Set	Positive	Negative	Total	Training	Test	SVM	Incremental SVM
adult	34014	11208	45222	20000	2000	0.7800	0.7680
mushroom	4208	3916	8124	7124	1124	0.9730	0.9728
PD00	445	595	1040	622	418	0.9761	0.9450
PD15mat	423	516	939	592	347	0.9683	0.9510
PD30mat	423	516	939	592	347	0.9579	0.9251
PM00mat	444	595	1039	629	419	0.9785	0.9642
PM15mat	422	516	938	590	348	0.9511	0.9368
PM30mat	422	516	938	590	348	0.9569	0.9397
PU00	445	595	1040	622	418	0.9593	0.9498
PU30	423	516	939	592	347	0.9683	0.9452
patents	303315	3192822	3496137	3000000	496137	0.8315	0.8864

number of training examples exceeds 1,200,000, the standard svm failed to go on. We can see that the accuracy of our method is higher than the standard svm in contrast with other cases, this is because the standard svm method can only train with 1,200,000 examples on the experimental machine, while by saving the kernel matrix into disk before training, our method can use all the training examples.

All experiments were carried out on a machine with 6GBytes of memory and 2TBytes of disk running Windows 7 Ultimate.

4.3   Complexity Analysis

The main advantage of our algorithm is the low cost of memory space. It can easily be inferred that in our algorithm, essentially you just need memory for one row of kernel matrix and the training label, you do not even have to store the training vectors. This can significantly reduce memory requirements in situations where the training vector has a relatively high dimensionality. On average, our method costs less than 1% memory space than the standard svm.

As we know, the time complexity of a standard SVM QP solver is $O(M^3)$, where M denotes the size of training set. If we use our method in a batch mode, two parts of our algorithm costs most of the training time: calculating the kernel matrix and testing the performance of after each iteration. The time complexity of the first part,i.e. calculating the kernel, is $O(nM^2)$, where n denotes the dimensionality training vector, while the time complexity of the second part,i.e. the iterative steps, is $O(tM^2)$, where t denotes the iterative steps, since in each iteration we need to adjust weights and bias for each training example, and the time complexity for each example is $O(M)$. In our experiments on all the data

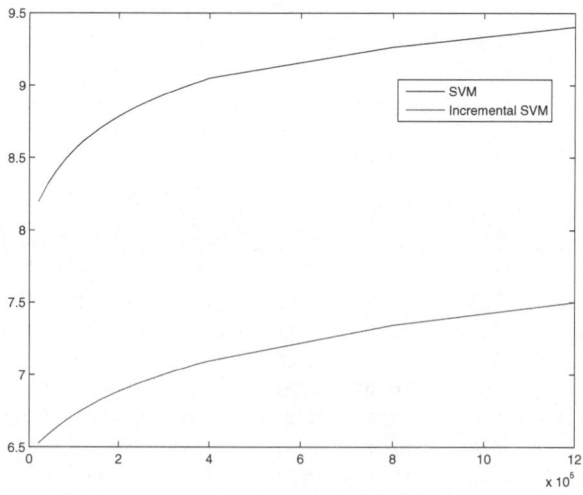

Fig. 1. Memory usage of incremental svm and our method on large data set

sets, both the dimensionality of training vector(n) and the iterative steps(t) are much less than the size of training set(M), as a result the time complexity of our algorithm is $O(M^2)$. What's more, the first part of our algorithm can be heavily parallelled, since each element of the kernel matrix is independent of the rest, using modern technology like cuda, the training time can be significantly reduced.

5   Conclusion

In this paper we proposed an incremental approach to incremental support vector machine learning. The experiment results presented show that our method can achieve performance approximately the same as batch SVM training while our method requires less memory and computational cost.

References

1. Liang, Z., Lia, Y.: Incremental support vector machine learning in the primal and applications. Neurocomputing 72(10-12), 2249–2258 (2009)
2. Zheng, J., Yu, H., Shen, F., Zhao, J.: An Online Incremental Learning Support Vector Machine for Large-scale Data. In: Diamantaras, K., Duch, W., Iliadis, L.S. (eds.) ICANN 2010. LNCS, vol. 6353, pp. 76–81. Springer, Heidelberg (2010)
3. Liu, X., Zhang, G., Zhan, Y., Zhu, E.: An Incremental Feature Learning Algorithm Based on Least Square Support Vector Machine. In: Preparata, F.P., Wu, X., Yin, J. (eds.) FAW 2008. LNCS, vol. 5059, pp. 330–338. Springer, Heidelberg (2008)
4. Vapnik, V.: The nature of statistical learning theory. Springer, New York (1999)
5. Ruping, S.: Incremental learning with support vector machines. Technical Report TR-18, Universitat Dortmund, SFB475 (2002)
6. Cauwenberghs, G., Poggio, T.: Incremental and decremental support vector machine learning. In: Leen, T.K., Dietterich, T.G., Tresp, V. (eds.) Advances in Neural Information Processing Systems, vol. 13, pp. 409–415. MIT Press (2001)
7. Shilton, A., Palaniswami, M., Ralph, D., Tsoi, A.C.: Incremental Training of Support Vector Machines. IEEE Transactions on Neural Networks 16(1) (January 2005)
8. Mitra, P., Murthy, C.A., Pal, S.K.: Data Condensation in Large Databases by Incremental Learning with Support Vector Machines. In: International Conference on Pattern Recognition (2000)
9. UC Irvine Machine Learning Repository, http://archive.ics.uci.edu/ml/

Multi-phase Fast Learning Algorithms for Solving the Local Minimum Problem in Feed-Forward Neural Networks

Chi-Chung Cheung[1], Sin-Chun Ng[2], and Andrew kwok-fai Lui[2]

[1] Department of Electronic and Information Engineering,
The Hong Kong Polytechnic University, Hunghom, Hong Kong
encccl@polyu.edu.hk
[2] School of Science and Technology, The Open University of Hong Kong,
30 Good Shepherd Street, Homantin, Hong Kong
scng@ouhk.edu.hk

Abstract. Backpropagation (BP) learning algorithm is the most widely supervised learning technique which is extensively applied in the training of multi-layer feed-forward neural networks. Many modifications of BP have been proposed to speed up the learning of the original BP. However, they all have different drawbacks and they cannot perform very well in all kinds of applications. This paper proposes a new algorithm, which provides a systematic approach to make use of the characteristics of different fast learning algorithms so that the learning process can converge to the global minimum. During the training, different fast learning algorithms will be used in different phases to improve the global convergence capability. Our performance investigation shows that the proposed algorithm always converges in different benchmarking problems (applications) whereas other popular fast learning algorithms sometimes give very poor global convergence capabilities.

Keywords: backpropagation, multi-phase learning algorithms, local minimum.

1   Introduction

Backpropagation (BP) learning algorithm [1] is the most popular supervised learning technique which is extensively applied in the training of multi-layer feed-forward neural networks. It is so popular because it is simple and it computational complexity is low. However, its convergence (learning) rate is slow, and it is easily trapped in local minima, especially for non-linearly separable problems such as the exclusive OR (XOR) problem [2, 3]. When a learning process is trapped into a local minimum and it cannot escape afterwards to go to the global minimum, it is called local minimum problem. Another problem to affect the converge rate and the global convergence capability (i.e., the capability to go to the global minimum) is "flat spot" problem. The main reason to have the "flat spot" problem is due to the premature saturation in the derivative of the activation function [4 – 7]. If a learning process is

J. Wang, G.G. Yen, and M.M. Polycarpou (Eds.): ISNN 2012, Part I, LNCS 7367, pp. 580–589, 2012.

trapped into a "flat spot" or a local minimum, the weight update of the learning process will become very slow or even unchanged (i.e., either the convergence rate is very small or the global convergence capability is poor). Many fast learning algorithms based on BP have been proposed to improve the performance of BP in terms of the convergence rate (i.e., speed up the learning process). But they seldom improve the global convergence capability [8 – 10]. Recently some new algorithms are proposed to address the local minimum problem [11, 12]. [11] proposed the Enhanced Two-Phase Method (E2P) to identify the existence of local minima and assign appropriate fast learning algorithms to speed up the learning rate with better global convergence capability. However, E2P still cannot completely the local minimum problem. In most cases, when the first fast learning algorithm cannot escape from a local minimum, the second algorithm can solve it (i.e., after switching to the second fast learning algorithm, the learning process can converge to the global minimum). However, occasionally in some cases, when the two fast learning algorithms cannot solve the problem, the learning process cannot converge. [12] proposed another approach called Fast Learning Algorithm with Promising Convergence Capability (PCC). According to the characteristics of different fast learning algorithms, PCC assigns them systematically in a learning process until it converges. In [12], PCC can always converge in two popular complicated applications with a fast learning rate, whereas many other popular fast learning algorithms give very poor global convergence capabilities in two applications. However, there are too many parameters required to set in the algorithm and some parameter settings are quite arbitrary, which not be applied in general applications.

In this paper, three different fast learning algorithms are assigned into the learning process systematically to solve the local minimum problem. The assignment of the fast learning algorithms is based on their characteristics. Through our simulation results, our proposed algorithm can always converge in different applications while other cannot.

This paper is organized as follows. Section 2 introduces the basic operations of three popular fast learning algorithms, which will be used in our proposed algorithm named as Local Minimum Solver (LMS). Moreover, their characteristics and limitations will be discussed. Section 3 describes our proposed algorithm. Section 4 compares its performance with the three popular fast learning algorithms. Finally, conclusions are described in Section 5.

2   Fast Learning Algorithms

In our proposed algorithm, three popular fast learning algorithms will be used and this section briefly describes their standard operations: Quickprop [8], RPROP [9] and MGFPROP [10]. Moreover, their characteristics and limitations will be discussed here.

2.1   Quickprop

The Quickprop algorithm was developed in [8] to improve the convergence of BP. Instead of using the gradient function of BP and the first order derivative of the overall error to update the current weights, Quickprop uses successive values of the gradient of the error surface in the weight space to estimate the location of a minimum. It then changes the weights to move directly towards this minimum. The main assumptions of the Quickprop algorithm are that the error surface is concave and locally quadratic.

Based on these assumptions, the weight update rule of the algorithm is:

$$\Delta\omega_{ij}(t) = \frac{E'(t)}{E'(t-1)-E'(t)}\Delta\omega_{ij}(t-1),\qquad(1)$$

where $\Delta\omega_{ij}(t)$ is the change of the weight connecting the ith and j^{th} nodes in a neural network at the tth iteration, $E(t)$ is the system error at t^{th} iteration, and $E'(t) = \partial E(t)/\partial\omega_{ij}(t)$. In Equation (1), the Quickprop algorithm will take an infinite step and the network will behave chaotically when the difference between $E'(t-1)$ and $E'(t)$ is very small. To avoid it happening, a parameter called the maximum growth factor, ϕ, is introduced to limit the growth of a step size, i.e.,

$$\Delta\omega_{ij}(t) = \max\left(\phi, \frac{E'(t)}{E'(t-1)-E'(t)}\right)\Delta\omega_{ij}(t-1).\qquad(2)$$

The major drawback of Quickprop is the local minimum problem. Quickprop always reaches the first minimum when it is found, whether it is a local minimum or the global minimum. That explains why it is easy to be trapped into a local minimum and its global convergence capability is very poor, especially when there are many local minima in an application.

Fig. 1 shows the learning process of Quickprop in the 5-bit Counting problem (this application will be described later in Section 4). Each learning curve shows one typical run (out of the 100 runs) in our experiment. The 5-bit Counting application has a number of local minima and thus fast learning algorithms are easily trapped into those local minima and are slow to proceed further. In Fig. 1, Quickprop was very fast at the beginning and very close to the error threshold at around 400 iterations. Then it is trapped into a local minimum and finally cannot converge.

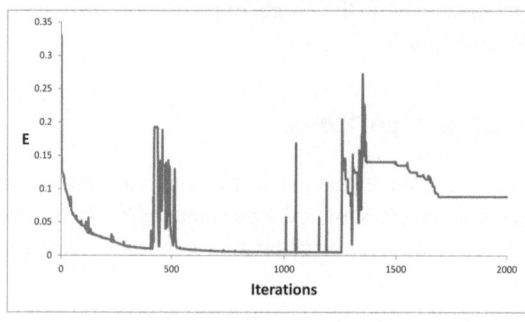

Fig. 1. The performance of Quickprop in the 5-bit counting problem

2.2   RPROP

'Resilient propagation' (RPROP) [9] is a variable step size algorithm. Each weight has its own variable update step being adapted throughout the algorithm to decrease the overall error. The update-value evolves as follows:

$$\Delta_{ij}^{(t)} = \begin{cases} \eta^+ \Delta_{ij}^{(t-1)}, & \text{if } \partial E^{(t-1)}/\partial \omega_{ij} \times \partial E^{(t)}/\partial \omega_{ij} > 0 \\ \eta^- \Delta_{ij}^{(t-1)}, & \text{if } \partial E^{(t-1)}/\partial \omega_{ij} \times \partial E^{(t)}/\partial \omega_{ij} < 0 \\ 0, & \text{otherwise} \end{cases} \tag{3}$$

$$\Delta \omega_{ij}^{(t)} = \begin{cases} -\Delta_{ij}^{(t-1)}, & \text{if } \partial E^{(t)}/\partial \omega_{ij} > 0 \\ +\Delta_{ij}^{(t-1)}, & \text{if } \partial E^{(t)}/\partial \omega_{ij} < 0 \\ 0, & \text{otherwise} \end{cases} \tag{4}$$

where $0 < \eta^- < 1 < \eta^+$, $\omega_{ij}^{(t+1)} = \omega_{ij}^{(t)} + \Delta \omega_{ij}^{(t)}$, and $\omega_{ij}^{(t+1)}$ is the weight from neuron j to neuron i at the tth iteration.

RPROP has the advantage of very fast convergence speed; it has been shown in [9] that RPROP outperforms BP and some other fast learning algorithms. RPROP is still a local search technique, however, and it suffers from the local minimum problem. Note that the global convergence capability of RPROP is usually very poor in many applications compared with other popular fast learning algorithms. Fig. 2 shows the learning process of the Iris problem when RPROP is applied. This application is very complicated and has many local minima. Thus, many fast learning algorithms including RPROP are easily trapped into them and therefore they have very poor global convergence capabilities in these two applications. In Fig. 2, RPROP is very fast at the beginning and closes to the error threshold very quickly because the step size of RPROP is big. However, since the step size is too big, it traps itself into local minima and finally cannot converge.

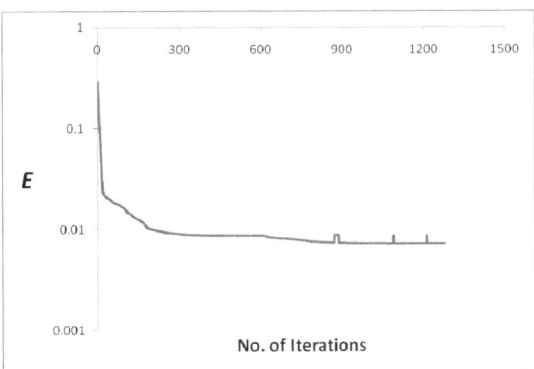

Fig. 2. The performance of RPROP in the Iris problem

2.3   MGFPROP

In BP, the back-propagated error signals $\delta_{pm}(i)$ and $\overline{\delta}_{pk}(i)$ at the ith iteration include the factors $o_{pm}(i)(1-o_{pm}(i))$ and $\overline{o}_{pk}(i)(1-\overline{o}_{pk}(i))$ respectively where $o_{pm}(i)$ and $\overline{o}_{pk}(i)$ are the outputs of the output node m and the hidden node k from the input pattern p at the ith iteration respectively. The characteristics of these factors cause BP to have a slow convergence rate. When $o_{pm}(i)$ or $\overline{o}_{pk}(i)$ approaches extreme values (i.e., 0 or 1), the error signals will become so small that the effect of the true error signal $t_{pm}-o_{pm}(i)$ is weak (t_{pm} is the desired target of the output neuron m from the input pattern p). Thus, if the learning process diverges, the magnitude of the factors becomes so small that the output cannot be effectively adjusted by the error signals, and the learning process becomes very slow or is even suppressed. This leads to the "flat spot" problem. To overcome this problem, MGFPROP (BP with Magnified Gradient Function) magnifies the factors $o_{pm}(i)(1-o_{pm}(i))$ and $\overline{o}_{pk}(i)(1-\overline{o}_{pk}(i))$ by using a power factor $1/S$ ($S \geq 1$), i.e.,

$$\delta_{pm}(i) = (t_{pm} - o_{pm}(i))\left[o_{pm}(i)(1-o_{pm}(i))\right]^{1/S} \tag{5}$$

$$\overline{\delta}_{pk}(i) = \left[\overline{o}_{pk}(i)(1-\overline{o}_{pk}(i))\right]^{1/S}\sum_{m=1}^{M}\delta_{pm}(i)\omega_{km}(i) \tag{6}$$

where $\omega_{km}(i)$ is the network weight for the hidden node k and the output node m at the ith iteration [10]. When compared with the standard BP algorithm, the gradient term of MGFPROP has a larger increment when the factors approaches zero and the effect of the true error signal is stronger. The simulation results in [10] show that MGFPROP has a faster convergence rate and better global convergence capability when compared with the standard BP and some modified BP algorithms. In Fig. 3, when MGFPROP is applied in the Iris problem, it is fast at the beginning but very slow after that because the step size of MGFPROP is small so that it is not easily

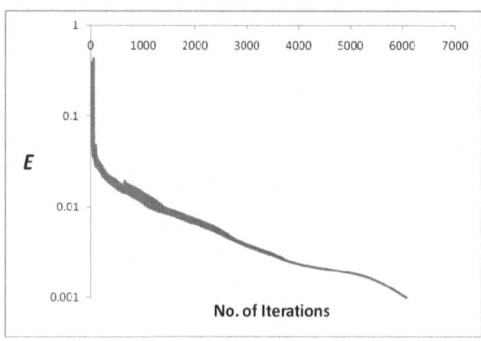

Fig. 3. The performance of MGFPROP in the Iris problem

trapped into local minima and, most of the time, it can converge to the global optimal solution smoothly. The major disadvantage of MGFPROP is that its convergence rate is not very fast, especially in complicated applications.

3   Local Minimum Solver (LMS)

Through the previous section, it is found that different fast learning algorithms have different characteristics and thus their performances are different in different applications. It can be concluded that it is almost impossible to have a single fast learning algorithm so that its performance is always the best in all different kinds of applications. Thus, instead of developing a fast learning algorithm with the best global convergence capability in all different kinds of applications, it is better to develop a systematic approach that makes use of the characteristics of existing fast learning algorithms to guide the learning process to converge in different benchmarking problems (applications). Based on this methodology, this paper proposes a systematic approach called Local Minimum Solver (LMS). The algorithm is shown in Fig. 4.

In this algorithm, the characteristics of three different fast learning algorithms are used to improve the global convergence capability: Quickprop is the fastest algorithm but it is very easily trapped into a local minimum; RPROP is also very fast but its performance is unstable, especially in some complicated applications; MGFPROP has a very good global convergence capability but its converge rate is not very fast.

Thus Quickprop is used at the beginning in our algorithm. When the learning process is trapped into a local minimum, RPROP is used and hope it can escape from such local minimum. If it does not work, MGFPROP is used. This procedure will be repeated until the learning process is converged. The equations used when the learning process is trapped into a local minimum are to force the learning curve to go to another minimum. If stored weights are greater than its current values (i.e., the value of the weight when it is trapped into a local minimum), the stored weights are increased by the equations, and vice versa. The parameters Δ and λ are the constants to construct the expanding distance (i.e., the factor which multiples stored weights. It is used to modify the value of a weight so that the difference between the updated weight and its current weight is larger than that between the original stored weight and its current weight.). If the number of times that the local minimum has been visited is large, the expanding distance should also be large and it is hoped that this time the expanding distance is long enough to escape from the local minimum. Note that its value is limited by N_{max} because the learning curve may diverge if n is too large. Moreover, the value of n is obtained from the smallest number of visits from such three fast learning algorithms.

In the final part of the algorithm, it is required to check whether it suffers from the "flat-spot" problem. If a fast learning algorithm cannot converge within sufficient long iterations, it is claimed that the fast learning algorithm cannot converge properly and so it is require switching to other methods.

Begin
  Record the initial weights
  Use Method Quickprop
  Repeat
  Calculate the change of the system error, ΔE
  If ($T \leq \Delta E \leq 0$) // Trap into a local minimum
    Determine the statistics of this local minimum
    If it has been visited before,
      Count the smallest number of visits of each method (say N)
      If there are more than one method with the same value of N,
        Select a fast learning method with the following priority:
            Quickprop > RPROP > MGFPROP
        Then apply the following equations to change the current
        weights:
            If ($\omega^{(S)}{}_{ij} > \omega^{(L)}{}_{ij}$) $k_{ij} \leftarrow \Delta$ else $k_{ij} \leftarrow -\Delta$
            If ($n > N_{max}$) $n \leftarrow N_{max}$
            $\omega_{ij} \leftarrow \omega^{(S)}{}_{ij} [1 + k_{ij} 2^{n/\lambda}]$
            ($n = 1$ if this is the first visit)
  If the fast learning algorithm goes back to the previous local minimum,
    It is claimed that it is a local minimum
    Determine the statistics of this local minimum
    If it has been visited before,
      Count the smallest number of visits of each method
      If there are more than one method with the same value of N,
        Select a fast learning method with the following priority:
            Quickprop > RPROP > MGFPROP
    If ($\omega^{(S)}{}_{ij} > \omega^{(L)}{}_{ij}$) $k_{ij} \leftarrow \Delta$ else $k_{ij} \leftarrow -\Delta$
    If ($n > N_{max}$) $n \leftarrow N_{max}$
    $\omega_{ij} \leftarrow \omega^{(S)}{}_{ij} [1 + k_{ij} 2^{n/\lambda}]$
  If a fast learning algorithm cannot converge the learning process
    within D iterations,
    // flat spot problem
    Switch to other method by following the rules
    below:
      Quickprop $\rightarrow$ RPROP
      RPROP $\rightarrow$ MGFPROP
      MGFPROP $\rightarrow$ Quickprop
  Until (converged)
End

Fig. 4. LMS algorithm

4   Numerical Results

This section reports a number of experiments that were conducted on four popular benchmarking problems (applications) — the XOR problem, the 5-bit Counting, Iris, and Breast Cancer applications (data sets from the UCI Machine Learning Repository [13]) — to investigate the performance of Quickprop, RPROP, MGFPROP, and our proposed algorithm. To apply MGFPROP algorithm, it is considered to apply in the output layer only because it is found that the effect is better than that applied in both layers. Brief descriptions of these four applications are shown in Table I where μ and α are the learning rate and the momentum of BP for these three applications respectively.

Note that N, K, and M represent the number of input, hidden, and output nodes respectively. The input and the target patterns for these two applications consist of 0s and 1s only. All fast learning algorithms in this paper were terminated when the mean square error E reached the error threshold 0.001 within 1,000,000 epochs, where

$$E = \sum_{p=1}^{P} \sum_{m=1}^{M} [t_{pm} - o_{pm}]^2 / PM . \tag{7}$$

Note that P is the total number of the input patterns. The initial weights were drawn at random from a uniform distribution between -0.3 and 0.3. Each experiment was performed 100 times for 100 different sets of initial weights.

Table 1. Problem Descriptions

Application	Description	Network Architecture $N - K - M$	Parameter Setting (μ, α)
XOR	Give 2 binary inputs a and b, and output $a \oplus b$.	$2 - 2 - 1$	$(0.5, 0.7)$
5-bit Counting	Count the number of 1s from the 5 input units [23].	$5 - 12 - 6$	$(0.1, 0.7)$
Iris	This may be the best known database to be found in the pattern recognition literature. The data set contains 3 classes of 50 instances each, where each class refers to a type of iris plant [23].	$4 - 15 - 3$	$(0.02, 0.05)$
Breast Cancer	These breast cancer databases were obtained from the University of Wisconsin Hospitals, Madison, from Dr. William H. Wolberg. The databases reflect this chronological grouping of the data [23].	$9 - 20 - 1$	$(0.005, 0.03)$

The numerical result is shown in Table II. The number under the algorithm is the average number of epochs to converge and the number inside a bracket is the global convergence capability. For example, the converge rate of Quickprop in the XOR application is 59.56 epochs on average and its global convergence capability is 50% (i.e., only 50% of the learning process can be converge).

Compared with all four fast learning algorithms, LMS always converge in all cases with reasonable convergence rate. The differences of the convergence rate of LMS may be quite large in Iris and Breast Cancer applications. However, the difference is big because the global convergence capability of the other three fast learning algorithms are too low and usually it takes more epochs to converge in such cases. In Breast Cancer, it can be seen that all three fast learning algorithms have very poor global convergence capability. But, in LMS, it makes use of these three algorithms systematically and so it can always converge.

Table 2. Performance Comparisons

Applications	Quickprop	RPROP	MGFPROP	LMS
XOR	59.56 (50%)	79.29 (42%)	1055.71 (98%)	2859.21 (100%)
Counting	479.90 (63%)	571.00 (4%)	4940.45 (100%)	1655.77 (100%)
Iris	- (0%)	4045.64 (22%)	57437.30 (100%)	77527.25 (100%)
Breast Cancer	1185.00 (5%)	2152.00 (2%)	4343.72 (18%)	24251.76 (100%)

5   Conclusions

This paper investigated the performance of some popular fast learning algorithms by conducting experiments on different learning problems (applications) Their performance is limited by too many local minima in these applications. To overcome such limitations, this paper proposed a fast learning algorithm called Local Minimum Solver (LMS). It provides a systematic approach to keep trying to escape from local minima. The simulation results revealed that the LMS always converges in four popular complicated applications with a reasonable fast convergence rate, where other popular fast learning algorithms give very poor global convergence capabilities. In the future, the algorithm will be further enhanced to have a faster convergence rate.

Acknowledgment. This project is funded by The Open University of Hong Kong Research Grant (Project No. 09/1.3).

References

[1] Rumelhart, D.E., Hinton, G.E., Williams, R.J.: Learning internal representations by error propagation. In: Parallel Distributed Processing: Exploration in the Microstructure of Cognition, vol. 1, MIT Press, Cambridge (1986)

[2] Blum, E.K., Li, L.K.: Approximation theory and feedforward networks. Neural Networks 4, 511–515 (1991)

[3] Gori, M., Tesi, A.: On the problem of local minima in back-propagation. IEEE Transactions on Pattern Analysis and Machine Intelligence 14(1), 76–86 (1992)

[4] Lee, Y., Oh, S.H., Kim, M.W.: An Analysis of Premature Saturation in Back Propagation Learning. Neural Networks 6, 719–728 (1993)

[5] Stager, F., Agarwal, M.: Three methods to speed up the training of feedforward and feedback perceptrons. Neural Networks 10(8), 1435–1443 (1997)

[6] Van Ooyen, A., Nienhuis, B.: Improving the convergence of the back-propagation algorithm. Neural Networks 5, 465–471 (1992)

[7] Vitela, J.E., Reifman, J.: Premature Saturation in Backpropagation Networks: Mechanism and Necessary Conditions. Neural Networks 10(4), 721–735 (1997)

[8] Fahlman, S.E.: Fast learning variations on back-propagation: An empirical study. In: Touretzky, D., Hinton, G., Sejnowski, T. (eds.) Proceedings of the 1988 Connectionist Models Summer School, Pittsburgh, pp. 38–51. Morgan Kaufmann, San Mateo (1989)

[9] Riedmiller, M., Braun, H.: A direct adaptive method for faster back-propagation learning: The RPROP Algorithm. In: Proceedings of International Conference on Neural Networks, vol. 1, pp. 586–591 (1993)

[10] Ng, S.C., Cheung, C.-C., Leung, S.H.: Magnified Gradient Function with Deterministic Weight Evolution in Adaptive Learning. IEEE Transactions in Neural Networks 15(6), 1411–1423 (2004)

[11] Cheung, C.-C., Ng, S.C., Lui, A.K., Shensheng, S.: Enhanced Two-Phase Method in Fast Learning Algorithms. In: Proceedings of IJCNN 2010, Barcelona, Spain (July 2010)

[12] Cheung, C.-C., Ng, S.C., Lui, A.K., Shensheng, S.: A Fast Learning Algorithm with Promising Convergence Capability. In: Proceedings of IJCNN 2011, San Jose, US (August 2011)

[13] Asuncion, A., Newman, D.J.: UCI machine learning repository. University of California, Irvine, School of Information and Computer Sciences (2007), http://archive.ics.uci.edu/ml/

Skull-Closed Autonomous Development: Object-Wise Incremental Learning*

Yuekai Wang[1,2], Xiaofeng Wu[1,2], and Juyang Weng[3,4]

[1] State Key Lab. of ASIC & System, Fudan University, Shanghai, 200433, China
[2] Department of Electronic Engineering, Fudan University, Shanghai, 200433, China
[3] School of Computer Science, Fudan University, Shanghai, 200433, China
[4] Dept. of Computer Sci. and Eng., Michigan State University,
East Lansing, MI 48824, USA

Abstract. The series of Where-What Networks (WWNs) is a brain-inspired developmental model that simulates the dorsal (where) stream and the ventral (what) stream that converge to the motor area in the frontal cortex. Since developmental learning is always incremental, the order of different stimuli should affect the outcome of learning. In contrast to the uniform distribution of stimuli across image frames used in prior WWN experiments, this work studies non-uniform distribution in the sense that during training one object is presented at all the image locations before another object is presented. A new mechanism called cell regenesis is introduced to enable a less-often used cell to recommit its neuronal resource to new stimuli. The experimental results shown in this paper indicate that WWN-6 can deal with object-wise incremental learning.

Keywords: Autonomous development, Incremental learning, Where-What Networks, Hebbian learning, Computer vision.

1 Introduction

A little child is able to learn one concept (or task) after another (i.e., incrementally) taught by teachers with the help of other sensory organs (e.g., eyes, arms), in which the mechanism of autonomous development is embodied [1,2]. Autonomous development indicates that the skull of the child should be closed so that the brain can only interact with the external environment by the eyes and arms (or other parts of the body). In our brain-inspired developmental model WWN-6 [3], a three-area structure corresponds to such framework, i.e., the internal "brain" of the network has been closed by getting rid of "pulvinar" existing widely in WWN-1 to WWN-5 [4,5], inside the skull, which is off limit to the

* This work was supported by Fund of State Key Lab. of ASIC & System (11M-S008) and the Fundamental Research Funds for the Central Universities to XW, Changjiang Scholar Fund of China to JW; The authors would like to thank Dr. Matthew Luciw for providing his WWN-3 source code to conduct the work here.

J. Wang, G.G. Yen, and M.M. Polycarpou (Eds.): ISNN 2012, Part I, LNCS 7367, pp. 590–597, 2012.

teachers (programmers) in the external environment except interactions with its sensory ends and motor ends.

For human being, people always learn concepts one by one throughout his/her life, no matter how many concepts he ever learned, and normally forget the known concepts scarcely used or reviewed. Therefore, incremental learning is more nature and plays an important role in autonomous development compared with batch learning. Since developmental learning is always incremental, the order of different stimuli should affect the outcome of learning. In all the prior WWN experiments, the batch learning was applied in which the distribution of stimuli across image frames is actually uniform. This work studies non-uniform distribution case in incremental learning of WWN-6 in the sense that during training one object is presented at all the image locations before another one is presented. A new mechanism of WWN-6, called cell regenesis, is introduced to enable a less-often used neuron to re-commit its resource to new stimuli.

In the remainder of the paper, Section 2 presents the details of WWN-6 including the structure and algorithms. Experimental results of incremental learning are reported in Section 3. Section 4 gives the conclusions and discussion.

2   Skull-Closed Developmental WWN-6

2.1   Network Structure

The structure of network (WWN-6) is shown as Fig. 1 which consists of three areas, X area (sensory ends), Y area (internal brain) and Z area (motor ends). X area receives the input signal, which is an image in our example. Z area is the effector, providing the actions of the network. Different actions (firing of the neurons) represent different concepts. Here, two categories of concepts are used by the teachers in the external background: the location of the foreground object in the image and the type of the foreground object, corresponding to Location Motor (LM) and Type Motor (TM). Of course, the concepts are not limited to these two (e.g., size of the object).

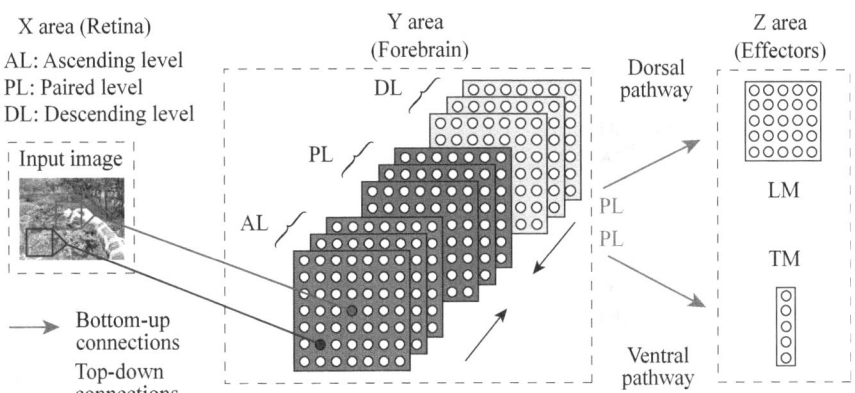

Fig. 1. The structure of WWN-6

Y area is regarded as the internal brain in the skull, which is off limit to the teachers in the external environment. Using a prescreening area for each source in Y area, before integration, results in three laminar levels: the ascending level (AL) that prescreenings the bottom-up input, the descending level (DL) that prescreenings the top-down input and paired level (PL) that combines the outputs of AL and DL. In each level, the same number of neurons are placed at a 3D position, r (rows) $\times c$ (columns) $\times d$ (depth). Besides, there exist two pathways and two connections in this model. Dorsal pathway refers to the stream $X \rightleftharpoons Y \rightleftharpoons \mathrm{LM}$, while ventral pathway refers to $X \rightleftharpoons Y \rightleftharpoons \mathrm{TM}$, where symbol "$\rightleftharpoons$" indicates two connections, one for each direction.

2.2   Concepts and Algorithms

Pre-response of the Neurons. Each area A in $\{X, Y, Z\}$ has a weight vector $\mathbf{v} = (\mathbf{v}_b, \mathbf{v}_t)$ (index b represents "bottom-up" while t represents "top-down"). Its pre-response value is:

$$r(\mathbf{v}_b, \mathbf{b}, \mathbf{v}_t, \mathbf{t}) = \dot{\mathbf{v}} \cdot \dot{\mathbf{p}} \tag{1}$$

where $\dot{\mathbf{v}}$ is the unit vector of the normalized synaptic vector $\mathbf{v} = (\dot{\mathbf{v}}_b, \dot{\mathbf{v}}_t)$, and $\dot{\mathbf{p}}$ is the unit vector of the normalized input vector $\mathbf{p} = (\dot{\mathbf{b}}, \dot{\mathbf{t}})$ ($\mathbf{b}$ and $\mathbf{t}$ represent the bottom-up and top-down input respectively). The inner product measures the degree of match between these two directions $\dot{\mathbf{v}}$ and $\dot{\mathbf{p}}$, because $r(\mathbf{v}_b, \mathbf{b}, \mathbf{v}_t, \mathbf{t}) = \cos(\theta)$ where θ is the angle between two unit vectors $\dot{\mathbf{v}}$ and $\dot{\mathbf{p}}$. This enables a match between two vectors of different magnitudes. The pre-response value ranges in $[-1, 1]$.

In other words, if the synaptic weight vector is considered as the object feature stored in the neuron, the pre-response measures the similarity between the input signal and the object feature.

Top-k Competition. Top-k competition takes place among the neurons in the same level in Y area, imitating the lateral inhibition which effectively suppresses the weakly matched neurons (measured by the pre-responses). Top-k competition guarantees that different neurons detect different features. The response $r'(t)$ after top-k competition is

$$r'(t) = \begin{cases} r(t)(r_q - r_{k+1})/(r_1 - r_{k+1}) & \text{if } 1 \le q \le k \\ 0 & \text{otherwise} \end{cases}$$

where r_1, r_q and r_{k+1} denote the first, qth and $(k+1)$th neuron's pre-response respectively after being sorted in descending order.

Two Types of Y Neurons. There exist two types of neurons in Y area according to their states, initial state neurons (ISN) and learning state neurons (LSN). After the initialization of the network, all the neurons are in the initial state. During the learning of the network, neurons may be transformed from the initial state into the learning state, depending on the pre-response of the neurons.

In our network, a parameter ϵ_1 is defined as the state transformation threshold. If the pre-response is over $1 - \epsilon_1$, the neuron is transformed into the learning state, otherwise, the neuron keeps the current state.

Hebbian-like Learning. Hebbian-like learning is described as:

$$\mathbf{v}_j(n) = w_1(n)\mathbf{v}_j(n-1) + w_2(n)r'(t)\dot{\mathbf{p}}(t) \tag{2}$$

where $r'(t)$ is the response of the neuron after top-k competition, n is the age of the neuron (related to the number of firings by the neuron), w_1 and w_2 are two parameters representing retention rate and learning rate with $w_1 + w_2 \equiv 1$. These two parameters are defined as following:

$$w_1(n) = 1 - w_2(n), \quad w_2(n) = \frac{1 + u(n)}{n}$$

where $u(n)$ is the amnesic function:

$$u(n) = \begin{cases} 0 & \text{if } n \leq t_1 \\ c(n - t_1)/(t_2 - t_1) & \text{if } t_1 < n \leq t_2 \\ c + (n - t_2)/r & \text{if } t_2 < n \end{cases} \tag{3}$$

where $t_1 = 20, t_2 = 200, c = 2, r = 10000$ [6].

Only the firing neurons will do Hebbian-like learning to update the synaptic weights according to the equation 2. In Y area, if a neuron in the learning state is one of the top-k winners and its pre-response is over $1 - \epsilon_2$, this neuron will be fired and implement Hebbian-like learning, with suppressing all the neurons in the initial state simultaneously. If there is no neurons in the learning state fired, all the neurons in the initial state will implement the hebbian-like learning. The age of the neurons in the learning state and the initial state is updated as

$$n(t+1) = \begin{cases} n(t) & \text{if the neuron is ISN} \\ n(t) + 1 & \text{if the neuron is top-k LSN.} \end{cases}$$

In general, a neuron with lower age has higher learning rate. That is to say, ISN is more capable to learn new concepts than LSN. If the neurons are regarded as resources of the brain of the network, ISNs are the idle resources while LSNs are the developed resources. So, the resources utilization (RU) in Y area can be calculated as

$$RU = \frac{N_{LSN}}{N_{LSN} + N_{ISN}} \times 100\%$$

where RU represents the resources utilization rate, N_{LSN} and N_{ISN} are the number of LSN and ISN.

Synapse Maintenance and Cell Regenesis. Synapse maintenance is a biologically inspired mechanism proposed to deal with the problem of leaked-in background pixels caused by the arbitrary contours of the object [7]. The mechanism is meant to adjust the receptive fields dynamically and automatically based on the statistics in nature that the patterns from foreground objects appear relatively more often than patterns of background.

In the learning stage, some neurons may fire frequently and some may not, which indicates the unbalanced load distribution of the resources: the loads of some neurons are too heavy while the others are almost wasted. Therefore, in WWN-6, a biologically inspired mechanism called cell regenesis is introduced to improve the resource utilization. For the firing neuron, the ages of its neighbor neurons (totally 6 neighbors in 3-D space) are checked, if the following conditions are satisfied, the corresponding neighbor neuron (neuron B) will die and revive (i.e., turn back to the initial state):

$$n_A(t) > t_1 \quad \text{and} \quad n_A(t) > 4n_B(t)$$

where A is a fired neuron, and B is one of its neighbors. $n(t)$ is the neuron age and $t_1 = 20$ (equation 3).

3   Experiments and Results

In all the prior experiments for the series of Where-What-Networks (WWNs), the learning mode applied to training the networks was batch learning, i.e., all the foreground objects to be learned are prepared before training and all the objects that appear at one location of the input image (the location for each object may be different) need to be learned before learning other cases (the foreground objects appear at other locations of the input image). This means that the distribution of stimuli across image frames is uniform for all the objects in every learning round. Unfortunately, developmental learning is always incremental and the distribution of stimuli is non-uniform for the objects to be learned in every round. In our incremental learning experiment (Table 1), the network is required to learn one object at all possible locations (chosen at random) in the image before another object is presented and never learns the previous one. Such incremental learning mode has not been discussed yet before. In this section, an experiment to study the WWN-6 with object-wise incremental learning are performed.

In details, each image for either network training or network testing in the experiment consists of two parts: foreground object and natural background. 8 foreground objects to be learned are selected from the MSU-25 image dataset [8] which are shown in Fig. 2. Background images are randomly extracted from 13 natural images[1] and randomly cropped into patches of 42×42 pixels. Fig. 3 visualizes some input images (composite images) as examples (the foreground object emerge in the unknown complex backgrounds). Only one object is learned in each epoch and the learned objects are not learned any more.

---

[1] Available from http://www.cis.hut.fi/projects/ica/imageica/

Cat   Dog   Truck   Pig   Duck   Elephant   Tiger   Tank

Fig. 2. The foreground objects to be learned

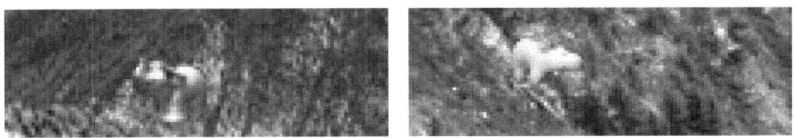

Fig. 3. Input images to the network

During training, the network is supervised by the external teacher (i.e., Z serves as the input and the firing of the neurons in LM and TM is imposed). But for testing, there is no imposed action, i.e., no teacher supervision, which means Z serves as the output of the network.

The performance of WWN-6 after each training epoch including recognition rate, location error and resources utilization (RU) is summarized in Table 1. From the preliminary results, two points can be concluded:

- The resources utilization (RU) increased when the number of objects to be learned increased, which indicates that more and more ISNs in the internal brain are turned into LSNs. When the network learned the 8th object, almost all the neurons turned into learning state.
- The recognition performance of learned objects became worse (the recognition rate dropped and the location error increased) when the number of objects to be learned increased. This phenomenon is similar to human, for the known things but not seen for a long time, people usually recognize them slowly even cannot remember or misrecognize.

In order to investigate the working procedure of WWN-6, the synaptic weights in different epochs are visualized in Fig. 5, (e) and (f) ((e) for epoch 6 and (f) for epoch 7). And two instances are chosen to illustrate the effects of the important mechanisms of WWN-6.

- Instance 1: (c) and (d). (c) shows that this neuron has learned the object "truck" and is in the learning state. (d) shows that the same neuron is turned back into the initial state. This state change (LSN → ISN) indicated that this neuron experienced "cell regenesis" .
- Instance 2: (a) and (b). (a) and (b) show that for the same neuron, the state of the neuron are the same (learning state) but the learned features are different, "dog" for (a) and "tank" for (b). This indicates that within one training epoch, the neuron state can change rapidly to learn new object (learning state → initial state → learning state).

Table 1. The performance of the network with the incremental learning. In the column "performance", "type" refers to the accuracy rate of the type recognition and the unit is %; "location" refers to the location error measured by the Euclidean distance with the correct location and the unit is pixel. In each epoch (Ep.), a new foreground object is added and the object with all possible locations of the background image is learned.

Object	Performance	Ep. 1	Ep. 2	Ep. 3	Ep. 4	Ep. 5	Ep. 6	Ep. 7	Ep. 8
Cat	Type	100	100	100	96.68	96.12	96.12	96.12	96.12
	Location	0.99	1.06	1.10	1.37	1.38	1.39	1.39	1.40
Dog	Type	×	100	100	100	99.72	99.72	99.72	99.72
	Location	×	0.73	0.86	0.95	1.03	1.03	1.03	1.04
Truck	Type	×	×	100	99.17	99.17	99.17	99.17	99.17
	Location	×	×	0.72	0.93	1.04	1.06	1.05	1.08
Pig	Type	×	×	×	100	98.61	98.61	98.61	98.61
	Location	×	×	×	1.04	1.15	1.25	1.26	1.29
Duck	Type	×	×	×	×	100	100	100	100
	Location	×	×	×	×	0.97	0.99	1.00	1.04
Elephant	Type	×	×	×	×	×	81.16	81.16	81.16
	Location	×	×	×	×	×	3.24	3.24	3.26
Tiger	Type	×	×	×	×	×	×	76.73	76.73
	Location	×	×	×	×	×	×	3.63	3.64
Tank	Type	×	×	×	×	×	×	×	51.80
	Location	×	×	×	×	×	×	×	5.44
RU		×	12.70%	25.62%	39.83%	47.77%	53.44%	68.71%	88.28%	99.77%

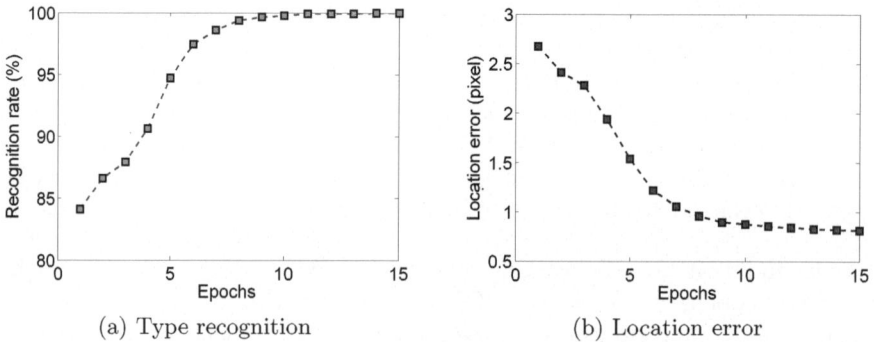

(a) Type recognition   (b) Location error

Fig. 4. Network performance in 15 epochs

Furthermore, an extra experiment to simulate the review stage in human learning is performed. The trained network by incremental learning continued to learn the same 8 objects once more for memory consolidation. The performance variation is shown in Fig. 4. Both recognition rate and location error become convergent after 10 epochs, which indicates that review is positive for the network performance similar to our human brain.

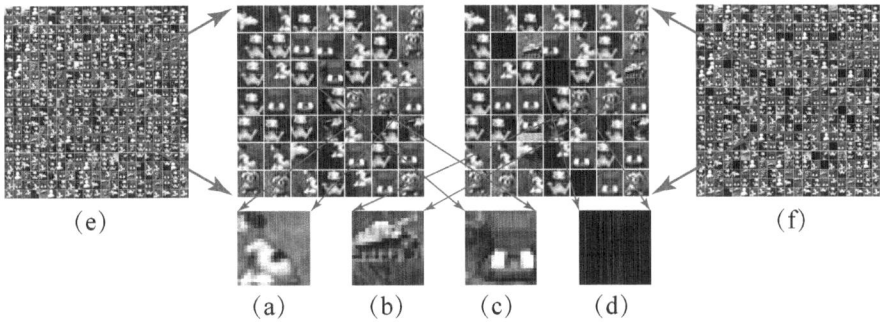

Fig. 5. The visualization of the bottom-up synaptic weights of some Y neurons

4 Conclusion

WWN faces a great challenge in incremental learning — the conflicting criteria of fast learning and long-term memory. The age-dependent learning rate in Hebbian learning enables a neuron to learn quickly but gradually turn mature to become a long-term memory. Cell regenesis enables a less useful neuron to recommit its neuronal resource. Our experimental results have shown that objects presented sequentially can be learned by WWN-6. Next, we will study how the entire resource of WWN can be dynamically shared by a dynamic number of objects.

References

1. Weng, J., McClelland, J., Pentland, A., Sporns, O., Stockman, I., Sur, M., Thelen, E.: Autonomous mental development by robots and animals. Science 291(5504), 599–600 (2001)
2. Weng, J.: Why have we passed "neural networks do not abstract well"? Natural Intelligence 1(1), 13–23 (2011)
3. Wang, Y., Wu, X., Weng, J.: Skull-Closed Autonomous Development. In: Lu, B.-L., Zhang, L., Kwok, J. (eds.) ICONIP 2011, Part I. LNCS, vol. 7062, pp. 209–216. Springer, Heidelberg (2011)
4. Ji, Z., Weng, J., Prokhorov, D.: Where-what network 1: "Where" and "What" assist each other through top-down connections. In: Proc. IEEE Int'l Conference on Development and Learning, Monterey, CA, August 9-12, pp. 61–66 (2008)
5. Luciw, M., Weng, J.: Where-what network 3: Developmental top-down attention for multiple foregrounds and complex backgrounds. In: Proc. IEEE International Joint Conference on Neural Networks, Barcelona, Spain, July 18-23, pp. 1–8 (2010)
6. Weng, J., Luciw, M.: Dually optimal neuronal layers: Lobe component analysis. IEEE Trans. Autonomous Mental Development 1(1), 68–85 (2009)
7. Wang, Y., Wu, X., Weng, J.: Synapse maintenance in the where-what network. In: Proc. Int'l Joint Conference on Neural Networks, San Jose, CA, July 31 - August 5, pp. +1–8 (2011)
8. Luciw, M., Weng, J.: Top-down connections in self-organizing Hebbian networks: Topographic class grouping. IEEE Trans. Autonomous Mental Development 2(3), 248–261 (2010)

MaxMin-SOMO: An SOM Optimization Algorithm for Simultaneously Finding Maximum and Minimum of a Function

Wu Wei and Atlas Khan

Department of Applied Mathematics,
Dalian University of Technology Dalian, China
wuweiw@dlut.edu.cn, atlas900@gmail.com

Abstract. An self-organizing feature map optimization (SOMO) algorithm was proposed by Mu-Chun Su et al [1,2] in order to find a wining neuron in the SOM network, through a competitive learning process, that stands for the minimum of an objective function. In this study, we generalizes the SOMO algorithm to a so called MaxMin-SOMO algorithm for simultaneously finding two winning neurons such that one winner stands for the minimum and the other for the maximum of the objective function. Numerical simulations show that, when we are interested in both maximum and minimum of an objective function, the MaxMin-SOMO algorithm works more effectively than SOMO algorithm.

Keywords: SOM-Based optimization (SOMO), SOFM algorithm.

1 Introduction

Self-Organizing Map (SOM) is an unsupervised learning algorithm proposed by Kohonen [3,4,5]. The principal goal of the SOM algorithm is to map an incoming pattern in a higher dimensional space into a lower (usually one or two) dimensional space, and perform this transforation adaptively in a topological ordered fashion. The applications of SOM range widely from simulations used for the purpose of understanding and modeling of computational maps in the brain to subsystems for engineering applications such as speech recognition, vector quantization and cluster analysis [3,4,5,6,7,8,9,10,11].

An SOM-Based optimization (SOMO) algorithm is introduced in Mu-Chun et al [1] for solving continuous optimization. The idea of SOMO algorithm is to find a winning neuron in the SOM network, through a competitive learning process, that stands for the minimum of an objective function. In [1], the SOM-Based optimization (SOMO) algorithm is compared with, and shown to be more efficient than, Genetic algorithms (GAs) [12,13] and Particle swarm optimization (PSO) algorithm [14,15,16] for continuous optimization. The purpose of this paper is to generalize the SOM-Based optimization (SOMO) to a so called MaxMin-SOMO algorithm for simultaneously finding two winning neurons such that one winner stands for the minimum and the other for the maximum of the objective

J. Wang, G.G. Yen, and M.M. Polycarpou (Eds.): ISNN 2012, Part I, LNCS 7367, pp. 598–606, 2012.

function. It is shown by numerical simulations that, if we are interested in both maximum and minimum of an objective function, the MaxMin-SOMO algorithm works more effectively than SOMO algorithm.

This paper is organized as follows. In Section 2, a brief introduction of the basic SOMO algorithm is given. The MaxMin-SOMO algorithm is proposed in Section 3. In Section 4, some computer simulations are provided to show the effectiveness of the MaxMin-SOMO algorithm.

2   Original SOM-Based Optimization (SOMO) Algorithm

In the below, let us describe the SOMO algorithm [1] used for finding the minimum point x^* of a function $f(x)$, $x \in R^n$. The SOMO algorithm network contains $M \times N$ neurons arranged as a two dimensional array. For each neuron (i, j), its weight $\underline{W}_{i,j}$ is a vector in R^n, where $1 \le i \le M$ and $1 \le j \le N$ for some positive integers M and N. For a special input $x = (x_1, ..., x_n)^T = (1, 1, \cdots, 1)^T \in R^n$, the winner out of all the neurons is defined as

$$
\begin{aligned}
(i^*, j^*) &= \underset{1 \le i \le M, 1 \le j \le N}{\arg} \min f(\underline{W}_{i,j} \times \underline{x}_1, ..., \underline{W}_{i,j} \times \underline{x}_n) \\
&= \underset{1 \le i \le M, 1 \le j \le N}{\arg} \min f(\underline{W}_{i,j} \times 1, ..., \underline{W}_{i,j} \times 1) \\
&= \underset{1 \le i \le M, 1 \le j \le N}{\arg} \min f(\underline{W}_{i,j})
\end{aligned}
\tag{1}
$$

The idea of SOM training is applied to the network such that the weight $\underline{W}_{i^*,j^*}$ of the winner will get closer and closer to the minimum point x^* during the iterative training process. The detail of the training process is as follows:

Step 1. Initialization

Step 1.1. Initialization of the neurons on the four corners

Let the two points $(l_1, l_2, ..., l_n)^T$ and $(h_1, h_2, ..., h_n)^T$ are randomly chosen and far enough from each other. The weight vectors of the neurons on the corners are initialized as:

$$
\underline{W}_{1,1} = (l_1, l_2, ..., l_n)^T
\tag{2}
$$

$$
\underline{W}_{M,N} = (h_1, h_2, ..., h_n)^T
\tag{3}
$$

$$
\underline{W}_{1,N} = (l_1, l_2, ..., l_{\lfloor \frac{n}{2} \rfloor}, h_{\lfloor \frac{n}{2} \rfloor + 1}, ..., h_n)^T
\tag{4}
$$

$$
\underline{W}_{M,1} = (h_1, h_2, ..., h_{\lfloor \frac{n}{2} \rfloor}, l_{\lfloor \frac{n}{2} \rfloor + 1}, ..., l_n)^T
\tag{5}
$$

Step 1.2 Initialization of the neurons on the four edges

The initialization of the weights of the neurons on the four edges as follows:

$$
\begin{aligned}
\underline{W}_{1,j} &= \tfrac{W_{1,N}-W_{1,1}}{N-1}(j-1) + \underline{W}_{1,1} \\
&= \tfrac{j-1}{N-1}\underline{W}_{1,N} + \tfrac{N-j}{N-1}\underline{W}_{1,1}
\end{aligned}
\tag{6}
$$

$$
\begin{aligned}
\underline{W}_{M,j} &= \tfrac{W_{M,N}-W_{M,1}}{N-1}(j-1) + \underline{W}_{M,1} \\
&= \tfrac{j-1}{N-1}\underline{W}_{M,N} + \tfrac{N-j}{N-1}\underline{W}_{M,1}
\end{aligned}
\tag{7}
$$

$$
\begin{aligned}
\underline{W}_{i,1} &= \tfrac{W_{M,1}-W_{1,1}}{M-1}(i-1) + \underline{W}_{1,1} \\
&= \tfrac{i-1}{M-1}\underline{W}_{M,1} + \tfrac{M-i}{M-1}\underline{W}_{1,1}
\end{aligned}
\tag{8}
$$

$$
\begin{aligned}
\underline{W}_{i,N} &= \tfrac{W_{M,N}-W_{1,N}}{M-1}(i-1) + \underline{W}_{1,N} \\
&= \tfrac{i-1}{M-1}\underline{W}_{M,N} + \tfrac{M-i}{M-1}\underline{W}_{1,N}
\end{aligned}
\tag{9}
$$

where $i = 2, ..., M-1$, $j = 2, ..., N-1$.

Step 1.3 Initialization of the remaining neurons

$$
\underline{W}_{i,j} = \tfrac{W_{i,N}-W_{i,1}}{N-1}(j-1) + \underline{W}_{i,1}
\tag{10}
$$

$$
= \tfrac{j-1}{N-1}\underline{W}_{i,N} + \tfrac{N-j}{N-1}\underline{W}_{1,N},
\tag{11}
$$

where $i = 2, ..., M-1$, $j = 2, ..., N-1$.

Step 1.4 Random noise

A small amount of random noise is added for each weight so as to keep the weight vectors from being linearly dependent:

$$
\underline{W}_{i,j} = \underline{W}_{i,j} + \underline{t}
\tag{12}
$$

for $1 \leq i \leq M$ and $1 \leq j \leq N$, where $\underline{t}$ denotes a small random noise.

Step 2. Winner finding

$$
(i^*, j^*) = \underset{1 \leq i \leq M, 1 \leq j \leq N}{\arg\ \min} f(\underline{W}_{i,j})
\tag{13}
$$

Step 3. Weights updating

The weights of the winner and its neighbors are adjusted by the following formula:

$$
\begin{aligned}
\underline{W}_{i,j}(t+1) = \ &\underline{W}_{i,j}(t) + \eta\beta(i^*,j^*,i,j)[\underline{W}_{i^*,j^*}(t) \\
&-\underline{W}_{i,j}(t)] + \lambda(1-\beta(i^*,j^*,i,j))\underline{p} \\
&for\ \ 1 \leq i \leq M, 1 \leq j \leq N
\end{aligned}
\tag{14}
$$

where the parameters η and λ are real valued constants, $d(i^*, j^*, i, j)$ is the lateral distance between winning neuron (i^*, j^*) and neuron (i, j), the vector $\underline{p}$ is called the perturbation vector, and

$$\beta(i^*, j^*, i, j) = 1 - \frac{d(i^*, j^*, i, j)}{\sqrt{M^2 + N^2}} \tag{15}$$

Step 4. Go to step 2 until a pre-specified number of generations is achieved or some kind of termination criterion is satisfied.

3   MaxMin-SOMO Algorithm

In this section we present the MaxMin-SOMO algorithm. Here we discuss the MaxMin-SOMO algorithm for finding one minimum and one maximum of a function simultaneously. It is an easy matter to generalize the algorithm for finding two or more minima and maxima. MaxMin-SOMO algorithm has the same training steps as those of original SOM-based optimization(SOMO) algorithm, except the step of weights updating process with m winners, which is as follows:

Step 1. The initialization of MaxMin-SOMO algorithm is the same as that of SOM-based optimization(SOMO).

Step 2. This step aims to find winning neurons, denoted by (i_1^*, j_1^*) and (i_2^*, j_2^*) with the best objective function values among the neurons:

$$(i_1^*, j_1^*) = \underset{1 \leq i \leq M, 1 \leq j \leq N}{\arg} \min f(\underline{W}_{i,j}), \tag{16}$$

$$(i_2^*, j_2^*) = \underset{1 \leq i \leq M, 1 \leq j \leq N}{\arg} \max f(\underline{W}_{i,j}), \tag{17}$$

Step 3. The weights updating rule
   The weights updating rule of the winners and its neighbors is as follows:
   For the neurons (i, j) in the neighborhood of the first winner (i_1^*, j_1^*) satisfying $p_1 \leq i \leq p_2$, $q_1 \leq j \leq q_2$, where

$$p_1 = \max(i_1^* - R_1, 1) \tag{18}$$

$$p_2 = \min(i_1^* + R_1, M) \tag{19}$$

$$q_1 = \max(j_1^* - R_1, 1) \tag{20}$$

$$q_2 = \min(j_1^* + R_1, N) \tag{21}$$

and R_1 is suitably chosen sizes of neighborhoods, the weights updating rule is

$$\underline{W}_{i,j}(t+1) = \underline{W}_{i,j}(t) + \eta_1 \beta_1(i_1^*, j_1^*, i, j)[\underline{W}_{i_1^*, j_1^*}(t)$$
$$- \underline{W}_{i,j}(t)] + \lambda_1(1 - \beta_1(i_1^*, j_1^*, i, j))\underline{p} \tag{22}$$

where

$$\beta_1(i_1^*, j_1^*, i, j) = 1 - \frac{d(i_1^*, j_1^*, i, j)}{\sqrt{M^2 + N^2}} \tag{23}$$

For the rest (i, j) neurons,

$$\begin{aligned}
\underline{W}_{i,j}(t+1) = \ & \underline{W}_{i,j}(t) + \eta_2 \beta_2(i_2^*, j_2^*, i, j)[\underline{W}_{i_2^*, j_2^*}(t) \\
& -\underline{W}_{i,j}(t)] + \lambda_2(1 - \beta_2(i_2^*, j_2^*, i, j))\underline{p}
\end{aligned} \tag{24}$$

where

$$\beta_2(i_2^*, j_2^*, i, j) = 1 - \frac{d(i_2^*, j_2^*, i, j)}{\sqrt{M^2 + N^2}} \tag{25}$$

We remark that in the above Step 2, we require the 2 winners, i.e., one winner stands for minimum and the second one for maximum, to be separated in two neighborhoods, such that the winners can spread around rather than accumulate into one point.

Step 4. Go to step 2 until a pre-specified number of generations is achieved or some kind of termination criteria is satisfied.

4   Simulation Results

4.1   Objective Functions

In this subsection we discuss the following functions. All these functions are minimized and maximized by using MaxMin-SOMO algorithm.
1. U_1 function:

$$f(\underline{x}) = 300 \sin(2\pi x) \sin(2\pi y) - \sin(\pi x) \sin(\pi y) \tag{26}$$

2. Giunta function:

$$\begin{aligned}
f(\underline{x}) = \sum_{i=1}^{30} & \left(\sin\left(\frac{16}{15}x_i - 1\right) + \sin^2\left(\frac{16}{15}x_i - 1\right) \right. \\
& \left. + \frac{1}{50}\sin[4\left(\frac{16}{15}x_i - 1\right)] \right) + 0.3
\end{aligned} \tag{27}$$

4.2   Parameters of Simulation

In table 1 we present the global minima, dimensions and the upper bound of the number of generations for optimization algorithms. For comparison purpose, we also present the parameters involved in the SOM-based optimization(SOMO) algorithm and MaxMin-SOMO. The neurons are arranged as a 30×30 array, namely $M = N = 30$. For the SOM-based optimization (SOMO) algorithm, we set $\eta = 0.2$ and $\lambda = 0.001$, for the MaxMin-SOMO algorithm, $\eta_1 = 0.2$, $\eta_2 = 0.35, \lambda_1 = 0.01$ and $\lambda_2 = 0.001$.

Table 1. Parameters for the two test functions

Test Function	Dimensions	Initial range	Number of generations
U_1 function	2	$0 \leq x_i \leq 10$	100
Giunta	30	$-10 \leq x_i \leq 10 \approx 0.9$	100

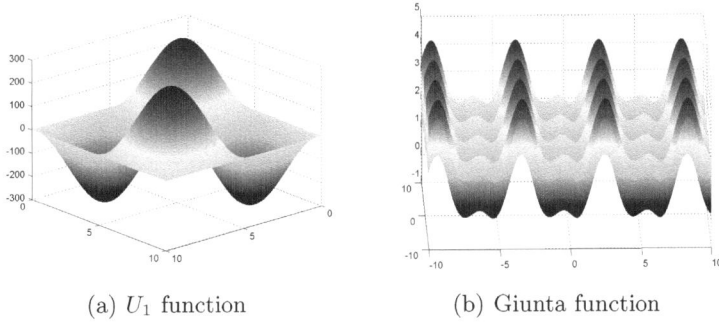

(a) U_1 function   (b) Giunta function

Fig. 1. Graphs of the two test functions

4.3 Simulations of MaxMin-SOMO Algorithm for One Minimum and One Maximum

In this subsection we present the simulation results for the case of finding one minimum and one maximum of a function simultaneously. For each function, each algorithm conducted 30 runs. The best solutions found for each run after pre-specified number of generations were recorded. Table 2 tabulates the comparison of the simulation results. The mean column and the standard deviation column represents the mean and the standard deviation of the best solutions of 30 runs. In table 2 we find the minimum and maximum of a function by running SOM-based optimization(SOMO) algorithm twice. But by MaxMin-SOMO algorithm we find the both minimum and maximum of a function simultaneously.

The figure 2 and figure 3 show the best performance curves by finding a minimum and a maximum of a function respectively. In figure 2 we compare the

Table 2. Comparison of MaxMin-SOMO and the original SOMO algorithms for finding two minima

Test Function	Algorithm	Mean	Standard deviation	Time(M)	Time(SD)
U_1 Function	SOMO				
	Minimum	-2.9999e+002	5.6843e-014	1.0642	1.0672
	Maximum	2.9999e+002	1.7184e-012	1.0518	1.0307
	MaxMin-SOMO				
	Minimum	-2.9999e+002	4.2246e-011	0.5538	0.5664
	Maximum	2.9999e+002	3.8216e-013		
Giunta	SOMO				
	Minimum	0.9670	1.4901e-09	1.0116	1.0049
	Maximum	69.0318	1.4807e-011	1.1512	1.1426
	MaxMin-SOMO				
	Minimum	0.9670	1.6565e-010	0.7372	0.6636
	Maximum	69.0318	2.2880e-011		

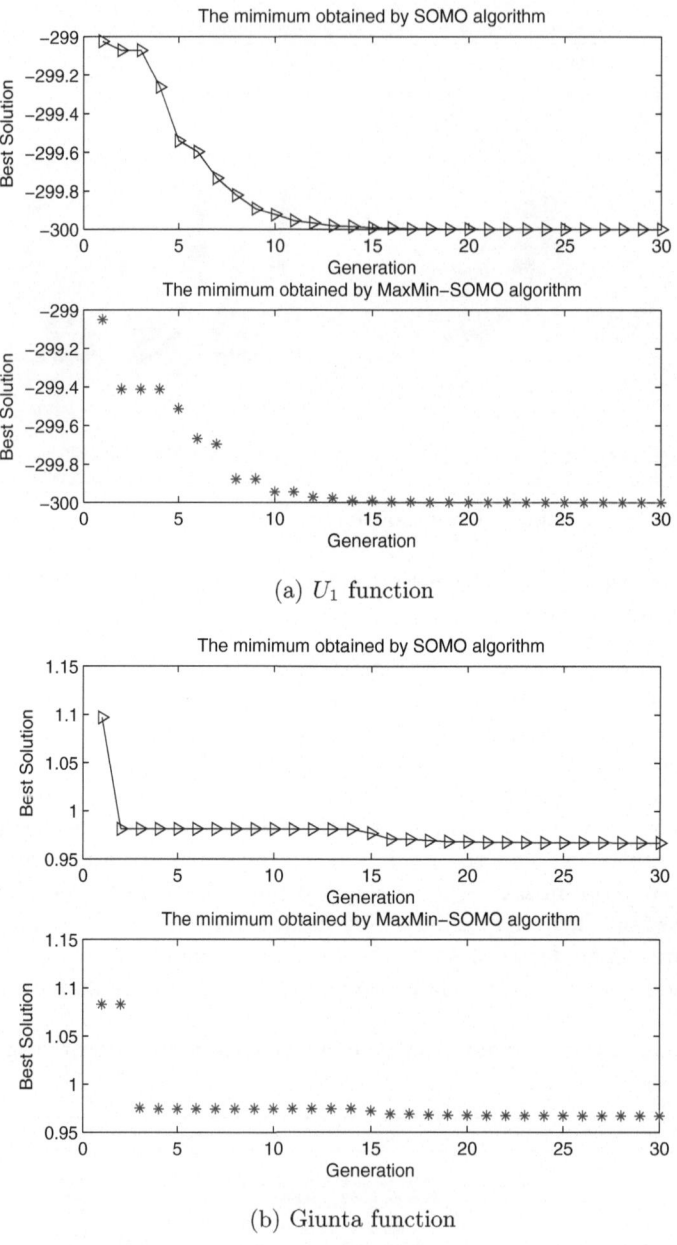

(a) U_1 function

(b) Giunta function

Fig. 2. Best performance curves corresponding to SOM-based optimization(SOMO) algorithm and MaxMin-SOMO algorithm for finding a minimum of a function

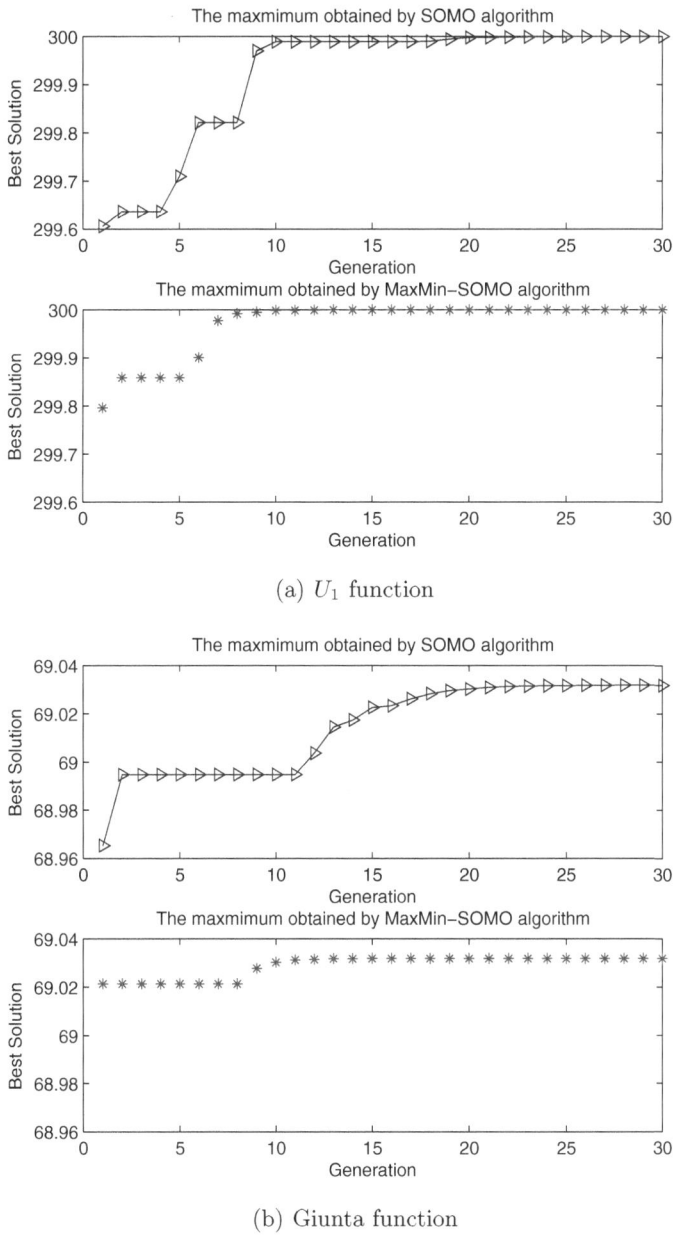

(a) U_1 function

(b) Giunta function

Fig. 3. Best performance curves corresponding to SOM-based optimization(SOMO) algorithm and MaxMin-SOMO algorithm for finding a maximum of a function

minimum of a function obtained by SOM-based optimization(SOMO) algorithm and MaxMin-SOMO algorithm respectively. In figure 3 we compare the maximum of a function obtained by SOM-based optimization(SOMO) algorithm and MaxMin-SOMO algorithm respectively. By SOM-based optimization(SOMO) algorithm, we find a minimum and a maximum of a function separately by running the algorithm twice. But by MaxMin-SOMO algorithm, we find a minimum and a maximum of a function simultaneously.

References

1. Su, M.-C., Zhao, Y.-X.: A variant of the SOM algorithm and its interpretation in the viewpoint of social influence and learning. Neural Comput Applic. (2009)
2. Su, M.C., Zhao, Y.X., Lee, J.: SOM-based optimization. In: IEEE International Joint Conference on Neural Networks, Budapest, pp. 781–786 (2004)
3. Kohonen, T.: Self-organization maps, 3rd extended edn. Springer, Heidelberg (2001)
4. Kohonen, T., Oja, E., Simula, O., Visa, A., Kangas, J.: Engineering application of the self-organizing map. Proc IEEE 84(10), 1358–1383 (1996)
5. Kohonen, T.: Self-organization and associative memory, 3rd edn. Springer, New York (1989)
6. Kohonen, T.: Self-Organizing Maps, 1st edn., 2nd edn., Springer Series in Information Sciences, vol. 30. Springer, Heidelberg (1995)
7. Kaski, S., Kangas, J., Kohonen, T.: Bibliography of selforganizing map (SOM) papers: 1981-1997. Neural Comput. Surv. 1, 102–350 (1998)
8. Oja, M., Kaski, S., Kohonen, T.: Bibliography of self-organizing map (SOM) papers: 1998-2001 addendum. Neural Comput. Surv. 3(1), 1–56 (2002); The self-organizing map. Proc IEEE 84(10), 1358, 1383 (2003)
9. Delgado, A.: Control of Nonlinear Systems Using a Self-Organising Neural Network. Neural Comput. & Applic. 9, 113–123 (2000)
10. Ahmad, N., Alahakoon, D., Chau, R.: Cluster identification and separation in the growing self-organizing map: application in protein sequence classification. Neural Comput. & Applic. 19, 531–542 (2010)
11. Valova, I., Beaton, D., Daniel, A.B.: MacLean Fractal initialization for high-quality mapping with self-organizing maps. Neural Comput. & Applic. 19, 953–966 (2010)
12. Holland, J.H.: Adaptation in natural and artificial systems. University of Michigan Press, Ann Arbor (1975)
13. Goldberg, D.E.: Genetic algorithms in search, optimization, and machine learning. Addison-Wesley, Reading (1989)
14. Kennedy, J., Eberhart, R.: Particle swarm optimization. In: IEEE International Conference on Neural Networks, vol. 4, pp. 1942–1948 (1995)
15. Eberhart, R., Kennedy, J.A.: New optimizer using particle swarm theory. In: Proceedings of the 6th International Symposium on Micro Machine and Human Science, pp. 39–43 (1995)
16. Kennedy, J., Eberhart, R.C., Shi, Y.: Swarm intelligence. Academic Press, New York (2001)

Hybrid Algorithm Based on Particle Swarm Optimization and Artificial Fish Swarm Algorithm

Jingqing Jiang[1,*], Yuling Bo[2], Chuyi Song[2], and Lanying Bao[2]

[1] College of Computer Science and Technology,
Inner Mongolia University for Nationalities, Tongliao 028000, China
[2] College of Mathematics, Inner Mongolia University for Nationalities,
Tongliao 028000, China
`jiangjingqing@yahoo.com.cn`

Abstract. A hybrid algorithm based on particle swarm optimization(PSO) and artificial fish swarm algorithm(AFSA) is proposed. It combines the advantages of PSO and AFSA. The improved AFSA is introduced into PSO at the iteration. The following behavior and swarming behavior of AFSA are performed on two sub-swarms simultaneously. The proposed algorithm increases the variety of the population and improves the accuracy of the solution.

Keywords: Particle Swarm Optimization, Artificial Fish Swarm Algorithm, Hybrid Algorithm, Function Optimization.

1   Introduction

Particle swarm optimization (PSO) was introduced by Kennedy and Eberhart[1] in 1995, who had been inspired by the research of the artificial livings. It is an evolutionary computational model based on swarm intelligence. Since PSO was proposed it has attracted broad attention in the fields of evolutionary computing, optimization and many other fields for the little parameters, faster convergence and easier performance.

The artificial fish swarm algorithm (AFSA) was presented by Li in 2002[2]. It is a kind of the intelligent optimization methods based on fish behaviors. It is designed from bottom to top and has no special requirements for the shape and property of the search space. AFSA starts from the constructing of the fish's simple behaviors. And then each fish performs the local optimization behavior. Finally, the global optimum appears. The implement of AFSA doesn't need to calculate the gradient value of objective function. This algorithm has good self-adaptive ability. It overcomes the local optimal value to obtain the global optimal value. It has the higher convergence speed and it is a robust parallel algorithm. It can be used to solve many optimization models. However AFSA has some disadvantages, such as the poor balance between developing and exploring, slower running speed and lower precision etc. These disadvantages affect the quality and efficiency of AFSA.

---

[*] Corespongding author.

J. Wang, G.G. Yen, and M.M. Polycarpou (Eds.): ISNN 2012, Part I, LNCS 7367, pp. 607–614, 2012.
© Springer-Verlag Berlin Heidelberg 2012

This paper analyses the properties of PSO and AFSA. And then introduces the improved AFSA into PSO. The hybrid algorithm overcomes the local optimization and improves the searching ability.

2   The Basic Theory of the Algorithm

2.1   Particle Swarm Optimization Algorithm

The PSO consists of a number of individuals refining their knowledge of the given search space. Individuals (particles) in the PSO have positions and velocities. The system is initialized firstly by a set of randomly generated potential solutions, and then performs the search for the optimum one iteratively. PSO finds the optimum solution by swarms following the best particle and has much profound intelligent background.

Suppose that the search space is D-dimensional and m particles form the colony. The ith particle represents a D-dimensional vector X_i ($i=1, 2, \ldots, m$). It means that the ith particle locates at $X_i = (x_{i1}, x_{i2}, \ldots, x_{iD})$ ($i=1, 2, \ldots, m$) in the search space. The position of each particle is a potential solution. We calculate the particle's fitness by putting its position into a designated objective function. When the fitness is higher, the corresponding X_i is "better". The ith particle's "flying" velocity is also a D-dimensional vector, denoted as $V_i = (v_{i1}, v_{i2}, \ldots, v_{iD})$ ($i=1, 2, \ldots, m$). Denote the best position of the ith particle as $P_i = (p_{i1}, p_{i2}, \ldots, p_{iD})$, and the best position of the colony as $P_g (p_{g1}, p_{g2}, \ldots, p_{gD})$, respectively. The PSO algorithm could be performed using the following equations

$$V_i(k+1) = wV_i(k) + c_1 r_1 (P_i - X_i(k))/\Delta t + c_2 r_2 (P_g - X_i(k))/\Delta t \tag{1}$$

$$X_i(k+1) = X_i(k) + V_i(k+1)\Delta t \tag{2}$$

where $i=1, 2, \ldots, m$, k represents the iterative number, w is the inertia weight, c_1 and c_2 are learning rates, r_1 and r_2 are random numbers between 0 and 1, Δt is the time step value.

2.2   Artificial Fish Swarm Algorithm

The details of the artificial fish behavior are as follows[2]:

An artificial fish denotes a vector $X = (x_1, x_2, \cdots, x_n)$, where $x_i (i = 1, 2, \cdots, n)$ is the variable that needed to optimize. The food consistence of the position which an artificial fish locate is denoted by $Y = f(X)$, where Y is the objective function value. The distance between two artificial fishes is denoted by $d_{i,j} = \|X_i - X_j\|$. The other properties of an artificial fish are the visual field ($visual$), crowded factor (δ), the largest number of every trying ($trynumber$).

Behavior statement

In a water field, fish could find the most nutrition position by itself or following other fishes. The most nutrition position has more fishes. The artificial fish swarm algorithm implements the optimization by simulate preying behavior, swarming behavior and following behavior.

(1) Preying behavior: set the current position of *ith* artificial fish is X_i. Select a position X_j in its visual field randomly. If $Y_i < Y_j$ (forward condition) then move a step to this direction. Otherwise randomly select a position X_j again, and then judge whether it satisfies the forward condition. Try *trynumber* times. If the forward condition is not yet satisfied then perform random moving behavior.

(2) Swarming behavior: Explore the partner number n_f in an artificial fish's neighborhood. If $n_f/N < \delta, (0 < \delta < 1)$, it shows that the center of partners has more foods and not crowded. In this case, if $Y_i < Y_j$ then the artificial fish moves a step to the center X_c. Otherwise perform random preying behavior.

(3) Following behavior: Explore the optimal neighbor X_{max} in its neighborhood. If $Y_i < Y_{max}$ and the partner number n_f in the neighborhood of X_{max} satisfies $n_f/N < \delta, (0 < \delta < 1)$, it shows that the position X_{max} have more food and not crowded. Then the artificial fish move a step to the position X_{max}. Otherwise performs preying behavior.

(4) Random behavior: The artificial fish selects a random position in its visual field and then move a step to this direction. It is a default behavior of preying behavior. It provides a random swimming in preying behavior when the *trynumber* is small. It also increases the variety of the swarm so that the artificial fish could jump out of the local optimal value.

(5) Behavior selection: According to the problem, artificial fish evaluates its current situation, and then selects a behavior. The selection criterion is having progress or fastest progress. Finally the artificial fishes will gather around the several local optimums. The global optimum will appear in these fields.

(6) Bulletin Board: Bulletin board is used to record the optimal artificial fish. In the optimization process, each artificial fish compares its position with the bulletin board after a moving. If its position is better than the bulletin board, the bulletin board is rewritten by this artificial fish. So the historical optimal position is written in bulletin board.

3   The Hybrid Algorithm Based on PSO and AFSA

This paper composes PSO and AFSA to remain their advantages. The idea comes from the PSO based preying operator proposed by Wang[3] and the improved PSO with swarming operator[4]. The following behavior and swarming behavior are performed on two sub-swarms simultaneously. The default behavior is preying behavior. PSO is the main flow in the proposed algorithm. After an iteration of PSO, the following behave and the swarming behavior is performed respectively. The algorithm compares the optimum obtained by following behavior and swarming behavior. The best optimum is regard as the global optimum. The PSO jumps out of the pre-maturity by performing artificial fish swarm algorithm. The proposed algorithm increases the variety of the population and improves the accuracy of the solution.

3.1   Algorithm Steps

The steps of the hybrid algorithm based on PSO and AFSA are as follows:

(1) Initialize the swarm size N, and initialize the position x_i and velocity v_i of each particle randomly. Set the learning rate c_1 and c_2 for particles. Set the visual field ($visual$), crowded factor (δ) and moving step ($step$) for artificial fish.

(2) Calculate the fitness of each particle. Calculate the best position p_{id} that the ith particle experienced and the present best global position p_{gd} that the particle swarm experienced. Initialize the bulletin board by the present best solution p_{gd} obtained through particle swarm optimization.

(3) Update the velocity and position of each particle by Eq. (1) and Eq. (2).

(4) Calculate the fitness of each particle. Update the best position p_{id} that the ith particle experienced and the present best global position p_{gd} that the particle swarm experienced.

(5) If the p_{gd} better than the bulletin board, update the bulletin board by p_{gd}. Partition the swarm into two equal sub swarms. One swarm performs the swarming behavior of AFSA and the other swarm performs the following behavior of AFSA.

(6) Compare the solutions of swarming behavior and following behavior. Update the bulletin board by the better solution. Compare the bulletin board with the best solution of particle swarm p_{gd}. If the bulletin board better than p_{gd}, update p_{gd} with bulletin board.

(7) If the objective function value satisfies the accuracy or the maximal iteration generation is achieved, output the solution. Otherwise go to (3).

The flow chart is given in Fig.1.

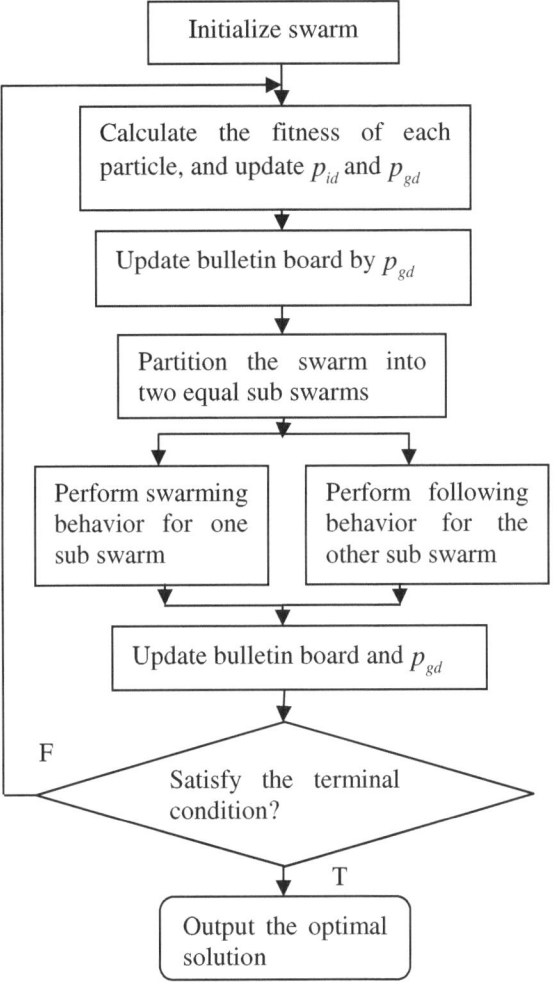

Fig. 1. Flow chart

4   Simulation Experience

In order to examine the effectiveness of the proposed hybrid algorithm we solve 7 problems. The testing functions are as followings:

(1) $f_1(x) = x_1^2 + x_2^2$, the minimal value is 0.

(2) $f_2(x) = 100(x_1^2 - x_2)^2 + (1 - x_1)^2$, the minimal value is 0.

(3) $f_3(x) = g(x)h(x)$, where

$$g(x) = [1 + (x_1 + x_2 + 1)^2 (19 - 14x_1 + 3x_1^2 - 14x_2 + 6x_1x_2 + 3x_2^2)];$$
$$h(x) = [30 + (2x_1 - 3x_2)^2 (18 - 32x_1 + 12x_1^2 + 48x_2 - 36x_1x_2 + 27x_2^2)], \text{ the}$$
minimal value is 3.

(4) $f_4(x) = (x_1^2 + x_2^2)^{\frac{1}{4}} [\sin(50(x_1^2 + x_2^2)^{0.1}) + 1.0]$, the minimal value is 0.

(5) $f_5(x) = a(x_2 - bx_1^2 + cx_1 - d)^2 + e(1 - f)\cos(x_1) + e$,

where $a = 1, b = 5.1/(4\pi^2), c = 5/\pi, d = 6, e = 10, f = 1/(8\pi)$,

$-100 \leq x_1, x_2 \leq 100$, the minimal value is 0.39788735772974.

(6) $f_6(x) = 4x_1^2 - 2.1x_1^4 + \frac{1}{3}x_1^6 + x_1x_2 - 4x_2^2 + 4x_2^4$,

$-5 \leq x_1, x_2 \leq 5$, the minimal value is -1.03162845348988.

(7) $f_7(x) = 1000[(x_1 - 1)^2 + (x_2 - 2)^2] + 1$,

$-2.08 \leq x_1, x_2 \leq 2.08$, the minimal value is 1.

All the programs are written in MATLAB7.0. The parameters for the hybrid algorithm are as follows: the swarm size N=40, the maximal iterative generation M=1000, the inertia weight $w=0.7$, learning rates $c_1 = c_2 = 2$, dimension $D = 2$, the visual field $visual = 3.5$, crowded factor $\delta = 1$, moving step $step=0.3$ and $Try\_number = 10$. The program is run on the testing functions for 20 times and the best results are showed in table1 to table 3.

Table 1. The comparison of global optimal values for function $f_1(x)$ and $f_2(x)$

Functions	Searching regions	Optimal function values x for optimal function in paper[5]	value of hybrid algorithm	Optimal function values of hybrid algorithm
$f_1(x)$	$x_1 \in (-5,5)$ $x_2 \in (-5,5)$	4.1429719958297e-008	(0.056908746651e-005, -0.304614922991e-005)	9.6028856754391e-012
$f_2(x)$	$x_1 \in (-5,5)$ $x_2 \in (-5,5)$	7.0950553507689e-011	(1.00000114544531, 1.00000219923578)	2.1521300375527e-012

It can be seen from table 1 that the optimal function values obtained through the proposed hybrid algorithm are better than those in paper [5]. $f_1(x)$ is an unimodal function. It reaches the minimum 0 at (0, 0). $f_2(x)$ is a singular non-convex functions. Its function value changes slowly and it reaches the minimum 0 at (0, 0). It is usually used to test the global searching ability for optimization algorithm.

Table 2. The comparison of global optimal values for function $f_3(x)$ and $f_4(x)$

Functions	Searching regions	Optimal function values in paper[6]	x for optimal function value of hybrid algorithm	Optimal function values of hybrid algorithm
$f_3(x)$	$x_1 \in (-2,2)$ $x_1 \in (-2,2)$	3.00000006455463	(0.00000575882895, -1.00000055703883)	3.00000000918428
$f_4(x)$	$x_1 \in (-100,100)$ $x_1 \in (-100,100)$	3.14955995514226e-015	(0.79702554479856, -0.36375290147197)	5.195880464128456e-016

Table 2 shows the comparison of global optimal values for function $f_3(x)$ and $f_4(x)$ with those in paper [6]. It can be seen that the optimal function values obtained through the propose hybrid algorithm are better than those in paper [6]. It is difficult to obtain the global optimal value for the multimodal functions such as $f_3(x)$ and $f_4(x)$. But the hybrid algorithm has the ability to jump out of the local optimum and obtains the global optimum. The results in this paper approximate the exact solution. It shows the effectiveness of the proposed algorithm.

Table 3. The comparison of global optimal values for function $f_5(x)$, $f_6(x)$ and $f_7(x)$

Functions	Optimal function values in AFSA	x for optimal function value of hybrid algorithm	Optimal function values of hybrid algorithm
$f_5(x)$	0.39788735974184	(9.42477619503795, 2.47499800967284)	0.39788735774496
$f_6(x)$	-1.03162845340261	(0.08977028425282, -0.71264366491184)	-1.03162843301603
$f_7(x)$	1.00000010705268	(0.99998720552940, 2.00000414260801)	1.00000018085968

Table 3 shows the comparison of global optimal values for function $f_5(x)$, $f_6(x)$ and $f_7(x)$ with those obtained by AFSA.

5   Conclusion

Analyzing the results in section 4, it can be seen that the proposed algorithm obtains better results in convergency and stability for both unimodal and multimodal functions. It not only avoids the pre-maturity of PSO but also increases the variety of the swarm. It enhances the balance ability between the exploring and developing of AFSA, and improves the accuracy of the result and the global searching ability.

Acknowledgement. This paper is supported by the National Natural Science Funds of China under Grant No. 61163034, the Science Research Project of High Education of Inner Mongolia Autonomous Region under Grant No. NJ10118, NJ10112 and NJZY11208, the Natural Science Foundation of Inner Mongolia Autonomous Region under Grant No. 2009MS0914.

References

1. Kennedy, J., Eberhart, R.C.: Particle Swarm Optimizer. In: Proceedings of the IEEE International Conference on Neural Networks Perth, pp. 1942–1948 (1995)
2. Li, X., Shao, Z., Qian, J.: An Optimizing Method Based on Autonomous Animats: Fish-swarm Algorithm. Systems Engineering-theory & Practice 22(11), 32–38 (2002)
3. Wang, L., Hong, Y., Zhao, F.: Particle Swarm Optimization Based on Prey Operator. Computer Applications and Software 26(11), 112–115 (2009)
4. Li, R., Chang, X.: New Hybrid Particle Swarm Optimization. Application Research of Computers 26(5), 1700–1702 (2009)
5. Qu, L., He, D.: Novel Artificial Fish-school Algorithm Based on Chaos Search. Computer Engineering and Applications 46(22), 40–42 (2010)
6. Luo, D., Zhou, Y., Huang, H.: Hybrid Optimization Algorithm Based on Particle Swarm and Artificial Fish Swarm Algorithm. Computers and Applied Chemistry 26(10), 1257–1261 (2009)

The High Degree Seeking Algorithms with k Steps for Complex Networks*

Minyu Feng, Hong Qu**, Yi Xu, and Xing Ke

Computational Intelligence Laboratory,
School of Computer Science and Engineering,
University of Electronic Science and Technology of China
hongqu@uestc.edu.cn

Abstract. Search in complex network is an open issue, lots of algorithms have been proposed, however, most of them have their own shortcomings such as stepping slow or checking too many nodes. This paper presents a new high degree seeking algorithm with k steps in order to solve this problems for scale-free networks. This algorithm not only enables fast access to distant nodes, but also reduce the average search steps and check fewer nodes. Simulations are carried out to illustrate the performance of the proposed method.

Keywords: high degree seeking, complex networks, average search steps, random walk, query information.

1 Introduction

In 1960s, Stanley Milgram social psychologist at Harvard University made a number of social surveys and concluded[1] the average distance between any two people on the planet is 6. This small-world experiment told us two facts: First, the average distance between any two people is very short even though the network itself is extremely huge. Second, the network is able to be searched which means people are likely to find a shorter path to a stranger no matter how many paths are linked between them or how different they are. Watts, Strogaz and Newman[2][3] proposed a small-world model by reconnecting the rules network or adding path to it. Their model shows that the average distance between any two people is able to be short as long as we add some new paths to the rules network. Barabái and Albert proposed[4] a new model called scale-free network. They found the degree distribution of this kind of network follows a power law distribution. Kleinberg first[5] studied the theory of complex networks in searching capabilities. Later, Watts did further research[6] on this issue. K Sneppen discussed[7] seeking in different kind of complex networks, and Ernesto Estrada proposed[8] communicability betweenness in it. All of them tell us the complex networks are able to be searched.

* This work was supported by National Science Foundation of China under Grant 60905037.
** Corresponding author.

J. Wang, G.G. Yen, and M.M. Polycarpou (Eds.): ISNN 2012, Part I, LNCS 7367, pp. 615–623, 2012.
© Springer-Verlag Berlin Heidelberg 2012

Since then, lots of search strategies are proposed such as random walk[9][10], high degree seeking[11][12] and greedy search[13]. However, all of them have their own disadvantages. The search steps of random walk are huge; The query information of high degree seek is large; The greedy search may not be optimal in spatial scale-free networks that have high heterogeneity in node degree. In order to reduce the average searching steps, check fewer nodes and be optimal, we introduce a new high degree seeking with k steps based on scale-free network model.

In this paper, scale-free network model is introduced in section II. Some classic search algorithms are described in section III. A new high degree seeking algorithm with K steps is presented in section IV. Simulation is presented in section V. Finally, conclusions are drawn in Section VI.

2   Scale-Free Network Model

Coupled rules networks are not small-world networks even with high clustering properties. On the other hand, Erdós and Rényi's random graph has a small average path length but without the high clustering properties. Therefore, these two types of networks model can not reproduce the characteristics of the real networks, after all, most of the them are neither completely rule nor entirely random. As a transition from a completely rule networks to entirely random graphs, Watts and Strogtz introduced[2] an interesting small-world network model called WS small-world network model. However, the random process of WS small-world model construction algorithm may destroy the network's connectivity, Newman and Watts[3] proposed a new small-world model called NW small-world model which 'adds edge randomly' instead of 'reconnecting randomly'.

No matter NW or WS small-world network model, they don't consider two characteristics of the real networks that are proposed by Barabái and Albert[4]:

1. **Growth characteristics:** the size of the network is constantly expanding just like every month a large number of new research articles published and the number of new pages produced on the WWW every day.
2. **Preferential attachment features:** the new nodes tend to connect to those 'big' node with a high degree. This phenomenon is also known as the 'rich get richer' or 'Matthew effect'. For example, new posts have been more inclined to quote some important documents widely cited, the new personal home page of the hypertext links are more likely to point to Sina, Yahoo and other famous sites.

Since this type of network connection degree to the node has no obvious characteristic length, we call it scale-free network. And Barabái and Albert proposed a new model called BA model to explain it, here is how they constructed it[4]:

1. **Growth**: from a node with the number of m_0, introducing each new node and connecting to existing nodes with the number of m, here $m \leq m_0$.
2. **Priority connections**: what the relationship between the probability of a new node connecting to an existing node i and the node i, node j's degrees satisfy is as following:

$$\Pi_i = \frac{k_i}{\sum\limits_j k_j}. \tag{1}$$

After t steps later, this algorithm produces a network, its numbers of nodes are $t+m_0$, meanwhile edges are mt. Now that the model is constructed,the followings are some of its statistical properties:

The clustering coefficient of BA small-world network is[14]:

$$C = \frac{m^2(m+1)^2}{4(m-1)}[\ln(\frac{m+1}{m}) - \frac{1}{m+1}]\frac{[\ln(t)]^2}{t}. \tag{2}$$

This indicates that it is similar with ER random graph, BA scale-free network model has no obvious clustering features when the scale of the network is huge enough.

The Average path length of BA scale-free network model is[15]:

$$L \propto \frac{logN}{loglogN}. \tag{3}$$

This indicates that BA scale-free network also has small world effect.

The similar results of degree distribution of the BA scale-free network model can get in different ways such as continuum theory[4], main equation method[16] and rate equation method[17]:

$$P(k) = \frac{2m(m+1)}{k(k+1)(k+2)} \propto 2m^2k^{-3}. \tag{4}$$

This indicates that the distribution function of BA network can be approximate described by a power law function that its power index is 3.

3   Classic Search Algorithms

Since the fast searching capabilities has been confirmed by Kleinberg, more and more searching algorithms are raised. A searching strategy of Complex networks is usually described by the process of message passing. From a given source node, according to certain rules to one or more of its neighbors to pass query information in order to find the information we need. The most typical ones are bread-first searching, random walking, greed search and high degree seeking.

Applying random walk to find a path from the source node i to the target node j:Start with node i, determine whether its neighbor node has the target node, stop searching if there is; Else, check a random neighbor'neighbors to see if there is. Repeat this process until any neighbors of the target node is found.

Compare with broadcast searching, the steps of random walking is much lager, however, check information one time each time, greatly reducing the network's message traffic.

A simple search algorithm in spatial networks is greedy search[13], where each node passes the message to the neighbor closest to the target node. Let d_i be the distance to the target node from each neighbor i and let k_i be the degree of the neighbor i.

Greedy search chooses the neighbor with the smallest d_i. This will ensure that the message is always going to the neighbor closest to the target node.

Random walking is a basic dynamic process, more and more people study it, here are three different random walking strategies[9][10]: unrestricted random walking, no-retracing random walking and self-avoiding random walking. People found that with different network topology, the efficiency of the search strategy is quite different. However, all the search strategies are not suitable for BA scale-free network model. Further, Martin Rosvall and Carl T.Bergsrom[18] use random walking on complex networks to reveal community structure.

Recently, Kim and others did the research[19] of using the high degree seeking in a power-law distribution network in the path finding problem, they proved the effectiveness of their high degree seeking in BA scale-free network model. The followings are the specific steps of the algorithm.

Consider the condition, each node is in the understanding of their neighbors and knows the neighbors'degrees:

Step 1: Initially, to determine the source node i and target node j;

Step 2: Starting from node i,to determine whether its neighbors include the target node: if not, the max degree of the neighbor node will be set to the current node; if so, then stop the search;

Step 3: We can visit the same node several times, but each edge can only be visited only once, if the current node's edges have been all visited, then return to the previous node;

Step 4: Repeat these two steps 2 and 3, until we find any neighbors of the target node, target node is found and the search is completed.

This gives us a complete path between i and j, remove the ring on this path, we can get the path between i and j.

4   A High Degree Seeking Algorithm with K Steps

As previously described, the original high degree seeking algorithm put forward by Adamic[11][12] can full use of node's degree but each step need to check the node's neighbors leads to step slow and check too many nodes. Later, Kim proposed a new high degree seeking algorithm based on scale-free networks which steps faster but still checks too many nodes and too slow to get the distant nodes. Here proposes a new high degree seeking algorithm with K steps. The followings are the detailed description of this algorithm.

Select n nodes from N nodes as the source node, the search steps for each selected source node i to target node j is t_{ij}, we can get the number of search steps from each n to the other $N - 1$:

$$T_i = \sum_{j=1, j\neq i}^{N} t_{ij}. \tag{5}$$

We define the average search steps:

$$\overline{T} = \sum_i \frac{T_i}{N(N-1)}. \tag{6}$$

We define the amount of query information as the times of query neighbor nodes.

Fewer the average search steps are, less the amount of information inquiries and better the algorithm is. Thus, the average search steps and the amount of query information are important statistical properties for measuring the quality of the algorithm.

Step 1: Initially, determining the source node and target node;
Step 2: From the current node, search k steps randomly;

>   *If* The current node is the target node *then*
>   Goto **step 4**;
>   *else*
>   Goto **step 3**.

Step 3: Starting from the current node get from **step 2**,

>   *If* The current node's neighbors include the target node *then*
>   Goto **step 4**;
>   *else*
>   Find the node with max degree in the neighbors, supposed
>   as node i;
>   Set i as current node ;
>   Goto **step 2**.

Step 4: Stop, write the final path.

The same node can be visited several times, but each edge can only be visited only once, if the current node's edges have been all visited, then return to the previous one. Obviously, when $k = 0$, the algorithm will degenerate into Kim's high degree seeking.

Fig.1 illustrates each step of this algorithm.

Fig.2 gives an example for high degree seeking with 2 steps. First,determine the source node i and target node j as (a). Then start random walking from node i to node 3 with 2 steps as (b) and (c), the current node is node 3. Apply the high degree seeking to it, none of its neighbor is the target node. Choose the max degree node 4 to be the current node from them as (d). Start random walking again from node 4 to node j with 2 steps as (e) and (f). After this, the target node j is reached and the seeking terminates.

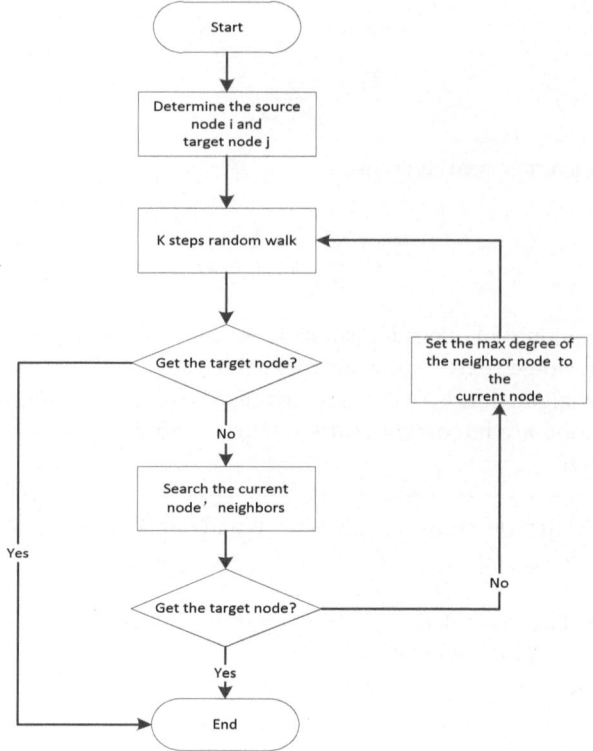

Fig. 1. Example for high degree seeking with k steps, search steps $T=5$

5   Simulation

The same as other high degree seeking, this high degree seeking with k steps is more suitable for BA scale-free network. So, the BA scale-free network model need to be randomly constructed. We start from five nodes, add another five nodes to them each step, and the number of final network N is 100. The constructed BA scale-free network model is presented in Fig.3.

Applying high degree seeking with k steps to this network while n is 88, the relationship between step k and average search steps is shown in Fig.4, the relationship between step k and the amount of query information is shown in Fig.5.

With the k growing, the average search steps rapid increase and finally trend levelling off. At the same time, the amount of query information fall quickly and finally trend levelling off. When $k = 0$, we can get the data of Kim's high degree seeking for comparing. Considering both average search steps and amount of query information, when about $k = 2$, this algorithm is better than Kim's. If only take the average search steps as standard, Kim's is still better. However, we have to consider them both in practical application. Table I shows the comparison.

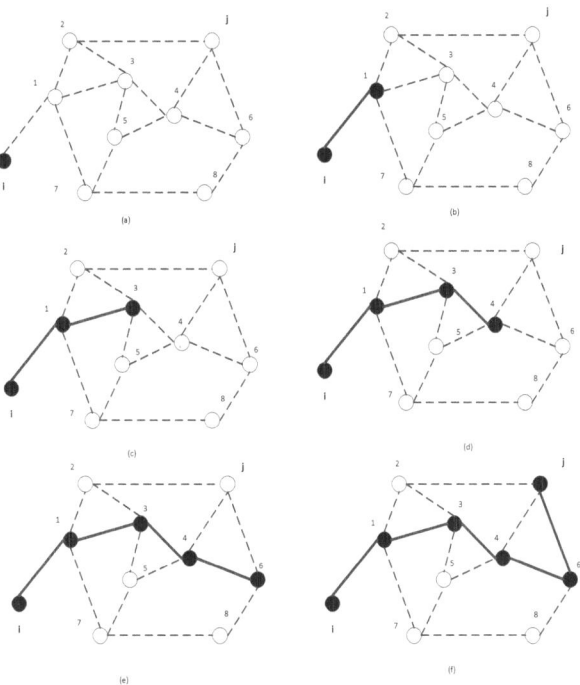

Fig. 2. Example for high degree seeking with k steps, search steps $T=5$

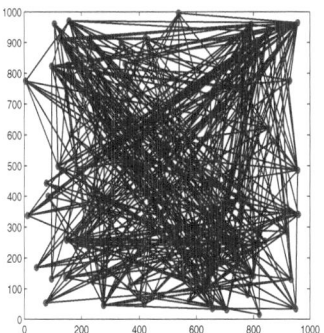

Fig. 3. BA scale-free network model

Along with the increase of k, the amount of query information is decreasing while average search step is increasing, so k is not the bigger the better, we have to control k's value according to the number of network'nodes N.

High degree seeking with k steps not only search forward fast but also full use information of node. In some cases such as two distant nodes with low degree, this algorithm is even better no matter in search steps or query information. We get the sparse matrix of Fig.3 and take node 3 and node 91 as an example, the

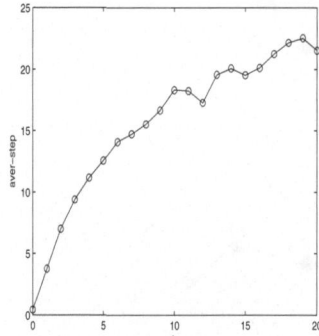

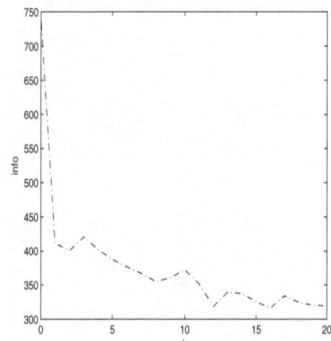

Fig.2. The relationship between k and average search steps

Fig.3. The relationship between step k and amount of query information

Table 1. The comparison of the different high degree seeking

step k	0	2	5	10	20
Average search steps	0.7	3.8	12.2	17.2	21.2
Query information	741	402	383	376	319

Table 2. The comparison between distant node 3 and node 91

step k	0	3
Average search steps	75	9
Query information	16	4

simulation results are: when $k = 0$ which is degenerate into Kim's high degree seeking, the average search steps are 75 and the amount of query information is 16; but when $k = 3$, the average search steps are 9 and the amount of query information is 4. The result is clearly presented in Table 2:

Although the simulation results have a certain randomness, but we can still see this algorithm's advantage of searching in two distant nodes with low degree. Consider both average search steps and amount of query information, high degree seeking with k steps is still an efficient strategy.

6   Conclusions

With the continuous rise of the network theory, network search gradually attracted people's attention. The high degree seeking with k steps in this paper not only search forward fast but also full use information of node. When k is a reasonable value according to N, this algorithm improves the search speed and reduces the amount of query information. Further, This algorithm can be widely used in social networking such as friend recommendation systems of social networking sites or tracing system to find someone who is weakly linked to you.

However, When k is the best value according to N and how to measure both average search steps and amount of query information is still a problem worthy of studying.

References

1. Milgram, S.: The small world problem. Psycholoy Today 60–67 (May 1967)
2. Watts, D.J., Strogatz, S.H.: Collective dynamic of 'small-world' networks. Nature 393(6684), 440–442 (1998)
3. Newman, M.E.J., Watts, D.J.: Renormalization group analysis of the small-world network model. Phys. Lett. A 263, 341–346 (1999)
4. Barabasi, A.L., Albert, R.: Emergence of scaling in random networks. Science 286(5439), 509–512 (1999)
5. Kleinberg, J.: Navigation in a small world. Nature 406, 845 (2000)
6. Watts, D.J., Dodds, P.S., Newman, M.E.J.: Identity and search in social networks. Science 296, 1302–1305 (2002)
7. Sneppen, K., Trusina, A., Rosvall, M.: Hide-and-seek on complex networks. Europhys. Lett. 69(5), 853–859 (2005)
8. Estradaa, E., Highamb, D.J., Hatanoc, N.: Communicability betweenness in complex networks. Physica A 388, 764–774 (2009)
9. Hughes, B.D.: Random Walks and Random Environments. Clarendon Press, Oxford (1996)
10. Jasch, F., Blumen, A.: Target problem on small-world networks. Phys. Rev. E 63, 041108 (2001)
11. Adamic, L.A., Lukose, R.M., Puniyani, A.R., Huberman, B.A.: Search in power-law networks. Phys. Rev. E 64, 046135 (2001)
12. Adamic, L.A., Lukose, R.M., Huberman, B.A.: Local search in unstructured networks. In: Bornholdt, S., Schuster, H.G. (eds.) Handbook of Graphs and Networks. Wiley-VCH, Berlin (2003)
13. Thadakamalla, H.P., Albert, R., Kumara, S.R.T.: Search in spatial scale-free networks. New Journal of Physics 9, 190 (2007)
14. Fronczak, A., Fronczak, P., Holyst, J.A.: Mean-field theory for clustering coefficients in Barabasi-Albert network. Phys. Rev. E 68, 046126 (2003)
15. Cohen, R., Havlin, S.: Scale-free networks are ultrasmall. Phys. Rev. Lett 90, 058701 (2003)
16. Dorogovtsev, S.N., Mendes, J.F.F., Samukhin, A.N.: Structure of growing networks with preferential linking. Phys. Rev. Lett. 85, 4633–4636 (2002)
17. Krapivsky, P.L., Redner, S., Leyvraz, F.: Connectivity of growing random networks. Phys. Rev. Lett. 85, 4629–4632 (2000)
18. Rosvall, M., Bergstrom, C.T.: Maps of random walks on complex networks reveal community structure. PNAS 105(4), 1123 (2008)
19. Kim, B.J., Yoon, C.N., Han, S.K., Jeong, H.: Path finding strategies in scale-free networks. Phys. Rev. E 65, 027103 (2002)

Improved PSO Algorithm with Harmony Search for Complicated Function Optimization Problems

Jian Yu[1,2] and Ping Guo[1]

[1] Image Processing and Pattern Recognition Laboratory,
Beijing Normal University, Beijing 100875, China
[2] College of Mathematics and Information Technology,
Hanshan Normal University, Chaozhou, Guangdong 521041, China
czyujian@163.com, pguo@ieee.org

Abstract. Improved particle swarm optimization algorithm with harmony search (IHPSO) is proposed in this paper. This algorithm takes particle swarm search direction estimation mechanism and harmony search (HS) approach to particle swarm optimization (PSO) algorithm, which increases the search capability of PSO algorithm considerably. The proposed algorithm initializes a new search with harmony pitch adjusting or random selection when PSO search direction is estimated incorrectly. This can provide further opportunities of finding better solutions for the particle swarm by guiding the entire particle swarm to promising new regions of the search space and accelerating the search. PSO, HPSO and IHPSO, as well as other advanced PSO procedures from the literature were compared on several benchmark test functions extensively. Statistical analyses of the experimental results indicate that the performance of IHPSO is better than the performance of PSO and HPSO.

Keywords: Particle swarm optimization, harmony search, function optimization.

1   Introduction

As an intelligent optimization algorithm, particle swarm algorithm (PSO) introduced by Kennedy and Eberhart [1] has been paid attention extensively, which was inspired by the social behavior of bird flocking to solve optimization problems. Similarly to other intelligent optimization algorithm like genetic algorithm (GA), PSO is a population-based optimizer based on the premise that social sharing of information. PSO has a memory for sharing information retained by all the particles and optimal solutions found by the particle swarm. PSO algorithm shows a promising performance on nonlinear function optimization [3]. However, PSO is inclined to trap into premature convergence for its poor local search capability, especially in the case complex multi-peak search problems [4]. Many improvements [8-13] have been proposed to overcome these disadvantages of PSO algorithm. In recent years, some researchers have improved the PSO algorithm by introducing the harmony search (HS) concepts.

J. Wang, G.G. Yen, and M.M. Polycarpou (Eds.): ISNN 2012, Part I, LNCS 7367, pp. 624–632, 2012.

HS algorithm conceptualized a behavioral phenomenon during music players' improvisation when musicians search for a better state of harmony with improving its tune in a natural musical performance processes [5,7]. The engineers seek for a global solution as determined by an objective function originated in an analogy between music improvisation and engineering optimization, just like the musicians seek to find musically pleasing harmony as determined by aesthetics [6].

PSO algorithm has strong direction of searching while harmony search algorithm has better local searching ability. The particle swarm harmony search (PSHS) is proposed by Geem [8], in which particle swarm algorithm is combined with the HS algorithm for the first time and is applied to solve the problem of water network design. Li and Liu [9] proposed harmony particle swarm algorithm (HPSO) to solve the problem of structural design optimization.

But facing complicated function optimization problems, the HPSO algorithm still traps into local minimum easily. For solving this kind of optimizations, IHPSO algorithm is proposed in this paper. The difference to HPSO [9] is that IHPSO introduced two parameters to evaluate the searching direction of particle swarm correctly or not, which results in further opportunities of finding better solutions for the particle swarm by guiding the entire particle swarm to promising new regions of the search space and accelerating the search.

To evaluate the performance of IHPSO in the optimization problems, the PSO and HPSO algorithms are included in the comparisons.

2   Method

2.1   Basic PSO Algorithm

PSO algorithm [1] is a population-based optimization method, where a population is called a swarm. A swarm consists of N particles moving around in a D-dimensional search space, and each particle in the swarm is the potential solution of the optimization problem. The position of the ith particle can be represented by $y_i = (y_{i1}, y_{i2}, \ldots, y_{iD})$. The velocity for the ith particle can be written as $v_i = (v_{i1}, v_{i2}, \ldots, v_{iD})$. The positions and velocities of the particles are confined within $[y_{min}, y_{max}]$ and $[v_{min}, v_{max}]$, respectively, where the y_{min} and y_{max} are the lower bounds and upper bounds of the search space, and the v_{min} and v_{max} are the lower bounds and upper bounds of velocities.

Particle swarm's fitness is determined by an object function. At each generation, each particle follows two best positions to update itself. One is called $pbest$. $pbest_i = (pbest_{i1}, pbest_{i2}, \ldots, pbest_{iD})$ is the best previous position yielding the best fitness value for the ith particle. The other is called $gbest$. $gbest = (gbest_1, gbest_2, \ldots, gbest_D)$ is the best position discovered by the whole population. The velocity v_{id} and position y_{id} updates of the dth dimension of the ith particle are presented below:

$$v_{id}(t+1) = w(t)v_{id}(t) + c_1 r_1 (pbest_{id} - y_{id}(t)) + c_2 r_2 (gbest_d - y_{id}(t)) \tag{1}$$

$$y_{id}(t+1) = y_{id}(t) + v_{id}(t+1) \tag{2}$$

where $v_i(t+1)$ respents the i particle's speed at $t+1$ iteration. r_1 and r_2 are two uniformly distributed random numbers in [0,1]. c_1 and c_2 are called acceleration constants and usually set at 2. $y_i(t+1)$ respents the i particle's position at $t+1$ iteration. w is inertia weight set at a random number in [0,1]. w controls the impact of the previous velocity of a particle on the position it remembered. In general, w is decreased linearly from 0.9 to 0.4 throughout the search process to effectively balance the local and global search abilities of the swarm [10]. The equation for the inertia weight w can be written as:

$$w = (w_{max} - w_{min}) \frac{(iter_{max} - iter_i)}{iter_{max}} + w_{min} \qquad (3)$$

In Eq.(3), w_{max} is 0.9, w_{min} is 0.4 , $iter_i$ is the number of generations, $iter_{max}$ is the maximum number of allowed iterations.

The steps in the procedure of basic PSO are as follows:

Step 1. Initial population: Each particle is randomly generated. All particles in the solution space are randomly generated with an individual position and velocity.

Step 2. Fitness evaluation: the fitness function of all particles is calculated.

Step 3. Velocity and position update: The particles move through the search space at each iteration using Eq.(1) and Eq.(2).

Step 4. Update *pbest* and *gbest*: At each iteration, each individual compares its current fitness value to its own *pbest* and global best solution *gbest*. The *pbest* and *gbest* values are updated if the new values are better than the old ones.

Step 5. Repeat Step 2–Step 4 until the termination condition is met.

2.2   Harmony Search Algorithm

HS algorithm is based on natural musical performance processes that occur when a musician searches for a better state of harmony improvisation [5]. This algorithm includes a number of optimization operators, such as the harmony memory (HM), the harmony memory size (HMS), the harmony memory consideration rate (HMCR), the pitch adjusting rate (PAR) and the pitch adjustment bandwidth (BW) [8]. In HS algorithm, the HM stores the feasible vectors, which are all in the feasible space. How the HS algorithm generates a new vector from its harmony memory and how it is used to improve the PSO algorithm will be discussed as follows [6].

When a musician improvises one pitch, usually one of three rules is used:

(1) playing any one pitch from his/her memory, i.e. choosing any one value from HM, defined as memory consideration;
(2) playing an adjacent pitch of one pitch in his/her memory, i.e., choosing an adjacent value of one value from HM, defined as pitch adjustments;
(3) playing totally random pitch from possible sound ranges, i.e. , choosing totally random value from the possible value range, defined as randomization .

Similarly, when each decision variable chooses one value in the HS algorithm, it can apply one of the above three rules in the whole HS algorithm. If a new harmony vector is better than the worst harmony vector in the HM, the new harmony vector replaces the worst harmony vector in the HM. This procedure is repeated until a stopping criterion is satisfied. The computational procedure of the basic HS algorithm can be summarized as follows:

Step 1. Initialize the problem and algorithm parameters, including HMS, HMCR, PAR and BW.

Step 2. Initialize the harmony memory (HM) from a uniform distribution in the possible ranges.

Step 3. Use one of the above three rules to generate a new harmony vector from the HM.

Step 4. Update the HM only if its fitness (measured in terms of the objective function) is better than the worst harmony.

Step 5. Check the stopping criterion (generally the number of iterations). If it is satisfied, computation is terminated. Otherwise, Step 3 and Step 4 are repeated.

2.3   IHPSO Algorithm

In this paper, a hybrid algorithm named improved PSO with harmony search (IHPSO) is proposed. It adopted the traits of fast speed and direction of searching in PSO and the traits of jumping out of local optimal solution with HS algorithm.

The main improvement in IHPSO algorithm is that two parameters were introduced to evaluate the searching direction of PSO correctly or not, which results in further opportunities of finding better solutions for the particle swarm by guiding the entire particle swarm to promising new regions of the search space and accelerating the search.

One is direction evaluation parameter *countf*. It is defined as the *gbest* fitness value (global optimum at each iteration) has not changed for a certain number of consecutive iterations, which means the direction of particle swarm searching is wrong. *countf* adhere to the following conditions:

$$f(gbest(t + 1)) < f(gbest(t)) \Rightarrow countf\,(t + 1) = countf\,(t) + 1,$$

$$f(gbest(t + 1)) > f(gbest(t)) \Rightarrow countf\,(t + 1) = 0.$$

Where $gbest(t + 1)$ respents the global optimum at $t+1$ iteration, $countf(t+1)$ denote the number of consecutive failures at $t+1$ iteration and the operator f is the fitness function of PSO.

The other one is threshold parameters ε. It is defined as the maximum of *countf*. When *countf* reach ε, the harmony pitch adjusting or random selection has been used in the PSO algorithm to avoid searching trapped in local solutions. The optimal choice of values for ε is problem-dependent. In this paper, ε is set to 6. And the HM used the same matrix with swarm matrix of PSO algorithm.

Pitch adjustment rate (PAR) was adopted with improvement in harmony search (IHS) algorithm proposed in paper [7] by dynamically varying PAR values with generation number as expressed as:

$$PAR = \frac{(PAR_{max} - PAR_{min})}{iter_{max}} iter_i + PAR_{min} \cdot \tag{4}$$

In Eq. (4), PAR_{min} is the minimum of pitch adjusting rate, PAR_{max} is the maximum pitch adjusting rate, $iter_i$ is the number of generations, $iter_{max}$ is the maximum number of allowed iterations. The other operators of HS have not been employed. In summary, the realization of IHPSO can be described as follows:

Step 1. Initial population: Each particle is randomly generated. All particles in the solution space are randomly generated with an individual position and velocity.

Step 2. Fitness evaluation: the fitness function of all particles is calculated.

Step 3. Search direction evaluation: the gbest fitness value has not changed for a certain number of consecutive iterations. if *countf* < ε, goto Step 4, otherwise goto Step 5.

Step 4. Velocity and position update: The particles move through the search space at each iteration using Eq.(1) and Eq.(2).

Step 5. Use one of the above three rules to generate a new harmony vector from the HM(the same to the swarm matrix of PSO algorithm).

Step 6. Update pbest and gbest: At each iteration, each individual compares its current fitness value to its own *pbest* and global best solution *gbest*. The *pbest* and *gbest* values are updated if the new values are better than the old ones.

Step 7. Repeat Step 2 - Step 6 until the termination condition is met.

3   Experiments

3.1   Benchmark Functions

In our experimental studies, a set of four benchmark functions [10] was employed to evaluate the IHPSO algorithm in comparison with others:

Sphere

$$f_1(x) = \sum_{i=1}^{D} x_i^2 \tag{5}$$

Rosenbrock

$$f_2(x) = \sum_{i=1}^{D-1} (100(x_{i+1} - x_i^2)^2 + (x_i - 1)^2) \tag{6}$$

Rostrigrin

$$f_3(x) = \sum_{i=1}^{D} (x_i^2 - 10\cos(2\pi x_i) + 10) \tag{7}$$

Griewark

$$f_4(x) = \frac{1}{4000} \sum_{i=1}^{D} x_i^2 - \prod_{i=1}^{D} \cos\left(\frac{x_i}{\sqrt{i}}\right) + 1 \tag{8}$$

Table 1. Basic characters of the Benchmark functions

Function	Trait	Feasible solution space	Global Optimum
Sphere	Uni-modal	[-100,100]	0
Rosenbrock	Uni-modal	[-100,100]	0
Rostrigrin	Multi-modal	[-10,10]	0
Griewark	Multi-modal	[-600,600]	0

3.2   Parameter Settings

The population size was set at 40. The acceleration constants c1 =1.2, c2 =1 0. The inertia weight w is critical for the convergence behavior of PSO. A suitable value for the inertia weight w usually provides a balance between global and local exploration abilities and consequently results in a better optimum solution. In our programming, w is set in Eq. (3), *PAR* is set to Eq. (4) and PAR_{max}=0.5, PAR_{min}=0.1.PSO, HPSO and IHPSO are all set to terminate after 5000 fitness evaluations.

3.3   Experimental Results and Discussion

To evaluate the performance of the proposed IHPSO, the dimensions were set to 10, 20 and 30, respectively. And the maximum number of generations (Gen.) was set to 5000. Each algorithm was run 50 times to get the mean value. The experimental results of PSO, HPSO and IHPSO are given in table 2, table 3, table 4 and table 5, respectively.

Table 2.   Mean function value for Sphere function

Dim.	PSO	HPSO	IHPSO
10	34.3004	4.6676e-006	4.2268e-008
20	133.5557	1.0795e-005	1.6355e-007
30	228.4396	1.0172e-005	1.4700e-007

Table 3. Mean function value for Rosenbrock function

Dim.	PSO	HPSO	IHPSO
10	4.4450e+004	6.3301e-004	4.8353e-006
20	2.7137e+005	0.0015	4.8268e-006
30	5.2824e+005	0.0021	7.7450e-006

Table 4. Mean function value for Rostrigrin function

Dim.	PSO	HPSO	IHPSO
10	93.5620	0.0015	8.1972e-006
20	238.0263	0.0039	2.1221e-005
30	418.5260	0.0032	3.9827e-005

Table 5. Mean function value for Griewark function

Dim.	PSO	HPSO	IHPSO
10	89.6577	9.5975	1.8549e-005
20	252.0123	0.0012	3.1299e-005
30	425.7015	0.0024	3.6127e-005

It is seen that the proposed IHPSO can find the best solutions successfully for these four functions at any dimensionalities facing complicated optimization functions, and its precision of solutions is much higher than PSO and HPSO at the same time.

Tables 2–5 indicate that IHPSO outperformed PSO and HPSO on Benchmark functions Sphere, Rosenbrock, Rastrigrin and Griewark.

Fig. 1 plot the mean best fitness in the form of logarithm values over the number of generations for PSO, HPSO, and IHPSO with 40 particles on ten 30-dimensional functions. Each algorithm was run 50 times to get the mean value. And for the sake of showing clearly the maximum number of generations (Gen.) was set to 1000.

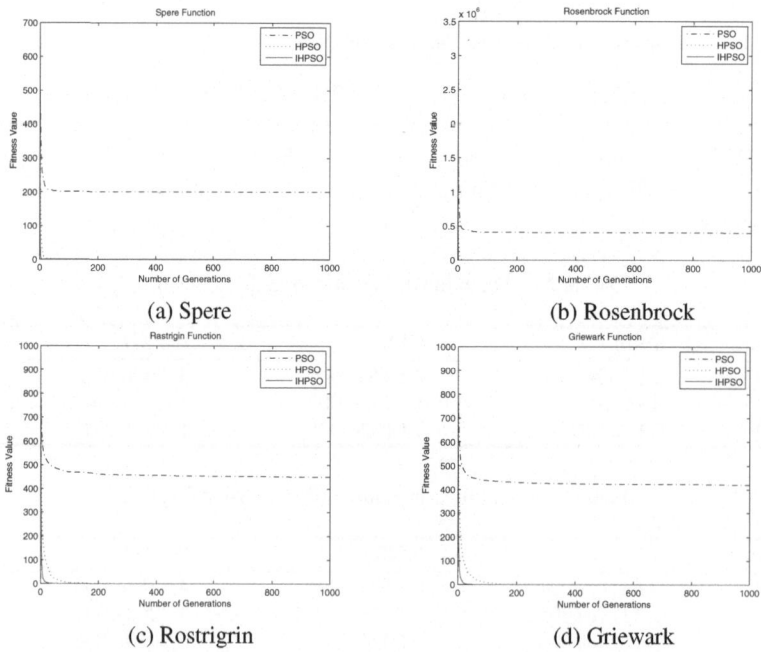

(a) Spere

(b) Rosenbrock

(c) Rostrigrin

(d) Griewark

Fig. 1. The four benchmark functions for PSO, HPSO and IHPSO

These figures clearly show that the search efficiency of IHPSO is superior to that of PSO, and HPSO on all four benchmark functions. At the same time, the best solution obtained by IHPSO is also superior to the best solution obtained by PSO or HPSO.

4   Conclusion

The proposed IHPSO algorithm takes particle swarm search direction estimation mechanism and harmony search approach to PSO algorithm. It initializes a new search with harmony pitch adjusting or random selection when particle swarm search direction is estimated incorrectly, which results in further opportunities of finding better solutions for the particle swarm by guiding the entire particle swarm to promising new regions of the search space and accelerating the search. That enhances the search capability of PSO considerably. Experiments with four complicated function optimization problems show that the proposed IHPSO algorithm is fairly effective and its search efficiency is superior to PSO or HPSO algorithm.

Acknowledgement. The research work described in this paper was fully supported by the grants from the National Natural Science Foundation of China (Project No. 90820010, 60911130513). Prof. Ping Guo is the author to whom the correspondence should be addressed, his e-mail address is pguo@ieee.org.

References

1. Kennedy, J., Eberhart, R.C.: Particle swarm optimization. In: Proceedings of IEEE International Conference on Neural Networks, Piscataway, NJ, pp. 1942–1948 (1995)
2. Elbeltagi, E., Hegazy, T., Grierson, D.: Comparison among five evolutionary-based optimization algorithms. Advanced Engineering Informatics 19, 43–53 (2005)
3. Liu, Y.Z., Qin, Z., Lu, S.J.: Center particle swarm optimization. Neuro Computing 70, 672–679 (2007)
4. Jiang, Y., Hu, T., Huang, C.C., Wu, X.: An improved particle swarm optimization algorithm. Applied Mathematics and Computation 193, 231–239 (2007)
5. Lee, K., Geem, Z.W.: A new meta-heuristic algorithm for continuous engineering optimization: Harmony search theory and practice. Computer Methods in Applied Mechanics and Engineering 194, 3902–3933 (2005)
6. Zhao, S.Z., Suganthan, P.N., Pan, Q.-K., Tasgetiren, M.F.: Dynamic Multi-Swarm Particle Swarm Optimizer with Harmony Search. Expert Systems with Applications 38, 3735–3742 (2011)
7. Omran, M.G.H., Mahdavi, M.: Global-best harmony search. Applied Mathematics and Computation 198(2), 643–656 (2008)
8. Geem, Z.W.: Particle-swarm harmony search for water network design. Engineering Optimization 41, 297–311 (2009)
9. Li, L., Liu, F.: Harmony Particle Swarm Algorithm for Structural Design Optimization. In: Geem, Z.W. (ed.) Harmony Search Algorithms for Structural Design Optimization. SCI, vol. 239, pp. 121–157. Springer, Heidelberg (2009)

10. Chuang, L.Y., Tsai, S.W., Yang, C.-H.: Chaotic catfish particle swarm optimization for solving global numerical optimization problems. Applied Mathematics and Computation 217, 6900–6916 (2011)
11. Yu, J., Guo, P.: Studies Of RBF Neural Network Model With Application Based On AQPSO Optimization Algorithm. Journal of Beijing Normal University(Natural Science) 43(6), 627–630 (2007) (in Chinese)
12. Yu, J.: Solving sequence alignment based on chaos particle swarm optimization algorithm. In: 2011 International Conference on Computer Science and Service System, Nanjing, China, pp. 3567–3569 (2011) (in Chinese)

An Improved Chaotic Ant Colony Algorithm[*]

Hongru Li, Shuzhuo Wang, and Mengfan Ji

College of Information Science and Engineering,
Northeastern University, Shenyang, 110819, P.R. China
lihongru@ise.neu.edu.cn

Abstract. Ant colony algorithm is a rising intelligent algorithm in recent years, which performs well in solving large-scale combinatorial optimization problem. On the basis of analyzing the advantages and disadvantages of ant colony algorithm, to solve the shortage of the basic ant colony algorithm, we present a chaotic ant swarm algorithm with strategy of return-trip optimization and elitist strategy. At first, make the basic ant colony algorithm into chaos initialization. When getting the mathematical solution, put into chaos interference factor to prevent from getting into the local minimum. Furthermore bring two improvement projects: strategy of return-trip optimization and elitist strategy into the ant colony algorithm to improve the quality of the solution. The simulation results indicate that the improved chaotic ant colony algorithm is a good solution to the shortages of the basic ant colony algorithm.

Keywords: Ant Colony Algorithm, Chaotic Ant Swarm, Strategy of Return-trip Optimization, Elitist Strategy.

1   Introduction

In the last few decades, nature has always been a rich source of human creativity, bio-simulation has received increasing attention and wide applications in a variety of fields. Nature is considered as a fertile source of concepts, principles, mechanism to solve complex computational problems.

Ant colony optimization (ACO) is a nature-inspired optimization algorithm motivated by the natural collective of real-world ant colonies [1]. Ants have no sense of sight, but they can deposit pheromone on the ground in order to mark their path that should be followed by other ants of their colonies. When they pass a new corner of process, will randomly choose a path forward, and then share their experience with the entire colony by updating a data structure. The data structure is called the pheromone. Ants leave the pheromone on the edge of the path. When following ants meet at this crossing again, it is more likely for them to choose the route with more pheromone. Then ants leave the pheromone again, it leads to a positive feedback system. The shorter routes obtain more and more pheromone, the pheromone of other

---

[*] This work is supported by national natural science foundation of P.R. China Grant # 61004083.

J. Wang, G.G. Yen, and M.M. Polycarpou (Eds.): ISNN 2012, Part I, LNCS 7367, pp. 633–640, 2012.

routes decrease as times go on, it eventually make ants find the most optimal path. This computational model was introduced by M. Dorigo and his colleague[2,3,4,5].

ACO is usually used to solve the traveling salesman problems (TSP), but there are many disadvantages such as the slow convergence rate, falling into local optimum. In such a context, chaotic ant swarm (CAS) is proposed, which is a very promising optimization tool, it describes the adaptation of the chaotic behavior of individual ant and the intelligent organization actions of ant colony to the solution of optimization problems. Based on chaos theory, chaotic ant swarm was developing in 2006[7].

This paper is organized as follows, we describe the algorithm of ACO in Section 1, the mathematics model of ACO is constructed in Section 2. In Section 3, we introduce chaotic ant swarm (CAS) [8,9], based on this, propose the further variants and improvements. The improved chaotic ant swarm (ICAS) contains two strategies (elitist strategy and strategy of return-trip optimization). In Section 4, the choice of the parameter values of our algorithms used in the test runs and the test instances. In Section 5, the conclusion is given.

2   Mathematics Model of ACO

It is important to calculate the pheromone for constructing the model. The proposed approach [5] aims to utilize a number of ants to search for constructing a pheromone matrix. Furthermore, the movements of the ants are steered by the pheromone. That is, the ants prefer to move towards positions with larger pheromone. The proposed approach starts from the initialization process and runs for iterations to construct the pheromone matrix by iteratively performing both the construction process, which constructs the pheromone matrix, and the update process, which updates the pheromone matrix. Each of the above process is presented in detail as follows.

We assume that $b_i(t)$ show the number of ants of the parameter i, $T_i(t)$ indicate the pheromone of the route (i,j), n is described as Sample size, m show the amount of ants, we can get $m = \sum_{i=1}^{n} b_i(t); \Gamma = \{\tau_{ij}(t) \mid c_i, c_j \subset C\}$ is the set of remained pheromone.

At initial time, the pheromone on each route is equal, we can assume that $\tau_{ij}(0) = const$,ants determine the direction based on the pheromone in the course of searching,, we define $tabu_k (k = 1, 2 ... m)$ to record the route of current parameter k ,the set is related to the $tabu_k$,we can calculate the probability distribution over $allowed_k$, the update is performed after the movement of each ant within each construction-step. Each component of the pheromone matrix is updated according to equation (1).

$$p^k_{ij} \begin{cases} \dfrac{[\tau_{ij}(t)]^\alpha [\eta_{ij}(t)]^\beta}{\displaystyle\sum_{s\subset allowed_k} [\tau_{is}(t)]^\alpha [\eta_{is}(t)]^\beta}, & \text{if } \quad j\in allowed_k \\ \\ 0, & others \end{cases} \tag{1}$$

The heuristic values $\eta_{ij}(t)$ can be computed as follows:

$$\eta_{ij}(t) = \frac{1}{d_{ij}} \tag{2}$$

The heuristic prefers jobs with a small due date from all jobs that would finish before their due date when scheduled next. Furthermore, of all those jobs that will be finished after their due date the jobs with short processing times are preferred. After an ant has selected the next job j, a local pheromone update is performed at element (i, j) of the pheromone matrix according to equation (3).

$$\tau_{ij}(t+n) = (1-\rho)*\tau_{ij}(t) + \Delta\tau_{ij}(t)$$
$$\Delta\tau_{ij}(t) = \sum_{k=1}^{m} \Delta\tau_{ij}^{k}(t) \tag{3}$$

Where $\Delta\tau_{ij}(t)$ is the amount of pheromone increment[5].

The algorithm stops when some stopping criterion is met a certain number of generations has been done or the optimal solution has not changed for several generations.

3   The Improved Chaotic Ant Swarm Algorithm

Each ant performs a chaotic exploration of its hunting positions and interacts with its neighbors. These ants search chaotically until they have been organized via pheromone trails (or visual landmarks), and then move to the position, which is the most successful one among the previously met hunting positions. These principles were used to implement heuristic algorithms for the search of a global optimum or near-optimum of a function in a search space.

3.1   Overview of Chaotic Ant Swarm

Chaotic ant swarm algorithm is a global optimization method based on swarm intelligence [8], as chaotic mapping can be described as nonlinear difference equation without any random factor, but the track may be completely random, at the same time, it has the ergodic property in the state space, Logistic mapping is the most popular chaotic mapping, it can be described as follows:

$$x_{n+1} = \mu x_n (1-x_n), 0 < \mu \le 4, 0 < x < 1 \tag{4}$$

When the parameters of initialization are based on ACO, the pheromone of each route is equal, ants choose the route with the same possibility, in this way, it is hard to search a better route from the complete ones in a short time, so it has a poor speed of converging, we assume that the pheromone is given a lot of illuminating pieces of information when initialized, it will speed up convergence rate.

The improved method is to use chaotic mapping[9], the initialization parameters are based on chaos. Each chaotic parameter is corresponding to one route, it will produce a lot of route. We choose some better routes with the inverse pheromone. Thus, the pheromone of each route is not equal in order to speed up the convergence.

In the second place, the pheromones are added to the chaotic disturbance, ACO makes use of the positive feedback principle[5], it speeds up the evolution process to a certain degree. But there are some defects, such as stagnant phenomenon, into the local optimal solution.   Adding the chaotic disturbance can improve stagnant phenomenon, the equation of updating pheromone is described as follows[10]:

$$z_{i+1} = \mu z_i (1 - z_i), i = 0, 1, 2 \dots , \mu \in (\ 2, 4] \tag{5}$$

$$z_i^` = 2 * z_i - 1 \tag{6}$$

$$\tau_{ij}^` = \rho * \tau_{ij} + \Delta \tau_{ij} + z_{i*n+j}^` \tag{7}$$

CAS improve the issue of stagnant phenomenon[11], into the local optimal solution, and accelerate the process of search, but the solution sink into the local, ants only consider the distance between the current and the candidate, not the distance between the current and the start. Based on this, we propose two strategies (strategy of return-trip optimization and elitist strategy).

3.2   Strategy of Return-Trip Optimization

The probability distribution in ant colony algorithm is only related to the pheromone and the distance between the current and the candidate. On the contrary, the distance between the current and the start is not under consideration, it leads to the span is so large, which makes the sum increase. Considering the return-trip route project is showed as figure 1. The second route will be chosen based on the strategy.

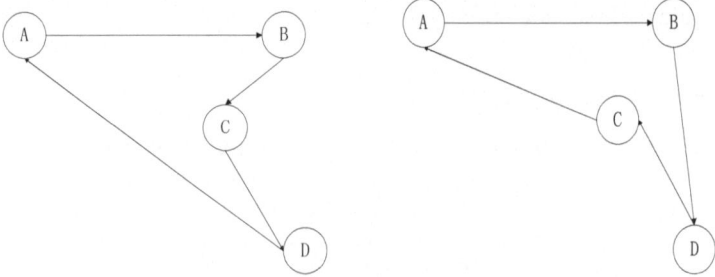

Fig. 1. The return-trip route project

3.3   Elitist Strategy

This paper introduces a parameter ($\mu_{ij} = d_{i0} + d_{0j} - d_{ij}$), it takes the distance between the current and the candidate into account. Also, the distance between the current and the start is considered, in this way, it improves the quality of the route.

$$P_{ij}^k(t) = \frac{[\tau_{ij}(t)]^\alpha [\eta_{ij}]^\beta [\mu_{ij}]^\gamma}{\sum_{s \in allowed} [\tau_{is}(t)]^\alpha [\eta_{is}]^\beta [\mu_{is}]^\gamma} \tag{8}$$

When ants finish the searching, the pheromone will get the related increment, even though in worst case. The pheromone disturb the later ants to search, which lead to inactive searching. Thus, the better routes should get the pheromone, that is, when the length of the path is less than a given value, it can obtain the increment, on the contrary, it get nothing. This method can accelerate the convergence speed of the algorithm.

The flow chat of ICAS with elitist strategy and strategy of return-trip optimization is present as figure 2.

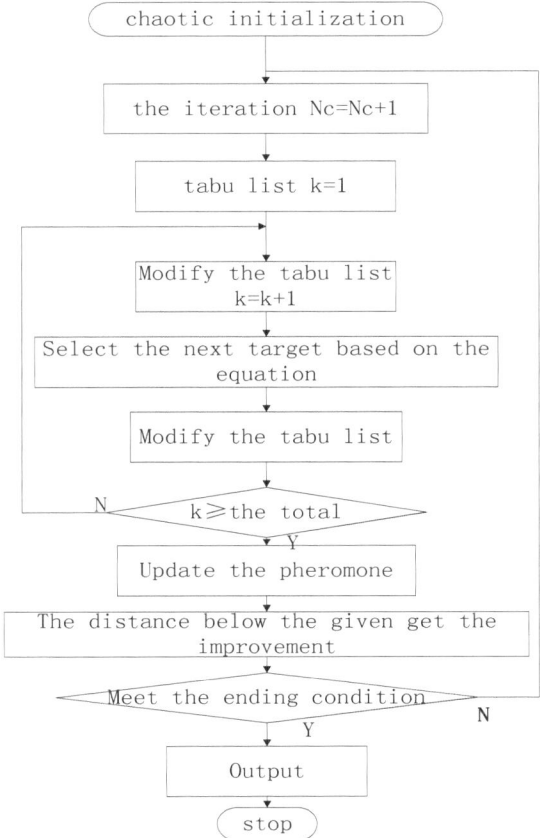

Fig. 2. The flow chat of ICAS

4   Simulation Experiments

The traveling salesman problem (TSP) is one of the typical combinatorial optimization problems. To better illustrate the effectiveness, we have chosen the most common test instances, according to the position of the provincial capital and municipality directly under the Central Government in China, we build the 31-city TSP, as the value of ants is close to or equal to the number of the city, the algorithm can get optimal solution in a minimum of iterations.

At the initialization step, we set the values of chaotic ant swarm parameter $N_{c_{max}} = 200$, the attenuation coefficient is rho=0.5;0<rho<1, the pheromone that ants release is Q=200. Because of limitation of space, we only give the simulation result of the example. A number of experimental results are present. Figure,3,5,7 show the best route in ACO, CAS and ICAS. Figure 4,6,8 indicate the shortest length of the tour(Solid line) and the average length of the tour(Dashed line) in ACO, CAS and ICAS.

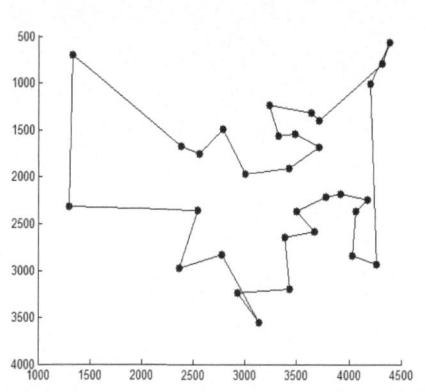

Fig. 3. The best route in ACO

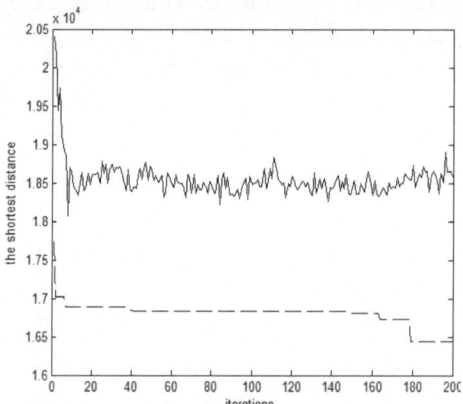

Fig. 4. Tour length in ACO

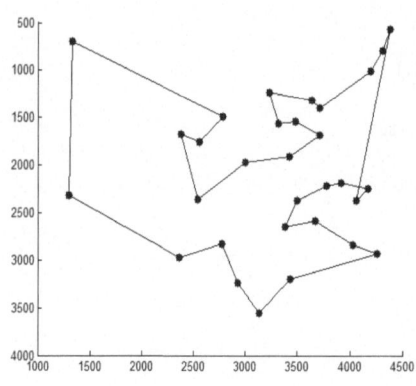

Fig. 5. The best route in CAS

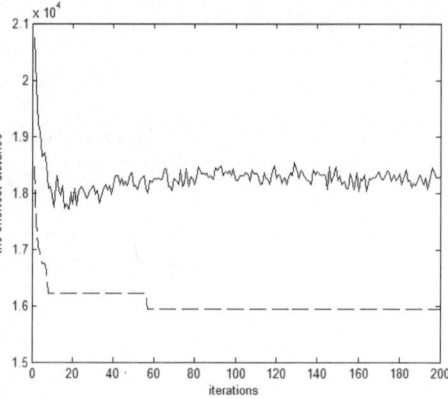

Fig. 6. Tour length in CAS

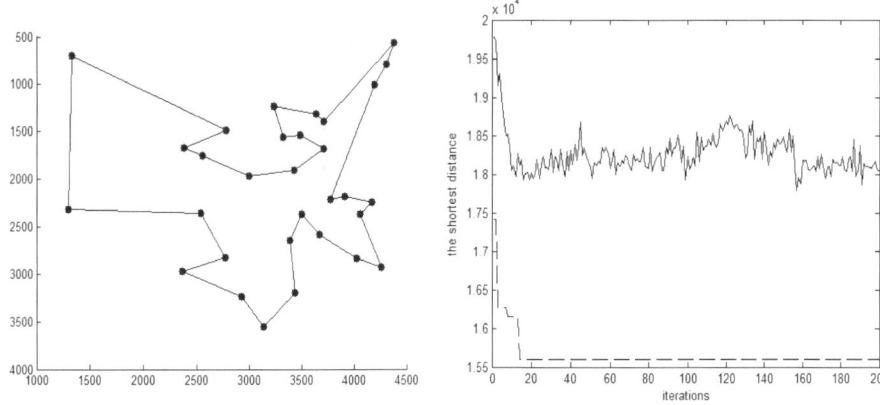

Fig. 7. The best route in ICAS   **Fig. 8.** Tour length in ICAS

In order to bring out the efficiency of ICAS algorithm, we use the same TSP problem to simulate the instance in computer, run the program 50 times and list the results in average of each method in Table 1. In iteration time, ICAS is close to CAS, and much less than ACO. In the distance of route, ICAS is the least. The simulation results show that the ICAS is much more effective than other algorithms, and strategy of return-trip optimization and elitist strategy have a greatly improve the performance in finding good solutions.

Table 1. Comparisons of ICAS with ACO and CAS

Method	ACO	CAS	ICAS
Iteration time(s)	178.3	50.3	50.1
Distance of Route	1.62e+04	1.59e+04	1.56e+04

5   Conclusion

To solve the shortages of the basic ant colony algorithm, we bring the knowledge of chaos dynamics into the basic ant colony algorithm, and apply strategy of return-trip optimization and elitist strategy to prevent from falling into the local minimum. Simulations used for the 31-city TSP show that the improved chaotic ant swarm can improve searching accuracy, increase convergence speed, and overcome the disadvantages of stagnant phenomenon and getting into the local optimal solution.

References

1. Dorigo, M., Gambardella, L.M.: Ant colony system: A cooperative learning approach to the traveling salesman problem. IEEE Trans. on Evolutionary Computation 1, 53–66 (1997)

2. Dorigo, M., Di Caro, G.: Ant colony optimization: a new meta-heuristic. In: Congress on Evolutionary Computation, vol. 2, pp. 1470–1477 (1999)
3. Dorigo, M., Stützle, T.: Ant Colony Optimization. MIT Press, Boston (2004)
4. Dorigo, M., Maniezzo, V., Colorni, A.: Positive feedback as a search strategy. Technical Report 91-016, Dipartimento di Elettronica, Politecnico di Milano, Milan, Italy (1991)
5. Dorigo, M., Gambardella, L.M., Middendorf, M., Stutzle, T.: Special Issue on Ant Colony Optimization. IEEE Transactions on Evolutionary Computation 6, 317–320 (2002)
6. Aydın, D.: An Efficient Ant-Based Edge Detector. In: Nguyen, N.T., Kowalczyk, R. (eds.) Transactions on Computational Collective Intelligence I. LNCS, vol. 6220, pp. 39–55. Springer, Heidelberg (2010)
7. Dorigo, M., Birattari, M., Stutzle, T.: Ant colony optimization. IEEE Computational Intelligence Magazine 1, 28–39 (2006)
8. Cai, J., Ma, X., Li, L., Yang, Y., Peng, H., Wang, X.: Chaotic ant swarm optimization to economic dispatch. Electr. Power Syst. Res. 77, 1373–1380 (2007)
9. Chen, L., Aihara, K.: Chaotic simulated annealing by a neural network model with transient chaos. Neural Netw. 8, 915–930 (1995)
10. Li, Y., Wen, Q., Li, L., Peng, H.: Hybrid chaotic ant swarm optimization. Chaos Solitons Fractals 42, 880–889 (2009)
11. Wang, K., Huang, L., Zhou, C., Pang, W.: Particle swarm optimization for traveling salesman problem. In: Proceedings of the Second International Conference on Machine Learning and Cybernetics, Xi'an, China, vol. 3, pp. 1583–1585. IEEE Press, New York (2003)

A Game Based Approach for Sharing the Data Center Network

Ying Yuan[1], Cui-rong Wang[2], and Cong Wang[2]

[1] School of Information Science and Engineering,
Northeastern University, Shenyang, 11004, China
yuanying1121@163.com
[2] Department of Information, Northeastern University at Qinhuangdao, 066004, China
wangcr@mail.neuq.edu.cn, Congw1981@gmail.com

Abstract. Current virtual datacenters in cloud computing have flexible mechanisms to partition compute resources but provide little control over how tenants share the network. This paper proposes a game based approach for sharing the network bandwidth between tenants. Leveraging network virtualization technology, we present a game model for virtual bandwidth allocation. In the game, the data center owner as a leader announces a price for bandwidth allocation that attempts to drive the tenant's virtual networks to the social optimal solution, each virtual network as a follower chooses a willingness-to-pay to maximize its own profit. Experimental results show that the bandwidth allocation between tenants is efficient and fair.

Keywords: Virtual data center, network slicing, multi tenant, virtual bandwidth allocation.

1 Introduction

Data centers which are built using virtualization technology with virtual machines as the basic processing elements are called virtual data centers (VDCs) [1]. Comparing with the traditional data centers, VDCs could provide some significant merits such as server consolidation, high availability and live migration, and provide flexible resource management mechanisms. Therefore, VDCs are widely used as the infrastructure of existing Cloud computing systems [2, 3].

To achieve cost efficiencies and on-demand scaling, VDCs are highly multiplexed shared environments, with VMs and tasks from multiple tenants coexisting in the same cluster. While VDCs provide many mechanisms to schedule local compute, memory, and disk resources [4], existing mechanisms for apportioning network resources fall short. End host mechanisms such as TCP congestion control are widely deployed to determine network sharing today via a notion of flow-based fairness. However, TCP does little to isolate tenants from one another: poorly-designed or malicious applications can consume network capacity, to the detriment of other applications which generate non TCP friendly flows. Thus, while resource allocation

J. Wang, G.G. Yen, and M.M. Polycarpou (Eds.): ISNN 2012, Part I, LNCS 7367, pp. 641–649, 2012.

using TCP is scalable and achieves high network utilization, it does not provide robust performance isolation.

Network virtualization can extenuate the ossifying forces of the current Ethernet and stimulate innovation by enabling diverse virtual networks belong to different tenants to cohabit on a shared physical link. In the main thought of network virtualization, virtual machines of same applications in data center are partitioned into same virtual networks by network slicing, but the virtual bandwidth allocation mechanism is not well considered.

This paper makes the case for virtual bandwidth allocation between virtual links in multi tenant VDCs to proactively prevent network congestion and provide more agility. Based on the idea of the Stackelberg [5] solution from non-cooperative game theory, this paper presents a hierarchical game theoretic model for dynamic bandwidth allocation between virtual networks to support bandwidth sharing between multi tenants in VDCs.

The rest of the paper is organized as follows. Network virtualization technique is briefly introduced in Section 2. In section 3, we first give a basic mode for bandwidth sharing between virtual networks of multi tenants, and then solve the overall problem in a distribute manner. Section 4 presents experimental evidence via a simulation implementation. Section 5 gives the conclusion.

2   Network Virtualization in VDC

Recently, the fair sharing of network bandwidth in VDC is being studied by datacenter researchers and some proposals are presented. Seawall [6] uses a hypervisor-based framework for bandwidth fair sharing among VM-pairs. It focuses on fair sharing and how resource allocation and bandwidth guarantee can be provided in the framework. For multiple tenants in the cloud, SecondNet [1] introduces a centralized VDC allocation algorithm for bandwidth guaranteed. It achieves scalability by distributing all the virtual-to-physical mapping, routing, and bandwidth reservation state in server hypervisors. The goal of our proposal is different from them. Leveraging network virtualization technique, physical network links in VDC can also be multi tenants, thus we can propose proper virtual bandwidth allocation algorithm on the virtualization architecture.

Network virtualization is a promising way to support diverse applications over a shared substrate by running multiple virtual networks, which customized for different performance objectives. Today, network virtualization is moving from fantasy to reality, as many major router vendors start to support both switch virtualization and switch programmability [7]. Fig. 1 depicts the substrate node architecture that is composed of three modules: substrate resources, virtual management, and virtual switch.

The substrate resources module comprises the physical resources of the real switch, such as network interfaces, RAM, IO (buffer), etc. The virtual management module is a middleware as an abstract of the substrate resource for the up layer. It contains the components of the adapted-control unit to dynamically build or modify parameters of virtual networks and a monitoring unit to monitor the running status of each virtual network.

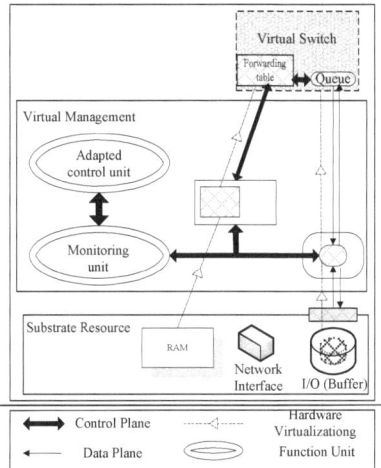

Fig. 1. Substrate switch architecture for virtualization

Based such virtual switch, VDC owner can slice the substrate network to many virtual networks and lease them to any service provider. Service provider can run their own service applications in the rental virtual network. VDC owner as substrate provider just need to control and monitoring the virtual networks running in data centers. With a commercial multi-tenancy strategy and a dynamic bandwidth allocation algorithm between virtual networks, which we will present in Section 3, the VDC owner can achieve best revenue and the service provider can also gain sufficient QoS guarantee in their virtual networks.

3   Virtual Bandwidth Sharing Algorithm

This section presents a hierarchical game theoretic model for dynamic bandwidth allocation between virtual networks in VDC. We first give a basic mode for bandwidth allocation between virtual networks of multi tenants, and proof that the global problem can be divided into sub-problems on rack switch's port, then we give the bandwidth sharing algorithm which based Stackelberg solution from non-cooperative game theory.

3.1   Basic Model

The virtual bandwidth sharing problem in this subsection is considered from the overall perspective of the system which contains virtual networks and substrate hardware resource in VDC under multi tenants market mechanism. Consider a substrate network with a set L of links, and let C_j be the capacity of substrate link $j \in J$. The network is shared by a set N of virtual networks and indexed by i. Define a vector b_{il} which denotes the allocated bandwidth of virtual network i in link *j*. Let $U_i(b_{il})$ be the utility of virtual network *i* as a function of his bandwidth b_{il}. Note that the utility $U_i(b_{il})$ should be an increasing, nonnegative, strictly concave and twice continuously differentiable function of b_{il} over the range $b_{il} \geq 0$. Assume further that utilities are additive. The bandwidth control problem can be formulated as the following optimal problem *P1*:

$$\text{MAX} \sum_{i=1}^{N} \sum_{l=1}^{L_i} U_i(b_{il})$$

$$s.t. \quad \forall i, \forall l, \quad b_{il} \geq 0,$$

$$\forall l \in L, \quad \sum_{i}^{N} b_{il} \leq C_l$$

For each virtual network, its bandwidth must be greater than or equal to 0, the total bandwidth of all virtual networks in physical link *l* does not exceed the maximum bandwidth C_l allowed by the hardware. Since the utility functions are strictly concave, and hence continuous, and the feasible solution set is compact then the above optimal problem has a unique optimal solution.

P1 is an overall problem with multiple constraints. Considering the fact that virtual networks on data centers are of non-cooperative nature in terms of their demand for networks resources, leveraging non-cooperative game theory, let the network announce a rental price per unit of bandwidth, then let all virtual networks play a non-cooperative game, the resulting bandwidth allocation at the Nash equilibrium point of the game solves the above optimal problem *P1*.

3.2   Distributed Implementation

The above problem *P1* for virtual bandwidth allocation in VDC is still a global issue. Obviously, it's impossible to manage vast amounts of virtual nodes in large-scale network as well as in VDC.

P1 can be split into several distributed problem. Recall the problem in the previous section, each b_{il} in vector $b_{il} = (b_{il}, l \in L)$ denotes the allocated bandwidth for virtual network *i* in link *l*. For any set of virtual network links L_i we have $L_i \subseteq L$. Then the overall optimal problem *P1* can be rewritten as:

$$\text{MAX} \sum_{i=1}^{N} \sum_{l=1}^{L_i} U_i(b_{il}) = \sum_{l=1}^{L_i} \sum_{i=1}^{N} U_i(b_{il})$$

$$= \sum_{i=1}^{N} U_i(b_{i1}) + \sum_{i=1}^{N} U_i(b_{i2}) + \dots\dots + \sum_{i=1}^{N} U_i(b_{iL}) \tag{1}$$

From equation (1) we can see the *P1* can be transformed into *L* sub optimization problems on each network port of rack switches. When the bandwidth allocation for every virtual network on each port of the rack switches in the physical network is optimal, the overall optimization problem *P1* can be solved simultaneously. This distributed solution in large-scale data center network was feasible, and can be easily achieved.

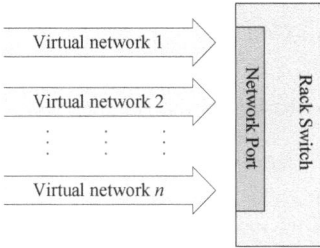

Fig. 2. Sharing the virtual bandwidth at network port of the rack switch

Then we can get the sub optimization problems on each network port of rack switches (as shown in Fig. 2):

$$\max \sum_{i=1}^{n} U_i(b_i)$$
$$s.t. \qquad \forall i,\ b_i \geq 0, \tag{2}$$
$$\sum_{i}^{n} b_{il} \leq C_l$$

Where n is the number of virtual networks, b_i denotes the allocated bandwidth for virtual network i at link l. $U_i(b_{il})$ is the utility function discussed in the previous section. Then we can build a Stackelberg game model for bandwidth allocation according to sub optimization problem (2). Giving the objective function of each virtual link:

$$F_i(x_i; p) = \omega_i \log(1+b_i) - p \bullet b_i \tag{3}$$

Where $\omega_i > 0$ is weight of virtual link i which determined by the practical market operation mechanism and set by the data center owner according to the share expectations of occupied bandwidth announced by all followers (virtual links on physical link l). p is a rental price per unit of bandwidth announced by the leader (data center hardware owner). $\omega_i \log(1+b_i)$ is the utility function of virtual link i. From equation (4) we have:

$$\max_{0 < x_i \leq k \bullet c - x_{-i}^*} F_i(x_i, x_{-i}; p) = \omega_i \log(1+b_i) - p \bullet b_i \tag{4}$$

Where $x_{-i} = \sum_j x_j - x_i$, $k \bullet c = C_a$ is the total quantity of bandwidth which the substrate owner determined to allocation to the tenants in link l, c is the norm unit of bandwidth in allocation, and k is a constant representing the partition granularity of bandwidth. Giving the price p, equation (4) define a non-cooperative game, at the Nash equilibrium point of the game the bandwidth allocation is optimal.

For leaders, the goal is to calculate an appropriate price p to drive followers' game to achieve a Nash equilibrium point efficiently, and make best profit for itself simultaneously. The objective function of leader is defined as follows:

$$\max_{p>0} L(p;\overline{b}^*), \quad L(p;\overline{b}) = p\cdot\overline{b} - \overline{b}\cdot e \tag{5}$$

Where $\overline{b} = \sum_j b_j$, $p\cdot\overline{b}$ is profit of the leader, $\overline{b}\cdot e$ is the cost of the leader for allocated bandwidth $\overline{b}$, e is a constant an always greater than zero. Till now, we can define a Stackelberg game model according equation (4) and (5), which has one leader and n followers. And we have the following theorem:

Theorem 1: Giving the above Stackelberg model, there exists a unique price p^* maximizes leader's profit, and for this p^* there exists a virtual bandwidth allocation strategy $b^* = (b_1^*, b_2^*, ..., b_n^*)$ which can drive the follower to archive Nash equilibrium, hence the follow also gain the best profit at the same time.

Proof

First, Adding a additional quantity to F_i will not affect the Nash equilibrium of the model, and hence the original game is equivalent to one where all users have the identical objective function:

$$F(x_1, x_2, ...x_n; p) = \sum_j \omega_i \log(1+b_i) - p\overline{b} \tag{6}$$

Thus, all followers will have same objective function F, for all $x_i, i \in N$, such that $\overline{x} < C$,

$$F_{x_i x_i} = -\frac{\omega_i}{(1+b_i)^2} < 0 \tag{7}$$

It is now easy to see that $b_i > 0$, and $\omega_i > 0$, hence F is strictly concave in the rage $b_i > 0$. So there exists a unique solution maximize the function F when $F' = 0$, thus the game has a unique Nash equilibrium point. At the equilibrium point the profit of each virtual network is maximized.

$$F_{x_i} = \frac{\omega_i}{1+b_i} - p = 0 \tag{8}$$

Using this in the first-order conditions $F_{x_i} = 0$, for any $i, j \in [1, n]$ we can obtain:

$$y_i = \frac{\omega_i}{\omega_j} y_j, \quad \forall i, j \in n \tag{9}$$

Where $y_i = 1 + x_i$, let $\overline{y} = \sum_j y_j$ and $\overline{\omega} = \sum_j \omega_j$, can y_i be expressed as:

$$y_i = \frac{\omega_i}{\overline{\omega}} \overline{y}, \quad \forall i \in n \tag{10}$$

Substitute equation (10) into equation (7):

$$g(\overline{y}) = \frac{\overline{\omega}}{\overline{y}} - p = 0 \tag{11}$$

Then consider objective function $L(p;\overline{b})$ of the leader. When the followers' game reaches Nash equilibrium, from equal (11) we can obtain: $p = \overline{\omega}/\overline{y}$, for $\overline{x} = \overline{y} - n$, we can rewrite L to:

$$L(\overline{y}) = (\frac{\overline{\omega}}{\overline{y}} - e)(\overline{y} - n) = \overline{\omega} - n\frac{\overline{\omega}}{\overline{y}} - e\overline{y} + ne \tag{12}$$

The second derivative of L is: $L^{''}(\overline{y}) = -\frac{2n\overline{y}\overline{\omega}}{(\overline{y})^4}$

For $\overline{\omega} > 0$, so in the interval $\overline{y} > 0$, L is strictly concave. Function L reach maximum value at $L' = 0$. i.e.

$L^{'}(\overline{y}) = \frac{n\overline{\omega}}{(\overline{y})^2} - e = 0$, then:

$$\overline{y}^* = (\frac{n\overline{\omega}}{e})^{\frac{1}{2}} \tag{13}$$

Introducing equation (16) into (14), we can calculate the price when the system achieves the Stackelberg equilibrium point.

$$p^* = (\frac{\overline{\omega}e}{n})^{\frac{1}{2}} \tag{14}$$

From the above derivation we can see that when leaders given a certain $\omega_i (i \in n)$ weight for each virtual link, there exists a unique p^* maximum the leader's profit; at the same time, n followers' game can reach the Nash equilibrium.

4   Performance Evaluation

As well-known in network congestion control problem, without using any virtual bandwidth control mechanism, when the two virtual machines do their best to send the traffic, so as to occupy the full bandwidth of the physical link. UDP traffic which is non TCP friendly is dominant, and TCP traffic just rarely able to successfully send few packets. The main cause of this situation is because due to TCP congestion control mechanisms, when network congestion occurs the sliding window will limit the sending rate to a small value.

In our sharing model, giving a priority for each tenant's virtual networks, when the follower reach Nash equilibrium of the game, each tenant has no reason to change its bandwidth demands, because it would make their earnings reduced. Therefore, the proposed model in this paper achieves a fair and stable virtual bandwidth allocation between virtual networks in data center. For friendly data traffic in virtual bandwidth competition, the proposed model can also solve apparently.

In practical implementation, the partition granularity of bandwidth will be crucial for fair sharing of network resource in VDCs. So we calculated the influence of the partition granularity k on the virtual bandwidth that each virtual network gained between two virtual networks i.e. $n=2$. The weight ratio which indicates the priority of each network is $n_1:n_2=1:2$.

The numeric result is shown in Fig.3, from which we can see that the bandwidth share ratio of the two virtual network infinitely close to their weight ratio when $k>50$. When $k<10$ the virtual network which has better priority will take up more bandwidth.

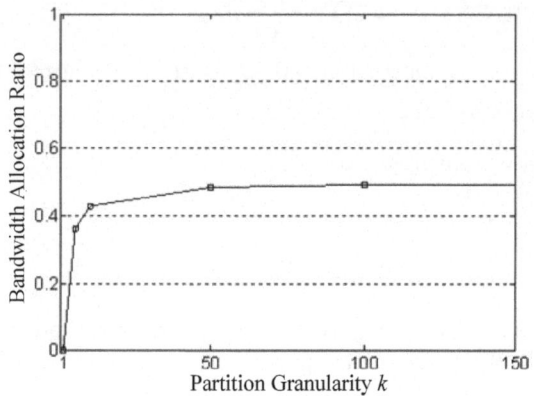

Fig. 3. Influence of the partition granularity k on the bandwidth allocation ratio between tow virtual networks

5   Conclusion

This paper introduced a game based virtual bandwidth allocation algorithm in VDC to provide multi tenants mechanism for network resource. We present an overall optimal problem and divide it into sub-problems which can be solved at network port of the rack switch. We believe that network virtualization and proper network resource sharing mechanism are more suitable for VDCs to support multi-tenancy mechanism in cloud computing environment.

References

1. Chuanxiong, G., Guohan, L., Helen, J.W., et al.: SecondNet: A Data Center Network Virtualization Architecture with Bandwidth Guarantees. In: ACM CoNEXT 2010, pp. 15:1–15:12. ACM, Philadelphia (2010)
2. VMware, VMware vCloud,
   http://www.vmware.com/technology/cloud-computing.html
3. Amazon, Amazon Elastic Compute Cloud (Amazon EC2),
   http://aws.amazon.com/ec2/

4. Ludmila, C., Diwaker, G., Amin, V.: Comparison of the three CPU schedulers in Xen. In: ACM SIGMETRICS 2007, vol. 35, pp. 42–51. ACM, New York (2007)
5. Meisam, R., Zhi-Quan, L., Paul, T., Jong-Shi, P.: A stackelberg game approach to distributed spectrum management. Mathematical Programming 129, 197–224 (2011)
6. Alan, S., Srikanth, K., Albert, G., Changhoon, K.: Seawall: Performance Isolation for Cloud Datacenter Networks. In: 2nd USENIX HotCloud 2010, pp. 1–1 (2010)
7. Cisco opening up IOS, http://www.networkworld.com/news/2007/121207-cisco-ios.html

Optimal Task and Energy Scheduling in Dynamic Residential Scenarios

Francesco De Angelis[1], Matteo Boaro[1], Danilo Fuselli[1],
Stefano Squartini[1], Francesco Piazza[1], Qinglai Wei[2], and Ding Wang[2]

[1] Dipartimento di Ingegneria dell'Informazione,
Universitá Politecnica delle Marche, Ancona, Italy
[2] State Key Laboratory of Management and Control for Complex Systems,
Institute of Automation, Chinese Academy of Sciences, Beijing, China

Abstract. Smart homes of the future will include automation systems that will provide lower energy consumption costs and comfortable environments to end users. In this work we propose an algorithm, based on the "Mixed-Integer Linear Programming" paradigm, able to find the optimal task and energy scheduling in realistic residential scenarios, in order to reduce costs and satisfy the user requirements at the same time. Both the static and the dynamic case studies have been addressed on purpose and results obtained from computer simulations seem to confirm the effectiveness of the idea.

1 Introduction

The smart grid concept covers a wide spectrum of the electrical power engineering, from generation to customer. Computation Intelligence techniques are surely useful on purpose [1,2]. In this paper an optimal task and energy scheduling for smart homes is presented using the "Mixed-Integer Linear Programming" (MILP) approach. In order to minimize the energy consumption, and related costs, tasks are scheduled on the basis of different electricity prices, task temporal constraints and forecasted renewable energy. Several methods have been developed to accomplished efficient energy or task scheduling: deterministic methods [3], Particle Swarm Optimization [4,5], Genetic Algorithms [6], and also Artificial Neural Networks [7], but they all consider task and energy scheduling separately.

The MILP technique can be used only for energy scheduling [8], but also to jointly achieve [9] optimal task and energy scheduling. In this work, inspired from [9], new features are proposed in order to improve performances of the optimization procedure: tasks can be or not interruptible, and can also be considered as a sequence of sub-tasks with different parameters, so a most detailed scenario can be simulated with low computational costs. The major difference from [9] is that also a dynamic procedure has been realized with success to face real-case optimization problems. The supposed residential scenario is composed by a storage system and renewable energy resources, so the system has to take decisions in order to find the best solution in terms of costs and renewable available energy, knowing task parameters and respecting the temporal constraints decided by the customer.

J. Wang, G.G. Yen, and M.M. Polycarpou (Eds.): ISNN 2012, Part I, LNCS 7367, pp. 650–658, 2012.

The analytical issues of the implemented algorithm are discussed in Section 2, whereas the related operational aspects, for the static and dynamic case studies, are pointed out in Section 3. Section 4 deals with the conducted computer simulations whereas Section 5 draws the work conclusions.

2   The Proposed Algorithm: Analytical Issues

The implemented algorithm is based on the "Mixed-Integer Linear Programming" (MILP) paradigm, which represents an evolution of the standard "linear programming" (LP) one. Its objective consists in maximizing or minimizing a given function, considering some constraints according to:

$$\max\ f(x) = c^T x \quad \text{or} \quad \min\ f(x) = c^T x$$
$$\text{subject to} \quad Ax \le b \quad \text{or} \quad A \ge b$$

where $x \ge 0$, $x \in R^{n \times 1}$, $A \in R^{m \times n}$, $b \in R^{m \times 1}$

Differently from LP, MILP considers both real and integer variables.

Cost Function

This is the cost function to be minimized:

$$Q = \sum_{t=1}^{num\ slot} \left\{ \sum_{i=1}^{num\ task} \left[(w_{i,t} P_i - S_{i,t}) C_t \right] + \right.$$

$$+ \sum_{m=1}^{num\ store-items} \left[(Pc_{m,t}\eta_m - Sst_{m,t})C_t - \frac{Pd_{m,t}}{\eta_m}(C_t - Cmb) \right] - Sex_t Cs_t \left. \right\} \quad (1)$$

where *num slot* is the temporal slots number; *num task* is the tasks number; *num store-items* is the number of storage items; $w_{i,t} = w_{i,t-1} + Ts_{i,t} - Te_{i,t}$ ($Ts_{i,t}$ is a bit for "start" slot for the i-th task, $Te_{i,t}$ is a bit for "end" slot of the i-th task) is a bit that shows if the i-th task is on or off; P_i is consumption of i-th task; for time t C_t is electricity cost; $Pc_{m,t}$ is m-th storage item charge; $Pd_{m,t}$ is the m-th storage item discharge; η_m is the efficiency of the m-th storage item; Cmb is the storage item maintenance cost; Cs_t is selling price; the total renewable resources $Stot_t$ is divided in three parts: $S_{i,t}$ (tasks), $Sst_{m,t}$ (storage items), Sex_t (selling). Differently from [9], this function considers three power flows and avoids a "biased" task scheduling, in which tasks are concentrated during the renewable energy peak levels instead of a uniform distribution.

Task Constraints

– Starting and ending time for each task:

$$\sum_{t \ge S_i}^{t_{last,i} - T_i} Ts_{i,t} = 1 \qquad \sum_{t \ge S_i + T_i}^{t_{last,i}} Te_{i,t} = 1 \qquad \forall i \qquad (2)$$

where $Ts_{i,t}$ is 1 if task i starts at time t, 0 otherwise; $T_{last,i}$ is the i-th task deadline decided by user, S_i is the i-th task earliest time decided by user, T_i is the i-th task time duration (task starts only one time); $Te_{i,t}$ is 1 if task i ends at time t, 0 otherwise (task ends only one time).

– Continuity for each task:

$$Ts_{i,t} = Te_{i,t+T_i} \qquad \forall i, S_i \le t \le t_{last,i} - T_i \qquad (3)$$

where T_i is the processing time for the i-th task. Tasks must operate continuously.

– On/off for each task in every temporal slot:

$$w_{i,t} = w_{i,t-1} + Ts_{i,t} - Te_{i,t} \qquad \forall i, 1 \le t \le T \qquad (4)$$

where T is the work horizon, $w_{i,t}$ is 1 if task i is on at time t, 0 otherwise.

– Some tasks must be off during some slots (e.g.: during sleeping period):

$$\sum_t Ts_{i,t} = 0 \qquad i \text{ and } t \text{ decided by user} \qquad (5)$$

– Consecutive tasks (j-th task is done before i-th task, e.g. washing machine):

$$\sum_{t=S_i}^{M} Ts_{i,t} + (M - S_i + 1)Te_{j,M+1} \le M - S_i + 1 \qquad i \ne j, \forall S_i \le M \le t_{last,i} - T_i \qquad (6)$$

Storage System Constraints

– Storage level for each item in the system:

$$SL_{m,MIN} \le SL_{m,t} \le SL_{m,MAX} \qquad 1 \le t \le T \qquad (7)$$

– Electricity stored in a storage item at time t:

$$SL_{m,t} = SL_{m,t-1} + Pc_{m,t}\eta_m - \frac{Pd_{m,t}}{\eta_m} \qquad 1 \le t \le T \qquad (8)$$

where at time t $Pc_{m,t}$ is the m-th storage item charge rate, $Pd_{m,t}$ is the m-th storage item discharge rate and η_m is the m-th storage item efficiency.

– Final electricity stored must be greater or equal to a well defined quantity:

$$SL_{m,t} \ge SL_{m,END} \qquad t = T \qquad (9)$$

– Charge and discharge rate can't exceed the electrical charge and discharge limits:

$$Pc_{m,t} \le Pc_{m,MAX} \qquad Pd_{m,t} \le Pd_{m,MAX} \qquad 1 \le t \le T \qquad (10)$$

– The storage item can discharge a smaller or equal quantity to load only when at least one task is on:

$$\sum_{i=1}^{num\,task} (w_{i,t}P_i - S_{i,t}) \geq \sum_{m=1}^{num\,store-items} Pd_{m,t} \qquad 1 \leq t \leq T \qquad (11)$$

Energy Constraints

– The total renewable energy is divided in three parts:

$$\sum_{i=1}^{num\,task} S_{i,t} + \sum_{m=1}^{num\,store-items} Sst_{m,t} + Sex_t \leq Stot_t \qquad 1 \leq t \leq T \qquad (12)$$

where at time t $S_{i,t}$ is for i-th task, $Sst_{m,t}$ is for m-th storage item, Sex_t is for sale.

– Imported energy from the grid ($3KW$ in our case):

$$\sum_{i=1}^{num\,task} (w_{i,t}P_i - S_{i,t}) +$$

$$+ \sum_{m=1}^{num\,store-items} (Pc_{m,t} - Sst_{m,t} - Pd_{m,t}) \leq 3KW \qquad 1 \leq t \leq T \qquad (13)$$

– We have renewable energy for a task only when the task is on:

$$w_{i,t} \geq \frac{S_{i,t}}{Stot_t} \qquad 1 \leq t \leq T \qquad (14)$$

– Renewables for a task can not exceed the task power:

$$w_{i,t}P_i - S_{i,t} \geq 0 \qquad \forall i, 1 \leq t \leq T \qquad (15)$$

– Renewable energy for storage can not exceed the storage system charge:

$$Pc_{m,t} - Sst_{m,t} \geq 0 \qquad \forall m, 1 \leq t \leq T \qquad (16)$$

Finally our system is modelled, and minimizing the cost function means minimizing the costs and optimizing the available energy.

3 The Proposed Algorithm: Operational Issues

3.1 The Static Case Study

By using cost profile, forecasted renewable energies and constraints defined by the user, the algorithm finds the best load profile for the scenario. The proposed cost function (1) is completely original and solves some problems that may occur with the function reported in [9]. Indeed its usage might "bias" the task scheduling: more tasks are scheduled concurrently during energy peak levels, and they are not distributed in a uniform way in a larger window with more renewables. In the new algorithm three terms about renewable energies are considered in order to have different energy flows: energy can meet the load demand, can charge the storage system or can be sold to the grid. With this form, MILP provides a more balanced behaviour for the whole scheduling.

Other features have been added to improve performances of [9] in a real case: *consequentiality* and *interruptibility*. A task can be interrupted when it does not need continuity to finish its work (in this case (3) can be ignored): this task type operates for the minimum resolution time (one slot) and can be stopped and restarted later. With regard to the consequentiality, unlike [9] we consider more complex task behaviours, because one task can be splitted in more sub-tasks in order to consider work "cycles" (e.g. washing machine or dishwasher) in the correct order.

3.2   The Dynamic Case Study

Whenever a change in the scenario occurs (new tasks or modification of the configuration), an external structure built upon MILP calls for a dedicated script: old constraints are traduced and added with the new conditions, and tasks parameters are put in a general list (updated externally to MILP) in order to trace the whole process from the start to the end. Obviously the algorithm maintains consequentiality of the tasks and all the constraints related to it: if a task has been already started in the previous optimization procedure, now it is forced to operate for the remaining time slots (if it is not interruptible) in order to finish the process, so the time-continuity and operability between various MILP algorithms are guaranteed because every time new equivalent groups of constraints are considered. The procedure includes also a dynamic work-horizon to allow completion of tasks, so the necessary longest process duration is used for launching the script: the work-horizon can be extended automatically whenever new tasks need it, or can be simply decreased step by step if the customer is not interested to have new optimizations in future. For this automatic system, changes in the scenario become interrupts that can be classified in three types:

- new *schedulable* tasks are added to the scenario;
- a new *not-schedulable* task starts;
- a *not-schedulable* task is finished.

Whenever one of these three conditions occurs, there is a new scheduling. We thus divide tasks in two categories: *schedulable* and *not-schedulable*.

A task is *schedulable* when the system can choose the processing time: $Te_i - Ts_i \geq T_i$ $\forall i$. The admitted interval of time is decided by the user, but obviously the algorithm chooses when it is more convenient, performing both energy and task scheduling. A task is *not-schedulable* when the system does not know the amount of the related time processing, because that is a "critic" task for the user (e.g. television), and it can not be never switched off automatically: only the user can shutdown the appliance when he prefers (depending on what the customer is doing at a certain time instant). The system considers the not-schedulable task like "always on" during the work horizon T, so it performs only energy scheduling and not task scheduling.

When an interrupt occurs, the system updates all the previous tasks, traces the amount of time for which a task operated in the past, deletes from the task list the completed ones, and after that new tasks are eventually added with their parameters: in this way the MILP algorithm provides the new task scheduling, related to the new scenario. Such a dynamic extension has been implemented, so the optimization algorithm can offer solutions step by step, whenever a scenario changes in terms of own characteristics. This results in an overall optimal task and energy system with remarkable reliability and robustness capabilities, especially in dynamic and not predictable real cases.

4   Computer Simulations

For our simulations the scenario consists of a photovoltaic system and one storage system; the sun profile is taken from [10], and the electricity cost from [11]. Tables below report the results for each temporal slot ($s1 = 7$ a.m., $s2 = 8$ a.m. ...): $\times$ means that task must be off, $\circ$ task can be on, $\bullet$ task is on; C_h is storage system charge, D_h is storage system discharge, SL is storage system level, R_{task} is renewable used for tasks, R_{store} is renewable used for storage system charge, R_{sell} is renewable sold to grid, R_{tot} is total renewable energy, En_{cost} is electricity price ($cents/kW$), I_{en} is power from the grid, $Load$ is the actual load demand; the maximum energy can be acquired from the grid is $3kW$, and energy selling price is $2.14\ dollarcent/kW$.

The scenario selected by the user in the **static case study** is described in Table 1 whereas the storage system parameters used for this simulation are shown in Table 2.

The results obtained by means of the proposed MILP based algorithm are detailed in Table 3. The total cost is only 0.355 $. If MILP and storage system are missing, tasks start in relation with user decisions (related to maximum power from grid), all renewables are sold to grid causing an higher cost: 0.526 $. It follows that a cost reduction of 32.5% is obtained by means of the employed algorithm.

Now let us move to consider the **dynamic case study**. storage system parameters are the same of the static case previously addressed, such as also renewables and cost profiles. After a first scheduling we suppose that an interrupt occurs at temporal slot 5 (so in the first table remaining underlined slots and values are not considered anymore): task 3 and task 4 are added as new schedulable tasks. It must be noted that continuity between different schedules is maintained

Table 1. Tasks and user constraints

	Task	$P_{(KW)}$	$T_{(hour)}$	T_{start}	T_{end}
Dishwasher	1	1	2	15:00	19:00
Washing machine	2	1	2	14:00	21:00
Cooker microwave	3	1	1	18:00	20:00
Cooker oven	4	1	1	15:00	18:00
Spin dryer	5	2	2	14:00	21:00

Table 2. Storage system parameters (in W):

η	SL_0	SL_{END}	SL_{MIN}	SL_{MAX}	Cap	Ch_{rate}	Dh_{rate}
100%	2000	1000	500	4500	5000	2000	2000

and previous temporal constraints are still valid for the next optimization stage. Overall simulation results attainable in this case study are reported in Table 4.

With MILP optimization the total cost is 0.118 \$. If MILP optimization and the storage system are missing the tasks start in the first valid slot for the customer (according to the available maximum load) and all the renewables are sold to the grid: in this case the total cost is 0.373 \$. So, using dynamic procedure a cost reduction of 68.4% is achieved. It can be seen that a consistent money

Table 3. MILP Optimization in the static case study

	P	T	$s1$	$s2$	$s3$	$s4$	$s5$	$s6$	$s7$	$s8$	$s9$	$s10$	$s11$	$s12$	$s13$	$s14$	$s15$
Task 1	1K	2	×	×	×	×	×	×	×	●	●	○	○	×	×	×	×
Task 2	1.2K	2	×	×	×	×	×	×	●	●	○	○	○	○	○	×	×
Task 3	1K	1	×	×	×	×	×	×	×	×	×	×	●	○	×	×	×
Task 4	1K	1	×	×	×	×	×	×	×	●	○	○	×	×	×	×	×
Task 5	2K	2	×	×	×	×	×	×	○	○	●	●	○	○	○	×	×
Ch	–	–	325	2	121	276	301	0	0	197	352	151	0	0	0	0	0
Dh	–	–	0	0	0	0	0	0	783	0	0	1796	1000	0	0	0	0
SL	–	–	2325	2327	2448	2724	3111	3530	2747	2944	3296	1500	500	500	500	500	1000
R_{task}	–	–	0	0	0	0	0	0	417	397	0	204	0	0	0	0	0
R_{store}	–	–	0	2	121	276	387	419	0	0	352	0	0	0	0	0	0
R_{sell}	–	–	0	0	0	0	0	0	0	0	0	0	0	0	0	0	0
R_{tot}	–	–	0	2	121	276	387	419	417	397	352	204	0	0	0	0	0
En_{cost}	–	–	5.42	6.58	5.70	5.60	5.60	6.12	5.99	5.09	5.37	5.53	6.54	6.67	6.74	6.97	4.73
I_{en}	–	–	325	0	0	0	0	0	0	3000	3000	0	0	0	0	0	500
$Load$	–	–	0	0	0	0	0	0	1200	3200	3000	2000	1000	0	0	0	0

Table 4. MILP Optimization in the dynamic case study

	P	T	s1	s2	s3	s4	s5	s6	s7	s8	s9	s10
$Task\,1$	1K	1	●	○	×	×	×	×	×	×	×	×
$Task\,2$	1.3K	2	×	○	○	●	●	×	×	×	×	×
Ch	−	−	314	2	121	0	0	419	81	0	0	0
Dh	−	−	0	0	0	1024	913	0	0	0	0	0
SL	−	−	2314	2316	2437	1413	500	919	1000	1000	1000	1000
R_{task}	−	−	0	0	0	276	387	0	0	0	0	0
R_{store}	−	−	0	2	121	0	0	419	81	0	0	0
R_{sell}	−	−	0	0	0	0	0	0	336	397	352	204
R_{tot}	−	−	0	2	121	276	387	419	417	397	352	204
En_{cost}	−	−	5.42	6.58	5.70	5.60	5.60	6.12	5.99	5.09	5.37	5.53
I_{en}	−	−	1314	0	0	0	0	0	0	0	0	0
$Load$	−	−	1000	0	0	1300	1300	0	0	0	0	0

	P	T	s1	s2	s3	s4	s5	s6	s7	s8	s9	s10
$Task\,2$	1.3K	1	●	×	×	×	×	×	×	×	×	×
$Task\,3$	800	1	○	○	●	×	×	×	×	×	×	×
$Task\,4$	1.4K	2	×	○	○	●	●	×	×	×	×	×
Ch	−	−	0	419	0	1308	0	204	0	0	0	0
Dh	−	−	913	0	383	0	1048	0	0	0	0	0
SL	−	−	500	919	536	1844	796	1000	1000	1000	1000	1000
R_{task}	−	−	387	0	417	397	352	0	0	0	0	0
R_{store}	−	−	0	419	0	0	0	204	0	0	0	0
R_{sell}	−	−	0	0	0	0	0	0	0	0	0	0
R_{tot}	−	−	387	419	417	397	352	204	0	0	0	0
En_{cost}	−	−	5.60	6.12	5.99	5.09	5.37	5.53	6.54	6.67	6.74	6.97
I_{en}	−	−	0	0	0	2311	0	0	0	0	0	0
$Load$	−	−	1300	0	800	1400	1400	0	0	0	0	0

saving is obtained with MILP especially in time-variant scenarios, because the best solution in terms of costs can be found for each different configuration.

5   Conclusions

In this work, a MILP based algorithm for task and energy scheduling in residential scenarios has been proposed. The algorithm is able to work not only in static but also in dynamic cases, thus extending what already appeared in a recent publication [9]. Some computer simulations have been performed on purpose and related results allowed the authors to positively conclude about the effectiveness of the idea and its suitability in presence of time-variant conditions, also from a pure monetary perspective.

Future efforts will be targeted to implement:

- plug-in hybrid electrical vehicles considered as storage systems, usable for load in some temporal slots but that must be charged at user-defined hours;
- models for the heating management to be included within the MILP algorithm for optimal scheduling;
- a suitable algorithm able to work in residential environments made of houses sharing the same renewable energy sources, always to minimize the overall amount of energy acquired from the grid.

References

1. Harley, R.G., Liang, J.: Computational Intelligence in Smart Grids. In: Symposium Series on Computational Intelligence (SSCI). CIASG (2011)
2. Venayagamoorthy, G.K.: Potentials and Promises of Computational Intelligence for Smart Grids. In: Power and Energy Society General Meeting. IEEE (2009)
3. Zhu, J.: Optimization of Power System Operation. Wiley-IEEE (2009)
4. Gudi, N., Wang, L., Devabhaktuni, V., Depuru, S.S.S.R.: Demand Response Simulation Implementing Heuristic Optimization for Home Energy Management. In: North American Power Symposium, NAPS (2010)
5. Pedrasa, M.A.A., Spooner, T.D., MacGilland, I.F.: Scheduling of Demand Side Resources Using Binary Particle Swarm Optimization. Transactions on Power Systems (2009)
6. Liang, R.H., Liao, J.H.: A Fuzzy-Optimization Approach for Generation Scheduling with Wind and Solar Energy Systems. Transactions on Power Systems (2007)
7. Vale, Z.A., Faria, P., Morais, H., Khodr, H.M., Silva, M., Kadar, P.: Scheduling distributed energy resources in an isolated grid An artificial neural network approach. Power and Energy Society General Meeting (2010)
8. Morais, H., Kádár, P., Faria, P., Vale, Z.A., Khodr, H.M.: Optimal scheduling of a renewable micro-grid in an isolated load area using mixed-integer linear programming. Renewable Energy - An International Journal (2009)
9. Zhang, D., Papageorgiou, L.G., Samsatli, N.J., Shah, N.: Optimal Scheduling of Smart Homes Energy Consumption with Microgrid. In: The First International Conference on Smart Grids, Green Communications and IT Energy-aware Technologies. IEEE (2011)
10. National Renewable Energy Laboratory (NREL): San Francisco, January 1 (1999), http://www.nrel.gov/rredc/
11. Huang, T., Liu, D.: Residential Energy System Control and Management using Adaptive Dynamic Programming. In: Conference on Neural Networks, San Jose, California, USA (2011)

Biogeography Based Optimization
for Multi-Knapsack Problems

Hongwei Mo[1], Zhenzhen Li[1], and Lulin Zhang[1]

Automation College, Harbin Engineering University, Harbin, 150001, China
Automation College, Harbin Engineering University
{honwei2004,zhezhenli,LLzhang}@126.com

Abstract. Biogeography-based Optimization Algorithm (BBOA) is a kind of new global optimization algorithm inspired by biogeography. It mimics the migration behavior of animals in nature to solve engineering problems. In this paper, BBOA based Multidimensional Knapsack Problem (MKPBBOA) is proposed. The migration strategy is designed to solve the combination optimization problem. It is tested on standard MKPs. The experiment results show that MKPBBOA is good at solving such problems.

Keywords: Biogeography optimization algorithm, Multi-knapsack problem, Combinatorial optimization.

1 Introduction

The science of biogeography can be traced to the work of nineteenth century naturalists such as Alfred Wallace [1] and Charles Darwin [2]. In the early 1960s, Robert MacArthur and Edward Wilson began working together on mathematical models of biogeography. Since their distinct work, biogeography has become a major area of research[3]. Simon presented the first approach on biogeography inspired algorithm for engineering[4]. It is called biogeography-based optimization algorithm(BBOA). It is modeled the process of immigration and emigration of species between islands in nature and good at global optimization. One characteristic of BBO is that the original population is not discarded after each generation. Simon introduced the main idea of how to use biogeography to design an optimization algorithm and gave us the basic definitions, steps of algorithms. He had tested the new algorithm on two kinds of problems, one is sensor selection for aircraft engine health estimation. The BBOA was compared with the other kinds of nature inspired computing. The experiments results showed that it is indeed effective in solving these problems.

Various versions of biogeography-based optimization models were proposed in [5][6][7], and it had been for different applications, such as complex economic load dispatch problem[8]. We have improved the performance of basic BBOA by combining the strategy of clone selection for function optimization[9]. And we have succeed in designing a new algorithm based on BBO to solve the traveling salesman problem [10], muti-objective optimization[11]. These research results showed that the

J. Wang, G.G. Yen, and M.M. Polycarpou (Eds.): ISNN 2012, Part I, LNCS 7367, pp. 659–667, 2012.

idea of biogeography is very useful for solving both general function optimization and combinatorial optimization problems.

The multidimensional 0–1 knapsack problem(MKP) is one of the most well-known integer programming problems and has received wide attention from the operational research community during the last four decades. Although recent advances have made possible the solution of medium size instances, solving this NP-hard problem remains a very interesting challenge, especially when the number of constraints increases[12]. In paper, we propose the method of using BBOA to solve the Multi-Knapsack Problems(MKPs). The paper is organized as follows. Section 2 introduces the procedure of MKPBBOA. Section 3 gives simulation results. Conclusions and further work are given in Section 4.

2   Biogeograpy Based Optimization Algorithm

2.1   Principle of BBOA

In geography, geographical areas that are well suited as residences for biological species are said to have a high habitat suitability index (HSI). Features that correlate with HSI include rainfall, diversity of vegetation, diversity of topographic features, land area, and temperature. The variables that characterize habitability are called suitability index variables (SIVs). SIVs can be considered the independent variables of the habitat, and HSI can be considered the dependent variable.

For using the principles of solving optimization problems, a good solution is analogous to an island with a high HSI, and a poor solution represents an island with a low HSI. High HSI solutions resist change more than low HSI solutions. By the same token, high HSI solutions tend to emmigrate their features with low HSI solutions to share good information for problem solving. The shared features remain in the high HSI solutions, while at the same time appearing as new features in the low HSI solutions, while high HSI solutions remain in their original habitat. Poor solutions accept a lot of new features from good solutions by immigration. This addition of new features to low HSI solutions may raise the quality of those solutions.

2.2   Procedure of MKPBBOA

In this section, we propose the approach of using BBOA to solve MKPs. It is called MKPBBOA. In MKPBBOA, each individual is still considered as a 'habitat', with a habitat suitability index (HSI), which is similar to the fitness of EAs, to measure the individual. A good MKP solution is analogous to an island with a high HSI, and a poor MKP solution indicates an island with a low HSI. High HIS MKP solutions tend to share their features with low HSI solutions. Low HSI MKP solutions accept a lot of new features from high HSI solutions. In MKPBBOA, each individual has its own immigration rate λ and emigration rate μ. A good solution has higher μ and lower λ, vice versa. The immigration rate and the emigration rate are functions of the number of species in the habitat. The immigration rate λ and the emigration rate μ are functions of the number of species in the habitat as shown in equation (1) and (2).

$$\mu_k = \frac{Ek}{n} \qquad (1)$$

$$\lambda_k = I\left(1 - \frac{k}{n}\right) \qquad (2)$$

where n is the total number of individuals in a population.

So according to (1) and (2), the immigration and emigration model are simple straight lines model giving a general description of the process of immigration and emigration. Consider the immigration model, as the number of species k increases, the habitat becomes more crowded, fewer species are able to successfully survive immigration to the habitat, and the immigration rate decreases. For the emigration, as the number of species increases, the habitat becomes more crowded, more species are able to leave the habitat to explore other possible residences, and the emigration rate increases.

Suppose that we have a global optimization problem and a population of candidate individuals. The individual is represented by a D-dimensional integer vector. The population consists of $NP = n$ parameter vectors. In MKPBBOA, there are two main operators, the migration and the mutation. They are implemented in step 7-9 and Step 10-11, respectively. The procedure of MKPBBOA is realized as follows.

Algorithm. The main procedure of MKPBBOA

```
1: Initialize m_max population size n , generation number N ,
     generate the initial habitats H^n randomly
2: Evaluate the HSI for each individual in H^n
3: Sort the population from best to worst
4: Initialize the generation counter t = 1
5: While the halting criterion is not satisfied do
6:    For each individual, map the HSI to the number of
       species
7:    Calculate the immigration rate λ_i and the emigration
       rate μ_i for each path H(i) according to (1) and (2)
8:      Calculate P_s
9:        If  rand< λ_i and μ_i <sum( μ_i )
            If habitat H(i) selected
               Crossover( H(i) , H(i+1))
            End if
          End for
10: Calculate mutation rate m_i
11: Mutate each habitat in H^n with mutation rate m_i
12: Evaluate H^n, update HSI
13: Sort H^n
```

```
14 :Keep the first two best individuals
15:  t = t + 1
16: End while
```

where rand(0,1) is a uniformly distributed random real number in (0, 1) and $H(i)$ is the i-th habitat. m_i is the mutation rate that is calculated as

$$m_i = m_{max}(1 - \frac{p_i}{p_{max}})\qquad(3)$$

where m_{max} is a user-defined parameter, and $P_{max} = \text{argmax } P_i$, $i = 1,...NP$. With the migration operator, MKPBBOA can share the information among solutions. Especially, poor solutions tend to accept more useful information from good solutions. This makes MKPBBOA be good at exploiting the information of the current population. Additionally, the mutation operator tends to increase the diversity of the population.

The emigration and immigration rates of each solution are used to probabilistically share information among habitats. In MKPBBOA, it is carried out by the operation of selection crossover(step 9). According to the model of λ and μ in (1) and (2),we can suppose that the solutions with lower λ and higher μ should be better than the other solutions. Emigration rates μ of the other solutions are used to decide whether a habitat $H(i)$ should be selected or not. If its μ value is bigger than the sum of the other habitats, then it is selected. It is used to crossover with its neighbor $H(i+1)$ to share its good information and produce more diverse habitats. The crossover operation is two-point crossover. This step is different from that of GA. As we know, two parents are selected to crossover to produce offspring in the population in GA. And the crossover operation is implemented after selection operation. In MKPBBO, only one habitat will be selected based on its λ and μ. And crossover operation is included in selection operation. In fact, it is a special migration process. It mimics the migration phenomena happening in biology. In biology, during the migration process, information will be shared among different habitats when animals migrate from one habitat to another.

Furthermore, to simulate the effect of cataclysmic events in biogeography, habitats which represent candidate solutions mutate with a mutation rate dependent on μ. Considering the specific characteristics in MKP,when mutation operation works, the n-bit binary string negates one of its bits; or the habitat negates the two bits chosen from one-value bits and zero-value bits respectively. Both of the two types of mutation have 50-percent probability to be executed.

3   Experiment Results

3.1   Multi-Knapsack Problem

Basically, the MKP is a resource allocation model which can be stated as[13]

$$\max \; z = \sum_{j=1}^{n} c_j x_j$$

$$s.t. \;\; \sum_{j=1}^{n} a_j x_j \le b_i, i \in M = \{1,2,...,m\} \tag{4}$$

$$x_j \in \{0,1\}, \; j \in N = \{1,2,...,n\} \tag{5}$$

where n is the number of items and m is the number of knapsack constraints with capacities b_i. Each item   requires a_{ij} units of resource consumption in the i th knapsack and yields c_j units of profit upon inclusion. The goal is to find a subset of items that yields maximum profit without exceeding the resource capacities. By its nature, all entries are nonnegative. More precisely, it can be assumed, without loss of generality, that $c_j > 0, b_i > 0, 0 \le a_{ij} \le b_i$ and $\sum_{j=1}^{n} a_{ij} > b_i$ for all $j \in N$ and for all $i \in M$ (since otherwise some or all of the variables can fixed to 0 or 1). Moreover, any MKP having at least one of these entries a_{ij} equal to 0, can be replaced by an equivalent MKP with positive entries.

For MKP, 0-1 binary representation is an appropriate choice. Hence, an n-bit binary string is used as the encoding way in our algorithm, where n is the number of variables in MKP.

However, an n-bit binary string may represent an infeasible solution, which means that at least one constraint in the MKP is violated. So we apply a penalty function to penalize the habitat suitability index (HSI) of any infeasible solution. HSI is similar to fitness used in most computing intelligence algorithm. Whenever there is at least one constraint is violated, the HSI of the habitat in MKP is calculated as follows.

$$HSI = \sum_{i=1}^{m} ((\sum_{j=1}^{n} a_{ij} x_i)/b_i) \tag{6}$$

3.2   Results and Discussion

Thiel and Voss [13] showed that a standard GA using a direct search in the complete search space is not able to obtain good solutions for the MKP, except for small problems. For a fair comparison, we investigate the performance of standard MKPBBOA searching the complete search space directly. The parameters of MKP BBOA are: habitat modification probability=1, maximum immigration and migration rates=1 for each habitat, maximum mutation rate=0.8.The proposed MKPBBOA is tested on MKP benchmarks selected from OR-Library [14] which has been solved in the literature. We realized the test by AMD T5250 1.5 G, Window XP and Matlab7.1 The tested instances are 2.28 with 28 objects and two constraints, and 5.100 with 100 objects and five constraints. In the test, computation stops after 3000 iterations. The number of habitats is 100, and each was solved 30 times to obtain the Avg, i.e., the average of the best solution in all the 30 runs.

Table 1. Test results on WEINGS

Problems	Avg.	Best	Time(s)
WEING1	141278	141278	0.5156
WEING2	130883	130883	0.9375
WEING3	95677	95677	14.6875
WEING4	119337	119337	0.4531
WEING5	98796	98796	1.7031
WEING6	130623	130623	28.2031

In Table 1, it shows the test results for 6 instances of benchmarks 2.28 known as WEING. To reveal the performance of standard MKPBBO, we first tested instances from WEING 1 to WEING 6. For each instance, the best known solutions from OR-Library, the best and average solutions found by standard MKPBBOA, and the average expenditure of time to obtain the best solution are reported in Table1. It shows that standard MKPBBOA can find all the best solution in Table 1. However, it takes more than ten seconds to solve WEING3 and WEING6 while less than two seconds are taken when dealing with the other 4 instances.

In Table 2, it shows the test results for 30 instances of benchmarks 5.100. For each instance, the table reports the best known solutions from OR-Library, the best and average solutions found by standard MKP_BBO, the best and average gap, and the average settling time. Gap is a measurement for the quality of the solution generated, i.e., (best known value--best solution value) / (best known value)%. Avg. represents the average settling time in each run. The settling time reflects the dynamic performance and it is used to represent the time for finding the best solution value in each loop to rise from 0% to 95% of the best known value. In table 2, BestGap is a static indicator and Avg. is a dynamic indicator. From the view point of BestGap, the algorithm found 3 optimal solutions for 3 instances and it is encouraging that standard MKPBBOA can find a better solution over the best known solution described in OR-Library for instance 5x100_03. In term of Avg., for most instances, the average settling time is within 3 seconds; even for some difficult instances, the average settling time does not exceed 8 seconds.

Table 2. Results of MKPBBOA on 5.100 instances

Problem	Best	Avg.	AvgGap	Best	BestGap	Avg(s)
5x100_00	**24381**	23981.97	1.64%	24227	0.63%	4.17
5x100_01	**24274**	23840.97	1.78%	24148	0.52%	3.64
5x100_02	**23551**	23196.80	1.50%	23480	0.30%	7.64
5x100_03	**23534**	23239.90	1.25%	**23538**	-0.02%	5.13
5x100_04	**23991**	23619.83	1.55%	23836	0.65%	3.88
5x100_05	**24613**	24185.63	1.74%	24449	0.67%	4.31
5x100_06	**25591**	25158.33	1.69%	25424	0.65%	4.98
5x100_07	**23410**	22983.87	1.82%	23308	0.44%	2.22
5x100_08	**24216**	23862.13	1.46%	24137	0.33%	4.50
5x100_09	**24411**	24007.07	1.65%	24295	0.48%	3.84
5x100_10	**42757**	42378.80	0.88%	**42757**	0.00%	1.94
5x100_11	**42545**	42175.30	0.87%	42433	0.26%	2.45
5x100_12	**41968**	41603.93	0.87%	41880	0.21%	1.67
5x100_13	**45090**	44718.27	0.82%	44941	0.33%	1.31
5x100_14	**42218**	41823.30	0.93%	42134	0.20%	1.88
5x100_15	**42927**	42603.43	0.75%	42845	0.19%	2.11
5x100_16	**42009**	41610.87	0.95%	41907	0.24%	2.44
5x100_17	**45020**	44589.70	0.96%	44901	0.26%	1.56
5x100_18	**43441**	42996.87	1.02%	43243	0.46%	2.67
5x100_19	**44554**	44233.23	0.72%	44458	0.22%	1.81
5x100_20	**59822**	59530.73	0.49%	**59822**	0.00%	0.72
5x100_21	**62081**	61810.27	0.44%	62019	0.10%	0.67
5x100_22	**59802**	59494.33	0.51%	59639	0.27%	0.67
5x100_23	**60479**	60227.47	0.42%	60457	0.04%	0.67
5x100_24	**61091**	60856.43	0.38%	61028	0.10%	1.03
5x100_25	**58959**	58714.60	0.41%	58921	0.06%	0.64
5x100_26	**61538**	61236.93	0.49%	61420	0.19%	0.89
5x100_27	**61520**	61260.57	0.42%	61421	0.16%	1.11
5x100_28	**59453**	59122.33	0.56%	**59453**	0.00%	1.70
5x100_29	**59965**	59690.30	0.46%	59910	0.09%	0.77

In Fig.1., we give the convergence of MKPBBO for problem 5x100_00 as an example. It can seen that it can convergence to optimal solution.

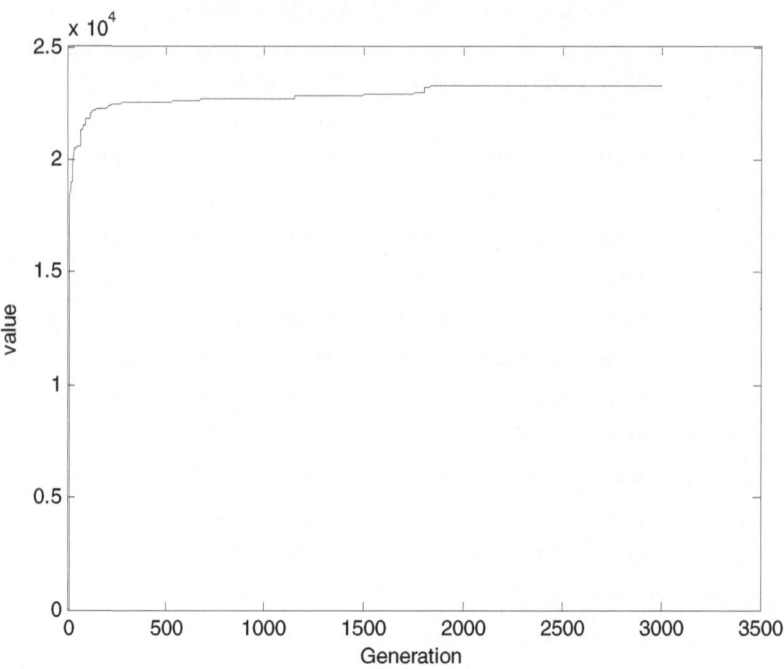

Fig. 1. The convergence of MKPBBOA for problem 5x100_00

4   Conclusions

In this paper, we proposed an approach MKPBBOA for multi-knapsack problems based on biogeography based optimization algorithm. It is tested on classical MKPs. From the results, it can bee seen that MKPBBOA showed excellent performance. It shows again that the idea of biogeography is very useful for solving engineering problems in practice. But there are still some problems to be solved. In further investigation, we will focus on more complex combination optimization problems and multi-objects optimization by our improved BBO and will research more effective ways for improving BBO, such as converging speed.

Acknowledgement. The work is supported by National Nature Science Foundation of China under grant No. 61075113, Excellent Young Teacher of Academy of Heilongjiang Province,China, No. 1155G18, and Excellent Young Teacher of Academy of Harbin Engineering University, No. HEUQG0809,the Fundamental Research Funds for the Central Universities No.HEUCF110441.

References

[1] Wallace, A.: The Geographical Distribution of Animals (Two Volumes). Adamant Media Corporation, Boston (2005)

[2] Darwin, C.: The Origin of Species. Gramercy, New York, USA (1995)

[3] Hanski, I., Gilpin, M.: Metapopulation Biology. Academic, New York (1997)

[4] Simon, D.: Biogeography-based optimization. IEEE Transactions on Evolutionary Computation 12, 702–713 (2008)

[5] Ergezer, M., Simon, D., Du, D.W.: Oppositional biogeography-based optimization. In: IEEE Conference on Systems, Man, and Cybernetics, San Antonio, TX, pp. 1035–1040. IEEE Press (2009)

[6] Du, D., Simon, D., Ergezer, M.: Biogeography-based optimization combined with evolutionary strategy and immigration refusal. In: IEEE International Conference on Systems, Man, and Cybernetics, San Antonio, TX, pp. 1023–1028. IEEE Press (2009)

[7] Ma, H., Chen, X.: Equilibrium species counts and migration model tradeoffs for biogeography-based optimization. In: 48th IEEE Conference on Decision and Control, Shanghai, China, pp. 3306–3310 (2009)

[8] Bhattacharya, A., Chattopadhyay, P.K.: Solving complex eeconomic load dispatch problems using bogeography-based otimization. Expert Systems with Applications 37, 3605–3615 (2010)

[9] Qu, Z., Mo, H.W.: Research of Hybrid Biogeography Based Optimization and Clonal Selection Algorithm for Numerical Optimization. In: Tan, Y., Shi, Y., Chai, Y., Wang, G. (eds.) ICSI 2011, Part I. LNCS, vol. 6728, pp. 390–399. Springer, Heidelberg (2011)

[10] Mo, H.W., Xu, L.F.: Biogeography migration algorithm for traveling salesman problem. International Journal of Intelligent Computing and Cybernetics 4(3), 311–330 (2011)

[11] Mo, H.W., Xu, Z.D.: Research of Biogeography-Based Multi-Objective Evolutionary Algorithm. Journal of Information Technology Research 4(2), 70–80 (2011)

[12] Freville, A.: The multidimensional 0–1 knapsack problem: an overview. European Journal of Operational Research 155, 1–21 (2004)

[13] Thiel, J., Voss, S.: Some experiences on solving multiconstraint zero–one knapsack problems with genetic algorithms. In: INFOR, vol. 32, pp. 226–242 (1994)

[14] Chu, P., Beasley, D.: A genetic algorithm for the multiconstrained knapsack problem. Journal of Heuristics 4, 63–86 (1998)

MRKDSBC: A Distributed Background Modeling Algorithm Based on MapReduce

Cong Wan, Cuirong Wang, and Kun Zhang

College of Information Science and Engineering,
Northeastern University, Shenyang 110044, China
10000cong@163.com

Abstract. Video surveillance is a widely used technology. Moving object detection is the most important content of video surveillance. Background modeling is an important method in moving object detection. However, background modeling algorithm is usually computationally intensive when the size of video is large. Kernel density estimation method based on Chebyshev inequality (KDSBC) is a new background modeling algorithm. This paper present MRKDSBC based on MapReduce which is a distributed programming model. Further more, we prove the correctness of the algorithm theoretically and implement it on Hadoop platform. Finally, we compare it with traditional algorithm.

Keywords: Chebyshev inequality, background modeling, Kernel density estimation, distributed, MapReduce, Hadoop.

1 Introduction

Video surveillance is widely used in video conferencing, image transmission as well as banking, transportation, community and other important field[1][2]. However, most of the traditional video surveillance only concern to save or transport the real-time video in stead of responding some abnormal event. Intelligent video surveillance has becoming an important and widely researched issue. Moving object detection is the most important content of video surveillance. There are two main methods, one is color identification that detective moving object through color matching, another is background subtraction that remove the pixels in background of the video through background model to achieve it [3].

In general video surveillance system, the camera position is fixed, so the background is the same and the characters, vehicles entering and leaving the scene. However, in face, the moving objects may stop and stay for a long time, the object stopped for a long time may move for some reason, and the scene changes in the weather, light, etc. Therefore, in different time periods, the background of the video is different.

It has been widely recognized that background modeling is computationally intensive when the size of video is large. It may be cost a long time on computation in

J. Wang, G.G. Yen, and M.M. Polycarpou (Eds.): ISNN 2012, Part I, LNCS 7367, pp. 668–677, 2012.

some case, and it's unable to accept. It is commonly believed that there are two ways to speed up algorithm: the first one is to optimizing the algorithm itself, whereas another one is to changing the algorithm and executing it on a parallel environment. The second way doesn't reduce the amount of calculation, but it do shorten the execute time. Moreover, a well-designed parallel algorithm could save more time with the expansion of the environment scale. There are some traditional parallel programming models such as MPI [4][5][6], which demand a high availability environment.

MapReduce is a distributed programming model focus on large data sets on clusters of computers introduced by Google [7], is also the core cloud computing programming model at present. MapReduce programming paradigm is inspired by the map and reduce functions commonly used in functional programming. It cut data into splits automatically according to user needs. The map function process separate split and generate key/value pairs as intermediate results. Key/value pairs with the same key will be fetched by the same reduce function and it will produce the final result. In the whole MapReduce execution process, there are multiple concurrent tasks during the map stage and reduce stage.

MapReduce shield the complexity of parallel processing details, greatly simplifies the design of parallel programs. Developers could focus on the specific application of Map and Reduce processing logic, while system will handle the complex concurrent transactions.

Apache Hadoop [8] is a software framework that supports data-intensive distributed applications, which implements Google's MapReduce and Google File System (GFS). It divided application into many small units, and executes these units on cluster nodes. In Hadoop, an application submitted to be processed is called a Job, and the work unit that separated from the job and running on a compute nodes is called Task. In addition, Hadoop Distributed File System (HDFS) is the primary storage system used by Hadoop applications. HDFS creates multiple replicas of data blocks and distributes them on compute nodes throughout a cluster to enable reliable, extremely rapid computations.

This paper present MRKDSBC based on MapReduce which is a distributed programming model. Further more, we prove the correctness of the algorithm theoretically and implement it on Hadoop platform. Finally, we compare it with traditional algorithm.

2   Related Works

Background subtraction is the most commonly used method in Background detection. It build video background model in a real-time and carry out difference to subtract the background. Background modeling-based approach can generally reflect the dynamic changes over time, and provide a more complete data. Currently, there are some related works [9][10].

Many researchers engaged in migrating the traditional algorithms to the MapReduce framework. K. Wiley et al. [11] discusses image coaddition which is a multi-stage image-processing pipeline could get a single image of higher quality from a set of images in the cloud using Hadoop. Support Vector Machine (SVM) techniques have been used extensively in automatic image annotation. N. K. Alham et al. [12] presents MRSMO, a high performance SVM algorithm for automatic image annotation, using MapReduce. The K-Means clustering is one of the most common methods in the field of pattern recognition, data mining and image processing. However, it is time-consuming and memory-consuming especially when both the size of input images and the number of expected classifications are large. Zhenhua Lv et al. [13] implements K-Means clustering algorithm using MapReduce. ISODATA is the most frequently used unsupervised classification algorithm. Bo Li et al. [14] propose parallel ISODATA clustering algorithm based on MapReduce. In order to In order to reduce the difficulty of the process, the original images will be transformed into other format, usually text, Before the algorithms based on MapReduce processing images[13][14]. When the image is relatively small in size, multiple images will be packaged. In addition, there are some other researchers committed to dealing with large-scale data using MapReduce. Some researchers have improved existing MapReduce model, making it more suitable for some special cases. Pan Wei et al. [15] present MapReduce Based on Message Passing. Yanfeng Zhang et al. [16] present iMapReduce that explicitly supports the implementation of iterative algorithms.

3   KDSBC Algorithm

Kernel density estimation method based on Chebyshev inequality algorithm described as follow:

Let set $X = \{x_1, x_2, x_3 ... x_N\}$ denotes a set of image samples, and $x_k(i, j)$ is the gray value of pixel on the position (i, j). $\overline{X}(i, j)$ denotes the Sample Mean of X, described as equations (1)

$$\overline{X}(i, j) = \frac{1}{N} \sum_{k=1}^{N} x_k(i, j) \tag{1}$$

$S^2(i, j)$ denotes the second-order centre distance of X, described as equations(2)

$$S^2(i, j) = \frac{1}{N} \sum_{k=1}^{N} (x_k(i, j) - \overline{X}(i, j))^2 \tag{2}$$

Moreover, $\mu(i, j)$ and $\sigma^2(i, j)$ denotes the mathematical expectation and variance of X, and their estimated value $\hat{\mu}(i, j) = \overline{X}(i, j)$, $\hat{\sigma}^2(i, j) = S^2(i, j)$.

Then, we describe the algorithm as follow steps:

1. Load all $x \in X$ and calculate the $\overline{X}$ and S^2 for all pixels. Thus $\hat{\mu}$ and $\hat{\sigma}^2$ are calculated.

2. Use piecewise function $M_1(k,i,j)$ divided pixels into three categories: background point, foregroundand point and undefined point. , described as equations (3)

$$M_1(k,i,j) = \begin{cases} 1 & (1-\dfrac{\sigma_k^2(i,j)}{\varepsilon^2}) \geq T_1 \\ -1 & T_2 < (1-\dfrac{\sigma_k^2(i,j)}{\varepsilon^2}) < T_1 \quad \varepsilon = \theta * \hat{\sigma} \\ 0 & (1-\dfrac{\sigma_k^2(i,j)}{\varepsilon^2}) \leq T_2 \end{cases} \tag{3}$$

In the previous equations, 1 means background point; 0 means foregroundand point; -1 means undefined. The Threshold T1, T2 and θ are empirical values.

3. Identify the undefined point. Described as equations (4) and (5)

$$P_r(x_k) = \frac{1}{N}\sum_{i=1}^{N}\frac{1}{\sqrt{2\pi\sigma^2}}e^{-\frac{1}{2}\frac{(x_k-x_i)^2}{\sigma^2}} \tag{4}$$

$$M_2(k,i,j) = \begin{cases} 1 & P_r(x_k) \geq T_3 \\ 0 & P_r(x_k) < T_3 \end{cases} \tag{5}$$

4. Generate background. $isBack(k,i,j)$ represent the background identification and $B(i,j)$ represent gray value of background described as equations (6)

$$B(i,j) = \begin{cases} \dfrac{\sum\limits_{k=1}^{N}[x_k(i,j)*isBack(k,i,j)]}{\sum\limits_{k=1}^{N}isBack(k,i,j)} & \sum\limits_{k=1}^{N}isBack(k,i,j) \neq 0 \\ 255 & \sum\limits_{k=1}^{N}isBack(k,i,j) = 0 \end{cases} \tag{6}$$

4   Algorithm Based on MapReduce

MapReduce [8] is a programming model and Hadoop [9] is an open source system that implements the MapReduce model. This model mainly consists of two functions: map and reduce that implemented by users.

In order to achieve better efficiency of parallel computation, we pack multiple images into a binary file as input data and each byte in the file represent a pixel gray value. The file has a nine bytes long header. The first byte response for the image number in the file, the next four response for image width and the last four response for image height.

The algorithm can be detailed as five steps. Each of them is a map/reduce process and each process use previous output as input. In another word, they are executed sequentially. The data flow diagram shown as Fig. 1

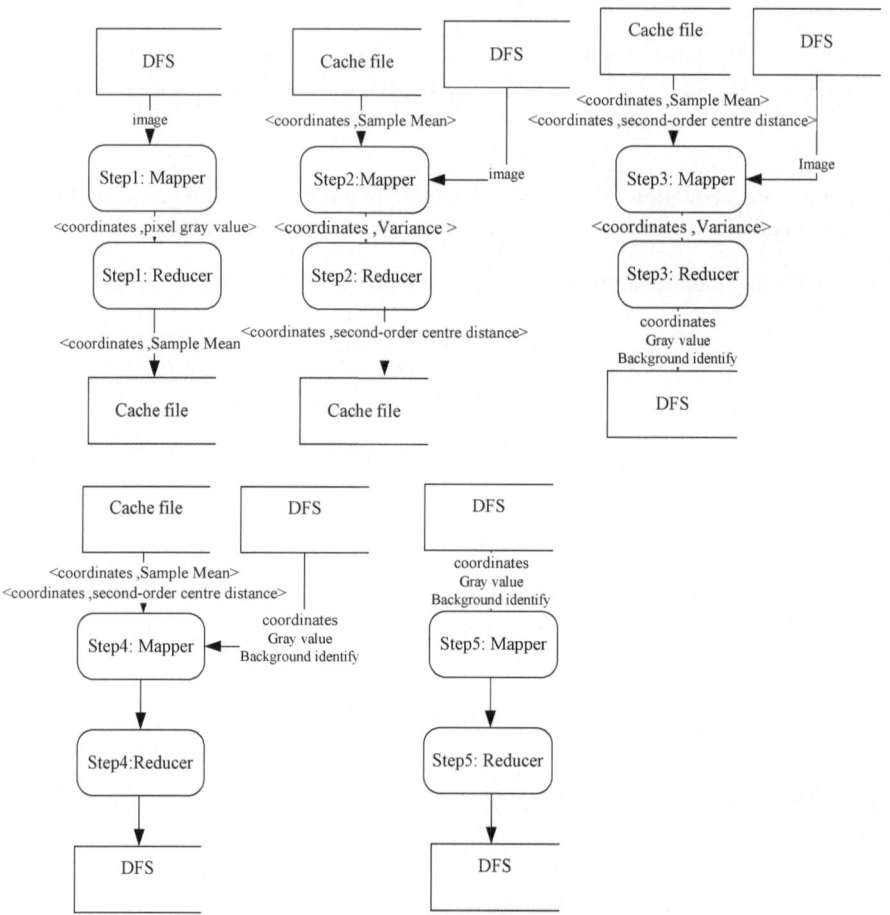

Fig. 1. The data flow diagram of algorithm based on MapReduce. It shows the data flow in the five step3 separately.

Step 1. Calculate the Sample Mean. We define a file that contains k images as a split. Given all the images having the same height and width, we can get the coordinates of the pixel in the image. The map function outputs pixel coordinates as key and pixel gray value as value. The Combiner function sums the pixel gray value and the total image number of the mapper. The reduce function collect the total number of images and the sum of pixel gray value and calculate sample mean of each pixel. Each of the reducer will calculate sample mean of a sub set of all the pixels and output to a separate file. Given Sample Mean is required by all the mappers, we put such files in a cache file that each nodes in the cluster would have a copy so that they can access it locally.

Step 2. Calculate the second-order centre distance. The map function calculates the Variance of each pixel and outputs pixel coordinates as key and Variance as value. The Combiner function sums the Variance and the total image number of the mapper. The reduce function collect the total number of images and the sum of Variance and calculate second-order centre distance of each pixel. As the previous step, we put the result in a cache file.

Step 3. Identify the background point for the first time using the Chebyshev inequality. The map function calculates and output a sample index and pixel coordinate as key and σ^2 as value. The reduce function identify the background according to equations (3), then the background identification of each pixel and pixel gray value would be saved to the DFS as a text format. Each line of the text recorded a pixel coordinates, gray value and background identification (1/0/-1).

Step 4. Identify the background point for the second time using the kernel density estimation. The map function receive a <key, value> pair as input, key is represented by coordinate and value is represented by a tuple (background identification, pixel gray value). For each pixel that background identification is -1, map function output coordinate as key and pixel gray value as value. The reduce function identify the background according to equations (5) and saved to the DFS as a text format.

Step 5. Calculate the background. The final step will calculate the background according to the data generated in the third and fourth step. For each pixel that background identification is 1, the map function read each line of the text and output coordinate as key and pixel gray value as value. The reduce function calculate the gray value of each pixel as a background according to equations (6).

5   The Proof

In the previous work, we present algorithm under the traditional platform and algorithm base-on MapReduce, and in this chapter we will prove that the two algorithms will get the same results. Let set X denotes of samples and set $P = \{i \mid 0 \leq i \leq iwidth\} \times \{j \mid 0 \leq j \leq iheight\}$ denotes of all the pixel coordinates. Iwidth means image width, Iheight means image height and SNum means the number of samples.

In the step1: let MapNum represent the number of mappers and RedNum represent the number of reducers. X_k is a subset of X, and $X_1 \cup X_2 \cup ... \cup X_{MapNum} = X$. P_l is a subset of P, and $P_1 \cup P_2 \cup ... \cup P_{RedNum} = P$.

In *mapper$_k$* , it processes that $N_k = |X_k|$ and $SumGray_k(i,j) = \sum x_m(i,j)$,

$x_m \in X_k, (i,j) \in P$

In *reducer$_l$* , it processes as equations (7)

$$\bar{X}_l(i,j) = \frac{\sum_{k=1}^{MapNum} SumGray_k(i,j),}{\sum_{k=1}^{MapNum} N_k} \quad (i,j) \in p_l \tag{7}$$

Because of $P_1 \cup P_2 \cup ... \cup P_{RedNum} = P$, $\bar{X}_1(i,j) \cup \bar{X}_1(i,j) \cup ... \cup \bar{X}_{RedNum}(i,j) = \bar{X}$.

In the step2:

In *mapper$_k$* , it calculates that $N_k = |X_k|$ and

$$SumS2_k(i,j) = \sum (x_m(i,j) - \bar{X}(i,j))^2 \quad , x_m \in X_k, (i,j) \in P$$

In *reducer$_l$* , it processes as equations (8)

$$\bar{X}_l(i,j) = \frac{\sum_{k=1}^{MapNum} SumS2_k(i,j)}{\sum_{k=1}^{MapNum} N_k}, (i,j) \in p_l \tag{8}$$

Because of $P_1 \cup P_2 \cup ... \cup P_{RedNum} = P$, $S_1^2(i,j) \cup S_2^2(i,j) \cup ... \cup S_{RedNum}^2(i,j) = S^2$.

In step3 calculate isBack1(k, i, j) for each point in the sample using equations (3), which k represent sample number and (i, j) represent coordinate. The value of isBack1(k, i, j) may be 1,0 or -1.

In step4 calculate isBack2(k, i, j) for the point isBack1(k, i, j)=-1

In step5, mappers are divided into two parts, processing result set from step3 and step4 separately. The background pixel at each coordinate is processed in two mappers belong to two parts. The first mapper compute $backSum1 = \sum x_m(i,j) * isBack3(m,i,j)$ Where isBack3 defined as follow equations (9)

$$isBack3 = \begin{cases} 1 & isBack1(m,i,j) \neq 1 \\ 0 & isBack1(m,i,j) = 1 \end{cases} \tag{9}$$

The next mapper compute $backSum2 = \sum x_m(i,j) * isBack2(m,i,j)$. In the reducer process background pixel gray value as follow equations (10)

$$B(i, j) = \frac{backSum1 + backSum2}{\sum\limits_{m=1}^{Snum} isBack2(m,i,j) + \sum\limits_{m=1}^{Snum} isBack3(m,i,j)} \qquad (10)$$

We have identified every point in the samples in the step three and step four, So isBack2 and isBack3 covers all the possible background point. Therefore, the result from traditional algorithm and algorithm based on MapReduce are the same.

6   Experiment

We implement KDSBC and MRKDSBC algorithm in the actual environment and compare the experimental results. We mainly consider the trend of time with the increase of the volumes of data and size of one image package.

For the MRKDSBC environment, we set up Hadoop on a computer cluster which has 1 NameNode and 5 DataNodes. Both NameNode and 5 DataNodes are composed of 2.93GHz Intel Core2 Duo CPU and 2GB memory, All nodes were connected by a gigabit switch. In terms of software, we implement the application using jdk-6u26-windows-i586 and eclipse-SDK-3.6.1. The operating system is Ubuntu10.04 and the Hadoop version is Hadoop-0.21.0.

For KDSBC, we implement the algorithm using jdk-6u26-windows-i586 and eclipse-SDK-3.6.1. And run this program with a environment of 2.93GHz Intel Core2 Duo CPU and 2GB memory under windows.

Experimental data comes from a 15 minute traffic surveillance video, it was split into ten thousand images. Each image is 352 pixels in width and 240 pixels in height and the size of each image file is about 12 Kilobyte. First of all, we validate the availability of the algorithm. The background produced by KDSBC and MRKDSBC with 100 images shown as Fig. 3. Fig 2(a) is randomly selected from the 1000 images. Fig 2(b) shows result processed by MRKDSBC and (c) is processed by KDSBC. Two images is the same, indicating that there is no difference in the results between two algorithms.

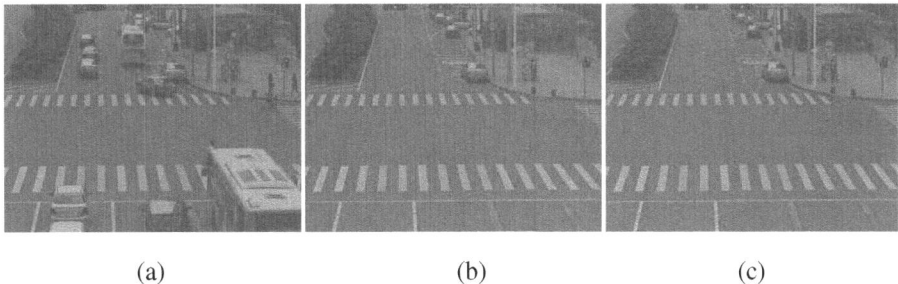

(a)   (b)   (c)

Fig. 2. The original image and processed images. (a) is the original image. (b) is processed by MRKDSBC. (c) is processed by KDSBC.

We packed 120 images in one package which have a size of 17.2 megabit. Fig. 3 shows the processing speed trend of two algorithms with increasing number images. With the expansion of data size, the MRKDSB shows the advantage.

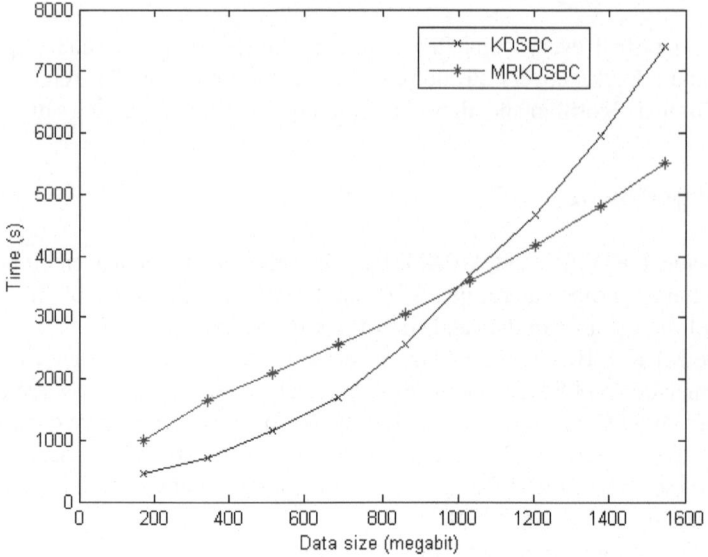

Fig. 3. processing speed trend of MRKDSBC and KDSBC

7   Conclusion and Future Work

In this paper, we have presented a MapReduce based distributed background modeling algorithm. Since there are many different between MapReduce programming model and traditional model, we prove the correctness of the algorithm theoretically and compare the experimental results. Meanwhile, the experiments show that MRKDSBC algorithm performed better than traditional algorithm. Because of some characteristics of Hadoop, we need to transform and pack images into a package instead of separate images. In addition, users need to manually upload images, invoke the application and download the result instead of easy-to-use interface. We will improve these two issues in the future work. Background modeling is only a part of moving object detection. In the future work, we will also continue to implement related algorithms based on MapReduce.

References

1. Collins, R.T., Lipton, A.J., Kanade, T.: Introduction to the special section on video surveillance. IEEE Transactions on Pattern Analysis and Machine Intelligence 22, 745–746 (2000)

2. Versavel, J.: Road safety through video detection. Intelligent, 1999. In: Proceedings of IEEE/IEEJ/JSAI International Conference on Transportation Systems, pp. 753–757 (1999)
3. Gang, L., et al.: New moving target detection method based on background differencing and coterminous frames differencing. Chinese Journal of Scientific Instrument 22(8), 961–964 (2006)
4. Jie, L., et al.: Applications of MPI parallel-computing on image processing. Infrared Laser Engineering 33(5), 496–499 (2004)
5. Plimpton, S.J., Devine, K.D.: MapReduce in MPI for Large-scale graph algorithms. Parallel Computing 37(9), 610–632 (2011)
6. Hoefler, T., Lumsdaine, A., Dongarra, J.: Towards Efficient MapReduce Using MPI. In: Ropo, M., Westerholm, J., Dongarra, J. (eds.) PVM/MPI. LNCS, vol. 5759, pp. 240–249. Springer, Heidelberg (2009)
7. Dean, J., Ghemawat, S.: MapReduce: simplified data processing on large clusters. Commun. ACM 51(1), 107–113 (2008)
8. Hadoop: Open source implementation of MapReduce, `http://hadoop.apache.org/`
9. Karmann, K.P., Brandt, A.: Moving object recognition using an adaptive background memory. In: Proceedings of the 3rd International Workshop on Time-Varying Image Processing and Moving Object Recognition 2, pp. 289–296 (1990)
10. Kilger, M.: A shadow handler in a video-based real-time traffic monitoring system. In: Proceedings IEEE Workshop on Applications of Computer Vision, pp. 11–18 (1992)
11. Keith, W., et al.: Astronomy in the Cloud: Using MapReduce for Image Coaddition. In: 20th Annual Conference on Astronomical Data Analysis Software and Systems, Boston 2010. Astronomical Society of the Pacific Conference Series, vol. 442, pp. 93–96 (2011)
12. Alham, N.K., et al.: A MapReduce-based distributed SVM algorithm for automatic image annotation. Computers and Mathematics with Applications 62(7), 2801–2811 (2011)
13. Lv, Z., Hu, Y., Zhong, H., Wu, J., Li, B., Zhao, H.: Parallel K-Means Clustering of Remote Sensing Images Based on MapReduce. In: Wang, F.L., Gong, Z., Luo, X., Lei, J. (eds.) WISM 2010. LNCS, vol. 6318, pp. 162–170. Springer, Heidelberg (2010)
14. Bo, L., Hui, Z., Zhenhua, L.: Parallel ISODATA Clustering of Remote Sensing Images Based on MapReduce. In: 2010 International Conference on Cyber-Enabled Distributed Computing and Knowledge Discovery, pp. 380–383 (2010)
15. Wei, P., et al.: Evaluating Large Graph Processing in MapReduce Based on Message Passing. Chinese Journal of Computers 34(10), 1768–1784 (2011)
16. Yanfeng, Z., et al.: iMapReduce: A distributed computing framework for iterative computation. In: 2011 IEEE International Symposium on Parallel & Distributed Processing, Workshops and Phd Forum, pp. 1112–1121 (2011)

Erratum: Research of Dynamic Load Identification Based on Extreme Learning Machine

Wentao Mao[1,2], Mei Tian[3], Guirong Yan[2], and Xianfang Wang[1]

[1] College of Computer and Information Technology, Henan Normal University, Xinxiang City, 453007, China
[2] State Key Laboratory for Strength and Vibration, Xi'an Jiaotong University, China
[3] Management Institute, Xinxiang Medical University, China
maowt.mail@gmail.com

J. Wang, G.G. Yen, and M.M. Polycarpou (Eds.): ISNN 2012, Part I, LNCS 7367, pp. 80–89, 2012.
© Springer-Verlag Berlin Heidelberg 2012

DOI 10.1007/978-3-642-31346-2_76

On page 89, in 'Acknowledgement', the foundation No. should read '122300410111' instead of '112300410111'.

_____

The original online version for this chapter can be found at
http://dx.doi.org/10.1007/978-3-642-31346-2_10

Author Index